Instant
Information

Instant Information

Editors
Joel Makower and Alan Green

A Tilden Press Book

Prentice Hall Press • New York

Published by Prentice Hall Press
A division of Simon & Schuster, Inc.
Gulf + Western Building
1 Gulf + Western Plaza
New York, New York 10023

PRENTICE HALL PRESS is a trademark of Simon & Schuster, Inc.

Library of Congress Cataloging-in-Publication Data

Instant Information

   "A Tilden Press book."
   Includes indexes.
   1. Information services—United States—
Directories. I. Makower, Joel, 1952-   .
II. Green, Alan, 1950-   . I. Makower, Joel.
Z674.5.U5I57 1987 020'.25'73 86-43169

ISBN 0-13-609413-9 (pbk.)

Manufactured in the United States of America
Phototypesetting by Chronicle Type and Design

10 9 8 7 6 5 4 3 2

Editorial and Research Staff

Laura A. Bergheim
Managing Editor

Philip Blair
Jim Dentzer
Barbara Dickens
Marilyn P. Fenichel
Brooke Gladstone
Bill Hogan
Peter Krasilovsky
Brian McArthur
Wendy Melillo
William Ragland
John Rankin
Thomas A. Robertson
Susan Santo
Laurie Stroblas
Melanie Wells
Robert Westgate

Thanks Also:

Barry Groves
Gerry Jones
John May
Steve Smith & Co.

Contents

Introduction

"Knowledge," Samuel Johnson once wrote, "is of two kinds. We know a subject ourselves, or we know where we can find information about it." Two centuries later, our body of knowledge has expanded in ways Johnson couldn't have imagined. Finding information is no longer that simple. As most researchers know, tracking down experts on an unfamiliar subject often means poring endlessly through specialized catalogs, directories, and reference books. With this book, however, Johnson's notion of knowledge may be a bit closer to reality.

There is information everywhere: trade associations, universities, government agencies, corporations, think tanks, historical societies, nonprofit groups, and on and on. Any one may be the best repository of both historical and up-to-date information on a given subject. But tracking down the best sources—particularly those that are ready, willing, and able to help you—usually is time consuming. Even worse, such searches often are futile.

Some researchers have had an important edge: the Library of Congress in Washington, D.C. Among the services available at the world's largest repository of information is a computer data base that can help refer users to appropriate resources. Unfortunately, that service is available only to those with the time to actually visit our nation's capital. And those who manage to get to one of the crowded terminals often find long, confusing entries that may lead them in many different directions. Even worse, there is no index to this information lode. If you don't know key terms to search, chances are you may come away having missed a number of potentially valuable sources.

This book solves those problems. We have taken that data base and condensed it, edited it, reorganized it, and added many new organizations. Moreover, we've created two comprehensive indexes to help you easily pinpoint subjects in which you have an interest.

How to use this book. This book is divided into three parts: a state-by-state listing of reference sources, an organization name index, and a subject index.

The listings include nearly 9,000 organizations, agencies, university programs, and public and private groups, arranged alphabetically by state. (Also included are organizations in Canada, Puerto Rico, and the Virgin Islands.) Each entry offers a brief description of the organization's main interests and purpose, including the types of information it makes available. When known, it is also noted whether there are costs for this information, along with restrictions on its use.

A few important notes: Although there are many state agencies included in the book, many others were not included. If a state has a unique feature—such as geological formations or key industries—appropriate state agencies are included. Generally, though, because state agencies are relatively easy to track down (and in order to keep this book to a manageable size), they were not included.

It is also important to note that each organization's entry was pared down to its essence. Not only were countless abbreviations used but rules of grammar were often suspended: articles were frequently dropped, sentences are truncated. Still, every attempt was made to offer enough information to provide the essentials of an organization's interest; in some cases, organizations have additional narrow interests not specifically noted here.

Ultimately, of course, there is no such thing as "instant information." Comprehensive research on any subject can involve seemingly endless hours of digging. One subject will offer an unwieldy number of potential information sources; another subject will have precious few. But the rewards of persistence can be gratifying.

Like so many other things worth finding, the search for good information sources usually requires equal parts inspiration and perspiration. We hope we've provided the inspiration in the pages that follow. The rest is up to you.

Organization Listings

Editors' Note

Although organizations are listed alphabetically by state, with each organization assigned its own unique five-digit identifying number, there are frequently gaps in the numbering sequence. These gaps in no way reflect errors. Listings were continually updated and verified throughout the editing process; during that time, organizations either closed their doors or, for a variety of reasons, were deemed inappropriate for this book. To ensure as accurate a book as possible, those listings were deleted from the data base, thus creating the numerical gaps.

Alabama

01001. AC-CU-MET, 2100 Marietta Ave, Muscle Shoals, AL 35661; (205) 383-117. Interest in synoptic meteorological summaries, wind prediction, weather forecasting, microcomputer applications. Provides advisory, consulting, translation services; conducts seminars, workshops.

01002. Air University Library, Maxwell Air Force Base, AL 36112; (205) 293-2888. Interest in aeronautics, aerospace management, military art and science, politics and government, social change. Permits use of collection to qualified researchers who obtain permission in advance.

01004. Alabama Agricultural Experiment Station, Auburn Univ, AL 36849; (205) 826-4840. Interest in agricultural science and research. Fills requests for research info, organizes fair exhibits, field days, and seminars; provides other services through plant breeding, foundation seed production, and soil testing activities.

01005. Alabama Citizens Action Programs, 3213 Lorna Rd (Hoover), Birmingham, AL 35216; (205) 979-1803. Provides consulting services, and seminars on drug, alcohol, tobacco education. Services free; contributions appreciated.

01006. Alabama Conservancy, 2717 Seventh Ave S, Ste 201, Birmingham, AL 35233; (205) 322-3126. Interest in all aspects of energy conservation, including strip mining reclamation, recycling, hazardous wastes, and pesticide control. Answers membership inquiries, provides resources to anyone seeking assistance on environmental problems. Services limited.

01007. Alabama Cooperative Fishery Research Unit, Fisheries Bldg, Auburn Univ, AL 36849; (205) 826-4786. Interest in fisheries, aquatic ecology, endangered species, taxonomy, systematics, ichthyofaunal surveys, spring-dwelling fishes, fish reproduction, exotic fishes. Conducts research, graduate level courses, and seminars. Services available to cooperating agencies only.

01008. Alabama Cooperative Wildlife Research Unit, Auburn Univ, Auburn, AL 36830; (205) 826-4796. Interest in wildlife management, animal ecology. Answers brief inquiries, makes referrals.

01010. Alabama Dept of Forensic Sciences, P.O. Box 231 (Wire Rd), Auburn, AL 36831-0231; (205) 887-7001. Serves as forensic science system for Ala. Answers inquiries. Few restrictions on info access for scientists in related fields; services to others limited. Services free to Ala. law enforcement agencies, district attorneys, courts, coroners, hospitals, medical doctors, and attorneys.

01011. Alabama Geological Survey, P.O. Box O, Univ Station, Tuscaloosa, AL 35486; (205) 349-2852. Interest in minerals, energy, water, and petroleum resources in Ala. Nominal cost for pamphlets, other materials.

Free library reference service. No restrictions to scientists in related fields, except for confidential info.

01012. Alabama Historical Commission, 725 Monroe St, Montgomery, AL 36130; (205) 261-3184. Interest in important historic, architectural, or archaeological sites in Ala. Provides advisory and reference services; onsite use of collections. Services free, except conferences, workshops, and publications.

01013. Alabama Humanities Resource Center, 6030 Monticello Dr, Montgomery, AL 36130; (205) 277-7330. Interest in literature, history, philosophy, ethics, comparative religions, and jurisprudence. Provides advisory services; distributes publications, films, videotapes, and exhibition materials; permits onsite use of collection. Free to out-of-school adult orgs, colleges, universities, Ala. libraries.

01014. Alabama Law Institute, P.O. Box 1425 (Law Center, Rm. 326), Tuscaloosa, AL 35486; (205) 345-9411. Interest in revision of Ala. statutes, law reform, legal research. Provides advisory services, seminars. Services provided free or at nominal cost, primarily to Ala. legislators.

01015. Alabama Legislative Reference Service, State Capitol, Ste 220, Montgomery, AL 36130; (205) 261-3023. Provides research reports, documents, court reports, etc. concerning Ala. legislation, govt, economics, and history. Answers inquiries; provides computerized subject index of pending legislation. Services primarily for legislators.

01016. Alabama Soil and Water Conservation Committee, P.O. Box 3336 (1445 Federal Dr), Montgomery, AL 36193; (205) 832-3727. Interest in soil and water conservation in Ala. Provides free conservation literature to school children, provides visual aid programs for church, civic, and school groups.

01017. Alabama Solar Energy Association, c/o Univ of Ala. Huntsville-JEEC, Huntsville, AL 35899; (205) 895-6257. Interest in solar energy, including architectural design, solar technology, heating systems, tax credits, window coatings. Answers inquiries, conducts seminars. Services primarily for members, but others assisted.

01018. Alabama Wildlife Federation, 25 Washington Ave, Ste 107, Montgomery, AL 36104; (205) 832-WILD. Devoted to conservation, wildlife preservation, pollution control, restoration, recreation of Ala. natural resources. Answers inquiries, provides free reference, other services.

01019. American Fertility Foundation, 2131 Magnolia Ave, Ste 201, Birmingham, AL 35256; (205) 251-9764. Assists physicians and consumers in obtaining info about human reproduction, especially infertility. Distributes pamphlets, documents; provides reference services. Services free, except pamphlets.

01022. American Porphyria Foundation, P.O. Box 11163, Montgomery, AL 36111 Nonprofit org that serves as info source about the rare disorder porphyria to patients and physicians. Supported by membership dues and donations.

01023. American Truck Historical Society, 201 Office Park Dr, Birmingham, AL 35223; (205) 879-2131 ext 590. Interest in history of trucks and trucking companies. Provides reproduction services, distributes publications, permits onsite use of collections. Services provided free to members, for a fee to others.

01025. Army Aeromedical Research Laboratory, P.O. Box 577, Fort Rucker, AL 36362; (205) 255-6907. Provides consultation on medical aspects of aviation. Provides reference, literature-searching services; makes interlibrary loans.

01026. Army Missile Laboratory, Army Missile Command, Redstone Arsenal, AL 35898; (205) 876-3251. Contains central collection of scientific info for the Army Missile Command and NASA Marshall Space Flight Center. Provides reference, translation services, provides info on handling and processing data and info, makes interlibrary loans. Services by special arrangement.

01027. Bass Anglers Sportsman Society of America, P.O. Box 17900 (1 Bell Rd), Montgomery, AL 36141; (205) 272-9530. Interest in bass fishing, fish management, pollution abatement. Answers inquiries, conducts seminars. Services free to members.

01028. Biocommunication Research Laboratory, Dept of Biocommunication, Univ of Ala. at Birmingham, Univ Station, Birmingham, AL 35294; (205) 934-4814. Studies oral anatomy and physiology of normal and disabled persons. Provides consulting services and computer software, research info and seminars, fabricates pseudopalates. Services free, except pseudopalates and computer software.

01030. Carver Research Foundation, Tuskegee Univ, Tuskegee, AL 36088; (205) 727-8246. Answers inquiries regarding food and nutritional science, agricultural, natural, and behavioral science research, and chemistry. Holdings include census data, anthropological, energy, and natl rural development data.

01031. Center for Aging, Univ of Ala. at Birmingham, OBSB Box 32 (933 S 19th St), Univ Station, Birmingham, AL 35223; (205) 934-3260. Info center on problems of aging, including Alzheimer's Disease. Offers educational programs at graduate level, initiates delivery of services to the elderly. Provides advisory services, conducts seminars. Some services free, others at cost.

01032. Center for Business and Economic Research, Coll of Commerce and Business Administration, Univ of Ala., P.O. Box AK, University, AL 35486; (205) 348-6191. Provides consulting, reference, and duplication services on business, economics, population. Also offers special tabulations from census summary tapes. Fees for data used in funded research.

01033. Civil Air Patrol National Headquarters, Aerospace Education Directorate, Maxwell Air Force Base, AL 36112; (205) 293-5371. Provides professional consultation services in aerospace education and training.

01034. Comet Information Center, Museum of Natural History, Univ of Ala., Box 5897 (Smith Hall, Rm 105), Tuscaloosa, AL 35486; (205) 348-7550. Interest in astronomy, Halley's comet, meteorites, stargazing. Provides free advisory, reference services.

01035. Dauphin Island Marine Repository, Marine Environmental Sciences Consortium, P.O. Box 369-370, Dauphin Island, AL 36528; (205) 861-2141. Interest in hydrography and ecology of estuaries, particularly Mobile Bay, Mississippi Sound, and adjacent continental shelf; zoogeography of northern Gulf of Mexico. Makes interlibrary loans with standard request form; duplication services for a fee.

01036. Department of Fisheries and Allied Aquacultures, Swingle Hall, Auburn Univ, AL 36849; (205) 826-4786. Interest in research, management of warm-water fish species. Answers inquiries, provides consulting services. Services available to scientists, fishery biologists, fish farmers.

01037. Ethnic American Art Slide Library, College of Arts and Sciences, Univ of South Ala., Univ Blvd, Mobile, AL 36699; (205) 460-6337. Sells duplicates of slides of 19th and 20th Century ethnic American art to educational institutions and individual researchers.

01038. Human Resources Development Center, Tuskegee Univ, P.O. Box 681, Tuskegee Institute, AL 36088; (205) 727-8764. Concerned with community, rural, and economic development, food and nutrition, youth leadership, and rural community education. Evaluates data, provides advisory, research, and current-awareness services.

01039. Institute of Higher Education Research and Services, Univ of Ala., P.O. Box 6293, Univ, AL 35486; (205) 348-6060. Interest in higher education, including manpower and community assessments. Answers inquiries, provides consulting services. Free to faculty, administrators, educational specialists in postsecondary education.

01040. International Association of Educators for World Peace, c/o Charles Mercieca, Ph.D., Exec V.P., P.O. Box 3282, Blue Spring Station, Huntsville, AL 35810; (205) 859-7429. Promotes intl understanding, world peace, human welfare, environmental protection through education. Provides advisory, reference services; conducts seminars, workshops; evaluates, analyzes data. Fee for some services.

01041. International Center for Aquaculture, Auburn Univ, Auburn, AL 36830; (205) 826-4786. Conducts surveys worldwide evaluating aquaculture potential, developing plans for increasing fish production in developing countries, and providing resident advisors for projects. Offers advisory services, info on R&D in progress; conducts seminars, workshops; analyzes data.

01042. International Fertilizer Development Center, P.O. Box 2040, Muscle Shoals, AL 35660; (205) 381-6600. Interest in improving fertilizer processing, manufacturing, marketing, effectiveness, and forecasting world fertilizer supply and demand. Provides literature-searching, training programs, data evaluation, other services. Some fees.

01043. Laboratory of Exocrine Physiology, Dept of Physiology and Biophysics, Univ of Ala. at Birmingham, Univ Station, Birmingham, AL 35294; (205) 934-4588. Interest in salivary gland physiology and growth, autonomic nervous system, autonomic regulation of electrolyte secretion, cystic fibrosis. Provides advisory and current-awareness services, info on research. Services free.

01044. Laboratory of Medical Genetics, School of Medicine, Univ of Ala. at Birmingham, Univ Station, Birmingham, AL 35294; (205) 934-4968. Interest in medical and biochemical genetics, cytogenetics, genetic counseling, birth defects, prenatal detection of genetic disorders. Provides reference, consulting, clinical services; conducts seminars. Services on sliding-fee basis available to referred patients, their families, and health professionals.

01045. Lister Hill Library of the Health Sciences, Univ of Ala. at Birmingham, Univ Station, Birmingham, AL 35294; (205) 934-5460. Interest in medicine, dentistry, nursing, public health, optometry, allied health sciences. Provides advisory, reference, literature-searching services, conducts seminars, permits onsite use of collections. Some services free, and available to Ala. health professionals.

01046. Ludwig von Mises Institute, Auburn Univ, 213 Thach Hall, Auburn, AL 36849; (205) 826-2500. Interest in free market school of economics. Permits onsite use of collections; conducts seminars, workshops. Services free, except publications.

01047. Maxillofacial Prosthetics Center, Univ of Ala. at Birmingham, 1717 Sixth Ave S, Birmingham, AL 35294; (205) 934-3356. Provides advisory services, seminars, on maxillofacial prosthetics, cancer rehabilitation, cleft-lip and palate prostheses, prosthetic rehabilitation of congenital, developmental, and acquired defects of the head and neck. Services free.

01048. Medical Rehabilitation Research and Training Center in Spinal Cord Dysfunction, School of Medicine, Univ of Ala. at Birmingham, Univ Station, Birmingham, AL 35294; (205) 934-3334. Interest in all physical, psychological, behavioral aspects of spinal cord injury or dysfunction. Provides advisory, consulting services and info on research, conducts workshops and seminars, evaluates data. Applicability of fees depends on service requested.

01049. Military Police Association Fund, USAMPS &

CS/TC & FM, Ft McClellan, AL 36205; (205) 238-3851. Answers inquiries from military, civilian law enforcement agencies and other interested parties. Services free.

01050. Mineral Resources Institute, State Mine Experiment Station, Univ of Ala., Drawer AY, Univ, AL 35486; (205) 348-6577. Interest in mineral resources, extraction, processing, evaluation. Answers inquiries, provides consulting services.

01051. Minerals and Materials Research, Bureau of Mines, Box L, Univ, AL 35486; (205) 758-0491. Provides technical consultation on industrial mineral, refractory, ceramic, and aqueous and gaseous waste problems; tests and evaluates clays.

01052. Multipurpose Arthritis Center, School of Medicine, Univ of Ala. at Birmingham, Univ Station, Birmingham, AL 35294; (205) 934-5304. Conducts research, provides training, offers education in diagnosis, control, and treatment of arthritis. Provides advisory, translation services, research info, conducts seminars. Fee for some services.

01053. National Fertilizer Library, Tennessee Valley Authority, Muscle Shoals, AL 35660; (205) 386-2871. Interest in fertilizer production, application, distribution and marketing, toxic impurities. Provides reference, reproduction, manual and computerized literature-searching services, permits onsite use of collection. Services free, except online searches and reproduction services.

01054. National Speleological Society, Cave Ave, Huntsville, AL 35810; (205) 852-1300. Maintains files covering every known cave in U.S. Provides consulting, reference, literature-searching services. Other than copying and mailing costs, services to govt free, depending on scope. Fees to private industry.

01055. National Tillage Machinery Laboratory, Agricultural Research Service, USDA, P.O. Box 792, (Donahue Dr and Samford Ave) Auburn, AL 36831-0792; (205) 887-8596. Interest in tillage, physical properties of soils, root growth, earth moving, soil dynamics. Provides informal consulting, in-house literature-searching services, lends materials, permits onsite use of collections.

01056. Nuclear Science Center, Auburn Univ, AL 36849; (205) 826-4230. Research and training facility interested in pure and applied aspects of nuclear science, radioisotope and radiation applications. Answers inquiries, provides consulting services.

01057. Professional Convention Management Association, c/o Roy B. Evans, 2027 First Ave N, Ste 1007, Birmingham, AL 35203; (205) 251-1717. Seeks to improve management of professional meetings in medicine, medical sciences, and allied professions. Provides consulting services, makes referrals.

01059. Society of Logistics Engineers, Park Plaza, 303 Williams Ave, Ste 992, Huntsville, AL 35801; (205)

539-3800. Interest in logistics engineering and management. Provides advisory, reference services; conducts symposia, seminars, annual convention. Services free to members and interested others.

01060. Southeastern Fish Cultural Laboratory, U.S. Fish and Wildlife Service, Rte 3, Box 86, Marion, AL 36756; (205) 683-6175. Researches husbandry, nutrition, genetics, and disease relating to warm-water and intermediate zone fishes, particularly striped bass and catfish. Answers inquiries, permits onsite use of collections.

01061. Southern Building Code Congress International, 900 Montclair Rd, Birmingham, AL 35213-1206; (205) 591-1853. Involved in administration, enforcement of building, fire regulations. Interest in model building codes, building construction, inspection, rehabilitation, historic preservation, swimming pools, energy conservation, amusement devices. Provides advisory and consulting services, some limited to membership.

01062. Southern Poverty Law Center, P.O. Box 2087 (1001 South Hull St), Montgomery, AL 36104; (205) 264-0286. Provides legal services for poor and minorities, including advisory, consulting, and current-awareness services about Ku Klux Klan, death penalty, poverty, voting rights, mental illness, legal issues. Answers inquiries free; fee for some services.

01063. Southern Research Institute, 2000 Ninth Ave S, Birmingham, AL 35205; (205) 323-6592. Provides info services concerning chemistry, engineering, physics, pharmacology, biological sciences, metallurgy, plastics, polymers, water desalination, cancer and virus chemotherapy. Makes photocopies of articles on fee basis, provides reference services, performs contract research, permits onsite use of collection during off-hours.

01064. Sparks Center for Developmental and Learning Disorders, Univ of Ala. at Birmingham, P.O. Box 313, (1720 Seventh Ave), Univ Station, Birmingham, AL 35294; (205) 934-5471. Offers training in interdisciplinary setting for professionals who work with developmentally disabled persons. Provides technical consulting to agencies and consumer groups, provides research info, evaluates data. Fee for some services.

01065. State Museum of Natural History, Univ of Ala., Box 5897, Smith Hall, Univ, AL 35486; (205) 348-7550. Interest in natural history, including paleontology, entomology, mammalogy, anthropology. Identifies specimens, permits onsite use of collections by qualified scientists.

01066. TVA Office of Agricultural and Chemical Development, Tennessee Valley Authority, National Fertilizer Development Ctr, Muscle Shoals, AL 35660; (205) 386-2601. Supplies technical material and info on all phases of fertilizer research, development, and use. Answers inquiries by correspondence.

01067. U.S. Army Aviation Museum, P.O. Box H, Fort Rucker, AL 36362; (205) 255-4507. Contains army avia-

tion aircraft and equipment, technical orders, manuals, documents, and photographs. Answers inquiries, provides limited reference services. Open to public.

01068. U.S. Army Safety Center, Ft Rucker, AL 36362; (205) 255-6510. Supports and assists army safety program by investigating and reporting aircraft/mishap reports. Gives presentations on accident prevention. Some safety-related materials provided free, others for a fee. Info requests must be in writing.

01069. USAF Historical Research Center, Maxwell Air Force Base, AL 36112; (205) 293-5958. Dedicated to history of U.S. Air Force. Provides advisory and reference services; interlibrary loan service limited almost completely to fed govt. Unclassified materials available to general public for onsite use.

01070. United States Sports Academy, P.O. Box 8650, Mobile, AL 36609; (205) 343-7700. Interest in sport management, medicine, fitness, coaching. Provides literature searches and copying services, makes interlibrary loans.

01071. University of Alabama Arboretum, Biology Dept, P.O. Box 1927, Univ, AL 35486; (205) 348-5960. Collects native and exotic plants. Answers inquiries, permits onsite use of collection, with special tours on request. Services free.

01072. University of North Alabama Planetarium and Observatory, Florence, AL 35632; (205) 766-4100 ext 284. Interest in astronomy and astronomy education. Answers inquiries, provides advisory and reference services. Planetarium shows for a fee. Observatory open to public.

01073. Von Braun Astronomical Society, P.O. Box 1142, Huntsville, AL 35807; (205) 539-0316. Interest in amateur astronomy. Conducts planetarium shows, star parties, and open-house showings for a fee.

01074. Water Resources Research Institute, 202 Hargis Hall, Auburn, AL 36849; (205) 826-5075. Interest in water resources and research, water supply and use, wells, hydraulics, water pollution, conservation, microbiology. Answers inquiries, makes referrals, permits onsite use of collection.

Alaska

02001. Alaska Agricultural Experiment Station, Univ of Alaska, Fairbanks, AK 99701; (907) 474-7188. Maintains reference collection for study of subarctic agriculture and horticulture. Answers inquiries, provides advisory and data evaluation services. Most services free to agricultural and related groups.

02002. Alaska Center for the Environment, 1069 W 6th Ave, Anchorage, AK 99501; (907) 274-3621. Provides info on environmental topics; works to protect public use lands, maintain environment. Provides general reference services, conducts seminars and workshops. Most services free.

02003. Alaska Cooperative Fishery Research Unit, Univ of Alaska, 138 Arctic Health Bldg, Fairbanks, AK 99701; (907) 474-7661. Conducts education, research programs on Alaskan freshwater ecosystems. Answers inquiries, provides consulting and other services, conducts seminars, permits onsite use of collection. Services free.

02004. Alaska Cooperative Wildlife Research Unit, Univ of Alaska, Fairbanks, AK 99701; (907) 474-7673. Researches Alaskan wildlife biology, ecology, animal behavior, population dynamics. Provides consulting, bibliographic, and wildlife identification services; permits onsite use of collections. Services primarily for students.

02005. Alaska Department of Transportation and Public Facilities, Div of Planning, 2301 Peger Rd (306 Tanana Dr, Univ of Alaska Campus), Fairbanks, AK 99701; (907) 479-2241. Tests, evaluates, develops highway, building construction and maintenance techniques for Dept of Transportation and Public Facilities. Answers inquiries, provides advisory services.

02006. Alaska Geographic Society, P.O. Box 4-EEE, Anchorage, AK 99509; (907) 274-0521. Maintains reference collection of periodicals about geography of Alaska and northwestern Canada. Answers inquiries free.

02007. Alaska Geological Society, P.O. Box 1288, Anchorage, AK 99510. Provides info on geology, related earth sciences; oil, gas, and mineral exploration. Distributes publications, makes referrals to other info sources. Services provided for fee.

02008. Alaska Historical Commission, Old City Hall, 524 W 4th Ave, Ste 207, Anchorage, AK 99501; (907) 274-6222. Provides advisory and evaluation services on Alaskan history. Conducts seminars, workshops; offers research, publications grants.

02009. Alaska Historical Library Collection, Alaska State Library, Pouch G (State Office Bldg), Juneau, AK 99811; (907) 465-2925. Maintains research collections covering all Alaskan and arctic topics, historical periods. Answers inquiries, provides citation and bibliographic services, permits onsite use of collection.

02010. Alaska Historical Society, 524 W 4th, No 208, Anchorage, AK 99501; (907) 276-1596. Provides current-awareness service about ongoing research of Alaskan history and archeology. Conducts seminars and workshops, makes referrals to other info sources. Services free.

02011. Alaska Historical and Transportation Museum, Box 920 (Mile 40.2 Glenn Hwy, Alaska State Fairgrounds), Palmer, AK 99645; (907) 745-4493. Promotes charitable, educational, research use of Alaskan industrial, transportation artifacts. Answers inquiries, provides tours and presentations. Open daily year-round at no charge.

02012. Alaska State Council on the Arts, 619 Warehouse Ave, Ste 220, Anchorage, AK 99501; (907) 279-1558. Provides grants and services to arts orgs and artists in Alaska. Provides advisory, consulting, reference services; conducts seminars, workshops. Services available to the public.

02013. Alaska State Museum, Pouch FM, Juneau, AK 99811; (907) 465-2901. Collects Alaskan artifacts, coordinates development of museums statewide. Provides general reference services. Permits onsite use of collections. Services free, available to public, nonprofit institutions.

02014. Arctic Environmental Information and Data Center, 707 A St, Anchorage, AK 99501; (907) 279-4523. Central referral center for Alaskan environmental knowledge and data. Provides general reference services, permits onsite use of collections. Services free, unless extensive.

02015. Bureau of Mines, Alaska Field Operations Center, P.O. Box 550 (Juneau Island, Douglas, AK), Juneau, AK 99802; (907) 364-2111. Conducts engineering, geological studies of mineral reserves and resources; studies production methods; develops conservation programs. Provides general reference services, permits onsite use of collection. Services free, most without restriction.

02016. Center for Cross-Cultural Studies, Univ of Alaska, Fairbanks, AK 99701; (907) 474-7143. Provides interdisciplinary instructional programs to improve public education in Alaska. Provides advisory, consulting, and referral services. Most services free.

02017. Elmer E. Rasmuson Library, Univ of Alaska, Fairbanks, AK 99701; (907) 479-7482. Contains reference materials relating to Alaska and polar regions. Provides advisory, reference, literature-searching, abstracting, other services. Onsite use of materials permitted. Restricts borrowing to univ cardholders.

02018. Geophysical Institute, Univ of Alaska, Fairbanks, AK 99701; (907) 474-7503. Studies geophysics, geochemistry, climatology. Provides consulting and literature-searching services. Fee for some services.

02019. Institute of Arctic Biology, Univ of Alaska, Fairbanks, AK 99701; (907) 474-7640. Studies tundra and taiga ecosystem, plant and animal physiology, biology, ecology. Provides analysis and referral services, distributes publications. Seminars free to public; workshops closed.

02021. Institute of Marine Science Library, Univ of Alaska, Fairbanks, AK 99701; (907) 479-7740. Provides reference info on ocean biology, chemistry and geology. Bibliographic instruction, data base searches, and other services available. Permits onsite use of collection.

02022. Institute of Social and Economic Research, Univ of Alaska, 707 A St, Anchorage, AK 99501; (907) 278-4621. Researches political, cultural, sociological, and economic aspects of arctic life. Answers inquiries, provides advisory services and statistical analyses. Services limited by staff capabilities.

02023. Institute of Water Resources/Engineering Experiment Station, Univ of Alaska, Fairbanks, AK 99775-1760; (907) 474-7775. Provides biological, chemical, and hydrologic info on Alaskan waters; studies problems of waste treatment. Answers inquiries free, provides advisory, consulting services for fee.

02024. Mineral Industry Research Laboratory, School of Mineral Engineering, Univ of Alaska, Fairbanks, AK 99701. Concerned with basic and applied research to develop Alaska mineral industry. Provides advisory, reference, literature-searching services; conducts seminars, workshops. Services free.

02025. Missing Children of America, P.O. Box 10-1938 (3136 Old Seward Hwy), Anchorage, AK 99503; (907) 272-8484. Aids missing children in the U.S. Educates public about child abduction, provides free advisory, consulting, referrals, other services.

02026. National Marine Fisheries Service, Auke Bay Fisheries Laboratory, NOAA, P.O. Box 210155, Auke Bay, AK 99821; (907) 789-7231. Maintains research areas and collections for study of marine biology, oceanography, ecology. Answers inquiries, lends specimens to recognized taxonomists associated with academic or govt orgs.

02027. National Marine Fisheries Service, Kodiak Investigations, NOAA, Box 1638, Kodiak, AK 99615; (907) 487-4961. Provides resources for study of marine and fishery biology of Gulf of Alaska and eastern Bering Sea. Answers inquiries, provides consulting, analyses, and referral services, permits onsite use of collections.

02029. Office of Earthquakes, Volcanoes, and Engineering, U.S. Geological Survey, College Observatory, 800 Yukon Dr, Fairbanks, AK 99701; (907) 479-6146. Records all components of Earth's magnetic field. Answers inquiries, provides reference services, evaluates and analyzes data. Data available on exchange basis to educational, scientific orgs.

02030. Trustees for Alaska, 725 Christensen Dr, Ste 4, Anchorage, AK 99501; (907) 276-4244. Public interest law firm specializing in Alaskan environmental issues. Monitors compliance with environmental regulations, advises citizen groups, litigates; offers free advisory and referral services.

02031. University of Alaska Museum, 907 Yukon Dr, Fairbanks, AK 99701; (907) 474-7505. Collection of natural and cultural Alaskan artifacts. Conducts educational and children's programs. Open to public.

Arizona

03001. Aerial Phenomena Research Organization, 3910 E Kleindale Rd, Tucson, AZ 85716; (602) 323-1825. Interest in reports and photos relating to UFOs. Publishes monthly bulletins, answers inquiries, provides consulting, reference, and duplication services. Services provided selectively; nominal fee usually charged.

03002. Agricultural Experiment Station, Univ of Ariz., Tucson, AZ 85721; (602) 621-7192. Studies agricultural economics, arid lands, entomology, related fields. Documents focus on arid land development. Publishes quarterly, technical bulletins. Answers inquiries, makes referrals, permits onsite use of collections.

03003. Agricultural Research Service, USDA, 2000 E Allen Rd, Tucson, AZ 85719; (602) 629-6881. Controls weeds and brush on grazing lands. Studies soil erosion, quantity, quality of runoff water. Maintains collection of books, periodicals, and reports. Answers inquiries, makes referrals, provides consulting and reference services.

03004. American Academy of Dental Practice Administration, c/o Exec Secty, 15609 Meadow, Park Dr, Sun City, AZ 85351; (602) 972-8405. Interest in all aspects of dental practice administration. Provides guidance, disseminates health info to dental profession and public. Tapes of annual conference presentations available for a fee.

03005. American Automatic Control Council, Secretariat, 1051 Camino Velasquez, Green Valley, AZ 85614; (602) 625-0401. Interest in automatic control and instrumentation of systems in fields of science, technology, and society. Answers inquiries about activities of Intl Federation of Automatic Control, conducts annual conference.

03007. American Burn Association, c/o Thomas L. Wach, M.D., Secty, 1130 E McDowell Rd, Ste B-2, Phoenix, AZ 85006; (602) 239-2391. Sponsors studies and research in treatment and prevention of burns. Publishes newsletters, standards, and directories, makes referrals to other sources. Fees vary.

03008. American Compensation Association, P.O. Box 1176 (6619 N Scottsdale Rd), Scottsdale, AZ 85252; (602) 951-9191. Researches compensation at all levels. Publishes newsletter, placement bulletin, technical reports. Answers inquiries, provides reference services, manages certification program for compensation professionals. Fee for some services.

03009. American Federation of Astrologers, P.O. Box 22040 (6535 S Rural Rd), Tempe, AZ 85282; (602) 838-1751. Interest in education and research on astrology. Publishes monthly bulletin, books, technical reports, standards, data compilations, and reprints. Makes referrals to other sources of info. Services generally free to members.

03010. American Graduate School of International Management, Thunderbird Campus, Glendale, AZ 85306; (602) 978-7232. Studies international commerce and foreign trade. Maintains collection of books and current periodicals. Answers inquiries and provides reference services. Faculty provides consulting services, usually for a fee.

03011. American Indian Consultants, 2070 E Southern Ave, Tempe, AZ 85282; (602) 945-2635. Develops capacity of Indian managers to use available resources. Answers inquiries, provides advisory, consulting, and technical assistance, conducts seminars and workshops. Services primarily under contract, but others assisted.

03012. American Science Fiction Association, P.O. Box 9010, Scottsdale, AZ 85252; (602) 677-2424. Specializes in fiction, science fiction, fantasy, and futuristic evaluations. Publishes *Androidian Magazine, SF Abstracts,* and related materials. Conducts seminars and workshops, makes referrals, makes interlibrary loans for nominal fee.

03013. American Video Association, 557 E Juanita, No 3, Mesa, AZ 85204; (602) 892-8553. Represents independent retailers of consumer video equipment. Answers inquiries, distributes publications, provides referral services. Services primarily for dues-paying members, but others assisted.

03014. Amerind Foundation, Dragoon, AZ 85609; (602) 586-3003. Interest in anthropology and archaeology of Americas, archaeological field work in Southwest, and material culture of native Americans. Extensive museum holdings. Museum, library, and photographic collections available for research by appointment.

03015. Appleton-Whittell Research Ranch Sanctuary, Box 44, Elgin, AZ 85611; (602) 455-5522. Dedicated to conservation and research of plant and animal life and habitats. Serves as outdoor laboratory for broad range of environmental and ecological studies. Answers inquiries and makes referrals. Self-guided tours in small groups.

03016. Applied Computer Research, P.O. Box 9280, Phoenix, AZ 85068; (602) 995-5929. Publishes computer and data processing related info, including monthly newsletters and semi-annual reference directories. Price list with content description available.

03017. Arabian Horse Owners Foundation, 4633 E Broadway, Ste 131, Tucson, AZ 85711; (602) 326-1515. Interest in heritage and use of Arabian horses. Answers inquiries, provides referrals services, conducts seminars and workshops, permits onsite use of collections. Services free, except research.

03018. Arizona Commission of Agriculture and Horticulture, 1688 W Adams St, Rm 421, Phoenix, AZ 85007; (602) 255-4373. Interest in regulation of agriculture and horticulture. Maintains related plant and entomological collections. Answers inquiries, provides consulting services, identifies insect and plant disease specimens, makes referrals, permits onsite use of collections.

03019. Arizona Commission on the Arts, 2024 N 7th St, Ste 201, Phoenix, AZ 85006; (602) 255-5882. Funds nonprofit arts projects, maintains resource center for artists and arts administration in visual arts, writing, and music. Publishes quarterly and related materials. Answers inquiries, conducts programs, makes referrals.

03020. Arizona Cooperative Fishery Research Unit, 210 Biological Sciences East, Univ of Ariz., Tucson, AZ 85721; (602) 621-1959. Researches fisheries biology, limnology, aquatic ecology, and water quality. Answers inquiries, provides consulting services, makes referrals to other sources of info. Services free.

03021. Arizona Cooperative Wildlife Research Unit, Univ of Ariz., Biological Sciences Bldg, Rm 214, Tucson, AZ 85721; (602) 621-7297. Interest in research projects on animal populations in Southwest. Publishes technical reports, books, and reprints. Answers inquiries, distributes publications, conducts seminars.

03023. Arizona Game and Fish Department, 2222 W Greenway Rd, Phoenix, AZ 85023; (602) 942-3000. Interest in wildlife and conservation. Publishes *Wildlife Views,* pamphlets, annual reports. Answers inquiries and makes referrals. Originates weekly radio programs.

03024. Arizona Historical Society Library, 949 E 2nd St, Tucson, AZ 85719; (602) 628-5774. Maintains books, historical photographs, and related materials on history of Ariz. and Southwest. Answers inquiries, provides duplication services, sells copies of photographs.

03025. Arizona Oil and Gas Conservation Commission, 1645 W Jefferson St, Ste 420, Phoenix, AZ 85007; (602) 255-5161. Interest in administration and enforcement of statutes, rules, and regulations relating to exploration of oil, gas, helium, and geothermal resources in Ariz. Answers inquiries, provides info, and permits onsite use of collections. Services free.

03026. Arizona Solar Energy Commission, Capitol Tower, Rm 502, 1700 W Washington St, Phoenix, AZ 85007; (602) 255-3682. Center for Ariz. solar energy effort. Publishes reports and workbooks for homeowners, builders, and others. Answers inquiries, provides limited reference services and info on R&D. Advises companies on marketing. Services free.

03027. Arizona State Museum, Univ of Ariz., Tucson, AZ 85721; (602) 626-1180. Interest in archaeology and ethnography of Indian cultures of Southwest and Mexico. Archaeological collections contain specimens and photographs, books, and archives. Access to scientific or academic researchers.

03028. Arizona Wildlife Federation, P.O. Box 15666 (3935 N 31st St), Phoenix, AZ 85060; (602) 946-6160. Promotes use and management of natural resources in Ariz. Publishes monthly, answers inquiries, makes referrals, and provides reference services. Services free to members, at cost to others.

03029. Arizona-Sonora Desert Museum, Rte 9, Box 900 (Kinney Rd, Tucson Mountain Park), Tucson, AZ 85743; (602) 883-1380. Interest in zoology, botany, and geology of Ariz., Sonora, and Baja Calif., with emphasis on Sonoran Desert. Publishes newsletters, annual report, bulletins. Answers inquiries, makes referrals, provides consulting. Access for nonmembers by permission.

03030. Armour Research Center Library, 15101 N Scottsdale Rd, Scottsdale, AZ 85260; (602) 998-6120. Interest in meats, dairy, and poultry products, sausage development, soaps, and floor care products. Maintains collection of related books and journals. Special collection of cookbooks dates back to 1800's. Provides photocopying services.

03031. Army Intelligence Center and School, Library, Ft Huachuca, AZ 85613; (602) 538-7930 or 538-7390. Interest in books, reports, periodicals on military intelligence, history, and intl relations. Answers inquiries, provides reference and bibliographic services. Services free, available by appointment.

03032. Art Libraries Society of North America, 3775 Bear Creek Circle, Tucson, AZ 85749; (602) 749-9112. Promotes use of art libraries and visual resources collections. Publishes newsletter and related materials. Answers inquiries, makes referrals, conducts conferences, seminars, and workshops. Nominal fees for publications and programs.

03033. Association for Fathers and Children Together, P.O. Box 7162, Phoenix, AZ 85011; (602) 247-9715. Interest in fathers' rights involving divorce and child custody. Publishes monthly newsletter, provides reference services. Membership open to all.

03034. Astronomical League, c/o Don Archer, Exec Secty, P.O. Box 12821, Tucson, AZ 85732. Interest in observation and education in astronomy. Publishes quarterly and books, answers inquiries regarding league activities, makes referrals, and advises on technical problems. Some program materials available on loans to members.

03035. Boyce Thompson Southwest Arboretum, P.O. Box AB, Superior, AZ 85273; (602) 689-2811. Interest in plants and animals of arid regions. Maintains specimens of living plants, shrubs, trees. Publishes quarterly journal on subjects related to arid land plants. Answers inquiries, provides consulting services.

03036. Bureau of Applied Research in Anthropology, Univ of Ariz., Tucson, AZ 85721; (602) 621-6282. Dedicated to basic research and application of anthropological approaches to practical problems. Answers inquiries, makes referrals, provides consulting services, permits onsite use of collections. Services free.

03037. Center for Arid and Tropical New Crop Applied Science and Technology, Div of Agriculture, Rm 221, Ariz. State Univ, Tempe, AZ 85287; (602) 965-1260. Conducts lab and field investigations, publishes technical reports, standards, and feasibility studies. Answers inquiries and provides assistance in developing businesses. Fees for extensive services.

03038. Center for Indian Education, Coll of Education, Ariz. State Univ, Farmer Education Bldg, Rm 302, Tempe, AZ 85287; (602) 965-6292. Provides graduate academic programs, research, and educational services related to education and American Indians. Permits onsite use of archives, publishes related materials, conducts programs, makes referrals. Services free.

03039. Center for Latin American Studies, Ariz. State Univ, Tempe, AZ 85281; (602) 965-5058. Supporting agency for schools offering degrees and/or undertaking research emphasizing Latin America. Answers inquiries, makes referrals, distributes publications. Services free, except publications.

03040. Center for Meteorite Studies, Ariz. State Univ, Tempe, AZ 85287; (602) 965-6511. Maintains collection of meteorite specimens and related reports. Answers inquiries, provides reference, literature-searching, and reproduction services, permits onsite use of collections. Services free to qualified investigators.

03041. Center for the Study of Deserts and Oceans, Dept of Ecology and Evolutionary Biology, Univ of Ariz., Tucson, AZ 85721; (602) 621-7287. Interest in research directed toward flora and fauna studies, ecology, and oceanography of Northern Gulf of Calif., with special programs in mariculture, ecology, behavior, physiology, etc. Answers inquiries, provides some consulting services at cost.

03042. Citizens for Decency Through Law, 2331 Royal Palm Rd, Ste 105, Phoenix, AZ 85026; (602) 995-2600. Combats obscenity and pornography. Provides legal assistance to those prosecuting obscenity and pornography. Answers inquiries, provides advisory and consulting services, conducts seminars and conferences. Services free.

03043. Colorado River Indian Tribes Public Library, Rte 1, Box 23-B, Parker, AZ 85344; (602) 669-9211 ext 211. Maintains general publications, collections, and microfilm related to history of Mohave and Chemehueve tribes. Answers inquiries, provides reference services, makes interlibrary loans. Services free.

03044. Commission on Accreditation of Rehabilitation Facilities, 2500 N Pantano Rd, Tucson, AZ 85715; (602) 886-8575. Interest in accountability authority and quality control intermediary for orgs and programs serving disabled. Sets standards, distributes publications, answers inquiries from public. Seminars and site surveys provided to rehabilitation facilities for a fee.

03045. Community Artists Project, 902 E Hampton St, Tucson, AZ 85719; (602) 622-1506. Consortium of nonprofit art orgs. Produces art events for disadvantaged and teacher training, provides advisory and reference services. Services and programs primarily for senior citizens and generally free, except for special events.

03046. Community Organization for Drug Abuse, Mental Health and Alcohol, 124 W Thomas Rd, No 110, Phoenix, AZ 85013; (602) 234-0096. Interest in community education and treatment planning of mental health, drug, and alcohol abuse. Publishes semimonthly newsletter, research papers, and directories, collects and evaluates data. Services for a fee.

03047. Consortium for International Development, 5151 E Broadway, Ste 1500, Tucson, AZ 85711; (602) 745-0455. Encourages involvement of member faculties in intl development of arid and subhumid climates. Provides technical assistance, research, consulting, and related services through contracts and grants with donor agencies and host-country govts.

03048. Cosanti Foundation, 6433 Doubletree Rd, Scottsdale, AZ 85253; (602) 948-6145. Interest in R&D of an alternative urban environment. Publishes books, journals, articles, and brochures, provides info on R&D in progress, makes referrals. Services free.

03049. Cotton Research Center of Agricultural Research Service, USDA, 4207 E Broadway, Phoenix, AZ 85040; (602) 261-4221. Interest in research in genetics, breeding, and physiology of cotton. Holds cotton varieties and germplasm accessions. Answers inquiries, makes referrals.

03050. Counselor Training Center, Col of Education, Ariz. State Univ, Tempe, AZ 85287; (602) 965-5067. Interest in physical, social, psychological, and vocational counseling. Maintains occupational info library. Answers inquiries and provides counseling services. Small fee charged per semester for clients.

03051. Court Club Enterprises, 8303 E Thomas Rd, Scottsdale, AZ 85251; (602) 945-0143. Interest in maintenance, management, and marketing of court clubs. Answers inquiries and provides free advisory services. Fee for consulting services, seminars, and publications.

03052. Crash Research Institute, Robertson Research, P.O. Box 968 (1024 E Vista Del Cerro), Tempe, AZ 85281; (602) 966-6690. Studies aircraft and auto accidents and injuries, teaches crash investigation. Collection includes Fed Aviation Administration computer data. Answers inquiries, makes referrals, conducts workshops for a fee.

03053. Dental Information, 2509 N Campbell, Tucson, AZ 85719. Stresses dental self-help. Publishes books, maintains files on mineral metabolism, provides advisory services and info on research in progress, conducts seminars and workshops. Permits onsite examination of holdings. Services free.

03054. Department of Geosciences, Univ of Ariz., Tucson, AZ 85721; (602) 621-6024. Interest in teaching and research in geosciences, with emphasis on economic geology. Publishes faculty materials. Answers inquiries, makes interlibrary loans, provides consulting and referral services. Information services free, except some maps.

03055. Department of Higher and Adult Education, Ariz. State Univ, Tempe, AZ 85281; (602) 965-6248. Interest

in preparation of adult educators in areas of instruction, program planning, and administration. Publishes monographs and occasional papers, provides consulting services.

03056. Desert Botanical Garden, 1201 N Galvin Parkway, Phoenix, AZ 85008; (602) 941-1217. Interest in study of desert plants. Distributes pamphlets and calenders of classes and other events. Answers inquiries, provides plant identification, reference, and consulting services, permits onsite use of collections.

03057. Do It Now Foundation, P.O. Box 5115 (2050 E Univ Dr, Ste 7), Phoenix, AZ 85010; (602) 257-0797. Intl nonprofit org for drug, alcohol, and health education. Answers inquiries, makes referrals, provides advisory services, distributes publications, radio spot announcements, and transit posters. Fee for reproduction services.

03059. Engineering Experiment Station, Univ of Ariz., Tucson, AZ 85721; (602) 626-4433. Publishes reports, bulletins, data, and nonprint materials on diverse modes of engineering. Answers inquiries, distributes publications, makes loans, provides consulting services for a fee.

03060. Environmental Research Laboratory, Univ of Ariz., Tucson Intl Airport, Tucson, AZ 85706; (602) 621-7962. Performs basic and applied research in desert regions in development of advanced technology systems of food and energy production. Answers inquiries, makes referrals, provides consulting services, permits onsite reference.

03062. Group for the Advancement of Psychiatry, c/o Secty, 30 Camino Espanol, Tucson, AZ 85716. Maintains 22 working committees, each concerned with specific aspects of psychiatry. Publishes reports. Inquiries referred to appropriate committee.

03063. Heard Museum of Anthropology and Primitive Art, 22 E Monte Vista Rd, Phoenix, AZ 85004; (602) 252-8840. Interest in North American Indians, with emphasis on Southwest, Mexico, and Indian art. Publishes newsletter, pamphlets, books. Answers inquiries, provides consulting and reference services, permits onsite use of collections. Admission charged.

03064. Herb Information, 2509 N Campbell Ave, No 9, Tucson, AZ 85719. Studies plants in medicine. Maintains data base on uses of wild plants and publishes reference book. Answers inquiries, provides advisory services, conducts seminars and workshops. Services free, except publications.

03065. Institute of Atmospheric Physics, Univ of Ariz., PAS Bldg, Rm 542, Attn: Librarian, Tucson, AZ 85721; (602) 626-1211. Researches climatology and aerosol physics. Publishes reports, answers inquiries, permits onsite reference.

03066. International Academy of Biological Medicine, P.O. Box 31313, Phoenix, AZ 85046; (602) 992-0589. Interest in biological alternatives to conventional therapies and drugs. Answers inquiries and publishes annual member directory, free with SASE.

03067. International Seal, Label, and Cigar Band Society, 8915 E Bellevue St, Tucson, AZ 85715; (602) 296-1048. Interest in collecting all types of labels and seals and conducting research on manufacturers and printers of such items. Answers inquiries, publishes quarterly newsletter, provides reference services at cost to non-members.

03068. International Society of Cryptozoology, P.O. Box 43070, Tucson, AZ 85733; (602) 884-8369. Interest in matters related to animals of unexpected form or size, or unexpected occurrence in time or space. Answers inquiries, provides advisory services, distributes publications for members. Limited services to nonmembers.

03069. Jojoba Growers Association, 3420 E Shea Blvd, No 125, Phoenix, AZ 85028; (602) 996-4563. Promotes jojoba industry. Publishes directory, survey of jojoba under cultivation, related data, and newsletters. Provides info on research in progress, conducts seminars and programs. Services free, except publications.

03070. Key Collectors International, P.O. Box 9397, Phoenix, AZ 85020; (602) 997-2266. Promotes lock and key collecting and history of locks. Publishes journal, conducts seminars and workshops, answers inquiries, provides advisory and referral services for a fee.

03071. Kitt Peak National Observatory Library, P.O. Box 26732 (950 N Cherry Ave), Tucson, AZ 85726; (602) 325-9295. Studies astronomy and astrophysics. Maintains collection of books, periodicals, and journal subscriptions. Answers inquiries, provides reproduction services for a fee, makes interlibrary loans, permits onsite use of collections.

03072. L-5 Society, 1060 E Elm St, Tucson, AZ 85719; (602) 622-6351. Interest in space colonization/industrialization and related concepts. Answers inquiries, supplies info on R&D in progress, provides visual materials for meetings. Services free, except reproduction.

03073. Laboratory of Tree-Ring Research, Univ of Ariz., Tucson, AZ 85721; (602) 621-2191. Interest in all aspects of dendrochronology. Publishes monographs and annual *Tree-Ring Bulletin*. Facilities and collections available to qualified scholars by special arrangement. Some service analyses for a fee.

03074. Lincoln Continental Owners Club, P.O. Box 549, Nogales, AZ 85628; (602) 281-8193. Interest in memorabilia of Lincoln Continentals, model years 1940-71. Publishes bimonthly and quarterly, answers inquiries, makes referrals free. Conducts natl meets and regional and local activities.

03075. Lowell Observatory, Mars Hill Rd, 1400 West, Flagstaff, AZ 86001; (602) 774-3358. Researches solar system, stars, and cosmology. Maintains extensive photographic records and sky surveys. Answers inquiries, permits onsite reference by qualified scientists.

03076. Lunar and Planetary Laboratory, Univ of Ariz., Tucson, AZ 85721; (602) 621-1131. Researches all aspects of solar system. Also interested in theoretical studies. Maintains library. No restrictions on access to info by scientists; limited services to others.

03077. Meteor Crater Museum of Astrogeology, 121 E Birch St, Ste 210, Flagstaff, AZ 86001; (602) 774-8350. Commercial collection of meteorites, tektites, shocked materials, minerals, and museum pieces. Maintains astronaut hall of fame. Answers inquiries, makes referrals. Admission fee for onsite use of collection.

03078. Middle East Studies Association of North America, Dept of Oriental Studies, Univ of Ariz., Tucson, AZ 85721; (602) 621-5850. Promotes study and understanding of Middle East. Answers inquiries, conducts seminars, workshops, and annual meeting. Distributes data, makes referrals. Services for a fee.

03079. Mohave Museum of History and Arts, 400 W Beale St, Kingman, AZ 86401; (602) 753-3195. Interest in history, anthropology, mining info, archaeology of Mohave County, Ariz. Maintains library of books, monographs, and journals. Answers inquiries, makes referrals, provides literature citations. Permits onsite use of collection. Services free.

03080. Museum of Northern Arizona, Route 4, P.O. Box 720 (Ft Valley Rd), Flagstaff, AZ 86001; (602) 774-5211. Interest in Northern Ariz. and Colo. Plateau anthropology, archaeology, biology, ethnology, geology, and art. Publishes journal, technical series, bulletins. Provides reference and loan services. Limited lab space available to visiting scientists.

03082. National Foundation for Asthma, P.O. Box 30069, Tucson, AZ 85751-0069; (602) 323-6046 Provides health services for asthmatics, funds educational programs, provides assistance to patients on basis of ability to pay, publishes booklets on asthma and other allergic diseases. Patients must be referred by a physician.

03083. National Indian Training and Research Center, 2121 S Mill Ave, Ste 218, Tempe, AZ 85282; (602) 967-9484. Trains American Indians for leadership roles, and orients professionals working in Indian communities. Answers inquiries, provides advisory services, conducts research. Services generally on contract.

03084. National Native American Cooperative, Box 5000, San Carlos, AZ 85550; (602) 244-8244 ext 1409. Provides Indian cultural programs for conventions and other meetings. Answers inquiries, provides advisory and referral services, permits onsite use of collections. Info and referrals free; other services for a fee.

03085. National Speakers Association, 4323 N 12th St, Ste 103, Phoenix, AZ 85014; (602) 265-1001. Publishes directory of over 2,000 speakers, including topic specialties. Answers inquiries, distributes directory and informative brochures.

03086. Native American Research Library, P.O. Drawer K, Window Rock, AZ 86515; (602) 871-6730. Archive of Navajo people and other Native American groups. Answers inquiries, provides reference and reproduction services, makes interlibrary loans. Services free.

03087. Navajo Code Talkers Association, P.O. Box 1182, Window Rock, AZ 86515. Interest in use of Navajo speakers as radio operators in World War II. Maintains collections of original documents, tapes, and interviews. Answers inquiries, permits onsite use of collections.

03088. Navajo Tribal Museum, P.O. Box 308, Window Rock, AZ 86515; (602) 871-6673. Collects all aspects of Navajo culture and archeology and history of Southwest. Maintains specimens of plants, fossils, and rocks. Distributes publications, answers brief inquiries, and makes referrals. Museum open to public.

03089. Office of Arid Lands Studies, Univ of Ariz., 845 N Park Ave, Tucson, AZ 85719;(602) 621-1955. Interest in documents, serials, data base dealing with various aspects of arid lands. Publishes newsletter, bibliographies, and environmental profiles. Answers inquiries and provides consulting services to qualified scientists.

03090. Papago Tribe of Arizona, P.O. Box 837, Sells, AZ 85634; (602) 383-2221. Interest in history and culture of Papago Indians. Has materials on Papago Indians and their culture and crafts. Answers inquiries, provides reproduction services at cost, makes referrals.

03091. Phoenix Art Museum, 1625 N Central Ave, Phoenix, AZ 85004; (602) 257-1222. Maintains encyclopedic collection from Renaissance to present, including paintings, graphics, sculptures. Answers inquiries, provides reference services, permits onsite use of collection and library.

03092. Pima Air Museum, 6400 S Wilmot Rd, Tucson, AZ 85706; (602) 574-0462. Interest in collection, preservation, and display of historically significant aircraft, related artifacts, and memorabilia. Inquiries answered and onsite use of materials available by arrangement.

03093. Poetry Center, Univ of Ariz., 1086 N Highland Ave, Tucson, AZ 85719; (602) 621-7941. Sponsors poetry and prose readings. Features tapes of poets reading from their own works. Answers inquiries, makes referrals, provides literature-searching sevices, permits onsite use of collections. Services free.

03094. Post-Tensioning Institute, 301 W Osborn Rd, Ste 3500, Phoenix, AZ 85013; (602) 265-9158. Advances use of fabricated post-tensioning construction materials. Publishes info for adoption of standards, answers inquiries, provides advisory and reference services. Services free to members; limited services to others.

03095. Productivity Institute, Coll of Business, Ariz. State Univ, Tempe, AZ 85287; (602) 965-7626. Liaison to business community for info on productivity improvement. Publishes monthly newsletter, helps orgs develop programs for improving productivity. Permits onsite use of collections. All services at cost.

03096. Pueblo Grande Museum, 4619 E Washington St, Phoenix, AZ 85034; (602) 275-3452. Interest in artifacts related to prehistoric Indians of Salt River Valley. Museum open to public. Lab facilities available to anthropologists and students for onsite use by appointment.

03097. Reading Reform Foundation, 7054 E Indian School Rd, Scottsdale, AZ 85251; (602) 946-3567. Interest in restoration of intensive phonics to beginning reading instruction. Publishes newsletter, technical reports and pamphlets, answers inquiries, provides literature citations, permits onsite use of collection.

03098. Second Harvest, Natl Foodbank Network, 1001 N Central, Ste 303, Phoenix, AZ 85004; (602) 252-1777. Assists food banks to redistribute unsold donated food to charitable organizations. Solicits food donations and provides training and technical assistance to agencies wishing to redistribute surplus food.

03099. Southwest Institute for Research on Women, 269 Modern Languages Bldg, Univ of Ariz., Tucson, AZ 85721; (602) 621-7338. Promotes research on women in Southwest. Maintains clearinghouse of ongoing research on women by scholars and issues publications. Answers inquiries, provides referrals, conducts conferences. Services free.

03100. Southwest Parks and Monuments Association, 221 N Court, Tucson, AZ 85701; (602) 622-1999. Aids and promotes educational and scientific activities of Natl Park Service. Publishes popular books, technical reports, maps, and other interpretive literature. Provides brief answers to technical inquiries and makes referrals.

03101. Southwest Research Station of The American Museum of Natural History, Portal, AZ 85632; (602) 558-2396. Interest in natural history and wildlife research. Maintains reference books and large map collection covering local and adjacent areas. Resources and lab facilities available to qualified scientists.

03102. Stein Engineering Services, 5602 E Monte Rosa, Phoenix, AZ 85018; (602) 945-4603. Interest in engineering of measuring systems, especially in field of experimental mechanics. Provides reference, bibliographic services and special educational programs. Provides review summaries on measuring techniques. Fee for services.

03103. Steward Observatory, Univ of Ariz., Tucson, AZ 85721; (602) 626-2288. Interest in research in fields of observational and theoretical astronomy, operation and development of telescopes and instrumentation for both ground-based and space applications. Answers inquiries, provides consulting services, conducts seminars.

03104. Sunlight Energy Corp., 4411 W Echo Lane, Dept. I, Glendale, AZ 85302; (602) 934-6492 or 949-9975. Commercial firm that designs photovoltaic systems. Publishes technical reports, standards, specifications, and brochures. Inquiries answered free; consulting services for a fee.

03105. U.S. Water Conservation Laboratory, Agricultural Research Service, USDA, 4331 E Broadway, Phoenix, AZ 85040; (602) 261-4356. Conducts research to increase conservation and efficient use of water in systems involving soils, plants, and the atmosphere. Answers inquiries, provides consulting and reference services, permits onsite use of collection.

03106. UFO Information Retrieval Center, Points West No 158, 3131 W Cochise Dr, Phoenix, AZ 85021; (602) 997-1523. Interest in sighting accounts of UFOs and collection of related materials. Answers inquiries, provides consulting and reference services, free to students, at cost to others.

03107. University Council for Educational Administration, 108 Farmer Bldg, Tempe, AZ 85287; (602) 965-6690. Consortium of univs preparing educational administrators. Publishes books, journals, abstracts, and instructional materials. Publications distributed at cost.

03108. University of Arizona Herbarium, 113 Agricultural Sciences Bldg, Tucson, AZ 85721; (602) 621-7243. Studies flora of Southwestern U.S. and Mexico, particularly Ariz. Maintains dried plant specimens. Provides consulting and reference services, identifies plants, lends material to recognized herbaria, permits onsite use of collection.

03109. Walking Association, P.O. Box 37228, Tucson, AZ 85740; (602) 742-9589. Supports walking for health and rights of walkers to a safe environment. Disseminates info, helps form local chapters.

03110. Water Resources Research Center, Univ of Ariz., Tucson, AZ 85721; (602) 621-7607. Coordinates research on all aspects of hydrology and water resources. Maintains reports, reprints, and pamphlets, mostly from state water research institutes. Answers inquiries, makes referrals, permits onsite use, makes interlibrary loans.

03111. Western Humor and Irony Membership, c/o Don L.F. Nilsen, English Dept, Ariz. State Univ, Tempe, AZ 85287. Maintains files on American humor and humorists arranged geographically and alphabetically. Publishes yearbook and reprints. Answers inquiries, provides reference services, sells publications.

03112. Western Single Side Band Association, P.O. Box 1568 (17802 N 132nd Ave), Sun City, AZ 85372. Interest in radio communication by use of suppressed carrier technique. Maintains display of pioneer communication equipment. Answers inquiries, makes referrals, provides consulting services.

03113. Whooping Crane Conservation Association, 3000 Meadowlark Dr, Sierra Vista, AZ 85635; (602) 458-0971. Interest in conservation of whooping cranes. Small reference collection of technical reports, books, and clippings. Publishes quarterly newsletter, answers inquiries.

03114. Yuma Proving Ground Technical Library, U.S. Army Test and Evaluation Command, Yuma, AZ 85365-9103. Maintains collection of military specifications and standards. Answers inquiries, provides advisory and reference services, primarily for Army Materiel Command and other govt agencies, but available to others.

Arkansas

04025. American Association for Rehabilitation Therapy, P.O. Box 93, N Little Rock, AR 72116. Paramedical professional society. Members include educational, manual arts, recreation, and rehabilitation therapists. Provides general reference services, distributes copies of free career information folders, provides article reprints.

04026. American Association of Bible Colleges, P.O. Box 1523, Fayetteville, AR 72701; (501) 521-8164. Natl accrediting agency for Bible colleges. Provides general reference services, distributes publications. Services free to members, at cost to others.

04028. Arkansas Agricultural Experiment Station, Univ of Ark., Fayetteville, AR 72701; (501) 575-2253. Interest in general agriculture, ag economics, entomology, rural sociology, home econ, ag engineering, horticulture, forestry, animal sciences, agronomy, plant pathology, pesticides. Provides general reference services, permits onsite and mail use of collections.

04029. Arkansas Arts Council, 225 E Markham, Ste 200, Little Rock, AR 72201; (501) 371-2539. Channels grants to state cultural orgs, programs, and projects. Technical assistance services limited to Ark. arts orgs; other services available to anyone.

04030. Arkansas Audubon Society, c/o Ellen Neaville, Pres, 8 Brooks Dr, Rogers, AR 72756; (501) 636-8731. Sponsors summer ecology camp and small research projects, and awards scholarships to natl Audobon camps. Provides reference services, speakers, films, educational materials. Services for a fee.

04031. Arkansas Bureau of Environmental Health Services, Radiation Control, and Emergency Management Programs, Ark. Dept of Health, 4815 W Markham St, Little Rock, AR 72201; (501) 661-2301. Interest in regulatory control of ionizing radiation within Ark. Answers inquiries free.

04032. Arkansas Forestry Commission, P.O. Box 4523 (3821 W Roosevelt Rd), Asher Station, Little Rock, AR 72214; (501) 664-2531. Interest in forest protection, fire control, forest insect and disease control, forest planning and improvement. Provides advisory and technical assistance services, distributes data and publications. Services free.

04033. Arkansas Game and Fish Commission, Little Rock, AR 72201; (501) 376-1317. Interest in hunting and fishing in Ark., fish and game mgmt, nongame, endangered species. Answers inquiries, makes referrals.

04034. Arkansas Genealogical Society, P.O. Box 908, Hot Springs, AR 71902. Interest in genealogy and family history. Provides speakers for meetings and historical and genealogical societies; provides general reference services. Brochures, ancestor charts, researchers lists, and other publications sent on request.

04035. Arkansas Geological Commission, 3815 W Roosevelt Rd, Little Rock, AR 72204; (501) 371-1646. Interest in geology, mineral resources, and hydrology of Ark. Answers inquiries, provides limited consulting services to municipalities, permits onsite use of collection.

04036. Arkansas History Commission, One Capitol Mall, Little Rock, AR 72201; (501) 371-2141. Interest in Ark. government, history, and genealogy. Provides general reference services. Collection open to public, manuscript indexes available to researchers.

04037. Arkansas Museum of Science and History, MacArthur Park, Little Rock, AR 72202; (501) 371-3521. Interest in cultural and natural history of Ark., with emphasis on anthropology and ecology. Provides environmental education and extensive educational outreach programming, and reference services. Permits onsite use of collections.

04038. Arkansas Natural and Scenic Rivers Commission, The Heritage Center, Ste 200, 225 E Markham St, Little Rock, AR 72201; (501) 371-8134. Interest in assisting riparian landowners of free-flowing streams, and development of a statewide system of streams. Answers inquiries, distributes publications. Services free, primarily to Ark. residents.

04039. Arkansas State Library, One Capitol Mall, Little Rock, AR 72201; (501) 371-1524. Interests include social, biological, physical sciences, and engineering appropriate to support state library system; children's books, library services for handicapped. Lends books, answers reference requests to county and public libraries, state employees; permits onsite use of collections by any individual.

04040. Arkansas State University Museum, Box 490, State Univ, AR 72467; (501) 972-2074. Interest in natural history, history, and anthropology of Ark., American military history, glass and chinaware, dolls, and buttons. Answers inquiries, makes direct and interlibrary loans, permits onsite use of collections.

04041. Army Office of the Chief of Engineers, U.S. Army Corps of Engineers, P.O. Box 867 (Federal Office Bldg, 700 Capitol Ave), Little Rock, AR 72203; (501) 378-5718. Interest in resources of White River and Ark. River Basins, including flood control, navigation, hydroelectric power, water supply, recreation, fish and

wildlife, development. Answers inquiries, lends materials.

04042. Arts Center of the Ozarks, P.O. Box 725 (216 W Grove St), Springdale, AR 72765; (501) 751-5441. Provides quality arts education and entertainment for northwest Ark. Provides advisory, reference services; conducts seminars, workshops. Fee for some services.

04043. Civil War Round Table Associates, c/o Jerry L. Russell, Natl Chair, P.O. Box 7388 (9 Lefever Lane), Little Rock, AR 72217; (501) 225-3996. Interest in preservation of historic sites of Civil War and American Civil War history. Services free.

04044. Cotton Belt Rail Historical Society, P.O. Box 2044, Pine Bluff, AR 71613; (501) 541-1802. Interest in railway memorabilia and artifacts of the Cotton Belt Railway. Makes referrals to other sources of info. Services at cost.

04045. Department of Entomology, Univ of Ark., Fayetteville, AR 72701; (501) 575-2451. Interest in all aspects of entomology, including biology, ecology, and taxonomic status of insects. Provides general reference services, distributes info on safe use of insecticides and mgmt of insect pests. Most services free.

04046. Engineering Experiment Station, Univ of Ark., W 20th St, Fayetteville, AR 72701; (501) 575-6407. Interest in agricultural, chemical, civil, computer science, electrical, industrial, and mechanical engineering. Answers inquiries, makes referrals, lends materials, permits onsite use of collection.

04047. Fish Farming Experimental Station, U.S. Fish and Wildlife Service, Box 860, Stuttgart, AR 72160; (501) 673-8761. Interest in parasites and diseases of catfish and commercial warmwater fish species. Provides diagnostic and other info on fish culture to federal, state, univ, and private interests.

04048. Graduate Institute of Technology, Univ of Ark. at Little Rock, 33rd and Univ, Little Rock, AR 72204; (501) 373-2720. Interest in process control, contamination, pollution, gas and liquid-solid chromatography, and physical chemistry. Answers inquiries, performs research and provides consulting services for a fee, permits onsite use of collection.

04049. Heifer Project International, P.O. Box 808 (825 W 3rd St), Little Rock, AR 72203; (501) 376-6836. Works at home and abroad through livestock development programs to alleviate hunger, malnutrition, and poverty. Provides free general reference services.

04050. Hot Springs National Park, P.O. Box 1860 (Corner of Central and Reserve Aves), Hot Springs, AR 71901; (501) 624-3383. Interest in Hot Springs National Park, including its geology and thermal waters. Answers inquiries relating to park and interprets park features.

04051. Klipsch and Associates, P.O. Box 688 (Oakhaven), Hope, AR 71801; (501) 777-6751. Interest in stereos, acoustics, loudspeaker design and construction. Answers inquiries, permits onsite reference.

04052. Midsouth Astronomical Research Society, P.O. Box 4145, N Little Rock, AR 72116; (501) 835-8476. Interest in astronomy, including amateur research, especially Mars, Jupiter, Saturn, and principal comets. Provides general reference services, permits onsite use of collection. Services free.

04053. National Center for Toxicological Research, Jefferson, AR 72079; (501) 541-4000. Conducts toxicological research in cancer, birth defects, and inherited defects caused by pesticides and environmental contaminants. Provides consultation and support to research programs; conducts training, workshops, symposia.

04054. National Education Program, Station A, Searcy, AR 72143. Seeks better understanding, greater appreciation of U.S. constitutional govt and private enterprise system, with Biblical morality. Provides general reference services, permits onsite use of collection. Fee for some services.

04055. National River Academy of the USA, P.O. Box 827, Helena, AR 72342; (501) 338-6701. Interest in attracting young people to careers in inland waterways transportation industry. Provides training courses, offers apprentice program and U.S. Coast Guard licensing. Provides general reference services.

04056. Ouachita River Valley Association, P.O. Box 913, Camden, AR 71701; (501) 836-9316. Interest in development and use of commercial waters in Ouachita River Basin in Ark. and La., navigation, flood control, hydroelectric power production, and water supply and quality. Provides general reference services.

04057. Ozark Folk Center, Mountain View, AR 72560; (501) 269-3851. Outdoor museum devoted to depicting traditional Ozark culture. Provides advisory and reference services, permits onsite use of collections. Services free, except for copying, available to those with scholarly interests.

04058. People's Action for a Safe Environment, 322 Watson, Fayetteville, AR 72701; (501) 442-9056. Interest in hazards of nuclear power in Ark. Evaluates and analyzes data, provides general reference services permits use of collections. Services free except printing costs.

04059. Southern Association on Children Under Six, Box 5403, Brady Station, Little Rock, AR 72215; (501) 227-6404. Interest in day care, nursery and kindergarten education, legislation and standards for care and education of children under six. Provides advisory and consulting services, distributes publications. Costs, availability of services, vary.

04060. Water Resources Research Center, Univ of Ark., 223 Ozark Hall, Fayetteville, AR 72701; (501) 575-4403. Interests include water resources, streamflow, aquatic ecology, electronic monitoring of water quality, waste disposal, pollution control, groundwater quality control and mgmt. Answers brief technical inquiries, makes referrals.

04061. Winrock International Institute for Agricultural Development, Route 3, Morrilton, AR 72110; (501) 727-5435. Works with agriculture around the world, collaborates with other institutions with similar interests, permits onsite use of collections. Services free to private and voluntary org personnel and selected others.

California

5018. ABC-Clio Information Services, P.O. Box 4397, 2040 Alameda Padre Serra, Santa Barbara, CA 93103; (805) 963-4221. Interest in world, U.S., and Canadian history, political science, related social sciences and humanities, library science. Sells publications. Databases available through DIALOG Information Services, Inc.

05019. AXIOS, 800 S Euclid St, Fullerton, CA 92632; (714) 526-2131. Acts as an info clearinghouse on the Orthodox Church in America and Orthodox Christian religion throughout the world. Provides general reference services, permits onsite use of collections. Most services free.

05020. Abalone Alliance, 2940 16th St, Ste 310, San Francisco, CA 94103; (415) 861-0592. Nonprofit org of 50 antinuclear/safe energy groups throughout Calif. involved in public education and direct action opposing nuclear power and weapons. Provides general reference services, conducts seminars, permits onsite use of collections. Services free.

05021. Academy of Dentistry International, 7804 Calle Espada, Bakersfield, CA 93309-2702; (805) 832-3236. Provides continuing education for dentists, provides clinicians and lecturers to countries seeking to upgrade the level of dentistry services. Answers inquiries, conducts seminars and workshops. Services free, available to dentists.

05022. Academy of Hospital Public Relations, 870 Market St, Ste 942, San Francisco, CA 94102; (415) 433-3400. Interest in health care public relations, marketing, development, and community relations. Publishes newsletter, standards, critiques of hospital publications. Answers inquiries, provides consulting services. Services provided for a fee to hospital public relations directors and administrators.

05023. Academy of Science Fiction, Fantasy, and Horror Films, 334 W 54th St, Los Angeles, CA 90037; (213) 752-5811. Presents awards of merit and recognition to and promotes science fiction, fantasy, and horror films. Answers inquiries, provides free reference and referral services.

05024. Academy of Scientific Hypnotherapy, P.O. Box 12041, San Diego, CA 92112-3041; (619) 427-6225. Interest in hypnotherapy and hypnotism. Provides advisory, reference, referral, and current-awareness services and research info; permits onsite use of collection. Services primarily for members, but public will be served on receipt of a SASE.

05026. Acoustic Emission Technology Corp. Technical Library, 1824J Tribute Rd, Sacramento, CA 95815; (916) 927-3861. Interest in acoustic emission monitoring technology, testing and applications. Provides general reference services, publishes and distributes materials, permits onsite use of collection. Services available to anyone, except commercial competitors, sometimes for a fee.

05027. Adoptee/Natural Parent Locators-International, P.O. Box 1283, Canyon Country, CA 91351; (805) 251-3536. Helps adoptees, natural parents, and adoptive parents locate one another. Administers special programs relating to adoption problems. Answers inquiries, makes referrals, provides advisory services. Services free to members.

05028. Adult Film Association of America, 1654 Cordova St, Los Angeles, CA 90007; (213) 463-3555. Interest in adult (X-rated) motion picture production, distribution, and exhibition; censorship ordinances and laws; First Amendment rights. Answers inquiries, provides legal advice and interpretations, conducts seminars, and workshops. Services free to members, selectively to others.

05029. Aerobics and Fitness Association of America, 15250 Ventura Blvd, Ste 802, Sherman Oaks, CA 91403; (818) 905-0040. Promotes fitness through aerobic exercise. Offers certification program for aerobic exercise instructors, publishes journal.

05030. Aerojet Ordnance Co., Technical Library, 2521 Michelle Dr, Tustin, CA 92680; (714) 730-6004 ext 368. Interest in ordnance, metallurgy, engineering. Makes interlibrary loans, provides copying services. Library not open to public.

05031. Aerojet-General Corp., Technical Information Center, P.O. Box 13400, Sacramento, CA 95813; (916) 355-4076. Interest in chemistry, rocketry, rocket propellants and propulsion, metallurgy, engineering, mathematics, aeronautics, astronautics. Permits onsite reference by govt employees.

05032. African Studies Association, 255 Kinsey Hall, Univ of Calif. at Los Angeles, 405 Hilgard Ave, Los Angeles, CA 90024; (213) 206-8011. Concerned with scholarly and professional interests in Africa. Publishes *African Studies Review, ASA News,* and related publications. Answers inquiries, provides consulting and reference services, makes referrals. Most services free. Various African studies mailing lists available for rent.

05033. African Studies Center, Univ of Calif., Los Angeles, CA 90024; (213) 825-3686. Answers inquiries on African studies, sponsors interdisciplinary colloquia, conducts seminars, and lectures, permits on site use of collection. Services mostly free.

05034. After Image, 3807 Wilshire Blvd, Ste 250, Los Angeles, CA 90010; (213) 480-1105. Provides photo research and assignment photography services. Maintains collection of over 400,000 photographs in file with additional thousands referenced. Permits onsite use of collections. Services available to those seeking copyright release to publish photographs.

05035. Agri-Silviculture Institute, c/o Paul J. Marks, Pres, Youth Resources, Inc., P.O. Box DD (14580 Mission St), Cabazon, CA 92230. Dedicated to developing tree crop agricultural systems suited to marginal and unproductive lands. Publishes *Experimental Tree Crops List* and state-of-the-art reviews. Invites correspondence and exchanges of info, reports, and seeds.

05036. Aid to Adoption of Special Kids, 3530 Grand Ave, Oakland, CA 94610; (415) 451-1748. Interest in advocacy on behalf of physically/emotionally handicapped children. Provides general reference services, conducts seminars and workshops, distributes publication. Services free.

05037. Air Force Flight Test Center, Technical Library, Stop 238, Edwards Air Force Base, CA 93523; (805) 277-3606. Interest in manned and unmanned aircraft testing, rocket research, propellants, parachute testing, satellite tracking, etc. Provides info on current research, makes interlibrary loans. Govt agencies and their contractors may use collections after obtaining proper clearance.

05038. Air Force Rocket Propulsion Laboratory, Edwards Air Force Base, CA 93523; (805) 277-5014. Interest in propellant and combustion technology, liquid, solid, and nuclear rocket technology. Answers inquiries within scope of laboratory's mission, publishes and distributes materials.

05039. Air Mail Pioneers, c/o Jerome Lederer, Pres, 468-D Calle Cadiz, Laguna Hills, CA 92653; (714) 581-6246. Publicizes accomplishments of Post Office Dept Air Mail Service from 1918 to 1927. Maintains collection of historical photographs and reports. Publishes periodical. Answers inquiries, provides reference services, distributes publication. Services free.

05040. Alexander Lindsay Junior Museum, 1901 First Ave, Walnut Creek, CA 94596; (415) 935-1978. Interest in natural history education, archives, exhibits. Provides general reference services, conducts a wide range of educational programs for children and adults, permits onsite use of collections, lends domestic animal pets.

05041. Alternative Energy Collective, Solar Station, 5829 Adeline St, Oakland, CA 94608; (415) 547-6307. Interest in energy self-reliance education and conservation, alternative energy resources, solar energy. Provides general reference services, evaluates data, conducts classes, permits onsite use of collection. Most services free.

05042. Amalgamated Flying Saucer Clubs of America, P.O. Box 39, Yucca Valley, CA 92284; (619) 365-1141. Interest in flying saucers, extraterrestrial contact and communication, electromagnetic propulsion, etc. Answers inquiries, makes referrals, provides consulting and general reference services.

05043. Amateur Athletic Foundation, L.A. Organizing Committee, 2141 W Adams Blvd, Los Angeles, CA 90018; (213) 730-9600. Interest in sports histories and personalities. Maintains collection of related photos and print materials. Answers inquiries, provides consulting, reference, and reproduction services. Distributes publications and makes referrals. Permits onsite use of collections. Charge for some services.

05044. American Academy of Medical Preventics, 6151 W Century Blvd, Ste 1114, Los Angeles, CA 90045; (213) 645-5350. Interest in preventive medicine, chelation therapy. Provides advisory and referral services, conducts seminars, permits onsite use of collection. Services free, except postage and handling.

05045. American Academy of Ophthalmology, 655 Beach St, P.O. Box 7424, San Francisco, CA 94105; (415) 561-8500. Publishes health educational leaflets, surveys, reports (single copies free) on various aspects of eye care. Answers inquiries, conducts correspondence course for medical assistants.

05046. American Academy of Sports Physicians, 28222 Agoura Road, #105, Agoura, CA 91301; (818) 991-6740. Org of medical doctors and osteopaths involved in clinical, academic, and research problems in sports medicine. Acts as clearinghouse for sports medicine research. Holds annual meeting.

05047. American Allergy Association, P.O. Box 7273, Menlo Park, CA 94026; (415) 322-1663. Serves needs of individuals suffering from allergies caused by various pollens, dust, and mold. Provides info about allergen-free diets, and coping with various commercial products.

05049. American Association for Artificial Intelligence, 445 Burgess Dr, Menlo Park, CA 94025; (415) 328-3123. Interest in artificial and machine intelligence. Provides reference and referral services, info on research, conducts conferences and tutorials. Services free.

05050. American Association for Crystal Growth, c/o Robert S. Feigelson, Center for Materials Research, Stanford Univ, Stanford, CA 94305; (415) 497-4007. Sponsors conferences in field of crystal growth, gives awards for achievements in research, sponsors young author award, conducts conferences, seminars, workshops. Services provided at cost.

05051. American Association for Health Promotion, P.O. Box 1654, Loma Linda, CA 92354; (714) 824-4598. Dedicated to assuring optimal quality in health promotion professional training and practice, emphasizing spiritual aspect of health promotion. Provides scholarship funding base. Anyone may apply for membership.

05052. American Association for Maternal and Child Health, 233 Prospect-P209, La Jolla, CA 92037; (619) 459-9308. Interest in maternal and child health. Answers inquiries, distributes publications. Services at cost.

05053. American Association for the Advancement of Slavic Studies, c/o Dorothy Atkinson, Exec Dir, 128 Encina Commons, Stanford Univ, Stanford, CA 94305; (415) 497-9668. Nonprofit org of Slavic scholars interested in advancement of scholarly study relating to Soviet Union, eastern Europe. Provides referral services and answers inquiries, publishes and distributes materials.

05054. American Association of Dental Victims, 3320 E 7th St, Long Beach, CA 90804; (213) 433-9649. Membership consists of individuals with iatrogenic dental injuries. Seeks to change state law and establish investigatory bodies of laypersons to recommend disciplinary actions to higher authorities in cases of professional negligence on part of dentists. Answers inquiries, evaluates data. Inquiries from the public must be accompanied by a legal-size SASE.

05055. American Auto Racing Writers and Broadcasters Association, c/o Norma "Dusty" Brandel, Exec Dir, 922 N Pass Ave, Burbank, CA 91505; (818) 842-7005. Specializes in writing about automobile racing and other motor sports. Makes annual selections to Auto Racing All-American and Auto Racing Hall of Fame. Answers inquiries, makes referrals. Services free.

05056. American Aviation Historical Society, 2333 Otis St, Santa Ana, CA 92704; (714) 549-4818. Interest in intl aviation history. Publishes journal and newsletter. Answers inquiries, makes referrals.

05057. American Bamboo Society, 1101 San Leon Court, Solana Beach, CA 92075; (619) 481-9869. Provides info on identification, propagation, utilization, and culture of bamboos. Seeks to preserve and increase number of bamboo species in U.S. Provides reference, literature-searching, reproduction services; conducts seminars, workshops. Fee for some services.

05058. American Behcet's Foundation, 110 E 16th Street, Santa Ana, CA 92701; (714) 542-8357. Works to find a cure for Behcet's disease. Funds research, gathers patient info, disseminates info. Also offers patients life insurance.

05059. American Buckskin Registry Association, P.O. Box 3850, Redding, CA 96049; (916) 223-1420. Promotes Buckskin horses. Interest in characteristics and genetics of the Buckskin, horse show events. Fee for some services.

05060. American Cetacean Society, P.O. Box 2639, San Pedro, CA 90731; (213) 548-6279. Maintains library on marine mammals (includes taped songs of humpback whale), provides consulting, reference services; conducts school programs, speakers' bureau, booth presentations. Services free.

05061. American Concrete Pumping Association, 1034 Tennessee St, Vallejo, CA 94590; (707) 553-1732. Interest in concrete pumping safety, standards for concrete pumping equipment, inspection and certification of concrete pumps and pump operators. Provides advisory, reference, referral and literature-searching services; lends materials. Services free.

05062. American Down Association Library Section, 3830 Watt Ave, Ste 10, Sacramento, CA 95821; (916) 971-1135. Interest in thermal characteristics of feathers and down, filling capacities, lofting properties, and flammability of feathers and down. Provides general reference services, evaluates data, conducts seminars. Services free to firms, govt agencies, and individuals dealing with feathers and down.

05063. American Endodontic Society, 1400 N Harbor Blvd, No 104, Fullerton, CA 92635; (714) 870-5590. Promotes a simplified and standardized procedure for root canal therapy. Answers inquiries, conducts seminars and workshops; distributes patient literature and publications. Services primarily for dentists.

05064. American Endurance Ride Conference, 701 High St, Ste 216, Auburn, CA 95603; (916) 823-2260. Natl sanctioning org for endurance horse rides. Provides advisory, reference, literature-searching, and current-awareness services; evaluates, analyzes data; conducts seminars, workshops. Some services may be restricted to membership, open to anyone.

05065. American Federation of Aviculture, P.O. Box 1568 (2208A Artesia Blvd), Redondo Beach, CA 90278; (213) 372-2988. Interest in care and breeding of birds, research and conservation of avian wildlife and habitats. Provides general reference services, conducts seminars, publishes and distributes materials. Services free to members and public schools.

05066. American Film Institute Library, P.O. Box 27999 (2021 N Western Ave), Los Angeles, CA 90027; (213) 856-7655. Interest in all aspects of film, TV, and theater business. Provides general reference services, conducts an annual Film/TV Documentation Workshop, permits onsite use of collections. Reference service free; other services subject to a fee.

05067. American Fuchsia Society, Hall of Flowers, Golden Gate Park, Ninth Ave and Lincoln Way, San Francisco, CA 94122. Interest in cultivation, registration, and usage of Fuchsias. Publishes bulletin, Checklist of Fuchsias Registered, Judging School Manual and A.F.S. Judging Rules. Answers inquiries, provides consulting and reference services. Services free or at cost.

05068. American Gold Association, P.O. Box 457 (263 Church St), Ione, CA 95640; (209) 274-2196. Interest in gold history, gold mining industry, gold in economics. Publishes and sells materials. Answers inquiries or refers inquirers to other sources of info free.

05069. American Handwriting Analysis Foundation, P.O. Box 6201, San Jose, CA 95150; (408) 377-6775. Provides info for educational and professional advancement of handwriting analysis. Provides advisory, reference, referral, literature-searching services; conducts research; conducts certification tests, lectures, and workshops. Services provided for a fee.

05070. American Herb Association, P.O. Box 353, Rescue, CA 95672 (916) 626-5046. Interest in herbs, ethnobotany, plant research and products, chemical analysis of medicinal plants. Provides advisory, consulting, referral, and reference services; evaluates data; conducts seminars, workshops. Services primarily for dues-paying members, but others may be assisted at cost.

05071. American Hypnotists' Association, c/o Rafael M. Bertuccelli, MD, Pres, Glanworth Bldg, Ste 6, 1159 Green St, San Francisco, CA 94109; (415) 775-6130. Interest in ethical hypnology, clinical psychology, and social work. Publishes newsletter and standards. Answers inquiries, makes referrals, conducts seminars. Services free to professionals in healing arts; charge to others.

05072. American Indian Historical Society, 1451 Masonic Ave, San Francisco, CA 94117; (415) 626-5235. Preserves and enhances Native American culture and disseminates info about it to the general population. Publishes various books. Answers inquiries, makes referrals; provides advisory and reference services; conducts research. Services provided for a fee.

05073. American Institute for Research Project Talent Data Bank, American Institutes for Research, P.O. Box 1113 (1791 Arastradero Rd), Palo Alto, CA 94302; (415) 493-3550. Interest in educational, policy, and population research, psychology, sociology, economics. Data provided researchers for specific studies on a cost basis.

05074. American Institute of Maintenance, P.O. Box 2068 (1120 E Chevy Chase Dr), Glendale, CA 91209; (818) 244-1176. Answers inquiries on contract building service, distributes pamphlets, makes referrals to other sources of info. Services for nonmembers limited according to time required.

05075. American Justice Institute, 705 Merchant St, Sacramento, CA 95814; (916) 443-4376. Interest in criminal and juvenile justice. Sells publications, permits onsite use of collection free.

05077. American Lupus Society, 23751 Madison Street, Torrance, CA 90505; (213) 373-1335. U.S.-Canadian society that assists lupus erythematosus patients and their families, promotes public awareness, and raises funds. Chapter services include patient support groups, publications, media releases, and programs.

05078. American Medical International Market Planning Associates, 433 N Camden Dr, Ste 800, Beverly Hills, CA 90210; (213) 205-5319. Interest in strategic planning, facility planning and design, and functional analysis for hospitals. Provides general reference services, permits limited onsite use of collection. Fees charged for literature searches and copying.

05079. American Medical Joggers Association, P.O. Box 4704, N Hollywood, CA 91607; (213) 985-0079. Encourages physicians to participate in jogging, running, and endurance exercises as a more healthful way to life. Publishes periodical, abstracts, indexes. Answers inquiries, makes referrals, provides advisory services. Services free, primarily for those in related medical fields.

05080. American Microsystems Corporate Info Center, 3800 Homestead Rd, Bldg 800, Santa Clara, CA 95051; (408) 554-2109. Manufacturing firm interested in integrated circuits, microelectronics, computer-aided design. Provides general reference services, makes interlibrary loans. Services free within limits of time and staff. Dealings with library representatives preferred.

05081. American Mosquito Control Association, 5545 E Shields Ave, Fresno, CA 93727; (209) 292-5329. Interest in mosquitoes, mosquito-transmitted diseases and their control. Provides general reference services. Services free, except advisory and consulting services.

05083. American Narcolepsy Association, P.O. Box 1187, San Carlos, CA 94070; (415) 591-7979. Works to solve problems associated with narcolepsy and related sleep disorders. Distributes info, funds and conducts research, provides volunteer work.

05084. American Osteopathic Academy of Sclerotherapy, c/o Rayma Kulik, Exec Secty, 2110 La Mesa Ct, Spring Valley, CA 92078; (619) 469-1198. Conducts teaching seminars and provides lecture-demonstrations about sclerotherapy. Answers inquiries, makes referrals free.

05086. American Physical Fitness Research Institute, 654 N Sepulveda Blvd, P.O. Box 49024, Los Angeles, CA 90049; (213) 476-6241. Promotes wellness in all parts of life. Produces radio and television spots on wellness topics, does special studies for labor and management on worksite health promotion, and distributes posters and charts for young people.

05087. American Plant Life Society, c/o R. Mitchell Beauchamp, Editor, P.O. Box 985 (843 E 16th St), National City, CA 92050; (619) 477-0295. Concerned with research and culture of Amaryllidaceae and allied plant families. Maintains plant life library. Answers inquiries, makes referrals; sells publications.

05088. American Prevention Institute, 1425 Engracia Ave, Torrance, CA 90501; (213) 328-6338. Teaches basic, advanced, and low-stress nutrition. Maintains small library collection of books and lecture notes. Answers inquiries, makes referrals, provides advisory services, conducts seminars, makes interlibrary loans. Services provided at cost.

05089. American Register of Lithium Babies, Dept of Psychiatry and Langley Porter Psychiatric Institute, 401 Parnassus Avenue, San Francisco, CA 94143; (415) 681-8080 ext 258. Provides info on risks of pregnancy for women who take lithium. Brochure available to general public. Physicians may obtain further info by phone.

05090. American Rheumatism Association Medical Information System, 701 Welch Rd, Ste 3301, Palo Alto, CA 94304; (415) 497-7331. Interest in arthritis, rheumatic diseases, connective tissue diseases, immunologic disease. Provides reference services, publishes and distributes materials. Services provided for a fee, available only to physicians.

05091. American River Touring Association, 445 High St, Oakland, CA 94601; (415) 465-9355. Sponsors whitewater rafting trips and educational programrams. Answers inquiries, provides reference services, conducts seminars, workshops, schools, cooperative trips. Fee for some services.

05092. American Shore and Beach Preservation Association, 412 O'Brien Hall, Univ of Calif., Berkeley, CA 94720; (415) 642-7341. Interest in preservation and development of shorelines of oceans, lakes, and rivers, beach and shore erosion. Answers inquiries, conducts seminars, distributes publications, makes referrals to other sources of info. Services provided at cost.

05093. American Shortwave Listeners Club, 16182 Ballad Lane, Huntington Beach, CA 92649; (714) 846-1685. Interest in worldwide shortwave radio broadcast stations. Has small collection of books on radio communications and electronic test equipment. Publishes monthly news bulletin, and directory, answers inquiries, makes referrals, provides advisory and reference services. Services generally free.

05095. American Social Health Association, 260 Sheridan Ave, Ste 307, Palo Alto, CA 94306; (800) 227-8922, in Calif. (800) 982-5803. Works to eliminate sexually transmitted diseases as a public health problem. Provides funding for research, lobbies fed officials, provides general reference services, maintains natl hotline for members.

05096. American Social Health Association, Herpes Resource Center, Box 100, Palo Alto, CA 94302; (415) 321-5134. Provides info and support services to persons who suffer from herpes. Sponsors local support groups, provides telephone counseling services, conducts info, research, and education projects.

05097. American Society for Enology and Viticulture, P.O. Box 1855, Davis, CA 95617; (916) 753-3142. Interest in enology, viticulture, wine and grape industries. Publishes quarterly journal and directory. Technical info sessions and exhibition each June open to public.

05098. American Society for Head and Neck Surgery, Div of Otolaryngology/Head and Neck Surgery, Stanford Univ Medical Center, Stanford, CA 94305; (415) 497-7104. Interest in surgery and care of patients with head and neck cancer. Publishes *AMA Archives of Otolaryngology*, journal articles. Answers inquiries, provides consulting services, conducts seminars. Services free to physicians.

05100. American Society of Bookplate Collectors and Designers, 605 N Stoneman Ave, No F, Alhambra, CA 91801; (213) 283-1936. Interest in bookplates and artists who design them, bookplate owners and collectors. Publishes *Bookplates in the News* (quarterly) and year book. Answers inquiries free.

05101. American Society of Cinematographers, P.O. Box 2230 (1782 N Orange Dr), Hollywood, CA 90078; (213) 876-5080. Interest in cinematography. Answers inquiries, provides advisory and reference services, permits onsite use of collection. Services free, except publications.

05102. American Society of Music Arrangers, P.O. Box 11, Hollywood, CA 90078; (213) 871-2762 or 545-4882. Affiliated with American Federation of Musicians, conducts workshops for members, and clinics and seminars open to anyone. Services available for a fee, with a reduction for members.

05104. American Society of Questioned Documents Examiners, 585 Tarryton Isle, Alameda, CA 94501-5643; (415) 865-2820. Interest in forged document examination, including identification of handwriting, typewriting, writing materials. Provides general reference services, performs professional questioned document services for a fee.

05105. American Society on Aging, 833 Market St, Ste 516, San Francisco, CA 94103; (415) 543-2617. Interest in advocacy for the elderly. Provides general reference services, publishes and distributes materials, permits onsite use of collection. Services available at cost; loans restricted to members.

05106. American Tax Reduction Movement, 6363 Wilshire Blvd, Ste 350, Los Angeles, CA 90048; (213) 658-5151. Interest in taxes, tax reduction legislation. Publishes *Taxing Times.* Answers inquiries free.

05107. American Tunaboat Association, One Tuna Lane, San Diego, CA 92101; (619) 233-6405. Membership of American tunaboat owners utilizing the purse seine. Provides free general reference services.

05108. American Viticultural Area Association, c/o Guenoc Winery, P.O. Box 1146, Middletown, CA 95461; (415) 995-7335. Provides public with info on viticultural. Answers inquiries, distributes publications.

05109. Americas Behavioral Research Corp., 1925 Page St, San Francisco, CA 94117; (415) 861-0197. Interest in bilingual education, educational equity for women. Provides general reference services, publishes and distributes materials, conducts seminars. Services generally subject to a fee.

05110. Ampex Corp. Technical Information Services, 401 Broadway, Redwood City, CA 94063; (415) 367-3368. Interest in magnetic recording and magnetic tape, nonmagnetic recording, electronics, sound, core memory systems, etc. Answers inquiries, publishes and distributes materials, makes interlibrary loans.

05113. Andrus Gerontology Center, Univ of Southern Calif., Univ Park, Los Angeles, CA 90089-0191; (213) 743-6060. Conducts training and research in human development and aging. Provides research and training at all levels. Operates reference library.

05114. Animal Protection Institute, P.O. Box 22505 (5894 S Land Park Dr), Sacramento, CA 95822; (916) 422-1921. Interest in animal protection and welfare, humane education. Provides general reference services, distributes publications. Services free, except some publications.

05115. Aquatic Research Institute, 2242 Davis Court, Hayward, CA 94545; (415) 785-2216. Interest in aquatic sciences, aquaculture/mariculture, aquarium sciences/industry, limnology, oceanography, water pollution, etc. Provides general reference services, identifies aquatic organisms, permits onsite use of collections. A fee may be charged for services.

05116. Armenian Educational Foundation, 517 E Wilson Ave, Ste 103B, Glendale, CA 91206; (213) 240-3257. Interest in Armenian education and schools in America and the Middle East. Publishes annual report. Answers inquiries, conducts symposia, sponsors cultural activities.

05117. Army Combat Developments Experimentation Command, Bldg 2925, Fort Ord, CA 93941; (408) 242-4706 or 242-3618. Interest in Army small unit org, weapons systems, and equipment. Provides general reference services, permits onsite use of collection by authorized personnel. Services free and generally available; selected materials restricted to U.S. govt agencies.

05118. Art Council Aids, P.O. Box 641, Beverly Hills, CA 90213. Commercial org interested in history of various art styles and forms from around the world. Publishes catalogs, sells slide series with commentaries to educational orgs in U.S. and abroad.

05119. Art Museum Association of America, 270 Sutter St, 4th Fl, San Francisco, CA 94108; (415) 392-9222. Sponsors exhibition of foreign art in U.S. Conducts annual museum management institute; offers other services. Services available to members — arts museums, univ museums and galleries, and community arts orgs — meeting security and insurance requirements for use of touring exhibitions.

05120. Arthur E. Guedel Memorial Anesthesia Center, P.O. Box 7999 (2395 Sacramento St), San Francisco, CA 94120; (415) 923-3240. Has comprehensive collection in field of anesthesiology, including books and journals. Provides reference and reproduction services, makes interlibrary loans.

05121. Asbestos Victims of America, P.O. Box 559, Capitola, CA 95010; (408) 476-3646. Provides medical, legal, and emotional counseling to asbestos victims, informs public about hazards of asbestos. Maintains a reference library.

05122. Asia Foundation, P.O. Box 3223 (550 Kearny St), San Francisco, CA 94119; (415) 982-4640. Interest in law and justice, rural and urban development, population of Asia. Publishes annual report. Answers inquiries, makes referrals.

05123. Asian American Psychological Association, c/o Herbert Z. Wong, Pres, RAMS, 3626 Balboa St, San Francisco, CA 94121; (415) 668-5955. Answers inquiries concerning psychology for and among Asian Americans. Service free.

05124. Asian Law Caucus, 1322 Webster St, Ste 410, Oakland, CA 94612; (415) 835-1474. Supplies legal services and community legal education to Asian Americans in the San Francisco area. Provides general reference services, publishes and distributes materials. Fees based on income and nature of request.

05125. Asian-American Studies Center, Institute of American Cultures, Univ of Calif., Los Angeles, CA 90024; (213) 825-2974. Interest in Asian-American studies. Researches and disseminates info through publications, seminars, and conference presentations, offers classes at UCLA, conducts an M.A. program in Asian-American studies.

05126. Asociacion Nacional Pro Personas Mayores, Library, Resource Center, 2727 W 6th St, Ste 270, Los Angeles, CA 90057 (213) 487-1922. Provides training and technical assistance, conducts social research on Hispanic elderly. Provides general reference services, publishes and distributes materials, permits onsite use of collections. Services available for a fee.

05127. Association for Childbirth at Home International, P.O. Box 39498, Los Angeles, CA 90039; (213) 667-0839. Interest in all aspects of making home birth an available and safe option. Provides general reference services, conducts seminars, publishes and distributes materials. Fee for some services.

05128. Association for Humanistic Psychology, 325 Ninth St, San Francisco, CA 94103; (415) 626-2375. Worldwide network for development of the human sciences. Provides general reference services, publishes and distributes materials, conducts seminars. Services provided for a fee, primarily for members.

05129. Association for Media Psychology, 228 Santa Monica Blvd, Ste 3, Santa Monica, CA 90401; (213) 394-4546. Stimulates research on ways media influence public attitude, behavior, and well-being. Encourages its use in prevention of physical and mental disorders, and aims to improve usefulness of mental health professions through use of media. Provides advisory, consulting, referral services, conducts convention and seminars. Fee for some services.

05130. Association for Women Geoscientists, P.O. Box 1005, Menlo Park, CA 94025. Devoted to furthering participation of women in the geosciences. Has several local chapters. Provides general reference services, publishes and distributes materials. Services primarily for members, but others assisted.

05131. Association of Applied Insect Ecologists, 5927 La Prada Terrace, Los Angeles, CA 90042; (213) 254-6580.

Implements research and education about benefits of integrated pest management. Publishes newsletter, produces video tapes. Answers inquiries, makes referrals, provides consulting services free. Conducts workshops and annual conference for a fee.

05132. Association of Balloon and Airship Constructors, P.O. Box 7, Rosemead, CA 91770. Interest in technical design and operational materials useful in airship design, construction, and operations. Provides general reference services, publishes and distributes materials. Services free, except analytical services and publications.

05133. Association of Human Resource Systems Professionals, P.O. Box 8040-A202, Walnut Creek, CA 94596; (415) 945-8428. Membership org of personnel, data processing, and other professional individuals who have interests in human resource systems. Conducts seminars, workshops, distributes publications and data compilations. Services available for a fee; members receive discounts.

05134. Association of Lunar and Planetary Observers, c/o Dr John E. Westfall, Dept of Geography, San Francisco State Univ, 1600 Holloway Ave, San Francisco, CA 94132; (415) 469-1149. Promotes study of the moon and galaxy by amateur astronomers. Holds annual meetings and cooperates with intl chapters. Publishes quarterly journal. Answers inquiries, makes referrals, provides advisory and current-awareness services. Services generally free.

05135. Association of Sleep Disorders Centers, P.O. Box 2604, Del Mar, CA 92014; (619) 455-8007. Encourages promotion of sleep disorders medicine as it pertains to clinics and clinicians. Distributes materials, conducts training courses. Membership limited.

05136. Association of University Architects, c/o James E. Westphall, Asst Vice Chancellor for Physical Planning and Development, 400 Golden Shore, Ste 228, Long Beach, CA 90802. Interest in campus planning, design and construction of buildings for higher education. Answers inquiries, makes referrals to other sources of info. Provides consultation on campus planning, fees determined individually.

05137. Association of Western Hospitals, 830 Market St, 8th Fl, San Francisco, CA 94102; (415) 421-8810. Interest in training and education of hospital executive and administrative personnel, management development. Provides general reference services, publishes and distributes materials, sponsors conferences.

05138. Astro-Science Laboratory, Diablo Valley Coll, 321 Golf Club Rd, Pleasant Hill, CA 94523; (415) 685-1230 ext 3465. Interest in undergraduate astronomy. Answers inquiries, provides advisory services. Services free.

05139. Astronomical Society of the Pacific, 1290 24th Ave, San Francisco, CA 94122; (415) 661-8660. Acts as clearinghouse for astronomical info, publishes journal, answers inquiries, provides advisory services, operates special hotline, conducts seminars, workshops, lectures.

05140. Audio-Digest Foundation, 1577 E Chevy Chase Dr, Glendale, CA 91206; (818) 245-8505. Interest in continuing medical education in various medical disciplines. Answers inquiries, prepares and sells tape recordings of lectures.

05141. Avenues, P.O. Box 5192, Sonora, CA 95370; (209) 533-1468. Nonprofit, natl support group for arthrogryposis multiplex congenita. Publishes newsletter, provides info.

05143. Batterers Anonymous, 1269 North E St, San Bernardino, CA 92405; (714) 884-6809. Self-help counseling org for men who batter their mates. Answers inquiries; provides advisory, referral, consulting services; conducts seminars, workshops. Services free.

05144. Bay Area Center for Law and the Deaf, Deaf Counseling Advocacy and Referral Agency (DCARA), 125 Parrot St, San Leandro, CA 94577; (415) 895-2430. Legal services agency for the deaf and hearing-impaired. Provides general reference services, publishes and distributes materials. All services free to deaf and hearing-impaired persons.

05145. Beatrice/Hunt-Wesson Foods, 1645 W Valencia Dr, Fullerton, CA 92634; (714) 680-2158. Maintains reference collection for study of food sciences. Answers inquiries, makes interlibrary loans, and referrals; permits onsite use of collection. Services free, available by prior appointment.

05146. Becker and Hayes, 2800 Olympic Blvd, Ste 103, Santa Monica, CA 90404; (213) 829-6866. Interest in design of info systems and associated products and services. Provides general reference services, publishes and distributes materials, conducts seminars, permits onsite use of collection. All services provided for a fee.

05147. Beckman Instruments Research Library, 2500 Harbor Blvd, Fullerton, CA 92634; (714) 871-4848 ext 358 or 359. Interest in scientific instruments, electronics, physics, optics, spectroscopy, gas chromatography, clinical chemistry, laboratory reagents, clinical laboratories. Permits onsite reference to unclassified material.

05148. Behavioral Therapy Institute, 1736 Old Grove Rd, Pasadena, CA 91107; (818) 791-7999. Provides forensic consulting, personality analysis, studies of human sexuality, and specialized info for attorneys concerning expert witness services. Answers inquiries, makes referrals, provides consulting, and testing services; conducts seminars and workshops for a fee.

05149. Benthic Invertebrate Collection, Scripps Institution of Oceanography, Aquarium Museum A-007, La Jolla, CA 92093; (619) 452-4820 or 452-2150. Holds specimens of benthic invertebrates. Publishes catalogs of collection, offers consulting services, loans specimens to qualified persons or gives them as gift to institutions.

05150. Berkeley Asian-American Studies Library, Univ of Calif., 3407 Dwinelle Hall (101 Wheeler Hall), Berkeley, CA 94720; (415) 642-2218. Collects materials on various aspects of Asian-American experience, especially history and contemporary issues. Answers inquiries, provides reference services, lends materials. Services free, primarily for Asian-American studies community.

05151. Berkeley Cancer Research Laboratory, Univ of Calif., 3510 Life Sciences Bldg, Berkeley, CA 94720; (415) 642-4711. Studies mammary cancer, vaginal cancer, tumor virus genetics. Maintains related collection of over 2,000 volumes, 100 dissertations, 1,000 slides and photographs. Conducts seminars, makes referrals, permits onsite use of collections. Services primarily for groups in biological sciences.

05152. Berkeley Center for Research in Management, Univ of Calif., 554 Barrows Hall, Berkeley, CA 94720; (415) 642-4041. Interest in research in management problems, managerial styles, techniques, and ethics and related topics. Provides general reference services, publishes and distributes materials, conducts seminars. Services free, except publications.

05154. Berkeley National Magnetic Fusion Energy Comp Center, Lawrence Livermore Natl Lab, P.O. Box 5509, Mail Code L-560 (7000 E Ave), Livermore, CA 94550; (415) 422-4017. Provides supercomputer services to programs sponsored by DoE and promotes sharing of computer programs among magnetic fusion researchers. Answers inquiries or makes referrals. Extensive services provided only for users authorized by Office of Fusion Energy.

05155. Berkeley Particle Data Group, Lawrence Berkeley Lab, Bldg 50, Rm 308, Univ of Calif., Berkeley, CA 94720; (415) 486-5885. Sponsored by U.S. Dept of Energy and Natl Science Foundation. Provides bibliographic searches for sponsoring agencies, their contractors, and physicists engaged in high-energy research.

05156. Berkeley Radio Astronomy Lab, Univ of Calif., Berkeley, CA 94720; (415) 642-6424. Supports Hat Creek Radio Astronomy Observatory, which houses a 26 meter-diameter radiotelescope and a 3-element millimeter-wavelength aperture synthesis interferometer. Answers inquiries, distributes tape copies of surveys and data compilations. Services free.

05157. Berkeley Shock Wave Data Center, Lawrence Livermore Natl Lab, H Div, Univ of Calif., P.O. Box 808, Livermore, CA 94550; (415) 442-7216. Interest in shock wave data on condensed systems. Answers inquiries concerning data from DoE and its contractors only. Info provided to others on exchange basis only.

05158. Bio Integral Resource Center, P.O. Box 7414 (1307 Acton St), Berkeley, CA 94706; (415) 524-2567. Interest in integrated pest management programs and technologies. Provides general reference services, publishes and distributes materials. Fees charged for publications and consultation.

05160. Bioagricultural Library, Univ of Calif., Riverside, CA 92521; (714) 787-3238 or 787-3701. Answers inquiries on life sciences, health sciences, arid lands research; provides reference, copying services for a fee; makes interlibrary loans; permits onsite use of collection.

05161. Biofeedback Research Institute, 6399 Wilshire Blvd, Ste 900, Los Angeles, CA 90048; (213) 933-9451. Manufactures and markets clinical computerized biofeedback instruments and provides professional training. Publishes and distributes materials. General reference services generally free.

05162. Biomedical Engineering Society, P.O. Box 2399, Culver City, CA 90231; (213) 206-6443. Promotes increase of biomedical engineering knowledge and its utilization. Provides general reference services, publishes and distributes materials. Services free, except publications.

05163. Biometric Project, Statistics Dept, Univ of Calif., Riverside, CA 92521; (714) 787-3774. Interest in statistical theory and applications in life, physical, and social sciences, agronomy. Answers inquiries, provides consulting services and short lists of literature citations, prepares analyses, permits onsite use of collection.

05164. Birth Control Institute, 1242 W Lincoln Ave, Ste 7-10, Anaheim, CA 92805; (714) 956-4630. Interest in education and medical services related to family planning, venereal disease testing, abortion. Provides general reference services, publishes and distributes materials, permits onsite use of collections. Fee for some services.

05165. Bob Bondurant School of High Performance Driving, Sears Point Intl Raceways, Inc., Hwys 37 and 121 Sonoma, CA 95476; (707) 938-4741. Provides advanced training for street, high performance, corporate, race car, and police drivers. Answers inquiries, makes referrals, provides advisory services, conducts workshops, analyzes data. Simple inquiries free, other services on a fee basis.

05166. Bowers Museum, 2002 N Main St, Santa Ana, CA 92706; (714) 972-1900. Interest in Orange County and Calif. anthropology, geography, geology, history; African, Oceanic, and Pre-Columbian cultures. Provides general reference services. Staff will authenticate and date artifacts.

05167. Braille Institute of America, 741 N Vermont Ave, Los Angeles, CA 90029; (213) 663-1111. Provides education and training for blind in southern Calif. Interest in programs, special services for blind. Provides info, counseling, books, volunteer assistance.

05169. Brain and Pituitary Foundation of America, 1360 Ninth Avenue, Ste 210, San Francisco, CA 94122; (209) 227-5466. Helps patients with brain and pituitary disorders. Sponsors educational program for medical professionals and the public, raises and distributes funds for research, provides info networks.

05170. Broadcast Designers' Association, 251 Kearney St, Ste 602, San Francisco, CA 94108; (415) 788-2324. Seeks to improve design process and quality of design product in television. Fosters continuous exchange of ideas, info, and experience. Provides reference services, conducts annual seminars and design competitions, operates an employment services bureau, other services. Services primarily for members, but others are assisted.

05171. Brooks Institute, Undersea Research Div, 2190 Alston Rd, Santa Barbara, CA 93108; (805) 969-2291. Publishes reports, specifications, films, photos; answers inquiries free; provides consulting, photographic exhibit production services for a fee; tests underwater photographic hardware for a fee.

05172. Burbank Public Library, Warner Research Collection, 110 N Glenoaks Blvd, Burbank, CA 91502; (818) 953-9743. Provides library and search service to motion picture and television industry in Burbank area. Provides advisory, consulting, reference, literature-searching, abstracting and indexing services; permits onsite use of collections. Services provided for a fee to those in motion pictures and TV, but freelance writers, artists, designers also assisted.

05173. Burn Institute, 3737 Fifth Ave, No 206, San Diego, CA 92103; (619) 291-4764. Offers private sessions for fire-setting children and their parents and provides reentry program for burned children. Provides advisory, consulting, other services free to San Diego/Imperial County residents, for a fee to others.

05174. Business Exchange, 4716 Vineland Ave, N Hollywood, CA 91602; (213) 985-8603. Computerized barter program for all types of businesses. Data base of over 16,000 member businesses offering over 100,000 products and services. Answers inquiries, provides advisory services, permits onsite use of data base for a fee. Service charges on purchases.

05175. C.G. Jung Institute Library, 10349 W Pico Blvd, Los Angeles, CA 90064; (213) 556-1193. Interest in analytical, Jungian, and child and adolescent psychology, Judeo-Christian and Oriental religions, fairy tales, occult. Provides general reference services, lends materials, permits onsite use of collections. Most services for members, but collections may be used onsite by public.

05176. C.I.T. Jet Propulsion Laboratory, Calif. Institute of Technology, 4800 Oak Grove Dr, Pasadena, CA 91103; (213) 354-6848. Interest in unmanned planetary spacecraft, displays featuring Deep Space Network. Publishes and distributes materials. Answers inquiries free.

05177. Cactus and Succulent Society of America, c/o Dr Ronald E. Monroe, Pres, Dept of Zoology, San Diego

State Univ, San Diego, CA 92182; (714) 265-4870. Interest in study and conservation of cactus and other succulents throughout the world. Publishes and distributes materials, provides general reference services free.

05178. Cal Poly School of Architecture and Environmental Design, Calif. Polytechnic State Univ, San Luis Obispo, CA 93407; (805) 546-1311. Provides advisory, consulting services, computer programs for architectural offices; publishes manufacturers' catalogs, specifications, project drawings. Some services free.

05179. California Academy of Sciences, Science Museum, Golden Gate Park, San Francisco, CA 94118; (415) 221-5100. Interest in natural history, paleontology, botany, ichthyology, zoology, geology, astronomy. Answers brief inquiries, provides consulting services, publishes and distributes materials, identifies and lends specimens. Museum open to public.

05180. California Academy of Sciences, Steinhart Aquarium, Golden Gate Park, San Francisco, CA 94118; (415) 221-5100. Interest in care and display of marine and fresh water specimens, aquarium administration and management. Provides general reference and limited consulting services, permits onsite use of literature collection by qualified personnel. Aquarium open to public.

05181. California Academy of Sciences, J.W.M., Jr. Memorial Library, Golden Gate Park, San Francisco, CA 94118; (415) 221-5100 ext 75. Interest in anthropology, biology, botany, geology, ichthyology, and paleontology, etc. of Pacific Basin, Calif., and Baja Calif. Provides reference services, makes interlibrary loans, permits onsite use of collection. Services intended for appropriate professional personnel.

05182. California Air Resources Board, P.O. Box 2815 (1131 S St), Sacramento, CA 95812; (916) 323-8377. Interest in air pollution: its control, environmental effects, research in photochemical reactions. Provides general reference services, publishes and distributes materials, permits onsite use of collection.

05183. California Committee of Two Million, P.O. Box 2046, San Francisco, CA 94126; (415) 392-8887. Statewide political action org that supports issues favoring protection of free-flowing rivers in Calif. Interested in water resources management. Makes free referrals to other sources of info.

05184. California Cooperative Fishery Research Unit, Humboldt State Univ, Arcata, CA 95521; (707) 826-3268. Interest in graduate student training in fisheries activities and aquatic ecology. Provides general reference services, conducts seminars, publishes and distributes materials, permits onsite use of collection. Services free, except seminars.

05185. California Date Administrative Committee, 81-855 Hwy 111, Rm 2-G, Indio, CA 92201; (619) 347-4510. Interest in date production and marketing statistics.

Publishes monthly bulletin, annual report. Distributes publications free.

05186. California Historical Society Library, 2099 Pacific Ave, San Francisco, CA 94109; (415) 567-1848. Interest in Calif. history and its various aspects. Answers brief mail and telephone inquiries free, makes referrals, publishes and distributes materials, permits onsite use of collections.

05187. California Institute of Technology Seismological Laboratory, Div of Geological and Planetary Sciences, Pasadena, CA 91125; (818) 356-6912. Teaches and conducts research in the seismological sciences. Answers inquiries, makes referrals, provides advisory services, permits onsite use of collections. Most services free to scientists. General earthquake info available for southern Calif., provided by phone or letter.

05188. California Inventors Council, P.O. Box 2036, Sunnyvale, CA 94087; (408) 732-4314. Encourages innovation and invention in use of technology. Provides inventors and manufacturers with pertinent info. Publishes quarterly magazines, answers inquiries, provides advisory services, conducts seminars, and conferences. Services primarily for members.

05189. California Medical Clinic for Headaches, 16542 Ventura Blvd, Ste 204, Encino, CA 91436; (213) 986-4248. Researches headaches. Publishes critical reviews, reprints. Answers inquiries, makes referrals, provides consulting services, conducts seminars. Services free, except consulting and seminars.

05190. California Primate Research Center, Univ of Calif., Davis, CA 95616; (916) 752-7333. Conducts human health-related research in which the nonhuman primate is the animal model of choice. Maintains primate colony for breeding and research. Publishes Annual Progress Report, related info. Answers inquiries, makes referrals, provides reference services. Services free.

05191. California Radiological Society, 1225 Eighth St, Ste 590, Sacramento, CA 95814; (916) 446-2028. Interest in clinical radiology, including its uses in medicine, physics, research, and such fields as veterinary work. Provides consulting, reference, and document services, primarily to members.

05192. California Raisin Advisory Board, P.O. Box 5335, Fresno, CA 93755; (209) 224-7010. Interest in production, marketing, and consumer acceptance of raisins and raisin products. Answers most inquiries free.

05193. California Redwood Association, 591 Redwood Hwy, Ste 3100, Mill Valley, CA 94941; (415) 381-1304. Interest in Calif. redwoods, including chemical, physical, and mechanical properties of redwood forests. Answers inquiries, provides reference and consulting services, permits onsite use of literature collection.

05194. California Self-Help Center, 2349 Franz Hall, 405 Hilgard Avenue, Los Angeles, CA 90024; (213) 825-

1799. Statewide consumer self-help group and reference service. Provides info, referral services.

05195. California Spanish Language Data Base, 604 William St, Oakland, CA 94612; (415) 893-8702. Interest in reference resource sharing for the Spanish-speaking community. Provides cataloging and related services, publishes and distributes materials. Services available at cost.

05196. California State Archives, 1020 "O" St, Room 130, Sacramento, CA 95814; (916) 445-4293. Interest in records created or accumulated by agencies of Calif. state govt. Brief questions answered without charge, and referrals made to other sources of info. Permits onsite use of collection. Copies of records can be furnished for a fee.

05198. California State Indian Museum, 2618 K St, Sacramento, CA 95816; (916) 324-0971 Interest in Calif. Indians, ethnology of Indians of North America. Provides general reference services, conducts interpretive programs for groups. Museum open to the public free.

05199. California State Library, P.O. Box 2037 (914 Capitol Mall), Sacramento, CA 95809; (916) 445-2585. Interest in all subjects except medicine, including Calif. history, accounting, social welfare, law, library science, urban planning. Provides general reference services to state govt and all libraries; library open to public.

05200. California Strawberry Advisory Board, P.O. Box 269 (41 Hangar Way), Watsonville, CA 95076; (408) 724-1301. Interest in advertisement and promotion of sale of Calif. strawberries, strawberry plant research. Provides general reference services, publishes and distributes materials. Services free, primarily for growers, consumers, and food services.

05201. California Water Resources Association, 245 E Olive Ave, Ste 503, Burbank, CA 91503; (213) 849-3120, 849-3129, or 848-9990. Interest in development of water resources of Calif. and West. Answers inquiries regarding water development by providing explanatory materials, provides speakers to civic groups, for television and radio features.

05202. Cancer Control Society, 2043 N Berendo St, Los Angeles, CA 90027; (213) 663-7801. Interest in educational materials pertaining to nontoxic cancer therapies. Library has 10,000 books and 100 periodical titles. Answers inquiries, makes referrals, provides reference services, permits onsite use of collection. Services free.

05203. Cancer Research Institute, School of Medicine, Univ of Calif., 1282-M, San Francisco, CA 94143; (415) 666-2201 or 666-4211. Consultant service for cancer care. Interest in cancer biology, research, education, and patient care. Provides general reference services, conducts seminars, permits onsite use of collection. Services free, limited to professionals in the field.

05204. Cancer Research Project, School of Medicine, Univ of Southern Calif., 1840 N Soto St, Los Angeles, CA 90032; (213) 224-7415. Interest in basic research on human and animal oncogenes. Maintains small collection of related materials. Answers inquiries, provides consulting services. Services basically to those in scientific and research fields.

05205. Canine Companions for Independence, P.O. Box 446(1215 Sebastopol Rd), Santa Rosa, CA 95402; (707) 528-0830. Trains dogs to assist disabled people to live independent and fulfilled lives. Provides advisory, reference, and referral services, evaluates data, conducts two-year dog training programs and two-week student training programs. Info services free; student training programs provided for a fee.

05206. Career Guidance Foundation College Catalog Library, Career Guidance Foundation, 8090 Engineer Rd, San Diego, CA 92111; (714) 560-8051, (800) 854-2670. Publishes microfiche college catalog collection and various other microfiche catalogs in education and related fields. Answers inquiries for purchasers of collections.

05207. Career Research Systems, P.O. Box 8969 (17371 Mt Wynne Circle), Fountain Valley, CA 92708. Disseminates info on current and projected employment opportunities for affirmative action and academic members. Maintains resource library of standard data pertinent to users and clients. Answers inquiries, makes referrals, provides advisory services. Conducts seminars and workshops.

05208. Carnation Research Laboratories Library, 8015 Van Nuys Blvd, Van Nuys, CA 91412; (818) 787-7820. Interest in dairy products, biochemisty, biological sciences, chemical engineering, nutrition, animal feeds, veterinary medicine. Answers inquiries, provides copying services at cost, makes interlibrary loans.

05209. Cecil and Ida Green Pinon Flat Observatory, Institute of Geophysics and Planetary Physics, Univ of Calif., Mail Code A-025, La Jolla, CA 92093; (619) 452-2889. Monitors deformations in the earth's crust. Publishes periodicals, technical reports, abstracts and indexes. Answers inquiries, provides info on R&D in progress, distributes data compilations. Services free, except certain materials.

05210. Center for Afro-American Studies, Institute of American Cultures, Univ of Calif., 3111 Campbell Hall, 405 Hilgard Ave, Los Angeles, CA 90024; (213) 825-7403. Conducts B.A. and M.A. programs in Afro-American Studies. Publishes and distributes materials, sponsors annual symposia, lecture series, and cultural events, permits onsite use of collection. Services free to public.

05211. Center for Astrophysics and Space, Univ of Calif., San Diego C-011, La Jolla, CA 92093; (619) 452-3933. Research center for high energy astrophysics, space and solar physics, solar wind, quasars, pulsars, x-ray and gamma ray astronomy, earth's magnetosphere.

Provides advisory, referral, and research services, evaluates data. Services free, unless extensive.

05213. Center for Attitudinal Healing, 19 Main Street, Tiburon, CA 94920; (415) 435-5022. Helps adults and children with life-threatening or catastrophic illnesses achieve peace of mind and relief. Provides support programs, hospital and home visits, volunteer training, educational materials and workshops. All services and programs free.

05214. Center for Chinese Studies, Univ of Calif., Berkeley, CA 94720; (415) 642-6510. Interest in social sciences, humanities, and literature concerning post-1949 China. Academic researchers provided reference services; some documents in collection may be reproduced.

05215. Center for Community Development, Humboldt State Univ, Arcata, CA 95521; (707) 826-3731. Assists community groups reassess and redeploy their skills, resources, and other assets. Interest in community development. Provides general reference services, publishes and distributes materials, permits onsite use of collection. Services provided at cost.

05216. Center for Computer/Law, P.O. Box 3549 (1112 Ocean Dr), Manhattan Beach, CA 90266; (213) 372-0198. Interest in computer and telecommunications law and its applications. Provides general reference services, publishes and distributes materials, conducts seminars. Except for answers to inquiries, services subject to a fee.

05217. Center for Economic Conversion, 222C View St, Mountain View, CA 94041; (415) 968-8798. Nonprofit research, education, and organizing org planning for conversion of military production to socially useful purposes. Provides general reference services, conducts seminars, evaluates data, permits onsite use of collections. Services for a fee.

05218. Center for Health Games and Simulations, San Diego State Univ, San Diego, CA 92182-0252; (619) 265-3696, 265-5528. Provides info on health simulations and games in education. Trains health professionals and educators in design and use of simulation technology. Conducts research and seminars, maintains database.

05219. Center for Human Information Processing, Univ of Calif., La Jolla, CA 92093; (619) 452-3005. Interest in research in human info processing, neuropsychology. Provides consulting services and conducts research on contract or grant basis, publishes and distributes materials, conducts seminars. Services primarily for professionals.

05220. Center for Laser Studies, Univ of Southern Calif., Univ Park, Los Angeles, CA 90007; (213) 743-6418. Interest in lasers, quantum electronics, optics, electrooptics. Provides general reference services, publishes and distributes materials, conducts seminars. Services available for a fee.

05221. Center for Marine Studies, San Diego State Univ, 5402 Coll Ave, San Diego, CA 92182; (619) 265-6523. Coordinates multidisciplinary marine studies program of instruction and research and provides special supporting services. Answers inquiries, provides advisory and reference services. Services generally free.

05222. Center for Marital and Sexual Studies, 5199 E Pacific Coast Hwy, Long Beach, CA 90804; (213) 597-4425. Interest in sexual research, marital counseling, training of professionals. Provides general reference services, publishes books and articles. Services provided to professionals and couples with problems; fees depend on ability to pay.

05223. Center for Process Studies, 1325 N Coll Ave, Claremont, CA 91711; (714) 626-3521 ext 224. Interest in process philosophy and theology, hermeneutic interfaith dialogue, historiography. Provides general reference services, publishes and distributes materials, permits onsite use of collections. Services available at cost.

05224. Center for Radar Astronomy, Space Telecommunications and Radioscience Lab, Stanford Electronics Labs, Stanford, CA 94305; (415) 497-3533. Involved in space flight radioscience research conducted on most NASA planetary missions. Provides general reference services, evaluates data. Services free, except postage, within limits of time and staff.

05226. Center for Solar Energy Applications, Dept of Environmental Studies, San Jose State Univ, San Jose, CA 95192; (408) 277-3107. Interest in solar energy applications, with emphasis on info, education, and architectural design of residential and commercial buildings. Has library collection of related materials. Conducts classes, permits onsite use of collection. Services free, except classes.

05227. Center for Studies in Higher Education, Univ of Calif., Berkeley, CA 94720; (415) 642-5040. Concerned with higher education, and with historical, comparative issues. Publishes occasional papers, answers inquiries, refers to other sources of info.

05228. Center for Survey Research, San Diego State Univ, San Diego, CA 92182-0350; (619) 265-5407. Interest in sample survey research. Provides consulting services and sample survey research on a fee basis.

05229. Center for Sutton Movement Writing, P.O. Box 7344 (2621 Blackthorn St), Newport Beach, CA 92658-7344; (714) 644-8342. Promotes use of sign languages used by deaf in cultural and recreational activities. Publishes newspaper and related materials. Answers inquiries, provides advisory and consulting services, conducts seminars and workshops. Services may involve a fee.

05230. Center for Ulcer Research and Education, c/o V.A. Wadsworth, Bldg 115, Room 217, Los Angeles, CA 90073; (213) 825-5091. Funds and conducts research on cause, cure, and prevention of peptic ulcers. Sponsors conferences and symposia on research developments.

05231. Center for the Partially Sighted, 919 Santa Monica Blvd, Ste 200, Santa Monica, CA 90405; (213) 458-3501. Offers rehabilitative services to partially sighted and legally blind, including evaluations, prescription of visual aids, orientation and mobility training, counseling, etc. Conducts research. Fees scaled to patients' incomes.

05232. Center for the Study of Comparative Folklore and Mythology, Univ of Calif., 1037 GSM, Library Wing, Los Angeles, CA 90024; (213) 825-4242. Interest in comparative folklore, mythology, folk tales, legends, etc. Answers inquiries, publishes and distributes materials, provides reference services, makes referrals.

05233. Center for the Study of Evaluation, Univ of Calif., Graduate School of Education, 145 Moore Hall, Los Angeles, CA 90024; (213) 825-4711. Publishes monographs, and reports, answers inquiries, provides copies of articles, refers users to ERIC data base system.

05234. Center for the Study of Parent Involvement, 303 Van Buren Ave, Oakland, CA 94610; (415) 465-3507. Interest in parent involvement, education, community participation. Provides general reference services, conducts seminars.

05235. Center on Administration of Criminal Justice, Univ of Calif., Davis, CA 95616; (916) 752-2893. Interest in criminal justice research and demonstration programs. Publishes technical reports and journal articles. Answers inquiries, provides advisory services, conducts seminars and workshops. Services generally free.

05236. Center on Deafness, Univ of Calif., San Francisco, 1474 Fifth Ave, San Francisco, CA 94143; (415) 731-9150. Interest in mental health services for the hearing-impaired. Provides general reference services, conducts seminars. Services available at cost.

05237. Ceramic Tile Institute of America, 700 N Virgil Ave, Los Angeles, CA 90029; (213) 660-1911. Provides complete promotional, technical, educational, and testing support for all ceramic tile and related products. Provides advisory, consulting, reference, referral, and literature-searching services and research info; evaluates and analyzes data; conducts seminars, workshops. Services, available to architects, specification writers, general contractors, tile contractors.

05238. Chevron Oil Field Research, Technical Information Services, P.O. Box 446 (3282 Beach Blvd), La Habra, CA 90631; (213) 694-7500. Interest in geosciences, petroleum engineering, physics, chemistry, mathematics. Publishes and distributes materials, makes interlibrary loans, permits onsite use of collections by prior arrangement. Services free.

05239. Chevron Research Co., Library, Technical Information Center, P.O. Box 1627 (576 Standard Ave), Richmond, CA 94802; (415) 620-2105. Collection of U.S. and foreign patents, books and other materials relating to petroleum products, chemical engineering, and environmental pollution. Publishes related materials. Answers inquiries, makes referrals, provides advisory services. Services free by appointment.

05240. Chicano Studies Research Library, Univ of Calif., 3121 Campbell Hall, 405 Hilgard Ave, Los Angeles, CA 90024; (213) 206-6052. Interest in Chicanos, bilingual education, Mexican immigration. Provides general reference services, conducts seminars, permits onsite use of collections. Most services free.

05241. Child Abuse Listening Mediation, P.O. Box 718, Santa Barbara, CA 93102; (805) 682-1366, 569-2255. Provides comprehensive, multi-modal treatment and prevention services to families in which sexual abuse, incest, or physical abuse has occurred. Answers professional inquiries, makes appropriate referrals. Distributes info.

05242. Child Amputee Prosthetics Project, Univ of Calif., UCLA Rehabilitation Center, 1000 Veteran Ave, Los Angeles, CA 90024; (213) 825-5201. Interest in new types of child prostheses, new methods of training child amputees, problems of child amputee. Provides consulting and reference services, publishes and distributes materials.

05243. Child, Youth and Family Services, 1741 Silverlake Blvd, Los Angeles, CA 90026; (213) 664-2937. Develops projects to help meet needs of children with special needs and their families. Provides general reference services, conducts seminars, evaluates data. Services free to agencies serving that population.

05244. Children's Cancer Research Institute, 2351 Clay Street, Ste 512, San Francisco, CA 94115; (415) 563-8777. Develops new techniques for treating children and young adults with cancer. Operates clinics, strives to maintain normal living environment for its patients, and emphasizes emotional rehabilitation.

05246. Children's Hospital of L.A. Hotline, 4650 Sunset Blvd, Los Angeles, CA 90054; (213) 669-2522 or 669-2153 (office); (213) 666-1015 (crisis line). Telephone crisis intervention service that gives callers emotional support and info free; refers callers to other agencies; provides training for community agency personnel for a fee.

05247. China Trade Development Corp. of Chicago, 2049 Century Park East, Ste 416, Los Angeles, CA 90067; (213) 556-8091. Conducts economic research and analysis on Asia and North America. Assists with direct sales, compensation trade, and joint venture proposals. Maintains map collections of urban areas worldwide. Answers inquiries, provides consulting and translation services. Services available for a fee.

05248. Chinese Historical Society of America, 17 Adler Pl (Off 1140 Grant Ave), San Francisco, CA 94133; (415) 391-1188. Interest in history of Chinese people in U.S. Provides limited reference services, unless extensive.

05249. Chinese for Affirmative Action, 17 Walter U. Lum Pl, San Francisco, CA 94108; (415) 982-0801. Nonprofit civil rights org interested in Chinese American issues. Provides free general reference services.

05250. Citizens Action League, 2988 Mission St, San Francisco, CA 94110; (415) 236-8232. Acts on neighborhood, city-wide, and state-wide issues. Answers inquiries, makes referrals, and distributes info packets. Services free.

05251. Citizens' Research Foundation, Univ of Southern Calif., Research Annex, 3716 S Hope St, Los Angeles, CA 90007; (213) 743-5440 or 743-5211. Provides info on financing of politics. Interest in campaign costs, fund raising, public attitudes. Answers technical inquiries, provides consulting services. Duplication services and onsite use of collection available by appointment.

05252. Classification Society, North American Branch, c/o Lawrence J. Hubert, Pres, Dept of Education, Univ of Calif., Santa Barbara, CA 93107; (805) 961-2734. Interest in pattern recognition, classification based on quantitative analysis of data. Provides general reference services, publishes and distributes materials. Services primarily for members, but others assisted.

05253. Clean Fuel Institute, 2936 McAllister St, Riverside, CA 92503; (714) 688-5474. Interest in hydrogen energy and technology, nonpolluting hydrogen fuel, societal advantages of hydrogen energy, hydrogenfueled vehicles. Provides general reference services, conducts seminars. Services free or at minimal cost.

05254. Clinical Pharmacology Research Institute, 2006 Dwight Way, No 208, Berkeley, CA 94704; (213) 841-5446. Interest in clinical pharmacology. Publishes reports, provides consulting services free to physicians and all govt agencies.

05255. Cloisonne Collectors Club, 1631 Mimulus Way, La Jolla, CA 92037; (619) 454-0595. Interest in antique cloisonne, historic and contemporary enameling, including champleve, bas-taille, grisaille, plique ajour, limoges, more. Provides general reference services, conducts exhibitions and tours. Services primarily for collectors.

05256. Club of the Friends of Ancient Smoothing Irons, c/o Edna Glissman, U.S. representative, P.O. Box 215 (4400 Park Dr), Carlsbad, CA 92008. (619) 729-1740. Interest in smoothing irons. Answers inquiries and provides reference services free if request accompanied by a SASE. Permits onsite use of collections.

05257. Coalition for the Medical Rights of Women, 1638-B Haight St, San Francisco, CA 94117; (415) 621-8030. Works to improve quality of health services for women while increasing public awareness of them. Publishes newsletter, critical reviews, and educational brochures. Answers inquiries, conducts seminars, provides info on R&D in progress. Publications available for a fee.

05258. Cointelpro Survivors, P.O. Box 246 (1439 E St), Napa, CA 94559; (415) 864-0475. Documents and publicizes allegations of abuse of power by Federal Bureau of Investigation. Acts as victim support group, networks with other watchdog committees, lobbies against FBI activities it believes violate civil liberties.

Provides free advisory, evaluation, referral and consulting services.

05259. College of Oceaneering, Jim Joiner, Pres, 272 S Fries Ave, Wilmington, CA 90744; (213) 834-2501. Nonprofit diver training school interested in all types and aspects of diving. Answers inquiries, publishes and distributes materials, conducts diving courses.

05260. Colorado River Association, 417 S Hill St, Ste 1024, Los Angeles, CA 90013; (213) 626-4621. Interest in water problems of 11 western states, especially as they relate to Colorado River. Answers inquiries, publishes and distributes materials, provides consulting services.

05261. Commission on Peace Officer Standards and Training, Calif. Dept of Justice, P.O. Box 20145 (4949 Broadway), Sacramento, CA 95820. Interest in police selection, and training, police science, public service personnel selection, regulatory law enforcement. Permits onsite use of collection. General reference services primarily for participating local govts.

05262. Committee for Freedom of Choice in Medicine, 146 Main St, Ste 408, Los Altos, CA 94022; (415) 948-9475. Interest in nontoxic therapies for cancer and related diseases, decriminalization of vitamin B17 (laetrile). Provides general reference services, publishes and distributes materials. Fee for some services.

05263. Committee for the Preservation of the Tule Elk, P.O. Box 3696, San Diego, CA 92103; (714) 485-0626. Interest in preservation and restoration of Tule elk and other endangered species. Provides general reference services free, except films and lectures.

05264. Committee of Small Magazine Editors and Publishers, P.O. Box 703 (2421 Buchanan St), San Francisco, CA 94101; (415) 922-9490. Trade assn of about 1,000 small book and periodical publishers and other interested persons in U.S. and abroad. Interest in small book and magazine publishing. Conducts annual conference for publishers. Answers inquiries free.

05265. Community Analysis Research Institute, School of Library Science, Univ of Southern Calif., Univ Park, Los Angeles, CA 90007; (213) 743-2385. Interest in library and info research, community analysis. Conducts institutes throughout U.S., provides consulting services to those conducting a community analysis. Costs of services vary.

05266. Community Economics, 1904 Franklin St, Ste 900, Oakland, CA 94612; (415) 832-8300. Interest in limited-equity cooperative housing developments and economic development. Provides general reference services, publishes and distributes materials, develops co-op housing. Services for a fee.

05267. Community Environmental Council, 924 Anacapa St, Ste B4, Santa Barbara, CA 93101; (805) 963-0583. Interest in local, state, and natl recycling and energy conservation; related topics. Provides general reference services, evaluates, and and analyzes data, conducts seminars. Services free.

05268. Comprehensive Cancer Center, U.S.C. Cancer Center, 1721 Griffin Ave, Rm 205, Los Angeles, CA 90031; (213) 224-6420. Disseminates cancer info through professional and public education programs. Provides general reference services, publishes and distributes materials, permits onsite use of collection. Services free.

05269. Consortium for International Crop Protection, 2288 Fulton St, Ste 310, Berkeley, CA 94704; (415) 642-9950. Assists developing nations in preventing crop losses through pest control. Provides advisory, reference, referral, literature-searching, copying services and info on current research; conducts seminars. Services often free to developing nations, at cost to others, primarily for those active in the field.

05270. Constitutional Rights Foundation, 601 S Kingsley Ave, Los Angeles, CA 90005; (213) 487-5590. Develops education programs and materials to educate youth in the law and the structure of our legal and governmental system. Provides general reference services, publishes and distributes educational materials. Services available for a fee.

05271. Consulting Chemists Association, P.O. Box 2360, Monrovia, CA 91016; (213) 627-8377. Encourages science and practice of consulting among chemists and chemical engineers. Works to inform public about members' activities. Publishes directory. Free referral service linking inquirers to independent member consultants.

05272. Contemporary Historical Vehicle Association, c/o Leland H. Greer, Pres, 45 Claremont Ave, Orinda, CA 94563; (415) 254-8175. Interest in restoration and preservation of all land vehicles 25 years of age, back to 1928. Provides general reference services, publishes and distributes materials.

05273. Cooperative National Park Resources Studies Unit, Institute of Ecology, Univ of Calif., 2148 Wickson Hall, Davis, CA 95616; (916) 752-7119. Coordinates univ, fed, and private researchers in 17 natl park areas within Calif. Provides general reference services, conducts seminars and workshops. Services generally free.

05274. Coordinating Commmittee on Pesticides, 1057 Solano Ave, Room 106, Albany, CA 94706; (415) 526-7141. Provides info to public and govt agencies about exposure to toxic substances. Organizes groups, provides referrals, public education, community action counseling, and library services.

05275. Council for Planning and Conservation, P.O. Box 228, Beverly Hills, CA 90213; (213) 276-2685. Concerned with all aspects of environmental concerns in southern Calif. Answers inquiries when accompanied by SASE.

05276. Council of Engineers and Scientists Organizations, 14140 Boach Blvd, Ste 114, Westminster, CA 92683; (714) 898-6603. Interest in labor relations for industrially employed engineers and scientists. Maintains collection of over 25,000 reports. Answers inquiries, provides free consulting and reference services.

05277. Cross & Cockade, The Society of World War I Aero Historians, 10443 S Memphis Ave, Whittier, CA 90604; (213) 944-4003. Interest in all aspects of World War I air war, including personal histories, technical evaluation of aircraft, etc. Provides general reference services, lends materials to members, permits onsite use of collection. Services primarily for members. Fees may be charged.

05278. Cystinosis Foundation, 477 15th Street, Ste 200, Oakland, CA 94612; (415) 834-7897. Seeks to raise awareness, funds for research into causes of cystinosis. Responds to inquiries from concerned individuals.

05279. D.A.T.A., P.O. Box 26875, San Diego, CA 92126; (619) 578-7600, (800) 854-7030. Interest in comprehensive data on worldwide, commercially-available semiconductors, discrete devices, integrated circuits, etc. Provides general reference services, distributes publications, provides marketing services.

05280. DFA of California, P.O. Box 270A (303 Brokaw Rd), Santa Clara, CA 95052; (408) 727-9302. Assn of dried fruit and tree nut processors. Interest in production and processing research, quality grading and distribution. Answers inquiries, provides consulting services to producers, packers, and distributors of food products.

05281. DIALOG Information Services, 3460 Hillview Ave, Palo Alto, CA 94304; (800) 227-1927, (415) 858-3785. Interest in interactive info retrieval system and in on-line access to the world's major bibliographic databases. Search services available on a cost-per-hour basis. Offline printing and mailing provided on a cost-per-record basis. Additional services also available.

05282. DoD Nuclear Information and Analysis Center, Kaman Tempo, 816 State St, Santa Barbara, CA 93102; (805) 965-0551. Serves as central collection point and reference center for all technical info pertinent to effects of nuclear explosions. Provides general reference services and computational support, conducts seminars.

05283. Datagraphix, P.O. Box 82449, San Diego, CA 92138; (619) 291-9960, 282-8479. Interest in computer output microfilm and laser page printing systems equipment, including related supplies and software. Answers inquiries, provides literature on products at no charge, provides photos, slides, and sample microfiche in limited quantities.

05284. Datatape Engineering Library, P.O. Bin 7014 (360 Sierra Madre Villa), Pasadena, CA 91109; (213) 796-9381 ext 2222. Interest in electronics, physics, instrumentation, mathematics, recording methods. Makes interlibrary loans, provides reproduction services, makes referrals to other sources of info.

05285. DeForest Memorial Archives, Electronics Museum, Foothill Coll, 12345 El Monte Rd, Los Altos Hills,

CA 94022; (415) 948-8590 ext 381. Interest in West Coast and early Bay Area electronics, early wireless and radio. Provides general reference services, permits onsite use of collection. Services available to qualified persons doing research or working on projects.

05287. Death Valley National Monument, Death Valley, CA 92328; (619) 786-2331. Interest in geology, biology, and history of Death Valley, Calif. and Nevada. Provides general reference services, permits onsite use of collections, sells informational material.

05288. Dental Research Institute, Center for the Health Sciences, Univ of Calif., Los Angeles, CA 90024; (213) 206-8045. Interest in multidisciplinary research in fields related to oral health and disease. Provides general reference services, publishes and distributes materials, conducts seminars. Services free.

05289. Department of Applied Mechanics and Engineering Science, Univ of Calif., La Jolla, CA 92093; (619) 452-3170. Interest in mechanical, structural, chemical engineering; bioengineering science, applied mechanics, applied ocean sciences, engineering physics, solid and structural mechanics, fluid mechanics. Provides advisory services, research info. Conducts seminars, workshops. Fee for some services.

05290. Department of Microbiology and Public Health, Calif. State Univ, 5151 State Univ Dr, Los Angeles, CA 90032; (213) 224-3531. Interest in food poisoning, contamination of milk and water, viral antigens and pathogenicity. Publishes reports, and reprints, provides consulting services.

05291. Department of Nutritional Sciences, Coll of Natural Resources, Univ of Calif., 119 Morgan Hall, Berkeley, CA 94720; (415) 642-6490. Interest in food chemistry and toxicology, nutrition, genetic engineering and enzyme technology, etc. Answers brief inquiries from state residents, makes referrals.

05292. Department of Psychology, Developmental Program, Stanford Univ, Stanford, CA 94305; (415) 497-1409. Interest in human motivation, including parent-child relationships, intrinsic motivation, development. Publishes books and journal articles by faculty members, answers inquiries free within limits of time and staff.

05293. Department of the Youth Authority, Division of Research, 4241 Williamsbourgh Dr, Sacramento, CA 95823; (916) 445-9626. Interest in info on youthful offenders committed to jurisdiction of Youth Authority, related evaluation. Approved users may obtain answers to questions and data tabulations. Assistance in interpreting info also provided.

05294. Desert Fishes Council, 407 W Line St, Bishop, CA 93514; (714) 872-2791 or 873-4095. Dedicated to preserving America's desert fishes and protection and management of their habitats. Publishes proceedings of annual symposium, progress reports on species preservation programs. Answers inquiries, makes referrals, provides advisory services. Most services free.

05295. Desert Protective Council, P.O. Box 4294, Palm Springs, CA 92263. Interest in desert areas, conservation, ecology. Answers inquiries, provides consulting services. Services free.

05296. Design International, P.O. Box 1803, Ross, CA 94957; (415) 457-8596. Interest in designers of architecture, ceramics, enameling, fashion design, fibre art, industrial design, photography, and the like. Conducts design seminars and forums in U.S. and abroad, distributes publications. Fee for some services.

05297. Direct Relief International, P.O. Box 30820 (2801-B De La Vina St), Santa Barbara, CA 93130; (805) 687-3694. Provides medical supplies and services to needy in locations around the world. Publishes quarterly newsletter, annual report. Answers all inquiries, makes referrals, operates a speakers bureau.

05298. Directors Guild of America, 7950 Sunset Blvd, Hollywood, CA 90046; (213) 656-1220. Represents directors, managers, coordinators for collective bargaining in motion picture and television industry. Answers inquiries, makes referrals.

05299. Disability Rights Education and Defense Fund, 2212 Sixth St, Berkeley, CA 94710; (415) 644-2555. Dedicated to integrating disabled persons into social, educational, economic, political mainstream. Provides advisory, legal services; conducts seminars, workshops; makes referrals. Services free to low-income persons and orgs representing them; others charged on sliding-fee basis. Priority given to disabled persons or victims of discrimination.

05300. Division of Biological Control, Univ of Calif., 1050 San Pablo Ave, Albany, CA 94706; (415) 642-7191. Answers inquiries on biological control of insects, spider mites, weeds; permits onsite use of museum collection of insect parasites, predators; publishes papers, reports, books; provides consulting services.

05301. Division of Laboratory Animal Medicine, Center for the Health Sciences, Univ of Calif., Los Angeles, CA 90024; (213) 825-7281. Publishes bibliography on lab animal medicine, answers inquiries, provides consulting services. Services available only to qualified scientists.

05302. Division of Perinatal Biology, Dept of Physiology, School of Medicine, Loma Linda Univ, Loma Linda, CA 92350; (714) 824-4325. Conducts research and teaching in physiology and biology of the developing fetus and newborn infant. Provides advisory services, makes referrals, conducts seminars. Services free.

05303. Document Engineering Co., 15210 Stagg St, Van Nuys, CA 91405; (213) 873-5566. Commercial org interested in current and obsolete Dept of Defense specification and standard documents. Provides military standard, qualified product list revision, library updating, and reproduction services. Services provided for a fee.

05305. Drug Information Analysis Service, Div of Clinical Pharmacy, School of Pharmacy, Univ of Calif., San

Francisco, CA 94143; (415) 666-4346. Answers inquiries on drugs, provides therapeutic recommendations, makes referrals to other sources of info, permits onsite use of collection. Services free, only to those in health care.

05306. Dry Lands Research Institute, Univ of Calif., Riverside, CA 92502; (714) 787-4554. Interest in dry lands research, land use, regional economic studies, archeology, geothermal energy. Publishes technical reports, answers inquiries free.

05307. Dystonia Medical Research Foundation, 9615 Brighton Way, Ste 416, Beverly Hills, CA 90210; (604) 668-5931, (213) 272-1925. Interest in finding causes of dystonia and related disorders. Supports workshops, doctor/patient education, and research grants; supplies referrals.

05308. EEG Systems Laboratory, 1855 Folsom St, San Francisco, CA 94103; (415) 621-8343. Interest in electroencephalography, magnetoencephalography, brain function imaging. Provides general reference services, conducts seminars. Services at cost to qualified professionals.

05309. ENKI Research Institute, 6660 Reseda Blvd, Ste 203, Reseda, CA 91335; (213) 708-0680. Interest in life science management and research with special emphasis on mental health services and systems. Provides general reference services, publishes and distributes materials. Services provided for a fee.

05310. ERIC Clearinghouse for Junior Colleges, Univ of Calif. at Los Angeles, 8118 Mathematical Sciences Bldg, Los Angeles, CA 90024; (213) 825-3931. Interest in all print materials relevant to community/junior college education. Provides general reference services, publishes and distributes materials, abstracts. Most services free.

05311. Earl Warren Legal Institute, Boalt Hall School of Law, Univ of Calif., 396 Boalt Hall, Berkeley, CA 94720; (415) 642-5880. Contributes to improved understanding and administration of laws and legal system. Provides general reference services, publishes and distributes materials, conducts seminars, permits onsite use of collection. Services free, except seminars and some publications.

05313. Earthmind, 4844 Hirsch Rd, Mariposa, CA 95338. Provides research and education in alternative sources of energy. Provides general reference services, publishes and distributes materials, permits onsite visits by written appointment only. Services free, except publications.

05314. Earthquake Engineering Research Institute, 2620 Telegraph Ave, Berkeley, CA 94704; (415) 848-0972. Works toward solving earthquake engineering problems. Publishes books, bibliographies, abstracts, brochures; sponsors seminars, workshops, conferences.

05315. East West Academy of Healing Arts, P.O. Box 31211, San Francisco, CA 94131; (415) 285-9400. Interest in cross-cultural health systems, holistic medicine, traditional Chinese medicine. Provides general reference services, sponsors U.S.-China professional exchange programs. Clinical services available to anyone.

05316. East-West Cultural Center, 2865 W 9th St, Los Angeles, CA 90006; (213) 480-8325. Helps integrate cultural, spiritual values of East and West with teachings of Sri Aurobindo. Conducts classes for a fee, lectures for donations; permits onsite use of collection.

05317. Eaton Corp. IMS Division Library, 31717 La Tienda Dr, Westlake Village, CA 91359; (818) 889-2211 ext 2357. Interest in computers, electronics, microwave technology, artificial intelligence, physics, mathematics, business management. Makes interlibrary loans, permits onsite reference at discretion of librarian.

05318. Ecology Action Educational Institute, P.O. Box 3895, Modesto, CA 95352; (209) 538-1689. Provides consulting, and reference services, presents lectures on ecology, permits onsite use of collection, publishes reports, and teaching units for secondary education. Fees charged for some services.

05319. Ecology Center, 1403 Addison St, Berkeley, CA 94702; (415) 548-2220. Interest in environmental policy, education, and protection. Provides general reference services, distributes publications, permits onsite use of collection. Services free.

05320. Ecology Center of Southern California, Educational Communications, Inc., P.O. Box 35473, Los Angeles, CA 90035; (213) 559-9160. Evaluates environmental impact reports, distributes data, and provides testimony at govt hearings. Provides advisory, consulting, referral, audiovisual services. Services free, except audiovisuals and publications.

05321. Education Voucher Institute, 24650 Crestview Ct, Farmington, CA 48024; (313) 471-6777. Conducts research and acts as a clearinghouse on educational vouchers and tax credits. Provides general reference services, conducts seminars, sells publications.

05322. Educational and Industrial Testing Service, P.O. Box 7234, San Diego, CA 92107; (714) 222-1666 or 488-1666. Commercial org interested in tests and books on education, psychology and in career guidance. Answers inquiries, provides reference services on a request basis.

05323. Edward L. Ginzton Physics Laboratory, W. W. Hansen Laboratories of Physics, Stanford Univ, Stanford, CA 94305; (415) 497-0100. Interest in microwave acoustics, quantum electronics and lasers, superconducting high-power transmission lines, fiber optics coupling, vacuum tunneling. Distributes copies of reports and journal articles at actual production cost in photocopy form.

05324. Electric Auto Association, 1249 Lane St, Belmont, CA 94002; (415) 591-6698. Promotes electric vehicles and transportation. Answers inquiries or makes referrals, conducts public electric vehicle exhibits and rallies. Services free.

05325. Electric Power Research Institute, P.O. Box 10412 (3412 Hillview Ave), Palo Alto, CA 94303; (415) 855-2411, 855-2000. Funds research and development of technology to meet electrical energy needs environmentally and economically. Maintains data base of research in progress. Answers inquiries. Services primarily for member electric utilities, but others assisted.

05326. Electronics Research Laboratory, Univ of Calif., 341 Cory Hall, Berkeley, CA 94720; (415) 642-7200. Interest in bioelectronics, biomedical electronics, and mathematical ecology, computer sciences, scanning electron microscopy, related areas. Answers inquiries, provides limited free copies of published articles.

05327. Elsa Wild Animal Appeal, P.O. Box 4572, N Hollywood, CA 91607; (213) 769-8388. Interest in conservation of wildlife, endangered species, development of wildlife education programs for children. Provides general reference services, publishes and distributes materials.

05328. Emotional Health Anonymous, 2420 San Gabriel Blvd, Rosemead, CA 91770; (213) 573-5482, 283-3574. Self-help program for emotionally ill persons based on 12 steps of Alcoholics Anonymous. Group meetings free and open to all. Meetings offer mutual support, acceptance, and exploration.

05329. Enamel Guild West, P.O. Box 721, La Jolla, CA 92038 (619); 454-0595. Interest in enameling and its many techniques; glass fired on copper, silver, gold, and steel; cloisonne, photo imagery, paillons, more. Provides general reference services, conducts exhibitions. Services primarily for members, but others will be assisted; fee may be charged. Permanent exhibition space and access to enamel studio equipment available.

05330. End Violence Against the Next Generation, 977 Keeler Ave, Berkeley, CA 94708; (415) 527-0454. Collects and disseminates info about effects of corporal punishment, promotes alternative methods of raising and educating children. Provides free advisory, referral and current-awareness services.

05331. Engineering-Science, 125 W Huntington Dr, Arcadia, CA 91006; (818) 445-7560. Interest in engineering design and research in water resources, treatment, hazardous and toxic waste management, etc. Answers limited inquiries, provides consulting services for a fee.

05332. Entrepreneurs Alliance, 1333 Lawrence Expressway, Ste 150, Santa Clara, CA 95051 (408) 246-1007. Interest in innovation, entrepreneurship, small companies, etc. Provides general reference services, publishes and distributes materials, conducts seminars. Some services free to members.

05333. Environmental Communications, 62 Windward Ave, Venice, CA 90291; (213) 392-4964. Produces and distributes slide sets and books. Maintains collection of 200,000 original slides with special emphasis on modern architecture. Provides consulting, reference, and current-awareness services; makes referrals. Fees charged for some services.

05334. Environmental Design & Research Center, 261 Port Royal Ave, Foster City, CA 94404. Interest in computer graphics applications in architecture, building design, and engineering. Provides consulting, training, distributes material, makes referrals at cost.

05335. Environmental Education Group, 5762 Firebird Court, Camarillo, CA 93010; (213) 342-4984. Interest in environmental quality, energy resources and alternatives. Provides general reference services, publishes and distributes materials, conducts seminars. Fee for some services.

05336. Environmental Toxicology Library, Univ of Calif., Davis, CA 95616; (916) 752-2562. Provides advisory, reference, copying services on contract basis; provides statistical summaries from pesticide data bank for a fee; publishes bibliography on pesticides. Onsite use of collection by special permision only.

05337. Esperanto Information Center, Box 1129, El Cerrito, CA 94530; (415) 653-0998. Interest in Esperanto, the international language, as a solution to the world language problem. Provides general reference services, publishes and distributes materials, permits onsite use of collection by appointment. Services primarily for members. Most materials sold.

05338. Exploratorium, 3601 Lyon St, San Francisco, CA 94123; (415) 563-7337. Science museum that maintains collection of 600 interactive exhibits. Answers inquiries, makes referrals, conducts school tours. Permits onsite use of collections. Admission fee for persons over 17.

05339. Extensions for Independence, 635-5 N Twin Oaks Valley Rd, San Marcos, CA 92069; (619) 744-4083. Designs and manufactures special equipment for functional independence of physically handicapped. Answers inquiries, provides advisory, consulting and referral services, conducts seminars and workshops. Services primarily for handicapped; others assisted for a fee.

05340. FMC Corp. Central Engineering Laboratories Library, P.O. Box 580 (1185 Coleman Ave), Santa Clara, CA 95052; (408) 289-2529 or 289-3493. Interest in aspects of engineering research and development applied to machinery manufacturing. Provides general reference services, publishes and distributes materials, permits onsite reference by appointment.

05342. Families Anonymous, P.O. Box 528 (14617 Victory Blvd, Ste 1), Van Nuys, CA 91408; (818) 989-7841. Interest in families with members with drug abuse, dependence, or addiction problems; emotional and behavioral consequences of drug problems in the family. Answers inquiries, conducts group meetings, makes referrals to local chapters, sources of info, and therapeutic resources. Except for publications, services free.

05344. Family Survival Project for Brain-Damaged Adults, 1736 Divisadero Street, San Francisco, CA 94115; (415) 921-5400. Helps those who care for adult victims of chronic brain disorders. Provides services including family consultations, legal and financial consultations, support groups, respite care, professional therapy, technical assistance, and a speakers bureau.

05345. Far West Lab for Educational Research and Development, 1855 Folsom St, San Francisco, CA 94103; (415) 565-3000. Interest in educational research and development, technical assistance to Far West region. Maintains info center for visitors, provides support services, publishes and distributes materials.

05346. Farallones Institute, Rural Center, 15290 Coleman Valley Rd, Occidental, CA 95465; (707) 874-3060. Interest in ecologically-sound, community-based technologies, land and resource use. Provides general reference services, offers courses for both credit and noncredit, distributes publications. Services provided at cost.

05347. Fargo Co., 577 10th St, San Francisco, CA 94103; (415) 621-4471. Interest in law enforcement and military equipment and support systems, security countermeasure systems. Answers inquiries, provides consulting services, conducts seminars in use of equipment.

05348. Fathers' Rights of America, P.O. Box 7596, Van Nuys, CA 91409; (818) 789-4435. Interest in fathers' rights, divorce, child support, child custody. Provides general reference services, conducts seminars. Services free to membership, open to anyone.

05349. Feldenkrais Guild, P.O. Box 11145, San Francisco, CA 94101; (415) 550-8708. Nonprofit educational org of teachers of Feldenkrais method of movement. Publishes directory, provides general reference services.

05350. Feminist History Research Project, P.O. Box 1156, Topanga, CA 90290; (213) 455-1283. Interest in women's history. Provides general reference services, conducts seminars, publishes and distributes materials, permits onsite use of collections. Services for a fee, primarily to qualified researchers.

05351. Fibonacci Association, c/o Dept of Mathematics, Univ of Santa Clara, Santa Clara, CA 95053; (408) 984-4525. Interest in Fibonacci and related numbers, including Lucas numbers, elementary number theory, Fibonacci numbers in nature. Answers inquiries, publishes and distributes materials, makes referrals, suggests areas of research.

05352. Film and Television Study Center, 6216 Yucca St, Hollywood, CA 90028; (213) 469-1917. Coordinates resources of all major film research and screening activities in the L.A. area. Provides general reference services, conducts seminars, permits onsite use of collections. Services to serious researchers.

05353. Firearms Research and Identification Association, 18638 Alderbury Dr, Rowland Heights, CA 91748; (213) 964-7885. Answers inquiries, provides consulting services. Issues certificates of authenticity and identity of firearms. Serves as expert witness in related matters under litigation. Services provided on a fee basis.

05354. Fisher Berkeley Corp., 5800 Christie Ave, Emeryville, CA 94608; (415) 655-9696. Interest in wired communications equipment and systems, intercoms, hospital communications and info systems. Answers inquiries, makes referrals, provides free wired communications design service to architects, engineers, and industrial/institutional users.

05355. Food Research Institute Library, Stanford Univ, Stanford, CA 94305; (415) 497-3943. Interest in economic aspects of production, trade, and prices of food, feed and fiber commodities worldwide. Provides limited reference and duplication services at cost, makes interlibrary loans, permits onsite use of collection.

05356. Ford Western Development Laboratories Library, Ford Aerospace & Communications Corp., M/S V-54, 3939 Fabian Way, Palo Alto, CA 94303; (415) 852-6993. Interest in aeronautics, antennas, astronautics, astronomy/astrophysics, space sciences, etc. Makes interlibrary loans.

05357. Foundation for American Communications, 3383 Barham Blvd, Los Angeles, CA 90068; (213) 851-7372. Conducts seminars for executives and journalists on the needs of media, and on current issues. Provides general reference services, publishes and distributes materials. Services free to media and public policy, academic, and nonprofit groups, at a fee to businesses.

05358. Foundation for Glaucoma Research, 490 Post Street, Ste 1101, San Francisco, CA 94102; (415) 986-3162. Supports medical research into causes and treatments of glaucoma. Welcomes inquiries and encourages public and professional education, but cannot offer referrals. Foundation has established community support groups for patients.

05359. Foundation for Health Research, P.O. Box 688 (212 W Foothill Blvd, 2nd Fl), Monrovia, CA 91016; (213) 357-2181. Depository for health and health freedom related materials. Provides grants for completion of selected research projects. Answers inquiries, provides library assistance, permits onsite use of collections.

05360. Francis Bacon Library, 655 N Dartmouth Ave, Claremont, CA 91711; (714) 624-6305. Interest in history of science, Tudor and Stuart literature, history, politics, 20th Century art, (especially Dada). Provides general reference services, provides duplication services for a fee, permits onsite reference by qualified persons.

05361. Francis I. Proctor Foundation for Research in Ophthalmology, Univ of Calif. Medical Center, 3rd and Parnassus Aves, San Francisco, CA 94143; (415) 666-1441. Interest in ophthalmology, trachoma, uveitis, toxoplasmosis, external diseases of the eye. Publishes newsletter and bibliographies, answers inquiries, provides consulting services. Services primarily for scientists and physicians.

05363. Friedreich's Ataxia Group in America, P.O. Box 11116, Oakland, CA 94611; (415) 658-7014. Natl org of Friedreich's ataxia patients, physicians, families. Provides mutual support for members, publishes a newsletter to keep public informed of progress being made, and supports research through voluntary contributions.

05364. Friends of the Earth, 1045 Sansome St, San Francisco, CA 94111; (415) 433-7373. Nonprofit, intl membership org interested in world environment, conservation, energy, population. Provides general reference services, publishes and distributes materials. Services free; members contribute $25 or more per year.

05365. Friends of the River, Fort Mason Center, Bldg C, San Francisco, CA 94123; (415) 771-0400. Seeks to preserve free-flowing streams of the West and encourage balanced use of nation's energy and water resources. Provides general reference services, permits onsite use of collection. Services free, except publications.

05366. Friends of the Sea Otter, P.O. Box 221220, Carmel, CA 93922; (408) 625-3290. Interest in preservation of Calif. sea otter and its habitat. Provides general reference services, publishes and distributes materials, conducts programs. Services free, except film rental.

05367. Fund for Human Ecology, P.O. Box 1, Olema, CA 94950. Interest in actual and philosophical aspects of man on earth. Provides advisory and consulting services, distributes publications. Broadcast tapes provided for a fee, except to educational stations. Other services and materials available for a fee.

05368. Gamblers Anonymous, 1543 W Olympic Blvd, Ste 531, Los Angeles, CA 90015; (213) 386-8789. Encourages self-help for compulsive gambling. Publishes monthly bulletin and annual directory, answers inquiries, conducts seminars. Services free.

05369. Gaucher's Disease Registry, 4418 E Chapman Ave, Ste 139, Orange, CA 92669; (714) 532-2212. Interest in Gaucher's disease, including rights of disabled, support groups, fund raising, and legislation. Provides free general reference services.

05370. Gauss Scientific Society, 116 South F St, Lompoc, CA 93436; (805) 736-2662. Interest in gravitation and gravity, including theories. Answers inquiries, ana-lyzes data, makes referrals to other sources of info. Services free.

05371. Gemological Institute of America, 1660 Stewart St, Santa Monica, CA 90404; (213) 829-2991. Interest in gemology, gem testing, diamond grading, jewelry designing, retailing, display, diamond setting. Provides general reference services, makes identification reports of pearls and gemstones, grades diamonds, provides consulting services for a fee.

05372. General Dynamics Corp., Convair Division Research Library, P.O. Box 85386, San Diego, CA 92138-5386; (619) 573-4876. Interest in aerodynamics, aircraft, communications, electrical engineering, material science, space vehicles. Makes interlibrary loans. Library may be used by outside visitors by appointment only.

05373. Geodex International Inc., P.O. Box 279 (669 Broadway), Sonoma, CA 95476; (707) 938-0001. Interest in soil mechanics, foundation engineering, rock mechanics, engineering geology, structural engineering. Publishes and sells materials.

05374. Geosat Committee, 153 Kearny St, Ste 209, San Francisco, CA 94108; (415) 981-6265. Dedicated to improvement of land observation satellite remote sensing for civilian applications. Provides advisory, consulting, reference, referral services; conducts biennial state-of-the-art workshop; evaluates data; permits onsite use of collections. Most services available to anyone -- often for a fee.

05375. Geoscience Information Service, P.O. Box 225, Chico, CA 95927. Interest in distribution of soil and vegetation in Calif. Publishes terrain analysis, geologic index, geologic map index. Answers inquiries, provides advisory, and consulting services. Selected indexes free to nonprofit institutions; other services and publications available for a fee.

05376. Geothermal Resources Council, P.O. Box 1350 (111 G St), Davis, CA 95617; (916) 758-2360. Encourages research, exploration, and development of geothermal energy. Provides general reference services, some on a cost basis.

05377. Geothermal World Corp., 5762 Firebird Court, Camarillo, CA 93010; (805) 482-6288 or 482-3068. Interest in all aspects of geothermal energy utilization and development. Publishes and distributes materials. General reference services provided for a fee.

05378. Gerontological Information Center, Ethel Percy Andrus Gerontology Center, Univ of Southern Calif., Univ Park, Los Angeles, CA 90089; (213) 743-5990. Interest in gerontology, human development and aging. Maintains collection of 9,000 print materials on life-span development. Answers inquiries, makes referrals, provides reference services and printed bibliographies, permits onsite use of collection. Services free.

05379. Get Oil Out!, P.O. Box 1513 (924 Anacapa St, B2.), Santa Barbara, CA 93102; (805) 965-1519. Interest in oil pollution: legislation, effects, causes, etc.; off-shore oil operations. Answers inquiries free, provides copying services for a fee, lends or sells slides and prints, permits onsite use of collections.

05380. Giannini Foundation of Agricultural Economics Library, 248 Giannini Hall, Univ of Calif., Berkeley, CA 94720; (415) 642-7121. Interest in agricultural economics, labor, marketing, water resources, pollution, erosion, desalination, rural development. Answers inquiries, permits onsite use of collection by qualified personnel. With certain restrictions, duplication services available.

05381. Global Geochemistry Corp., 6919 Eton Ave, Canoga Park, CA 91303; (818) 992-4103. Conducts experimental research in earth and environmental sciences. Provides advisory, consulting, literature-searching, referral, reference services; conducts seminars and workshops; generates, evaluates, analyzes data. Services provided for a fee.

05382. Grantsmanship Center, 1031 S Grand Ave, Los Angeles, CA 90015; (213) 749-4721. Interest in training and publishing in grantsmanship, fund raising, proposal writing. Maintains library of fed documents, foundation and nonprofit agency reports. Publishes bimonthly newsletter, various monographs. Conducts 250 training programs each year. Services available for a fee.

05383. Ground Systems Technical Library, Hughes Aircraft Co., P.O. Box 3310 (Bldg 600/MS C222, 1901 W Malvern Ave), Fullerton, CA 92634; (714) 732-3506. Answers inquiries for local librarians on electrical engineering, provides reference, and literature-searching services, permits limited onsite reference under supervision.

05384. Guide Dogs for the Blind, P.O. Box 1200 (350 Los Ranchitos Rd), San Rafael, CA 94915; (415) 479-4000. Provides qualified, legally blind persons with guide dogs. Publishes *The Guide Dog News* quarterly. Answers inquiries, makes referrals, provides reference services, evaluates data.

05386. Hancock Library of Biology and Oceanography, Allan Hancock Foundation, Univ of Southern Calif., Los Angeles, CA 90089-0371; (213) 743-6005. Interest in marine biology and oceanography. Maintains collections of 95,000 volumes. Publishes monographs, technical reports. Answers inquiries, provides reference services. Makes interlibrary loans, permits onsite use of collection.

05387. Hastings Research, 126 Hyde St, San Francisco, CA 94102; (415) 673-2888. Provides legal research assistance to attorneys. Interest in research on law of any jurisdiction in the U.S. or its territories. Provides legal research services on a fee basis.

05389. Hemlock Society, P.O. Box 66218, Los Angeles, CA 90066-0218; (213) 391-1871. Supports active, voluntary euthanasia for the terminally ill. Works to raise public awareness of issue, and to clarify existing laws on suicide and assisted suicide; sells publications.

05390. Hereditary Disease Foundation, 606 Wilshire Blvd, Ste 504, Santa Monica, CA 90401; (213) 458-4183. Supports research in hereditary diseases by way of grant support, interdisciplinary workshops, educational programs, and maintenance of tissue banks. Answers inquiries, makes referrals. Services free, but restricted to physicians, researchers, and families with history of hereditary disease.

05392. Herpes Resource Center, P.O. Box 100 (260 Sheridan Ave), Palo Alto, CA 94302; (415) 328-7710. Provides info on treatment and research of herpes infections. Publishes quarterly newsletter and research summaries. Answers inquiries, makes referrals, provides advisory and reference services free. Conducts seminars, distributes publications for members.

05393. High Energy Physics Laboratory, Stanford Univ, Stanford, CA 94305; (415) 497-0280. Interest in nuclear and high energy physics, free electron laser physics, radio frequency superconductivity. Answers brief inquiries, makes referrals, provides reprints of journal articles, permits onsite use of collection.

05394. Higher Education Research Institute, Univ of Calif., Moore Hall, Room 320, Los Angeles, CA 90024; (213) 825-1925. Interest in empirical research into postsecondary and higher education, including fed financial aid and related topics. Provides general reference services, analyzes data, conducts seminars.

05395. Hollywood Archives, P.O. Box 1566, Apple Valley, CA 92307; (619) 242-8569. Specializes in hard-to-find movie info. Publishes directories and guides, provides general reference services. Fee for some services.

05396. Holt Atherton Center for Western Studies, Univ of the Pacific, Stockton, CA 95211; (209) 946-2404. Interest in history of the American West, especially Calif. Provides general reference services, publishes and distributes materials, permits onsite use of collection. Most services free.

05398. Homosexual Information Center, 6758 Hollywood Blvd, No 208, Los Angeles, CA 90028; (213) 464-8431. Promotes open discussion and understanding of homosexuality. Maintains library covering all aspects of homosexuality. Provides general info and specialized resources for scholars and professionals.

05399. Hoover Institution on War, Revolution, and Peace, Stanford Univ, Stanford, CA 94305; (415) 497-2058. Research org and repository of materials that conducts research programs on contemporary intl problems and domestic policy, extends grant support to selected scholars. Provides general reference services to qualified personnel, makes interlibrary loans. Provides research consultation.

05400. Hopkins Marine Station, Stanford Univ, Pacific Grove, CA 93950; (408) 373-6658. Interest in marine biology in its widest sense, including biochemistry, ecology, evolution, embryology. Provides general reference services. Qualified scientists may have access to specimen collections. Onsite use of library's collections permitted by appointment only.

05401. Hormone Research Laboratory, Univ of Calif., Health Sciences West, Room 1088, San Francisco, CA 94143; (415) 666-2624. Conducts basic endocrine research and provides teaching at graduate and postgraduate levels. Provides general reference services, publishes and distributes materials. Services free for those active in the field.

05402. Horseless Carriage Club of America, P.O. Box 1000 (312 E Las Tunas Dr), San Gabriel, CA 91776; (818) 286-3123. Interest in preservation of historical motor vehicles and their accessories. Publishes bimonthly magazine, answers inquiries, makes referrals. Services primarily for members, but others assisted as time allows.

05403. Horticultural Crops Research Laboratory, Agricultural Research Service, USDA, 2021 S Peach Ave, Fresno, CA 93727; (209) 487-5334. Interest in research on horticultural crops related to yield, quality, resistance to insects and diseases, etc. Staff members cooperate with other fed and state agencies, univs, and various commodity orgs.

05404. House Ear Institute, George Kelemen Library, 256 S Lake St, Los Angeles, CA 90057; (213) 483-4431. Serves as world center for research into disorders of ear, training of ear specialists, and for clinical treatment. Provides advisory, reference, literature-searching, abstracting, indexing, referral, and reproduction services; conducts seminars and symposia. Inquirers assisted as time allows.

05405. Human Factors Society, P.O. Box 1369, Santa Monica, CA 90406; (213) 394-1811. Answers inquiries; publishes journal, newsletter, index on human factors, human engineering, bioengineering, user-machine systems design, cybernetics, bionics, medical electronics.

05406. Human Sexuality Program, School of Medicine, Univ of Calif. Medical Center, 400 Parnassus Ave, A841, San Francisco, CA 94143; (415) 666-4787. Interest in human sexuality training for medical students and other professionals. Provides general reference services, publishes and distributes materials. Fees vary.

05407. Hunger Project Communications and Information Department, 2015 Steiner St, San Francisco, CA 94115; (415) 346-6100. Seeks to end world hunger by mobilizing public attitudes. Provides general reference services, conducts seminars and briefing sessions. Services free, except briefings.

05408. Huntington Medical Research Institutes, 734 Fairmount Ave, Pasadena, CA 91105; (213) 440-5432. Interest in development of human cell lines, experimental cardiology, medical cytogenetics. Answers inquiries, provides info on R&D in progress. Makes interlibrary loans, permits onsite use of collections. Services available without charge to physicians and scientists in related fields.

05409. Hydrocephalus Parent Support Group, Div of Neurosurgery, H-893, Univ of Calif. Medical Center, 225 Dickinson Street, San Diego, CA 92103-9981; (619) 695-3139, (619) 726-0507. Provides info on hydrocephalus and related conditions to parents and health care professionals, provides support for parents, holds social functions for hydrocephalic children and their parents.

05410. IEEE Computer Society, Publications Office, 10662 Los Vaqueros Circle, Los Alamitos, CA 90720; (714) 821-8380. Interest in computers, software engineering, component and system design and testing. Provides reference services, conducts seminars, distributes publications. Services provided at cost.

05411. Indian Training Network, 36292 Berkshire Pl, Newark, CA 94560; (415) 797-8341. Interest in training, organizational development, program evaluation, cultural awareness, and support systems of interest to Native American community orgs. Provides general reference services, conducts seminars, evaluates data, designs training programs, permits onsite use of collection. Services free to certain community orgs, at cost to others.

05412. Infant Stimulation Education Association, c/o Dr S. Ludington, Dir, UCLA Center for Health Sciences, Factor 5-942, Los Angeles, CA 90024; (213) 825-9402. Disseminates info about infant stimulation techniques, tools, and programs to professionals and parents. Provides general reference services, conducts seminars, permits onsite use of bibliography. Services free, except educational materials. Info packet mailed to persons sending a SASE.

05416. Information Systems Security Association, P.O. Box 71926, Los Angeles, CA 90071. Conducts seminars on info systems, computer, and data security; security techniques, disaster recovery planning. Makes free referrals.

05417. Information on Demand, P.O. Box 9550 (2116 Berkeley Way), Berkeley, CA 94709; (415) 644-4500 (800) 227-0750. Interest in document delivery and bibliographic research, especially in chemistry, medicine, biology, engineering, humanities, and social sciences. Provides research and consulting services at cost to all.

05418. Institute for Antiquity and Christianity, 831 N Dartmouth Ave, Claremont, CA 91711; (714) 621-8066. Conducts basic research in cultural heritage of Western civilization. Supplies photographs, conducts seminars makes referrals. Services available for a fee.

05419. Institute for Child Behavior Research, 4182 Adams Ave, San Diego, CA 92116; (714) 281-7165. Info clearinghouse on childhood psychoses and other severe learning and behavior disorders. Interest in autism, related disorders. Provides general reference services, publishes and distributes materials, conducts seminars. Services free.

05420. Institute for Contemporary Studies, 785 Market St, Ste 750, San Francisco, CA 94103; (415) 543-6213. Publishes quarterly journal on public policy issues. Answers inquiries, evaluates data, distributes data compilations and publications.

05421. Institute for Creation Research, P.O. Box 2667, El Cajon, CA 92021; (619) 440-2443. Interest in "scientific" creationism research and education. Provides general reference services, conducts seminars, publishes and distributes materials. Services free, except some publications and seminars.

05422. Institute for Food and Development Policy, 1885 Mission St, San Francisco, CA 94103; (415) 864-8555. Nonprofit public education center focusing on world hunger and development issues. Provides general reference services, publishes and distributes materials, permits onsite use of collections on restricted basis. Services provide at cost.

05423. Institute for Information Management, 510 Oakmead Parkway, Sunnyvale, CA 94086; (408) 749-0133. Degree-granting institution offering education, research, consulting, and publications to the info systems management community. Provides general reference services, conducts seminars, distributes data compilations and publications.

05424. Institute for Marine Information, P.O. Box 91033, Pasadena, CA 91109; (213) 258-6929. Answers inquiries concerning marine museums, biological, maritime, and historical data concerning the seas, Pacific Ocean Basin, natural history. Services free.

05425. Institute for Mathematical Studies in the Social Sciences, Stanford Univ, Ventura Hall, Stanford, CA 94305; (415) 497-3111. Interest in computer-based instruction in a variety of subjects at all levels, special education for disadvantaged. Provides general reference services, permits onsite use of collection.

05426. Institute for Reality Therapy, 7301 Medical Center Dr, Ste 202, Canoga Park, CA 91307; (818) 888-0688. Publishes newsletter, brochure on theory of Reality Therapy; answers inquiries, provides advisory services, conducts workshops. Services free, except workshops.

05427. Institute for Research in Social Behavior, Broadway-Grand Plaza, 456 22nd St, Oakland, CA 94612; (415) 465-2791. Conducts studies in mental health, education, public health, and social welfare. Provides general reference services, distributes materials. Services provided at cost.

05428. Institute for Scientific Analysis, 2410 Lombard St, San Francisco, CA 94123 (415) 921-4987. Conducts evaluation and demonstration projects in social sciences. Provides general reference services. Consult-

ing services available on a grant basis; other services free to govt agencies, for a fee to others.

05429. Institute for Studies of Destructive Behaviors and the Suicide Prevention Center, 1041 S Menlo Ave, Los Angeles, CA 90006; (213) 386-5111. Interest in study of destructive behaviors, mental health responses, crisis intervention. Provides general reference services, publishes and distributes materials, conducts seminars, permits onsite use of collection. Services free to legitimate users.

05430. Institute for the Advancement of Human Behavior, 4370 Alpine Road, Ste 205, Portola Valley, CA 94025; (415) 851-8411. Provides continuing education and conducts seminars for health care professionals. Concentrates on communicating under pressure, pain control, dealing with problem patients, guided imagery.

05431. Institute for the Future, 2740 Sand Hill Rd, Menlo Park, CA 94025; (415) 854-6322. Performs sponsored research, conducts seminars, and teleconferences on wide range of topics, answers inquiries, provides consulting services, publishes reports.

05432. Institute for the Interdisciplinary Applications of Algebra and Combinatorics, Univ of Calif., Santa Barbara, CA 93106; (805) 961-3002. Interest in mathematics, linear algebra, matrix theory, multilinear algebra, combinatorics, scientific communication. Provides general reference services, publishes and distributes materials, conducts seminars. Services provided at cost.

05433. Institute for the Study of Economic Systems, c/o Kelso & Co., Inc., Embarcadero Center 3, Ste 1760, San Francisco, CA 94111; (415) 788-7454. Interest in two-factor economic theory, financing techniques. Publishes journal irregularly and distributes it to members free, to others at cost.

05434. Institute for the Study of Sexual Assault, 403 Ashbury Street, San Francisco, CA 94117; (415) 861-2048. Conducts research on various aspects of sexual assault, provides training and consultation. Operates library, conducts research for a fee, operates speakers bureau, administers grants.

05435. Institute of Archaeology, Univ of Calif., 405 Hilgard Ave, Los Angeles, CA 90024; (213) 825-4169. Interest in archeology, excavations, cuneiform signs. Provides general reference services, conducts seminars, publishes and distributes materials, permits onsite use of collections. Fees charged for publications and literature searches.

05436. Institute of Business and Economic Research, Univ of Calif., 156 Barrows Hall, Berkeley, CA 94720; (415) 642-1922. Interest in research into problems of economics and business, with emphasis on Calif. and Pacific Coast. Answers inquiries, makes referrals, provides info on research in progress, conducts seminars. Services generally free.

05437. Institute of Chemical Biology, Univ of San Francisco, San Francisco, CA 94117-1080; (415) 666-6415. Interest in biochemistry, toxicology and carcinogenicity of inorganic substances, organic synthesis. Answers inquiries and provides consulting services.

05438. Institute of Ecology, Univ of Calif., Davis, CA 95616; (916) 752-3026. Publishes monographs, proceedings on water quality in Lake Tahoe Basin, answers inquiries, conducts research, makes referrals to other sources of info.

05439. Institute of Environmental Stress, Univ of Calif., Santa Barbara, CA 93106; (805) 961-2350, 961-2361, or 961-2179. Provides data derived from research on environmental control, answers inquiries, provides consulting, reference services, and research facilities. Some services free.

05440. Institute of Geophysics and Planetary Physics, Univ of Calif., Riverside, CA 92521; (714) 787-4503. Interest in measurement of solar neutrons and gamma-rays, geothermal resources studies, earthquake studies, laboratory experiments. Provides general reference services, publishes and distributes materials. Services free, except consulting.

05441. Institute of Governmental Studies, Univ of Calif., 109 Moses Hall, Berkeley, CA 94720; (415) 642-1472. Conducts extensive and varied research and service programs in such fields as public policy, politics and urban-metropolitan problems. Provides general reference services, permits onsite use of its collection.

05442. Institute of Human Origins, 2453 Ridge Rd, Berkeley, CA 94709; (415) 845-0333. Publicly supported foundation that promotes original anthropological research. Provides general reference services, conducts seminars and an annual symposium, evaluates data. Services free.

05443. Institute of Industrial Relations, Univ of Calif., 2521 Channing Way, Berkeley, CA 94720; (415) 642-1705. Interest in industrial psychology and sociology. Has selective collection of standard works, statistical compilations, govt documents. Provides free reference services, onsite use of collections.

05444. Institute of Noetic Sciences, 475 Gate Five Rd, Ste 300, Sausalito, CA 94965; (415) 331-5650. Interest in psychic research and related topics. Provides general reference services, publishes and distributes materials. Services primarily for members, but some are free to public.

05445. Institute of Risk Management Consultants, 58 Diablo View Dr, Orinda, CA 94563; (415) 254-9472. Interest in risk management, encompassing property and liability insurance, self-insurance funding, and related loss prevention techniques. Provides talks or articles explaining risk management consulting.

05446. Institute of Transportation Studies Library, Institute of Transportation Studies, Univ of Calif., 412 McLaughlin Hall, Berkeley, CA 94720; (415) 642-3604.

Interest in transportation planning, economics, and engineering, highway engineering, airport engineering. Provides general reference services, permits onsite use of collections.

05447. Institute of Urban and Regional Development, Univ of Calif., Wurster Hall, Room 316, Berkeley, CA 94720; (415) 642-4874. Research and publishing institute for urban studies, policy analysis, and policies planning, program evaluation of social services. Info provided primarily through publications, available on request.

05448. Inter-American Tropical Tuna Commission, c/o Scripps Institution of Oceanography, La Jolla, CA 92093; (714) 453-2820 ext 301. Interest in biology and ecology of tropical tunas and associated marine mammals of eastern Pacific Ocean and commonly used bait fish. Publishes research reports, and bibliographies, answers inquiries, makes interlibrary loans. Primarily for academic and scientific orgs, but others assisted.

05449. Inter-Financial Association, 21 Tamal Vista Blvd, Corte Madera, CA 94925; (415) 924-1930 Natl, multi-industry org devoted to development of unified financial services industry. Provides a meeting forum for representatives of all financial industries, conducts educational conferences and symposia. Most services free. Memberships available for an annual fee.

05450. Interfaith Center to Reverse the Arms Race, 132 N Euclid Ave, Pasadena, CA 91101; (213) 681-4292. Interest in reversing nuclear arms race through education and programs for religious community. Provides advisory, reference, referral services; evaluates, analyzes data; conducts conferences, film festivals. Fees for film rental and some educational materials. Services intended primarily for clergy and religious congregations, but available to anyone.

05451. Intermediate Technology, 556 Santa Cruz Ave, Menlo Park, CA 94025; (415) 328-1730. Promotes education, research, and development in low capital technology. Maintains resource center for intermediate technology materials and experience. Answers simple inquiries free, makes referrals, provides advisory services.

05452. International Academy at Santa Barbara Environmental Studies Institute, Riviera Campus, 2074 Alameda Padre Serra, Santa Barbara, CA 93103; (805) 965-5010. Interest in current political affairs, environmental/ecological topics. Provides general reference services, permits onsite use of collections. Services generally free.

05454. International Association for Enterostomal Therapy, 5000 Birch Street, Ste 400, Newport Beach, CA 92660; (714) 476-0269. Promotes high standards for care and rehabilitation of ostomy patients, patients with pressure sores, incontinence, and related skin conditions. Provides education and certification, publishes a journal, conducts research.

05455. International Association for Personnel Women, 5820 Wilshire Blvd, Ste 500, Los Angeles, CA 90036. (213) 937-9000. Conducts conferences on human resources management and women in human resources management. Conferences open to all upon payment of registration fees. Membership open to professionals in same or related fields.

05456. International Association for the Physical Sciences of the Ocean, c/o Dr Eugene C. LaFond, Secty General, LaFond Oceanic Consultants, P.O. Box 7325, San Diego, CA 92107; (619) 222-3680. Interest in physical oceanography, marine geology and geophysics, marine pollution. Organizes meetings, makes referrals to other sources of info.

05457. International Association of Business Communicators, Communication Bank, 870 Market St, Ste 940, San Francisco, CA 94102; (415) 433-3400. Info and resource network to communicators and related professionals. Interest in nonbroadcast video. Provides general reference services, publishes and distributes materials, permits onsite use of collections. Services available for a fee.

05459. International Association of Cancer Victims and Friends, 7740 W Manchester Avenue, Ste 110, Playa del Rey, CA 90291; (213) 822-5032. Disseminates educational materials concerning prevention and control of cancer through nontoxic therapies. Publishes info relating to cancer-causing factors in environment, food, cancer prevention, cancer detection, and nontoxic cancer treatments.

05460. International Association of Plumbing and Mechanical Officials, c/o Tom Higham, Exec Dir, 5032 Alhambra Ave, Los Angeles, CA 90032; (213) 223-1471. Promotes uniform codes for standardization of manufactured equipment, installation methods, and inspection procedures. Provides general reference services, publishes and distributes materials. Services primarily for members, but some provided for a fee to others.

05461. International Bicycle Touring Society, 2115 Paseo Dorado, La Jolla, CA 92037; (714) 454-6428. Organizes bicycle tours for adults who can afford staying in hotels and eating in restaurants. Publishes journal articles, and directories, answers inquiries free.

05462. International Biotoxicological Center, 23000 Grand Terrace Rd, Colton, CA 92324; (714) 825-4773. Reference and documentation org interested in biotoxicology, poisonous and medicinal plants, environmental pollutants, immunology. Provides general reference services, permits onsite use of collections. Services provided for a fee.

05463. International Bird Rescue Research Center, Aquatic Park, Berkeley, CA 94710; (415) 841-9086. Interest in rehabilitation of oiled birds and related causes. Provides general reference services, publishes and distributes materials, permits onsite use of collection. Fees charged for consulting and duplication services.

05464. International Bundle Branch Block Association, 6631 W 83rd St, Los Angeles, CA 90045-2899; (213) 670-9132. Serves as info center for professionals and as a support group for patients with bundle branch block, a heart dysfunction. Provides reference services, permits onsite use of collection. Fees levied on an ability-to-pay basis. Services available to professionals and concerned laity.

05465. International Center for Dance Orthopaedics and Dance Therapy, 9201 Sunset Blvd, Ste 317, Hollywood, CA 90069; (213) 276-5440. Interest in musculoskeletal problems of classical dancers and others engaging in dance activity. Provides general reference services, conducts symposia, permits onsite use of collections. Services available at cost.

05466. International College of Applied Nutrition, P.O. Box 386, La Habra, CA 90631; (213) 697-4576. Ph.D's engaged in practice of and/or research in nutrition and its allied fields. Answers inquiries free, sells publications, conducts seminars and symposiums for professional and prospective members.

05467. International Conference of Building Officials, 5360 S Workman Mill Rd, Whittier, CA 90601; (213) 699-0541. Interest in model building code development, inspector certification programs, training programs, and structural safety. Provides related consulting services, training.

05468. International Council for Development of Underutilized Plants, 18 Meadow Park Court, Orinda, CA 94563; (415) 254-9212. Supports domestication and commercialization of underutilized plants. Provides general reference services, sponsors research, publishes and distributes materials, permits onsite use of collection. Services free, except mailing charges.

05469. International Documentary Association, 8489 W 3rd St, Los Angeles, CA 90048; (213) 655-7089. Supports and honors work of documentary and nonfiction film and video makers around the world. Provides advisory, referral, and reference services; conducts seminars, other events; operates a job referral program. Services free to members. Job referral program free to employers; prospective employees chosen from membership.

05470. International Ecosystems University, 310 Oakvue Rd, Pleasant Hill, CA 94523; (415) 932-4499 or 946-1500. Publishes journal examining environmental problems in an interdisciplinary way; holds conference, workshops. Provides consulting services at cost to some users, free to others.

05471. International Foundation for Telemetering, 21031 Ventura Blvd, Ste 1001, Woodland Hills, CA 91364; (818) 884-9567. Holds annual fall telemetry conference in southwestern U.S., at which educational tutorial sessions are conducted. Answers inquiries, provides reference, consulting services.

05472. International Guiding Eyes, P.O. Box 4875, Sylmar, CA 91342; (818) 362-5834 (818) 362-6877. Trains blind persons in use of guide dogs, trains and provides guide dogs free of charge to certain blind persons over 16 years of age. Recipients spend four weeks at school in training with their dogs.

05473. International Human Powered Vehicle Association, P.O. Box 2068, Seal Beach, CA 90740; (213) 420-9817. Administers competition for first one-man human powered vehicle to exceed 65 mph. Conducts seminars, workshops; sanctions races and vehicle competitions. Fee for some services.

05474. International Institute of Municipal Clerks, 160 N Altadena Dr, Pasadena, CA 91107; (818) 795-6153. Maintains collection of municipal ordinance files, clerk manuals, and related materials. Answers inquiries, makes referrals, provides advisory services, permits onsite use of collections. Services free to members, at cost to others.

05475. International Joseph Diseases Foundation, 1832 Holmes Street, Bldg E, P.O. Box 2250, Livermore, CA 94550; (415) 455-0706. Nonprofit intl org of patients and health care professionals interested in striatonigral disease. Conducts clinics, provides counseling, promotes research and works to educate medical profession and public.

05476. International Naturopathic Association, 874 N Beverly Glen Blvd, Los Angeles, CA 90077; (213) 479-1945. Interest in natural therapy, herbs, massage, selective dieting. Provides general reference services, conducts seminars, permits onsite use of collection. Services generally free.

05477. International Palm Society, c/o James Mintken, Secty, P.O. Box 27, Forestville, CA 95436; (707) 887-7723. Intl clearinghouse for info about palm plant family. Answers inquiries, makes referrals, provides advisory services, publishes quarterly journal. Provides seeds to members for nominal handling charge. Services primarily for members.

05478. International Project for Soft Energy Paths, Friends of the earth Foundation, 124 Spear St, San Francisco, CA 94105; (415) 495-4770. Encourages development of soft energy systems that are renewable, efficient, diverse, and environmentally benign. Publishes *Soft Energy Notes* 6 times a year. Answers inquiries, makes referrals, provides reference services. Services free, except publication.

05479. International Remote Sensing Institute, Exec Airport, 6151 Freeport Blvd, Sacramento, CA 95822; (916) 422-9631. Publishes special reports on remote sensing applications to environmental monitoring, answers inquiries, provides consulting, and reference services, sponsors seminars, and symposia for a fee.

05480. International Right of Way Association, 6133 Bristol Parkway, Ste 270, Culver City, CA 90230; (213) 649-5323. Interest in govt real estate and right-of-way matters, relocation assistance, property management. Answers inquiries or refers inquirers to other sources of info free, sells publications.

05481. International Society for Astrological Research, P.O. Box 38613 (838 S 5th Ave), Los Angeles, CA 90038; (213) 465-1408. Interest in astrology and its use as a tool for psychological understanding of the individual. Conducts seminars, makes referrals. Fee for some services.

05482. International Society for Geothermal Engineering, P.O. Drawer 4743, Whittier, CA 90607; (213) 699-3780. Seeks to advance useful service of terrestrial heat sources through teaching, publishing, and audiovisual work. Provides general reference services, conducts seminars, sells slide presentations.

05483. International Society for the Arts, Sciences and Technology, c/o Journal Leonardo, Art Dept, San Francisco State Univ, 1600 Holloway Ave, San Francisco, CA 94132. Promotes interactions between artists, scientists, and engineers. Provides intl education and charitable assistance to artists. Conducts conferences, seminars, and workshops, makes referrals. Services free.

05484. International Society of Biorheology, Dept of Physiology and Biophysics, Univ of Southern Calif. School of Medicine, 2025 Zonal Ave, Los Angeles, CA 90033; (213) 224-7244. Interest in biorheology, hemorheology, tissue and cell mechanics, bio-fluids, in vivo, in vitro rheology, clinical hemorheology. Answers inquiries or makes referrals for free, conducts seminars, workshops, and intl congresses.

05485. International Toxic Shock Syndrome Network, P.O. Box 1248, Beverly Hills, CA 90213-1248; (213) 274-1061. Support group for toxic shock syndrome victims and their families. Provides counseling, info. Works with other groups to establish standards and testing for tampons.

05486. International Transactional Analysis Association, c/o Susan Sevilla, Exec Dir, 1772 Vallejo St, San Francisco, CA 94123; (415) 885-5992. Promotes and assists in research on transactional analysis theory and therapy. Maintains files of current research projects. Answers inquiries, makes referrals, provides reference services. Services free and available primarily to members, but others assisted.

05487. Interstitial Cystitis Association of America, Box 151323, San Diego, CA 92115; (619) 486-4497. Supports patients with interstitial cystitis. Promotes knowledge and understanding of disease conditions, supports research, accepts donations.

05488. Inventors Assistance League, 345 W Cypress St, Glendale, CA 91204; (213) 246-6540. Interest in marketing and research of patents, trademarks, copyrights. Answers inquiries, provides consulting services. Offers patent application assistance. Initial interview and counseling free, with subsequent optional services provided at cost.

05489. Inventors Workshop International Education Foundation, P.O. Box 251, Tarzana, CA 91356; (818) 344-3375. Teaches protection, development, and market testing of products. Publishes *The Lightbulb* bimonthly and *Inventors Guidebook*. Members receive free consultation services, evaluation of their ideas, and advice.

05491. Janus Information Facility, 1952 Union St, San Francisco, CA 94123; (415) 567-8197. Serves as liaison between individual transsexuals and health and legal channels. Publishes pamphlets, booklets, treatment centers list. Answers inquiries, provides consulting services, distributes publications. $20 donation requested.

05492. Japanese American Citizens League, 1765 Sutter St, San Francisco, CA 94115; (415) 921-5225. Promotes civil rights and equal opportunity advocacy through research, planning, and program development. Publishes weekly newspaper, directories, bibliographies. Answers inquiries, provides advisory, and reference services. Services free, primarily for members.

05493. Japanese American Cultural and Community Center, 244 S San Pedro St, Los Angeles, CA 90012; (213) 628-2725. Promotes activities that serve to preserve and encourage appreciation of Japanese culture and Japanese-American heritage. Provides general reference services, conducts seminars, makes direct and interlibrary loans, permits onsite use of collections. Services available on payment of membership fee.

05494. Jet Propulsion Laboratory Library, Calif. Institute of Technology, 4800 Oak Grove Dr, Pasadena, CA 91109; (818) 354-4200. Interest in lunar, planetary, and deep-space unmanned scientific missions, tracking and data acquisition techniques and equipment, etc. Answers inquiries, makes referrals to other sources of info. Services limited to approved personnel.

05495. Josephine D. Randall Junior Museum, 199 Museum Way, San Francisco, CA 94114; (415) 863-1399. Interest in Calif. ecology, zoology, geology, anthropology, arts and crafts, photography, industrial arts, seismology, computer education. Provides general reference services, permits onsite use of collections. Services free, except cost of materials.

05496. Journalism Association of Community Colleges, c/o Modesto Junior Coll, Modesto, CA 95350; (209) 575-6224. Exchanges teaching ideas and materials among Calif. community colls. Publishes bimonthly newsletter, semiannual Idea Exchange for student publication ideas, annual directory. Answers inquiries, makes referrals.

05497. Judah L. Magnes Memorial Museum, Western Jewish History Center, 2911 Russell St, Berkeley, CA 94705; (415) 849-2710. Interest in western U.S. Jewish history. Provides general reference services, publishes and distributes materials, permits onsite use of collections. Publications, reference services for a fee, others free.

05498. Jules Stein Eye Institute, UCLA Center for Health Sciences, 800 Westwood Plaza, Los Angeles, CA 90024; (213) 825-5051. Promotes and conducts vision research, patient care, and ophthalmic education. Provides general reference services, publishes and distributes materials, conducts seminars on a fee basis for health care professionals only.

05499. Julie Moore & Associations, P.O. Box 5156, Riverside, CA 92517; (714) 943-3863. Commercial org that creates and disseminates wildlife info, especially bibliographic entries. Provides advisory, consulting, literature-searching, abstracting, indexing, and referral services for a fee.

05500. Kaiser Aluminum and Chemical Corp. Library, P.O. Box 877, Pleasanton, CA 94566; (415) 847-4572. Interest in aluminum technology. Answers inquiries, provides reference services. Services available to govt agencies, industry, and students only.

05501. Kestrel Institute, 1801 Page Mill Rd, Palo Alto, CA 94304; (415) 493-6871. Involved in research in computer program synthesis, codification of programming knowledge, program transformations, and development of a programming environment. Provides advisory, consulting, referral services. Services primarily for special groups.

05502. Kinnetic Laboratories, P.O. Box 1040, Santa Cruz, CA 95061; (408) 462-6200. Provides commercial oceanographic/marine biological consulting. Maintains small collection of related books and papers. Publishes technical reports, critical reviews, data compilations. Conducts oceanographic investigations, evaluates data. Services provided for a fee.

05503. Labor Occupational Health Program, Institute of Industrial Relations, Univ of Calif., 2521 Channing Way, Berkeley, CA 94720; (415) 642-5507. Provides education in occupational safety and health to labor and management. Provides general reference services, conducts workshops, evaluates data. Workshops, technical assistance primarily for labor unions and labor-management groups, provided at negotiated rates.

05504. Laboratory for Comparative Biochemistry, 4620 Santa Fe St, San Diego, CA 92109; (714) 274-5401. Performs research in the biomedical sciences and offers educational opportunities for advanced students. Answers inquiries, provides advisory services, conducts seminars. Services free, restricted to professionals.

05505. Lawrence Berkeley Laboratory Isotopes Project, Nuclear Science Div., Univ of Calif., Berkeley, CA 94720; (415) 486-6152. Interest in nuclear structure and decay data, including properties of radioisotopes, stable nuclei, and nuclear reactions. Answers requests for data within limits of staff and time, publishes and distributes materials.

05506. League to Save Lake Tahoe, P.O. Box 10110 (2197 Lake Tahoe Blvd), S Lake Tahoe, CA 95731; (916) 541-5388. Interest in preserving environmental balance, scenic beauty, and outdoor recreational opportunities of Lake Tahoe Basin. Publishes quarterly newsletter, answers inquiries free.

05507. Legal Economic Evaluations, 1010 Corporation Way, Ste 201, Palo Alto, CA 94303; (800) 221-6826, (415) 969-7682. Economic consulting firm specializing in litigation. Provides consulting services and economic expert testimony to attorneys in U.S. and Canada.

05508. Legal Services for Children, 149 Ninth St, San Francisco, CA 94103; (415) 863-3762. Law office serving minors. Interest in legal and other matters affecting minors' rights and welfare. Provides advice on establishing similar service for minors elsewhere.

05509. Lepidopterists' Society, c/o Julian P. Donahue, Secty, Natural History Museum, 900 Exposition Blvd, Los Angeles, CA 90007; (213) 744-3364. Intl nonprofit org that promotes study of insects and facilitates exchange of specimens and ideas by professional worker and amateurs. Provides reference, referral services; conducts conferences, seminars, workshops; rents mailing list. Services primarily for members, but others will be assisted within limits of time and staff. Some fees may be charged.

05510. Letterman Army Institute of Research, Presidio of San Francisco, San Francisco, CA 94129-6800; (415) 561-2600 or 561-4767. Interest in dermatology research, blood research, info science, laser research, pesticides, trauma and shock research. Provides general reference services, publishes and distributes materials, permits onsite use of collections.

05511. Library Information Services, 1563 Trestle Glen Rd, Oakland, CA 94610; (415) 444-1998. Info specialist in engineering, architecture, business, and economics. Answers inquiries, provides advisory services. Arranges interlibrary loans, plans and organizes special libraries. Services available for a fee.

05512. Lillian Paley Center for the Visual Arts, 1515 Webster St, Ste 425 443, Oakland, CA 94612; (415) 451-6300. Nonprofit service org for artists, galleries, consultants, collectors, and scholars interested in contemporary visual arts. Provides general reference services, conducts seminars, sponsors exhibitions of members' works, permits onsite use of collections. Fee for some services.

05513. Linus Pauling Institute of Science and Medicine, 440 Page Mill Rd, Palo Alto, CA 94306; (415) 327-4064. Interest in research in cancer, aging, and nutrition. Answers inquiries and distributes publications. Services free within limits of time and staff.

05514. Little People of America, P.O. Box 633, San Bruno, CA 94066; (415) 589-0695. Interest in dwarfism, related problems. Provides general reference services, publishes and distributes materials, conducts annual meetings. Services generally provided through membership fee.

05516. Litton Industries Guidance and Control Systems, 5500 Canoga Ave, Woodland Hills, CA 91364; (818) 716-3171. Interest in engineering, mathematics, physics, data processing, instrumentation, computer technology, guidance and control. Answers inquiries, makes referrals, makes interlibrary or intercompany loans and searches outside data banks.

05517. Los Angeles Communications Law Program, School of Law, Univ of Calif., Los Angeles, Los Angeles, CA 90024; (213) 825-6211. Interest in communications law and telecommunications. Publishes journal, conducts symposia. Services available for a fee.

05518. Los Angeles Rubber Group Foundation, Dept of Chemical Engineering, HED 211, Univ of Southern Calif., Los Angeles, CA 90089-1211; (213) 743-2573. Interest in rubber and polymer technology, elastomers, plastics, coatings. Answers inquiries, makes referrals, permits onsite use of collection, conducts courses. Director provides private consulting services.

05519. Luckey Laboratories, 7252 Osbun Rd, San Bernardino, CA 92404; (714) 884-6235. Interest in alcohol and its effects on driving and related endeavors, manufactures alcohol testing devices. Answers inquiries, provides consulting and reference services, provides expert testimony in court cases involving alcohol. Fee charged for services.

05520. Luso-American Education Foundation, P.O. Box 1768, Oakland, CA 94604; (415) 452-4465. Perpetuates Portuguese culture in America. Provides advisory and reference services. Assists school districts in setting up language and literature courses. Makes referrals, permits onsite use of collections. Services free to Calif. residents only.

05521. Manuscript Society, c/o David R. Smith, Exec Dir, 350 N Niagara St, Burbank, CA 91505; (213) 845-3011. Interest in autograph and manuscript collecting. Publishes quarterly journal, newsletter, and directories, answers inquiries. Not involved in appraising, purchasing, selling, or authenticating manuscripts.

05522. Mare Island Naval Shipyard Technical Library, Code 202.13, Stop T 4 (Bldg 483, 4th Fl), Vallejo, CA 94592; (707) 646-4306. Interest in analytical chemistry, materials testing, mechanical engineering, nuclear, and electrical engineering, nuclear chemistry. Answers inquiries, provides interlibrary loans, permits onsite use of collections subject to security clearance.

05523. Marin Wildlife Center, P.O. Box 957 (76 Albert Park Lane), San Rafael, CA 94915-0957; (415) 454-6961. Interest in natural sciences, (with emphasis on S.F. Bay area), nature education, ecology, wildlife. Answers inquiries, conducts classes and field trips, presents exhibitions on natural history, ecological, and environmental subjects.

05524. Marine Bioassay Laboratories, 1234 Hwy 1, Watsonville, CA 95076. Researches chemical oceanography and related physical and marine biology. Publishes technical reports, critical reviews, data compilations. Conducts marine bioassay tests and computerized analysis of chemical field results.

05525. Marine Ecological Institute, 811 Seaport Blvd, Redwood City, CA 94063; (415) 364-2760. Interest in marine science education, especially ecology of S.F. Bay region. Provides general reference services, publishes and distributes materials, conducts biological survey work. Services provided for a fee.

05526. Marine Science Institute, Univ of Calif., Santa Barbara, CA 93106. Concerned with marine science. Publishes brochure, research studies, annual reports; answers inquiries, refers inquirers to other sources of info, provides presentations on research.

05527. Marineland, 6610 Palos Verdes Dr South, Rancho Palos Verdes, CA 90274; (213) 377-1571. Interest in ichthyology, mammalogy, marine mammals, research and education. Answers inquiries, lends films, permits onsite observation of live collections. Qualified scientists may be granted access to all collections.

05528. Media Alliance, Fort Mason, Bldg D, San Francisco, CA 94123; (415) 441-2557. Nonprofit membership org with resource center for community interested in uses and analysis of media. Provides advisory and referral services, conducts seminars and workshops. Services primarily for members, but others assisted within limits of time and staff.

05530. Medic Alert Foundation International, P.O. Box 1009, 2323 Colorado, Turlock, CA 95381; (209) 668-3333, (800) 344-3226. Provides emergency medical identification system, including a 24-hour worldwide emergency answering service. Also conducts medical training for public and emergency personnel.

05531. Medication Information Service, South Bay Free Clinic, 1807 Manhattan Beach Blvd, Manhattan Beach, CA 90266; (213) 376-3000. Offers info on, or answers to, questions about drugs of all kinds. Aims to educate consumers about drugs and their proper use. Accepts inquiries by telephone only.

05532. Meiklejohn Civil Liberties Institute, P.O. Box 673 (1715 Francisco St), Berkeley, CA 94701; (415) 848-0599. Operates research library interested in human rights and social justice. Provides general reference services, distributes publications, permits onsite use of collection.

05533. Memorial Cancer Research Foundation of Southern California, 9808 Venice Blvd, Culver City, CA 90230; (213) 559-3550. Involved in investigational protocol studies in cancer treatment. Answers inquiries free.

05534. Men's Rights, P.O. Box 163180, Sacramento, CA 95816; (916) 484-7333. Interest in sexism and men's problems. Provides general reference services, conducts seminars, permits onsite use of collections. Seminars provided on a fee basis, other services at cost.

05535. Mental Health Information Service, Neuropsychiatric Institute, Center for the Health Sciences, Univ of Calif., Los Angeles, CA 90024; (213) 825-0597 or 825-0374. Library interested in mental health services, cultural anthropology, neurology, mental illness, alcoholism, psychoanalysis, social work, etc. Provides general reference services, consultation to professional community.

05536. Mental Research Institute, 555 Middlefield Rd, Palo Alto, CA 94301; (415) 321-3055. Provides research, training, and service institute for interactional study of the individual, the family, and the community. Publishes semestrial training brochures, newsletter. Answers inquiries, provides consulting services, conducts seminars. Minimum fee charged.

05537. Mental Retardation Research Center, Univ of Calif., 760 Westwood Plaza, Los Angeles, CA 90024; (213) 825-5542. Interest in mental retardation, developmental biology, related fields. Provides general reference services, publishes and distributes materials. Services free.

05538. Mexican American Community Services Agency, 332 N 2nd St, San Jose, CA 95112; (408) 275-8506. Conducts human service, social, and educational research on Mexican-American communities. Provides general reference and translation services, conducts seminars, permits onsite use of collection. Services free.

05539. Microbeam Analysis Society, c/o Gordon Cleaver, Pres, General Electric Corp., Vallecitos Nuclear Center, Pleasanton, CA 94566. Interest in x-ray and electron physics. Publishes quarterly, proceedings of annual meetings, and bibliographies, answers inquiries, conducts meetings and workshops, provides literature-searching services. Services provided at cost.

05540. Milieu Information Service, P.O. Box 6536 (1863 Shulman Ave), San Jose, CA 95150; (408) 287-4071. Publishes books, research reports, college textbooks on environmental subjects; provides weather forecasting, free reference services, consulting services, speakers.

05541. Model A Ford Club of America, 250 S Cypress, La Habra, CA 90631. Interest in preservation and restoration of Model A Fords. Maintains technical and historical data on Model A Fords, 1928 through 1931. Answers inquiries, makes referrals, provides consulting services, distributes publications. Services available primarily to members, but others assisted.

05542. Morab Horse Registry of America, P.O. Box 143 (144 Baron Ave), Clovis, CA 93613; (209) 297-7491. Collects, verifies, records, and preserves pedigrees of the Morab horse. Publishes newsletter and fact sheets. Answers inquiries, makes referrals, provides advisory services, evaluates data. Newsletters available to members, other services free.

05543. Moss Landing Marine Laboratories, P.O. Box 223, Moss Landing, CA 95039; (408) 633-3304. Educational and research institution interested in marine sciences, environmental relations of marine organisms, etc. Answers to inquiries limited by time and effort required, permits onsite reference by appoinment.

05544. Motorcycle Safety Foundation Research Department, P.O. Box 5044 (Airway Ave), Costa Mesa, CA 92628; (714) 241-9251. Interest in motorcycle safety, licensing, and rider education. Provides general reference services, conducts seminars and workshops, evaluates data, lends materials. Services provided for a fee.

05545. Mount Wilson and Las Campanas Observatories Library, 813 Santa Barbara St, Pasadena, CA 91101; (213) 577-1122. Interest in astronomy, astrophysics, history of science. Permits onsite use of collections. Library welcomes research in astrophysics and history of astronomy by qualified scholars. Service available at discretion of librarian.

05546. Multi-Focus, 1525 Franklin St, San Francisco, CA 94109; (415) 673-5100. Interest in human sexuality, including education and therapy. Publishes *The Yes Books of Sex*. Lends nonprofit materials at set fees to persons in education, therapy, research, and counseling only.

05547. Museum of Systematic Biology, School of Biological Sciences, Univ of Calif., Irvine, CA 92717; (714) 856-7420. Interest in biota of southern Calif., southern Ariz., and Baja, Calif. Publishes Research Series, answers inquiries, provides reference services, permits onsite use of specimen collection.

05548. Museum of Vertebrate Zoology, Univ of Calif., Berkeley, CA 94720; (415) 642-3567. Interest in vertebrate zoology, including systematics, morphology, physiology, ecology, and behavior of animals. Provides general reference service, identifies specimens, permits onsite use of collections. Services available to qualified persons.

05549. Mutilation Data Center, 4623 E Washington, Apt. 20, Orange, CA 92669; (714) 639-5273. Provides info about animal mutilation, kidnapping, child abuse, drug trafficking and abuse, serial murders, terrorism, cults, political extremists. Evaluates, distributes data; answers inquiries. Services free to law enforcement agencies, humane societies, child welfare agencies, and other researchers on an exchange basis.

05550. NASA Ames Research Center Library, 202-3, Moffett Field, CA 94035; (415) 694-5157. Interest in aerospace technology, interplanetary probes, extraterrestrial intelligence, computational physics. Provides general reference services, permits onsite use of collections by govt agencies, their contractors and univs. Services free to qualified users.

05551. NASA Industrial Application Center, Univ of Southern Calif., 3716 S Hope St, 2nd Fl, Los Angeles, CA 90007; (213) 743-6132. Provides info and assistance in technology utilization to public. Interest in applications of research leading to technology transfer. Offers online data searches, provides document delivery services, conducts special projects.

05552. NEUS, P.O. Box 99219, San Diego, CA 92109. Interest in small business assistance, technical publi-

cations. Provides general reference services, publishes and distributes materials, conducts data bank searches, assists in holding conferences and meetings on any subject.

05553. Narcotic Educational Foundation of America, 5055 Sunset Blvd, Los Angeles, CA 90027; (213) 663-5171. Interest in preventing abusive drug use. Publishes films, brochures, posters; provides consulting, reference services; disseminates literature (single copies free), lends material; operates speakers bureau.

05555. Narcotics Anonymous, World Service Office, 16155 Wyandotte St, Van Nuys, CA 91406; (818) 780-3951. Worldwide voluntary membership society of recovered drug addicts offering help to others seeking recovery. Provides general reference services. Some services confidential and provided only to self-help groups; others free.

05556. National Acupuncture Association, P.O. Box 24509, Los Angeles, CA 90024; (213) 477-4343. Coordinates info on acupuncture in U.S. Answers inquiries, provides consulting services, conducts seminars. Services at cost.

05557. National Aeronautic Association, U.S. Hang Gliding Association, P.O. Box 66306 (11423 Washington Blvd), Los Angeles, CA 90066; (213) 390-3065. Supervises hang gliding activities such as record attempts and competition. Interest in hang gliding safety and instruction. Provides general reference services, publishes and distributes materials. Services free, except postage.

05559. National Alopecia Areata Foundation, P.O. Box 5027, Mill Valley, CA 94941; (415) 383-3444. Provides support network for victims of alopecia areata (baldness). Disseminates info, raises funds for research, provides names of local support groups.

05560. National Association for Children of Alcoholics, 31706 Coast Hwy, Ste 201, S Laguna, CA 92677; (714) 499-3889. Supports and serves as a resource for children of alcoholics. Operates clearinghouse for info, hosts conferences, increases public awareness, provides training.

05561. National Association for Sickle Cell Disease, 3460 Wilshire Blvd, Ste 1012, Los Angeles, CA 90010; (213) 731-1166. Promotes natl awareness about sickle cell anemia and its impact on society. Provides general reference services, conduct seminars. Services free, except some educational materials.

05562. National Association for Sickle Cell Disease, 4221 Wilshire Blvd, Ste 360, Los Angeles, CA 90010-3505; (213) 936-7205, (800) 421-8453. Educates public about sickle cell disease, identifies carriers of disease, promotes interests of sickle cell patients. Makes recommendations, raises funds, provides financial aid and training.

05563. National Association of Composers-USA, Box 49652, Barrington Station, Los Angeles, CA 90049;

(213) 451-8213. Concerned with advancing professional, musical, and social status of American composers. Provides general reference services, conducts classes. Info services generally restricted to members.

05564. National Association of Dance and Affiliated Artists, P.O. Box 8, San Bruno, CA 94066; (415) 583-7662. Interest in all forms of dance and prevention of dance injuries. Answers inquiries, conducts seminars and youth programs. Some services subject to a fee; some restricted to members.

05565. National Association of Hispanic Nurses, 2014 Johnston St, Los Angeles, CA 90031; (213) 221-7156. Serves health care needs of the Hispanic community. Publishes quarterly newsletter, natl directory, brochure. Consults with Hispanic nurses, collaborates with other Hispanic health professionals.

05566. National Association of Human Services Technologies, 11th and L Bldg, Ste 321, Sacramento, CA 95814; (916) 444-3772. Promotes natl certification of professionals and paraprofessionals in human services. Provides advisory services, conducts seminars, and workshops. Most services free.

05567. National Association of Miniature Enthusiasts, P.O. Box 1178 (351 Oak Pl, Ste E.), Brea, CA 92622; (714) 529-0900. Seeks to stimulate and maintain natl interest in miniature collecting and building. Answers inquiries free, conducts seminars and workshops in conjunction with conventions, which require a registration fee.

05568. National Association of Physical Therapists, P.O. Box 367 (1325 S Hills Dr), W Covina, CA 91793; (818) 919-7836 or 332-7755. Involved in representation, education, and accreditation of physical therapists. Provides general reference services, evaluates data, conducts seminars, permits onsite use of collection. Services free, except some publications.

05570. National Association of Underwater Instructors, P.O. Box 14650 (4650 Arrow Hwy, Ste F-1), Montclair, CA 91763; (714) 621-5801. Trains and certifies underwater diving instructors. Interest in skin and scuba diving, underwater diving safety. Permits onsite use of collection. General reference services free to members, for a fee to others.

05571. National Athletic Health Institute, 575 E Hardy St, No 104, Inglewood, CA 90301; (213) 674-1600. Conducts basic and clinical research on athletic and recreational activities. Provides fellowships, conducts seminars and a sports injury clinic, serves as a clearinghouse in sports medicine info, evaluates data, lends materials. Fee for some services.

05572. National Center for Computer Crime Data, 4053 JFK Library—CSULA, 5151 State Univ Dr, Los Angeles, CA 90032; (213) 225-1364. Interest in prevention of computer crimes. Provides general reference services, conducts seminars, publishes and distributes materials, permits onsite use of collections. Research done on an hourly fee-plus-cost basis.

05573. National Center for Health Education, Office of School Health Programs, 1130 Burnett Avenue, Ste G, Concord, CA 94520; (415) 676-2813. Improves health education of American public. Conducts research on evaluation of health education, provides info, conducts seminars. Technical consultation on a fee-for-service or retainer basis.

05574. National Center for Youth Law, 1663 Mission St, 5th Fl, San Francisco, CA 94103; (415) 543-3307. Interest in all aspects of juvenile legal advocacy. Consultation, representation, and info dissemination free. Training available for cost of expenses incurred. Onsite use of library permitted.

05575. National Clearinghouse on Marital Rape, 2325 Oak St, Berkeley, CA 94708; (415) 548-1770. Interest in criminalization of marital, cohabitation, and date rape. Sells printed publications, provides consulting services, conducts workshop and seminars. Fees charged. Inquiries must include a SASE.

05576. National Council on Crime and Delinquency, 77 Maiden Lane, 4th Fl, San Francisco, CA 94108; (415) 956-5651. Promotes alternatives to juvenile incarceration. Provides general reference services, publishes and distributes materials, permits onsite use of collection. Services generally free.

05577. National Energy Research and Information Institute, Univ of La Verne, 1950 Third St, La Verne, CA 91750; (714) 593-9570. Researches accurate energy info. Interested in communication of energy info to the public and nation's decision makers. Provides general reference services for a fee.

05578. National Federation of Independent Business, 150 W 20th Ave, San Mateo, CA 94403; (415) 341-7441. Interest in regulations and legislation affecting small business at local, state, and natl levels. Provides Congress with collected data, informs public on concerns of small business, offers educators a clearinghouse of resources and info.

05579. National Field Archery Association, Rte 2, Box 514 (31419 Outer Interstate 10), Redlands, CA 92373; (714) 794-2133. Sponsors annual natl and sectional championship field archery tournaments. Interest in field archery and bow-hunting. Publishes and distributes materials, answers inquiries or refers inquirers to other sources of info.

05580. National Film Information Service, Academy of Motion Picture Arts and Sciences, 8949 Wilshire Blvd, Beverly Hills, CA 90211; (213) 278-8990. Interest in history and technology of motion pictures and motion picture industry. Provides general reference services, publishes and distributes materials, permits onsite use of library's collections, makes referrals to other info sources.

05581. National Foundation of Wheelchair Tennis, 3857 Birch St, No 411 (4000 MacArthur Blvd, Ste 420), Newport Beach, CA 92660; (714) 831-0958 or 851-1707. Promotes and fosters wheelchair tennis for the handicapped. Provides general reference services, conducts seminars. Services free, except some publications.

05582. National Foundation to Fight Political Corruption, 530 E Cypress St, Glendale, CA 91205. Conducts research and public education on political corruption with special attention to organized crime. Provides general reference services, publishes and distributes materials, permits onsite use of collections. Services free.

05583. National Geothermal Information Resource, Lawrence Berkeley Laboratory, Univ of Calif., Berkeley, CA 94720; (415) 486-4294. Provides info on geothermal development and related activities at identified resource. Provides general reference services, analyzes data for a fee.

05584. National Health Federation, P.O. Box 688 (212 W Foothill Blvd), Monrovia, CA 91016; (213) 357-2181 or 359-8334. Interest in education in anticompulsory vaccination, holistic health, alternative therapies, environmental legislation. Provides general reference services, publishes and distributes materials, sponsors meetings and symposia.

05585. National Health Federation, P.O. Box 688, Monrovia, CA 91016; (818) 357-2181, 359-8334. Advocates civil liberty of freedom of choice in matters of personal health, provides educational programs, legislative activities and legal defense fund. Sponsors conventions and seminars, maintains library.

05586. National Health Law Program, 2639 S LaCienega Blvd, Los Angeles, CA 90034; (213) 204-6010. Specializes in health problems of the poor. Responds to requests for background info, model statutes, litigation assistance. Maintains health law library. Answers inquiries, makes referrals, provides advisory services. Priority given to Legal Services attorneys and clients.

05587. National Hot Rod Association, P.O. Box 150 (10639 Riverside Dr), N Hollywood, CA 91603; (818) 985-6472. Conducts organized drag racing competitions, with emphasis on safety and mechanical innovation programs. Publishes *National Dragster* newsweekly, Official Drag Rules. Answers inquiries, provides consulting services, conducts seminars. Most services free and available to members.

05588. National Housing Law Project, 1950 Addison, Ste 200, Berkeley, CA 94704; (415) 548-9400, 548-2600. Provides assistance to Legal Services attorneys, community development corps and govt orgs. Provides general reference services, distributes publications, permits onsite use of collection by appointment. Services free, except publications.

05589. National Ichthyosis Foundation, P.O. Box 252, Belmont, CA 94002-0252; (415) 591-1653. Raises funds, promotes research on ichthyosis, a skin disease. Provides advice, guidance, and support among sufferers, distributes educational material.

05590. National Institute for Management Research, P.O. Box 3727 (1714 18th St), Santa Monica, CA 90403. Interest in education for managers and professional staff of business, govt, science, and professional orgs in financial info systems, personal business computers, human resource management, and related fields. and schedule control systems. Conducts seminars and conferences. Services available for a fee.

05591. National Intercollegiate Flying Association, c/o Harold S. Wood, Exec Dir, P.O. Box 9910, San Diego CA 92109; (619) 270-7114. Interest in aviation and aviation education in institutions of higher learning. Publishes bimonthly newsletter, answers inquiries, makes referrals, conducts seminars.

05592. National Inventors Foundation Library, 345 W Cypress St, Glendale, CA 91204; (818) 246-6540. Interest in creating, developing, protecting, and marketing of inventions and new products. Maintains large collection of books, journals, and pamphlets on inventing. Answers inquiries, makes referrals, provides reference services, permits onsite use of collection.

05593. National Lupus Erythematosus Foundation, 5430 Van Nuys Blvd, Ste 206, Van Nuys, CA 91401; (818) 885-8787. Interest in Lupus Erythematosus, including medical research, patient care, and public education. Publishes booklet, leaflets, other printed material for lay and professional understanding. Answers inquiries, conducts seminars, provides counseling services for patient and/or family.

05594. National Lupus Erythematosus Foundation, 5430 Van Nuys Blvd, Ste 206, Van Nuys, CA 91401; (818) 885-8787. Funds research to control lupus, a skin disease. Has developed comprehensive research program involving geneticists, immunologists, and virologists; publishes pamphlets, reports on research results.

05595. National Office Machine Service Association, P.O. Box 762, San Fernando, CA 91340; (818) 892-9673. Interest in office automation equipment, service and repair. Provides general reference services, conducts seminars, identifies sources for office machine parts and supplies. Services free to members, at cost to others.

05596. National Safety Management Society, 3871 Piedmont Avenue, Oakland, CA 94611; (415) 653-4148. Promotes new concepts of accident prevention and loss control, safety management. Provides research and education. Membership open to anyone with managerial responsibilities.

05597. National Senior Citizens Law Center, 1636 W 8th St, Ste 201, Los Angeles, CA 90017; (213) 388-1381. Natl resource center for legal problems affecting elderly. Drafts pleadings, answers inquiries, and writes memoranda on request from Legal Services programs. Publishes legislative newsletter and educational brochures. Services only to local Legal Services offices.

05598. National Stuttering Project, 1269 Seventh Ave, San Francisco, CA 94122; (415) 566-5324. Offers info on stuttering to people with speech difficulties and general public. Answers inquiries, provides advisory and referral services, conducts seminars and meetings. Services generally free.

05599. National Task Force on Prostitution, P.O. Box 26354, San Francisco, CA 94126; (415) 381-3881. Works for natl and intl decriminalization of prostitution. Answers inquiries, makes referrals, provides advisory services, conducts seminars and workshops. Services free, except publications and speakers.

05600. National Valentine Collectors Association, P.O. Box 1404, Santa Ana, CA 92702; (714) 547-1355. Promotes interest in old valentines. Provides advisory, reference, literature-searching, and reproduction services; conducts seminars, workshops, auctions, and natl shows. Fee for some services.

05601. National/International Scholarship Research Service, Box 2516 (122 Alto St), San Rafael, CA 94912; (415) 456-1577. Interest in info on scholarships, fellowships, grants, loans from private sources. Provides general reference services, distributes data compilations. Services for a fee to students.

05602. Native American Studies Library, Univ of Calif., 3415 Dwinelle Hall (103 Wheeler), Berkeley, CA 94720; (415) 642-2793. Interest in North American Indians, American history, Indian history and culture. Provides free reference, referral services, permits onsite use of collections. Loans limited to Univ of Calif. faculty and students.

05603. Natural History Museum of Los Angeles County, 900 Exposition Blvd, Los Angeles, CA 90007; (213) 744-3414. Interest in zoology, botany, ethnology, archaeology, paleontology, geology, U.S. history and technology. Provides general reference services, publishes and distributes materials, permits onsite research by qualified personnel, rents exhibit materials, sponsors lectures, etc.

05604. Naval Biosciences Laboratory, Naval Supply Center, Bldg 844, Oakland, CA 94625; (415) 832-5217. Interest in recombinant DNA technology, monoclonal antibodies, immunobiology, microbiology, pollution. Answers document requests. Service primarily for naval personnel and others having a legitimate need-to-know.

05605. Naval Ocean Systems Center Technical Library, San Diego, CA 92152; (714) 225-6623 or 225-6171. Interest in electrical engineering, physics, mathematics, statistics, oceanography, undersea technology, and related areas. Publishes and distributes materials, permits visitors with appropriate need-to-know and security clearance.

05606. Naval Weapons Center, Library Div, Technical Information Dept, China Lake, CA 93555; (619) 939-2507. Interest in naval ordnance, missiles, propulsion systems, and infrared technology, pyrotechnics, ballistics, aerodynamics, electronics. Makes interlibrary loans, provides library services to center personnel and contractors with security clearance and need-to-know.

05607. Navy/Government-Industry Data Exchange Program, GIDEP Program Dir, GIDEP Operations Center, Corona, CA 91720; (714) 736-4677. Interest in technical data exchange among govt agencies and industry. Provides participants with data, notifies participants of potential problems, makes referrals.

05608. New Games Foundation, P.O. Box 7901, San Francisco, CA 94120; (415) 526-7774. Interest in personal growth through play that focuses on participation, creativity, and community. Provides general reference services, conducts seminars. Services availble for a fee.

05609. New Hope Pain Center, Section of Algology, Dept of Neurosurgery, USC School of Medicine, 55 E Calif. Blvd, Pasadena, CA 91105-3202; (818) 405-8000. Interest in pain treatment and clinical research in areas of patients with chronic intractable pain syndromes. Answers inquiries, provides advisory services, conducts seminars. Patient treatment on a fee basis.

05610. Newport Aeronautical Sales, P.O. Box 1845, Newport Beach, CA 92660; (714) 631-8250. Supplier of U.S. unclassified military and commercial aircraft engineering drawings and technical manuals in both microform and hard copy. Maintains collection of over 20,000 military technical manuals and 100,000 engineering drawings. Sells manuals, drawings, and other publications.

05611. Noble Oil Laboratories, 873 Linden Ave, Carpinteria, CA 93013; (805) 684-1611. Educates commercial industries on uses of jojoba oil while serving the needs of jojoba grower. Answers inquiries, provides reference and literature-searching services. Provides advisory services concerning planting, hulling, and oil extraction. Fee for some services.

05612. Non Destructive Testing Management Association, 1605 Sonoma Ave, Albany, CA 94707; (415) 526-5587. Assists member companies to improve common problem areas in nondestructive testing industry. Answers inquiries, distributes publications. Services provided through membership, available to nondestructive testing laboratories, shops, and companies.

05613. North American Committee of Enamel Creators, P.O. Box 721, La Jolla, CA 92038; (619) 454-0595. Interest in enamelling, history of enamelling, American and Canadian enamellers, education of public about enameling. Provides general reference services, evaluates data, conducts seminars. Services primarily for enamellers or their sponsors, but others assisted. A fee may be charged for some services.

05614. North American Films, P.O. Box 919, Tarzana, CA 91356; (213) 340-1328. Interest in educational and industrial motion pictures. Rents and sells films. Answers questions, provides advisory or consulting services, and makes referrals. Fees may be charged.

05615. North American Radio Archives, c/o Ronald E. Staley, Pres, 333 N Berendo, Apt 333, Los Angeles, CA 90004; (213) 662-7617. Promotes and preserves old-time radio programs. Maintains collection of related materials, including 6,000 taped radio programs. Publishes quarterly journal. All inquiries answered, reference services provided, and referrals made. Modest fees may be charged to nonmembers.

05616. Norton Simon Museum, 411 W Colorado Blvd, Pasadena, CA 91105; (818) 449-6840. Interest in art from early Renaissance through 20th Century, Indian and Southeast Asian sculpture. Provides general reference services, conducts private guided tours of exhibits. Museum open to public.

05617. Nuclear Free Zone Registry, P.O. Box 172, Riverside, CA 92502; (714) 674-6576. Info, resource, and intl networking center on Nuclear Free Zones. Provides general reference services, evaluates and analyzes data, conducts seminars. Services free, except for slides, promotional materials, and printed materials in bulk.

05618. Nuclear Test Effects and Geologic Data Bank, Earth Sciences Dept, Lawrence Livermore Natl Lab, Univ of Calif., P.O. Box 808, L-222, Livermore, CA 94550; (415) 422-6491. Contains info on geology of Energy Dept's Nevada test site. Answers inquiries, makes referrals, provides advisory services. Services free in reasonable quantities.

05619. Oakland Museum, Natural Sciences Department, 1000 Oak St, Oakland, CA 94607; (415) 273-3884. Interest in natural environment, interrelationships between organisms and their environment. Provides general reference services, conducts seminars, and field trips, permits onsite use of collections. All services free, except seminars and field trips.

05620. Oceanic Society, Bldg E, Fort Mason, San Francisco, CA 94123; (415) 441-1104. Intl membership org that promotes informed and sensible management of ocean and coastal resources. Provides general reference services, conducts seminars. Services generally free unless special research required.

05621. Organization of Women Architects and Design Professionals, P.O. Box 26570, San Francisco, CA 94126; (415) 550-6051. Aims to improve professional standing of women in architecture and related fields. Maintains library and slide collection. Publishes newsletter and brochure; conducts seminars. Answers inquiries, makes referrals, provides consulting services.

05622. Oriental Healing Arts Institute, 1945 Palo Verde Ave, Ste 208, Long Beach, CA 90815; (213) 431-3544. Nonprofit educational org dedicated to advancement of traditional Chinese medicine. Provides general reference services, conducts seminars, permits onsite use of collection. Services free, except publications, consulting and translation services.

05623. Orientation/Media International, P.O. Box 424, Pacific Grove, CA 93950; (408) 649-8215. Interest in transcultural training for persons preparing for intl work in U.S. or abroad. Has collection of games, literature, and techniques from many countries. Provides consultation on transcultural policy setting and training programs. Fees charged for all services.

05624. Orthomolecular Medical Society, 6151 W Century Blvd, Ste 1114, Los Angeles, CA 90045; (213) 417-7917. Scientific, educational, and research org interested in orthomolecular medicine, advanced nutritional medicine. Emphasizes megadose vitamin therapy and amino acids. Varying types of membership available.

05625. Overeaters Anonymous, P.O. Box 92870, Los Angeles, CA 90009 (2190 W 190th St, Torrance, CA.); (213) 320-7941. Interest in obesity control and recovery based on 12 steps of Alcoholics Anonymous program. Answers inquiries or refers inquirers to other sources of info free.

05626. Owner Builder Center, 1516 Fifth St, Berkeley, CA 94710; (415) 526-9222. Teaches people how to build, remodel, and repair their homes. Provides general reference services, helps other orgs get started, conducts seminars, workshops and training sessions. Services free, except classes and consulting services.

05627. PKU Parents, c/o Dale Hillard, 8 Myrtle Lane, San Anselmo, CA 94960; (415) 457-4632. Self-help org of parents and professionals that provides support and education for parents of children with phenylketonuria. Helps families with newly diagnosed PKU children cope with initial shock and provides info; conducts annual conferences.

05628. PYRAMID, 1777 N Calif. Blvd, Ste 200, Walnut Creek, CA 94596; (415) 939-6666. Provides info, technical assistance, and other services to persons and programs involved in drug abuse prevention. Services include program planning and evaluation, networking and community support. Provides general reference services, distributes publications.

05629. Pacific Coast Entomological Society, Calif. Academy of Sciences, Golden Gate Park, San Francisco, CA 94118-9961; (415) 221-5100. Interest in entomology, with emphasis on insects of western North America, insect taxonomy, morphology. Persons with serious interests may borrow material or use collection onsite.

05630. Pacific Gas and Electric Co., Corporate Library, 77 Beale St, Room 1220, San. Francisco, CA 94106; (415) 972-2573. Interest in public utility economics, energy engineering. Provides general reference services primarily for company employees; limited services provided to others.

05631. Pacific Grove Museum of Natural History, 165 Forest Ave, Pacific Grove, CA 93950; (408) 372-4212. Interest in natural history of Monterey County, Calif., including Indians. Publishes pamphlets, answers brief inquiries, makes referrals. Museum open to public.

05632. Pacific Information Inc., 11684 Ventura Blvd, Ste 295, Studio City, CA 91604; (818) 797-7654. Provides info management services and publications for business and industry, general reference and consultation services, conducts seminars. Services for a fee.

05633. Pacific Maritime Association, P.O. Box 7861 (635 Sacramento St), San Francisco, CA 94120; (415) 576-3200. Interest in West Coast maritime labor contracts and collective bargaining. Provides general reference services, permits onsite use of file material, (subject to limitations), conducts seminars.

05635. Pacific Seabird Group, c/o Point Reyes Bird Observatory, 4990 Shoreline Hwy, Stinson Beach, CA 94970. Interest in marine birds of the Pacific and the world, wildlife conservation. Answers inquiries, conducts annual meeting and workshops. Services free, unless extensive. Publications for sale.

05636. Pacific Southwest Forest and Range Experiment Station, U.S. Forest Service, P.O. Box 245 (1960 Addison St), Berkeley, CA 94701; (415) 486-3382. Interest in forestry, timber and watershed management, forest fires, forest products utilization and marketing, range management. Answers inquiries, provides consulting, reference, and document services, permits onsite use of literature collection.

05637. Pacific Studies Center, 222B View St, Mountain View, CA 94041; (415) 969-1545. Makes info available on current events, including social, political, and economic events to activists, journalists, students. Provides general reference services, conducts seminars, permits onsite use of collections.

05638. Packard Automobile Classics, P.O. Box 2808, Oakland, CA 94618. Interest in collection, preservation, restoration, maintenance, and operation of Packard automobiles and equipment. Publishes quarterly magazine, news bulletin. Answers inquiries, makes referrals, conducts national tour. Services for members only, but membership open to all.

05639. Palo Alto Medical Foundation Library, 860 Bryant St, Palo Alto, CA 94301; (415) 326-8120. Interest in medicine and basic science, medical research. Provides reference services to physicians and scientists.

05640. Pan American Association of Ophthalmology, c/o H. Dunbar Hoskins, Jr., MD, Secty-Treas, 267 Miller Ave, Ste 2, Mill Valley, CA 94941. Disseminates scientific ophthalmological info; promotes friendship among ophthalmologists of Western Hemisphere. Answers inquiries, makes referrals, provides free consulting and reference services.

05641. Parenting in the Nuclear Age, P.O. Box 3479, Berkeley, CA 94703; (415) 848-8744. Interest in helping families cope with their children's nuclear fears. Provides general reference services, conducts seminars. Services free to families and those working with children.

05643. Parents Anonymous, 7120 Franklin Avenue, Los Angeles, CA 90046; (213) 876-9642 (800) 421-0353, Calif. (800) 352-0386. Provides treatment and/or prevention of child abuse. Hot-line telephone service available 24 hours a day. Sponsors regular local meetings.

05644. Parkinson's Educational Program USA, 1800 Park Newport, Ste 302, Newport Beach, CA 92660; (714) 640-0218, (800) 344-7872. Promotes research on, and develops coping techniques for people afflicted with Parkinson's disease, Parkinson's syndrome. Provides public education, research promotion, and rights protection, offers referral and counseling services.

05645. Peace Exchange, 1985 Louis Rd, Palo Alto, CA 94303; (415) 856-6662. Sponsored by Northern Calif. Conference of United Church of Christ, interested in Soviet-American relations, Soviet-American citizens' exchanges. Provides advisory and referral services, conducts seminars, workshops. Services free.

05646. Peace and Common Security, Fort Mason Center, San Francisco, CA 94123; (415) 673-8866. Interest in origins of human conflict, intl security and peace, arms control, related topics. Provides general reference services, conducts seminars. Some services free; others at cost.

05647. Pediatric Projects, P.O. Box 1880, Santa Monica, CA 90406; (213) 459-7710. Advocates mental health care for chronically ill, disabled, children and their families. Publishes and distributes materials, disseminates info.

05648. People for Energy Progress, P.O. Box 777, Los Gatos, CA 95031; (408) 226-9429. Monitors legislative activities and educates public on energy-related matters. Provides general reference services, evaluates and distributes data, provides speakers for schools, clubs, and others. Services free, except speakers' travel expenses.

05649. Performing Tree, 1320 W 3rd St, Los Angeles, CA 90017; (213) 482-8830 or 625-6285. Dedicated to childrens' needs for art, music, dance, and theater as essential elements in their basic education. Offers educational performances, provides general reference services, evaluates data, conducts seminars. Services for a fee to parents, educators, and artists.

05650. Permag Pacific Corp., 10631 Humbolt St, Los Alamitos, CA 90720; (213) 594-6515. Interest in design, manufacture, and application of metallic and ceramic permanent magnets, technical ferrites and ceramics, etc. Provides general reference services, provides consulting services, permits onsite reference.

05651. PharmChem, 3925 Bohannon Dr, Menlo Park, CA 94025; (415) 328-6200. Provides factual info about illicit and licit drugs, drug use trends, and current topics of interest in related health fields. Publishes *PharmChem* Newsletter 6 times a year. Answers inquiries.

05652. Pharmacists' Planning Service, P.O. Box 1336, Sausalito, CA 94966; (415) 332-4066. Promotes public health education and awareness campaigns. Also active in protecting pharmacists' rights and professional roles.

05653. Philip L. Boyd Deep Canyon Desert Research Center, Dept of Biology, Univ of Calif., Riverside, CA 92521; (714) 787-5917. Interest in biology of desert organisms. Answers inquiries, publishes and distributes materials, provides consulting services. Services free to qualified personnel.

05654. Physics Library, Stanford Univ, Stanford, CA 94305; (415) 497-4342. Interest in all phases of physics, with emphasis on graduate and research level, astronomy, astrophysics, applied physics. Lends materials to qualified persons, makes interlibrary loans.

05655. Pioneer Fund, P.O. Box 33 (28 Kehoe Way), Inverness, CA 94937; (415) 669-1122. Supports documentary filmmakers and education policy projects. Conducts seminars and workshops, evaluates data, makes referrals. Services free to grant seekers in appropriate categories.

05656. Planetary Society, 65 N Catalina Ave, Pasadena, CA 91109; (818) 793-5100. Promotes planetary exploration and search for extraterrestrial life. Provides general reference services, conducts seminars. Services free and primarily for members, but others may be assisted.

05657. Popular Rotorcraft Association, P.O. Box 570 (11852 Western Ave), Stanton, CA 90680; (714) 898-6500. Interest in construction, safety, and operation of privately-owned, noncommercial rotorcraft. Publishes *Popular Rotorcraft Flying* bimonthly. Answers inquiries, makes referrals; conducts contests, fly-ins, seminars, and workshops. Services free.

05658. Population Research Laboratory, Dept of Sociology and Anthropology, Univ of Southern Calif., Univ Park (3716 S Hope St), Los Angeles, CA 90007; (213) 743-2950. Interest in demography as related to environment and to social disorganization. Collects census materials, related materials. Answers inquiries, makes referrals, provides consulting services. Permits onsite use of collections. Services available to local agency personnel, free.

05659. Premenstrual Syndrome Action, P.O. Box 19669, Irvine, CA 92713; (714) 752-6355. Provides info on symptoms and treatment of premenstrual syndrome. Services include info and referral, consultation, training for health and social service professionals, public speaking, and publications. Fees set on a sliding scale.

05660. Price-Pottenger Nutrition Foundation, P.O. Box 2614, La Mesa, CA 92041; (619) 582-4168 or 582-4873. Distributes info on nutrition and preventive medicine research. Provides advisory, reference, referral, literature-searching, and copying services, conducts seminars, makes interlibrary loans, permits onsite use of collections. Services free.

05661. Private Islands Unlimited, 17538 Tulsa St, Granada Hills, CA 91344; (818) 360-8683. Provides info on islands and island properties worldwide. Provides advisory, abstracting and indexingr services for a fee.

05662. Product Safety Association, P.O. Box 91236, Los Angeles, CA 90009; (213) 978-6186. Represents product safety professionals and provides voluntary standards for industry and govt. Provides advisory and current-awareness services; prepares standards for clients; conducts seminars, workshops, training courses; evaluates data. Services provided at cost.

05663. Professional Engineering Institute, P.O. Box 639, San Carlos, CA 94070; (415) 593-9731. Promotes professional registration (licensing) of engineers. Provides general reference services, conducts seminars. Services free, except seminars and publications, primarily for practicing engineers and engineering students, but others will be assisted.

05664. Professional and Technical Consultants Association, 1190 Lincoln Ave, Ste 3, San Jose, CA 95125; (408) 287-8703. Assists individuals and companies in locating consultants with specific capabilities. Conducts seminars. Fee for some services.

05665. Project Concern International, P.O. Box 85323 (3550 Afton Rd), San Diego, CA 92138; (619) 279-9690. Interest in development of primary and basic health care programs in developing countries and disadvantaged areas in U.S. Provides general reference services. Advisory and consulting services for a fee, others free.

05666. Project Concern International, 3550 Afton Road, San Diego, CA 92123; (619) 279-9690. Provides primary and preventive care, community health education for needy worldwide. Provides referral and recruitment services for health care programs worldwide.

05667. Project Jonah, P.O. Box 40280, San Francisco, CA 94140; (415) 285-9846. Studies population and behavior of Cetacea. Educates public on need to preserve whales, dolphins, and porpoises. Distributes "Project Jonah Teaching Kit." Answers inquiries, provides consulting and literature-searching services, conducts research. Donation requested for services.

05668. Project on Linguistic Analysis, Machine Translation Group, Univ of Calif., 2222 Piedmont Ave, Berkeley, CA 94720; (415) 642-5937. Interest in research and development of Chinese-to-English translation by computer. Answers inquiries, provides consultation, makes referrals to other sources of info.

05669. Psoriasis Research Association, 107 Vista Del Grande, San Carlos, CA 94070; (415) 593-1394 or 593-2374. Interest in psoriasis and related diseases. Supports clinical and laboratory research, rehabilitation centers, fund raising. Answers inquiries, provides consulting services, prepares analyses and evaluations, makes referrals.

05670. Public Management Institute, 358 Brannan St, San Francisco, CA 94107; (415) 896-1900. Commerrcial org interested in all aspects of nonprofit and public agency management, especially fund-raising techniques. Provides general reference services, publishes and distributes materials. Services primarily for nonprofit orgs for a fee.

05671. Public Policy Research Organization, Univ of Calif., Irvine, CA 92717; (714) 856-5449. Concerned with public policy on technology. Maintains data on usage of info technologies, answers inquiries, provides advisory services. Services available at cost.

05672. Puppeteers of America, 5 Cricklewood Path, Pasadena, CA 91107; (213) 979-5748. Nonprofit membership org with affiliated guilds in 29 cities interested in puppetry. Provides general reference services, publishes and distributes materials, holds festivals. Services free, primarily for members.

05673. Quality Circle Institute, P.O. Box Q (1425 Vista Way), Red Bluff, CA 96080; (916) 527-6970. Commercial org interested in use of quality circles as a participatory management concept. Provides general reference services, conducts training programs, and seminars. Services for a fee.

05674. Quality of Working Life and Human Resource Management, Institute of Industrial Relations, Univ of Calif. at Los Angeles, 405 Hilgard Ave, Los Angeles, CA 90024; (213) 825-1095. Interest in labor-management cooperation. Provides general reference services, publishes and distributes materials. Questions answered free, other services subject to a fee, available to managers and union officials.

05675. Quantum Institute, Univ of Calif., Santa Barbara, CA 93106; (805) 961-2582 Research unit designed to assist govt agencies, private industry, and foundations in applied physical sciences. Provides general reference services, conducts seminars, and R & D. Services provided at cost plus fee.

05676. R. M. Hutchins Center for Study of Democratic Institutions, P.O. Box 4068, Univ of Calif., Santa Barbara, CA 93103; (805) 961-2611. Interest in problems facing democracy. Info provided through center's publications.

05677. R.H. Lowie Museum of Anthropology, Univ of Calif., Berkeley, CA 94720; (415) 642-3681 Interest in ethnology of Africa, Asia, North America, South America, and Oceania; archeology of North America and Mediterranean. Info services available to professional anthropologists by appointment. Loan and duplication services also available.

05678. Racing Driver's Club, P.O. Box 404, Fremont, CA 94357; (415) 793-2514. Provides assistance to road racing drivers. Interested primarily in sports car road race (not oval track or offroad) drivers. Provides general reference services free to anyone, but membership invited.

05679. Rand Corp. Library, 1700 Main St, Santa Monica, CA 90406; (213) 393-0411. Interest in policy analysis of various widely diversified fields. Provides general reference services, permits onsite use of collections by special arrangement. Services free to serious scholars.

05680. Raytheon Co., Engineering Library, 6380 Hollister Ave, Goleta, CA 93117; (805) 967-5511 ext 3004. Interest in electronics, electrical engineering, electronic countermeasures, radar. Services provided for noncompany personnel limited to interlibrary loans and issuance of some documents.

05681. Redwood Inspection Service, 591 Redwood Hwy, Ste 3100, Mill Valley, CA 94941; (415) 381-1304. Interest in specifications or grading rules for redwood lumber, shakes, and shingles. Publishes *Standard Specifications for Grades of Calif. Redwood Lumber*. Answers questions relating to publication.

05682. Regional Cancer Foundation, 15th Ave and Lake St, Bldg 1805, Presidio of San Francisco, San Francisco, CA 94129; (415) 221-2132. Interest in cancer prevention, treatment, education, and rehabilitation. Provides general reference services, conducts seminars, lends materials. Services free, except online computer access.

05683. Rehabilitation Research and Training Center on Aging, Univ of Southern Calif., c/o Rancho los Amigos Hospital, 7600 Consuelo St, Downey, CA 90242; (213) 722-7402. Conducts research, disseminates info, and trains students and practitioners in rehabilitation of the older adult. Provides general reference services, conducts seminars and workshops. Services free to nonprofit service centers.

05684. Reiss-Davis Child Study Center Research Library, Reiss-Davis Child Study Center, 3200 Motor Ave, Los Angeles, CA 90034; (213) 204-1666 ext 359. Interest in interdisciplinary aspects of child mental health psychiatry, and community education for trainees and professionals. Provides general reference services, makes interlibrary loans, permits onsite use of collection.

05685. Remote Sensing Research Program, Univ of Calif., 260 Space Sciences Laboratory, Berkeley, CA 94720; (415) 642-2351. Interest in remote sensing research, satellite and high altitude aerial imagery. Provides general reference services, permits onsite use of collection. Services free except computer processing, charged by the hour.

05687. Resource Center for Nonviolence, P.O. Box 2324 (515 Broadway), Santa Cruz, CA 95063; (408) 423-1626. Interest in nonviolence as a force for personal and social change, political and economic noncooperation, draft and resistance, nuclear disarmament, more. Conducts public educational programs, including workshops, study groups, workcamps, and residency, internship, and training programs; permits onsite use of collections. Services free, except for those items rented.

05688. Resource Information Network for Cancer, c/o American Cancer Society, 2975 Wilshire Blvd, Ste 200, Los Angeles, CA 90010; (213) 386-7660. Coop program interested in cancer materials and resources. Provides free general reference services, within limits of staff time.

05689. Reuben H. Fleet Space Theater and Science Center, P.O. Box 33303, San Diego, CA 92103; (619) 238-1233. Planetarium and audiovisual center interested in science education, astronomy, atomic physics, lasers, vision, etc. Answers inquiries free, provides consulting services at cost.

05690. Rockwell International Corp. Technical Information Center, Rocketdyne Div, 6633 Canoga Ave, Canoga Park, CA 91304; (818) 710-2575. Provides technical support services for all Rocketdyne employees, other Rockwell libraries, and general public. Provides literature-searching services, makes referrals and interlibrary loans. Permits onsite use of collection. Services to nonemployees by appointment only.

05691. Roeding Park Zoo, 894 W Belmont Ave, Fresno, CA 93728; (209) 488-1549. Interest in exotic animals, animal pathology, zoo animal medicine. Answers inquiries, provides consulting and literature-searching services, makes referrals, permits onsite reference.

05692. Rotary Natural Science Center, Dept of Visitor Services, Oakland Office of Parks and Recreation, 1520 Lakeside Dr, Oakland, CA 94612; (415) 273-3739. Interest in native waterfowl, including migration, mammals, reptiles, plants, conservation, local natural history. Provides general reference services, conducts seminars, permits onsite use of collections.

05693. Ryukyu Philatelic Specialist Society, P.O. Box 4092, Berkeley, CA 94704; (415) 841-5797. Interest in history and development of the postal system of the Ryukyu Islands under U.S. admin from 1945 to 1972. Provides general reference services, publishes and distributes materials. Services may be subject to a fee.

05694. SAFE Association, 15723 Vanowen St, Box 246, Van Nuys, CA 91406; (818) 994-6495. Interest in environmental safety, and life-support equipment and education in areas of aerospace, hydrospace, automotive, and medicine. Answers inquiries, makes referrals, provides speakers for meetings and seminars, permits onsite reference.

05695. SRI International, Chemical Information Services, 333 Ravenswood Ave, Menlo Park, CA 94025; (415) 326-6200 ext 3900. Interest in chemical industry economics. Compilation of market research info since 1950. Publishes *Chemical Economics Handbook*, related materials. All info services available only to program participants, who pay a basic a fee. Participants have consulting privileges with professional staff.

05696. SRI International, Computer Science Laboratory, 333 Ravenswood Ave, Menlo Park, CA 94025; (415) 859-4172. Conducts research into application of computer science techniques to development of computer systems. Provides advisory, consulting, referral services, conducts research, seminars and workshops. Services free, unless extensive.

05697. SRI International Life Sciences Div, 333 Ravenswood Ave, Menlo Park, CA 94025; (415) 326-6200. Conducts research in the life sciences. Publishes books, technical reports, journal articles, state-of-the-art reviews, research summaries. Provides advisory, and consulting services. Conducts seminars and workshops. Services primarily under contract.

05698. SRI International, Artificial Intelligence Center, Computer Science and Technology Div, 333 Ravenswood Ave, Menlo Park, CA 94025; (415) 859-2311. Conducts research in artificial intelligence. Provides advisory, consulting, referral, info service at cost.

05699. SRI International, Library and Research Information Services Department, 333 Ravenswood Ave, Menlo Park, CA 94025; (415) 859-2634. Interest in physical sciences, electronics and radio sciences, info sciences and engineering, economics, management systems, etc. Makes interlibrary loans. Library open to non-staff by appointment only.

05700. Saber Laboratories, 577 10th St, San Francisco, CA 94103; (415) 431-4707. Manufactures security and countermeasure systems. Provides general reference services, publishes and distributes materials, permits onsite use of collection. Services at cost to some users, free to others, and restricted to corps, govt agencies.

05701. Sacramento Valley Museum Association, Rte. 1, Box 240 (1495 Williams Ave), Williams, CA 95989; (916) 473-2978. Interest in history of Sacramento Valley. Answers inquiries. Museum open to public.

05702. Salinity Laboratory, Agricultural Research Service, USDA, 4500 Glenwood Dr, Riverside, CA 92501; (714) 683-0170. Interest in research in salinity in agriculture, soil science, plant tolerance to salinity, irrigation systems, water quality in agriculture. Answers inquiries, distributes publications and reprints. Services free within limits.

05703. Salk Institute for Biological Studies, P.O. Box 85800, San Diego, CA 92138; (619) 453-4100. Interest in basic research in neuroscience and molecular and cellular biology. Maintains library of 13,000 books, and monographs and journals. Publishes newsletters and research reports for lay audiences. Answers inquiries.

05704. San Diego Museum of Man, 1350 El Prado, Balboa Park, San Diego, CA 92101; (714) 239-2001. Interest in man in western Americas, including ethnology, archeology, and physical anthropology. Provides general reference services, presents educational programs, permits onsite use of collections. Scientific library open for reference by appointment.

05705. San Diego Natural History Library, P.O. Box 1390 (Balboa Park), San Diego, CA 92112; (714) 232-3821. Interest in natural history, including biology, paleontology, botany, geology, Provides general reference services, distributes materials, permits onsite use of collections. Services free, except loans and reproductions, by appointment.

05706. San Francisco Crafts and Folk Art Museum Reference Library, 626 Balboa St, San Francisco, CA 94118; (415) 668-0406. Interest in world folk arts, traditional and contemporary crafts, all craft media. Provides reference, and referral services, conducts seminars and workshops, permits onsite use of collections. Fee for some services.

05707. San Francisco Port Commission, Ferry Bldg, San Francisco, CA 94111; (415) 391-8000. Interest in port and ocean traffic, maritime facilities, commercial waterfront property management, traffic services and charges. Provides general reference services, publishes and distributes materials.

05708. San Francisco Society for the Prevention of Cruelty to Animals, 2500 16th St, San Francisco, CA 94013; (415) 621-2174. Trains dogs for deaf and hearing-impaired. Provides free advisory, reference, referral, current-awareness, and translation services.

05709. Sanitary Engineering and Environmental Health Research Laboratory, Univ of Calif., Richmond Field Station, 47th and Hoffman Blvd, Bldg 112, Richmond, CA 94804; (415) 231-9449. Conducts environmental and health-related research and training in areas of water, solid wastes, and air resources. Answers inquiries, makes reports and publications available at nominal fees or on loan basis.

05710. Sansum Medical Research Foundation, 2219 Bath St, Santa Barbara, CA 93105; (805) 682-7638. Conducts biochemical research in diabetes and alcoholism. Publishes journal articles, reviews. Answers inquiries, provides consulting services, conducts classes. Services free.

05711. Santa Barbara Museum of Natural History, 2559 Puesta del Sol Rd, Santa Barbara, CA 93105; (805) 682-4711. Interest in all aspects of life and earth sciences, prehistoric civilizations of western North America/Santa Barbara area. Provides general reference services, loans materials, permits onsite use of collection on request. Museum open to public.

05712. Santa Fe Railway Historical Society, P.O. Box 60178, Los Angeles, CA 90060; (714) 775-7029. Interest in info, drawings, and photographs pertaining to locomotives, rolling stock, trackage, structures, operation, and corporate history of Atchison, Topeka, and Santa Fe Railway Co. Provides free reference, literature-searching, and referral services. Fee for copying and postage.

05713. Save-the-Redwoods League, 114 Sansome St, Room 605, San Francisco, CA 94104; (415) 362-2352. Answers inquiries related to redwood forest preservation. Permits onsite use of films, slides, photos collection; publishes bulletins; refers inquirers to other sources of info.

05714. Screen Actors Guild, 7750 Sunset Blvd, Hollywood, CA 90046; (213) 876-3030. Labor org that negotiates and enforces wages and working conditions for actors in motion picture/television industry. Answers inquiries, advises members on rights, responsibilities, and benefits.

05715. Scripps Clinic and Research Foundation, 10666 N Torrey Pines Rd, La Jolla, CA 92037; (619) 455-9100. Involved in diagnosis and treatment of pain patients. Conducts research on pain problems as well as its psychological and physiological aspects. Answers inquiries and provides advisory and consulting services free to medical groups and individuals. Standard fees charged patients.

05716. Scripps Marine Geological Collection, A-020, Scripps Institution of Oceanography, 8602 La Jolla Shores Dr, La Jolla, CA 92093; (619) 452-4386 or 452-2037. Interest in sediment samples and dredged rocks from ocean floor, especially the Pacific. Answers inquiries, provides samples, permits onsite use of collections, makes referrals to other sources of info. Services free to qualified users.

05717. Scripps Physical and Chemical Oceanographic Data Facility, Scripps Institution of Oceanography, Mail Code S-001, La Jolla, CA 92093; (714) 452-4420. Collects and analyzes physical and chemical oceanographic data. Interest in physical and chemical oceanographic data. Provides general reference services, distributes data compilations. Services available at cost.

05718. Scripps Zooplankton Invertebrate Collection, c/o A. Fleminger, Curator, A.001, Scripps Institution of Oceanography (Ritter Hall, Room 230), La Jolla, CA 92093; (619) 453-2071. Interest in marine invertebrate zooplankton accumulated in support of studies on systematic zoology, marine biogeography, etc. Access to collection can be arranged. Material provided to institutions. Consulting services available.

05719. Sea Shepherd Conservation Society, P.O. Box 70005, Redondo Beach, CA 90277; (213) 399-6713. Interest in protection and conservation of marine wildlife, especially whales and seals. Provides general reference services, publishes and distributes materials. Services free, but donations accepted.

05720. Search Group, 925 Secret River Dr, Sacramento, CA 95831; (916) 392-2550. Interest in applications of modern technology to needs of criminal justice community. Provides general reference services, publishes and distributes materials. Most services free to related institutions.

05721. Self-Help for the Elderly, 640 Pine St, San Francisco, CA 94108; (415) 982-9171. Interest in needs of, and services for elderly. Provides general reference services free to those interested in field of aging.

05722. Semiconductor Industry Association, 4320 Stevens Creek Blvd, Ste 275, San Jose, CA 95120; (408) 246-1181. Trade org for U.S. semiconductor manufacturers. Provides general reference services, supplies technical training videotapes on lease basis. Other services available to member companies only.

05723. Sensory Aids Foundation, 399 Sherman Ave, Ste 12, Palo Alto, CA 94306; (415) 329-0430. Interest in employment-related needs of handicapped persons. Provides general reference services, conducts seminars. Fees charged for workshops and training programs; other services free.

05724. Sequoia Natural History Association, Three Rivers, CA 93271; (209) 565-3341 ext 68. Interest in natural history, human history, and general info relating to Sequoia and Kings Canyon Natl Parks. Sells publications, answers inquiries.

05725. Sequoia-Turner Corp., 755 Ravendale Dr, Mountain View, CA 94043; (415) 969-5533. Interest in fluorometry and spectrophotometry and their applications in analytical chemistry. Provides general reference services, conducts seminars, distributes publications. Services available to those in chemical analysis, mostly free.

05726. Sexaholics Anonymous, P.O. Box 300, Simi Valley, CA 93062. Promotes sexual restraint. Does not offer treatment or therapy. Provides support group philosophy taken directly from Twelve Steps and Twelve Traditions of Alcoholics Anonymous.

05727. Shakespeare Society of America, 1107 N Kings Rd, Los Angeles, CA 90069; (213) 654-5623. Reproduces Shakespeare's plays. Provides general reference services, publishes and distributes journal, permits onsite use of collection. Services free to members only; membership open to anyone.

05728. Sherman Grinberg Film Libraries, 1040 N McCadden Pl, Hollywood, CA 90038; (213) 464-7491. Commercial org involved in research and licensing of archival film and tape. Provides reference services, makes referrals, permits onsite use of collection by appointment only. Services primarily for filmmakers, film researchers, etc., for a fee.

05729. Sidney R. Frank Group and SRF Research Institute, 444 David Love Pl, Goleta, CA 93117. Interest in applied meteorological research, including environmental pollution, meteorological research, field surveys, etc. Answers brief inquiries, provides consulting and operational services on a contract or grant basis, provides expert-witness testimony in court, lends some materials.

05730. Sierra Club, 530 Bush St, San Francisco, CA 94108; (415) 981-8634. Interest in conservation of natural resources, environmental policy, energy policy, outdoor recreation. Provides general reference services, permits onsite use of collection. Services available at minimal cost.

05731. Silverado Museum, P.O. Box 409 (Library Ln), St Helena, CA 94574; (707) 963-3757. Interest in life and works of Robert Louis Stevenson. Maintains collec-

tion of 7,600 related items. Answers inquiries, makes referrals, provides consulting services, conducts tours and gives talks. Museum open to public. Services free.

05732. Simon Wiesenthal Center, Yeshiva Univ of Los Angeles, 9760 W Pico Blvd, Los Angeles, CA 90035; (213) 553-9036 or 553-4478. Interest in materials pertaining to Jewish life, philosophy, and history. Publishes semiannual magazine and newsletters. Answers inquiries, makes referrals, conducts seminars, lend materials, permits onsite use of collections. Services generally free, copying at cost.

05733. Singer Co. Librascope Technical Library, 833 Sonora Ave, Glendale, CA 91201; (213) 244-6541. Interest in computer systems, optical systems, ASW systems, fire control systems, acoustics, sonar, signal processing. Provides general reference services. Users must have security clearance; access to unclassified materials permitted with escort.

05734. Sleep Disorders Clinic, Dept of Neurology, UCLA School of Medicine, 710 Westwood Plaza, Room 1184, Los Angeles, CA 90024; (213) 206-8005. Interest in sleep and sleep disorders. Provides general reference services, conducts seminars. Fees charged for consultations and testing.

05735. Sleep Disorders Clinic and Research Center, Stanford Univ Medical Center, Administrative Offices, Edwards Bldg, R-303, Stanford, CA 94305; (415) 497-7458. Interest in evaluation, diagnosis, and treatment services for sleep disorders. Provides some reference services, publishes and distributes materials. Patients seen on referral of a physician; polysomnograph services available.

05736. Sleep Research Society, Exec Secty, c/o Dept of Psychiatry (M003), Univ of Calif., San Diego, La Jolla, CA 92093; (619) 452-2137. Stimulates info exchange among professional researchers in both clinical and basic aspects of sleep. Provides consulting, abstracting, and indexing services, conducts seminars. Services provided, on an hourly fee basis, to other sleep researchers.

05737. Smith-Kettlewell Institute of Visual Sciences, 2232 Webster St, San Francisco, CA 94115; (415) 561-1619. Develops sensory aids for blind and deaf-blind. Provides advisory, consulting, referral, and reference services, conducts electronics training program for blind, lends materials, other services. Services free.

05738. Smithkline Bio-Science Laboratories Library, 7600 Tyrone Ave, Van Nuys, CA 91405; (213) 989-2520. Interest in chemical and microbiological analyses of biological fluids and drugs, karyotyping of cell chromosomes. Answers inquiries, makes interlibrary loans on a cooperative basis, permits onsite use of collection.

05739. Soaring Society of America, P.O. Box 66071, Los Angeles, CA 90066-0071; (213) 390-4440. Promotes and regulates sport of gliding and soaring. Provides general reference services, publishes and distributes materials, conducts seminars, permits onsite use of collections. Most services free, except publications.

05740. Social Science Research Lab, Coll of Arts and Letters, San Diego State Univ, San Diego, CA 92182-0436; (619) 265-5845. Promotes instruction, interdisciplinary exchanges, and cooperation concerning research and instruction in the social sciences. Provides general reference services, conducts seminars, permits onsite use of collection. Services free.

05742. Society for Adolescent Medicine, P.O. Box 3462, Granada Hills, CA 91344; (818) 368-5996. Promotes research and disseminates info on adolescent medicine. Holds one scientific meeting a year, identifies careers in adolescent medicine, plans professional education, makes physician referrals.

05743. Society for Computer Simulation, P.O. Box 2228 (1010 Pearl St, Ste 3.), La Jolla, CA 92038; (714) 459-3888. Interest in all aspects of simulation and modeling. Publishes monthly magazines covering applications and techniques of simulation and modeling. Answers inquiries. Provides copies and reprints of papers in SCS publications for a fee.

05744. Society for Creative Anachronism, P.O. Box 743, Milpitas, CA 95035-0743; (408) 262-5250. Studies, exchanges info on pre-17th Century Western culture, including medieval and renaissance dance, heraldry, and armor. Provides free inquiry and referral services, sells publications.

05745. Society for Investigative Dermatology, c/o Ervin H. Epstein, Jr., MD, Secty/Treas, Univ of Calif. Dermatology Service, San Francisco General Hospital, Bldg 100, Room 269, 1001 Potrero St, San Francisco, CA 94122. Interest in dermatologic research and communications. Publishes monthly *Journal of Investigative Dermatology*. Refers inquiries to appropriate individual. Service available only to scientists.

05746. Society for Nutrition Education, 1736 Franklin St, Ste 900, Oakland, CA 94612; (415) 444-7133. Interest in nutrition education, disease and nutrition, fitness, pregnancy and nutrition, etc. Provides general reference services, publishes and distributes materials, permits onsite use of collection. Services primarily for members, on a contract basis to others.

05748. Society for Psychophysiological Research, c/o Robert W. Levenson, Secty-Treas, Univ of Calif., 401 Parnassus Ave, San Francisco, CA 94143; (415) 681-8080 ext 207. Publishes journal on relationship between physiological processes and behavior.

05750. Society for Public Health Education, 703 Market Street, Ste 535, San Francisco, CA 94103; (415) 546-7601. Dedicated to health promotion through research, professional education, and standards settings. Examines natl health legislation, stimulates research on health education programs, provides communications link among health education orgs.

05751. Society for Surgery of the Alimentary Tract, Dept of Surgery, Univ of Calif. at Los Angeles, School of Medicine, Los Angeles, CA 90024; (213) 825-9425. Promotes exchange of knowledge among alimentary tract surgeons. Meets regularly to discuss surgical problems. Promotes training opportunities, encourages research, and publishes scientific papers.

05752. Society for the Advancement of Material and Process Engineering, P.O. Box 2459 (843 W Glentana St), Covina, CA 91722; (818) 331-0616. Interest in materials science, process engineering. Answers inquiries, conducts conferences and symposia, publishes and distributes materials. Services free.

05753. Society for the Preservation of Birds of Prey, P.O. Box 891, Pacific Palisades, CA 90272. Interest in protection, conservation, and public attitudes relating to birds of prey. Publishes *The Raptor Report*, 1-3 times a year. Answers inquiries from adults, advises orgs, makes referrals to raptor experts. Info free, but donations suggested.

05754. Society of Allied Weight Engineers, c/o Fred H. Wetmore, Exec Secty, 344 E J St, Chula Vista, CA 92010. Interest in mass properties engineering, weight and balance procedures and requirements. Provides general reference services, publishes and distributes materials, conducts seminars. Services provided at cost, but not available to Iron Curtain countries.

05755. Society of Biological Psychiatry, 2010 Wilshire Blvd, Los Angeles, CA 90057; (213) 483-7863. Publishes journal, books, directory on field of biological psychiatry. Answers inquiries, provides consulting services, makes referrals. Fee may be charged for some services.

05756. Society of Critical Care Medicine, 223 E Imperial Hwy, Ste 110, Fullerton, CA 92635; (714) 870-5243. Seeks to improve care of those afflicted with life-threatening illnesses, monitor care offered by treatment facilities, and standardize training of professionals. Conducts seminars and annual meetings, provides current-awareness and referral services. Services free, except publications and tapes.

05757. Society of Research Administrators, 1505 Fourth St, Ste 203, Santa Monica, CA 90401; (213) 393-3137. Professional org interested in research administration. Provides general reference services, conducts seminars, publishes and distributes materials. Most services free.

05758. Society of Vertebrate Paleontology, c/o Dr David Whistler, Los Angeles County Museum of Natural History, Exposition Blvd, Los Angeles, CA 90007; (213) 744-3411. Intl assn of professionals and amateurs interested in vertebrate paleontology, evolution, comparative anatomy, and taxonomy. Provides some general reference services, publishes and distributes materials.

05759. Society to Preserve and Encourage Radio Drama, Variety, and Comedy, P.O. Box 1587, Hollywood, CA

90028. Interest in radio drama, variety, and comedy shows. Provides general reference services, publishes and distributes materials, permits onsite use of collections. General info to anyone, other services limited to paying members.

05760. Solar Turbines Inc. Technical Information Center, E-1, P.O. Box 80966, San Diego, CA 92138; (714) 238-5992. Interest in gas turbine design, test, and manufacture, applied research in high-temperature metals and processes, gas compressors. Provides reference services, lends some materials in literature collection.

05761. Solar Use Now for Resources and Employment, 961 Embarcadero Delmar, Isla Vista, CA 93117; (805) 685-1624. Advocates use of solar energy through lobbying and provision of info services. Maintains collection of related materials. Answers inquiries, provides advisory services, makes referrals, conducts slide shows, and seminars. Services free on payment of membership fee.

05762. Songwriters Resources and Services, 6772 Hollywood Blvd, Hollywood, CA 90028; (213) 463-7178. Promotes protection and education of songwriters. Provides general reference services, and group legal services, evaluates songs, conducts workshops, permits onsite use of collections. Some services free or at cost; others limited to membership.

05763. Southeast Asia Resource Center, P.O. Box 4000-D, Berkeley, CA 94704; (415) 548-2546. Interest in research on Southeast Asia and U.S. policy toward those countries. Publishes and distributes materials. General reference services generally free, primarily for Congress and news media, but others assisted.

05764. Southern California Academy of Sciences, c/o Los Angeles County Museum of Natural History, 900 Exposition Blvd, Los Angeles, CA 90007; (213) 744-3384. Museum interested in biology, invertebrate, experimental, and vertebrate zoology, botany, anthropology, geology, paleontology. Answers inquiries as time permits. Library accessible to public for reference.

05765. Southern California Meter Association, P.O. Box 460, Ste C5, Downey, CA 90241; (213) 927-6739. Interest in fluid measurement and control instrumentation, remote control and telemetering, microcomputers, control valves and actuators. Holds monthly meetings, annual instrumentation short course at Los Angeles Harbor Coll, for a fee.

05766. Southwest Regional Lab for Educational Research and Development, 4665 Lampson Ave, Los Alamitos, CA 90720; (213) 598-7661. Interest in basic skills instruction, education for handicapped, comprehensive arts and media education, related topics. Answers inquiries, publishes and distributes materials.

05767. Soyfoods Center, P.O. Box 234 (1021 Dolores Dr), Lafayette, CA 94549; (415) 283-2991. Interest in soyfoods, soyfoods industry and market. Provides document search and delivery, permits onsite use of collections, answers inquiries. Fee for some services.

05768. Specialty Automotive Manufacturers Association, c/o Dick Wells and Associates, 4340 Campus Dr, Ste 213, Newport Beach, CA 92660; (714) 850-1418. Serves interests of manufacturers and suppliers of kit cars and related components, as well as vehicle owners (hobbyists). Answers inquiries or makes referrals without cost.

05769. Specialty Equipment Market Association, 11540 E Slauson Ave, Whittier, CA 90606; (213) 692-9402. Represents auto manufacturing industry with govt leaders, consumer groups; disseminates info to educate public; provides advisory services. Services free.

05770. Speech Technology Laboratory, 3888 State St, Santa Barbara, CA 93105; (805) 687-0110. Commercial org that conducts basic and applied research on technical aspects of speech and language. Provides advisory, consulting, and referral services, provides info on R&D programs, evaluates data, conducts seminars and workshops. Services for a fee.

05771. Spiritual Counterfeits Project Information and Referral Service, P.O. Box 4308, Berkeley, CA 94704; (415) 540-5767. Researches and critiques effects and influences of new religions and psychological movements. Provides general reference services, distributes publications. Services free, except publications.

05772. Stanford Center for Chicano Research, Stanford Univ, P.O. Box 9341 (Bldg 170, Central Campus), Stanford, CA 94305; (415) 497-3914. Interest in Chicano urban populations and conditions. Provides general reference services, conducts seminars, conducts research on contract or grant basis. Services primarily for scholars and policymakers.

05773. Stanford Environmental Law Society, c/o Stanford Law School, Stanford, CA 94305; (415) 497-4421. Interest in environmental law. Provides general reference services, publishes and distributes material, permits onsite use of collections. Services free to some nonprofit orgs, at a fee to students and professionals.

05774. Stanford Linear Accelerator Center, Stanford Univ, P.O. Box 4349, Stanford, CA 94305; (415) 854-3300 ext 2204. Publishes reports on accelerators, high energy physics. Answers inquiries, provides stock reference photos, permits onsite reference of collection, gives prearranged tours.

05775. Stanford Univ, Technical Information Service, Green Library, Room 151, Stanford Univ Libraries, Stanford, CA 94305; (415) 497-9418. Interest in various fields of sciences and engineering, social sciences and humanities. For commercial and industrial orgs. Lends books and provides copying services.

05776. Starlight Foundation, 9021 Melrose Avenue, Ste 204, Los Angeles, CA 90069; (213) 205-0631. Dedicated to making wishes of terminally and chronically ill children come true.

05777. Statewide Air Pollution Research Center, Univ of Calif., Riverside, CA 92521-0312; (714) 787-5124. Interest in air pollution, photochemistry, atmospheric interactions, mutagenic pollutants. Provides free reprints of technical articles by research staff, permits free access to collections, duplicates reprint and microfilm articles for a fee.

05778. Statistical/Biomathematical Consulting Clinic, Univ of Calif., Center for the Health Sciences, Room AV-617, Los Angeles, CA 90024; (213) 825-3296. Provides consulting services to biological and medical researchers for a fee; consults by telephone to remedy problems on use of batch mode data processing software.

05779. Stonehenge Study Group, 2821 De La Vina St, Santa Barbara, CA 93105; (805) 687-9350. Conducts research on and expeditions to photograph and measure megalithic sites in England, Wales, Scotland, Ireland, Sweden, France, and Malta. Provides reference, referral, consulting services; conducts expeditions, seminars, workshops. Fee for some services.

05780. Structural Engineers Association of California, 217 Second St, San Francisco, CA 94105; (415) 974-5147. Interest in structural engineering, effect of earthquakes on buildings, seismology, building design and materials, building code provisions. Answers inquiries, makes referrals.

05781. Strybing Arboretum and Botanical Garden, 9th Ave and Lincoln Way, Golden Gate Park, San Francisco, CA 94122; (415) 558-3622. Interest in horticulture, especially in Mediterranean climates, botany, Calif. native plants, New World cloud forests. Provides general reference services, conducts tours, lectures. Open free to public.

05782. Stucco Manufacturers Association, 14006 Ventura Blvd, Sherman Oaks, CA 91423; (213) 789-8733. Interest in use of colored stucco. Answers inquiries free or for a fee, depending on request.

05783. Student Assistance Council of America Scholarship Search, 407 State St, Santa Barbara, CA 93101; (805) 963-1311. Interest in scholarships, grants, and financial aid for undergraduate college students. Conducts computer searches to locate sources of financial aid for college students on payment of a processing fee. Computerized data bank holds about 250,000 private-sector financial sources.

05784. Substance Abuse Librarians and Information Specialists, 1816 Scenic Ave, Berkeley, CA 94709; (415) 642-5208. Assn of individuals and orgs interested in alcohol/drug/substance abuse. Provides general reference services, publishes and distributes materials. Fees vary according to each member org.

05785. Sunkist Growers Research Library, 760 E Sunkist St, Ontario, CA 91761; (714) 983-9811 ext 454. Interest in postharvest citrus fruit and citrus products technology, organic, analytical, and food chemistry. Answers inquiries, provides reference and copying services without charge. Onsite use of collection permitted on request.

05786. Surgical Eye Expeditions International, 1216 State St, Ste 310, Santa Barbara, CA 93102; (805) 963-3303. Org of ophthalmologists in private practice who provide free eye care, establish eye surgery and free glasses clinics for presbyopic patients. Services free, except consultation, to medical, civic, health authorities, govts, service club groups, and others.

05787. Surrogate Parent Foundation, 8447 Wilshire Blvd, Ste 306, Beverly Hills, CA 90211; (213) 506-1804. Interest in surrogate parenting, reproductive technology, embryo and ovum transfer, in vitro insemination. Provides free general reference services.

05788. Survey Research Center, State Data Program/Survey Research Center, Univ of Calif., 2538 Channing Way, Berkeley, CA 94720; (415) 642-6571. Interest in sample survey materials on political, social, and economic topics covering many topics. Magnetic tape and codebooks reproduced for researchers at standard rates. Sells catalog of data holdings.

05789. Swords to Plowshares, 2069-A Mission St, San Francisco, CA 94110; (415) 552-8805. Offers employment, outreach, info, counseling, and financial assistance services to veterans. Provides general reference services, plus job placement assistance. Services available to veterans and veterans' groups.

05791. System Safety Society, 14252 Culver Dr, Ste A261, Irvine, CA 92714; (714) 551-2463. Interest in safety assurance in complex systems and products. Publishes *Hazard Prevention* bimonthly, conference proceedings, reprints. Answers inquiries regarding membership, sponsored conferences, and publications. Reprints available.

05792. TRW Electronics and Defense Sector, Technical Information Center, One Space Park, S/1930, Redondo Beach, CA 90278; (213) 536-2631. Interest in defense and space systems engineering, design, development, and fabrication, microelectronics research and development, systems engineering for civil programs such as environmental and energy studies. Makes interlibrary loans, permits onsite use of collection by arrangement.

05793. Technical Marketing Society of America, P.O. Box 7275 (3711 Long Beach Blvd, Ste 609), Long Beach, CA 90807; (213) 595-0254. Fosters development of marketing info and new ideas for science and technology professionals. Publishes *Market Outlook* and bimonthly newsletter. Answers inquiries, conducts seminars, provides info on employment opportunities. Services to nonmembers for a fee.

05794. Tel-Med, P.O. Box 1768 (952 S Mt Vernon), Colton, CA 92324; (714) 825-6034. Provides telephone access to a library of concise, physician-approved, 3 to 5-minute tape recordings on health care topics. Basic health info free to all users within a toll-free dialing area in almost 400 cities.

05796. Teledyne Ryan Aeronautical, Technical Information Services, P.O. Box 80311 (2701 N Harbor Dr), San Diego, CA 92138; (619) 291-7311 ext 1067. Interest in aerodynamic engineering, materials characteristics, and applications related to production of air vehicles. Answers inquiries, makes referrals, provides reference services, lends materials. Limited onsite use of collection permitted.

05797. Telesensory Systems, P.O. Box 7455, Mountain View, CA 94039; (415) 960-0920. Develops, manufactures, and markets sophisticated electronic aids for the blind and visually impaired. Publishes newsletter and R&D progress reports. Answers product inquiries.

05799. Thera Institute, P.O. Box 1090, Aptos, CA 95003; (408) 688-0358 or 426-1378. Involved in adaption of high technology to smaller-scale systems.Maintains files on relevant technologies and biological research. Answers inquiries, makes referrals, provides advisory and reference services. Conducts seminars and workshops and research on relevant ideas.

05800. Thomas Jefferson Research Center, 1143 N Lake Ave, Pasadena, CA 91104; (213) 789-0791. Seeks workable solutions to human problems of individuals, orgs, and society and develops training and developmental materials. Answers inquiries free, provides consulting services, conducts seminars, publishes and distributes materials for a fee.

05801. Toastmasters International, P.O. Box 10400 (2200 N Grand Ave), Santa Ana, CA 92711; (714) 542-6793. Devoted to promoting effective speaking through its member clubs. Provides inquiry and referral servies, conducts seminars and workshops. Services primarily for members, but others assisted within limits of time and staff.

05802. Training Media Distributors Association, 1258 N Highland Ave, Los Angeles, CA 90038. Interest in copyright protection of training media. Answers inquiries, sells pamphlet.

05803. TreePeople/California Conservation Project, 12601 Mulholland Dr, Beverly Hills, CA 90210; (818) 769-2663 (213) 273-8733. Encourages individuals to care for and improve environment. Provides general reference services, assists in organizing community tree plantings, conducts workshops. Services free, but membership encouraged.

05804. Trust for Public Land, 82 Second St, San Francisco, CA 94105; (415) 495-4014. Interest in urban revitalization, land conservation. Provides general reference services, publishes and distributes materials, conducts seminars and workshops. Services free, except consulting.

05805. Tustin Institiute of Techology, 22 E Los Olivos St, Santa Barbara, CA 93105; (805) 682-7171. Private engineering school that specializes in training in vibration, shock, and acoustics. Offers regular and correspondence courses. Provides consulting services, distributes publications. Services provided at cost to all users.

05806. Twinline, P.O. Box 10066, Berkeley, CA 94704; (415) 644-0861. Provides support services to help parents cope with stresses and issues involved in care of multiple birth children. Operates telephone advice, info service; provides general reference services. Services free.

05807. U.S. Air Force Western Space and Missile Center Technical Library, AFL 2827 (PMET), Vandenberg Air Force Base, CA 93437; (805) 866-9745. Interest in aerospace test and evaluation, radar, telemetry, optics, data automation, electrical engineering, computer science. Provides library services to Dept of Defense agencies and their contractors only.

05808. U.S. Borax Research Corp., Research Library, P.O. Box 4111 (9412 Crescent Way), Anaheim, CA 92803; (714) 774-2670. Interest in boron chemistry, chemistry and certain aspects of mining and ceramics, metallurgy, glass. Answers inquiries, provides reference services, makes interlibrary loans, permits limited onsite reference by request.

05809. U.S. Metric Association, 10245 Andasol Ave, Northridge, CA 91325; (213) 363-5606. Promotes conversion to metric system of measurement. Provides assistance to industry, business, govt; answers inquiries free if SASE furnished (fee charged for extensive research).

05810. U.S. Navy Pacific Missile Test Center Technical Library, Code 1018, Bldg 36, Point Mugu, CA 93042; (805) 989-7401. Interest in radar, guidance systems, guided missiles, aerodynameting services.

05811. U.S. Nuclear-Free and Independent Pacific Network, 942 Market St, Room 711, San Francisco, CA 94102; (415) 434-2988. Disarmament, church, environmental, and human rights orgs interested in military activity of the U.S., Pacific Ocean and its islands. Provides general reference services, conducts seminars, permits onsite use of collection. Some services free.

05813. U.S.D. Corp., 3323 W Warner Ave, Santa Ana, CA 92702; (714) 540-8010. Interest in underwater sports equipment, diving gear, respirators, and self-contained breathing apparatus. Answers inquiries, provides consulting and bibliographic services, permits onsite reference.

05814. UCLA Jonsson Comprehensive Cancer Center, Information Service, Reference Div, Biomedical Library, UCLA 12-077 CHS, Los Angeles, CA 90024; (213) 206-8016. Interest in info services for cancer research, diagnosis, therapy, and prevention. Provides general reference services, publishes and distributes materials, permits onsite use of collections.

05815. UCLA Map Library, Univ of Calif., 405 Hilgard Ave, Los Angeles, CA 90024; (213) 825-3526. Interest in maps and related cartographic literature, with emphasis on Pacific Ocean and islands, Africa, and Latin America. Answers inquiries, provides reference and photocopy services, makes limited interlibrary loans, permits onsite use of collection.

05816. UPDATA Publications, 1746 Westwood Blvd, Los Angeles, CA 90024; (213) 474-5900. Gathers material from a variety of sources, reduces it to microfiche, and provides subject and title indexes. Also provides online data bases to all items. Info provided primarily through publications, which are for sale, and computer literature searches.

05817. USC Program in Information Technology, Center for Futures Research, Univ of Southern Calif., Los Angeles, CA 90007; (213) 743-5229. Interest in technological innovation processes, info technology. Provides general reference services, publishes and distributes materials. Services provided at cost.

05818. Umbrella Associates, P.O. Box 3692, Glendale, CA 91201; (818) 797-0514. Interest in contemporary artists worldwide and in museums, galleries, books featuring their works. Provides general reference services, publishes and distributes materials, permits onsite use of collections. Services for a fee.

05819. Union of American Physicians and Dentists, 1730 Franklin St, Ste 200, Oakland, CA 94606; (415) 839-0193. Represents physician and dentist members in dealings with hospitals, insurance companies, govt programs, and other health orgs. Answers inquiries, provides data evaluation, literature-searching and other services, conducts seminars, and workshops. Most services free.

05820. United Ministries in Education National Career Development Project, c/o Richard N. Bolles, Dir, P.O. Box 379, Walnut Creek, CA 94597; (415) 935-1865. Natl clearinghouse for career changers and job hunters. Provides general reference services, publishes and distributes materials, conducts seminars. Services free, except newsletter and workshops.

05821. United New Conservationists, P.O. Box 362, Campbell, CA 95008; (408) 295-2009. Interest in protecting environmental quality of life. Maintains collection of literature on conservation and environment. Leased land developed for community gardens. Answers inquiries, makes referrals, provides free advisory, reference, and literature-searching services.

05822. United Ostomy Association, 2001 W Beverly Blvd, Los Angeles, CA 90057; (213) 413-5510. Voluntary health agency interested in ileostomy, colostomy, and urostomy care and management. Answers inquiries, provides advisory services, distributes publications. Services free, except publications.

05826. United States Divorce Reform, P.O. Box 243, Kenwood, CA 95452; (707) 833-2550. Interest in removal of divorce from the courts, reorganization of state govts to replace divorce courts with executive agencies. Publishes and distributes materials, answers inquiries.

05827. Urban Studies Program, Center for Politics, Policy, and Public Administration, San Francisco State Univ, 1600 Holloway Ave, San Francisco, CA 94132; (415) 469-1178. Interest in undergraduate urban education, social policy planning, environment, public interest law, community org. Provides general reference services, publishes and distributes materials, teaches courses and conducts seminars.

05828. Varian Associates Technical Library, 611 Hansen Way, Palo Alto, CA 94303; (415) 493-4000. Interest in electronics, mathematics, chemistry, physics and nuclear physics, metallurgy, linear accelerators, etc. Provides general reference services, permits onsite use of collection by qualified visitors. Evidence of security clearance and need-to-know required.

05829. Violin Society of America, P.O. Box 139, Idyllwild, CA 92349; (714) 659-4203. Holds annual convention and sponsors international competition for violin, viola, and cello makers biennially. Interest in matters pertaining to stringed instruments. Provides general reference services, publishes and distributes materials. Services free.

05830. Visibility Lab, Scripps Institution of Oceanography, P-003, Univ of Calif., La Jolla, CA 92093; (619) 294-3680. Publishes technical reports on optics, answers inquiries, provides consulting services,(free unless extensive). Digital image processing computer facility available to qualified users.

05831. Vocational and Occupational Information Center for Educators, Calif. Dept of Education, 721 Capitol Mall, 4th Fl Sacramento, CA 95814; (916) 445-0401. Has info and papers on all aspects of vocational education. Provides hard copy documents or audiovisuals on a 3-week loan basis. Makes referrals to resource persons and orgs. Services free.

05832. Volunteers in Asia, P.O. Box 4543 (The Clubhouse, Old Union, Stanford Univ), Stanford, CA 94305; (415) 497-3228 or 326-7672. Involved in volunteer work in Indonesia, Taiwan, the Philippines, Korea, Japan, and People's Republic of China, primarily in teaching English as a second language. Provides general reference services. Services free, except publications.

05833. W. M. Keck Lab of Hydraulics and Water Resources, Keck Bldg, Calif. Institute of Technology, 1201 E Calif. Blvd, Pasadena, CA 91125; (818) 356-6811. Interest in water resources, hydraulic engineering, water pollution control, sediment transportation. Provides general reference services, publishes and distributes materials. Individual faculty members may provide consulting services for a fee.

05834. Western Association of Fish and Wildlife Agencies, c/o Sandra J. Wolfe, Secty, Dept of Fish and Game, 1416 Ninth St, Rm 1236-8, Sacramento, CA 95814; (916) 445-7613. Interest in fish and wildlife research and management, including ecology, biology, limnology, and analytical methods. Publishes annual, answers inquiries.

05835. Western Bird Banding Association, c/o Howard L. Cogswell, Treas, 1548 East Ave, Hayward, CA 94541. Interest in ornithology, birds, bird banding. Publishes

North American Bird Bander quarterly, answers inquiries, provides info about R&D in progress. Services available only to subscribers.

05836. Western Gerontological Society, 833 Market Street, Ste 516, San Francisco, CA 94103; (415) 543-2617. Improves lives of older persons through education, training, policy analysis, and advocacy. Provides general reference services on age-related topics, conducts research and training programs for gerontology students, professionals.

05837. Western Interpreters Association, Attn: Doug Bryce, P.O. Box 28366, Sacramento, CA 95828; (916) 381-4620. Interest in natural and cultural environment interpretation and protection. Provides general reference services, publishes and distributes materials, conducts seminars. Services free, except seminars and publications.

05838. Western States Advertising Agencies Association, 2410 Beverly Blvd, No 1, Los Angeles, CA 90057; (213) 387-7432. Interest in advertising agency management, public education in advertising, legislation affecting advertising, media marketing. Provides general reference services, conducts seminars.

05839. Western States Black Research Center, 3617 Mont Clair St, Los Angeles, CA 90018; (213) 737-3292. Seeks to preserve history and cultural heritage of Americans of African descent. Offers grants to black filmmakers. Provides advisory, reference, referral, literature-searching, magnetic tape, and reproduction services; evaluates data and provides programs for cable TV. Fee for some services.

05840. Western Water Education Foundation, 1007 Seventh St, Ste 315, Sacramento, CA 95814; (916) 444-6240. Interest in water issues in Calif., environmental pollution, conservation, education. Provides general reference services free.

05841. Whale Center, 3929 Piedmont Ave, Oakland, CA 94611; (415) 654-6621. Seeks to end commercial whaling and protect whale habitats. Provides general reference services, conducts research, publishes and distributes materials. Fee for some services.

05842. Wilderness Travel Resource Center International, American Guides Association, Inc., Box 935 (Rd 94-B S Hwy 16.), Woodland, CA 95695; (916) 662-6824. Interest in qualified wilderness guides worldwide, primitive areas suitable for wilderness travel. Provides general reference services, publishes and distributes materials, conducts seminars and training courses. Info free, other services generally at cost.

05843. Wildlife Conservancy, 909 12th St, Ste 207, Sacramento, CA 95814; (916) 442-2666. Interest in conservation and restoration of wildlife and habitat in Calif. Provides advisory and reference services, makes referrals. Conducts workshops and symposia, evaluates data.

05844. Wine Institute, c/o Joan Ingalls, Librarian, 165 Post St, San Francisco, CA 94108; (415) 986-0878. Interest in wine, winemaking enology, grapes, viticulture, wine and grape economics, wine law and regulation, wine history. Answers nontechnical inquiries, provides reference services to producer members, permits onsite use of library collection by media by appointment only.

05845. Women Library Workers, 2027 Parker St, Berkeley, CA 94704; (415) 540-5332. Aids career and educational interests of women working in fields of library and info science. Provides general reference services, publishes and distributes materials. Services generally free to members, at cost to others.

05846. Women in Cell Biology, c/o Dr Alina Lopo, Dept of Biological Chemistry, Univ of Calif. School of Medicine, Davis, CA 95616; (916) 752-3310. Interest in women in science, with special interest in field of cell biology. Answers inquiries, conducts workshops, distributes publications. Services free, except publications.

05848. Women's History Research Center, 2325 Oak Street, Berkeley, CA; (415) 548-1770. Works to make marital rape a punishable offense in all states. Provides general reference services, publishes pamphlet. Clearinghouse's director tours country speaking on marital rape.

05850. Women's Sports Foundation, 195 Moulton St, San Francisco, CA 94123; (415) 563-6266 (800) 227-3988. Interest in participation of women and girls in all legitimate sporting activities. Provides general reference services, conduct seminars, permits onsite use of collections. Services free.

05851. World Institute on Disability, 1720 Oregon St, Ste 4, Berkeley, CA 94702; (415) 486-8314. Focuses on major problems of disabled people, including attendant care, public education, and development of independent living. Provides advisory, referral, and reference services; conducts seminars, workshops. Services free to individuals and small self-help groups, at cost to govt and large orgs.

05852. World International Nail and Beauty Association, 518 W Katella Ave, Orange, CA 92667; (714) 532-2553. Interest in nail and skin care, makeup, cosmetics, beauty culture. Provides general reference services, conducts seminars, evaluates data.

05853. World Plan Exec Council, Institute for Social Rehabilitation, 17310 Sunset Blvd, Pacific Palisades, CA 90272; (213) 459-4387. Interest in transcendental meditation for use in rehabilitation programs. Provides general reference services, conducts seminars, permits onsite use of collection. Fee for some services.

05854. World Print Council, Box 26010, San Francisco, CA 94126; (415) 776-9200. Info and advocacy service for fine art printmakers. Provides general reference services, publishes and distributes materials, permits onsite use of collections. Some services may be subject to a fee.

05855. World Without War Council, 1730 Martin Luther King, Jr. Way, Berkeley, CA 94709; (415) 845-1992. Interest in world politics, war, weapons, and strategies, arms control and disarmament, world community and human rights, religious and ethical thought on war. Provides advisory and referral services, conducts seminars and workshops, permits onsite use of collections. Services free, but contributions requested.

05856. Wyatt Technology Co., P.O. Box 3003 (350 S Hope Ave), Santa Barbara, CA 93105; (805) 682-0512. Commercial org interested in design and development of instrumentation based on differential light scattering technique. Provides general reference services, publishes and distributes materials, permits onsite use of collection. Services for a fee.

05857. XonTech Engineering Department, 6862 Hayvenhurst Ave, Van Nuys, CA 91406; (818) 787-7380. Provides info about explosive detection technology, pesticide monitoring via gas chromatography, Doppler Acoustic Radar technology. Answers inquiries free.

05858. Yesterday's Children, 5945 Fiddletown Pl, San Jose, CA 95120; (408) 268-5654. Aids people searching for their historical pasts. Provides counsel and assistance in search for biological families; reference, literature-searching, evaluation and referral services. Fee for some services.

05859. Yosemite Museum and Research Library, P.O. Box 577, Yosemite National Park, CA 95389; (209) 372-4461 ext 280 (Library), (209) 372-4461 ext 281. Interest in Yosemite Natl Park: history, photography, ethnology, geology. Answers inquiries, provides consulting and reference services, permits onsite use of library collections. Use of collections available by prior arrangement only. Copying services available for a fee.

05860. Yosemite Natural History Association, P.O. Box 545, Yosemite National Park, CA 95389; (209) 372-4532. Dedicated to Yosemite Natl Park, in cooperation with Natl Park Service. Answers inquiries; publishes bulletin, natural history pamphlets, books; provides research library.

05861. Youth Science Institute, 16260 Alum Rock Ave, San Jose, CA 95127; (408) 258-4322 or 258-7382. Interest in biological sciences as they relate to Calif., ecology, geology, water and energy conservation, computer education. Provides general reference services, conducts seminars, permits onsite use of collections. Services at cost.

05862. Zoological Society of San Diego, P.O. Box 551, San Diego, CA 92112; (714) 231-1515 ext 420 or 421. Interest in zoology, veterinary medicine, horticulture, zoological gardens. Provides general reference services, provides consulting services, conducts educational programs. Library not open to public.

Colorado

07006. AMC Cancer Research Center and Hospital Medical Library, 1600 Pierce St, Lakewood, CO 80214; (303) 233-6501. Interest in all aspects of cancer treatment and research. Maintains books, bound periodicals, journals, pamphlets, reprints. Answers inquiries, makes referrals, provides consulting.

07008. Academy of Parapsychology and Medicine, P.O. Box 36121, Denver, CO 80227. Interest in conditions under which total healing is possible through the study of all forms of paranormal and unorthodox healing. Publishes symposium transcripts and technical reports, answers inquiries, provides reference services.

07010. Aeronomy Laboratory, NOAA Environmental Research Laboratories, Plasma Physics Bldg, Rm 24-2102, Boulder, CO 80303; (303) 497-3216. Interest in radar studies of atmospheric dynamics. Publishes research reports and technical memoranda. Provides consultation and info on laboratory-related subjects.

07011. Affiliated Inventors Foundation, 501 Iowa Ave, Colorado Springs, CO 80909; (303) 635-1234. Encourages and assists inventors by providing educational materials and specific services. Answers inquiries, provides preliminary evaluations and minimum consulting services free. Provides patent searches for a fee.

07012. Agricultural Experiment Station, Colo. State Univ, Ft Collins, CO 80523; (303) 491-5371. Interest in agricultural engineering. Maintains seed reference collection, insect reference collection, plant herbarium, Colo. weed reference collection. Publishes bulletins and progress reports, answers inquiries, makes referrals.

07013. American Academy of Forensic Sciences, 225 South Academy Blvd, No 201, Colorado Springs, CO 80910; (303) 596-6006. Interest in study of standards in the field of forensic sciences. Publishes quarterly, answers inquiries by referral to selected individuals associated with the academy. Provides consulting services; provides expert referral service for small fee.

07014. American Association for Protecting Children, American Humane Association, P.O. Box 1266 (9725 East Hampden), Denver, CO 80201; (303) 695-0811. Promotes improved child protective services through program evaluation, consultation, training, research, and publications. Answers inquiries, provides consulting and reference services, sells publications, makes referrals.

07017. American Association of Suicidology, 2459 South Ash, Denver, CO 80222. Promotes study of suicide and improvement of suicide prevention services. Seeks to increase public awareness of the suicide problem and preventive resources. Provides advisory and reference services, distributes publications, makes referrals. Most services free.

07018. American Boarding Kennels Association, 311 North Union Blvd, Colorado Springs, CO 80909; (303) 635-7082. Interest in commercial pet boarding. Publishes magazine and newsletter, conducts educational programs for kennel operators, answers inquiries, makes referrals, provides advisory services on a fee basis.

07019. American Holistic Nurses Association, Box 116, Telluride, CO 81435. Promotes principles and practices of holistic health through education. Provides forum for exchange of ideas. Activities include meetings and conferences, publications, speakers bureau.

07020. American Homebrewers Association, P.O. Box 287 (734 Pearl St), Boulder, CO 80306-0287; (303) 447-0816. Promotes public awareness and appreciation of beer. Publishes directory and trade magazines. Answers inquiries, makes referrals, provides advisory and reference services, conducts conferences and seminars. Services free, except conferences, seminars, and publications.

07022. American Institute of Timber Construction, 333 West Hampden Ave, Englewood, CO 80110; (303) 761-3212. Interest in construction standards for engineered timber structures. Publishes timber construction manual, construction standards, and other technical data, answers inquiries.

07023. American Meteorite Lab, P.O. Box 2098 (7891 Oceola St, Westmister, Colo.), Denver, CO 80201; (303) 428-1371. Provides identification of meteorites. Publishes related materials. Services free.

07024. American Mobile Home Association, P.O. Box 710 (12929 West 26th St), Golden, CO 80401; (303) 232-6336. Interest in lobbying and counseling activities for people who live in mobile homes. Publishes monthly magazine and handbook. Answers inquiries, provides counseling, makes referrals, conducts seminars and workshops. Services primarily for members, but others assisted.

07025. American Numismatic Associations, P.O. Box 2366, Colorado Springs, CO 80903; (303) 632-2646. Library and museum dedicated to coins and currency. Publishes *The Numismatist* monthly and periodical indices. Answers inquiries, provides advisory and copying services, conducts certification program. Lends library materials to members only.

07026. American Reye's Syndrome Association, National Office, 701 South Logan, Ste 203, Denver, CO 80209; (303) 777-2592. Interest in Reye's Syndrome info, early recognition aids and counseling. Fosters research into causes, treatment, and prevention. Answers inquiries, provides reference services, maintains 24-hour hotline. Services provided at cost.

07028. American School Food Service Association, 4101 East Iliff St, Denver, CO 80222; (303) 757-8555. Works to expand scope of child nutrition programs and increase professional competence of individuals involved. Publishes periodicals and newsletters related to topic. Answers inquiries, conducts seminars, makes referrals. Services may be provided for a fee.

07029. American Society for Environmental History, c/o J. Donald Hughes, Dept of History, Univ of Denver, Denver, CO 80210; (303) 871-2347, 871-2958, or 871-2952. Interest in environmental studies in a cross-disciplinary historical context. Publishes quarterly, newsletter; answers inquiries and provides advisory services; conducts meetings, symposia, and programs. Some services may be provided for a fee.

07030. American Society for Surgery of the Hand, 3025 South Parker Rd, Ste 65, Aurora, CO 80014; (303) 755-4588. Furnishes leadership and fosters advances in hand surgery. Maintains library and museum, publishes *Journal of Hand Surgery* bimonthly. Answers inquiries, provides continuing education, makes referrals. Services free.

07032. American Society of Andrology, c/o Rupert Amann, Secty, Animal Reproduction Laboratory, Colo. State Univ, Ft Collins, CO 80523; (303) 491-6666. Interest in clinical and lab research pertinent to structure and function of the male reproductive system and male gametes. Publishes *Journal of Andrology* monthly, newsletter; conducts seminars, workshops, and annual meetings. Services available for a fee.

07033. American Society of Bariatric Physicians, 7430 East Caley Ave, Ste 210, Englewood, CO 80111; (303) 779-4833. Encourages excellence in the practice of bariatric medicine through interchange of info, research, and continuing education. Maintains small collection of books. Answers inquiries, makes referrals, conducts seminars, and provides cassette tapes of post-graduate education courses.

07035. American Society of Farm Managers and Rural Appraisers, c/o Exec Vice Pres, 950 South Cherry St, Ste G-16, Denver, CO 80222; (303) 758-3513. Devoted to management of farms and ranches and appraisal of rural real estate as a service for a fee. Answers inquiries, conducts seminars, provides consulting and reference services. Primarily for persons in agriculture, but others may be assisted. Fees charged for some services.

07036. American Society of Parasitologists, c/o Dr Gerald D. Schmidt, Secty-Treas, Dept of Biological Sciences, Univ of Northern Colo, Greeley, CO 80639; (303) 351-2467. Interest in ecology of parasites. Individual members maintain their own collections. Publishes bimonthly journal, answers inquiries free.

07037. American Society of Sugar Beet Technologists, P.O. Box 1546 (1311 South College St), Ft Collins, CO 80522; (303) 482-8250. Interest in research related to sugar beet industry. Maintains collection of journals and reports, including foreign literature and data, publishes journal. Answers technical inquiries, makes referrals. Nominal charge for volume orders.

07038. American Solar Energy Society, 2030 17th St, Boulder, CO 80302; (303) 443-3130. Develops and promotes solar energy as a source of heat for crop improvement, energy plantations, thermoelectric devices. Maintains collection of related materials. Publishes monthly magazine, quarterly and membership directory; answers inquiries; conducts seminars; makes referrals.

07039. American Tax Token Society, c/o George Van Trump, Jr., Secty, P.O. Box 26523, Lakewood, CO 80226; (303) 985-3508. Collects sales tax-related items. Encourages and facilitates research and publication of data on sales taxes and sales tax items. Publishes quarterly newsletter, answers inquiries. Services primarily for members, but others assisted.

07040. American Water Works Association, 6666 West Quincy Ave, Denver, CO 80235; (303) 794-7711. Interest in management, operation, and maintenance of public water supply utilities. Maintains specialized library of water information. Answers inquiries, makes referrals, provides reference services, conducts seminars. Fees charged for most services, with member discounts.

07041. American Wilderness Alliance, 7600 Arapahoe Rd, Ste 114, Englewood, CO 80112; (303) 771-0380. Interest in U.S. wilderness, wildlife habitat, and wild river resources. Publishes newsletter, answers inquiries, provides advisory services, conducts seminars and workshops. Services may be subject to a fee.

07042. Arabian Horse Registry of America, 3435 South Yosemite, Denver, CO 80231; (303) 750-5626. Interest in registration of Arabian horses. Maintains small collection of books, computerized data base of horses and owners. Publishes reports, stud books, newsletter; provides reference, literature-searching services; provides progeny and pedigree searches. Most services provided for a fee.

07044. Arthropod-borne Animal Diseases Research Laboratory, Agricultural Research Service, USDA, Denver Federal Center, Building 45-S-3, Box 25327, Denver, CO 80225; (303) 236-7953. Engages in basic and applied research on animal diseases transmitted by insects. Maintains small collection of books, periodicals, and reports. Answers inquiries.

07045. Associated Business Writers of America, c/o National Writers Club, 1450 South Havana St, Aurora, CO 80012; (303) 751-7844. Builds communication among freelance business writers, editors, and other business writing clients. Publishes bulletin and membership directory, answers inquiries, provides advisory and consulting services for free.

07046. Association for Experiential Education, c/o Richard J. Kraft, Exec Dir, Box 249-CU, Boulder, CO 80309; (303) 492-1547. Provides forums to address contemporary issues in experiential education. Answers inquiries, provides reference service, conducts seminars and annual conference. Services free, except for seminars, workshops, and publications.

07047. Association of Audio-Visual Technicians, P.O. Box 9716, Denver, CO 80209; (303) 733-3137. Interest in audiovisual production technology and repair. Has library of manuals and several self-teach programs available for rental. Answers inquiries, provides reference services, sponsors seminars, publishes newsletter. Services free, except for publications.

07048. Association of Family and Conciliation Courts Research Unit, 1720 Emerson St, Denver, CO 80218; (303) 837-1555. Conducts basic and applied research studies dealing with family law issues. Answers inquiries, provides consulting services, evaluates data, distributes publications. Info services free.

07049. Association of Operating Room Nurses, 10170 East Mississippi Ave, Denver, CO 80231; (303) 755-6300. Interest in operating room nursing education. Answers inquiries, provides technical consultation and reference services. Library services primarily for headquarters staff. Services of education dept for assn members only.

07051. Association of Surgical Technologists, Caller E, Littleton, CO 80120; (303) 978-9010. Interest in professional development of the surgical technologist through certification, continuing education. Publishes bimonthly journal, answers inquiries, makes referrals, provides reference services. Most services free.

07053. Beet Sugar Development Foundation, P.O. Box 1546 (1311 South College Ave), Ft Collins, CO 80522; (303) 482-8250. Supports or conducts research in beet sugar production and processing. Answers inquiries, conducts institute to improve fundamental background information for processing and management personnel. Services may be provided at cost.

07054. Behavior Genetics Association, c/o Dr Robert Plomin, Secty, Institute for Behavioral Genetics, Box 447, Univ of Colo, Boulder, CO 80309; (303) 492-7362. Interest in implications of interrelationships between genetic mechanisms and human and animal behavior. Educates and trains researchers and informs the public. Publishes bimonthly journal, answers inquiries, sponsors seminars, makes referrals. Services generally free.

07055. Behavioral Research Institute, 2305 Canyon Blvd, Boulder, CO 80302; (303) 444-1682. Conducts basic and program evaluation research on social problem behavior with emphasis on juvenile populations. Answers inquiries, provides advisory services, conducts seminars and workshops, permits onsite use of collection. Services provided at cost.

07056. Bibliographical Center for Research, Rocky Mountain Region, 1777 South Bellaire, Ste G-150, Denver, CO 80222; (303) 691-0550. Regional network linking libraries to automated literature data bases. Publishes newsletter, answers inquiries, provides consulting, reference, and literature-searching services. Services provided on contractual basis.

07057. Biofeedback Society of America, c/o Dr Francine Butler, Exec Dir, 4301 Owens St, Wheat Ridge, CO 80033; (303) 422-8436. Studies biofeedback and self-regulation. Answers inquiries, provides advisory and reference services at cost, primarily for professionals.

07059. Blind Outdoor Leisure Development, 533 E Main St, Aspen, CO 81612; (303) 925-2086. Sponsors recreational activities for the blind. Answers inquiries free and provides opportunities for holidays in the Rockies for visually impaired, with some financial aid available. Services available to visually impaired of any age.

07062. Brain Technologies Corp., 414 Buckeye St, Ft Collins, CO 80524; (303) 493-9210. Addresses usefulness of brain research and the studies of creativity, innovation, and human values to organization management. Answers inquiries, provides consulting services, conducts seminars. Services available for a fee.

07063. Bureau of Mines, Denver Research Center, U.S. Dept of the Interior, Building 20, Denver Federal Center, Denver, CO 80225; (303) 236-0697. Interest in rock mechanics as applied to ground control. Publishes reports, answers inquiries, makes referrals.

07064. Business Research Division, College of Business and Administration, Univ of Colo, Campus Box 420, Boulder, CO 80309; (303) 492-8227. Interest in business and economic research on recreation and leisure. Has extensive reference collection on travel research and Colo. business. Answers inquiries, makes referrals, provides consulting services, permits onsite use of collection.

07065. Center for Community Development and Design, Coll of Design and Planning, Univ of Colo. at Denver, 1100 14th St, Denver, CO 80202; (303) 629-2816. Provides architectural, planning, design, and community development assistance to urban neighborhoods and small towns. Answers inquiries, makes referrals, provides consulting services and reports at cost.

07066. Center for Judaic Studies, Univ of Denver, Denver, CO 80208; (303) 753-2068. Emphasizes history of Judaism, Jews, and Israel. Answers inquiries, provides advisory services, makes referrals, permits onsite use of collections. Services may be subject to a fee.

07067. Center for Mass Communications Research and Policy, Dept of Mass Communications, Univ of Denver Denver, CO 80210; (303) 753-2166. Conducts formative and evaluative research on creation of effective public service mass communications. Answers inquiries, provides consulting services, conducts seminars, analyzes data, produces films, filmstrips, slide shows, and TV presentations. Services at cost.

07068. Center for Research and Education, 900 28th St, Ste 200, Boulder, CO 80303; (303) 449-8440. Offers economic development program design, evaluation, and management. Answers inquiries, provides advisory and consulting services, conducts seminars and workshops. Services provided at cost.

07069. Center for Research in Ambulatory Health Care, Library Resource Center, 1355 South Colo. Blvd, Ste 900, Denver, CO 80222; (303) 753-1111. Interest in management of medical group practices, health maintenance organizations, and evolving forms of medical care in which group practice is key component. Answers inquiries and makes referrals, permits onsite use of collections.

07070. Center for Research on Judgment and Policy, Institute of Cognitive Science, Campus Box 344, Univ of Colo, Boulder, CO 80309; (303) 492-8122. Develops quality of decision making and policy formation. Explores ways of using techniques of judgment analysis. Maintains library of related books and materials. Provides advisory services, distributes publications. Services free, except for mailing costs.

07071. Central Great Plains Agricultural Research Station, Agricultural Research Service, USDA, P.O. Box K (County Rd GG NO 40345), Akron, CO 80720; (303) 345-2259. Conducts research on management and conservation of soil and water resources. Answers inquiries, makes referrals, provides info on research in progress. Services free.

07072. Child Health Associationiate Program, School of Medicine, Box C219 (4200 East 9th Ave), Univ of Colo, Denver, CO 80262; (303) 394-7963. Prepares nonphysician health professsionals to provide comprehensive health care for children. Answers inquiries, makes referrals, provides consulting and advisory services. Services free to physicians, educators, administrators, and program applicants.

07073. Classic Jaguar Association, c/o Richard T. Trenk, Chairman and Tech Ed, 13568 West Mississippi Court, Lakewood, CO 80228; (303) 986-1909. Provides technical, parts, and historical info on Jaguars and SS cars. Has large library of parts catalogs, owner manuals, etc. Answers inquiries, provides advisory, consulting, and reference services. Nominal consultant fee charged to authors using data for commercial gain.

07074. Collaborative Radiological Health Laboratory, Colo. State Univ, Ft Collins, CO 80523; (303) 491-8522. Interest in delayed effects of irradiation. Answers inquiries, provides research and consulting services to university and federal agencies, and other orgs.

07075. College Music Society, Regent Box 44, Univ of Colo, Boulder, CO 80302; (303) 449-1611. Concerned with philosophy and practice of music in colleges and universities. Publishes bibliographies, directory, and related reports. Answers inquiries, distributes publications. Services available for a fee.

07077. Colorado College, Charles Leaming Tutt Library, Colo. Coll, Colorado Springs, CO 80903; (303) 473-2233 ext 670. Interest in literature of American West and Southwest. Maintains collection of books and related materials. Provides computer-assisted research and copying, permits onsite use of collections by some business and professional people.

07079. Colorado School of Mines Arthur Lakes Library, Golden, CO 80401; (303) 273-3665 (reference service); (303) 273-3665 (interlibrary loan); (303) 273-3697 (maps). Studies geology, geophysics, and metallurgy. Makes interlibrary loans, provides photocopy and microfiche duplication services, permits onsite reference by members of the scientific and technical community.

07080. Colorado School of Mines, Research Institute, 5920 McIntyre St, Golden, CO 80403; (303) 279-2581. Interest in slurry pipeline studies and geological exploration. Has small reference collection of books. Answers inquiries.

07081. Colorado Wildlife Federation, 1560 Broadway, Ste 895, Denver, CO 80202; (303) 830-2557. Protects habitat, soil, and water, by fostering wise management and enhancing status of wildlife. Publishes *Colorado Wildlife* monthly. Answers inquiries, provides free advisory services.

07082. Cooperative Institute for Research in Environmental Sciences, Univ of Colo, Campus Box 449, Boulder, CO 80309; (303) 492-8028. Researches atmospheric chemistry, atmospheric physics, geophysics, and climate dynamics. Answers inquiries, distributes publications, makes referrals.

07083. Cooperative Wildlife Research Unit, Colo. State Univ, 201 Wagar Bldg, Ft Collins, CO 80523; (303) 491-5396. Interest in wildlife management and research. Answers inquiries, provides advice and info on grad research programs, makes referrals.

07084. Denver Botanic Gardens, Helen Fowler Library, 909 York St, Denver, CO 80206; (303) 297-2548 ext 24 or 26. Maintains collections on orchids and bromeliads. Answers inquiries, provides advisory and reference services, conducts seminars, permits onsite use of collections. Nonmembers charged admission to gardens and library.

07085. Denver Wildlife Research Center, U.S. Fish and Wildlife Service, Building 16, Federal Center, Denver, CO 80225; (303) 236-7873. Researches wildlife ecology and animal behavior. Maintains library and publishes technical reports and reprints. Answers inquiries; provides advisory and and reference services, info on research in progress; makes interlibrary loans, referrals. Permits onsite use of collections.

07086. Department of Communication Disorders and Speech Science, Univ of Colo, Campus Box 409, Boulder, CO 80309; (303) 492-6445. Concerned with speech science and phonetics. Answers inquiries, provides advisory and reference services, permits onsite use of collection. Services at cost.

07087. Department of the Interior, Western Technical Office, Brooks Towers, 1020 15th St, Denver, CO 80202; (303) 844-2451. Assists states in developing, regulating, and enforcing nationwide program to protect environment from adverse effects of coal mining. An-swers inquiries, makes referrals, provides free advisory, reference, and copying services.

07088. Domestic Technology International, P.O. Box 2043 (6726 Happy Hill Rd), Evergreen, CO 80439; (303) 674-1597. Conducts research, education, and training in domestic lifestyle alternatives and domestic solar energy technology. Provides advisory and consulting services and conducts training programs. Assesses and plans research, education, and training programs. Services available at cost.

07089. Dude Ranchers Association, P.O. Box 471, La-Porte, CO 80535; (303) 493-7623. Interest in dude ranches. Publishes biennial magazine and *Dude Ranch Vacation Directory.* Answers inquiries, provides literature-searching services, distributes publications. Magazine available for a fee; other services, including directory, free.

07090. EPA, National Enforcement Investigations Center, Denver Federal Center, Building 53, Box 25227, Denver, CO 80225; (303) 234-5765. Interest in enforcement of laws on water pollution, air pollution, pesticides, toxic substances, and effluent. Answers inquiries, provides reference services, permits onsite use of collection.

07091. Education Commission of the States Clearinghouse, Lincoln Tower, Room 300, 1860 Lincoln St, Denver, CO 80295; (303) 830-3600. Interest in states' education policies. Answers inquiries, makes referrals, provides free consulting, reference, and copying services.

07092. Educational Media Center, Univ of Colo. at Boulder, Stadium Bldg 360, Box 379, Boulder, CO 80309; (303) 492-7341. Markets series of alternative energy sources materials. Produces films, filmstrips, audio and video cassettes, and study guides. Catalog of materials available. Distributes materials for a fee.

07093. Engineering Research Center, Coll of Engineering and Applied Science, Campus Box 423, Univ of Colo, Boulder, CO 80309; (303) 492-7427. Interest in aerospace engineering sciences. Answers inquiries, makes referrals, provides consulting services and reprints of professional papers as available.

07094. Environmental Action Resource Service, P.O. Box 8, Farisita, CO 81037; (303) 746-2252. Centralized source of info regarding feasibility of alternative energy sources. Answers inquiries, distributes publications, permits onsite use of collection. Services free, donations appreciated.

07096. Exanimo Press, P.O. Box 18 (23520 Highway 12), Segundo, CO 81070. Prepares and distributes special columns for periodicals and technical orgs. Has library of books and maps relating to prospecting, small mining, professional occupations. Answers inquiries, provides advisory services, makes referrals free.

07097. Federal Legal Information Through Electronics, Denver, CO 80279; (303) 370-7531. Legal research service center for Dept of Defense. Research attorneys have access to full-text legal info storage and retrieval system. Advisory services provided to federal, state, and local govt agencies.

07098. Federal Railroad Administration, National Test Center, P.O. Box 11130, Pueblo, CO 81001; (303) 545-5660. Tests and evaluates transportation equipment and systems for U.S. agencies, foreign governments, and private agencies. Maintains collection of technical books, reports, and articles. Answers inquiries, provides consulting and testing services for a fee.

07099. Fish and Wildlife Service Editorial Office, Aylesworth Hall, Colo. State Univ, Ft Collins, CO 80523. Editorial service for Fish and Wildlife Service's publications. Data base contains citations from *Sport Fishery Abstracts and Wildlife Review*. Office attempts to answer inquiries within its capacity.

07100. Forensic Sciences Foundation, 225 South Academy Blvd, Ste 201, Colorado Springs, CO 80910; (303) 596-6006. Conducts research on procedures and standards utilized in forensic sciences. Publishes bimonthly publication and several related materials. Answers inquiries and provides advisory services. Services primarily for those in law enforcement but others assisted. Costs vary.

07101. Fort Carson Museum of the Army in the West, Ft Carson, CO 80913-5000; (303) 579-2908, 579-4348, or 579-3237. Interest in American military history, arms, and edged weapons. Maintains historical items regarding contributions of military to society. Answers inquiries, permits onsite use of collections, including reference library.

07102. Fort Logan Mental Health Center, 3520 West Oxford Ave, Denver, CO 80236; (303) 761-0220. Interest in hospital-based psychiatric treatment and community psychiatry. Medical library contains books and related materials. Library makes interlibrary loans, provides duplication services, and permits onsite use of its collections.

07103. Four Corners Geological Society, P.O. Box 1501, Durango, CO 81301; (303) 247-7834. Interest in exploration and research of petroleum and mineral exploration. Publishes books and info reports. Answers inquiries, conducts seminars, distributes publications, makes referrals. Services provided at cost.

07104. Fragile X Foundation, PO Box 30233, Denver, CO 80203. Interest in education and research of children and families with X-linked mental retardation. Sponsors lectures for health professionals to increase awareness of syndrome. Assists in forming parent support groups.

07105. Frank J. Seiler Research Laboratory, USAF Academy, CO 80840; (303) 472-3120. Interest in electrochemistry and energetic materials. Publishes bibliographies and reports, answers inquiries, provides advisory and consulting services. Services available to govt agencies and authorized contractors and grantees.

07106. Gem Village Museum, 39671 Highway 160, Bayfield, CO 80112; (303) 884-2811. Interest in geological and archaeological material from San Juan Basin area. Maintains collection of geological specimens; has library of books, journals, technical reports, pamphlets, photos, maps, and charts. Answers inquiries, makes referrals, permits onsite use of collections.

07107. Geological Society of America, P.O. Box 9140 (3300 Penrose Pl), Boulder, CO 80301; (303) 447-2020. Interest in geology and geophysics. Publishes and sells newsletters, maps, books, and a monograph series.

07108. Hip Society, 3535 Cherry Creek North Drive, Denver, CO 80209. Provides organized exchange of info about new ideas and techniques in diagnosis and management of hip problems. Issues bound volume of articles annually.

07109. Hoffman Pilot Center, Jeffco Airport Exec Bldg, Ste 7, Broomfield, CO 80020; (303) 469-3333. Airplane and helicopter pilot school. Has collection of books, periodicals, technical reports, and papers; publishes newsletter, bibliographies, training manuals. Answers inquiries, makes referrals, provides advisory services for a fee.

07110. Information Handling Services, 15 Inverness Way East, Englewood, CO 80150; (303) 790-0600. Gathers, organizes, indexes, and disseminates info in economical and easy-to-use microforms. Provides advisory, consulting, reference, indexing, microform, and magnetic tape services; conducts seminars, workshops; makes referrals. Services provided on subscription or fee basis.

07111. Institute for Behavioral Genetics, Univ of Colo, Boulder, CO 80309; (303) 492-7362. Concerned with inheritance of behavioral characteristics. Publishes books, journal articles, critical reviews. Answers inquiries, makes referrals, provides consulting services, conducts seminars. Services free, except consulting services.

07112. Institute for Telecommunication Sciences, National Telecommunications and Info Administration, 325 Broadway, Boulder, CO 80303; (303) 497-3572. Interest in communication sciences and info policy analysis. Publishes reports and other publications. Answers inquiries of a scientific or technical nature, consults with mutually interested groups or individuals.

07113. Institute of Arctic and Alpine Research, Univ of Colo, Campus Box 450, Boulder, CO 80309; (303) 492-6387. Interest in multidisciplinary approach to the study of environmental processes in arctic and alpine regions. Maintains library of books, periodicals, maps, and pamphlets and related materials. Reprints available.

07115. Institute of Certified Financial Planners, 3443 South Galena, Ste 190, Denver, CO 80231; (303) 751-7600. Promotes professional ethics and standards of practice for financial planners. Publishes monthly newsletter and quarterly journal, answers inquiries, makes referrals to member planners. Services available for a fee.

07117. International Association of Geophysical Contractors, 5335 West 48th Ave, Ste 400, Denver, CO 80212. Interest in geophysical, gravity, and magnetic surveys. Publishes quarterly newsletter for members. Answers inquiries and makes referrals to other sources of info. Services free.

07118. International Concerns Committee for Children, 911 Cypress Dr, Boulder, CO 80303; (303) 494-8333. Sponsors homeless children abroad. Answers inquiries, makes referrals, provides counseling services, distributes publications. Services available for donation.

07119. International Health Society, c/o Franklin L. Bowling, M. D., Secty-Treas, 1001 East Oxford Lane, Englewood, CO 80110; (303) 789-3003. Dedicated to continuing medical education of health professionals in public and international health. Publishes quarterly bulletin. Sponsors and cosponsors meetings and scientific assemblies on public and intl health.

07120. International Meteorology Aviation and Electronics Institute, P.O. Box 3341, Boulder, CO 80307; (303) 469-3335. Interest in training in aspects of airborne weather modification. Collects periodicals, books, and scientific reports pertaining to aviation, meteorology, electronics, and weather modification. Answers inquiries, provides advisory, consulting, and reference services.

07121. International Research Center for Energy and Economic Development, 216 Economics Bldg, Box 263, Univ of Colo, Boulder, CO 80309-0263; (303) 492-7667. Monitors research related to energy and development. Provides some advisory services free to governmental agencies and nonprofit entities. Permits onsite use of collections.

07122. International Society of Women Airline Pilots, P.O. Box 38644, Denver, CO 80238. Idea and info exchange group of women airline pilots. Maintains computerized info bank of women flight crew members helping other women. Answers inquiries, provides advisory services, conducts seminars and annual conference. Services free.

07123. JILA Atomic Collisions Data Center, Univ of Colo, Boulder, CO 80309; (303) 492-7801. Collects, evaluates, and distributes data on collisions of electrons, photons, atoms, and molecules. Answers inquiries, prepares evaluated compilations for modeling ionized gases. Services for scientists and engineers in relevant areas.

07124. Kempe National Center for the Prevention and Treatment of Child Abuse and Neglect, Dept of Pediatrics, Health Sciences Center, Univ of Colo, 1205 Oneida St, Denver, CO 80220; (303) 321-3963. Conducts research and demonstrates innovative programs on diagnosis, evaluation, and treatment of child abuse and neglect.

Answers inquiries; provides consulting and reference services, technical assistance for professionals.

07126. Laboratory for Atmospheric and Space Physics, Campus Box 392, Univ of Colo, Boulder, CO 80309; (303) 492-7677. Interest in solar physics, planetary atmospheres. Publishes technical reports, conducts seminars open to public.

07128. Manville Service Corp., R&D Information Center, P.O. Box 5108 (10100 West Ute Ave, Littleton, Colo.), Denver, CO 80217; (303) 978-5471. Interest in energy conservation in buildings; study of materials containing glass fibers, foams, alkali. Makes loans, permits onsite use of collection.

07129. Medical Group Management Association, c/o Dr Richard V. Grant, Exec Dir, 1355 South Colo. Blvd, Ste 900, Denver, CO 80222; (303) 753-1111. Interest in administration of medical group practices. Publishes monthly newsletter and bimonthly journal. Offers educational programs, conducts research. Answers inquiries, provides consulting services, makes referrals.

07130. Medical Rehabilitation Research and Training Center, Univ of Colo. Health Sciences Center, Box C-2424 (200 East 9th Ave), Denver, CO 80262; (303) 394-5144. Conducts research and implements clinical services. Publishes books, technical reports and R&D summaries; answers inquiries and conducts seminars. Services for a fee.

07131. Menu -- The International Software Database, 1520 South Coll Ave, Ft Collins, CO 80524; (303) 482-5000, (800) 843-6368 (in Colo.). Provides details on software dealing with any subject or application. Updates online data base of software packages, publishes software catalogs. Customized reports may be ordered by telephone. Services available for a fee.

07132. Mine Safety and Health Administration Health and Safety Analysis Center, P.O. Box 25367 (730 Simms St, Lakewood, Colo.), Denver Federal Center, Denver, CO 80225; (303) 236-2729. Compiles and publishes data of injury/illness and employment reports from mineral industries. Answers queries of administrators, Congress, industry, labor and govt groups. Qualified users are govt offices, Congress, mining industry, and union personnel.

07133. Mineral Information Institute, 425 South Cherry St, Ste 200, Denver, CO 80222; (303) 393-7211. Disseminates info to improve public's awareness of mineral and energy resources. Publishes quarterly newsletter and annual info catalog, answers inquiries, provides advisory and reference services--often for a fee.

07134. Model Interstate Science and Technology Information Clearinghouse, National Conference of State Legislatures, 1125 17th St, Ste 1500, Denver, CO 80202; (303) 292-6600. Gathers info for state lawmakers on scientific and technological aspects of public policy issues. Answers inquiries and provides info on research in progress, makes referrals and conducts seminars. Services primarily for state legislators and their staffs; others assisted.

07135. Morris Animal Foundation, 45 Inverness Dr East, Englewood, CO 80112; (303) 790-2345. Makes grants for research projects on the health problems of dogs, cats, horses, and zoo/wild animals. Collects books, periodicals, and technical reports, answers inquiries, makes referrals, permits onsite use of collections.

07136. Mountain Administrative Support Center, Library Division, RAS/MC5, National Oceanic and Atmospheric Administration, 325 Broadway, Boulder, CO 80303; (303) 497-3271. Interest in telecommunications and atmospheric sciences. Has collection of books, reports, microfiche, and related materials. Provides literature-searching and bibliographic services, makes interlibrary loans.

07137. Museum of Western Colorado, 4th and Ute Sts, Grand Junction, CO 81501; (303) 242-0971. Interest in social/natural history of western Colo. with emphasis on settlement history and paleontology. Maintains archives and special collections. Answers inquiries, provides copying services. Services free, but by appointment.

07138. Muslim Bibliographic Center, American Institute of Islamic Studies, P.O. Box 10398, Denver, CO 80210; (303) 936-0108. Large specialized collection on Islam and Muslim world. Answers inquiries, provides advisory, reference, and reproduction services for a fee.

07139. NCSC Institute for Court Management, 1331 17th St, Ste 402, Denver, CO 80202; (303) 293-3063. Interest in education, research, and training programs to improve management of the nation's federal and state trial and appellate courts. Answers inquiries, provides advisory services, conducts seminars. Most services free.

07140. National Archery Association of U.S., 1750 East Boulder St, Colorado Springs, CO 80909; (303) 578-4576. Selects and trains U.S. archery teams. Answers inquiries, provides advisory services, conducts seminars, makes referrals. Services free to membership, open to anyone.

07141. National Association of Counsel for Children, 1205 Oneida St, Denver, CO 80220; (303) 321-3963. Provides self-training and education for attorneys, guardians ad litem, and other advocates of children. Publishes quarterly newsletter and related books. Answers inquiries, makes referrals, provides advisory services, conducts seminars. Services included in membership fee.

07142. National Asthma Center LUNG LINE Information Service, National Jewish Hospital/National Asthma Center, 3800 East Colfax Ave, Denver, CO 80206; (800) 222-5864; (303) 398-1477 (in Colo.). Experienced nurses answer questions and make referrals. Provides advisory and reference services, info on research in progress. Most services free.

07143. National Bureau of Standards, Boulder Laboratories, 325 Broadway, Boulder, CO 80303; (303) 497-3244. Interest in standards and material properties relating to electromagnetics, geophysical dynamics. Answers general inquiries, makes referrals. Provides speakers, services without charge on contract basis to other govt agancies, the scientific community, and industry.

07144. National Center for American Indian Education, P.O. Box 18329 (941 East 17th St), Capitol Hill Station, Denver, CO 80218; (303) 861-1052. Interest in counseling, guidance, and placement service offering scholarship assistance to American Indian students. Answers inquiries, makes referrals, provides consulting services.

07145. National Center for Atmospheric Research, Univ Corporation for Atmospheric Research, P.O. Box 3000 (1850 Table Mesa Dr), Boulder, CO 80307; (303) 497-1650. Seeks to extend range and quality of weather prediction. Maintains library of technical reports, meteorological data, journals, and texts. Answers inquiries, makes loans, provides free advisory sevices.

07147. National Center for Audio Tapes, Academic Media Services, Univ of Colo. at Boulder, Stadium Bldg, Campus Box 379, Boulder, CO 80309; (303) 492-7341. Depository of noncopyright audio educational materials. Collections includes over 15,000 audio tape programs. Sells reproductions of tapes at cost. Tapes may be copied by purchasers.

07148. National Center for Higher Education Management Systems, P.O. Drawer P, Boulder, CO 80302; (303) 497-0357. Interest in enhancing effectiveness and efficiency of higher education orgs fostering improved management. Publishes technical reports, R&D summaries, and related materials, distributes publications and software, answers inquiries and makes referrals.

07149. National Conference of State Legislatures, 1125 17th St, Ste 1500, Denver, CO 80202; (303) 292-6600. Represents state legislatures at natl level in policy issues and state-federal relations. Answers inquiries, provides access to online info system, conducts workshops.

07150. National Crop Insurance Association, South Bldg, Ste 322, 2860 South Circle Dr, Colorado Springs, CO 80906; (303) 576-5111. Interest in development of insurance adjustment procedures and forms. Has extensive slide library, educational/training materials, loss adjustment instruction manuals for crops. Answers inquiries, provides reference services, makes referrals.

07151. National Earthquake info Center, U.S. Geological Survey, Stop 967, Denver Federal Center, Box 25046, Denver, CO 80225; (303) 236-1500. Interest in routine location of earthquakes worldwide and publication of hypocenter parameters and all associated data. Answers inquiries, provides info on current earthquake activity, makes referrals.

07152. National Environmental Health Association, 1200 Lincoln St, Ste 704, Denver, CO 80203; (303) 861-9090. Interest in air and water pollution control. Answers inquiries regarding professional development and education in environmental health.

07154. National Farmers Union, Office of National Coordinator, 12025 East 45th Ave, Denver, CO 80251; (303) 371-1760. Researches vertical integration resource development, development of rural areas, political action education. Publishes newsletter, pamphlets, reports, books; answers inquiries; makes referrals.

07155. National Indian Health Board, 1602 South Parker Road, Ste 200, Denver, CO 80231. Advocates high quality health care for American Indians. Reviews Indian health budget materials and various Indian-related govt activities. Conducts annual conference including workshops, general assemblies, educational exhibits, and health fair.

07156. National Indian Law Library, Native American Rights Fund, 1506 Broadway, Boulder, CO 80302-6296; (303) 447-8760. Publishes *National Indian Law Library Catalog* and related indexes and directories. Answers inquiries, provides reference and copying services, makes referrals, performs limited research. Fees charged for copying.

07157. National Institute of Judicial Dynamics, c/o Albert B. Logan, Esq., Dir, 411 Lakewood Circle, Ste B711, Colorado Springs, CO 80910; (303) 574-2082. Interest in improvement of American justice system. Has library on legal aspects of alcoholism. Answers inquiries, makes referrals, provides consulting services, distributes publications. Services available to professionals and students.

07159. National Oceanic and Atmospheric Administration, Air Resources Laboratory, 325 Broadway, Boulder, CO 80303; (303) 497-3000. Determines baseline values of atmospheric quantities from four baseline stations to determine changes in global weather and climate. Answers inquiries, provides free consulting services to scientific groups engaged in similar or related activities.

07160. National Oceanic and Atmospheric Administration, Environmental Sciences Projects Office, Physical Science Research Bldg 3, 30th and Marine Sts, Boulder, CO 80302; (303) 497-6382. Interest in weather modification and flash floods. Answers specific inquiries of scientific or technical nature related to work.

07161. National Oceanic and Atmospheric Administration, Geophysical Data Center, National Environmental Satellite, Data, and iInformation Service, Boulder, CO 80303; (303) 497-6215. Interest in solar-terrestrial physics, solid earth sciences, marine geology, and geophysics. Maintains major computerized and microfilmed collections of related data. Answers inquiries, assists scientists, reproduces data, conducts seminars.

07162. National Onion Association, 1 Greeley National Plaza, Ste 510, Greeley, CO 80631; (303) 353-5895. Interest in promotion and protection of onion industry. Maintains statistics and info, publishes newsletters. Answers inquiries free; provides reference and literature-searching services free to members, for a fee to others.

07163. National School Orchestra Association, 7142 South Newport Court, Englewood, CO 80112; (303) 770-0574. Produces programs and literature for directors of school orchestras and music teachers. Answers inquiries, provides advisory services, conducts seminars and an annual composition contest. Services free or at cost to members.

07164. National Seed Storage Laboratory, Agricultural Research Service, USDA, Colo. State Univ Campus, Ft Collins, CO 80523; (303) 484-0402. Studies genetic shifts in seeds. Maintains computerized data bank containing records on seed germ plasm accessions. Answers inquiries, provides consulting and reference services primarily for scientists involved in agricultural and horticultural crop breeding.

07165. National Stroke Association, 1420 Ogden Street, Denver, CO 80218. Provides info exchange system and support network for stroke victims and their families and physicians. Provides library and audiovisual clearinghouse, info hotline, and rehabilitation and aftercare centers.

07166. National Wheelchair Athletic Association, 2107 Templeton Gap Rd, Ste C, Colorado Springs, CO 80907; (303) 632-0698. Promotes growth and development of wheelchair sports for physically disabled in U.S. Publishes quarterly newsletter, answers inquiries, provides limited reference services. Services free, unless extensive.

07168. National Writers Club, 1450 South Havana, Ste 620, Aurora, CO 80012; (303) 751-7844. Interest in all phases of creative writing for magazines, book publication, and play production. Has collection of 1,400 titles dealing with creative writing, extensive library of motion picture and television working scripts. Onsite use of collections permitted. Personal assistance provided members only.

07169. Natural Hazards Research and Applications Information Center, IBS No 6, Campus Box 482, Univ of Colo, Boulder, CO 80309; (303) 492-6818. Promotes interaction of info between researchers and users. Answers inquiries, makes referrals, provides advisory services, permits onsite use of collections.

07170. North American Aerospace Defense Command, U.S. Air Force, Peterson AFB, CO 80914; (303) 554-3523. Interest in ballistic missile early warning systems. Maintains launch and decay info on most satellites. Publishes fact sheets, answers inquiries, provides advisory and reference services to govt agencies and bona fide news media representatives.

07171. North American Guild of Change Ringers, c/o Martin Meier, Public Relations Officer, P.O. Box 2048, Woodland Park, CO 80863; (303) 687-6656. Studies bells and ringing. Publishes quarterly journal, answers inquiries, conducts ringing courses.

07172. Nuclear Physics Laboratory, Univ of Colo., Boulder, CO 80309; (303) 492-7483. Interest in nuclear physics and ion-induced reactions. Publishes annual progress report, technical articles in scientific periodicals. Answers technical inquiries from scientists.

07173. Obesity Foundation, 7430 East Caley Ave, Ste 210, Englewood, CO 80111; (303) 779-4834. Educates health professionals and general public on obesity. Researches causes and effects of obesity. Maintains small collection of reprint articles on obesity and associated conditions. Answers inquiries, makes referrals.

07174. Orphan Voyage, 2141 Road 2300, Cedaredge, CO 81413; (303) 856-3937. Gives voice to adopted adults, original parents, and adoptive parents. Maintains literature collection written about orphans, academic papers. Distributes publications, answers inquiries, provides consulting, permits onsite use of collections.

07176. Paul de Haen International, 2750 South Shoshone St, Englewood, CO 80110; (303) 781-6683; (800) 438-0296. Interest in all aspects of drug info, including synthesis of new compounds and pre-marketing and post-marketing data. Drug info systems published in microfiche format. Answers inquiries, makes referrals, provides data base-searching services on individual request basis.

07177. Petroleum Information Corp., P.O. Box 2612, 4100 East Dry Creek Rd, Denver, CO 80201; (303) 740-7100. Petroleum reporting service company offering daily or weekly reports that cover drilling activity in most states and western Canada. Provides consulting, reference, abstracting, indexing, and duplication services, all for a fee.

07178. Potato Board, c/o Robert L. Mercer, Exec V.P., 1385 South Colo. Blvd, Ste 512, Denver, CO 80222; (303) 758-7783. Promotes virtues of potatoes and directs consumer advertising and public relations activities. Answers inquiries, provides reference services and info on research in progress, distributes publications. Services free.

07179. Potential Gas Agency, Institute for Energy Resource Studies, Colo. School of Mines, Campus Box 13, Golden, CO 80401; (303) 279-4320. Approves criteria and methods insuring maintenance of standards and objectivity in gas supply reports. Publishes supply guides and resource maps, answers inquiries, sells publications.

07180. Professional Engineers of Colorado, 2701 Alcott St, Ste 263, Denver, CO 80211; (303) 458-0465. Concerned with professional engineering relating to aspects of legislation, ethics, engineering registration, and education. Publishes *Colorado Engineering*. Answers inquiries free.

07181. Professional Rodeo Cowboys Association, National Media Department, 101 Pro Rodeo Dr, Colorado Springs, CO 80919; (303) 593-8840. Maintains large collection of books on rodeo. Publishes biweekly and related guides, answers inquiries, permits onsite use of collections. Some services for a fee.

07182. Research High Altitude Observatory Library, National Center for Atmospheric Research, P.O. Box 3000, Boulder, CO 80307; (303) 497-1516. Interest in solar physics, astronomy, astrophysics, and electronics. Maintains collection of books and bound journals and online catalog of holdings. Provides reference and duplication services to scientific personnel and graduate students only.

07183. Roaring Fork Energy Center, P.O. Box 9950 (110 East Hollam, Office No. 7), Aspen, CO 81612; (303) 925-8885. Promotes exploration of alternative energy sources and design considerations through education. Facilitates a variety of symposia, workshops, college-level courses, and citizen-participation programs; answers inquiries; provides advisory and consulting services at cost.

07184. Rocky Mountain Association of Geologists, 1220 Univ Bldg, 910 16th St, Denver, CO 80202; (303) 573-8621. Interest in exploration and development of fossil fuels and other minerals. Publishes *Mountain Geologist* quarterly. Provides consulting and reference services, conducts seminars, distributes publications. Services free, except for publications and seminars.

07185. Rocky Mountain Forest and Range Experiment Station, U.S. Forest Service, 240 West Prospect St, Ft Collins, CO 80526; (303) 221-4390. Interest in forestry management. Publishes technical reports, handbooks, monographs, bibliographies, literature reviews, bulletins. Answers inquiries, provides consulting, reference, and document services, permits onsite use of literature collection.

07186. Rocky Mountain Hydraulic Laboratory, Rallenspark, CO 80510. Studies hydraulics and protection of off-shore structures from underscour. Publishes reports, films, and technical papers. Answers brief inquiries, provides consulting services, disseminates reprints of papers and reports.

07187. Rocky Mountain Mineral Law Foundation, Fleming Law Bldg, B-405, Univ of Colo, Boulder, CO 80309; (303) 492-6545. Interest in legal problems affecting exploration and development of water, gas, and land resources. Publishes newsletters and related materials. Answers inquiries, sponsors annual institute devoted to oil and gas, mining, water, and environmental law. Services primarily for members.

07188. Rolf Institute, P.O. Box 1868, Boulder, CO 80306; (303) 449-5903. Promotes Rolfing. Interest in training and certification of Rolfers. Publishes books, directories, videotapes, film, and reprints. Answers inquiries, makes referrals, conducts seminars and classes.

Seminars limited to certified teachers; other services open. Fees charged for most services.

07189. Rural Education Association, c/o Dr Joseph Newlin, Exec Dir, Office for Rural Education, 300 Education Bldg, Colo. State Univ, Ft Collins, CO 80523; (303) 491-7022. Offers educational service agency programs for small schools, migratory agricultural workers, American Indians. Answers inquiries, provides consulting services, makes referrals. Conducts natl conference anually.

07190. Sheep Industry Development Program, American Sheep Producers Council, Inc., 200 Clayton St, Denver, CO 80206; (303) 399-8130. Provides total marketing services to sheep producers. Has collection of posters, recipes, films, and sheep production materials. Publishes handbook, directory, and related materials, answers inquiries, provides advisory and reference services for a fee.

07191. Society for Range Management, 2760 West 5th Ave, Denver, CO 80204; (303) 571-0174. Interest in management and use of range ecosystems. Answers brief inquiries, frequently by referral to member specialists. Provides reference services.

07192. Society for the Study of Evolution, c/o Jeffry B. Mitton, Exec V.P., Dept of Environmental, Population, and Organismic Biology, Campus Box 334, Univ of Colo, Boulder, CO 80309; (303) 492-8956. Promotes study of organic evolution. Integrates fields of science concerned with evolution through publications and annual meetings.

07193. Society of Photo-Technologists, P.O. Box 9634, Denver, CO 80209; (303) 698-1820; (800) 525-9710. Interest in theory and techniques involved in camera repair and modifications. Maintains microfiche library of service manuals. Answers inquiries, makes referrals, provides free consulting services.

07194. Solar Energy Applications Laboratory, Coll of Engineering, Colo. State Univ, Ft Collins, CO 80523; (303) 491-8617. Interest in development of high performance solar heating and solar cooling systems using advanced components. Publishes technical reports, journal articles, bibliographies, and reprints. Answers inquiries and makes referrals, permits onsite use of collections. Services provided at cost.

07197. Space Environment Laboratory, National Oceanic and Atmospheric Administration, Radio Bldg, Rm 3050, 325 Broadway, Boulder, CO 80303; (303) 497-3311. Interest in forecasting of space environment and polar cap events. Maintains data base of recent solar-geophysical data. Provides daily forecasts and immediate warning of solar-geophysical activity via telephone, teletype, and commercial satellite broadcast.

07198. Sports Car Club of America, 6750 South Emporia St, Englewood, CO 80112; (303) 790-1044. Interest in motor sports administration. Offers a variety of info brochures. Answers inquiries, provides advisory

services, makes referrals. Services provided at nominal charge, depending on those rendered.

07199. Standard & Poor's Compustat Services, 7400 South Alton Ct, Englewood, CO 80112; (303) 771-6510; (800) 525-8640. Interest in publicly reported financial data. Has library of financial and statistical info on over 6,000 publicly traded U.S. and Canadian corps. Answers inquiries, provides consulting, reference, and magnetic tape services, distributes publications. Subscription fees charged.

07200. State Historical Society of Colorado, Documentary Resources Department, 1300 Broadway, Denver, CO 80203; (303) 866-2305. Interest in Colo. history. Has collection of books and pamphlets, photos, serials, and related materials. Publishes guides, indexes, calendars. Answers factual inquiries, makes referrals, provides reference, advisory, and duplication services, permits onsite use of collections.

07201. State Legislators Arts, Tourism and Cultural Resources Project, National Conference of State Legislatures, 1125 17th St, Ste 1500, Denver, CO 80202; (303) 292-6600. Conducts legislative info services, research and education activities in the arts, tourism, and historic preservation. Publishes in-house magazine and related materials. Answers inquiries, provides advisory and reference services, primarily for legislators and their staffs.

07202. Supersensonic Energy Technologies, P.O. Box 66, Boulder Creek, CO 95006; (408) 338-2161. Researches holistic uses of life energy and develops instrumentation to measure subtle energy fields. Researches and develops new psychotronic instruments. Answers inquiries, provides advisory services, conducts seminars.

07204. Therapeutic Recreation Information Center, Dept of Physical Education and Recreation, Univ of Colo, Box 354, Boulder, CO 80302; (303) 492-5429. Info clearinghouse concerned about recreational opportunities for handicapped and aging persons. Answers inquiries and provides computerized searching services. Provides consulting services, makes referrals, permits onsite use of collection. Fees for some services.

07205. Thorne Ecological Institute, 4860 Riverbend Rd, Boulder, CO 80301; (303) 443-7325. Dedicated to application of ecological principles to stewardship of natural resources. Collects books, periodicals, reports, and clippings. Answers inquiries, makes referrals, permits onsite use of collections.

07206. Toxic Element Research Foundation, P.O. Box 38579, Colorado Springs, CO 80937. Promotes research and disseminates info on heavy metal toxicities, especially that of mercury from dental fillings.

07207. U.S. Committee on Irrigation, Drainage and Flood Control, P.O. Box 15326, Denver, CO 80215; (303) 234-3006. Interest in irrigation practices and systems. Publishes annual report, monthly bulletin, transactions of intl congresses on irrigation and drainage. Answers inquiries on limited basis, provides minor reference services.

07208. U.S. Cycling Federation, c/o U.S. Olympic Committee, 1750 East Boulder St, Building 4, Colorado Springs, CO 80909; (303) 578-4581. Interest in amateur bicycle racing. Publishes *Cycling USA* monthly, rule book, and pamphlets. Answers inquiries, provides advisory and reference services, conducts seminars and workshops. Services provided for a fee.

07209. U.S. Figure Skating Association Museum, 20 First St, Colorado Springs, CO 80906; (303) 635-5200. Interest in figure skating. Maintains library with repository of memorabilia. Answers inquiries and permits onsite use of collections. Services free.

07210. U.S. Olympic Committee, 1750 East Boulder St, Colorado Springs, CO 80909; (303) 632-5551. Interest in Olympic Games. Publishes pamphlet on history and organization of the games. Answers inquiries, provides reference services. Services free.

07212. Ute Indian Museum, P.O. Box 1736, 17253 Chipeta Dr, Montrose, CO 81401; (303) 249-3098. Interest in history and culture of Ute Indians. Has collection of artifacts, guns, life-sized figures, dioramas. Answers brief inquiries, permits onsite use of collections and minimal reference materials. Museum open to the public May 15-Oct 15.

07213. Wave Propagation Laboratory, NOAA ERL R/E/WP, 325 Broadway, Boulder, CO 80303; (303) 497-6451. Interest in remote sensing of atmosphere and ocean. Provides research and consulting services and advice on lab-related subjects to govt and industry.

07214. Webb-Waring Lung Institute, 4200 East 9th Ave, Denver, CO 80262; (303) 394-8231. Interest in research and research training in acute and chronic pulmonary diseases. Answer inquiries, provides copies of published articles, conducts seminars and lectures. Services primarily for scientists, physicians, and health-related orgs.

07215. Western Interstate Commission for Higher Education, P.O. Drawer P, Boulder, CO 80302; (303) 497-0200. Coordinates work of 13 member states in providing West's education and manpower needs. Clearinghouse responds to inquiries for info free. Provides special research reports.

07216. Western Interstate Energy Board, 6500 Stapleton Plaza, 3333 Quebec St, Denver, CO 80207; (303) 377-9459. Serves advisory capacity on energy, natural resources, and environmental law. Primary mission centers on federal and state statutory and regulatory activities. Publishes newsletter, answers inquiries, provides limited referrals. Services free, except for publications.

07217. Western Museum of Mining and Industry, 4520 North Park St (125 North Gate Rd), Colorado Springs, CO 80907; (303) 598-8850. Interest in artifacts relating to mining industry and American West. Publishes catalogs on museum's artifact collection. Answers inquiries, makes referrals, permits onsite use of collections. Services free.

07218. Western Nuclear, 134 Union Blvd, No. 640, Lakewood, CO 80228; (303) 986-4571. Interest in exploration for and mining and milling of black oxide. Maintains library materials and data bases on exploration projects. Info of a nonproprietary nature freely given regarding discovery, development, mining, and recovery of black oxide.

07219. Western and English Manufacturers Association, 789 Sherman St, Ste 360, Denver, CO 80203; (303) 837-1280. Interest in statistics and surveys of manufacturing and distribution industries dealing in Western and English apparel, saddlery, tack, hardware, and rodeo equipment. Answers inquiries, makes referrals, provides reference services, distributes publication. Simple inquiries answered free.

07220. Wildlife World Museum, P.O. Box 1000 (18725 Monument Hill Rd), Monument, CO 80132; (303) 488-2460. Dedicated to showing man's relationship to wildlife through art. Maintains collection of 2,200 pieces of animal-related art. Answers inquiries, provides advisory and consulting services, conducts seminars, workshops, and other programs. Services for a fee.

07221. World Data Center A: Glaciology (Snow and Ice), CIRES, Campus Box 449 (30th and Marine Sts), Univ of Colo, Boulder, CO 80309; (303) 492-5171. Interest in frozen ground studies and all aspects of glaciology. Answers inquiries, makes referrals, provides reference and copying services, permits onsite use of collections. Services provided on cost recovery basis.

07222. World Data Center A: Solar-Terrestrial Physics, National Geophysical Data Center, NOAA, E/GC2, 325 Broadway, Boulder, CO 80303; (303) 497-6323. Has major collections of magnetograms, ionograms, all-sky auroral imagery, and data tabulations. Answers inquiries, provides consulting and reference services, permits onsite use of collections. Standard charges for reproducing data and providing services.

07223. World Data Center A: Solid Earth Geophysics, National Geophysical Data Center, NOAA, 325 Broadway, Boulder, CO 80303; (303) 497-6521. Interest in seismology, geomagnetism, and heat. Has copies of 5 million seismograms, info on 500,000 earthquakes, observational data. Answers inquiries, makes referrals, provides advisory and reference services, conducts seminars, lends materials. Services provided at cost.

07224. World Sign Association, 200 Fillmore St, Ste 407, Denver, CO 80206; (303) 355-3559. Interest in sign engineering, manufacturing, marketing, and maintenance. Publishes technical reports, reviews, and directories. Answers inquiries, makes referrals, conducts annual meetings. Some services provided at cost.

Connecticut

08007. Aetna Life & Casualty, Corporate Communications, 151 Farmington Ave, Hartford, CT 06156; (203) 273-2843. Distributes public service films on health, safety, and general education. Films loaned free, except return mailing charges, to some groups and television stations in continental U.S.

08008. American Budgerigar Society, c/o Corienne P. Traver, 141 Hill St Ext, Naugatuck, CT 06770; (203) 729-4810. Interest in budgerigar housing, health, breeding, and exhibition. Provides general reference services, sells leg bands. Info services free and primarily for members, but others assisted.

08009. American CB Radio Association, 184 Windsor Ave, Windsor, CT 06095; (203) 236-6035. Interest in citizens' band radio operation and equipment. Provides general reference services free to members, and answers written requests from nonmembers.

08010. American Driving Society, P.O. Box 1852, Lakeville, CT 06039 (Reservoir Rd, Millerton, NY); (518) 789-6169. Supplies horse show organizers with show forms and data. Conducts seminars, distributes publications, makes referrals. Except for publications, services for a fee, restricted to members. Membership open to all.

08011. American Indian Archaeological Institute, P.O. Box 260 (Route 199), Washington, CT 06793; (203) 868-0518. Interest in history and archeology of the Indians of the Northeast Woodlands. Provides general reference services, conducts seminars, permits onsite use of collections. Fee for services.

08012. American Nuclear Insurers Library, The Exchange, Ste 245, 270 Farmington Ave, Farmington, CT 06032; (203) 677-7305 ext 380. Provides insurance for the nuclear industry. Answers inquiries, distributes publications. Services free and available by special request.

08013. American Radio Relay League, 225 Main St, Newington, CT 06111; (203) 666-1541. Interest in amateur radio communications. Answers inquiries, provides training courses, and info on the amateur space satellite program. Services free, except major publications.

08014. American Registry of Medical Assistants, P.O. Box 39 (2 Nevins Ave), Enfield, CT 06082; (203) 745-8238. Interest in medical assistants. Answers inquiries, makes referrals.

08015. Animal Rights Network, P.O. Box 5234 (49 Richmondville Ave), Westport, CT 06881; (203) 226-8826. Promotes animal rights awareness. Answers inquiries, distributes publications. Services free, except publications.

08017. Area Cooperative Educational Services Library, 295 Mill Rd, North Haven, CT 06473; (203) 234-0130. Interest in education and social sciences. Provides general reference services, permits onsite use of collections, trains persons for info utilization.

08018. Association for Fitness in Business, 1312 Washington Blvd, Stamford, CT 06902; (203) 359-2188. Provides continuing education for and research in health and fitness. Provides general reference services, conducts seminars. Services available to anyone; fee charged to nonmembers.

08019. Association of Bridal Consultants, 200 Chestnutland Rd, New Milford, CT 06776-2521; (203) 355-0464. Improves professionalism of wedding organizers, provides info on wedding planning. Provides references and evaluations, distributes publications. Fees may be charged to nonmembers.

08020. Association of Clinical Scientists, c/o Secty-Treas, Univ of Conn. School of Medicine, P.O. Box G, Farmington, CT 06032; (203) 674-2328. Promotes education and research in clinical science. Holds scientific meetings in the spring and fall, for which registration fee is required. Publishes journal, available by subscription.

08021. Association of Executive Search Consultants, 151 Railroad Ave, Greenwich, CT 06830; (203) 661-6606. Catalogs demand for executives, publishes code of ethics, and membership directory, conducts seminars. Services free.

08022. Audubon Council of Connecticut, Route 4, Sharon, CT 06069; (203) 364-0520. Initiates and supports programs to advance the protection of Conn. wildlife. Provides general reference services, sponsors field trips. Services free.

08023. Automation Industries/Sperry Products Division, P.O. Box 3500 (1000 Shelter Rock Rd), Danbury, CT 06810; (203) 796-5000. Interest in nondestructive testing services and equipment/systems for evaluating materials using modern techniques. Provides general reference services.

08024. Belding Heminway Co., P.O. Drawer 28, Putnam, CT 06260 (203) 928-2784. Interest in textiles and polymer science, related areas of physical science. Lends some literature materials, provides limited duplication services, permits onsite use of collection by arrangement.

08025. Belgian American Educational Foundation, 195 Church St, New Haven, CT 06510; (203) 777-5765. Sponsors multidisciplinary educational exchanges between the U.S. and Belgium. Conducts seminars, distributes reports, permits onsite use of collections. Services free.

08026. Book Manufacturers Institute, 111 Prospect St, Stamford, CT 06901; (203) 324-9670. Natl trade assn for book manufacturers. Interest in book printing and binding. Provides free general reference services. Services primarily for members and allied industries.

08027. Burndy Library, Norwalk, CT 06856; (203) 852-6294. Interest in history of science, provides research in rare books in science. Library open to public.

08028. Center for Direct Marketing, 11 Commerce St, Norwalk, CT 06850; (203) 227-8435. Seminar-conducting org interested in direct mail marketing, advertising, credit. Conducts seminars for a fee; discount to nonprofit orgs.

08029. Center for Farm and Food Research, P.O. Box 88, Falls Village, CT 06031. Studies relationship of food production to economic, political, and military policy. Publishes various materials, conducts seminars. Services free, except consulting and seminars.

08030. Center for the Advancement of Human Communications, Graduate School of Corporate and Political Communications, Fairfield Univ, Fairfield, CT 06430; (203) 255-5411 ext 2527. Interest in research and education in human communications. Provides free general reference services, conducts seminars for a fee.

08031. Center for the Environment and Man, 275 Windsor St, Hartford, CT 06120; (203) 549-4400. Interest in environmental sciences and management. Performs research on negotiated contract basis.

08032. Children's Campaign for Nuclear Disarmament, 14 Everit St, New Haven, CT 06511; (203) 787-5262. Educates children on dangers of the nuclear arms race. Provides reference services and referrals, distributes publications. Except for large numbers of publications, services free.

08033. Clairol Research and Development Division, 2 Blachley Rd, Stamford, CT 06902; (203) 357-5073. Interest in research on hair, hair and skin care products, and chemical treatments. Answers inquiries free.

08034. Coast Guard, International Ice Patrol, Avery Point, Groton, CT 06340; (203) 445-8501. Interest in surveillance of iceberg population off Newfoundland coast. Provides free general reference services.

08035. Coblentz Society, Perkin-Elmer Corp., M.S. 903, Norwalk, CT 06856; (203) 762-6127. Interest in infrared spectroscopy, Raman spectroscopy. Provides general reference services, conducts symposia. Services free, except workshops and reference data compilations.

08036. Combustion Engineering Power Systems Library, Dept 6435-405, 1000 Prospect Hill Rd, Windsor, CT 06095; (203) 688-1911 ext 6519. Interest in all forms of energy systems, physics, metallurgy, chemistry, computer science, engineering, mathematics, environmental science, and relevant business applications. Provides limited reference services.

08037. Company of Fifers and Drummers, P.O. Box 318, Westbrook, CT 06898. Interest in early American martial music. Provides general reference services, conducts seminars distributes publications, permits onsite use of collections. Services for a fee.

08039. Connecticut Aeronautical Historical Association, Bradley Air Museum, Bradley International Airport, Windsor Locks, CT 06096; (203) 623-3305. Promotes restoration of aeronautical records and objects of historical interest. Provides general reference services, permits onsite viewing of collections for a fee. Services available within limits of time and staff.

08040. Connecticut Agricultural Experiment Station, P.O. Box 1106 (123 Huntington St), New Haven, CT 06504-1106; (203) 789-7265. Interest in plant sciences and ecology. Provides general reference services.

08042. Connecticut Historical Society, 1 Elizabeth St, Hartford, CT 06105; (203) 236-5621. Interest in Conn. history and genealogy. Provides general reference services, conducts seminars, distributes publications, permits free onsite use of collections. Other services subject to a fee.

08043. Connecticut Justice Academy, Saybrook Rd, Haddam, CT 06438; (203) 345-4547. Interest in criminal justice, management development, psychology, mental health, penology. Provides general reference services, conducts seminars, permits onsite use of collections. All services free to Conn. residents, some at cost or not available to out-of-state users.

08045. Connecticut Wildlife Federation, 27 Washington St, Middletown, CT 06457; (203) 347-1291. Interest in conservation of forest, mineral, and wildlife resources. Provides general reference services, sponsors Natl Wildlife Week in Conn., operates Junior Conservation Camp. Services free.

08046. Copper Development Association, Greenwich Office Park 2, Box 1840, Greenwich, CT 06836; (203) 625-8210. Interest in properties and applications of copper, brass, and bronze. Answers inquiries, disseminates reports and data sheets.

08047. Cornelia de Lange Syndrome Foundation, 60 Dyer Ave, Collinsville, CT 06022. Supports parents and children affected by CdLS, disseminates info, conducts seminars. Services free and available to anyone, but memberships encouraged.

08048. Creative Arts in Education, 305 Great Neck Rd, Waterford, CT 06385; (203) 443-7139. Umbrella org for several art and theater projects. Provides consulting services, conducts seminars, permits onsite use of collections. Services for a fee to membership, which is open to schools and agencies.

08049. Cryogenic Consulting Service, P.O. Box 215, Westport, CT 06880; (203) 227-3305. Interest in industrial applications of cryogenics. Publishes technical papers, answers inquiries, provides consulting and R&D services. Fees for all services.

08050. Cytogenetics Research Laboratory, Johnson Memorial Hospital, Chestnut Mountain Rd, Stafford Springs, CT 06076; (203) 749-2201. Interest in cytogenetics and genetic counseling. Answers inquiries, provides consulting and reference services, makes referrals. Services at cost.

08051. DMS, 100 Northfield St, Greenwich, CT 06830; (203) 661-7800. Market research and publishing firm. Provides defense and govt intelligence reports; interest in all aspects of global defense. Provides specific reference services at cost to industry and non-Communist govts.

08052. Data Entry Management Association, P.O. Box 16722, Stamford, CT 06905; (203) 967-3500. Provides info on data management techniques, data entry technology. Conducts conferences, and seminars, distributes publications. Some services free.

08054. Division of Perinatal Medicine at Yale, Dept of Pediatrics, Yale Univ School of Medicine, 333 Cedar St, New Haven, CT 06510; (203) 436-3193. Provides general reference services for the biotechnology industry and community. Conducts seminars. Services primarily for academics and physicians and may be provided for a fee.

08055. Dorr-Oliver, 77 Havemeyer Lane, Stamford, CT 06904; (203) 358-3550, 358-3770. Interest in chemical and sanitary engineering, pulp, and paper, food processing, mining, biotechnology, business. Provides general reference services, permits onsite use of collection by appointment. Services free, primarily for staff.

08057. Eno Foundation for Transportation, P.O. Box 2055 (270 Saugatuck Ave), Westport, CT 06880; (203) 227-4852. Interest in all forms of transportation. Provides general reference services, permits onsite use of collection.

08058. Family Television Research and Consultation Center, Dept of Psychology, Yale Univ, 405 Temple St, New Haven, CT 06511; (203) 432-4286. Provides research, consultation on effects of television on children and youth. Conducts workshops, distributes publications. Some services free.

08059. Farrel Company, Emhart Machinery Group, 25 Main St, Ansonia, CT 06401; (203) 734-3331. Interest in machinery and productivity systems for various industrial processes. Answers inquiries, permits onsite use of collection by request.

08060. Forum for Resources on Federal Lands Foundation, Box 219, Old Greenwich, CT 06870; (203) 323-4516. Interest in physical constraints on global environment and behavioral constraints on social environment. Provides free general reference services.

08061. Futures Group, 76 Eastern Blvd, Glastonbury, CT 06033; (203) 633-3501. Research and management consulting company. Interest in forecasting, technology assessment, energy, transportation, consumer goods, health, policy analysis, new product development. Provides general reference services at cost.

08062. Gesell Institute of Human Development, 310 Prospect St, New Haven, CT 06511; (203) 777-3481. Operates clinical services for children and family practice and consultation medical service. Provides some reference services, conducts workshops, permits limited onsite use of collection.

08063. Godfrey Memorial Library, 134 Newfield St, Middletown, CT 06457; (203) 346-4375. Interest in genealogy, local history, and biography. Answers inquiries

on fee basis, makes limited interlibrary loans, permits onsite use of collection.

08064. Handweavers Guild of America, 65 La Salle Rd, West Hartford, CT 06107; (203) 233-5124. Promotes fiber arts. Provides general reference services, conducts biennial conference. Fee for some services.

08065. Haskins Laboratories, 270 Crown St, New Haven, CT 06510; (203) 436-1774. Conducts research on all aspects of speech perception, physiology, and computer speech analysis. Provides general reference services, free for researchers involved in speech and linguistic studies.

08066. Health Care Exhibitors Association, 49 Locust Ave, Ste 107, New Canaan, CT 06840; (203) 966-6909. Provides health care marketing, publishes handbook, conducts seminars. Services free to members, at cost to nonmembers.

08068. Hocker International Federation, 54 Miller St, Fairfield, CT 06430; (203) 255-5907, (800) 243-4141. Interest in hocker, a team sport similar to soccer. Provides general reference services, distributes publications. Services available for a fee.

08069. Human Lactation Center, 666 Sturges Highway, Westport, CT 06880; (203) 259-5995. Conducts research, disseminates info, and provides fieldwork training in the field of human lactation. Provides general reference services available to scientific researchers, some at cost.

08071. Human Relations Area Files, P.O. Box 2054, Yale Station (755 Prospect St), New Haven, CT 06520; (203) 777-2334. Interest in worldwide anthropology, various social sciences. Provides limited reference services. Scholars may have access to files.

08072. Indian and Colonial Research Center, Main St, Old Mystic, CT 06372; (203) 532-9771. Interest in local history, Indians, area genealogy. Provides general reference services, permits onsite use of collections. Donation requested.

08073. Industrial Risk Insurers, 85 Woodland St, Hartford, CT 06102; (203) 525-2601; (203) 525-2601 ext 412. Association of insurance companies providing specialized insurance coverage. Interest in research, and design in insurance protection. Provides general reference services.

08075. Innovation International, 356 Newtown Turnpike, Wilton, CT 06897; (203) 762-3465. Interest in inventions and patent applications, related marketing and funding. Provides free general reference services.

08077. Institute of Materials Science, Univ of Conn., Box U-136, Storrs, CT 06268. Performs graduate research and training in materials science with main emphasis on metallurgy and polymer science. Publishes technical papers, conducts seminars and workshops. Services available at cost plus indirect univ cost.

08079. International Association of Campus Law Enforcement Administrators, 638 Prospect Ave, Hartford, CT 06105; (203) 233-4531. Interest in administration, planning, operation, and maintenance of security, police, safety, and traffic departments at univ level. Provides general reference services. Services available for a fee.

08080. International Conference of Police Chaplains, c/o Secty, 4 Holly Dr, Old Saybrook, CT 06475; (203) 388-4560. Promotes and supports police chaplaincy. Provides advisory and consulting services, distributes publications. Services free.

08082. International Ozone Association, 83 Oakwood Ave, Norwalk, CT 06850; (203) 847-8169. Nonprofit scientific and educational org interested in ozone technology. Provides general reference services, conducts seminars. Services for a fee to nonmembers as time and staff permit.

08083. International Resource Development, 6 Prowitt St, Norwalk, CT 06855; (203) 866-7800. Management consulting and publishing firm specializing in studies related to corporate strategy, product planning, and market research. Distributes publications for a fee; price lists available.

08084. International Sand Collector's Society, 43 Highview Ave, Old Greenwich, CT 06870; (203) 637-2801. Interest in collection, classification, and retention of sand samples from the world's beaches. Provides general reference services, permits onsite use of collection. Services free.

08085. International Society on Toxinology, Dept of Pharmacology, Univ of Conn., Storrs, CT 06268; (203) 486-2213. Interest in pharmacology, biochemistry, immunology of animal, plant, and microbial toxins and venoms. Provides general reference services for a fee.

08086. Life Insurance Marketing and Research Association, Box 208, Hartford, CT 06141; (203) 677-0033. Intl research and consulting org of insurance companies. Provides general reference services, conducts seminars, permits onsite use of collection. Services primarily for members; some materials available to nonmembers for a fee.

08087. Lupus Network, 230 Ranch Drive, Bridgeport, CT 06606; (203) 372-5795. Nonprofit educational org that provides info to those concerned with lupus. Gathers data about systemic lupus erythematous patients.

08088. Malignant Hyperthermia Association of the U.S., P.O. Box 3231, Darien, CT 06820; (203) 655-3007. Provides info to Malignant Hyperthermia-susceptible (MHS) families and their physicans. Operates a 24-hour inquiry "hotline," conducts seminars, distributes publications. Services free.

08089. Marble Collectors Society of America, P.O. Box 222 (51 Johnson St), Trumbull, CT 06611; (203) 261-3223. Furthers hobby of marble collecting through various educational activities and publications. Pro-

vides references, conducts surveys. Services available on a cost-recovery basis.

08090. Marine Sciences Institute, Univ of Conn., Avery Point, Groton, CT 06340; (203) 446-1020 ext 214. Assists in graduate education, research, and public service in marine science. Provides advisory services, conducts seminars. Fee for some services.

08091. Massenet Society and Lovers of French Music, 4775 Durham Rd (Route No. 77), Guilford, CT 06437. Interest in operas of Jules Massenet and French music composed by teachers and students of Massenet. Provides general reference services, sponsors concerts and lectures. Services available for a membership fee.

08092. Meckler Publishing, 11 Ferry Lane West, Westport, CT 06880; (203) 226-6967. Interest in library science, microform and computer equipment for libraries, videodiscs and optical disk for educational and corporate use. Provides general reference services at cost.

08093. Medical Research Laboratories, Hartford Hospital, 80 Seymour St, Hartford, CT 06115; (203) 524-2937. Interest in medical research involving granulocytic function and regulators, antibiotic pharmacokinetics. Answers inquiries, provides consulting services. Limited services available to scientific researchers.

08094. Mid-America Research Institute, 645 Farmington Ave, Hartford, CT 06105; (203) 233-3230. Analyzes motor vehicle accident data. Answers inquiries, provides advisory and reference services, conducts research, makes referrals to other info sources. Services for a fee.

08095. Mystic Seaport Museum/G.W. Blunt White Library, Greenmanville Ave, Mystic, CT 06355; (203) 572-0711. Interest in 19th-Century U.S. maritime history. Provides general reference services, permits onsite use of collections. Services free, except photocopying.

08097. Nabisco Brands, Technical Information Center, 15 River Rd, Wilton, CT 06897; (203) 762-2500. Collects materials in food science, analytical chemistry, biochemistry, nutrition, microbiology. Makes direct and interlibrary loans, referrals to other sources of info, permits onsite use of collection. Services free.

08098. National Association for Drama Therapy, 19 Edwards St, New Haven, CT 06511; (203) 624-2146. Assn interested in promoting and studying benefits of drama therapy. Distributes publications, provides advice, holds annual conference. Regular membership restricted. Services may be subject to a fee.

08099. National Association for the Advancement of Humane Education, Box 362, East Haddam, CT 06423; (203) 434-8666. Interest in humane education. Provides general reference services, conducts seminars, permits onsite use of collection. Services free, except seminars and major publications.

08100. National Organization for Rare Disorders, Fairwood Professional Building, 100 Route 37, Box K,

New Fairfield, CT 06812; (203) 746-6518. Coalition of health orgs dedicated to those suffering rare diseases. Promotes research and cooperation.

08101. National Shooting Sports Foundation, 1075 Post Rd, Riverside, CT 06878; (203) 637-3618. Interest in shooting sports and wildlife conservation. Provides general reference services. Services free, except nominal charges for publications.

08102. Natural Science for Youth Foundation, 763 Silvermine Rd, New Canaan, CT 06840; (203) 966-5643. Dedicated to wildlife and conservation management promotion nationally. Provides consulting and administrative services to museums, conducts training programs. Services for members and those seeking membership.

08103. Nature Center for Environmental Activities, P.O. Box 165 (10 Woodside Lane), Westport, CT 06881; (203) 227-7253. Interest in natural sciences, wildlife, environmental education. Provides general reference services, lends animals to local schools, permits onsite use of collections.

08104. Naval Submarine Medical Research Laboratory, Box 900, Groton, CT 06349; (203) 449-3263. Interest in psychophysiology of hearing and vision, human factors engineering, and related studies. Answers inquiries, makes limited interlibrary loans.

08105. Naval Underwater Systems Center, New London Laboratory (Code 021311), New London, CT 06320; (203) 447-4276. Interest in underwater acoustics, undersea warfare, ocean surveillance. Makes interlibrary loans, permits onsite reference, subject to security clearance and librarian approval.

08106. Navy Submarine Force Library and Museum, Building 83, Box 16, Groton, CT 06349; (203) 449-3174. Interest in submarine history and development. Answers short inquiries, provides facility for onsite reference by prior arrangement.

08108. NewsBank, 58 Pine St, New Canaan, CT 06840; (203) 966-1100. Publishing company specializing in providing indexes to current info materials. Provides general reference services. Publications available by subscription.

08109. Northeast Fisheries Center, Milford Laboratory, National Marine Fisheries Service, NOAA, 212 Rogers Ave, Milford, CT 06460-6499; (203) 783-4200. Interest in environmental studies and molluscan aquaculture. Answers inquiries, provides consulting services, makes interlibrary loans, permits onsite reference.

08110. Northeast Utilities Service Co., Library, P.O. Box 270, Hartford, CT 06141; (203) 665-5141. Interest in electrical and mechanical engineering, public utility economics. Answers inquiries, lends materials, permits onsite use of collection.

08111. Northeastern Research Center for Wildlife Diseases, Dept of Pathobiology, Univ of Conn., Box U-89, Storrs, CT 06268; (203) 486-4000. Cooperative research facility serving New England states, N.Y., Pa., and N.J. Interest in mercury and lead poisoning and diseases to wildlife. Answers inquiries, provides consulting services free to participating states.

08112. Northeastern Weed Science Society, c/o Richard A. Ashley, Secty, Plant Science Dept, U-67, Univ of Conn., Storrs, CT 06268. Interest in weed science and weed control. Provides general reference services, holds annual conference.

08113. Odyssey Institute Corp., 817 Fairfield Ave, Bridgeport, CT 06604; (203) 334-3488. Interest in drug abuse, child abuse, services to women in distress, parent education. Provides general reference services, conducts training programs. Services for a fee.

08115. Out-of-Home Measurement Bureau, P.O. Box 1201 (100 Barnegat Rd), New Canaan, CT 06840; (203) 966-0130. Audits pedestrian and vehicular traffic to out-of-home advertising displays, recommends industry standards. Distributes publications, makes referrals. Services primarily for members, fees may be charged.

08116. Packaging Institute, U.S.A., 20 Summer St, Stamford, CT 06810; (203) 325-9010. Interest in any matters having to do with packaging. Provides general reference services, permits onsite use of library. Services on cost basis with member and nonmember rates.

08117. Pfizer Central Research Laboratories, Library, Eastern Point Rd, Groton, CT 06340; (203) 441-3688. Interest in organic chemistry, biochemistry, medically-related fields. Permits use of collections by area students and scientists.

08118. Promoting Enduring Peace, P.O. Box 5103 (112 Beach Ave), Woodmont, CT 06460; (203) 878-4769. Provides info on peace education, disarmament, nuclear weapons effects. Conducts seminars and workshops; distributes reprints. Services free.

08119. Quality Bakers of America Cooperative, 70 Riverdale Ave, Greenwich, CT 06830; (203) 531-7100. Interest in all phases of the baking and food industry. Provides general reference services on cost basis (members receive some services free and discount on other services).

08120. Rogers Corp., Lurie Library, One Technology Dr, Rogers, CT 06263; (203) 774-9605 ext 319 or 406. Interest in plastics and rubber, circuitry and ceramics, chemical engineering. Makes interlibrary loans, provides limited photocopying services,.

08121. Roper Center, Univ of Conn., Box U-164R, Storrs, CT 06268; (203) 486-4441. Interest in public opinion surveys on social and political questions in the U.S. and other countries. Provides general reference services. Hourly fee charged for staff time, duplications at cost.

08122. Sar-assist, One Island Lane, Greenwich, CT 06830; (203) 869-1322. Commercial consulting firm interested in rescue, survival, safety, worldwide disaster response. Inquiries that can be answered from files free, consulting services for a fee.

08123. Save the Children, Library, 54 Wilton Rd, Westport, CT 06880; (203) 226-7271. Serves staff at headquarters and field offices of Save the Children in the U.S. and Third World countries. Provides references, permits onsite use of collections. Services free.

08124. Sea Grant-Marine Advisory Service, Cooperative Extension Service, Coll of Agriculture and Natural Resources, Univ of Conn., Groton, CT 06340; (203) 445-8664. Disseminates educational and reserach results relating to marine issues to public. Provides general reference services, conducts seminars and workshops, distributes publications. Services generally free.

08125. Selectrons, P.O. Box 115 (137 Mattatuck Heights Rd), Waterbury, CT 06725; (203) 755-9900. Interest in metal repair, restoration, and processing. Provides general reference services, conducts training courses, distributes publications. Fee for some services.

08126. Selenium-Tellurium Development Association, P.O. Box 3096, Darien, CT 06820; (203) 655-0470. Interest in developments in the use of chemicals, electronics, explosives, medicine, metallurgy. Provides free general reference services. Abstracts only to qualified individuals.

08127. Sibling Information Network, Dept of Educational Psychology, Univ of Conn., Box U-64, Storrs, CT 06268; (203) 486-4034. Info clearinghouse for families of disabled persons. Answers inquiries, makes referrals. Services free to membership, open to all.

08129. Sikorsky Aircraft, Public Relations, North Main St, Stratford, CT 06602; (203) 386-4000 ext 6088. Interest in all aspects of air transportation systems. Answers nontechnical inquiries, lends films, provides speakers, makes interlibrary loans of unclassified and nonproprietary material.

08130. Skip Barber Racing School, Route 7, Canaan, CT 06018; (203) 824-0771. Interest in race car driving, competition driving, defensive driving. Answers inquiries, provides advisory services, conducts schools. Services free, except schools.

08131. Society for Cinema Studies, c/o Secty-Treas, P.O. Box 236, Washington, CT 06793; (212) 737-2715. Intl org that serves univ cinema and film studies depts. Provides info, conducts seminars, distributes publications. Services free to members.

08132. Society for Experimental Stress Analysis, 14 Fairfield Dr, Brookfield Center, CT 06805; (203) 775-6373. Interest in experimental mechanics, measurement of stresses and strains in metals and composites. Answers inquiries. Services free.

08133. Society for Values in Higher Education, 409 Prospect St, New Haven, CT 06510; (203) 865-8839. Interest in interdisciplinary study of educational values. Pro-

vides advisory services and info, conducts seminars, distributes publications. Services free to members, at cost to others.

08134. Society of Plastics Engineers, 14 Fairfield Dr, Brookfield Center, CT 06805; (203) 775-0471. Interest in plastics and polymers, their uses and properties. Answers or refers inquiries and provides career and educational info in plastics and polymers. Services free.

08135. Sporting Arms and Ammunition Manufacturers' Institute, P.O. Box 218, Wallingford, CT 06492; (203) 265-3232. Represents leading American producers of sporting firearms, sporting ammunition. Answers inquiries on firearms, ammunition, and propellants related to safety in their use, handling, storage, transportation, and manufacture.

08137. Stowe-Day Foundation, Stowe-Day Foundation, 77 Forest St, Hartford, CT 06105; (203) 522-9258, 522-9259. Interest in Victorian literature, particularly works of Harriet Beecher Stowe and Mark Twain, 19th-Century arts and architecture. Answers inquiries and permits free onsite use of collections.

08138. Talcott Mountain Science Center for Student Involvement, Montevideo Rd, Avon, CT 06001; (203) 677-8571. Instructs students and community in environmental sciences and research. Provides general reference services. Hourly fee charged for onsite programs or in-school services. Journals furnished for nominal fee.

08139. Terri Gotthelf Lupus Research Institute, P.O. Box 486, Ridgefield, CT 06877; (301) 258-9211. Supports, coordinates, and conducts research concerning lupus and related diseases. Grants fellowships, disseminates info.

08140. U.S. Coast Guard Academy, Library, New London, CT 06320; (203) 444-8510. Interest in Coast Guard history and related subjects. Provides general reference services. Services primarily for cadets and academy faculty, but limited services to others.

08141. Uniroyal, Technical Library, World Headquarters, Research Bldg, Middlebury, CT 06749; (203) 573-4509. Interest in chemistry, physics, mathematics, engineering, rubbers (natural and synthetic), plastics and resins, fibers and textiles. Makes limited interlibrary loans.

08142. United States Tobacco Museum, 96 West Putnam Ave, Greenwich, CT 06830; (203) 869-5531. Interest in tobacco-related art, artifacts, and historical materials. Provides general reference services, permits onsite use of collections. Services free by appointment.

08143. United Technologies Corp., Library System, Silver Lane, East Hartford, CT 06108; (203) 727-7120. Interest in aeronautics, related fields. Provides reference services, makes interlibrary loans, makes unclassified and nonproprietary info available to scientific and educational community.

08144. Van Vleck Observatory, Wesleyan Univ, Middletown, CT 06457; (203) 347-9411 ext 303. Interest in astronomy, astrophysics, and related fields. Answers inquiries, makes referrals to other sources of info, provides consulting services.

08145. Veteran Motor Car Club of America, c/o Walter O. MacIlvain, Editor, 17 Bonner Rd, Manchester, CT 06040. Interest in antique automobiles and related items. Provides general reference services at cost to nonmembers.

08146. Vietnam Veterans Agent Orange Victims, 93 Prospect Street, Stamford, CT 06901; (203) 323-7478. Supports those exposed to Agent Orange while serving in Vietnam war. Distributes medical info packages and surveys.

08148. Wire Association, P.O. Box H (1570 Boston Post Rd), Guilford, CT 06437; (203) 453-2777. Interest in wire and wire products. Provides general reference services. Sponsors meetings worldwide.

08149. World Association for Public Opinion Research, c/o The Roper Center, Yale Univ, P.O. Box 1732, Yale Station, New Haven, CT 06520; (203) 436-8186. Interest in survey research, public opinion and communication research. Provides general reference services, conducts annual conferences.

08150. Yale Arbovirus Research Unit, Dept of Epidemiology and Public Health, Yale School of Medicine, 3333 (60 Coll St), New Haven, CT 06510; (203) 436-3595. Conducts research and serves as the Intl Reference Center for Arboviruses of WHO and FAO. Provides general reference services, permits onsite use of collections. Services free, all available to research scientists and orgs.

08151. Yale Economic Growth Center Collection, Yale Univ, Box 1958, New Haven, CT 06520 (203) 436-8411 (research staff), (203) 436-3412 (library). Interest in theoretical analysis of a natl economy. Provides general reference services, permits onsite use of collection. Services primarily for scholars.

08152. Yale-China Association, Box 905A, Yale Station (442 Temple St), New Haven, CT 06520; (203) 436-4422. Interest in political, economic, and social aspects of contemporary China, educational exchanges, trade, and investment between China and U.S. Provides general reference services. Services available to anyone, most free to members.

Delaware

09003. Alfred I. DuPont Institute, Medical Library, P.O. Box 269, Wilmington, DE 19899; (302) 651-5820. Orthopedic hospital and outpatient clinic for handicapped children with extensive referral services. Library has 20,000 bound volumes and 320 periodicals and is open to the public.

09004. College of Marine Studies, Univ of Del., Newark, DE 19711; (302) 738-2841. Researches shoreline processes, marine biology, ocean engineering. Holds extensive technical references. Open to qualified scientists; materials available by interlibrary loan. Inquiries answered.

09005. Delaware Academy of Medicine, Lewis B. Flinn Library, 1925 Lovering Ave, Wilmington, DE 19806; (302) 656-1629. Interest in medicine and dentistry. Permits onsite reference by public, provides staff-operated photocopy service, makes interlibrary loans for a fee. Technical inquiries not answered.

09008. Delaware Council on Crime and Justice, 701 Shipley St, Wilmington, DE 19801; (302) 658-7174. Studies and plans programs involving criminal justice system and victim services. Seminars and workshops conducted free; referral service and library available for onsite use.

09009. Delaware Development Office, P.O. Box 1401 (99 Kings Highway), Dover, DE 19903; (302) 736-4271. Interest in promotion and budgeting of Del. industrial, economic, and small business development and travel promotion. Handles inquiries, provides advisory services at no charge.

09012. Delaware Geological Survey, Univ of Del., 101 Penny Hall, Newark, DE 19716; (302) 451-2833. Interest in geology of Del. and related subjects. Answers inquiries on state geology and water resources; provides consulting services to govt agencies, industries, individuals; distributes publications.

09014. Delaware Poultry Research Lab, Agricultural Research Service, USDA, Rte 2, Box 600, Georgetown, DE 19947; (302) 856-0047. Studies regulation of fat deposition and muscle development in poultry. Scientific reports and articles produced, with limited reprints available. Inquiries answered.

09017. Delaware Wildlife Federation, P.O. Box 8111, Wilmington, DE 19713; (302) 998-7532. Publishes monthly newsletter, answers inquiries. Conducts seminars, workshops, hunter safety education classes in high schools; sponsors hunter and water safety programs. Services free.

09018. Department of Entomology and Applied Ecology, Coll of Agricultural Sciences, Univ of Del., Newark, DE 19711; (302) 451-2526. Interest in biological control, plant-insect interactions, basic ecology, evolution and natural selection, wildlife management. Inquiries answered, consulting services available to individuals and agencies.

09019. Department of Mechanical and Aerospace Engineering, Univ of Del., Newark, DE 19716; (302) 738-2421. Interests include heat transfer, thermodynamics, fluid mechanics, gas dynamics, and related fields. Permits limited onsite use of collection.

09020. Disaster Research Center, Univ of Del., Newark, DE 19716; (302) 451-2581. Interest in community preparations for natural and technological disasters. Holdings in several languages make up world's most extensive library on subject. Library open to public; special services available for a fee.

09021. Forward Lands, 2800 Pennsylvania Ave, Wilmington, DE 19806; (302) 655-2151. Acquires and receives gifts of lands for charitable, educational, recreational, or scientific purposes. Publishes newsletter, provides consulting services, answers inquiries.

09022. Hagley Museum and Library, P.O. Box 3630, Wilmington, DE 19807; (302) 658-2401. Holds manuscripts, images, and periodicals on iron and steel, chemical, and petroleum industries. Reference and photocopying services, interlibrary loans available.

09023. Haskell Laboratory for Toxicology and Industrial Medicine, E.I. du Pont de Nemours and Co., P.O. Box 50, Newark, DE 19714; (302) 366-5225. Specializes in toxicology, industrial hygiene, occupational medicine. Library contains info from lab investigations and other sources. Info exchanged with research orgs, supplied to customers through manufacturing depts.

09024. Henry Francis du Pont Winterthur Museum, Winterthur, DE 19735; (302) 654-1548. Displays period settings of American decorative arts made or used between 1640-1840. Library has related books, periodicals, archival materials. Library and museum open to public.

09025. Historical Society of Delaware, 505 Market St Mall, Wilmington, DE 19801; (302) 655-7161. Del. history and genealogy org that publishes semiannual journal, answers inquiries, provides advisory, genealogical, reference, reproduction services. Fee charged for genealogical research and reproductions.

09026. Institute for Neuroscience and Behavior, Univ of Del., Newark, DE 19711; (302) 738-1191. Conducts neuroscience research. Inquiries answered and publications and reprints distributed at cost.

09027. International Reading Association, P.O. Box 8139 (800 Barksdale Rd), Newark, DE 19714; (302) 731-1600. Interest in educational psychology focusing on development of reading skills. Reference-index guide to assn articles, studies, and reports available. Info exchange services available.

09028. Mount Cuba Astronomical Observatory, P.O. Box 3915 (Hillside Mill Rd), Greenville, DE 19807; (302) 654-6407. Collection includes photometry of celestial bodies, maps, periodicals, surveys. Onsite reference by members and others on request. Six-session "overview of modern astronomy" offered, referrals made.

09029. Music Resource Center, Dept of Music, Univ of Del., Newark, DE 19711; (302) 738-8130. Specializes in opera and large ensemble music. Maintains recordings, scores, books, audio and video tapes, and periodicals. Answers inquiries; allows free use of facilities as time permits.

09030. Produce Marketing Association Information Center, 700 Barksdale Plaza, Newark, DE 19711; (302) 738-7100. Provides free economic, regulatory, technical data about fresh fruits, nuts, vegetables, floral products. Provides reference, reproduction, microfilm services. Publications at cost to members, at increased fee to others.

09031. Rodel, 451 Bellevue Rd, Newark, DE 19713; (302) 366-0500. Synthetic leather "poromerics" for all applications made by commercial manufacturer. Provides technical reports and procedural info on products.

09032. Water Resources Center, Univ of Del., Newark, DE 19716; (302) 451-2191. Interest in water and water resources. Maintains reports of center's research projects. Issues periodic newsletter and annual report, makes referrals, answers inquiries.

District of Columbia

10021. ACTION, Off of Policy and Planning, 806 Connecticut Ave NW, Washington, DC 20525; (202) 254-8523. Collects statistical info concerning Volunteers in Service to America (VISTA), Young Volunteers in ACTION (YVA), Foster Grandparents Program (FGP), Retired Senior Volunteer Program (RSVP), and Senior Companion Program (SCP). Answers inquiries.

10022. AFL-CIO Community Services Department, 815 16th St NW, Washington, DC 20006; (202) 637-5189. Interest in community service programs, including disaster assistance, retirement, unemployment, debt counseling, hospital and medical services, etc. Answers inquiries or makes referrals. Services primarily for members, but others assisted.

10023. AFL-CIO Department for Professional Employees, 815 16th St NW, Washington, DC 20006; (202) 638-0320. Interest in unionization of professional and technical employees, technological change, productivity, professional women, labor and the arts. Publishes newsletter, answers inquiries, provides speakers.

10024. AT International Library, 1331 H St NW, Washington, DC 20005; (202) 879-2900. Promotes appropriate technology in Third World thru funding, research, info exchange, projects. Publications list available. Provides inquiry, reference services; permits onsite use of collections by appointment.

10025. Academy for Educational Development, Clearinghouse on Development Communication, 1255 23rd St NW, Washington, DC 20037; (202) 862-1900. Provides assistance and info to educators, researchers, and practitioners working in development communications. Provides general reference services, conducts seminars, distributes publications, permits onsite use of collection. Fees charged to cover cost of publications.

10026. Academy for Educational Development, Systems Services Division, 1255 23rd St NW, Washington, DC 20037; (202) 862-1900. Collects info on higher education's administration, systems, and strategic planning. Answers inquiries, provides consulting and reference services, makes referrals, conducts seminars.

10027. Academy for State & Local Government, 444 N Capitol St NW, Ste 349, Washington, DC 20001; (202) 638-1445. Public policy center of natl orgs of public officials. Assists local govts in mobilizing and applying expert knowledge to emerging problems. Answers inquiries, provides advisory services, distributes publications, makes referrals. Services at cost.

10028. Academy for State & Local Government, International Center, Academy for State and Local Government, 444 N Capitol St NW, Ste 349, Washington, DC 20001; (202) 638-1445. Serves local govt as its "window on the world" and promotes the intl exchange of practical experience in dealing with urban problems. Answers inquiries, provides reference services, conducts seminars, distributes publications, and makes referrals. Fees may be charged.

10029. Accreditation Council for Services for Mentally Retarded & Other Developmentally Disabled Persons, 4435 Wisconsin Ave NW, Room 202, Washington, DC 20016; (202) 363-2811. Natl accrediting body for agencies serving mentally retarded, developmentally disabled. Provides consultinga, onsite prog evaluation; conducts workshops. Inquiries free; other services for a fee.

10030. Action on Smoking & Health, 2013 H St NW, Washington, DC 20006; (202) 659-4310. Nonprofit legal action antismoking group. Provides general reference services. Services free, except publications, to any antismoking person.

10031. Administration for Children, Youth & Families, Off of Human Development Services, 400 Sixth St SW, Rm 5030, Washington, DC 20201; (202) 755-7762. Operates Head Start and related demonstration and experimental programs, administers child welfare and adoption assistance grant-in-aid programs. Answers inquiries, provides reference and consulting services.

10032. Administrative Conference of the U.S., 2120 L St NW, Ste 500, Washington, DC 20037; (202) 254-7020. Seeks to develop improvements in legal procedures by which fed agencies administer regulatory, benefit, and other governmental programs. Answers inquiries, distributes publications, makes referrals, permits onsite use of collections. Services free.

10034. Administrative Office of the U.S. Courts, 811 Vermont Ave NW, Washington, DC 20544; (202) 633-6094. Administrative center of U.S. courts (except Supreme Court). Answers inquiries, lends statistical data, makes referrals, distributes publications.

10035. Advisory & Learning Exchange, Edmondes School Bldg, 9th and D Sts NE, Washington, DC 20002; (202) 547-8030. Interest in teaching and learning, preschool through high school; education theory and practice. Answers inquiries; conducts workshops; provides consulting services; permits onsite use of collection.

10036. Advisory Council on Historic Preservation, 1100 Pennsylvania Ave NW, Rm 809, Washington, DC 20004; (202) 786-0503. Acts as policy advisor to govt in field of historic preservation, providing the president and Congress with an annual report on the state of preservation activities in U.S. Answers public inquiries, distributes publications, makes referrals, and offers a training course.

10037. Aerospace Industries Association of America, 1725 DeSales St NW, Washington, DC 20036; (202) 429-4600. Natl trade assn of companies engaged in research, manufacturing of aerospace products. Publishes journal, annual reference book, studies; provides info on research in progress.

10038. Aerospace Medical Association, Washington Natl Airport, Washington, DC 20001-4977; (703) 892-2240. Studies aerospace medicine, life sciences, and bioastronautics, primarily the medical aspects of flying and adaptation of man to flight. Publishes a journal, answers inquiries, provides reference services.

10039. African-American Labor Center, 1400 K St NW, Ste 700, Washington, DC 20005; (202) 789-1020. Interest in assistance to African trade unions in union development and leadership training, workers' education, vocational training, cooperatives and credit unions, health, etc. Answers inquiries, distributes publications, makes referrals.

10040. Afro-Hispanic Institute, 3306 Ross Pl NW, Washington, DC 20008; (202) 966-7783. Interest in blacks in Spanish-speaking countries. Publishes scholarly materials. Provides inquiry, reference, translation services; permits onsite use of collections. Publications sold; other services free or at cost.

10041. Agency for International Development, Bureau for External Affairs, 320 21st St NW, Washington, DC 20523; (202) 655-4000. Source of general info relating to economic assistance programs of U.S. Answers inquiries or makes referrals.

10042. Agency for International Development Library, 320 21st St NW, Rm 105 SA-18, Washington, DC 20523; (703) 235-1000 or 235-8936. AID encourages economic and social development of less developed countries, particularly in agriculture, health, education, and nutrition. Library services provided to non-AID users as resources permit. Publications can be borrowed. Limited reproduction services.

10043. Agency for International Development, Office of Nutrition, S&T/N AID Rm 320, RPC, Washington, DC 20523; (703) 235-9062. Interest in alleviating malnutrition in lesser-developed countries, combatting nutrition-related health problems, promoting food technology, etc. Provides reference and consulting services, conducts seminars. Services available to persons and orgs active in the field of nutrition; free to those in developing countries.

10044. Agency for International Development, Office of Women in Development, New State, Rm 3725-A, 320

21st St NW, Washington, DC 20523; (202) 632-3992. Seeks to integrate women into the AID program in less developed countries so they may participate as equal partners. Answers inquiries, provides reference services, conducts seminars, distributes publications, and makes referrals. Services and publications provided free.

10045. Agricultural Cooperative Service, U.S. Dept of Agriculture, Rm 3405, South Bldg, 14th St and Independence Ave, SW, Washington, DC 20250; (202) 447-8870. Provides business services and cooperative organizations for use by farmers; conducts related studies. Provides info.

10047. Agricultural Marketing Service, Dept of Agriculture, Rm 3071, South Bldg, 14th St and Independence Ave, SW, Washington, DC 20250; (202) 447-5115. Provides regulatory and standardization services for agricultural producers, administers marketing programs, publishes materials.

10048. Agriculture Council of America, 1250 Eye St NW, Ste 601, Washington, DC 20005; (202) 602-9200. Nonprofit org that develops agricultural policy, coordinates public education programs on agriculture. Provides inquiry and referral services, conducts workshops and meetings. Most services free.

10049. Air Conditioning Contractors of America, 1228 17th St NW, Washington, DC 20036; (202) 296-7610. Publishes technical manuals and interactive computer programs on heating, air conditioning, ventilation systems. Conducts seminars and workshops, makes referrals to other sources of info.

10050. Air Force Federal Computer Performance Evaluation & Simulation Center, U.S. Air Force Communications Command, FEDSIM/CC (6118 Franconia Rd, Alexandria, VA), Washington, DC 20330; (202) 274-8065. Provides computer and communication system performance evaluation and simulation services to all fed govt agencies. Answers only general inquiries from public.

10051. Air Force, Office of Air Force History, HQ USAF/CHO, Building 5681, Bolling Air Force Base, Washington, DC 20332-6098; (202) 767-4712; (202) 767-5089 (Library). Maintains histories of Air Force organizations, from pre- through post-World War II, including the Korean and Vietnam wars. Answers inquiries, provides reference and copy services, makes referrals. Services free, except copying, to U.S. citizens.

10052. Air Force, Office of Scientific Research, Bolling Air Force Base, Washington, DC 20332. Awards grants and contracts for research in science and engineering related to natl security and the U.S. Air Force. Answers inquiries on AFOSR technical reports and their availability through the DTIC-NTIS systems. Staff scientists consult on Air Force problems.

10053. Air Transport Association of America Library, 1709 New York Ave NW, Washington, DC 20006; (202) 626-4184. Owns statistical reports of transportation regulatory agencies, congressional documents, industry

studies. Publishes annual report, permits onsite use of collection, makes interlibrary loans.

10054. Airport Operators Council International, 1700 K St NW, Washington, DC 20006; (202) 296-3270. Interest in civil airport mgmt (operation, development, economics, law, technology). Publishes tech reports, sells other data. Provides reference, update services; conducts seminars. Services free.

10055. Alban Institute, 4125 Nebraska Ave NW, Washington, DC 20016; (202) 244-7320. Interest in organizational, religious dynamics of congregations. Publications list available. Provides inquiry, advisory, consulting services; conducts seminars, workshops. Services for a fee.

10056. Alcohol & Drug Problems Association of North America, 444 N Capitol St, Ste 181, Washington, DC 20001; (202) 737-4340. Promotes concern for alcoholism and drug problems with emphasis on legislation, education, social work, research, and treatment. Answers inquiries, provides reference services and makes referrals. Extensive services provided to members only.

10057. Alexander Graham Bell Association for the Deaf, 3417 Volta Pl NW, Washington, DC 20007; (202) 337-5220 (Voice and TTY). Owns technical reports, clippings, journals on deafness. Publishes magazine with reviews of current research, answers inquiries, permits onsite use of collection by appointment.

10058. Alliance For Justice, 600 New Jersey Ave NW, Washington, DC 20001; (202) 624-8390. Natl assn of public interest orgs seeking to maintain funding for, and access to, courts and agencies for public interest lawyers. Answers inquiries, provides consulting services, distributes publications, makes referrals. Most services free.

10059. Alliance for Environmental Education, P.O. Box 1040 (3421 M St NW), Washington, DC 20007; (202) 797-4530. Coordinates cooperation among nongovt orgs involved in environmental education; acts as a clearinghouse for environmental education materials. Provides general reference services. Membership and most services limited to regional or natl environmental educational orgs.

10060. Alliance to Save Energy, 1925 K St NW, Ste 206, Washington, DC 20006; (202) 857-0666. Promotes efficient energy use by conducting research and demonstration projects, and by providing education and advocacy. Provides limited advisory services, distributes publications, and makes referrals. Services free, except publications, with priority to members.

10061. Aluminum Association, 818 Connecticut Ave NW, Washington, DC 20006; (202) 862-5100 (General inquiries); (202) 862-5192 (Info Ctr); (202) 862-5156 (Publications). Publishes pamphlets, handbooks, reference books, abstracts, proceedings, monographs, journals on aluminum technology, standards; permits onsite use of collection by appointment only.

10062. Aluminum Recycling Association, 900 17th St NW, Ste 504, Washington, DC 20006; (202) 785-0550. Publishes industry brochures on recycled aluminum specification alloys, casting, and foundry alloys. Answers inquiries, provides quarterly shipment statistics.

10063. Amateur Chamber Music Players, 633 E St NW, Washington, DC 20004. Nonprofit org of about 4,000 members worldwide formed to encourage, facilitate the playing of chamber music by helping amateurs meet one another. Publishes directories of members. Services available to members.

10064. America the Beautiful Fund, 219 Shoreham Bldg, Washington, DC 20005; (202) 638-1649. Nonprofit org interested in American cultural heritage, conservation, charitable gardening, environmental arts and design. Answers inquiries, provides consulting services and seed grants for qualified projects. Services free to some, at cost to others.

10065. American Academy of Actuaries, 1720 Eye St NW, 7th Fl, Washington, DC 20006; (202) 223-8196. Represents actuaries in life, health, liability, property, and casualty insurance, as well as pensions and govt insurance companies, consulting actuarial firms, govt, academic institutions, and a growing number of industries. Answers inquiries, makes referrals.

10066. American Academy of Child Psychiatry, 3615 Wisconsin Ave NW, Washington, DC 20016; (202) 966-7300. Interest in all aspects of child psychiatry and mental health, social policy, legal issues, training. Provides general reference services, distributes publications, acts as an info resource to fed govt and Congress.

10067. American Academy of Facial Plastic & Reconstructive Surgery, 1101 Vermont Ave NW, Ste 404, Washington, DC 20005; (202) 842-4500; (800) 332-FACE (Toll-free USA); (800) 523-FACE (Toll-free Canada). Intl medical society that stimulates study, research, and scientific advancement of head and neck surgery. Interest in plastic and reconstructive surgery of head and neck. Answers inquiries, sells brochures.

10068. American Academy of Judicial Education, 2025 Eye St NW, Rm 903, Washington, DC 20006; (202) 775-0083. Nonprofit educational institution that provides judicial education programs and services to those in criminal justice training. Services and faculty available for in-state judicial conferences. Fees paid by individual state offices of judicial education.

10069. American Academy of Optometry, 5530 Wisconsin Ave NW, Ste 745, Washington, DC 20815; (301) 652-0905. Publishes monthly journal on optometry, optics; conducts continuing education courses, diploma programs, annual research meeting for optometrists and vision scientists.

10070. American Academy of Otolaryngology-Head and Neck Surgery, c/o Jerome C. Goldstein, MD, Exec V.P., 1101 Vermont Ave NW, Ste 302, Washington, DC 20005; (202) 289-4607. Serves as info center for otolaryngology. Publishes journal, newsletter, monographs, correspondence courses, patient education leaflets; offers courses, exhibits.

10071. American Academy of Thermology, c/o Margaret R. Abernathy, Exec Dir, Georgetown Medical Ctr, 3800 Reservoir Rd NW, Washington, DC 20007; (202) 625-7748 or 625-7409. Interest in thermography, thermographic diagnosis, thermographic screening, thermal emission, heat transfer. Answers inquiries, conducts seminars and workshops, distributes newsletter.

10072. American Advertising Federation, 1400 K St NW, Washington, DC 20005; (202) 898-0089. Promotes better understanding of function and value of advertising and seeks to improve environment in which advertising operates. Answers inquiries, provides reference services, distributes publications, makes referrals. Services free.

10073. American Agricultural Economics Documentation Center, c/o Dr Wayne Rasmussen, Economic Research Service, USDA, 1301 New York Ave NW, Washington, DC 20250; (202) 786-1724. Creates and maintains computerized bibliographic data base, AG-ECON, containing citations of agricultural economics literature. Answers inquiries, makes referrals, permits onsite use of collection. Services free.

10074. American Agriculture Movement, 100 Maryland Ave NE, Ste 500A, Washington, DC 20002; (202) 544-5750. Works for parity for agricultural commodities, preserving the family farm. Lobbies on agricultural issues. Publishes periodical, answers inquiries, conducts workshops. Services free.

10075. American Airship Association, P.O. Box 43184, Attn: Frank G. McGuire, Washington, DC 20010; (301) 986-9202. Interest in aerostatic science as it relates to lighter-than-air craft airships, dirigibles, zeppelins, blimps, balloons. Answers inquiries, provides advisory services free. Newsletter available by subscription.

10076. American Anthropological Association, 1703 New Hampshire Ave NW, Washington, DC 20009; (202) 232-8800. Publishes journal, newsletter, special publications on cultural, social, physical, and applied anthropology, archaeology; makes referrals for scholars, media; provides career info.

10077. American Archives Association, 449 Washington Bldg, 15th St and New York Ave NW, Washington, DC 20005; (202) 737-6090. Interest in forensic genealogy, intl probate research. Answers inquiries, provides reference and general genealogical research, permits onsite use of collection by the public. Services free, except research, to qualified researchers.

10078. American Assembly of Collegiate Schools of Business, 1755 Massachusetts Ave NW, Washington, DC 20036; (202) 483-0400. Interest in business administration and mgmt education, school accreditation, intl and governmental affairs, corporate/univ relations.

Provides general reference services, free to members and at modest charge to nonmembers.

10079. American Association for Adult & Continuing Education, 1201 16th St NW, Ste 230, Washington, DC 20036; (202) 822-7866. Provides leadership in advancing learning as a lifelong process by concentrating on adult education. Publishes newsletter, answers inquiries, provides some consulting and research services, conducts seminars.

10080. American Association for Clinical Chemistry, 1725 K St NW, Washington, DC 20006; (202) 857-0717. Interest in clinical chemistry, clinical chemistry standards and education. Answers inquiries, provides advisory services, conducts an employment clearinghouse. Services free to members; a small fee may be charged to nonmembers.

10081. American Association for Dental Research, 1111 14th St NW, Ste 1000, Washington, DC 20005; (202) 898-1050. Promotes dental research. Publishes journal, answers inquiries, provides advisory and microfilm services, distributes publications. Most services free.

10082. American Association for Higher Education, 1 Dupont Circle NW, Washington, DC 20036; (202) 293-6440. Concerned with all aspects of higher education. Publishes a bulletin and magazine, answers inquiries and makes referrals.

10083. American Association for Hospital Planning, 1101 Connecticut Ave NW, Ste 700, Washington, DC 20036; (202) 857-1162. Interest in hospital planning, services, design, construction, and financing; fed legislation concerning hospitals. Provides general reference services, conducts annual conferences. Services free and primarily for members, but others assisted.

10084. American Association for Marriage & Family Therapy, 1717 K St NW, Room 407, Washington, DC 20006; (202) 429-1825. Dedicated to professional marriage and family therapy, and field of marriage and family relations. Provides general reference services, conducts annual conference, distributes publications. Services free, except some publications.

10085. American Association for Medical Systems & Informatics, 1101 Connecticut Ave NW, Ste 700, Washington, DC 20036; (202) 857-1199. Interest in development of medical, scientific, and educational programs and dissemination of related info, promotion of development of systems for health care. Answers inquiries, publishes newsletter, holds annual conference.

10086. American Association for World Health, U.S. Committee for the World Health Organization, 515 22nd St NW, Washington, DC 20037; (202) 861-4322. Interest in world health problems and multilateral and bilateral intl health agencies working to solve these problems. Answers inquiries, provides advisory services, conducts seminars, distributes publications. Services free to members, at cost to others.

10087. American Association for the Advancement of Science Library, 1333 H St NW, Washington, DC 20005; (202) 326-6610. Seeks to further the work of scientists, facilitate cooperation among them, foster scientific freedom and responsibility. Answers nontechnical inquiries only, permits use of collection by appointment.

10088. American Association for the Advancement of Science, Project on the Handicapped in Science, Off of Opportunities in Science, 1776 Massachusetts Ave NW, Washington, DC 20036. Advocacy, info resource for disabled scientists, students of science. Maintains data base, answers inquiries, distributes publications, conducts workshops. Services free, except some publications.

10089. American Association of Airport Execs, 2301 M St NW, Washington, DC 20037; (202) 331-8994. Publishes journal, bulletins on airport operation; owns standards, specifications; provides consulting services; permits onsite use of collection. Services to nonmembers limited.

10090. American Association of Black Women Entrepreneurs, 1326 Missouri Ave NW, Ste 4, Washington, DC 20011; (202) 231-3751. Promotes black female entrepreneurship. Holds statistical data; provides inquiry, advisory, consulting services; conducts seminars, workshops. Services to nonmembers for a fee.

10091. American Association of Children's Residential Centers, 440 First St NW, Ste 310, Washington, DC 20001; (202) 638-1604. Supports residential treatment for emotionally disturbed children. Provides inquiry, advisory, referral services; conducts annual conference; distributes publications.

10092. American Association of Colleges for Teacher Education, 1 Dupont Circle NW, Washington, DC 20036; (202) 293-2450. Natl assn of colleges, universities provides consulting services. Develops accreditation standards; permits onsite use of collection. Fee for some services.

10093. American Association of Colleges for Teacher Education, ERIC Clearinghouse on Teacher Education, 1 Dupont Circle NW, Ste 610, Washington, DC 20036; (202) 293-2450. Acquires, abstracts, and disseminates info on significant aspects of teacher education, health education, and physical education. Provides info from the ERIC system, distributes publications, makes referrals.

10094. American Association of Colleges of Nursing, 1 Dupont Circle, Ste 530, Washington, DC 20036; (202) 463-6930. Seeks to improve professional nursing through advancing the quality of education, promoting research, developing leadership. Answers inquiries free, provides consulting services, conducts seminars, distributes publications, and makes referrals for members.

10095. American Association of Community & Junior Colleges, 1 Dupont Circle NW, Ste 410, Washington, DC

20036; (202) 293-7050. Nonprofit natl professional org interested in community and junior colleges, including curriculum development, tuition, etc. Provides general reference services, permits onsite use of collection. Services free to member institutions and their staffs, others charged.

10096. American Association of Dental Schools, 1619 Massachusetts Ave NW, Washington, DC 20036; (202) 667-9433. Source of data on preprofessional, professional, and post-doctoral dental education and training of auxiliary personnel. Answers inquiries, publishes journal, provides consulting services. Services primarily for members.

10097. American Association of Homes for the Aging, 1129 20th St NW, Ste 400, Washington, DC 20036; (202) 296-5960. Concerned with care of elderly and standards in facilities serving the elderly. Answers inquiries, provides assistance to administrators of nonprofit homes for the aging, conducts public info programs and educational conferences.

10098. American Association of MESBICS, 915 15th St NW, Ste 700, Washington, DC 20005; (202) 347-8600. Represents Minority Enterprise Small Business Investment Co. (MESBIC) sector of financial community. Helps find capital sources. Provides inquiry, consulting, referral services; conducts workshops. Most services free.

10099. American Association of Motor Vehicle Administrators, 1201 Connecticut Ave NW, Ste 910, Washington, DC 20036; (202) 296-1955. Assn of state and provincial officials enforcing motor vehicle laws in U.S. and Canada. Publishes handbooks, provides consulting services, reviews motor vehicle safety equipment to ensure compliance with standards.

10100. American Association of Museums, 1055 Thomas Jefferson St NW, Washington, DC 20007; (202) 338-5300. Publishes annual official museum directory, accounting handbook, standards, bimonthly news magazine, reprints, reports; answers inquiries; provides reference services.

10101. American Association of Nurserymen, 1250 Eye St NW, Ste 500, Washington, DC 20005; (202) 789-2900. Publishes horticultural industry info bulletins, career leaflets, nursery stock standards, industry operating cost statistics; refers to specialists at state land grant colleges.

10102. American Association of Poison Control Centers, c/o Secty-Treas, 2025 Eye St NW, Ste 105, Washington, DC 20006. Intl org interested in poison control, toxic substances. Conducts meetings, seminars; provides visual aids on the prevention of accidental poisoning; distributes data compilations; makes referrals.

10103. American Association of Psychiatric Services for Children, 1001 Connecticut Ave NW, Ste 800, Washington, DC 20036; (202) 833-9775. Publishes newsletter on child psychiatry, answers inquiries, provides consulting services, makes referrals. Services primarily for academic and professional persons.

10104. American Association of Retired Persons, Institute of Lifetime Learning, 1909 K St NW, Washington, DC 20049; (202) 662-4895. Supports adult education adapted to needs and interests of older persons, emphasizing nontraditional education, gerontology, and technology. Answers inquiries, helps establish discussion groups and disseminates info on institutions offering free or reduced tuition to older persons.

10105. American Association of Retired Persons, National Gerontology Resource Center, 1909 K St NW, Washington, DC 20049; (202) 728-4880. Concerned with gerontology, particularly research in social gerontology, welfare for the aging, retirement planning, housing, health care, education, employment, and social security. Makes interlibrary loans, permits onsite use of the collection, answers inquiries.

10106. American Association of Retired Persons, Widowed Persons Service, 1909 K St NW, Washington, DC 20049; (202) 728-4370. Provides support services to newly widowed. Answers inquiries, provides consulting, conducts seminars, distributes publications, and makes referrals. Services free, except publications to nonmembers.

10107. American Association of Sex Educators, Counselors, & Therapists, 11 Dupont Circle NW, Ste 220, Washington, DC 20036; (202) 462-1171. Natl nonprofit org that works to develop competency standards for sex educators and therapists. Interest in training and research in sex education. Provides general reference services, conducts seminars, distributes publications. Services generally free, primarily for members.

10108. American Association of State Highway & Transportation Officials, 444 N Capitol St, Ste 225, Washington, DC 20001; (202) 624-5800. Fosters development and operation of a nationwide transportation system. Publishes a quarterly, answers inquiries, conducts seminars, distributes publications. Services normally free.

10109. American Association of University Administrators, 1133 15th St NW, Washington, DC 20005; (202) 429-9440. Interest in admin of higher education, college and univ administration, professional administration standards. Provides general reference services, conducts seminars, distributes publications. Services primarily for members, others assisted on time-available basis.

10110. American Association of University Women, Educational Foundation Library, 2401 Virginia Ave NW, Washington, DC 20037; (202) 785-7700. Concerned with education and achievements of women and their status in society. Answers inquiries, provides reference services, makes interlibrary loans. Services primarily for members.

10111. American Association of University Women, Public Policy Department, 2401 Virginia Ave NW, Washington, DC 20037; (202) 785-7712. Works on women's education, retirement; peace, natl security issues. Publishes newsletter, info packets; answers inquiries; conducts seminars, workshops. Most services free or at cost.

10112. American Astronomical Society, 1816 Jefferson Pl NW, Washington, DC 20036; (202) 659-0134. Interest in dynamical astronomy, high energy astrophysics, planetary sciences, solar physics, galactic structure and stellar motions, etc. Answers inquiries, distributes publication, provides career info and faculty lecturers to small colleges.

10113. American Bankers Association Library, 1120 Connecticut Ave NW, Washington, DC 20036; (202) 467-4180 (Library); (202) 467-4101 (general info). Publishes journal, index, books, pamphlets, newsletters, audiovisual materials; owns collection on banking, mgmt, law; provides onsite use of collection; makes interlibrary loans.

10114. American Bar Association, Mental Disability Legal Resource Center, Commission on the Mentally Disabled, 1800 M St NW, Washington, DC 20036; (202) 331-2240. Supports legal rights of the disabled, mentally retarded, developmentally disabled. Provides limited advisory, reference, and reproduction services, distributes publications. Most services free.

10116. American Battle Monuments Commission, Pulaski Bldg, Rm 5127, 20 Massachusetts Ave NW, Washington, DC 20314; (202) 272-0533. Responsible for construction and maintenance of U.S. military cemeteries and memorials on foreign soil and certain memorials on American soil. Provides exact location of place of internment of war dead and advice on visits to cemeteries.

10118. American Bus Association, 1025 Connecticut Ave NW, Washington, DC 20036; (202) 293-5890. Natl org of intercity bus industry. Publishes journal, annual report, safety regulations, travel dictionary, pamphlets; answers inquiries; permits limited onsite use of collection.

10119. American Catholic Philosophical Association, Catholic Univ of America, Washington, DC 20064; (202) 635-5518. Promotes philosophical inquiry and study of science, law, religion, metaphysics, and ethics. Answers inquiries, conducts research, distributes publications. Placement service available to members.

10120. American Chain Association, 1133 15th St NW, Washington, DC 20005-4979; (202) 429-9440. Interest in chains for power transmission, conveying and elevating. Publishes manuals and handbooks for sale to educational institutions and industry.

10121. American Chemical Society, 1155 16th St NW, Washington, DC 20036; (202) 872-4600. Provides info on chemical technology; publishes newsletter on chemical and engineering news, journals, monographs, reference books; makes interlibrary loans; permits onsite reference.

10122. American Chemical Society, Women Chemists Committee, 1155 16th St NW, Washington, DC 20036; (202) 872-4456. Assn for women in chemistry and chemical engineering. Answers inquiries, distributes publications, makes referrals. Operates members' job referral service for women chemists. Many services free.

10123. American Civil Liberties Union, Foundation National Prison Project, 1616 P Street NW, Ste 340, Washington, DC 20036; (202) 331-0500. Interest in prison conditions, law, corrections, prisoner's rights. Provides general reference services, distributes publications, permits onsite use of collections. Services free, except publications and reproduction services, by appointment.

10124. American Coal Ash Associates, 1819 H St NW, Ste 510, Washington, DC 20006; (202) 659-2303. Promotes utilization of coal byproducts produced by electric coal burning power plants. Publishes newsletter, answers inquiries, provides advisory services, conducts seminars, distributes publications. Services free to members.

10125. American Coalition of Citizens with Disabilities, 1012 14th St NW, Ste 901, Washington, DC 20005; (202) 628-3470. Promotes interests of all disabled persons in U.S. Publishes books, directories (hardcopy, cassettes); answers inquiries; conducts workshops. Most services free.

10126. American Coll Theatre Festival, c/o John F. Kennedy Ctr for the Performing Arts, Washington, DC 20566; (212) 254-3437. Seeks to honor college and univ theatre productions and to encourage students to take an active part in college theatre. Produces annual festival at Kennedy Center, answers inquiries, conducts workshops.

10127. American College of Foot Orthopedists, 1377 K St NW, Room 202, Washington, DC 20005. Publishes newsletter on foot orthopedics; provides consulting services; examines applicants for fellowship; supports residency program in podiatric medicine colleges.

10128. American College of Nuclear Physicians, 1101 Connecticut Ave NW, Ste 700, Washington, DC 20036; (202) 857-1135. Interest in nuclear medicine. Answers inquiries, distributes publications. Services free, except publications.

10129. American College of Nurse-Midwives, 1522 K St NW, Ste 1120, Washington, DC 20005; (202) 347-5445. Represents certified nurse-midwives in U.S. Interest in nurse-midwifery service and education. Answers inquiries, provides consulting services, distributes publications, Services free, except consulting, publications, and approval visits.

10130. American College of Obstetricians & Gynecologists, Resource Center, 600 Maryland Ave SW, Ste 300 East, Washington, DC 20024; (202) 638-5577. Interest in obstetrics and gynecology, maternal and child health, health care delivery. Answers inquiries, provides reference and literature-searching services, publishes and distributes materials, permits onsite use of collection.

10131. American College of Preventive Medicine, 1015 15th St NW, Washington, DC 20005; (202) 789-0003. Promotes academic progs in preventive medicine; advocates cost-effective prevention progs. Publishes newsletter, scholarly materials; answers inquiries; conducts seminars, research. Services provided for a fee.

10132. American Committee for International Conservation, c/o Secretariat, Natural Resources Defense Council, 1350 New York Ave NW, No 300, Washington, DC 20006. Assists and coordinates interests of U.S. orgs in intl wildlife conservation activities such as conservation treaties, parks and reserves, ecological research.

10133. American Committee on East-West Accord, 109 11th St SE, Washington, DC 20003; (202) 546-1700. Seeks to improve East-West (especially U.S.-Soviet) relations. Distributes publications, film; provides inquiry, advisory services; lends materials; provides speakers. Services free, except publications.

10134. American Council for Capital Formation, 1850 K St NW, Ste 520, Washington, DC 20006; (202) 293-5811. Directs public attention to low rate of capital formation in U.S.; advocates response. Publishes newsletter, reports, books; answers inquiries; sponsors meetings, seminars; distributes newsletter. Services free.

10135. American Council for Construction Education, 1015 15th St NW, Ste 700, Washington, DC 20005; (202) 347-5875; (301) 593-7284. Administers a program on accreditation of baccalaureate programs in construction education. Answers inquiries, conducts seminars, distributes publications, makes referrals. Services provided as part of accreditation process.

10136. American Council for University Planning & Academic Excellence, P.O. Box 9478, Washington, DC 20016. Researches educational, academic, administrative needs of univs. Provides inquiry, advisory, ref services; conducts seminars; distributes publications; permits onsite use of resources. Services at cost, only for U.S. residents.

10137. American Council of Independent Laboratories, 1725 K St NW, Washington, DC 20006; (202) 887-5872. Publishes directory of member scientific labs; answers inquiries; conducts seminars, workshops; makes referrals to members. Services free.

10138. American Council of Life Insurance, 1850 K St NW, Washington, DC 20006; (202) 862-4000; (202) 862-4050. Concerned with life and health insurance. Publishes pamphlets, audiovisual materials; provides data tabulations, repros, consulting services; permits onsite use of collection.

10139. American Council of Young Political Leaders, 426 C St NE, Washington, DC 20002; (202) 546-6010. Provides U.S. and foreign young political leaders study

tours. Publishes newsletter, answers inquiries. Services free, available selectively.

10140. American Council of the Blind, 1211 Connecticut Ave NW, Ste 506, Washington, DC 20036; (202) 833-1251. Promotes interests of blind, handicapped persons. Awards college scholarships to the blind. Provides inquiry, advisory, referral services; conducts seminars. Services free.

10141. American Council on Cosmetology Education, 1990 M St NW, Ste 650, Washington, DC 20036; (202) 331-9550. Interest in postsecondary education in cosmetology arts, science. Publishes newsletter, directories; provides inquiry, advisory services; conducts seminars. Most services free or at cost.

10142. American Council on Education, Center for Leadership Development, 1 Dupont Circle NW, Washington, DC 20036; (202) 833-4780. National in-service orientation program for college and univ administrators who deal with responsibilities of academic leadership and decision-making. Conducts meetings and programs for college and univ administrators. Fees are charged.

10143. American Council on Education, Division of Policy Analysis & Research, 1 Dupont Circle NW, Washington, DC 20036; (202) 833-4744. Conducts educational research, compiling computerized data on more than 1.5 million new freshmen entering college annually since 1966. Info files for research purposes on a cost basis.

10144. American Council on Education, Office on Educational Credit & Credentials, 1 Dupont Circle, Washington, DC 20036; (202) 833-4770. Monitors educational credit and credentialing policies for postsecondary education. Answers inquiries, provides advisory services, makes referrals to other sources of info, conducts conference.

10145. American Cultured Dairy Products Institute, 888 16th St NW, Washington, DC 20006; (202) 223-1931. Acts as clearinghouse for technical info related to product development of cultured milk products. Answers inquiries, conducts training, distributes publications. Most services free.

10146. American Educational Research Association, 1230 17th St NW, Washington, DC 20036; (202) 223-9485. Conducts research in any aspect of education. Answers inquiries within limits of time, distributes publications, makes referrals.

10147. American Enterprise Institute for Public Policy Research, 1150 17th St NW, Washington, DC 20036; (202) 862-5800. Fosters research; publishes newsletter, legislative and public opinion analyses, monographs; holds panel discussions, conferences; allows onsite use of collection with permission.

10148. American Epilepsy Society, c/o Charlotte McCutchen, MD, Secty, Dept of Neurology, Washington, DC Veterans Admin Med Ctr, 50 Irving St NW, Washington, DC 20422. Publishes bimonthly journal on epilepsy, including clinical, research aspects; makes referrals; provides short lists of literature citations in response to written inquiries.

10149. American Farmland Trust, 1717 Massachusetts Ave NW, No 601, Washington, DC 20036; (202) 332-0760. Seeks to preserve agricultural land, soil, farming opportunities. Provides inquiry, consulting, referral services; conducts seminars; publishes newsletter, tech reports. Most services free.

10150. American Federation of Government Employees, 80 F St NW, Washington, DC 20001; (202) 737-8700. Answers inquiries on labor organization of govt employees; publishes journal; provides consulting services; prepares analyses. Services to researchers on unionism in govt.

10151. American Federation of Home Health Agencies, 429 N St SW, Ste S-605, Washington, DC 20024; (202) 554-0526. Promotes use of home care services. Publishes monthly newsletter, legislative, regulatory reports; provides inquiry, advisory, consulting, referral services.

10152. American Federation of Police, 1000 Connecticut Ave NW, Ste 9, Washington, DC 20036; (202) 293-9088; Records Ctr: 1100 Northeast 125th St, N Miami, FL 33161 (305) 891-1700. Educational assn of police and sheriffs that seeks civil preparedness for disasters. Has library of printed, AV materials. Answers inquiries, conducts seminars, distributes publications, rents films. Some services free, others for a fee.

10153. American Federation of Teachers, 555 New Jersey Ave NW, Washington, DC 20001; (202) 879-4400. AFL-CIO affiliate concerned with education at all levels, collective bargaining and working conditions for teachers. Publishes newspaper; answers inquiries free for teachers, unionists, educators, and media.

10154. American Film Institute Resource Center, John F. Kennedy Ctr, Washington, DC 20566; (202) 828-4088. Studies history and criticism of film, video, media arts. Library for onsite use. Publishes journal, reference, AV materials; provides inquiry, reference, referral services free, by appt.

10155. American Folklore Society, 1703 New Hampshire Ave NW, Washington, DC 20009; (202) 232-8800. Interest in U.S. folklore, folklife, folk culture. Publishes journal, answers inquiries, distributes publications. Services free, except publications.

10156. American Foreign Policy Institute, 499 S Capitol St, Ste 500, Washington, DC 20003; (202) 484-1676. Interest in defense-related foreign policy issues. Publishes special studies and undertakes studies for sponsors, provides consulting services, conducts seminars. Services normally provided at cost.

10157. American Forest Council, 1250 Connecticut Ave NW, Suite 320, Washington, DC 20036; (202) 463-2455. Publishes bibliography of teaching aids, reviews; provides reference, consulting services; sells films, slides; permits onsite reference to forestry statistics, natl tree farm records.

10158. American Forestry Association, 1319 18th St NW, Washington, DC 20036; (202) 467-5810. Publishes journal, reports, pamphlets related to forestry, books on tree identification. Answers inquiries, makes referrals to other source of info, permits onsite use of collection.

10159. American Genetic Association, 818 18th St NW, Washington, DC 20006; (202) 659-2096. Publishes journal, acts as clearinghouse for info on heredity. Photos in journal for use in illustrating textbooks. Reference service free to members.

10160. American Geophysical Union, 2000 Florida Ave NW, Washington, DC 20009; (202) 462-6903. Concerned with theoretical, applied sciences dealing with earth. Publishes research journals, monographs, translations; answers inquiries; sponsors conferences.

10161. American Health Care Association, Department of Research & Education, 1200 15th St NW, Washington, DC 20005; (202) 833-2050. Represents long-term health care facilities before Congress, fed regulatory agencies, and other professional and trade associations. Publishes journal, answers inquiries, provides advisory services, conducts seminars, distributes publications. Services free.

10162. American Health Planning Association, 1110 Vermont Ave NW, Ste 950, Washington, DC 20005; (202) 861-1200. Supports health planning activities across the country and represents their interests to Congress, the Administration, and other groups and orgs. Provides general reference services. Most services free to member agencies; nominal charges to other groups.

10163. American Hiking Society, 1701 18th St NW, Washington, DC 20009; (202) 234-4609. Promotes walking, interests of hikers, footpath maintenance, related research. Maintains file on trails, clubs, publications. Answers inquiries; conducts seminars, workshops. Services free.

10164. American Historic & Cultural Society, Honor America Program, 926 Natl Press Bldg, Washington, DC 20045; (202) 628-7481 or 628-3400. Sponsors educational programs to honor American values of citizenship and the national heritage. Creates educational and historical feature material for the media. Services free.

10165. American Home Economics Association, Public Relations Dept, 2010 Massachusetts Ave NW, Washington, DC 20036; (202) 862-8300. Seeks to improve quality and standards of individual and family life through education, research, cooperative programs, and public info. Answers inquiries, provides consulting and reference services, primarily for assn members.

10166. American Horse Council, 1700 K St NW, Washington, DC 20006; (202) 296-4031. Dedicated to development of American equine industry. Interest in all aspects of horse ownership and use. Provides general reference services, sells publications, permits limited onsite use of collection.

10167. American Horse Protection Association, P.O. Box 53399 (1902-B T St NW), Washington, DC 20009; (202) 745-0611. Dedicated to the welfare of horses, both wild and domestic. Publishes newsletter; answers inquiries; provides advisory, consulting, and reference services; distributes publications. Services free.

10168. American Hot Dip Galvanizers Association, 1101 Connecticut Ave NW, Ste 700, Washington, DC 20036; (202) 857-1119. Promotes use of products hot dip galvanized after fabrication. Conducts seminars; publishes reports, standards and specifications; sells repros; provides free reference service.

10169. American Institute for Conservation of Historic & Artistic Works, c/o Martha Morales, Exec Secty, 3545 Williamsburg Lane NW, Washington, DC 20008; (202) 364-1036. Nonprofit professional org seeking to maintain high standards among conservators of historic and artistic works. Answers inquiries, distributes list of certified paper conservators, makes referrals. Services free to members, for a fee to others.

10170. American Institute of Architects, 1735 New York Ave NW, Washington, DC 20006; (202) 626-7300. Answers inquiries on architecture; publishes magazines, specifications, technical reports, proceedings; provides reference, copying services; permits onsite use of collection.

10171. American Institute of Biological Sciences, 730 11th St NW, Washington, DC 20001; (202) 628-1500. Studies all aspects of biological sciences, including biological education. Answers inquiries, provides consulting services and career info.

10172. American Institute of Cooperation, 1800 Massachusetts Ave NW, Ste 508, Washington, DC 20036; (202) 296-6825. Educational assn of farmer cooperatives in U.S. Publishes newsletter, answers inquiries, sponsors conferences.

10173. American Institute of Homeopathy, 1500 Massachusetts Ave NW, Ste 41, Washington, DC 20005; (202) 223-6182. Interest in homeopathy and homeopathic therapeutics. Publishes journal; provides consulting, reference, translating, document services; owns collection of books, reports.

10174. American Institute of Merchant Shipping, 1625 K St NW, Ste 1000, Washington, DC 20006; (202) 783-6440. Answers inquiries on world shipping industry; publishes annual report, newsletter, reprints of govt documents, bulletins; permits onsite reference by request.

10176. American International Automobile Dealers Association, 1128 16th St NW, Washington, DC 20036; (202) 775-0761. Interest in impact of imported automobile industry in U.S., trade legislation, proposals affecting imported auto industry. Answers inquiries.

10177. American Iron & Steel Institute, 1000 16th St NW, Washington, DC 20036; (202) 452-7100. Promotes iron and steel industry. Publishes reports, referral materials; answers inquiries; conducts seminars. Services generally free.

10178. American Maritime Association, 1211 Connecticut Ave NW, Ste 414, Washington, DC 20036; (202) 833-8864. Serves interests of unsubsidized U.S. flag ships in merchant marine. Prepares congressional testimony, research papers; presents legal briefs; answers inquiries. Services free.

10179. American Meat Institute, P.O. Box 3556 (1700 N Moore St, Ste 1600; Arlington, VA), Washington, DC 20007; (703) 841-2400. Publishes newsletter, reports, conference proceedings, statistical summaries; answers inquiries; conducts seminars. Services generally free.

10180. American Mining Congress, 1920 N St NW, Ste 300, Washington, DC 20036; (202) 861-2800. Interest in mining and mineral processing operations, including govt regulation, modernization, economics, environmental quality, safety. Provides general reference services, permits onsite use of collection. Special reports provided to members.

10181. American National Metric Council, 1010 Vermont Ave NW, Ste 320-21, Washington, DC 20005; (202) 628-5757. Serves private sector as a planning, coordinating, and info center for metric activities and developing conversion plans. Answers inquiries, publishes a monthly, conducts conferences, and distributes publications.

10182. American Near East Refugee Aid, 1522 K St NW, No 202, Washington, DC 20005; (202) 347-2558. Interest in economic aid; health assistance; educational, social development; refugee aid in the West Bank, Gaza Strip, Lebanon. Publishes newsletter. Answers inquiries. Services mostly free.

10183. American Newspaper Publishers Association Library, P.O. Box 17407, Dulles Airport (11600 Sunrise Valley Dr, Reston, VA), Washington, DC 20041; (703) 648-1000. Interest in newspaper publishing, freedom of the press, journalism, etc. Provides general reference services, makes interlibrary loans, permits onsite use of collections. Services free and primarily for ANPA members and newspaper librarians.

10184. American Newspaper Publishers Association, Technical Research Department, P.O. Box 17407, Dulles Intl Airport (11600 Sunrise Valley Dr, Reston, VA), Washington, DC 20041; (703) 648-1000. Owns project records, standards and specifications, films, photos, abstracts; publishes research reports; answers inquiries; provides consulting services to members for a fee.

10185. American Ornithologists' Union, c/o Natl Museum of Natural History, Smithsonian Institution, Washington, DC 20560; (202) 357-2051. Seeks to advance and improve the science of ornithology. Conducts seminars and workshops, distributes publications. Services provided at cost.

10186. American Patent Research Corp., 1377 K St NW, No 400, Washington, DC 20005; (202) 628-4332. Commercial org interested in inventions, inventors, patents, marketing. Maintains natl data base for invention licensing, followup legal work. Provides consulting, referral services on percentage or cost-sharing basis.

10187. American Petroleum Institute, 1220 L St NW, Washington, DC 20005; (202) 682-8000. Answers inquiries free; provides repro services for a fee; publishes petroleum data book, statistical bulletins, reports; permits onsite use of collection.

10188. American Pharmaceutical Association, 2215 Constitution Ave NW, Washington, DC 20037; (202) 628-4410. Interest in pharmacy student education, health sciences education, health team development, manpower programs, integration of services. Provides general reference services, distributes data compilations. Fees vary with services rendered.

10190. American Planning Association, 1776 Massachusetts Ave NW, Washington, DC 20036; (202) 872-0611. Interest in planning at all levels of govt. Conducts research; publishes journals, books; answers questions on field of comprehensive planning; makes referrals.

10191. American Podiatric Medical Association, 20 Chevy Chase Circle, Washington, DC 20015; (202) 537-4900. Provides info on foot health, education in podiatry, data on fed and state laws and insurance. Answers inquiries.

10192. American Psychiatric Association, Div of Public Affairs, 1400 K St NW, Washington, DC 20005; (202) 682-6000. Sponsors medical education for psychiatrists; promotes prevention of mental illness; advances standards of treatment; publishes journals, books, reports; supplies repros for a fee.

10193. American Public Health Association, 1015 15th St NW, Washington, DC 20005; (202) 789-5600. Studies public health aspects of dental health, environment, epidemiology, food and nutrition, gerontological health and administration. Provides consulting and reference services.

10194. American Public Health Association, Clearinghouse on Infant Feeding & Maternal Nutrition, Intl Health Programs, 1015 15th St NW, Washington, DC 20005; (202) 789-5600. Promotes improved nutrition for mothers, infants in Third World; breast feeding. Has collection of documents (for onsite use); provides inquiry, referral services. Services free, except copying.

10195. American Public Power Association, 2301 M St NW, Washington, DC 20037; (202) 775-8300. Answers inquiries on planning, construction, operation of municipally owned electric systems; publishes journal, newsletter, safety manual; provides consulting service.

10196. American Public Transit Association, 1225 Connecticut Ave NW, Washington, DC 20036; (202) 828-2800. Disseminates general info on transit industry to public; publishes annual fact book; permits onsite reference to files by qualified persons; provides inquiry service for members.

10197. American Public Welfare Association, 1125 15th St NW, Washington, DC 20005; (202) 293-7550. Conducts policy analysis in income maintenance, social services, medicaid, and food stamps. Answers inquiries; provides consulting, abstracting and indexing services; conducts seminars; distributes publications. Some services at cost.

10198. American Pulpwood Association, 1619 Massachusetts Ave NW, Washington, DC 20036; (202) 265-0670. Publishes reports, safety guides, statistical reviews, training guides, film directory; answers inquiries; provides consulting services to subscribers; holds regional meetings.

10199. American Railway Engineering Association, 2000 L St NW, Ste 403, Washington, DC 20036; (202) 835-9336. Advances scientific, economical mgmt of railroads. Publishes bulletins, manuals, tech reports, reference materials; answers inquiries. Services free, except some publications.

10200. American Recreation Coalition, 1901 L St NW, Ste 700, Washington, DC 20036; (202) 466-6870. Interest in recreation program mgmt, funding, policy. Answers inquiries, provides reference services, evaluates data, conducts seminars and workshops, distributes publications. Fee for some services.

10201. American Red Cross Blood Services, 17th and D Sts NW, Washington, DC 20006; (202) 857-3413. Promotes integrated, nonprofit blood supply for U.S. using only volunteer donors; regional blood services; basic, applied blood research. Provides inquiry and referral services, generally free.

10202. American Red Cross Library, 17th and D St NW, Washington, DC 20006; (202) 857-3491. Furnishes volunteer aid to the armed forces and victims of war and provides national and intl relief to mitigate suffering caused by natural disasters. Answers inquiries, provides reference services, makes referrals. Services primarily for staff, students, scholars, and writers.

10203. American Rivers Conservation Council, 322 Fourth St NE, Washington, DC 20002; (202) 547-6900. Natl org dedicated to preservation of America's wild, scenic rivers. Publishes newsletter; provides inquiry, advisory services; conducts seminars. Services free to members, small donation requested of others..

10204. American Road & Transportation Builders Association, 525 School St SW, Washington, DC 20024; (202) 488-2722. Seeks improvement of transportation systems in U.S. Answers inquiries without charge unless extensive services required, makes referrals to other sources of info.

10205. American Running & Fitness Association, 2420 K St NW, Washington, DC 20037; (202) 965-3430. Promotes physical fitness through running, athletics, and preventive medicine. Answers inquiries, provides reference services, conducts seminars, distributes publications, makes referrals. Services free to members.

10206. American Seed Research Foundation, 1030 15th St NW, Ste 964, Washington, DC 20005; (202) 223-4080. Publishes technical reports on basic research on seed physiology, provides info on research in progress. Services free to contributors, at cost to others.

10207. American Seed Trade Association, 1030 15th St NW, Ste 964, Washington, DC 20005; (202) 223-4080. Promotes business interests of the seed industry. Publishes (and sells) newsletter, yearbook, conference proceedings. Answers inquiries, conducts seminars. Services free.

10208. American Short Line Railroad Association, 2000 Massachusetts Ave NW, Washington, DC 20036; (202) 785-2250. Interest in rail transportation short lines. Provides general reference and consulting services, permits onsite use of collection. Services generally only to members and govt.

10209. American Ski Federation, 499 S Capitol St, Ste 406, Washington, DC 20003; (202) 484-6260. Represents ski industry. Publishes newsletter; provides inquiry, advisory, referral services; conducts seminars. Services free, except seminars and publications.

10210. American Society & Academy of Microbiology, 1913 Eye St NW, Washington, DC 20006; (202) 833-9680. Professional, nonprofit component of ASM concerned with professional standards and conduct and public understanding of the profession of microbiology. Provides free general reference services.

10211. American Society for Engineering Education, 11 Dupont Circle NW, Ste 200, Washington, DC 20036; (202) 293-7080. Publishes journals, monographs, reports, case studies on education for engineering; answers inquiries; provides consulting services; permits onsite use of collection.

10212. American Society for Information Science, 1010 16th St NW, Washington, DC 20036; (202) 659-3644. Provides reference, career info, consulting services on info science; publishes journals, monographs; provides repros for a fee.

10213. American Society for Microbiology, 1913 Eye St NW, Washington, DC 20006; (202) 833-9680. Promotes knowledge of microbiology. Monitors govt policies; publishes nine journals, books, pamphlets, abstracts; provides documents on request for minimal charge.

10214. American Society for Training & Development, 600 Maryland Ave SW, Ste 305, Washington, DC 20024; (202) 484-2390. Devoted to expansion of skills and standards of professionals in training and human resource development. Answers inquiries, provides ad-

visory and reference services, conducts seminars, distributes publications. Services free to members.

10215. American Society of Allied Health Professions, 1 Dupont Circle NW, Ste 300, Washington, DC 20036; (202) 293-3422. Interest in all aspects of allied health education and service delivery, including advocacy for the handicapped. Provides general reference services, some career info. Fees may be charged for consulting services.

10216. American Society of Appraisers, c/o Paul L. O'Brien, Exec Dir, P.O. Box 17265, (11800 Sunrise Valley Dr, Reston, VA) Washington, DC 20041; (703) 620-3838. Answers inquiries on valuation, appraisals, and estimating; publishes journal, appraisal manual; provides consulting, reference, literature-searching services; conducts seminars.

10217. American Society of Association Executives, 1575 Eye St NW, Washington, DC 20005; (202) 626-2723. Professional society for those who manage trade, educational, technical, business, and professional associations and societies. Serves as clearinghouse for info on assn mgmt; answers inquiries; provides advisory and reference services; conducts seminars; sells publications.

10218. American Society of Electroplated Plastics, 1133 15th St NW, Washington, DC 20005; (202) 429-9440. Interest in electroplated plastics, electromagnetic interference, electronic shielding. Publishes a bulletin, answers inquiries, makes referrals.

10219. American Society of Internal Medicine, c/o William R. Ramsey, Exec V.P., 1101 Vermont Ave NW, Ste 500, Washington, DC 20005; (202) 289-1700. Interest in socioeconomic aspects of health care, including improved modes of payment, improved means of care delivery, etc. Provides general reference services free within limitation of time and staff, distributes publications free to members only.

10220. American Society of International Law Library, 2223 Massachusetts Ave NW, Washington, DC 20008; (202) 265-4313. Interest in public intl law. Provides duplication services for a fee, makes interlibrary loans. Library open to public.

10221. American Society of Landscape Architects, 1733 Connecticut Ave NW, Washington, DC 20009; (202) 466-7730. Promotes landscape architecture, environmental planning, education and skill in the art as a part of public welfare. Answers inquiries, provides consulting, reference and employment services. Manages the Landscape Architecture Foundation. Services primarily for those in the profession.

10222. American Society of Notaries, 810 18th St NW, Washington, DC 20006; (202) 347-7303. Interest in law relating to notary publics. Answers inquiries, makes interlibrary loans, publishes and distributes materials, permits onsite use of collection. Services generally free.

10223. American Society of Travel Agents, 4400 MacArthur Blvd NW, Washington, DC 20007; (202) 965-7520; W Coast Regional Off: 4420 Hotel Circle Ct, Ste 230; San Diego, CA 92108; (619) 298-5065). Promotes travel agency industry, safeguards public against fraud, encourages worldwide tourism. Answers inquiries, handles complaints, provides reference services, conducts seminars, distributes publications, makes referrals. Some services free.

10224. American Sociological Association, 1722 N St NW, Washington, DC 20036; (202) 833-3410. Encourages cooperative relations among persons engaged in scientific study of society; publishes magazines on sociology, teaching newsletter; answers inquiries; makes referrals.

10225. American Statistical Association, 806 15th St NW, Washington, DC 20005; (202) 393-3253. Source of data on statistics and statistical applications in economics, engineering, and physical, biological, and social sciences. Answers inquiries, publishes monthly, distributes publications.

10226. American Symphony Orchestra League, Orchestra Services Div, 633 E St NW, Washington, DC 20004; (202) 628-0099. Represents, promotes symphonies and symphonic music. Publishes magazine, reference materials; provides inquiry, advisory, technical assistance and referral services; conducts seminars, workshops. Some services free to all; fees, restrictions for others.

10227. American Textile Manufacturers Institute, 1101 Connecticut Ave NW, Ste 300, Washington, DC 20036; (202) 862-0500. Publishes reports, news releases on textile manufacturing; answers inquiries; provides reference services. Services to nonmembers limited according to time and effort required.

10228. American Veterans Committee, 17171 Massachusetts Ave NW, Washington, DC 20036; (202) 639-8886. Acts as a watchdog in veteran and military affairs; is active in World Veterans Federation. Publishes a quarterly, answers inquiries, conducts seminars, distributes publications, and makes referrals. Most services free.

10229. American Wire Producers Association, 1101 Connecticut Ave NW, Ste 700, Washington, DC 20036; (202) 857-1155. Interest in statistics regarding import/export of wire and wire rod, trade legislation, regulations, U.S. Trade Representative negotiations. Answers inquiries. Statistics and membership lists to members only.

10230. American Youth Hostels, 1332 Eye St NW, Ste 800, Washington, DC 20005; (202) 783-6161. Interest in low-cost accommodations, travel, and transportation in U.S. and abroad. Answers inquiries, distributes publications, plans trips, offers training courses, distributes ID card and handbook.

10231. American Youth Work Center, 1522 Connecticut Ave NW, 4th Floor, Washington, DC 20036; (202) 785-0764. Org for youth service agencies and workers committed to helping communities develop services for youth that encourage their participation. Answers inquiries, provides consulting and reference services, makes referrals, organizes exchange programs.

10232. Americans for Democratic Action, 1411 K St NW, Ste 850, Washington, DC 20005; (202) 638-6447. Liberal political org committed to progressive social change. Campaigns for liberal candidates and conducts lobbying on domestic and foreign policy issues. Publishes newsletter, answers inquiries, conducts seminars, distributes publications. Most services free.

10233. Americans for Energy Independence, 1629 K St NW, Washington, DC 20006; (202) 466-2105. Nonprofit coalition for effective natl energy policies, energy supply measures. Publications list available. Answers inquiries; conducts workshops; presents radio prog. Most services free.

10234. Americans for Indian Opportunity, 1010 Massachusetts Ave NW, Ste 200, Washington, DC 20001; (202) 371-1280. Advocacy group for U.S. Indian tribes and individuals. Interest in Indians, economic and resources development, justice, and education. Provides general reference services, conducts seminars, publishes and distributes materials. Technical assistance is provided to Indian people only.

10235. Animal Damage Control Program, Fish and Wildlife Service, Dept of the Interior, Washington, DC 20240; (202) 632-7463. Publishes reports, info circulars, brochures, articles on animal damage control; answers inquiries; provides consulting services, technical planning assistance to other agencies.

10236. Animal Welfare Institute, P.O. Box 3650, Georgetown Station (1686 34th St NW), Washington, DC 20007; (202) 337-2332. Concerned with humane treatment of laboratory animals, marine mammals, and endangered species. Answers inquiries and provides consulting services, distributes manuals free.

10237. Antarctica Project, 624 Ninth St NW, Ste 500, Washington, DC 20001; (202) 737-3600. Promotes conservation of Antarctic thru educational progs. Holds AV materials; publications list available. Answers inquiries, provides reference services, conducts workshops. Fee for some services.

10238. Antitrust Division, Dept of Justice, 10th St and Constitution Ave, Washington, DC 20530; (202) 633-2401, 633-2481. Enforces corporate compliance with antitrust legislation. Answers inquiries, makes referrals, conducts seminars.

10239. Appalachian Regional Commission, 1666 Connecticut Ave NW, Washington, DC 20235; (202) 673-7893. Concerned with issues affecting Appalachia, including: hwy and other transportation, public health, education, libraries, housing, energy, the environment. Answers inquiries, makes referrals, provides technical assistance and consulting services to Appalachian states.

10240. Appropriate Technology Program, State and Local Assistance Programs, Off of Asst Secty for Conservation and Renewable Energy, U.S. Dept. of Energy, 1000 Independence Ave SW, Washington, DC 20585; (202) 252-9104. Interest in renewable energy, energy conservation. Publishes tech reports, R&D summaries, data compilations; answers inquiries; conducts seminars. Services free.

10241. Architectural & Transportation Barriers Compliance Board, Switzer Bldg, Rm 1010, 330 C St SW, Washington, DC 20202; (202) 245-1591. Deals with physical access problems in fed facilities. Maintains library, publishes reference materials, answers inquiries, provides some technical services, conducts seminars and workshops. Services free.

10242. Armed Forces Institute of Pathology, 14th St and Alaska Ave NW, Washington, DC 20306; (202) 576-2934. Joint agency of Army, Navy, and Air Force under mgmt of Surgeon General of the Army, concerned with all aspects of pathology. Answers inquiries, provides consulting services, conducts course, lends materials. Services primarily for pathologists. Medical Museum is open daily.

10243. Arms Control & Foreign Policy Caucus, 501 House Annex 2, Washington, DC 20515; (202) 226-3440. Bipartisan group of members of U.S. Senate and House of Representatives concerned with foreign and military policy. Open to any member seeking world peace, intl cooperation, and arms control through legislative action. Answers inquiries and makes referrals.

10244. Arms Control Association, 11 Dupont Circle NW, Ste 900, Washington, DC 20036; (202) 797-6450. Nonpartisan national org dedicated to promoting public understanding of effective policies and programs in arms control and disarmament. Provides general reference services free, except copying and publications.

10245. Army Corps of Engineers, Public Affairs, Dept of the Army, Rm 8137, 20 Massachusetts, Ave NW, Washington, DC 20314; (202) 272-0011. Serves as liaison between Corps and the public. Provides general reference services; distributes publications; provides info on current civil works projects, permit requirements, etc.

10246. Army Institute of Dental Research, Walter Reed Army Medical Ctr, Washington, DC 20307; (202) 576-3116. Interest in dental research, excluding caries and cancer. Special projects include wound healing, biodegradable bandages, drug delivery, bacterial identification, preventive dentistry, etc. Answers inquiries, provides consulting services, provides reprints of published articles.

10247. Army Joint Medical Library, Off of the Surgeons General, Pentagon, Rm 1B-473, Washington, DC 20310; (202) 695-5752. Library with holdings covering medical specialties, medical personnel, hospital administration, nursing, public health, military medical history. Answers inquiries, provides reference services, makes referrals.

10248. Arrow, Inc. Foundation, 1000 Connecticut Ave NW, Ste 401, Washington, DC 20036; (202) 296-0685. Seeks improvement of the lives of American Indians at the reservation level, embracing direct aid, education, health, and training. Answers inquiries.

10249. Artists Equity Association, Inc., P.O. Box 28068, Central Station (920 F St NW), Washington, DC 20038; (202) 628-9633. Natl, nonprofit, esthetically nonpartisan org for visual artists. Strives for economic, social, and legislative change that benefits artists. Answers inquiries, provides consulting, conducts seminars, distributes publications, makes referrals. Services free to members.

10250. Assistant Secretary for Trade Development, Dept of Commerce, 14th St and Constitution Ave NW, Rm 1104, Washington, DC 20230; (202) 566-6767. Investigates economics of service industries, retail and whholesale trade, personal and business services, business crime, and franchising. Answers inquiries, provides advisory and reference services, conducts seminars, distributes publications. Services free.

10251. Associate Administrator for Airports, Fed Aviation Admin, ARP-1, 800 Independence Ave SW, Washington, DC 20591; (202) 755-9471. Administers airport planning and development grant programs and certifies airports for safety purposes. Answers inquiries, makes referrals, provides technical advice.

10252. Associated General Contractors of America, 1957 E St NW, Washington, DC 20006; (202) 393-2040. Concerned with building, highway, municipal, utilities, and industrial construction. Publishes monthly journal, weekly newsletter; answers inquiries, makes referrals.

10253. Associated Pharmacologists & Toxicologists, 5510 16th St NW, Washington, DC 20011; (202) 882-3811. Interest in pharmacology, toxicology (especially applied). Publishes scholarly materials; provides inquiry, advisory, referral services; conducts seminars. Services provided on a sliding-scale fee.

10254. Associated Publishers, Inc., 1401 14th St NW, Washington, DC 20005; (202) 667-2822. Studies Afro-American life and history, role of Afro-American in American history, economic and social aspects of Afro-American in the modern world. Provides info primarily through its publications, most for sale.

10255. Associates for Renewal in Education, Inc., Edmonds School Bldg, 9th and D Sts NE, Washington, DC 20002; (202) 547-8030. Provides training and education programs targeted to various groups. Interest in teens, senior citizens, community development. Provides general reference services, conducts workshops, distributes publications, permits onsite use of collection. Services free, except workshops.

10256. Association for Educational Communications & Technology, 1126 16th St NW, Washington, DC 20036; (202) 466-4780. Professional org composed of educators and others concerned with learning process and instructional technology. Provides general reference and consulting services, primarily to members; sponsors annual convention.

10257. Association for Educational Data Systems, 1201 16th St NW, Washington, DC 20036; (202) 822-7845. Studies impact of the computer and related processes on the field of education. Answers inquiries, makes referrals, conducts workshops and annual convention.

10258. Association for Gerontology in Higher Education, 600 Maryland Ave SW, W Wing 204, Washington, DC 20024; (202) 484-7505. Promotes gerontology as field in higher education. Publishes newsletter, reference materials; provides inquiry, advisory, referral services; conducts seminars, conferences. Most services free.

10259. Association for Hospital Medical Education, 1101 Connecticut Ave NW, No 700, Washington, DC 20036; (202) 857-1196. Nonprofit org that promotes sound programs of medical education in teaching hospitals. Monitors legislation affecting medical education, etc. Provides general reference services, conducts seminars, distributes publications. Services free, except seminars and consulting.

10260. Association for Recorded Sound Collections, P.O. Box 75082, Washington, DC 20013; (703) 684-8244. Serves scholars, collectors interested in recorded sound. Working on data base on commercial disc recordings, 1894 to mid-1950's. Publishes newsletter, journal, reference materials; provides inquiry, referral services to members.

10261. Association for Women in Science, 2401 Virginia Ave NW, Ste 303, Washington, DC 20037; (202) 833-1998. Concerned with women in science, career development, affirmative action for women, sexism, and legislation. Publishes newsletter, answers inquiries, provides consulting and reference services, operates registry service for employers, makes referrals for jobs and speakers.

10262. Association for Workplace Democracy, 1747 Connecticut Ave NW, Washington, DC 20009; (202) 265-7727. Promotes democratic ownership, mgmt of enterprises. Publishes research, provides inquiry and referral services, sponsors conferences. Services mostly for members, some to others.

10263. Association for the Advancement of Psychology, 1200 17th St NW, Ste 400, Washington, DC 20036; (202) 466-5757. Works toward increased govt support in education, training, and use of psychological manpower. Answers inquiries, publishes a monthly legislative summary, provides reference services, makes referrals to other sources of info.

10264. Association for the Care of Children's Health, 3615 Wisconsin Ave NW, Washington, DC 20016; (202) 244-1801. Interest in social and emotional aspects of pediatric care of children in hospitals, clinics, and the community. Provides free general reference services, charge for publications and conferences.

10265. Association for the Study of Afro-American Life and History, 1401 14th St NW, Washington, DC 20005; (202) 667-2822. Publishes journal, bulletin on black history; owns books, journals, photos, display materials, correspondence, maps, charts, data compilations; makes referrals to other sources.

10266. Association of Academic Health Centers, 11 Dupont Circle NW, Ste 210, Washington, DC 20036; (202) 265-9600. Provides interdisciplinary focus on total health manpower education. Answers inquiries, provides advisory services, conducts seminars, distributes publications, makes referrals. Services free to specialists in the field.

10267. Association of American Chambers of Commerce in Latin America, 1615 H St NW, Washington, DC 20062; (202) 463-5485. Interest in U.S.-Latin American trade, investment, policies, private enterprise. Provides inquiry and referral services, conducts seminars, evaluates data, distributes publication. Services free.

10268. Association of American Geographers, 1710 16th St NW, Washington, DC 20009; (202) 234-1450. Publishes geography journals, monographs, reports, maps; serves as channel for acquisition of geographic journals through exchange program with foreign countries.

10270. Association of American Law Schools, 1 Dupont Circle NW, Ste 370, Washington, DC 20036; (202) 296-8851. Interest in legal education. Answers inquiries, distributes publications, permits onsite use of collection. Computer-based info provided for a fee; other services free, except publications.

10271. Association of American Medical Colleges, 1 Dupont Circle NW, Ste 200, Washington, DC 20036; (202) 828-0400. Advances medical education, research by publishing journal, reports, bibliographies, surveys, books; provides consulting services; permits onsite use of collection by researchers.

10272. Association of American Railroads, 50 F St NW, Washington, DC 20001; (202) 639-2300. Acts as link among public, press, and broadcast media, and others interested in railroad industry. Answers inquiries, provides reference services, distributes publications, makes referrals. Services free.

10274. Association of American Railroads, Hazardous Materials Section, 50 F St NW, Washington, DC 20001; (202) 639-2232. Publishes standards, specifications, info on emergency handling of hazardous materials; provides free consulting, reference services. Extensive research provided at nominal rate.

10275. Association of American Railroads, Research & Test Department, 50 F St NW, Washington, DC 20001; (202) 639-2100. Conducts research pertaining to problems of rail carriers and analysis and study of all phases of rail transportation. Answers inquiries, provides consulting and reference services.

10276. Association of Bank Holding Companies, 730 15th St NW, Rm 820, Washington, DC 20005; (202) 393-1158. Assn of companies registered with Fed Reserve Board. Publishes bibliographies of bank holding company references, state bank holding company statutes; answers inquiries.

10277. Association of Catholic Colleges & Universities, Natl Catholic Educational Assn, 1 Dupont Circle, Ste 650, Washington, DC 20036; (202) 293-5954. Facilitates exchange among, and represents, Catholic institutions of higher education. Publishes newsletter and journal, provides inquiry and advisory services, conducts seminars. Services free.

10278. Association of Collegiate Schools of Architecture, 1735 New York Ave NW, Washington, DC 20006; (202) 785-2324. Advances architectural education. Interest in architecture, including credentials in design professions, curriculum statistics, intl liaisons. Answers inquiries, provides reference services, sells some publications.

10279. Association of Federal Investigators, 1612 K St NW, Ste 202, Washington, DC 20006; (202) 466-7288. Interest in investigation, law enforcement, security activities in fed govt. Publishes newsletter, journal; conducts seminars (for a fee); testifies on legislative matters.

10280. Association of Former Members of Congress, 1755 Massachusetts Ave NW, Washington, DC 20036; (202) 332-3532. Conducts Congressional Fellow programs, promotes legislative exchanges, liaison services for foreign leaders, publishes comparative studies. Provides some reference services. Services primarily for former members of Congress.

10281. Association of Governing Boards of Universities and Colleges, 1 Dupont Circle, Ste 400, Washington, DC 20036; (202) 296-8400. Publishes monthly newsletter, bimonthly journal, brochure; responds to inquiries on matters of trusteeship and governance in higher education. Preference given to members.

10282. Association of Jesuit Colleges & Universities, 1424 16th St NW, Ste 300, Washington, DC 20036; (202) 667-3889. Represents Jesuit colleges, univs; provides communications network; coordinates special projects. Publishes newsletter, referral materials; provides inquiry, referral services at cost.

10283. Association of Maximum Service Telecasters, 1735 DeSales St NW, Ste 400, Washington, DC 20036; (202) 347-5412. Interest in television, including interference, service coverage, and allocations; spectrum mgmt, etc. Answers inquiries, distributes publications, makes referrals to other sources of info. Fees charged on an individual basis.

10284. Association of Oil Pipe Lines, 1725 K St NW, Ste 1205, Washington, DC 20006; (202) 331-8228. Works with other assns and legislators on legislative, regulatory matters affecting oil pipeline industry. Publishes annotated bibliography, answers inquiries free.

10285. Association of Petroleum Re-refiners, 2025 Pennsylvania Ave NW, Ste 1111, Washington, DC 20006; (202) 833-2694. Intl assn of companies that re-refine, reclaim, process, supply petroleum. Answers inquiries; conducts seminars, intl conferences; distributes publications. Most services free.

10286. Association of Research Libraries, Center for Chinese Research Materials, 1527 New Hampshire Ave NW, Washington, DC 20036; (202) 387-7172. Center for info on contemporary Chinese studies: history, literature, politics, economics, sociology, philosophy, business, and trade. Answers inquiries, provides consulting and reference services, makes referrals. Most material is in Chinese for academicians, libraries, and fed agencies.

10287. Association of Research Libraries, Systems & Procedures Exchange Center, Off of Mgmt Studies, 1527 New Hampshire Ave NW, Washington, DC 20036; (202) 232-8656. Interest in library mgmt and operation. Provides general reference and on-demand survey services, lends materials. Services provided free or at cost to member institutions, on a cost-plus basis to others.

10288. Association of Science-Technology Centers, 1413 K St NW, 10th Fl, Washington, DC 20005-3405; (202) 371-1171. Engages in natl projects to advance public understanding of science. Provides general reference services free to members, at cost to others.

10289. Association of State & Territorial Solid Waste Management Officials, 44 N Capitol St, Rm 343, Washington, DC 20001; (202) 624-5828. Surveys state needs in solid waste mgmt programs, legislation. Publishes data compilations, reports; answers inquiries; provides free referral services.

10290. Association of Trial Lawyers of America, 1050 31st St NW, Washington, DC 20007; (202) 965-3500. Interest in torts; environmental, criminal, railroad, aviation, maritime law. Provides general reference services, sponsors the National College of Advocacy. Services free, or at variable cost. Priority given to members, legal profession.

10291: Association of Trial Lawyers of America, Products Liability--Medical Malpractice Exchange, 1050 31st St NW, Washington, DC 20007; (202) 965-3500. Provides medical, technical, and legal references for use by member attorneys representing plaintiffs in products liability and medical negligence actions. Service provided on a fee basis, only to ATLA members.

10292. Association of the Wall & Ceiling Industries, 25 K St NE, Ste 300, Washington, DC 20002; (202) 783-2924. Sponsors a foundation and research library on painting, plastering, drywall, lathing, and other wall structures. Publishes newsletter, answers inquiries, provides consulting and reference services, conducts workshops, and distributes publications. Services free.

10293. Association on Third World Affairs, 1712 Corcoran St NW, Washington, DC 20009; (202) 265-7929. Interest in Third World economic, political, social issues. Publishes newsletter; provides inquiry, advisory, reference, translation services; conducts seminars. Some services free, some at cost.

10294. Association to Unite the Democracies, Inc., P.O. Box 75920 (313 E Street NE), Washington, DC 20002; (202) 544-5150. Dedicated to supporting creation of an intl fed union of democratic nations. Provides general reference services, conducts seminars, distributes publications, permits onsite use of collection.

10295. Asthma & Allergy Foundation of America, 1302 18th St NW, Ste 303, Washington, DC 20036; (202) 293-2950. Studies public health and medical educational aspects of allergic disease, ranging from asthma to insect stings. Answers inquiries, provides consulting and reference services, assists in chapter development.

10296. Atlantic Council of the U.S., 1616 H St NW, Washington, DC 20006; (202) 347-9353. Bipartisan, nonprofit org formulating recommendations affecting members of the Atlantic Community, Australia, and Japan. Distributes publications at cost and permits onsite use of library.

10297. Atlantic States Marine Fisheries Commission, 1717 Massachusetts Ave NW, Ste 703, Washington, DC 20036; (202) 387-5330. Represents 15 Atlantic Seaboard states and administers Interstate Fisheries Management Program. Publishes reports and provides reference services.

10298. Automotive Dismantlers and Recyclers Association, 1133 15th St NW, Ste 1100, Washington, DC 20005; (202) 429-9440. Offers info to improve business systems of companies recycling used automotive parts, scrap metal. Publishes journal, provides consulting services. Services to nonmembers limited.

10299. Aviation & Fire Management Staff, Forest Service, USDA, Washington, DC 20250. Investigates forest wildfire mgmt techniques, crew organizations, plans and training, aircraft and ground equipment. Answers inquiries, distributes publications, makes referrals.

10302. Baptist World Alliance, 1628 16th St NW, Washington, DC 20009; (202) 265-5027. Offers fellowship and assistance in evangelism, education, financial aid, and communication among Baptists of the world. Provides disaster relief, answers inquiries, provides reference services, distributes data compilations, makes referrals. Services free.

10303. Barrier Islands Coalition, c/o Natl Wildlife Federation, 1412 16th St NW, Washington, DC 20036; (202)

797-6866. Coalition of local and national environmental and conservation organizations formed to conserve resources of the nation's barrier islands and barrier beaches. Acts as an info exchange, answers inquiries or makes referrals free.

10304. Better Hearing Institute, Box 1840, Washington, DC 20013 (5021-B Backlick Rd, Vienna, VA); (703) 642-0580; (800) 424-8576. Interest in hearing, hearing help, hearing loss, rehabilitation, and hearing conservation. Answers inquiries, provides advisory services, publishes and distributes publications, makes referrals. Services free, except bulk publications.

10305. Bicycle Manufacturers Association of America, 1101 15th St NW, Ste 304, Washington, DC 20005; (202) 452-1166. Assn of domestic bicycle producers, promoting bicycling and encouraging legislation on safety and bikeways. Answers inquiries, provides advisory services, distributes brochures, makes referrals. Some services free.

10306. Biomass Energy Research Association, c/o Institute of Gas Technology, 1825 K St NW, Ste 218, Washington, DC 20006; (202) 785-2856. Promotes biomass energy research, public awareness of biomass energy. Publishes newsletter, scholarly materials; provides inquiry, consulting services; conducts seminars, workshops. Services primarily for members.

10307. Biometric Society, P.O. Box 269, Ben Franklin Station (806 15th St NW), Washington, DC 20044; (202) 783-1880. Answers inquiries on statistics and mathematics of biology; publishes journal, proceedings of intl meetings; refers inquirers to other sources of info free.

10308. Biometrics Division, Off of Info Mgmt and Statistics, Veterans Admin, 810 Vermont Ave NW, Washington, DC 20420; (202) 389-3458. Holds medical, demographic info on patients treated in Veterans Administration hospitals, nursing homes; publishes reports; answers inquiries from biomedical researchers.

10309. Bituminous Coal Operators' Association, 303 World Ctr Bldg, 918 16th St NW, Washington, DC 20006; (202) 783-3195. Answers special-purpose inquiries on bituminous coal industry; owns reports, periodicals, govt publications; makes referrals.

10310. Board for Certification of Genealogists, P.O. Box 19165, Washington, DC 20036. Certifies persons competent to do professional genealogical research and writing and genealogical record searching. Makes referrals to certified genealogists.

10311. Board for International Broadcasting, Ste 1100, Connecticut Ave NW, Washington, DC 20036; (202) 254-8040. Supervises broadcasts from Radio Liberty and Radio Free Europe. Provides info, annual reports.

10312. Board on Geographic Names, Defense Mapping Agency, Bldg 56, Naval Observatory, Washington, DC 20305; (202) 254-4453. Establishes uniformity in geographic nomenclature and orthography for use throughout fed govt. Answers inquiries, distributes publications.

10313. Brazilian-American Cultural Institute, 4103 Connecticut Ave NW, Washington, DC 20008; (202) 362-8334. Promotes Brazilian culture, Portuguese language. Offers wide range of programs. Provides inquiry, reference, AV services; conducts seminars, language classes. Fee for some services.

10314. Bread for the World, 802 Rhode Island Ave NE, Washington, DC 20018; (202) 269-0200. Nonprofit Christian movement to influence public policy on hunger, poverty. Publishes newsletter, books; provides inquiry, advisory, update services; conducts seminars. Most services free.

10315. Broadcast Education Association, 1771 N St NW, Washington, DC 20036; (202) 429-5355. Assn of colleges and univs with programs in broadcasting, interested in education for careers in broadcasting. Provides general reference services, distributes publications, conducts seminars. Some services free, limited to communications-oriented groups.

10316. Brookings Institution, 1775 Massachusetts Ave NW, Washington, DC 20036; (202) 797-6000. Publishes books, journals, annual report; conducts research; holds conferences; offers repros; provides computing services to nonprofit orgs engaged in social science research.

10317. Building Development Counsel International, 1511 K St NW, Ste 1100, Washington, DC 20005; (202) 628-2760. Interest in buildings and their design, with emphasis on the fed sector and foreign markets. Provides consulting services to architects and engineers on a fee basis.

10318. Building Owners & Managers Association, International Research Department, 1250 Eye St NW, Ste 200, Washington, DC 20005; (202) 289-7000. Assists members in operating high-rise buildings efficiently by providing specific info and services. Answers inquiries, provides reference and reproduction services, conducts seminars, distributes publications, makes referrals. Nonmembers are charged a fee.

10319. Bureau of African Affairs, Public Affairs, Dept of State, Rm 3509, 2201 C St NW, Washington, DC 20520; (202) 632-0362. Creates regional profiles (including background notes, historical and ethnographic data, current policy speeches), and studies U.S. policy matters relating to Sub-Saharan African countries. Provides info, answers inqiries. Most services free; will respond according to ability.

10320. Bureau of East Asian and Pacific Affairs, Public Affairs, Dept of State, Rm 5310, 2201 C St NW, Washington, DC 20520; (202) 632-2538. Creates regional profiles and studies U.S. policy matters relating to East Asian and Pacific countries. Provides info, answers inquiries. Most services free; will respond according to ability.

10321. Bureau of Economic Analysis, Dept of Commerce, 1401 K St NW, Washington, DC 20230; (202) 523-0777. Studies U.S. economy, gross national product, national income, capital stock, and plant and equipment expenditures. Answers inquiries and makes referrals. Professionals may have direct access to the data collection.

10322. Bureau of Economic and Business Affairs, Dept of State, Rm 6828, 2201 C St NW, Washington, DC 20520; (202) 632-1486. Interest in intl finance and development, trade policies, copyright and patent laws, and transportation and telecommunications. Provides info, answers inquiries. Most services free; will respond according to ability.

10323. Bureau of Economic and Business Affairs, Office of East-West Trade, Dept of State, Rm 3819, 2201 C St NW, Washington, DC 20520; (202) 632-0964. Interest in policy regarding trade between U.S. and communist nations. Provides info, answers inquiries. Most services free; will respond according to ability.

10325. Bureau of Engraving & Printing, Public Affairs Section, Program Analysis and External Affairs Staff, 14th and C Sts SW, Washington, DC 20228; (202) 447-0193. Provides info on the design, engraving, and printing of U.S. govt securities, particularly currency and postage stamps. General info free, a fee charged for involved inquiries. Uncut sheets of currency in one- and two-dollar denominations for sale.

10326. Bureau of European Affairs, Dept of State, Rm 5229, 2201 C St NW, Washington, DC 20520; (202) 632-0850. Creates regional profiles and studies U.S. policy matters relating to European countries and Canada; disseminates info on most European/intl treaty organizations, and science and trade councils. Most services free; will respond according to ability.

10327. Bureau of Higher and Continuing Education, Dept of Education, 400 Maryland Ave, SW, Washington, DC 20202; (202) 245-9758. Interest in continuing education, other adult student and community services, minority and women's assistance. Provides info, training, referrals.

10328. Bureau of Human Rights and Humanitarian Affairs, Dept of State, 2201 C St NW, Washington, DC 20520; (202) 632-0334. Studies U.S. policy relating to matters of intl human rights and humanitarian causes, including political asylum in the U.S. Provides info; answers inqiries. Most services free; will respond according to ability.

10329. Bureau of Indian Affairs, Dept of the Interior, 18th and E Sts NW, Washington, DC 20245; (202) 343-1100, 343-7445. Promotes independent development of Indian peoples, their cultural and economic advancement. Answers inquiries, provides referrals, publications.

10330. Bureau of Industrial Economics, Dept of Commerce, Rm 4878, 14th St and Connecticut Ave NW, Washington, DC 20230; (202) 377-1405. Evaluates and analyzes specific industry performance. Provides expert info, answers inquiries, publishes materials, makes referrals.

10331. Bureau of InterAmerican Affairs, Public Affairs, Dept of State, Rm 6913A, 2201 C St NW, Washington, DC 20520; (202) 632-3048. Creates regional profiles and studies U.S. policy matters relating to South and Central American countries; oversees American delegation and info dissemination for the Organization of American States. Provides info, answers inqiries. Most services free; will respond according to ability.

10332. Bureau of International Organization Affairs, Dept of State, 2201 C St NW, Washington, DC 20520; (202) 632-9600. Interest in various activities and issues involving intl orgs, including conferences, delegations, human rights affairs, etc. Provides info answers inqiries. Most services free; will respond according to ability.

10333. Bureau of Land Management, 18th and C Sts NW, Washington, DC 20240; (202) 343-4151. Manages public lands, conducts surveys, keeps various records. Answers inquiries, makes referrals.

10334. Bureau of Mines, Division of Industrial Minerals, Columbia Plaza, Rm 870, 2401 E St NW, Washington, DC 20241; (202) 634-1102. Collects, interprets, and disseminates statistical and technical info on industrial minerals. Answers inquiries, provides advisory and reference services, some free.

10335. Bureau of Mines, Helium Operations, Columbia Plaza, Rm 939, 2401 E St NW, Washington, DC 20241; (202) 634-4734. Carries out all Bureau of Mines activities concerned with identification, conservation, production, and utilization of helium. Answers inquiries free. Computerized gas analyses files available from Natl Technical Info Service.

10336. Bureau of Mines, Office of Technical Information, Columbia Plaza, Rm 1033, 2401 E St NW, Washington, DC 20241; (202) 634-1004. Source of info on mineral conservation, mine health and safety research, mining technology research and metallurgy. Answers inquiries, distributes info and films.

10337. Bureau of Motor Carrier Safety, Fed Hwy Admin, 400 Seventh St SW, Washington, DC 20590; (202) 426-1790. Online system containing info on medical, technical, economic, financial, and risk data as it relates to commercial motor carriers and drivers and vehicle safety regulations. Answers inquiries and conducts training at state level.

10338. Bureau of Near Eastern and South Asian Affairs, Public Affairs, Dept of State, Rm 4515, 2201 C St NW, Washington, DC 20520; (202) 632-5150. Creates regional profiles and studies U.S. policy matters relating to Near Eastern and South Asian countries. Provides info, answers inqiries. Most services free; will respond according to ability.

10339. Bureau of Oceans and International and Scientific Affairs, Dept of State, Rm 7831, 2201 C St NW, Washington, DC 20520; (202) 632-6491. Examines foreign policy impact on intl environment, health matters, energy, and science and technology development. Provides info, answers inqiries. Services free; will respond according to ability.

10340. Bureau of Politico-Military Affairs, Dept of State, Rm 7317, 2201 C St NW, Washington, DC 20520; (202) 632-7327. Studies and develops policy related to U.S. security, arms control and disarmament, arms trade with foreign countries, and military assistance programs. Provides info, answers inqiries. Most services free; will respond according to ability.

10341. Bureau of Prisons, Dept of Justice, 320 First St NW, Washington, DC 20534; (202) 724-3029. Source of info on crime, criminals, juvenile delinquency, corrections. Answers inquiries, collections are accessible for onsite use by professional personnel and adult students.

10342. Bureau of Prisons, National Institute of Corrections, Dept of Justice, 320 First St NW, Rm 200, Washington, DC 20534; (202) 724-3106. Seeks to improve correctional practices at state, local, and fed levels. NIC Info Center, Boulder, Colo., answers inquiries, and makes referrals free. Technical aid available to correctional agencies.

10343. Bureau of Public Affairs, Dept of State, 2201 C St NW, Washington, DC 20520; (202) 647-6575. Represents interests of the U.S. in foreign affairs, history of diplomacy, the Dept of State and the Foreign Service. Conducts foreign policy conferences, provides speakers, holds seminars, distributes publications, answers inquiries.

10344. Bureau of Reclamation, Dept of the Interior, C St bet 18th and 19th Sts NW, Rm 7644, Washington, DC 20240; (202) 343-4662. Promotes economic growth through development of water and related land and energy resources in the 17 contiguous western states. General info and technical inquiries should be directed to Bureau of Reclamation, Attention: 200, P.O. Box 25007, Denver, CO 80225, (303) 234-2041.

10345. Bureau of Social Science Research, 1990 M St NW, Washington, DC 20036; (202) 223-4300. Analyzes data on social sciences; publishes research reports; provides consulting services, bibliographies for a fee; distributes newsletter free. Data available to approved researchers.

10346. Bureau of the Census, Dept of Commerce, Washington, DC 20233; (301) 763-4100. Statistical agency that collects, processes, compiles, and disseminates data covering a range of subjects. Provides statistical info based on regular censuses, conducts special censuses at the request and expense of local communities. Special tabulations are on a cost basis.

10347. Bureau of the Census, Center for International Research, Dept of Commerce, Washington, DC 20233;

(301) 763-2870. Maintains demographic info for all developing countries, conducts research, prepares computer programs, and represents the Bureau of the Census in intl statistical activities. Responds to requests for specific demographic info. Makes projections on request. Provides online access to the International Data Base for fed agencies.

10348. Bureau of the Census, Information Services Program, Field Div, Washington, DC 20233; (202) 763-5830. Provides info on bureau's programs, products, services. Holds all Census publications. Provides inquiry, consulting services; info on research in progress. Conducts workshops. Services provided through regional offices.

10349. Bureau of the Census, International Statistical Programs Center, Washington, DC 20233; (301) 763-2832. Plans and conducts bureau's foreign consultation, technical assistance, and training programs. Consults and maintains liaison with other govt agencies and with foreign govts and intl orgs; disseminates descriptions of research to other countries.

10350. Bureau of the Census, Agriculture Div, Washington, DC 20233; (301) 763-5230. Compiles agricultural production statistics for counties, states, U.S., and outlying areas. Answers inquiries free, provides special data tabulations at cost.

10351. Bureau of the Census, Industry Division, Washington, DC 20233; (301) 763-5850. Compiles manufacturing and mining statistics covering U.S. Answers inquiries free, provides special tabulations of data at cost.

10352. Bureau of the Mint, Dept of the Treasury, 501 13th St NW, Washington, DC 20220; (202) 376-0837. Publishes annual report; works with other govt branches; answers inquiries on mint functions, including manufacture and distribution of coins, medals; provides historical info.

10353. Business & Professional Women's Foundation Resource Center, 2012 Massachusetts Ave NW, Washington, DC 20036; (202) 293-1200 ext 39. Interest in women in the economy, education and sex roles, status of women, occupational segregation, sexual harassment. Provides general reference services, distributes publications, permits onsite use of collections. Most services free, except publications.

10354. Business Advisory Council on Federal Reports, 1625 Eye St NW, Washington, DC 20006; (202) 331-1915. Council composed of business firms and trade assns that advises Office of Management and Budget, other fed agencies on improving report forms, questionnaires, statistical programs.

10355. Business Council for International Understanding Institute, Amer Univ, 3301 New Mexico Ave NW, Ste 244, Washington, DC 20008; (202) 686-2771. Trains and develops U.S. and foreign nationals to cope and function effectively in other cultures. Interest in intercultural communication and adaptation. Provides

general reference services on a cost-plus-overhead basis, primarily for special corporate groups.

10356. Business Executives for National Security, 21 Dupont Circle, Ste 401, Washington, DC 20036; (202) 429-0600. Monitors defense issues from business perspective. Publishes newsletter, reports; provides inquiry, advisory, reference services; conducts seminars. Services to members.

10358. CSR Power Information Center, 1400 Eye St NW, Ste 600, Washington, DC 20005; (202) 842-7600. Publishes looseleaf project briefs of govt-sponsored projects in advanced power field; provides info on research in progress. Fee charged to all nongovt requesters.

10361. Can Manufacturers Institute, 1625 Massachusetts Ave NW, Washington, DC 20036; (202) 237-4677. Publishes technical reports, voluntary standards, newsletter, legislative reviews on can manufacturing industry; provides info on research. Services provided for a fee.

10362. Capitol Historical Society, 200 Maryland Ave NE, Washington, DC 20515; (202) 543-8919. Interest in all aspects of U.S. Capitol and Congress, including funding artwork, public education, D.C. history. Answers or refers requests for info, distributes publications. Society cannot fulfill extensive research requests.

10363. Capitol Services Incorporated, 415 Second St NE, Ste 200, Washington, DC 20002; (202) 546-5600. Concerned with all subjects covered in *Congressional Record* and *Federal Register*. Answers inquiries, provides abstracting, indexing, and online retrieval services. Makes referrals and distributes publications. Services provided at cost.

10364. Carnegie Institution of Washington, Rock Information System, Geophysical Laboratory, 2801 Upton St NW, Washington, DC 20008; (202) 966-0334. Interest in chemical composition of Cenozoic volcanic rocks. Provides computer literature-searching and reduction services. Services free upon written request.

10365. Cartographic & Architectural Archives Branch, Special Archives Div, Natl Archives and Records Admin, Washington, DC 20408; (703) 756-6700. Interest in fed cartographic and architectural records. Provides general reference services, legal certification of authenticity of reproductions for a fee. Selected maps and aerial photographs may be examined onsite.

10366. Catholic Biblical Association of America, c/o Catholic Univ of America, 620 Michigan Ave NE, Washington, DC 20064; (202) 635-5519. Facilitates the study of scripture and related fields by those who specialize in these areas. Only those specialists qualify for membership. Services primarily for members, but publications available for purchase.

10367. Center for Applied Linguistics, 1118 22nd St NW, Washington, DC 20037; (202) 429-9292. Involved in study of language and in application of linguistics to educational, cultural, and social concerns. Answers inquiries; provides consulting, abstracting and reference services, sometimes free.

10369. Center for Applied Research in the Apostolate, 3700 Oakview Terrace NE, Washington, DC 20017; (202) 832-2300. Promotes application of modern techniques to the church's social and religious mission in the world. Answers inquiries; provides consulting, reference, and duplication services; conducts research and seminars; sells publications. First consultations are free.

10370. Center for Auto Safety, 2001 S St NW, Ste 410, Washington, DC 20009; (202) 328-7700. Interest in design and assembly defects in new cars, legal rights of owners of defective cars, safety designing, self-help tactics. Answers inquiries, sells publications, allows photocopying for a fee.

10371. Center for Corporate Public Involvement, 1850 K St NW, Washington, DC 20006; (202) 862-4047. Provides info, guidance, research capability to member health, life insurance companies. Provides inquiry, advisory, consulting, referral services; distributes publications (single copies free).

10372. Center for Defense Information, 600 Maryland Ave SW, Ste 303 West, Washington, DC 20024; (202) 484-9490. Provides independent, informed analyses of U.S. defense policies available to journalists, scholars, govt officials, and the public. Provides general reference services, conducts seminars, permits onsite use of collections. Most services free.

10373. Center for Development Policy, 418 10th St SE, Washington, DC 20003; (202) 547-6406. Monitors U.S. relations with Third World. Provides analyses of impact of U.S. development policies overseas. Has extensive library. Publishes research; provides inquiry, advisory, referral services free, unless extensive.

10374. Center for Environmental Education, 624 Ninth St NW, Ste 500, Washington, DC 20001; (202) 737-3600. Nonprofit org working to conserve marine species (especially whales, seals, sea turtles), their habitats. Conducts, sponsors research; provides inquiry, referral services; conducts conferences; sponsors radio, TV series. Most services free.

10375. Center for Food Safety & Applied Nutrition, HFF-37, Food and Drug Admin, 200 C St SW, Rm 3321, Washington, DC 20204; (202) 245-1236. Respository of info on nutrition, foods, food additives, food technology. Answers limited inquiries, but not on FDA policy; permits onsite use of collection.

10376. Center for Hellenic Studies, 3100 Whitehaven St NW, Washington, DC 20008; (202) 234-3738. Interest in all aspects of ancient Greece. Has extensive library for onsite use, publishes monograph series. Limited services available to interested scholars.

10377. Center for International Policy, 236 Massachusetts Ave NE, Ste 505, Washington, DC 20002; (202) 544-

4666. Concerned with U.S. foreign policy on Third World--its impact on human rights, needs. Answers inquiries, provides speakers, conducts seminars. Services free, except publications.

10378. Center for Law & Social Policy, 1751 N St NW, Washington, DC 20036; (202) 872-0670. Clinical and legal educational org interested in problems of the poor, minorities, civil rights enforcement, health care advocacy. Provides general reference services, distributes publications, permits limited onsite use of collection. Most services free.

10379. Center for Multinational Studies, 1625 Eye St NW, Washington, DC 20006; (202) 331-1978. Seeks to determine facts, clarify issues, and relate the multinational corporation to the broader global economy. Advisory services available chiefly for member companies, although some outside inquiries are answered.

10380. Center for National Policy Review, Catholic Univ School of Law, Washington, DC 20064; (202) 832-8525. Conducts research and review of natl policies with urban and civil rights implications. Interest in enforcement of civil rights laws, race and sex discrimination. Provides general reference services, distributes publications. Services free or at cost to regular-paying clients.

10381. Center for National Security Studies, 122 Maryland Ave NE, Washington, DC 20002; (202) 544-5380. Monitors national security issues within U.S. govt, provides expert testimony, assistance on reform proposal and Freedom of Info Act. Provides reference assistance, conducts seminars, makes referrals.

10382. Center for Peace Studies, Georgetown Univ, Maguire Bldg, Rm 410, Washington, DC 20067; (202) 625-4240. Academic prog in peace studies. Seeks to integrate faith, research, action in peacemaking. Provides ref services; conducts seminars, workshops; distributes printed, AV resources for peace teaching.

10383. Center for Population Options, International Center on Adolescent Fertility, 2031 Florida Ave NW, Washington, DC 20009; (202) 387-5091. Confronts problems of early childbearing in developing countries. Provides info, tech assistance (in English, Spanish, French). Services free to persons, orgs in developing countries; for a fee to others.

10384. Center for Radiation Research, Natl Measurement Laboratory, Natl Bur of Standards, Washington, DC 20234; (301) 921-2551. Provides info on units and standards of light (including ultraviolet and infrared), spectroscopy (visible through far ultraviolet), atomic radiation, and collision data for plasmas. Answers inquiries, provides consulting services to govt, commercial, and scientific agencies on a contract or no-cost basis.

10385. Center for Renewable Resources/Solar Lobby, 1001 Connecticut Ave NW, Ste 510, Washington, DC 20036; (202) 466-6880 or 466-6350. Researches, advocates prudent natl energy policy, solar applications.

Provides inquiry, referral services. Most services free to all; charge for publications, seminars, conferences.

10387. Center for Responsive Governance, 1000 16th St NW, Washington, DC 20036; (202) 223-2400. Provides research, education to make institutions more accessible, accountable to citizens. Publishes journal, research; answers inquiries; conducts seminars, symposia. Services free or at cost.

10388. Center for Science in the Public Interest, 1501 16th St NW, Washington, DC 20036; (202) 332-9110. Works to improve quality of the American diet through research and public education. Provides advisory services and referral assistance free, distributes publications at cost. Most services aimed at local citizen groups and health professionals.

10389. Center for Strategic and International Studies, Georgetown Univ, 1800 K St NW, Ste 400, Washington, DC 20006; (202) 887-0200. Coordinates data exchange system linking Soviet scholars in North America and Europe; publishes reports; conducts conferences, seminars bringing together specialists from govt, business, press, univ.

10390. Center for Women Policy Studies, 2000 P St NW, Ste 508, Washington, DC 20036; (202) 872-1770. Nonprofit org that provides an interdisciplinary approach to the identification, analysis, and solution of the problems related to status of women in society. Answers inquiries, makes referrals for a nominal charge, conducts research under contract.

10391. Center for the Study of Pre-Retirement& Aging, Catholic Univ of America, 208 St John's Hall, Washington, DC 20064; (202) 635-5483. Provides education, research, training on problems of the elderly to local community, especially churches. Publishes newsletter; provides inquiry, consulting, referral services and outreach programs. Fee for some services.

10392. Center of Concern, 3700 13th St NE, Washington, DC 20017; (202) 635-2757. Interest in worldwide social justice issues in policymaking, population and food policy, new intl economic order, labor movement. Answers inquiries free, provides advisory and consulting services, distributes publications for a fee.

10393. Central Intelligence Agency, Washington, DC 20505; (202) 351-7676. Collects and analyzes foreign intelligence, provides advice to U.S. govt based on intelligence evaluations. Provides info, sells various publications.

10394. Central Office Film Library, Veterans Admin, 810 Vermont Ave NW, Washington, DC 20420; (202) 389-2793. Owns collection of films, other audiovisual materials produced by Veterans Administration, other govt agencies. Publishes catalog, lends films free.

10395. Central Station Electrical Protection Association, 1120 19th St NW, Ste LL20, Washington, DC 20036; (202) 296-9595. Source of data on central station electrical alarm industry, burglar, and fire alarms. An-

swers inquiries, provides reference services, distributes publications, makes referrals. Services free.

10396. Chamber of Commerce of the U.S., 1615 H St NW, Washington, DC 20062; (202) 659-6000. Monitors legislation and regulations of interest to the business community, concentrating on specific areas such as agriculture, education, technology, energy, consumer affairs, environment, transportation. Publishes newspaper and magazine, answers inquiries, makes referrals.

10397. Charlin Jazz Society, 201 Eye St SW, Rm 104, Washington, DC 20024; (202) 484-1697. Promotes jazz as classical, African-American art form. Provides opportunities for musicians, internship program for young performers. Provides calendar for local area; offers consulting, workshops for a fee.

10398. Chemical Specialties Manufacturers Association, 1001 Connecticut Ave NW, Ste 1120, Washington, DC 20036; (202) 872-8110. Does legislative reporting; develops specifications, testing methods for aerosol spray products; performs surveys; conducts seminars. Some services for members only.

10399. Children's Bureau Clearinghouse on Child Abuse & Neglect Information, Dept of Health and Human Services, P.O. Box 1182 (400 Sixth St SW), Washington, DC 20013; (202) 245-2856. Source of info on child abuse and neglect, child abusers, child protection services, and on treatment and prevention. Answers inquiries, provides reference and magnetic tape services, conducts seminars, and distributes publications. Some services free.

10400. Children's Defense Fund, 122 C St NW, Washington, DC 20001; (202) 628-8787; (800) 424-9602 (toll-free). Created to provide long-range and systematic advocacy on behalf of the nation's children. Publishes newsletter, answers inquiries, provides advisory services and legal aid, distributes publications, makes referrals. Services free.

10401. Children's Foundation, 815 15th St NW, No 928, Washington, DC 20005; (202) 347-3300. Monitors administration of programs for children and families, especially the Child Care Food Program. Answers inquiries, provides advisory services, conducts seminars, distributes publications, makes referrals. Some services free.

10402. Children's Hospital National Medical Center, Department of Adolescent & Young Adult Medicine, 111 Michigan Ave NW, Washington, DC 20010; (202) 745-2178. Provides health care, conducts training prog in adolescent medicine. Provides free inquiry, consulting, referral services, primarily for health professionals.

10403. Children's Legal Rights Information & Training Program, 2008 Hillyer Pl, Washington, DC 20009; (202) 332-6575. Provides legal info, training to those who deliver services to children, youth, their families. Answers inquiries free; conducts workshops; distributes print, AV materials for a fee.

10404. Children's Literature Center, Library of Congress, 10 First St SE, Washington, DC 20540; (202) 287-5535. Contains info relating to children's informational and recreational media needs, books, films, games, etc. Answers reference and research inquiries, provides bibliographic info but does not serve children.

10406. Children's Theatre Association of America, c/o Amer Theatre Assn, 1010 Wisconsin Ave NW, Washington, DC 20007. Promotes use of children's theater, creative drama in education. Publishes journal, newsletter, referral materials, curriculum aids; provides inquiry, advisory, referral services; conducts workshops; provides speakers. Services free to members.

10407. Citizens Against Nuclear War, 1201 16th St NW, Washington, DC 20036; (202) 822-7483. Coalition to prevent nuclear war thru verifiable, bilateral freeze on testing, production, deployment of nuclear weapons. Conducts seminars, distributes publications, provides speakers. Most services free.

10408. Citizens for the Treatment of High Blood Pressure, 1140 Connecticut Ave NW, Ste 606, Washington, DC 20036; (202) 296-4435. Researches policy, funding for high blood pressure control; encourages private sector participation. Provides inquiry, advisory services; conducts seminars. Services usually free.

10409. Citizens' Energy Project, 1110 Sixth St NW, No 300, Washington, DC 20001; (202) 289-4999. Conducts research and info gathering on solar energy, renewable energy resources, and nuclear power issues. Answers inquiries, provides reference services, conducts seminars, distributes publications, makes referrals. Services free, except publications.

10410. Civil Rights Division, Dept of Justice, Rm 5643, 10th St and Constitution Ave NW, Washington, DC 20530; (202) 633-2151. Works to eliminate discrimination as provided by fed law. Answers inquiries, makes referrals, distributes materials.

10411. Clean Water Action Project, 733 15th St NW, Ste 1110, Washington, DC 20005; (202) 638-1196. Promotes public interest in water, toxics, and public works issues thru national consensus and citizen outreach and training. Answers technical inquiries, distributes publications, makes referrals. Services free, primarily for activist groups.

10412. Clear Channel Broadcasting Service, 1776 K St NW, Ste 1100, Washington, DC 20006; (202) 429-7020. Represents its members before Fed Communications Comm and Congress in matters affecting clear-channel allocations. Answers inquiries, distributes publications, makes referrals, permits onsite use of collections. Services free, unless extensive.

10413. Clearinghouse on the Future, H2-555, Washington, DC 20515; (202) 226-3434. Encourages congressional awareness of the impact of its decisions on the future and provides Congress with info on trends and emerging issues. Answers inquiries, publishes newsletter, provides reference service, makes referrals. Services primarily for members of Congress.

10414. Coal Exporters Association, 1130 17th St NW, Washington, DC 20036; (202) 463-2625. Studies coal and coke, coal export, coal imports. Distributes publication at cost to nonmembers.

10415. Coalition for Common Sense in Government Procurement, 1990 M St NW, Ste 400, Washington, DC 20036; (202) 331-0975. Monitors fed procurement procedures. Has library of regulations, policies, legislation. Publishes newsletter, reference materials; provides inquiry, advisory, referral services; conducts seminars. Services primarily for members.

10416. Coalition for a New Foreign & Military Policy, 712 G St SE, Washington, DC 20003; (202) 546-8400. Promotes arms control, disarmament, human rights, self-determination, reordered fed spending priorities. Publishes journal, reports, AV materials; provides inquiry, advisory services.

10417. Coast Guard Bridge Administration Div, Off of Navigation, Coast Guard, 2100 Second St SW, Washington, DC 20593; (202) 426-0942. Interest in administration of laws relating to the approval of location and plans of bridges to be constructed across the navigable waters of U.S. Answers inquiries, distributes publication.

10418. Coast Guard National Response Center, Headquarters Command Ctr Div (G-TGC), Off of Command, Control, and Communication, Coast Guard, 2100 Second St SW, Washington, DC 20593; (202) 426-1105. Acts as focal point for reporting of hazardous substance/ material spills. Interest in oil and hazardous substance/material pollution. Publishes statistics, provides emergency advice and info on spills.

10419. Coast Guard, Office of Boating, Public, & Consumer Affairs, Commandant (G-B), Coast Guard, Washington, DC 20593; (202) 426-1088. Promotes recreational boating safety, including boat standards and regulations, compliance and defect notification, equipment requirements, public education. Answers general inquiries, provides consulting services.

10420. Coast Guard, Search & Rescue Division, Commandant (G-OSR), Off of Operations, Coast Guard, 2100 Second St SW, Rm 3222-I, Washington, DC 20593; (202) 426-1948. Compiles records on search and rescue operations, which may be viewed onsite by appointment. Reproduction services limited to copies of specific search and rescue records.

10421. Cold Regions Bibliography Project, Science and Technology Div, Library of Congress, 10 First St SE, Washington, DC 20540; (202) 287-5668. Publishes monthly bulletin on Antarctic research, annual bibliography; provides reference, abstracting services primarily for sponsoring agencies; small services performed free for others.

10422. College & University Personnel Association, 11 Dupont Circle, Ste 120, Washington, DC 20036; (202) 462-1038. Follows legal, legislative, regulatory developments in personnel administration in higher education. Has data bank of annual compensation surveys. Offers publications; provides inquiry, advisory services. Services free or at cost.

10423. Color Marketing Group, 1133 15th St NW, Washington, DC 20005; (202) 429-9440. Members develop colors and supply samples to nonmembers for a fee; provide color marketing info, education, and marketing assistance. Answers inquiries.

10424. Commerce Department Library, 14th St and Constitution Ave, Washington, DC 20230; (202) 377-2161. Repository for many U.S., foreign business and economic references. Provides free info, referrals, reference services.

10425. Commercial Development Association, 1133 15th St NW, Washington, DC 20005; (202) 429-9440. Interest in professional and commercial development of industrial products. Conducts educational programs among its members, sponsors technical meetings, distributes publications.

10426. Commission of Fine Arts, 708 Jackson Pl NW, Washington, DC 20006; (202) 566-1066. Provides govt agencies with expert advice on matters relating to art and approves plans for buildings and monuments. Answers inquiries, provides advisory and reference services, distributes publications and makes referrals. Some services at cost.

10427. Commission on Civil Rights, 1121 Vermont Ave NW, Washington, DC 20425; (202) 376-8177. Interest in discrimination, prejudice; promotes equal opportunity, voting rights, observance of fed civil rights laws. Provides info, library services, free publications.

10428. Commission on Presidential Scholars, U.S. Dept of Education, 400 Maryland Ave SW, Rm 2079, Washington, DC 20202; (202) 245-7793. Selects students of outstanding scholastic accomplishment and leadership ability to be Presidential Scholars. Answers inquiries.

10429. Committee for National Security, 2000 P St NW, Ste 515, Washington, DC 20036; (202) 833-3140. Educates opinion leaders on reducing risks of nuclear war. Holds annual women's conference; manages speakers bureau; organizes educational, outreach activities; produces educational materials.

10430. Committee for the Preservation of the White House, 1100 Ohio Dr SW, Washington, DC 20242; (202) 426-6622. Reports to the President and advises director of Natl Park Service on the preservation of the museum character of ground floor and public rooms of the White House. Answers inquiries and makes referrals.

10450. Committee on the Present Danger, 905 16th St NW, Washington, DC 20006; (202) 628-2409. Interest in strategic military balance between U.S. and USSR.

Publications list available. Provides inquiry, advisory services; conducts seminars, workshops. Services free, available selectively.

10451. Commodity Credit Corporation, Dept of Agriculture, Rm 5071 South Bldg, 14th St and Independence Ave, SW, Washington, DC 20250; (202) 447-8165. Aids in commodity distribution, protects prices, stabilizes commodity supply.

10452. Commodity Management Division, Off of Procurement (FC), Fed Supply and Services, General Services Admin, Washington, DC 20406; (703) 557-7901. Develops specifications, standards, and commercial item descriptions for fed procurement and conducts market research. Publishes federal standardization handbook, answers inquiries, makes referrals.

10453. Common Carrier Bureau, Fed Communications Comm, 1919 M St NW, Rm 500, Washington, DC 20554; (202) 632-6910. Administers licensing of radio for common carrier communication facilities, including satellite, wire, and cable in interstate and foreign service. Answers inquiries; makes referrals; provides info on tariffs, accounting methods, operating practices, services and facilities.

10454. Communications Satellite Corp. Central Library, 950 L'Enfant Plaza South, SW, Washington, DC 20024; (202) 863-6834. Source of info on electrical engineering, telecommunications, communications satellites, corporate business. Publishes brochures and makes interlibrary loans.

10456. Community Nutrition Institute, 2001 S St NW, Washington, DC 20009; (202) 462-4700. Dedicated to establishment of a national food policy by info community orgs, consumer groups, and local officials of fed food programs. Answers inquiries; provides consulting, conducts seminars; distributes publications. Services at cost.

10457. Composite Can and Tube Institute, 1742 N St NW, Washington, DC 20036; (202) 223-4840. Publishes directory, industry standards and specifications for composite cans; answers inquiries; makes referrals to local manufacturers for those interested in specific products.

10459. Comptroller of the Currency, Dept of the Treasury, 490 L'Enfant Plaza East, Washington, DC 20219; (202) 447-1810. Examines, regulates, and supervises the national banking system. Answers inquiries, provides info on banking laws and regulations. Library open to public, photocopying services available.

10460. Computer & Business Equipment Manufacturers Association, 311 First St NW, Washington, DC 20001; (202) 737-8888. Nonprofit, cooperative org of manufacturers of data processing and business equipment and associated products interested in mutual industry objectives and problems. Answers inquiries from the press and public; makes referrals.

10461. Computer Institute, Natl Defense Univ, Washington Navy Yard, Washington, DC 20374; (202) 433-2011 or 433-2012. Element of NDU interested in all aspects of automated info systems and instruction in their use. Services primarily for employees of DoD. Educational services extended to other govt agencies on a space-available basis with a minimal tuition fee.

10462. Concern, Inc., 1794 Columbia Rd NW, Washington, DC 20009; (202) 328-8160. Provides environmental info, encourages community activism. Interest in groundwater, pesticides, acid rain, hazardous waste mgmt, etc. Answers inquiries; makes referrals; organizes conferences, workshops, and exhibits; sells publications.

10463. Conference Board of the Mathematical Sciences, 1529 18th St NW, Washington, DC 20036; (202) 293-1170. Publishes books, surveys, reports on mathematical sciences, including applied mathematics, mathematical logic, statistics, computer science; answers inquiries.

10464. Conference on Alternative State & Local Policies, 2000 Florida Ave NW, Washington, DC 20009; (202) 387-6030. Provides forum for progressive elected officials, activists, experts interested in alternative policies, progs at state, local level. Publishes journal, model legislation, policy memoranda. Answers inquiries.

10465. Congressional Budget Office, Office of Intergovernmental Relations, House Annex 2, 2nd and D Sts SW, Washington, DC 20515; (202) 226-2600. Provides Congress with budget-related info, analyses of alternative fiscal, budgetary, progmatic policies. Publications list issued annually. Answers inquiries. Services free.

10466. Conservation & Environmental Protection Division, Agricultural Stabilization and Conservation Service, Dept of Agriculture, 14th St and Independence Ave SW, Washington, DC 20250; (202) 447-6221. Studies application of conservation practices, control of agricultural water pollution, soil erosion, forest and wildlife mgmt. Answers inquiries.

10467. Conservation Foundation, 1255 23rd St NW, Washington, DC 20037; (202) 797-4300 or 293-4800. Conducts research and educational programs to encourage human conduct to sustain and enrich life on earth. Publishes newsletter, conducts research and policy studies. Library open to public.

10469. Consumer Product Safety Commission, National Injury Information Clearinghouse, (Westwood Towers Bldg, Rm 625, 5401 Westbard Ave, Bethesda, MD) Washington, DC 20207; (301) 492-6424. Interest in injury data on accidents associated with consumer products. Answers inquiries, provides injury data and summaries of accident investigation reports. Services free, but under the Freedom of Info Act, there is a charge for costs over $25.

10470. Consumer Product Safety Commission, Office of the Secretary, Washington, DC 20207; (301) 492-6800; (800)

638-2772 (toll-free for gen inquiries from all 50 states, P.R., and V.I.). Interest in hazardous consumer products, flammable fabrics, poison prevention packaging, electrical safety, athletic products, power equipment safety, home insulation safety, toy safety. Provides general reference services. Limited quantities of consumer info available free.

10472. Consumers for World Trade, 1001 Connecticut Ave NW, Ste 800, Washington, DC 20036; (202) 785-4835. Interest in promotion of liberal trade policies (decreasing tariffs and quotas and export disincentives) on behalf of the American consumer. Serves as clearinghouse for channeling info to, and coordinating activities on, trade matters. Distributes booklets free.

10473. Continental Association of Funeral & Memorial Societies, 2001 S St NW, Ste 530, Washington, DC 20009; (202) 745-0634. Org of those that help people preplan funerals. Encourages dignified, simple, and economical funerals, provides education, and promotes legislative reforms. Answers inquiries, provides advisory services, conducts seminars, distributes publications. Most services free.

10474. Conveyor Equipment Manufacturers Association, 1133 15th St NW, Washington, DC 20005; (202) 429-9440. Publishes and sells bimonthly bulletin, standards, news releases, yearbook, data compilations, films, brochures on design, installation, and use of conveyers.

10475. Cooperative Education Association, c/o Jan Rundlett Speed, Exec Secty, 655 15th St NW, Ste 300, Washington, DC 20005; (202) 639-4770. Interest in all phases of cooperative education. Conducts seminars and workshops, distributes publications, makes referrals to other sources of info. Services primarily for members, but others assisted within limits of time and staff.

10476. Cooperative Forestry Staff, Forest Service, USDA, P.O. Box 2417, Washington, DC 20013; (703) 235-2212. Studies forest mgmt and forest products utilization, urban forestry, timber stand improvement, tree genetics and seedling production. Answers inquiries, provides advice, makes referrals.

10477. Copyright Office, Library of Congress, 10 First St SE, Washington, DC 20559; (202) 287-8700. Serves U.S. as registry for claims to copyright in literary, artistic, and musical works and sound recordings, and as repository of records of copyright ownership. Answers inquiries, permits onsite use of records, provides search services for $10 an hour.

10478. Cordage Institute, 444 N Capitol St, Ste 711, Washington, DC 20001; (202) 638-7030. Nonprofit assn interested in the manufacture and sales of rope and twine. Provides general reference services, often free.

10479. Corn Refiners Association, 1001 Connecticut Ave NW, Washington, DC 20036; (202) 331-1634. Interest in corn and corn refining industry. Answers inquiries, provides reference services, distributes publications. Services free, except some publications.

10480. Corporation for Public Broadcasting, 1111 16th St NW, Washington, DC 20036; (202) 293-6160. Private nonprofit corporation that advances public broadcasting and provides increased services to the public. Answers inquiries, conducts seminars. Fee for some services.

10481. Cosmetic, Toiletry & Fragrance Association, 1110 Vermont Ave NW, Ste 800, Washington, DC 20005; (202) 331-1770. Represents manufacturers of finished products in the cosmetic, toiletry, and fragrance industry, and suppliers of ingredients used in the production and marketing. Answers inquiries, makes referrals. Services primarily for members.

10482. Council for Advancement & Support of Education, 11 Dupont Circle NW, Ste 400, Washington, DC 20036; (202) 328-5900. Promotes public and alumni relations and fundraising for higher education. Answers inquiries, provides reference services and placement listings, makes referrals. Fees may be charged.

10483. Council for American Private Education, 1625 Eye St NW, Ste 822, Washington, DC 20006; (202) 659-0016. Promotes sound public policy on private schools at all levels, communications, research within the private school community. Provides inquiry, advisory, referral services free.

10484. Council for Educational Development & Research, 1518 K St NW, Ste 206, Washington, DC 20005; (202) 638-3193. Interest in education R&D. Publishes journal, answers inquiries, conducts seminars and workshops. Services free.

10485. Council for International Exchange of Scholars, 11 Dupont Circle NW, Washington, DC 20036; (202) 833-4950. Principal private agency in U.S. assisting in administration of the exchange program for univ lecturers and research scholars authorized under the Fulbright-Hays Act. Answers inquiries and makes referrals.

10486. Council for Responsible Nutrition, 2100 M St NW, Ste 602, Washington, DC 20037; (202) 872-1488. Trade assn of nutrient supplement manufacturers. Publishes newsletter (for members only); provides inquiry, advisory services free.

10487. Council for a Livable World, 100 Maryland Ave NE, Ste 500B, Washington, DC 20002; (202) 543-4100. Nonprofit educational, political, and lobbying org that supports Senate candidates; publishes newsletters, surveys of Senate races, candidate profiles, fact sheets; does lobbying.

10488. Council of Chief State School Officers, Resource Center on Sex Equity, 400 N Capitol St, Ste 379, Washington, DC 20001; (202) 393-8159. Seeks to eliminate sexism and sex role stereotyping in education. Answers inquiries, provides advisory services, conducts seminars. Services primarily for educators, sometimes for a fee.

10489. Council of Economic Advisers, 17th St and Pennsylvania Ave NW, Washington, DC 20500; (202) 395-5084. Analyzes the national economy and advises the President on economic development and on the economic impact of policy. Answers inquiries.

10490. Council of Graduate Schools in the U.S., 1 Dupont Circle NW, Washington, DC 20036; (202) 223-3791. Furnishes technical assistance, consulting services to univs, colleges for fee; publishes newsletter, reports, annual proceedings, position papers; answers inquiries free.

10491. Council of Independent Colleges, 1 Dupont Circle NW, Ste 320, Washington, DC 20036; (202) 466-7230. Sponsors natl public info campaigns in support of independent higher education. Answers inquiries, publishes newsletter, provides consulting services, administers a national mgmt info system.

10492. Council of Professional Associations on Federal Statistics, 806 15th St NW, Ste 440, Washington, DC 20005; (202) 783-5808. Provides research, educational services on fed statistics, statistical issues. Publishes newsletter, research; provides inquiry, advisory, referral services; conducts seminars. Services free.

10493. Council of State Administrators of Vocational Rehabilitation, 1055 Thomas Jefferson St NW, Ste 401, Washington, DC 20007; (202) 638-4634. Interest in rehabilitation of physically and mentally handicapped individuals. Provides general reference services, distributes publications. Services free for state rehabilitation agencies and agencies for the blind.

10494. Council of State Housing Agencies, 444 N Capitol St, No 118, Washington, DC 20001; (202) 624-7710. Represents state housing finance agencies. Maintains data base, publishes materials (for members only), answers inquiries, conducts seminars and workshops. Most services free.

10495. Council of State Planning Agencies, Natl Governors Assn, 444 N Capitol St, Ste 291, Washington, DC 20001; (202) 624-5386. Interest in state planning in the fields of economic development, executive mgmt, social services, renewable resource mgmt. Answers inquiries; provides advisory, consulting services for a fee.

10496. Council of Tree & Landscape Appraisers, 1250 Eye St NW, Ste 504, Washington, DC 20005; (202) 789-2592. Natl public info org for horticultural appraisals. Publishes reference and promotional materials; provides inquiry, advisory, update services; distributes publications, AV programs. Most services free.

10497. Council on Environmental Quality, 722 Jackson Pl NW, Washington, DC 20006; (202) 395-5700. Develops and recommends to the President and Congress policies that promote environmental quality. Answers inquiries, provides speakers, analyzes environmental data.

10498. Council on Hemispheric Affairs, 1612 20th St NW, Washington, DC 20009; (202) 745-7000. Promotes common interests of the hemisphere, constructive U.S. policy on Latin America. Publishes newsletter, research; provides inquiry, advisory, referral services; permits onsite use of collections. Services free, except publications.

10499. Council on International Nontheatrical Events, 1201 16th St NW, Washington, DC 20036; (202) 785-1136 or 785-1137. Selects short films from the U.S. for submission to intl film events. Film entrants pay a fee. Answers inquiries and provides reference services free.

10500. Council on Library Resources, 1785 Massachusetts Ave NW, Washington, DC 20036; (202) 483-7474. Private foundation that aids in solving library problems. Publishes newsletter, annual report, reports of studies; answers inquiries; makes referrals; distributes publications free.

10501. Council on Postsecondary Accreditation, 1 Dupont Circle, Ste 305, Washington, DC 20036; (202) 452-1433. Interest in monitoring agencies that accredit postsecondary educational institutions and programs. Answers inquiries, provides advisory services, makes referrals, publishes and distributes materials. Services free.

10502. Council on Synthetic Fuels, 1301 Pennsylvania Ave NW, Ste 301, Washington, DC 20004; (202) 347-7069. Trade assn for synthetic fuels producers, supporting industries. Publishes reports, papers, proceedings; Answers inquiries; conducts seminars. Most services free.

10503. Crime Prevention Coalition, 805 15th St NW, Rm 705, Washington, DC 20005; (202) 393-7141. Mobilizes citizens to reduce crime, fear of crime. Has data base on programs. Answers inquiries; provides tech assistance, training, educational materials; conducts conferences. Fee for some services.

10504. Cued Speech Program, Gallaudet Coll, 7th St and Florida Ave NE, Washington, DC 20002; (202) 651-5527. Interest in cued speech (method of communication for the deaf), problems of language acquisition, lipreading of the deaf, etc. Provides general reference services, conducts workshops, lends materials. Services free, except some materials.

10505. Customs Service Public Information Division, U.S. Treasury Dept, P.O. Box 7407 (1301 Constitution Ave NW), Washington, DC 20044; (202) 566-8195 or 566-5286. Provides info on Customs Service programs, operations, requirements, regulations, imports, tariffs, and quotas. Answers inquiries, provides advisory services, distributes some publications.

10506. Customs Service, Carriers, Drawback & Bonds Division, U.S. Treasury Dept, 1301 Constitution Ave NW, Washington, DC 20229; (202) 566-5732. Administers customs laws governing the control of carriers arriving and departing from U.S. and their movement point-to-point, including vessels, aircraft, trucks, and containers. Answers inquiries, makes referrals, provides advisory services.

10508. Decimal Classification Division, Library of Congress, 10 First St SE, Washington, DC 20540; (202) 287-5265. Source of info on library subject classification, classified bibliography, Dewey Decimal Classification and Relative Index. Answers inquiries, makes referrals, provides advisory services.

10510. Defenders of Wildlife, 1244 19th St NW, Washington, DC 20036; (202) 659-9510. Natl nonprofit wildlife advocacy org interested in endangered species, wildlife mgmt and legislation, intl wildlife treaties. Disseminates info, responds to public inquiries free or for a nominal fee, publishes and distributes materials.

10511. Defense Audiovisual Agency, Still Photographic Depository, Bldg 168, NDW, Anacostia Naval Station, Washington, DC 20374; (202) 433-2166. Collection of two million photographs having historical and documentary interest or a continuing use. Provides info on availability of Army, Navy, Air Force, and Marine Corps photographs. Prints free to govt agencies, for a fee to public.

10512. Defense Mapping Agency, Hydrographic/Topographic Center, ATTN: SDS, 6500 Brookes Lane, Washington, DC 20315; (202) 227-2080. Operates and maintains Dept of Defense Libraries of Topographic Maps, Nautical Charts, Geodetic Data, Bathymetric Data, and Foreign Place Names. Answers inquiries, provides limited reproduction services at cost, makes referrals for DoD and authorized agencies.

10514. Defense Security Assistance Agency, Dept of Defense, Pentagon, Washington, DC 20301; (202) 695-3291. Assists military in foreign countries, runs Foreign Military Sales (FMS) program. Provides info and publications on military sales, assistance, and education.

10515. Denver Wildlife Research Center Museum, Natl Museum of Natural History, Smithsonian Institution, 10th St and Constitution Ave NW, Washington, DC 20560; (202) 357-1930. Studies the taxonomy, ecological distribution, community interactions, and life histories of North American birds, mammals, amphibians, and reptiles. Provides authoritative info, identifies specimens or limited remains, permits onsite use of specimen collections by scientists.

10516. Department of Anthropology, Natl Museum of Natural History, Smithsonian Institution, 10th St and Constitution Ave NW, Washington, DC 20560; (202) 357-2363. Library of physical anthropology, including human variation and adaptation, cultural and biological factors in human evolution. Answers inquiries, distributes publications, provides consulting services. Library accessible to qualified researchers upon application.

10517. Department of Botany, Natl Museum of Natural History, Smithsonian Institution, 10th St and Constitution Ave NW, Washington, DC 20560; (202) 357-2534. Studies plant taxonomy, ecology, anatomy, and morphology. Answers or refers inquiries on botanical subjects, lends specimens to research institutions. Space is provided to researchers.

10518. Department of Commerce, 14th St and Constitution Ave NW, Washington, DC 20230; (202) 377-2000. Responsible for promoting U.S. economic development and foreign trade. Encourages minority business development. Conducts research; provides studies, consulting, free info and publications.

10519. Department of History of Science & Technology, Natl Museum of Amer History, Smithsonian Institution, Constitution Ave between 12th and 14th Sts NW, Washington, DC 20560; (202) 357-1963. Studies American science, technology, and engineering from colonial times to present. Staff identifies objects, provides consultation and info about the collections. Researchers may have access to study collections.

10520. Department of Invertebrate Zoology, Natl Museum of Natural History, Smithsonian Institution, 10th St and Constitution Ave NW, Washington, DC 20560; (202) 381-5262. Studies the systematics, ecology, histology, life history, and zoo-geography of invertebrates, emphasizing marine animals and excluding insects. Answers public inquiries relevant to research, provides info on collections to qualified individuals.

10521. Department of Mineral Sciences, Natl Museum of Natural History, Smithsoniann Institution, 10th St and Constitution Ave NW, Washington, DC 20560; (202) 357-2039. Studies systematic mineralogy and petrology; composition, constituents, and textures of meteorites and tektites; volcanology; submarine geology; crystal structures of minerals. Answers inquiries, identifies specimens, provides consulting services.

10522. Department of Paleobiology, Natl Museum of Natural History, Smithsonian Institution,, 10th St and Constitution Ave NW, Washington, DC 20560; (202) 357-2162. Studies sediments and fossil organisms (osteology, morphology, paleo-environments, stratigraphy, ecology, evolution, systematics). Answers inquiries, provides consulting services regarding the collections.

10523. Department of Social & Cultural History, Natl Museum of Amer History, Smithsonian Institution, Constitution Ave between 12th and 14th Sts NW, Washington, DC 20560; (202) 381-6230. Studies the material culture of everyday life in U.S. from its settlement to present. Staff identifies objects, provides consultation on the collections and general info. Researchers may have access to study collections.

10524. Department of State Library, 2201 C St NW, Washington, DC 20520; (202) 647-0486. Concerned with all areas of the world and their peoples, diplomatic history, intl political and economic conditions

and policies. Within security limits, library facilities are open for scholarly research.

10525. Department of State Visa Office, Dept of State, 2401 E St NW, Washington, DC 20520; (202) 647-1972. Supervises administration of U.S. immigration laws relating to issuance of visas to aliens visiting or immigrating to U.S. Answers inquiries, provides info and statistical data relating to U.S. immigration laws.

10526. Department of Vertebrate Zoology, Natl Museum of Natural History, Smithsonian Institution, 10th St and Constitution Ave NW, Washington, DC 20560; (202) 357-2740. Concerned with systematics, distribution, ecology, and evolution of mammals, birds, reptiles, amphibians, and fishes. Answers inquiries, provides consulting services, identifies vertebrate specimens. Encourages onsite reference use of collections by qualified investigators.

10527. Development Group for Alternative Policies, 1010 Vermont Ave NW, Ste 521, Washington, DC 20005; (202) 638-2600. Facilitates aid to Third World poor. Publishes tech reports and journal articles, answers inquiries, conducts workshops, distributes publications. Services for a fee to aid orgs.

10528. Development Resources, 2426 Ontario Rd, Washington, DC 20009; (202) 797-9610. Foundation that provides tech assistance to projects in developing countries, U.S. for the poor. Provides inquiry and consulting services on a sliding-scale fee, conducts workshops. Awards some grants.

10529. Directorate for Astronomical, Atmospheric, Earth, and Ocean Sciences, Division of Polar Programs, Natl Science Found, 1800 G St NW, Rm 627, Washington, DC 20550; (202) 357-7817. Conducts research program; publishes journal; serves as clearinghouse of info on Antarctic records, files, documents, maps maintained within executive agencies, nongovt orgs.

10530. Directorate for Biological, Behavioral, and Social Sciences, Division of Biotic Systems and Resources, Natl Science Found, 1800 G St NW, Washington, DC 20550; (202) 357-7332. Concerned with ecology, ecosystems, systematic biology, population biology. Marine ecology is excluded. Answers inquiries or refers inquirers to other info sources free.

10531. Directorate for Biological, Behavioral, and Social Sciences, Division of Molecular Biosciences, Natl Science Found, 1800 G St NW, Washington, DC 20550; (202) 357-9400. Interest in biochemistry, biophysics, prokaryotic genetics, metabolic biology. Answers inquiries or refers inquirers to other info sources free.

10532. Disability Rights Center, 1616 P Street NW, Ste 435, Washington, DC 20036; (202) 328-5198. Interest in rights of the disabled, including fed policies, actions, affirmative action. Publishes, sells reports and reprints of testimony, legal resource guides, equipment resource guide.

10533. Disabled American Veterans, 807 Maine Ave SW, Washington, DC 20024; (202) 554-3501. Represents all wounded, disabled U.S. veterans, their survivors and dependents. Publishes magazine; provides inquiry, advisory services free to veterans, survivors, dependents. Membership not required.

0534. Displaced Homemakers Network, 1010 Vermont Ave NW, Ste 817, Washington, DC 20005; (202) 628-6767. Provides communications, assistance, data collection, referrals, and legislative monitoring for displaced homemakers. Answers inquiries, provides consulting and referrals, conducts seminars, distributes publications. Some services free.

10535. Distilled Spirits Council of the U.S., 1250 Eye St NW, Washington, DC 20005; (202) 628-3544. Publishes annual statistical review of distilled spirits industry; provides reference services; permits onsite use of library collection by appointment. Most services free.

10536. Division of Astronomical Sciences, Natl Science Found, 1800 G St NW, Washington, DC 20550; (202) 357-9488. Conducts research in galactic and extragalactic astronomy, the solar system, stars and their evolution, astronomical instrumentation. Answers inquiries or makes referrals free.

10537. Division of Behavioral & Neural Sciences, Natl Science Found, 1800 G St NW, Washington, DC 20550; (202) 357-7564. Investigates neurobiology, sensory physiology, perception, psychobiology, memory, and cognitive processes. Answers inquiries and makes referrals free.

10538. Division of Biomass Energy Technology, Off of Renewable Energy Technology, Off of the Asst Secty for Conservation and Renewable Energy, Dept of Energy, 1000 Independence Ave SW, Washington, DC 20585; (202) 252-5275. Interest in biomass energy feedstocks (trees, herbaceous crops, aquatic species) and their thermo/biochemical conversion to fuels. Publishes tech reports. Answers inquiries. Services free.

10539. Division of Employment & Unemployment Analysis, Bur of Labor Statistics, Dept of Labor, 441 G St NW, Rm 2486, Washington, DC 20212; (202) 523-1944 or 523-1371. Compiles monthly statistics on labor force status of the civilian noninstitutional population 16 years of age and over, cross-classified by a variety of social and economic characteristics. Answers inquiries, provides consulting services and data compilations. Most services free.

10540. Division of Fishery Research, Fish and Wildlife Service, Dept of the Interior, Washington, DC 20240; (202) 653-8772. Conducts research and development of new and improved concepts and techniques for the preservation and mgmt of freshwater sport fisheries. Answers inquiries and makes referrals.

10541. Division of Forest Fire & Atmospheric Sciences Research, Forest Service, USDA, P.O. Box 2417 (Rosslyn Plaza East, Rm 606-F; 1621 N Kent St, Arlington,

VA), Washington, DC 20013; (703) 235-8195. Studies forest meteorology, remote sensing, fire science, prescribed uses of fire, fire control. Answers inquiries or makes referrals.

10542. Division of Geothermal & Hydropower Technologies, Dept of Energy, 1000 Independence Ave SW, Washington, DC 20585; (202) 633-8906. Supports development of new technologies for cost-effective and environmentally acceptable utilization of geothermal energy. Answers inquiries, conducts seminars, distributes publications, makes referrals. Services free.

10543. Division of Industrial Prices & Price Indexes, Off of Prices and Living Conditions, Bur of Labor Statistics, Dept of Labor, 600 E St NW, Washington, DC 20212; (202) 272-5113. Compiles statistics on producer prices and price indexes, indexes for the output of selected industries, and producer price indexes for net output of industry. Distributes monthly reports of industrial prices and indexes. Descriptions, procedures, and uses of indexes are provided on request.

10544. Division of International Prices, Off of Prices and Living Conditions, Bur of Labor Statistics, Dept of Labor, Washington, DC 20212; (202) 272-5020. Tracks price changes for U.S. exports and imports, current and past. Makes comparisons of U.S. export indexes with those of West Germany and Japan. Answers inquiries and publishes reports. Individual company and product data are confidential.

10545. Division of Materials Research, Natl Science Found, 1800 G St NW, Washington, DC 20550; (202) 357-9794. Does research into solid state physics and chemistry, low-temperature physics, condensed matter theory, metallurgy, polymers, and ceramics. Answers inquiries or makes referrals free.

10546. Division of Monthly Industry Employment Statistics, Off of Employment Structure and Trends, Bur of Labor Statistics, Dept of Labor, 441 G St NW, Rm 2089, Washington, DC 20212; (202) 523-1446. Compiles data on employment in nonagricultural industries, hours and earnings of production of nonsupervisory workers, conduct of payroll surveys generating these data. Answers inquiries, provides consulting and duplication services. Machine-readable data is provided at cost.

10547. Division of Ocean Energy Technology, Off of Solar Electric Technology, Dept of Energy, 1000 Independence Ave SW, Rm 5E098, Washington, DC 20585; (202) 376-5517. Interest in alternative renewable ocean thermal energy resources, solar energy. Publishes tech reports, reprints. Answers inquiries, conducts seminars and workshops. Most services free.

10548. Division of Ocean Sciences, Natl Science Found, 1800 G St NW, Washington, DC 20550; (202) 357-9639. Concerned with biological and physical oceanography, marine chemistry, submarine geology, and geophysics. Answers inquiries and makes referrals free.

10549. Division of Physics, Natl Science Found, 1800 G St NW, Washington, DC 20550; (202) 357-7985. Investigates atomic, molecular, plasma, particle, gravitational, theoretical, and nuclear physics. Answers inquiries and makes referrals free.

10550. Division of Refuge Management, Fish and Wildlife Service, Dept of the Interior, 18th and C Sts NW, Washington, DC 20240; (202) 343-4311. Seeks to protect, preserve, and manage a network of lands and waters in the National Wildlife Refuge System to encourage wildlife conservation. Publishes and distributes documents for Congress, govt, and the public.

10551. Division of Wildlife Research, Fish and Wildlife Service, Dept of the Interior, Washington, DC 20240; (202) 653-8762. Supervises and coordinates research relating to mammals, migratory and nonmigratory birds, and endangered species, and animal damage control research. Answers inquiries and makes referrals.

10552. Document Room, Hart Senate Off Bldg, Rm B-04, Washington, DC 20510; (202) 224-7860. Provides limited number of free copies of House and Senate documents, including bills, resolutions, presidential messages to Congress, most committee reports, and public laws.

10554. Drug Enforcement Administration, Dept of Justice, 1405 Eye St NW, Washington, DC 20537; (202) 633-1249. Enforces U.S. anti-drug policies involving illegal and prescription drugs. Answers inquiries, makes referrals.

10555. ERIC Clearinghouse on Higher Education, George Washington Univ, 1 Dupont Circle NW, Ste 630, Washington, DC 20036; (202) 296-2597. Collects, processes, and disseminates literature related to higher education and produces reviews or state-of-the-art papers on critical issues in the field. Answers inquiries, provides consulting and reference services. Supplier of ERIC services. Fee for some services.

10556. Economic Development Administration, Dept of Commerce, Rm 7800B, 14th Street and Constitution Ave NW, Washington, DC 20230; (202) 377-5113, 377-5081. Provides economic development assistance to depressed areas and to firms threatened by foreign imports. Provides info about grants, loans, etc.

10557. Economic Research Service, Dept of Agriculture, 500 12th Street SW, Washington, DC 20250; (202) 447-8104. Makes agricultural projections based on economic research, provides studies and evaluations to policymakers. Provides free publications list.

10558. Economic Research Service, International Economics Division, Dept of Agriculture, 500 12th St SW, Rm 348, Washington, DC 20250; (202) 447-8474. Conducts, publishes research on intl food and fiber outlook; implications for U.S., world agriculture. Maintains automated data bases.

10559. Economic Statistics Bureau of Washington, P.O. Box 10163, Washington, DC 20018; (202) 393-5070. Publishes monthly handbook of basic economic statistics (by subscription); provides consulting services for a fee.

10560. Edison Electric Institute, 1111 19th St NW, Washington, DC 20036; (202) 828-7400. Answers inquiries, provides reference services on electric utility business, publishes reports, provides repros for a fee, makes interlibrary loans. Library open to public by appointment.

10561. Education & Research Institute, 517 Second St NE, Washington, DC 20002; (202) 546-1710. Trains prospective journalists in basic skills in context of traditional values. Publishes reports, newsletter; answers inquiries; conducts seminars, workshops.

10562. Education Department, Information Branch, Office of Public Affairs, Rm 2097, 400 Maryland Ave, SW, Washington, DC 20202; (202) 245-8564. Provides info, publications, referrals regarding dept programs, functions, and policies.

10563. Eisenhower Foundation, 1990 M St NW, Ste 200, Washington, DC 20036; (202) 429-0440. Supports community self-help by inner-city residents to combat crime. Publishes studies, promotional materials, newsletter; provides inquiry, advisory services; distributes publications. Services free.

10564. Eisenhower Institute for Historical Research, Natl Museum of Amer History, Constitution Ave between 12th and 14th Sts NW, Washington, DC 20560; (202) 357-2263 or 357-2183. Assists American and foreign researchers in military history. Acts as a liaison between museum and official military service historians. Provides free general reference services to any serious researcher in military history.

10565. Electricity Consumers Resource Council, 1828 L St NW, Washington, DC 20036; (202) 466-4686. Represents industrial users of electricity. Maintains library, data base on electricity consumption; answers inquiries; conducts workshops. Most services free.

10566. Electronic Industries Association, 2001 Eye St NW, Washington, DC 20006; (202) 457-4900. Represents electronics industry. Develops voluntary standards; sponsors seminars, conferences; publishes technical reports, proceedings; provides reference services.

10567. Electronic Industries Association, Joint Electron Device Engineering Councils, 2001 Eye St NW, Washington, DC 20006; (202) 659-2200. Interest in industry-sponsored and registered defining data covering all categories of electron tubes and semiconductors. Sells publications or photocopies of individual registration data release files.

10568. Electronic Industries Foundation, 1901 Pennsylvania Ave NW, Ste 700, Washington, DC 20006; (202) 955-5810. Promotes use of electronics for public benefit, especially for disabled. Researches public policy on the field. Provides inquiry, advisory, consulting services; conducts seminars, workshops.

10569. Emergency Committee for American Trade, 1211 Connecticut Ave NW, Ste 801, Washington, DC 20036; (202) 659-5147. Acts as lobby for freer intl trade and investment that represents the interests of its 64 corporate members. Provides general reference services; permits onsite use of materials. Services generally free, except certain publications.

10570. Employee Relocation Council, 1627 K St NW, Washington, DC 20006; (202) 857-0857. Develops and circulates studies and info to member corporations on the many aspects involved in employee relocation. Answers inquiries, provides advisory and reference services, distributes publications. Most services only to members.

10571. Employment & Training Administration, Office of Public Affairs, Dept of Labor, 200 Constitution Ave NW, Rm S-2322, Washington, DC 20210; (202) 376-6270. Source of info on employment and training, unemployment insurance, testing, work-experience programs, job placement, and counseling. Answers inquiries, provides advisory services, distributes publications, makes referrals.

10572. Employment and Training Administration, Bureau of Apprenticeship and Training, Dept of Labor, 601 D St NW, Washington, DC 20213; (202) 376-7139. Holds statistical data on apprenticeship, training programs; publishes standards, reports; provides reference, consulting services to employer assns, natl companies, labor unions, vocational schools.

10574. Energenics Systems, 1100 17th St NW, Ste 505, Washington, DC 20036; (202) 463-8620. Commercial org involved with development, ownership of innovative projects in alternative energy resources. Provides inquiry, advisory, consulting services, usually on contract basis.

10575. Energy Information Administration, Dept of Energy, 1000 Independence Ave, SW, Washington, DC 20585; (202) 252-2363. Collects, evaluates, disseminates various energy data. Answers inquiries, distributes reports and publications.

10576. Environmental & Energy Study Conference, H2-515, Washington, DC 20515; (202) 226-3300. Bipartisan legislative service org of U.S. Congress for research, analysis of environmental, energy, natural resources issues. Publishes bulletin, briefs, reports. Bulletin available by subscription.

10577. Environmental Action, 1525 New Hampshire Ave NW, Washington, DC 20036; (202) 745-4870. Lobbies on national legislation and fed regulation and works to elect good environmentalists to Congress. Distributes legislative alerts and other publications to members.

10579. Environmental Design & Surveys Branch, Hwy Design Div, HNG-22, Off of Engineering, Fed Hwy Admin, 400 Seventh St SW, Washington, DC 20590; (202) 426-0306. Applies aerial surveys to highway engineering, public transportation, and environmental design. Answers inquiries, provides consulting and reference services.

10580. Environmental Educators, 2100 M St NW, Washington, DC 20037; (202) 466-3055. Commercial org engaged in program consulting, membership development, and direct response advertising for nonprofit conservation orgs. Provides consulting services on a fee basis.

10581. Environmental Fund, 1325 G St NW, Ste 1003, Washington, DC 20005; (202) 879-3000. Publicizes overpopulation, its effects on environment, natural resources, quality of life in U.S. Library available for onsite use. Publishes newsletter, monographs, papers; provides computer projections, graphics.

10582. Environmental Law Institute, 1616 P St NW, Ste 200, Washington, DC 20036; (202) 328-5150. Fosters dialogue among environmental professionals. Interest in environmental law research. Provides info primarily through its publication (sold by subscription). Offers access to data bases on a fee basis, conducts annual conference. Library open by appointment.

10583. Environmental Policy Institute, 218 D St SE, Washington, DC 20003; (202) 544-2600. National info center on energy, environmental issues. Publications list available. Provides inquiry, consulting services; conducts seminars. Most services free.

10584. Equal Employment Advisory Council, 1015 15th St NW, Ste 1220, Washington, DC 20005; (202) 789-8650. Represents views held by business, industry on equal employment opportunity, affirmative action. Publishes materials; conducts seminars, workshops. Fee for some services.

10585. Equal Employment Opportunity Commission Library, 2401 E St NW, Rm 242, Washington, DC 20507; (202) 634-6990. Administers Title VII of the Civil Rights Act of 1964 and investigates charges of employment discrimination. Answers inquiries, provides advisory and technical assistance.

10586. Esperantic Studies Foundation, 6451 Barnaby St NW, Washington, DC 20015; (202) 362-3963. Devoted to research and education on intl language problems. Provides general reference services; permits onsite use of collection. Most services free.

10587. Ethics & Public Policy Center, 1030 15th St NW, Ste 300, Washington, DC 20005; (202) 682-1200. Interest in relation of ethical, religious values to public policy issues. Provides inquiry, advisory services free, within limits of time and staff; conducts seminars, workshops.

10588. Ethiopian Community Center, 1929 18th St NW, Ste 1, Washington, DC 20009; (202) 328-3102. Sponsors cultural, educational, social development progs for Ethiopian community in U.S. Provides inquiry, advisory, reference, translation services; conducts seminars. Services free, except translations.

10589. European Communities Commission Information Service, 2100 M St NW, Ste 707, Washington, DC 20037; (202) 862-9500. Publishes magazine, brochures, films on European economic community. Makes interlibrary loans; answers inquiries free. Library open to public.

10590. Export-Import Bank of the U.S., 811 Vermont Ave NW, Washington, DC 20571; (202) 566-8320. Aids in financing and facilitates export of U.S. goods. Answers inquiries, provides advisory services, but not advice on how to establish an export business. Library services available to researchers with permission of librarians.

10591. Extension Service, Deputy Administrator for Natural Resources & Rural Development, Dept of Agriculture, 5925 South Bldg, Washington, DC 20250; (202) 447-7947. Concerned with natural resource policy carried out in cooperation with State Cooperative Extension Services. Answers inquiries or makes referrals, provides consulting services to State Extension Services.

10592. Farm Labor Research Committee, 1901 L St NW, Ste 804, Washington, DC 20036; (202) 296-0078. Interest in farm labor-mgmt relations, legislation. Publishes newsletter (by subscription), news releases; answers inquiries. Most services free.

10593. Farmers Home Administration, Rm 5014, South Bldg, 14th St and Independence Ave, SW, Washington, DC 20250; (202) 447-7967. Provides credit to U.S. farmers unable to obtain it elsewhere.

10594. Federal Bar Association, 1815 H St NW, Ste 408, Washington, DC 20006; (202) 638-0252. Professional assn of attorneys in fed govt, or interested in fed law. Publishes materials; provides phone info, calendar, job bank; conducts continuing legal education. Most services for lawyers, some free.

10595. Federal Bureau of Investigation, National Crime Information Center, Technical Services Div, 10th St and Pennsylvania Ave NW, Washington, DC 20535; (202) 324-2606. Has computerized data base, telecommunications network that links criminal justice agencies in U.S., Canada to FBI. Provides inquiry, advisory services; conducts seminars. Services free, available only to agencies.

10596. Federal Communications Commission, 1919 M St NW, Washington, DC 20554; (202) 632-7000. Oversees and regulates radio, TV, cable services, promotes fair telephone rate structures, provides broadcast licensing services. Provides info, makes referrals.

10597. Federal Crop Insurance Corporation, Rm 4096, South Bldg, 14th St and Independence Ave, SW, Washington, DC 20250; (202) 447-6795. Provides crop insurance, promotes agricultural stability.

10598. Federal Deposit Insurance Corp., 550 17th St NW, Washington, DC 20429; (202) 389-4221. Protects bank deposits and safeguards nation's money supply in the event of bank failure. Answers inquiries, makes referrals, distributes publications, provides a reporting service. Services limited according to time and effort required.

10599. Federal Election Commission, 1325 K St NW, Washington, DC 20463; (202) 523-4089, 523-4068. Promotes fair election campaign procedures by enforcing compliance with related fed laws. Provides info, makes referrals, distributes free publications.

10600. Federal Election Commission, National Clearinghouse on Election Administration, 1325 K St NW, Washington, DC 20463; (202) 523-4183; (800) 424-9530 (toll free). Administers Federal Election Campaign Act, including campaign disclosure requirements and expenditure limitations of presidential nominating conventions and elections. Answers inquiries, provides advisory services, distributes publications, conducts seminars, makes referrals.

10601. Federal Emergency Management Agency, 500 C St SW, Washington, DC 20472; (202) 287-0300; (800) 638-6620 (toll-free for flood insurance inquiries). Provides point of contact in the fed govt for emergency mgmt activities and provision of comprehensive disaster relief. Answers inquiries, distributes publications, lends films. Materials may be purchased from the Natl Audiovisual Center (Washington, DC 20409) or the Natl Technical Info Service (Springfield, VA 22161).

10602. Federal Energy Regulatory Commission, Office of Public Information, 825 N Capitol St, Washington, DC 20426; (202) 357-8118. Independent regulatory agency with many functions of the former Federal Power Commission, but also including pipeline regulation. Answers inquiries, provides reference services, distributes publications and makes referrals.

10603. Federal Grain Inspection Service, Rm 1628, South Bldg, 14th St and Independence Ave, Washington, DC 20250; (202) 382-0219. Provides and maintains U.S. standards for grain, conducts inspections, administers grain-weighing program at ports of entry and exit. Answers inquiries.

10604. Federal Highway Administration, National Ridesharing Information Center, 400 Seventh St SW, Rm 3301, Washington, DC 20590; (202) 426-0210. Provides info on ridesharing. Publishes newsletter, directories, brochures, reports; answers inquiries. Services free.

10605. Federal Home Loan Bank Board, 1700 G St NW, Washington, DC 20552; (202) 377-6296. Establishes policies, issues regulations, and supervises operations of the Federal Home Loan Bank System, the Federal Savings and Loan Insurance Corporation, and the Federal Home Loan Mortgage Corporation. Answers inquiries and makes referrals.

10606. Federal Information Centers, General Services Admin, 18th and F Sts NW, Washington, DC 20405; (202) 566-1937. Source of basic info on govt services and programs, located in 70+ major cities across the country. Intended to eliminate maze of referrals, centers in Iowa, Kansas, Missouri, and Nebraska that can be reached on a toll-free hotline; other centers have local numbers.

10607. Federal Judicial Center, Dolley Madison House, 1520 H St NW, Washington, DC 20005; (202) 633-6011. Promotes development and adoption of improved judicial administration in fed courts. Answers inquiries, makes referrals. Onsite use of the collection permitted, limited loans allowed. Further services provided to judicial personnel only.

10608. Federal Labor Relations Authority, 500 C St SW, Washington, DC 20424; (202) 382-0711. Maintains labor-mgmt relations within fed govt. Answers inquiries, publishes annual report, investigates complaints, makes referrals.

10609. Federal Library & Information Center Committee, c/ o Library of Congress, Washington, DC 20540; (202) 287-6055 or 287-6454. Provides coordination and fosters cooperation among fed libraries and info centers to establish a channel of communication and solve fed library problems. Answers inquiries, makes referrals, provides consultation, conducts seminars.

10610. Federal Maritime Commission, 1100 L St NW, Washington, DC 20573; (202) 523-5764. Regulates waterborne shipping in offshore commerce of U.S. Answers inquiries regarding subjects of commission interest, searches records and info on an hourly charge basis, copies and certifies or validates documents on a cost-per-page or document basis.

10611. Federal Mediation & Conciliation Service, 2100 K St NW, Washington, DC 20427; (202) 653-5290. Assists labor-mgmt disputants in industries affecting interstate commerce to settle their differences through conciliation and mediation. Answers inquiries, makes referrals, provides consulting and reference services, provides speakers.

10612. Federal Reserve System Board of Governors, C St bet 20th and 21st Sts NW, Washington, DC 20551; (202) 452-3000. Administers domestic credit and monetary policies, regulates and supervises banks and bank holding companies and the intl monetary system. Freedom of Info Office and Office of Public Affairs provide info and records inspection services.

10613. Federal Reserve System, Division of Consumer & Community Affairs, C St bet 20th and 21st Sts NW, Washington, DC 20551; (202) 452-2631. Concerns itself with a number of consumer-oriented programs mandated to the Board of Governors by Congress. Answers inquiries, makes referrals, distributes pamphlets. Services free.

10614. Federal Trade Commission, Public Reference Branch, 6th St and Pennsylvania Ave NW, Rm 130, Washington, DC 20580; (202) 523-3598. Interest in trade laws and policy, enforcement of antitrust laws, trade competition, consumer protection, advertising, etc. Answers inquiries, distributes publications, makes referrals to other sources of info, permits onsite use of collections. Services free.

10615. Federal Trade Commission, Office of Consumer Education, 6th St and Pennsylvania Ave NW, Rm 108, Washington, DC 20580; (202) 523-3575. Communicates FTC-enforced laws, trade regulation rules, other concerns thru the media. Publishes consumer info, industry education manuals; print, radio, TV public service.

10616. Federal Voting Assistance Program, Off of the Secty of Defense, Dept of Defense, Pentagon, Rm 1B457, Washington, DC 20301; (202) 694-4928. Administers certain fed voting legislation involving military personnel and U.S. citizens living overseas. Publishes books and technical reports, answers inquiries, provides ombudsman-type assistance to citizens, conducts seminars. Services free.

10617. Federation for American Immigration Reform, 1424 16th St NW, 7th Fl, Washington, DC 20036; (202) 328-7004. Interest in immigration to U.S. (law, policies, reform); illegal immigration; refugees. Publishes newsletter; provides free inquiry, advisory, referral services; conducts workshops.

10618. Federation of American Scientists, 307 Massachusetts Ave NE, Washington, DC 20002; (202) 546-3300. Interest in science and public policy, freedom of expression for scientists. Publishes magazine, answers inquiries. Services free, except publications.

10619. Federation of National Associations, 1350 New York Ave NW, Ste 615, Washington, DC 20005; (202) 393-1778. Trade assn for greeting card, candle, gift wrappings, and tyings industries. Has collection of antique greetings; publishes market list, bibliographies; answers inquiries. Services free.

10620. Federation of Organizations for Professional Women, 1825 Connecticut Ave NW, Room 403, Washington, DC 20009; (202) 328-1415. Assn committed to attaining equal opportunity for women in education and employment. Answers inquiries, conducts seminars, distributes publications, makes referrals. Services free, primarily for members.

10621. Feminist Alliance Against Rape, P.O. Box 21033, Washington, DC 20009; (202) 462-3717. Distributes publications regarding feminist anti-rape projects and crisis centers, rape prevention, domestic violence, child sexual assault, sexual harassment, antipornography, related subjects.

10622. Fertilizer Institute, 1015 18th St NW, Washington, DC 20036; (202) 861-4900. Answers technical inquiries on soil fertility and plant nutrition, industry production statistics; publishes journal; makes referrals. Info provided for use in U.S. only.

10623. Financial Management Service, Dept of the Treasury, Pennsylvania Ave and Madison Pl NW, Washington, DC 20226; (202) 566-2780. Oversees mgmt of financial resources and operations of fed govt, including central disbursing, check claims and reconciliation, central accounting and financial reporting. Answers inquiries and provides consultation to fed agencies.

10624. Fire Marshals Association of North America, Natl Fire Protection Assn, 1110 Vermont Ave NW, Ste 1210, Washington, DC 20005; (202) 667-7441. Works on fire prevention, education. Maintains statistics data base; answers inquiries; provides inquiry, referral services. Fee for some services; seminars, publications limited to members.

10625. Fish and Wildlife Service, Dept of the Interior, 18th and C Sts NW, Washington, DC 20240; (202) 343-5634. Responsible for conservation of fish and wildlife resources such as endangered species. Publishes monthly bulletin, journals, annual research report; answers inquiries.

10626. Fishery Resources Program, Fish and Wildlife Service, Dept of the Interior, 18th and C Sts NW, Rm 3251, Washington, DC 20240; (202) 343-6394. Coordinates planning, work selection, and funding of fish production, research, and technical assistance directed to a variety of anadromous and freshwater species of fish. Answers inquiries and makes referrals. Services free.

10627. Flexible Packaging Association, 1090 Vermont Ave NW, Ste 500, Washington, DC 20005; (202) 842-3880. Interest in mgmt, finance, economics, and marketing in flexible packaging industry; legislation on fair packaging and labeling; food additives, sanitation, and safety. Distributes publications, some on cost basis.

10628. Food & Agriculture Organization of the United Nations, c/o Roger A. Sorenson, Dir, 1001 22nd St NW, Ste 300, Washington, DC 20437; (202) 653-2402. Interest in agricultural development, world agricultural economics and statistics, food and agricultural legislation, etc. Answers nontechnical inquiries, distributes FAO newsletter, permits prearranged onsite use of collection and index.

10629. Food & Drug Law Institute, 1701 K St NW, Ste 904-906, Washington, DC 20006; (202) 833-1601. Membership org of firms interested in laws and regulations applicable to the food, drug, cosmetic, and related industries. Provides general reference services; conducts legal research; sponsors graduate fellowships in food and drug law at New York and George Washington Univs.

10630. Food Marketing Institute, 1750 K St NW, Washington, DC 20006; (202) 452-8444. Assn of supermarket operators, grocery wholesalers. Publishes news-

letter, bulletin, research reports; answers inquiries; prepares analyses; permits onsite use of collection.

10631. Food Processing Machinery and Supplies Association, 1828 L St NW, Ste 700, Washington, DC 20036; (202) 833-1790. Publishes convention/exposition directory, newsletters for food processing industry; answers inquiries; makes referrals; provides consulting, marketing info.

10632. Food Processors Institute, 1401 New York Ave NW, Ste 400, Washington, DC 20005; (202) 393-0890. Source of data on food processing, including quality control and govt regulations. Conducts seminars and distributes publications. Services provided for a fee.

10633. Food Research & Action Center, 1319 F St NW, Washington, DC 20004; (202) 393-5060. Works to improve, expand fed food programs. Involved in publication, research, training, fieldwork; legal aspects and legislative advocacy regarding food. Provides inquiry, advisory, referral services. Most services free.

10634. Food Safety & Inspection Service, Information Division, Dept of Agriculture, 14th St and Independence Ave SW, Washington, DC 20250; (202) 447-9113. Handles mandatory inspection of meat, poultry. Publishes consumer info, referral materials; answers inquiries, refers inquirers to specialists. Some data, reports available to researchers.

10635. Foodservice Consultants Society International, 1000 Connecticut Ave NW, Ste 9, Washington, DC 20036. Owns technical reports on food facilities engineering; publishes journal, newsletter for members, glossary, brochures; answers inquiries; provides consulting services for a fee.

10637. Foreign Agricultural Service, Rm 5071 South Bldg, 14th St and Independence Ave, SW, Washington, DC 20250; (202) 447-3935. Promotes U.S. agricultural exports, analyzes foreign markets and agricultural situations, conducts trade negotiations. Answers inquiries, maintains data base.

10638. Foreign Claims Settlement Commission of the U.S., 1111 20th St NW, Washington, DC 20579; (202) 653-5883. Determines merits of claims of U.S. nationals against foreign govts for losses and injury sustained by them within aegis of the International Claims Settlement Act of 1949, War Claims Act of 1948, and Czechoslovakian Claims Settlement Act of 1981. Answers inquiries.

10639. Foreign Trade Zones Board, Dept of Commerce, 14th St and Constitution Ave NW, Washington, DC 20230; (202) 377-2862. Administers Foreign Trade Zones Act, which provides for establishment and operation of customs-free zones in U.S. and Puerto Rico. Answers inquiries, provides info on foreign-trade zone benefits and application procedures, makes referrals.

10640. Forest Insect & Disease Research Staff, Forest Service, USDA, P.O. Box 2417 (Rosslyn Plaza East,

Rm 1211; 1621 N Kent St, Arlington, VA), Washington, DC 20013; (703) 235-8065. Pursues research on all aspects of forest and wood products, insects and diseases, including biology, ecology, and pest mgmt. Answers inquiries and makes referrals.

10641. Forest Pest Management Staff, Forest Service, USDA, P.O. Box 2417 (Rosslyn Plaza East, Rm 204; 1611 N Kent St, Arlington, VA), Washington, DC 20013; (703) 235-1560. Concerned with biological and impact evaluations, and prevention and suppression of forest insect and disease outbreaks, pesticide use and environmental pollutants. Answers inquiries, makes referrals, distributes brochures and reprints.

10642. Forest Service, Forest Products & Harvesting Research Staff, Forest Service, USDA, P.O. Box 2417, Washington, DC 20013; (703) 235-1203. Studies forest products utilization, timber and wood quality, processes and product development, wood chemistry and fiber products. Inquiries referred to the appropriate Forest Experiment Station.

10643. Forest Service, Office of Information, USDA, P.O. Box 2417, Washington, DC 20013; (202) 447-3760. Publishes reports, pamphlets, bulletins, bibliographies related to forestry; provides consulting, reference services. Distributes single copies of publications free.

10644. Forest Service, Watershed & Air Management Staff Unit, USDA, P.O. Box 2417 (Rosslyn Plaza East, Rm 1210; 1621 N Kent St, Arlington, VA), Washington, DC 20013; (703) 235-8096. Interest in soil, water, air resource mgmt on Natl Forest System lands. Has collection of computer progs, other tools for watershed mgmt. Publishes materials, answers inquiries free.

10645. Foundation for Cooperative Housing, 2501 M St NW, No 450, Washington, DC 20037; (202) 887-0700. Nonprofit org that develops low-cost housing in U.S. and developing countries. Interest in community development, social services, etc. Provides general reference services, conducts seminars, distributes publications. Info services free, except some publications.

10646. Foundation for Public Affairs Resource Center, 1255 23rd St NW, Washington, DC 20037; (202) 872-1750. Concerned with corporate public affairs, public interest groups, and public policy issues affecting business. Publishes a monthly, answers inquiries, provides advisory and reproduction services, distributes publications, makes referrals. Most services free.

10647. Foundry Equipment & Materials Association, 1133 15th St NW, Ste 1000, Washington, DC 20005; (202) 429-9440. Assn of manufacturers of foundry equipment, including blast cleaning and tumbling, dust and fume control equipment, flasks, furnaces, and accessories. Answers inquiries and makes referrals.

10648. Free Congress Research & Education Foundation, Child & Family Protection Institute, 721 Second St NE, Washington, DC 20002; (202) 546-3004. Monitors trends in U.S. family situation, policy. Publishes journal, answers inquiries, conducts seminars. Services free, except publications.

10649. Freedom of Information Clearinghouse, Ctr for the Study of Responsive Law, Public Citizen, P.O. Box 19367 (2000 P St NW, Ste 700), Washington, DC 20036; (202) 785-3704. Provides info on U.S., state open govt laws to public. Serves as resource for litigation, keeps files on the issue. Provides inquiry, advisory, referral services; conducts workshops. Services free.

10650. Freer Gallery of Art, Smithsonian Institution, Jefferson Dr and 12th St SW, Washington, DC 20560; (202) 357-2104. Conducts research and exhibit programs to contribute to a better understanding of the artistic achievements of Far and Near Eastern civilizations. Answers inquiries about the collections. Experts available for consultation. Library and gallery open to public.

10651. Friends Committee on National Legislation, 245 Second St NE, Washington, DC 20002; (202) 547-6000; (202) 547-4343 (24-hour legislative update tape). Monitors congressional action on U.S. foreign policy, foreign economic policy, disarmament, military spending, and many other issues. Publishes newsletter, answers inquiries, provides consulting and reference services, conducts briefings.

10652. Frontlash, 815 16th St NW, Rm 203, Washington, DC 20006; (202) 783-3993. Interest in voter registration, attitudes, voter education, youth political attitudes, labor political action. Answers inquiries free, distributes publications--some for a fee.

10654. Futures Industry Association, 1825 Eye St NW, Ste 1040, Washington, DC 20006; (202) 466-5460. Interest in commodity futures exchanges and trading and improvement of the financial strength and ethics of the industry. Answers brief inquiries, provides advisory and consulting services, makes referrals.

10655. Gallaudet University, 800 Florida Ave NE, Washington, DC 20002; (202) 651-5480. Liberal arts college for deaf students, with a graduate school that provides professional training for teachers, counselors, and audiologists who work with deaf people. Provides general reference services. Some fees, other costs negotiable.

10656. Garden Centers of America, 1250 Eye St NW, Ste 500, Washington, DC 20005; (202) 737-4060. Functions to bring retail garden center business to a higher level of efficiency and customer service. Provides general reference services, conducts seminars, distributes publications. Services provided free to members and at cost to nonmembers.

10657. General Accounting Office, 441 G St NW, Rm 7015, Washington, DC 20548; (202) 275-2812. Provides the media info about activities of the Comptroller General of U.S. and General Accounting Office. Answers inquiries from press and public, distributes publications to the press, conducts computerized data searches.

10658. General Aviation Manufacturers Association, 1400 K St NW, Ste 801, Washington, DC 20005; (202) 393-1500. Interest in general aviation. Provides general reference services, distributes publications, conducts seminars, makes referrals to other sources of info, makes motion pictures available. Services largely free.

10659. General Conference of Seventh-day Adventists, Department of Public Affairs & Religious Liberty, G6840 Eastern Ave NW, Washington, DC 20012; (202) 722-6681. Concerns itself with church-state affairs, religious liberty issues, including fed aid, Sunday laws, religion in public schools, and law. Answers inquiries, provides reference services, conducts seminars, distributes publications. Services may be provided at cost.

10660. General Services Administration, Consumer Information Center, 18th and F Sts NW, Washington, DC 20405; (202) 566-1794. Encourages release of consumer info accumulated as a byproduct of govt research, development, and procurement activities. Produces press releases and bilingual radio scripts, distributes publications.

10661. General Services Administration, Office of Public Affairs, Off of the Administrator, 18th and F Sts NW, Washington, DC 20405; (202) 566-1231. Concerned with fed building design, construction, mgmt, and maintenance. Answers inquiries, makes referrals.

10663. Gerontological Society of America, 1411 K St NW, Ste 300, Washington, DC 20005; (202) 393-1411. Interest in research, education, and practice for professionals in the field of aging, including housing projects. Provides general reference services, conducts annual seminars, sells publications. Services available to any interested professional.

10664. Global Water, 1629 K St NW, Ste 500, Washington, DC 20006; (202) 466-3528. U.S.-based org looking to conserve, improve worldwide water supplies, sanitation. Provides inquiry, referral services; country-specific info on projects in developing countries. Services free.

10665. Gold Institute, 1026 16th St NW, Ste 101, Washington, DC 20036; (202) 783-0500. Worldwide nonprofit assn of gold miners, refiners, fabricators, manufacturers. Provides inquiry, consulting, referral services free to members, for a fee to others.

10666. Gorgas Memorial Institute of Tropical & Preventive Medicine, 2001 Wisconsin Ave NW, Washington, DC 20007; (202) 338-9330. Conducts research on tropical diseases, host-parasite-vector relationships, epidemiology, control and treatment. Qualified scientists may have access to collections and other facilities. Identification of insect vectors available. Research services provided on contract.

10667. Government Accountability Project, 1555 Connecticut Ave NW, Ste 202, Washington, DC 20036; (202) 232-8550. Assists govt, corporate whistleblowers. Publishes books, produces films; provides inquiry, advisory, legal training services; conducts workshops. Most services free.

10668. Government Research Corp., 1250 Connecticut Ave NW, Ste 600, Washington, DC 20036; (202) 223-0222. Interest in fed govt policy monitoring, analyzing, and in providing advice concerning public policy in a variety of areas. Provides general reference services, interlibrary loans, permits onsite use of its collections by appointment. Services provided for a fee to all users.

10669. Grocery Manufacturers of America, 1010 Wisconsin Ave NW, Ste 800, Washington, DC 20007; (202) 337-9400. Interest in grocery industry, food and non-food issues, nutrition, labeling, safety, and quality of food products, marketing regulation and distribution of grocery products. Answers inquiries, makes referrals, distributes publications. Services free and primarily for members.

10670. Ground Zero, 806 15th St NW, Ste 421, Washington, DC 20005; (202) 638-7402. Nonprofit org that works to prevent nuclear war. Publishes promotional, scholarly materials; answers inquiries. Services at cost.

10671. HUD Library, Dept of Housing and Urban Development, 451 Seventh St SW, Rm 8141, Washington, DC 20410; (202) 755-6370. Owns written materials on urban renewal, city, county, state planning; provides consulting, reference, repro services; makes interlibrary loans; permits onsite use of collection.

10672. HUD Office of the Special Advisor for Disability Issues, Dept of Housing and Urban Development, Rm 10142, Washington, DC 20410; (202) 426-6030 (V/TDD). Interest in govt policies on the disabled, HUD programs for the disabled. Provides inquiry, advisory, referral services, info on research in progress. Services free.

10673. Handgun Control, Inc., 1400 K St NW, Ste 500, Washington, DC 20005; (202) 898-0792. Nonprofit citizens' lobby for handgun control. Comprehensive file of articles, research papers, legislative info, govt reports, statistical data, litigation procedures. Answers inquiries. Services free.

10674. Health & Energy Institute, 236 Massachusetts Ave NE, Ste 506, Washington, DC 20002; (202) 543-1070. Interest in health effects of ionizing radiation. Publishes materials; provides inquiry, consulting services; conducts seminars; permits onsite use of library. Fee for some services.

10675. Health Care Financing Administration, Office of Public Affairs, Dept of Health and Human Services, North Bldg, Rm 4244, 330 Independence Ave SW, Washington, DC 20201; (202) 245-6183. Has oversight of Medicare, Medicaid, and related federal programs. Publishes brochure; provides inquiry, advisory services for free.

10676. Health Occupations Students of America, 1250 Eye St NW, Ste 303, Washington, DC 20005. Interest in health occupations education. Publishes newsletter, reference materials; provides free inquiry, advisory services.

10677. Hearing Industries Association, c/o Carole M. Rogin, Dir of Market Development, 1255 23rd St NW, Washington, DC 20037; (202) 833-1411. Represents interests of hearing aid manufacturers and distributors as well as manufacturers of component parts. Answers inquiries, distributes publications, compiles statistics, makes referrals. Services free, primarily for those concerned with hearing problems.

10678. Hebraic Section, African and Middle Eastern Div, Library of Congress, 10 First St SE, Washington, DC 20540; (202) 287-5422. Maintains holdings on Israel, Jews, and Judaism in all parts of the world, Jewish history, the Bible, Hebrew, Yiddish, and Amharic literature. Answers inquiries, makes referrals, provides reference services. Materials for onsite use only.

10679. High Frontier, 1010 Vermont Ave NW, No 1000, Washington, DC 20005; (202) 737-4979. Promotes outer space technology for nonnuclear commercial, military purposes. Answers inquiries, conducts seminars, operates speakers' bureau, distributes print and AV materials. Services free to some, at cost to others.

10680. Highway Loss Data Institute, 380 Watergate, 600 New Hampshire Ave NW, Ste 650, Washington, DC 20037; (202) 333-6200. Contributes to crash loss reduction research by providing up-to-date data about loss characteristics of automobiles through analysis of vehicle collision insurance, injury policy, and claims data. Answers inquiries and distributes publications free.

10681. Highway Research Information Service, Transportation Research Board, NRC-NAS-NAE-IOM, 2101 Constitution Ave NW, Washington, DC 20418; (202) 334-3250. Offers transportation administrators, engineers, researchers info on highway, urban transit-related research; publishes journal of abstracts. Services provided for fee.

10682. Highway Users Federation for Safety and Mobility, 1776 Massachusetts Ave NW, Washington, DC 20036; (202) 857-1200. Publishes news releases and bulletins on highway-related natl legislation, answers inquiries, assists govt programs to increase safety of highway traffic. Fee charged for extensive assistance.

10683. Historic House Association of America, 1600 H St NW, Washington, DC 20006; (202) 673-4025. Interest in historic buildings and historic preservation; legislation, govt progs. Provides consulting and referral services, publishes a monthly, conducts seminars and workshops. Some services free.

10684. History of Earth Sciences Society, c/o Ellis L. Yochelson, Secty, Museum of Natural History, Rm E-501, Washington, DC 20560; (202) 343-3232. Fosters scholarship, public interest in history of earth sciences. Publishes journal, calendar; answers inquiries; conducts seminars, workshops. Services free, except journal.

10685. Home & School Institute, Trinity Coll, Washington, DC 20017; (202) 466-3633. Nonprofit educational org that helps families better teach their children, and assists educators and others to work more effectively with parents and community. Provides general reference services, conducts courses, distributes publications. Fees for courses and publications.

10686. Horticultural Research Institute, 1250 Eye St NW, Ste 500, Washington, DC 20005; (202) 789-2900. Nonprofit org devoted to support of research necessary for the advancement of nursery industry. Provides general reference services, evaluates data. Members receive all services free; nonmembers receive limited services free.

10687. House Committee on Agriculture, Rm 1301, Longworth House Office Bldg, Washington, DC 20515; (202) 225-2171. Subcommittees: Conservation, Credit and Rural Development; Cotton, Rice and Sugar; Dept Operations, Research and Foreign Agriculture; Domestic Marketing, Consumer Relations, Nutrition; Forests, Family Farms and Energy; Livestock, Daily and Poultry; Tobacco and Peanuts; Wheat, Soybeans and Feed Grains.

10688. House Committee on Appropriations, Rm H-218, Capitol Bldg, Washington DC 20515; (202) 225-2771. Subcommittees: Agriculture, Rural Development and Related Agencies; Commerce, Justice, and State, the Judiciary and Related Agencies; Defense; District of Columbia; Energy and Water Development; Foreign Operations; Interior and Related Agencies; Labor, Health and Human Service, Education, and Related Agencies; Legislative Branch; Military Construction; Transportation and Related Agencies; Treasury, Postal Service, and General Government.

10689. House Committee on Armed Services, Rm 2120, Rayburn House Office Bldg, Washington, DC 20515; (202) 225-4151. Subcommittees: Investigations; Military Installations and Facilities; Military Personnel and Compensation; Procurement and Military Nuclear Systems; Readiness; Research and Development; Seapower and Strategic Critical Materials.

10690. House Committee on Banking, Finance, and Urban Affairs, Rm 2129, Rayburn House Office Bldg, Washington, DC 20515; (202) 225-4247. Subcommittees: Consumer Affairs and Coinage; Domestic Monetary Policy; Economic Stabilizations; Financial Institutions Supervision, Regulation and Insurance; General Oversight and Investigations; International Development Institutions and Finance; International Finance, Trade and Monetary Policy.

10691. House Committee on Education and Labor, Rm 2181, Rayburn House Office Bldg, Washington, DC 20515; (202) 225-4527. Involved in forming education and labor legislation, including vocational rehabilitation, minimum wage legislation, and school lunch programs. Subcommittees: Elementary, Secondary, and Vocational Education; Employment Opportunities; Health and Safety; Human Resources; Labor-Management Relations; Labor Standards; Postsecondary Education; Select Education.

10692. House Committee on Energy and Commerce, Rm 2125, Rayburn House Office Bldg, Washington, DC 20515; (202) 225-2927. Subcommittees: Commerce, Transportation and Tourism; Energy Conservation and Power; Fossil and Synthetic Fuels; Health and the Environment; Oversight and Investigations; Telecommunications, Consumer Protection and Finance; Ad Hoc Subcommittee on Trade with China.

10693. House Committee on Foreign Affairs, Rm 2170, Rayburn House Office Bldg, Washington, DC 20515; (202) 225-5021. Subcommittees: Africa; Asian and Pacific Affairs; Europe and the Middle East; Human Rights and International Organizations; International Economic Policy and Trade; International Operations; Arms Control, International Security and Science; Western Hemisphere Affairs.

10694. House Committee on Government Operations, Rm 2157, Rayburn House Office Bldg, Washington, DC 20515; (202) 225-5051. Subcommittees: Commerce, Consumer and Monetary Affairs; Environment, Energy and National Resources; Government Activities and Transportation; Government Info, Justice and Agriculture; Intergovtal Relations and Human Resources; Legislation and National Security; Employment and Housing.

10695. House Committee on House Administration, Rm H-236, Capitol Bldg, Washington, DC 20515; (202) 225-2061. Involved in House administration and mgmt, fed election legislation, Library of Congress, and the Smithsonian Institution. Subcommittees: Accounts; Procurement and Printing; Office Systems; Personnel and Police; Services; Elections.

10696. House Committee on Interior and Insular Affairs, Rm 1324, Longworth House Office Bldg, Washington, DC 20515; (202) 225-2761. Subcommittees: Energy and the Environment; General Oversight, Northwest Power, and Forest Management; Mining and Natural Resources; National Parks and Recreation; Public Lands; Water and Power Resources.

10697. House Committee on Merchant Marine and Fisheries, Rm 1334, Longworth House Office Bldg, Washington, DC 20515; (202) 225-4047. Studies issues and formulates measures related to the regulation and protection of fisheries and wildlife, the Coast Guard, merchant marine and Panama Canal. Subcommittees: Coast Guard and Navigation; Fisheries and Wildlife Conservation and the Environment; Merchant Marine; Oceanography; Oversight and Investigations; Panama Canal/Outer Continental Shelf.

10698. House Committee on Public Works and Transportation, Rm 2165, Rayburn House Office Bldg, Washing-

ton, DC 20515; (202) 225-4472. Studies issues and formulates measures related to public bldgs and roads, bridges and dams, flood control, rivers and harbors, watershed development, mass transit, surface transportation excluding railroads, and civil aviation. Subcommittees: Aviation; Economic Development; Investigations and Oversight; Public Bldgs and Grounds; Surface Transportation; Water Resources.

10699. House Committee on Rules, Rm H-312 Capitol Bldg, Washington, DC 20515; (202) 225-9486. Studies issues and formulates measures governing the disposition of business on the House floor and most rules of the House, and waivers relating to legislative deadlines imposed by the Congressional Budget Act. Subcommittees: Legislative Process; Rules of the House.

10700. House Committee on Science and Technology, Rm 2321, Rayburn House Office Bldg, Washington, DC 20515; (202) 225-6371. Subcommittees: Energy Development and Application; Energy Research and Production; Investigations and Oversight; Natural Resources, Agriculture Research and Environment; Science, Research and Technology; Space Science and Applications; Transportation, Aviation and Materials.

10701. House Committee on Small Business, Rm 2361, Rayburn House Office Bldg, Washington, DC 20515; (202) 225-5821. Studies issues and formulates measures related to small business in general, and to the Small Business Administration. Subcommittees: Antitrust and Restraint of Trade Activities Affecting Small Business; Energy, Environment, and Safety Issues Affecting Small Business; Export Opportunities and Special Small Business Problem; General Oversight; SBA and SBIC Authority, Minority Enterprise and General Small Business Problems; Tax, Access to Equity Capital and Business Opportunities.

10702. House Committee on Standards of Official Conduct, Rm HT-2 Capitol Bldg, Washington DC 20515; (202) 225-7103. Involved in enforcing the Code of Official Conduct. Has no permanent subcommittees.

10703. House Committee on Veterans' Affairs, Rm 335 Cannon House Office Bldg, Washington, DC 20515; (202) 225-3527. Subcommittees: Compensation, Pension and Insurance; Education, Training and Employment; Hospitals and Health Care; Housing and Memorial Affairs; Oversight and Investigations.

10704. House Committee on Ways and Means, Rm 1102, Longworth House Office Bldg, Washington, DC 20515; (202) 225-3625. Studies issues and formulates measures regarding taxation, social security, tariffs, and health care programs financed through payroll taxes. Subcommittees: Health; Oversight; Public Assistance and Unemployment Compensation; Select Revenue Measures; Social Security; Trade.

10705. House Committee on the Budget, Rm 214, House Annex #1, Washington, DC 20515; (202) 225-7200. Involved in the coordination of spending and revenues in fed budget. Has no permanent subcommittees.

10706. House Committee on the District of Columbia, Rm 1310, Longworth House Office Bldg, Washington, DC 20515; (202) 225-4457. Studies issues and formulates measures regarding municipal affairs and the administration of the District of Columbia. Subcommittees: Fiscal Affairs and Health; Government Operations and Metropolitan Affairs; Judiciary and Education.

10707. House Committee on the Judiciary, Rm 2137, Rayburn House Office Bldg, Washington, DC 20515; (202) 225-3951. Studies issues and formulates measures related to fed courts, constitutional amendments, immigration and naturalization, Presidential succession, antitrust and monopolies, impeachment resolutions, patents, trademarks, and copyrights. Subcommittees: Administrative Law and Governmental Relations; Civil and Constitutional Rights; Courts, Civil Liberties and Administration of Justice; Crime; Criminal Justice; Immigration, Refugees, and International Law; Monopolies and Commercial Law.

10708. House Committee on the Post Office and Civil Service, Rm 309, Cannon House Office Bldg, Washington, DC 20515; (202) 225-4054. Studies issues and formulates measures related to the postal service, civil service, and fed statistics. Subcommittees: Census and Population; Civil Service; Compensation and Employee Benefits; Human Resources; Investigations; Postal Operations and Services; Postal Personnel and Modernization.

10709. Housing Assistance Council, 1025 Vermont Ave NW, Ste 606, Washington, DC 20005; (202) 842-8600. Interest in rural low-income housing, community development, rural and public housing production, research, Indian and migrant housing. Provides general reference services, conducts workshops, lends materials, permits onsite use of collection. Services may be provided at cost.

10711. Howard University, Center for Sickle Cell Disease, 2121 Georgia Ave NW, Washington, DC 20059; (202) 636-7930. Promotes education, patient care, and research in sickle cell disease and related syndromes. Publishes newsletter, answers inquiries, provides advisory services, conducts seminars, distributes publications. Services free.

10712. Howard University, Moorland-Spingarn Research Center, Founders Library, Rm 109, 500 Howard Pl NW, Washington, DC 20059; (202) 636-7239. Library for reference, bibliography, and research related to Afro-American history and culture and African history. Answers inquiries; provides advisory, reference, photographic, microform, and copying services; conducts seminars; makes referrals. Most services free.

10713. Howard University, Small Business Development Center, School of Business and Public Admin, P.O.

Box 748 (2600 Sixth St NW), Washington, DC 20059; (202) 636-5150. Provides mgmt training, counseling, and assistance to small business executives and staff and conducts women's and veterans' programs. Answers inquiries, provides free advisory and reference services, conducts seminars.

10714. Human Environment Center, 810 18th St NW, Washington, DC 20006; (202) 393-5550. Promotes confluence of social, environmental progress. Provides free inquiry, advisory, referral services; conducts seminars, conferences.

10715. Human Rights Internet, 1338 G St SE, Washington, DC 20003; (202) 543-9200. Internatl clearinghouse for human rights. Maintains computerized data base, library (for onsite use). Publishes journal; provides inquiry, advisory, referral services; conducts workshops. Services free or at cost.

10716. Humane Society of the U.S., 2100 L St NW, Washington, DC 20037; (202) 452-1100. Dedicated to prevention of cruelty to animals. Investigates incidents of animal abuse, conducts studies, and collects data. Answers inquiries, provides advisory and reference services, conducts seminars, distributes publications and films. Some services for a fee.

10719. Immigration and Naturalization Service, Dept of Justice, 425 Eye St NW, Washington, DC 20536; (202) 633-4330 (Info Off); (202) 633-3053 (Statistics Branch). Maintains stastistics on admission, exclusion, deportation, and naturalization of aliens. Answers inquiries.

10720. Independent Petroleum Association of America, 1101 16th St NW, Washington, DC 20036; (202) 857-4722. Interest in domestic crude oil and natural gas exploration and production. Provides free general reference services, distributes publications.

10721. Independent Sector, 1828 L St NW, Washington, DC 20036; (202) 223-8100. Seeks to preserve and enhance the tradition of giving, volunteering, and not-for-profit initiative. Conducts meetings and seminars, distributes publications, makes referrals, provides reference services. Services for members and subscribers only.

10722. Indian Arts and Crafts Board, Dept of the Interior, 18th and C Sts NW, Rm 4004, Washington, DC 20240; (202) 343-2773. Promotes development of traditional and innovative Native American arts and crafts. Answers inquiries, makes referrals, provides consulting services to Native American groups and individuals.

10723. Indian Education Programs, Dept of Education, 400 Maryland Ave SW, Washington, DC 20202; (202) 732-1887. Interest in educational opportunities for Indian students, adults. Provides inquiry, advisory, referral services; conducts seminars, workshops. Services free to Indian students, schools, orgs.

10724. Indochina Project, Ctr for Intl Policy, 236 Massachusetts Ave NE, Ste 505, Washington, DC 20002;

(202) 546-8181. Concerned with developments in Indochina, relations with U.S. Answers inquiries, provides speakers, conducts seminars, distributes publications. Services free, except publications.

10725. Information & Statistics Division, Off of Mgmt Systems, AMS-200, Fed Aviation Admin, 800 Independence Ave SW, Washington, DC 20591; (202) 426-3791. Compiles statistics relating to civil aircraft, airmen and airports, measures of activity, type or kind of aircraft, age and type of pilots. Answers inquiries.

10726. Information Center for Handicapped Individuals, 605 G St NW, Washington, DC 20001; (202) 347-4986. Links handicapped with available resources, services; advocates needed new services. Publishes referral materials; provides inquiry, advisory, reference, legal services; conducts workshops. Services free.

10727. Information Industry Association, 316 Pennsylvania Ave SE, Ste 400, Washington, DC 20003; (202) 544-1969. Trade assn for companies whose products and services are designed to meet info needs in virtually all phases of activity. Interest in management of info as a resource. Provides general reference services, conducts seminars, sells directory and special publications.

10729. Information/Documentation, P.O. Box 17109, Dulles Intl Airport, Washington, DC 20041; (703) 979-5363; (800) 336-0800. Commercial org that distributes public U.S. govt documentation, data bases for a fee. Provides inquiry, advisory, consulting, document delivery, reference, bibliographic services; conducts seminars, workshops.

10730. Institute for Local Self-Reliance, Information Access Section, 2425 18th St NW, Washington, DC 20009; (202) 232-4108. Encourages the nation's cities to pursue self-reliance as a development strategy. Answers inquiries; provides advisory, consulting, and reference services; conducts seminars; distributes publications. Most services free, primarily for municipal govts.

10731. Institute for Palestine Studies, P.O. Box 25697 (3501 M St NW), Washington, DC 20007; (202) 342-3990. Promotes understanding of Palestine, Middle East problems. Publishes scholary materials, provides free inquiry and referral services.

10732. Institute for Policy Studies, 1901 Q St NW, Washington, DC 20009; (202) 234-9382. Conducts research into domestic public policy, foreign and military policies, intl economic order. Answers inquiries, provides consulting and copying services, conducts seminars. Services at cost.

10733. Institute for Policy Studies, Project on Conventional Arms & Interventionism, 1901 Q St NW, Washington, DC 20009; (202) 234-9382. Fosters research, education in military, foreign policy issues. Provides inquiry, advisory, ref services; conducts seminars; distributes publications; permits onsite use of collection. Fee for some services.

10734. Institute for Research on the Economics of Taxation, 1331 Pennsylvania Ave NW, Ste 515, Washington, DC 20004; (202) 347-9570. Does empirical, theoretical analysis of govt tax, fiscal activities; economic policy. Publishes papers and data, answers inquiries, conducts seminars and conferences. Most services free.

10735. Institute for Sino-Soviet Studies, School of Public and Intl Affairs, George Washington Univ, 2130 H St NW, Ste 601, Washington, DC 20052; (202) 676-6340. Interest in Russian-Soviet, East European, East Asian studies. Has library of primary, secondary materials, including current Russian, Chinese press (for authorized onsite use). Publishes journal, conducts seminars and workshops.

10736. Institute for Soviet-American Relations, 2738 McKinley St NW, Washington, DC 20007; (202) 244-4725. Encourages alternatives to polarization between U.S. and USSR: cultural, scientific, business, educational, tourist interchanges. Answers inquiries. Fee for some services.

10737. Institute for the Development of Indian Law, 2100 M St NW, Ste 602, Washington, DC 20037; (202) 293-6141. Interest in selective litigation involving Indian treaty rights, historical research. Answers inquiries and permits onsite use of collection free, sells publications.

10738. Institute for the Study of Anxiety in Learning, Fund for Education and Human Services, 1802B T St NW, Washington, DC 20009; (202) 667-5291. Provides guidance, info on reentry into math. Publishes materials; provides inquiry, consulting, referral services; conducts seminars, workshops for a fee. Most services free.

10739. Institute of Applied Natural Science, 3000 Connecticut Ave NW, Ste 308, Washington, DC 20008; (202) 387-7749. Nonprofit educational and research org that conducts research in hypnosis and its effects. Provides general reference services, conducts seminars and lectures. Charges for private appointments, seminars, and educational courses.

10740. Institute of Criminal Law & Procedure, Law Ctr, Georgetown Univ, 25 E St NW, Washington, DC 20001; (202) 662-9550. Interest in criminal justice, corrections. Archives include data from natl studies (for onsite use). Provides inquiry, advisory services, conducts seminars. Services available to researchers; a fee may be charged.

10741. Institute of Laboratory Animal Resources, Natl Research Council, 2101 Constitution Ave NW, Washington, DC 20418; (202) 334-2590. Answers inquiries free on animal stocks used in biological and medical research, testing, teaching; publishes directory of sources of animals for research; reports on care of lab animals.

10742. Institute of Makers of Explosives, 1575 Eye St NW, Ste 550, Washington, DC 20005; (202) 789-0310. Publishes pamphlets on safety in manufacture, storage, transportation, use of commercial explosives; provides blasting cap safety education posters; answers inquiries; makes referrals.

10743. Institute of Navigation, 815 15th St NW, Ste 832, Washington, DC 20005; (202) 783-4121. Coordinates knowledge of navigators, scientists, equipment developers; publishes journal; permits onsite use of collection; exchanges info with navigation societies in other countries.

10744. Institute of Scrap Iron and Steel, 1627 K St NW, Ste 700, Washington, DC 20006; (202) 466-4050. Publishes journal, handbook with specifications, technical reports on metallic scrap; answers inquiries; makes referrals; lends materials. Services mostly free.

10745. Institute of Shortening & Edible Oils, 1750 New York Ave NW, Washington, DC 20006; (202) 783-7960. Promotes food fats and oils, technology, regulation, statistics, nutrition, etc. Answers inquiries free.

10746. Institute of Transportation Engineers, 525 School St SW, Ste 410, Washington, DC 20024; (202) 554-8050. Publishes handbook, journal, newsletter, standards and specifications, reports; provides reference services, but not those offered by traffic engineering consultants.

10747. Insulation Contractors Association of America, 905 16th St NW, Washington, DC 20006; (202) 347-2791. Represents and develops standards for insulation industry; promotes energy conservation. Publications price list available. Answers inquiries, conducts workshops. Services usually free.

10748. Insurance Institute for Highway Safety, 300 Watergate, 600 New Hampshire Ave NW, Washington, DC 20037; (202) 333-0770. Answers inquiries on highway loss reduction techniques; gives info on research; publishes newsletter; makes available films, testimony before congressional committees and fed agency hearings.

10749. Inter-American Bar Foundation, 1819 H St NW, Ste 310, Washington, DC 20006; (202) 293-1455. Interest in administration of justice in Western Hemisphere countries. Publishes materials, answers inquiries; conducts seminars. Most services free.

10750. Inter-American Commission on Human Rights, Organization of Amer States, 1889 F St NW, Washington, DC 20006; (202) 789-6000. Promotes observance and protection of human rights in the Americas and serves as consultative organ of the OAS in these matters. Answers inquiries, distributes publications. Services free.

10751. Inter-American Development Bank, 808 17th St NW, Washington, DC 20577; (202) 634-8000. Interest in social and economic development in Latin America. Provides general reference services, analyzes data, conducts seminars, permits onsite use of library. General services free; seminars and training only for preselected individuals.

10752. Inter-American Nuclear Energy Commission, Organization of Amer States, 1889 F St NW, Washington, DC 20006; (202) 789-3368, 789-3369, or 789-3370. Interest in peaceful uses of nuclear energy in Latin America. Publishes reports, answers inquiries, provides reference services free, makes referrals to other sources of info.

10753. Interfaith Action for Economic Justice, 110 Maryland Ave NE, Washington, DC 20002-5694; (202) 543-2800; (800) 424-7292 (for legislative updates). Cooperative effort of religious agencies to influence legislation on hunger, poverty in U.S., abroad. Answers inquiries, distributes publications. Most services provided at cost.

10754. Intergovernmental Health Policy Project, 2100 Pennsylvania Ave NW, Ste 616, Washington, DC 20037; (202) 872-1445. Clearinghouse for state health legislation. Publishes newsletter, research, legislative reports; conducts seminars; provides inquiry, referral services free to state, U.S. officials, others served at cost.

10755. Internal Revenue Service Library, Rm 4324, 1111 Constitution Ave NW, Washington, DC 20224; (202) 566-6342. Library of taxation and law. Open to govt personnel for official business; provides interlibrary loans to other govt libraries.

10756. Internal Revenue Service, Public Affairs Division, 1111 Constitution Ave NW, Rm 1111, Washington, DC 20224; (202) 566-4054. Major source of info on fed tax laws, their administration and enforcement. Provides info on tax laws to the general and special interest media.

10757. Internal Revenue Service, Statistics of Income Division, 1111 Constitution Ave NW, Washington, DC 20224; (202) 376-0216. Compiles annual statistics on the operation of income tax laws as required by the Internal Revenue Code. Answers factual inquiries, provides advice, furnishes special tabulations and public use of files at cost. Bona fide researchers may have direct access to some of the data.

10758. International Association for Dental Research, 1111 14th St NW, Ste 1000, Washington, DC 20005; (202) 898-1050. Holds computerized info on 6,000 dental researchers around world; publishes monthly dental research journal, newsletters; answers inquiries; makes referrals.

10759. International Association of Cooking Schools, 1001 Connecticut Ave NW, Rm 800, Washington, DC 20036; (202) 293-7716. Represents cooking schools, interests of the industry. Publishes cookbook, directory; answers inquiries; conducts seminars, workshops. Services free to members; to nonmembers for a fee.

10760. International Association of Fire Chiefs, 1329 18th St NW, Washington, DC 20036; (202) 833-3420. Assn consisting of fire chiefs, physicians, instructors, marshals, commissioners, and other fire fighters. Answers inquiries, provides consulting services, distributes publications, makes referrals. Fees for services.

10761. International Association of Fire Fighters, 1750 New York Ave NW, Washington, DC 20006; (202) 872-8484. Affiliated with AFL/CIO and Canadian Labour Congress. Publishes journal, annual survey of wages and working conditions, pamphlets, research reports; conducts seminars.

10762. International Association of Fish & Wildlife Agencies, 1412 16th St NW, Washington, DC 20036; (202) 232-1652. Interest in coordination, conservation among fish and wildlife agencies in North America, Canada, Mexico. Answers inquiries, provides limited consulting services, permits onsite use of collection. Services free, except publications.

10763. International Association of Hydrological Sciences, 2000 Florida Ave NW, Washington, DC 20009; (202) 462-6903. Promotes the study of hydrology and water resources and initiates research into problems that require intl cooperation. Answers inquiries free, conducts symposia, distributes publications for a fee.

10764. International Association of Ice Cream Manufacturers, 888 16th St NW, Washington, DC 20006; (202) 296-4250. Publishes annual and various bulletins on ice cream production, merchandising, distribution, fed standards. Answers inquiries, makes referrals.

10765. International Association of Machinists and Aerospace Workers, 1300 Connecticut Ave NW, Washington, DC 20036; (202) 857-5200. Affiliate of AFL-CIO publishes newspaper, annual reports, films, pamphlets, bulletins. Provides literature citations in response to inquiries. Services provided to scholars.

10766. International Bridge, Tunnel, and Turnpike Association, 2120 L St NW, Ste 305, Washington, DC 20037; (202) 659-4620. Interest in toll facility and highway design, financing, and operations. Publishes monthly newsletter, reports, surveys, meeting proceedings; permits onsite use of collection.

10768. International Center for Research on Women, 1717 Massachusetts Ave NW, Room 501, Washington, DC 20036; (202) 797-0007. Interest in the socioeconomic roles of women in developing countries. Answers inquiries, provides advisory and reference services, conducts seminars, makes referrals, permits onsite use of literature collection. Services free, except consulting.

10769. International City Management Association, 1120 G St NW, Washington, DC 20005; (202) 626-4600. Concerned with urban affairs. Publishes journals, directory of local govts; provides reference, consulting services to subscribing cities for a fee, offers statistical reports at cost.

10770. International Cogeneration Society, 1700 K St NW, Ste 1300, Washington, DC 20006; (202) 659-1552. Conducts, publishes research on integrated energy systems. Maintains data base on industrial plants; provides inquiry, advisory, referral services; conducts seminars. Services free to members, at cost to others.

10771. International Cotton Advisory Committee, 1225 19th St NW, Ste 650, Washington, DC 20036; (202) 463-6660. Assn of govts interested in production, export, import, and consumption of cotton. Answers inquiries, sells publications.

10772. International Council on Education for Teaching, 1 Dupont Circle, Rm 616, Washington, DC 20036; (202) 857-1830; (202) 659-5810. Interest in teacher training, educational development and policy, higher education worldwide. Provides inquiry, reference, consulting services; tech assistance (especially in Third World). Most services free to members, at cost to others.

10773. International Downtown Executives Association, 915 15th St NW, Ste 900, Washington, DC 20005; (202) 783-4963. Professional org of specialists on development, revitalization of downtowns and adjacent neighborhoods. Publishes materials; provides inquiry, advisory, consulting services. Fees charged to nonmembers.

10774. International Economic Policy Association, 1625 Eye St NW, Washington, DC 20006; (202) 331-1974. Concerned with U.S. intl economic policies. Provides congressional testimony; publishes reports, overseas surveys. Info services generally not available to public.

10775. International Economic Studies Institute, 1400 Eye St NW, Ste 510, Washington, DC 20005; (202) 898-2022. Sponsors and conducts statistical, economic, and scientific research concerning intl economic issues.

10776. International Energy Information Center, 909 M St NW, Washington, DC 20001; (202) 737-5454. Interest in fossil and nuclear energy, coal mining, energy transport. Holds research data; distributes publications; provides inquiry, consulting, referral services at cost.

10777. International Exchange Service, Smithsonian Institution, Washington, DC 20560; (202) 357-2073. Acts as forwarder for packages of scientific, cultural, and literary publications from individuals, societies, universities, and other U.S. orgs for transmittal to other countries, and vice versa. Answers inquiries on forwarding services.

10778. International Exhibitions Foundation, 1700 Pennsylvania Ave NW, Ste 580, Washington, DC 20006; (202) 737-4740. Organizes, circulates art exhibitions of highest quality to museums, galleries in U.S., abroad. Publishes scholarly catalogs, answers inquiries. Exhibitions available to qualifying orgs on a fee basis.

10779. International Federation for Family Life Promotion, 1511 K St NW, Ste 333, Washington, DC 20005; (202) 783-0137. Provides guidance, education in family, and natural family planning. Publications list available.

Provides inquiry and consulting services, permits onsite use of collection. Services generally free, except consulting.

10780. International Federation on Aging, 1909 K St NW, Washington, DC 20049; (202) 662-4927. Interest in social, comparative gerontology. Maintains extensive files (for onsite use); publishes scholarly materials; provides free inquiry, advisory services; conducts seminars.

10781. International Food Policy Research Institute, 1776 Massachusetts Ave NW, Washington, DC 20036; (202) 862-5614. Conducts research on policy problems affecting production, consumption, and distribution of food in the developing world. Publishes a quarterly, answers inquiries, sponsors seminars, provides reference services, distributes publications, makes referrals.

10782. International Franchise Association, 1025 Connecticut Ave NW, Ste 707, Washington, DC 20036; (202) 659-0790. Represents franchisors before govt bodies. Answers inquiries, provides limited reference services, conducts symposia, distributes publication. Services for members.

10783. International Hajji Baba Society, 1524 T St NW, Washington, DC 20009; (703) 560-3765. Promotes interest in pre-1900 oriental rugs, textiles. Publishes newsletter, exhibition catalogs; provides inquiry, consulting services free, if not extensive.

10784. International Hospital Federation, 444 N Capitol St NW, Ste 500, Washington, DC 20001; (202) 638-1100. Interest in hospital and health care mgmt. Provides advice and assistance, arranges hospital visits in any member country, provides literature-searching and translation services, conducts seminars. Most services free to any org that deals with hospitals.

10785. International Human Rights Law Group, 733 15th Street NW, Ste 1000, Washington, DC 20005; (202) 639-8016. Nonprofit org of lawyers for human rights. Publishes guides, legal materials; provides inquiry, legal, advisory services (most free); conducts seminars; permits onsite use of collections. Most services free.

10786. International Institute for Environment & Development, 1717 Massachusetts Ave NW, Ste 302, Washington, DC 20036; (202) 462-0900. Intl nonprofit org interested in links between environment, mgmt of the world's natural resources and development, and human and economic needs. Provides general reference services, conducts seminars, distributes publications, permits occasional onsite use of collection.

10787. International Institute of Site Planning, 914 11th St NW, Washington, DC 20001; (202) 737-2227. Info center for research onsite planning. Organizes lectures, exhibits; provides inquiry, advisory, referral services; distributes publications; lends materials. Services provided at cost.

10788. International Law Institute, 1920 N St NW, Washington, DC 20036; (202) 463-7979. Offers a combination of research and practical training focusing on legal aspects of intl trade, investment, and business. Students, friends of the institute, visiting scholars, researchers, and AID-sponsored foreign govt officials have access to the collections.

10789. International Masonry Institute, 815 15th St NW, Washington, DC 20005; (202) 783-3908. Conducts promotional programs in U.S. and Canada. Answers inquiries, publishes newsletter, provides consulting and reference services, conducts seminars, distributes publications. Most services free.

10790. International Monetary Fund, Bureau of Statistics, 700 19th St NW, Washington, DC 20431; (202) 477-2963. Fund is sponsored by member govts. Interest in intl finance, intl trade, balance of payments, govt finance statistics. Distributes publications and data. Services free to member govts, for a fee to others.

10791. International Numismatic Society, P.O. Box 66555 (1100 17th St NW, Ste 1000), Washington, DC 20035; (202) 223-4497. Coordinates numismatic research worldwide. Maintains library, publishes scholarly materials, answers inquiries, provides advisory and photographic services. Most services for a fee.

10792. International Personnel Management Association, 1850 K St NW, Washington, DC 20006; (202) 833-5860. Owns records of public personnel agencies. Publishes journals, reports; provides consulting, testing services; permits onsite use of collection. Limited services to nonmembers.

10793. International Resources Consultants, 1025 15th St NW, Ste 500, Washington, DC 20005; (202) 638-2002. Interest in mgmt consulting in agriculture, health research, engineering, systems mgmt, etc. Provides general reference services, conducts workshops, analyzes data, permits onsite use of collection. Services primarily for special groups, provided for fees.

10794. International Road Federation, 525 School St SW, Washington, DC 20024; (202) 554-2106. Publishes journal, reports on planning, maintenance, operation of natl, intl highway networks; answers brief inquiries from nonmembers; permits onsite use of collection.

10795. International Sculpture Center, 1050 Potomac St NW, Washington, DC 20007; (202) 965-6066. Service org for professional sculptors, those interested in sculpture. Provides inquiry, advisory, referral services; sponsors conferences; distributes journal. Services available to all, but preference to members.

10796. International Slurry Seal Association, 1101 Connecticut Ave NW, Ste 700, Washington, DC 20036; (202) 857-1160. Promotes increased use of asphalt slurry seal for efficient pavement surfacing. Publishes magazine, referral materials; answers inquiries; conducts seminars, workshops. Most services free.

10797. International Society for Labor Law & Social Security, c/o Leroy S. Merrifield, George Washington Univ, Natl Law Ctr, Washington, DC 20052; (202) 676-6745. Concerned with labor law; labor relations; and social legislation, domestic and foreign. Answers inquiries, publishes a quarterly,and makes referrals.

10798. International Student Pugwash, 505B Second St NE, Washington, DC 20002; (202) 544-1784. Educates youth on ethical dilemmas at interface of science, technology, society. Publication list available. Provides reference services, resource lists. Services at cost, chiefly to students.

10799. International Systemology Institute, P.O. Box 8606 (5605 16th St NW), Washington, DC 20011; (202) 723-0698. Conducts research in field of systemology (study of living organisms viewed as whole systems). Answers inquiries from professionals on cost-recovery basis.

10800. International Trade Administration, Office of Textiles & Apparel, Dept of Commerce, 15th St and Constitution Ave NW, Rm 3001, Washington, DC 20230; (202) 377-5078. Negotiates, implements bilateral textile, apparel restraint agreements; other programs for the industry. Publishes data, answers inquiries, conducts seminars. Most services free.

10801. International Trade Administration, Statutory Import Programs Staff, Deputy Asst Secty for Import Admin, Dept of Commerce, 14th St and Constitution Ave NW, Rm 1523, Washington, DC 20230; (202) 377-4216. Processes applications for duty-free entry of scientific instruments under provisions law. Permits onsite inspection of holdings. Copies of documents supplied for a fee.

10802. International Trade Administration, Trade Opportunities Program, Off of Trade Info Services, Dept of Commerce, 14th St and Constitution Ave NW, Rm 1324, Washington, DC 20230; (202) 377-2208. Provides U.S. firms with specific live foreign trade leads, using computer-assisted system. Offers bulletin by subscription, rapid-mail notices. Also provides info on tape.

10803. International Trade Administration, Marketing Publications & Services Div, Export Promotion Services, Dept of Commerce, 14th St and Constitution Ave NW, Rm 2106, Washington, DC 20230; (202) 377-5367. Focal point for promoting interest in exporting by the business community and providing it with info and assistance. Answers inquiries, provides free consulting and reference services, distributes publications.

10804. International Trade Administration, Office of Eastern Europe & Soviet Affairs, Deputy Asst Secty for Europe, Dept of Commerce, 14th St and Constitution Ave NW, Rm 3414, Washington, DC 20230; (202) 377-2645. Counsels and assists companies on East-West trade with Communist countries. Answers inquiries, provides consulting services, conducts seminars, makes referrals. Services free.

10805. International Union of Operating Engineers, 1125 17th St NW, Washington, DC 20036; (202) 429-9100. Concerned with construction, stationary engineer industries. Owns safety material, surveys, slides, films; publishes journal; answers brief inquiries; makes referrals.

10806. International Visitors Information Service, 733 15th St NW, Ste 300, Washington, DC 20005; (202) 783-6540. Assists intl visitors in Washington, D.C. Maintains info centers, provides multilingual escorts for sightseeing, operates Language Bank. Available to all visitors. Professional appointments arranged by prior request only.

10807. International Water Resources Association, P.O. Box 42360, Washington, DC 20015; (703) 768-4638. Interest in water resources in all aspects. Answers inquiries, provides advisory services, makes referrals to other sources of info. Services free.

10808. Interstate Commerce Commission, 12th St and Constitution Ave NW, Washington, DC 20423; (202) 275-7252 (Public Affairs); (202) 275-7119 (Info). Interest in interstate commerce by railroads, trucks, buses, barge operations and coastal shipping, freight forwarders, and transportation brokers. Answers inquiries.

10809. Interstate Commerce Commission, Office of Compliance & Consumer Assistance, 12th St and Constitution Ave NW, Washington, DC 20423; (202) 275-7844. Assists public with complaints on surface transport (rail, truck, bus, interstate movers). Publishes consumer info; provides free inquiry, advisory, referral services.

10810. Interstate Conference of Employment Security Agencies, 444 N Capitol St, Ste 126, Washington, DC 20001; (202) 628-5588. Seeks to improve public employment service, unemployment insurance programs, manpower programs. Answers inquiries, permits onsite use of collections. Services free.

10811. Interstate Conference on Water Problems, 1620 Eye St NW, Ste 800, Washington, DC 20006; (202) 466-7287. Interest in state water mgmt, natl water policy, fed water quantity and quality programs. Answers inquiries from states and individuals, conducts conferences. Services provided at cost to some users.

10812. Interstate Natural Gas Association of America, 1660 L St NW, Washington, DC 20036; (202) 293-5770. Owns periodicals, newsletters covering natural gas industry and other energy developments; publishes weekly report; answers inquiries as time permits; makes referrals.

10813. Investment Company Institute, 1775 K St NW, Washington, DC 20006; (202) 293-7700. Assn of mutual fund and investment mgmt firms and their advisors and underwriters. Answers inquiries, provides reference services, conducts seminars, distributes publications. Some services free.

10814. Investor Responsibility Research Center, 1319 F St NW, Ste 900, Washington, DC 20004; (202) 833-3727. Conducts research and publishes impartial reports and newsletters on corporate governance with emphasis on shareholder resolutions proposed to major corporations. Answers inquiries for subscribers, provides consulting, and reference services, conducts seminars, sells publications.

10815. Ion Energetics Data Center, Ctr for Chemical Physics, Natl Measurement Laboratory, Natl Bur of Standards, Washington, DC 20234; (301) 921-2439. Collects and disseminates info on ionization and appearance potentials, proton and electron affinities by all techniques, including spectroscopy. Answer inquiries, provides consulting services, makes referrals. Services for professionals in the field.

10816. Island Resources Foundation, 1718 P St NW, Ste T-4, Washington, DC 20036; (202) 265-9712. Works to solve unique problems of island systems worldwide. Interest in coastal zone mgmt, water pollution control, tropical reef ecology. Provides general reference services at variable fees.

10817. Japan Economic Institute, 1000 Connecticut Ave NW, Rm 211, Washington, DC 20036; (202) 296-5633. Publishes weekly report on economic, political relations of U.S. and Japan (available by subscription); free newsletter, pamphlets; answers inquiries; permits onsite use of library.

10818. Japan Information & Culture Center, Embassy of Japan, 917 19th St NW, Washington, DC 20006; (202) 234-2266 ext 416. Publishes newsletter; provides inquiry, referral services; conducts exhibits, performances, other activities; provides speakers. Services free.

10819. Japan-America Society of Washington, 606 18th St NW, Washington, DC 20006; (202) 289-8290. Interest in improvement of American understanding of Japanese society, economy, polity, and culture. Conducts Japanese language school, other programs; provides general reference services; permits onsite use of collections. Services free within limits.

10820. Jobs in Energy, 815 15th St NW, Washington, DC 20005; (202) 347-5590. Publicizes, supports programs in energy, jobs, community economic development, especially for the poor, disadvantaged. Provides consulting services; conducts seminars, workshops. Services free, except consulting.

10821. Johns Hopkins University, Center of Canadian Studies, School of Advanced Intl Studies, 1740 Massachusetts Ave NW, Washington, DC 20036; (202) 785-6292. Interest in Canadian politics, economics, and external and defense relations, especially Canadian-American relations; Quebec. Provides general reference services, permits onsite use of collections. Most services free to senior and graduate students and other professionals.

10822. Joint Agricultural Weather Facility, Natl Weather Service, NOAA, South Bldg, Rm 5844, Dept of Agriculture, Washington, DC 20250; (202) 447-7917. Provides NOAA support to Dept of Agriculture for crop assessing and monitors weather in major agricultural regions of U.S. and foreign countries. Answers inquiries, publishes a bulletin, permits onsite use of collection.

10823. Joint Center for Political Studies, 1301 Pennsylvania Ave NW, Ste 400, Washington, DC 20004; (202) 626-3500. Provides research and info on black politics and issues. Interest in black political participation, govt policies, etc. Provides reference services, distributes materials, conducts seminars, offers internships, permits onsite use of collections. Services free, except publications.

10824. Joint Committee on Printing, Congressional Record Index Office, N Capitol and H Sts NW, Rm C738, Washington, DC 20402; (202) 275-9007. Source of info on debates and statements of Congress as reported in *Congressional Record* and the history of bills reflecting all action on legislation. Publishes *Index to Congressional Record*, answers inquiries regarding issues raised since last appearance of the Index.

10825. Joint Council on Educational Telecommunications, c/o Corp for Public Broadcasting, 1111 16th St NW, Washington, DC 20036; (202) 293-6160. Consortium of national and regional orgs and assns working in education, info science, and public broadcasting. Answers inquiries, provides consulting services—primarily to members.

10827. Judicial, Fiscal, & Social Branch, Civil Archives Div, Natl Archives and Records Admin, Pennsylvania Ave and 8th St NW, Rm 5-W, Washington, DC 20408; (202) 523-3089. Interest in records of a variety of fed agencies, including U.S. Postal Service, Coast Guard, Supreme Court. Answers inquiries, makes referrals, provides copying services for a fee.

10828. Justice Department Library, Rm 5400, 10th St and Pennsylvania Ave NW, Washington, DC 20530; (202) 633-3775. Provides general reference services.

10829. Kennedy Institute of Ethics Library, Ctr for Bioethics, Kennedy Institute, Georgetown Univ, 3520 Prospect St NW, 3rd Fl, Washington, DC 20057; (202) 625-2383. Interest in ethics, bioethics, medicine and the law, medical and professional ethics, ethics and the life sciences. Provides general reference services, permits onsite use of collection. Services free, except copying services.

10830. Kinship, P.O. Box 23641, L'Enfant Station, Washington, DC 20026-0641; (202) 543-6996. Researches adoption issues. Maintains data bases on law, search and support groups. Provides free inquiry, reference services; conducts conferences, workshops (for small fee).

10831. Land Development Institute, 1401 16th St NW, Washington, DC 20036; (202) 232-2144. Specializes in real estate law. Publishes reference materials; price list available. Provides inquiry, consulting, reference services; conducts seminars; permits onsite use of library. Fee for services.

10832. Landscape Architecture Research & Information Clearinghouse, 1733 Connecticut Ave NW, Washington, DC 20009; (202) 223-6229. Provides info on landscape architecture, land-use design. Maintains database, archives, library (for onsite use); provides inquiry, reference services; conducts seminars; distributes publications. Services for a fee.

10833. Lawyers' Committee for Civil Rights Under Law, 1400 Eye St NW, Ste 400, Washington, DC 20005; (202) 371-1212. Dedicated to concept that all Americans are entitled to equal rights under law and that lawyers should help solve serious modern problems through processes of the law. Answers inquiries, provides advisory and legal services, conducts seminars, distributes publications. Most services free.

10834. Leadership Conference on Civil Rights, 2027 Massachusetts Ave NW, Washington, DC 20036; (202) 667-1780. Coalition to advance civil rights thru fed legislation. Publishes newsletter, reports; answers inquiries; conducts seminars, workshops; permits onsite use of library. Some services for a fee.

10835. League for International Food Education, c/o Albert Meisel, Exec Dir, 915 15th St NW, Ste 915, Washington, DC 20005; (202) 331-1658. Consortium of professional societies whose members volunteer to work on nutrition and food technology problems in the developing world. Answers inquiries, conducts seminars, locates personnel, makes referrals. Services free to agencies working in the field.

10836. League of Historic American Theatres, 1600 H St NW, Washington, DC 20006; (202) 289-1494. Promotes preservation, use of America's historic theatre buildings. Publishes newsletter, reference materials. Provides inquiry, consulting, reference services; conducts seminars. Some services available to all; others to members only.

10837. League of Women Voters Education Fund, 1730 M St NW, Washington, DC 20036; (202) 429-1965. Interest in citizen participation and citizens right to know, govt processes, election laws and voting rights, policy issues. Answers inquiries or refers inquirers to other sources of info free, sells publications.

10839. Lebanese Information & Research Center, 1926 Eye St NW, Washington, DC 20006; (202) 347-5810; (202) 638-5250 (newsline, updated daily). Funded by Lebanese sources. Interest in Lebanon, Middle East. Publishes papers, newsletter; answers inquiries; maintains phone newsline, library; provides free advisory, referral services.

10840. Legal Services Corporation, Public Affairs Office, 1733 15th St NW, Washington, DC 20005; (202) 272-4030. Provides info on the programs and functions of the Legal Services Corporation, which provides financial aid to qualified individuals, programs, firms, corps, orgs and state and local govts to fund legal assistance programs for eligible low-income clients. Answers inquiries according to abilities.

10841. Legislative & Diplomatic Branch, Civil Archives Div, Natl Archives and Records Admin, Pennsylvania Ave and 8th St NW, Rm 5-E, Washington, DC 20408; (202) 523-3174. Interest in records of U.S. Congress, diplomatic records between U.S. and other nations, fed documents relating to the American Revolution, internal records of Dept of State. Answers inquiries, makes referrals, provides copying services for a fee.

10842. Let's-Play-To-Grow, 1701 K St NW, Ste 205, Washington, DC 20006; (202) 331-1346. Works with families, others to enhance physical, social development of handicapped children. Publishes info, recreation materials in English, Spanish; provides inquiry, advisory services; conducts workshops; provides speakers. Most services free.

10843. Lettumplay, 418 Seventh St NW, Washington, DC 20005; (202) 724-4493. Promotes noncommerical jazz performances, study, outreach programs. Maintains archive (with recordings), museum; provides consulting services; conducts seminars, workshops. Fee for services.

10844. Libraries Museum Reference Center, 2235 Arts and Industries Bldg, Smithsonian Institution, Washington, DC 20560; (202) 357-3101. Clearinghouse on museology. Has book, journal collections; extensive subject files; computerized data bases. Provides inquiry, referral services; makes interlibrary loans. Services free.

10846. Library & Printed Archives Branch, National Archives & Records Administration, Pennsylvania Ave and 8th St NW, 2nd Fl, Washington, DC 20408; (202) 523-3286. Interest in American history, politics, govt, and biography and the special fields of archival science, records, and manuscripts. Permits onsite use of holdings, makes interlibrary loans library holdings only .

10847. Library of Congress, Exchange & Gift Division, 10 First St SE, Washington, DC 20540; (202) 287-5243. Acquires library materials by exchange, gift, other nonpurchase means for Library of Congress; disposes of surplus materials. Answers inquiries.

10848. Library of Congress, Exhibits Office, 10 First St SE, Deck 38, Washington, DC 20540; (202) 287-5223. Organizes, executes exhibitions for the Library of Congress, including traveling exhibitions, loans of items. Publishes catalogs, answers inquiries. Charges rental fees for traveling exhibits.

10849. Library of Congress, Information Office, 10 First St SE, Washington, DC 20540; (202) 287-5180. Library with holdings of 80 million items covering every field except clinical medicine and technical agriculture, which are specialties of the two other national libraries. Info office answers inquiries about the library, its activities, services, and hours.

10851. Library of Congress, New Serial Titles Section, Serial Record Div, Library of Congress, 10 First St SE, Washington, DC 20540; (202) 287-5300. Interest in serial publications in all languages; bibliographic, location info on them. Publishes monthly union list, answers inquiries. Services free.

10852. Library of Congress, Science & Technology Division Technical Reports Section, Library of Congress, 10 First St SE, Washington, DC 20540; (202) 287-5655. Identifies, locates tech reports, other nonconventional scientific lit (from 1940). Services 3+ million items. Provides inquiry, search services; item identification. Most services free.

10853. Library of the National Museum of American Art & National Portrait Gallery, Smithsonian Institution, Washington, DC 20560; (202) 357-1886. Library of fine arts, with emphasis on American paintings, sculpture, graphics, portraiture, and photography. Answers inquiries, provides reference and copying services, makes referrals. Services available to Smithsonian staff, qualified adults, students.

10854. Lighting Research Institute, 1015 15th St NW, Ste 802, Washington, DC 20005; (202) 347-7474. Sponsors and promotes research on photobiology and vision with an emphasis on those research areas with direct human application. Answers inquiries, conducts symposia.

10855. Linguistic Society of America, 3520 Prospect St NW, Washington, DC 20007; (202) 298-7120. Interest in linguistics, including univ programs in U.S. and abroad, employment opportunities, and individual linguists and their fields of competence. Publishes a quarterly, answers inquiries.

10856. Lipid Research Clinic, George Washington Univ Medical Ctr, 2150 Pennsylvania Ave NW, Washington, DC 20037; (202) 676-4152. Conducts research into relationship between blood lipids and lipoproteins and coronary artery disease. Provides consultation in the diagnosis and treatment of hyperlipidemia, answers inquiries, makes referrals. Patients are charged for medical services rendered.

10857. Lombardi Cancer Research Center, Georgetown Univ School of Medicine, 3800 Reservoir Rd NW, Washington, DC 20007; (202) 625-7721. Involved in multidisciplinary basic and clinical research, serving as a resource for cancer diagnosis, treatment, and control. Answers inquiries, provides advisory services, distributes publications, makes referrals. Services free.

10858. MDS Industry Association, 1725 N St NW, Washington, DC 20036; (202) 639-4410. Represents interests of multipoint distribution service industry. Answers inquiries; provides consulting, legal services (members only); conducts seminars (for a fee). Some services free.

10859. Machinery and Allied Products Institute, 1200 18th St NW, Rm 400, Washington, DC 20036; (202) 331-8430. Economic research org for capital goods and allied product industries. Publishes executive letter series covering significant industrial trends, current govt developments; answers inquiries.

10860. Mainstream Information Network, 1200 15th St NW, Washington, DC 20005; (202) 833-1198. Concerned with employment of the handicapped, including legal aspects. Publishes, sells newsletter, guides; provides inquiry, advisory, reference, update services free.

10861. Malaysian Tin Bureau, 1625 Eye St NW, Ste 913, Washington, DC 20006; (202) 331-7550. Info source sponsored by Tin Industry (Research and Development) Board, Kuala Lumpur, Malaysia. Answers inquiries, distributes publications, makes referrals. Services free.

10862. Man-Made Fiber Producers Association, 1150 17th St NW, Washington, DC 20036; (202) 296-6508. Prepares educational materials on manmade fibers for teachers and students in textile, clothing, and home economics classes at all levels. Answers inquiries, provides reference and publications services. Services free, except some publications.

10863. Marine Corps, History & Museums Division, Marine Corps Headquarters (Code HD), 8th & Eye Sts SE, Washington, DC 20380; (202) 433-3838. Maintains operational archives of U.S. Marine Corps. Interest in Marine Corps history, amphibious warfare. Provides general reference services, permits onsite use of collections. Services free to U.S. govt agencies.

10864. Marine Engineers Beneficial Association, c/o J.M. Calhoon, Pres, Research and Development Dept, 444 N Capitol St, Ste 800, Washington, DC 20001; (202) 347-8585. Publishes magazine on marine engineering, answers inquiries, provides consulting services, evaluates ship construction, provides training for marine industry.

10865. Marine Mammal Commission, 1625 Eye St NW, Rm 307, Washington, DC 20006; (202) 653-6237. Develops and reviews policy to insure objectives of the Marine Mammal Protection Act of 1972 are attained. Supports research, answers inquiries, provides info, conducts seminars, makes referrals. Reports distributed through Natl Technical Info Service at cost.

10866. Marine Technology Society, 1730 M St NW, Ste 412, Washington, DC 20036; (202) 659-3251. Publishes conference transactions, journal, newsletter on marine science and technology, such as undersea vehicles. Answers inquiries, makes referrals, permits onsite use of collection.

10867. Maritime Administration, Office of Research & Development, Dept of Transportation, 400 Seventh St SW, Washington, DC 20590; (202) 382-0360. Promotes maritime research and development, new ship designs, navigation aids, ship operations procedures.

Answers inquiries, makes referrals. Some info only on a need-to-know basis.

10868. Mass Media Bureau, Fed Communications Commission, 1919 M St NW, Rm 314, Washington, DC 20554; (202) 632-6460. Administers licensing and regulation of radio and television broadcasting stations, including network and cable. Answers inquiries or refers inquirers to other sources of info.

10870. Mathematical Association of America, 1529 18th St NW, Washington, DC 20036; (202) 387-5200. Publishes monthly, bimonthly magazines on mathematics, info booklet, books, monographs, reports; answers limited inquiries; makes referrals.

10871. Meat Machinery Manufacturers Institute, 1919 Pennsylvania Ave NW, Ste 300, Washington, DC 20006; (202) 872-1990. Trade assn of manufacturers of industrial meat cutting and meat processing machinery in U.S. Refers inquirers to its member companies free.

10872. Mental Health Law Project, 2021 L St NW, Washington, DC 20036-4909; (202) 467-5730. Investigates legal rights of mentally and developmentally disabled persons through test-case litigation, training, publications, policy, and legal advocacy. Provides copying services and makes referrals to attorneys free.

10873. Merit Systems Protection Board, 1120 Vermont Ave NW, Washington, DC 20419; (202) 653-7124. Responsible for enforcing fed personnel and department rights and duties as they relate to the Civil Service Reform Act. Provides info, referrals, library services, free publications.

10874. Microform Reading Room, Library of Congress, 10 First St SE, Washington, DC 20540; (202) 287-5471. Library's collection of microreproductions of titles selected from general book collections and reproduced under its Preservation Program, with one significant collection in each major area of library's holdings. Answers inquiries, provides reading machines.

10875. Middle East Institute, 1761 N St NW, Washington, DC 20036; (202) 785-1141. Publishes journal on Middle East, books, studies, bibliographies; provides reference, consulting services; sponsors conferences, seminars; offers classes in Arabic, Turkish, Farsi, Hebrew.

10876. Migrant Legal Action Program, 2001 S St NW, Ste 310, Washington, DC 20009; (202) 462-7744. Provides litigative and other assistance to attorneys representing migrant farmworkers. Provides general reference services, conducts seminars, permits onsite use of collections. Services free to legal services programs, at cost to others.

10877. Milk Industry Foundation, 888 16th St NW, 2nd Fl, Washington, DC 20006; (202) 296-4250. Publishes special research project reports on fresh milk and fresh milk products, answers inquiries, refers inquirers to other sources of info.

10878. Mineralogical Society of America, 2000 Florida Ave NW, Washington, DC 20009; (202) 462-6913. Publishes journal, reviews, special papers on mineralogy, publishes abstracts jointly with Mineralogical Society of Great Britain and Ireland, makes referrals.

10879. Minority Business Development Agency Information Clearinghouse, Dept of Commerce, Washington, DC 20230; (202) 377-2414. Disseminates info on establishing and successfully operating minority-owned business enterprises. Refers minority business owners to sources of specific management and technical assistance; provides guidance to minority firms on how to get on fed and private bidders' lists.

10880. Modern Military Headquarters Branch, Military Archives Div, Natl Archives and Records Admin, Pennsylvania Ave and 8th St NW, Room 11-W, Washington, DC 20408; (202) 523-3340. Interest in U.S. military records from World War II to the 1960's and captured German and other foreign records mainly from 1920 through World War II. Answers inquiries, makes referrals, provides copying services for a fee.

10881. Monsour Medical Foundation Commission for the Advancement of Public Interest Organizations, 1875 Connecticut Ave NW, Ste 1010, Washington, DC 20009; (202) 462-0505. Promotes cooperation among groups and individuals in to develop strategies for resolving specific, current public interest problems. Sponsors workshops, distributes publications, and makes referrals. Services free.

10882. Mortgage Bankers Association of America Library, 1125 15th St NW, Washington, DC 20005; (202) 861-6580. Interest in mortgage banking activities, including single-family loans, income property finance, agricultural credit, etc. Answers inquiries, makes limited interlibrary loans, permits limited onsite use of collection. Services free and primarily for members and govt agencies.

10883. Motion Picture Association of America, 1600 Eye St NW, Washington, DC 20006; (202) 293-1966. Represents largest companies producing, distributing theatrical films, TV material in U.S., worldwide. Publishes reports. Answers inquiries. Services free.

10884. Motion Picture, Broadcasting & Recorded Sound Division, Library of Congress, 10 First St SE, Washington, DC 20540; (202) 287-5840. Repository of films, television and radio programs and sound recordings representing the full history of these media. Supports researcher's activities. Listening and viewing services available by advance appointment to qualified scholars. Some copying services available.

10886. Museum Consultants International, 1716 17th St NW, Washington, DC 20009; (202) 462-2380. Nonprofit clearinghouse of museum, museum-related expertise (over 250 consultants). Provides inquiry, advisory, referral services; conducts seminars, workshops. Services generally available for a fee.

10887. Museum of the City of Washington, Rutherford B. Hayes Bldg, 5th and K Sts NE, Washington, DC 20002; (202) 544-7424. Interest in local Washington history, community, neighborhood history. Sponsors traveling exhibit, small library. Answers inquiries; distributes publications. Most services free.

10888. Music Division, Library of Congress, 10 First St SE, Washington, DC 20540; (202) 287-5504. Library's collection of material on music of western civilization and its history, American music and its documentation. Composer's manuscripts and correspondence are in the collection as well as an assembalge of rare and valuable musical instruments. Answers inquiries, makes referrals, provides consulting and reference services. Limited onsite use of collections.

10889. National Abortion Federation, 900 Pennsylvania Ave SE, Washington, DC 20003; (202) 546-9060. Fosters the provision of quality abortion services so that they may be accessible to all women. Answers inquiries, provides advisory and reference services, makes referrals, supports a hotline: (800) 772-9100. Special services provided for a fee.

10890. National Abortion Rights Action League, 1424 K St NW, Washington, DC 20005; (202) 347-7774. Nonprofit lobbying and political action org dedicated to keeping abortion legal and accessible. Interest in legal status of abortion at natl and state levels. Answers inquiries, distributes publications, makes referrals. Services free and primarily for members.

10891. National Academy of Public Administration, 1120 G St NW, Suite 540, Washington, DC 20005; (202) 347-3190. Affiliated with the Natl Institute of Public Affairs and concerned with all aspects of public administration and governance. Answers inquiries, provides consulting services, conducts conferences.

10892. National Accrediting Commission of Cosmetology Arts & Sciences, 1990 M St NW, Suite 650, Washington, DC 20036; (202) 331-9550. Official accrediting agency for cosmetology schools in U.S. Interest in accreditation of cosmetology schools in U.S. and Canada. Answers inquiries free, publishes and distributes materials.

10893. National Advisory Council on Women's Educational Programs, 2000 L St NW, Suite 500, Washington, DC 20036; (202) 634-6105. Advises on legislative programs and other matters concerning educational equity for women. Distributes some publications (some sold by Govt Printing Office), makes referrals. Services free.

10894. National Aeronautic Association, 1400 Eye St NW, No 550, Washington, DC 20005; (202) 898-1313. Seeks to keep the public informed of the importance of aviation and space flight to national security, economic progress, and international understanding. Publishes a newsletter, answers inquiries, and makes referrals free.

10895. National Aeronautics & Space Administration, History Office, Mgmt Support Off (LBH), Off of External Relations, Washington, DC 20546; (202) 453-8303. Makes history of NASA available to policy makers, scholars. Holds collections for onsite use. Publishes studies, referral materials. Provides inquiry, referral services. Most services free; available by arrangement.

10896. National Aeronautics and Space Administration, News and Information Branch, Public Affairs Div, 400 Maryland Ave SW, Washington, DC 20546; (202) 453-8400. Publishes journal on aerospace technology, puts out list of films produced by NASA, supplies photographs and slides to news media, handles media requests for nontechnical info on NASA.

10897. National Agricultural Aviation Association, 115 D St SE, Suite 103, Washington, DC 20004; (202) 546-5722. Interest in agricultural aviation, aerial application of pesticides, fertilizer, and seeds. Provides general reference services, lobbies for agricultural aviation, distributes publications. Services at cost.

10898. National Agricultural Chemicals Association, 1155 15th St NW, Washington, DC 20005; (202) 296-1585. Collects info on agricultural chemicals, pesticides, toxicology. Answers inquiries and makes referrals to other sources of info.

10899. National Agricultural Lands Center, 318 Fourth St NE, Washington, DC 20002; (202) 546-7407. Promotes effective resource management projects, progs. Maintains current catalog of projects needing funding. Provides inquiry, advisory services; conducts seminars; evaluates data. Services for a fee.

10900. National Air & Space Museum Library, 7th St and Independence Ave SW, Washington, DC 20560; (202) 357-3133. Interest in aeronautics and astronautics, early pioneers of flight and early aircraft, astronomy, earth and planetary sciences. Provides general reference services, distributes brochure, permits onsite use of collections. Services free, unless extensive.

10901. National Air Carrier Association, 1730 M St NW, Suite 710, Washington, DC 20036; (202) 833-8200. Represents interests of some scheduled and charter airlines, air freight forwarders, and airport authorities before U.S. govt agencies and Congress. Answers inquiries, distributes data compilations and publication, makes referrals. Service fees charged.

10902. National Air Transportation Association, 1010 Wisconsin Ave NW, Suite 405, Washington, DC 20007; (202) 965-8880. Represents interests of airport service orgs throughout U.S., publishes newsletter, handbooks, reports, brochures; answers inquiries, gives info on industry trends to members.

10904. National Alliance for the Mentally Ill, 1200 15th St NW, No 400, Washington, DC 20005; (202) 833-3530. Interest in mental illness, law, patient rights, accountability. Publications pricelist available. Provides inquiry, advisory services, referrals.

10905. National Aquarium Society, Dept of Commerce Bldg, Room B-037, 14th St and Constitution Ave NW, Washington, DC 20230; (202) 377-2826. Operates aquarium, has referral library for onsite use. Answers inquiries; lends educational materials, including slide progs, teaching boxes, pamphlets. Admission fee.

10906. National Architectural Accrediting Board, 1735 New York Ave NW, Washington, DC 20006; (202) 783-2007. Interest in accreditation of academic progs in architecture. Answers inquiries free, distributes list of accredited progs, first copy free.

10907. National Archives Federal Archives & Records Center, 7th St and Pennsylvania Ave NW, Washington, DC 20408; (202) 724-1614. Maintains noncurrent records of U.S. govt including records of former fed civilian and military personnel. Many records available to qualified researchers subject to statutory or security restrictions. Documents authenticated and copies supplied for a small fee.

10908. National Archives, Military Service Branch, Military Archives Div, Pennsylvania Ave and 8th St NW, Room 8-E, Washington, DC 20408; (202) 523-3223. Interest in military service records, from Revolutionary War to date. Provides inquiry, copying services for a fee.

10909. National Archives, Still Picture Branch, Special Archives Div, Pennsylvania Ave and 8th St NW, Room 18-N, Washington, DC 20408; (202) 523-3236. Interest in still pictures created by, for, about U.S. agencies or owned by them. Over 5 million items for onsite use. Publishes referral materials. Provides inquiry, referral services; can copy photographs for a fee.

10910. National Archives for Black Women's History, 1318 Vermont Ave NW, Washington, DC 20005; (202) 332-1233 or 332-9201. Archives for history of black women in U.S. Answers inquiries, provides referral services, permits onsite use of collections. Services free.

10911. National Assembly of Local Arts Agencies, 1785 Massachusetts Ave NW, Suite 413, Washington, DC 20036; (202) 483-8670. Represents local arts agencies; promotes their programs. Publishes newsletter. Provides inquiry, referral services, conducts seminars, workshops. Services for a fee to nonmembers, free or at discount to members.

10912. National Assembly of National Voluntary Health & Social Welfare Organizations, 1319 F Street NW, Suite 601, Washington, DC 20004; (202) 347-2080. Interest in cooperation among national voluntary health and social welfare orgs on program services, public policy, and agency management. Answers inquiries, makes referrals. Services free.

10913. National Association for Child Care Management, 1800 M St NW, Washington, DC 20036; (202) 452-8100. Represents interests of privately owned and operated child care centers and preschool educational institutions. Answers inquiries, provides reference services, conducts seminars. Services free to members.

10914. National Association for Foreign Student Affairs, 1860 19th St NW, Washington, DC 20009; (202) 462-4811. Membership org of professionals and volunteers working in intl educational exchange. Interest in intl education standards, responsibilities. Provides general reference services, conducts workshops, distributes publications. Services free, except for publications, workshops.

10915. National Association for Home Care, Research Division, 519 C St NE, Washington, DC 20002; (202) 547-7424. Monitors legislative activity on hospice, home health care; promotes research. Publishes newsletters, referral materials. Provides inquiry and referral services, conducts seminars. Services free.

10916. National Association for Human Development, 1620 I St NW, Room 517, Washington, DC 20006; (202) 331-1737. Interest in human development needs. Publishes printed, media materials; tests instruments. Provides inquiry, consulting services, conducts seminars, workshops. Services available for a fee.

10917. National Association for Search & Rescue, P.O. Box 50178, Washington, DC 20004. Supports, develops, promotes, and implements search and rescue capabilities. Answers inquiries, provides advisory, consulting, reference services; conducts seminars, distributes publications, makes referrals. Fees for some services.

10918. National Association for the Education of Young Children, 1834 Connecticut Ave NW, Washington, DC 20009; (202) 232-8777. Acts on behalf of the needs, rights, and well-being of young children, with primary focus on the provision of educational services and resources to adults who work with and for children. Publishes journal, answers inquiries, makes referrals.

10919. National Association of Activity Therapy & Rehabilitation Program Directors, c/o Occupational Therapy, St Elizabeth's Hospital, William A. White Div, 2700 Martin Luther King, Jr. Ave SE, Washington, DC 20032; (202) 574-7566. Investigates issues of mental health, rehabilitation, and occupational therapy. Answers inquiries, provides reference services, conducts seminars, distributes publications, and makes referrals. Services free.

10920. National Association of Area Agencies on Aging, 600 Maryland Ave SW, Rm 208, Washington, DC 20024; (202) 484-7520. Natl org of area agencies interested in advocacy for the elderly, services to them. Computerized data bank. Answers inquiries; provides referral services. Services at low cost.

10922. National Association of Black-Owned Broadcasters, 1730 M St NW, Suite 412, Washington, DC 20036; (202) 463-8970. Trade assn of black owners of radio, TV, cable TV companies. Publishes newsletter, directories. Provides inquiry, advisory, consulting, referral services; conducts seminars, workshops. Services for a fee.

10923. National Association of Broadcasters, 1771 N St NW, Washington, DC 20036; (202) 293-3500 (General), (202) 293-3579 (Library). Interest in broadcast industry. Limited free reference service available. Library open to public by appointment, but materials do not circulate and no public copying facilities available.

10924. National Association of Business & Educational Radio, 1330 New Hampshire Ave NW, Washington, DC 20036; (202) 659-8334. Interest in land mobile communications, two-way radio systems, including legislation, rules, and regulations governing use of two-way radio; radio frequency allocations. Answers inquiries, makes referrals. Services free.

10925. National Association of College & University Business Officers, 1 Dupont Circle, Ste 500, Washington, DC 20036; (202) 861-2500. Serves business, financial, management interests of univ administrators. Library for onsite use. Publishes magazine, referral materials. Provides inquiry, advisory, referral services; conducts seminars. Services free, except publications.

10926. National Association of Community Health Centers, 1625 Eye St NW, Ste 420, Washington, DC 20006; (202) 833-9280. Natl advocate for community health centers, ambulatory care progs. Publishes newsletters, referral materials. Provides inquiry, consulting services; tech assistance. Fee for some services.

10927. National Association of Cosmetology Schools, 1990 M St NW, Ste 650, Washington, DC 20036; (202) 775-0311. Interest in cosmetology, hair care, beautician, manicurist training. Publishes newsletter, directory. Provides inquiry, referral services. Services free, except seminars and workshops.

10928. National Association of Counties, 440 First St NW, Washington, DC 20001; (202) 393-6226. Provides consulting, reference services on all aspects of local govt, conducts seminars, permits onsite use of collection. Extensive services available to subscribing counties.

10929. National Association of County Planning Directors, 440 First St NW, Washington, DC 20006; (202) 393-6226. Interest in county planning and resource and growth management. Answers inquiries, makes inquiries, furnishes documents on cost basis. Services to county govts.

10930. National Association of Criminal Defense Lawyers, 1815 H St NW, Suite 550, Washington, DC 20006; (202) 872-8688. Supports attorneys actively defending persons accused of crimes. Provides brief bank, expert hotline (for members only). Publishes magazine, manuals, reviews. Conducts seminars for a fee.

10931. National Association of Criminal Justice Planners, 1500 Massachusetts Ave NW, Suite 129, Washington, DC 20005; (202) 223-3171. Fosters criminal justice planning, improvement at all levels of govt. Publishes reviews, directories, data. Provides inquiry, advisory services. Conducts conferences. Services primarily for members; fee for others.

10932. National Association of Developmental Disabilities Councils, 1234 Massachusetts Ave NW, Suite 203, Washington, DC 20005; (202) 347-1234. Org of state, territorial developmental disabilities councils. Publishes newsletter, reports, data. Answers inquiries, conducts seminars, workshops. Services free.

10933. National Association of Dredging Contractors, 1625 Eye St NW, Suite 321, Washington, DC 20006; (202) 223-4820. Publishes annual reports, technical material (for members' use only) on channel dredging and waterfront construction, book on waterways of U.S.; answers inquiries, makes referrals.

10934. National Association of Evangelicals, Office of Public Affairs, 1430 K St NW, Ste 900, Washington, DC 20005; (202) 628-7911. Provides united voice for evangelical Christian churches in U.S. Publishes magazine, newsletter, reports. Provides inquiry, advisory services, conducts seminars. Many services free.

10935. National Association of Federal Credit Unions, P.O. Box 3769 (1111 N 19th St, No 708; Arlington, VA), Washington, DC 20007; (703) 522-4770. Lobbies Congress, U.S. agencies on behalf of federally-chartered credit unions. Publishes newsletter, magazine, directories. Answers inquiries; conducts seminars, workshops. Some services free, some for members only.

10936. National Association of Federal Veterinarians, 1522 K St NW, Ste 836, Washington, DC 20005; (202) 223-3590. Interest in veterinary public health and preventive medicine, food hygiene and inspection, food animal disease control, food animal drug safety. Answers inquiries, conducts seminars, distributes newsletter, makes referrals. Services free, except newsletter.

10937. National Association of Housing Cooperatives, 2501 M St NW, Ste 451, Washington, DC 20037; (202) 887-0706. Supports the cooperative housing movement. Maintains liaison among cooperative housing orgs and promotes their interests. Answers inquiries, provides consulting services for housing cooperatives, distributes publications, makes referrals. Some services available to nonmembers for a fee.

10938. National Association of Housing and Redevlopment Officials, Watergate Bldg, Rm 404, 2600 Virginia Ave NW, Washington, DC 20037; (202) 333-2020. Publishes journal, studies, reports on public housing, urban renewal; answers inquiries, provides consulting services, furnishes data tabulations. Services for members only.

10939. National Association of Life Underwriters, 1922 F St NW, Washington, DC 20006-4387; (202) 331-6000. Trade assn represents state and local assns of life insurance agents, general agents, and managers. Interest in legal reserve life insurance. Provides general reference services, distributes publications. Services free.

10940. National Association of Margarine Manufacturers, 1625 I St NW, Ste 1024-A, Washington, DC 20006;

(202) 785-3232. Promotes interest in margarine and food spreads and their manufacture. Answers inquiries and makes referrals. Services free within limits of time and personnel available.

10941. National Association of Minority Contractors, 1250 Eye St NW, Ste 505, Washington, DC 20005; (202) 347-8259. Helps minorities enter mainstream of American economic life through the construction industry. Provides general reference services; sponsors educational seminars. Services membership funded and primarily for the construction industry.

10942. National Association of Neighborhoods, 1650 Fuller St NW, Washington, DC 20009; (202) 332-7766. Seeks to provide neighborhoods with means for formation of public policy and provide exchange of knowledge and experience between neighborhoods. Answers inquiries, provides advisory services, conducts seminars, and distributes publications. Services provided free and primarily for members.

10943. National Association of Private Industry Councils, 810 18th St NW, Ste 705, Washington, DC 20006; (202) 223-5640. Involved in planning, implementation of employment, training policies. Publishes ref, update materials. Provides inquiry, advisory services; conducts seminars. Services available to nonmembers for a fee, on limited basis.

10944. National Association of Professional Educators, 900 17th St NW, Ste 300, Washington, DC 20006; (202) 293-2142. Interest in alternative to teacher unions. Has computerized info on educational practices. Publishes newsletter. Answers inquiries, conducts seminars, workshops. Most services free.

10945. National Association of Railroad Passengers, 417 New Jersey Ave SE, Washington, DC 20003; (202) 546-1550. Interest in rail passenger service improvement, including long distance, short distance, and commuter services. Publishes monthly newsletter, answers inquiries, provides advisory and reference services. Services free.

10946. National Association of Real Estate Investment Trusts, 1101 17th St NW, Ste 700, Washington, DC 20036; (202) 485-8717. Interest in real estate investment, finance; real estate investment trusts. Publishes newsletter, referral works. Provides inquiry, advisory, consulting services. Some services for a fee to nonmembers.

10947. National Association of Realtors Department of Economics & Research, 777 14th St NW, 12th Fl, Washington, DC 20005; (202) 383-1061 or 383-1062. Provides economic data and research concerning the existing home market, mortgage and real estate industry. Distributes publications, and makes referrals. Services at cost.

10948. National Association of Regional Councils, 1700 K St NW, Washington, DC 20006; (202) 457-0710. Fosters city-county-state regional cooperation; represents regional councils of govt (COGs). Provides tech assis-

tance; educational, inquiry, referral services. Conducts workshops; distributes publications. Some services at cost to nonmembers.

10949. National Association of Regulatory Utility Commissioners, P.O. Box 684 (1102 ICC Bldg), Washington, DC 20044; (202) 628-7324. Org serves consumer interest by seeking to improve the quality and effectiveness of public regulation in America. Answers inquiries free, sells publications.

10950. National Association of Rehabilitation Facilities, P.O. Box 17675 (8200 Greensboro Dr, Ste 900; McLean, VA), Washington, DC 20041; (703) 556-8848. Provides info on rehabilitation hospitals, units, and centers and sheltered workshop orgs and management. Answers inquiries, provides consulting and reference services, conducts seminars. Services for those conducting rehabilitation programs.

10951. National Association of Retired Federal Employees, 1533 New Hampshire Ave NW, Washington, DC 20036; (202) 234-0832. Promotes general welfare of civil service annuitants and their survivors through support of legislation and preretirement counseling. Publishes magazine, answers inquiries, provides reference services, conducts seminars, distributes publications. Services free, within reason.

10952. National Association of Schools of Public Affairs & Administration, 1120 G St NW, Ste 520, Washington, DC 20005; (202) 628-8965. Center for info on education progs, developments in public administration. Publishes directory, referral materials. Answers inquiries, conducts annual conference on public service education.

10953. National Association of Securities Dealers, 1735 K St NW, Washington, DC 20006; (202) 728-8000. Self-regulatory org for over-the-counter market. Holds databases on securities; securities firms, personnel. Publishes ref materials. Provides inquiry, ref services; conducts conferences. Some services at cost.

10954. National Association of Small Business Investment Companies, 1156 15th St NW, Ste 1101, Washington, DC 20005; (202) 833-8230. Collects data on the small business investment company industry. Answers inquiries and makes referrals.

10955. National Association of State Approved Colleges & Universities, 3843 Massachusetts Ave NW, Washington, DC 20016; (202) 363-3607. Promotes administration, teaching in colleges, univs in U.S., Canada. Publishes journal, tech reports, data. Provides inquiry, advisory, ref services; conducts seminars. Services provided at cost.

10956. National Association of State Aviation Officials, 1300 G St NW, Ste 400, Washington, DC 20005; (202) 783-0587. Interest in state aviation programs, including airport construction and development, air transportation, transfer of certain fed aviation functions to state agencies. Provides general reference services, permits onsite use of collection. Services free, unless extensive.

10957. National Association of State Departments of Agriculture, 1616 H St NW, Washington, DC 20006; (202) 628-1566. Represents state agriculture agencies before Congress, U.S. agencies. Monitors legislation. Publishes newsletter, directories. Provides inquiry, referral services; conducts seminars. Services free, within limits.

10958. National Association of State Mental Health Program Directors, 1001 Third St SW, Ste 114, Washington, DC 20024; (202) 554-7807. Coordinates the actions of state mental health agencies with other state agencies, national citizen voluntary assns and their state affiliates. Answers inquiries, provides consulting services, distributes data. Fees for nonmembers.

10959. National Association of State Units on Aging, 600 Maryland Ave SW, Ste 208, Washington, DC 20024; (202) 484-7182. Natl org for info, tech assistance, professional development support to state units on aging. Maintains computerized data base. Provides inquiry, consulting services; conducts seminars. Fee for some services.

10961. National Association of State Universities & Land-Grant Colleges, 1 Dupont Circle NW, Ste 710, Washington, DC 20036; (202) 778-0818. Assists U.S. black public colleges and universities in increasing their visibility by promotion of their activities. Distributes publications free, except for multiple copies.

10962. National Association of Student Financial Aid Administrators, 1776 Massachusetts Ave NW, Rm 100, Washington, DC 20036; (202) 785-0453. Nonprofit corp of institutions of postsecondary education and others promoting effective administration of student financial aid. Answers inquiries, provides consulting services, distributes publications, and makes referrals. Most services free.

10963. National Association of Towns & Townships, 1522 K St NW, Ste 730, Washington, DC 20005; (202) 737-5200. Offers tech assistance, training, support to local govt officials; researches public policy for rural govts, small towns. Publications list available. Fee for some services.

10964. National Association of Trade & Technical Schools, 2251 Wisconsin Ave, Ste 200, Washington, DC 20007; (202) 333-1021. Interest in private vocational education, including accreditation procedures. Publishes newsletter, answers inquiries, provides consulting and reference services, makes referrals.

10965. National Association of Urban Flood Management Agencies, 1015 18th St NW, Ste 200, Washington, DC 20036; (202) 293-4844. Advocates effective local, federal urban flood control policies, practices. Publishes bulletins, newsletter. Answers inquiries; conducts conferences. Services generally free.

10966. National Association of Wheat Growers, 415 Second St NE, Ste 300, Washington, DC 20002; (202) 547-7800. Interest in public policy issues affecting wheat industry. Answers inquiries; distributes publications free to members, by subscription to others; permits onsite use of collection.

10967. National Association of Wholesaler-Distributors, 1725 K St NW, Washington, DC 20006; (202) 872-0885. Interest in wholesale distribution, including laws and legislation affecting wholesaler-distributors, taxation, profits, inventory costs, etc. Provides general reference services, conducts seminars, permits onsite use of collection. Services free, unless extensive, and primarily for members.

10968. National Biomedical Research Foundation, Georgetown Univ Medical Ctr, 3900 Reservoir Rd NW, Washington, DC 20007; (202) 625-2121. Performs research on computer use in biology, medicine; provides reference services; conducts seminars, workshops; permits onsite use of collection. Some services free.

10969. National Black Caucus of Local Elected Officials, 1301 Pennsylvania Ave NW, Ste 400, Washington, DC 20004; (202) 626-3500. Independent coalition of black local elected officials; works for goals, priorities of minority constituents. Provides free inquiry service; conducts seminars, workshops for black elected officials, others.

10970. National Black Child Development Institute, 1463 Rhode Island Ave NW, Washington, DC 20005; (202) 387-1281. Monitors and analyzes public policy as it relates to black children's development and education. Answers inquiries or refers inquirers to other sources of info. Services free.

10971. National Black Media Coalition, 516 U St NW, Washington, DC 20001; (202) 387-8155. Conducts research in and advocacy for activities necessary to build upon the black presence in mass communications, including television, radio, and advertising. Publishes magazine, answers inquiries, conducts seminars, distributes publications, offers internships.

10972. National Board of Trial Advocacy, 1050 31st St NW, Washington, DC 20007; (202) 965-3500 ext 287 or 384. Aids public in choosing effective counsel; certifies trial specialists (attorneys). Maintains computerized data base. Publishes directory. Answers inquiries. Services free.

10973. National Bowling Council, 1919 Pennsylvania Ave NW, Ste 504, Washington, DC 20006; (202) 659-9070. Fosters greater participation in bowling. Publishes data, bibliographies. Answers inquiries. Services free.

10974. National Broiler Council, c/o W.P. Roenigk, Dir of Economic Research, 1155 15th St NW, Washington, DC 20005; (202) 296-2622. Conducts public affairs and consumer education programs, including natl chicken cooking contest. Answers inquiries, conducts seminars, distributes publications. Services free.

10976. National Burglar and Fire Alarm Association, 1120 19th St NW, Ste LL20, Washington, DC 20036; (202) 296-9595. Issues publications and materials on false alarm prevention, public relations and marketing, legal and regulatory aspects; answers inquiries; makes referrals.

10977. National Cable Television Association, 1724 Massachusetts Ave NW, Washington, DC 20036; (202) 775-3550. Publishes newsletter on cable technology, directory of cable training schools, studies, conference proceedings, data compilations, videotapes; answers inquiries, makes referrals.

10978. National Campaign for a World Peace Tax Fund, 2121 Decatur Pl NW, Washington, DC 20008; (202) 483-3751. Lobbies for legislative solution for persons opposed to use of their taxes for military purposes. Provides inquiry, ref services; conducts workshops. Services at cost.

10979. National Campground Owners Association, 804 D St NE, Washington, DC 20002; (202) 543-6260. Represents small recreation businesses. Publishes magazine, statistics. Provides inquiry, advisory services; conducts seminars, workshops. Fee for some services.

10980. National Capital Area Paralegal Association, P.O. Box 19505, Washington, DC 20006; (202) 659-0243. Promotes paralegal profession; offers continuing legal education. Publishes newsletter, referral materials. Provides inquiry, consulting, reference, job referral services. Fee for some services.

10981. National Capital Planning Commission, 1325 G St., N.W., Washington, DC 20576; (202) 724-0174. Acts as central govt planning agency for overall natl capital area. Provides publication, info, referral services.

10982. National Catholic Conference for Interracial Justice, 1200 Varnum St NE, Washington, DC 20017; (202) 529-6480. Promotes relations within a multiracial, multicultural society, especially in Catholic community. Provides inquiry, advisory services; conducts workshops. Services free, except workshops.

10983. National Catholic Educational Association, 1077 30th St NW, Ste 100, Washington, DC 20007; (202) 293-5954. Concerned with all aspects of Catholic education from early childhood through the univ. Publishes a quarterly and a newsletter, answers inquiries, provides consulting services for a fee.

10984. National Catholic Educational Association, Department of Special Education, c/o Sr. Suzanne Hall, SND, Ph.D., Dir of Special Ed, 1077 30th St NW, Ste 100, Washington, DC 20007; (202) 293-5954. Provides info on Catholic services in special education of persons .with major physical and mental disabilities. Answers inquiries, publishes newsletter, provides advisory services. Services free, primarily for members.

10985. National Caucus & Center on Black Aged, 1424 K St NW, Ste 500, Washington, DC 20005; (202) 637-8400. Works to improve quality of life for older blacks thru advocacy, volunteerism, services (employment, housing, training). Conducts seminars, workshops; distributes publications. Most services at cost.

10986. National Center for Clinical Infant Programs, 733 15th St NW, Ste 912, Washington, DC 20005; (202) 347-0308. Nonprofit org on infant health, mental health, development. Publishes materials. Answers inquiries, conducts training progs for professionals (fellowships available). Services geared to professionals.

10987. National Center for Education in Maternal & Child Health, Georgetown Univ, 3520 Prospect St NW, Ground Fl, Washington, DC 20007; (202) 625-8400. Educates public, professionals on maternal & child health, human genetics. Publishes, distributes print, AV materials; research. Provides inquiry, ref, update services. Services free.

10988. National Center for Export-Import Studies, Georgetown Univ, Washington, DC 20057; (202) 625-4797. Interest in trade policies, mechanisms, regulations, policy. Publications list is available. Carries out research. Provides inquiry, referral services. Services for a fee.

10989. National Center for Housing Management, 1275 K St NW, Ste 700, Washington, DC 20005; (202) 872-1717. Interest in improving the quality of housing management in U.S. by working with federal, state, local govts; private enterprise. Publications. Conducts research. Provides advisory services at cost.

10990. National Center for Job-Market Studies, P.O. Box 3651 (1629 K St NW), Washington, DC 20007; (202) 229-4885. Develops progs to improve job market. Provides inquiry, consulting services; conducts seminars, workshops; distributes publications. Services for a fee to job applicants, employers, counselors, educators.

10991. National Center for Neighborhood Enterprise, 1367 Connecticut Ave NW, Washington, DC 20036; (202) 331-1103. Interest in urban community development; grassroots organization. Publishes journal, research. Provides inquiry, advisory services; conducts seminars, workshops.

10992. National Center for Preservation Law, 2101 L St NW, Washington, DC 20037; (202) 466-8960. Provides free legal services to public agencies, nonprofit historic preservation orgs. Provides advisory, ref services free to public agencies, nonprofit local preservation orgs.

10993. National Center for Statistics & Analysis, Natl Hwy Traffic Safety Admin, NRD-33, 400 Seventh St SW, Washington, DC 20590; (202) 426-4844. Compiles national statistics on motor vehicle accidents and fatalities, crash severity, injury, research development and testing. Answers inquiries, makes referrals to NHTSA experts, permits access to data files by qualified users.

10994. National Center for Therapeutic Riding, P.O. Box 42501 (Rock Creek Park Horse Ctr), Washington, DC 20015; (202) 966-8004. Provides specialized riding prog for special education classes in school system; teacher training in therapeutic riding; inquiry, advisory, reference services. Conducts courses, seminars. Services free.

10995. National Center for Urban Ethnic Affairs, P.O. Box 33279, Washington, DC 20033; (202) 232-3600. Interest in neighborhood decentralization and economic revitalization, ethnic affairs, intercultural education, city planning, etc. Provides consulting services at cost, makes referrals free, distributes publications.

10996. National Center on Arts & the Aging, 600 Maryland Ave SW, West Wing 100, Washington, DC 20024; (202) 479-1200 ext 387. Improves access to art for older citizens. Publishes referral materials. Provides inquiry, consulting, referral services; conducts workshops; permits onsite use of library. Fee for some services.

10998. National Citizens' Coalition for Nursing Home Reform, 1825 Connecticut Ave NW, Ste 417B, Washington, DC 20009; (202) 797-0657. Interest in nursing homes, nursing care reform. Publishes journal, other materials. Provides inquiry, advisory, consulting, referral services; conducts seminars, workshops. Fees to nonmembers.

10999. National Clay Pipe Institute, 1015 15th St NW, Ste 1250, Washington, DC 20005; (202) 789-1630. Concerned with sanitation and stream pollution control, sewer and drainage systems. Answers inquiries, provides advisory services, lends motion pictures, makes referrals.

11001. National Clean Air Coalition, 530 Seventh St SE, Washington, DC 20003; (202) 543-8200. Lobbies for strong natl clean air legislation. Answers inquiries, provides info on research in progress, conducts seminars. Services free.

11002. National Clearinghouse Library, Commission on Civil Rights, 1121 Vermont Ave NW, Washington, DC 20425; (202) 254-6600 (Info Off), (202) 254-6636 (Library). Independent bipartisan fact-finding agency that investigates violations of civil rights and serves as a clearinghouse for civil rights info.

11003. National Coal Association, Coal Bldg, 1130 17th St NW, Washington, DC 20036; (202) 463-2625. Answers inquiries free on bituminous coal use, production; publishes newsletter, journals, booklets, speeches, engineering publication; loans documents; provides repros at cost.

11004. National Coalition for Jail Reform, 1828 L St NW, Ste 1200, Washington, DC 20036; (202) 296-8630. Assn of natl orgs dealing with issues of jail reform. Answers inquiries, provides advisory services, conducts seminars. Services free to members, at cost to others.

11005. National Coalition of Independent College & University Students, 1 Dupont Circle, Ste 540, Washington, DC 20036; (202) 659-1747. Nationwide lobbying org that researches education issues. Provides inquiry, advisory, referral services; conducts seminars. Services free to member schools, at cost to others.

11006. National Coalition to Ban Handguns, 100 Maryland Ave NE, Washington, DC 20002; (202) 544-7190. Interest in weapons; education, law, research. Publishes printed, AV materials; provides inquiry, consulting, referral services; offers onsite use of library; conducts workshops. Some services for a fee.

11007. National Commission on Working Women, 2000 P St NW, Ste 508, Washington, DC 20036; (202) 872-1782. Advocacy project for women in nonprofessional occupations (sales, service, clerical, factory). Publishes newsletter, research; Aaswers inquiries. Services free, except some publications.

11008. National Committee For Adoption, 2025 M St NW, Ste 512, Washington, DC 20036; (202) 463-7559. Interest in all aspects of adoption. Publishes newsletter; provides inquiry, expert consultant, referral services; conducts workshops; operates hotline. Services mostly for members; to others for a fee.

11009. National Committee for Responsive Philanthropy, 810 18th St NW, Ste 408, Washington, DC 20006; (202) 347-5340. Seeks to make private philanthropy more accessible and accountable to minority, women's, and public interest groups. Answers inquiries, provides advisory services, distributes publications. Most services free.

11010. National Committee on Cultural Diversity in the Performing Arts, Kennedy Ctr for the Performing Arts, Washington, DC 20566; (202) 872-0466, 254-6470. Maintains network of artists, orgs, to foster cultural diversity. Provides tech assistance, consulting services; natl research unit on minorities in performing arts. Services to those in the field.

11011. National Committee on the Treatment of Intractable Pain, P.O. Box 9553, Friendship Station, Washington, DC 20016-1553; (301) 983-1710. Seeks to end bureaucratic obstruction, ignorance, and professional resistance to providing effective drugs and methods in treatment of pain, including making heroin available to terminal patients. Answers inquiries, provides references services, distributes publications.

11012. National Committee, Arts with Handicapped, Education Off, John F. Kennedy Ctr for the Performing Arts, Washington, DC 20566; (202) 332-6960 (voice); (202) 293-3989 (TTY). Natl agency for progs in arts and the handicapped. Has library of printed, AV materials. Publications available. Provides inquiry, advisory, referral services; conducts workshops. Most services free.

11014. National Community Education Association Clearinghouse, 1201 16th St NW, Ste 305, Washington, DC 20036; (202) 466-3530. Acts an info exchange for topics related to community education. Collects and disseminates info on community education. Answers inquiries, provides reference, referral and publications services. Services free, primarily for community education practitioners.

11016. National Congress for Community Economic Development, 2025 Eye St NW, Ste 901, Washington, DC 20006; (202) 659-8411. Publishes newsletter and other materials; provides inquiry, advisory, referral services; analyzes public policy; monitors legislation. Services free to members, at cost to others.

11017. National Congress of American Indians, 804 D St NE, Washington, DC 20002; (202) 546-9404. Promotes and protects American Indian rights. Publishes newsletter, other materials; provides inquiry, advisory, referral services; conducts seminars. Services free, except some publications.

11018. National Constructors Association, 1101 15th St NW, Ste 1000, Washington, DC 20005; (202) 466-8880. Publishes newsletter, safety standards for industrial construction work; answers inquiries; makes referrals to other source of info. Services free.

11019. National Consumers League, 600 Maryland Ave SW, Ste 202 West, Washington, DC 20024; (202) 554-1600. Publishes bimonthly bulletin, consumer guides to health care; owns books, journals, reports; sponsors conferences, seminars, workshops; refers to other sources of info.

11020. National Corporation for Housing Partnerships, 1133 15th St NW, Washington, DC 20005; (202) 857-5700. Interest in creation of housing by private enterprise for families of low and moderate income, supplying equity capital and joint venture funds to local builders/developers. Answers inquiries free, publishes and distributes materials.

11021. National Cotton Council of America, 1030 15th St NW, Ste 700, Washington, DC 20005; (202) 833-2943. Promotes cotton and related aspects of economic and market research, production, and processing technology. Answers inquiries, provides reference and limited consulting services.

11022. National Council for Alternative Work Patterns, 1925 K St NW, Ste 308A, Washington, DC 20006; (202) 466-4467. Provides info concerning reduced work hours and flexible schedule policies and arrangements. Answers inquiries, provides reference services, conducts conferences, sells publications.

11023. National Council for International Health, 2100 Pennsylvania Ave NW, Ste 740, Washington, DC 20037; (202) 466-4740. Promotes cooperation and communication in intl health work. Publishes materials; provides inquiry, consulting services; conducts workshops, conferences. Most services free, for those in intl health.

11024. National Council for International Visitors, 1630 Crescent Pl NW, Washington, DC 20009; (202) 332-1028. Council of nongovt orgs interested in short-term visitors from abroad traveling in U.S. for professional or other serious purposes. Provides general reference services, conducts conferences, distributes publications. Services free, except some publications, for nonprofit use.

11025. National Council for U.S.-China Trade, 1050 17th St NW, Ste 350, Washington, DC 20036; (202) 429-0340. Interest in U.S.-China trade, China's economy, Sino-American relations. Provides general reference services, conducts seminars, distributes publications, permits onsite use of collections with restrictions. Fees for some services.

11026. National Council for Urban Economic Development, 1730 K St NW, Ste 1009, Washington, DC 20006; (202) 223-4735. Interest in industrial and commercial economic development, public/private development. Answers inquiries or makes referrals; provides in-depth advisory, consulting, and research services to members only.

11027. National Council for the Social Studies, 3501 Newark St NW, Washington, DC 20016; (202) 966-7840. Provides info on social studies programs; publishes magazine, newsletter; allows onsite use of collection; conducts research, survey programs, conferences, workshops, seminars.

11028. National Council for the Traditional Arts, 806 15th St NW, Washington, DC 20005; (202) 639-8370. Supports traditional arts in U.S. Conducts research, training progs. Holdings include AV, printed materials. Provides inquiry, consulting services; conducts workshops. Services free, except consulting.

11029. National Council of Architectural Registration Boards, 1735 New York Ave NW, Ste 700, Washington, DC 20006; (202) 783-6500. Nonprofit org of all state architectural registration boards. Publishes standards, newsletters, exam handbooks. General info free on request.

11030. National Council of Commercial Plant Breeders, 1030 15th St NW, Ste 964, Washington, DC 20005; (202) 223-4082. Promotes interests of plant breeders, fosters cooperation with public agencies to recognize individual achievements in the field and advance plant breeding as a career. Answers inquiries, provides germ plasm data, conducts workshops. Services free to members, at cost to others.

11031. National Council of Farmer Cooperatives, 1800 Massachusetts Ave NW, Ste 604, Washington, DC 20036; (202) 659-1525. Represents local cooperative businesses owned by farmers. Publishes newsletter, congressional handbook, pamphlets; conducts workshops. Services mostly free.

11032. National Council of Higher Education Loan Programs, c/o Frohlicher & Frohlicher, 1009 Independence Ave SE, Washington, DC 20003; (202) 547-1571. Org of directors of nonprofit agencies that administer the guaranteed student loan program in U.S. Answers inquiries, provides advisory services, conducts seminars, distributes publications, makes referrals. Services free.

11033. National Council of La Raza, 20 F St NW, 2nd Fl, Washington, DC 20001; (202) 628-9600. Devoted to working towards equal opportunities for Hispanic Americans by using private sector funds. Answers inquiries, provides technical and advisory services, conducts seminars, distributes publications, makes referrals free to the Hispanic community.

11034. National Council of Senior Citizens, 925 15th St NW, Washington, DC 20005; (202) 347-8800. Works for interests of senior citizens. Publishes periodical and data, provides free inquiry and advisory services, conducts seminars.

11035. National Council of Technical Service Industries, 1850 K St NW, Ste 1190, Washington, DC 20006; (202) 861-0200. Represents providers of tech services to fed govt. Holds data on govt competition with private sector. Publishes papers and analyses, provides free inquiry and reference services.

11036. National Council of University Research Administrators, c/o Natalie A. Kirkman, Dir, Natl Off, 1 Dupont Circle, Ste 618, Washington, DC 20036. Studies administration of research, education, and training activities at colleges and universities. Publishes newsletter, answers inquiries, makes referrals, conducts workshops and annual conference.

11037. National Council on Vocational Education, 2000 L St NW, Ste 580, Washington, DC 20036; (202) 634-6110. Advises the president, secty of Education, and Congress on progress of vocational and occupational education, employment, and training throughout the nation. Answers public inquiries free.

11038. National Council on the Aging, 600 Maryland Ave SW, W Wing 100, Washington, DC 20024; (202) 479-1200. Publishes journals, reports; conducts research; provides training, technical assistance; provides reference, abstracting services; permits free onsite use of collection.

11039. National Crafts Clearinghouse & Complaint Center, 2719 O St NW, Washington, DC 20007; (202) 338-5613. Provides info on crafts, aids low-income craftsmen. Provides inquiry, advisory, consulting, reference services, sometimes for a fee.

11041. National Credit Union Administration, 1776 G St NW, Washington, DC 20456; (202) 357-1000, 357-1050. Supervises, charters, examines fed credit union operations and their insurance funds. Provides info, referral services, publishes materials.

11042. National Criminal Justice Association, 444 N Capitol St, Ste 608, Washington, DC 20001; (202) 347-4900. Membership org of criminal justice practitioners that advises state governors on substantive criminal justice issues. Answers inquiries; provides advisory, training, and copying services; conducts research; distributes publications. Services primarily for members.

11043. National Demonstration Water Project, 1725 DeSales St NW, Ste 402, Washington, DC 20036; (202) 659-0661. Conducts natl prog for better delivery of water and sanitation services to low-income rural residents. Publications list available. Answers inquiries. Some services free.

11044. National Ecumenical Coalition, P.O. Box 3554, Georgetown Station (2059 N Woodstock St, Ste 305; Arlington, VA), Washington, DC 20007; (703) 524-4503. Coalition of religious orgs seeking to guarantee civil and constitutional rights for citizens of all countries by improving intl relations and strengthening the U.N. Answers inquiries; provides advisory, reference, and expert witness services; conducts seminars; publishes and distributes publications. Some services for a fee.

11045. National Education Association, Instruction & Professional Development, 1201 16th St NW, Washington, DC 20036; (202) 822-7350. Promotes educational technology, student evaluation, teacher evaluation, education, preparation and certification. Answers inquiries, makes referrals, maintains liaison with govt agencies and other orgs. Services primarily for members.

11046. National Electrical Manufacturers Association, 2101 L St NW, Washington, DC 20037; (202) 457-8400. Publishes standards and specifications, books; compiles statistical data on production, marketing of electrical products. Requests for data must be made in person.

11047. National Endowment for the Arts, 1100 Pennsylvania Ave NW, Washington, DC 20506; (202) 682-0536. Promotes artistic excellence thru grants and other programs. Answers inquiries, provides publications and referrals.

11048. National Endowment for the Arts, Office for Special Constituencies, 1100 Pennsylvania Ave NW, Washington, DC 20506; (202) 682-5532; (202) 682-5496 (TTY). Conducts advocacy, tech assistance programs to make the arts accessible to the handicapped, elderly, institutionalized. Provides free inquiry, advisory, referral services.

11049. National Endowment for the Humanities, 1100 Pennsylvania Ave NW, Washington, DC 20506; (202) 786-0438. Promotes interest in the humanities through grants and other programs. Provides info, distributes publications, makes referrals.

11050. National Energy Information Center, Energy Info Admin, DOE, EI-20, Forrestal Bldg, 1000 Independence Ave SW, Rm 1F-048, Washington, DC 20585; (202) 252-8800. Provides energy info, assistance in support of fed, state, and local govts, as well as academic community, industrial and commercial orgs, and general public. Develops and implements info mgmt tools, an online index of EIA publications, and provides training sessions. Answers inquiries. Services free, except publications.

11051. National Environmental Satellite, Data, and Information Service, NOAA, Washington, DC 20233; (301) 763-8111. Provides imagery from natl environmental satellite system; provides cloud cover images, atmospheric soundings, wind measurements, sea surface temperature; publishes satellite data.

11052. National Executive Committee for Guidance, c/o ASEE, 11 Dupont Circle, Ste 200, Washington, DC 20036; (202) 293-7080. Interest in academic guidance in engineering for secondary school students. Publishes promotional materials, provides free inquiry services.

11053. National Federation of Community Broadcasters, 1314 14th St NW, Washington, DC 20005; (202) 797-8911. Works with community licensed, noncommercial radio stations to provide info, programming, and technical support. Publishes newsletter, answers inquiries, provides consulting and reference services, conducts seminars, distributes data and publications. Initial services free.

11054. National Federation of Local Cable Programmers, 906 Pennsylvania Ave SE, Washington, DC 20003; (202) 544-7272. Interest in community antenna TV, cable TV. Has library of videotapes, print materials. Publishes printed, video materials; provides inquiry, advisory services; conducts seminars, workshops. Services for members.

11055. National Flight Data Center, Air Traffic Service (ATO-259), Fed Aviation Admin, 800 Independence Ave SW, Washington, DC 20591; (202) 426-8856. Responsible for requirements, design standards, and specifications of U.S. civil aeronautical charts and flight info products. Answers inquiries.

11056. National Food Processors Association, 1133 20th St NW, Washington, DC 20036; (202) 331-5900. Publishes newsletter, canned food statistics, annual report, labeling manual; makes interlibrary loans; gives info to scientists in related fields; answers brief inquiries.

11057. National Football League Players Association, 1300 Connecticut Ave NW, Ste 407, Washington, DC 20036; (202) 463-2200. Represents NFL players in collective bargaining. Publishes newsletter, magazine; answers inquiries; provides paid sports reporting service, chiefly for attorneys and players' agents.

11058. National Forest Products Association Information Center, 1250 Connecticut Ave NW, Washington, DC 20036; (202) 463-2700. Interest in comprehensive forest mgmt. Provides free general reference services to anyone 18 years or older; permits onsite use of collections by appointment. Extensive searching for nonmembers provided on a fee basis.

11059. National Gallery of Art, 6th St and Constitution Ave NW, Washington, DC 20565; (202) 737-4215. Supports research in the fields of art history, art conservation, and art education. Answers inquiries, lends motion picture films and color slides, permits onsite use of collections. Gallery open to public.

11060. National Gallery of Art, Center for Advanced Study in the Visual Arts, 6th St and Constitution Ave NW, Washington, DC 20565; (202) 842-6480. Promotes study of history, theory, criticism of art, architecture, urbanism by historians, critics, art theorists, others. Sponsors fellowships, publishes research, conducts seminars for specialists.

11061. National Genealogical Society, 1921 Sunderland Pl NW, Washington, DC 20036; (202) 785-2123. Library of genealogy, local history, heraldry, and biography. Provides copying services and home study course on genealogy, conducts seminars, distributes publications, makes referrals. Fees for nonmembers.

11062. National Grain & Feed Association, Library & Information Center, P.O. Box 28328 (725 15th St NW), Washington, DC 20005; (202) 783-2024. Concerned with grain science and technology, food marketing policy, animal science, economics, and other agricultural matters. Publishes newsletters, answers inquiries, provides reference services, distributes publications, makes referrals. Services at cost.

11063. National Grange, 1616 H St NW, Washington, DC 20006; (202) 628-3507. Publishes pamphlets and legislative newsletter on agriculture, provides consulting services, makes referrals to other sources of info, permits onsite use of collection.

11065. National Health Information Clearinghouse, P.O. Box 1133 (1555 Wilson Blvd, Ste 700; Rosslyn, VA), Washington, DC 20013; (703) 522-2590; (800) 336-4797. Maintains automated data base on resources in health promotion and education. Maintains library for onsite use, provides free referral services.

11066. National Health Policy Forum, 2100 Pennsylvania Ave NW, Ste 616, Washington, DC 20037; (202) 872-1390. Conducts educational progs for health specialists in govt: seminars, site visits (by invitation); distributes publications. Inquiries, referrals free.

11067. National Highway Traffic Safety Administration, Associate Administrator for Enforcement, 400 Seventh St SW, Washington, DC 20590; (202) 426-9700; (800) 424-9135 (hearing-impaired). Assures compliance by domestic and foreign motor vehicle and equipment manufacturers with fed motor vehicle safety standards. Answers inquiries, provides consultation and info, maintains toll-free hotline: (800) 424-9393.

11068. National Home Study Council, 1601 18th St NW, Washington, DC 20009; (202) 234-5100. Provides accreditation to home study schools; publishes magazine, annual directory; answers inquiries; permits onsite use of library; conducts conferences and workshops open to public.

11069. National Housing Rehabilitation Association, 1025 Connecticut Ave NW, Ste 707, Washington, DC 20036; (202) 466-8760. Interest in regulation of housing rehabilitation, adaptive re-use, neighborhood revitalization. Provides inquiry, advisory, referral services; conducts seminars, workshops. Services free to members, fees charged to others.

11070. National Human Studies Film Archive, Off of the Asst Secty for Science, Smithsonian Institution, 955 L'Enfant Plaza SW, Washington, DC 20024; (202) 287-3349. Interest in multidisciplinary, multicultural studies of the human condition through the visual medium. Answers inquiries, makes referrals to other sources of info. Serious researchers permitted onsite use of the research film materials.

11071. National Immigration, Refugee, & Citizenship Forum, 533 Eighth St SE, Washington, DC 20003; (202) 544-0004. Provides multiethnic, multiracial, and multi-institutional approach to immigration issues. Answers inquiries, conducts briefings, provides analyses of govt developments.

11072. National Industrial Transportation League, 1090 Vermont Ave NW, Ste 410, Washington, DC 20005; (202) 842-3870. Interest in industrial traffic and transportation matters; motor, rail, air, and barge rates; represents shippers before Congress, regulatory agencies, and courts. Answers inquiries, distributes publications, makes referrals.

11073. National Information Center for Handicapped Children & Youth, P.O. Box 1492 (1555 Wilson Blvd, Rosslyn, VA), Washington, DC 20013; (703) 522-3332. Acts as national info clearinghouse for parents of handicapped children, disabled adults, and professionals. Answers inquiries and distributes newsletters. Services free.

11074. National Initiative for Glaucoma Control, 1140 Connecticut Ave NW, Ste 606, Washington, DC 20036; (202) 466-4555. Seeks to prevent glaucoma thru research, treatment, screening, education. Inquiries answered free; consulting, seminars for a fee.

11075. National Institute for Citizen Education in the Law, 605 G St NW, Washington, DC 20001; (202) 624-8217. Fosters widespread understanding of the law and legal system by developing curriculum on practical law for use in schools and by corrections departments and other agencies. Answers inquiries, provides names of programs and leaders. Some services free.

11076. National Institute for Music Theater, Kennedy Ctr for the Performing Arts, Washington, DC 20566; (202) 965-2800. Dedicated to the support of all forms of music theater in U.S. Publishes newsletter, answers inquiries, sponsors national colloquia on subjects of current concern to the field.

11077. National Institute for Work & Learning, 1200 18th St NW, No 316, Washington, DC 20036; (202) 887-6800. Collaborates with business, education, labor, and govt to enhance occupational education. Answers inquiries, provides advisory services, conducts seminars, distributes publications, makes referrals. Fee for some services.

11078. National Institute for the Conservation of Cultural Property, Arts and Industries Bldg, Rm 2225, Smithsonian Institution, Washington, DC 20560; (202) 357-2295. Interest in conservation of cultural property; natl policies, technology. Answers inquiries, conducts seminars (by invitation). Services free, except postage for publications.

11079. National Institute of Building Sciences, 1015 15th St NW, Ste 700, Washington, DC 20005; (202) 347-5710. Works to improve bldg regulatory environment, introduce new technology. Publishes journal, reports; provides inquiry, consulting, reference services; conducts conferences. Some services free, chiefly for members.

11080. National Institute of Education, Educational Reference Center, 1200 19th St NW, Rm 208, Washington, DC 20208; (202) 254-7934. Provides research and retrieval services in the area of education and education-related literature to members of the Dept of Education. Answers inquiries, provides assistance to ERIC users, makes referrals. Services free.

11081. National Institute of Education, Publications & Administrative Management Division, 1200 19th St NW, Washington, DC 20208; (202) 254-5800. Interest in educational research and development. Answers inquiries, distributes publications. Services free.

11082. National Institute of Handicapped Research, Dept of Education, Code 2305, 400 Maryland Ave SW, Washington, DC 20202; (202) 732-1134. Administers grant program for rehabilitation research and training centers and rehabilitation engineering centers in U.S. Answers inquiries and makes referrals. Reports of research available.

11083. National Institute of Independent Colleges & Universities, 122 C St NW, Ste 750, Washington, DC 20001; (202) 383-5964. Conducts public policy research and legal services for independent colleges, univs. Provides data bases (usually charges fee). Publications price list available. Services available to all in higher education.

11084. National Institute of Oilseed Products, 1725 K St NW, Washington, DC 20006; (202) 223-5475. Publishes annual trading rules, weekly newsletter on seeds, their oils, and meals; owns books, periodicals, reports; answers inquiries; makes referrals to other sources of info.

11085. National Interreligious Service Board for Conscientious Objectors, 800 18th St NW, Ste 600, Washington, DC 20006; (202) 393-4868. Serves needs and advocates rights of conscientious objectors. Publishes newsletter, manual, info packets; provides inquiry, advisory, reference services; conducts seminars. Services free, except literature.

11086. National Investor Relations Institute, 1730 M St NW, Ste 806, Washington, DC 20036; (202) 861-0630. Fosters development of professionals engaged in investor relations activities. Interest in investor relations and corporate, shareholder communications. Provides general reference services, conducts workshops, distributes publications. Services primarily for members; fees may be charged.

11087. National Italian-American Foundation, 666 11th St NW, Suite 800, Washington, DC 20036; (202) 293-1713. Promotes interests of Italian-Americans. Publishes newsletter and books; provides inquiry, advisory, reference services; conducts seminars. Services free, except publications.

11088. National Labor Relations Board, 1717 Pennsylvania Ave NW, Washington, DC 20570; (202) 632-4950. Administers and enforces National Labor Relations Act, including unfair labor practices by employers and unions. Answers inquiries, provides advisory and consulting services.

11089. National League of Cities, 1301 Pennsylvania Ave NW, Washington, DC 20004; (202) 626-3000. Provides info on municipal govt and administration, citizen participation, community development, environmental quality, health and housing. Answers inquiries, provides consulting and reference services. Services primarily for members.

11090. National Legal Aid & Defender Association, 1625 K St NW, 8th Fl, Washington, DC 20006; (202) 452-0620. Works on behalf of legal services, legal aid, and public defender programs and attorneys for the indigent in civil and criminal matters. Answers inquiries, provides advisory services, makes referrals to other sources of info. Services free.

11091. National Legal Center for the Public Interest, 1101 17th St NW, Washington, DC 20036; (202) 296-1683. Natl resource center, clearinghouse on public interest law. (Does not litigate.) Publishes reports, monographs, proceedings; answers inquiries; conducts seminars. Services free.

11092. National Library Service for the Blind and Physically Handicapped, Library of Congress, 1291 Taylor St NW, Washington, DC 20542; (202) 287-5100. Owns braille and recorded books, magazines, music scores; publishes journals; provides reference services; provides bibliographic services, reading materials through regional libraries.

11093. National Measurement Laboratory, Center for Analytical Chemistry, Natl Bur of Standards, Washington, DC 20234; (301) 921-2851. Natl reference lab for measurements in analytical chemistry. Provides info on different kinds of analysis; publishes annual reports and technical journals; provides consulting services.

11094. National Meat Association, 734 15th St NW, Washington, DC 20005; (202) 347-1000. Interest in meat packing/processing industry, including congressional and regulatory issues affecting the industry. Answers inquiries or makes referrals free.

11096. National Mediation Board, 1425 K St NW, Washington, DC 20572; (202) 523-5920. Handles labor-related disputes in railroad and airline industries, works to

avoid travel disruption. Provides info, publications, referrals. Info provided on request, but limited.

11097. National Medical Association, 1012 10th St NW, Washington, DC 20001; (202) 347-1895. Professional society of black physicians. Publishes monthly medical journal and abstracts, answers inquiries, provides advisory services, conducts seminars. Services free, except journal.

11098. National Multi Housing Council, 1250 Connecticut Ave NW, Ste 620 Washington, DC 20036; (202) 659-3381. Interest in multifamily housing (rent control, condominiums, tax law, production). Publishes bibliography, reports; provides advisory, inquiry, reference services free; permits onsite use of collections.

11099. National Museum of African Art, Smithsonian Institution, 316 A St NE, Washington, DC 20560; (202) 287-3490. Interest in art and culture of Africa, black America, Afro-American painters and sculptors. Provides general reference services, makes interlibrary loans, permits onsite use of collections. Services by appointment.

11100. National Museum of American Art, Smithsonian Institution, 8th and G Sts NW, Washington, DC 20560; (202) 357-3176 or 357-2247. Center for the study, conservation, and presentation of American art through exhibitions, lectures, research programs, education and special activities for children. Answers inquiries on the collections, advises on conservation, conducts special tours.

11101. National Museum of American History, Smithsonian Institution Libraries, Constitution Ave between 12th and 14th Sts NW, Washington, DC 20560; (202) 357-2036. Collection of info on American history, history of science and technology, decorative arts, electricity, numismatics and philately. Answers inquiries, provides copying services, makes referrals, permits onsite use of collections.

11102. National Museum of Natural History, Smithsonian Institution Libraries, 10th St and Constitution Ave NW, Washington, DC 20560; (202) 357-1496. Source of data on systematic biology, invertebrate and vertebrate zoology, paleobiology, minerology, oceanography, entomology and ethnography. Answers inquiries, provides copying services, makes referrals. Services for Smithsonian staff and qualified researchers.

11103. National Museum of Natural History, National Anthropological Archives, 10th St and Constitution Ave NW, Washington, DC 20560; (202) 357-1976. Collection of records on anthropology, including ethnology, ethnohistory, archaeology, physical and applied anthropology. Provides reference and copying services, makes referrals, permits onsite use of collections. Services free, except copying.

11104. National Network in Solidarity with the Nicaraguan People, 2025 Eye St NW, Ste 1117, Washington, DC 20006; (202) 223-2328. Works to end U.S. govt intervention in Nicaragua, Central America. Publishes newsletter; provides inquiry, advisory, reference services; conducts seminars, aid campaigns, tours. Fees charged for some services.

11105. National Newspaper Association, 1627 K St NW, Ste 400, Washington, DC 20006; (202) 466-7200. Interest in journalism and the legal, legislative, managerial, and technical aspects of the community daily and weekly newspaper business. Provides general reference services, analyzes data. Services generally free and primarily for members, but others assisted.

11106. National Nutrition Consortium, 24 Third St NE, Ste 200, Washington, DC 20002; (202) 547-4819. Stimulates involvement of scientists in national nutrition policy to enhance presentation of accurate info to legislators, regulators, and others interested in food and nutrition. Answers inquiries and makes referrals.

11107. National Ocean Industries Association, 1050 17th St NW, Ste 700, Washington, DC 20036; (202) 785-5116. Trade assn of offshore and ocean-related companies engaged in development and use of marine resources. Answers inquiries, publishes newsletter.

11108. National Office for Black Catholics, 810 Rhode Island Ave NE, Washington, DC 20018; (202) 635-1778. Encourages black Catholic participation in Roman Catholic Church to eradicate racism within church. Answers inquiries, provides advisory services, conducts seminars, distributes publications, makes referrals. Simple inquiries and referrals free.

11109. National Organization for Victim Assistance, 1757 Park Rd NW, Washington, DC 20010; (202) 232-8560. Nonprofit org for victims' and witnesses' rights, compensation, assistance. Provides publications and training packages for criminal justice professionals, consulting and reference services at cost.

11110. National Organization for the Reform of Marijuana Laws, 2001 S St NW, Room 640, Washington, DC 20004; (202) 483-5500. Seeks a noncriminal approach to marijuana use. Interest in reform of marijuana laws in U.S. Provides general reference services, conducts seminars, distributes publications. Services generally free, but actual costs may be assessed.

11111. National Park Service, National Register of Historic Places Branch, Interagency Resources Div, Dept of the Interior, 1100 L St NW, Rm 6209, Washington, DC 20240; (202) 343-9536. Recognizes resources that contribute to an understanding of the historical and cultural foundations of the nation. Answers inquiries, provides reference services, conducts seminars, makes referrals. Services free, except copying.

11112. National Park Service, Natural Landmarks Branch, Div of Interagency Resources (413), Dept of the Interior, 1100 L St NW, Washington, DC 20240; (202) 343-9525. Interest in natlly significant natural areas, in public or private ownership, designated by the Secty of the Interior as Natl Natural Landmarks. Provides info on request.

11113. National Park Service, Office of Public Affairs, 18th and C Sts NW, Washington, DC 20240; (202) 343-6843 (Off of Public Affairs); (202) 343-7394 (Media Div). Publishes maps, posters, natural history studies, reports, guide for handicapped visitors, series on remote sensing in archaeology; answers inquiries; makes photos available to media.

11114. National Parking Association, 1112 16th St NW, Ste 2000, Washington, DC 20036; (202) 296-4336. Publishes journals on design, construction, operation of parking facilities, govt affairs and state legislative reports; provides reference services for a fee.

11115. National Parks & Conservation Association, 1701 18th St NW, Washington, DC 20009; (202) 265-2717. Publishes bimonthly journal, reports on preservation of natural, cultural resources in natl parks, wilderness areas of U.S.; informs on conservation issues. Library open to public.

11116. National Petroleum Council, 1625 K St NW, 6th Fl, Washington, DC 20006; (202) 393-6100. Provides advisory services on petroleum to Dept of Energy. Publishes reports, answers inquiries, makes interlibrary loans. Services mostly free.

11117. National Petroleum Refiners Association, 1899 L St NW, Ste 1000, Washington, DC 20036; (202) 457-0480. Answers inquiries; publishes newsletter, reports, proceedings, fed regulations on petroleum refining, petrochemicals; provides consulting services; conducts surveys.

11118. National Planning Association, 1606 New Hampshire Ave NW, Attn: Martha Lebenz, Editor, Washington, DC 20009; (202) 265-7685. Publishes quarterly newsletter, books, natl and regional series giving economic projections; provides info primarily through publications.

11119. National Radio Broadcasters Association, 2033 M St NW, Ste 506, Washington, DC 20036; (202) 466-2030. Provides info on radio broadcasting (commercial and noncommercial). Answers inquiries, provides reference services, makes referrals, conducts seminars, distributes publications.

11120. National Railroad Passenger Corporation (Amtrak), 400 N Capitol St, Washington, DC 20001; (202) 383-3860. Provides info on Amtrak passenger services and programs. Answers inquiries according to abilities.

11121. National Rehabilitation Information Center, 4407 Eighth St NE, Catholic Univ of America, Washington, DC 20017; (202) 635-5826. Provides support to professionals and others involved in rehabilitation of physically and mentally disabled. Provides data, answers inquiries, makes referrals. Fees for some services.

11122. National Resource Center for Consumers of Legal Services, 3254 Jones Ct, Washington, DC 20007; (202) 338-0714. Promotes development of legal service plans to avert spiraling costs and poor quality of prepaid employee benefits. Publishes newsletter, answers inquiries, provides technical assistance, distributes publications, makes referrals. Services at cost.

11123. National Restaurant Association, 311 First St NW, Washington, DC 20001; (202) 638-6100. Interest in foodservice industry: legislation, promotion, mgmt development, statistics, and training. Provides general reference services (members given priority).

11124. National Rifle Association of America, 1600 Rhode Island Ave NW, Washington, DC 20036; (202) 783-6505. Interest in firearms safety education, marksmanship instruction, shooting range construction, hunting, wildlife mgmt, more. Provides general reference services, analyzes criminal justice data, distributes publications, lends films, etc. Services generally free, except publications, primarily for members.

11125. National Rural Electric Cooperative Association Library, 1800 Massachusetts Ave NW, Washington, DC 20036; (202) 857-9787. Publishes journals on rural electrification, provides reprints, makes interlibrary loans, permits onsite use of collection. Services free by appointment.

11126. National Rural Housing Coalition, 1016 16th St NW, Washington, DC 20036; (202) 775-0046. Supports legislation to end bad housing in rural America. Interest in rural housing legislation. Provides general reference services; sends copies of congressional testimony, special analyses, etc. on request.

11127. National Science Foundation, Division of Civil & Environmental Engineering, 1800 G St NW, Washington, DC 20550; (202) 357-9545. Supports civil and environmental engineering research (especially on earthquakes). Publishes tech reports, books; provides inquiry, reference, referral services to researchers, the public. Some services free.

11128. National Science Foundation, Division of Electrical, Computer, & Systems Engineering, 1800 G St NW, Washington, DC 20550; (202) 357-9618. Funds research in electrical, computer, systems engineering. Publishes tech reports, other materials; answers inquiries. Services usually free.

11129. National Science Foundation, Division of Industrial Science & Technological Innovation, 1800 G St NW, Washington, DC 20550; (202) 357-9666. Interest in industrial incentives to increase technological innovation, small business research, univ/industry cooperative research projects and centers, productivity research. Answers inquiries free.

11130. National Science Foundation, Division of Mechanical Engineering & Applied Mechanics, 1800 G St NW, Washington, DC 20550; (202) 357-9542. Supports research in mechanical engineering. Publishes tech reports, research findings; provides info on current programs, grantee findings, research in progress. Services for researchers and the public usually free.

11131. National Science Foundation, Public Information Branch, 1800 G St NW, Washington, DC 20550; (202)

357-9498. Answers inquiries regarding NSF activities; publishes annual report, magazine, guide to programs; makes referrals; sponsors info booths at professional society meetings.

11132. National Science Teachers Association, 1742 Connecticut Ave NW, Washington, DC 20009; (202) 328-5800. Affiliated with American Assn for Advancement of Science. Maintains employment registry for teachers, publishes journals, answers inquiries, provides consulting services.

11133. National Security Industrial Association, 1015 15th St NW, Ste 901, Washington, DC 20005; (202) 393-3620. Assn of manufacturing, research, service companies related to natl security. Conducts seminars, conferences. Services limited according to time required.

11134. National Serials Data Program, Library of Congress, Washington, DC 20540; (202) 287-6452. Responsible for all aspects of the assignment of Intl Standard Serial Numbers (ISSN) to U.S. serials. Interest in natl and intl identification, cataloging, and control of serial titles. Answers inquiries about program, identifies serial titles and provides the ISSN.

11135. National Sheriffs' Association, 1250 Connecticut Ave NW, Washington, DC 20036; (202) 872-0422. Provides assistance to fed, state, and local govts in corrections and law enforcement areas. Answers inquiries, provides advisory services, conducts seminars, distributes publications, makes referrals. Some services only to members.

11136. National Social Science & Law Center, 1825 Connecticut Ave NW, Ste 401, Washington, DC 20009; (202) 797-1100. Specializes in social science research methodologies, surveys, data compilation, analysis, and computer applications. Answers inquiries, provides advisory and publication services, makes referrals. Services free to legal services orgs.

11137. National Society for Children & Adults with Autism, 1234 Massachusetts Ave NW, Ste 1017, Washington, DC 20005; (202) 783-0125. Interest in autism and other severe disorders of communication and behavior, advocacy for victims of autism. Provides general reference services, publishes and distributes materials, permits onsite use of collection. Services free, except some materials.

11138. National Society for Medical Research, 1029 Vermont Ave NW, Ste 700, Washington, DC 20005; (202) 347-9565. Acts as clearinghouse on problems concerning biomedical research such as ethical aspects of using animals, cadavers. Publishes monthly bulletin, annual report, reprints, brochures.

11139. National Soft Drink Association, 1101 16th St NW, Washington, DC 20036; (202) 463-6732. Issues publications on history of soft drinks, soft drink ingredients, container deposit proposals. Answers inquiries.

11140. National Solid Wastes Management Association, 1120 Connecticut Ave NW, Ste 930, Washington, DC 20036; (202) 659-4613. Interest in all aspects of waste mgmt, including refuse collection, processing, disposal, hazardous waste, etc. Provides general reference services, conducts seminars, certifies equipment. Services free; priority given to assn members and govt.

11141. National Soybean Processors Association, 1800 M St NW, Ste 1030, Washington, DC 20036; (202) 452-8040. Interest in soybean processing industry, research for better soybean yield. Answers inquiries; other info services to members only.

11142. National Space Institute, 600 Maryland Ave SW, W Wing Ste 203, Washington, DC 20024; (202) 484-1111; (202) 484-3802 (Hotline). Dedicated to informing U.S. public about benefits of space exploration. Answers inquiries, makes referrals, publishes material. Services free, unless extensive. Space Hotline provides telephone access to space events.

11143. National Stone Association, 1415 Elliot Pl NW, Washington, DC 20007; (202) 342-1100. Interest in crushed stone and related engineering, marketing, education and training, community relations, and governmental affairs. Provides general reference services free to members and most other users, unless extensive.

11144. National Sudden Infant Death Syndrome Clearinghouse, 8201 Greensboro Drive, Ste 600, McLean, VA 22102; (703) 821-8955. Provide info on Sudden Infant Death Syndrome, its effects on families. Maintains core library (for onsite use), publishes newsletter and reference materials, answers inquiries. Services free.

11145. National Taxpayers Union, 713 Maryland Ave NE, Washington, DC 20002; (202) 543-1300. Seeks to reduce govt waste, improve govt accounting, amend Constitution to outlaw deficit spending. Publishes periodicals, answers inquiries. Most services free.

11146. National Technical Association, P.O. Box 27787 (4014 Georgia Ave NW, Washington, DC 20038; (202) 826-6100. Seeks to integrate black technical input into the scientific process and make blacks aware of their contributions. Answers inquiries, provides consulting and reference services, conducts seminars, distributes publications. Fee for some services.

11147. National Telecommunications & Information Administration, Dept of Commerce, Washington, DC 20230; (202) 377-1800. Serves as President's principal advisor on telecommunications and info, develops national policies for communications, represents executive branch views on communications matters. Answers short, specific info requests.

11148. National Tire Dealers & Retreaders Association, 1250 Eye St NW, Ste 400, Washington, DC 20005; (202) 789-2300. Interest in retail tire, automotive service, and tire retreading and repairing, including mgmt. Provides retread inspection program and consulting

services for a fee; conducts training programs, seminars; evaluates data.

11149. National Transportation Safety Board, 800 Independence Ave SW, Washington, DC 20594; (202) 382-6600. Independent agency interested in accident investigation of all modes of transportation. Sells data base tapes and computer programs, permits onsite use of hardcopy materials. Publications sold by Natl Technical Info Service. Reproduction services at cost.

11150. National Trust for Historic Preservation, 1785 Massachusetts Ave NW, Washington, DC 20036; (202) 673-4000. Promotes preservation of sites, buildings, objects; publishes magazine, books; offers advisory services, conferences, workshops. Onsite use of collection restricted to members.

11151. National Trust for Historic Preservation, National Main Street Center, 1785 Massachusetts Ave NW, Washington, DC 20036; (202) 673-4219. Works to revitalize business districts thru private initiative, broad participation. Publishes AV materials, manuals, newsletter; provides inquiry, advisory, consulting, referral services.

11152. National Urban Coalition, 1120 G St NW, Ste 900, Washington, DC 20005; (202) 628-2990. Works to improve the lives of people in American cities. Answers inquiries, provides data base, conducts seminars, distributes publications, makes interlibrary loans, permits onsite use of collection. Services free, except publications.

11153. National Urban League, Research Department, 425 13th St NW, Ste 515, Washington, DC 20004; (202) 783-0220. Analyzes conditions in U.S. from a black perspective. Interest in U.S. social and economic conditions, blacks, minorities. Provides general reference services, permits onsite use of collection. Services free, except publications.

11154. National Victims' Resource Center, Dept of Justice, Rm 1386, 633 Indiana Ave NW, Washington, DC 20531; (202) 272-6500. Natl clearinghouse for victim services. Provides general reference services, distributes materials, makes referrals.

11155. National Wildlife Federation, 1412 16th St NW, Washington, DC 20036; (202) 797-6800. Owns books on conservation of wildlife, natural resources; publishes journals; answers inquiries; provides reference services; makes interlibrary loans. Federation's Institute for Wildlife Research (8925 Leesburg Pike; Vienna, VA), conducts research and maintains library, open to public.

11157. National Women's Education Fund, 1410 Q St NW, Washington, DC 20009; (202) 462-8606. Promotes women's access to public policy process. Publishes printed, AV materials; answers inquiries; conducts training programs. Fees charged for some services.

11158. National Women's Health Network, 224 Seventh St SE, Washington, DC 20003; (202) 543-9222. Maintains clearinghouse (for members only, by appointment). Publishes newsletter and books, answers inquiries, conducts conferences. Services mostly free.

11159. National Wooden Pallet and Container Association, 1619 Massachusetts Ave NW, Washington, DC 20036; (202) 667-3670. Intl clearinghouse for data unitization of goods, palletization, use of wooden containers. Publishes handbooks, specifications; provides technical advice.

11160. National Zoological Park, Smithsonian Institution, 3000 Block of Connecticut Ave NW, Washington, DC 20008; (202) 673-4717. Displays exhibits of live mammals, birds, reptiles. Publishes guidebook, films, slides, annual report, brochures; provides consulting services. Library answers inquiries, provides copying services, makes interlibrary loans, makes referrals, permits onsite use of collections.

11161. National Zoological Park, Department of Pathology, Smithsonian Institution, 3000 Block of Connecticut Ave NW, Washington, DC 20008; (202) 673-4869. Makes pathology diagnoses of zoo animals by organ, species, and disease syndromes. Answers inquiries and permits onsite use of collections. Services free to professionals and students in medical fields.

11163. Natural Resources Defense Council, 1350 New York Ave NW, Ste 300, Washington, DC 20005; (202) 783-7800. Interest in environmental law, environmental quality. Answers inquiries, provides advisory services. Services generally free and primarily for citizens groups, but others assisted as time permits.

11164. Naval Historical Foundation, Bldg 57, Washington Navy Yard, Washington, DC 20374; (202) 433-2005. Operates library, archives, and store in Navy Memorial Museum. Interest in Naval history. Answers inquiries, provides limited reference services, makes referrals, permits onsite use of collections. Services free.

11165. Naval Observatory, Massachusetts Ave and 34th St NW, Washington, DC 20390; (202) 653-1499 (Library). Owns rare books on astronomy and mathematics; publishes almanacs, list of U.S. Naval Observatory publications; makes interlibrary loans; permits onsite reference of collection.

11166. Navy Memorial Museum, Bldg 76, Washington Navy Yard, Washington, DC 20374; (202) 433-2651. Museum of naval history from 1776 to present, including naval ships, weapons, and personnel, naval customs and scientific exploration. Answers inquiries, distributes publications, makes referrals, permits onsite use of collections. Services free.

11167. Naval Historical Center, Operational Archives, Bldg 44, Washington Navy Yard, Washington, DC 20374; (202) 433-3171. Maintains records on recent U.S. naval operations, strategy, and policy, office files of senior naval officers and naval biography. Answers inquiries, provides consulting and reference services,

makes referrals. "Declassified Records in the Operational Archives" available on request.

11168. Naval Intelligence Support Center Library, 4301 Suitland Rd, Washington, DC 20390; (301) 763-1606. Library of science and technology as they apply to Naval intelligence. Answers inquiries, makes referrals, permits onsite use of collection by govt personnel with proper security clearance.

11169. Near East Section, African and Middle Eastern Div, Library of Congress, 10 First St SE, Washington, DC 20540; (202) 287-5421. Collection of materials on cultures and languages of an area extending from Afghanistan to Morocco, and from Turkey and Central Asia to Sudan, excluding Israel. Answers inquiries, makes referrals, provides reference services. Special materials for onsite use only.

11170. Nephrology Division, Georgetown Univ Medical Ctr, 3800 Reservoir Rd, Rm 2212, Washington, DC 20007; (202) 625-7257. Source of info on kidney disease, renal physiology, dialyzable poisons, homotransplantation, and other issues of kidney treatment. Answers brief inquiries, but provides extensive services only to members of American Society of Nephrology and Intl Congress of Nephrology.

11173. North American Telecommunications Association, Research Department, 2000 M St NW, Ste 550, Washington, DC 20036; (202) 296-9800. Represents business telephone equipment manufacturers, vendors; promotes competitive market. Publishes annual statistical review; provides inquiry, referral services. Services free, primarily for members.

11174. Northeast-Midwest Institute, 218 D St SE, Washington, DC 20003; (202) 544-5200. Conducts, publishes research on regional economic impacts of U.S. policy (esp on Northeast and Midwest). Maintains economic, statistical info; provides inquiry, advisory, research, referral services; conducts seminars. Many services free.

11175. Nuclear Control Institute, 1000 Connecticut Ave NW, Rm 406, Washington, DC 20036; (202) 822-8444. Monitors nuclear programs in U.S., elsewhere; opposes spread of nuclear weapons. Publishes newsletter, reports; provides inquiry, advisory services; conducts seminars. Most services free.

11176. Nuclear Information & Resource Service, 1616 P St NW, Suite 160, Washington, DC 20036; (202) 328-0002. Provides info on nuclear energy, including a bimonthly magazine. Answers inquiries, provides reference services, distributes publications, makes referrals. Fee for mailing and copying.

11177. Nuclear Regulatory Agency, Public Document Room, 1717 H St NW, Left Lobby, Washington, DC 20555; (301) 634-3273. Maintains documents related to agency's work, open to public. Reference, computer search, document processing, and microfiche services provided by staff. Provides info, answers inquiries according to abilities. Most services free.

11178. Nuclear Regulatory Commission, Office of Public Affairs, 1717 H St NW, Left Lobby, Washington, DC 20555; (202) 492-7715. Provides info on regulation of nuclear industry, power reactor and materials licensing, storage, handling, and transport of nuclear materials and reactor safety research. Issues press releases, answers inquiries, makes referrals.

11179. OEF International, 2101 L St NW, Ste 916, Washington, DC 20037; (202) 466-3430. Works overseas to promote participation of Third World women in socioeconomic development; provides development education in U.S. Conducts training progs.

11180. OPERA America, 633 E St NW, Washington, DC 20004; (202) 347-9262. Nonprofit service org for professional opera companies. Publishes reference materials; provides inquiry, advisory, consulting, referral services; conducts conferences, auditions. Services free to member companies, for a fee to others.

11181. Occupational Safety & Health Review Commission, Office of Information, 1825 K St NW, Washington, DC 20006; (202) 634-7943. Interest in adjudication of Labor Dept enforcement actions alleging health and/or safety violations in the workplace and proposing penalties contested by employers. Answers inquiries, permits onsite use of case files.

11183. Office for Civil Rights, Dept of Health and Human Services, 330 Independence Ave SW, Washington, DC 20201; (202) 245-6700. Seeks to eliminate unlawful discrimination and ensure equal opportunities for the beneficiaries of fed financial assistance. Answers inquiries and compiles data. Services free.

11184. Office of Acid Deposition, Environmental Monitoring, & Quality Assurance, RD-680, Environmental Protection Agency, 401 M St SW, Washington, DC 20460; (202) 382-5763. Develops agencywide quality assurance for data. Publishes tech reports, answers inquiries, provides info on quality assurance, makes referrals to other sources of info. Services free.

11185. Office of Air & Radiation, Environmental Protection Agency, Mail Code ANR-45S, Washington, DC 20460; (202) 382-7645. Implements Title II of Clean Air Act and determines compliance of mobile sources with emission control regulations. Info furnished in response to FOIA requests, according to EPA's published fee schedule.

11186. Office of American Studies, Smithsonian Institution, Barney Studio House, Washington, DC 20560; (202) 673-4872. Conducts graduate programs in American civilization and interdepartmental research in the material culture of U.S. Coordinates univ graduate programs in American civilization and Smithsonian's own resources.

11187. Office of Aviation Medicine, Fed Aviation Admin, AAM-1, 800 Independence Ave SW, Washington, DC 20591; (202) 426-3535. Source of data on civil aviation medicine applications in aviation safety, occupational health, biomedical research. Answers inquiries and distributes publications. Services free.

11188. Office of Aviation Policy & Plans, APO-110, Fed Aviation Admin, 800 Independence Ave SW, Washington, DC 20591; (202) 426-3103. Provides forecasts for all phases of airlines, airport operations, and air traffic industry pertinent to FAA planning. Answers inquiries, provides copying services, conducts seminars, distributes publications, makes referrals. Services free, except some publications.

11189. Office of Bilingual Education & Minority Languages Affairs, Dept of Education, 400 Maryland Ave SW, REP 421, Washington, DC 20202; (202) 245-2600. Funds development, operation of bilingual education programs. Provides data bases; publishes reference materials; provides free inquiry, advisory, referral services; conducts seminars, workshops.

11190. Office of Building Energy Research & Development, Off of Asst Secty for Conservation and Renewable Energy, Department of Energy, Rm GF-231, 1000 Independence Ave SW, Washington, DC 20585; (202) 252-9444. Interest in energy conservation R&D related to residential and commercial buildings. Provides general reference services. Services primarily for groups within the building industry, but also available to others, and usually free.

11191. Office of Business Liaison, Dept of Commerce, Rm 5898C, Washington, DC 20230; (202) 377-3176. Expedites access of the business community to govt resources and maintains open channels of communication. Answers inquiries, provides advisory services, conducts seminars, makes referrals. Services free.

11192. Office of Business Loans, Small Business Admin, 1441 L St NW, Washington, DC 20416; (202) 653-6570. Provides info and guidance to small firms seeking loans from SBA.

11193. Office of Civil Rights, Dept of Education, 400 Maryland Ave, SW, Washington, DC 20202; (202) 426-6426. Enforces compliance with civil rights laws dealing with education. Provides info.

11194. Office of Civilian Radioactive Waste Management, Dept of Energy, Rm 5A085, 1000 Independence Ave, SW, Washington, DC 20585; (202) 252-6842. Conducts R&D on civilian waste mgmt, alternative methods of nuclear waste storage. Provides info, publishes materials, makes referrals.

11195. Office of Communication & Education Services, Commodity Futures Trading Commission, 2033 K St NW, Washington, DC 20581; (202) 254-8630. Regulates trading of futures and option contracts on domestic commodity exchanges and certain off-exchange commodity transactions. Answers inquiries, distributes publications, makes referrals. Services free, except reproductions.

11196. Office of Compliance & Consumer Assistance, Interstate Commerce Commission, Washington, DC

20423; (202) 275-7849. Responsible for compliance and enforcement functions of the Interstate Commerce Act. Answers inquiries, provides advisory services, distributes publications, provides assistance to consumers. Services free.

11197. Office of Computer Software and Systems, Dept of Defense, Pentagon, Washington, DC 20301; (202) 694-0210, 694-0208. Manages software technology, ADA computer language. Provides general info and public data base file, collects and distributes documentation.

11198. Office of Educational Research and Improvement, Dept of Education, Rm 722 Brown Bldg, 1200 19th St NW, Washington, DC 20208; (202) 254-8251. Conducts R&D for dept, provides grants for school improvement. Publishes materials, answers inquiries, disseminates info.

11199. Office of Elementary and Secondary Education, Dept of Education, Rm 2189, 400 Maryland Ave, SW, Washington, DC 20202; (202) 245-8720. Interest in policy for elementary, preschool, and high school instruction, racial discrimination, education grants for disadvantaged students. Answers inquiries, makes referrals.

11200. Office of Endangered Species, Fish and Wildlife Service, Dept of the Interior, Washington, DC 20240; (703) 235-1975 (Branch of Biological Support); (703) 235-2407 (Technical Info Staff). Manages implementation of Endangered Species Act of 1973 through conservation of endangered and threatened animal and plant species and their natural ecosystems. Answers inquiries, distributes publications, makes referrals. Services free.

11201. Office of Family Assistance, Social Security Admin, Dept of Health and Human Services, 2100 Second St SW, Rm 404, Washington, DC 20201; (202) 245-2000. Responsible for administration of the Aid to Families with Dependent Children program and U.S. Repatriate Program. Answers inquiries, distributes publications. Most services free.

11202. Office of Folklife Programs, Smithsonian Institution, 2600 L'Enfant Plaza, Washington, DC 20560; (202) 287-3424. Works to create a national cultural milieu in which authentic folk expression can thrive and develop. Answers inquiries, coordinates research and performance activities, makes referrals.

11203. Office of Fusion Energy, Dept of Energy, Washington, DC 20045; (301) 353-4941. Interest in fusion energy; research in supporting fields (plasma physics, materials science, nuclear technology). Publishes tech reports, answers inquiries, conducts seminars. Services free.

11204. Office of Grants and Program Systems, Dept of Agriculture, Rm 324, Administrative Bldg, 14th St and Independence Ave, SW, Washington, DC 20250; (202) 475-5720. Awards grants for agricultural research, programs to small/minority businesses, schools, etc. Answers inquiries, makes referrals.

11205. Office of Human Development Services, Administration on Aging, Dept of Health and Human Services, 330 Independence Ave SW, Washington, DC 20201; (202) 245-1826. Center within fed govt for collection, analysis, and dissemination of info related to needs, problems, and interests of older persons. Answers inquiries, provides reference services, makes referrals. Services free.

11206. Office of Industrial Programs, Off of the Asst Secty for Conservation and Renewable Energy, 6G-030, Dept of Energy, 1000 Independence Ave SW, Washington, DC 20585; (202) 252-2072. Promotes R&D for industrial energy conservation technologies that offer large potential for saving scarce fuels. Answers inquiries, distributes publications, makes referrals. Services free.

11207. Office of Information & Consumer Affairs, Employment Standards Admin, Dept of Labor, 3rd St and Constitution Ave NW, Washington, DC 20210; (202) 523-8743. Oversees administration of the Fair Labor Standards Act, Title III of Consumer Credit Protection Act, Davis-Bacon Acts, Walsh-Healey Public Contracts Act, and other statutory enactments that provide compensation to workers. Answers inquiries, makes referrals, provides advisory services.

11208. Office of Information Resources Management, General Services Admin, 18th and F Sts NW, Washington, DC 20405; (202) 566-1000. Manages Federal Telecommunications System, fed agencies' data processing policies and programming. Answers inquiries, provides engineering and consulting services. Some services to fed agencies only, others available to public at cost.

11209. Office of Information, Department of Labor, 200 Constitution Ave NW, Washington, DC 20210; (202) 523-9711. Disseminates info about Labor Dept's programs, offices, policies, and services. Answers inquiries according to ability; most services, except some publications, free.

11210. Office of International Affairs & Energy Emergencies, Dept of Energy, 1000 Independence Ave SW, Washington, DC 20585; (202) 252-5800. Responsible for developing and implementing intl energy policy and coordinating DoE's energy emergency preparedness program. Answers inquiries and makes referrals. Services free.

11211. Office of International Aviation, Fed Aviation Admin, AIA-1, 800 Independence Ave SW, Washington, DC 20591; (202) 426-3213. Compiles data on intl aviation, including aviation aspects of foreign policy, intl aviation orgs. Provides consulting services to foreign govts on traffic control, airports, training, and similar subjects. Answers brief inquiries for the public.

11212. Office of International Cooperation and Development, Dept of Agriculture, 14th St and Independence Ave SW, Washington, DC 20250; (202) 447-3157. Focuses on sharing knowledge of agriculture through both development assistance and cooperation with other countries. Answers inquiries, provides consulting services, makes referrals, permits onsite use of collection.

11213. Office of Metric Programs, Dept of Commerce, Herbert C. Hoover Bldg, Rm 4082, 14th and E Sts NW, Washington, DC 20230; (202) 377-0944. Plans, coordinates increasing use of the metric system in U.S. Answers inquiries, provides reference services, permits onsite use of data collection. Services free, unless extensive.

11214. Office of Naval Architecture and Engineering, Maritime Admin, 400 Seventh St SW, Washington, DC 20590; (202) 426-5733. Owns photos, slides, project records, technical reports, standards, specifications on naval architecture, marine engineering. Answers inquiries, provides repros for a fee.

11215. Office of Nondestructive Evaluation, Natl Measurement Laboratory, Natl Bur of Standards, Washington, DC 20234; (301) 921-3331. Investigates nondestructive materials evaluation methods, including x-radiography, ultrasonics, eddy currents, small angle neutron scattering, acoustic emission, resonance neutron radiographs. Answers inquiries, provides consulting services, conducts symposia.

11216. Office of Patent and Trademark Services, Patent Search Div, Washington, DC 20231; (703) 557-2276 (Search Rm); (703) 557-2977 (Record Rm). Microfilm collection of U.S. patents and documents dealing with Patent and Trademark Office. Patent search advisors give advice on fields of search and the files. Original files and papers of issued patents available without restriction.

11217. Office of Pension and Welfare Benefit Programs, Dept of Labor, 3rd St and Constitution Ave NW, Rm N5471, Washington, DC 20216; (202) 523-8921. Enforces minimum standards established by Employee Retirement Income Security Act of 1974 for employee benefit plans involving vesting, funding, and conduct for plan fiduciaries. Provides info on ERISA, distributes publications, answers inquiries.

11218. Office of Personnel Management Staffing Group, 1900 E St NW, Washington, DC 20415; (202) 632-6005. Provides info on recruitment of candidates for civil service positions, competitive civil service examinations, and fed employment. Publishes manuals and pamphlets, answers inquiries.

11219. Office of Postsecondary Education, Dept of Education, 7th and D Sts, SW, Washington, DC 20202; (202) 245-9274. Provides financial support and grants for public and private postsecondary education; implements related policy. Answers inquiries, makes referrals.

11220. Office of Procurement and Technical Assistance, Small Business Admin, 1441 L St NW, Washington, DC 20416; (202) 653-6588. Owns computerized list of 110,000 small businesses. Answers inquiries; helps small business firms procure contracts from larger firms, govt agencies; helps lease govt property.

11221. Office of Productivity, Technology and Innovation, Dept of Commerce, Rm 4816, 14th St and Constitution Ave, Washington, DC 20230; (202) 377-1093. Acts as liaison between small businesses, local and state govts. Promotes technological advancement through R&D, financing, training. Provides general reference services, distributes publications. Fees charged for financial models.

11222. Office of Public Affairs, Fish and Wildlife Service, Dept of the Interior, Washington, DC 20240; (202) 343-5634. Fed agency interested in fish, wildlife, and their habitats, especially migratory birds, sport fisheries, and endangered species, natl wildlife refuges, etc. Provides general reference services, publishes and distributes materials, operates a photo lending library.

11223. Office of Public Affairs, Department of Agriculture, Rm 402-A, 14th and Independence Ave, SW, Washington, DC 20250; (202) 447-7454. Disseminates info on USDA's programs and offices, which are involved in farm policy, rural development, agriculture science, nutrition, food supply, marketing of agricultural products, protection of natural resources, related areas. Answers inquiries, makes referrals, provides publications, some free.

11224. Office of Public Affairs, Department of Transportation, Rm 10413, 40 7th St, SW, Washington, DC 20590; (202) 426-4321. Disseminates info to public about functions, offices, and policies of the Transportation Dept. Answers inquiries and provides info; most services free.

11225. Office of Public Affairs, Department of the Interior, Rm 7211, 18th and C Sts NW, Washington, DC 20240; (202) 323-3171. Provides info regarding dept's policies, programs, and functions. Answers inquiries, makes referrals, distributes publications.

11226. Office of Public Affairs, Federal Bureau of Investigation, Rm 7116, 9th St and Pennsylvania Ave, Washington, DC 20535; (202) 324-5353. Provides info about FBI programs, Ten Most Wanted Fugitives list; answers inquiries.

11227. Office of Public Programs & Exhibits, Natl Archives and Records Admin, Pennsylvania Ave and 8th St NW, Rm G-12, Washington, DC 20408; (202) 523-3216. Interest in public programs and exhibits of the Natl Archives and Records Administration. Produces curricular materials and a variety of exhibits, guided tours, and educational programs for the general public.

11228. Office of Public Records, 232 Hart Senate Office Bldg, Washington, DC 20510; (202) 224-0322. Maintains records required by Federal Election Campaign Act relating to candidates for U.S. Senate and committees supporting such candidates. Records may be examined in the office.

11229. Office of Radiation Programs, Environmental Protection Agency, Washington, DC 20460; (703) 557-9710. Interest in health hazards associated with exposure to ionizing and nonionizing radiation, public health aspects of nuclear energy, etc. Answers inquiries; provides info to govt agencies, scientific orgs, industries; makes referrals; publishes and distributes materials.

11230. Office of Refugee Resettlement, Family Support Admin, Dept of Health and Human Services, 330 C St SW, Washington, DC 20201; (202) 245-0403 or 245-0418. Concerned with resettlement of refugees, education, English language training, health services, employment, and welfare. Answers inquiries and makes referrals.

11231. Office of Research & Development, Fed Railroad Admin, U.S. Dept of Transportation, 400 Seventh St SW, RRD-1, Washington, DC 20590; (202) 426-0955. Conducts railroad safety research. Answers inquiries or refers inquirers to other sources.

11232. Office of Rural Development Policy, Dept of Agriculture, Rm 5042, South Bldg, 14th St and Independence Ave, Washington, DC 20250; (202) 447-6795. Assists in rural development policy implementation. Answers inquiries.

11233. Office of Science and Technology, Drug Enforcement Administration, Dept of Justice, 1405 Eye St NW, Washington, DC 20537; (202) 633-1211. Conducts research relating to law enforcement, developing specialized, covert equipment and methodologies for forensic drug chemistry. Publishes newsletter, answers inquiries, performs drug analyses for those in the criminal justice system.

11234. Office of Science and Technology, Federal Communications Commission, 2025 M St NW, Rm 7202, Washington, DC 20554; (202) 632-7060. Answers inquiries on regulatory aspects of radio, television, telephone, telegraph; publishes reports, lists of frequency assignments, radio equipment acceptable for licensing.

11235. Office of Small Business Research & Development, Natl Science Found, 1800 G St NW, Rm 1250, Washington, DC 20550; (202) 357-7464. Promotes interests of small businesses performing research in the physical, astronomical, atmospheric, oceanographic, earth, biological, and other sciences. Serves as clearinghouse for info on NSF support of scientific and engineering research by small companies.

11238. Office of Solid Waste & Emergency Response, Off of Emergency and Remedial Response (WH-548-B), Environmental Protection Agency, 401 M St SW, Washington, DC 20460; (202) 245-3045. Makes assessments of potential danger that a discharge of oil or hazardous substances may present within constraints of the "Superfund" law. Provides tape and microfiche data and distributes compilations. Services provided for a fee.

11239. Office of Special Education & Rehabilitative Services, Clearinghouse on the Handicapped, Dept of Education, Switzer Bldg, Rm 3132, 330 C St SW, Washington, DC 20202; (202) 732-1241. Seeks to improve the lives of handicapped individuals by enhancing the flow of info. Publishes a directory, answers inquiries, distributes publications, makes referrals. Services free.

11240. Office of Strategic Petroleum Reserve, Dept of Energy, 1000 Independence Ave SW, MS 3G052, Washington, DC 20585; (202) 252-4410. Interest in procurement, storage of petroleum to reduce U.S. vulnerability to supply interruption. Publishes reports, petroleum reserve plan; answers inquiries. Services free.

11241. Office of Student Financial Assistance, Dept of Education, P.O. Box 84 (400 Maryland Ave SW), Washington, DC 20044; (202) 245-8595. Source of info on financial aid for eligible students in postsecondary education, fed grants, loans, and work-study programs. Provides info on grants and makes referrals. Services free.

11242. Office of Technology Assessment, 600 Pennsylvania Ave SE, Washington, DC 20510; (202) 226-2115 (Public Affairs); (202) 226-2160 (Info Ctr); (202) 224-8996 (Publications). Provides Congress with nonpartisan and expert analyses of complex issues involving science and technology. Supplies info on reports in progress and distributes publications. Published results are disseminated to the public as appropriate.

11243. Office of Technology Assessment & Forecast, Patent and Trademark Off (2221 Jefferson Davis Hwy; Crystal Plaza 6, Rm 1225; Arlington, VA), Washington, DC 20231; (703) 557-4115. Seeks to enhance use of patent files by assembling, analyzing, and making available meaningful data from these files. Answers inquiries, provides reports tailored to individual needs, distributes publications, makes referrals.

11244. Office of Terminal [Nuclear] Waste Disposal & Remedial Action, Dept of Energy, Washington, DC 20545; (301) 353-5006. Handles radioactive waste problems. Maintains integrated data base on radioactive waste inventories, projections. Publishes reports, data; provides inquiry, advisory, referral services. Services may be limited.

11246. Office of Vehicle & Engine R&D, Dept of Energy, CE-13, Forrestal Bldg, Rm 5G-030, 1000 Independence Ave SW, Washington, DC 20585; (202) 252-9118. Projects transportation demands to the year 2000 and estimates energy savings resulting from transportation energy alternatives. Evaluates data and distributes publications.

11247. Office of Vocational and Adult Education, Rm 5102, ROB #3, 7th and D sts., SW, Washington, DC 20202; (202) 245-8166. Interest in rural education, education training, vocational education. Administers grants, provides info.

11248. Office of Wages & Industrial Relations, Bur of Labor Statistics, 441 G St NW, Washington, DC 20212; (202) 523-1383. Studies all aspects of trends and structures of wages, salaries, and employee benefits, including professional, administrative, technical, and clerical categories. Answers inquiries, provides reference services, makes referrals.

11249. Office of Weights & Measures, Natl Bur of Standards, Washington, DC 20234; (301) 921-2401. Repository of info on fed, state, and local weights and measures laws, regulations, and commercial measurement practices. Answers inquiries, distributes publications, makes referrals. Services free.

11250. Office of the Assistant Secretary for Fossil Energy, Dept of Energy, 1000 Independence Ave SW, Washington, DC 20585; (202) 252-4700. Coordinates efforts in developing technologies for increasing the supply of domestic fossil fuels. Responsible for managing Strategic Petroleum and Naval Petroleum and Oil Shale Reserves. Answers inquiries, provides advisory services, distributes publications.

11251. Office of the Assistant Secretary for Nuclear Energy, U.S. Dept of Energy, 1000 Independence Ave SW, Washington, DC 20585; (202) 252-6450. Interest in nuclear power systems, R&D on nuclear power technology, nuclear safety, etc. Provides general reference services, distributes publications. Services free, except when otherwise required by the DOE pricing manual.

11252. Office of the Assistant Secretary of Defense, Public Affairs, Dept of Defense, Pentagon, Washington, DC 20301; (202) 697-5737. Provides info, referrals, publications on DoD services and functions.

11253. Office of the Consumer Adviser, Dept of Agriculture, Rm 232W, Administrative Bldg, 14th St and Independence Ave, Washington, DC 20250; (202) 382-9681. Interest in consumer-related issues, serves as liaison between consumer and dept. Provides info, makes referrals.

11254. Office of the Federal Register, Natl Archives and Records Admin, 1100 L St NW, Washington, DC 20408; (202) 523-5240. Publishes daily *Federal Register*, weekly *Compilation of Presidential Documents*; answers inquiries; provides certified copies of *Federal Register* documents for small fee.

11255. Office of the Liaison for Minorities & Women in Higher Education, Dept of Education, 400 Maryland Ave SW, Washington, DC 20202; (202) 472-1357. Interest in participation of minorities, women in higher education; black colleges, univs. Provides free inquiry, advisory services; permits onsite use of collections.

11256. National Archives & Records Administration, 8th & Pennsylvania Ave NW, Washington, DC 20408; (202) 523-3218 (Reference Services Branch); (202) 523-3000 (Recorded general info), (202) 523-3204 (genealogical info). Source of info on the National Archives' holdings of textual, cartographic, audiovisual, and machine-readable records produced by the fed govt. Answers general inquiries, makes referrals, and assists researchers from fed agencies, scholars, and the public.

11257. Office of the Postmaster General, Postal Service, 475 L'Enfant Plaza W SW, Rm 10206, Washington, DC 20260; (202) 245-5343. Maintains history of Post Office Dept and U.S. Postal Service, its programs, personnel, biographies, organizations, and accomplishments. Answers inquiries and makes referrals.

11258. Office of the Superintendent of Documents, Govt Printing Off, N Capitol St between G and H Sts NW, Washington, DC 20402; (202) 783-3238. Provides info regarding subjects, availability, sales, prices of govt publications and sells them to public. Provides info about administration of Federal Depository Library Program.

11259. Office of the Surgeon General, Dept of the Army, Pentagon, Washington, DC 20310; (202) 697-1358. Seeks to improve military health plans and policies, personnel management, army health standards, and military medical research. Answers army health care inquiries. Reference services are limited by time and effort required.

11260. Office of the U.S. Trade Representative, Exec Off of the Pres, 600 17th St NW, Washington, DC 20506; (202) 395-4647 or 395-5140. Advises and assists the President in administering the trade agreements program, develops intl trade policy, and has lead responsibility for conducting all intl trade negotiations. Answers inquiries and distributes data.

11261. Oil, Chemical, & Atomic Workers International Union Citizenship, AFL-CIO, 1126 16th St NW, Washington, DC 20036; (202) 223-5770. Investigates energy research, occupational health and safety problems of workers in U.S., collective bargaining and human relations. Answers inquiries, provides consulting and reference services, makes referrals.

11262. Optical Society of America, 1816 Jefferson Pl NW, Washington, DC 20036; (202) 223-8130. Owns journals, state-of-the-art reviews of astronomical, aeronautic, space optics; publishes journals, translation of Russian journal; answers inquiries; makes referrals.

11263. Organization of American States, Library, 17th St and Constitution Ave NW, Washington, DC 20006; (202) 789-6037 or 789-6040. Has holdings on history, culture, and development of OAS member states. Library open to public. Published materials available through interlibrary loan. Limited copying for a fee.

11264. Organization of American States, Pan American Highway Congresses, 1889 F St NW, No 350 G, Washington, DC 20006; (202) 789-3193. Promotes, coordinates highway development in OAS member states, including adoption of uniform standards for highway design and construction. Distributes publications free to members and at cost to others; conducts regional conventions.

11265. Organization of Chinese American Women, 1525 O St NW, Washington, DC 20005; (202) 328-3185. Seeks to integrate Chinese-American women into mainstream of women's activities. Publishes newsletter, answers inquiries, conducts workshops. Services primarily for Asian-American women; fees vary.

11267. Outboard Boating Club of America, 2550 M St NW, Washington, DC 20037; (202) 296-4588. Provides info on recreational boating law, cruising, insurance. Provides free inquiry, advisory, referral services; distributes publications.

11268. Outdoor Power Equipment Institute, 1901 L St NW, Ste 700, Washington, DC 20036; (202) 296-3484. Trade assn comprised of lawn and garden equipment manufacturers. Provides industry statistics, develops voluntary standards, publishes reports, answers brief inquiries.

11269. Overseas Citizens Services, Dept of State, Bureau of Consular Affairs, 2201 C. St NW, Washington, DC 20520; (202) 632-3444. Provides info, including travel advisories and emergency financial, legal, and medical aid to U.S. citizens travelling abroad; helps in search for missing Americans. Info free to the public.

11270. Overseas Development Council, 1717 Massachusetts Ave NW, Ste 501, Washington, DC 20036; (202) 234-8701. Seeks to increase American understanding of the problems faced by developing countries and importance of these countries to U.S. Conducts seminars and distributes publications.

11271. Packaging Machinery Manufacturers Institute, 1343 L St NW, Washington, DC 20005; (202) 347-3838. Members make packaging machinery and packaging-related converting machinery. Answers inquiries from machinery users free; sponsors packaging machinery and materials exhibition.

11272. Paleontological Society, Natl Museum of Natural History, Rm E-501, Smithsonian Institution, 10th & Constitution Ave NW, Washington, DC 20560; (202) 343-5097. Interest in paleontology. Answers inquiries, publishes and distributes materials.

11273. Pan American Health Organization, Documentation & Health Information Office, 525 23rd St NW, Washington, DC 20037; (202) 861-3300. Concerned with prevention and control of communicable diseases, emergency preparedness, and disaster relief coordination, epidemiological surveillance. Provides free reference service using PAHO-LINE computerized system. Documents available in microfiche.

11274. Panama Canal Commission, Public Information Office, 425 13th St NW, Washington, DC 20004; (202) 724-0104. Provides info on the activities of the Panama Canal Commission, which operates and maintains the Panama Canal and is involved in certain civil protec-

tion and housing programs in the Republic of Panama. Answers inquiries according to abilities.

11275. Paperboard Packaging Council, 1101 Vermont Ave NW, Ste 411, Washington, DC 20005; (202) 289-4100. Disseminates info on paperboard packaging industry, its marketing, safety standards, and environmental regulations. Distributes info on packaging in the food distribution system and how packaging affects marketing and economic development. Conducts seminars and evaluates data.

11276. Paralyzed Veterans of America, 801 18th St NW, Washington, DC 20006; (202) 872-1300. Nonprofit veterans service org that promotes research, rehabilitation, and education for persons with spinal cord injury or other disabilities. Provides free general reference services, distributes publications.

11278. Partners of the Americas, 1424 K St NW, Washington, DC 20005; (202) 628-3300. Promotes economic, social, and humanitarian development in the American hemisphere. Answers inquiries, provides consulting services. Services free.

11279. Partnership for Productivity, 2441 18th St NW, Washington, DC 20009; (202) 483-0067. Fosters intl network of agencies for small enterprise development, entrepreneurship. Publishes newsletter, tech reports; provides advisory, consulting, training, evaluation services. Services for a fee.

11281. Pattern Recognition Society, c/o Natl Biomedical Research Found, Georgetown Univ Medical Ctr, 3900 Reservoir Rd NW, Washington, DC 20007; (202) 625-2121. Seeks to advance theory, application, and practice of pattern recognition. Distributes publication by subscription.

11282. Peace Corps, Information Collection and Exchange Program, Rm 701, 806 Connecticut Ave NW, Washington, DC 20525; (202) 254-7386. Disseminates info gathered by Peace Corps volunteers about practical technology and project planning for Third World countries. Provides info, answers inquiries according to abilities.

11283. Peace Corps, Office of Public Affairs, Rm M-1214, 806 Connecticut Ave NW, Washington, DC 20526; (202) 254-5010. Provides info on programs, policies, and functions of the Peace Corps, which provides volunteers and programs to better the quality of life in Third World countries. Answers inquiries.

11284. Peace through Law Education Fund, 421 New Jersey Ave SE, Washington, DC 20003; (202) 544-2152. Seeks to provide Congress and the public info and approaches to crucial problems of intl cooperation. Sponsors a food-and-population and World Military and Social Expenditures speaker series. Also makes referrals.

11285. Pension Benefit Guaranty Corporation, Branch of Coverage and Inquiries, Insurance Operations Dept, Rm 5314, 2020 K St NW, Washington, DC 20006; (202) 254-

4817. Provides info on services and functions of the Pension Benefit Guaranty Corporation, which ensures payment of private pension plan benefits if those programs are terminated without payment capabilities. Answers inquiries according to abilities.

11286. Pension Rights Center, 1701 K St NW, Ste 305, Washington, DC 20006; (202) 296-3778. Promotes fair, responsive retirement income system. Publications price list available. Answers inquiries, provides tech assistance. Most services free.

11287. Pentagon Library, Rm 1A518, Washington, DC 20310-6000; (202) 697-4301. Library of military art and science, history, political science, foreign affairs, and other matters of interest to Dept of Defense. Library is for official use only. Material with security classification only to properly authorized persons in DoD.

11288. People for the Ethical Treatment of Animals, P.O. Box 56272 (406 Cedar St NW), Washington, DC 20011; (202) 726-0156. Nonprofit org for humane treatment of animals, animal rights. Library of printed, AV materials. Publishes newsletter; provides inquiry, referral services; conducts seminars. Services generally free.

11289. Pet Industry Joint Advisory Council, 1710 Rhode Island Ave NW, Washington, DC 20036; (202) 452-1525. Interest in animal welfare, animal transport, research on human/companion animal bond, law affecting pet industry. Publishes newsletter, answers inquiries. Services free.

11290. Pharmaceutical Manufacturers Association, 1100 15th St NW, Washington, DC 20005; (202) 835-3400. Concerned with prescription drug industry. Publishes weekly newsletter for members; answers inquiries from press, public; provides online search service to member firms.

11291. Philanthropon House, C.G. Jung Library & Information Center, 2948 Brandywine St NW, Washington, DC 20008; (202) 363-7766. Interest in wide range of psychology topics, especially C.G. Jung and related writers, marriage counseling, occult subjects. Provides general reference services, permits onsite use of collections, distributes publications. Services for members only; membership open to anyone.

11292. Photoduplication Service, Library of Congress, 10 First St SE, Washington, DC 20540; (202) 287-5640. Library's master negative microform collection, totaling over 310,000 microfilm reels and 130,000 microfiche on a broad range of subjects. Photoreproductions avilable for a fee, inquiries are answered, descriptions of the collection on request.

11294. Police Executive Research Forum, 2300 M St NW, Ste 910, Washington, DC 20037; (202) 466-7820. Promotes professionalism of police staff; research, open debate on criminal justice issues. Provides inquiry, consulting, referral services; conducts seminars, workshops. Services free.

11295. Police Foundation, Communications Office, 1001 22nd St NW, Ste 200, Washington, DC 20037; (202) 833-1460. Analyzes the police, law enforcement, arrest productivity, police mgmt and administration. Answers inquiries, conducts seminars, sells publications, makes referrals. Services primarily for those in the field.

11296. Population Association of America, P.O. Box 14182, Benjamin Franklin Station (806 15th St NW), Washington, DC 20044; (202) 393-3253. Scientific society that publishes newsletter, bibliographic journal, quarterly journal with articles relating to population. Makes referrals to other sources of info.

11297. Population Crisis Committee, 1120 19th St NW, Washington, DC 20036; (202) 659-1833. Seeks to stimulate other orgs to give higher priority to population affairs, raise funds, and encourage new programs worldwide. Info is disseminated through committee's free publications.

11298. Population Institute, 110 Maryland Ave NE, No 207, Washington, DC 20002; (202) 544-3300. Pursues the goal of bringing world population into balance with world resources. Answers inquiries free, distributes publications by subscription.

11299. Population Reference Bureau, 777 14th St NW, Washington, DC 20005; (202) 639-8040. Disseminates info about population trends, publishes data sheets, provides consulting services for fee, permits onsite use of collection free, makes interlibrary loans.

11300. Postal Rate Commission, Rm 500, 2000 L St NW, Washington, DC 20268; (202) 254-3880. Provides info on postal rates, classifications, services, regulations, and practices. Answers inquiries according to abilities.

11301. Potomac Institute, 1501 18th St NW, Washington, DC 20036; (202) 332-5566. Concerned with equality of opportunity in American life. Answers inquiries, provides consulting and reference services, makes referrals, conducts seminars.

11302. Power Marketing Administration, Dept of Energy, Rm 6B104, 1000 Independence Ave, SW, Washington, DC 20585; (202) 252-1040. Markets hydroelectricity from fed plants. Answers inquiries, provides info.

11303. Preservation Office, Library of Congress, 10 First St SE, Washington, DC 20540; (202) 287-5213. Interest in preservation of books, manuscripts, prints, drawings, photographs, maps. Answers inquiries, provides telephone consulting services, assists in preservation problems.

11304. President's Commission on White House Fellowships, 712 Jackson Pl NW, Washington, DC 20500; (202) 395-4522. Conducts an annual national competition which selects 14 to 20 outstanding men and women to become White House Fellows. Commission answers inquiries and provides advisory services.

11305. President's Committee on Employment of the Handicapped, Vanguard Bldg, 1111 20th St NW, Washington, DC 20036; (202) 653-5044. Seeks to develop a climate of acceptance and maximum opportunities for employment of handicapped persons. Answers inquiries, provides advisory services, makes referrals.

11306. President's Committee on Mental Retardation, 330 Independence Ave SW, Washington, DC 20201; (202) 245-7634. Advises the President on mental retardation programs and needs, acts as a liaison among orgs serving in the mental retardation field, and promotes public understanding. Publishes newsletter, answers inquiries, makes referrals.

11307. President's Council on Physical Fitness and Sports, 450 Fifth St NW, Rm 7103, Washington, DC 20001; (202) 272-3421. Develops, implements, and coordinates a national program for physical fitness and sports. Prepares articles alerting the public to the need for physical fitness, which are supplied to magazines and journals.

11308. Pretrial Services Resource Center, 918 F St NW, Ste 500, Washington, DC 20004; (202) 638-3080. Interest in pretrial alternatives, alternatives to prosecution for adults. Maintains library, data bank on U.S. programs; publishes materials; provides inquiry, referral services.

11309. Privacy Journal, P.O. Box 15300, Washington, DC 20003; (202) 547-2865. Clearinghouse of materials on the right to privacy, computer records, security, and surveillance. Answers inquiries; provides consulting, abstracting, indexing, and reference services; distributes publications; makes referrals. Some services free.

11310. Private Radio Bureau, Fed Communications Commission, 2025 M St NW, Rm 5002, Washington, DC 20554; (202) 632-6930. Develops, regulates, and licenses radio services including aviation, marine, private operational fixed microwave, and industrial. Answers inquiries, makes referrals, distributes publications, permits onsite use of the collections.

11311. Psychological Abstracts Information Service, 1200 17th St NW, Washington, DC 20036; (202) 955-7600. Provides ways to access the world's literature in psychology and related sciences. Provides tape edition of PsycINFO data base from 1967 to present. Distributes publications, answers inquiries, conducts seminars. Aside from courtesy assistance, there is a charge for all products.

11312. Public Affairs Information, 1000 Potomac St, Room 401, Washington, DC 20007; (202) 342-3950. Reports, monitors proposed legislation, regulations in all states. Maintains online data base. Provides inquiry, advisory, consulting, referral services; conducts seminars, workshops. Services for a fee.

11313. Public Broadcasting Service, 475 L'Enfant Plaza SW, Washington, DC 20024; (202) 488-5000. National membership org of public television stations primarily responsible for providing multiple national program services for its member stations. Answers inquiries, rents or sells videocassettes, makes referrals.

11314. Public Citizen Congress Watch, 215 Pennsylvania Ave SE, Washington, DC 20003; (202) 546-4996. Public interest congressional watchdog that works with groups associated with the Public Citizen network. Answers inquiries, publishes newsletter, provides advisory services, distributes publications, makes referrals. Services free.

11315. Public Citizen, Critical Mass Energy Project, 215 Pennsylvania Ave SE, Washington, DC 20013; (202) 546-4996. Consumer watchdog group on energy issues, least-cost energy planning. Provides inquiry, advisory, reference, legal services; conducts seminars, workshops; sells publications. Fees charged.

11316. Public Citizen, Health Research Group, 2000 P St NW, Ste 708, Washington, DC 20036; (202) 872-0320. Focuses on fed legislation and regulatory activities of the Food and Drug Administration and the Occupational Safety and Health Administration. Answers inquiries, makes referrals, distributes publications on cost basis.

11317. Public Citizen, Tax Reform Research Group, 215 Pennsylvania Ave SE, Washington, DC 20003; (202) 546-4996. Monitors Internal Revenue Service, lobbys Congress, assists local groups to advance progressive tax reform. Answers inquiries free, but fees may be charged for copying and mailing. Publishes and distributes materials.

11319. Public Information, Department of the Treasury, 15th and Pennsylvania Ave NW, Washington, DC 20220; (202) 566-2041. Disseminates info about the functions, offices, and policies of the Treasury Dept. Answers inquiries, provides info. Most services free.

11320. Public Inquiries, Department of Energy, 1000 Independence Ave, SW, Washington, DC 20585; (202) 252-5575. Provides info regarding DoE programs, policies, and functions. Answers inquiries, makes referrals, distributes publications.

11322. Public Lands Institute, 1350 New York Ave NW, Washington, DC 20005; (202) 783-7800. Promotes conservation, wise use of public land resources. Publishes newsletter; provides inquiry, advisory, reference services; conducts workshops. Services free, unless extensive.

11323. Public Law Education Institute, 1601 Connecticut Ave NW, Suite 407, Washington, DC 20009; (202) 232-1400. Conducts legal research on military law and justice and the selective service. Interest in selective service, veterans, etc. Sells publications, provides photocopies for a fee, makes interlibrary loans, makes referrals. Library open to the public.

11324. Publishing Office, Library of Congress, 10 First St SE, Washington, DC 20540; (202) 287-5093. Carries out the planning, editing, design, production, and marketing of the publications of Library of Congress. Answers inquiries about current, forthcoming, and out-of-print publications.

11325. RARE, 1601 Connecticut Ave NW, Washington, DC 20009; (202) 745-7364. Promotes environmental education in Latin America and the Caribbean. Provides advisory services free.

11326. Radio Technical Commission for Aeronautics, 1 McPherson Square, Ste 500, 1425 K St NW, Washington, DC 20005; (202) 682-0266. Nonprofit assn of govt, industry orgs involved in aeronautics. Publishes reports; conducts seminars, workshops. Services primarily for members, but will provide to others.

11327. Radio Television News Directors Association, 1735 DeSales St NW, Washington, DC 20036; (202) 737-8657. Gathers info and monitors matters affecting broadcast journalism, and seeks to raise the standards and ethics of the profession. Provides general reference services free, except publications.

11328. Rare Book & Special Collections Division, Library of Congress, 10 First St SE, Washington, DC 20540; (202) 287-5434. Library's collection of rare books, first editions, fine printing, color plate and illustrated books, fine bindings, and other rarities. Inquiries are answered and onsite use of the collections by the public is permitted.

11329. Reading Is Fundamental, 600 Maryland Ave SW, Rm 500, Smithsonian Institution, Washington, DC 20560; (202) 287-3220. Provides technical assistance to autonomous local reading motivation programs. Operates the Inexpensive Book Distribution Program. Answers inquiries, conducts seminars, publishes and distributes materials. Services free.

11330. Recreation Management Staff Unit, Forest Service, USDA, P.O. Box 2417 (S Agriculture Bldg, Rm 4243; 12th St and Independence Ave SW), Washington, DC 20013; (202) 447-3706. Concerned with public outdoor recreation, its mgmt, and balancing outdoor recreation with other uses of forest lands. Answers inquiries, provides limited consulting services, makes referrals.

11331. Regulatory Information Service Center, New EOB, 726 Jackson Pl NW, Rm 5216, Washington, DC 20503; (202) 395-4931. U.S. govt center. Compiles, disseminates info on fed regulatory activity; abstracts, compiles regulatory activity; publishes reference materials; provides inquiry, referral services. Services primarily for U.S. officials.

11332. Rehabilitation Engineering Society of North America, 1101 Connecticut Ave, NW, Ste 700, Washington, DC 20036; (202) 857-1199. Org of rehabilitation engineering community. Promotes engineering solutions to physical disability problems. Publishes newsletter, answers inquiries, conducts seminars.

11333. Rehabilitation Research & Training Center, Dept of Psychiatry and Behavioral Sciences, George Washington Univ Medical Ctr, 2300 Eye St NW, Ste 613, Washington, DC 20037; (202) 676-2624. Explores the role of family, school, and workplace in the rehabilitation of adolescents and adults with severe disabilities, to improve services offered to them. Answers inquiries, provides consulting services, conducts seminars, distributes publications. Fee for services.

11334. Religious Coalition for Abortion Rights, 100 Maryland Ave NE, Washington, DC 20002; (202) 543-7032. Religious coalition seeking to preserve the option of legal abortion. Conducts seminars, distributes publications, makes referrals. Services free, except some publications.

11335. Renwick Gallery, Natl Museum of Amer Art, Smithsonian Institution, Washington, DC 20560; (202) 357-2531. Presents curatorial changing exhibitions and other public programs on creative achievements of craftsmen and designers in U.S., past and present. Offers tours and lectures, sells books and related mdse.

11336. Reporters Committee for Freedom of the Press, 800 18th St NW, Ste 300, Washington, DC 20006; (202) 466-6313. Provides legal research and defense for the news media, print and electronic, in areas involving First Amendment protections. Publishes newsletter, answers inquiries, provides advisory and reproduction services. Services free, primarily for those in media.

11337. Reserve Officers Association of the U.S., 1 Constitution Ave NE, Washington, DC 20002; (202) 479-2200. Interest in personnel mgmt within the Armed Forces, problems in recruiting, force structures, military unionization, etc. Answers inquiries, conducts seminars, distributes publications, makes referrals. Services provided free to members, at cost to others.

11338. Resource Policy Institute, 5108 MacArthur Blvd NW, Washington, DC 20016; (202) 363-6133. Researches energy, environment, resource policy. Provides inquiry, advisory services; conducts seminars, water resource auditing prog; distributes publications. Most services free or at cost.

11339. Resources for the Future, 1616 P St NW, Washington, DC 20036; (202) 328-5000. Nonprofit research org concerned with conservation of natural resources. Owns documents of Ford Foundation Energy Policy Project (limited access to scholars); publishes bulletin, books; conducts conferences, seminars.

11340. Revenue Sharing Advisory Service, 1725 K St NW, Ste 200, Washington, DC 20006; (202) 872-1766. Publishes materials on revenue sharing, fed assistance progs; geared to state, local govt officials. Provides advisory, consulting, referral services to subscribers; conducts seminars.

11342. Rubber Manufacturers Association, 1901 Pennsylvania Ave NW, 6th Fl, Washington, DC 20006; (202)

682-4800. Publishes standards, specifications, manuals, bulletins, charts, statistical reports on tire shipments and rubber consumption; answers inquiries involving nonproprietary info.

11343. Rural America, 1302 18th St NW, No 302, Washington, DC 20036; (202) 659-2800. Natl program of policy-oriented research, education, and advocacy designed to improve human opportunities in rural areas. Provides general reference services, conducts workshops, distributes publications. Services free, except consulting services and publications.

11344. Rural Electrification Administration, Dept of Agriculture, 14th St and Independence Ave SW, Washington, DC 20250; (202) 382-1255. Provides financial, technical assistance for rural electric and telephone systems. Publishes bulletins, answers inquiries, handles Freedom of Info requests.

11345. SANE, Committee for a Sane Nuclear Policy, 711 G St SE, Washington, DC 20003; (202) 546-7100. Works to cut military expenditures in order to free funds for domestic needs, for arms control and disarmament, and for a civilian economy. Provides general reference services, permits onsite use of collection. Services free, except publications.

11348. Scientific Apparatus Makers Association, 1101 16th St NW, Washington, DC 20036; (202) 223-1360. Publishes brochures, technical product standards for scientific instruments and laboratory apparatus. Owns collection of reports, technical guides; answers inquiries.

11349. Scientific Manpower Commission, 1500 Massachusetts Ave NW, Washington, DC 20005; (202) 223-6995. Provides data on science and engineering manpower; publishes annual data resource report on minorities, summary of salary surveys; provides affirmative action counseling for fee.

11350. Scientific, Economic & Natural Resources Branch, Civil Archives Div, Natl Archives and Records Admin, Pennsylvania Ave and 8th St NW, Rm 13-E, Washington, DC 20408; (202) 523-3238. Interest in activities of fed agencies in agriculture, business, economics, environment, labor, science. Provides info. With some exceptions, holdings for onsite use; copies provided for a fee.

11351. Securities Investor Protection Corp., 900 17th St NW, Ste 800, Washington, DC 20006; (202) 223-8400. Seeks to provide specific limited protections to customers of securities firms that are forced to liquidate. Answers inquiries, distributes publications, makes referrals. Services free.

11352. Securities and Exchange Commission, Office of Public Affairs, 450 Fifth St NW, Washington, DC 20549; (202) 272-2650. Administers laws designed to protect the investing public. Answers inquiries and makes referrals. Info also available from regional and branch offices.

11353. Selective Service System, Public Affairs Office, 1023 31st St NW, Washington, DC 20435; (202) 724-0970. Provides info on the services and functions of the Selective Service System, which administers military draft programs. Answers inquiries according to abilities.

11354. Senate Committee on Agriculture, Nutrition, and Forestry, Rm 328A, Russell Senate Office Bldg, Washington, DC 20510; (202) 224-2035. Subcommittees: Agricultural Credit and Rural Electrification; Agricultural Production, Marketing and Stabilization of Prices; Agricultural Research, Conservation, Forestry and Gen. Legislation; Rural Development, Oversight and Investigations; Foreign Agricultural Policy; Nutrition.

11355. Senate Committee on Appropriations, Rm S-128, Capitol Bldg, Washington, DC 20510; (202) 224-3471. Subcommittees: Agricultural, Rural Development and Related Agencies; Commerce, Justice, State, the Judiciary, and Related Agencies; Defense; District of Columbia; Energy and Water Develop.; Foreign Operations; HUD-Independent Agencies; Interior and Related Agencies; Labor, Health and Human Services, Education, and Related Agencies; Legislative Branch; Military Construction; Transportation and Related Agencies; Treasury, Postal Service and General Government.

11356. Senate Committee on Armed Services, Rm 222, Russell Senate Office Bldg, Washington, DC 20510; (202) 224-3871. Studies issues and formulates measures relating to military and defense matters. Subcommittees: Defense Acquisition Policy; Manpower and Personnel; Military Construction; Perparedness; Seapower and Force Projection; Strategic and Theater Nuclear Forces.

11357. Senate Committee on Banking, Housing and Urban Affairs, Rm SD534, Dirksen Senate Office Bldg, Washington, DC 20510; (202) 224-7391. Studies issues and formulates measures relating to banks and other financial institutions, public and private housing, fed monetary policy, urban development, mass transit, and certain foreign trade matters. Subcommittees: Economic Policy; Financial Insitutions and Consumer Affairs; Housing and Urban Affairs; International Finance and Monetary Policy; Securities.

11358. Senate Committee on Commerce, Science and Transportation, Rm 508, Dirksen Senate Office Bldg, Washington, DC 20510; (202) 224-5115. Subcommittees: Aviation; Business, Trade and Tourism; Communications; Consumer; Merchant Marine; Science, Technology and Space.

11359. Senate Committee on Energy and Natural Resources, Rm 358, Dirksen Senate Office Bldg, Washington, DC 20510; (202) 224-4971. Studies regulation, conservation research and development of energy, mining, natl parks, wilderness and historical areas, and U.S. territorial possessions. Subcommittees: Energy, Regulation and Conservation; Energy Research and Development; Natural Resources Development; Public Lands, Reserved Water and Resource Conservation; Water and Power.

11360. Senate Committee on Environment and Public Works, Rm 410, Dirksen Senate Office Bldg, Washington, DC 20510; (202) 224-6176. Studies environmental protection, water resources and flood control, public works and buildings, highways, and noise pollution. Subcommittees: Environmental Pollution; Nuclear Regulation; Water Resources; Transportation; Toxic Substances and Environmental Oversight; Regional and Community Development.

11361. Senate Committee on Finance, Rm SD219, Dirksen Senate Office Bldg, Washington, DC 20510; (202) 224-4515. Subcommittees: Energy and Agricult. Taxation; Estate and Gift Taxation; Health; International Trade; Oversight of the IRS; Savings, Pensions and Investment Policy; Social Security and Income Management Programs; Taxation and Debt Management.

11362. Senate Committee on Foreign Relations, Rm 446, Dirksen Senate Office Bldg, Washington, DC 20510; (202) 224-4651. Studies issues relating to foreign policy, treaties, diplomatic affairs and the United Nations. Subcommittees: International Economic Policy, Oceans and Environment; African Affairs; European Affairs; E Asian and Pacific Affairs; Near Eastern and S Asian Affairs; Western Hemisphere.

11363. Senate Committee on Governmental Affairs, Rm 340, Dirksen Senate Office Bldg, Washington, DC 20510; (202) 224-4751. Subcommittees: Civil Service, Post Office and General Services; Energy, Nuclear Proliferation, and Government Processes; Governmental Efficiency and the District of Columbia; Intergovtal Relations; Oversight of Governmental Management; Permanent subcommittee on Investigations.

11364. Senate Committee on Labor and Human Resources, Rm 4230, Dirksen Senate Office Bldg, Washington, DC 20510; (202) 224-5375. Studies issues relating to education, labor, health, and public welfare. Subcommittees: Aging; Children, Family, Drugs and Alcoholism; Education, Arts and the Humanities; Handicapped; Labor.

11365. Senate Committee on Rules and Administration, Rm 305, Russell Senate Office Bldg, Washington, DC 20510; (202) 224-6352. Involved in overseeing the rules of the Senate, mgmt of the Senate and Senate employees, fed elections, Presial succession, Smithsonian Institution, and the Library of Congress; no subcommittees.

11366. Senate Committee on Small Business, Rm 428A, Russell Senate Office Bldg, Washington, DC 20510; (202) 224-5175. Creates measures relating to small businesses. Subcommittees: Urban and Rural Economic Development; Government Procurement; Productivity and Competition; Innovation and Technology; Export Promotion and Market Development; Entrepre-

neurship and Special Problems Facing Small Business; Small Business: Family Farm.

11367. Senate Committee on Veterans Affairs, Rm 414, Russell Senate Office Bldg, Washington, DC 20510; (202) 224-9126. Interest in veterans affairs, including pensions, medical care, life insurance, education, and rehabilitation. No permanent subcommittees.

11368. Senate Committee on the Budget, 6th floor, Dirksen Senate Office Bldg, Washington, DC 20510; (202) 224-0642. Involved in the coordination of appropriations and revenues in the fed budget; has no permanent subcommittees.

11369. Senate Committee on the Judiciary, Rm 224, Dirksen Senate Office Bldg, Washington, DC 20510; (202) 224-5225. Studies fed courts and judges, civil rights and civil liberties, legislative apportionment, antitrust, immigration. Subcommittees: Adminstrative Practise and Procedure; Constitution; Courts; Criminal Law; Immigration and Refugee Policy; Juvenile Justice; Patents, Copyrights and Trademarks; Security and Terrorism.

11370. Senate Special Committee on Aging, Dirksen Senate Off Bldg, Rm G-33, Constitution Ave and 1st St NE, Washington, DC 20510; (202) 224-5364. Concerned with problems of and opportunities for the elderly, including health, employment, retirement income, housing, and medical and social services. Makes committee records available and provides info on fed legislation on aging.

11371. Sensory Communication Research Lab & Rehabilitation Engineering Center for the Hearing-impaired, Gallaudet Univ, 7th St and Florida Ave NE, Washington, DC 20002; (202) 651-5440. Interest in research to improve speech communication for persons with impaired hearing; research on speech technology; etc. Answers inquiries, makes referrals. Services only to qualified research and clinical persons.

11372. Serial and Government Publications Division, Library of Congress, 10 First St SE, Washington, DC 20540; (202) 287-5647 (Div Off); (202) 287-5690 (Newspaper and Current Periodical Rm). Answers inquiries on serial publications; provides reference services, list of newspapers received. Requests requiring extensive search referred to private researchers.

11373. Service Corps of Retired Executives, 1111 18th St NW, Ste 625, Washington, DC 20417; (202) 634-6200. Group of retired people who offer their services, without pay, to assist small business orgs in overall mgmt. Answers inquiries, provides consulting services, conducts seminars, distributes publications. Services free, primarily for those in small businesses.

11374. Shipbuilders Council of America, 1110 Vermont Ave NW, Ste 1250, Washington, DC 20005; (202) 775-9060. Trade assn of shipbuilding, ship repair industry in U.S. Publishes newsletter and statistics, answers inquiries, permits onsite use of collection. Services free.

11376. Signed English Project, Ctr for Studies in Education and Human Development, Gallaudet Research Institute, Washington, DC 20002; (202) 651-5281. Interest in signed English. Answers inquiries, provides consulting services. Services usually free, except some publications.

11377. Silver Institute, 1026 16th St NW, Ste 101, Washington, DC 20036; (202) 783-0500. Worldwide nonprofit assn of silver miners, refiners, and manufacturers. Interest in silver and promotion of its uses. Provides general reference services, conducts seminars, distributes publications, permits onsite use of collection. Services free to members.

11378. Single Service Institute, 1025 Connecticut Ave NW, Washington, DC 20036; (202) 347-0020. Promotes the concept of disposability for cups and plates in food service and packaging; represents industry in communications with govt. Answers inquiries, distributes publication, provides training aids to public health departments at cost.

11379. Slurry Transport Association, 1800 Connecticut Ave NW, Washington, DC 20009; (202) 332-5751. Fosters exchange of info and encourages investigation and research into pipeline delivery of solids. Answers inquiries, conducts conferences, distributes publications, makes referrals. Most services free.

11380. Small Business Administration, Information Office, 1441 L St NW, Washington, DC 20416; (202) 653-6600. Publishes booklets, leaflets on small business mgmt; provides info services through field offices; answers inquiries; provides consulting, referral services.

11381. Small Business Administration, Office of Advocacy, 1441 L St NW, Washington, DC 20416; (202) 634-7600 or 653-7561; (800) 368-5855 (Answer desk). Keeps small business informed of issues, regulations, conferences. Publications list available. Operates a toll-free "Answer Desk" for problems with govt. Services free.

11382. Small Business Administration, Office of Women's Business Ownership, 1441 L St NW, Rm 414, Washington, DC 20416; (202) 653-8000. Helps women start, expand their own businesses, enter mainstream of the economy. Provides advisory, counseling services.

11383. Small Scale Technology Branch, Energy Mgmt and Extension Div, 1000 Independence Ave, CE-24, Washington, DC 20585; (202) 252-9104. Decides on providing govt aid for energy-related inventions (administrative support, contracts, grants to inventors). Provides inquiry, advisory, consulting services.

11384. Small-Scale Hydropower Branch, Div of Geothermal and Hydropower Tech (CE-324), Dept of Energy, 1000 Independence Ave SW, Washington, DC 20585; (202) 252-4198. Interest in small-scale hydroelectric resource development. Publishes tech reports, other materials; answers inquiries; provides info on R&D in progress. Services free.

11385. Smithsonian Institution, Office of Printing & Photographic Services, MHT CB-054 OPPS, Washington, DC 20560; (202) 357-1933 or 357-1803. Maintains Smithsonian collections that may be photographed. Answers inquiries; provides advisory, reference, reproduction services for a fee; makes referrals.

11388. Social Security Administration, Welfare Management Institute, Off of Family Assistance, 2100 Second St SW, Washington, DC 20201; (202) 245-3418. Serves as referral center, distribution point for tech assistance in mgmt of welfare programs. Publishes research, training materials; provides inquiry service; conducts seminars, workshops. Services free.

11389. Society for Information & Documentation, Federal Republic of Germany, 1990 M St NW, Ste 680, Washington, DC 20036; (202) 466-2808 or 466-2809. Develops the West German scientific and technical info infrastructure. Answers or refers inquiries free, provides at cost West German documents to American requesters and American documents to West German requesters. Services to noncommercial requesters only.

11390. Society for Intercultural Education, Training, & Research, 1414 22nd St NW, Ste 101, Washington, DC 20037; (202) 296-4710. Concerned with intercultural communication and cooperation. Answers inquiries, publishes newsletter, provides consulting and reference services, conducts seminars, distributes publications, makes referrals. Services free, primarily for members.

11391. Society for Neuroscience, 11 Dupont Circle NW, Washington, DC 20036; (202) 462-6688. Promotes an understanding of the function of nervous systems. Interest in nervous systems, research and education in the neurosciences. Answers inquiries, makes referrals free. Sells publications.

11393. Society for Technical Communications, 815 15th St NW, Ste 516, Washington, DC 20005; (202) 737-0035. Interest in technical communication in all media, standards, publications. Distributes publications for a fee.

11394. Society for the History of Technology, Natl Museum of Amer History, Rm 5008, Smithsonian Institution, Washington, DC 20560; (202) 357-3301. Encourages research and education in the history of technology and culture. Interest in inventions, science-technology relationships. Conducts seminars, distributes publications to members, makes referrals. Services free.

11395. Society of Federal Linguists, P.O. Box 7765, Washington, DC 20044. Interest in promotion of the professional status and competence of fed govt linguists and establishment of professional standards and training programs. Answers inquiries, makes referrals, conducts meetings. Most services free.

11396. Society of Prospective Medicine, 1101 Connecticut Ave NW, Ste 700, Washington, DC 20036; (202) 857-1199. Identifies health hazards and develops risk assessment and reduction programs. Answers inquiries, provides reference services, conducts seminars, distributes publications, makes referrals. Services free, primarily for medical personnel.

11397. Society of Toxicology, 1133 15th St NW, No 620, Washington, DC 20005; (202) 293-5935. Studies all aspects of toxicology. Inquiries are referred to society committees by the Exec Secty.

11398. Soil Conservation Service, Dept of Agriculture, P.O. Box 2890, Washington, DC 20013; (202) 447-4543. Publishes bulletins, handbooks on soil and water conservation; answers inquiries; makes referrals to other sources of info; permits onsite use of collection by approved visitors.

11399. Soil Conservation Service, National Cooperative Soil Survey, P.O. Box 2890, Washington, DC 20013; (202) 382-1819. Publishes soil surveys for all land areas in the nation. Interest in soil resources of U.S., including soil maps, soil descriptions, soil classification. Provides general reference services, distributes publications.

11400. Solar Energy Industries Association, 1717 Massachusetts Ave NW, Ste 503, Washington, DC 20036; (202) 483-6225. Source of data on active and passive solar energy, photovoltaics, solar thermal energy conversion, industrial process heat. Publishes newsletter, answers inquiries, conducts seminars, distributes publications, makes referrals. Most services free for govt and industry only.

11402. Solar Rating & Certification Corp., 1001 Connecticut Ave NW, Ste 800, Washington, DC 20036; (202) 452-0078. Nonprofit org for certification programs, natl rating standards for solar energy equipment. Publishes reference materials. Answers inquiries. Services, except directories, free.

11403. Soy Protein Council, 1255 23rd St NW, Ste 850, Washington, DC 20037; (202) 467-6610. Represents the food protein industry, promoting the acceptance of food protein products and keeping members informed about govt actions. Answers inquiries and distributes brochures. Services free.

11405. Special Olympics, 1350 New York Ave NW, Ste 500, Washington, DC 20005; (202) 628-3630. Intl prog of athletic activities, competition for the mentally retarded. Offers grants, program materials, insurance coverage to chapters in U.S., and throughout the world (list available).

11406. Sport Fishing Institute, 1010 Massachusetts Ave NW, Ste 100, Washington, DC 20001; (202) 898-0770. Publishes reports on fish conservation, answers inquiries, provides consulting services. Services provided free to members, govt agencies; at cost to others.

11407. Standard & Poor's Corp., 900 17th St NW, Washington, DC 20006; (202) 296-3990. Publishes financial info, stock and bond market data, industry surveys, and info on corporations and securities. Provides consulting, reference, and magnetic tape services through vendors, distributes publications, makes referrals. General info is free.

11408. Statistical Reporting Service, USDA, S Agriculture Bldg, Rm 5809, Washington, DC 20250; (202) 447-7017. Publishes crop and livestock statistical reports (sold by subscription), answers inquiries, provides consulting services, copies magnetic tape for nominal charge.

11409. Student Loan Marketing Association (Sallie Mae), 1050 Thomas Jefferson St NW, Washington, DC 20007; (202) 333-8000. Provides secondary market and warehousing facility to lenders under the Guaranteed Student Loan Program. Answers inquiries free. Inquiries about secondary market programs should be addressed to the Marketing Dept, (202) 965-7700.

11410. Student Press Law Center, 800 18th St NW, Washington, DC 20006; (202) 466-5242. Seeks to protect First Amendment rights for student journalists. Acts as a clearinghouse for info on censorship and provides legal support. Answers inquiries, provides free advisory and reference services, distributes publications, makes legal referrals for students and teachers.

11412. Sulphur Institute, 1725 K St NW, Washington, DC 20006; (202) 331-9660. Owns books, journals, films on chemistry, agronomy, soil science, animal nutrition; publishes technical bulletins; provides reference services; permits onsite use of collection.

11413. Supreme Court of the U.S., Office of the Clerk, 1st and E Capitol Sts NE, Washington, DC 20543; (202) 479-3011. Acts as source of info on judicial practice and procedures before Supreme Court, status of pending cases, calendar of cases and activities of the court. Answers inquiries and provides guidance on recent decisions. Inquiries from news media are answered by the Press Office (202) 479-3211.

11414. Tanners' Council of America, 2501 M St NW, Washington, DC 20037; (202) 785-9400. Trade assn of leather tanning industry. Maintains research lab; publishes newsletter, statistics, reports, standards and specifications; provides reference, consulting services.

11415. Tax Foundation, 1 Thomas Circle NW, Ste 500, Washington, DC 20005; (202) 822-9050. Answers inquiries on research, fiscal, mgmt aspects of govt; publishes journals, books, pamphlets; permits onsite use of collection.

11416. Teachers of English to Speakers of Other Languages, 1118 22nd St NW, Suite 205, Washington, DC 20037; (202) 625-4569. Interest in English as a second or foreign language, bilingual education, applied linguistics. Provides general reference services, distributes placement info, permits onsite use of collection. Services free, except professional consulting services.

11417. Technical Reference Division, National Highway Traffic Safety Administration, 400 Seventh St SW, Rm 5108-NAD-52, Washington, DC 20590; (202) 426-2768. Studies all areas of motor vehicle and highway safety, including automotive and highway engineering and design. Answers inquiries, makes referrals, provides reference services. Technical records available for public inspection and copying.

11418. Technology Utilization and Industry Affairs Division, Terrestrial Applications Off, Code LGT-1, Natl Aeronautics and Space Admin, 400 Maryland Ave SW, Washington, DC 20546; (202) 755-6280. Promotes widespread use outside aerospace community of technological innovations resulting from NASA programs. Sponsors meetings, symposia; arranges conferences at NASA field installations.

11419. Telecommunications Research & Action Center, 1530 P St NW, Washington, DC 20005; (202) 462-2520. Concerned with telecommunications research and reform, issues such as fairness in the media, children's programming, cable and new technologies. Publishes magazine and newsletter, answers inquiries, makes referrals.

11420. Territorial and International Affairs, Dept of Interior, 18th and C Sts NW, Washington, DC 20240; (202) 343-4822. Encourages development of U.S. Trust Territories and Dependencies, supports U.S. foreign policy. Provides info, answers inquiries, publishes materials.

11421. Thread Institute, 1101 Connecticut Ave NW, Ste 300, Washington, DC 20036; (202) 862-0518. Natl trade assn representing manufacturers, converters, and distributors of thread and thread products in U.S. Provides general reference services, conducts seminars.

11422. Timber Management Staff, Forest Service, USDA, P.O. Box 2417 (S Agriculture Bldg, Rm 3207; 12th St and Independence Ave SW), Washington, DC 20013; (202) 447-6893. Conducts timber sales planning, preparation, appraisal, and contract administration and studies silvicultural systems. Answers inquiries, provides consulting services, makes referrals.

11424. Trade Relations Council of the U.S., 1001 Connecticut Ave NW, Washington, DC 20036; (202) 785-4185. Interest in economic statistics and industry foreign trade data. All services provided for cost. Data base available on tape at reproduction cost.

11425. Traffic Safety Programs, Natl Hwy Traffic Safety Admin, 400 Seventh St SW, Washington, DC 20590; (202) 426-0837. Establishes performance standards and technical guidelines for State Hwy Safety Programs funded by matching grants-in-aid. Distributes publications, answers inquiries, provides advisory and technical services.

11426. Transportation Data Coordinating Committee, 1101 17th St NW, Ste 708, Washington, DC 20036; (202) 293-5514. Serves as clearinghouse for the coordination of business data, codes, formats, and systems used in computer-based data transmission systems. Answers inquiries, provides consulting services to members. Services provided to nonmembers at cost.

11427. Transportation Policy Associates, 810 18th St NW, Rm 508, Washington, DC 20006; (202) 638-5244. Concerned with natl policies affecting carriers, users, suppliers of transport equipment. Publishes annual statistical analysis; answers inquiries from press, research groups.

11428. Transportation Research Board, Railroad Research Information Service, National Academy of Science, 2101 Constitution Ave NW, Washington, DC 20418; (202) 334-3251. Promotes planning, regulation, building, maintenance, and operation of rail transportation systems worldwide. Provides reference services, distributes publications, makes referrals. Services for a fee.

11429. Travel Data Center, 1899 L St NW, Ste 610, Washington, DC 20036; (202) 293-1040. Improves quality and range of statistical info on travel, tourism, and recreation activities of Americans. Answers inquiries from members, conducts special studies, surveys and seminars, distributes publications. Services at cost.

11430. Travel Industry Association of America, 1899 L St NW, Washington, DC 20036; (202) 293-1433. Covers all components of the travel industry, including suppliers and sales in all geographic areas. Answers inquiries, provides advisory services, conducts seminars, distributes publications, makes referrals. Services free to members, for a fee to others.

11431. Traveling Exhibition Service, Smithsonian Institution, Arts and Industries Bldg, Rm 2170, Washington, DC 20560; (202) 357-3168. Organizes, circulates exhibitions on art, history, science to institutions in U.S., abroad. Publishes books, training materials; produces educational materials. Price lists available.

11432. Treasurer of the United States, Dept of the Treasury, 15th St and Pennsylvania Ave NW, Washington, DC 20220; (202) 566-2843. Supervises the issue, retirement, and destruction of currency of U.S. and compiles historical facts and statistics relating to U.S. currency and coinage. Answers inquiries.

11433. U.S. Advisory Commission on Public Diplomacy, U.S. Info Agency, 301 Fourth St SW, Washington, DC 20547; (202) 485-2457. Concerned with U.S. public diplomacy, including intl informational, educational, and cultural activities. Answers inquiries concerning commission's activities.

11434. U.S. Arms Control and Disarmament Agency, Library, State Dept Bldg, Rm 5851, 320 21st St NW, Washington, DC 20451; (202) 632-1592. Responsible for conducting research to support arms control and disarmament policy formulation, and for conducting intl negotiations in arms control and disarmament field. Answers inquiries, provides reference services primarily for fed govt personnel.

11435. U.S. Army Center of Military History, Attn: DAMH-HS, Pulaski Bldg, Rm 4229, 20 Massachusetts Ave NW, Washington, DC 20314; (202) 272-0295. Interest in U.S. Army military history, art, museums, foreign military history (limited). Provides reference service on subjects in U.S. military history, permits onsite use of holdings. Most services free.

11436. U.S. Beet Sugar Association, 1156 15th St NW, Ste 1019, Washington, DC 20005; (202) 296-4820. Publishes statistical data, teaching kit for upper elementary, junior high levels; provides general, nontechnical, nonscientific info about sugar beet industry.

11437. U.S. Botanic Gardens, 1st St and Maryland Ave SW, Washington, DC 20024; (202) 225-8333. Maintains U.S. Botanic Gardens Park. Publishes plant culture sheets, holds free courses open to public, provides free group tours by appointment, presents special shows of flowering plants.

11439. U.S. Catholic Conference, Division of Elementary & Secondary Education, 1312 Massachusetts Ave NW, Washington, DC 20005; (202) 659-6652. Concerned with Catholic and nonpublic, elementary and secondary education. Answers inquiries, provides consulting services.

11440. U.S. Catholic Mission Association, 1233 Lawrence St NE, Washington, DC 20017; (202) 832-3112. Charitable, religious org for global missionary work. Maintains data on Catholic missionaries. Answers inquiries, conducts seminars, distributes publications. Most services free.

11441. U.S. Committee for Refugees, 815 15th St NW, Ste 610, Washington, DC 20005; (202) 667-0782. Advocate of the refugee in development of U.S. public policy. Publishes newsletter, reference materials; provides inquiry, referral services; permits onsite use of collections. Fee for some services.

11442. U.S. Conference of Local Health Officers, 1620 Eye St NW, Washington, DC 20006; (202) 293-7330. Reports activities of Congress, U.S. agencies of interest to local health depts. Answers inquiries; conducts seminars, training sessions. Services free to members, some available to nonmembers.

11443. U.S. Conference of Mayors, Labor-Management Relations Service, 1620 Eye St NW, 4th Fl, Washington, DC 20006; (202) 293-7330. Serves the labor and employee relations needs of local and state govts. Provides general reference services, distributes materials, conducts seminars. Services primarily for members of the sponsoring org and subscribers.

11444. U.S. Hide, Skin, & Leather Association, 1707 N St NW, Washington, DC 20036; (202) 833-2405. Interest in hide industry; marketing of cattlehides and skins; leather. Provides gerneral reference services, semi-annual conventions, regional meetings. Services primarily for members, but others assisted when possi-

ble. Handling and mailing charge for materials sent to nonmembers.

11445. U.S. Information Agency, Office of Public Liaison, U.S. Info Agency, 301 Fourth St SW, Washington, DC 20547; (202) 485-2355. Source of info on agency activities. Answers inquiries concerning educational and cultural exchange programs; however, agency is prohibited by law from disseminating program materials prepared for use overseas.

11446. U.S. International Trade Commission, Library, 701 E St NW, Washington, DC 20436; (202) 523-0013. Maintains holdings on commercial policy, foreign trade, general and economic statistics, with emphasis on trade. Answers inquiries, makes referrals. Limited photocopying service for a fee.

11447. U.S. Migratory Bird Conservation Commission, Dept of the Interior, 1717 H St NW, Rm 524, Washington, DC 20240; (202) 653-7653. Approves of and fixes the prices on lands recommended by the Secty of the Interior as refuges under the Migratory Bird Conservation Act of February 18, 1929. Answers inquiries and makes referrals free.

11449. U.S. National Focal Point-UNEP/Infoterra, c/o U.S. Environmental Protection Agency, 401 M St SW, Rm 2903B WSM (PM 211-A), Washington, DC 20460; (202) 382-5917. Part of a network of intl focal points engaged in developing and operating directories of environmental info under auspices of the U.N. Environment Program. Referrals free.

11451. U.S. Postal Service, Communications Department, 475 L'Enfant Plaza West, SW, Washington, DC 20260; (202) 245-4144. Publishes annual report of Postmaster General, monthly newsletter sent to businesses, pamphlets, brochures; responds to inquiries from media; develops natl public relations programs.

11452. U.S. Savings Bond, Office of Public Affairs, Treasury Dept, Washington, DC 20226; (202) 634-5389. Promotes U.S. Savings Bonds, their sale and special programs. Answers inquiries, makes referrals, provides brochures, works with media on Savings Bond articles.

11453. U.S. Synthetic Fuels Corp.,Information Management Group, 2121 K St NW, Ste 350, Washington, DC 20586; (202) 822-6377. Maintains tech info base on synthetic fuels. Provides info, referral services. Primary user audience is U.S. Synthetic Fuels Corp. staff. Some public info.

11454. U.S. Tax Court, 400 Second St NW, Washington, DC 20217; (202) 376-2754; (202) 376-2707. Adjudicates fed tax controversies involving income, gift, estate, and excise taxes and penalties imposed on private foundations; renders declaratory judgments on retirement plans, exempt organizations, Section 367 exchanges, and the status of certain govt obligations.

11455. U.S. Travel & Tourism Administration, Dept of Commerce, 14th & Constitution Ave. NW, Washington, DC 20230; (202) 377-4028. Promotes travel to U.S. and seeks to improve the reception, services, and hospitality extended to foreign visitors. Distributes publications. Services free, except data compiled from intl inflight survey, available by subscription.

11457. USDA Graduate School, Dept of Agriculture, Rm 129, Capital Gallery Bldg, 600 Maryland Avenue SW, Washington, DC 20024; (202) 447-4419. Offers non-degree courses on a variety of subjects for relatively little cost. Answers inquiries, distributes publications.

11458. Underseas Cable Engineers, 5206 Manning Pl NW, Washington, DC 20016; (202) 362-3127. Holds extensive data bases on intl telecommunications routes, sea cable systems, and world's fleet of cableships. Provides consulting services, lectures for a fee.

11459. Union of American Hebrew Congregations, Religious Action Center, 2027 Massachusetts Ave NW, Washington, DC 20036; (202) 387-2800. Liaison between Reform Jewish movement, U.S. govt. Publishes resource, program manuals; reports. Provides inquiry, reference services; conducts leadership, advocacy training seminars.

11460. United Campuses to Prevent Nuclear War, 220 Eye St NE, Room 130, Washington, DC 20002; (202) 543-1505. Promotes U.S. univ programs on arms control, nuclear war. Holds collection of syllabuses. Publishes info, promotional materials (price list on request); answers inquiries. Most services free.

11461. United Nations Information Center, 1889 F St NW, Ground Fl, Washington, DC 20006; (202) 289-8670. Serves as liaison between U.N. and U.S. govt and cooperates with nongovtl orgs in disseminating info about issues before the UN. Provides media relations, publications, films, graphics, exhibitions, public liason, and reference.

11462. United Service Organizations (USO), 601 Indiana Ave NW, Washington, DC 20004; (202) 783-8121. Operates in U.S. and overseas to enhance general well-being of military personnel and their families. Answers inquiries; provides advisory, welfare, recreational, and entertainment services; and distributes publications. Most services free to military.

11463. United States International Development Cooperation Agency, 320 21st St NW, Washington, DC 20523; (202) 632-9170. Provides info on the agency's services and functions, which include advising on U.S. intl economic and bilateral development policy and assistance programs. Answers inquiries according to abilities.

11464. United States Railway Association, Public Affairs Office, 955 L'Enfant Plaza N., SW, Washington, DC 20595; (202) 488-8777, ext 530. Provides info on services and functions of the Railway Association, which authorizes and oversees maintenance of the railway system in the midwest and northeast regions of the U.S. Answers inquiries according to abilities.

11466. United States-South Africa Leader Exchange Program, 1700 17th St NW, Ste 508, Washington, DC 20009; (202) 232-6720. Promotes peaceful, just solution to problems of South Africa. Sponsors exchanges, training; publishes newsletter; provides inquiry, advisory services; conducts conferences. Services generally free.

11467. Urban Institute, Library, 2100 M St NW, Washington, DC 20037; (202) 857-8688. Collects materials bearing on urban policy, economic development, public finance, housing, transportation, employment and labor policy. Answers phone inquiries, distributes publications, makes interlibrary loans. Library open to public by appointment only.

11468. Urban Land Institute, 1090 Vermont Ave, Ste 300, Washington, DC 20005; (202) 289-8500. Publishes journals, books, project reference file on urban land use, planning; provides reference service free; permits onsite use of library by appointment. Priority given to members.

11469. Urban Mass Transportation Administration, Dept of Transportation, 400 Seventh St SW, Washington, DC 20590; (202) 426-4043. Source of info on urban mass transit. Answers inquiries, provides reference services, permits onsite use of collection.

11470. Utility Data Institute, 2011 Eye St NW, Ste 700, Washington, DC 20006; (202) 466-3660. Manages and provides comparative utility data on power plants, transmission lines, pipelines, mining, waste mgmt, etc. Answers inquiries, provides abstracting, indexing, and reproduction services for a fee.

11471. Veterans Administration, Research Division, Off of Info Mgmt and Statistics, 810 Vermont Ave NW, Washington, DC 20420; (202) 389-2458. Researches, publishes surveys, estimates, projections of veteran population, its demographic, socioeconomic characteristics. Responds to inquiries.

11472. Veterans Day National Committee, Veterans Admin, 810 Vermont Ave NW, Washington, DC 20420; (202) 389-5386. Directs the planning, promotion, and operation for Veterans Day observances on national, regional, and local levels. Answers inquiries, provides advisory services.

11474. Volunteers in Overseas Cooperative Assistance, 1800 Massachusetts Ave NW, Ste 301, Washington, DC 20036; (202) 223-2072. Povides short-term technical help through unpaid volunteers to cooperatives and govt agencies responsible for cooperative development overseas. Answers inquiries, lends available materials, permits onsite use of collection. Services free.

11475. Volunteers in Service to America (VISTA), Public Information, Rm 303 PAR, 806 Connecticut Avenue NW, Washington, DC 20525; (202) 634-9424. Helps rural or urban U.S. poor through volunteer service programs. Answers inquiries, makes referrals.

11476. Walter Reed Army Medical Center, Health Physics Office, Bldg 188, Forest Glen Section, Washington, DC 20307; (301) 427-5107. Interest in health physics, protection of personnel and environment from unwarranted radiation exposure. Answers inquiries. There are no restrictions on info for scientists in related fields, but services for others limited according to time and effort required.

11479. Washington Office for Social Concern, Unitarian Universalist Assn of Churches and Fellowships in North America, 100 Maryland Ave NE, Rm 106, Washington, DC 20002; (202) 547-0254. Interest in denominational education and social action on public policy and legislative issues such as nuclear disarmament, etc. Provides general reference services, publishes periodical, conducts seminars. Services free for Unitarian Universalist churches and fellowships.

11480. Washington Office on Africa, 110 Maryland Ave NE, Room 112, Washington, DC 20002; (202) 546-7961. Lobbys, educates for progressive U.S. foreign policy on southern Africa. Has library for onsite use. Publishes materials; provides inquiry, referral services; conducts seminars. Most services free.

11481. Washington Peace Center, 2111 Florida Ave NW, Washington, DC 20008; (202) 234-2000. Organizes peace education, action in Washington, D.C., metro area. Publishes monthly newsletter; answers inquiries; provides draft, military counseling; conducts seminars. Services free.

11484. Water Pollution Control Federation, 2626 Pennsylvania Ave NW, Washington, DC 20037; (202) 337-2500. Publishes journal, technical manuals on clean water issues; provides reference services; permits onsite use of collection by appointment. Services mostly free.

11485. Wheat Flour Institute/Millers National Federation, 600 Maryland Ave SW, Washington, DC 20024; (202) 484-2200. Provides info on wheat flour, nutrition and diet, milling, wheat flour use in baked goods. Answers inquiries and distributes publications for small charge.

11486. Wider Opportunities for Women, 1325 G St NW, Washington, DC 20005; (202) 638-3143. Nonprofit women's employment advocacy org interested in equal employment opportunities for women. Provides technical assistance and programs for low-income women. Offers general reference services, publishes and distributes materials.

11487. Wilderness Society, 1400 Eye St NW, Washington, DC 20005; (202) 842-3400. Seeks preservation of America's public lands. Conducts educational programs; publishes magazine; provides consulting, limited literature-searching services.

11488. Wildlife & Fisheries Staff, Forest Service, USDA, P.O. Box 2417 (Rosslyn Plaza East, Rm 607 RP-E; 1621 N Kent St, Arlington, Va.), Washington, DC 20013;

(703) 235-8015. Studies wildlife and wildlife habitat, fish and fish habitat, water quality, balancing wildlife mgmt with other uses of forest lands. Answers inquiries and makes referrals.

11489. Wildlife Management Institute, 1101 14th St NW, Ste 725, Washington, DC 20005; (202) 371-1808. Promotes wildlife restoration projects. Provides consulting services to state conservation commissions for a fee, conducts annual conference open to public.

11491. Women in Information Processing, Lock Box 39173 (2400 Wisconsin Ave NW), Washington, DC 20016; (202) 328-6161. Serves members in info processing, allied fields. Maintains data bank of female professionals, managers. Publishes newsletter; provides referral services; conducts seminars, meetings. Services provided for a fee.

11492. Women's Bureau, Dept of Labor, 200 Constitution Ave NW, Washington, DC 20210; (202) 523-6652. Concerned with welfare of wage-earning women, including expansion of opportunities for profitable employment in nontraditional jobs, equitable working conditions, and elimination of sex discrimination in employment. Answers inquiries, makes referrals, provides advisory services.

11493. Women's Campaign Fund, 815 15th St NW, Ste 601, Washington, DC 20005; (202) 638-3900. Political committee that provides financial, tech assistance to progressive women candidates. Answers inquiries, conducts seminars for women candidates for a fee.

11494. Women's College Coalition, 1101 17th St NW, Ste 1001, Washington, DC 20036; (202) 466-5430. Promotes women's colleges. Maintains data base and clearinghouse for research. Publications price list available. Provides inquiry, referral services; permits onsite use of collections. Most services free.

11495. Women's Equity Action League, 1250 Eye St NW, Ste 305, Washington, DC 20005; (202) 898-1588. Interest in rights and status of women, women and taxes, employment of women, women and the military, women and sports. Answers some inquiries free, distributes publications on fee basis. Priority given to WEAL members. Membership is open.

11496. Women's Institute for Freedom of the Press, 3306 Ross Place NW, Washington, DC 20008; (202) 966-7783. Researchs women's use of mass and women-owned media. Answers inquiries, offers advisory services, distributes publications, conducts seminars and workshops. Permits onsite use of collections. Services at cost.

11497. Women's Medical Center of Washington, D.C., 1712 Eye St NW, Ste 704, Washington, DC 20006; (202) 298-9227. Promotes affordable health services for women of all economic levels. Provides inquiry, consulting, referral services; conducts seminars. Some services free, others for a fee.

11498. Women's Research & Education Institute, 204 Fourth St SE, Washington, DC 20003; (202) 546-1010. Research arm of bipartisan Congressional Caucus for Women's Issues. Has data base on research. Answers inquiries; conducts conferences, briefings. Services free, except publications.

11499. Woodrow Wilson International Center for Scholars Library, Smithsonian Institution Bldg, 1000 Jefferson Dr, Washington, DC 20560; (202) 357-2567. Studies major issues confronting man in last decades of the 20th century. Interest in intl affairs and security. Makes interlibrary loans and permits onsite use of collection by prearrangement. Services free.

11500. Workers' Institute for Safety & Health, 1126 16th St NW, Washington, DC 20036; (202) 887-1980. Labor-supported org in occupational health, industrial hygiene. Provides inquiry, advisory, reference services; evaluates work site health, safety conditions; conducts workshops. Services mostly restricted to labor orgs, related groups.

11501. Work Force Analysis & Statistics Div, Asst Dir for Workforce Info, Compliance and Investigations Group, Off of Personnel Mgmt, 1900 E St NW, Washington, DC 20415; (202) 632-9527. Controls direction of the work force statistical compilation, analysis, and publication program of the Office of Personnel Management. Answers inquiries and provides data on the fed work force.

11502. World Agricultural Outlook Board, Dept of Agriculture, 14th St and Independence Ave SW, Washington, DC 20250; (202) 447-6030. Tracks domestic, intl markets for agricultural, food commodities; global factors affecting world commodity market. Publishes research for subscribers. Answers inquiries.

11503. World Bank, Publications Department, 1818 H St NW, Washington, DC 20043; (202) 334-8093. Provides technical assistance and makes loans to less developed countries for the express purpose of raising living standards. Distributes publications, some free and some at cost.

11504. World Data Center, Coordination Office, Natl Academy of Sciences, 2101 Constitution Ave NW, Washington, DC 20418; (202) 389-6478. Makes available data collected during Intl Geophysical Year. Answers inquiries on data interchange as a whole. Inquiries concerning data in specific disciplines should be addressed to appropriate subcenter.

11505. World Data Center, Oceanography, Natl Oceanic and Atmospheric Admin, 2001 Wisconsin Ave NW, Rm 414, Washington, DC 20235; (202) 634-7249. Collects oceanographic data, including observations from shore, ships, and other mobile platforms; publications dealing with the marine sciences; inventories of marine data. Provides data compilation and makes referrals. Services generally free of charge.

11506. World Data Center, Rotation of Earth, U.S. Naval Observatory, Time Service Div, Washington, DC 20390; (202) 653-1529. Studies location of the instantaneous pole of rotation and the instantaneous rotation rate of the earth. Answers inquiries, assists scientists in obtaining data, maintains Telephone Digital Communications Data Service.

11507. World Federalists Association, 418 Seventh St SE, Washington, DC 20003; (202) 546-3950. Seeks abolition of war through just and enforceable world laws. Answers inquiries, provides advisory services, conducts seminars, distributes publications, makes referrals. Services free.

11508. World Federation of Public Health Associations, c/o Dr Susi Kessler, MD, Amer Public Health Assn, 1015 15th St NW, Washington, DC 20005; (202) 789-5600. Seeks to exchange technical info with and strengthen national public health assns. Represents public health interests and consults with the World Health Org. Provides general reference services.

11509. World Hunger Education Service, 1317 G St NW, Washington, DC 20005; (202) 347-4441. Nonprofit org concerned with hunger and poverty, appropriate technology, economic development, and food policy. Answers inquiries, provides advisory services, conducts a food policy program, distributes publications. A fee for services.

11510. World Peace Through Law Center, 1000 Connecticut Ave NW, Ste 800, Washington, DC 20036; (202) 466-5428. Nongovtal org devoted to continued development of intl law and legal maintenance of world order. Answers inquiries, distributes publications.

11511. World Population Society, 1111 14th St NW, 4th Fl, Washington, DC 20005; (202) 463-6606. Advocacy org that initiates, stimulates, and helps support research and communicates info on population change and its impact on man's capacity to meet human needs. Provides general reference services at cost to nonmembers.

11512. World Wildlife Fund/the Conservation Foundation, 1255 23rd St NW, Washington, DC 20037; (202) 293-4800. Publishes newsletter on wildlife conservation, provides reprints, sponsors conferences, permits onsite use of collection by arrangement. Services generally free and available to writers, conservation/scientific pros, students.

11514. Worldwatch Institute, 1776 Massachusetts Ave NW, Washington, DC 20036; (202) 452-1999. Identifies emerging global issues and brings them to the attention of the press and public. Distributes Worldwatch Paper Series, makes referrals. Some services free, primarily for journalists and policymakers.

11515. Writing Instrument Manufacturers Association, 1625 Eye St NW, Washington, DC 20006; (202) 331-1429. Represents writing instrument manufacturing industry. Publishes directory, bulletin, legislative letters; answers inquiries free.

11516. Youth for Understanding International Exchange, 3501 Newark St NW, Washington, DC 20016; (202) 966-6808. Fosters intl awareness and better understanding among people through intl exchange of high school students. Answers inquiries concerning exchange programs and host family info; distributes publications.

11517. Zero Population Growth, 1601 Connecticut Ave NW, 4th Fl, Washington, DC 20009; (202) 332-2200. Works to mobilize broad public support for population stabilization in U.S. and worldwide. Publishes newspaper and answers inquiries.

Florida

13002. Agricultural Research Center, 1305 E Main St, Lakeland, FL 33801; (813) 686-1017. Nonprofit org engaged in practical and limited basic research on soil analysis and fertilization, including fertilization of citrus groves, Fla. agriculture, pesticides, herbicides. Answers inquiries, provides limited consulting services.

13003. Air Force Armament Laboratory, Eglin Air Force Base, FL 32542; (904) 882-3212. Primary Air Force org for research and development in all types of nonnuclear weapons, especially guided missiles and munitions, and a major resource for analysis of weapons effects. Answers inquiries regarding munitions R&D, furnishes technical library services, makes referrals.

13004. Air Force Space Museum, ESMC/PA, Patrick Air Force Base (Cape Canaveral Air Force Station), FL 32925; (305) 494-5933. Devoted to history of missile launches and space projects at Cape Canaveral. Holds missiles, rockets, blockhouse control rooms and equipment, other exhibits. Answers inquiries free. Open to military personnel (active or retired), guests with proper identification, Sundays only.

13005. American Academy of Medical Directors, One Urban Centre, Ste 648, 4830 W Kennedy Blvd, Tampa, FL 33609; (813) 873-2000. Natl assn for physicians in mgmt positions. Provides info and data on medical mgmt and administrative medicine. Operates an info-communications computerized network. Most services to physician managers. Some services to non-members for a fee.

13006. American Accounting Association, c/o Paul L. Gerhardt, Exec Dir, 5717 Bessie Dr, Sarasota, FL 33583; (813) 921-7747. Interest in accounting education. Answers general (not technical) inquiries within limits of time and personnel, makes referrals to other sources of info.

13007. American Association of Certified Orthoptists, c/o Barbara Cassin, Pres, Dept of Ophthalmology, Box J-284, J. Hillis Miller Health Center, Gainesville, FL 32610; (904) 392-3111. Assn of certified orthoptists working under supervision of ophthalmologists, testing eye muscles, binocular vision, related disorders

including strabismus, amblyopia. Answers inquiries, distributes brochures free.

13008. American Association of Religious Therapists, c/o Dr Dale H. Ratliff, Exec Secty, 7175 SW 45th St, Ste 303, Ft Lauderdale, FL 33314. Interest in religious therapy, pastoral psychology, clergy postgraduate education. Answers brief inquiries, provides consulting services for a fee, makes referrals.

13009. American Beekeeping Federation, c/o Frank A. Robinson, Secty-Treas, 13637 NW 39th Ave, Gainesville, FL 32606; (904) 332-0012. Represents U.S. beekeeping industry. Interest in bees and bee products (honey, beeswax, bee venom, pollen, propolis, and pollination). Inquiries answered free within limits of resources.

13010. American Board of Dental Public Health, Box J-404 JHMHC, Gainesville, FL 32610; (904) 392-2671. Natl examining and certifying agency for specialty practice of dental public health. Concerned with dental epidemiology, standards and priorities for treatment of dental diseases, disease prevention. Individual inquiries answered free. Publications provided to specialists only.

13011. American Board of Pathology, P.O. Box 25915 (Lincoln Center, 5401 W Kennedy Blvd), Tampa, FL 33622; (813) 879-4864. Serves as examining and certifying body for the medical specialty of pathology. Answers inquiries or refers inquirers to other sources of info.

13012. American Coll of Podiatric Radiologists, c/o Dr Irving H. Block, Secty, 1 Lincoln Rd Bldg, No 308, Miami Beach, FL 33139; (305) 531-9866. Focuses on radiology of the lower extremities, education in podiatric radiology, radiological health and protection. Answers inquiries, conducts seminars, provides info on current research, lends materials. Services free and available to specialized groups.

13013. American Council of the International Institute of Welding, P.O. Box 351040 (550 NW LeJeune Rd), Miami, FL 33135; (305) 443-9353. Distributes documents and info about welding processes, testing, terminology, research, health and safety, weldability of metals, pressure vessels, boilers and pipelines, more. Answers inquiries, sells publications. Services primarily for members, but others assisted.

13014. American Dinner Theatre Institute, P.O. Box 2537, Sarasota, FL 33578; (813) 365-1754. Membership org of dinner theater owner/operators. Publishes newsletter, membership directory, cookbook, and bartender's guide, answers inquiries, provides advisory and consulting services. Services free, except for consulting, open to current and potential dinner theater producers.

13015. American Electroplaters' Society, Central Fla. Research Park, 12644 Research Pkwy, Orlando, FL 32826; (305) 281-6441. Interest in electroplating and surface finishing, corrosion prevention, paints. Answers inquiries, conducts training programs, conferences, distributes publications, makes referrals. Fee for some services.

13016. American Health and Wellness Association, 781 W Oakland Park Blvd, Ste 273, Ft Lauderdale, FL 33311; (305) 761-1279. Natl clearinghouse for info on health and wellness, with interests in nutrition, fitness and exercise, smoking cessation, high blood pressure, more. Permits onsite use of collection. Services primarily for members, but others assisted. Fees for some services.

13017. American Hibiscus Society, c/o Sue J. Schloss, Exec Secty, P.O. Drawer 5430, Pompano Beach, FL 33064. Devoted to cultivation and nomenclature of Hibiscus, particularly H. rosa sinensis. Answers inquiries, refers inquirers to other info sources, sponsors public flower shows. Services primarily for members, but others assisted.

13018. American Natural Hygiene Society, 12816 Race Track Rd, Tampa, FL 33625; (813) 855-6607. Promotes better health through natural living, particularly natural hygiene, nutrition, exercise, ecology, fasting, organic gardening. Answers inquiries, conducts seminars and annual convention, distributes publications. Services free, some materials at cost.

13019. American Orchid Society, 6000 S Olive Ave, W Palm Beach, FL 33405; (305) 585-8666. Interest in orchids, their culture, breeding, botany and classification, ecology, phylogeny, conservation, and uses as art subjects and items of trade. Answers inquiries, provides consulting and reference services.

13020. American Society for Artificial Internal Organs, P.O. Box C, Boca Raton, FL 33429; (305) 391-8589. Interest in artificial internal organs and their utilization, bioengineering, clinical dialysis, gas exchange, organ transplantation and perfusion, cardiac assist devices. Conducts annual meeting and seminar open to public for registration fee, sells publications, awards annual fellowship.

13021. American Society of Ichthyologists and Herpetologists, c/o Carter R. Gilbert, Secty, Fla. State Museum, Univ of Fla., Gainesville, FL 32611; (904) 392-1721. Interest in systematics, distribution, evolution, anatomy, ecology, and physiology of fishes, amphibians, and reptiles. Services on a limited basis.

13022. American Water Ski Association, P.O. Box 191 (799 Overlook Dr SE), Winter Haven, FL 33882; (813) 324-4341. Org of boating and ski equipment manufacturers and individuals that serves as governing body of organized (tournament) water skiing in the U.S. and as natl public relations clearinghouse for water ski info. Services free, except for publications.

13023. American Welding Society, 550 NW Le Jeune Rd, Miami, FL 33126; (305) 443-9353. Professional technical society for promotion of welding and related technology including soldering, brazing, etc. Answers in-

quiries, provides limited consulting, reference, custom data base searching services, permits onsite use of collection.

13024. Antarctic Marine Geology Research Facility and Core Library, Dept of Geology, Fla. State Univ, Tallahassee, FL 32306; (904) 644-2407. Collects and researches oceanic bottom samples, marine geology, Antarctic waters, sediment core samples. Answers inquiries, provides reference services, permits onsite use of collections. Services free; samples available only with NSF approval.

13025. Aquatic Weed Program, 2183 McCarty Hall, Univ of Fla., Gainesville, FL 32611; (904) 392-1799. Serves as an intl info retrieval system on the topic of freshwater aquatic macrophytes, and provides technical assistance to less developed countries with aquatic weed problems. Answers inquiries, provides reference services. Services free.

13026. Army Tropic Test Center, P.O. Drawer 942, Attn: Technical Information Center, APO Miami (Fort Clayton, Panama Canal Area), FL 34004; (313) 285-5910. Conducts tropic environmental testing of Army equipment and material. Interest in climatology, micrometeorology, terrain, tanks, ordnance, physical anthropometry, human engineering. Info services to Dept of Defense. Unclassified reports sold to public.

13027. Association for Institutional Research, c/o Jean C. Chulak, Exec Secty, 314 Stone Bldg, Fla. State Univ, Tallahassee, FL 32306; (904) 644-4470. Devoted to research and analysis leading to the improved understanding, planning, mgmt, and operation of postsecondary education institutions and agencies. Answers inquiries.

13028. Association for Medical and Health Alternatives, P.O. Box 112 (1505 N Fort Harrison Ave), Clearwater, FL 33517; (813) 734-9016. Provides info on alternative treatments for health problems. Has computerized data bank of treatment alternatives for cancer, heart disease, arthritis, more. Permits onsite use of collections. Services for a fee.

13029. Association for Multi-Image International, c/o Marilyn J. Kulp, Exec Dir, 8019 N Himes Ave, Ste 401, Tampa, FL 33614; (813) 932-1692. Promotes multi-image production and utilization as a medium for education, communications, entertainment. Answers inquiries, provides advisory, reference, abstracting, indexing services, permits onsite use of collections. Services primarily for members, others assisted for a fee.

13030. Association of American State Geologists, c/o C.W. Hendry, Jr., Secty-Treas, Bureau of Geology, 903 W Tennessee St, Tallahassee, FL 32304. Sponsored by all state geological surveys, interested in geology, mineral, water, and energy resources, and mapping of the U.S. Answers inquiries, provides advisory services, distributes publication. Services free.

13031. Association of Birth Defect Children, 3526 Emerywood Lane, Orlando, FL 32806; (305) 859-2821. Interest in birth defects caused by drugs, chemicals, radiation, other environmental agents. Answers inquiries, provides advisory services, networking for parents of children with birth defects, conducts seminars and workshops. Services free.

13033. Associated Public-Safety Communications Officers, P.O. Box 669 (105 1/2 Canal St), New Smyrna Beach, FL 32070; (904) 427-3461. Fosters development of public safety communications and greater correlation of town, state, and fed activities for the rapid dissemination of public safety communications. Answers inquiries free, distributes publications for a fee. Services to anyone in public safety field.

13034. Athletic Institute, 200 Castlewood Dr, N Palm Beach, FL 33408; (305) 842-3600. Interest in sports, physical education, health, dance, recreation programs. Answers inquiries, provides reference services, films and publications for sale.

13035. Atlantic Oceanographic and Meteorological Laboratory, NOAA, 4301 Rickenbacker Causeway, Miami, FL 33149; (305) 361-4400. Focuses on research on hurricanes to improve description of their structure, dynamics, and energetics, increase understanding of their multiscale interactive processes, improve their predictability. Answers inquiries, exchanges data with govt agencies and scientists.

13036. Black Resources Information Coordinating Services, 614 Howard Ave, Tallahassee, FL 32304; (904) 576-7522. Focuses on info by and about blacks, Hispanic Americans, Asian-Americans, and American Indians. Provides consulting, employment exchange info, exhibit services for groups, conducts genealogical research, permits onsite use of collection. Charges made for searches.

13037. Bonsai Clubs International, c/o V. Ellermann, 800 W Virginia St, No 501, Tallahassee, FL 32304. Devoted to creation, care, display, and improvement of bonsai (miniature trees), including saikei, suiseki (rock sculptures from nature), Japanese gardens. Answers inquiries free, provides reference services and info on current R&D, all on limited basis. Provides advisory services to bonsai clubs.

13038. Boost Alcohol Consciousness Concerning Health of Students, 124 Tigert Hall, Univ of Fla., Gainesville, FL 32611; (904) 392-1261. Promotes alcohol education programs on college campuses. Answers inquiries, provides advisory and reference services, conducts workshops, distributes publications. Fees charged for publications and workshops, other services free on campuses with BACCHUS chapters, fees charged to others.

13039. Bureau of Marine Research, Fla. Dept of Natural Resources, 100 Eighth Ave SE, St Petersburg, FL 33701; (813) 896-8626. Conducts research to advise on mgmt of marine crustacean, shellfish, finfish resources, salt water fisheries, endangered species assessment and recovery. Answers inquiries, permits onsite use of collections of invertebrates, fishes, plants by prior arrangement. Library open to all.

13040. Camera M.D. Studios Library Division, 8290 NW 26th Pl, Ft Lauderdale, FL 33322; (305) 741-5560. Offers over 250,000 professional color transparencies and black and white pictures covering health and biological sciences. Answers inquiries, provides reference, reproduction services, distributes catalog. Services free, except for catalog and use of specific photographs.

13041. Cancer Information Service, Fla. Comprehensive Cancer Center, P.O. Box 016960 (D8-4) (1475 NW 12th Ave), Miami, FL 33101; (800) 4-CANCER. Operates toll-free, bilingual (English and Spanish) telephone service to answer inquiries about cancer. Over 400 publications on cancer (some in Spanish) available free. Also provides advisory and reference services free.

13042. Caribbean Conservation Corp., c/o Dr Archie Carr, Technical Dir, Dept of Zoology, Univ of Fla., Gainesville, FL 32611; (904) 392-1250. Focuses on life history studies, preservation, restoration of sea turtles, especially the Atlantic Green Turtle (Chelonia mydas) population and related problems of Caribbean ecology. Answers inquiries.

13043. Center for Applied Gerontology, College of Social and Behavioral Sciences, Univ of South Fla., 4202 Fowler Ave, Tampa, FL 33620; (813) 974-2414. Concerned with economics of aging, demographic analyses, midlife, social policy. Answers inquiries, provides advisory and tech assistance, permits onsite use of materials. Services free on a limited basis to state and local nonprofit orgs, extensive services for a fee.

13044. Center for Climacteric Studies, Univ of Fla., 901 N 8th Ave, Ste B-1, Gainesville, FL 32601; (904) 392-3184. Promotes preventive health care for women, ages 35-65. Emphasis on osteoporosis screening, cardiovascular fitness assessment, more. Provides advisory, consulting, reference services, available for a fee to consumers and health care professionals.

13045. Center for Design Planning, 3695 St Gaudens Rd, Miami, FL 33133; (305) 448-8422. Nonprofit group involved in planning of public spaces, street furniture research and design, streetscape, urban revitalization, growth mgmt. Answers inquiries, provides advisory and design services, evaluates data. Services at cost to professional or public orgs only.

13046. Center for Information Research, Univ of Fla., 339 Larsen Hall, Gainesville, FL 32611. Provides info about computer-based automation and machine intelligence. Offers software library, advisory and consulting services, seminars and workshops. Fee for some services.

13047. Center for Neurobiological Sciences, Univ of Fla., Gainesville, FL 32610; (904) 392-6555. Researches neurosciences, including neuroanatomy, neurophysiology, neurochemistry, neuroendocrinology, psychobiology, and neuropharmacology. Provides advisory, consulting services, and info on current research at the discretion of center, subject to a fee.

13048. Center for Policy and Law in Education, School of Education, Univ of Miami, Box 8065, Coral Gables, FL 33143; (305) 284-2891. Interest in civil, contract, and criminal law for schools and colleges with emphasis on policies to minimize chances of litigation. Answers inquiries, provides advisory, consulting services, conducts training programs, permits onsite use of collection. Services for a fee to all.

13049. Center for Research in Mining and Mineral Resources, Univ of Fla., 161 Rhines Hall, Gainesville, FL 32611; (904) 392-6670. Interest in the mineral industry, particularly in Fla., including mineral processing, mineral engineering, and environmental studies. Answers inquiries, provides advisory services, distributes data. Services free to Fla. state agencies and at cost to private users.

13050. Center for Tissue Trauma Research and Education, 408 NE Alice Ave, Jensen Beach, FL 33457-6099; (305) 692-9266. Researches decomposing human flesh, tissue trauma, including bedsores, diabetic and decubitus ulcers, burns, tissue trauma therapy. Answers inquiries, provides reference services, conducts education programs. Services free, primarily for health care professionals, but others assisted.

13051. Center for Tropical Agriculture, Institute of Food and Agricultural Sciences, Univ of Fla., 3028 McCarty Hall, Gainesville, FL 32611; (904) 392-1965. Provides technical assistance overseas in tropical agriculture. Interest in plant, animal, soil and crop science, animal feeds. Answers inquiries, permits onsite use of collection. Services generally free, except for reproduction costs and publications.

13052. Center of Intelligent Machines and Robotics, Coll of Engineering, Univ of Fla., Gainesville, FL 32611. Interest in further development of robotics systems for use in industry and medicine. Provides consulting and technology assessment services on a contract basis.

13053. Children's Rights of America, 2069 Indian Rocks Rd, Largo, FL 33544; (813) 584-0888. Assists parents in recovery of missing children. Answers inquiries, provides advisory and reference services, evaluates data, makes referrals. Services free.

13054. Climacteric Outreach, 901 NW 8th Ave, Ste B-1, Gainesville, FL 32601. Promotes well-being and a healthier way of life in the middle years (35-65) by taking research findings and applying them to people's daily lives, with an emphasis on consumer education.

13055. Collector Circle, P.O. Box 12600 (1313 S Killian Dr), Lake Park, FL 33403; (305) 845-6075. Interest in history of thimble manufacturing and design, use of thimble as sewing tool, thimbles as collectibles, other sewing tools. Answers inquiries, provides advisory, reference sevices at cost.

13056. Correctional Industries Association, c/o Paul A. Skelton, Jr., Exec Secty, 706 Middlebrook Circle, Tallahassee, FL 32312; (904) 385-4878. Org of persons employed in correctional (prison) field interested in mgmt and operations of correctional industries. Answers inquiries, provides reference, consulting services, seminars, data, publications. Services free, except consulting and publications,.

13057. Cuban National Planning Council, 300 SW 12th Ave, Penthouse, Miami, FL 30130; (305) 541-4590. Identifies social, economic, and cultural needs of Cubans in the U.S. Answers inquiries, provides counseling, manpower training services, conducts workshops. Responses to requests for info, counseling, and referrals generally free. Available to all, unless restricted by govt guidelines.

13058. Dance Masters of America, 328 N 4th Ave, Wauchula, FL 33873; (813) 773-2417. Interest in dance, dance education. Answers inquiries, conducts workshops, makes referrals to other sources of info. Services free, except workshops,.

13059. Department of Communicology, College of Social and Behavioral Science, Univ of South Fla., Tampa, FL 33610; (813) 974-2006. Specializes in study of speech pathology, audiology, deaf education. Answers inquiries, provides consulting, diagnostic, therapy services. Services free.

13060. Department of Marine Science, Univ of South Fla., St Petersburg, FL 33701; (813) 893-9130. Interest in all aspects of marine science with emphasis on Fla. coastal processes, marine geology, algae, plankton ecology of region, deep sea sedimentation, more. Answers inquiries, provides consulting services, analyzes data, distributes publications. Services for a fee, available to all.

13061. Department of Ocean Engineering, Fla. Atlantic Univ, 500 NW 20th St, Boca Raton, FL 33431; (305) 393-3430. Interest in basic and engineering sciences, ocean engineering, oceanography, ocean structures, hydrodynamics. Holds 700,000-book library. Answers inquiries, makes referrals, provides individual consulting. Limited services free, regular or detailed services on fee basis.

13062. Department of Pharmacology, Univ of Miami School of Medicine, P.O. Box 016189 (1600 NW 10th Ave), Miami, FL 33101; (305) 350-6643. Interest in cardiovascular pharmacology, clinical pharmacology, receptors and neuropharmacology, molecular and pharmacological properties of ionophores, pharmacology of smooth muscle, interaction of membranes and drugs. Provides consulting services to any interested org.

13063. Drug Information and Pharmacy Resource Center, Univ of Fla., J. Hillis Miller Health Center, Box J-4, Gainesville, FL 32610; (904) 392-3576. Supplies unbiased point-of-use drug info for health professionals. Answers drug info requests, provides other pharmacy-related references and resources. Services primarily for pharmacists, physicians, other allied health professionals.

13064. E-Systems, ECI Division, P.O. Box 12248 (1501 72nd St, North), St Petersburg, FL 33733; (813) 381-2000 ext 2182. Specializes in defense systems development, electronic countermeasures, microwave devices, electronic communication technology. Provides brief literature searches, photocopies, permits onsite use of collections. Special requirements for access to classified info.

13065. Electrical Generating Systems Association, P.O. Box 9257, Coral Springs, FL 33065; (305) 755-2677. Interest in standard specifications for standby engine-driven or tractor-driven electrical generating systems, performance standards for transfer switches used with engine generators, codes for emergency power by states, more. Answers inquiries, offers training programs, publications.

13066. Embry-Riddle Aeronautical Univ, Learning Resources Center, Regional Airport, Daytona Beach, FL 32014; (904) 252-5561 ext 1377. Interest in aviation education, including aeronautical engineering, aircraft maintenance, airframe and powerplant mechanic training, subsonic aerodynamics, pilot training and simulation research. Answers inquiries, provides consulting services, referrals to other info sources.

13067. Emphysema Anonymous, P.O. Box 66, Fort Myers, FL 33902; (813) 334-4226. Interest in emphysema and related breathing problems, education, treatment, care of patient. Answers inquiries, provides advisory, reference services, conducts seminars and workshops on breathing, distributes publications. Services free.

13069. Engineering and Industrial Experiment Station, Coll of Engineering, Univ of Fla., 300 Weil Hall, Gainesville, FL 32611; (904) 392-0941. Conducts technical research programs in such areas as biomedical engineering, implants, lasers, building codes, wind and wave studies, oil recovery, hybrid-electric vehicles, waste treatment, more. Answers inquiries, provides engineering news to publications.

13070. Environmental Management Association, 1019 Highland Ave, Largo, FL 33540; (813) 586-5710. Interest in industrial and institutional sanitation maintenance mgmt, including housekeeping, building maintenance, food industry sanitation, and training, certification standards for professionals. Answers inquiries, provides consulting, reference, job referral services.

13071. Epilepsy Concern International Service Council, 1282 Wynnewood Drive, W Palm Beach, FL 33409. Starts and maintains small self-help groups of people seeking help in dealing with epilepsy. Members mostly people with epilepsy and their families. Provides opportunity for people with epilepsy to pool resources, talents, share activities. Publishes pamphlets, newsletter.

13072. Everglades National Park, National Park Service, P.O. Box 279, Homestead, FL 33030; (305) 247-6211. Interest in population dynamics and natural history, endangered species, marine and terrestrial invertebrates, exotic plant invasions, the Everglades. Answers inquiries, provides reference services, permits onsite use of collections. Services free, available to public on premises.

13073. Expertise Institute, P.O. Box 38-1494 (130 NW 79th St), Miami, FL 33138; (305) 472-0165. Org of independent Miami-based scientists that consults on efficient fuel usage, alcohol production, security devices development. Also interested in engineering, chemistry, metallurgy, microbiology, toxicology, medicine, and furnishing expert witness assistance. Services for a fee.

13074. Fairchild Tropical Garden, 10901 Old Cutler Rd, Miami, FL 33156; (305) 667-1651. Library and exhibits feature tropical botany and horticulture. Answers inquiries, makes referrals, permits onsite use of literature collection. Exhibits open daily to public. Admission fee charged.

13075. Federal-State Agricultural Weather Service (Florida), 1408 24th St SE, Ruskin, FL 33570; (813) 645-2181. Provides daily agricultural weather forecasts for Fla. Special interest in frost warnings, microclimate for agriculture, methods for protecting crops from frost and freeze damage. Answers inquiries, makes referrals, provides consulting services in the area of agricultural meteorology.

13076. Fennell Orchid Co. Orchid Jungle, 26715 SW 157th Ave, Homestead, FL 33031; (305) 247-4824. Collects specimens and info on orchids, other rare tropical pot plants, mostly epiphytes, bromeliads, ferns, aroids, and cryptostegia, horticulture, tissue culture. Answers inquiries, provides consulting services for a fee, makes referrals, permits onsite use of collections by known researchers.

13077. Florida Agricultural Research Institute, P.O. Box 9326 (505 Avenue A NW, Ste 305), Winter Haven, FL 33883-9326; (813) 293-4827. Trade assn of fertilizer, pesticide, agricultural limestone suppliers, representing the industry in legislative, regulatory, public affairs activities. Answers inquiries, conducts seminars and workshops, evaluates data. Services free, primarily for members, but others assisted as time permits.

13078. Florida Audubon Society, 1101 Audubon Way, Maitland, FL 32751; (305) 647-2615. Interest in environmental sciences and ornithology, energy. Answers inquiries, provides consulting, reference services, permits onsite use of collection of books, reports, periodicals.

13079. Florida Bureau of Coastal Data Acquisition, Div of Beaches and Shores, Fla. Dept of Natural Resources, 3900 Commonwealth Blvd, Tallahassee, FL 32303; (904) 488-3180. Conducts coastal engineering studies, inlet studies, erosion surveys along sand beaches of Atlantic Ocean and Gulf of Mexico. Answers inquiries, permits onsite use of collections. Services free, primarily for beach-front owners and local govt, others served as resources permit.

13080. Florida Bureau of Criminal Justice Assistance, Fla. Div of Public Safety Planning and Assistance, 2571 Exec Center Circle East, Tallahassee, FL 32301; (904) 488-0090. Interest in criminal justice, especially juvenile justice, crime and the elderly, jails and prisons, juvenile delinquency and its prevention, career criminals. Serves as centralized resource for natl, state, and local criminal justice statistical info. Free to appropriate individuals.

13081. Florida Conservation Foundation, 1203 Orange Ave, Winter Park, FL 32789; (305) 644-5377. Concentrates on environmental issues of importance to Fla., including energy, water quality, waste mgmt, wildlife, public works, citizen action. Answers inquiries, provides advisory services, permits onsite use of collection. Services to anyone, free to sponsors.

13082. Florida Defenders of the Environment, 1523 NW 4th St, Gainesville, FL 32608; (904) 372-6965. Nonprofit org of biologists, economists, land planners, lawyers interested in assessing environmental problems in Fla. Answers inquiries, provides advisory and reference services, permits onsite use of collection. Fee for some services.

13083. Florida Dept of Citrus, P.O. Box 148 (1115 E Memorial Blvd), Lakeland, FL 33802; (813) 682-0171. Interest in citrus: flavor, essences, new products, color, microbiology, testing methods, quality assurance, juice products, by-products of citrus fruits and juices, mechanical harvesting, pre- and post-harvest physiology, and fresh fruit handling. Answers inquiries in most cases.

13084. Florida Entomology Society, c/o Dr David F. Williams, Secty, P.O. Box 12425, Univ Station, Gainesville, FL 32604; (904) 373-6701. Interest in basic and applied research in entomology, with emphasis on Fla. entomology, insect behavior, taxonomy, morphology, physiology. Answers inquiries, provides reference services.

13085. Florida Epidemiology Research Center, Office of Laboratory Services, Fla. Dept of Health and Rehabilitative Services, 4000 W Buffalo Ave, Tampa, FL 33614; (813) 272-2316. Monitors surface, ground, and potable waters for viruses and freshwater lakes and ponds for pathogenic Naegleria amoeba in Fla. Answers inqui-

ries, conducts arbovirus diagnostic and surveillance work. Info services free with a SASE.

13086. Florida Historical Society, c/o Gary R. Mormino, Exec Dir, Special Collections Dept, Univ of S Fla. Library, Tampa, FL 33620; (813) 974-2731. Interest in Fla. history, anthropology, archeology, historic preservation. Answers inquiries, provides reference and reproduction services, conducts seminars, sponsors activities in public schools. Permits onsite use of collections. Answers to mail inquiries and onsite use are free.

13087. Florida Institute of Oceanography, 830 First St, South, St Petersburg, FL 33701; (813) 893-9100. State org for coordinating the oceanography teaching, research, and contract and grant programs of 12 Fla. colleges, univs, state agencies. Supervises programs, provides advisory services and info on R&D in progress. Services generally available to any responsible agent.

13088. Florida Institute of Phosphate Research, 1855 W Main St, Bartow, FL 33830; (813) 533-0983. Researches phosphate, minerals processing, phosphogypsum, clays, radon, radiation, fertilizers, reclamation. Provides advisory, reference services, permits onsite use of collections. Services generally free.

13089. Florida Institute of Technology, P.O. Box 1150, Melbourne, FL 32901; (305) 723-3701 ext 302. Interest in physical, chemical, biological, geological/geophysical, and bioenvironmental oceanography, ocean engineering, coastal resources. Answers inquiries, provides consulting services, permits onsite use of collection. Services at minimum incurred cost to all users.

13090. Florida Solar Energy Center, 300 State Rd 401, Cape Canaveral, FL 32920; (305) 783-0300. Focuses on all aspects of solar energy, including education and demonstration projects, low-energy building design. Answers inquiries, provides limited reference services, conducts workshops, permits onsite use of collections. Services generally free.

13091. Florida State Museum, Univ of Fla., Museum Dr, Gainesville, FL 32611; (904) 392-1721. Operates as research center with special interest in systematic biology, nonsystematic natural history, general history of Caribbean area. Answers inquiries, consults, refers, identifies specimens. Qualified persons may borrow materials and use collections onsite. Museum open to public free.

13092. Florida Water Resources Research Center, 424 A.P. Black Hall, Univ of Fla., Gainesville, FL 32611; (904) 392-0840. Interest in Fla. water resources, aquatic biology, aquifers, canals, desalination, estuaries, eutrophication, fluid mechanics, groundwater, hydrogeology, irrigation, wastes and waste treatment, more. Answers inquiries, makes referrals, permits onsite use of literature collection.

13093. Florida Wildlife Federation, 4080 N Haverhill Rd, W Palm Beach, FL 33407; (305) 683-2328. Dedicated to wetland protection, environmental education, conservation education, resource mgmt. Answers inquiries, conducts seminars and workshops, distributes publications. Services free.

13094. Food, Drug, and Medical Device Databank, P.O. Box 19656 (999 Woodcock Rd, Ste 306), Orlando, FL 32814; (305) 898-7793. Informs public and medical profession of food, drugs, or devices that are recalled or otherwise found to have problems. Answers inquiries, provides advisory, reference services, permits onsite use of collections. Services free to public, at cost to professionals, hospitals.

13095. Goodwin Institute for Cancer Research, 1850 NW 69th Ave, Plantation, FL 33313; (305) 587-9020. Conducts research in germfree methodology, breeding colonies of germ-free animals, experimental chemotherapy and carcinogenesis, tumor immunology, hyperbaric environments, recombinant virology, viral vaccines. Answers inquiries.

13096. Gulf and Caribbean Fisheries Institute, 4600 Rickenbacker Causeway, Miami, FL 33149; (305) 361-4190. Interest in fisheries, including biology, marketing, mgmt, socioeconomics, product evaluation, geopolitics of fisheries, fishery treaty org, and regional fishery problems. Answers inquiries, conducts annual meeting, specialized workshops.

13097. Humanities Exchange, P.O. Box 1608, Largo, FL 34294; (813) 581-7328. Org of museums, historical societies, universities, corporations, etc. interested in traveling exhibitions. Provides info, cross-referenced by category, region, fees, organizer, on traveling exhibitions. Individual questions answered free, other services only to membership.

13098. Huxley Institute/American Schizophrenia Association, 900 N Federal Hwy, Boca Raton, FL 33432; (305) 393-6167, (800) 847-3802. Promotes orthomolecular psychiatry and medicine as a treatment for some mental and physical illnesses, including alcoholism, allergies, schizophrenia, manic depression. Answers inquiries, provides reference services, physician referrals, public use of collections onsite.

13099. Independent Battery Manufacturers Association, 100 Larchwood Dr, Largo, FL 33540; (813) 586-1408. Represents battery manufacturers, promotes development of standards of quality, sound business practices, disseminates info. Answers inquiries, provides advisory, reference services, conducts meetings, makes referrals. Fee for some services.

13100. Insect Attractants, Behavior and Basic Biology Laboratory, Agricultural Research Service, USDA, P.O. Box 14565 (1700 SW 23rd Dr), Gainesville, FL 32604; (904) 374-5701. Interest in providing alternatives to and improving use patterns for pesticides, using behavioral manipulation, insect hormones, insect olfaction, genetics. Provides advisory and reference services, permits onsite use of collection. Free, except offsite advisory services.

13101. Institute for Advanced Study of the Communication Processes, 63 ASB, Univ of Fla., Gainesville, FL 32611; (904) 392-2046. Interest in all aspects of human communication, including phonetics, linguistics, neurology, acoustics, forensic applications, speech pathology, audiology. Provides consulting services, permits onsite use of collection. Services free to anyone on mailing list, at cost to others.

13102. Institute for Molecular and Cellular Evolution, Univ of Miami, 521 Anastasia Ave, Coral Gables, FL 33134; (305) 284-5181. Interest in reconstruction of the origin of reproductive cells on earth, solar energy utilization, evolution of behavior. Provides reference services, answers inquiries. Services free and generally available only to the scientific community.

13103. Institute of Business Appraisers, P.O. Box 1447, Boynton Beach, FL 33435; (305) 433-0908. Interest in the valuation and appraisal of businesses, professional certification and standards, code of ethics for appraisers. Answers inquiries, evaluates data, permits onsite use of collection. Some services restricted to members, most available free.

13104. Institute of Food and Agricultural Sciences, Univ of Fla., Route 4, Box 63, Monticello, FL 32344; (904) 997-2596. Conducts research on horticultural crops, especially pecans, peaches, and woody ornamentals, plant pathology, breeding, physiology, and entomology. Inquiries answered.

13105. Institute of Internal Auditors, 249 Maitland Ave, Altamonte Springs, FL 32701; (305) 830-7600. Conducts seminars on basics of operational auditing, complex techniques, new developments, auditing with computers. Sponsors Certified Internal Auditor program. Answers brief inquiries, offers literature-searching services, permits onsite use of collection.

13106. Institute of Molecular Biophysics, Fla. State Univ, Call St, Tallahassee, FL 32306; (904) 644-4764. Interest in molecular biophysics, including molecular electronic spectroscopy to study molecular energy transformation and biological reaction mechanisms, crystallization, polymer chemistry, recombinant DNA technology, more. Answers inquiries, provides references to researchers, academics.

13107. Inter American Press Association, 2911 NW 39th St, Miami, FL 33142. Collects technical info for publishing, especially in Spanish-language newspapers, magazines. Answers inquiries, provides consulting, translation services, distributes publications, rents mailing list of all Spanish publications. Services free (except where expenses incurred) to all.

13108. International Affiliation of Independent Accounting Firms, 2000 S Dixie Hwy, Ste 206, Miami, FL 33133; (305) 856-1593. Provides group representation to independent accounting firms. Interest in intl accountancy, auditing, marketing methods. Answers inquiries, provides advisory and reference services, evaluates data. Services free.

13109. International Association for Hydrogen Energy, P.O. Box 248266, Univ of Miami, Coral Gables, FL 33124; (305) 284-4666. Develops technologies for a hydrogen-based energy system as alternative to fossil fuel-based energy systems. Answers inquiries, conducts intl forums and workshops, distributes data compilations. Services free, except for publications, primarily for members, but others assisted.

13110. International Association of Marine Science Libraries and Information Centers, Harbor Branch Foundation, Inc., R.R. 1, Box 196, N Old Dixie Hwy, Fort Pierce, FL 33450; (305) 465-2400. Provides info services on marine science and oceanography. Answers inquiries, conducts annual conference, distributes publications, makes referrals to other sources of infor. Services free, except for conferences and publications.

13111. International Association of Telecomputer Networks, 517 E Hwy 434, Ste A, Winter Springs, FL 32708; (305) 327-3270. Represents telecomputer networks, manufacturers, software vendors, agents. Provides info on FCC regulations, legislation, markets, hardware, software. Maintains vendor list, promotes standards and policy. Answers inquiries, holds conferences. Services for a fee to all.

13112. International Council of Associations of Surfing, Surf House, Box 2174, Palm Beach, FL 33480; (305) 736-4277. Governs amateur and professional, saltwater, freshwater, winter-snow surfing. Provides info and materials on all aspects of surfing. Conducts annual conference, seminars, workshops. Fee for some services.

13113. International Game Fish Association, 3000 E Las Olas Blvd, Ft Lauderdale, FL 33316; (305) 467-0161. Represents interests of anglers worldwide. Provides world record catch info and intl angling rules. Answers inquiries, accumulates data on game fish and fishing results, permits onsite use of collections. Services on payment of membership fee.

13114. International Oceanographic Foundation, 3979 Rickenbacker Causeway, Miami, FL 33149; (305) 361-5786. Provides public education on marine resources, ocean currents, energy sources, geology, chemistry, physics, engineering, pollution control. Holds permanent exposition. Answers inquiries, makes referrals, provides consulting services, books, loans films. Services free to members.

13115. International Swimming Hall of Fame, 1 Hall of Fame Dr, Ft Lauderdale, FL 33316; (305) 462-6536. Nonprofit educational shrine and research center for swimming. Hosts natl and intl swimming and diving meets, provides reference services, conducts swimming and diving shows. Library open to public for research free. Fee charged for admission to museum.

13116. Iron Overload Diseases Association, 224 Datura St, Ste 912, W Palm Beach, FL 33401. Serves hemochromatosis patients and families, promotes research, presses for earlier diagnosis, more effective treatment of iron overload disease which assn believes to be underdiagnosed. Organizes self-help groups, fundraising for research, screening programs and patient referrals.

13117. John and Mable Ringling Museum of Art, P.O. Box 1838 (5401 Bayshore Rd), Sarasota, FL 33578; (813) 355-5101. Contains 10,000 paintings, drawings, prints, decorative arts from the medieval period through 20th Century, ancient art from Greece and Cyprus. Permits onsite use of collections. Services free, except for reproduction services.

13118. Joint Center for Environmental and Urban Problems, 1515 W Commercial Blvd, Ft Lauderdale, FL 33309; (305) 776-1240. Addresses urban, environmental problems such as land use, water quality, comprehensive planning, coastal zone mgmt, mass transit, etc. Answers inquiries, provides advisory, consulting, reference services, permits onsite use of collections. Most info services free.

13119. Kennedy Space Center Library, Cape Canaveral, FL 32899; (305) 867-3600. Interest in testing, launching of space vehicle systems, facilities and ground-support equipment for manned and unmanned launches, history of Kennedy Space Center. Onsite reference for govt agencies and contractors. Authorized students and researchers are permitted in open literature area only.

13120. Marine Laboratory, Univ of Fla., 313 Bartram West, Gainesville, FL 32611; (904) 392-1097. Interest in marine biology, particularly ecological, physiological, and life history studies of marine animals, environmental impact studies. Answers brief inquiries, identifies regional marine animals, permits onsite use of collection.

13121. Marineland Research Laboratory, RFD 1, Box 122 (about 18 miles south of St Augustine on Rte A1A), St Augustine, FL 32084; (904) 829-5607. Collects specimens and info on marine mammals, fishes, invertebrates, mariculture, anatomy, and drugs as they relate to behavior of marine mammals, vocalization, shock, parasites, general pathology. Answers inquiries, identifies strange fishes, ambergris, etc.; makes referrals.

13122. Medical Passport Foundation, P.O. Box 820, DeLand, FL 32721; (904) 734-0639. Nonprofit org created to promote and distribute a uniform system of medical records, promote better medical care, education, research on the causes and prevention of congenital defects. Answers inquiries free, distributes publications at cost.

13124. Miami Geological Society, P.O. Box 144156, Coral Gables, FL 33114; (305) 233-5515. Publicizes geological info of the Caribbean and Miami areas and provides scholarships to geology students. Answers inquiries, conducts lectures and field trips, distributes publications. Fees charged for publications and field trips.

13125. Miami Serpentarium Laboratories, 12655 S Dixie Hwy, Miami, FL 33156; (305) 235-5722. Interest in venomous snakes, venoms, antivenoms, use of biological derivations of snake venoms as pharmaceuticals for treatment of neurological and inflammatory diseases. Answers inquiries, provides reference services, makes referrals, arranges demonstrations, lectures on venoms.

13126. Missing Children Help Center, 410 Ware Blvd, Ste 400, Tampa, FL 33619; (813) 623-KIDS, (800) USA-KIDS (outside Fla.). Acts as coordinator among missing children, parents, law enforcement. Promotes public awareness through educational programs, distributes vital info and photographs of missing children nationwide. Answers inquiries, provides advisory services. Services free.

13127. Modern Talking Picture Service, 5000 Park St North, St Petersburg, FL 33709; (813) 541-7571. Distributes free-loan 16mm, 35mm films, videocassette programs to schools, community groups, etc. on science, engineering, physical education, driver education, public health, business education, vocational guidance, more. Free catalog describes films, which are available to anyone. Only cost is return postage.

13128. Morikami Museum of Japanese Culture, 4000 Morikami Park Rd, Delray Beach, FL 33446; (305) 499-0631. Interest in Japanese and Japanese-American culture; folk arts, including pottery, paper wares, furniture; history of the Yamato colony of Japanese farmers in south Fla. Answers inquiries, permits onsite use of collections. Services free, except for workshops and publications.

13129. Morton Collectanea, P.O. Box 248204 (Univ of Miami, Main Campus), Coral Gables, FL 33124; (305) 284-3741. Interest in economic botany, including fuelwood trees, honeybee plants, tropical fruits, medicinal, poisonous, and edible wild plants. Answers inquiries, provides literature-searching and duplication services for a fee, prepares surveys, investigations, reports, holds lectures.

13130. Mote Marine Laboratory, 1600 City Island Park, Sarasota, FL 33577; (813) 388-4441. Interest in marine research, including toxic organic chemicals, cancer in sharks, benthic marine organisms, red tide, wetland ecology, snook aquaculture, manatee surveys, sea turtles. Conducts research, provides reference and consulting services.

13131. Mount Sinai Pain Center, Dept of Anesthesiology, Miami Beach, FL 33140; (305) 674-2070. Interest in diagnosis and mgmt of chronic pain problems. Answers inquiries, provides advisory and consulting services, conducts seminars and workshops, diagnoses and treats chronic pain. Services for a fee, ex-

cept to indigent patients, and available to medical and lay groups.

13132. Museum of Arts and Sciences, 1040 Museum Blvd, Daytona Beach, FL 32014; (904) 255-0285. Museum of science, astronomy, local natural history, Cuban fine and ethnic arts, paleontology. Includes exhibits, planetarium, library, prehistory of Fla. wing. Answers inquiries, provides consulting and reference services, sponsors trips, films. Nonmembers pay small admission fee.

13133. Museum of Science and Industry, 4801 E Fowler Ave, Tampa, FL 33617; (813) 985-5531. Interest in science, industry, natural and human history, primarily of the Fla. region. Includes collections of minerals, fossils, historical objects, ethnological basketry, research archives. Provides advisory services, permits onsite use of collections and archive by qualified persons.

13134. Museum of Science and Space Transit Planetarium, 3280 S Miami Ave, Miami, FL 33129; (305) 854-4242. Conducts participatory science activities on south Fla.'s natural history, astronomy, meteorology, chemistry, physics, biology, technology, mineralogy, aerospace history, conchology. Answers inquiries, conducts science camp and classes, permits limited onsite use of collections.

13135. Music Industry Educators Association, c/o School of Music, Univ of Miami, P.O. Box 248165, Coral Gables, FL 33124. Org of music educators, students, music industry firms interested in music publishing, record production, talent mgmt, marketing, recording techniques, curriculum development. Answers inquiries, provides advisory, reference services, speakers. Most services free.

13136. National Association of Federally Licensed Firearms Dealers, 2801 E Oakland Park Blvd, Ft Lauderdale, FL 33306; (305) 561-3505. Pro-firearm org that provides info on firearm legislation, production, sales. Answers inquiries, provides reference and magnetic tape (dealer listing) services, distributes publications. Services free, except magnetic tape service and some publications.

13137. National Entrepreneurial Development Center, School of Business and Industry, Fla. A&M Univ, Tallahassee, FL 32307; (904) 599-3589. Researches problems facing black entrepreneurs, provides executive training, talent search, financial, info and broker services to minority entrepreneurs and businessmen. Info services to minority entrepreneurs, some provided at cost.

13138. National Foundation for Advancement in the Arts, 100 N Biscayne Blvd, Miami, FL 33132; (305) 371-9470. Awards cash grants to young artists active in dance, music, theater, writing, visual arts. Answers inquiries, provides advisory services, conducts seminars and workshops, distributes publications.

13139. National Golf Foundation, 200 Castlewood Dr, N Palm Beach, FL 33408; (305) 844-2500. Org supported by major golf manufacturers, golf assns, etc. Interest in market research, design and construction of golf courses, driving ranges, miniature golf courses. Has access to data on all U.S. golf courses. Answers inquiries, provides various services free or at cost to all.

13140. National Hurricane Center, Natl Weather Service, NOAA, Gables One Tower, Rm 631, 1320 S Dixie Hwy, Coral Gables, FL 33146; (305) 666-0413. Interest in tropical cyclones, hurricanes, weather forecasts, storm warnings. Holds computerized data tracking cyclones dating from 1886. Answers inquiries, provides info on current research, permits onsite use of collections. Most services free.

13141. National Network of Youth Advisory Boards, P.O. Box 402036, Ocean View Beach, Miami Beach, FL 33140; (305) 532-2607. Nonprofit assn devoted to enhancing communication between youth and city or town govt. Interest in juvenile justice, education, recreation, drug abuse, more. Answers inquiries, provides advisory, consulting, reference services. Services generally free.

13142. National Parkinson Foundation, Bob Hope Rd, 1501 NW 9th Ave, Miami, FL 33136; (305) 547-6666. Univ of Miami School of Medicine's nonprofit org that provides outpatient diagnostic, treatment, and rehabilitation services, research funds for Parkinson's disease, neurological disorders. Answers inquiries, provides free consulting, reference services.

13144. Navy Underwater Sound Reference Detachment, Naval Research Laboratory, P.O. Box 8337 (755 Gatlin Ave), Orlando, FL 32856-8337; (305) 859-5120. Conducts research on underwater sound and underwater sound transducers, standards, electronic measurement and control systems. Answers inquiries, makes referrals, provides consulting, measurement, and loan of standard transducers, permits onsite use of collection. Services primarily for Dept of Defense.

13145. Nutrition Co., P.O. Box 11102, Tallahassee, FL 32302; (904) 222-8745. Info clearinghouse that serves professionals in dietetics, nutrition, and related health fields. Answers inquiries, provides consulting, reference, data, abstracting and indexing services, conducts workshops, distributes publications. Services for a fee.

13146. Operation PAR, 6613 49th St North, Pinellas Park, FL 33565; (813) 527-5866. Provides substance abuse prevention, education, and treatment services. Conducts in-jail, outpatient, primary prevention programs, more. Answers inquiries, offers consulting services, operates speakers bureau. Services for a fee.

13147. Orlando Science Center, 810 E Rollins St, Orlando, FL 32803-1291; (305) 896-7151. Interest in physical and life sciences, anthropology, natural history of Fla. Conducts tours, lectures, film series, classes, planetarium and multimedia presentations, field trips, tours and expeditions. Planetarium and observatory open to public, admission fees charged.

13148. P.K. Yonge Library of Florida History, Univ of Fla. Libraries, 404 Library West, Gainesville, FL 32611; (904) 392-0319. Interest in Fla. history from its discovery to the present, history of the Southeast Borderlands in the colonial period. Permits onsite use of collections, which are largest in U.S. Services free, available to adult public.

13149. Pain and Back Rehabilitation Program, Comprehensive Pain Center, Dept of Neurological Surgery, Univ of Miami School of Medicine, P.O. Box 016960 (1501 NW 9th Ave), Miami, FL 33101; (305) 547-6946. Involved in pain research, emphasizing multidisciplinary treatment of chronic pain problems, including low back pain. Answers inquiries, provides advisory services on case-by-case basis. Services free.

13151. Panama Canal Commission Library, Panama Canal Commission, APO (Building 0610, Gaillard Hwy, Ancon, Republic of Panama; 52-7884), Miami, FL 34011. Collects materials related to Panama Canal, shipping, engineering. Covers planning, construction, operation, maintenance of canal, early interoceanic canal surveys, French Panama canal attempt. Limited onsite, offsite reference available to public as time and staff permit.

13152. Papanicolaou Cancer Research Institute, P.O. Box 6188 (1155 NW 14th St), Miami, FL 33123; (305) 324-5572. Conducts basic biochemical/biophysical research on cancer and related conditions, cytology, immunology, molecular structure and interactions, electron microscopy, enzymology, more. Answers inquiries, makes interlibrary loans, permits onsite use of collection. Services at cost.

13153. Phytochemical Society of North America, c/o Dr J.T. Romeo, Biology Dept, Univ of South Fla., Tampa, FL 33620; (813) 974-2336. Interest in phytochemistry, natural plant products, plant biochemistry, drugs. Brief questions and referrals handled free, negotiable fee for services requiring substantial time.

13154. Railway Engineering Maintenance Suppliers Association, 5600 Marina Dr, Holmes Beach, FL 33510; (813) 778-4121. Interest in engineering, maintenance of way, signal, and communications equipment used by domestic and foreign railroads. Refers technical inquiries to assn members for reply, or to other orgs or individuals without charge. Holds periodic exhibits of equipment.

13155. Raptor Research Foundation, c/o Dr Jeffrey L. Lincer, Pres, 4718 Dunn Dr, Sarasota, FL 33583; (813) 365-1000 ext 2402. Coordinates research on the biology and mgmt of birds of prey. Answers inquiries, provides advisory services, info on R&D in progress, conducts seminars, evaluates data. Services generally free.

13156. Real Estate Data, 2398 NW 119th St, Miami, FL 33167; (305) 685-5731. Holds real property map and corresponding ownership info on over 275 counties in U.S. Provides reference, abstracting, and microform services, conducts seminars and workshops, evaluates and distributes data, permits onsite use of publications. Services for a fee to all.

13157. Remote Sensing Laboratory, Dept of Mechanical Engineering, Coll of Engineering, Univ of Miami, Box 248003, Coral Gables, FL 33124; (305) 284-3881. Studies applications of radar and satellites to meteorological analysis and research, with emphasis on tropics, subtropics, instrumentation for hydrological applications, propagation of radar microwaves in atmosphere, more. Permits onsite use of literature collection, lends materials.

13158. Rosenstiel School of Marine and Atmospheric Science, Univ of Miami, 4600 Rickenbacker Causeway, Miami, FL 33149; (305) 361-4000. Focuses on marine biology, geology and geophysics, estuarine research, physical and chemical oceanography, dynamics of the Gulf Stream, fauna of the Caribbean, subsea cementation of reefs, microalgae, etc. Answers inquiries, provides reference services, permits onsite use of collections.

13159. SCM Corp. Organic Chemicals Technical Library, P.O. Box 389 (Foot of W 61st St), Jacksonville, FL 32201; (904) 764-1711 ext 336 or 368. Focuses on organic chemistry, engineering, business. Permits onsite reference by arrangement.

13160. Shared Parenting Association, P.O. Box 430306 (6510 SW 93rd Ave), Miami, FL 33143. Devoted to cause of equal status and responsibilities in parenting for fathers and mothers after divorce. Answers inquiries, provides advisory services, conducts seminars and workshops. Services free, but donations suggested.

13161. Silicon Beach Consultancy, 2000 W Glades Rd, Ste 200, Boca Raton, FL 33431; (305) 368-4752. Interest in corporate planning, early warning systems, futurism, and the psychological and philosophical barriers to setting up futures groups in large and small companies. Provides consulting, reference services, conducts seminars, workshops. Services for a fee.

13162. Society of American Magicians, International, c/o Joyce Zachary, Natl Secty, P.O. Box 368, Mango, FL 34262-0368; (813) 689-9772. Seeks to advance magic as an art in the fields of amusement, entertainment, and education. Interest in magic, including its instruction, performance, sales, and advancement. Answers inquiries and distributes a publication free.

13163. Solar Energy and Energy Conversion Laboratory, Dept of Mechanical Engineering, Coll of Engineering, Univ of Fla., 325 MEB, Gainesville, FL 32611; (904) 392-0812. Researches solar energy use, energy conservation, industrial testing of energy-related materials and equipment. Answers inquiries, provides info on

R&D in progress, industrial testing services, conducts workshops.

13164. Southeast Archeological Center Library, National Park Service, P.O. Box 2416, Tallahassee, FL 32304; (904) 222-1167. Devoted to archaeology, ethnology, history of the southeastern U.S. Answers inquiries, makes referrals to other sources of info. Services free to SEAC-sponsored students and employees and to other fed and state agencies. Other requests for info considered on individual basis.

13165. Southeastern Fisheries Association, 312 E Georgia St, Tallahassee, FL 32301; (904) 224-0612. Researches commercial fishing in the southeastern U.S., seafood marketing, fisheries extension. Provides advisory and reference services and info on R&D in progress, evaluates and analyzes data, permits onsite use of collections. Services at cost.

13166. Southeastern Geological Society, P.O. Box 1634, Tallahassee, FL 32302. Interest in geology in southeastern U.S., including paleontology, stratigraphy, sedimentology, sedimentary petrology, geomorphology, petroleum geology. Answers inquiries, provides reference services, conducts field trips. Services free, except for publications.

13167. Southern Pine Inspection Bureau, 4705 Scenic Hwy, Pensacola, FL 32504; (904) 434-2611. Supported by Southern Pine lumber industry, bureau promulgates lumber grading standards, provides quality control to Southern Pine lumber manufacturers and pressure treating plants. Answers inquiries, distributes publications. Services at cost to all users.

13168. Space Astronomy Laboratory, Univ of Fla., 1810 NW 6th St, Gainesville, FL 32609; (904) 392-5450. Devoted to optical and microwave experiments and nuclear astrophysics, also operates a night-sky observatory on Maui, Hawaii. Answers inquiries, provides info on research in progress, permits onsite use of collections. Services free.

13169. Sporting Goods Manufacturers Association, 200 Castlewood Dr, North Palm Beach, FL 33408; (305) 842-4100. Interest in all aspects of sporting goods industry, including product standards and safety, marketing, legislation and regulation, economic and legal aspects of licensing. Answers inquiries, evaluates and analyzes data. Services subject to a fee, may be restricted to specific groups.

13170. Subtropical Horticulture Research Station, Agricultural Research Service, USDA, 13601 Old Cutler Rd, Miami, FL 33158; (305) 238-9321. Conducts research to protect horticultural crops from deterioration and damage from insects, diseases, other hazards during storage and marketing. Answers inquiries, provides consulting services, referrals, published reports. Onsite use of collections restricted to qualified researchers.

13171. Tall Timbers Research, Rte. 1, Box 678, Tallahassee, FL 32312; (904) 893-4153. Nonprofit foundation with interest in mgmt of habitats for wildlife, game animals, plants, natural history, ecological research, fire ecology, ornithology. Answers inquiries, permits onsite use of collections. Services at cost.

13172. Textile Rental Services Association of America, P.O. Box 1283 (1250 E Hallandale Beach Blvd), Hallandale, FL 33009; (305) 457-7555. Interest in laundry industry, including linen supply, industrial and commercial laundering, machinery, promotion, sales, production standards, industry statistics. Answers inquiries, provides consulting services, makes referrals, permits onsite reference. Services for assn members only.

13173. Towing and Recovery Association of America, P.O. Box 2517 (717 Exec Dr), Winter Park, FL 32790; (305) 647-8588. Promotes automotive towing-storage-recovery operators through legislative lobbying and natl trade show. Answers inquiries, provides reference services, evaluates data. Services free to members and govt officials, at cost to nonmembers in industry and others.

13174. Virology Laboratory, Dept of Microbiology, Univ of Miami School of Medicine, P.O. Box 016960 (1550 NW 10th Ave), Miami, FL 33101; (305) 547-6568. Conducts research in the biological and medical disciplines, including virology, immunochemistry, congenital defects, oncology, more. Answers inquiries, provides consulting, reference services, permits onsite observation of research techniques. Services to qualified persons.

13175. Women Band Directors National Association, 3580 Rothschild Dr, Pensacola, FL 32503; (904) 432-2887. Org of women band directors, school music supervisors, etc. that sponsors awards and scholarships, conducts workshops, summer courses. Interest in band music, performance art, music therapy, teacher training. Info free, other services generally for a fee.

13176. Wood and Synthetic Fling Institute, 108 Dania Circle, LeHigh Acres, FL 33936; (813) 369-2262. Provides standards and specifications for the installation and maintenance of wood and synthetic floors. Answers inquiries, conducts seminars, distributes publications, makes referrals. Services free to architects, nominal charge to others.

Georgia

14005. Alternate Lifestyles, 5263 Bouldercrest Rd, Ellenwood, GA 30049; (404) 961-0102. Church group interested in recovery and preservation of values and practices from the past that contribute to more human relationships. Provides general reference services, conducts seminars, distributes publications. Services free, except publications.

14006. American Academy of Dental Radiology, c/o Dr William R. Wege, School of Dentistry, Medical Coll of Georgia, Augusta, GA 30902; (404) 828-2935. Interest in dental radiology (x-rays, radioisotopes), radiation protection. Maintains library; publishes journals; provides inquiry, consulting services, primarily for members of dental, medical professions.

14007. American Association for Vocational Instructional Materials, 120 Engineering Center, Univ of Georgia, Athens, GA 30602; (404) 542-2586. Interest in preparation, distribution of vocational instructional materials related to farm and rural industry. Provides general reference services, distributes publications. Sells materials, provides other services free.

14008. American Association of Occupational Health Nurses, 3500 Piedmont Rd, Suite 400, Atanta, GA 30305-1513; (404) 262-1162. Assn of registered professional nurses working with workers. Maintains library, archives; publishes journal, other materials; provides inquiry, some advisory services free; holds conferences, other meetings.

14010. American Association of Public Health Dentistry, c/o Dr E. Joseph Alderman, 99 Butler St SE, Atlanta, GA 30303; (404) 572-2601. Interest in dental public health, preventive and community dentistry. Provides free general reference services, distributes publications.

14011. American Association of Zoo Veterinarians, c/o Morton S. Silberman, DVM, Executive Secretary, 214 WMB, Emory Univ, Atlanta, GA 30322; (404) 329-7423. Interest in veterinary medicine, emphasizing preventive medicine, husbandry, scientific research on captive wild animals, exotic animal diseases. Answers inquiries, provides consulting services, conducts seminars, makes referrals. Services free.

14012. American Camellia Society, P.O. Box 1217, Fort Valley, GA 31030; (912) 967-2358. Researches genus Camellia: culture, pest control, varieties, breeding. Has plant collections and library for onsite use of printed, visual materials; publishes journal; provides reference, consulting services.

14013. American Electroencephalographic Society, 2579 Melinda Dr, Atlanta, GA 30345; (404) 934-1620. Interest in electroencephalography (EEG), evoked potentials. Publishes journal, newsletter, guidelines in EEG, syllabuses; makes referrals to specialists on request; sponsors AMA-accredited courses.

14014. American Osteopathic College of Dermatology, 1847-A Peeler Rd, Atlanta, GA 30338; (404) 399-6865. Provides postdoctoral training to osteopathic physicians in osteopathic medicine, dermatology. Provides general reference services, conducts seminars. Services provided at cost.

14015. American Protestant Correctional Chaplains' Association, c/o Rev. Ralph Graham, Executive Director, 5235 Greenpoint Dr, Stone Mountain, GA 30088. Provides certification and promotes institutional standards for religious programming and chaplaincy. Provides general reference services, distributes newsletter. Services free, except newsletter and certification costs, to those in the field.

14016. American Rafting Association, 75 Third St NW, Atlanta, GA 30308; (404) 875-7238. Nonprofit corp interested in rafting competition, water safety, preservation of waterways. Provides free general reference services, distributes publications.

14017. American Society of Heating, Refrigerating, & Air-Conditioning Engineers, 1791 Tullie Circle NE, Atlanta, GA 30329; (404) 636-8400. Interest in all aspects of heating, refrigeration, air conditioning, ventilation, insulation. Publishes journal, handbook, standards, tech papers; answers inquiries.

14018. American String Teachers Association, Univ of Georgia Station, Box 2066, Athens, GA 30612-0066; (404) 542-5254 ext 48. Nonprofit org that promotes professional and amateur string and orchestra study, teacher education, research; sponsors exchange performances. Answers inquiries, conducts seminars and workshops, distributes publications. Services generally available for a fee.

14022. Arthritis Foundation, 1314 Spring St, NW, Atlanta, GA 30309; (404) 872-7100. Supports research on causes, prevention, cure of all forms of arthritis. Local chapters serve patients, families, medical profession, public with clinics, home visits, psychological support, classes, speakers.

14023. Association of Environmental Engineering Professors, c/o Dr F. Michael Saunders, Civil Engineering, Georgia Tech Univ, Atlanta, GA 30332. Interest in environmental engineering education. Answers inquiries free, publishes materials.

14024. Business Council of Georgia, 1280 South Omni International, Atlanta, GA 30335; (404) 223-2264. Interest in industrial development in Ga., including relevant legislation, labor relations, educational development. Publishes monthly newsletter, statistics, directories, legislative bulletin; provides technical, site-finding services.

14025. Callaway Gardens, Pine Mountain, GA 31822; (404) 663-2281. Interest in horticultural, nature, and environmental study. Provides general reference services, conducts symposia and seminars, permits onsite reference. Educational services free, others available at nominal fee.

14026. Calorie Control Council, 5775 Peachtree-Dunwoody Rd, Suite 500-D, Atlanta, GA 30342; (404) 252-3663. Sponsors research, represents dietary foods and beverages industry and its customers. Provides general reference services, conducts seminars, distributes publications. Fees charged for services only in exceptional cases.

14028. Carl Vinson Institute of Government, Univ of Georgia, Terrell Hall, Athens, GA 30602; (404) 542-2736. Interest in training, research, educational services relating to local and state govt in Georgia and beyond. Provides general reference and consulting services, publishes materials, permits onsite study. Services primarily for Ga. govt; free to some, at cost to others.

14029. Carpet & Rug Institute, P.O. Box 2048 (310 South Holiday Dr), Dalton, GA 30720; (404) 278-3176. Interest in carpets, rugs. Has extensive library for onsite use. Publishes reports, consumer info (price list available); answers inquiries. Services free, if not extensive.

14030. Center of Rehabilitation Medicine, School of Medicine, Emory Univ, 1441 Clifton Rd NE, Atlanta, GA 30322; (404) 329-5507. Interest in all aspects of research, education, and patient care relating to rehabilitation medicine. Provides general reference services and consulting, conducts seminars, sells videotape copies. Patient care for a fee to referred patients.

14031. Centers for Disease Control, Office of Public Affairs, Atlanta, GA 30333; (404) 329-3286. Responds to public inquiries on preventive medicine, occupational safety, family planning, health education. Maintains statistics on disease, disability, deaths linked to environmental, workplace hazards.

14032. Centers for Disease Control, Center for Health Promotion & Education, Bldg 1, SSB249, 1600 Clifton Rd, NE, Atlanta, GA 30333; (404) 329-3492. Offers technical assistance, expertise in health promotion, education--especially nutrition, reproduction, violence epidemiology. Maintains data base of health education literature, program info for community health educators.

14033. Chickamauga & Chattanooga National Military Park, National Park Service, P.O. Box 2128, Fort Oglethorpe, GA 30742; (404) 866-9241. Interest in Chickamauga campaign, Civil War battles around Chattanooga. Answers inquiries, makes referrals, identifies Civil War artifacts, provides genealogical info on Civil War soldiers.

14034. Coca-Cola, Technical Information Services, P.O. Drawer 1734 (310 North Ave), Atlanta, GA 30313; (404) 676-2008. Interest in beverages, soft drinks, chemistry, nutrition, food science and technology, packaging. Provides copying services, makes loans, permits onsite reference. Services free to those who cannot find a specific publication in their library.

14035. Concrete Sawing & Drilling Association, 3130 Maple Dr, Suite 7, Atlanta, GA 30305; (404) 257-1177. Interest in diamond sawing and drilling. Provides general reference services, conducts seminars, distributes publications. Services free, except mailing costs.

14036. Demographic Research & Training Laboratory, Department of Sociology, Emory Univ, Atlanta, GA 30322; (404) 329-7510. Involved in demographic research and training. Provides general reference services, conducts seminars and workshops, distributes data compilations, permits onsite reference. Services may be provided for a fee.

14037. Doctors Ought to Care, 302 Turner-McCall Blvd, Rome, GA 30161; (404) 291-2075. Natl, nonprofit org that provides education on preventable illness, especially those related to smoking and alcohol/drug abuse. Provides general reference and consulting services, conducts seminars and advertising campaigns, distributes publications. Services free, except for printed materials.

14038. Educanetic Consulting Associates, 258 Midvale Dr NE, Atlanta, GA 30342; (404) 255-9270. Interest in behavioral consulting related to fear of flight, aircraft passenger fear and anxiety, etc. Provides general reference services and consulting, conducts seminars, distributes publications. Brief inquiries answered free, fees charged for other services.

14039. Environmental Resources Center, Ga. Institute of Technology, Atlanta, GA 30332; (404) 894-2375. Interest in conservation, development, planning, management of natural resources, especially research on Ga. water resources. Publishes reports, books; provides inquiry, consulting, extension services.

14040. Families in Action, National Drug Information Center, Families in Action, 3845 North Druid Hills Rd, Suite 300, Decatur, GA 30033; (404) 325-5799. Community education group interested in all aspects of drug and alcohol abuse, parent/child relationships, etc. Provides general reference services, conducts workshops, distributes publications, permits onsite reference. Services free, except publications and copying.

14041. Fernbank Science Center Library, 156 Heaton Park Dr, Atlanta, GA 30307; (404) 378-4311. Museum and educational facility interested in natural and health sciences, outdoor education. Provides general reference services, consulting; conducts programs, seminars; distributes publications; permits onsite reference. Services provided at cost.

14042. Find-Me, P.O. Box 1612 (205 North Chilton Ave), La Grange, GA 30241; (404) 884-7419. Nonprofit org that counsels families, advises public about missing persons phenomenon. Provides general reference services, conducts seminars, distributes publications. Services free.

14043. Forest Farmers Association, 4 Executive Park East, NE, Atlanta, GA 30329; (404) 325-2954. Interest in growing, processing of timber in southern U.S. Publishes magazine, manuals. Answers inquiries, provides reference services, permits onsite use of materials.

14044. Fred R. Crawford Witness to the Holocaust Project, Emory Univ, Atlanta, GA 30322; (404) 329-7525. Collects oral, video, and written testimony of witnesses to German concentration camps of World War II. Provides general reference services, sells publications, permits onsite reference. Services generally free.

14045. Future Aviation Professionals of America, 4291 J Memorial Dr, Decatur, GA 30032; (404) 294-0226; (800) 538-5627. Commercial org that provides career aviation employment info for pilots, flight attendants, and aviation mechanics. Provides general reference, resume, and consulting services, distributes publications. Services provided for a fee.

14047. Georgia Conservancy, 3110 Maple Dr, Suite 407, Atlanta, GA 30305; (404) 262-1967. Interest in environmental protection of natural and urban areas in Ga. Provides general reference services, distributes publications, permits onsite reference. Services free, except bulk publications.

14048. Georgia Council on Moral & Civic Concerns, c/o Dr J. Emmett Henderson, Executive Director, 2930 Flowers Rd South, Atlanta, GA 30341; (404) 451-9361. Interest in pastoral counseling of alcoholics and drug-dependent persons, related issues. Provides general reference services, conducts seminars and civic group programs, distributes publications. Services free.

14049. Georgia Department of Archives & History, Dept of Georgia Office of Sec of State, 330 Capitol Ave SE, Atlanta, GA 30334; (404) 656-2350. Interest in Georgia colonial, state, and local history, govt, genealogy. Provides general reference services, conducts seminars, permits onsite reference. Services free, except reproductions.

14050. Georgia Historical Society, 501 Whitaker St, Savannah, GA 31499; (912) 944-2128. Interest in history of Ga., especially Savannah. Collection has 30,000 vols, journals, periodicals, 2,200 manuscript collection, maps, photos, microfilm (for onsite use). Publishes journal, manuscripts; provides inquiry, reference services.

14051. Georgia Humanities Resource Center, c/o Georgia Southern Coll Library, Statesboro, GA 30460-8074; (912) 681-5482. Interest in social trends, art in society, biography, urban development, Southern history. Lends materials, permits onsite reference. Loans subject to a fee, onsite use free. Services available for nonprofit purposes.

14052. Georgia Institute of Technology Bioengineering Center, Office of Interdisciplinary Programs, Georgia Institute of Technology, 225 North Ave, Atlanta, GA 30332; (404) 894-2375. Educational coordination center interested in bioengineering, biomedical instrumentation, computer applications in rehabilitation research. Provides general reference services, conducts seminars. Services free.

14053. Georgia Solar Coalition, P.O. Box 5506 (1083 Austin Ave NE), Atlanta, GA 30307; (404) 525-7657. Nonprofit coalition that promotes use of renewable energy resources. Provides general reference services, conducts seminars, distributes publications. Most services free.

14054. Glutamate Association, 5775 Peachtree-Dunwoody Rd, Suite 500-D, Atlanta, GA 30342; (404) 252-3663. Assn of manufacturers, natl marketers, and processed food users of glutamic acid and its salts, such as MSG. Answers inquiries free, distributes single copies of publications free.

14055. Heartlife, P.O. Box 54305, Atlanta, GA 30308; (404) 523-0826; (800) 241-6993. Supports heart patients, their families. Assists local chapters to organize. Exchanges info thru magazine, toll-free phone number.

14056. Hoya Society International, P.O. Box 54271, Atlanta, GA 30308; (404) 787-3260. Interest in plant genus Hoya, Hoya nomenclature and taxonomy. Provides general reference services, translations; distributes data, publication, and color slides. Services provided at cost.

14057. Industrial Development Research Council, 1954 Airport Rd NE, Atlanta, GA 30341; (404) 458-6026. Works in industrial development; plant location, planning; geoeconomics. Library holds relevant materials. Publishes compilations and reports, answers inquiries, conducts conferences. Fees may be charged.

14058. Infant Formula Council, 5775 Peachtree-Dunwoody Rd, Suite 500-D, Atlanta, GA 30342; (404) 252-3663. Manufacturers' assn interested in infant formulas, infant feeding and nutrition. Answers inquiries, distributes brochures, loans film, makes referrals. Services free, except bulk copies of the brochures free.

14059. Institute for Behavioral Research, Univ of Georgia, 548 Graduate Studies Research Center, Athens, GA 30602; (404) 542-1806. Interest in family interaction, divorce and adolescent adjustment, cognitive studies, research on deviance, etc. Provides consultation and survey research, biographical data.

14062. Institute of Ecology, Univ of Georgia. Ecology Bldg, Athens, GA 30602; (404) 542-2968. Interest in ecosystems, environmental design, applied ecology, environmental impact analysis, tropical ecology, wetlands ecology. Answers inquiries; offers consulting services to corps, govt, individuals.

14064. Inter-American Council for Medical Assistance, Education & Research, 320 Doctors Bldg, Columbus, GA 31901; (404) 322-2547. Provides medical and biological info to medical schools and univs throughout Latin America. Provides general reference services, translations; distributes data. Services available only to special groups--at cost to some, free to others.

14065. International Association for Financial Planning, 5775 Peachtree Dunwoody Rd, Suite 120-C, Atlanta, GA 30342; (404) 252-9600. Nonprofit org interested in financial planning, financial services and products. Provides general reference services, conducts seminars and conventions, distributes publications. Services provided on sliding-fee scale.

14066. International Association on Water Pollution Research & Control, c/o Dr Frederick G. Pohland, Chairman, U.S. National Committee, IAWPRC, School of Civil Engineering, Georgia Institute of Technology, Atlanta, GA 30332; (404) 894-2265. Interest in all aspects of water quality management. Publishes monthly journal, proceedings; provides inquiry, reference services; consulting services to intl agencies. Sponsors intl conferences, natl symposia.

14067. International Council for Small Business -- U.S.A., c/o Vivian Edwards, Executive Secretary, Small Business Development Center, Univ of Georgia, Athens, GA 30602. Interest in small business management, entrepreneurial development, education, and research. Holds conferences.

14068. International Food Additives Council, 5775 Peachtree-Dunwoody Rd, Suite 500-D, Atlanta, GA 30342; (404) 252-3663. Interest in regulatory, scientific, and educational issues surrounding direct and indirect food additives. Answers inquiries free, distributes brochure at cost.

14069. International Paper Company Southlands Experiment Forest, Route 1, Box 571, Bainbridge, GA 31717; (912) 246-3642. Interest in management of forests, wildlife, outdoor recreation. Maintains small library; publishes newsletter, reports, research notes; answers inquiries within limits of time, staff.

14070. Inventors Clubs of America, P.O. Box 450261 (4005 Brown Rd, Tucker, GA), Atlanta, GA 30345; (404) 938-5089. Nonprofit club interested in help for inventors, including R&D, engineering, manufacturing, marketing, patent protection. Provides general reference services, conducts seminars, distributes publication and data. Services provided for a fee.

14071. Law Engineering Testing Company, Bldg E-5150, 1140 Hammond Dr, Atlanta, GA 30328; (404) 396-8000. Civil, geological, chemical engineering firm with offices across U.S. Answers inquiries; provides consulting services on a fee basis; permits onsite use of collection of unpublished reports, other records.

14072. Lockheed-Georgia Company, Technical Information Department, Dept. 72-34, Zone 7, Marietta, GA 30063; (404) 424-2928. Interest in all aspects of aerospace technology. Extensive holdings of internal reports, other materials on paper, microform, film. Provides reference services; has own online interactive info retrieval system.

14073. Lupus Foundation of America, c/o Virginia J. Masters, Secretary, 4434 Covington Hwy, Decatur, GA 30035; (404) 289-7453. Provides info and counseling for patients with Lupus erythematosus, supports research, develops clinics. Provides general reference services, conducts seminars, distributes publications. Fees charged for most services, except those to hospitals.

14074. MAP International Learning Resource Center, MAP International, Box 50 (2200 Glynco Parkway), Brunswick, GA 31520; (912) 653-6010; (912) 265-6010. Interest in health education, agriculture, maternal and child health, sanitation, nutrition, hunger. Provides general reference services, conducts seminars, distributes publications, permits onsite reference. Fees charged for services to Americans, foreign requests free.

14075. MEGA Systems, 620 Peachtree St NE, Atlanta, GA 30308; (404) 892-6342. Commercial org interested in all aspects of new business development: financing, mergers, divestment, management and employee development, etc. Provides technical services, conducts workshops, evaluates data. Services provided for a fee.

14077. Marine Institute, Univ of Georgia, Sapelo Island, GA 31327; (912) 485-2276. Interest in salt marsh and estuarine ecology, coastal ocean ecology. Answers inquiries, makes interlibrary loans.

14078. Martin Luther King, Jr. Center for Nonviolent Social Change, 449 Auburn Ave NE, Atlanta, GA 30312; (404) 524-1956. Interest in American civil rights movement, use of nonviolent strategies for social change. Provides general reference and consulting services, conducts seminars, permits onsite reference. Services provided at cost, available to persons with legitimate research purposes.

14079. Medical College of Georgia Comprehensive Sickle Cell Center, Protein Chemistry Laboratories, Medical Coll of Georgia, Augusta, GA 30912; (404) 828-3091. Interested in sickle cell anemia, hemoglobin synthesis, structure, function, gene mapping, thalassemia. Provides general reference services, conducts seminars, courses, and counseling, distributes publications. Services free.

14080. Modern Talking Picture Service, 4705-F Bakers Ferry Rd, Atlanta, GA 30336; (404) 696-2025. Offers films, videos (on food, dentistry, chemicals, alcohol abuse, the handicapped, environment) provided by producers, sponsors, including trade assns, U.S. govt. List available.

14081. NASA Computer Software Management & Information Center, 112 Barrow Hall, Univ of Georgia, Athens, GA 30602; (404) 542-3265. Maintains library of computer progs (and documentation) developed by and for NASA. Publishes annual software catalog. Provides copies of programs, documentation for a fee; searches for programs for defined needs.

14082. National Automotive Parts Association, 2999 Circle 75 Parkway, Atlanta, GA 30339; (404) 956-2200. Interest in automotive parts. Answers inquiries, provides marketing and info services for NAPA distribution centers for use by NAPA parts stores, makes referrals.

14083. National Coalition for Marine Conservation, P.O. Box 23298, Savannah, GA 31403; (912) 234-8062. Nonprofit coalition that promotes legislative, administrative action protecting marine resources. Conducts annual symposium on fisheries, provides free general reference services.

14084. National Committee on Certification of Physician's Assistants, 3384 Peachtree Rd, NE, Suite 560, Atlanta, GA 30326; (404) 261-1261. Gives certifying exams for physicians' assistants (PAs). Decides eligibility, standards; verifies, renews certificates; publishes lists of certified PA's; assists state medical boards with PA-related legislation.

14085. National Dimension Manufacturers Association, 101 Village Parkway, Suite 202 (2002 Richard Jones Rd), Marietta, GA 30067; (404) 953-2242. Interest in wood component parts, their manufacture, standards. Library holds standards, specifications. Publishes standards, specifications, consumer guide; answers inquiries.

14086. National Institute for Occupational Safety & Health, 1600 Clifton Rd, NE, Bldg 1, Room 3106, Atlanta, GA 30333; (404) 329-3778. Answers nontechnical queries on occupational safety and health. Works with Clearinghouse for Occupational Safety & Health Info, Cincinnati. Maintains toxic substances data base, searchable via MEDLARS system.

14087. National Interfaith Coalition on Aging, P.O. Box 1924 (298 South Hull St), Athens, GA 30603; (404) 353-1331. Interest in religion and aging, spiritual health of the elderly, natl policies on aging, aging education, etc. Provides general reference and consulting services, conducts seminars, distributes publications, permits onsite reference. Services subject to a fee, some for members only.

14088. Nuclear Assurance Corp., 5720 Peachtree Parkway, Norcross, GA 30092; (404) 447-1144. Commercial org interested in world nuclear fuel market, flow of nuclear fuel cycle, related consulting services. Provides general reference services, conducts seminars and workshops, distributes publications. Services provided at cost.

14089. Pain Control Center, Center of Rehabilitation Medicine, School of Medicine, Emory Univ, 1441 Clifton Rd NE, Atlanta, GA 30322; (404) 329-5492. Interest in medical and psychological aspects of chronic pain, impairment and disability, pain and litigation. Answers inquiries, provides advisory services, conducts seminars. Fees generally charged for services.

14090. Parent Resources Institute on Drug Education, 100 Edgewood Ave, Suite 1216, Atlanta, GA 30303; (404) 658-2548. Resource center interested in adolescent drug abuse, drug culture, marijuana, other drugs. Provides general reference services, conducts workshops, distributes publications, permits onsite reference.

14091. Potash & Phosphate Institute, 2801 Buford Highway NE, Suite 401, Atlanta, GA 30329; (404) 634-4274. Interest in potash, phosphorus in fertilizers. Publishes magazine and newsletter, answers inquiries, provides consulting and limited bibliographic services.

14092. Price Gilbert Memorial Library, Georgia Institute of Technology, Atlanta, GA 30332-0900; (404) 894-4511. Provides bibliographic assistance to business, industry, and govt nationwide. Provides general reference services, translations, online data base services. Services provided to off-campus users on fee or contract basis.

14094. Public Health Service, Centers for Disease Control, U.S. Public Health Service, 1600 Clifton Rd NE, Atlanta, GA 30333; (404) 329-3534. Undertakes programs for prevention, control of infectious diseases, malnutrition. Publishes statistics, training materials. Refers queries to proper programs.

14096. Savannah Science Museum, 4405 Paulsen St, Savannah, GA 31405; (912) 89. Interest in natural and physical sciences. Provides general reference and consulting services, conducts programs, lends materials. Museum open to public.

14097. Skidaway Institute of Oceanography Library, P.O. Box 13687 (McWhorter Dr, Skidaway Island), Savannah, GA 31416-0687; (912) 356-2474. Interest in physical, chemical, geological, biological oceanography, especially estuaries, Gulf Stream. Maintains extensive library for onsite use. Answers inquiries, makes interlibrary loans.

14098. Southeastern Power Administration, Samuel Elbert Bldg, Elberton, GA 30635; (404) 283-3261. Interest in transmission, marketing of hydroelectric power; water resources development. Answers inquiries.

14099. Southern Association of Colleges & Schools Commission on Colleges, 795 Peachtree St NE, Atlanta, GA 30365; (404) 897-6127. Interest in regional accreditation of colleges and universities in the South. Answers inquiries, publishes materials.

14100. Southern Forest Institute, 2900 Chamblee Tucker Rd, Bldg 5, Atlanta, GA 30341; (404) 451-7106. Interest in forest conservation, forest products industries of southern U.S. Maintains library, answers inquiries, provides photos.

14102. Southern Regional Education Board, 1340 Spring St NW, Atlanta, GA 30309; (404) 875-9211. Interest in education in the South: financing, legislation, statistics, regional cooperation. Publishes reports, newsletters; provides consulting and analyses, primarily for key officials of member states.

14105. U.S. Army National Infantry Museum, Fort Benning, GA 31905; (404) 545-2958. Collects, preserves, exhibits artifacts (weapons, uniforms,manuscripts, insignia) to record history of U.S. Army Infantry since 1755. Answers inquiries; permits onsite use of collections, archives, library.

14106. USDA National Peanut Research Laboratory, Agricultural Research Service, USDA, 1011 Forrester Dr, SE, Dawson, GA 31742; (912) 995-4441. Researches peanut quality, handling, environmental aspects. Has

small reference collection of books, periodicals, reports; answers inquiries.

14108. USDA Southeast Poultry Research Laboratory, Agricultural Research Service, USDA, 934 College Station Rd, Athens, GA 30605; (404) 546-3434. Researches characterization, definition, detection, prevention of poultry diseases. Maintains library, answers inquiries, distributes reprints. No diagnostic services provided.

14109. USDA Stored-Product Insects Research & Development Laboratory, Agricultural Research Service, USDA, P.O. Box 22909, Savannah, GA 31403; (912) 233-7981. Researches biology, chemistry, environmental aspects, and control (physical, pesticides) of stored-product insects. Maintains 22,000-vol library. Answers inquiries, provides consulting services.

14110. Vermiculite Association, c/o Leslie W. Thornbury, Dir, American Vermiculite Corp., 52 Executive Park South, Atlanta, GA 30329; (404) 321-7994. Interest in research into vermiculite products and new uses of vermiculite. Provides general reference and consulting services, distributes publications, conducts seminars. Services free.

14111. Voter Education Project, 52 Fairlie St NW, Atlanta, GA 30303; (404) 522-7495. Interest in nonpartisan voter registration and education, promotion of minority political participation, primarily in South. Provides general reference services, conducts seminars, awards grants, distributes publications. Services free, except publications.

14112. Yerkes Regional Primate Research Center, Emory Univ, Atlanta, GA 30322; (404) 329-7764. Interest in primate anatomy, physiology, and behavior. Has library for onsite use by qualified researchers. Provides limited reference services, disseminates reprints of articles by center personnel.

Hawaii

15001. Bernice P. Bishop Museum Library, P.O. Box 19000A (1525 Bernice St), Honolulu, HI 96819. Devoted to archeology, ethnology, linguistics, voyages and explorations, history, bibliography, and biological sciences of Pacific region. Answers reference questions as time permits, provides limited copying services, permits onsite reference by students and researchers.

15002. Cancer Research Center of Hawaii, 1236 Lauhala St, Honolulu, HI 96813; (808) 548-8415. Conducts comprehensive research in epidemiology, basic science, clinical science, and cancer control. Answers inquiries, conducts seminars for health professionals, operates cancer communications network and cancer info line. Services generally free.

15003. Chamber of Commerce of Hawaii, 735 Bishop St, Honolulu, HI 96813; (808) 531-4111. Source of comprehensive info on Hawaii, including economics, commerce, industry, business, agriculture, trade, fisheries, manufacturing, and marketing. Provides reference services for free or a fee as time and personnel allow.

15004. Chinese History Center, 111 North King St, Room 410, Honolulu, HI 96817; (808) 521-5948. Interested in history of Chinese in Hawaii. Answers inquiries, provides advisory, reference, literature-searching, current-awareness, and translation services; makes direct and interlibrary loans. Services provided at cost to some, free to others.

15005. East-West Center, East-West Center, 1777 East-West Rd, Honolulu, HI 96848; (808) 944-7555. Interest in relationships of food, energy, and raw materials among nations, family planning. Provides advisory and reference services; evaluates, analyzes data.

15006. Environmental Center, Univ of Hawaii, Crawford 317, 2550 Campus Rd, Honolulu, HI 96822; (808) 948-7361. Coordinates service efforts related to ecological relationships, natural resources, and environmental quality, with special relation to human needs and social institutions in Hawaii. Provides free advisory and current-awareness services, makes referrals.

15007. Hawaii Volcanoes National Park, HI 96718; (808) 967-7311. Provides info on large, active, major volcanoes; geology, plants, and animals in Kilauea crater area; volcanology; seismology. Answers inquiries, provides consulting services, permits onsite use of collections.

15008. Hawaiian Academy of Science, P.O. Box 19073 (150 South Vineyard Blvd), Honolulu, HI 96819; (808) 537-1330. Nonprofit society of scientists and laymen interested in advancement of science and science education in Hawaii. Permits onsite use of collection; sponsors science fairs, visiting scientists' programs, student science seminars, and occasional symposia and lectures. Membership open to anyone.

15009. Hawaiian Botanical Society, c/o Botany Dept, Univ of Hawaii, 3190 Maile Way, Honolulu, HI 96822; (808) 948-8369. Interest in plant life, horticulture in Hawaiian Islands. Answers inquiries, makes referrals, distributes publications. Services free, primarily for members, but others assisted.

15010. Hawaiian Historical Society, 560 Kawaiahao St, Honolulu, HI 96813; (808) 537-6271. Interest in history of Hawaii and Pacific. Provides reference, research, and copying services, permits onsite use of collections. Services free, except research and copying.

15011. Hawaiian Sugar Planters' Association, 99-193 Aiea Heights Dr, Aiea, HI 96701; (808) 487-5561. Provides info on cultivation and manufacture of sugar cane and its by-products. Answers questions, provides limited reference services, makes interlibrary loans. Services primarily for research staff and members of assn; others must have permission from director.

15012. Historic Hawaii Foundation, P.O. Box 1658 (119 Merchant St), Honolulu, HI 96806; (808) 537-9564. Provides reference services and info on architectural history of Hawaii, historic preservation, rehabilitation, adaptive reuse, and restoration; registration process for historic bldgs, more. Info, referrals free; a fee for workshops.

15014. Institute of Tropical Agriculture and Human Resources, Univ of Hawaii, 3050 Maile Way, Honolulu, HI 96822; (808) 948-8131. Interest in general and tropical agriculture, food science and human nutrition, animal science, fashion design, textiles, and merchandizing, human development, home economics, more. Provides consulting services, computerized literature-searching services.

15015. International Tsunami Information Center, P.O. Box 50027, Honolulu, HI 96850; (808) 546-2847. Seeks to ensure effective dissemination and collection of tsunami warnings and info, research, and exchange of scientific data and personnel among nations participating in Intl Tsunami Warning System in Pacific Ocean. Provides advisory services.

15016. James K. K. Look Laboratory of Oceanographic Engineering, Dept of Ocean Engineering, Univ of Hawaii, 811 Olomehani St, Honolulu, HI 96813; (808) 533-6412. Specializes in ocean engineering research and education, water waves, wave forecasting, shore protection, etc. Provides advisory and consulting services, permits onsite use of collections. Some services provided free on exchange-of-info basis, other services provided at cost.

15017. Law of the Sea Institute, William S. Richardson School of Law, Univ of Hawaii, 2515 Dole St, Honolulu, HI 96822; (808) 948-6750. Interested in intl law of sea, including naval and strategic aspects, intl fisheries policy, ocean policy and politics. Answers inquiries, provides referrals, sponsors annual conference and regional workshops, permits onsite use of collection.

15018. Life of the Land, 250 South Hotel St, Room 211, Honolulu, HI 96813; (808) 521-1300. Nonprofit environmental research and action org concerned with environmental impacts of uncontrolled development, population growth, and governmental inaction. Answers inquiries, permits onsite use of materials. Services free, primarily for Hawaiian citizens, but others assisted.

15019. Natural Energy Institute, Univ of Hawaii at Manoa, 2540 Dole St, Honolulu, HI 96822; (808) 948-8890. Promotes research, development, demonstration of natural energy resources in Hawaii and ways of helping state achieve energy self-sufficiency. Provides advisory, reference services and info on R&D in progress; conducts seminars, workshops. Most services free.

15020. Oceanic Institute, Makapuu Point, Waimanalo, HI 96795; (808) 259-7951. Nonprofit org specializing in

R&D of aquacultural opportunities and marine ecology. Answers inquiries, makes referrals. Services provided free to collaborating scientists. Pamphlets available on request. Extensive services subject to fee.

15021. Outdoor Circle, 200 North Vineyard Blvd, Room 502, Honolulu, HI 96817; (808) 521-0074. Dedicated to civic improvement. Interested in state billboard regulations and county sign regulations, beautification, urban blight control. Answers inquiries, makes referrals.

15022. Pacific Biomedical Research Center, Univ of Hawaii, 1993 East West Rd, Honolulu, HI 96822; (808) 948-8838. Interest in cell biology, neurobiology, and comparative learning. Provides collaborative and contractual research services. Staff members provide some consulting services on an individual basis to outside, profitmaking orgs for a fee.

15023. Pacific Fisheries Development Foundation, P.O. Box 2359 (335 Merchant St, Room 248), Honolulu, HI 96804; (808) 548-3469. Involved in development of fisheries resources in U.S. Pacific. Answers inquiries, provides advisory, consulting, reference, and copying services, evaluates data. Services provided at cost to outside users.

15024. Pacific Science Association, P.O. Box 17801 (Bishop Museum, 1525 Bernice St), Honolulu, HI 96817; (808) 847-3511. Intl org promoting study of scientific problems relating to Pacific region, particularly those affecting prosperity and well-being of Pacific peoples. Answers inquiries, conducts seminars and intl congresses. Services free, except publications.

15025. Pacific Submarine Museum, U.S. Naval Submarine Base, Pearl Harbor, HI 96860; (808) 471-0632. Dedicated to submarine history, warfare, research, underwater rescue, salvage, development of submersibles, World War II history. Provides advisory and other services. Services free and available to anyone by reservation.

15026. Pacific Telecommunications Council, 1110 Univ Ave, Suite 308, Honolulu, HI 96826; (808) 941-3789. Provides exchange of info, ideas, and viewpoints between suppliers, carriers, users, govts, academics, and intl bodies of telecommunications users in Pacific area. Answers inquiries, conducts conferences, seminars, and workshops. Services provided for a fee.

15027. Population Genetics Laboratory, Office of Research Administration, Univ of Hawaii, 1980 East West Rd, Honolulu, HI 96822; (808) 948-7186. Conducts research, analyzes human genetic data. Offers seminars, distributes publications, provides magnetic tape services. Services provided at cost by prior agreement.

15028. Tropical Fruit and Vegetable Research Laboratory, Agricultural Research Service, USDA, P.O. Box 2280 (2727 Woodlawn Dr), Honolulu, HI 96804; (808) 988-2158. Conducts fundamental and applied research for controlling and eradicating infestations of three tephritid fruit flies in Hawaii. Answers inquiries, provides consulting services, distributes publications. Services free.

15029. Videodocumentary Clearinghouse, Harbor Square, Suite 2201, 700 Richards St, Honolulu, HI 96813; (808) 523-2882. Provides videotaped documentaries depicting leaders in business and administration discussing current thinking and forecasts of future developments. Tapes and workshops for prospective editors and producers of similar video documentaries. Fee for services.

15030. Waikiki Aquarium, 2777 Kalakaua Ave, Honolulu, HI 96815; (808) 923-9741. Interest in Indo-Pacific marine biology, aquariology, marine education, research on sharks and fish larvae, Hawaiian cultural relationships with sea. Identifies area marine specimens, conducts guided tours (Japanese and English). Aquarium open to public daily.

15031. Water Resources Research Center, Univ of Hawaii, 2540 Dole St, Honolulu, HI 96822; (808) 948-7847. Interest in water resources of Hawaiian Islands, including hydrologic, engineering, and social aspects, precipitation and storms, soil-water relationships, more. Provides consulting aand bibliographic services, makes referrals, permits onsite reference.

Idaho

16002. Appaloosa Horse Club, P.O. Box 8403, Moscow, ID 83843; (208) 882-5578. Interest in Appaloosa horses. Maintains small collection of books. Publishes monthly magazine and several technical books. Answers inquiries, provides advisory services. Services generally free.

16004. Council of Graphological Societies, HCR-01, Box 208A, Naples, ID 83847; (208) 267-5818. Promotes research in graphology and conducts educational programs for members. Individual members and member groups maintain collections that may be accessed. Answers inquiries and makes referrals free, conducts seminars and workshops for a fee.

16005. Department of Veterinary Medicine, Univ of Idaho, Moscow, ID 83843; (208) 885-7081. Concerned with rehabilitation of sick and injured raptors. Answers inquiries, makes referrals, provides advisory and consulting services. Services free if used for educational purposes, otherwise provided at cost.

16006. Energy Inc. Technical Information Services, Box 736 (One Energy Dr), Idaho Falls, ID 83402; (208) 529-1000 ext 266. Interest in nuclear engineering and computer sciences. Maintains collection of 1,500 books, 150,000 reports on microfiche, and related materials. Makes loans, answers inquiries, provides copying services. Permits onsite use of collections.

16007. Forest, Wildlife, and Range Experiment Station, Univ of Idaho, Moscow, ID 83843; (208) 885-6442. Interst in forestry, wildlife and range management. Has small reference collection of journals and reports, series of station notes, bulletins, technical reports. Answers technical inquiries, provides consulting services.

16011. Idaho National Engineering Lab, Technical Library, P.O. Box 1625 (Univ Pl), Idaho Falls, ID 83415; (208) 526-1196. Furthers energy-related research conducted at Natl Engineering Lab. Maintains collection of 675,000 technical reports, permits onsite use of collections and interlibrary loans. Literature searches provided only for INEL personnel.

16012. Idaho Park Foundation, 1020 West Franklin St, Boise, ID 83702; (208) 344-7141. Solicits gifts of property having park, recreation, or open space potential. Publishes land trust management studies, materials on grant writing and nonprofit fundraising. Answers inquiries, makes referrals, provides advisory services.

16013. Idaho State Historical Society, 610 North Julia Davis Dr, Boise, ID 83702-7695; (208) 334-3356 (Library and Archives). Archival holdings of Idaho and Northwest history. Museum houses archaeological specimens and historical artifacts. Publishes quarterly historical journal and related materials, makes interlibrary loans, permits onsite use of collections.

16014. Idaho State Library, 325 West State St, Boise, ID 83702; (208) 334-2150. Research collection supports Idaho govt, history, the Northwest. Answers brief inquiries, provides consulting services, makes referrals, permits interlibrary loans. Services primarily for state agencies, public libraries.

16015. Idaho Water Resources Research Institute, Univ of Idaho, Moscow, ID 83843; (208) 885-6429. Interest in problems related to water resources. Maintains collection of related materials. Publishes technical reports, info bulletins, annual report; answers inquiries, makes referrals; provides consulting services; permits onsite use of collections.

16016. Idaho Wildlife Federation, P.O. Box 371, Meridian, ID 83642; (208) 888-9492. Interest in conservation, aesthetic appreciation, and restoration of wildlife and other natural resources. Publishes bimonthly newspaper and technical reports, answers inquiries, makes referrals, provides advisory services, conducts seminars. Services free.

16017. International Clarinet Society, Box 8099, Pocatello, ID 83209; (208) 236-3108. Supports projects benefitting clarinet performance. Library contains over 1,700 titles, scores, and parts. Answers inquiries, makes referrals, conducts seminars, permits onsite use of collections. Services free to membership, which is open.

16018. Postharvest Institute for Perishables Information Center, Library Room 314, Univ of Idaho, Moscow, ID 83843; (208) 885-7059. Interest in studies of postharvest commodities, with focus on developing countries and appropriate technology. Maintains collections of 8,000 related documents. Reference and document delivery services avilable. Provides teams of experts for consultation.

16019. Snake River Regional Studies Center, College of Idaho, Caldwell, ID 83605; (208) 459-5214. Interest in environment, human, and natural resources of Snake River Basin. Maintains bibliography of 5,000 info sources. Answers inquiries, provides consulting services. Fees may be charged for extensive services.

16020. Western Regional Environmental Education Council, c/o Richard Kay, Idaho Dept of Education, L.B. Jordan Bldg, Boise, ID 83720; (208) 334-2281. Develops and coordinates interdisciplinary environmental education programs. Publishes technical reports, directories, curriculum publications; conducts in-service training for members. Services primarily for schools and community agencies.

16021. Wilderness Education Association, Route 1, Box 3400, Driggs, ID 83422; (208) 354-8384. Certifies leaders in outdoor-related fields. Publishes *Wilderness Handbook*, reviews, and training curriculum, conducts seminars and leadership training courses, answers inquiries, makes referrals free.

Illinois

17002. ARCO Metals Co. Technical Information Center, 3205 N Frontage Rd, Arlington Heights, IL 60004; (312) 577-5527. Answers inquiries on metallography, metallurgy; refers to other sources of info; permits onsite use of collection by univ, industrial personnel by appointment only.

17003. ASA Education Foundation, 221 N LaSalle St, Ste 738, Chicago, IL 60601; (312) 236-4082. Answers inquiries on training opportunities in plumbing, heating, cooling, and piping industry. Provides info on research, conducts workshops. Fee for services.

17004. Academy for Implants and Transplants, 1737 W Howard St, Chicago, IL 60626; (312) 764-0350. Promotes art and science of implant and transplant dentistry. Provides advisory, consulting services; conducts seminars, workshops. Services free.

17005. Academy of General Dentistry, 211 E Chicago Ave, Chicago, IL 60611; (312) 440-4308. Represents interests of dentists. Provides microform services, conducts seminars and workshops, distributes dental health info to media. Services at cost.

17006. Accent on Information, P.O. Box 700 (Gillum Rd and High Dr), Bloomington, IL 61701; (309) 378-2961. Nonprofit org making living easier for handicapped. Publishes books, answers inquiries free, provides literature-searching services for a fee.

17007. Accreditation Association for Ambulatory Health Care, Westmoreland Bldg, Old Orchard Rd, Skokie, IL

60077; (312) 676-9610. Provides assistance to agencies that license ambulatory health care orgs. Conducts seminars, training programs. Fee for some services.

17008. Adhesives Manufacturers Association, 111 E Wacker Dr, Chicago, IL 60601; (312) 644-6610. Interest in paper converting and packaging assembly adhesives. Answers inquiries, refers inquirers to other sources of info free.

17009. Air Diffusion Council, 230 N Michigan Ave, Ste 1200, Chicago, IL 60601; (312) 372-9800. Publishes standards and specifications, textbook, press releases on air circulation, airflow regulators and distribution hardware. Answers inquiries, makes referrals.

17010. Air Force Office of Public Affairs, Military Airlift Command, Scott Air Force Base, IL 62225-5001; (618) 256-5309. Helps military airlift commanders maintain morale and effectiveness of personnel; manages internal and public info programs. Answers inquiries free.

17011. Air Force Weather Service Technical Library, Environmental Technical Applications Center, Scott Air Force Base, IL 62225; (618) 256-4044. Collects info on how atmospheric environment affects military plans. Provides advisory, reference, abstracting, copying services; permits onsite use of collection. Services available to Dept of Defense personnel.

17012. Air Movement and Control Association, 30 W Univ Dr, Arlington Heights, IL 60004; (312) 394-0150. Answers inquiries free on air circulation equipment. Publishes standards, ratings guides, directory of licensed products; lab test facility available.

17013. All-America Selections, 628 Exec Dr, Willowbook, IL 60521; (312) 655-0010. Evaluates newly bred varieties for home garden use. Answers inquiries, provides free general reference services, lends materials.

17014. Alliance of American Insurers, 1501 Woodfield Rd, Ste 400 West, Schaumburg, IL 60195-4980; (312) 490-8500. Distributes pamphlets on developments in property-casualty insurance; makes available info to news media, govt, regulatory sources. Training, audiovisual materials available for a fee.

17015. Alternative Schools Network, 1105 W Lawrence Ave, Rm 210, Chicago, IL 60640; (312) 728-4030. Acts as clearinghouse for alternative schools; assists in presenting grant proposals. Provides advisory, reference services; conducts seminars, workshops; permits onsite use of collection.

17016. Alzheimer's Disease and Related Disorders Association, 70 E Lake St, Chicago, IL 60601; (312) 853-3060; (800) 621-0379. Supports research on Alzheimer's disease; organizes support groups; advises govt agencies. Provides advisory, reference services; conducts seminars. Services generally free.

17017. America's Society of Separated and Divorced Men, 575 Keep St, Elgin, IL 60120; (312) 695-2200. Intl org that assists men going through separation or divorce.

Provides advisory, consulting, reference services; makes referrals to pro-male attorneys.

17018. American Academy of Pediatrics, P.O. Box 927 (141 Northwest Point Blvd), Elk Grove, IL 60007; (312) 228-5005, (800) 433-9016. Publishes reports, bibliographies, periodicals on pediatrics, continuing medical education. Answers inquiries; provides consulting, limited reference services.

17019. American Academy of Periodontology, 211 E Chicago Ave, Rm 924, Chicago, IL 60611; (312) 787-5518. Publishes registry of periodontics education, reprints, slides with tapes. Provides consulting services to professional groups, provides dental referral services. Most services free.

17020. American Academy of Physical Medicine and Rehabilitation, 30 N Michigan Ave, Ste 922, Chicago, IL 60602; (312) 236-9512. Publishes standards on physical medicine, rehabilitation. Provides advisory services; conducts seminars, workshops. Most services free, available to health professionals.

17021. American Architectural Manufacturers Association, 2700 River Rd, Ste 118, Des Plaines, IL 60018; (312) 782-8256. Acts as technical resource center by maintaining library containing voluntary specifications. Publishes certification program directory, consumer info literature, technical reports.

17022. American Assembly for Men in Nursing, c/o Coll of Nursing, Rush Univ, 600 S Paulina, 474-H, Chicago, IL 60612; (312) 942-7117. Provides info pertinent to male nurses; recruits men into profession. Answers inquiries, conducts seminars and workshops. Services primarily to members, but others assisted.

17023. American Association for Automotive Medicine, 40 Second Ave, Arlington Heights, IL 60005; (312) 640-8440. Answers inquiries on driver safety precautions. Publishes proceedings of annual meetings, conducts seminars, suggests speakers for interested groups.

17024. American Association for Laboratory Animal Science, 210 N Hammes Ave, Ste 205, Joliet, IL 60435; (815) 729-1161. Publishes directory of certified technologists; lends slides; conducts certification program, seminars, workshops.

17025. American Association for the Study of Headache, 5252 N Western Ave, Chicago, IL 60625; (312) 878-5558. Answers inquiries; provides consulting, reference services; conducts seminars; analyzes data on causes of headache. Services to physicians, dentists, and Ph.D's only.

17026. American Association of Endodontists, 211 E Chicago Ave, Ste 830, Chicago, IL 60611. Answers inquiries on endodontics (root canal therapy); has library of classical textbooks on endodontics; publishes journal, pamphlets.

17027. American Association of Hospital Dentists, 211 E Chicago Ave, Chicago, IL 60611; (312) 440-2661. Org of dentists treating special patients. Publishes directories, provides consulting services, conducts seminars. Services generally free.

17028. American Association of Individual Investors, 612 N Michigan Ave, Ste 317, Chicago, IL 60611; (312) 280-0170. Answers inquiries about financial planning and investment. Conducts seminars and workshops, provides info on current research. Fee for services.

17029. American Association of Law Libraries, 53 W Jackson Blvd, Chicago, IL 60604; (312) 939-4764. Publishes proceedings, statutes, manuals dealing with law library administration. Provides info on educational opportunities for law librarians; sponsors institutes, workshops.

17030. American Association of Medical Assistants, 20 N Wacker Dr, Ste 1575, Chicago, IL 60606; (312) 899-1500. Org representing allied health profession. Publishes newsletters, monographs, reports; distributes accredited program list; helps set up postsecondary medical assisting programs.

17031. American Association of Neurological Surgeons, c/o Carl H. Hauber, Exec Dir, 22 S Washington St, Ste 100, Park Ridge, IL 60068; (312) 692-9500. Answers inquiries on neurological surgery, pain control; head and spinal trauma. Publishes bibliographies, periodicals.

17032. American Association of Neuroscience Nurses, 22 S Washington St, No. 203, Park Ridge, IL 60068. Conducts workshops in neuroscience nursing; provides reference services; operates speaker's bureau. Most services free.

17033. American Association of Nurse Anesthetists, 216 Higgins Rd, Park Ridge, IL 60068; (312) 692-7050. Advances science of anesthesiology. Develops educational programs, provides consulting services, evaluates data. Most services free.

17034. American Association of Oral and Maxillofacial Surgeons, 211 E Chicago Ave, Ste 930, Chicago, IL 60611; (312) 642-6446. Publishes pamphlets on oral surgery; conducts meetings open to health pros for a fee; provides advisory, reference services. Most services free.

17035. American Association of School Librarians, 50 E Huron St, Chicago, IL 60611; (312) 944-6780. Improves library media services in elementary, secondary schools. Provides consulting, reference services, short lists of literature citations in response to specific inquiries.

17036. American Bar Association, Information Services, 750 N Lake Shore Dr, Chicago, IL 60611; (312) 988-5158. Answers brief inquiries, publishes journal, makes referrals to lawyer referral agencies. Does not give legal advice, do research on legal questions, or recommend attorneys.

17037. American Bar Association, Section of Family Law, 1155 E 60th St, Chicago, IL 60637; (312) 947-4000. Publishes quarterly journal on family law, including divorce law; answers inquiries. Services to ABA members, law students, scholars.

17038. American Bar Association, Standing Committee on Lawyer Referral Service, 1155 E 60th St, Chicago, IL 60637; (312) 947-3971. Provides advice to help state, local bar assns organize, improve lawyer referral services. Publishes natl directory, answers inquiries. Fee charged for promotional materials.

17039. American Bar Association, Traffic Court Program, Judicial Administration Div, 1155 E 60th St, Chicago, IL 60637; (312) 947-3981. Provides films on traffic court procedure; answers inquiries; conducts seminars, workshops; permits onsite use of collection. Most services free.

17040. American Bar Foundation, 750 N Lake Shore Dr, Chicago, IL 60611; (312) 988-6500. Publishes newsletter on current research, monographs, reports on administration of justice. Newsletter and annual report free on written request.

17041. American Board of Medical Specialties, One American Plaza, Ste 805, Evanston, IL 60201; (312) 491-9091. Interest in standards used to certify physicians. Publishes directories by specialty; provides free consulting, reference services.

17042. American Board of Orthopaedic Surgery, 444 N Michigan Ave, Chicago, IL 60611; (312) 822-9572. Conducts investigations, examinations of voluntary candidates in orthopaedic surgery. Publishes rules and procedures, answers inquiries.

17043. American Bryological and Lichenological Society, c/o Barbara Crandall-Stotler, Secty-Treas, Southern Ill. Univ, Carbondale, IL 62901. Answers inquiries free on mosses, lichens, liverworts, hornworts. Publishes journal, books, monographs; refers inquirers to other sources of info.

17044. American Can Co., Technical Information Center, Barrington Technical Center, 433 N Northwest Hwy, Barrington, IL 60010; (312) 381-1900 ext 433. Concerned with food canning and processing, materials engineering, machinery design. Provides access to computerized data bases, makes interlibrary loans.

17045. American College of Chest Physicians, c/o Alfred Soffer, MD, Exec Dir, 911 Busse Hwy, Park Ridge, IL 60068; (312) 698-2200. Publishes numerous quarterly brochures on medical education and research in diseases of chest. Answers brief inquiries from physicians, makes referrals to one of College's committees.

17046. American College of Legal Medicine, 213 W Institute Pl, Ste 412, Chicago, IL 60610; (312) 440-0080. Does research in medicine and law, answers inquiries, conducts seminars. Most questions answered free; other services for a fee.

17047. American College of Radiology, 20 N Wacker Dr, Rm 1660, Chicago, IL 60606; (312) 236-4963. Answers inquiries on radiology, including radiation hazards and protection, technician training, research programs. Publishes monthly bulletin, provides consulting services.

17048. American College of Surgeons, c/o C. Rollins Hanlon, MD, Dir, 55 E Erie St, Chicago, IL 60611; (312) 664-4050. Owns rare books on history of surgery; publishes catalog of films; provides reference, referral services free to surgeons, researchers. Collection must be used on premises.

17049. American Concrete Pavement Association, 2625 Clearbrook Dr, Arlington Heights, IL 60005; (312) 640-1020. Publishes newsletter, technical bulletins, reports on design, construction, maintenance of concrete pavement. Provides free advisory services.

17050. American Congress of Rehabilitation Medicine, 30 N Michigan Ave, Ste 922, Chicago, IL 60602; (312) 236-9512. Answers inquiries, provides consulting services, conducts seminars and postgraduate courses. Services to physicians, paramedical personnel.

17051. American Council on Industrial Arts Teacher Education, c/o Dr Everett N. Israel, Secty, Industrial Technology Dept, 210 Turner Hall, Ill. State Univ, Normal, IL 61761; (309) 438-3661. Answers inquiries on industrial arts teacher education; publishes annual directory, monographs; makes referrals to other sources of info. Services at cost to nonmembers.

17052. American Council on Pharmaceutical Education, 311 W Superior St, Chicago, IL 60610; (312) 664-3575. Answers inquiries on accreditation of colleges and providers of continuing education in pharmacy, makes referrals to other sources of info.

17053. American Dairy Science Association, 309 W Clark St, Champaign, IL 61820; (217) 356-3182. Publishes monthly journal on dairy science (available by subscription), answers inquiries. Services primarily for members, but will assist others.

17054. American Dental Association, 211 E Chicago Ave, Chicago, IL 60611; (312) 440-2500. Lends books, journals on dentistry to members free to nonmembers for nominal charge. Provides consulting services, publishes dentists' desk reference book.

17055. American Dental Hygienists' Association, 444 N Michigan Ave, Chicago, IL 60611; (312) 440-8900. Answers inquiries; publishes standards, specifications; provides advisory and reference services, info on research; conducts seminars, workshops. Services for dental hygienists at cost.

17056. American Dental Society of Anesthesiology, 211 E Chicago Ave, Ste 948, Chicago, IL 60611. Publishes journal, newsletter on anesthesiology in dentistry, including psychological approach to patient. Answers brief inquiries, provides advisory services, makes referrals.

17057. American Dialect Society, c/o Allan Metcalf, Exec Secty, English Dept, MacMurray Coll, Jacksonville, IL 62650 ; (217) 245-6151 ext 297. Preparing dictionary of American regional English. Holds collection of proverbs; publishes journal, monographs; answers inquiries. Membership open.

17058. American Dietetic Association, 430 N Michigan Ave, Chicago, IL 60611; (312) 280-5000. Provides direction for research on health through nutrition. Conducts seminars, workshops; serves as accrediting agency for dietetic programs. Fee for services.

17059. American Divorce Association of Men, 1008 W White Oak St, Arlington Heights, IL 60005; (312) 870-1040. Provides advisory, reference services; offers legal consultation and mediation; makes referrals to pro-male attorneys. Services to members.

17060. American Dry Milk Institute, 130 N Franklin St, Chicago, IL 60606; (312) 782-4888. Coordinates dry milk industry activities, including research. Provides advisory, reference, abstracting services; conducts seminars, workshops. Services free.

17062. American Egg Board, 1460 Renaissance Dr, Park Ridge, IL 60068; (312) 296-7044. Sponsored by egg producers, provides consumer education, promotion. Answers inquiries, distributes publications at cost.

17063. American Fabricating Institute of Technology, 7811 N Alpine Rd, Rockford, IL 61111-3199; (815) 654-1902. Answers inquiries on education on production, research, management of metal manufacturing. Provides reference services, conducts seminars and workshops. Most services free.

17065. American Federation of Small Business, 407 S Dearborn St, Chicago, IL 60605; (312) 427-0206. Publishes data compilations on small business, govt regulations; publishes petitions to Congress. Answers inquiries, evaluates data. Services free.

17066. American Foundrymen's Society, Golf and Wolf Rds, Des Plaines, IL 60016; (312) 824-0181. Answers inquiries; provides library on cast metals technology; publishes abstracts, indexes, bibliographies, pamphlets; provides literature-searching, duplication services.

17067. American Hardboard Association, 887-B Wilmette Rd, Palatine, IL 60067; (312) 934-8800. Distributes various publications, such as standards and specifications, on hardboard. Answers inquiries, provides single copies of all literature free on request.

17068. American Hardware Manufacturers Association, 931 N Plum Grove Rd, Schaumburg, IL 60195; (312) 885-1025. Answers inquiries on hardware products, antitrust developments, state taxation of interstate commerce, foreign trade; makes referrals; permits on-site reference by request.

17069. American Home Lighting Institute, 435 N Michigan Ave, Ste 1717, Chicago, IL 60611; (312) 644-0828. Publishes guidelines for residential lighting, directory of manufacturers; answers inquiries; provides reference services. Fee for some services.

17070. American Hospital Association, 840 N Lake Shore Dr, Chicago, IL 60611; (312) 280-6000. Interest in health care administration. Prepares literature index, bibliography; offers consultation, general reference services. Services to members for a fee.

17071. American Hospital Management Systems Society, 840 N Lake Shore Dr, Chicago, IL 60611; (312) 280-6023. Provides current-awareness services on hospital management systems. Publishes annual conference proceedings, conducts seminars, answers inquiries free.

17072. American Institute of Real Estate Appraisers, 430 N Michigan Ave, Chicago, IL 60611; (312) 329-8559. Interest in real estate valuation. Publishes books, reports, bibliographies, pamphlets; answers inquiries; conducts courses, seminars, workshops.

17073. American Institute of Steel Construction, 400 N Michigan Ave, Chicago, IL 60611; (312) 670-2400. Answers inquiries on fabricated structural steel and its application to buildings; makes referrals to other sources of info; provides reference, abstracting and indexing services.

17074. American Judicature Society, 25 E Washington St, Ste 1600, Chicago, IL 60602; (312) 558-6900. Answers inquiries, publishes bibliographies and reports on the administration of justice. Provides consulting, reference services; permits onsite use of collection. Services at cost.

17076. American Library Association, Resources and Technical Services Division, 50 E Huron St, Chicago, IL 60611; (312) 944-6780. Interest in acquisition, cataloging, preservation of library materials. Publishes quarterly journal, answers inquiries, provides consulting services, makes referrals.

17078. American Marketing Association, 250 S Wacker Dr, Chicago, IL 60606; (312) 648-0536. Publishes marketing newsletter, research journal, annual proceedings, bibliographies, monographs; provides reference services. Services free as time permits.

17079. American Meat Science Association, 444 N Michigan Ave, 18th Fl, Chicago, IL 60611; (312) 467-5520. Publishes conference proceedings, provides advisory services, conducts seminars and workshops, permits onsite use of collection. Fee for services.

17080. American Medical Association, Division of Library and Archival Services, 535 N Dearborn St, Chicago, IL 60610-4377; (312) 645-4818. Provides info on history, sociology of medicine, medical research. Provides literature searches, loan materials. Services for members; others may use library on approval of application.

17081. American Medical Association, Food and Nutrition Program, 535 N Dearborn St, Chicago, IL 60610; (312) 645-5070. Publishes books, reports, pamphlets on clinical nutrition, nutrition education in medicine, food-borne illness; answers inquiries.

17082. American Medical Association, Human Behavior Program, 535 N Dearborn St, Chicago, IL 60610; (312) 645-5083. Publishes reports on psychiatry, mental

health, alcoholism and drug dependence; provides consulting, reference services, primarily to members and allied health groups.

17083. American Medical Record Association, 875 N Michigan Ave, Ste 1850, Chicago, IL 60611; (312) 787-2672. Improves medical record services in health facilities nationwide. Provides reference service, training, independent study program. Most services for a fee.

17084. American Medical Technologists, c/o Chester B. Dziekonski, Exec Dir, 710 Higgins Rd, Park Ridge, IL 60068; (312) 823-5169. Offers certification of clinical laboratory personnel. Answers inquiries free, conducts continuing education programs for a fee.

17085. American Music Conference, 1000 Skokie Blvd, Wilmette, IL 60091; (312) 251-1600. Promotes music, especially amateur participation, in home, school, church, community. Answers inquiries, provides consulting to orgs with related goals.

17087. American Nuclear Society, 555 N Kensington, Lagrange Park, IL 60525; (312) 352-6611. Operates info center on nuclear standards. Provides access to computerized data bases; publishes standards, monographs, reviews, journals on nuclear science, engineering, technology.

17088. American Occupational Medical Association, 2340 S Arlington Heights Rd, Arlington Heights, IL 60005; (312) 228-6850. Answers inquiries on occupational and preventive medicine; provides reference services.

17089. American Oil Chemists' Society, 508 S 6th St, Champaign, IL 61820; (217) 359-2344. Answers inquiries on industrial technology of fats, oils; dispenses standard supplies; conducts natl technical meeting, courses, intl conferences; certifies chemists.

17090. American Orthopaedic Society for Sports Medicine, 70 W Hubbard St, Ste 202, Chicago, IL 60610; (312) 644-2623. Answers inquiries on sports medicine education and research; conducts seminars, workshops; makes referrals to other sources of info. Fee for some services.

17091. American Osteopathic Association, 212 E Ohio St, Chicago, IL 60611; (312) 280-5800. Publishes directory of osteopathic physicians; provides consulting, reference services; prepares analyses; permits limited onsite use of collection by qualified researchers.

17092. American Osteopathic College of Rehabilitation Medicine, c/o Julie E. Pickett, Exec Asst, P.O. Box 6014, Evanston, IL 60204; (312) 491-0984. Answers inquiries, provides consulting services, conducts seminars on osteopathic medicine. Some services free to health professionals, rehab-related agencies.

17093. American Police Center and Museum, 1130 S Wabash Ave, Chicago, IL 60605; (312) 431-0005. Interest in history of police work. Displays police uniforms, artifacts, photographs. Free to public.

17095. American Prosthodontic Society, 919 N Michigan Ave, Ste 2108, Chicago, IL 60611; (312) 944-7618. Conducts seminars, workshops, annual two-day sessions on prosthodontics; distributes publications. Services at cost.

17096. American Protestant Health Association College of Chaplains, 1701 E Woodfield Rd, Ste 311, Schaumburg, IL 60195; (312) 843-2701. Promotes professional growth of chaplains through certification. Provides advisory and reference services, conducts seminars. Most services free.

17097. American Public Works Association, Information Service, 1313 E 60th St, Chicago, IL 60637; (312) 667-2200. Publishes reports, handbooks, journal on design, construction, maintenance, administration of public works; provides photocopies.

17098. American Rabbit Breeders Association, P.O. Box 426 (1925 S Main St), Bloomington, IL 61701; (309) 827-6623. Interest in rabbit industry. Publishes journal, show rules, cookbook; answers inquiries; provides advisory, reference services. Services free; membership open.

17099. American Railway Car Institute, Governors Office Park I, 20280 Governors Hwy, Ste 101, Olympia Fields, IL 60461; (312) 747-0511. Answers brief inquiries on economic and financial trends in railroad industry. Publishes statistical reports, makes referrals. Services primarily for members and affiliates.

17100. American Society for Concrete Construction, c/o George B. Southworth, Exec Dir, World of Concrete Center, Addison, IL 60101; (312) 543-2999. Publishes periodicals, books on construction with concrete; provides advisory, reference, abstracting, indexing services. Services for a fee to nonmembers.

17101. American Society for Hospital Engineering, 840 N Lake Shore Dr, Chicago, IL 60611; (312) 280-6144. Advances development of hospital engineering. Publishes conference papers, provides advisory and reference services, conducts seminars.

17102. American Society for Hospital Food Service Administrators, American Hospital Assn, 840 N Lake Shore Dr, Chicago, IL 60611; (312) 280-6416. Publishes manuals for health care institutions; conducts educational programs; permits onsite use of materials. Services to food service administrators.

17103. American Society for Hospital Marketing and Public Relations, American Hospital Association, 840 N Lake Shore Dr, Chicago, IL 60611; (312) 280-6359. Distributes info about hospital public relations. Provides advisory and reference services, conducts workshops, permits onsite use of collection. Services to public at cost.

17104. American Society for Hospital Materials Management, c/o Marcie Anthony, Dir, American Hospital Assn, 840 N Lake Shore Dr, Chicago, IL 60611; (312) 280-6137. Provides general reference services on hospital materials management, including purchasing, inventory, and distribution. Conducts seminars, workshops. Most services free to members.

17105. American Society for Hospital Personnel Administration, American Hospital Assn, 840 N Lake Shore Dr, Chicago, IL 60611; (312) 280-6434. Answers inquiries on management in health care institutions. Conducts seminars and workshops, makes referrals to other sources of info. Services at discount to members.

17106. American Society for Nursing Service Administrators, American Hospital Assn, 840 N Lake Shore Dr, Chicago, IL 60611; (312) 280-6409. Provides info on nursing administration. Provides advisory, reference services; conducts seminars, workshops; permits onsite use of collection. Services at cost.

17107. American Society of Anesthesiologists, Library Museum, 515 Busse Hwy, Park Ridge, IL 60068; (312) 825-5586. Interest in anesthesia. Provides reference, abstracting, indexing, copying services; holds rare books on history of anesthesia. Services at cost.

17108. American Society of Artists, P.O. Box 1326 (N Michigan Ave, Chicago), Palatine, IL 60078; (312) 751-2500. Provides reference services on arts and crafts; conducts lectures, demonstrations; helps purchase supplies; presents art and craft shows.

17109. American Society of Clinical Hypnosis, 2250 E Devon Ave, Ste 336, Des Plaines, IL 60018. Publishes journal, newsletter, abstracts on clinical uses of hypnosis; answers brief inquiries; makes referrals; provides short lists of literature citations.

17110. American Society of Clinical Pathologists, 2100 W Harrison St, Chicago, IL 60612; (312) 738-1336. Publishes journal on clinical pathology, manuals, reference volumes, video cassettes; provides news to media; distributes brochures. Reference library available to members, scientists.

17111. American Society of Contemporary Medicine and Surgery, 211 E Chicago Ave, Chicago, IL 60611; (312) 787-3335. Provides conferences, seminars, audiovisuals on medical profession; answers inquiries. Services only to physicians and persons in related fields.

17112. American Society of Contemporary Ophthalmology, 211 E Chicago Ave, Chicago, IL 60611; (312) 787-3335. Provides continuing education to ophthalmologists through lectures, conferences, workshops, seminars, publications, audiovisuals; operates computerized info network.

17113. American Society of Dentistry for Children, 211 E Chicago Ave, Ste 920, Chicago, IL 60611; (312) 943-1244. Promotes dental health of children by dispensing info. Provides advisory services; conducts seminars, workshops. Most services free to health professionals.

17114. American Society of Golf Course Architects, 221 N LaSalle St, Chicago, IL 60601; (312) 372-7090. Answers inquiries on golf course architecture. Publishes brochures, provides free reference and literature-searching services.

17115. American Society of Lubrication Engineers, 838 Busse Hwy, Park Ridge, IL 60068; (312) 825-5536. Publishes monthly journal on lubrication engineering, with index in January issues; makes referrals to other sources of info.

17116. American Society of Neuroradiology, c/o Peter E. Weinberg, MD, Secty, 1415 W 22nd St, Ste 1150, Oak Brook, IL 60521. Publishes neuroradiology journal, placement listing of institutions needing neuroradiologists; answer inquiries. Services free, but limited.

17117. American Society of Plastic and Reconstructive Surgeons, 233 N Michigan Ave, Ste 1900, Chicago, IL 60601; (312) 856-1818. Answers inquiries on plastic and reconstructive surgery free; conducts seminars, workshops for a fee (restricted to doctors and those in associated fields such as medical research).

17118. American Society of Safety Engineers, 1800 E Oakton St, Des Plaines, IL 60018-2187; (312) 692-4121. Provides info for professionals in accident prevention fields; refers inquirers to safety engineering consultants when technical questions require considerable research on specialized area.

17119. American Society of Transplant Surgeons, 716 Lee St, Des Plaines, IL 60016; (312) 824-5700. Encourages info exchange to promote clinical transplantation. Provides consulting, reference services; conducts seminars. Services free.

17120. American Sod Producers Association, 4415 W Harrison St, Ste 309-C, Hillside, IL 60162; (312) 449-2890. National assn that seeks to improve production of better quality sod and to promote proper use of sod. Answers inquiries, distributes publications. Many services free.

17121. American Spinal Injury Association, 250 E Superior, Rm 619, Chicago, IL 60611; (312) 908-3425. Provides forum for exchange of info among physicians treating spinal cord injury. Provides consulting services, info on research; conducts seminars. Most services free.

17122. American Student Dental Association, 211 E Chicago Ave, No. 840, Chicago, IL 60611; (312) 440-2795. Answers inquiries on dentistry and dental education; makes referrals to other sources of info. Services free.

17123. American Theological Library Association, c/o Albert E. Hurd, Exec Secty, 5600 S Woodlawn Ave, Chicago, IL 60637; (312) 947-8850. Interest in administration of theological libraries. Publishes indexes, bibliographies, annual proceedings; answers inquiries; provides custom online searches.

17124. American Vocational Education Research Association, c/o Connie J. Ley, Dept of Home Economics, 144 Turner Hall, Ill. State Univ, Normal, IL 61761. Interest in research, evaluation of vocational education. An-

swers inquiries, makes referrals to other sources of info. Services free.

17125. Americans for Effective Law Enforcement, 5519 N Cumberland, No 1008, Chicago, IL 60656; (312) 372-0404. Nonprofit org that provides legal research assistance, advisory and reference services; conducts workshops. Most services free, available to attorneys, police.

17126. Amusement and Music Operators Association, 2000 Spring Rd, Ste 200, Oak Brook, IL 60521; (312) 654-2662. Provides info on coin-operated phonographs and amusement games industry. Analyzes data, conducts seminars and workshops, distributes publications. Services to public for a fee.

17127. Ancient Astronaut Society, 1921 St Johns Ave, Highland Park, IL 60035; (312) 432-6230. Searches for evidence of visits to earth by extraterrestrial intelligent beings in prehistoric times. Conducts seminars open to public (free to members).

17129. Argonne National Laboratory, Energy Software Center, 9700 S Cass Ave, Argonne, IL 60439; (312) 972-7250. Provides U.S. Dept of Energy's software exchange with other govt agencies, acquisition of commercial software. Distributes software packages to govt contractors, univs.

17131. Association for Business Communication, English Bldg, 608 S Wright St, Univ of Ill., Urbana, IL 61801; (217) 333-1006. Fosters education in written, oral, graphic communications of business, industry, govt. Acts as clearinghouse for research; answers inquiries. Most services free.

17132. Association for Library Service to Children, American Library Assn, 50 E Huron St, Chicago, IL 60611; (312) 944-6780. Provides pamphlets on improving library services for children. Makes available info on Newbery, Caldecott, Wilder, Batchelder awards; provides advisory services.

17133. Association for the Anthropological Study of Play, c/o Dr Gary Chick, Child Research Center, Rm 56, Univ of Ill., Champaign, IL 61820; (217) 333-6434. Assn of anthropologists, psychologists, sociologists, physical educators interested in study of play. Conducts annual conference, seminars, workshops. Services to members only.

17134. Association of College and Research Libraries, 50 E Huron St, Chicago, IL 60611; (312) 944-6780. Publishes reports, reviews, bibliographies, abstracts, directories; provides consulting, reference services; operates job placement service. Services generally free to members.

17135. Association of Home Appliance Manufacturers, 20 N Wacker Dr, Chicago, IL 60606; (312) 984-5800. Conducts statistical studies on home appliance industry; cosponsors panel solving consumer problems; publishes product standards, certification directories. Most services free.

17136. Association of Management Consultants, c/o Bonnie Poirier, Exec Dir, 500 N Michigan Ave, Ste 1400, Chicago, IL 60611; (312) 266-1261. Answers inquiries free on member firms and management consulting services. Publishes directory, makes referrals, conducts annual consultants workshop and regional meetings.

17137. Association of Official Seed Analysts, c/o Jim Lair, Secty/Treas, 801 Sangamon Ave, Springfield, IL 62701-1001; (217) 785-8487. Publishes annual proceedings, newsletter on seed analysis; provides short lists of literature citations in response to inquiries; makes referrals; supplies literature at cost.

17138. Association of Rehabilitation Nurses, 2506 Gross Point Rd, Evanston, IL 60201; (312) 475-7300. Provides advisory, consultation, reference, duplication services; conducts conferences, seminars, workshops, certified rehab registered nurse program.

17139. Association of Specialized and Cooperative Library Agencies, American Library Assn, 50 E Huron St, Chicago, IL 60611; (312) 944-6780. Serves as info clearinghouse for state and specialized library agencies. Publishes reports, directories, bibliographies; provides reference services.

17141. Automotive Service Councils, 188 Industrial Dr, Ste 112, Elmhurst, IL 60126; (312) 530-2330. Conducts technical and business management seminars, workshops for owners of automotive repair services; provides names of members to consumers. Reference service available free.

17142. Bakery Equipment Manufacturers Association, 111 E Wacker Dr, Chicago, IL 60601; (312) 644-6610. Provides directory of bakery equipment, ovens, other products produced by members; distributes directory free.

17143. Balzekas Museum of Lithuanian Culture, 4012 Archer Ave, Chicago, IL 60632; (312) 847-2441. Interest in Lithuanian history, culture. Provides advisory, translation services; permits onsite use of collection of 16th Century books. Most services free.

17144. Bank Administration Institute, 60 Gould Center, 2550 Golf Rd, Rolling Meadows, IL 60008; (312) 228-6200. Publishes journals, manuals, reports on banking industry. Answers inquiries, provides educational services to members, permits limited onsite use of collection.

17145. Bank Marketing Association, Information Center, 309 W Washington St, Chicago, IL 60606; (312) 782-1442. Answers inquiries on bank marketing practices. Provides reference services, lends materials, conducts online database searching, permits onsite use of collections. Services to nonmembers for a fee.

17146. Barren Foundation, c/o Richard Blandau, MD, Pres, 6 E Monroe St, Chicago, IL 60603; (312) 346-4038. Answer inquiries on infertility research. Publishes brochures; provides reference services; conducts medical seminars, support groups. Fee for services.

17147. Battery Council International, 111 E Wacker Dr, Chicago, IL 60601; (312) 644-6610. Interest in quality standards for automobile batteries. Publishes manuals, reports; answers inquiries; provides reference services. Services free to members, govt agencies.

17148. Biological Photographic Association, 1 Buttonwood Court, Indian Head Park, IL 60525. Intl org interested in natural sciences photography. Publishes journal; conducts conferences, tutorials, meetings, certification programs.

17149. Blind Service Association, 28 E Jackson Blvd, Chicago, IL 60604; (312) 987-0099. Answers inquiries on reading, recording services to blind and visually impaired adults, recreation programs for blind children. Makes referrals to other sources of info.

17150. Blue Cross and Blue Shield Association, 676 N St Clair St, Chicago, IL 60611; (312) 440-6000;. Promotes acceptance of nonprofit prepayment of health services; administers fed health programs; conducts programs on health care issues; provides limited reference services.

17151. Brain Research Foundation, 208 S LaSalle St, Ste 1427, Chicago, IL 60604; (312) 782-4311. Provides financial assistance for brain research at Univ of Chicago. Publishes reprints, provides free reference services.

17152. Brewery and Soft Drink Workers Conference U.S.A. and Canada, c/o Charles Klare, Dir, 1400 Renaissance Dr, Ste 406, Park Ridge, IL 60068; (312) 299-3406. Affiliated with Intl Brotherhood of Teamsters, Chauffeurs, Warehousemen. Answers brief inquiries on labor relations, refers inquirers to other sources of info.

17153. Building Officials and Code Administrators International, 4051 W Flossmoor Rd, Country Club Hills, IL 60477-5795; (312) 799-2300. Performs studies on new products; examines building plans for a fee; makes consulting surveys on contract basis; offers training.

17154. Business History Conference, c/o Jeremy Atack, Secty-Treas, Dept of Economics, Univ of Ill., Champaign, IL 61820; (217) 333-7300. Interest in history of economics. Publishes and sells papers of annual meeting, answers inquiries, makes referrals to other sources of info. Routine services free.

17155. CORPUS, P.O. Box 2649, Chicago, IL 60690; (312) 764-3399. Provides info on job opportunities for resigned priests. Provides advisory, general reference services; conducts seminars, workshops. Services free.

17156. Cancer Center Communications Program, McGaw Pavilion, 303 E Chicago Ave, Chicago, IL 60611; (312)

266-5260. Coordinates cancer-related research at McGaw Medical Center. Provides advisory, consulting, reference services; conducts seminars, workshops; permits onsite use of collections. Services free.

17157. Cancer Research Center, Pritzker School of Medicine, Univ of Chicago, 5841 S Maryland Ave, Chicago, IL 60637; (312) 962-6180. Publishes annual report on basic cancer research; answers inquiries; conducts seminars, workshops. Services primarily for doctors; fees depend on scope of request.

17158. Ceilings and Interior Systems Contractors Association, 1800 Pickwick Ave, Glenview, IL 60025; (312) 724-7700. Interest in sound absorption, interior lighting, air control, fire control. Publishes bimonthly journal, answers inquiries, refers inquirers to other sources of info free.

17159. Center for Children's Books, Univ of Chicago Library, 1100 E 57th St, Chicago, IL 60637; (312) 753-3450. Publishes journal reviewing trade books for children; has access to Center for Research Libraries; provides reference services. Approved individuals may use collections onsite.

17160. Center for Community and Social Concerns, World Correctional Service, 2849 W 71st St, Chicago, IL 60629; (312) 925-6591. Volunteer org that provides current-awareness services on criminal justice, info on research in progress. Services generally free.

17161. Center for Craniofacial Anomalies, Univ of Ill., Coll of Medicine, P.O. Box 6998 (808 S Wood St), Chicago, IL 60680; (312) 996-6979. Provides consulting services, info on research on craniofacial anomalies. Conducts seminars, permits onsite use of collection. Services to qualified professionals for a fee.

17162. Center for Health Administration Studies, Univ of Chicago, 5720 S Woodlawn Ave, Chicago, IL 60637; (312) 962-7753. Provides info services on health services research, health care programs. Publishes occasional bulletin, research series. Approved researchers have access to data.

17164. Center for Research Libraries, 6050 S Kenwood Ave, Chicago, IL 60637; (312) 955-4545. Collects materials not generally available in libraries and lends those materials to member libraries. Nonmembers served infrequently for a fee.

17165. Center for Research in Law and Justice, Dept of Criminal Justice, Coll of Liberal Arts and Sciences, Univ of Ill., P.O. Box 4348, Chicago, IL 60680; (312) 996-4632. Conducts research on criminal justice. Provides advisory, reference, abstracting services; conducts seminars, workshops. Most services provided on grant or contract basis.

17166. Center for Social Research in the Church, Concordia Coll, 7400 Augusta St, River Forest, IL 60305; (312) 771-8300 ext 299. Provides survey design, administration, analysis; provides consulting services; conducts

workshops; permits onsite use of collection. Fee for services.

17167. Center for Study of Multiple Birth, 333 E Superior St, Ste 476, Chicago, IL 60611; (312) 266-9093. Nonprofit foundation that fosters research on multiple birth. Provides advisory, reference services; conducts seminars, workshops. Services free.

17168. Center for UFO Studies, 1955 John's Dr, Glenview, IL 60025; (312) 724-2480. Nonprofit org with computerized catalog of UFO sightings. Provides factsheet, advisory and reference services; exchanges info with other research orgs; permits onsite use of collection.

17169. Center for Urban Economic Development, School of Urban Planning and Policy, Univ of Ill., P.O. Box 4348, Chicago, IL 60680; (312) 996-5240. Provides technical assistance in economic development to community orgs. Publishes technical reports and manuals on market studies, provides info to public.

17170. Center for Zoonoses and Comparative Medicine, Coll of Veterinary Medicine, Univ of Ill., 131 Veterinary Medicine Bldg, Urbana, IL 61801; (217) 333-2760. Interest in diseases that can be transmitted from animals to humans. Answers inquiries; provides advisory, consulting services. Services at cost.

17171. Center for the Study of Crime, Delinquency, and Corrections, Southern Ill. Univ, Carbondale, IL 62901; (618) 453-5701. Publishes training manuals for correctional personnel; provides consulting services and info on research; permits onsite use of collection. Fees charged to cover costs.

17172. Center for the Study of Ethics in the Professions, Ill. Institute of Technology, IIT Center, Chicago, IL 60616; (312) 567-3017. Provides advisory, consulting services relating to ethics code construction. Provides reference services, conducts symposia, permits onsite use of collections. Most services free.

17173. Center for the Study of Population and Social Organization, Dept of Sociology, Univ of Chicago, 5848 S Univ Ave, Chicago, IL 60637; (312) 962-3604. Evaluates data on urban social organization, survey methodology. Conducts seminars, workshops; permits onsite use of collection. Fees charged for some services.

17174. Central Electric Railfans' Association, P.O. Box 503 , Chicago, IL 60690; (312) 346-3723. Nonprofit technical educational assn that publishes books on rapid transit railways. Conducts meetings, inspection trips to electric railways. Most services free.

17175. Charles E. Merriam Center for Public Administration Library, 1313 E 60th St, Chicago, IL 60637; (312) 947-2162. Special library that provides limited reference service to natl assns concerned with public administration. Provides consulting, online searching services for a fee.

17176. Chemical Search Service, 18851 W Circle Court, Grayslake, IL 60030; (312) 223-8081. Answers inquiries on sources of rare chemicals. Provides consulting, literature-searching services; supplies chemicals on request. Fee for services.

17177. Chicago & North Western Historical Society, 8242 N Knox Ave, Skokie, IL 60076; (312) 982-1398. Offers historical info on Chicago & North Western Railroad. Provides advisory, reference services; permits onsite use of collection. Most services free.

17178. Chicago Academy of Sciences, 2001 N Clark St, Chicago, IL 60614; (312) 549-0606. Publishes research on natural history of Chicago. Loans collections to institutions; holds classes for schools; displays exhibits to public; provides library for onsite reference. Services designed for amateur naturalists.

17179. Chicago Board of Trade Public Relations, Marketing, and Education Information, 141 W Jackson Blvd, Chicago, IL 60604; (312) 435-3500. Commodity futures exchange org that publishes books, audiovisual aids, statistical annuals; handles press relations, tours, conferences; operates Commodities Institute.

17180. Chicago Council on Fine Arts, 78 E Washington St, Chicago, IL 60602; (312) 744-6630. Evaluates legislation affecting arts in Chicago; provides advisory, reference services; conducts seminars, workshops; permits onsite use of collection. Most services free.

17181. Chicago Historical Society Research Collections, Clark St at North Ave, Chicago, IL 60614; (312) 642-4600. Holds research and exhibition materials on Chicago history. Provides reference, copying services; permits onsite use of collection. Services generally free.

17182. Children's Memorial Hospital, Division of Genetics, 2300 Children's Plaza, Chicago, IL 60614; (312) 880-4462. Answers inquiries on genetic disorders. Provides advisory and consulting services, conducts seminars, evaluates data. Most services free.

17183. Chronic Epstein-Barr Virus Support Group, MINANN, Inc., P.O. Box 582, Glenview, IL 60025. Nonprofit org that acts as media liaison publicizing Chronic Epstein-Barr Virus that causes infectious mononucleosis. Forms local chapters.

17184. Citizen/Labor Energy Coalition, 600 W Fullerton Ave, Chicago, IL 60614; (312) 975-3680. Interest in benefits of price controls on oil and gas. Answers inquiries, conducts seminars and workshops. Most services free.

17185. Civil Aviation Medical Association, 801 Green Bay Rd, Lake Bluff, IL 60044; (312) 234-6330. Enlarges and disseminates knowledge by which civil aviation medicine safeguards public safety. Sponsors training in civil aviation medicine, answers inquiries free.

17186. Clearinghouse for Hospital Management Engineering, American Hospital Assn, 840 N Lake Shore Dr, Chicago, IL 60611; (312) 280-6023. Provides literature-searching services on hospital management engineering; conducts seminars, workshops; distributes material. Services at cost.

17187. Clearinghouse for Sociological Literature, Dept of Sociology, Northern Ill. Univ, DeKalb, IL 60115; (815) 753-0301. Acts as depository for sociological research; holds microfiche of papers deposited by authors and accepted for publication in abstract form; provides copies for a fee.

17188. Coal Extraction and Utilization Research Center, Southern Ill. Univ, Carbondale, IL 62901; (618) 536-5521. Coordinates responses to problems of coal fuel cycle. Answers reference requests, provides info, lends material, permits onsite use of collection.

17189. College of American Pathologists, 7400 Skokie Blvd, Skokie, IL 60077; (312) 677-3500. Interest in quality control in clinical labs. Provides advisory services, conducts seminars and workshops, evaluates data. Services at cost.

17190. College of Generalists in Dentistry, 1737 W Howard St, Rm 422, Chicago, IL 60626; (312) 764-0350. Motivates dentists to embark on expanded learning programs; educates public. Provides free advisory, reference services; conducts seminars, workshops.

17191. Comparative Education Center, Univ of Chicago, 5835 Kimbark Ave, Chicago, IL 60637; (312) 753-2922. Publishes papers on relationships between education and society; conducts studies; offers consultation on research. Approved academic users given access to material by appointment.

17192. Compassionate Friends, P.O. Box 3696, Oak Brook, IL 60522-3696; (312) 323-5010. Nationwide voluntary org for bereaved parents that provides help and suppport.;Conducts annual meeting. Each chapter has own resources, newsletter, and library.

17193. Concrete Reinforcing Steel Institute, 933 N Plum Grove Rd, Schaumburg, IL 60195; (312) 490-1700. Interest in reinforced concrete. Publishes books and computer programs, answers inquiries free, sells publications.

17195. Conference on College Composition and Communication, 1111 Kenyon Rd, Urbana, IL 61801; (217) 328-3870. Org of college composition and communication teachers. Answers inquiries; provides reference, abstracting, placement services; conducts seminars. Info available.

17196. Congress of Organizations of the Physically Handicapped, 16630 Beverly Ave, Tinley Park, IL 60477. Represents interests of physically handicapped in dealings with natl rehabilitation, research agencies. Answers inquiries, provides advisory services. Services free.

17197. Council for Research in Music Education, c/o School of Music, Univ of Ill., Urbana, IL 61801; (217)

333-1027. Answers inquiries on music education. Provides advisory and reference services, permits onsite use of collection. Services free.

17198. Council for the Advancement of Science Writing, c/o William J. Cromie, Exec Dir, 618 N Elmwood St, Oak Park, IL 60302; (312) 383-0820. Interest in science reporting and writing as a career. Answers inquiries; provides training programs, career info; conducts seminars.

17200. Council of Logistics Management, 2803 Butterfield Rd, Oak Brook, IL 60521; (312) 655-0985. Develops understanding of logistics and physical distribution process. Answers inquiries, conducts seminars and workshops. Fees for all services.

17202. Council on Rehabilitation Education, 185 N Wabash Ave, Rm 1617, Chicago, IL 60601; (312) 346-6027. Sets educational standards for rehab counselor education programs. Answers inquiries, provides advisory services, conducts seminars. Fee for some services.

17203. Court Counselor Program, 228 Northeast Jefferson, Peoria, IL 61603; (309) 672-6020. Renders counseling for rehabilitation of offenders, provides advisory reference services, evaluates data, permits onsite use of collections. Services free, primarily for law offenders.

17204. Cryogenic Society of America, c/o Werner K. Huget, Records Secty, 1033 S Blvd, Oak Park, IL 60302; (312) 383-7053. Publishes annual conference proceedings on applications of cryogenic technology. Answers inquiries free; conducts seminars, workshops for a fee.

17205. Cystic Fibrosis Research Center, Northwestern Univ, Children's Memorial Hospital, 2300 Children's Plaza, Chicago, IL 60614; (312) 649-4354. Conducts research on cystic fibrosis. Offers medical care; provides advisory, reference services; conducts seminars. Services free.

17206. Dadant & Sons, 51 S 2nd St, Hamilton, IL 62341; (217) 847-3324. Commercial firm that manufactures and distributes beekeeping supplies. Publishes beekeeping info, answers inquiries free, sells publications.

17207. Dairy Research Foundation, 6300 N River Rd, Rosemont, IL 60018; (312) 696-1020. Provides access to computerized data bases on dairy food sciences and technology; provides reference, literature-searching services. Services to dairy industry on limited basis.

17208. Data Processing Management Association, 505 Busse Hwy, Park Ridge, IL 60068; (312) 825-8124. Conducts research on info processing; offers films, self-study courses; sponsors annual intl conference and business exposition; offers onsite seminars.

17210. Decalogue Society of Lawyers, 179 W Washington St, Ste 350, Chicago, IL 60602; (312) 263-6493. Operates Jewish lawyer referral service; sponsors scholarships; provides advisory services; sponsors seminars, workshops. Services free.

17211. Department of Atmospheric Sciences, 1101 W Springfield Ave, Urbana, IL 61801; (217) 333-2046. Answers inquiries on education and research in atmospheric sciences. Provides advisory services, conducts seminars and workshops. Fee for services.

17212. Department of Pharmacology and Experimental Therapeutics, Medical Center, 2160 S 1st Ave, Maywood, IL 60153; (312) 531-3261. Answers inquiries on basic research in pharmacology, toxicology. Publishes reports, reviews; provides consulting services; sends reprints of publications on request.

17213. Dermatology Foundation, 820 Davis St, Evanston, IL 60201; (312) 328-2256. Natl nonprofit health agency that awards fellowships, grants in support of research and education in dermatology. Answers inquiries, refers inquirers to other sources of info.

17214. Diabetes Research and Training Center, Div of Biological Sciences, Pritzker School of Medicine, Univ of Chicago, 920 E 58th St, Chicago, IL 60637; (312) 962-9661. Answers inquiries on diabetes research; provides advisory, consulting services; conducts seminars, workshops. Services free to physicians, scientists.

17215. Disease Detection Information Bureau, 1165 N Clark St, Ste 311, Chicago, IL 60610; (312) 664-9780. Offers guidelines for diabetes detection. Provides advisory, reference services; distributes data compilations. Services free.

17216. Distribution Sciences, 1350 E Touhy Ave, Des Plaines, IL 60018; (312) 635-0200. Data processing services org catering to transportation/distribution industry. Provides info on research; provides consultative services on contractual basis.

17218. Door Operator and Remote Controls Manufacturers Association, c/o Frank S. Fitzgerald, Exec Secty, Park Place, Ste 201, 655 Irving Park at Lake Shore Dr, Chicago, IL 60613; (312) 525-2644. Manufacturers' trade assn whose members provide automatic electric-powered door operators for vehicular doors. Publishes spec data sheet, answers inquiries.

17219. Ducks Unlimited, Public Relations Office, One Waterfowl Way at Gilmer Rd, Long Grove, IL 60047; (312) 438-4300. Perpetuates waterfowl populations by improving wetland habitats. Answers inquiries free, operates film rental library.

17220. ERIC Clearinghouse on Elementary and Early Childhood Education, Univ of Ill., 805 W Pennsylvania Ave, Urbana, IL 61801; (217) 333-1386. Evaluates, disseminates info on elementary education. Conducts workshops, permits onsite use of collection. Fee for some services.

17221. ERIC Clearinghouse on Reading and Communication Skills, Natl Council of Teachers of English, 1111 Kenyon Rd, Urbana, IL 61801; (217) 328-3870. Disseminates info on teaching English, journalism. Provides reference, abstracting, copying services; permits on-site use of collection. Services free.

17222. Eagle Valley Environmentalists, P.O. Box 155, Main St, Apple River, IL 61001; (815) 594-2305. Holds proceedings of intl symposium on bald eagle. Provides reference, advisory services for a fee, conducts environmental education workshops.

17223. Educational Foundation for Nuclear Science, 5801 S Kenwood Ave, Chicago, IL 60637; (312) 363-5225. Acts as forum for scientists to express views to public on science and world affairs through publications. Answers inquiries.

17224. Electronic Data Processing Auditors Association, 373 S Schmale Rd, Carol Stream, IL 60188; (312) 682-1200. Conducts conferences, seminars, workshops on electronic data processing system control problems and techniques to eliminate them. Fee for services.

17225. Energy Resources Center, Univ of Ill., P.O. Box 4348, Chicago, IL 60680; (312) 996-4490. Provides info on energy technology and policy. Conducts research, provides free advisory and reference services, conducts seminars.

17226. Engine Manufacturers Association, 111 E Wacker Dr, Chicago, IL 60601; (312) 644-6610. Provides legislative reporting, engine statistical compilations, marketing data. Answers inquiries, refers inquirers to other sources of info free.

17227. Eterna International, P.O. Box 1344, Oak Brook, IL 60521. Works for adoption of unwanted handicapped children. Offers info on treatment, care, education; publishes surveys; gathers data for use by researchers.

17228. Executime Systems, P.O. Box 631, Lake Forest, IL 60045; (312) 362-0016. Answers inquiries on mail order advertising and direct marketing; provides advisory, consulting services; conducts seminars. Fee for services.

17229. Fabricating Manufacturers Association, 7811 N Alpine Rd, Rockford, IL 61111; (815) 654-1902. Answers inquiries on fabricating technology; provides advisory, consulting, reference services. Fee for services.

17230. Farm and Industrial Equipment Institute, 410 N Michigan Ave, Chicago, IL 60611; (312) 321-1470. Owns reports on farm and industrial machinery; publishes weekly newsletter, equipment specifications, booklets, monthly sales reports. Answers inquiries, provides reference services.

17231. Fats and Proteins Research Foundation, 2250 E Devon Ave, Des Plaines, IL 60018; (312) 827-0139. Answers inquiries on animals byproducts industries, detergent and chemical industries. Publishes and provides copies of research reports (duplication fee may be charged).

17232. Fermi National Accelerator Laboratory Technical Information Group, P.O. Box 500, Batavia, IL 60510; (312) 840-3401. Conducts research on structure of matter. Provides reference services, makes interlibrary loans, permits onsite use of collection. Services at cost to nonemployees.

17233. Fibre Box Association, 5725 N E River Rd, Chicago, IL 60631; (312) 693-9600. Advises fed govt on preparing standards, specifications for corrugated and solid fibreboard boxes. Publishes recommended practices, voluntary standards.

17234. Fisheries Research Laboratory, Southern Ill. Univ, Carbondale, IL 62901; (618) 536-7761. Interest in fish management and culture; is involved in fisheries science activities. Maintains lab, answers inquiries free, provides consulting services for a fee.

17235. Forest Park Foundation, 5823 N Forest Park Dr, Peoria, IL 61614; (309) 688-6631. Nonprofit org that grants financial assistance to projects on design, construction, operation of parks for conservation education, outdoor recreation. Provides consulting services free.

17236. Fusion Bonded Coaters Association, 21 Spinning Wheel Rd, Hinsdale, IL 60521; (312) 920-1411. Makes available info on corrosion protective systems. Provides advisory, consulting services; conducts seminars, workshops; distributes data. Services free.

17238. Gas Research Institute Technical Communications, 8600 W Bryn Mawr Ave, Chicago, IL 60631; (312) 399-8100. Nonprofit org that does research on natural gas. Conducts seminars, provides reference services, allows onsite use of resources, loans materials.

17239. Ghost Research Society, P.O. Box 205, Oaklawn, IL 60454-0205; (312) 425-5163. Seeks to establish existence of ghosts and paranormal phenomena. Provides advisory services, evaluates data, conducts seminars and workshops. Services free.

17240. Gould Information Center, 40 Gould Center, Rolling Meadows, IL 60008; (312) 640-4424. Commercial org that provides marketing info on electronics. Provides advisory, consulting, reference services; permits onsite use of collection. Services free.

17241. Government Finance Officers Association of the U.S. and Canada, c/o Jeffrey L. Esser, Exec Dir, 180 N Michigan Ave, Ste 800, Chicago, IL 60601; (312) 977-9700. Publishes periodicals, reports, bibliographies on govt accounting. Answers inquiries, provides reference services, permits onsite use of collection. Services free.

17242. Gypsum Association, 1603 Orrington Ave, Ste 1210, Evanston, IL 60201; (312) 491-1744. Publishes reports, specifications, slides, recommended practices for gypsum products' use; provides advisory services. Services free.

17244. Historical Pictures Service, 601 W Randolph St, Chicago, IL 60606; (312) 346-0599. Lends historical photos to publishers, television and movie producers, advertising agencies; collects engravings, drawings, paintings, maps. Photocopies mailed on request for a fee.

17245. Home Ventilating Institute, 30 W Univ Dr, Arlington Heights, IL 60004; (312) 394-0150. Answers inquiries on static and powered ventilation; provides reference services. Services at cost primarily for contractors, home builders, building code officials.

17246. Horizons for the Blind, 7001 N Clark St, Chicago, IL 60626; (312) 973-7600. Nonprofit corp that enables blind to enjoy cultural institutions. Provides advisory services, conducts training programs for institution personnel, permits onsite use of collections. Services free to some users.

17247. Hospital Research and Educational Trust, 840 N Lake Shore Dr, Chicago, IL 60611; (312) 280-6620. Supports and conducts research to improve health care services. Publishes quarterly research journal, education and training manuals. Info provided primarily through publications.

17249. Human Ecology Action League, 7330 N Rogers Ave, Rogers Park, IL 60626; (312) 761-7006. Disseminates info on clinical ecology. Provides advisory, reference services; conducts seminars, workshops. Services free to members, $1 for others.

17250. Human Ecology Research Foundation, 505 N Lake Shore Dr, Chicago, IL 60611; (312) 828-9480. Supports medical research in human ecology. Sponsors training programs for physicians, answers inquiries free.

17252. IIT Research Institute, Water Research Center, 10 W 35th St, Chicago, IL 60616; (312) 567-4270. Publishes reports for fed govt on water pollution assessment and control. Answers inquiries, provides contract research for a fee.

17253. IIT Research Institute, Tactical Weapon Guidance and Control Information Analysis Center, 10 W 35th St, Chicago, IL 60616; (312) 567-4519. Makes available info on research in tactical weapon guidance and control. Provides general reference, technical support services. Services restricted to those under contract to U.S. govt.

17254. Illinois Archaeological Survey, Univ of Ill., Davenport Hall, Rm 109, Urbana, IL 61801; (217) 333-1708. Publishes info and holds records on Ill. archeological surveys. Answers brief inquiries, provides consulting services, conducts workshops.

17256. Illinois Institute of Technology, Department of Environmental Engineering, 3300 S Federal St, Chicago, IL 60616; (312) 567-3535. Answers inquiries on air and water pollution control, pollution laws. Provides consulting, literature-searching services. Fees charged depend on nature of services requested.

17258. Illinois Railway Museum, P.O. Box 431 (Olson Rd), Union, IL 60180; (815) 923-4391. Operates muse-um with steam, diesel, electric railroad; provides reference services; conducts seminars, workshops. Services free to members, at cost to others.

17259. Illinois State Historical Library, Old State Capitol, Springfield, IL 62706; (217) 782-4836. Answers inquiries on Ill. history. Provides advisory, reference services; conducts seminars, workshops; permits onsite use of collections. Services free.

17260. Illinois State Library, Centennial Bldg, 3rd Fl, Springfield, IL 62756; (217) 782-5430. Publishes lists of Ill. state publications; provides free reference services through Ill. Library and Info Network. Photocopying fees charged when copies exceeds certain limits.

17261. Information Alternative, 600 S Dearborn St, Ste 1510, Chicago, IL 60605; (312) 461-0890. Provides lawyers and legal orgs with nonlegal info, trains lawyers in nonlegal research; organizes law libraries. Conducts workshops, seminars; provides consulting services.

17262. Information Retrieval Research Laboratory, Univ of Ill., 5-135 Coordinated Sciences Laboratory, 1101 W Springfield St, Urbana, IL 61801; (217) 333-1074. Does research on info science; provides consulting, online searching, abstracting services; conducts seminars, workshops. Services on contract or grant basis.

17263. Institute for Association Management, c/o Gartner & Associates, 2 N Riverside Plaza, Ste 2400, Chicago, IL 60606; (312) 454-0282. Answers inquiries on administrative skills for nonprofit assn managers. Provides advisory, consulting, reference services; conducts seminars, conferences. Fee for services.

17264. Institute for Certification of Computer Professionals, 2200 E Devon, Des Plaines, IL 60018; (312) 299-4227. Self-supporting org that develops, administers testing programs and certification for computer profession; provides info on programs. Testing services provided for a fee.

17265. Institute for Environmental Management, Coll of Arts and Sciences, Western Ill. Univ, Waggoner Hall, Rm 381, Macomb, IL 61455; (309) 298-1265. Supports, develops, and administers research, teaching, and service programs on environmental subjects. Answers inquiries free.

17266. Institute for Fluitronics Education, P.O. Box 106 (1000 Grandview Dr), Elm Grove, IL 63122; (414) 782-0410. Conducts seminars on fluid power technology for industry, govt agencies. Provides advisory, reference services at cost.

17267. Institute for Interconnecting and Packaging Electronic Circuits, 3451 Church St, Evanston, IL 60060; (312) 677-2850. Develops guidelines for electronic packaging industry. Answers inquiries, analyzes data, conducts seminars and workshops. Fee for services.

17268. Institute for Psychoanalysis, McLean Library, 180 N Michigan Ave, Chicago, IL 60601; (312) 726-6300. Owns psychoanalytic journals; rents films to institutions; offers literature searches at cost; translates from German for a fee. Services to members; library open to public.

17269. Institute for Psychosomatic and Psychiatric Research and Training, Michael Reese Hospital and Medical Center, 2959 S Cottage Grove Ave, Chicago, IL 60616; (312) 791-3826. Provides Univ of Chicago students' training; conducts research in psychiatry. Provides advisory, reference services; conducts seminars. Fee for some services.

17270. Institute of Business Designers, 1155 Merchandise Mart, Chicago, IL 60654; (312) 467-1950. Org of commercial interior designers does research, conducts seminars and workshops, and increases public awareness of services of interior designers. Nonmembers charged for some services.

17271. Institute of Environmental Sciences, 940 E Northwest Hwy, Mount Prospect, IL 60056; (312) 255-1561. Promotes research, design criteria in environmental sciences. Conducts seminars, provides reference services and info on current research. Fee for some services.

17272. Institute of Food Technologists, 221 N LaSalle St, Ste 2120, Chicago, IL 60601; (312) 782-8424. Intl society of food technologists, scientists. Publishes reference materials, provides abstracting services, conducts seminars and workshops.

17273. Institute of Gas Technology, Technical Information Services, 3424 S State St, Chicago, IL 60616 ; (312) 567-3871. Publishes newsletter on intl gas technology; provides reference, literature- and patent-searching, bibliographic, duplication services for a fee; permits onsite reference.

17274. Institute of Nuclear Materials Management, 8600 W Bryn Mawr Ave, Ste 720-S, Chicago, IL 60631; (312) 693-0990. Advances nuclear materials management to safeguard nuclear fuel facilities. Promotes research, provides reference services, conducts seminars. Services free to members, students, allied assns; at cost to others.

17275. Institution for Tuberculosis Research, Univ of Ill., Health Sciences Center, 904 W ADams St, Chicago, IL 60607; (312) 996-4688. Answers inquiries on BCG anti-tuberculosis vaccine (Tice strain). Publishes standards, specifications, biennial report; provides consulting services; disseminates reprints on request.

17276. Inter-University Seminar on Armed Forces and Society, Social Science Bldg, Univ of Chicago, 1126 E 59th St, Chicago, IL 60637; (312) 962-8694. Acts as focal point for communication among academics, military personnel conducting research. Publishes conference papers, gives researchers free access to archive.

17277. International Academy of Cytology, 5841 S Maryland Ave, HM 449, Chicago, IL 60637; (312) 962-6569, (312) 962-6577 (Editorial Office). Answers inquiries on exfoliative cytology (diagnoses, techniques, research). Provides consulting, reference, literature-searching services, primarily for members.

17278. International Agency for Apiculture Development, 3201 Huffman Blvd, Rockford, IL 61103; (815) 877-6266. Nonprofit corp that promotes methods of beekeeping in developing countries. Provides advisory, reference services; conducts seminars, workshops. Fee for services.

17279. International Association for Orthodontics, 211 E Chicago Ave, No 915, Chicago, IL 60611; (312) 642-2602. Publishes directory of orthodontics practitioners; provides consulting, reference services; sponsors seminars, conferences, workshops; lends audiovisual materials. Services at cost to nonmembers.

17280. International Association of Assessing Officers, 1313 E 60th St, Chicago, IL 60637; (312) 947-2069. Organized to improve tax assessment practices. Provides consulting services, conducts training programs, publishes research reports and bibliographies. Library open to public.

17281. International Association of Auditorium Managers, 500 N Michigan Ave, Ste 1400, Chicago, IL 60611; (312) 661-1700. Answers inquiries on auditorium management, including convention complexes and performing arts centers. Conducts seminars, industrial trade shows. Services at cost to some users.

17282. International Association of Electrical Inspectors, 930 Busse Hwy, Park Ridge, IL 60068; (312) 696-1455. Interest in standards for safe installation, use of electricity. Answers inquiries; provides reference, bibliographic services without charge; permits onsite use of collection.

17283. International Association of Hospital Central Service Management, 213 W Institute Pl, Ste 412, Chicago, IL 60610; (312) 440-0078. Offers certification to central service technicians. Provides consulting, reference services; conducts research, seminars. Services free.

17284. International Coroners and Medical Examiners Association, c/o Herbert H. Buzbee, Exec Secty-Treas, Courthouse, Room 24, Peoria, IL 61602; (309) 672-6050. Interest in investigations conducted by medico-legal officers. Conducts annual meetings, answers brief inquiries, provides consulting services to members.

17285. International Food Information Service, c/o Calvert L. Willey, Exec Dir, Institute of Food Technologists, 221 N LaSalle St, Ste 2120, Chicago, IL 60601; (312) 782-8424. Abstracts and indexes journals dealing with food science and technology. Provides general reference and translation services, conducts seminars. Fee for services.

17286. International Graphoanalysis Society, 111 N Canal St, Chicago, IL 60606; (312) 930-9446. Interest in handwriting analysis. Publishes journal, posters, reports; provides consulting, analytical services; permits onsite use of collection. Fees charged for services to public.

17287. International Institute of Ammonia Refrigeration, 111 E Wacker Dr, Ste 600, Chicago, IL 60601; (312) 644-6610. Promotes education and standards for safe use of ammonia as a refrigerant. Provides general reference services, conducts seminars and workshops. Fee for services.

17288. International Jensen, 4136 N United Parkway, Schiller Park, IL 60176; (312) 671-5680. Commercial org involved in manufacturing home and auto stereo equipment. Provides consulting services, info on research in progress. Services free.

17289. International Language and Commmunication Centers, 33 N Dearborn St, Ste 1300, Chicago, IL 60602; (312) 236-3366. Provides multiple language services such as translations, typesetting and graphic arts for technical foreign language publications. Services for a fee to all users.

17290. International Material Management Society, 650 E Higgins Rd, Ste 17 South, Schaumburg, IL 60195; (312) 310-9570. Interest in material management. Answers inquiries, certifies individuals, conducts courses, meetings, and conferences.

17291. International Museum of Surgical Science and Hall of Fame, International Coll of Surgeons, 1516 N Lake Shore Dr, Chicago, IL 60610; (312) 642-3555. Contains medical exhibits on relationship between culture and science. Conducts lectures, permits onsite use of collection, offers scholarships. Museum admission free.

17292. International Occultation Timing Association, 6 N 106 White Oak Lane, St Charles, IL 60174; (312) 584-1162. Disseminates info on occultations and eclipse phenomena; organizes scientific expeditions. Provides advisory and reference services, conducts seminars. Services free.

17293. International Pipe Association, 7811 N Alpine Rd, Rockford, IL 61111; (815) 654-1905. Works with regulatory and advisory agencies to develop practical materials and engineering standards for piping technology. Provides advisory, consulting, reference services.

17294. International Polka Association, 4145 S Kedzie Ave, Chicago, IL 60632; (312) 254-7771. Responsible for annual festival that includes induction of individuals into Polka Music Hall of Fame. Answers inquiries. Services free.

17295. International Sanitary Supply Association, 5330 N Elston Ave, Chicago, IL 60630; (312) 286-2575. Promotes public health, safety through training programs, legislative action; helps generate ideas on manufacture of cleaning products. Conducts annual convention, seminars.

17296. International Society for Pediatric Neurosurgery, c/o Dr Raimondi, 2800 N Lakeshore Dr, Ste 3802, Chicago, IL 60657; (312) 472-7355. Provides info on current research in pediatric neurosurgery. Answers inquiries, provides consulting services, conducts seminars and workshops.

17297. International Society of Appraisers, P.O. Box 726 (1950A Kenilworth), Hoffman Estates, IL 60195; (312) 882-0706. Assn of personal property appraisers. Provides info on research in progress, conducts education/testing/certification programs. Fee for most services.

17298. International Society of Bassists, c/o School of Music, Northwestern Univ, Evanston, IL 60201; (312) 492-7228. Org of bassists that participates in intl conferences; provides advisory, reference services; conducts seminars, workshops. Fee for services.

17299. International Society of Fine Arts Appraisers, P.O. Box 280, River Forest, IL 60305; (312) 848-3340. Dedicated to promoting science of fine arts appraising. Provides advisory, reference services; conducts seminars. Fee for services.

17300. International Society of Preretirement Planners, 2400 S Downing, Westchester, IL 60153; (312) 531-9140. Provides advisory, counseling, reference services on preretirement planning. Fee for services, intended for companies preparing employees for retirement.

17302. Investigations Institute, 53 W Jackson Blvd, Chicago, IL 60604; (312) 939-6050. Interest in training of fire and explosions investigators. Answers inquiries; provides advisory, consulting, reference services; conducts seminars, workshops. Services free to members and most govt agencies.

17303. Iron Castings Society, Cast Metals Federation Bldg, 455 State St, Des Plaines, IL 60016; (312) 299-9160. Publishes buyers' guide, manuals, films on iron castings; provides advisory, reference, translation, abstracting services. Services free and primarily for members; some available to industry, foreign orgs.

17306. John Howard Association, 67 E Madison St, Ste 1216, Chicago, IL 60603; (312) 263-1901. Nonprofit assn devoted to preventing crime and delinquency. Monitors prison conditions throughout Ill.; advocates system-wide prison reforms. Provides survey, consulting services for a fee.

17307. Joint Commission on Accreditation of Hospitals, 875 N Michigan Ave, Chicago, IL 60611; (312) 642-6061. Nonprofit org that conducts surveys for accreditation of hospitals, hospice programs, ambulatory health care orgs, psychiatric facilities. Conducts conferences, publishes manual of standards. Fee for services.

17308. Kenya Pyrethrum Information Centre, Paul A. Keane, 2100 Lincoln Park West, 10 DN, Chicago, IL 60614; (312) 935-4999. Publishes reports on Kenya Pyrethrum plant. Provides research, consulting, reference, abstracting services; conducts seminars, workshops. Services generally free.

17310. Laboratory for Atmospheric Probing, Dept of Geophysical Sciences, Univ of Chicago, 5734 S Ellis Ave, Chicago, IL 60637; (312) 962-8125. Answers inquiries on radar meteorology, cloud and precipitation physics. Publishes reports, provides consulting services for a fee.

17311. Lake Michigan Federation, 8 S Michigan Ave, No 2010, Chicago, IL 60603; (312) 263-5550. Promotes citizen participation in govt policy needed to protect Lake Michigan. Conducts workshops, permits onsite use of collection. Fees for copying services, publications.

17313. Land Improvement Contractors of America, P.O. Box 9 (1300 Maybrook Dr), Maywood, IL 60153; (312) 344-0700. Org of contractors, manufacturers who help farmers conserve natural resources. Publishes directories, provides advisory services. Most services free.

17314. Learning Corp. of America, c/o Simon & Schuster, Distributor, 108 Wilmot Rd, Deerfield, IL 60015; (800) 323-6301. Rents and sells films/cassettes for all levels of education on topics such as language arts, social studies, art, music, history, science. Publishes film catalogs, discussion guides.

17315. Learning Exchange, 2940 N Lincoln Ave, Chicago, IL 60657; (312) 549-8383. Interest in innovative teaching. Publishes newsletter and how-to manual, answers inquiries, provides referral services. Services to members only.

17316. Library of International Relations, 77 S Wacker Dr, Chicago, IL 60606; (312) 567-5014. Serves as reference, research facility on intl relations. Publishes annotated bibliography, makes interlibrary loans, provides copying services, conducts literature searches.

17317. Lightning Protection Institute, P.O. Box 406 (48 N Ayer St), Harvard, IL 60033; (815) 943-7211. Evaluates data on equipment designed to protect from lightning. Publishes reports, provides reference services, conducts seminars and workshops. Fee for some services.

17318. Lincoln Owners Club, c/o N. Kenneth Pearson, Editor, 821 W Chicago St, Algonquin, IL 60102; (312) 658-4588. Answers inquiries on restoration, operation of Lincoln automobiles. Provides consulting services, advertises parts wanted by inquirers. Services free.

17319. Major Appliance Consumer Action Panel, 20 N Wacker Dr, Chicago, IL 60606; (312) 984-5858; (800) 621-0477. Receives comments, complaints from appliance owners; advises industry how to improve service; reports to consumers. Services free.

17320. Management Advisory Services, Pannell Kerr Forster, 150 N Michigan Ave, Ste 3700, Chicago, IL 60601; (312) 781-0002. Commercial firm that provides consulting, reference services on market research in health care, hospitality, real estate, data processing industries. Fee for services.

17321. Management Contents, P.O. Box 3014 (2265 Carlson Dr), Northbrook, IL 60062; (312) 564-1006, (800) 323-5354. Commercial org that publishes biweekly compilation of current management journals' table of contents pages; sells subscriptions to publications.

17323. Maple Flooring Manufacturers Association, 8600 W Bryn Mawr Ave, Chicago, IL 60631; (312) 693-0990. Answers inquiries on maple flooring, including questions on research and development. Publishes standard specification manual, approved floor finish products list, research reports; distributes free literature to schools.

17324. Marketing Research Association, 111 E Wacker Dr, No 600, Chicago, IL 60601; (312) 644-6610. Answers inquiries on marketing research for business sector. Publishes directories, standards, reviews; conducts seminars. Services at cost.

17325. Marking Device Association, c/o Thomas H. Brinkmann, Exec Secty, 708 Church St, Evanston, IL 60201; (312) 328-3540. Interest in marking tools and methods. Answers inquiries, provides free reference services.

17326. Mason Contractors Association of America, 17W601 14th St, Oakbrook Terrace, IL 60181; (312) 620-6767. Answers inquiries on masonry construction; makes referrals to other sources of info; conducts courses in masonry estimating, financial planning.

17327. Materials and Methods Standards Association, 315 S Hicks Rd, Palatine, IL 60067. Establishes quality standards of materials for use by ceramic tile and dimensional stone industries. Conducts seminars, workshops. Services free.

17329. McCook Research Laboratories Library, AKZO Chemie America, 8401 W 47th St, McCook, IL 60525; (312) 442-7100 ext 242. Provides reference services on organic chemistry. Makes interlibrary loans, publishes accessions list, state-of-the-arts review, bibliography.

17330. Medical Library Association, 919 N Michigan Ave, Ste 3208, Chicago, IL 60611; (312) 266-2456. Answers inquiries, conducts seminars and workshops, provides info on health sciences library field. Workshops and publications available to nonmembers for a fee.

17331. Medical-Dental-Hospital Bureaus of America, 111 E Wacker Dr, Chicago, IL 60601; (312) 644-6610. Answers brief inquiries free on economics of health professions; provides short lists of literature citations. Members provide consulting, management services for a fee.

17332. Metal Lath/Steel Framing Association, 221 N La-Salle St, Chicago, IL 60601; (312) 346-1600. Publishes manual, specifications on lathing and plastering. Answers inquiries, provides consulting and literature-searching services, lends documents, permits onsite use of collection.

17333. Metro-Help National Runaway Switchboard, 2210 N Halsted St, Chicago, IL 60614; (800) 621-4000 (National hotline), (800) 972-6004 (Ill.), (312) 880-9860 (general business). Toll-free referral service that provides info on where runaways can seek help. Helps runaways contact families, distributes brochures for cost of postage, provides consulting services.

17334. Mid-America Legal Foundation, 20 N Wacker Dr, Ste 842, Chicago, IL 60606; (312) 263-5163. Nonprofit corp that studies effect of law on free enterprise. Provides free advisory services, conducts seminars and workshops.

17335. Military Miniature Society of Illinois, c/o Richard Pielin, Editor, 7230 W Balmoral, Chicago, IL 60656; (312) 775-2587. Provides reference services on military history; makes referrals to other sources of info; permits onsite use of collection. Services free.

17336. Mill Mutuals, One Pierce Pl, Itasca, IL 60143; (312) 250-8600. Provides info on research on agribusiness loss prevention. Publishes safety signs, bulletins, films, slides; provides abstracting, indexing services. Services free to insured.

17337. Money Management Institute, Household Finance Corp., 2700 Sanders Rd, Prospect Heights, IL 60070; (312) 564-6291. Helps individuals and families manage financial affairs more effectively. Publishes, distributes booklets and filmstrips. Fees charged for postage and handling.

17338. Monon Railroad Historical-Technical Society, c/o Edward J. Lewnard, Secty-Treas, 410 S Emerson St, Mt. Prospect, IL 60056. Provides free info on equipment, operations of Monon Railroad; serves as resource center for historical data. Publications provided to nonmembers for a fee.

17339. Monument Builders of North America, 1612 Central St, Evanston, IL 60201. Org of retailers and suppliers of funerary memorials. Provides advisory, reference services; conducts seminars, workshops; lends materials. Fee for services.

17340. Museum of Contemporary Art, 237 E Ontario St, Chicago, IL 60611; (312) 280-2660. Interest in modern art in all media. Conducts lectures, film showings, senior citizen outreach, volunteer, and intern programs; permits onsite use of collection.

17342. National Accrediting Agency for Clinical Laboratory Sciences, 547 W Jackson Blvd, Ste 608, Chicago, IL 60606; (312) 461-0333. Provides advice on operating existing programs, developing new programs in clinical laboratory sciences (onsite consultations arranged at cost); conducts regional workshops.

17343. National Animal Poison Control Center, Coll of Veterinary Medicine, Univ of Ill., 2001 S Lincoln, Urbana, IL 61801; (217) 333-3611. Hotline that receives telephone calls pertaining to poisoning or chemical contamination of animals. Services to veterinarians, poison control centers.

17344. National Anti-Vivisection Society, 100 E Ohio St, Chicago, IL 60611; (312) 787-4486. Dessiminates info on animal experimentation. Provides advisory and reference services, conducts seminars, permits onsite use of collection. Services free.

17345. National Association for the Cottage Industry, P.O. Box 14850, Chicago, IL 60614; (312) 472-8116. Provides advisory, reference services for home-based businesses. Evaluates and analyzes data, conducts seminars and workshops. Fee for services.

17346. National Association of Anorexia Nervosa and Associated Disorders, P.O. Box 271, Highland Park, IL 60035; (312) 831-3438. Provides reference, advisory services on eating disorders. Conducts workshops, conferences; helps form self-help groups. Services free.

17347. National Association of Architectural Metal Manufacturers, 221 N LaSalle St, Chicago, IL 60601; (312) 346-1600. Represents fabricators of hollow, architectural, ornamental metal products, metal flagpoles, metal bar grating. Publishes manuals, standards, specifications; answers inquiries.

17348. National Association of Boards of Pharmacy, 1300 Higgins Rd, Ste 103, Park Ridge, IL 60068; (312) 698-6227. Provides for interstate reciprocity of licensure of pharmacists. Provides advisory and reference services, conducts seminars. Most services free.

17349. National Association of College Admissions Counselors, c/o Dr Charles A. Marshall, Exec Dir, 9933 Lawler Ave, Ste 500, Skokie, IL 60077; (312) 676-0500. Conducts conferences, seminars, workshops on college admissions; operates nationwide college search hotline. Services free to members.

17350. National Association of Dealers in Antiques, c/o Shirley Kowing, 5859 N Main Rd, Rockford, IL 61103; (815) 877-4282. Answers inquiries from researchers on antique glass, china, furniture, art objects characterized by handicraft or historic interest; publishes bulletin. Services free.

17351. National Association of Fire Investigators, 53 W Jackson Blvd, Room 300, Chicago, IL 60604; (312) 939-6050. Provides advisory, reference services; conducts seminars; certifies fire investigators. Services free.

17352. National Association of Future Women, 7900 Cass Ave, Ste 115, Darien, IL 60559; (312) 960-2528. Provides networking to enhance women's potential for career and personal growth. Provides reference services, conducts seminars. Services free.

17353. National Association of Health Services Executives, 840 N Lake Shore Dr, 7th Fl/E Wing, Chicago, IL

60611; (312) 280-6697. Evaluates quality of health care services to disadvantaged and poor. Provides advisory and job referral services, conducts seminars, workshops. Fee for services.

17354. National Association of Juvenile Correctional Agencies, c/o Donald G. Blackburn, Secty-Treas, 36 Locksley Lane, Springfield, IL 62704; (217) 787-0690. Interest in prevention, treatment of juvenile delinquency; accreditation standards for training schools. Answers inquiries, provides reference services.

17355. National Association of Power Engineers, 2350 E Devon Ave, Ste 115, Des Plaines, IL 60018; (312) 298-0600. Answers inquiries on qualifications of power engineers, training programs, licensure requirements; conducts educational programs. Fee for some services.

17356. National Association of Professional Band Instrument Repair Technicians, P.O. Box 51 (8 Ardith Dr), Normal, IL 61761; (309) 452-4257. Upgrades knowledge of repair, restoration, maintenance of band instruments. Provides advisory, reference services; conducts seminars, workshops. Most services free.

17357. National Association of Public/Private Employer Negotiators and Administrators, 805 W Wolfram St, Unit 6, Chicago, IL 60657; (312) 528-1605. Provides consulting, reference services; conducts training seminars, workshops in contract negotiation. Services for a fee to management in public and private sectors.

17358. National Association of Service Merchandising, 221 N LaSalle St, 8th Fl, Chicago, IL 60601; (312) 368-1278. Provides info on distributing and merchandising general consumer goods, health and beauty aids sold through mass markets. Services to professional orgs.

17360. National Association of Women Business Owners, 500 N Michigan Ave, Ste 1400, Chicago, IL 60611; (312) 661-1700. Provides sources for marketing, technical assistance to women business owners. Publishes public policy position statements, conducts seminars, workshops. Most services free.

17361. National Automobile Theft Bureau, Public Relations Dept, 10330 S Roberts Rd, Palos Hills, IL 60465; (312) 430-2430. Implements policies for preventing vehicle theft, arson, and fraud, locates and identifies stolen vehicles. Services free.

17362. National Clearinghouse for Legal Services, 407 S Dearborn, Ste 400, Chicago, IL 60605; (312) 939-3830. Provides free info to attorneys representing poor. Publishes manuals, bibliographies; provides reference, copying services. Services for a fee to non-attorneys.

17363. National Coalition on Television Violence, P.O. Box 2159 (406 N Romine, Urbana, IL), Champaign, IL 61820 ; (217) 384-1920. Studies problems caused by use of violence to entertain. Provides free advisory and reference services, conducts seminars, permits onsite use of collection. Services free.

17364. National Committee for Prevention of Child Abuse, 332 S Michigan Ave, Ste 1250, Chicago, IL 60604; (312) 663-3520. Interest in prevention of child abuse. Answers inquiries, provides consulting services, publishes booklets and pamphlets. Fees charged for all services.

17365. National Committee on Uniform Traffic Laws and Ordinances, P.O. Box 1409 (405 Church St), Evanston, IL 60204; (312) 491-5280. Provides brief answers to inquiries on promotion of uniformity in traffic laws and ordinances. Prepares analyses, permits onsite use of collection by special arrangement.

17367. National Confectioners Association, 645 N Michigan Ave, Ste 1006, Chicago, IL 60611; (312) 280-1460. Answers inquiries on candy manufacturing technology. Sponsors research programs, seminars, annual convention, and triannual exposition of candymaking equipment and services.

17368. National Conference of Commissioners on Uniform State Laws, 645 N Michigan Ave, Ste 510, Chicago, IL 60611; (312) 321-9710. Publishes model state laws, handbook of natl conference of commissioners on uniform state laws, pamphlets of uniform acts. Answers inquiries free, provides duplication services at cost.

17369. National Council for Geographic Education, c/o Western Ill. Univ, Macomb, IL 61455; (309) 298-2470. Publishes journal, books, leaflets, newsletter on geographic education, environmental education, related fields. Answers inquiries, makes referrals to other sources of info.

17370. National Dairy Council Library, 6300 N River Rd, Rosemont, IL 60018; (312) 696-1020. Nonprofit org interested in dairy science and dairy products. Conducts research, develops educational materials, provides reference and copying services, permits onsite use of collection. Most services free.

17371. National Downs Syndrome Congress, 1640 W Roosevelt Rd, Chicago, IL 60608; (312) 226-0416; (800) 446-3835. Promotes public awareness of Downs syndrome. Provides info and referral services through parent groups nationwide. Services free.

17372. National Electronic Distributors Association, 1420 Renaissance Dr, Park Ridge, IL 60068; (312) 298-9747. Publishes annual survey, journal on electronic merchandising for distributors, suppliers; provides data on sales performance. Answers inquiries; provides advisory services.

17373. National Employee Services and Recreation Association, 2400 S Downing Ave, Westchester, IL 60153; (312) 562-8130. Develops employee services and recreation programs for business, industry. Provides advisory services; conducts conferences, workshops, exhibits.

17374. National Eye Research Foundation, 899 Skokie Blvd, Northbrook, IL 60062; (312) 564-4652. Sponsors research on eye care. Provides advisory, reference services; conducts public info programs. Services generally free.

17375. National Family Business Council Resource Center, 8600 W Bryn Mawr Ave, Ste 720, Chicago, IL 60631; (312) 693-0990. Promotes common interests of family-owned businesses. Provides consulting services, conducts seminars. Services free to members, at cost to others.

17376. National Fertilizer Solutions Association, 8823 N Industrial Rd, Peoria, IL 61615; (309) 691-2870. Conducts research on behalf of fertilizer industry; acts as liaison between industry, govt, public. Distributes audiovisual materials. Reference services free.

17377. National Garden Bureau, 628 Exec Dr, Willowbrook, IL 60521; (312) 655-0010. Disseminates gardening info. Publishes data sheets; provides advisory, consulting, reference services; lends materials. Services free to garden communicators.

17378. National Hearing Association, 721 Enterprise Dr, Oak Brook, IL 60521; (312) 323-7200. Nonprofit assn that provides info on research on treating hearing impairment. Provides advisory and reference services, conducts seminars. Most services free.

17379. National Housewares Manufacturers Association, 1324 Merchandise Mart, Chicago, IL 60654; (312) 644-3333. Publishes business survey of American housewares industry. Distributes films, press releases, history book; sponsors semiannual National Housewares Exposition. Services to schools, libraries, community groups.

17380. National Institute for the Foodservice Industry, 20 N Wacker Dr, Ste 2620, Chicago, IL 60606; (312) 782-1703. Provides advisory, reference services; conducts seminars, workshops; permits onsite use of collection. Services at cost to food service industry personnel, teachers, students.

17381. National LP-Gas Association, 1301 W 22nd St, Oak Brook, IL 60521; (312) 986-4800. Answers inquiries; maintains data bank of training resources available to industry; provides consulting, reference services. Services at nominal charge.

17382. National Live Stock and Meat Board, 444 N Michigan Ave, Chicago, IL 60611; (312) 467-5520. Nonprofit service org of livestock and meat industry. Distributes educational publications and audiovisual aids, provides reference services. Most materials provided at cost.

17383. National Marine Exhaust Research Council, 401 N Michigan Ave, Chicago, IL 60611; (312) 836-4747. Conducts studies on effects of marine engine usage on aquatic environments. Publishes abstracts, answers inquiries. Services free in small quantities.

17384. National Marine Manufacturing Association, 401 N Michigan Ave, Chicago, IL 60611; (312) 836-4747. Answers inquiries on pleasure craft manufacturing. Publishes technical reports; provides marketing, consulting, bibliographic services; permits onsite use of collection.

17385. National Merit Scholarship Corp., One American Plaza, Evanston, IL 60201; (312) 866-5100. Nonprofit org that administers competitions for Natl Merit and Natl Achievement Scholarship Program for Outstanding Negro Students; establishes eligibility requirements; selects winners.

17386. National Migraine Foundation, 5252 N Western Ave, Chicago, IL 60625; (312) 878-7715. Sponsors headache research; acts as resource center for migraine sufferers. Provides consulting, reference services; conducts seminars; analyzes data.

17387. National Nurses Society on Addictions, 2506 Gross Point Rd, Evanston, IL 60201; (312) 475-7300. Advocates programs to improve treatment of persons addicted to alcohol. Answers inquiries, evaluates data, conducts seminars and workshops. Services at cost.

17388. National Opinion Research Center, Univ of Chicago, 6030 S Ellis Ave, Chicago, IL 60637; (312) 962-1213. Conducts research on survey methodology; provides consultation for questionnaire design. Researchers may apply for access to collection. Answers to substantive questions provided at cost.

17389. National Osteopathic Foundation, 212 E Ohio St, Chicago, IL 60611; (312) 280-5850, (800) 621-1773. Provides low-cost student loans, info on osteopathic research. Provies advisory services, conducts seminars, lends materials. Free services available to physicians and patients.

17391. National Research Bureau, 310 S Michigan Ave, Ste 1150, Chicago, IL 60604; (312) 663-5580. Provides detailed data on shopping centers in U.S. Answers inquiries, distributes publications, makes referrals to other sources of info.

17392. National Roofing Contractors Association, 8600 Bryn Mawr Ave, Chicago, IL 60631; (312) 693-0700. Interest in roofing application techniques. Publishes magazine and technical reports, provides consulting services, conducts seminars. Services at cost to nonmembers.

17393. National Safe Transit Association, 625 N Michigan Ave, Chicago, IL 60611; (312) 337-7462. Nonprofit org that establishes, promotes performance criteria for preshipment testing of packaged products; publishes test procedures for package manufacturers, package testing labs.

17394. National Safety Council, Campus Safety Association, 444 N Michigan Ave, Chicago, IL 60011; (312) 527-4800 ext 290. Disseminates info on accident prevention to college campuses; sponsors natl safety awards. Provides advisory and reference services, awards scholarships. Some services free.

17395. National Safety Council, Safety Research Information Service, 444 N Michigan Ave, Chicago, IL 60611; (312) 527-4800. Makes available research reports on accident prevention (related to industrial, traffic, home, school, or farm safety); provides literature-searching services; makes referrals.

17396. National Safety Council, Research Department, 444 N Michigan Ave, Chicago, IL 60611; (312) 527-4800. Interest in studies on accident prevention and mitigation of injury and economic loss. Answers inquiries, provides consulting services, makes referrals.

17397. National Sash and Door Jobbers Association, 205 W Touhy, Ste 211, Park Ridge, IL 60068; (312) 823-6300. Publishes standards for woodwork products used in house construction. Provides audiovisual program, conducts correspondence course. Services generally free.

17398. National Sisters Vocation Conference, 1307 S Wabash Ave, Ste 350, Chicago, IL 60605; (312) 939-6180. Deepens understanding of women apostolates. Publishes studies; provides consulting, reference services; conducts seminars, conferences, workshops. Most services free.

17399. National Sporting Goods Association, 1699 Wall St, Mount Prospect, IL 60056; (312) 439-4000. Answers inquiries on sporting goods retailing. Analyzes data, conducts seminars and workshops, permits onsite use of collection. Fee for some services.

17400. National Standards Council of American Embroiderers, P.O. Box 8578, Northfield, IL 60093; (404) 256-1079 (Pres), (412) 279-0299 (School). Promotes art of embroidery. Provides exhibition opportunities; conducts seminars, workshops, correspondence school; lends materials. Services free.

17401. National Training and Information Center, 954 W Washington Blvd, Chicago, IL 60607; (312) 243-3035. Dedicated to neighborhood preservation. Provides onsite consultation, conducts training courses, conducts research. Fee for services.

17402. National Tuberous Sclerosis Association, P.O. Box 612, Winfield, IL 60190; (312) 668-0787. Interest in research on tuberous sclerosis. Provides advisory, reference services; conducts seminars, workshops; operates speakers bureau. Services free.

17403. National Woman's Christian Temperance Union Memorial Library, 1730 Chicago Ave, Evanston, IL 60201; (312) 864-1396. Answers inquiries on temperance reform. Provides reference services, conducts seminars and workshops, permits onsite use of collection. Most services free.

17404. National Wood Tank Institute, 848 Eastman St, Chicago, IL 60622; (312) 664-4272. Answers inquiries on specifications and recommended practice for wood tanks and continuous stave wood pipe. Distributes publications. Services free.

17405. National Woodwork Manufacturers Association, 205 W Touhy Ave, Park Ridge, IL 60068; (312) 823-6747. Publishes reports, directories; provides advisory services; administers seal of approval programs for hardwood doors. Technical standards free to architects, builders, govt agencies.

17406. Natural Land Institute, c/o George B. Fell, Exec Dir, 320 S 3rd St, Rockford, IL 61108; (815) 964-6666. Owns herbarium of northern Ill. plants. Provides free advisory and reference services; permits onsite use of collection.

17407. Naval Dental Research Institute, Bldg 1-H, Great Lakes, IL 60088; (312) 688-4678. Conducts research on dental health problems in Navy and Marine Corps populations. Provides consulting services. Services free and available to univs, research labs, govt agencies.

17408. Non-Ferrous Founders' Society, 455 State St, Ste 100, Des Plaines, IL 60016; (312) 299-0950. Interest in quality control, marketing of castings. Provides advisory services; publishes reports, conducts seminars and workshops. Fee for services.

17409. North American Professional Driver Education Association, 4935 W Foster Ave, Chicago, IL 60630; (312) 777-9605; Lending Library: P.O. Box 341; Fargo, ND 58107; (701) 293-7691. Publishes training, research, legislative affairs bulletins; provides single copies free of difficult-to-find research studies on driver education; lends materials by mail.

17410. North American Society of Adlerian Psychology, c/o Neva L. Hefner, Exec Secty, 159 N Dearborn St, Chicago, IL 60601; (312) 346-3458. Publishes books, research journal, newsletter, tapes on clinical psychology, psychiatry; answers inquiries; provides consulting services; makes referrals to other sources of info.

17412. Northeastern Illinois Planning Commission Library, 400 W Madison St, Chicago, IL 60606; (312) 454-0400. Provides demographic info on northeastern Ill. and profession of regional planning. Provides reference services, lends materials. Onsite use of collections available.

17413. Northern Hardwood and Pine Manufacturers Association, 8600 W Bryn Mawr Ave, Ste 720-South, Chicago, IL 60631; (312) 693-0990. Publishes newsletter, grading rules for northern hardwood, softwood logs. Provides consulting services, conducts seminars and workshops. Fee for services.

17415. Open Lands Project, 53 W Jackson Blvd, Chicago, IL 60604; (312) 427-4256. Promotes land preservation for conservation, recreation, scientific purpose. Engages in environmental education, conducts workshops. Most services free.

17416. Oriental Institute, Univ of Chicago, 1155 E 58th St, Chicago, IL 60637; (312) 962-9514. Conducts research on ancient Near East; does archeological excavations. Provides advisory, reference services; conducts seminars, workshops. Services at cost.

17417. Overseas Sales and Marketing Association, 3500 Devon Ave, Chicago, IL 60659; (312) 679-6070. Acts as forum for exchange of views and as clearinghouse for contacts with manufacturers, overseas buyers, and govt agencies.

17418. Pain Clinic, Coll of Medicine, 840 S Wood St, Rm 425, Chicago, IL 60612; (312) 996-7516. Answers inquiries; provides advisory, reference services on pain control through nerve blocking; conducts seminars; evaluates data. Most services free.

17419. Paper Industry Management Association, 2400 E Oakton Rd, Arlington Heights, IL 60005; (312) 956-0250. Publishes paper mill catalog and engineering handbook; answers inquiries; prepares in-depth reviews of selected papermaking processes; organizes training seminars.

17420. Parmly Hearing Institute, Loyola Univ of Chicago, 6525 N Sheridan Rd, Chicago, IL 60626; (312) 508-2710. Conducts auditory research. Answers inquiries, provides general reference services, conducts seminars, evaluates data. Services free, provided at discretion of institute.

17421. Paul Weir Co., Library, 20 N Wacker Dr, Ste 2828, Chicago, IL 60606; (312) 346-0275. Answers inquiries about coal mining engineering. Provides reference services, permits onsite use of collection. Services free to users in Chicago Library System, at cost to others.

17422. Percussive Arts Society, 214 W Main, Urbana, IL 61801; (217) 367-4098. Answers inquiries on music education and literature. Publishes reports, provides reference services, makes referrals to other sources of info.

17423. Physicians Forum, 220 S State St, Ste 1322, Chicago, IL 60604; (312) 922-1968. Membership org concerned with promotion of natl health system. Provides brief answers to inquiries about legislation, social programs; provides speakers; analyzes legislation.

17424. Pilot Guide Dog Foundation, 1123 W Wolfram St, Chicago, IL 60657; (312) 871-1336. Provides pilot guide dogs free to all qualified blind persons. Answers inquiries, provides advisory services. Services free, available only to blind persons.

17425. Polish American Historical Association, 984 Milwaukee Ave, Chicago, IL 60622; (312) 384-3352. Interest in history and culture of Poles in U.S. Answers inquiries; provides advisory, copying, microform services. Most services free.

17426. Polyurethane Manufacturers Association, 800 Roosevelt Rd, Bldg C, Ste 20, Glen Ellyn, IL 60137; (312) 858-2670. Publishes standards, directories, technical papers, videotapes on manufacture of polyurethane products; conducts workshops. Most services free.

17427. Portland Cement Association, 5420 Old Orchard Rd, Skokie, IL 60077; (312) 966-6200. Publishes reports, reviews, design data handbooks, quality control practices, bibliographies, films, slides pertaining to concrete projects; permits onsite use of collection.

17428. Powder Actuated Tool Manufacturers Institute, c/o T. David McFarland, Exec Dir, 435 N Michigan Ave, Ste 1717, Chicago, IL 60611; (312) 644-0828. Publishes standards and specifications for powder actuated fastening tools. Offers advisory services to govt, construction trades, labor councils, industries, contractors.

17429. Power Conversion Products Council International, P.O. Box 637 (17730 W Peterson Rd), Libertyville, IL 60048; (312) 362-3201. Disseminates info on power conversion products, including magnetic components, transformers, reactors, amplifiers, coils; conducts seminars, workshops. Fee for services.

17430. Power Tool Institute, 5105 Tollview Dr, Rolling Meadows, IL 60008; (312) 577-8350. Nonprofit assn of electric and battery operated power tool manufacturers. Answers inquiries, provides general reference services. Most services free.

17431. Pressure Sensitive Tape Council, c/o Carl A. Wangman, Exec Dir, 1800 Pickwick Ave, Glenview, IL 60025; (312) 724-7700. Publishes products directory on pressure sensitive tape and uses. Answers inquiries; consults with specification writing agencies to establish test methods and standard nomenclature.

17432. Prestressed Concrete Institute, 201 N Wells St, Chicago, IL 60606; (312) 346-4071. Publishes reports, design handbook on applications of prestressed concrete. Answers inquiries, makes referrals to other sources of info, permits onsite use of collection.

17433. Pro & Con Screening Board, 203 N Wabash, Ste 1804, Chicago, IL 60601; (312) 221-1231. Helps minorities understand how negative images on film, television affect self-esteem, vocational outlook. Conducts seminars, workshops. Fee for services.

17434. Professional Photographers of America, 1090 Exec Way, Des Plaines, IL 60018; (312) 299-8161. Answers inquiries on professional photography: portrait, commercial, or industrial. Publishes directory, refers inquirers to other sources of info, provides info on careers.

17435. Profit Sharing Council of America, 20 N Wacker Dr, Ste 722, Chicago, IL 60606; (312) 372-3411. Promotes profit sharing among employers; publishes annual survey. Provides free reference services, conducts seminars and workshops, permits onsite use of collection.

17436. Profit Sharing Research Foundation, 1718 Sherman Ave, Evanston, IL 60201; (312) 869-8787. Publishes info on profit sharing; provides reference, abstracting, copying service; conducts seminars, workshops; permits onsite use of collection. Services free.

17437. Program for Collaborative Research in the Pharmaceutical Sciences, Coll of Pharmacy, Univ of Ill., Health Sciences Center, 833 S Wood St, Chicago, IL 60612; (312) 996-7253. Provides literature searches from computer bank on all aspects of natural products; holds bibliography on chemical compounds isolated from living organisms.

17438. Property Loss Research Bureau, 1501 Woodfield Rd, Ste 400 West, Schaumburg, IL 60195-4978; (312) 490-8653. Natl membership org consisting of property and casualty insurers. Provides basic services to members only, but will give brief answers to technical inquiries.

17439. Radiological Society of North America, c/o Adele Swenson, Exec Dir, 1415 W 22nd St, Oak Brook, IL 60521; (312) 920-2670. Publishes radiology journals, reports, reviews; provides abstracting, indexing, microform services; conducts seminars, workshops. Services at cost to nonmembers.

17440. Railroad Retirement Board, 844 Rush St, Chicago, IL 60611; (312) 751-4500. Administers Railroad Retirement and Railroad Unemployment Insurance Acts. Conducts seminars, annual conferences; answers inquiries about retirement, health insurance activities; offers free employment service to qualified railroad workers.

17441. Recovery, The Association of Nervous and Former Mental Patients, 802 N Dearborn St, Chicago, IL 60610; (312) 337-5661. Demonstrates self-help methods to prevent relapses in former mental patients. Answers inquiries, publishes bimonthly magazine.

17442. Rehabilitation Engineering Program, 345 E Superior St, Rm 1441, Chicago, Il 60611; (312) 649-8560. Involved in research on prosthetics, orthotics, and total joint replacement. Answers inquiries, provides advisory and reference services. Fee for services.

17443. Rehabilitation Institute of Chicago, Learning Resources Center, 345 E Superior St, Chicago, IL 60611; (312) 908-2859. Answers inquiries on rehab of physically disabled. Provides advisory and reference services, permits onsite use of collection. Services free.

17444. Reinforced Concrete Research Council, c/o Portland Cement Assn, 5420 Old Orchard Rd, Skokie, IL 60077; (312) 966-6200. Publishes technical reports on reinforced concrete research and design; answers inquiries free.

17445. Research Resources Center, Health Sciences Center, 1940 W Taylor St, Chicago, IL 60612; (312) 663-7600. Publishes papers on electronic instrumentation, nuclear magnetic resonance spectroscopy. Owns research instruments; provides consulting, reference services to univs.

17446. Research-in-Aging Laboratory, Veterans Administration Medical Center, 151G, N Chicago, IL 60064; (312) 688-1900 ext 3078. Stores info on aging and developmental defects. Provides advisory and reference services, conducts seminars, permits onsite use of collection. Services at cost.

17447. Roof Coatings Manufacturers Association, 8600 W Bryn Mawr Ave, Chicago, IL 60631; (312) 693-0990. Develops standards and specifications for cold process protective roof coatings. Answers inquiries, conducts seminars and workshops. Services at cost.

17448. SEARCHLINE, P.O. Box F (4914 Columbia Ave), Lisle, IL 60532-0188; (312) 964-0127. Specializes in unconventional searches involving chemistry, engineering, biomedicine, environmental science. Offers consulting services for a fee.

17449. SHARE, c/o St John's Hospital, 800 E Carpenter St, Springfield, IL 62769; (217) 544-6464. Offers support for parents grieving loss of infant. Provides advisory services, conducts workshops, makes referrals to other sources. Most services free.

17451. Salmon Unlimited, c/o Roy Mueller, Pres, 4322 W Lawrence Ave, Chicago, IL 60630; (312) 736-5757 (office), (312) 729-2800 (hotline). Nonprofit corp that answers inquiries, provides consulting services free to anyone interested in Great Lakes sport fishery. Conducts seminars, provides speakers.

17452. Scoliosis Research Society, 222 S Prospect, Park Ridge, IL 60068; (312) 822-0970. Promotes and develops knowledge of causes, cures, prevention of scoliosis; conducts seminars for orthopaedic surgeons. Services, some at cost, restricted to orgs in field.

17453. Screen Manufacturers Association, c/o June G. Fitzgerald, Exec Secty, Ste 201 Park Place, 655 Irving Park, Chicago, IL 60613; (312) 525-2644. Publishes newsletter, standards, specifications for screening industry; answers inquiries.

17454. Second Harvest, Communications Department, 343 S Dearborn St, Ste 516, Chicago, IL 60604; (312) 341-1303. Distributes surplus food to food banks nationwide. Provides advisory, reference services; conducts seminars. Most services free.

17455. Self-Help Center, 1600 Dodge Ave, Ste S-122, Evanston, IL 60201; (312) 328-0470. Encourages self-help groups for persons with health problems. Provides advisory and reference services, conducts workshops, permits onsite use of collection. Fee for services.

17456. Shore Line Interurban Historical Society, P.O. Box 346, Chicago, IL 60690. Educates and promotes interest in three electric interurban railways of Chicago. Answers inquiries, makes referrals to other sources of info. Most services free.

17457. Slavic and East European Library, 1408 W Gregory Dr, Urbana, IL 61801; (217) 333-1349. Provides reference services on Slavic studies. Conducts seminars and workshops, permits onsite use of collection. Most services free.

17458. Sleep Laboratory, Dept of Psychiatry, Univ of Chicago, 5741 S Drexel Ave, Chicago, IL 60637; (312) 753-2353. Conducts research on physiology and function of sleep. Answers inquiries, performs literature sources, permits onsite use of collection. Services free to scientists.

17459. Small Homes Council, One E Saint Mary's Rd, Champaign, IL 61820; (217) 333-1801. Answers inquiries free on construction methods for low-rise housing. Conducts seminars and workshops for a fee, publishes reports, permits onsite use of collection.

17460. Small Motor Manufacturers Association, P.O. Box 637 (17730 W Peterson Rd), Libertyville, IL 60048; (312) 362-3201. Provides info on technical and industry data on fractional and subfractional horsepower motors. Conducts seminars, workshops. Fee for services.

17461. Society for the Study of Reproduction, 309 W Clark St, Champaign, IL 61820; (217) 356-3182. Composed of researchers in obstetrics, gynecology, urology, zoology. Publishes journals and bibliographies, conducts meetings. Services to professionals only.

17462. Society of Actuaries, 500 Park Blvd, Itasca, IL 60143; (312) 773-3010. Interest in actuarial science. Publishes educational texts, mortality tables, reports, research studies, career info; answers inquiries; provides reference services; makes referrals.

17463. Society of American Archivists, 600 S Federal St, Ste 504, Chicago, IL 60605; (312) 922-0140. Publishes standards, reviews, directories, bibliographies of archives profession; provides advisory, reference, abstracting services; conducts seminars, workshops; provides info on research; lends materials.

17464. Society of Die Casting Engineers, 2000 N 5th Ave, River Grove, IL 60171; (312) 452-0700. Owns books, journals, reports concerning metallurgy; publishes bimonthly magazine, reports, proceedings, reference books; answers inquiries; provides copying services for a fee.

17465. Society of Professional Business Consultants, 221 N LaSalle St, Chicago, IL 60601; (312) 346-1600. Answers inquiries on business consultation for physicians, dentists. Provides reference services, conducts seminars and workshops. Most services free, available to medical professionals.

17466. Society of Real Estate Appraisers, 645 N Michigan Ave, Chicago, IL 60611; (312) 346-7422. Provides info primarily through journal, guides, books, courses on real estate appraising, planning, and finance. Some publications free.

17467. Society of University Otolaryngologists, c/o Edward Applebaum, MD, 1855 W Taylor, Chicago, IL 60612; (312) 996-6582. Publishes abstracts on research in otolaryngology; answers inquiries. Service free.

17468. Solution Mining Research Institute, 812 Muriel St, Woodstock, IL 60098; (815) 338-8579. Acts as technol-

ogy center for solution mining industry. Provides advisory and reference services, disseminates info on current research. Fee for services.

17469. Sonia Shankman Orthogenic School, Univ of Chicago, 1365 E 60th St, Chicago, IL 60637; (312) 753-8682. Interest in emotional disturbances of childhood and adolescence. Answers inquiries free.

17470. Special Services Center, 809 W Madison St, Ste 602, Chicago, IL 60607; (312) 226-7990. Interest in reintegrating ex-offenders into community. Provides advisory, consulting, reference services. Some services free.

17471. Speech and Hearing Research Laboratory, Dept of Speech and Hearing Science, Univ of Ill., 901 S 6th, Champaign, IL 61820; (217) 333-2230. Interest in physiology of speech production. Answers inquiries; provides access to computerized data bases; offers consulting, magnetic tape services; conducts seminars.

17472. Spertus Museum of Judaica, 618 S Michigan Ave, Chicago, IL 60605; (312) 922-9012. Answers inquiries about Jewish culture, art. Provides reference services, conducts seminars and workshops, permits onsite use of collection. Services at cost.

17473. Spina Bifida Association of America, 343 S Dearborn St, Chicago, IL 60604; (312) 663-1562; (800) 621-3141. Funds research on spina bifida. Provides list of resources offering financial support to families; conducts seminars. Services generally free.

17474. Spring Manufacturers Institute, 380 W Palatine Rd, Wheeling, IL 30090; (312) 520-3290. Interest in precision mechanical springs and allied products. Publishes handbook of spring design, history of spring industry; answers brief inquiries; refers inquirers to member companies.

17475. Stan A. Huber Consultants, 200 N Cedar Rd, New Lenox, IL 60451; (815) 485-6161. Conducts seminars, courses on nuclear medicine technology. Provides consulting, reference services; performs nuclear equipment calibrations. Fee for services.

17476. Standard Oil Co. Indiana, Central Research Library, Amoco Research Center, P.O. Box 400, Naperville, IL 60566; (312) 420-5545. Makes interlibrary loans of books, reports on petroleum refining and chemistry, petroleum products, fuels research; provides access to computerized data bases.

17477. Steel Bar Mills Association, 1221 Locust St, Ste 405, St Louis, IL 63103; (314) 231-2011. Provides info on current research concerning problems in steelmaking. Evaluates data, conducts seminars and workshops. Services free, most limited to members.

17478. Steel Founders' Society of America, Cast Metals Federation Bldg, 455 State St, Des Plaines, IL 60016; (312) 299-9160. Publishes manuals, research reports, proceedings, standards and specifications on steelcastings; answers inquiries for anyone, but priority given to members and large users of steelcastings.

17479. Steel Plate Fabricators Association, 1250 Exec Pl, Ste 401, Geneva, IL 60134; (312) 232-8750. Publishes directory of metal plate fabricators, pamphlets, brochures, safety rules for fabricating shops; answers inquiries. Publications available for onsite reference.

17480. Steel Tank Institute, 666 Dundee Rd, Northbrook, IL 60062; (312) 644-6610. Interest in specifications, installation, use of corrosion-resistant underground steel liquid storage tanks. Answers inquiries free.

17481. Sun Foundation Center for Advancement in the Sciences, Art, and Education, R.R. 2, Washburn, IL 61570; (309) 246-8403. Increases access to arts, sciences, health, education. Provides reference services, conducts workshops, permits onsite use of collections. Most services free.

17482. Swedish-American Historical Society Archives, 5125 N Spaulding Ave, Chicago, IL 60625; (312) 583-5722. Answers inquiries on history of Swedes in U.S. with concentration on Chicago area. Permits onsite use of collection. Services generally free.

17483. Swiss-American Historical Society, c/o Prof. Marianne Burkhard, Pres, German Dept, Univ of Ill., Urbana, IL 61801; (217) 333-1288. Interest in history of Swiss immigrants to U.S. Answers inquiries, makes referrals to other sources of info. Services free.

17485. Therapeutic Communities of America, 624 S Michigan Ave, Chicago, IL 60605; (312) 663-1130. Provides advisory, reference services on treating substance abusers. Sets standards for licensing, conducts workshops. Most services provided for a fee.

17486. Touch of Nature Environmental Center, Southern Ill. Univ, Carbondale, IL 62901; (618) 529-4161. Answers inquiries on conservation and environmental education, special populations recreation and camping. Provides advisory services, makes referrals to other sources of info.

17487. Traffic Institute, P.O. Box 1409 (405 Church), Evanston, IL 60204; (312) 491-5476. Provides advisory, consulting, reference, abstracting services on traffic law. Provides info on research, conducts seminars and workshops. Fee for services.

17488. Tutorials of Cytology, 5841 S Maryland Ave, HM 449, Chicago, IL 60637; (312) 962-6577. Maintains close ties to Univ of Chicago and cytologic organizations. Provides consulting, reference services to members; conducts courses on cytologic topics.

17489. U.S. Psychotronics Association, 3459 Montrose Ave, Chicago, IL 60618; (312) 478-7715. Promotes free exchange of info on theories, practices related to psychotronics. Answers inquiries, conducts seminars and workshops. Fee for services.

17490. USA Toy Library Association, 1800 Pickwick Ave, Glenview, IL 60025; (312) 724-7700. Increases awareness of value of play; helps establish toy libraries. Provides reference services, conducts seminars and workshops. Most services free.

17491. USA-ROC Economic Council, P.O. Box 517 (200 S Main St), Crystal Lake, IL 60014; (815) 459-5875. Fosters business relations between U.S. and Taiwan.; Answers inquiries, identifies business opportunities. Services free to members.

17492. Underwriters Laboratories, 333 Pfingsten Rd, Northbrook, IL 60062; (312) 272-8800. Provides reference services on testing of products, equipment, methods for public safety. Publishes safety standards, annual directories of products. Catalog available on request.

17493. Union Carbide Corp., Films-Packaging Division Technical Library, 6733 W 65th St, Chicago, IL 60638; (312) 496-4286. Owns journals, abstracts, dissertations on high polymer chemistry, food science, technology. Makes interlibrary loans, permits onsite reference.

17494. United Parkinson Foundation, 360 W Superior St, Chicago, IL 60610; (312) 664-2344. Interest in Parkinson's disease. Provides consulting, reference services; conducts seminars, workshops; makes medical referrals for patients; permits onsite use of collection. Services free.

17495. University Film and Video Association, c/o Dept of Cinema and Photography, Southern Ill. Univ, Carbondale, IL 62901; (618) 453-2365. Intl org concerned with film. Answers inquiries, provides advisory and reference services. Most services free.

17496. University of Illinois Historical Survey, Library, 1408 W Gregory Dr, Urbana, IL 61801; (217) 333-1777. Answers inquiries on Ill. state and local history. Provides reference services, permits onsite use of collections. Services free.

17497. Upper Mississippi River Conservation Committee, 1830 Second Ave, Rock Island, IL 61201; (309) 793-5800. Sponsored by U.S. Fish and Wildlife Service, promotes conservation of natural resources of upper Mississippi River; publishes research reports.

17498. Vance Bibliographies, P.O. Box 229, Monticello, IL 61856; (217) 762-3831. Interest in public administration, architecture, city and regional planning. Sells bibliographies (pricelist available).

17499. Vibration Institute, 101 W 55th St, Clarendon Hills, IL 60514; (312) 654-2254. Promotes exchange of info on vibration technology. Provides advisory, reference, translation services; conducts seminars. Services at cost.

17500. Vitamin Information Bureau, 664 N Michigan Ave, Chicago, IL 60611; (312) 751-2223. Mail-order publishing firm devoted to better understanding of vitamins. Publishes booklets, filmstrips; distributes publications (most at nominal cost, some free in single copies).

17501. W.R. Grace and Co., Dearborn Chemical Library, 300 Genesee St, Lake Zurich, IL 60047; (312) 438-8241 ext 653. Holds books, periodicals, patents on chemical engineering, anticorrosion, boiler water treatment, water and air pollution control. permits onsite use of collection.

17502. Water Quality Association, 4151 Naperville Rd, Lisle, IL 60532; (312) 369-1600. Nonprofit assn with members involved in design, production, sale of equipment providing water to residential, commercial, industrial establishments. Answers inquiries free.

17503. Water Quality Research Council, 4151 Naperville Rd, Lisle, IL 60532; (312) 369-1600. Research and educational org that publishes books, technical reports, directories, on water quality. Answers inquiries. Most services free.

17504. Water Systems Council, 221 N LaSalle St, Attn: Charles Stolberg, Exec Dir, Chicago, IL 60601; (312) 346-1600. Answers inquiries on design, manufacture, installation, operation of farm and urban water systems. Publishes water systems handbook, pamphlets; makes referrals.

17506. Whey Products Institute, 130 N Franklin St, Chicago, IL 60606; (312) 782-5455. Represents whey products industry. Conducts research, provides advisory services, conducts seminars and workshops. Services free to members, univs, govt agencies.

17507. Women Employed Institute, 5 S Wabash Ave, Ste 415, Chicago, IL 60603; (312) 782-3902. Research division of org of working women. Provides advisory, consulting services; conducts conferences, educational programs. Fee for services.

17508. Wood Truss Council of America, 111 E Wacker Dr, Chicago, IL 60601; (312) 644-6610. Promotes interests of structural wood component manufacturers and suppliers. Conducts workshops and conferences. Fee for some services.

17509. Woodstock Institute, 417 S Dearborn St, Ste 400, Chicago, IL 60605; (312) 427-8070. Nonprofit org that revitalizes urban neighborhoods to benefit low-income residents. Provides advisory, consulting services; conducts seminars, workshops. Fee based on ability to pay.

Indiana

18001. Aerospace Research Applications Center, 611 N Capitol Ave, Indianapolis, IN 46204; (317) 264-4644. One of six similar centers set up by NASA to help find industrial uses for space research. Has complete file of NASA open literature on microfiche and computerized access to over 5 million articles, reports, etc. Fees for all reference services, but some at cost or less.

18002. Afro-American Arts Institute, Ind. Univ, 109 N Jordan Ave, Bloomington, IN 47405; (812) 335-9501. Interest in black music, dance, history. Answers inquiries, provides advisory and reference services, lends materials, permits onsite use of collections. Services free.

18003. Agency for Instructional Technology, P.O. Box A (1111 W 17th St), Bloomington, IN 47402-0120; (812) 339-2203, (800) 457-4509. U.S.-Canadian org that develops instructional materials using TV and computers. Acquires and distributes variety of TV and related printed materials for use as major learning resources. Has film/video archive, publishes annual catalog and guide. Extensive services for a fee.

18004. Alliance of Information and Referral Systems, 1100 W 42nd St, Suite 310, Indianapolis, IN 46208; (317) 923-8727. Offers professional umbrella for info and referral providers in public and voluntary agencies. Has data base of info and referral agencies in U.S. and Canada, publishes newsletter and directory, answers inquiries. Services generally available to members, others as resources permit.

18005. Alternative Technologies Association, P.O. Box 27246, Indianapolis, IN 46227; (317) 784-7744. Interest in alternative energy sources, energy conservation, home insulation. Publishes info sheets on insulation, answers inquiries, provides reference services, distributes publications. Most services free; SASE requested for mail replies.

18006. Amateur Athletic Union of the United States, 3400 W 86th St, Indianapolis, IN 46268; (317) 872-2900. Promotes and improves amateur sports in U.S., junior olympics, physical fitness programs. Publishes various sports handbooks, answers inquiries, provides advisory services. Services free, except for publications.

18007. American Animal Hospital Association, P.O. Box 768 (204 Lincoln Way East), Mishawaka, IN 46544; (219) 256-0280. Provides continuing ed for small animal veterinarians, sets standards for animal hospitals and clinics, disseminates consumer info on pet care. Publishes journals, books, brochures. Services free, except for some publications and requests requiring extensive time.

18008. American Camping Association, Bradford Woods, Martinsville, IN 46151; (317) 342-8456. Strives to assure highest professional practices for administration of organized camping. Has computerized listing of all organized camps in U.S., publishes magazine and annual guide. Answers inquiries, makes referrals. Some services for a fee.

18009. American College of Sports Medicine, P.O. Box 1440, Indianapolis, IN 46206; (317) 637-9200. Professional society interested in all medical and scientific aspects of physical activity. Publishes Sports Medicine Bulletin (quarterly), various monographs and position statements. Info free to those with professional interest in sports medicine; other services for a fee.

18010. American Institute of Parliamentarians, c/o B. Leiman, Exec Dir, 124 W Washington Blvd, Fort Wayne, IN 46802; (219) 422-3680. Promotes effective, democratic parliamentary practice; teaching of parliamentary procedure, training, certification, wider use of parliamentarians. Publishes quarterly journal, newsletter. Official opinions free to members; other services for a fee to all users.

18011. American Landrace Association, P.O. Box 671 (Interstate 65 at State Rte. 32), Lebanon, IN 46052; (317) 482-3042. Interest in Landrace breed of swine. Publishes monthly magazine, answers inquiries, provides advisory services. Info generally free to breeders.

18012. American Society for Geriatric Dentistry, c/o Dr William Borman, Exec Secty, 1121 W Michigan St, Ind. Univ, Indianapolis, IN 46202. Dedicated to maintenance and improvement of oral health of elderly. Has Arthur Elfenbaum Memorial Library of Geriatric Dentistry. Publishes authorized manual for professionals that is a guide for dental programs in nursing homes, answers inquiries, operates speakers bureau.

18014. American Society of Professional Ecologists, R-1, P.O. Box 269, Clayton, IN 46118; (317) 539-4653. Interest in environmental control, including air and water pollution, solid waste disposal, noise abatement, toxic substances, industrial wastes. Answers inquiries, distributes publications, makes referrals to other sources of info. Services free, except consulting to industry.

18015. Applied Stochastics Laboratory, School of Mechanical Engineering, Purdue Univ, W Lafayette, IN 47907; (317) 494-9775. Interest in applied stochastics, earthquake and wind engineering, with emphasis on instrumentation, dynamic measurement, and analysis. Publishes technical reports and research summaries, answers inquiries. Short inquiries free; charge for larger tasks.

18016. Archives of Traditional Music, Ind. Univ, Maxwell Hall, Room 057, Bloomington, IN 47405; (812) 335-8632. Interest in sound recordings of traditional music and verbal data from many geographical and cultural areas. Holdings include about 350,000 items, including film and videotapes. Tape copies and accompanying documentation may be available through purchase, exchange, or interlibrary loan.

18017. Arts Unlimiting, 1605 E 86th St, Indianapolis, IN 46240; (317) 253-5504. Provides arts-related training and info to orgs and individuals giving services to disabled persons. Publishes teaching materials and reprints; answers inquiries. Provides advisory and technical assistance services, conducts seminars and workshops. Services free.

18018. Association for Comparative Economic Studies, c/o Dr R. Skurski, Exec Secty, Dept of Economics, Univ of Notre Dame, Notre Dame, IN 46556; (219) 239-7016. Interest in economics and comparative economic studies. Publishes quarterly journals, distributed for a fee.

18019. Association for Continuing Higher Education, c/o Exec V.P., College of Graduate and Continuing Studies, Univ of Evansville, P.O. Box 329, Evansville, IN 47702; (812) 479-2471. Interest in adult education at college level and all aspects of evening college programs. Publishes quarterly journal, annual membership directory. Answers inquiries, provides consulting and reference services, makes referrals to other sources of info.

18020. Association of College Unions International, 400 E 7th St, Bloomington, IN 47405; (812) 332-8017. Interest in student activity and service centers. Has computerized data bank on union facilities and operations and small collection of books, periodicals, and reports. Publishes annual directory of members. Reference and referral services for a fee to nonmembers.

18021. Botanical Society of America, c/o David Dilcher, Secty, Biology Dept, Ind. Univ, Bloomington, IN 47405; (812) 335-9455. Interest in all aspects of botany and botanical education. Publishes monthly and quarterly journals, answers written inquiries within limits of staff time. Telephoned inquiries not accepted.

18022. Center for Governmental Services, Ind. State Univ, Terre Haute, IN 47809; (812) 232-6311 ext 5783. Interest in state and local administration in politics, election administration, and public access law. Publishes occasional newsletter, answers inquiries. Provides consulting, training, and reference services free to state agencies, at cost to others.

18023. Center for Information and Numerical Data Analysis and Synthesis, Purdue Industrial Research Park, 2595 Yeager Rd, W Lafayette, IN 47906; (317) 494-6300, 463-1581. Interest in collection, analysis, and correlation of thermophysical, electronic, electrical, magnetic, and optical property data for broad range of materials. Has computerized data base, about 200,000 unclassified technical papers. Reference services at cost.

18024. Center for Innovation in Teaching the Handicapped, School of Education, Ind. Univ, 2805 E 10th St, Bloomington, IN 47405; (812) 335-5847. Interest in design, development, evaluation of instructional materials for teacher trainers and preservice teachers of mildly handicapped and learning disabled children and adolescents. Services for a fee, except general inquiries, primarily for teachers of handicapped.

18025. Center for Urban and Regional Analysis, Ind. Univ, Poplars Bldg, Room 403, Bloomington, IN 47401; (812) 337-7874. Interest in urban and regional planning and research, econometric modeling, housing, transportation. Has large collection of housing and transportation research material. Provides advisory services for a fee, primarily for govt agencies or other urban and regional research centers.

18026. Center for the Study of the Future, 925 W Michigan St, Indianapolis, IN 46202; (317) 264-3984, 264-4796.

Devoted to exploring alternative futures. Answers inquiries, provides advisory and reference services; distributes publications, some provided for a fee.

18027. Clay Minerals Society, P.O. Box 2295, Bloomington, IN 47402; (812) 332-9600. Encourages and publishes research results on clays. Publishes bimonthly, answers inquiries, makes referrals to other sources of info. Fee for some services.

18028. Conservation Tillage Information Center, Exec Park, 2010 Inwood Dr, Fort Wayne, IN 46815; (219) 426-6642. Clearinghouse for info on conservation tillage. Interested in conservation tillage techniques, including no-till, ridge-till, strip-till, mulch-till, reduced-till, and fallow. Provides computerized abstract searches and distributes publications.

18029. Council of Administrators of Special Education, Ind. Univ, ES 3108, 902 W New York St, Indianapolis, IN 46223; (317) 264-3403. Interest in implementation of education programs and special education services for individuals with handicapping conditions. Publishes newsletter, answers inquiries. Provides services to legislative and regulatory agencies, school systems, colleges, and study commissions.

18030. Credit Research Center, Krannert Graduate School of Management, Purdue Univ, W Lafayette, IN 47907; (317) 494-4380. Conducts research on issues of public policy, consumer behavior, and managerial decision systems in consumer credit and mortgage credit. Answers inquiries, Provides computerized searching and reference services and info on research in progress. Services free.

18031. Cystic Fibrosis Research Center, Dept of Pulmonary Diseases, Riley Hospital, Ind. Univ, 702 Barn Hill Dr, Indianapolis, IN 46223; (317) 264-7208. Nonprofit org interested in cystic fibrosis and related pulmonary diseases. Answers inquiries, provides reference services, distributes publications. Services free, unless extensive.

18032. Developmental Training Center, Ind. Univ, 2853 E 10th St, Bloomington, IN 47405; (812) 335-6508. Provides interdisciplinary training, service, applied research for developmentally disabled. Has instructional and training materials, newsletters, videotapes, etc. Most reference services free, primarily for Ind. residents; others served on time-available basis.

18033. Electronic Music Consortium, School of Music, Ball State Univ, Muncie, IN 47306; (317) 285-5537. Sponsored by American Society of University Composers. Interest in electronic music, music composition, music engineering, electroacoustic performance, computer applications in music composition. Answers inquiries, provides advisory and tape services at cost.

18034. Electronics Technicians Association, International, Rt. 3, Box 564, Greencastle, IN 46135; (317) 653-3849.

Primary interest is continuing education in electronics technology. Has data base of practicing electronics technicians, computerized bank of electronics technology exam questions. Publishes monthly newsletter, annual directory. Routine inquiries answered free, other services subject to a fee.

18035. Eli Lilly and Co., Scientific Library, Lilly Corporate Center, Indianapolis, IN 46285; (317) 261-4030. Interest in biological, chemical, pharmacological, and pharmaceutical R&D; medicine. Has approximately 1.7 million cards of drug product info, pamphlets, promotional materials, clippings. Permits onsite use of collections with special permission. Services free to all users.

18036. Entomological Research Collection, Dept of Entomology, Purdue Univ, W Lafayette, IN 47907; (317) 494-4598. Interest in insects, with emphasis on insect fauna of Indiana; biosystematic and ecological research on aquatic insects, with emphasis on Ephemeroptera and Odonata. Has approximately one million insect specimens. Permits onsite use of collection. Reference services free.

18037. Environic Foundation International, P.O. Box 88, Notre Dame, IN 46556; (219) 233-3357. Initiates and sponsors educational activities in promotion of environmental awareness. Has files and slides on geotecture, thalatecture, nesotecture, synecotecture, psammotecture, hypsotecture, physiotecture. Services free, except for consulting.

18038. Eugene V. Debs Foundation, P.O. Box 843, Terre Haute, IN 47808; (812) 232-2163. Interest in life and work of American Socialist Eugene Debs, labor history, socialism. Maintains Debs home as museum, open to public. Distributes brochures, permits onsite use of collections. Services free.

18039. Food Research Library, Central Soya Co. Inc., P.O. Box 1400 (1946 W Cook Rd), Fort Wayne, IN 46801-1400; (219) 425-5906. Commercial firm interested in agribusiness, food processing, soybeans, lecithin, refined oils, microbiology, enzymology. Answers inquiries, provides reference services, distributes publications. Services free, except literature-searching and outside reprints.

18040. Gesneriad Society International, P.O. Box 102, Greenwood, IN 46142. Interest in Gesneria and Saintpaulia. Answers inquiries, provides advisory services, distributes seeds and newsletter. Services only to members or associated groups. Fee charged for seeds to cover postage.

18041. Girls Clubs of America, National Resource Center, 441 W Michigan St, Indianapolis, IN 46202. Provides info on girls, their growth and development, issues that have impact on women of tomorrow. Publishes newsletter, answers inquiries, distributes publications. Services free, except copying, available to youth-serving orgs; special services to those serving girls.

18042. Handy-Cap Horizons, 3250 E Loretta Dr, Indianapolis, IN 46227; (317) 784-5777. Nonprofit org interested in travel and recreation for handicapped, elimination of architectural barriers for handicapped in employment and housing, education of public on needs of handicapped. Publishes newsletter, magazine. Most services only for members.

18043. Haynes-Apperson Owners Club, c/o Mr. Wallace S. Huffman, President, 2125 S Webster St, Kokomo, IN 46901; (317) 453-6373. Interest in maintenance and preservation of Haynes-Apperson automobiles. Has catalogs, sales literature, pictures, letters, and related info on Haynes-Apperson autos and manufacturing. Reference services primarily for owners, on a limited basis to others, some free.

18044. Helen Kellogg Institute for International Studies, Univ of Notre Dame, 121 Decio Faculty Hall, Notre Dame, IN 46556; (219) 239-6580. Interest in research, education, outreach activities related to Third World development, especially of Latin America. International Documentation Center maintained in Memorial Library; contains newspapers, periodicals, pamphlets, clippings, reprints, etc. List of publications available.

18045. Hover Club of America, Box 216, Clinton, IN 47842-0216; (812) 466-2303. Promotes interest in hovercraft for sporting, recreational, and commercial purposes; affiliated with intl hovercraft clubs and orgs. Publishes quarterly newsletter, literature and general info, sends publications in response to inquiries; list of manufacturers available.

18046. Hudson Institute, P.O. Box 648 (620 Union Dr), Indianapolis, IN 46206. Supplements decision-makers' traditional sources of advice and ideas by providing independent analyses of issues, projecting long-range problems and changes, and suggesting alternative means to cope with them. Provides advisory and consulting services for a fee, distributes some reports.

18047. Hurty-Peck Library of Beverage Literature, 5650 W Raymond St, Indianapolis, IN 46241; (317) 243-3521. Interest in beverages: beer, ale, liquor, soft drinks, tea, wine, coffee, cocoa. Has world's largest collection of beverage literature (in English). Answers inquiries, permits onsite use of collection. Services free, except interlibrary loans and extensive copying.

18048. Indiana Historical Bureau, State Library and Historical Bldg, Room 408, 140 N Senate Ave, Indianapolis, IN 46204; (317) 232-2537. State agency interested in history of Ind. and Northwest Territory. Publishes monthly bulletin, maps, charts, and pamphlets for school and instructional uses. Disseminates info primarily through its publications, but sometimes will furnish other assistance to serious researchers.

18049. Indiana Limestone Institute of America, 400 Stone City Bank Bldg, Bedford, IN 47421; (812) 275-4426. Trade assn with membership east of Rocky Mountains engaged in quarrying, fabrication, and sale of Ind. limestone. Has motion pictures, photos, slides, pamphlets, related technical info, samples. Provides consulting services to architects, building owners, and engineers.

18050. Indiana State Library, 140 N Senate Ave, Indianapolis, IN 46204; (317) 232-3675. Interest in Ind. documents, history, government, politics, corps, library development, genealogy. Has more than 1 million items; serves as an Ind. Data Center and provides access to Ind. Information Retrieval System (INDIRS) data base. Permits onsite use of collections.

18051. Indianapolis Center for Advanced Research, 611 N Capitol Ave, Indianapolis, IN 46204; (317) 635-7666. Not-for-profit facility for scientific and engineering research, environmental-quality policy consultation. Publishes technical reports and R&D summaries, answers inquiries, makes referrals to other sources of info free.

18052. Institute for Child Study, Ind. Univ, Bypass 46, Bloomington, IN 47405; (812) 335-1732. Interest in language development, dialects, reading comprehension, and other aspects of school psychology of children; teaching of reading; use of psychometric instruments. Has 3,000 research reports, 1,000 govt documents. Approved academic users may have access to collection.

18053. Institute for Comprehensive Planning, P.O. Box 185, Valparaiso, IN 46383. Interest in statistics by state, county, and other geographical entities for handicapped, undereducated, unemployed. Answers inquiries, distributes publications. Services free to those with responsibilities in field, at cost to others.

18054. Institute for Environmental Health Studies, Purdue Univ, Lafayette, IN 47907; (317) 494-1436. Explores biological effects and toxicology of environmental toxicants. Particular attention is directed toward environmental causes of cancer, response of target tissue to environmental carcinogens. Answers inquiries, makes referrals, provides consulting services.

18055. Institute of Advanced Sanitation Research International, c/o Prog-Secty, 106 Drury Lane, W Lafayette, IN 47906; (317) 463-9203. Fellowship of doctoral and professional scientists and engineers in various nations, dedicated to science and technology of advancing sanitation research. Distributes publications, makes referrals to other sources of info. Services often free.

18056. Institute of Psychiatric Research, Dept of Psychiatry, School of Medicine, Ind. Univ, 1100 W Michigan St, Indianapolis, IN 46223; (317) 264-2375. Conducts basic and applied research in animals and man to explain mechanisms of neural function for application to clinical studies of mental disease. Answers inquiries, provides advisory and consulting services, distributes publications. Services free under most circumstances.

18057. International Buckskin Horse Association, c/o Exec Secty, P.O. Box 357, St John, IN 46373; (219) 365-8326. Preserves and records pedigrees of Buckskin, Dun, and Grulla horses. Collects data on Dun factor and genetics of Dun-type horse. Has registry of these horses, publishes information booklet. Services free, except subscription magazine.

18058. International John Steinbeck Society, c/o Dr Tetsumaro Hayashi, Pres, English Dept, Ball State Univ, Muncie, IN 47306; (317) 285-4044. Promotes interest in John Steinbeck's literature and biographical and bibliographical sources on him. Publishes quarterly, answers inquiries, and provides reference services to members. Users charged at cost.

18059. International League Against Rheumatism, 2211 Woodstock Place, Bloomington, IN 47401; (812) 333-1134. Assn of professional orgs in 69 countries that promotes intl cooperation for study, control, treatment of rheumatic diseases.

18060. International Society for Stereology, c/o Dr A-M Carpenter, V.P. for the Americas, N.W.C. Med. Ed., 3400 Broadway, Glen Park, IN 46408; (219) 980-6563. Interest in stereology applications in any discipline, including materials science, biology, forestry, and image analysis. Answers inquiries, provides advisory, consulting, and reference services, distributes publications. Fee for some services.

18061. Joint Highway Research Project, Civil Engineering Bldg, Purdue Univ, W Lafayette, IN 47907; (317) 494-2159. Interest in highway engineering, highway and transportation planning, urban planning, highway safety, traffic studies, public transportation. Has access to computerized Highway Research Information Service. Answers inquiries, permits onsite use of collection, lends research reports.

18062. Kinsey Institute for Research in Sex, Gender, and Reproduction, Ind. Univ, 416 Morrison Hall, Bloomington, IN 47405; (812) 335-7686. Interest in human sexual behavior, gender, reproduction. Has about 20,000 sexual case histories, along with manuscript items, photos, graphic arts, etc. Most holdings available for research purposes to bona fide scholars. Consulting services available; fees for all services.

18063. Laboratory for Applications of Remote Sensing, Purdue Univ, 1291 Cumberland Ave, W Lafayette, IN 47906; (317) 494-6305. Interest in remote sensing and its applications in agriculture, agronomy, forestry, geology, etc.; spectral measurement of soils, native vegetation. Publishes technical reports and R&D summaries. Small quantities of publications distributed free; other services at cost.

18064. Lowe's Syndrome Association, 222 Lincoln St, W Lafayette, IN 47906; (317) 743-3634. Fosters communication among families of boys with this genetic disease. Also provides info on the syndrome and encourages research.

18065. Magnavox Electronic Systems Corp. Library, 1313 Production Rd, Fort Wayne, IN 46808; (219) 482-4411. Interest in military electronics, including antisubmarine warfare, armament, communication, radar, and missile guidance, industrial electronics. Publishes reports and handbooks, provides reference services to employees and Defense Dept personnel. For others, access subject to approval.

18066. Medieval Institute, Univ of Notre Dame, 715 Memorial Library, Notre Dame, IN 46556; (219) 239-6603. Interest in research and instruction in Christian civilization of Middle Ages, medieval intellectual history. Has extensive collection of books, manuscripts, photos, etc. Answers inquiries, provides advisory, reference, computer searching, reproduction, and microform services.

18067. Mobil Electronics Research Laboratories, 5300 Alexandria Pike, Anderson, IN 46011-9598; (317) 642-7976. Interest in radio communications, wireless power, gravitation by electromagnetics, weather control by electromagnetic means, automatic signalling and control devices, radiant energy devices. Answers brief inquiries, provides consulting services for a fee.

18068. Musical Box Society, International, c/o Clarence W. Fabel, Secty, Box 205, Route 3, Morgantown, IN 46160. Historical, educational, and museum org dedicated to preservation and restoration of mechanical musical instruments. Has collection of books on mechanical musical items, publishes nontechnical newsletter, answers inquiries. Services free.

18069. National Association of Allied Health Schools, c/o Richard Miller, Pres, Elkhart Institute of Technology, 516 S Main St, Elkhart, IN 46514; (219) 295-5900. Enhances proper business ethics and proper training programs for schools accredited to train medical lab technicians and assistants. Answers inquiries, provides consulting services, distributes publications. Services free.

18070. National Association of Relay Manufacturers, P.O. Box 1505, Elkhart, IN 46515; (219) 264-9421. Interest in electromechanical, reed, thermal, solid state, and hybrid relays; standardization of technical ratings, nomenclature, and testing methods. Publishes reports, standards, and specifications, answers inquiries. Limited reference service on technical questions.

18071. National Flute Association, P.O. Box 834, Elkhart, IN 46515; (817) 387-9472. Interest in increasing excellence in flute performance and teaching and encouraging composition and publication of flute music. NFA Library of Flute Music is housed at Univ of Ariz. in Tucson. Info available to anyone; newsletter sent to schools and libraries by subscription.

18072. Naval Avionics Center Technical Library, Indianapolis, IN 46219-2189, (317) 353-7765. Interest in avionics, aeronautics, aerospace engineering, optics, electrical engineering, metallurgy. Has 30,000 reports, Visual Search Microfilm File (VSMF) of Defense Dept military specifications and drawings and vendor/product info. Makes interlibrary loans of books and periodicals.

18073. Neoteric—USA, Fort Harrison Industrial Park, Terre Haute, IN 47804; (812) 466-2303. Commercial org interested in light hovercraft industry, including build-it-yourself hovercraft. Has records and literature on all aspects of this technology (1957 on), publishes build-it-yourself plan packs, info packs. Services other than general info for a fee.

18074. New Call to Peacemaking, Box 1245, Elkhart, IN 46515; (219) 294-7536. Interest in Christian teaching and traditions about peace, threat of nuclear war, war and military taxes, nonviolent methods of resolving conflict. Services free, except for publications.

18075. Parentele, 5538 N Pennsylvania St, Indianapolis, IN 46220; (317) 259-1654. Nonprofit org designed to link parents of handicapped persons together in a nationwide communication system. Publishes quarterly newsletter, answers inquiries, holds annual national conference. Services on payment of membership dues.

18076. Peace Studies Institute and Program in Conflict Resolution, Manchester College, North Manchester, IN 46962; (219) 982-2141 ext 343. Interest in peace studies. Has complete files of Lemberg Center for the Study of Violence (formerly at Brandeis Univ), 34 file drawers of clippings, reports, interviews, taped interviews, etc. Answers inquiries, conducts seminars, rents AV materials. Services for a fee.

18077. Poynter Center, Ind. Univ, 410 N Park Ave, Bloomington, IN 47405; (812) 335-0261. Studies value basis and morality of contemporary American institutions: government, legal system, science, medicine, media, university, business, organized religion. Reference services generally free to college-age students and adults, within limits of staff availability.

18078. Program for Neural Sciences, Ind. Univ, Psychology Bldg, Room 320, Bloomington, IN 47401; (812) 335-1383. Interest in neuroanatomy, neurophysiology, neurochemistry, neuropsychology, sensory systems, neural mechanisms of hearing and vision. Answers inquiries, provides research info to other scientists.

18079. Public Health Entomology Laboratory, Dept of Physiology and Health Science, Ball State Univ, 2000 Univ Ave, Muncie, IN 47306; (317) 285-1343, 285-5961. Conducts research and provides public service in medical and public health entomology. Has 2,400 specimens of mosquitoes, other insects of medical importance. Answers inquiries, lends specimens, permits onsite use of collections. Services free to Ind. residents, at cost to others.

18080. Quantum Chemistry Program Exchange, Chemistry Dept, Ind. Univ, Bloomington, IN 47405; (812) 337-4784. Interest in computing, chemistry computer program, quantum chemistry computer programs. Holdings include computer programs, systems, and routines. Publishes annual research catalog, provides duplication services, permits onsite reference.

18081. Radiation Chemistry Data Center, Radiation Laboratory, Univ of Notre Dame, Notre Dame, IN 46556; (219) 239-6527. Interest in radiation chemistry and photochemistry. Has computer-based bibliographic data base covering 70,000 documents, computerized numeric data bases for kinetic and spectroscopic data on transients in solution. Reference services available to scientists interested in field.

18082. Religious Conference Management Association, One Hoosier Dome, Ste 120, Indianapolis, IN 46225; (317) 632-1888. Interest in religious conventions and meetings, convention management. Publishes periodic newsletter, answers inquiries, provides advisory and consulting services at cost.

18083. Research Center for Language and Semiotic Studies, Ind. Univ, P.O. Box 10 (701 E 8th St), Bloomington, IN 47402, (812) 335-6193. Interest in communication sciences, general linguistics, psycholinguistics, ethnolinguistics, animal communication, nonverbal communication, ethnology. Has technical reports, newsletters, and reprints. Answers inquiries, makes referrals, permits onsite use of collection. Headquarters of Semiotic Society of America; membership open.

18084. Riley Child Development Program, James Whitcomb Riley Hospital for Children, 702 Barnhill Dr, Indianapolis, IN 46223; (317) 264-4464. Meets needs of developmentally handicapped children and their families through patient care, training of professionals, research, and evaluation of services. Inquiries and referrals free, other services for a fee.

18085. Russian and East European Institute, Ind. Univ, Bloomington, IN 47405; (812) 335-7309. Interest in Russian, Soviet, and East European studies. Has maps, charts, books, journals, abstracts, indexes, newsletters, etc. in Russian, English, Polish, Czech, Rumanian, Serbo Croatian, and other languages. Individual faculty will answer inquiries in their areas of expertise.

18087. Specialized Center of Research-Hypertension, Dept of Medicine, School of Medicine, Ind. Univ, 1100 W Michigan St, Indianapolis, IN 46223; (317) 264-8153. Interest in research on hypertension. Has extensive biochemical and physiological data bases on normal and hypertensive subjects. Publishes books, reports and reprints, answers inquiries, makes referrals to other sources of info. Most services free to physicians, scientists, students.

18088. Thermal Sciences and Propulsion Center, School of Mechanical Engineering, Purdue Univ, W Lafayette, IN 47907; (317) 494-1500. Interest in propulsion, laser-doppler interferometry in transonic, supersonic, and mixing flows, combustion. Holdings include 7,000 reports, 300 journals. Answers inquiries, permits onsite use of literature collection, furnishes contractor reports as available.

18089. Thermophysical Properties Research Center, Purdue Univ, Purdue Industrial Research Park, 2595 Yeager Rd, W Lafayette, IN 47906; (317) 463-1581, 494-6300. Interest in thermophysical properties of matter, including thermal conductivity, accommodation coefficient, viscosity. Has over 100,000 unclassified technical papers, most on microfiche. Performs theoretical and experimental research. Nominal fees requested for some services.

18090. United Cancer Council, P.O. Box 40307 (650 E Carmel Dr, Suite 340), Indianapolis, IN 46240; (317) 844-6627. Voluntary federation of local United Way-funded cancer agencies. Has audiovisual library for member agencies, distributes educational pamphlets and educational radio and TV spot announcements.

18091. United States Gymnastics Federation, 1099 N Meridian, Suite 380, Indianapolis, IN 46204; (317) 638-8743. Natl governing body for sport of gymnastics in U.S. Responsible for creation, interpretation, and administration of rules and policies of gymnastics competition. Publishes monthly magazine and technical manuals, answers inquiries, makes referrals to other sources of info, sometimes for a fee.

18092. Veach, Nicholson, Griggs Associates, 1830A W Franklin St, Evansville, IN 47712; (812) 424-2936. Interest in concrete; soils; consulting civil engineering on highways, airports, and water-sewage treatment. Answers brief inquiries, provides consulting services for a fee. Soils lab identifies soil samples, performs tests on concrete and soils.

18093. Vector Biology Laboratory, Dept of Biology, Univ of Notre Dame, Notre Dame, IN 46556; (219) 283-7366. Conducts research on mosquito-borne diseases, especially arboviruses spread by Aedes mosquitoes. Serves as WHO International Reference Centre for Aedes mosquitoes, maintains computerized data bank on literature on mosquitoes. Services to those doing research.

Iowa

19001. Airpower Museum, R.R. 2, Antique Airfield, Ottumwa, IA 52501; (515) 938-2773. Interested in antique aircraft, aircraft restoration and preservation, aviation history. Answers inquiries, provides consulting and reference services. Museum open to the public. Services free, but donations accepted.

19002. Alcohol Studies Unit, Dept of Psychiatry, College of Medicine, Univ of Iowa, 500 Newton Rd, Iowa City, IA 52242; (319) 353-4537. Investigates social/psychological aspects of the alcohol problem. Answers inquiries, provides consulting services. Services free or for negotiated fee.

19003. Amana Heritage Society, Box 81, Amana, IA 52203; (319) 622-3567. Interest in history of the Amana colonies. Answers inquiries. Museum open to visitors for a fee; library open to researchers by appointment.

19004. American Agricultural Economics Association, c/o Raymond R. Beneke, Secty-Treas, Dept of Economics, Iowa State Univ., Ames, IA 50011; (515) 294-8700. Interest in agricultural economics, rural and resource development, policy. Answers inquiries within limits, operates info retrieval service and registry, conducts seminars and annual meeting. Services primarily for members.

19005. American College Testing Program, P.O. Box 168 (2201 North Dodge), Iowa City, IA 52243; (319) 337-1000. Interest in educational and vocational guidance, assessment, and research in secondary and higher education. Provides natl guidance-oriented assessment services, provides info, consulting services. Library open to the public with restrictions.

19007. American Council on Alcohol Problems, 2908 Patricia Dr, Des Moines, IA 50322; (515) 276-7752. Functions as lobbying group to affect federal and state legislation related to alcoholic beverages. Produces educational materials; is not a counseling org.

19008. American Society of Electroencephalographic Technologists, 6th at Quint, Dept GL, Carroll, IA 51401; (712) 792-2978. Professional society interested in EEG technology, evoked potential testing, neurodiagnostics. Answers inquiries free, conducts seminars and distributes publications for a fee.

19009. Archives of the American Lutheran Church, 333 Wartburg Pl, Dubuque, IA 52001; (319) 589-0320. Interest in history of American Lutheran Church. Provides general reference services, data tabulations, translations; loans made with prior approval. Fees charged for services.

19010. Balloon Federation of America, P.O. Box 264, Indianola, IA 50125; (515) 961-8809. Interest in lighter-than-air craft, ballooning. Provides general reference services, conducts seminars, distributes publications, some on cost basis. Services primarily for members, but general info, seminars, and onsite use of museum available to anyone.

19011. CONDUIT, Univ of Iowa, Oakdale Campus, Iowa City, IA 52242; (319) 353-5789. Nonprofit org that publishes educational computer software in biology, chemistry, economics, languages, music, political science, etc. Distributes educational software, makes referrals. Services provided for a fee.

19012. Center for Agricultural and Rural Development, Iowa State Univ, 578 Heady Hall, Ames, IA 50010; (515) 294-3133, 294-1183. Conducts agricultural economic policy and modeling research. Answers inquiries, conducts seminars, sells publications, makes referrals.

19013. Center for Educational Experimentation, Development and Evaluation, Coll of Education, Univ. of Iowa, N310 Oakdale Hall, Oakdale Campus, Oakdale, IA

52319; (319) 353-4200. Conducts research on computers in education, develops educational materials and programs. Provides general reference services, conducts seminars, distributes data. Services provided on sliding-fee basis.

19014. Center for Industrial Research and Service, Iowa State Univ. of Science and Technology, 205 Engineering Annex, Ames, IA 50011; (515) 294-3420. Interest in physical, biological, engineering, social, business, and management sciences of concern to Iowa business and industry. Provides general reference services, sponsors extension courses. Services free, except extension courses.

19015. Comparative Legislative Research Center, Dept of Political Science, Univ. of Iowa, 306 Schaeffer Hall, Iowa City, IA 52242; (319) 353-5040. Gathers data as part of cross-natl research projects. Interest in foreign legislatures and legislators. Provides general reference services, conducts seminars, distributes publications, permits onsite reference. Services provided at cost to non-affiliated persons.

19016. Council for Agricultural Science and Technology, c/o Dr William W. Marion, P.O. Box 1550, Iowa State Univ. Station, Ames, IA 50010-1550; (515) 292-2125. Public foundation interested in scientific production, utilization of food and fiber, environmental impacts. Services supplied to public limited to publications, other available info.

19017. Council on Chiropractic Education, 3209 Ingersoll Ave, Des Moines, IA 50312; (515) 255-2184. Natl accrediting agency interested in chiropractic education, standards, physicians and paraprofessionals. Provides general reference services, conducts workshops, distributes publications. Services free except workshops, accreditation, consulting, and bulk copies.

19018. Davenport Diocesan Volunteer Program, P.O. Box 38, Davenport, IA 52805; (319) 289-5736, 324-1911. Nonprofit Catholic program that sends volunteers to Third World and poverty areas of U.S. Provides general reference services, conducts workshops and seminars, distributes publications, permits onsite reference. Services free, unless extensive.

19019. Department of Animal Ecology, Coll of Agriculture, Iowa State Univ. of Science and Technology, Ames, IA 50011; (515) 294-6148. Conducts research on habitats of fish and wildlife, lake and stream eutrophication, pesticide accumulation. Provides general reference services, conducts seminars, distributes publications, permits onsite reference. Services free, except literature-searching and evaluations.

19020. Department of Orthopaedic, Surgery Biomechanics Laboratory, School of Medicine, Univ. of Iowa, Iowa City, IA 52242; (319) 356-2340. Conducts research on muscle and joint forces during locomotion, computer simulation of surgery. Answers inquiries from research groups interested in gait.

19021. Energy and Mineral Resources Research Institute, Ames Laboratory, Iowa State Univ. of Science and Technology, Ames, IA 50011; (515) 294-1856. Interest in chemistry, R&D studies, mechanical engineering, research in solid state metallurgy, mathematics and computer science research. Permits onsite use of reports only, makes reprints available on request.

19022. Energy and Self-Reliance Center, Citizens United for Responsible Energy, 3500 Kingman Blvd, Des Moines, IA 50311; (515) 277-0253. Encourages use of renewable energy sources. Provides general reference services, conducts workshops, lends materials to members only, permits onsite reference. Services primarily for members, but others assisted; fees may be charged.

19023. Fine Particle Society, c/o J.K. Beddow, Secty, 1153 Coll of Engineering, Univ. of Iowa, Iowa City, IA 52242. Interest in identification, characterization, behavior of fine particulates, aerosols. Holds annual meeting in U.S., publishes materials.

19024. Golden American Saddlebred Horse Association, Rte. 1, Box 67, Oxford Junction, IA 52323; (319) 486-2072. Service club that promotes golden-colored American saddlebred horse for show, additional use, and breeding. Answers inquiries, provides advisory and reference services free.

19025. Grout Museum of History and Science, 503 South St, Waterloo, IA 50701; (319) 234-6357. Interest in Iowa state and county history. Provides general reference services and reproductions; conducts planetarium shows, tours; permits onsite reference. Services free, except reproductions.

19026. Herbert Hoover Presidential Library, West Branch, IA 52358; (319) 643-5301. Interest in public service career and presidential administration of Herbert Hoover, emphasizing policy issues from 1914-64. Permits onsite reference upon written application to director. Inquiries answered, bibliographic services provided, nonrestricted items duplicated for a fee.

19027. Human Relations Area Files, c/o Dr Michael Chibnik, Dept of Anthropology, Univ. of Iowa, Iowa City, IA 52242; (319) 353-5831. Interest in ethnographic info relevant to comparative study of human beliefs and behaviors. Provides general reference services, translations; permits onsite reference. Services free.

19028. Indian Youth of America, P.O. Box 2786 (4509 Stone Ave), Sioux City, IA 51106; (712) 276-0794. Conducts counseling, substance abuse prevention, and placement programs for American Indian youth. Provides general reference services, conducts seminars and workshops, permits onsite reference. Services free, primarily for Indian youth and families.

19029. Institute of Agricultural Medicine and Occupational Health, Coll of Medicine, Univ. of Iowa, Iowa City, IA 52240; (319) 353-4720. Interest in preventive and occupational medicine, public health in industry and rural areas, transmissible animal diseases, hazards from farm chemicals, industrial hygiene. Lends documents, permits onsite reference, provides duplication services.

19030. Institute of Hydraulic Research, Univ. of Iowa, Iowa City, IA 52242; (319) 353-4962. Interest in engineering hydraulics, fluid mechanics, hydrology, geophysics, bioengineering, sediment transport, water resources, ecological monitoring and engineering. Answers inquiries, provides consulting services, produces educational films.

19031. International Association of Milk, Food and Environmental Sanitarians, P.O. Box 701, Ames, IA 50010; (515) 232-6699. Interest in safety, hygiene, sanitation, technology of all foods, milk products, procedure for investigation of diseases. Answers inquiries.

19032. International Association of Tool Craftsmen, 1915 Arrow Line Court, Bettendorf, IA 52722; (319) 332-6147. Interest in labor relations in toolmaking and diemaking industries; apprenticeships, journeymen. Answers inquiries.

19033. International Silo Association, 815 Office Park Rd, Ste 2, West Des Moines, IA 50265; (515) 225-0643. Interest in farm and industrial tower silos, ensiling of forages and grains, livestock feed storage structures, manure structures. Provides general reference services, conducts seminars and workshops, distributes publications. Services primarily for members, others assisted for a fee.

19035. Iowa Natural Heritage Foundation, Insurance Exchange Bldg, Ste 830, 505 Fifth Ave, Des Moines, IA 50309; (515) 288-1846. Interest in Iowa's natural resources, lands held for conservation and recreation, land management, etc. Provides general reference and consulting services, conducts seminars, distributes materials. Services free, except consulting, seminars, and materials.

19036. Iowa Ornithologists' Union, 235 McClellan Blvd, Davenport, IA 52803; (319) 355-7051. Interest in bird life in Iowa, ornithology, protection of birds, bird surveys. Provides general reference services, conducts conferences, distributes publications, permits onsite reference. Services generally free.

19037. Iowa State Historical Department, Office of the Museum, East 12th and Grand Ave, Des Moines, IA 50319; (515) 281-5240. Interest in Iowa history, U.S. history as reflected in natural and artifact history. Provides general reference services, preservation of artifacts, copying services for a fee.

19038. Maharishi International University Library, Fairfield, IA 52556; (515) 472-6745. Intl univ that emphasizes integration of traditional academic study with systematic study and development of consciousness, Transcendental Meditation. Answers inquiries, makes loans, permits limited onsite use of collection. Services free.

19039. Men's Garden Clubs of America, 5560 Merle Hay Rd, Johnston, IA 50131; (515) 278-0295. Natl men's club interested in gardening, horticulture, floriculture. Provides general reference services, conducts seminars, distributes publications, permits onsite reference.

19040. Midwest Plan Service, 122 Davidson Hall, Iowa State Univ. of Science and Technology, Ames, IA 50011; (515) 294-4337. Interest in agricultural engineering, design and construction of livestock, family housing, storages, livestock equipment, waste management, planning, utilities. Answers inquiries, sells publications.

19041. National Animal Disease Center, P.O. Box 70, Ames, IA 50010; (515) 239-8200. Interest in veterinary sciences, related pathology, physiology, biochemistry, microbiology, immunology, livestock diseases occurring in U.S. Answers inquiries, makes interlibrary loans, permits onsite reference by trained personnel.

19042. National Association of Atomic Veterans, 1109 Franklin St, Burlington, IA 52601; (319) 753-6112. Strives to help atomic veterans and widows with service-connected disability claims based on radiation exposure. Provides free general reference services, distributes newsletter.

19043. National Association of County Engineers, c/o Milton L. Johnson, P.E., Secty-Treas, 326 Pike Rd, Ottumwa, IA 52501; (515) 654-6928. Interest in county road planning, construction, maintenance, and management; county-level engineering. Answers inquiries.

19044. National Association of Hospital Purchasing Materials Management, P.O. Box 2436, Des Moines, IA 50311; (515) 270-8201. Interest in educational programs in hospital purchasing management and materials management. Provides general reference services, consulting; conducts seminars, conferences for a fee; distributes materials. Fee for some services.

19045. National Farmers Organization, 720 Davis Ave, Corning, IA 50841; (515) 322-3131. Nonpartisan org of farmers seeking reasonable prices for farm commodities through collective bargaining. Provides general reference services, conducts workshops. Services provided at cost.

19046. North American Gamebird Association, c/o John M. Mullin, Info Officer and Publications Editor, Goose Lake, IA 52750; (319) 577-2267. Interest in game bird breeding, hunting preserve operation, nature trails, hunting dogs, outdoor recreation. Provides general reference services, consulting for a fee; conducts meetings and short courses.

19047. North American Lily Society, c/o Dorothy B. Schaefer, Exec Secty, Box 476, Waukee, IA 50263; (515) 987-1371. Interest in cultivation of lilies. Answers inquiries, sells publications, conducts an annual show, which is open to the public.

19048. Norwegian-American Museum, 502 West Water St, Decorah, IA 52101; (319) 382-9682. Interest in Norwegian-Americans: genealogy, handicrafts, history, culture. Provides general reference services, conducts workshops, permits onsite reference. Fees charged for workshops, research, and admission to museum. Publications distributed to members only.

19049. Office of the State Historical Society, Iowa State Historical Dept, 402 Iowa Ave, Iowa City, IA 52240; (319) 338-5471. Interest in Iowa history and genealogy, U.S. history. Provides general reference and copying services, conducts seminars. Fees charged for out-of-state genealogical questions and all photocopying.

19050. Quill and Scroll Society, School of Journalism, Univ. of Iowa, Iowa City, IA 52242; (319) 353-4475. Intl honor society for high school journalists. Answers inquiries, makes referrals, distributes publications, conducts annual quiz and natl contest for high school students.

19051. Radiation Research Laboratory, 14 Medical Laboratories, Univ. of Iowa, Iowa City, IA 52240; (319) 353-3747. Interest in radiation effects, radioisotope methodology, radiological and health physics, immunodiagnosis of cancer. Provides consulting services to other univ and govt research laboratories.

19052. Rare-Earth Information Center, Energy and Mineral Resources Research Institute, Iowa State Univ. of Science and Technology, Ames, IA 50011; (515) 294-2272. Collects, stores, evaluates, disseminates info on rare earth metals, alloys, elements, and compounds. Provides general reference services, permits onsite use of collection. Minimum charge of $50 required from nonsponsoring companies for computer searches.

19053. Regional Social Science Data Archive, Laboratory for Political Research, Univ. of Iowa, 321A Schaeffer Hall, Iowa City, IA 52240; (319) 353-3945. Interest in empirical research and research methodology in political science, history, related disciplines. Unrestricted data and documentation may be obtained. Inquiries should be directed to Data Librarian.

19054. Remote Sensing Laboratory, Iowa Geological Survey, 123 N Capitol St, Iowa City, IA 52242; (319) 338-1173. Interest in remote sensing imagery to provide info and interpretation in geologic mapping, soils, floodplain identification, etc. Provides general reference and consulting services, distributes publications, permits onsite reference. Services free, except materials.

19055. Social Documents Collection, Univ. of Iowa Libraries, Iowa City, IA 52242; (319) 353-4854. Interest in publications by non-Marxist, ephemeral political orgs in U.S., primarily right-wing or conservative. Answers inquiries; provides literature-searching, duplications; permits onsite use of collection.

19056. Soil Conservation Society of America, 7515 Northeast Ankeny Rd, Ankeny, IA 50021; (515) 289-2331.

Nonprofit scientific and educational org interested in development and promotion of soil and water conservation, sound land use practices. Answers inquiries, conducts conferences, distributes position statements, sells publications.

19057. Spangler Geotechnical Laboratory, Engineering Research Institute, Iowa State Univ. of Science and Technology, Ames, IA 50010; (515) 294-3936. Interest in geotechnical engineering, highway and foundation engineering, materials testing, chemical soil stabilization. Answers inquiries, makes referrals. Specialized services performed on contract/fee basis; routine tests referred to commercial labs.

19058. Stanley Foundation, 420 East 3rd St, Muscatine, IA 52761; (319) 264-1500. Interest in study, research, education in intl relations and orgs. Sponsors conferences and seminars, publishes materials, sponsors noncommercial radio series and intl education model.

19059. State Archives of Iowa, Iowa State Historical Dept, East 7th and Court Ave, Des Moines, IA 50319; (515) 281-3007. Interest in Iowa history as reflected in official public records of the state, U.S. history, and genealogy. Provides general reference services, photocopies. Nominal fees charged for reference services.

19060. Studebaker Cars' Club, c/o George D. Krem, Pres, 1248 Esther Court, Iowa City, IA 52240; (800) 527-3452. Interest in acquisition, preservation, restoration, and operation of Studebaker cars and trucks. Provides general reference and consulting services, conducts seminars and meetings, distributes publications, lends materials. Services available on cost basis.

19061. Suzuki Association of the Americas, P.O. Box 354, Muscatine, IA 52761; (319) 263-3071. Promotes music education methods of Shinichi Suzuki, sponsors related performances. Provides general reference services, translations; conducts seminars, workshops; distributes publications. Services available to members.

19063. Veterinary Diagnostic Laboratory, College of Veterinary Medicine, Iowa State Univ. of Science and Technology, Ames, IA 50010; (515) 294-1950. Interest in analytical chemistry, poisons, pesticides, food additives, veterinary toxicology, parasitology. Provides general reference and consulting services free, except under special contract. Extensive services provided to veterinary, medical professionals only.

19064. Wildlife Disease Association, P.O. Box 886, Ames, IA 50010; (515) 233-1931. Nonprofit intl org interested in effects of infectious, parasitic, toxic, genetic, and physiologic diseases on wild animals, their relationship to man. Answers inquiries; sponsors intl and sectional meetings, conference; sells publications.

19065. World Food Institute, Iowa State Univ, Ames, IA 50011; (515) 294-7699. Interest in food, world food trade, food production and policy, intl food education, research and extension. Provides general reference services, conducts seminars, distributes publications, nominates scholars for resident study. Services generally free.

Kansas

20001. American Alfalfa Processors Association, 10100 Santa Fe, No. 305, Overland Park, KS 66212; (913) 648-6800. Publishes newsletters, slides on processing of alfalfa for use in livestock, poultry feeds; disseminates single pamphlets free. Extensive services only to members.

20002. American Association of Housing Educators, c/o Dept of Family Economics, Justin Hall, Kan. State Univ, Manhattan, KS 66506; (913) 532-5515. Publishes journal, newsletter, books on research related to housing. Answers inquiries, conducts seminars and workshops, makes referrals to other sources. Services at cost.

20003. American Association of Zoo Keepers, c/o Topeka Zoological Park, 635 Gage Blvd, Topeka, KS 66606; (913) 272-5821. Interest in care of captive exotic animals. Publishes brochures, answers inquiries, provides advisory services, conducts seminars and workshops. Most services free.

20004. American Institute of Baking, 1213 Bakers Way, Manhattan, KS 66502; (913) 537-4750. Research and education org for baking. Provides advisory, reference, copying services; makes interlibrary loans; permits onsite use of collection. Services at cost.

20005. American Society of Certified Engineering Technicians, P.O. Box 7789, Shawnee Mission, KS 66207; (913) 451-4938. Promotes certification and seeks to upgrade status of engineering technicians. Publishes bimonthly journal; conducts correspondence courses, salary surveys; sponsors scholarships.

20006. Association of Records Managers and Administrators, 4200 Somerset Dr, Suite 215, Prairie Village, KS 66208; (913) 341-3808. Publishes journal, newsletter, correspondence course on records management, owns small technical reference library with audiovisual aids, answers inquiries, maintains speakers' bureau.

20007. Association of Systematics Collections, Univ of Kan., Lawrence, KS 66045; (913) 864-4867. Intl nonprofit org that provides advisory services, info on permit requirements for biological collections; conducts seminars, workshops. Services free to individuals in member institutions.

20008. Athletes United for Peace, P.O. Box 1776 (901 Kentucky St), Lawrence, KS 66044; (913) 843-6435. Promotes peaceful competition between U.S. and Soviet Union through intl sporting events. Provides free advisory, copying services; conducts seminars and workshops; permits onsite use of collection.

20009. Aviation Data Service, P.O. Box 913 (312 E Murdock), Wichita, KS 67201; (316) 262-1491. Commercial

org that conducts market research in general aviation aircraft sales, especially business turbine aircraft. Provides advisory, magnetic tape services. Services at cost.

20010. Bureau of Educational Measurements, Data Processing and Educational Measurements Center, Emporia State Univ, Emporia, KS 66801; (316) 343-1200 ext 102. Publishes educational tests, technical reports, educational norms. Answers inquiries, provides consulting services, conducts testing programs, analyzes data, permits onsite use of collection.

20011. Center for Community and Regional Planning, Kan. State Univ, 302 Seaton Hall, Manhattan, KS 66506; (913) 532-5958. Conducts pilot projects on community planning, development for a fee. Publishes reports, specifications, and standards, provides advisory and reference services, permits onsite use of collection.

20012. Center for Latin American Studies, Univ of Kan., Lawrence, KS 66045; (913) 864-4213. Permits onsite use of collection on Caribbean and Central America, including history, geography, anthropology, languages. Makes interlibrary loans. Services free.

20013. Cerebral Palsy Research Foundation of Kansas, 2021 N Old Manor, Wichita, KS 67208; (316) 688-1888. Provides rehab services to physically handicapped. Publishes research summaries, provides advisory and reference services, conducts seminars. Services mostly free.

20014. Chisholm Trail Museum, 502 N Washington St, Wellington, KS 67152; (316) 326-2174. Owns archival materials on Chisholm Trail, history of Sumner County. Provides literature-searching, repro services; permits onsite use of collection. Services at cost.

20015. Communication Research Center, Univ of Kan., 3120 Wescoe Hall, Lawrence, KS 66045; (913) 864-3633. Publishes reports, bibliographies, data compilations on research on communication problems. Provides consulting, reference services; conducts seminars. Services at cost.

20016. Dwight D. Eisenhower Library, National Archives and Records Administration, Abilene, KS 67410; (913) 263-4751. Owns papers of former Pres. Dwight D. Eisenhower, oral history transcripts. Permits onsite access to collection upon written application. Provides bibliographic, repro service; makes interlibrary loans.

20017. Evapotranspiration Laboratory, Kan. State Univ, Manhattan, KS 66506; (913) 532-5731. Publishes technical journal articles on evapotranspiration, water use efficiency, soil moisture. Answers inquiries free.

20018. Flat Glass Marketing Association, 3310 Harrison St, Topeka, KS 66611; (913) 266-7013. Publishes specifications, manuals on glass, glazing, sealant. Answers inquiries, provides reference services, conducts seminars, workshops. Services at cost.

20019. Fort Larned Historical Society Santa Fe Trail Center, Route 3, Larned, KS 67550; (316) 285-2054. Owns unpublished histories of counties along Santa Fe Trail, historic sheet music. Provides free reference and copying services, permits onsite use of collection.

20020. Glass Tempering Association, 3310 Harrison St, Topeka, KS 66611; (913) 266-7064. Publishes standards and specifications for all uses of tempered glass, engineering standards manuals, product directory, consumer and technical brochure; answers inquiries.

20021. Golf Course Superintendents Association of America, 1617 St Andrews Dr, Lawrence, KS 66044; (913) 841-2240. Publishes journal, proceedings on turfgrass science and golf course management, including maintenance of tees, greens, trees, shrubs. Answers inquiries, sponsors annual intl conference.

20022. Grassland Heritage Foundation, 5450 Buena Vista, Shawnee Mission, KS 66205; (913) 677-3326. Promotes interest in prairie grasslands. Obtains land tracts for educational purposes, publishes newsletters, conducts workshops. Services mostly free.

20023. Hall Laboratory of Mammalian Genetics, Dept of Physiology and Cell Biology, Univ of Kan., Lawrence, KS 66045; (913) 864-4183. Publishes research journals on mammalian genetics, lab animal science. Provides access to literature collection and unique inbred strains of mice by qualified investigators.

20024. Hertzler Research Foundation Library, 4th and Chestnut Sts, Halstead, KS 67056; (316) 835-2241 ext 355. Owns books, periodicals on medical science. Answers inquiries, provides reference, literature-searching services. Offers repro services at cost to some, lends materials.

20026. Institute for Computational Research in Engineering, Kan. State Univ, Manhattan, KS 66506; (913) 532-5610. Publishes reports on simulation, numerical analysis, multiple computer programming. Answers inquiries, provides advisory services. Services free.

20027. Institute for Research in Learning Disabilities, Univ of Kan., 313 Carruth-O'Leary Hall, Lawrence, KS 66045; (913) 864-4780. Publishes reports on learning disabilities. Provides advisory and consulting services, info on research in progress; conducts workshops. Services mostly free.

20028. Institute for Systems Design and Optimization, Dept of Chemical Engineering, Durland Hall, Kan. State Univ, Manhattan, KS 66506; (913) 532-5584. Publishes reports on subjects such as systems engineering, synthesis, analysis. Provides advisory, reference services; conducts research. Fee for some services.

20029. Institute of Logopedics, 2400 Jardine Dr, Wichita, KS 67219; (800) 835-1043. Provides diagnostic, therapeutic, educational, social development services for multiple-handicapped children. Conducts research, offers advisory services. Info services free.

20030. International Academy of Preventive Medicine, 34 Corporate Woods, Suite 469, 10950 Grandview, Overland Park, KS 66210. Furthers education, research in preventive medicine. Provides diagnostic assistance to members, conducts natl conferences. Services for a fee to professionals.

20031. International Academy of Preventive Medicine, P.O. Box 25276, Shawnee Mission, KS 66225; (913) 648-8720. Furthers education and research on preventive medicine. Sponsors seminars and natl conferences providing continuing education credits, refers patients to member health care professionals.

20032. International Association for Mathematical Geology, c/o John C. Davis, Secty Gen, Kan. Geological Survey, 1930 Constant Ave, Lawrence, KS 66044; (913) 864-4991. Publishes journals on geomathematics, geostatistics, computer applications in earth sciences. Conducts seminars, provides literature-searching services free to professionals.

20033. International Association for Philosophy of Law and Social Philosophy, c/o Rex Martin, Dept of Philosophy, Univ of Kan., Lawrence, KS 66045; (913) 864-3976. Publishes newsletter, conference papers on philosophy of law, social philosophy. Free referral of inquiries to members with expertise in various topics.

20034. International Reference Organization in Forensic Medicine and Sciences, c/o William G. Eckert, M.D., Editor, P.O. Box 8282, Wichita, KS 67206; (316) 689-3707. Publishes annual intl bibliography. Indexes table of contents of forensic journals. Provides consulting, reference, literature-searching services; sponsors conferences.

20035. International Wheat Gluten Association, 10100 Santa Fe Dr, Suite 206, Overland Park, KS 66212; (913) 341-1155. Publishes technical reports, journals, standards, specifications, and directories. Provides advisory, reference services; conducts seminars. Services at cost to public.

20037. Kansas Cosmosphere and Discovery Center, 1100 N Plum St, Hutchinson, KS 67501; (316) 662-2305. Displays NASA space artifacts (space suits, Mercury, Gemini, and Apollo spacecraft, lunar module), has OMNIMAX theater, planetarium. Exhibits open free; admission charged for shows.

20038. Kansas Crop Improvement Association, 205 Call Hall, Kan. State Univ, Manhattan, KS 66506; (913) 532-6118. Owns 250 varieties of crop seeds. Publishes newsletters, standards; provides advisory, consulting services. Seed certification at cost to members; info free.

20039. Kansas State Historical Society, Center for Historical Research, 120 W 10th St, Topeka, KS 66612; (913) 296-3251. Publishes newsletters, monographs, books. Provides literature-searching, copying services, identifies documents, permits onsite use of library by public. Fee for extensive research by staff.

20040. Kansas State Library, State Capitol, Topeka, KS 66612; (913) 296-3296. Owns govt documents, online Kansas legislative info system, card index of bills. Provides advisory, reference services, permits onsite use of collection by public, answers inquiries.

20041. Kansas University Affiliated Facility, Bureau of Child Research, Univ of Kan., 348 Haworth, Lawrence, KS 66045; (913) 864-4950. Publishes periodicals, technical reports on developmental disabilities. Provides advisory, reference, repro services; conducts seminars. Services mostly free.

20042. Learning Resources Network, 1554 Hayes Dr, Manhattan, KS 66502; (913) 539-5376. Provides technical assistance to noncredit programs in various disciplines. Provides advisory, consulting, reference services; conducts seminars, workshops. Services for a fee.

20043. Lefthanders International, 3601 SW 29th St, Topeka, KS 66614; (913) 273-0680. Publishes lefthanders' catalog of mail-order products, directory of researchers on lefthandedness. Provides advisory, reference services. Most services free.

20044. Low Temperature Physics Laboratory, Dept of Physics and Astronomy, Univ of Kan., Lawrence, KS 66045; (913) 864-4889. Owns reprints of articles covering Lab's work in cryogenics, low temperature physics, magnetism, spin-lattice relaxation. Provides consulting services free, unless extensive.

20045. Menninger Foundation Professional Library, P.O. Box 829 (5600 W 6th St), Topeka, KS 66601; (913) 273-7500. Permits onsite use of collection on psychiatry, psychology, family therapy. Provides document delivery, literature searches for a fee. Services primarily for professionals.

20046. Mennonite Library and Archives, Bethel College, N Newton, KS 67117; (316) 283-2500. Publishes magazine on Mennonite life. Answers inquiries, provides translating and copying services, authenticates documents, owns correspondence and sermons of Mennonite leaders and missionaries.

20047. Mid-America Association of Educational Opportunity Program Personnel, c/o Wichita State Univ, P.O. Box 94, Wichita, KS 67208; (316) 689-3019. Publishes journal on providing access to postsecondary education for persons from low-income, minority, handicapped backgrounds. Provides advisory services, conducts seminars.

20048. Museum of Independent Telephony, 412 S Campbell, Abilene, KS 67410; (913) 263-2681. Nonprofit org that provides literature-searching services, conducts tours, permits onsite use of collection. Fees for extensive research.

20049. Museum of Invertebrate Paleontology, Lindley Hall, Univ of Kan., Lawrence, KS 66045; (913) 864-4974. Permits onsite use of collection of Pennsylvanian and Permian invertebrates, lower Paleozoic inarticulate brachiopods. Provides consulting services, mostly free.

20050. Museum of Natural History, Univ of Kan., Lawrence, KS 66045; (913) 864-4540. Provides taxonomic identification of fossil and recent Kansas vertebrates, North American native mammals, New World tropical reptiles and amphibians. Provides consulting services for a fee, permits access of collection to qualified scientists.

20051. National Association of Geology Teachers, c/o Allen Press, P.O. Box 368, Lawrence, KS 66044; (913) 843-1234. Seeks to improve teaching of earth sciences at all levels. Provides reference services, conducts field trips, curriculum development. Services mostly free.

20052. National Association of Jazz Educators, P.O. Box 724 (1335 Anderson), Manhattan, KS 66502; (913) 776-8744. Conducts composition contest and research, participates in intl conferences. Provides advisory and reference services, conducts workshops. Provides speakers. Services at cost.

20053. National Board for Respiratory Care, c/o Steven K. Bryant, Exec Dir, 11015 W 75 Terrace, Shawnee Mission, KS 66214; (913) 268-4050. Certification board for respiratory therapists, technicians, pulmonary technologists. Publishes study guides, answers inquiries free, conducts seminars for a fee.

20054. National Cleft Palate Association, Route 1, Buhler, KS 67552; (316) 665-3507. Educates public on cleft palate. Encourages research funding, monitors relevant legislation. Promotes cooperation with related orgs, serves as clearinghouse for info and resources.

20055. National Collegiate Athletic Association, P.O. Box 1906 (Nall Ave at 63rd St), Mission, KS 66201; (913) 384-3220. Owns data, publications, and films on natl collegiate play. Publishes newsletter, rules, statistical compilations. Provides advisory services, answers inquiries.

20057. National Organization on Legal Problems of Education, 3601 SW 29th St, Ste 223, Topeka, KS 66614; (913) 273-3550. Publishes journal, books, reviews, bibliographies. Provides advisory, reference, abstracting, copying services; conducts seminars, workshops. Services at cost.

20058. Neutron Activation Analysis Laboratory, Dept of Nuclear Engineering, Kan. State Univ, Manhattan, KS 66506; (913) 532-2654. Publishes books, journals on neutron activation analysis and environmental monitoring. Provides advisory, sample analysis services for a fee. Services primarily for colleges, univs.

20059. Organic Acidemia Association, 1532 S 87th Street, Kansas City, KS 66111; (913) 442-7080. Fosters communication between families and professionals who deal with rare metabolic disorders, such as organic acidemias; combats feeling of isolation of those with these disorders.

20060. Population Research Laboratory, Dept of Sociology, Kan. State Univ, Manhattan, KS 66506; (913) 532-

5984. Owns Kan. census tapes; migration, community studies. Answers inquiries, publishes reports, provides advisory services. Services generally for a fee.

20061. Postharvest Documentation Service, Food and Feed Grain Institute, Kan. State Univ, Farrell Library, Room 411, Manhattan, KS 66506; (913) 532-6516 ext 25. Provides computerized searches of data base on grain storage, marketing. Services for a fee, but emphasis is on service to developing countries eligible for U.S. assistance.

20062. Puritan-Bennett Corp., 9401 Indian Creek Parkway, Overland Park, KS 66225; (913) 649-0444. Publishes catalogs on equipment for medical use. Provides consulting, bibliographic services; permits onsite use of collection. Services primarily for medical, paramedical personnel.

20063. Research and Training Center on Independent Living, Bureau of Child Research, Univ of Kan., 348 Haworth Hall, Lawrence, KS 66045; (913) 864-4950. Publishes books, journals, bibliographies on independent living for disabled. Provides advisory, reference services; conducts workshops. Services for a fee.

20064. Smith Mental Retardation Research Center, Medical Center, Univ of Kan., 39th St and Rainbow Blvd, Kansas City, KS 66103; (913) 588-5970. Conducts research on mental retardation, reproduction biology, speech and cognition development. Provides consulting services, conducts seminars. Services mostly free.

20065. Snow Entomological Museum, Univ of Kan., Lawrence, KS 66045; (913) 864-4538. Permits onsite use of insect collections. Provides advisory, reference, specimen identification services; lends materials. Services generally free.

20066. Tallgrass Prairie Alliance, P.O. Box 557, Topeka, KS 66001; (913) 357-4681. Dedicated to preserving tallgrass prairie ecosystem. Provides speakers, films for schools. Conducts workshops, permits onsite use of collection. Services for a fee.

20067. U.S. Grain Marketing Research Laboratory, Agricultural Research Service, 1515 College Ave, Manhattan, KS 66502; (913) 776-2700. Publishes articles for journals on preventing insect infestation in grain, wheat utilization quality research. Answers inquiries, conducts oral presentations and lab tours.

20068. University of Kansas Center for Research, Nichols Hall, 2291 Irving Hill Dr, Campus West, Lawrence, KS 66045; (913) 864-3441. Owns Landsat and radar imagery, particularly of Kan. and Midwest. Publishes research reports; provides consulting, literature-searching services; sponsors seminars, conferences.

Kentucky

21001. American Dove Association, P.O. Box 21, Milton, KY 40045; (502) 268-3240. Publishes books, newsletter, standards, directories, reprints on doves; answers in-

quiries; conducts seminars, workshops; makes referrals. Services available to members.

21002. American Forage and Grassland Council, c/o J. Kenneth Evans, Exec Dir, 2021 Rebel Rd, Lexington, KY 40503; (606) 278-0177. Publishes reports, books, journal, annual proceedings, special publications on all phases of forages and grasslands. Answers inquiries, refers inquirers to other sources of info free.

21003. American Printing House for the Blind, Department of Educational Research, P.O. Box 6085 (1839 Frankfort Ave), Louisville, KY 40206; (502) 895-2405. Private, nonprofit org that publishes braille books, large-type books, talking books, bibliographies, catalogs of educational materials, etc. Answers inquiries free, provides advisory, reference, and copying services for a fee.

21004. American Society of Transportation and Logistics, P.O. Box 33095, Louisville, KY 40232; (502) 451-8150. Publishes journal, newsletter, correspondence courses, bibliography; administers program leading to certification in transportation and logistics; permits onsite use of collection.

21005. Area Business Databank, P.O. Box 829 (1018 South 4th St), Louisville, KY 40201; (502) 589-9666. Natl reference service that selects articles from business publications for reproduction on microfiche with index. Permits onsite use of data base. Services available for a fee.

21006. Army Armor School Library, Gaffey Hall, Old Ironside Ave, Fort Knox, KY 40121; (502) 624-6231. Owns books, periodicals, reports on military history. Provides advisory, reference, copying, literature-searching services; makes interlibrary loans. Services provided free.

21007. Association for Maternal and Child Health and Crippled Children's Programs, 275 East Main St, Frankfort, KY 40621; (502) 564-4830. Assn founded to work toward improvement of maternal and child health services administered by state agencies. Holds annual meeting; publishes proceedings, ad hoc committee reports.

21008. Association of American Plant Food Control Officials, c/o Div. of Regulatory Services, Univ of Ky., Lexington, KY 40546; (606) 257-2668. Publishes journals on legislation that regulates production, labeling, sale, and use of fertilizers; agricultural liming materials. Answers inquiries, conducts workshops. Services mostly free.

21009. C&I/Girdler Inc., Library, 1930 Bishop Lane, Louisville, KY 40232; (502) 456-4220. Owns books and bibliographies on engineering, chemistry, computer programming, instrumentation. Provides reference, copying services; makes interlibrary loans. Services available to technical libraries only.

21010. Celanese Technical Center, Celanese Plastics and Specialties Co., P.O. Box 99038 (9800 Bluegrass Parkway), Jeffersontown, KY 40299; (502) 585-8053. Owns over 100,000 chemical patents. Provides reference and copying services for a fee, makes interlibrary loans, permits onsite use of collection by special request, performs online searches.

21011. Center for Business and Economic Research, College of Business and Economics, Univ of Ky., 302 Mathews Bldg, Lexington, KY 40506-0047; (606) 257-7675. Research unit that publishes journal and technical reports, provides advisory services, conducts seminars and workshops, permits onsite use of collection. Services free.

21014. Council of State Governments, P.O. Box 11910 (Iron Works Pike), Lexington, KY 40578; (606) 252-2291. Provides and technical assistance to state officials and legislators. Conducts workshops, conferences; studies issues such as meeting health needs of elderly, state rural health services.

21015. Data Courier, 620 South 5th St, Louisville, KY 40202; (502) 582-4111, (800) 626-2823. Summarizes, indexes significant info in fields of business and management. Distributes data bases online, leases magnetic tape services, conducts workshops. Most services for a fee.

21016. Environmental Alternatives, 818 East Chestnut St, Louisville, KY 40204; (502) 587-3028. Provides tours, workshops, demonstrations on energy efficiency, alternative energy sources. Provides advisory, reference, repro services; permits onsite use of collection.

21017. Federal Correctional Institution, Bureau of Prisons, U.S. Dept of Justice, P.O. Box 2000, Lexington, KY 40512; (606) 255-6812. Publishes training manuals on treatment of inmates. Answers inquiries; provides tours by prior arrangement (limited to groups above high school age); owns books, periodicals, reports.

21018. Frontier Nursing Service, c/o D.M. Hatfield, Dir, Hyden, KY 41749; (606) 672-3162. Publishes bulletin on primary health care through medicine, nursing. Evaluates data, conducts workshops, provides info on research in progress.

21020. Government Law Center, Univ of Louisville, Gardner Hall, Room 340, Louisville, KY 40292; (502) 588-6508. Publishes textbooks, studies, directories; provides consulting, reference, abstracting, legislation analysis services at cost to anyone pursuing public objective.

21021. Human Development Program-University Affiliated Facility, Univ of Ky., 107 Porter Bldg, Lexington, KY 40506; (606) 257-1714. Provides technical assistance on ability-to-pay basis for persons with developmental disabilities. Provides advisory, reference services; conducts workshops; permits onsite use of collection.

21022. Institute for Mining and Minerals Research, Univ of Ky., P.O. Box 13015, Lexington, KY 40512; (606) 252-5535. Conducts research to promote use of Ky. fossil fuel. Provides chemical analysis services, conducts

annual oil shale symposium, permits onsite use of collection. Most services for a fee.

21023. International Museum of the Horse, Ky. Horse Park, 4089 Iron Works Pike, Lexington, KY 40511; (606) 233-4303 ext 232. Exhibits horse-related artifacts; provides advisory, reference services; permits onsite use of collection; conducts educational programs. Services mostly free.

21024. International Prisoners Aid Association, c/o Dr Badr-El-Din Ali, IPAA Exec Dir, Dept of Sociology, Univ of Louisville, Louisville, KY 40292; (502) 588-6836. Helps nongovernmental orgs in different countries rehabilitate offenders. Publishes intl directory of prisoners' aid agencies, provides advisory services, conducts seminars. Services available to anyone involved in offender rehab.

21025. James Graham Brown Cancer Center, Univ of Louisville, 529 South Jackson St, Louisville, KY 40202; (502) 588-6905. Governed by Regional Cancer Center Corp and Univ of Louisville. Conducts cancer treatment, research; publishes books, journals; conducts seminars, outreach educational programs.

21026. Keeneland Library, P.O. Box 1690 (Keeneland Race Course), Lexington, KY 40592; (606) 254-3412 ext 223. Owns books, periodicals, clippings, negatives related to thoroughbred breeding, racing. Answers inquiries, provides references services, permits onsite use of collection.

21028. Kentucky Derby Museum, P.O. Box 3513 (704 Central Ave at Churchhill Downs), Louisville, KY 40201; (502) 637-1111. Permits onsite use of collection of Kentucky Derby memorabilia. Answers inquiries, provides reference services, conducts tours. Services available for entrance fee.

21029. Kentucky Historical Society, Library, P.O. Box H, Old Capitol Annex, Broadway, Frankfort, KY 40602; (502) 564-3016. Permits onsite use of collection on Ky. history. Publishes journals, books, and art prints; provides advisory, reference, record restoration, and copying services; conducts seminars. Services available for a fee.

21030. Kentucky Research and Services, 2005 Newman Rd, Lexington, KY 40503; (606) 272-1907. Publishes technical reports, data compilations; provides advisory, reference, videotaping services; conducts seminars, workshops. Lobbying services available to interest groups in Ky.

21031. Kentucky State Library Services, Ky. Dept for Libraries and Archives, P.O. Box 537 (300 Coffee Tree Rd), Frankfort, KY 40602; (502) 875-7000. Publishes reports, bibliographies, and directories, answers inquiries, provides consulting, reference, and copying services, makes referrals, lends materials, permits onsite use of collection.

21032. Louisville Twin Study, Child Development Unit, Univ of Louisville, Health Sciences Center, Louisville,

KY 40292; (502) 588-5134. Owns psychometric and other data on twins. Publishes journals and newsletters, provides consulting services, answers inquiries, permits onsite use of collection by arrangement.

21033. Meat Laboratory, Dept of Animal Science, College of Agriculture, Univ of Ky., Lexington, KY 40546; (606) 257-3822. Publishes research papers, abstracts on meat science. Provides consulting services and extension services to state producer, consumer groups. Services free to Ky. residents.

21035. National Association for State Information Systems, P.O. Box 11910, Lexington, KY 40578; (606) 252-2291. Nonprofit corp concerned with problems faced by all levels of govt. Publishes newsletter, technical reports, and directories; provides reference services free to govts.

21036. National Carousel Association, P.O. Box 307 (955 Maple Dr), Frankfort, KY 40602; (317) 654-5807. Nonprofit org that promotes preservation, appreciation of classic wooden carousel. Publishes magazine, provides info on history of carousel, makes referrals to people who do restoration work.

21037. National Conference of Lieutenant Governors, P.O. Box 11910, Lexington, KY 40578; (606) 252-2291. Publishes newsletter, provides advisory services, conducts seminars and workshops. Services generally provided free to govts, nonprofit and public interest users; at cost to others.

21038. National Consortium for Black Professional Development, 2307 Taylorsville Rd, Rear Bldg, Louisville, KY 40205; (502) 451-8199. Publishes magazine on employment of minorities in science and engineering. Provides advisory, reference services; conducts seminars, workshops. Services for a fee.

21039. National Council for Environmental Balance, P.O. Box 7732 (4169 Westport Rd), Louisville, KY 40207; (502) 896-8731. Nonprofit org that provides analyses of technical material on energy, environment in lay language. Services available free to students, school libraries; for a fee to others.

21040. National Crime Prevention Institute Information Center, School of Justice Administration, Coll of Urban and Public Affairs, Univ of Louisville, Shelby Campus, Louisville, KY 40292; (502) 588-6987. Natl clearinghouse for crime prevention literature. Provides advisory, reference, literature-searching services; evaluates data; conducts seminars, workshops. Services for a fee.

21041. National Society of the Sons of the American Revolution Genealogy Library, 1000 South 4th St, Louisville, KY 40203; (502) 589-1776. Publishes books on American Revolution; owns museum of antiques, paintings. Provides reference and copying services, permits onsite use of collection. Services for a fee.

21042. National Wheelchair Basketball Association, 110 Seaton Bldg, Univ of Ky., Lexington, KY 40506; (606) 257-1623. Interest in wheelchair basketball. Publishes newsletters, directory, and rules; provides advisory services to member teams, conference officers, and those establishing teams.

21043. North American Falconers' Association, c/o Roger Thacker, Pres, Troy Park, Windhover Farm, Versailles, KY 40383. Interest in care, welfare, and training of raptorial bird species. Publishes periodicals, answers inquiries, provides consulting services. Services free.

21044. North American Trackless Trolley Association, c/o Harry R. Porter, Pres, 1042 Bardstown Rd, No. 2, Louisville, KY 40204; (502) 459-5261. Interest in statistical and historical data on trackless trolley vehicles and systems. Publishes and distributes current events publications.

21045. Oscar Getz and Bardstown Historical Museums Board of Trustees, Spalding Hall, P.O. Box 41, Bardstown, KY 40004; (502) 348-2999. Conducts tours; permits onsite use of collection of whiskey artifacts, advertising memorabilia, and patent drawings. Provides free reference services.

21046. Science Editors, P.O. Box 7185 (149 Thierman Lane), Louisville, KY 40207; (502) 897-5310. Distributes publication summarizing articles from medical, pharmacological journals reporting adverse drug reactions, drug interaction. Answers inquiries free, provides consulting services.

21047. Society for General Systems Research, c/o Dr John A. Dillon, Jr., Secty-Treas, Systems Science Institute, Univ of Louisville, Louisville, KY 40292; (502) 588-6996. Affiliate of American Assn for Advancement of Science. Publishes bulletin and yearbook on general systems theory, answers inquiries, makes referrals, holds annual meeting with AAAS.

21048. Society of Psychologists in Addictive Behaviors, c/o Curtis L. Barrett, Secty-Treas, P.O. Box 35070-Psychiatry, Louisville, KY 40232; (502) 562-8851. Encourages communication among psychologists working in prevention, treatment of substance abuse. Provides consulting services, conducts workshops. Services provided at cost.

21049. Tennessee Valley Authority, Land Between the Lakes, Tennessee Valley Authority, Golden Pond, KY 42231; (502) 924-5602. Publishes field guides to flora and fauna; provides advisory services; conducts environmental education programs; permits onsite use of collection. Services free.

21050. Tobacco and Health Research Institute, Scientific Information Section, Tobacco and Health Research Institute, Univ of Ky., Cooper and Univ Drs., Lexington, KY 40546; (606) 257-2877. Owns journals, patents, and abstracts on tobacco and health. Provides reference and copying services, lends materials, permits onsite use of collection. Services generally free to anyone.

21051. US Ecology, P.O. Box 7246 (9200 Shelbyville Rd, Ste 526)), Louisville, KY 40207; (502) 426-7160. Publishes pamphlets, standards, and specifications on radioactive chemical and hazardous waste management. Answers inquiries; provides technical, regulatory consulting services.

21052. United Catalysts Inc., Library, P.O. Box 32370 (1227 South 12th St), Louisville, KY 40232; (502) 637-9751. Owns books and periodicals on subjects such as inorganic and analytical chemistry, petrochemicals, catalysis. Lends materials, permits onsite use of collection.

21053. United Professional Horsemen's Association, 181 North Mill St, Lexington, KY 40507; (606) 252-6888. Publishes quarterly newsletter on show horse industry. Answers inquiries, provides advisory and reference services, conducts seminars and clinics. Services mostly free.

21054. Urban Shelter Associates, 1252 South Shelby St, Louisville, KY 40203; (502) 635-7928. Teaches volunteers how to weatherstrip homes of the poor and elderly. Provides advisory services and narrated slide show on energy house construction. Services available for a fee.

21055. Urban Studies Center, Gardencourt Campus, Univ of Louisville, Louisville, KY 40292; (502) 588-6626. Nonprofit agency that owns population, housing, health status data for Ky. Publishes research reports, provides consulting services, conducts research, permits onsite use of collection.

21057. Wenner-Gren Aeronautical Research Laboratory, Univ of Ky., Rose St, Lexington, KY 40506-0070; (606) 257-2782. Holds data on bioengineering, including bioastronautics, biomechanics, and cardiovascular dynamics. Publishes technical reports, journals; provides consulting, advisory services.

21058. World Airline Hobby Club, 3381 Apple Tree Lane, Erlanger, KY 41018; (606) 342-9039. Seeks to preserves history of commercial aviation from 1930s to present. Publishes journal, evaluates data, conducts seminars and workshops, answers inquries. Services provided at cost.

Louisiana

22001. ASM Division of Aquatic and Terrestrial Microbiology, American Society for Microbiology, c/o Dr Samuel P. Meyers, Dept of Food Science, La. State Univ, Baton Rouge, LA 70803; (504) 388-5206. Interest in marine, freshwater, and soil microbiology, microbiology of water pollution. Answers inquiries, makes referrals to member specialists.

22002. Advocacy Center for the Elderly and Disabled, 1001 Howard Ave, Suite 300-A, New Orleans, LA 70113; (504) 522-2337, (800) 662-7705 (in La.). Interest in sociolegal problems of the elderly, community-based services for the elderly and disabled, services to the developmentally disabled. Provides general reference services, conducts seminars. Services free to elderly clients and groups.

22003. American Rose Society, P.O. Box 30000 (Jefferson-Paige Rd), Shreveport, LA 71130; (318) 938-5402. Educational org involved in all facets of rose culture. Answers inquiries, provides consulting services, distributes publications, makes referrals.

22004. American Society for Handicapped Physicians, 137 Main St, Grambling, LA 71245; (318) 255-2675. Nonprofit membership org that supports and promotes handicapped physicians. Works to assist them develop employment opportunities during their education. Serves as clearinghouse for info. Membership open to physicians, interested persons.

22005. Amistad Research Center, 400 Esplanade Ave, New Orleans, LA 70116; (504) 522-0432. Interest in history of America's ethnic minorities, race relations in the U.S. Provides general reference services, permits onsite use of collections. Services free, except photocopying.

22006. Animal Behavior Society, c/o Terry Christenson, Secty, Dept of Psychology, Tulane Univ, New Orleans, LA 70118. Interest in animal behavior, promotes the biological study of animal behavior at all levels. Answers inquiries, provides career guidance in field of animal behavior, distributes info sheets.

22007. Association for Conservation Information, P.O. Box 426, Ferriday, LA 71334; (318) 757-4571. Interest in conservation info, conservation education. Provides general reference services, conducts seminars and workshops, distributes publications. Services except for workshops and seminars free; some restricted to members.

22008. Bee Breeding and Stock Center Laboratory, Agricultural Research Service, USDA, 1157 Ben Hur Rd, Baton Rouge, LA 70820; (504) 766-6064. Interest in research in honeybee breeding and bee genetics. Answers inquiries, distributes some publications free. Services available to anyone; bee stocks available only to research scientists.

22009. Cartographic Information Center, Dept of Geography and Anthropology, La. State Univ, Baton Rouge, LA 70803; (504) 388-6247. Interest in maps and related materials for natural, physical, cultural, social sciences, especially in Southeastern U.S., Latin America. Provides general reference services and consulting, permits onsite reference. Duplications provided at cost.

22010. Center for Energy Studies, La. State Univ, Baton Rouge, LA 70803-0301; (504) 388-4400. Interest in energy sources, conservation, energy policy, environmental sciences, Louisiana energy sources. Provides general reference services, conducts seminars, distributes publications, permits onsite study. Fee for some services.

22011. Center for Louisiana Studies, Univ of Southwestern La., P.O. Box 40831, Lafayette, LA 70504; (318) 231-6027. Interest in La. history, culture, and folklore. Provides general reference services, permits onsite use of collections. Services free to anyone requiring under one hour of staff time.

22012. Coastal Studies Institute, Center for Wetland Resources, La. State Univ, Baton Rouge, LA 70803; (504) 388-2395. Interest in technical aspects of world's coastal areas, including geology, sedimentation, chemistry, and surf zone processes. Answers brief inquiries, provides advisory services, disseminates reprints and technical reports.

22013. College of Design Resource Center, La. State Univ, Baton Rouge, LA 70803; (504) 388-2665. Interest in environmental design, including architecture, landscape, regional and urban planning, interior, graphic design, etc. Lends materials by special arrangement to persons in related fields, permits onsite study.

22014. Cordell Hull Foundation for International Education, c/o Ralph Severio, TESL Institute, Tulane Univ, New Orleans, LA 70118; (504) 865-4461. Interest in exchanges of students and teachers between U.S. and Central and South American countries, bilingual education. Answers inquiries, provides grant and loan assistance. Services free to English- and Spanish-speaking individuals.

22015. Council for the Development of French in Louisiana, P.O. Box 3936 (217 West Main St), Lafayette, LA 70502; (318) 233-1020. Interest in promotion and development of French language and culture in La. Provides general reference and translation services, conducts workshops, permits onsite study, offers French exchange programs abroad. Info services free, except workshops.

22016. Cystic Fibrosis Center and Pediatric Pulmonary Center, Dept of Pediatrics, School of Medicine, Tulane Univ, 1430 Tulane Ave, New Orleans, LA 70112; (504) 588-5601. Conducts research, training, treatment in pediatric pulmonary diseases. Interest in cystic fibrosis, asthma, etc. Provides general reference and consulting services, conducts seminars.

22017. Delta Regional Primate Research Center, Tulane Univ, Covington, LA 70433; (504) 892-2040 ext 223. Interest in research in infectious diseases, neurobiology, biochemistry, reproductive physiology, urology, veterinary science. Provides general reference services and consulting, permits onsite use of collection. Services primarily for core scientists and graduate students.

22018. Department of Rural Sociology Research, Agricultural Center, La. State Univ, Baton Rouge, LA 70803; (504) 388-5101. Interest in rural sociology research relating to La., rural and community development. Answers inquiries, provides advisory services, evaluates data, distributes publications.

22019. Eighteenth Century Short Title Catalogue for North America, c/o Dr Henry Snyder, Director, Coll of Arts and Sciences, La. State Univ, Baton Rouge, LA 70803; (504) 388-8625. Interest in creating data base with records of all books printed in Great Britain, its colonies during the 18th century. Provides reference, cataloging, bibliographical services; distributes publications. Data available online for a fee.

22020. Enviro-Med Laboratories, 1874 Dallas Dr, Baton Rouge, LA 70806; (504) 928-0232. Interest in environmental, biomedical, and chemical analysis of waste waters, potable water, hazardous wastes, air. Provides general reference services, conducts seminars, leases air and water sampling devices. Services provided for a fee.

22022. Gulf South Research Institute, P.O. Box 14787, Baton Rouge, LA 70898; (504) 766-3300. Interest in Gulf South economy, physical sciences, public health sciences, pollution abatement, human resources, oceanography, toxicology, urban development. Answers inquiries, makes referrals free, provides consulting, literature-searching services for a fee.

22023. International Association of Clerks, Recorders, Election Officials, and Treasurers, P.O. Box 790, Vidalia, LA 71373; (318) 336-8752. Interest in all elected or appointed clerks, recorders, election officials, treasurers, and other officials performing.similar duties. Answers inquiries, conducts workshops, distributes publication. Services free to anyone.

22024. International Double Reed Society, 626 Lakeshore Dr, Monroe, LA 71203-4032; (318) 343-5715. Interest in oboes, English horns, bassoons, contra-bassoons. Answers inquiries, conducts annual intl conferences, lends library materials. Services provided at cost.

22025. International Marketing Institute, Univ of New Orleans, Lakefront Campus, New Orleans, LA 70122; (504) 283-0279. Assists in the study, promotion of intl commerce. Provides general reference services, conducts seminars, distributes publications. Fees charged for seminars, directory; other services generally free.

22026. Lake Ponchartrain Laboratories, Gulf South Research Institute, P.O. Box 26518 (5010 Leroy Johnson Dr), New Orleans, LA 70186; (504) 283-4223. Interest in analytical chemistry, environmental technology, process engineering, polymer science, membrane technology, toxicology, etc. Provides consulting services and research work for fees.

22027. Louisiana Agricultural Experiment Station, La. State Univ Agricultural Center, P.O. Drawer E, Baton Rouge, LA 70803-5602; (504) 388-4181. Interest in general agriculture, chemistry, agricultural engineering, economics, agronomy, animal science, dairy science, entomology, feed and fertilizers, food science and technology. Answers inquiries, makes referrals.

22028. Louisiana Arts and Science Center, P.O. Box 3373 (Old Governor's Mansion, 502 North Blvd), Baton Rouge, LA 70821; (504) 344-9463. Interest in art, astronomy, science, history. Answers inquiries, provides advisory services, conducts guided tours, programs, and workshops, provides speakers, permits onsite study. Services free, except public planetarium shows.

22029. Louisiana Cooperative Fishery Research Unit, Parker Coliseum, Room 247, La. State Univ, Baton Rouge, LA 70803; (504) 388-6051. Interest in swamp, riverine, and estuarine ecology; early life histories of fishes. Answers inquiries, provides consulting services. Services generally free. Biological studies performed on a grant basis.

22030. Louisiana Cooperative Wildlife Research Unit, La. State Univ, Baton Rouge, LA 70803; (504) 388-4131. Interest in wildlife management and ecology, pesticides, wetland ecology, wildlife diseases. Provides general reference and consulting services, identifies specimens, permits onsite reference.

22031. Louisiana Geological Survey, Box G, Univ Station, Baton Rouge, LA 70893; (504) 342-6754. Interest in depth, quantity, quality of groundwater, protection of freshwater sands against pollution, general hydrology, geology, etc. Answers inquiries, publishes materials, makes referrals.

22032. Louisiana Historical Association, Univ of Southwestern La., P.O. Box 42808 (HLG 519), Lafayette, LA 70504; (318) 231-6871. Interest in history of La. Provides general reference services, conducts seminars, distributes publications. Services free, except publications.

22034. Louisiana Oil Marketers Association, P.O. Box 1 (509 Marshall St, Suite 1615), Shreveport, LA 71161; (318) 221-4113. Nonprofit trade assn for wholesale distributors of petroleum products. Interest in marketing of gasoline, other petroleum products. Answers inquiries, provides consulting services. Services free to assn members, at cost to others.

22035. Louisiana Universities Marine Consortium, Star Route Box 541, Chauvin, LA 70344; (504) 594-7552. Research org interested in biological oceanography, systematics and taxonomy, physiological ecology, marine pollution, etc. Provides general reference services, conducts seminars, permits onsite study. Services free, except consulting and computer searches.

22037. Museum of Geoscience, La. State Univ, Baton Rouge, LA 70803; (504) 388-2931. Interest in curation, research, and exhibition in geology, paleontology, archaeology, and folk life. Provides general reference services, distributes publications, permits onsite study. Services free to state agencies, at cost to others.

22038. National Association of Pipe Coating Applicators, 717 Commercial National Bank Bldg, Shreveport, LA 71101; (318) 227-2769. Interest in protective pipe coatings, plant-applied pipe coating specifications. Answers inquiries, distributes publications. Services free, except guidebook and specifications.

22039. National Hansen's Disease Center, Carville, LA 70721; (504) 642-7771. Natl facility for research and treatment of Hansen's Disease, also known as leprosy.

22040. Nematology Research Laboratory, Life Sciences Bldg, La. State Univ, Baton Rouge, LA 70803; (504) 388-1464 ext 40. Interest in nematode diseases of plants. Answers inquiries, identifies plant parasitic nematodes, makes referrals, permits onsite use of literature collection.

22041. New Orleans Society for Adolescent Psychiatry, c/o Dr Lincoln D. Paine, President, 1419 Amelia St, New Orleans, LA 70115; (504) 899-5111. Interest in psychotherapy for adolescents, social agencies serving adolescents, psychopathology of adolescents. Answers inquiries, conducts workshops, makes referrals. Services other than workshops free.

22042. Nuclear Science Center, La. State Univ, Baton Rouge, LA 70803-5820; (504) 388-2163. Interest in nuclear technology, engineering, radioisotope applications, health physics, nondestructive testing. Provides R&D services on cost-recovery basis, irradiation services. Services for educational purposes performed for minimum charges.

22043. Office of Air Quality and Nuclear Energy, La. Dept of Environmental Quality, P.O. Box 14690 (4845 Jamestown Ave), Baton Rouge, LA 70898-4690; (504) 925-4518. Interest in radiation in general, peaceful uses of nuclear energy, emergency plans for fixed nuclear facilities, radioactive waste. Provides computer listings, disseminates reports, permits onsite reference, makes referrals to other sources of info.

22044. Office of Sea Grant Development, Center for Wetland Resources, La. State Univ, Baton Rouge, LA 70803; (504) 388-1558. Develops, administers statewide, worldwide programs on environmental and coastal zone issues. Provides consulting services, conducts research and seminars, distributes publications, makes referrals. Some info services free.

22045. Population Food Fund, c/o Dr C.M. Cargille, 409 Sixth St, Mamou, LA 70554; (318) 639-2822. Conducts programs in public education, policy, and fund-raising. Interest in population, food, environment, resources policy. Answers inquiries free, conducts seminars on a fee basis.

22046. River Oaks Foundation, 1800 Jefferson Hwy, New Orleans, LA 70121; (504) 835-2661, 835-5017. Interest in psychotherapy, psychoanalysis, and other mental health-related subjects. Provides general reference services, conducts seminars, permits onsite use of collections. Services generally limited to mental health professionals, and may be subject to a fee.

22047. Rudolph Matas Medical Library, Tulane Univ, 1430 Tulane Ave, New Orleans, LA 70112; (504) 588-5155. Interest in medical sciences, public health, history of medicine. Provides general reference services, permits onsite study. Full services available only to

Tulane Univ faculty and students and local professionals. Fees charged for automated services.

22048. Scope Research and Development, P.O. Box 1135 (953 Julia St), Baton Rouge, LA 70821; (504) 344-7709. Interest in educational, sociological, and psychological research; marketing, consumer, and opinion surveys; criminal justice research. Provides general reference services, conducts seminars. General info services provided free.

22049. Southeastern Association of Fish and Wildlife Agencies, c/o Joe L. Herring, Secty-Treas, La. Dept of Wildlife and Fisheries, P.O. Box 15570, Baton Rouge, LA 70895; (504) 342-5881. Interest in fish and game management and conservation, including law enforcement info and education, wildlife and fish diseases, statistical methods of wildlife management. Answers inquiries or makes referrals.

22051. Southern Forest Products Association, P.O. Box 52468, New Orleans, LA 70152; (504) 443-4464 Trade assn of lumber manufacturers from 12 Southern states. Answers inquiries, distributes publications, makes referrals. Services available to those interested in forest management.

22052. Southern Regional Research Center, Agricultural Research Service, USDA, P.O. Box 19687 (1100 Robert E. Lee Blvd), New Orleans, LA 70179; (504) 589-7072. Interest in basic, utilization research on cotton, cottonseed, Southern-grown vegetables, food safety, mycotoxins, crop protection, and seed germination. Provides general reference services, reprints of papers; permits onsite study by trained personnel.

22053. Southwest Louisiana Geophysical Society, P.O. Box 51463--OCS, Lafayette, LA 70505. Interest in geophysical studies of southwest La., petroleum and other mineral exploration. Answers inquiries, conducts seminars and workshops. Services provided at cost to all users.

22054. USL-New Iberia Research Center, 100 Ave D, New Iberia, LA 70560; (318) 365-2411. Interest in toxicology, primate research and breeding, drug metabolism, residue analysis, teratology, pharmacokinetics, etc. Answers brief inquiries, publishes reports.

22055. Water Resources Center, La. Tech Univ, Ruston, LA 71272; (318) 257-3546. Interest in hydraulics, hydrology, water supply and quality; wastewater treatment, disposal; water resources; zoology; bacteriology. Answers inquiries, provides speakers on environmental subjects.

22056. William Ransom Hogan Jazz Archives, Howard-Tilton Memorial Library, Tulane Univ, New Orleans, LA 70118; (504) 865-5688. Interest in history of New Orleans jazz. Answers inquiries, provides consulting and reference services, permits onsite use of collection. Fees charged for duplication; services limited by copyright restrictions and handling.

Maine

23001. Americans for Customary Weight and Measure, Old Stone Farm, Wiscasset, ME 04578; (207) 882-5037. Opposes conversion to metric system from customary system of weights and measures. Interest in conversion costs, related policies and legislation. Provides general reference services, conducts seminars, distributes publications. Services free, except publications.

23002. Association of Railway Museums, Attn: Michael C. Lennon, Pres, P.O. Box 3454, Portland, ME 04104. Interest in electric and steam railway museums, railway equipment. Answers inquiries or makes referrals free, sells publication. Services available within limits of time.

23003. Bigelow Laboratory for the Ocean Sciences, Northeastern Research Found, McKown Point, West Boothbay Harbor, ME 04575; (207) 633-2173 ext 26. Lab, marine research facility interested in marine biology and chemistry, planktonic research, oceanography, estuarine biology. Provides general reference services, conducts seminars. Services provided for fees, negotiated on individual basis.

23004. Carriage Association of America, c/o H.K. Sowles, Jr, Exec V.P., P.O. Box 3788, Portland, ME 04104; (207) 781-4020. Promotes knowledge, collecting, restoring, driving, and research of horse-drawn vehicles. Answers inquiries, sponsors annual conference, makes referrals. Services free, primarily for members.

23005. Carrier Reports, P.O. Box 39, Lubec, ME 04652; (207) 733-2856. Commercial org interested in general info, financial data on air, rail, bus carriers. Provides general reference services, distributes pubblications and data compilations. Services free.

23006. Fisheries Research Laboratory, McKown Point, Maine Dept of Marine Resources, West Boothbay Harbor, ME 04575; (207) 633-5572. Interest in effects of algal, bacterial oil; oil emulsifier; thermal, pesticidal, and metallic ion pollution on fish, shellfish, crustacea, and seaweeds; population dynamics; effects of environmental variables on species abundance; etc. Answers inquiries, makes referrals, permits onsite use of collection.

23007. Ira C. Darling Center for Research, Teaching and Service, Univ of Maine at Orono, Walpole, ME 04573; (207) 563-3146. Interest in research in planktology, benthic ecology, aquaculture, ichthyology, micropaleontology, marine geology, chemistry, etc. Provides general reference services, conducts seminars, permits onsite use of collection. Services free, primarily for academic community.

23008. Jackson Laboratory, Bar Harbor, ME 04609; (207) 288-3371; (207) 288-5845. Mammalian genetics research institution interested in biomedical research with emphasis on cancer, other constitutional diseases. Provides general reference services, lends printed materials, permits onsite use of collection. Services free. Fee for bibliography searching.

23009. Joan Staats Library, Bar Harbor, ME 04609; (207) 288-3371. Interest in origin, characteristics, and uses of inbred strains of mice; mammalian genetics; biology, genetics of abnormal growths; molecular genetics; etc. Provides general reference services, permits onsite use of collection by qualified visitors. Fee charged for computer costs.

23010. Lumberman's Museum, Box 300, Patten, ME 04765; (207) 528-2650. Interest in history of logging in Maine from early 1800's to 1930's, with some reference to modern logging. Provides general reference services, distributes publications; permits onsite use of collections. Fee for some services.

23011. Maine Aquaculture Association, P.O. Box 535, Damariscotta, ME 04543; (207) 829-5567. Interest in marine and fresh water aquaculture in Maine; biological, environmental requirements of cultured species. Provides general reference services, distributes newsletter by subscription. Services available within limits of time and staff.

23012. Maine Coast Heritage Trust, P.O. Box 426, Northeast Harbor, ME 04662; (207) 276-5156. Interest in land conservation and protection in Maine, particularly Maine islands, coastline; economic benefits of land conservation. Provides general reference services, conducts seminars, evaluates data, distributes publications, lends materials, permits onsite use of collections.

23013. Maine Cooperative Fish and Wildlife Research Unit, Univ of Maine (Wildlife Unit, 240 Nutting Hall), Orono, ME 04469; (207) 581-2870. Fisheries Office: 313 Murray Hall; (207) 581-2580. Conducts research, provides technical assistance in wildlife and fish ecology, biology. Provides general reference services, conducts seminars, distributes publications. Services, generally free, primarily for wildlife and fisheries professionals, orgs, and govt agencies.

23015. Maine Department of Marine Resources, Marine Resources Lab, West Boothbay Harbor, ME 04575; (207) 633-5572. Interest in marine and anadromous fish and shellfish management, sanitation; fisheries inspection; environmental monitoring for biotoxins, oil, salinity, and climatology; etc. Provides general reference services, conducts seminars, evaluates data. Services free.

23017. Maine Historical Society, 485 Congress St, Portland, ME 04101; (207) 774-1822. Interest in Maine history and genealogy. Answers inquiries, permits onsite use of collections. Services available for a fee to nonmembers.

23018. Maine Organic Farmers and Gardeners Association, Box 2176, Augusta, ME 04330; (207) 622-3118. Interest in organic farm certification, farming, gardening education; food marketing; agricultural land preservation. Provides general reference services, conducts seminars, distributes publication. Services free, except newspaper.

23019. Marine Research Laboratory and Hydrocarbon Research Center, Bowdoin Coll, Brunswick, ME 04011; (207) 725-8731 ext 602. Interest in marine ecology, zooplankton and mussels, role of oil and hydrocarbons, effect of drill muds on marine organisms, effect of metal ions on marine animals. Answers inquiries, makes free referrals, performs oil sampling, analyses on sea water and marine organisms for a fee.

23020. Moosehorn National Wildlife Refuge, U.S. Fish and Wildlife Service, P.O. Box X, Calais, ME 04619; (207) 454-3251. Interest in wildlife, woodcock, spruce budworm, black duck management and research. Answers inquiries, provides advisory services. Services primarily for students in field, other researchers/managers, and landowners.

23021. Mount Desert Island Biological Laboratory, Salsbury Cove, ME 04672; (207) 288-3605. Interest in renal physiology, epithelial transport, developmental biology, North Atlantic fauna and flora, etc. Furnishes research facilities and logistic support for scientists to conduct their own investigations during summer months. Services provided for a fee.

23022. National Association of School Nurses, Box 1300, Scarborough, ME 04074; (207) 883-2117. Provides leadership in promotion and delivery of adequate health services to all children and youth by qualified school nurses. Initiates projects; represents assn interests in federal, state policy-making; monitors federal legislation pertaining to school health.

23023. Northeast Archives of Folklore and Oral History, Dept of Anthropology, Univ of Maine at Orono, South Stevens Hall, Orono, ME 04469; (207) 581-1891. Interest in folklore, folklife, lumbering, fishing, hunting, and forestry in New England and Atlantic Provinces of Canada. Provides general reference services, conducts seminars, permits onsite use of collections. Services available for a fee.

23024. Northeastern Lumber Manufacturers Association, c/o Stephen S. Clark, Exec V.P., 4 Fundy Rd, Falmouth, ME 04105; (207) 781-2252. Interest in manufacturing and marketing of Northeastern hardwood and softwood lumber, grading of softwood lumber. Provides general reference services. Fee only for technical grading services examinations.

23025. Nutting Memorial Library, Maine Maritime Academy, Castine, ME 04420; (207) 326-4311 ext 260. Interest in maritime technology, ocean and marine engineering, naval architecture, oceanography, navigation. Provides reference services, makes direct and interlibrary loans, permits onsite use of collection. Services free to anyone with identification card to allow direct borrowing.

23026. Penobscot Marine Museum, Church St, Searsport, ME 04974; (207) 548-6634. Interest in Maine maritime history. Answers inquiries, provides literature-searching services, permits onsite use of collection. Services free.

23027. Shelter Institute, 38 Center St, Bath, ME 04530; (207) 442-7938. Resource center for owner-built housing engineered for efficiency. Offers courses in theory and practice of physics, engineering in application to individual housing situations. Provides general reference services, evaluates data, conducts seminars. Services available for a fee.

23028. Society for the Preservation of Old Mills, P.O. Box 435, Wiscasset, ME 04578. Nonprofit org interested in preservation, restoration, adaptive use of old mills. Provides general reference services, makes direct and interlibrary loans, distributes publications. Services free.

23029. TRANET, P.O. Box 567, Rangeley, ME 04970; (207) 864-2252. Network for appropriate/alternative technologies that provides info on appropriate, alternative, and intermediate technologies, solar energy, wind power, village technology, rural technology, future studies, citizen action. Provides general reference services, distributes publications.

23030. Wilson Museum, Perkins St, Castine, ME 04421; (207) 326-8753. Interest in prehistory, anthropology, archaology worldwide, geology, local history. Answers brief inquiries, permits onsite use of collections by qualified researchers. Exhibits open to public.

Maryland

24010. AAI Corp. Technical Library, P.O. Box 6767, Baltimore, MD 21204; (301) 628-3193. Collects info on electronics for marine and industrial applications, ordnance, ATE equipment, and solar energy. Answers inquiries, makes referrals and interlibrary loans, permits onsite use of collection by persons with a need to know.

24012. Acacia Group, 6011 Executive Blvd, Suite 306, Rockville, MD 20852; (301) 881-7610. Commercial org involved in financial and estate planning, civil service, military and social security benefits, investments, life's hazards, and venture capital. Answers inquiries, provides advisory services, conducts seminars, makes referrals. Services free.

24013. Academy of American Franciscan History, P.O. Box 34440, W Bethesda, MD 20817; (301) 365-1763. Sponsored by Order of Franciscan Friars, interested in history of Catholic Church and Franciscan Order in Latin America. Answers inquiries, provides consulting and reference services, distributes publications, and makes referrals.

24014. Adoptees in Search, P.O. Box 41016, Bethesda, MD 20814; (301) 656-8555. Nonprofit corp composed of adult adoptees, adoptive parents, birth parents, and others. Publishes a newsletter, answers inquiries, provides advisory and reference services, distributes publications, makes referrals. Services for members.

24015. Agricultural Environmental Quality Institute, Ag Research Service, USDA, Bldg 001, Room 233, Beltsville, MD 20705; (301) 344-3030. Conducts research devoted to minimizing environmental damage by improving agricultural practices. Answers inquiries, provides consulting services, makes referrals. Services free.

24016. Agricultural and Environmental Information Retrieval and Indexing Services, P.O. Box 20939 (1915 Plyers Mill Rd), Silver Spring, MD 20902; (301) 649-4871. Provides info in agricultural, biological, medical, economic, and physical sciences. Answers inquiries, provides advisory and reference services, distributes publications and data compilations, makes referrals. Services provided on a sliding-fee scale.

24017. Aircraft Owners and Pilots Association, 421 Aviation Way, Frederick, MD 21701; (301) 695-2000. Concerned with general aviation, including ultralight aircraft operations, pilot training, airports, aircraft, and safety. Provides consulting and reference services, makes referrals, charts routes and makes flight plans for clients, distributes manuals and guides.

24018. Alcohol, Drug Abuse and Mental Health Administration, Public Health Service, Dept of Health and Human Services, Parklawn Bldg, Room 12C-15, 5600 Fishers Ln, Rockville, MD 20857; (301) 443-3783. Handles inquiries on mental health, drug abuse or alcohol. Requests for publications filled.

24019. Alcolac Research Library, 3440 Fairfield Rd, Baltimore, MD 21226; (301) 355-2600. Industrial org interested in monomers, surfactants and their synthesis. Answers inquiries, provides advisory and reference services, makes referrals, permits onsite use of collection. Services free, provided on a need-to-know basis.

24020. Alliance for Engineering in Medicine and Biology, 4405 East-West Hwy, Suite 402, Bethesda, MD 20814; (301) 657-4142. Promotes enlightened introduction and use of advanced technology in life science research and clinical practice. Answers inquiries, provides consulting services, distributes publications, conducts seminars, makes referrals. Services on a cost basis.

24021. Alloy Phase Diagram Data Center, Gaithersburg, MD 20899; (301) 921-2917. Investigates metals, alloys, semimetallic materials, and intermetallic compounds. Answers inquiries, makes referrals to other sources of info, permits onsite use of collection.

24022. American Academy of Environmental Engineers, P.O. Box 269 (3 Church Circle), Annapolis, MD 21404; (301) 267-9377. Concerned with environmental engineering related to water supply and waste water, industrial hygiene, radiation, air pollution, and general sanitation. Answers inquiries free, locates experts and conducts seminars for a fee.

24023. American Academy of Podiatric Sports Medicine, 1729 Glastonberry Rd, Potomac, MD 20854; (301) 424-7440. Nonprofit membership org concerned with podiatric sports medicine, physiology, kinesiology, and biomechanics. Answers inquiries, provides reference services, conducts seminars, distributes publications, makes referrals. Services free to members, at cost to others.

24024. American Academy of Psychiatry and the Law, 1211 Cathedral St, Baltimore, MD 21201; (301) 539-0379. Nonprofit org concerned with current issues in forensic psychiatry, penology, and criminology. Answers inquiries free.

24025. American Academy of the History of Dentistry, c/o H. Berton McCauley, 3804 Hadley Square East, Baltimore, MD 21218; (301) 243-5744. Seeks to stimulate interest, study, and research in history of dentistry. Answers inquiries, provides advisory free.

24026. American Association of Colleges of Osteopathic Medicine, 6110 Executive Blvd, Suite 405, Rockville, MD 20852; (301) 468-0990. Promotes educational opportunities in osteopathic medicine, including opportunities for minority and disadvantaged groups. Answers inquiries.

24027. American Association of Colleges of Pharmacy, 4720 Montgomery Ln, Suite 602, Bethesda, MD 20814; (301) 654-9060. Org representing pharmaceutical education in U.S. Answers inquiries, provides advisory services, distributes publications, makes referrals, permits onsite use of collection. Nonmembers may receive some info free.

24028. American Association of Colleges of Podiatric Medicine, 6110 Executive Blvd, Suite 204, Rockville, MD 20852; (301) 984-9350. Promotes podiatric medical education. Answers inquiries, provides reference services and career information. Informational services free.

24029. American Association of Immunologists, 9650 Rockville Pike, Bethesda, MD 20814; (301) 530-7178. Conducts research into immunology. Answers inquiries, provides advisory services, distributes journal, makes referrals. Services free.

24030. American Association of Nurse Attorneys, 113 W Franklin St, Baltimore, MD 21201; (301) 752-3318. Works to educate public on matters of nursing, health care, and law. Answers inquiries, conducts seminars, makes referrals, participates in nursing and health care litigation by filing of "amicus" briefs.

24031. American Association of Pathologists, 9650 Rockville Pike, Bethesda, MD 20814; (301) 530-7130. Oriented to medical school teaching and research in experimental pathology. Pamphlets distributed in answer to career info inquiries. Referrals sometimes made to other orgs and individuals.

24032. American Association of Physics Teachers, c/o Dr Jack M. Wilson, 5110 Roanoke Pl, Suite 101, College Park, MD 20740. Promotes physics education at all levels, from elementary through graduate school. Answers inquiries, arranges short courses and workshops, provides an exhibit of educational materials, distributes publications.

24033. American Association of University Affiliated Programs for Persons with Developmental Disabilities, 8605 Cameron St, Suite 406, Silver Spring, MD 20910. Promotes development and dissemination of technical knowledge on preventing and treating developmental disabilities. Answers inquiries, distributes publications, makes referrals. Services free.

24034. American Bladesmith Society, P.O. Box 68, Braddock Heights, MD 21714; (301) 371-7543. Preserves art of hand-forged blade. Publishes a newsletter, answers inquiries, provides advisory and reference services, conducts seminars, operates a rating system for apprentice, journeyman, and master smith. Services available to members.

24035. American Clinical and Climatological Association, c/o Richard J. Johns, MD, 522 Traylor Bldg, 720 Rutland Ave, Baltimore, MD 21205; (301) 955-3646. Medical society with an interest in era when climatological factors were considered important in management of disease, particularly pulmonary disease. Distributes publication for a fee.

24036. American College Health Association, 15879 Crabbs Branch Way, Rockville, MD 20855; (301) 963-1100. Seeks development of comprehensive health programs at institutions of higher education. Answers inquiries, provides consulting and reference services, makes referrals. Services primarily for members.

24038. American College of Cardiology Extended Learning, 9111 Old Georgetown Rd, Bethesda, MD 20814; (301) 897-5400. Involved in continuing education in cardiovascular disease, offering taped clinical discussions aimed at assisting practicing physician dealing with patients. Sells publications to physicians, nurses, medical schools, libraries, and hospitals.

24039. American College of Health Care Administrators, 8120 Woodmont Ave, Suite 200, Bethesda, MD 20814; (301) 652-8384. Concerned with nursing homes, geriatrics, gerontology, institutional long-term care insurance, and social security. Answers inquiries, provides advisory services, conducts seminars, distributes publications, makes referrals. Services free to members, for a fee to others.

24040. American College of Radiology, 6900 Wisconsin Avenue, Chevy Chase, MD 20815; (301) 654-6900. Seeks to advance the science of radiology and represent interests of radiologists. Services include publications, meetings, educational accreditation, seminars, professional placement, and management consultation. A charge for some publications.

24041. American Correctional Association, 4321 Hartwick Rd, Suite L-208, College Park, MD 20740; (301) 699-7600. Concerned with care, supervision, education, training, employment, treatment, and post-release adjustment of prisoners. Answers inquiries, provides reference and consulting services, conducts seminars and training workshops.

24042. American Council for Drug Education, 6193 Executive Blvd, Rockville, MD 20852; (301) 984-5700. Seeks to educate public about health hazards associated with use of marijuana and other psychoactive substances. Answers inquiries, provides consulting and reference services, conducts workshops, distributes publications, makes referrals.

24043. American Dance Therapy Association, 2000 Century Plaza, Columbia, MD 21044; (301) 997-4040. Seeks to maintain high standards of professional education and competence in field of dance therapy. Answers mail inquiries free if a legal-sized SASE is enclosed.

24044. American Deafness and Rehabilitation Association, 814 Thayer Ave, Silver Spring, MD 20910; (301) 589-0880. Promotes development and expansion of professional rehabilitation and human service delivery to adult deaf persons. Answers inquiries, provides consulting services, distributes publications, conducts seminars, makes referrals. Some services are free.

24045. American Digestive Disease Society, 7720 Wisconsin Ave, Bethesda, MD 20854; (301) 652-9293. Seeks to increase public awareness of digestive diseases and stimulate interest in digestive health. Answers inquiries, distributes publications, makes referrals, operates "Gutline" and "Gut Talk." Most services free, some are only for members.

24046. American Fisheries Society, 5410 Grosvenor Ln, Bethesda, MD 20814; (301) 897-8616. Professional society representing fisheries scientists. Answers inquiries and makes referrals free.

24047. American Humor Studies Association, c/o L.E. Mintz, American Studies, Univ of Md., College Park, MD 20742. Studies historical, cultural, sociological, and psychoanalytic perspectives on American humor in literature, graphic arts, news media, and society. Answers inquiries, provides consulting services, conducts seminars. Services available for a fee.

24048. American Institute for Design and Drafting, 966 Hungerford Dr, Suite 10B, Rockville, MD 20850; (301) 294-8712. Concerned with modern design and drafting, including integration with computer control, photodrafting, and certification of design and drafting schools. Publishes a newsletter, answers inquiries, conducts seminars, assists educational institutes in updating design-drafting curricula.

24050. American Institute of Nutrition, 9650 Rockville Pike, Bethesda, MD 20814; (301) 530-7050. Promotes research in nutrition and facilitates communication among nutrition researchers. Holds meetings, presents awards for outstanding research, publishes professional journals.

24051. American Institute of Ultrasound in Medicine, 4405 East-West Hwy, Bethesda, MD 20814; (301) 656-6117. Assn of physicians, engineers, physicists, technicians, manufacturers, and medical students concerned with diagnostic and therapeutic uses of high-frequency sonic energy. Answers inquiries, provides advisory, reference, and referral services. Services for those in the field.

24052. American Kidney Fund, 7315 Wisconsin Avenue, Suite 203E, Bethesda, MD 20814; (800) 638-8299. Provides direct financial assistance to kidney patients who cannot afford cost of treatment-related expenses. Promotes organ donations, supports professional education, distributes research grants, participates in community service activities.

24053. American Land Resource Association, 5410 Grosvenor Ln, Room 205, Bethesda, MD 20814; (301) 493-9140. Concerned with conservation, management, protection, and use of land resources. Provides advisory services, conducts seminars, distributes publications. Services free.

24054. American Lumber Standards Committee, P.O. Box 210, Germantown, MD 20874; (301) 972-1700. Acts as regulatory body to approve rules and to certify grading agencies as to competency, reliability, and adequacy of service performed. Answers inquiries, provides govt and private agencies with information on lumber standards.

24055. American Medical Care and Review Association, 5410 Grosvenor Ln, Suite 210, Bethesda, MD 20814; (301) 493-9552. Promotes competitive forms of health care delivery that offer comprehensive insurance programs guaranteeing quality of care with predictable cost. Answers inquiries, provides consulting and reference services, makes referrals. Services for a fee.

24056. American Medical Writers Association, 5272 River Rd, Suite 410, Bethesda, MD 20816; (301) 986-9119. Assn of medical communicators. On an informal basis, inquiries from public answered or referrals made to sources of info within the assn.

24058. American Occupational Therapy Association, 1383 Piccard Drive, Rockville, MD 20850; (301) 948-9626. Accredits training programs for occupational therapists. Sponsors workshops and maintains computerized files containing demographic info about AOTA members.

24059. American Physiological Society, c/o Dr Martin Frank, 9650 Rockville Pike, Bethesda, MD 20814; (301) 530-7164. Concerned with all branches of physiology except plant physiology. Answers inquiries.

24060. American Polygraph Association, P.O. Box 1061, Severna Park, MD 21146; (301) 779-5530. Promotes polygraph science, standards, research, and training. Publishes a newsletter, answers inquiries, provides advisory and reference services, conducts seminars, distributes publications. Services may be provided for a fee.

24061. American Society for Clinical Nutrition, 9650 Rockville Pike, Bethesda, MD 20814; (301) 530-7110. Promotes education in clinical nutrition and fosters exchange of research findings among nutritionists. Publishes a monthly, distributes publications, provides curricula info to medical community.

24063. American Society for Deaf Children, 814 Thayer Avenue, Silver Spring, MD 20910; (301) 585-5400. Provides info about deafness to parents and general public, and refers parents to local contacts. Has a library and develops position papers. Biennial conventions held for deaf persons, professionals, and family and friends of deaf people.

24064. American Society for Parenteral and Enteral Nutrition, 8605 Cameron St Suite 500, Silver Spring, MD 20910; (301) 587-6315. Provides educational activities for health care professionals, sponsors certification and self-assessment programs, and develops standards of care for nutritional assessment and support of patients.

24065. American Society for Pharmacology and Experimental Therapeutics, 9650 Rockville Pike, Bethesda, MD 20014; (301) 530-7060. Studies pharmacology and toxicology. Conducts occasional seminars, distributes publications, makes referrals. Services free, except for some publications.

24066. American Society of Biological Chemists, 9650 Rockville Pike, Bethesda, MD 20814; (301) 530-7145. Studies biochemistry and molecular biology. Answers inquiries, provides advisory services, distributes publication, makes referrals. Some services provided for a fee.

24067. American Society of Hospital Pharmacists, 4630 Montgomery Ave, Bethesda, MD 20814; (301) 657-3000. Studies hospital pharmacy practice, including intrahospital drug distribution systems and drug info services. Answers inquiries, provides reference, consulting, and on-line services, makes referrals. Library open to qualified individuals by request.

24068. American Society of Human Genetics, c/o Gerry Gurvitch, 15501-B Monona Dr, Derwood, MD 20855; (301) 424-4120. Concerned with human genetics, including basic research, teaching, clinical application; social, ethical, and legal issues. Answers inquiries.

24069. American Society of Plant Physiologists, P.O. Box 1688, Rockville, MD 20850; (301) 251-0560. Professional org of plant physiologists and plant biochemists engaged in teaching and research. Conducts seminars, distributes publications, makes referrals. Services provided at cost.

24070. American Speech-Language-Hearing Association, 10801 Rockville Pike, Rockville, MD 20852; (301) 897-5700. Encourages basic scientific study of the processes of individual human communication, with special reference to speech, hearing, and language. Answers

inquiries, distributes publications, provides consulting services for a fee, makes referrals, accredits clinical service facilities.

24071. American Trauma Society, P.O. Box 13526, Baltimore, MD 21203; (301) 528-6304. Seeks to mobilize public support to reduce suffering, death, and disability from injury and improve trauma care. Answers inquiries, provides reference services, conducts seminars, distributes publications, sells films, makes referrals. Some services free.

24072. American Type Culture Collection, 12301 Parklawn Dr, Rockville, MD 20852; (301) 881-2600. Collects, preserves, and distributes cultures of microorganisms and plant and animal cells. Sells cultures, answers inquiries, maintains patent culture depository, provides advisory services, distributes publications. Services available only to qualified microbiologists.

24073. American Urological Association, 1120 N Charles St, Baltimore, MD 21201; (301) 727-1100. Promotes interest in urology and urological research. Answers written inquiries, conducts seminars, distributes publications and educational materials.

24074. American Water Resources Association, 5410 Grosvenor Ln, Suite 220, Bethesda, MD 20814; (301) 493-8600. Concerned with all aspects of water resources, including water pollution, irrigation, meteorology, and drainage. Makes referrals to specialists in water resources field.

24075. American Wood Preservers Association, P.O. Box 849, Stevensville, MD 21666; (301) 643-4163. Investigates materials, methods, and principles involved in economic design, location, construction, maintenance, and operation of wood preserving. Sells publications.

24076. Animal Parasitology Institute, Ag Research Service, USDA, Bldg 1040, Beltsville, MD 20705; (301) 344-2202. Studies internal parasites of livestock and poultry, their life cycles and modes of transmission. Answers inquiries, lends specimens to research workers, who may also visit institute to study specimens and consult index-catalogue.

24077. Animal-Human Nutrition and Postharvest Sciences Staff, Ag Research Service, USDA, Bldg 005, Room 136, Beltsville, MD 20705; (301) 344-4050. Concerned with evaluation and planning of natl programs in animal and human nutrition. Provides info on R&D in progress, makes referrals to other sources of info. Services free.

24078. Architecture and Engineering Performance Information Center, 3907 Metzerott Rd, College Park, MD 20742; (301) 935-5545. Seeks to prevent structural and material failures by providing performance info to designers, builders, and inspectors. Provides advisory, reference, and abstracting services; conducts seminars; permits onsite use of computerized data. Services often for a fee.

24079. Armed Forces Radiobiology Research Institute Library, Defense Nuclear Agency, DoD, Bethesda, MD 20814; (301) 295-1330. Data collection on radiobiology, physiology, biochemistry, pathology, immunology, psychology, dosimetry, health physics, and nuclear medicine. Provides reference services, makes interlibrary loans, permits onsite use of collection. Services available to those with a need-to-know.

24080. Army Ballistic Research Laboratory, Aberdeen Proving Ground, MD 21005; (301) 278-3981. Collects data on weapons, ballistics, and related sciences. Provides info services to Dept of Defense and other govt agencies. Library answers inquiries and provides reference services to U.S. govt and govt contractors.

24081. Army Chemical Research and Development Center, Technical Library, Aberdeen Proving Ground, MD 21010; (301) 671-3935. Conducts programs in training, detection, and identification of, and develops warning systems for, chemical and biological agents. Provides interlibrary loan, reference, and referral services to U.S. govt agencies and their contractors.

24082. Army Medical Bioengineering Research and Development Laboratory Library, Fort Detrick, Frederick, MD 21701; (301) 663-2502. Conducts engineering research and development of military medical equipment for Army and on an "as required" basis for Navy and Air Force. Answers inquiries, provides reference services primarily for laboratory's research staff.

24083. Army Medical Research Institute of Infectious Diseases Library, Frederick, MD 21701; (301) 663-2720. Collects data on medical defense against biological warfare. Answers inquiries, provides reference and copying services, makes referrals. Services available to authorized recipients of defense info.

24084. Asphalt Institute, Asphalt Institute Bldg, Univ of Md. Campus, College Park, MD 20740; (301) 277-4258. Promotes asphalt and asphalt products, road, street, highway, and airfield paving. Answers inquiries.

24085. Associated Information Managers, 1776 E Jefferson St, Suite 470S, Rockville, MD 20852. Professional assn of directors and managers of information, administration, marketing, corporate, and strategic planning. Publishes newsletter, answers inquiries, provides reference services, conducts placement services, conducts seminars. Services for a fee.

24086. Associated Specialty Contractors, 7315 Wisconsin Ave, Bethesda, MD 20814; (301) 657-3110. Works with several other construction assns to develop procedures and guidelines on construction contracts and bidding. Answers inquiries, distributes publications, makes referrals. Services primarily for construction-oriented groups.

24087. Association for Childhood Education International, 11141 Georgia Ave, Suite 200, Wheaton, MD 20902; (301) 942-2443. Concerned with education and child development, infancy to early adolescence. Answers inquiries, makes referrals, permits onsite use of collection. Fees for materials sent to nonmembers.

24088. Association for Creative Change Within Religious and Other Social Systems, P.O. Box 219, Frederick, MD 21701. Assn of consultants, educators, counselors, clergy, and administrators and their clients interested in how applied behavioral science relates to religious and other systems. Answers inquiries, provides reference services, distributes publications, makes referrals to members.

24089. Association for Information and Image Management, 1100 Wayne Ave, Silver Spring, MD 20910; (301) 587-8202. Collects materials in info management, computer-aided design and manufacture, micrographics, and office automation. Answers technical inquiries, publications available for purchase.

24090. Association for International Practical Training, 217 American City Bldg, Columbia, MD 21044; (301) 997-2200. Enables college and univ students and others to obtain on-the-job training in a foreign country. Answers inquiries, makes referrals free. A registration fee for American students.

24091. Association for Small Business Advancement, c/o Charles E. Hilton, 7507 Standish Pl, Rockville, MD 20855. Seeks ways in which small business gains greater financial recognition and becomes more profitable. Answers inquiries, provides advisory services, conducts seminars, distributes publications, makes referrals. Services may be provided for a fee.

24092. Association for Women in Computing, 407 Hillmoor Dr, Silver Spring, MD 20901. Concerned with professional development and advancement of women in computing and computer education for women. Publishes newsletter, answers inquiries, provides advisory, consulting, and reference services, conducts seminars and makes referrals.

24093. Association of Consulting Foresters, 5410 Grosvenor Ln, Suite 120, Bethesda, MD 20814; (301) 530-6795. Concerned with forest management. Answers inquiries, provides consulting services for a fee, makes referrals, conducts and sponsors Practicing Foresters Institute.

24094. Association of Interpretive Naturalists, 6700 Needwood Rd, Derwood, MD 20855; (301) 948-8844. Membership org serving park naturalists, teachers of natural and cultural science, historians, curators, astronomers, wildlife managers, students, and others. Answers inquiries and makes referrals. Services primarily for members.

24095. Association of Physical Fitness Centers, 5272 River Road, Bethesda, MD 20816; (301) 656-5060. Trade assn that informs public about economics and ethics of physical fitness centers. Runs a clearinghouse of matters of interest to spa industry and issues a bimonthly newsletter.

24098. Atomic Energy Levels Data Center, Atomic & Plasma Radiation Div, National Bureau of Standards, A167 Physics Bldg, Gaithersburg, MD 20899; (301) 921-2011. Provides critical compilations of data on atomic spectra. Answers inquiries, provides consulting and reference services, distributes publications.

24099. Atomic Industrial Forum, 7101 Wisconsin Ave, Bethesda, MD 20814; (301) 654-9260. Collects data on nuclear insurance and indemnity, radiation and radioisotopes, atomic energy legislation, health and safety standards. Library is open only to member companies and orgs, but librarian will refer researchers to other appropriate sources of info.

24100. Atomic Transition Probabilities Data Center, Atomic & Plasma Radiation Div, National Bureau of Standards, A267 Physics Bldg, Gaithersburg, MD 20899; (301) 921-2071. Collects and catalogs relevant literature, analyzes numerical data, prepares and publishes bibliographies and tables of "best" atomic transition probabilities. Answers inquiries, provides consulting and reference services to scientists with professional interest in the field.

24101. Automotive Parts and Accessories Association, 5100 Forbes Blvd, Lanham, MD 20706; (301) 459-9110. Service-oriented assn for automotive aftermarket industry. Answers inquiries, provides consulting and reference services, conducts seminars, makes referrals. Most services free.

24102. Bakery, Confectionery and Tobacco Workers International Union, 10401 Connecticut Ave, Kensington, MD 20895; (301) 933-8600. Affiliated with AFL-CIO and Canadian Labour Congress. Answers inquiries, makes referrals.

24103. Baltimore & Ohio Railroad Historical Society, P.O. Box 13578, Baltimore, MD 21203-3578; (301) 744-4138. Conducts research and educates public concerning history and economic impact of American railroads, with emphasis on the B&O. Publishes a newsletter, answers inquiries, provides reference services, distributes publications. Services free.

24105. Beltsville Human Nutrition Research Center, Ag Research Service, USDA, Rm 223, Bldg 308, Beltsville, MD 20705; (301) 344-2157. Studies metabolism and requirements for nutrients. Answers inquiries or makes referrals.

24106. Bernan Associates, Government Publications Service, Jerome M. Frumkin, 9730/E George Palmer Hwy, Lanham, MD 20706. Commercial org with interest in govt publications (U.S., U.N., Canada). Provides a standing order service on over 1,000 publication series sold through Govt Printing Office and the Natl Technical Info Service. Similar services are offered for foreign agency publications.

24107. Bethesda Pain Control Program, 7315 Wisconsin Ave, Suite 615N, Bethesda, MD 20814; (301) 951-4466. A multispecialty org that assesses and treats chronic pain. Group also conducts projects with govt and industry on long-term disability and pain. Answers inquiries, provides advisory and consulting services, conducts seminars, distributes publications, makes referrals.

24108. Better Sleep Council, PO Box 275, Burtonsville, MD 20866; (703) 979-3550. Informs public about sleep and sleep disorders, and encourages scientific research in the field. Maintains a list of clinics and sleep laboratories to aid persons with sleep problems.

24109. Breast Cancer Advisory Center, P.O. Box 224, Kensington, MD 20895. Provides a mail service offering referrals to health professionals and info about detection, diagnosis, treatment, and physical and psychological rehabilitation for patients with breast cancer.

24110. Breast Cancer Program, Organs System Section, 8300 Colesville Rd, Silver Spring, MD 20918; (301) 427-8818. Concerned with human and animal breast cancer, epidemiology, biology of normal and malignant mammary tissue, research, and therapy. Publishes a bulletin, provides reference services, distributes publications, makes referrals. Services primarily for people working in the field.

24111. Brotherhood of Railway, Airline and Steamship Clerks, Freight Handlers, Express and Station Employes, 3 Research Pl, Rockville, MD 20850; (301) 948-4910. Affiliate of AFL-CIO for transportation and labor unions. Answers inquiries, provides consulting and reference services, conducts seminars, distributes publications. Services free.

24112. Bureau of Business and Economic Research, 4118 Tydings Bldg, College Park, MD 20742; (301) 454-2303. Conducts research in state and local public finance and in regional, urban, environmental, and natural resource economics. Answers inquiries, provides consulting services, makes referrals. A forecasting model is available. Services primarily for govt agencies.

24113. Bureau of Health Care Delivery and Assistance, Health Resources & Services Administration, Public Health Service, Parklawn Bldg, Room 705, 5600 Fishers Ln, Rockville, MD 20857; (301) 443-2320. Helps assure that health care services are provided to persons living in medically underserved areas. Answers inquiries, provides professional and technical consultation, makes referrals. Services free.

24114. Bureau of Health Care Delivery and Assistance, Division of Maternal and Child Health, Health Resources & Services Administration, Public Health Service, Parklawn Bldg, Room G-05, 5600 Fishers Ln, Rockville, MD 20857; (301) 443-2170. Concerned with maternal and child health and nutrition. Answers inquiries, provides reference services, makes referrals.

24116. Bureau of Health Professions, Health Resources & Services Administration, Public Health Service, Parklawn Bldg, Room 8A-03, 5600 Fishers Ln, Rockville, MD 20857; (301) 443-5794. Provides financial support to institutions for development of health professionals, targeting areas of high natl priority. Distributes publications, provides technical info services. Services primarily for those in the field.

24118. Bureau of Mines, Avondale Research Center, Dept of the Interior, 4900 LaSalle Rd, Avondale, MD 20782-3393; (301) 436-7501. Provides info on flotation fundamentals, mineral and metal recovery in fine particulate systems, experimental electrolysis, particulate mineralogy. Answers inquiries, provides consulting services, lends reports for short periods.

24120. Calendar Reform Foundation, 6210 Massachusetts Ave, Bethesda, MD 20816; (301) 229-6066. Promotes public education on various proposals for rationalizing Gregorian calendar. Answers inquiries, provides consulting services, conducts seminars, distributes a brochure. Services free.

24121. Calvert Marine Museum, P.O. Box 97 (Route 2), Solomons, MD 20688; (301) 326-2042. Dedicated to interaction between culture and marine environment of Chesapeake Bay and Patuxent River estuary. Answers inquiries, conducts tours, provides reproduction services, distributes publications, permits onsite use of collections. Services may be provided for a fee.

24122. Cambridge Scientific Abstracts, 5161 River Rd, Bldg 4, Bethesda, MD 20816; (301) 951-1400. Provides comprehensive coverage of world's literature in abstract form in areas of microbiology, biochemistry, zoology, environment, and other scientific and technical fields. All publications are available on a subscription basis; individual journals or data available on magnetic tape or through on-line computer systems.

24124. Cello Corp., 1354 Old Post Rd, Havre de Grace, MD 21078; (301) 939-1234. Compiles data on chemical specialties, including alkyl benzene, chelation, remote chromatography, cleaners, disinfectants, waxes, polishes, insecticides, and aerosol products. Answers inquiries, makes referrals, permits onsite reference.

24125. Center for Alternatives to Animal Testing, 615 N Wolfe St, Baltimore, MD 21205; (301) 955-3343. Serves as a natl resource in development of innovative in vitro methods to evaluate safety of commercial and therapeutic products. Answers inquiries, publishes a newsletter, provides consulting services, conducts seminars, makes referrals. Services free.

24126. Center for Applied Mathematics, National Bureau of Standards, Gaithersburg, MD 20899; (301) 921-2541. Investigates statistical methods, numerical analysis, and computer algorithms. Provides consulting services, makes interlibrary loans to govern-ment agencies, permits onsite use of collections.

24128. Center for Chemical Physics, Electrolyte Data Center, National Bureau of Standards, Chemistry B-348, Gaithersburg, MD 20899; (301) 921-2108. Collects thermodynamic data on aqueous electrolytes, with emphasis on equilibrium thermodynamic properties of aqueous electrolyte systems. Answers inquiries, provides compilations and critical reviews. Some services available to public.

24129. Center for Devices and Radiological Health, Food & Drug Administration, 1901 Chapman Avenue, Rockville, MD 20857; (301) 443-4190. Answers consumer inquiries by telephone or mail on general issues relating to medical devices or radiological health, and informs public about good health care.

24130. Center for Drugs and Biologics, Office for Consumer and Professional Affairs, Food & Drug Administration, 5600 Fishers Ln, Rockville, MD 20857; (301) 443-1016. Responds to inquiries covering entire spectrum of drug issues and develops responses to drug info requests under Freedom of Information Act.

24131. Center for Electronics and Electrical Engineering, Natl Bureau of Standards, Gaithersburg, MD 20899; (301) 921-3357. Investigates electronic materials and devices, including semiconductors, cryoelectronics, and optoelectronics. Answers inquiries, provides consulting services to govt agencies, scientific, academic, and electronics communities.

24132. Center for Fire Research, Information Services, Natl Bureau of Standards, Gaithersburg, MD 20899; (301) 921-3249. Provides a central document repository and a technical service on fire research. Makes interlibrary loans, permits onsite use of collection.

24134. Center for Mental Health Studies of Emergencies, National Institute of Mental Health, 5600 Fishers Ln, Room 6C12, Rockville, MD 20857; (301) 443-1910. Coordinates NIMH activities re-lating to mental health needs of persons in emergency conditions; administers crisis counseling programs in areas that have been declared disaster areas by President.

24136. Center for Research for Mothers and Children, National Institutes of Health, 7910 Woodmont Ave, Room 7C03, Bethesda, MD 20892; (301) 496-5133. Conducts research and training concerned with investigations of reproductive processes in man and animals. Answers inquiries.

24137. Center for Social Organization of Schools, 3505 N Charles St, Baltimore, MD 21218; (301) 366-3582. Concerned with social organization of schools and influence of schools' social and administrative organization on learning. Answers inquiries, makes referrals, lends materials. Services provided primarily to educators and researchers.

24138. Center for Studies of Antisocial and Violent Behavior, National Institute of Mental Health, 6C-15 Parklawn Bldg, 5600 Fishers Ln, Rockville, MD 20857; (301) 443-3728. Funds grants of benefit to particular agencies and jurisdictions investigating anti-social behavior, violence, mental health, and law. Answers inquiries, provides advisory services, makes referrals.

24140. Center on Aging, 1120 Francis Scott Key Hall, University of Maryland, College Park, MD 20742;

(301) 454-5856. Performs teaching, community training, research, and technical assistance on applied gerontology. Answers inquiries, provides advisory and consulting services, conducts seminars. Services for a fee to professionals.

24141. Chain Saw Manufacturers Association, 4340 East-West Hwy, Suite 1008, Bethesda, MD 20814; (301) 652-0774. Collects data on gasoline- and electric-powered chain saws. Answers inquiries or refers inquirers to other sources of info.

24142. Chemical Propulsion Information Agency, Applied Physics Laboratory, Johns Hopkins Rd, Laurel, MD 20707; (301) 953-7100. Acquires, compiles, analyzes, and disseminates pertinent data on chemical rocket, ramjet, space, and gun propulsion technology. Answers technical inquiries, provides consulting and reference services, permits onsite use of collection. Services only for qualified users.

24143. Chesapeake Bay Foundation, 162 Prince George St, Annapolis, MD 21401; (301) 268-8816. Seeks to involve citizens in care of natural resources of Chesapeake Bay region. Answers inquiries, provides advisory and reference services, makes referrals, permits onsite use of collection. Some services provided at cost.

24144. Chesapeake Bay Institute, 4800 Atwell Rd, Shady Side, MD 20764; (301) 867-7550. Library of oceanography and chemical, physical, and biological properties of estuarine, continental shelf, and oceanic environment. Answers inquiries. Technical publications provided at cost.

24145. Chesapeake Biological Laboratory, P.O. Box 38, Solomons, MD 20688; (301) 326-4281. Collects data on microbiology, plankton biology, finfish biology, toxicology, and systems ecology. Analytical services in nutrient chemistry and environmental toxicology available through special arrangements.

24146. Chessie System Railroads, Public Relations and Advertising Department, Pratt and Poppleton Sts, Baltimore, MD 21223; (301) 237-2387. Studies progress of rail transportation, railroad history, and all aspects of present-day railroading. Answers inquiries, provides reference services, makes referrals. Copies of library materials available for a fee. Railroad Museum open to public.

24147. Clearinghouse on Health Indexes, Center Bldg, Room 2-27, 3700 East-West Hwy, Hyattsville, MD 20782. Studies methodological aspects of developing and applying composite measures of health status and health-related quality of life. Distributes publication, answers inquiries, makes referrals, permits onsite use of collections. Services free.

24148. Coastal Society, 5410 Grosvenor Ln, Suite 110, Bethesda, MD 20814; (301) 897-8616. Promotes understanding and wise use of coastal environments. Publishes a bulletin, conducts seminars open to anyone.

24149. Collaborating Centre for Reference on Tumours of Laboratory Animals, NIH, Landow Bldg, Room 1 D20, 7910 Woodmont Bldg, Bethesda, MD 20892; (301) 496-6047. Provides materials and info on representative cancers and other lesions of lab animals. Answers inquiries, provides advisory services, distributes data compilations, lends slides of histologic sections, permits onsite use of collections. Services for qualified investigators.

24150. Combined National Veterans' Association of America, c/o Raymond J. Williams, 2303 Musgrove Rd, Silver Spring, MD 20904. Assn of veterans and military orgs seeking to solve problems of mutual interest, usually in legislative area. Answers inquiries, conducts seminars. Services free.

24151. Commission on Accreditation for Corrections, 6110 Executive Blvd, Suite 600, Rockville, MD 20852; (301) 770-3097. Administers voluntary correctional accreditation program, only natl program of its kind. Answers inquiries, provides consulting and reference services, conducts seminars, distributes publications, makes referrals. Services primarily for persons working in field.

24152. Committee for Single Adoptive Parents, P.O. Box 15084, Chevy Chase, MD 20815. Acts as info service to present and prospective single adoptive parents of both sexes. Publishes handbook, answers inquiries, provides advisory services, makes referrals. Services free, except for publications.

24153. Committee on Noise as a Public Health Hazard, 10801 Rockville Pike, Rockville, MD 20852; (301) 897-5700. Studies noise exposure, noise effects on hearing, physiological responses, sleep, performance, annoyance, and voice communication. Answers inquiries free.

24154. Community Health Centers Program, Parklawn Bldg, Room 7A-55, 5600 Fishers Ln, Rockville, MD 20857; (301) 653-2010. Assists states in becoming ready to assume responsibility for Community Health Centers under Primary Care Block Grant. Answers inquiries, provides consulting services, makes referrals. Services free, publications are available to anyone.

24156. Community Relations Service, Department of Justice, 5550 Friendship Blvd, Chevy Chase, MD 20815; (301) 492-5939. Provides assistance to communities in preventing and resolving community conflicts involving racial and ethnic minorities. Answers inquiries or makes referrals, distributes publications.

24158. Comsat Laboratories, Technical Library, 22300 Comsat Dr, Clarksburg, MD 20871; (301) 428-4512. Collection of data on electronics, satellite communications, mathematics, physics, and computer science. Answers inquiries, provides reference and duplication services, makes interlibrary loans. Services primarily for staff of Comsat Laboratories.

24160. Congressional Information Service, 4520 East-West Hwy, Bethesda, MD 20814; (301) 654-1550;. Commercial indexer and micropublisher of govt documents and other publications. Provides info through its publications, available by subscription, and its on-line data bases.

24161. Conservation and Renewable Energy Inquiry and Referral Service, P.O. Box 8900, Silver Spring, MD 20907; (800) 523-2929. Source of info on energy conservation and renewable energy technologies, including solar, photovoltaics, wind, wood, ocean energy, and bioconversion. Operates toll-free hotline, makes referrals.

24162. Consumer Credit Counseling and Educational Service of Greater Washington, 11426 Rockville Pike, Suite 105, Rockville, MD 20852; (301) 231-5833. Provides free counseling service for families and individuals with financial problems. Answers inquiries, provides debt counseling services, makes referrals.

24163. Continental Divide Trail Society, P.O. Box 30002, Bethesda, MD 20814; (301) 493-4080. Concerned with planning, development, and maintenance of Continental Divide Trail. Answers inquiries free; provides advisory services and distributes publications for a fee.

24164. Cooperative State Research Service, Current Research Information System, USDA, Natl Agricultural Library Bldg, 5th Floor, Beltsville, MD 20705; (301) 344-3846. Database designed to improve communications among agricultural research scientists, especially with regard to current research. Provides abstracts of ongoing research to specific inquiries. Requests from private individuals or orgs not honored.

24165. Council for Adult and Experiential Learning, Suite 203, 10840 Little Patuxent Parkway, Columbia, MD 21044. Assn of colleges, universities, service agencies, corporations, and individuals who share a philosophical commitment to experiential learning. Answers inquiries, provides training, distributes publications, leases software for assessment of learning. Some services free.

24166. Council for Educational Freedom in America, 2105 Wintergreen Ave, Forestville, MD 20747; (301) 350-0979. Concerned with freedom of education from govt control. Answers inquiries, conducts seminars, makes referrals. Services available for a contribution.

24167. Council of Biology Editors, Philip L. Altman, 9650 Rockville Pike, Bethesda, MD 20814; (301) 530-7036. Sets standards for editing, managing, or publishing biological periodicals. Conducts workshops and makes referrals.

24168. Council of Communication Societies, P.O. Box 1074, Silver Spring, MD 20910; (301) 953-5000 ext 4765. Nonprofit org concerned with human communication, including language, linguistics, speech, and writing. Answers inquiries or refers inquirers to other sources of info free.

24169. Cystic Fibrosis Foundation, 6000 Executive Blvd, Suite 510, Rockville, MD 20852; (301) 881-9130. Supports research and training in all aspects of cystic fibrosis. Answers inquiries, provides consulting services, distributes most publications free, makes referrals.

24170. DES ACTION/Washington, P.O. Box 5311 (4910 Macon Rd), Rockville, MD 20851; (301) 468-2170. Nonprofit org formed to fill needs of persons exposed to drug diethylstilbestrol (DES). Answers inquiries, provides consulting and reference services, conducts seminars, distributes publications, makes referrals, permits onsite use of collection. Services free.

24171. Dairy and Food Industries Supply Association, 6245 Executive Blvd, Rockville, MD 20852; (301) 984-1444. Concerned with sanitary standards for food and dairy processing equipment and materials. Technical inquiries answered by assn staff or referred to specialists. Pertinent reprints of published individual standards furnished in reply to inquiries.

24172. Data Collection on Atomic Line Shapes and Shifts, Natl Bureau of Standards, Gaithersburg, MD 20899; (301) 921-2071. Maintains collection of cataloged literature on broadening and shift of atomic spectral lines. Answers inquiries, provides consulting and reference services, permits onsite use of collection. Services available to scientists with professional interest in field.

24174. David W. Taylor Naval Ship Research and Development Center, Technical Information Center, Code 5220, Bethesda, MD 20084; (202) 227-1309. Collects data on naval architecture, including ship, submarine, and missile design and ship powering, stability, and control. Makes interlibrary loans. Onsite use is restricted to center personnel and other govt employees on approval.

24175. Disclosure, 5161 River Rd, Bethesda, MD 20816; (301) 951-1300. Commercial org providing dissemination services for Securities and Exchange Commission. Answers inquiries, provides copies of reports on-line or in paper or microform, distributes index. Services available for a fee.

24177. Drug Abuse Warning Network, National Institute on Drug Abuse, Parklawn Bldg, Room 11A55, 5600 Fishers Ln, Rockville, MD 20857 (301) 443-6637. Gathers, interprets, and disseminates statistical info on drug abuse. Can provide systemwide and regional profiles of types of drug abuse and drug abusers, identifying patterns and trends. Primary audience is govt agencies, legislators, pharmaceutical industry, and researchers.

24178. EG&G Washington Analytical Services Center, 1396 Piccard Dr, Rockville, MD 20850; (301) 840-3243. Investigates acoustics, electronics, and physics with particular interest in design, fabrication, installation, and maintenance of cable systems. Answers inquiries, makes limited interlibrary loans, provides consulting services for a fee, makes referrals.

24179. Economic Research Council, 7315 Wisconsin Ave, Suite 727-E, Bethesda, MD 20814; (301) 951-1072. Conducts research and publishes capital budget analyses of U.S. companies. Publishes a monthly, provides advisory and reference services, distributes publications, makes referrals. Fees charged for all services except referrals.

24180. Emergency Programs Information Center, 6505 Belcrest Rd, Hyattsville, MD 20782; (301) 436-8087. Studies foreign animal diseases. Answers inquiries, provides reference and microform services, distributes data compilations, permits onsite use of collections. Services free on written request.

24181. Endocrine Society, 9650 Rockville Pike, Bethesda, MD 20814; (301) 530-9660. Conducts research on fundamental physiology and clinical aspects of endocrine glands. Answers inquiries, conducts seminars, makes referrals. Services free.

24183. Enoch Pratt Free Library, 400 Cathedral St, Baltimore, MD 21201; (301) 396-5430. Has documents from federal govt, state of Md., city of Baltimore, and other city and state govts. Adults may have direct access to all materials except Mencken Collection, which is available only to academic researchers. Reference services available.

24184. Entomological Society of America, 4603 Calvert Rd, College Park, MD 20740; (301) 864-1334. Conducts studies in entomology, including systematics, morphology, and evolution. Answers inquiries, makes referrals, permits onsite use of collections.

24186. Epilepsy Foundation of America, 4351 Garden City Drive, Suite 406, Landover, MD 20785; (301) 459-3700. Represents interests of people with epilepsy by initiating federal programs, providing scientific knowledge about epilepsy, and acting as an advocate. Services include parent and patient information, counseling and referrals, employment assistance, medical services, and low-cost drugs.

24187. Equity Policy Center, 4818 Drummond Ave, Chevy Chase, MD 20815; (301) 656-4475. Seeks to ensure that impact of natl and intl programs is equitable, regardless of sex, age, health, or nationality. Answers inquiries, provides consulting services, conducts seminars, distributes publications, makes referrals. Materials distributed at cost.

24188. Expanded Shale, Clay and Slate Institute, 4905 Del Ray Ave, Suite 210, Bethesda, MD 20814; (301) 654-0140. Studies uses of rotary kiln lightweight shale, clay or slate aggregate. Answers inquiries, disseminates single copies of publications free.

24189. F.A.C.E., P.O. Box 28058, Northwood Station, Baltimore, MD 21239; (301) 799-2100. Devoted to support, encouragement, and dissemination of info about adoption. Publishes newsletter, answers inquiries, provides advisory and reference services. SASE requested for written response.

24190. Federation of American Societies for Experimental Biology, 9650 Rockville Pike, Bethesda, MD 20014; (301) 530-7026. Investigates genetics and cytology, reproduction, development, and growth. Sells publications.

24191. Filterite/Brunswick, Technetics Division, 2033 Greenspring Dr, Timonium, MD 21093; (301) 252-0800. Concerned with liquid and gas filtration, primarily cartridge type. Answers inquiries, provides consulting services, makes referrals, permits onsite reference.

24192. Flickinger Foundation for American Studies, 300 St Dunstan's Rd, Baltimore, MD 21212; (301) 323-6284. Investigates ideas and interrelationships of people in charitable, scientific, and cultural activities. Answers inquiries, provides advisory and reference services, conducts seminars, makes referrals. Services free for those qualified.

24194. Fogarty International Center, Natl Institutes of Health, Bldg 38A, Room 604, 9000 Rockville Pike, Bethesda, MD 20892; (301) 496-4627. Furthers intl collaboration in health and behavioral sciences. Programs include postdoctoral fellowships for American biomedical scientists to study abroad and for scientists from other countries to study in U.S.

24196. Food and Drug Administration, Consumer Inquiries, 5600 Fishers Ln, Rockville, MD 20857; (301) 443-3170. Provides consumer-oriented info on safety and efficacy of foods, drugs, cosmetics, and medical devices. Answers inquiries, distributes publications. Services free.

24197. Futures Network, 10533 Green Mountain Circle, Columbia, MD 21044; (301) 730-3310. Seeks a synthesis of economics, politics, psychology, spirituality, science, and technology to create a future commensurate with our capacities. Answers inquiries, provides advisory and reference services, conducts seminars, distributes publications, makes referrals. Fees are charged.

24198. General Electric Co., Lanham Center Operations, 4701 Forbes Blvd, Lanham, MD 20706; (301) 459-2900. Provides systems and services for earth resources programs to agencies that require remotely sensed data from spacecraft and aircraft. Provides remotely sensed images and image analysis, advisory and magnetic tape services. Services for a fee.

24199. Genetics Society of America, c/o Gerry Gurvitchy, 15501-B Monona Dr, Derwood, MD 20855; (301) 762-1424. Interest in genetics and genetics research. Answers inquiries, distributes publications, makes referrals. Services free, except for publications.

24200. Geomet Technologies, 1801 Research Blvd, Rockville, MD 20850; (301) 424-9133. Provides industry, labor, and govt with a comprehensive approach to environmental health concerns. Answers inquiries, makes interlibrary loans. Services provided for a fee.

24201. Germplasm Resources Laboratory, Agriculture Research Service, USDA, Bldg 001, Room 322, Beltsville, MD 20705; (301) 344-3328. Collects seeds and plants for researchers in federal, state, commercial, and private facilities. Answers inquiries, provides assistance with quarantine aspects for plant germplasm, acts as natl contact point for info on plant introduction and exchange.

24202. Gillette Medical Evaluation Laboratories, Information Center, 1413 Research Blvd, Rockville, MD 20850; (301) 424-2000. Commercial org interested in organic chemistry, particularly polymer and colloid chemistry. Answers questions and requests from libraries, makes interlibrary loans, permits onsite use of collections by professionals.

24203. Glenn L. Martin Wind Tunnel, Bldg 081, Univ of Md., College Park, MD 20742; (301) 454-2413. Studies low speed aerodynamics and relatively large scale subsonic wind tunnel testing. Answers inquiries, makes referrals, furnishes low speed wind tunnel testing services and research in incompressible flow.

24204. Golden Radio Buffs of Maryland, c/o Gene Leitner, 7506 Iroquois Rd, Baltimore, MD 21219. Dedicated to preservation on disc and tape of old-time radio programs and recognition of broadcast pioneers of radio's Golden Age. Answers inquiries, provides reference services, lends tapes, permits limited onsite use of collection. Services primarily for members.

24205. Goodwill Industries of America, 9200 Wisconsin Ave, Bethesda, MD 20814; (301) 530-6500. Strives to achieve full participation in society of disabled people and others with special needs. Employs field representatives for onsite consultation, provides expert congresssional testimony on issues of concern.

24206. Government Institutes, 966 Hungerford Dr, No 24, Rockville, MD 20850; (301) 251-9250. Sponsors interdisciplinary forums on energy and environmental topics of govt-related interest. Conducts seminars, provides newsletter preparation and production services, publishes and sells books.

24207. Governmental Refuse Collection and Disposal Association, Technical Information Center, P.O. Box 7219, Silver Spring, MD 20910; (301) 585-2898. Educational assn concerned with providing efficient, economically sound solid waste-management services. Publishes newsletter, answers inquiries, provides advisory and reference services, conducts seminars, distributes publications, makes referrals.

24208. Great Northern Railway Historical Society, 815 Stoneleigh Rd, Baltimore, MD 21212; (301) 377-8212. Studies history, operation, and memorabilia of Great Northern Railway. Answers inquiries, distributes publications, makes referrals. Services free.

24209. Group Against Smokers' Pollution, P.O. Box 632, College Park, MD 20740 (9811 Lanham-Severn Rd, Lanham); (301) 577-6427. Concerned with elimination of smoking in places used by nonsmokers. Answers inquiries, provides advisory services, conducts seminars, distributes publications, makes referrals. Services free.

24210. Gypsy Lore Society, c/o Sheila Salo, 2104 Dexter Ave, No 203, Silver Spring, MD 20902; (301) 681-3123. Promotes study of gypsy peoples and analogous itinerant or nomadic groups. Answers inquiries, provides reference services, distributes publications, makes referrals. Most services free.

24211. HUD USER, P.O. Box 280, Germantown, MD 20874-0280; (301) 251-5154. Offers a computer-based info service of results of research sponsored by Dept of Housing and Urban Development.

24212. Haviland Maritime Library, 4129 Roland Ave, Baltimore, MD 21211; (301) 889-5142. Consultant to Steamship Historical Society of America; Peabody Museum, Salem, Mass; The Mariners Museum, Newport News, Va.; and Maine State Museum. Answers inquiries or makes referrals, permits onsite use of collections. Services for specialists.

24213. Hazardous Materials Control Research Institute, 9300 Columbia Blvd, Silver Spring, MD 20910; (301) 587-9390. Dedicated to establishment and maintenance of a reasonable balance between expanding industrial productivity and an acceptable environment. Answers inquiries, conducts seminars, makes referrals. Services for a fee.

24214. High Blood Pressure Information Center, 2121 Wisconsin Ave NW, Suite 410, Washington, DC; (202) 496-1809. Promotes interest in hypertension and high blood pressure education. Answers inquiries, provides free advisory and reference services, makes referrals.

24215. Holly Society of America, Catherine F. Richardson, 304 N Wind Rd, Baltimore, MD 21204. Acts as official authority for registration of new varieties of holly. Answers inquiries; provides advisory, reference, and reproduction services; conducts seminars; makes referrals. Services available to anyone interested in holly.

24216. Horn Point Environmental Laboratories, P.O. Box 775 (Horn Point Rd), Cambridge, MD 21613; (301) 228-8200. Studies invertebrate biology, coastal and estuarine ecology, physical oceanography, and coastal geology in seafood processing. Answers inquiries, provides advisory services. Services free to Md. residents.

24217. Human Growth Foundation, 4607 Davidson Ln, Chevy Chase, MD 20815; (301) 656-7540. Voluntary health agency that provides funds to scientists for study of growth retardation. Answers inquiries, distributes educational materials, provides advisory services, makes referrals. Services free.

24218. Human Nutrition Information Service, Food & Consumer Services, USDA, 6505 Belcrest Rd, Hyattsville, MD 20782; (301) 436-7725. Studies food consumption levels, nutritive value, and economy of diets of various population groups. Answers inquiries. Survey data and food composition data available through Natl Technical Information Service.

24219. Human Resources Management Corp., 8775 Cloud Leap Crt, Suite 222, Columbia, MD 21045; (301) 730-6000. Provides professional services in training, conference management, and program development. Answers inquiries, provides advisory and consulting services, distributes publications. Services primarily for govt agencies and private corporations.

24220. Humor Communication Co., 8902 Maine Ave, Silver Spring, MD 20910; (301) 588-3561. Interest in use of humor in communication and interpersonal relationships; benefits of humor in workplace. Answers inquiries, conducts classes, makes referrals. Some services free.

24221. Hydronautics, 7210 Pindell School Rd, Attn: Gerrity, Laurel, MD 20707; (301) 776-7454. Collects data on hydrodynamics, hydrofoils, propellers, propulsion, ground effects, and fluid mechanics. Answers inquiries, provides consulting and research services for a fee, makes interlibrary loans, permits onsite reference by individuals from orgs.

24222. Hypoglycemia Association, 18008 New Hampshire Avenue, Ashton, MD 20861; (202) 544-4044. Nonprofit educational org established to help hypoglycemics understand and control their symptoms. Holds monthly meetings, publishes bulletins and additional literature for physicians, patients, and public.

24223. IIT Research Institute, Technical Information Services Library, ECAC Bldg 120, Annapolis, MD 21402; (301) 267-2251. Library of electronic and electrical engineering. Makes interlibrary loans of books and periodicals. Other info services are available to qualified Dept of Defense personnel only.

24224. Immune Deficiency Foundation, PO Box 586, Columbia, MD 21045; (301) 461-3127. Promotes and supports research into causes, prevention, treatment, and cure of immunodeficiency diseases. Supported by grants and donations from concerned individuals and groups.

24225. Imperial Glass Collectors Society, Attn: Ward Russell, 14700 Peach Orchard Rd, Silver Spring, MD 20904. Collects glassware manufactured by Imperial Glass Corp., Bellaire, Ohio. Publishes newsletter, answers inquiries, provides reproduction services, conducts seminars, distributes publications, permits onsite use of collections. Services may be subject to a fee.

24227. Indian Health Service, Health Resources & Services Admin, Parklawn Bldg, Room 5A-55, 5600 Fishers Ln, Rockville, MD 20857; (301) 443-1083. Develops and directs a program of comprehensive health services for eligible American Indians and Alaska Natives. Answers inquiries, provides reference services, makes referrals.

24228. Industrial Biotechnology Association, 2115 E Jefferson St, Rockville, MD 20852; (301) 984-9598. Trade assn of commercial biotechnology firms, both foreign and domestic. Publishes a newsletter, answers inquiries, provides reference services, makes referrals. Services free.

24229. Informatics General Corp., Fish and Wildlife Reference Service, 1776 E Jefferson St, 470S, Rockville, MD 20852; (800) 582-3421. Computerized info retrieval system providing access to state research on American fish and wildlife. Answers inquiries; provides consulting, reference, and abstracting services; makes referrals. Services for researchers in fish and wildlife management.

24231. Information for Partially Sighted, 9012 Old Georgetown Road, Bethesda, MD 20814; (301) 493-6300. Nonprofit info and referral service for anyone with failing vision, partial sight, progressive eye disease, or fluctuating vision. Offers info on aids and appliances, helps clients obtain certification for library and reading services, and serves homebound.

24232. Innovative Learning, 8808 Sonya Rd, Randallstown, MD 21133; (301) 922-2945. Advocates educational rights of handicapped, operation of special schools for learning disabled, and educational diagnosis and assessment. Answers inquiries, provides diagnostic and reference services, operates a school, makes referrals. Services provided for a fee.

24233. Insect Control and Research, 1330 Dillon Heights Ave, Baltimore, MD 21228; (301) 747-4502. Studies entomology, plant pathology, and plant protection and makes environmental assessments of entomological and tropical disease programs. Answers inquiries, provides consulting services for a fee, conducts laboratory and field testing of pesticides.

24234. Institute for Alternative Agriculture, 9200 Edmonston Rd, Suite 117, Greenbelt, MD 20770; (301) 441-8777. Research and info clearinghouse on low-energy, low-chemical agriculture. Publishes a newsletter, answers inquiries, provides reference services, conducts seminars, distributes publications, permits onsite use of collection. Services provided at cost.

24235. Institute for Child Study, Harold R.W. Benjamin Bldg, Room 3304, Univ of Maryland, College Park, MD 20742; (301) 454-2034. Concerned with biological, sociological, and psychological aspects of human growth and development. Answers inquiries or makes referrals, provides consulting services, workshops, and other programs.

24236. Institute of Human Performance, 7676 New Hampshire Ave, Langley Park, MD 20783; (301) 445-0900. Commercial org concerned with physical fitness, occupational health, body composition analysis, aging, and health surveillance systems. Answers inquiries; provides advisory, copying, and magnetic tape services; conducts seminars; distributes publications. Services provided for a fee.

24237. International Association for Aquatic Animal Medicine, c/o Robert L. Jenkins, Pier 3, 501 E Pratt St, Baltimore, MD 21202. Studies aquatic animal medicine (marine mammals as well as fish). Answers inquiries and provides consulting services free to anyone involved with aquatic animal medicine.

24238. International Association of Chiefs of Police, 13 Firstfield Rd, Gaithersburg, MD 20878; (301) 948-0922. Concerned with police management, operations, communications, and technology. Answers inquiries, provides bibliographic assistance and photocopy services, makes interlibrary loans. Services provided to police personnel.

24239. International Association of Pupil Personnel Workers, 9825 Docena Dr, Gaithersburg, MD 20879; (301) 977-9509. Studies compulsory school attendance laws of U.S. and Canada, pupil personnel services, and school social work. Answers inquiries, provides advisory services, conducts seminars, distributes publication. Services available to members.

24240. International Aviation Theft Bureau, 421 Aviation Way, Frederick, MD 21701; (301) 695-2022. Seeks to create an awareness of aviation theft problem, acts as a clearinghouse for aviation theft info, and encourages manufacturers to develop antitheft designs. Answers inquiries, provides advisory and abstracting services, makes referrals. Services provided at cost.

24241. International Cancer Research Data Bank Program, NIH, Bldg 82, Room 103, Bethesda, MD 20892; (301) 496-7483. Seeks to promote exchange of info between cancer scientists and dissemination of info about cancer. Answers inquiries, provides advisory and reference services, distributes publications, makes referrals. Services primarily for cancer researchers.

24242. International Clearinghouse on Science and Mathematics Curricula Developments, H.J. Benjamin Bldg, Univ of Maryland, College Park, MD 20742; (301) 454-4028. Studies new curricular developments in science and mathematics. Answers inquiries, provides consulting and reference services, makes referrals to other sources of info, permits onsite use of collections.

24243. International Commission on Ilumination, U.S. National Committee, c/o Klaus D. Mielenz, Natl Bureau of Standards, Gaithersburg, MD 20899; (301) 921-3864. Seeks to promote science and art of lighting, exchange lighting info among countries, and prepare intl agreements and recommendations. Provides free reference services and makes referrals. Services free.

24244. International Commission on Radiation Units and Measurements, 7910 Woodmont Ave, Suite 1016, Bethesda, MD 20814; (301) 657-2652. Seeks to formulate recommendations that represent consensus of intl scientific opinion on radiation. Evaluates data, provides info on research in progress, sells publications.

24245. International Consultants Foundation, 11612 Georgetowne Crt, Potomac, MD 20854; (301) 983-2709. Seeks to utilize multinatl professional consultants from behavioral and management sciences to provide expertise for orgs worldwide. Referral and consulting assistance available for specific assignments by country, language, and areas of expertise. Sells publications.

24246. International Council of Societies of Pathology, 7001 Georgia St, Chevy Chase, MD 20815; (301) 654-0095. Provides professional aids to pathology societies. Answers inquiries, provides advisory services, conducts seminars, makes referrals. Services free.

24247. International Eye Foundation, 7801 Norfolk Ave, Bethesda, MD 20814; (301) 986-1830. Promotes education of foreign and U.S. eye doctors to help meet developing world's eye care needs. Publishes a newsletter, answers inquiries, provides consulting services free.

24248. International Fabricare Institute, Research Division, 12251 Tech Rd, Silver Spring, MD 20904; (301) 622-1900. Conducts research on drycleaning and laundry processes and equipment and on textiles as related to laundering and drycleaning. Publishes a bulletin, answers inquiries, provides advisory services, distributes publications. Services primarily for members.

24249. International Guild of Candle Artisans, c/o Shirley Caplin, 9248 Brush Run, Columbia, MD 21045; (301) 730-8284. Seeks to perpetuate and improve art of candlemaking. Answers inquiries, conducts demonstrations, makes referrals. Services primarily for members.

24252. International Information Management Congress, P.O. Box 34404, Bethesda, MD 20817 (14 Accord Crt, Potomac, Md); (301) 983-0604. Intl federation of orgs and individuals engaged in furthering progress and application of document-based info systems. Answers inquiries, provides advisory and reference services, conducts seminars, makes referrals. Services free to members, at cost to others.

24253. International Institute for Resource Economics, 6210 Massachusetts Ave, Bethesda, MD 20816; (301) 229-6066. Interest in resource economics, with emphasis on mineral economics, agriculture, and energy problems. Conducts studies and provides consulting, reference, abstracting,and indexing services, answers inquiries, conducts seminars. Fees charged for all services.

24254. International Institute of Safety and Health, 5010 Nicholson Ln, Suite A, Rockville, MD 20852; (301) 984-8969. Serves professionals in safety and health field through education, training, and research. Answers inquiries, provides consulting, training and placement services, conducts seminars, makes referrals. Services provided for a fee.

24255. International Museum of Airlines, 805 Malta Ln, Silver Spring, MD 20901; (301) 593-2242. Compiles histories of airlines and airliners. Answers inquiries, permits onsite use of collections. Services free, except for copying.

24256. International Rett's Syndrome Association, 8511 Rose Marie Drive, Fort Washington, MD 20744; (301) 248-7031. Provides direct support to parents of children with Rett's Syndrome. Encourages research in prevention, treatment, and eradication of disorder.

24257. International Rural Water Resources Development Laboratory, Univ of Md., College Park, MD 20742; (301) 454-2213. Develops and tests technology appropriate to water resources, implements results in developing countries, and assists in local manufacturing. Answers inquiries, provides advisory and consulting services. Services directed primarily at Third World.

24258. International Society for Chronobiology, c/o Dr. Dora K. Hayes, Sec-Treas, Bldg 307, Room 120, Beltsville, MD 20705; (301) 344-2474. Concerned with time structure, physiological and statistical evaluation of rhythms, growth, development, aging, and other predictable changes in life forms.

24259. International Society on Thrombosis and Haemostasis, c/o James M. Stengle, MD, 9650 Rockville Pike, Bethesda, MD 20814. Fosters and encourages research, exchange of research information, and professional and public education on thrombosis and haemostasis. Answers inquiries, conducts seminars, distributes publications, makes referrals. Services provided at cost to all users.

24260. Intersociety Committee on Pathology Information, 4733 Bethesda Ave, Suite 735, Bethesda, MD 20814; (301) 656-2944. Informs medical and lay audiences about contributions of pathologists to diagnosis, therapy, research, and education and provides info about pathology as a career. Answers inquiries and provides reference services. Services primarily for health professionals.

24261. Irrigation Association, 13975 Connecticut Ave, Suite 205, Silver Spring, MD 20906; (301) 871-1200. Source of info on irrigation in agriculture and on turf, sprinkler irrigation as used in land treatment of wastewater, its standards and specifications. Answers inquiries, conducts seminars, lends materials, distributes publications, makes referrals. Most services free.

24263. Laboratory for Radiation and Polymer Science, Univ of Md., College Park, MD 20742; (301) 454-2435. Studies radiation chemistry, effects of ionizing radiation on chemical systems, source technology including gamma-ray sources and electron beam generators. Answers inquiries, provides advisory and consulting services, distributes publications.

24264. Laboratory of Molecular Genetics, National Institute of Neurological, Communicative Disorders, NIH Bldg 6, Room 408, Bethesda, MD 20892; (301) 496-4448. Conducts research into molecular processes involved in transmission of genetic information and its regulated expression during growth and differentiation. Answers inquiries, provides advisory services, makes referrals. Services free to research personnel.

24265. Laboratory of Molecular Hematology, National Heart, Lung & Blood Institute, NIH Bldg 10, Room 7D-18, Bethesda, MD 20892; (301) 496-5844. Investigates Cooley's anemia, thalassemia, sickle cell anemia, molecular biology, and genetics. Answers inquiries, provides advisory services, conducts seminars, distributes publications, makes referrals. Services free.

24266. Lacrosse Foundation, Newton H. White Athletic Center, Homewood, Baltimore, MD 21218. Supports and promotes lacrosse through events and services and acts as central clearinghouse for info. Answers inquiries free, rents films.

24267. Laurence-Moon-Biedl Syndrome Network, 122 Rolling Road, Lexington Park, MD 20653; (301) 863-5658. Brings together individuals with LMBS and their families for mutual support. Plans of network include increasing public and professional awareness of LMBS and encouraging research into cause, early detection, and treatment of syndrome.

24268. Law Enforcement Standards Laboratory, National Bureau of Standards, Route 270 and Quince Orchard Rd, Gaithersburg, MD 20899; (301) 921-3161. Investigates standards of performance of law enforcement, criminal justice, and crime prevention equipment. Answers inquiries and makes referrals.

24269. League of American Wheelmen, P.O. Box 988 (6707 Whitestone Rd, Suite 209), Baltimore, MD 21203; (301) 944-3399. Natl org interested in all areas of bicycling, except racing. Answers inquiries, provides advisory and reference services, distributes publications. Services for members.

24270. Les Amis du Vin, 2302 Perkins Pl, Silver Spring, MD 20910; (301) 588-0980. Studies history, origin, consumption patterns, and taste character of wines. Publishes magazine, answers inquiries, provides advisory services, conducts seminars, distributes publication. Services free to members.

24271. Lister Hill National Center for Biomedical Communications, 8600 Rockville Pike, Bethesda, MD 20894; (301) 496-4441. Studies application of computers, communications, audio-visual, and other technology to health care delivery. Answers inquiries, provides consulting services. Info directed primarily at biomedical community.

24272. Logistics Management Institute, 6400 Goldsboro Rd, Bethesda, MD 20817-5886; (301) 320-2000. Collects data on logistics, procurement, acquisition, and contracting. Answers brief inquiries. Services primarily for Dept of Defense and LMI research staff.

24273. Lovely Ln Museum, 2200 St Paul St, Baltimore, MD 21218; (301) 889-4458. Studies United Methodist history and biography, including early Methodist preachers in America. Manuscript materials available to researchers. Other materials may be borrowed through interlibrary loan or reproduced.

24274. Mail Advertising Service Association International, 7315 Wisconsin Ave, Suite 440-W, Bethesda, MD 20814; (301) 654-6272. Trade org representing firms that perform production services in mail advertising. Answers inquiries.

24275. Maryland Center for Productivity and Quality of Working Life, Univ of Md., College Park, MD 20742; (301) 454-6688. Concerned with productivity and its measurement, management development, quality of working life, and labor-management cooperation. Answers inquiries, provides consulting services, conducts seminars, distributes newsletter, makes referrals. Most services subject to a fee.

24276. Maryland Commission on Hereditary Disorders, 201 W Preston St, Baltimore, MD 21201; (301) 383-7035. Makes policy decisions about programs for detection and management of hereditary disorders. Answers inquiries, provides reference services, distributes publications, makes referrals. Services free.

24277. Maryland Department of Natural Resources, Library, Tawes State Office Bldg, Annapolis, MD 21401; (301) 269-3015. Library of natural resources of Md., its geology, water quality, environment, and Chesapeake Bay. Answers inquiries, provides free photocopy service on interlibrary loan requests, makes referrals, permits onsite use of collections.

24278. Maryland Governor's Committee on Migratory and Seasonal Farm Labor, c/o Leon Johnson, UMES, Princess Anne, MD 21852; (301) 651-2200. Monitors state regulations regarding housing, health, hygiene, transportation, education ,and welfare of agricultural migratory workers. Distributes publication and makes referrals. Services free.

24279. Maryland Hall of Records Commission, P.O. Box 828 (St John St & College Ave), Annapolis, MD 21404; (301) 269-3915. Collects and maintains Md., state, county, local, institutional, and private records deemed to have historical or administrative value. Answers inquiries; provides advisory, reference and reproduction services; permits onsite use of collections.

24280. Maryland Historical Society, Library, 201 W Monument St, Baltimore, MD 21201; (301) 685-3750. Library of Md. history, art, and architecture. Open to general public for reference use only. Reference and identification services provided for researchers.

24281. Masonic Service Association of the United States, 8120 Fenton St, Suite 207, Silver Spring, MD 20910⊧4785. Concerned with Freemasonry and its allied, appendant, and concordant bodies, degrees, and rites. Answers inquiries, provides reference services, conducts seminars, distributes publications. Services primarily for Masonic jurisdictions.

24282. Mechanical Contractors Association of America, 5410 Grosvenor Ln, Suite 120, Bethesda, MD 20814; (301) 897-0770. Concerned with installation of pipes and piping systems, including pipe welding for heating, cooling, ventilating, air conditioning, and plumbing. Answers inquiries, provides reference services. Services primarily for assn members.

24284. Microbiological Associates, 5221 River Rd, Bethesda, MD 20016; (301) 654-3400. Compiles data on virology, immunology, biochemistry, molecular biology, and biotechnology. Info regarding specific areas can be forwarded on request; other services restricted according to time and effort required.

24285. Mid Atlantic States Arts Consortium, 11 E Chase St, Suite 7-B, Baltimore, MD 21202; (301) 685-1400. Assists in development of the arts and provides support to artists, arts orgs, and arts institutions in an 8-state area. Answers inquiries, provides mailing lists and arts resource directories to public at cost for nonprofit uses.

24286. Munsell Color, 2441 N Calvert St, Baltimore, MD 21218; (301) 243-2171. Provides color standards for use in any given application. Answers inquiries, provides consulting and reference services, distributes publications. Services other than general inquiries provided for a fee.

24287. Murphy Center for the Codification of Human and Organizational Law, Box 80, Garrett Park, MD 20896; (301) 942-5798. Collects humorous and offbeat rules, definitions, principles, proverbs, aphorisms, diagrams, tests, explanations, and quotations. Answers inquiries free, distributes publications for a fee.

24288. Music Critics Association, 6201 Tuckerman Ln, Rockville, MD 20852; (301) 530-9527. Acts as an educational medium for promotion of high standards of music criticism in U.S., Canada, and elsewhere. Answers inquiries, conducts summer institutes. Services available to all music critics evaluated by committee.

24289. NAHB Research Foundation, P.O. Box 1627 (627 Southlawn Ln), Rockville, MD 20850; (301) 762-4200. Conducts market and technological contract research, development, and testing in light construction for govt and industry. Answers inquiries, provides consulting and reference services, conducts seminars, makes referrals. Services provided on a fee basis.

24290. NIDA Addiction Research Center, P.O. Box 5180, Baltimore, MD 21224; (301) 955-7502. Collects info on drug addiction, drug abuse, pharmacology, psychopharmacology, neuropharmacology, and neurochemistry. Answers inquiries, provides consulting services, makes interlibrary loans.

24291. National 4-H Council, 7100 Connecticut Ave, Chevy Chase, MD 20815; (301) 656-9000. Educational org that uses private resources to help expand and strengthen the 4-H program. Answers inquiries, provides advisory and reference services, conducts seminars, distributes publications. Most services are free.

24292. National Agricultural Library, Science & Education, USDA, 10301 Baltimore Blvd, Beltsville, MD 20705; (301) 344-3756. Serves research needs of USDA personnel and worldwide agricultural community. Offers search and printout services from AGRICOLA and other files to USDA personnel. For others, NAL answers inquiries or makes referrals.

24293. National Agricultural Library, Food and Nutrition Information Center, Science & Education, USDA, Room 304, 10301 Baltimore Blvd, Beltsville, MD 20705; (301) 344-3719. Specialized info center for food and nutrition professionals throughout U.S. Provides reference and referral services, including computer searching of data bases.

24294. National Aquarium in Baltimore, Pier 3, 501 E Pratt St, Baltimore, MD 21202; (301) 576-3800. Seeks to make known unity of life through water by providing a balance of recreation and education programs. Answers inquiries, conducts workshops, distributes publications. Services provided free or at minimal cost. The Aquarium open to public for a fee.

24295. National Archives and Records Administration, National Audio Visual Center, 8700 Edgeworth Dr, Capitol Heights, MD 20743-3701; (301) 763-1896. Repository of all unclassified audiovisual materials produced by or for federal govt agencies for interagency or public use. Answers inquiries, rents some materials and sells others. Free consultation and limited technical assistance provided.

24296. National Asphalt Pavement Association, P.O. Box 517 (6811 Kenilworth Ave), Riverdale, MD 20737; (301) 779-4880. Promotes asphalt pavement, including development of quality improvement techniques. Answers inquiries, provides consulting and reference services.

24298. National Association for Hearing and Speech Action, 10801 Rockville Pike, Rockville, MD 20852; (301) 897-8682, (800) 638-8255. Provides advocacy and public info activities for benefit of persons with hearing, speech, and language disorders. Toll-free helpline is available to receive telephone calls, both voice and TTY.

24299. National Association for Rural Mental Health, 6101 Montrose Road, Suite 360, Rockville, MD 20852; (301) 984-6200. Seeks to enhance delivery of mental health services to rural areas. Arranges educational programs and publishes a newsletter.

24300. National Association of Area Labor-Management Committees, P.O. Box 1398, Cumberland, MD 21502; (301) 777-8700. Concerned with industry, job retention and community and economic development through labor-management cooperation. Answers inquiries, provides advisory and consulting services, conducts seminars, makes referrals. Some services may be subject to a fee.

24301. National Association of Marine Services, 17509 Lafayette Dr, Olney, MD 20832; (301) 774-0217. Concerned with commercial shipping, marine supplies and services, and customs regulations. Publishes newsletter, answers inquiries, provides advisory services. Services free.

24303. National Association of School Security Directors, c/o Edgar B. Dews, Jr, P.O. Box 31338, Temple Hills, MD 20748. Concerned with safety and security of students, teachers, school employees, and educational facilities and equipment. Publishes a newsletter, answers inquiries, provides advisory and reference services, distributes publications. Some services are free.

24304. National Association of Social Workers, 7981 Eastern Ave, Silver Spring, MD 20910; (301) 565-0333. Seeks advancement of sound public social policies and programs and professional improvement. Answers inquiries, provides consulting services, permits onsite use of collection.

24305. National Association of Women Hwy Safety Leaders, 7206 Robinhood Dr, Upper Marlboro, MD 20870; (301) 868-7583. Works with leading natl women's orgs to reduce traffic injuries and deaths by supporting standards developed by U.S. Dept of Transportation's Natl Hwy Traffic Safety Administration. Answers inquiries, makes referrals. Services free.

24306. National Association of the Deaf, 814 Thayer Ave, Silver Spring, MD 20910; (301) 587-1788. Concerned with general welfare of the deaf in economic and educational fields, including the right to drive. Answers inquiries, provides consulting services, makes referrals.

24307. National Bureau of Standards, Center for Building Technology, Gaithersburg, MD 20899; (301) 921-3377. Compiles data on computer-integrated construction, structural loads and reliability, geotechnical engineering, and nondestructive evaluation methods for concrete structures. Provides consulting services.

24308. National Bureau of Standards, Center for Manufacturing Engineering, Gaithersburg, MD 20899; (301) 921-3421. Concerned with manufacturing engineering, automated manufacturing, robotics, production engineering, and automation and control technology. Provides limited consulting services free or, under special circumstances, on a contract basis. Provides calibration services for a fee.

24309. National Bureau of Standards, Chemical Kinetics Data Center, Center for Chemical Physics, Gaithersburg, MD 20899; (301) 921-2174. Studies chemical kinetics, rates of homogeneous chemical reactions in gaseous, liquid, and solid phases. Answers brief inquiries, provides info on published research, permits onsite use of collection. Services available to all scientists and technical personnel with professional interests.

24310. National Bureau of Standards, Chemical Thermodynamics Data Center, Center for Chemical Physics, A162 Chemistry Bldg, Gaithersburg, MD 20899; (301) 921-2111. Collects data on thermochemical and thermodynamic properties of pure chemical substances in gas, liquid, and solid phases and their aqueous solutions. Answers inquiries, provides consulting services. Services for those in the field.

24311. National Bureau of Standards, Crystal Data Center, Reactor Radiation Division, Gaithersburg, MD 20899; (301) 921-2744. Collects crystallographic data. Answers inquiries or makes referrals, provides X-ray crystallographic data. Services available to scientific and technical personnel.

24312. National Bureau of Standards, Diffusion in Metals Data Center, Metallurgy Division, Gaithersburg, MD 20899; (301) 921-3354. Collects data on diffusion in metals and their alloys, diffusion coefficients and activation energies for diffusion. Answers inquiries, provides consulting services. Services available for those in the field.

24313. National Bureau of Standards, Electricity Division, Center for Basic Studies, Gaithersburg, MD 20899; (301) 921-2701. Concerned with electrical standards, realization of electrical units in terms of mechanical units, dissemination of units of electrical measure, fundamental physical constants, and instrumentation. Calibrates precision electrical standards and measuring apparatus for a fee.

24314. National Bureau of Standards, Information Resources and Services Division, Patricia W. Berger, Gaithersburg, MD 20899; (301) 921-2318. Repository of basic measurement standards, engineering standards, and materials research. Provides limited service to public, disseminates scientific findings and info to scientists and industry.

24315. National Bureau of Standards, Metallurgy Division, Institute for Materials Science & Engtineering, Gaithersburg, MD 20899; (301) 921-2811. Studies physical metallurgy, chemical metallurgical defect and flaw characterization, and structure characterization. Answers inquiries, provides consulting services without charge or under contract to govt agencies, the scientific community, and industry.

24316. National Bureau of Standards, Photon and Charged Particle Data Center, Gaithersburg, MD 20899; (301) 921-2685. Collects data on electrons, positrons, protons, and other charged particles. Answers inquiries, permits onsite use of collection by persons with a professional interest in the field.

24317. National Bureau of Standards, Temperature and Pressure Division, Center for Basic Studies, Gaithersburg, MD 20899; (301) 921-3315. Establishes standards of temperature and pressure and calibration of practical standards. Answers inquiries, provides consulting services to govt, commercial, and scientific agencies on a contract or no-cost basis.

24318. National Cancer Institute, Office of Cancer Communications, NIH Bldg 31, Room 10A18, Bethesda, MD 20892; (301) 496-5583. Conducts research and training related to cause, prevention, detection, diagnosis, treatment, and rehabilitation of cancer. Written inquiries are answered, toll-free telephone service is available at 1-800-4-CANCER.

24319. National Center for Health Services Research, Publications and Information Branch, Public Health Service, Parklawn Bldg, Room 146, 5600 Fishers Ln, Rockville, MD 20857; (301) 443-4100. Supports and stimulates a natl program of health services research and development. Answers inquiries, provides consulting and reference services, distributes publications, makes referrals. Services free.

24320. National Center for Health Statistics, Public Health Service, Center Bldg, Room 1-57, 3700 East-West Hwy, Hyattsville, MD 20782; (301) 436-8500. Collects, analyzes, and disseminates statistics on and develops programs in health and demographics. Answers requests for data, provides consulting services. Standardized data tapes available for purchase.

24321. National Center for Standards and Certification Information, National Bureau of Standards, Gaithersburg, MD 20899; (301) 921-2587. Catalogs voluntary engineering standards, certification systems, federal and military standards and specifications. Answers inquiries, provides lists of standards in response to requests, provides names of orgs where standards may be obtained.

24322. National Center for Surrogate Parenting, 5530 Wisconsin Ave, Suite 940, Chevy Chase, MD 20815; (301) 656-7577. Provides surrogate mothers for infertile couples and studies psychological, medical, and legal ramifications. Services provided for a fee, available to infertile couples.

24323. National Center for Toxicological Research, Food & Drug Administration, 5600 Fishers Ln, Rockville, MD 20857; (301) 443-3155. Conducts research programs to study biological effects of potentially toxic chemical substances found in man's environment. Answers inquiries, provides info on R&D in progress, makes referrals.

24324. National Center for the Prevention and Control of Rape, National Institute of Mental Health, Parklawn Bldg, Room 6C-12, 5600 Fishers Ln, Rockville, MD 20857. Supports research on causes of rape and sexual assault and mental health consequences of such acts. Answers inquiries, distributes publications, makes referrals. Services free.

24325. National Child Support Enforcement Reference Center, Office CSE, Dept of HHS, 6110 Executive Blvd, Room 820, Rockville, MD 20852; (301) 443-5106. Investigates child support enforcement management practices, enforcement techniques, statistics, legislation ,and court decisions. Answers inquiries, lends materials, distributes publications, makes referrals. Services intended primarily for those in the field.

24326. National Classification Management Society, c/o Eugene Suto, 6116 Roseland Dr, Rockville, MD 20852; (301) 231-9191. Concerned with all aspects of security classification management of sensitive defense info. Publishes a bulletin, answers inquiries and provides advisory service. General info is free; publications available to nonmembers on a subscription basis.

24327. National Clearinghouse for Alcohol Information, P.O. Box 2345 (1776 E Jefferson St), Rockville, MD 20852; (301) 468-2600. Under govt contract, collects info from worldwide sources on studies and programs pertaining to all aspects of alcohol abuse. Responds to individual inquiries, makes referrals, distributes publications. Info services free.

24328. National Clearinghouse for Commuter Programs, 1195 Adele H. Stamp Union, Univ of Md., College Park, MD 20742. Studies characteristics and needs of college and university students living off campus. Answers inquiries, provides advisory and reference services, distributes publications, makes referrals. Services free to members.

24329. National Climate Program Office, 108 Rockwall Bldg, 11400 Rockville Pike, Rockville, MD 20852. Seeks to establish, coordinate, and manage a natl program intended to assist nation in understanding and responding to climate processes and their implications. Answers inquiries, conducts seminars, distributes publications. Services free.

24331. National Committee for Citizens in Education, Wilde Lake Village Green, Suite 410, Columbia, MD 21044; (301) 997-9300. Encourages parents and citizens to become involved in public school affairs and to influence schools to become more responsive to needs of the community. Answers inquiries, provides consulting and reference services, distributes publications.

24332. National Council for Therapy and Rehabilitation Through Horticulture, 9041 Comprint Court, Suite 103, Gaithersburg, MD 20877; (301) 948-3010. Promotes and encourages development of horticulture and related activities for therapy and rehabilitation. Publishes a newsletter, answers inquiries, provides professional consultation service, maintains a placement service. Some services at cost.

24334. National Council of Community Mental Health Centers, 6101 Montrose Road, Suite 360, Rockville, MD 20852; (301) 984-6200. Represents interests of community mental health centers in areas of legislation, regulations, and funding. Provides a variety of insurance

programs for mental health centers, a natl technical assistance program, monthly info packets, and training programs.

24336. National Council on Radiation Protection and Measurements, 7910 Woodmont Ave, Suite 1016, Bethesda, MD 20814; (301) 657-2652. Collects, analyzes, and disseminates info and recommendations about radiation protection and measurement. Public education efforts conducted primarily through release of reports on research conducted by the council.

24337. National Criminal Justice Reference Service, National Institute of Justice, Box 6000 (1600 Research Blvd), Rockville, MD 20850; (301) 251-5500. Serves as a clearinghouse for exchange of info on improvement of law enforcement and criminal justice. Answers inquiries, conducts computerized data base searches, distributes publications, makes referrals. Services primarily for criminal justice professionals.

24338. National Diabetes Information Clearinghouse, Box: NDIC, Bethesda, MD 20892; (301) 468-2162. Collects and disseminates info about materials, programs, and research in treatment of diabetes. Publishes newsletter, answers inquiries, distributes publications, permits onsite use of collections. Services intended primarily for health professionals.

24339. National Digestive Diseases Education and Information Clearinghouse, NIH, Westwood Bldg, Room 3A-17A, Bethesda, MD 20892; (301) 496-9707. Supplies educational materials on gastrointestinal function and pathophysiology of digestive diseases. Answers inquiries and makes referrals. Services free.

24340. National Eye Institute, Office of Scientific Reporting, Natl Institutes of Health, Bethesda, MD 20892; (301) 496-5248. Conducts research on causes, prevention, and treatment of disorders of the eye and visual system. Answers inquiries, distributes scientific reports.

24341. National Federation of Parents for Drug-Free Youth, 8730 Georgia Avenue, Suite 200, Silver Spring, MD 20910; (301) 585-5437, (800) 554-5437. Helps concerned parents prevent adolescent drug use. Assists in forming parent groups, provides education, distributes materials to Congress, and has a toll-free telephone number for emergency contact.

24342. National Federation of the Blind, 1800 Johnson St, Baltimore, MD 21230; (301) 659-9314. Concerned with all aspects of blindness and removal of legal, economic, and social discrimination against the blind. Answers inquiries, provides consulting and reference services, makes referrals.

24343. National Foundation for Cancer Research, 7315 Wisconsin Ave NW, Suite 332W, Bethesda, MD 20814; (301) 654-1250. Conducts basic cancer research at some 80 laboratories in 14 nations. Conducts seminars, distributes publications, makes referrals. Services free.

24344. National Geodetic Information Center, NOAA, 6001 Executive Blvd, Rockville, MD 20852; (301) 443-8631. Conducts geodesy, photogrammetry, and surveying. Answers inquiries, makes holdings available through sale, loan, or free distribution.

24345. National Health Planning Information Center, Public Health Service, Parklawn Bldg, Room 9A-33, 5600 Fishers Ln, Rockville, MD 20857; (301) 443-2183. Provides access to methodological info relevant to health planning, especially to meet needs of health planning agencies. Answers inquiries, provides reference services, distributes publications. Services free to health planning agencies.

24347. National Health Screening Council for Volunteer Organizations, 9411 Connecticut Avenue, Kensington, MD 20895; (301) 942-6601. Conducts volunteer efforts to coodinate existing health education and health screening services. Does not provide health info directly to individuals.

24348. National Heart, Lung and Blood Institute, Sickle Cell Diseases Branch, National Institutes of Health, 7550 Wisconsin Ave, Bethesda, MD 20892; (301) 496-6931. Supports research into sickle-cell disease. Answers inquiries; provides advisory, reference, abstracting, indexing, and copying services; distributes info kits and lends films; permits onsite use of collection. Services free.

24349. National Heart, Lung, and Blood Institute, Public Inquiries and Reports Branch, National Institutes of Health, Bethesda, MD 20892; (301) 496-4236. Conducts research and training related to causes, prevention, diagnosis, and treatment of diseases of the heart and circulation and of chronic lung diseases. Answers inquiries.

24351. National Hormone and Pituitary Program, 201 W Fayette Street, Suite 501-9, Baltimore, MD 21201; (301) 837-2552. Seeks to increase availability of human growth hormone by collecting human pituitary glands from hospitals and medical centers and organizing extraction and distribution of hormone for use in clinical growth research programs. Answers requests for info from public.

24352. National Information Standards Organization, Library-E106, Natl Bureau of Standards, Gaithersburg, MD 20899. Devoted to standards development in library and info sciences and related publishing practices. Answers inquiries or refers inquirers free.

24353. National Injury Information Clearinghouse, Consumer Product Safety Commission, 5401 Westbard Avenue, Room 625, Bethesda, MD 20207; (301) 492-6424. Collects, investigates, analyzes, and disseminates injury data and info relating to causes and prevention of death, injury, and illness associated with consumer products. Info requests answered.

24354. National Institute for Urban Wildlife, 10921 Trotting Ridge Way, Columbia, MD 21044; (301) 596-3311. Conducts research on impact of urbanization and other major works of man on natural systems, with emphasis on wildlife. Answers inquiries, provides advisory services, conducts seminars, makes referrals. Services primarily for planners, builders, engineers, and architects.

24355. National Institute of Allergy and Infectious Diseases, Office of Research Reporting and Public Response, NIH Bldg 31, Room 7A32, Bethesda, MD 20892; (301) 496-5717. Conducts research and training in allergic, immunologic, infectious, and parasitic diseases. Answers inquiries.

24356. National Institute of Arthritis, Diabetes, Digestive and Kidney Diseases, 9000 Rockville Pike, Bethesda, MD 20892; (301) 496-3583. Conducts research in arthritis and related diseases, metabolic and digestive diseases, kidney, liver, and urologic diseases. Answers inquiries.

24357. National Institute of Child Health and Human Development, Office of Research Reporting, NIH, Bldg 31, Room 2A32, 9000 Rockville Pike, Bethesda, MD 20892; (301) 496-5133. Conducts research and research training concerned with human development. Responds to inquiries.

24358. National Institute of Dental Research, Public Inquiries and Reports Section, NIH, Bldg 31, Room 2C35, Bethesda, MD 20892; (301) 496-4261. Conducts research and related training on dental caries. Answers inquiries.

24359. National Institute of Mental Health, Division of Biometry and Epidemiology, 5600 Fishers Ln, Rockville, MD 20857; (301) 443-3648. Provides info on epidemiology of mental disorders, research in mental health, and provision of mental health care. Publications distributed and inquiries answered.

24360. National Institute of Mental Health, Project Sleep, 5600 Fishers Ln, Room 9C-09, Rockville, MD 20857; (301) 443-3948. Seeks to improve diagnosis of sleep disorders, improve public knowledge of problem, and identify research needs. Answers inquiries, provides reference services, conducts seminars, distributes publications. Services free.

24361. National Institute of Neurological and Communicative Disorders and Stroke, Bethesda, MD 20892; (301) 496-5751. Conducts research and training relating to causes, prevention, diagnosis, and treatment of neurological and communicative disorders. Inquiries answered, publications distributed, referrals made.

24362. National Institute on Aging, Information Office, NIH, Bldg 31, Room 5C35, 9000 Rockville Pike, Bethesda, MD 20892; (301) 496-1752. Conducts biomedical, behavioral, and social research on the aging process and diseases and other special problems and needs of the aged. Answers inquiries, distributes publications, makes referrals. Services free.

24363. National Institute on Drug Abuse, Office of Science, 5600 Fishers Ln, Room 10-16, Rockville, MD 20857;

(301) 443-6480. Investigates scientific aspects of drugs of abuse, ranging from chemistry of abused substances to psychological characteristics of user groups. Answers inquiries, provides consulting services. Services are primarily for the scientific community.

24364. National Institutes of Health, Cancer Information Clearinghouse, NIH Bldg 31, Room 10A18, 9000 Rockville Pike, Bethesda, MD 20892; (301) 496-4070. Enhances communications within Natl Cancer Program by collecting and disseminating info concerning programs and materials for use in patient and public education. Services free to all health professionals; public and patients are referred to appropriate sources.

24365. National Institutes of Health, Division of Public Information, 9000 Rockville Pike, Bethesda, MD 20892; (301) 496-5787. Acts as central coordinating org for various public info units of Natl Institutes of Health. Answers inquiries of a general nature. Specific inquiries are referred to info unit of the bureau, institute, or division best qualified to respond.

24366. National Institutes of Health, Research Resources Information Center, Office of Research Services, 1601 Research Blvd, Rockville, MD 20892; (301) 984-2870. Conducts biomedical, human health and disease research and animal research related to both animal health and human disease. Answers inquiries, distributes publications. Services free to biomedical researchers.

24368. National Library of Medicine, National Institutes of Health, 8600 Rockville Pike, Bethesda, MD 20894; (301) 496-6308. Serves as medical info resource for orgs and individuals engaged in medical education, research, and services. Materials are accessible for use at library daily, except Sunday. Inter-library loans made and on-line data service available.

24369. National Measurement Laboratory, Molecular Spectra Data Center, Natl Bureau of Standards, B268 Physics Bldg, Gaithersburg, MD 20899; (301) 921-2021. Publishes evaluated tabulations of microwave and infrared absorption lines. Answers inquiries from scientists with a professional interest.

24370. National Measurement Laboratory, Office of Standard Reference Data, Natl Bureau of Standards, Gaithersburg, MD 20899; (301) 921-2228. Compiles data on physical and chemical properties of well characterized substances. Answers inquiries, makes referrals, permits onsite use of collections, administers Natl Standard Reference Data System.

24371. National Meteorological Center, NOAA, 5200 Auth Rd, Camp Springs, MD 20033; (301) 763-8016. Collects worldwide weather data on a continuous time schedule, processes these data using both manual and computer techniques into meteorological analyses describing current state of the atmosphere. Distributes weather data to meterologists.

24372. National Oceanic and Atmospheric Administration, Library and Information Services Division, Dept of Commerce, 6009 Executive Blvd, Rockville, MD 20852; (301) 443-8287. Library of mathematics, geodetic astronomy, nautical and aeronautical cartography, geodetic and hydrographic surveying. Answers inquiries, provides reference and copying services, makes interlibrary loans, permits onsite use of collections.

24373. National Organization of Mothers of Twins Clubs, 5402 Amberwood Ln, Rockville, MD 20853; (301) 460-9108. Sponsors education to encourage individuality of each twin and helps new parents of twins find educational materials and support. Answers inquiries, provides reference services, makes referrals, conducts seminars, distributes publications. Services may be provided for a fee.

24374. National Particleboard Association, 18928 Premiere Court, Gaithersburg, MD 20879; (301) 670-0604. Maintains liaison with all aspects of state and federal govt concerning wood product industry interests in U.S. Answers inquiries, provides reference services, makes referrals. Services generally free to consumers.

24375. National Sea Grant College Program, NOAA, 6010 Executive Blvd, Rockville, MD 20852; (301) 443-8923. Supervises grants to colleges, universities, and other research institutions for programs and projects to develop and conserve America's marine resources. Answers inquiries about grants procedures.

24376. National Space Science Data Center, Goddard Space Flight Center, NASA, Code 601, Greenbelt, MD 20771; (301) 344-6695. Provides means for further analysis and dissemination of satellite experimental space science and applications data. Answers inquiries, provides consulting and reference services, makes referrals, permits onsite use of collections.

24377. National Standards Association, 5161 River Rd, Bethesda, MD 20816; (301) 951-1310. Publisher, distributor, and info center on standards used by govt and industry. All holdings and publications are for sale. Assn's TECHINFO department provides reference services on a cost basis.

24378. National Student Speech Language Hearing Association, 10801 Rockville Pike, Rockville, MD 20852; (301) 897-5700. Encourages professional interest among college and univ students in study of normal and disordered human communication behavior. Answers inquiries, sells publications, makes referrals. Services primarily for members.

24379. National Sudden Infant Death Syndrome Foundation, 2 Metro Plaza, Suite 104, 8240 Professional Pl, Landover, MD 20785; (301) 459-3388. Investigates sudden infant death syndrome and provides support systems for families with children on home monitors. Answers inquiries, provides consulting and referral services, primarily to parents of SIDS victims and of high-risk infants.

24380. National Tooling and Machining Association, 9300 Livingston Rd, Fort Washington, MD 20744; (301) 248-6200. Source of info on capacities and capabilities of 4,000 companies in contract tooling and machining industry. Provides general info, including skills training, distributes publications and conducts seminars on fee basis.

24381. National Weather Association, 4400 Stamp Rd, Suite 404, Temple Hills, MD 20748; (301) 899-3784. Studies meteorology, weather forecasting, marine and aviation weather, and weather satellites. Answers inquiries, conducts seminars, makes referrals. Services primarily for members.

24382. National Weather Service, NOAA, 8060 13th St, Gramax Bldg, Silver Spring, MD 20910; (301) 427-7622. Provides meteorological services for general public, and for aviation, agricultural, forest, and wildlands management and marine interests. Answers inquiries or makes referrals.

24383. National Women's Studies Association, c/o Lefrak Hall, Univ of Maryland, Room 0218, College Park, MD 20742; (301) 454-3757. Concerned with women's studies, feminist education, academic women as victims of sex discrimination in employment. Publishes a newsletter, answers inquiries, provides reference services, distributes publications, makes referrals. Services may be subject to a fee.

24384. Nautical Research Guild, c/o Merritt Edson, 6413 Dahlonega Rd, Bethesda, MD 20816; (301) 229-0473. Studies history of ship types and their development. Answers inquiries, makes referrals, provides consulting services, identifies ship models.

24385. Naval Academy Museum, U.S. Naval Academy, Annapolis, MD 21402; (301) 267-2108. Collects, maintains, uses in public exhibits, and makes available for research objects, graphics, and manuscripts related to naval history. Answers inquiries, permits onsite examination of collections, makes referrals. Most services are free.

24386. Naval Air Test Center, Naval Air Test Center, Patuxent River, MD 20670; (301) 863-1700. Studies military aircraft and aircraft weapons systems. Answers inquiries, makes referrals to specialists, subject to security restrictions and routine public release clearance.

24388. Naval Medical Research Institute, Information Services Branch, 8901 Wisconsin Ave, Bethesda, MD 20814; (202) 295-2186. Collects data on behavior and work performance in saturation divers. Aids other govt agencies and scientific community as time and facilities permit.

24389. New Ventures, 2614 Kenhill Dr, Bowie, MD 20716; (301) 464-2622. Supports women coping with changes in lifestyle. Answers inquiries, provides consulting services, conducts workshops, provides counseling, operates a job bank. Services provided on a fee basis.

24390. New Windsor Service Center, SERRV Program, P.O. Box 365 (500 Main St), New Windsor, MD 21776; (301) 635-6464. Provides a market for self-help handicrafts, working worldwide with religious, cooperative, artisan, and developmental orgs. Answers inquiries, provides advisory services, evaluates handicraft samples, makes referrals. Services free.

24391. Nimitz Library, U.S. Naval Academy, Annapolis, MD 21402; (301) 267-2208. Library of naval history, technology, and intl law. Makes interlibrary loans. Services primarily for midshipmen and faculty members of Naval Academy, but collections are accessible for onsite use by serious researchers.

24392. Nitinol Technology Center, Naval Surface Weapons Center, Code R-32, Silver Spring, MD 20903-5000; (301) 394-2468. Investigates nitinol (alloy exhibiting shape memory effects), its manufacturing technology and its applications. Answers inquiries, provides advisory services, conducts seminars. Some services are free.

24393. North American Apiotherapy Society, 15621 Aitcheson Ln, Laurel, MD 20707; (301) 253-5313. Studies apiotherapy and therapeutic effects and uses of honey bee products. Answers inquiries, provides reference services, lends materials, distributes publications. Services may be provided for a fee.

24394. North American Bluebird Society, P.O. Box 6295 (2 Countryside Crt), Silver Spring, MD 20906; (301) 384-2798. Promotes protection of and research on Eastern, Western, and Mountain Bluebirds and other native cavity-nesting birds. Answers inquiries, distributes publication. Services free. Requests should be accompanied by a SASE.

24395. Nuclear Free America, 2521 Guilford Ave, Baltimore, MD 21218; (301) 235-3575. Acts as an intl clearinghouse and resource center for Nuclear Free Zones. Answers inquiries, provides advisory and consulting services, conducts seminars, distributes publications. Most services are free.

24396. Nutrition Today Society, P.O. Box 1829, Annapolis, MD 21404; (301) 267-8616. Dedicated to increase and dissemination of nutrition knowledge. Publishes educational packets that include slides and syllabi; videotaped debate on benefits of vitamin C is also available.

24397. Office for Protection from Research Risks, NIH Bldg 31, Room 4B07, 9000 Rockville Pike, Bethesda, MD 20892; (301) 496-7005. Administers HHS policy for protection of human subjects of biomedical and behavioral research and PHS policy for laboratory animal welfare. Answers inquiries, distributes copies of regulations, conducts an educational program. Services free.

24398. Office of Beneficiary Services, Health Care Financing Administration, Dept of HHS, Room 648 EHR, 6325 Security Boulevard, Baltimore, MD 21207; (301) 594-8131. Serves as focal point for info for Medicaid and Medicare beneficiaries. Assists in understanding and securing program benefits; distributes materials describing programs and their application to disabled or dialysis patients.

24399. Office of Health Maintenance Organizations, Health Care Financing Administration, 5600 Fishers Ln, Room 9-11, Rockville, MD 20857; (301) 443-4106. Provides technical assistance to developing and qualified health maintenance organizations (HMOs), reviews applications for and makes recommendations on qualification. Info available from the office includes procedures, current listings of HMOs, and materials on HMOs.

24400. Office of Health Planning, Health Resources & Services Administration, Parklawn Bldg, Room 13A-56, 5600 Fishers Ln, Rockville, MD 20857. Provides natl leadership and administration of a program of federal, state, and areawide health planning and health delivery systems. Answers inquiries, provides consulting services, makes referrals. Services available to health planning agencies.

24401. Office of International Health, Office of the Surgeon General, Parklawn Bldg, Room 18-87, 5600 Fishers Ln, Rockville, MD 20857; (301) 443-1774. Provides support to Asst Secty for Health and Secty of Dept of Health and Human Services in developing policy and coordinating activities of Public Health Service in field of intl health. Several desk officers serve as experts on various regions of the world.

24402. Office of Migratory Bird Management, U.S. Fish & Wildlife Service, Patuxent Wildlife Research Center, Laurel, MD 20811; (301) 776-4880. Studies migratory bird population dynamics, bird migration, distribution, and abundance. Limited interlibrary loans and onsite reference available.

24403. Office of Sea Grant and Extramural Programs, Marine Advisory Service, NOAA, 6010 Executive Blvd, Rockville, MD 20852; (301) 443-8923. Serves as link between known marine resources and marine-related clientele who require assistance. Answers inquiries or refers inquirers to other sources of info. Advisory services provided primarily at local level. Services free.

24404. Office on Smoking and Health, Centers for Disease Control, Park Bldg, Room 1-10, 5600 Fishers Ln, Rockville, MD 20857; (301) 443-1575. Collects and disseminates scientific and technical info in biomedical sciences as it relates to smoking. Publishes a bulletin, answers inquiries, makes referrals. Single copies of most items in collection available for research purposes.

24405. Optometric Council of the National Capital Region, 35 Wisconsin Circle, Suite 414, Chevy Chase, MD 20815; (301) 656-8650. Concerned with optometry. Answers inquiries, provides advisory and reference services, makes referrals. Services free.

24406. Organization for Use of the Telephone, P.O. Box 175, Owings Mills, MD 21117-0175; (301) 655-1827. Represents hearing aid users in negotiations with telephone companies, hearing aid manufacturers, and govt agencies. Publishes newsletter, answers inquiries, intervenes with telephone companies to acquire compatible phones. All info provided free.

24407. Orton Dyslexia Society, 724 York Rd, Baltimore, MD 21204; (301) 296-0232. Disseminates info on study and treatment of dyslexia. Answers inquiries; provides reference, abstracting and indexing services; distributes publications. Services provided to anyone interested in dyslexia.

24408. PYRAMID, 7101 Wisconsin Avenue, Suite 612, Bethesda, MD 20814; (301) 654-1194. Provides info, technical assistance, and other services to persons and programs across the country actively involved in drug abuse prevention. Provides packets of materials, telephone assistance, referrals, or onsite assistance from a consultant.

24412. Parkinsonian Support Groups of America, c/o Ida Raitano, 11376 Cherry Hill Rd, No 204, Beltsville, MD 20705. Represents those afflicted with Parkinson's disease, their families, and friends. Answers inquiries; provides advisory, consulting, and reference services; conducts seminars, exercise groups and summer camp for patients; distributes publications; makes referrals. Services free.

24413. Parklawn Health Library, Public Health Service, 5600 Fishers Ln, Room 13-12, Rockville, MD 20857; (301) 443-2673. Studies social and economic aspects of health and health sciences. Answers inquiries, provides reference and computer services, makes referrals, permits onsite use of collection. Services for official use.

24414. Phobia Society of America, 6181 Executive Blvd, Rockville, MD 20852; (301) 231-9350. Serves as a natl clearinghouse for info and referrals about phobia treatment. Publishes a newsletter, answers inquiries, provides reference services, conducts seminars, distributes publications, makes referrals. Most services are free.

24415. Plant Physiology Institute, Beltsville Ag Research Center, USDA, Bldg 001, Room 221, Beltsville, MD 20705; (301) 344-3036. Conducts research on growth and production of agricultural plants and greenhouse and climate-controlled growth facilities. Answers inquiries, provides consulting services, conducts seminars, makes referrals. Services free.

24416. Plant Physiology Institute, Hydrology Laboratory, Beltsville Ag Research Center, USDA, Bldg 007, Room 139, BARC-West, Beltsville, MD 20705; (301) 344-3490. Studies expected streamflow from agricultural watersheds, expressed in the form of watershed models and application of remote sensing to hydrology and water resources. Research info available to anyone.

24417. Plant Physiology Institute, Plant Stress Laboratory, Beltsville Ag Research Center, USDA, Bldg 001, Room 206, Beltsville, MD 20705; (301) 344-4528. Studies effects of ozone, sulfur dioxide, and other gaseous air pollutants on cellular metabolism and plant productivity. Answers technical inquiries and provides advisory services.

24418. Plant Protection and Quarantine Library, USDA, Federal Center Bldg 1, Room 628A, Hyattsville, MD 20782; (301) 436-5240. Concerned with protection of American agriculture from foreign and domestic plant and animal pests and diseases. Distributes brochures and program aids, makes referrals, provides consulting services. Copies of materials are free.

24419. Policy Research Institute, Health Futures Project, 2500 St Paul St, Baltimore, MD 21218. Concerned with alternative health care system futures and health technology assessment. Answers inquiries, provides advisory and consulting services, conducts seminars and distributes publications. Fees may be charged for services.

24420. Potency Restored, c/o Dr. Giulio I. Scarzella, 8630 Fenton St, Suite 218, Silver Spring, MD 20910; (301) 588-5777. Encourages public awareness of use of prostheses to cure impotence. Publishes a newsletter, answers inquiries, provides advisory and reference services, conducts seminars, makes referrals. Services free.

24422. Practitioner Reporting System, United States Pharmacopeial Convention, 12601 Twinbrook Parkway, Rockville, MD 20852; (800) 638-6725. Detects problems with medical specific products and drugs. Also detects trends to suggest product improvements and effect product recalls in serious cases.

24423. Professional Grounds Management Society, 7 Church Ln, Pikesville, MD 21208; (301) 653-2742. Society of superintendents and managers of grounds seeking professional advancement and improvement of grounds management. Answers inquiries and provides consulting services free to members, at cost to others.

24424. Public Gaming Research Institute, P.O. Box 1724 (51 Monroe St), Rockville, MD 20850; (301) 279-7000. Private org serving govt and industry in area of public gaming, including lotteries, horse race betting, bingo, Jai-Alai, and casino gambling. Answers inquiries, makes referrals, provides consulting services, conducts seminars, sells publications.

24426. Pyrotechnics Guild International, 5415 Bangert St, White Marsh, MD 21162; (301) 256-5144. Fosters legal and safe use of fireworks for celebration of natl holidays. Answers inquiries, provides reference services, conducts seminars, makes referrals. Services free. A publication is available by subscription.

24427. Quantum Metrology Group, Room A-141, National Bureau of Standards, Gaithersburg, MD 20899; (301) 921-2061. Studies fundamental constants, extension, and refinement of electromagnetic scale, basic symmetrics, and invariances, X-ray spectroscopy of atoms, molecules, and simple solids. Answers inquiries, provides consulting services to govt and scientific agencies on a contract or no cost basis.

24428. R P Foundation Fighting Blindness, 1401 Mt Royal Ave, 4th Floor, Baltimore, MD 21217; (301) 225-9400;. Seeks cause, prevention, and treatment for retinitis pigmentosa and allied retinal degenerative diseases. Answers inquiries, provides reference services, makes referrals, distributes publications. Services free.

24429. R. E. Gibson Library, Applied Physics Lab, The Johns Hopkins Univ, Johns Hopkins Rd, Laurel, MD 20707; (301) 953-5000 ext 5151. Data collection on computing sciences, electrical engineering, mathematics, physics, electronics, space science, and biomedical engineering. Makes interlibrary loans. Book and journal collections are available for scholarly research.

24430. Rachel Carson Council, 8940 Jones Mill Rd, Chevy Chase, MD 20815; (301) 652-1877. Intl clearinghouse on environment, emphasizing research and public education on chemical contamination, especially pesticides. Answers inquiries, conducts seminars, distributes publications, makes referrals. Services and publications available at a nominal fee.

24431. Reactor Radiation Division, Bldg 235, Room A-100, National Bureau of Standards, Gaithersburg, MD 20899; (301) 921-2421. Investigates molecular dynamics of solids and liquids. Answers inquiries and provides consulting services.

24432. Refrigeration Research Foundation, 7315 Wisconsin Ave, Bethesda, MD 20814; (301) 652-5674. Studies refrigerated warehouse storage of food. Answers inquiries, provides copying services at cost to nonmembers, permits onsite use of library.

24434. Registry of Interpreters for the Deaf, 814 Thayer Ave, Silver Spring, MD 20910; (301) 588-2406. Professional assn of interpreters working with deaf people. Answers inquiries and makes referrals. Services primarily for interpreters and persons interested in working with the deaf.

24435. Remington Farms, RD 2, Box 660, Chestertown, MD 21620; (301) 778-1565. Demonstrates how, through wise land use, wildlife habitat can be improved in a manner compatible with normal farming operations. Answers inquiries, conducts seminars and guided tours, distributes publications. Services free.

24436. Renewable Natural Resources Foundation, 5410 Grosvenor Ln, Bethesda, MD 20814-2193; (301) 493-

9101. Promotes advancement of research, education, scientific practice, and policy formulation for conservation and replenishment of the earth's renewable natural resources. Services available to anyone having a demonstrable need. Fees may be charged.

24437. Research Resources, Biological Carcinogenesis Branch, National Cancer Institute, Landow Bldg, Room A-22, 7910 Woodmont Ave, Bethesda, MD 20892; (301) 496-1951. Provides research resources and logistical support for the biological carcinogenesis research program. Answers inquiries, provides advisory services. Services free.

24438. Resilient Floor Covering Institute, 966 Hungerford Dr, Suite 12-B, Rockville, MD 20850; (301) 340-8580. Concerned with asphalt and vinyl composition tile, solid vinyl tile, and sheet vinyl floorings. Answers inquiries and makes referrals.

24439. Ridexchange, 6411 Sundown Rd, Laytonsville, MD 20879; (301) 963-3911. Matches vehicle providers with riders through a network of licensees who provide local service and access a common data base. Services provided for a $3-to-$5 fee per transaction, available to traveling public.

24440. SCM Pigments Division, Research Center Library, 3901 Glidden Rd, Baltimore, MD 21226; (301) 355-3600 ext 294. Provides data on pigments for paper, plastics, rubber, and paint. Answers brief inquiries, makes referrals, permits onsite use of collection by prior arrangement.

24441. Scientists Center for Animal Welfare, 4805 St Elmo Ave, Bethesda, MD 20814; (301) 654-6390. Conducts educational programs for scientists on humane issues of biomedical, agricultural, and wildlife research on animals. Conducts conferences and workshops, answers inquiries, provides advisory services, makes referrals. Services free.

24443. Self Help for Hard of Hearing People, 7800 Wisconsin Avenue, Bethesda, MD 20817; (301) 657-2248. Educates hearing impaired and public about hearing loss and its management, and to promote interests of the hearing impaired. Provides self-help programs, social activities, referrals, conferences, advocacy, research, and publications.

24444. Shakespeare Oxford Society, P.O. Box 16254, Baltimore, MD 21210; (301) 235-8719. Collects evidence indicating that Edward de Vere, 17th Earl of Oxford, wrote those works generally attributed to William Shakespeare. Answers reasonable inquiries by mail, makes referrals. Services provided as time and circumstances permit; fees may be charged.

24445. Sick Kids Need Involved People, 216 Newport Drive, Severna Park, MD 21146; (301) 647-0164. Volunteer org dedicated to helping children who, as a result of disease, handicap, or injury, are dependent on medical technology to maintain their health. Has 25 chapters around U.S.

24446. Smithsonian Institution, Environmental Research Center, 12441 Parklawn Dr, Rockville, MD 20852; (301) 443-2306. Conducts research concerned with physical, chemical, and biological interactions in environmental settings and determines mechanisms that measure biological systems. Answers inquiries, provides consulting services.

24447. Society for Applied Spectroscopy, P.O. Box 1438, Frederick, MD 21701; (301) 694-8122. Conducts studies in spectroscopy. Assists technical inquirers by providing referral service or references to Society publications.

24448. Society for Computer Applications in Engineering, Planning and Architecture, 358 Hungerford Dr, Rockville, MD 20850; (301) 762-6070. Seeks to further effective application of computers in engineering, architecture, and related fields. Answers inquiries, provides advisory services, conducts seminars, makes referrals. Services primarily for members, but others will be assisted.

24449. Society for Epidemiologic Research, 624 N Broadway, Room 225, Baltimore, MD 21205; (301) 955-3441. Studies epidemiology, chronic and infectious disease, health services and biostatistics. Answers brief inquiries free.

24450. Society for the Advancement of Chicanos and Native Americans in Science, P.O. Box 30040, Bethesda, MD 20814; (517) 355-4600. Promotes recruitment and advancement of Chicanos and native Americans in scientific careers. Answers inquiries, provides advisory, consulting and reference services, conducts seminars and distributes publications. Services may be subject to a fee.

24451. Society for the Application of Free Energy, 1315 Apple Ave, Silver Spring, MD 20910; (202) 882-4000. Studies natural sources of energy, including sun and wind as well as unconventional energies, such as mind power as a form of electrical energy and electronic force in plants and animals. Answers inquiries, provides advisory services, makes referrals. Services at cost.

24452. Society of American Foresters, 5400 Grosvenor Ln, Bethesda, MD 20814; (301) 897-8720. Natl org representing all segments of forestry profession in U.S. General inquiries answered by staff, technical inquiries referred to member specialists or other orgs or individuals. Onsite use of reference collection is permitted.

24453. Society of Eye Surgeons, 7801 Norfolk Ave, Bethesda, MD 20814; (301) 986-1830. Seeks cure and prevention of blindness through advancement of medical science and intl exchange of medical knowledge. Answers inquiries or refers inquirers to other sources of info. Services free.

24454. Society of State Directors of Health, Physical Education and Recreation, c/o Simon A. McNeely, 9805 Hillridge Dr, Kensington, MD 20895; (301) 949-2226. Collects data on school health services and health education. Answers inquiries, provides consulting services, evaluates physical education and recreation programs, permits onsite use of collection. Services primarily for members.

24455. Specific Diagnostic Studies, 11600 Nebel St, Suite 130, Rockville, MD 20852; (301) 468-6616. Specializes in recognition and understanding of learning differences through diagnostic testing and evaluation. Answers inquiries, provides advisory and reference services, conducts seminars, makes referrals. Most services free.

24456. Stepfamily Association of America, 28 Allegheny Ave, Suite 1307, Baltimore, MD 21204; (301) 823-7570. Acts as a support network and natl advocate for stepparents, remarried parents and their children. Answers initial inquiries free, provides consulting services to chapters. A quarterly bulletin is provided free to members, on a subscription basis to others.

24457. Sterling Silversmiths Guild of America, 600 Wyndhurst Ave, Baltimore, MD 21210; (301) 532-7062. Source of info on sterling silverware, flatware, hollowware, sterling jewelry, tarnish research, and silver design. Answers brief inquiries.

24458. Students Against Drunken Driving, 10812 Ashfield Road, Adelphi, MD 20783; (301) 937-7936. Attempts to combat deaths caused by drinking and driving. Offers community awareness programs, a high school curriculum, help in forming chapters, and a student-parent contract.

24459. Surratt Society, Surratt House & Museum, P.O. Box 427 (9110 Brandywine Rd), Clinton, MD 20735; (301) 868-1121. Maintains a program on site's involvement in the Lincoln assassination and mid-19th century life in Southern Md. Publishes a newsletter, answers inquiries, conducts tours, distributes publications, permits onsite use of library collections. Services free.

24461. Survivors of Incest Anonymous, 7702 Dunmanway, Baltimore, MD 21222; (301) 282-3400. Self-help group of men and women, 18 years or older, who have been victims of incest. Works to help victims realize they are not responsible for what happened. Meetings are confidential. Members are encouraged to seek professional therapy. Services free.

24462. Tissue Culture Association, 19110 Montgomery Village Ave, Suite 300, Gaithersburg, MD 20879; (301) 869-2900. Studies all aspects of cell biology and tissue culture (mammalian, plant, invertebrate, vertebrate). Answers inquiries. Maintains collection of films on plant and animal cell and organ culture and related fields, including cytology, cell biology, immunology, virology and genetics. Catalog available on request, rents films to orgs.

24464. Toxicology Information Program, National Institutes of Health, 8600 Rockville Pike, Bethesda, MD 20894; (301) 496-1131. Responsible for creation and development of a group of toxicologically-oriented online databases. Answers in-depth inquiries about toxicology and chemicals, provides customized reference services, primarily for scientific community and govt orgs.

24465. U.S. Army Environmental Hygiene Agency, Aberdeen Proving Ground, MD 21010; (301) 671-4236. Provides worldwide support for preventive medicine and environmental programs of the Army. Responds to inquiries from all of military services and other federal agencies.

24466. Undersea Medical Society, 9650 Rockville Pike, Bethesda, MD 20814; (301) 530-9225. Provides a forum for professional scientific communication among individuals and groups involved in life sciences and human aspects of undersea environment, and in hyperbaric medicine. Answers inquiries or makes referrals, conducts seminars, distributes publications.

24467. Unit for Research on Behavioral Systems, NIH, Bldg 110, Room 117, Poolesville, MD 20837; (301) 496-9556. Studies population dynamics, info managment, and simulation of biological brain function in preparation of manuscripts. Answers inquiries, distributes reprints of scientific papers.

24468. Unitarian and Universalist Genealogical Society, 10605 Lakespring Way, Cockeysville, MD 21030; (301) 628-2490. Clearinghouse for data and research on genealogical records of Unitarians, Universalists, and other religious liberals. Answers inquiries, provides reference services, makes referrals, permits onsite use of collections. Services primarily for members.

24469. United States Naval Institute, Annapolis, MD 21402; (301) 268-6110. Assn of active and retired military officers and civil servants interested in advancement of knowledge of naval and maritime services. Answers inquiries, permits use of collections by researchers, sells photographs of ships and aircraft of U.S. Navy and Coast Guard (black and white only).

24470. United States Police Canine Association, 8616 Trumps Hill Rd, Upper Marlboro, MD 20772; (301) 952-0040. Concerned with training of police dogs and related matters. Answers inquiries, provides advisory and reference services, conducts seminars, distributes publications, makes referrals. Services available to police officers and law enforcement agencies only.

24471. United Telegraph Workers, 701 E Gude Dr, Rockville, MD 20051; (301) 762-4444. Union affiliated with AFL-CIO and Canadian Labour Congress. Answers brief inquiries from public.

24472. Vegetarian Information Service, P.O. Box 5888 (10005 Clue Dr), Bethesda, MD 20814; (301) 530-1737. Seeks to enlighten public on merits of vegetarianism in enhancing human health, relieving animal suffering and world hunger, reducing food costs, and improving environmental quality. Answers inquiries, distributes publications, makes referrals. Most services are free.

24474. White Lung Association, 1114 Cathedral Street, Baltimore, MD 21201; (301) 727-6029. Nonprofit org dedicated to education of public about hazards of asbestos exposure. Maintains a collection of print and audio-visual materials on asbestos.

24475. Wildlife Society, 5410 Grosvenor Ln, Bethesda, MD 20814; (301) 897-9770. Promotes wildlife research, management, and science. Answers brief inquiries and makes referrals.

24477. World Data Center A: Rockets and Satellites, NASA, Goddard Space Flight Center, Code 601, Greenbelt, MD 20771; (301) 982-6695. Provides rocket and satellite data and info. Answers inquiries, assists scientists in obtaining data from NSSDC and other sources, distributes documents. Services free, except for document reproduction.

24478. World Future Society, 4916 St Elmo Ave, Bethesda, MD 20814-5089; (301) 656-8274. Educational org that forecasts possible technological and social developments. Answers inquiries and makes referrals free, conducts regional meetings and courses. Services available to members.

24479. World's Poultry Science Association, United States Branch, 11711 Roby Ave, Beltsville, MD 20705; (301) 937-3692. Promotes poultry science and technology and production, processing, and marketing of poultry meat and eggs. Answers inquiries.

Massachusetts

25003. ACCION International/AITEC, 1385 Cambridge St, Cambridge, MA 02139; (617) 492-4930. Concerned with small business development, credit and guarantee mechanisms, etc. among low-income populations. Provides general reference services, conducts seminars, permits onsite study. Services other than brief inquiries charged for.

25004. ARTS Computer Products, 145 Tremont St, Suite 407, Boston, MA 02111; (617) 482-8248. Interest in computers, equipment for the handicapped, software, programs. Provides general reference services, consulting. Services free.

25005. Abt Associates Inc., 55 Wheeler St, Cambridge, MA 02138; (617) 492-7100. Social science research org that conducts policy-oriented research, operates various social service programs, management studies. Provides general reference services, conducts seminars, distributes publications, permits onsite study. Services provided for fees.

25006. Action for Children's Television, 46 Austin St, Newtonville, MA 02160; (617) 527-7870. Natl nonprofit consumer org interested in television and its relationship to children, commercialism and children, etc. Answers inquiries, provides speakers for meetings.

25007. Adaptive Environments Center, Mass. Coll of Art, 621 Huntington Ave, Boston, MA 02115; (617) 739-0088. Interest in architectural accessibility in homes, public buildings, cultural programs, space planning. Provides general reference services, conducts seminars, distributes publications. Inquiries answered free, other services provided for a fee.

25008. Advanced Technology Publications, Laser Focus the magazine of Electro-Optics Technology, 119 Russell St, Littleton, MA 01460; (617) 486-9501. Interest in lasers and laser-related products and systems, electro-optic products and systems, fiberoptic products and systems. Provides marketing reports for a fee, publishes materials, makes referrals.

25009. African Studies Center, 125 Bay State Rd, Boston, MA 02215; (617) 353-3673. Interest in African economics, history, political science, sociology, anthropology, languages, religion, geography, etc. Performs general reference services; makes available materials to schools, the media, community groups in New England area.

25010. Aid to Artisans, 64 Fairgreen Pl, Chestnut Hill, MA 02167; (617) 277-7220. Nonprofit org promoting the welfare of craft communities in U.S. and less developed countries. Inquiries answered free; a fee for specialized consultation. Small grants offered.

25011. Air Force Atmospheric Sciences Division, U.S. Air Force Geophysics Lab (LY), Hanscom AFB, Bedford, MA 01731; (617) 861-2975. Interest in various meteorological subjects, including Doppler radar, numerical weather prediction, climatology, cloud physics, mesoscale forecasting, satellite meteorology and instrumentation. Answers inquiries, publishes reports.

25012. Air Force Balloon Design and Flight Analysis Branch, Aerospace Instrumentation Div, U.S. Air Force Geophysics Lab, Hanscom AFB, Bedford, MA 01731; (617) 861-3005. Interest in balloon materials, design, flight, and ground support instrumentation, sensing elements and operational techniques, zero pressure free balloons and tethered balloons. Provides consulting services by appointment to agencies and individuals.

25013. Air Force, Space Physics Division, U.S. Air Force Geophysics Lab, Hanscom Air Force Base, Bedford, MA 01731. Interest in space environment research, including data collection and analysis, preparation of models, and theoretical work. Info services generally restricted to USAF personnel. In-house publications available on request.

25014. Alden Research Laboratory, Worcester Polytechnic Institute, 30 Shrewsbury St, Holden, MA 01520; (617) 829-4323. Interest in hydraulics, hydraulic structures, hydraulic and steam-electric power installations, sewerage and water treatment plants, etc. Answers inquiries, provides consulting, conducts research and testing.

25015. Alliance for the Prudent Use of Antibiotics, P.O. Box 1372, Boston, MA 02117; (617) 956-6764. Interest in prudent use of antibiotics, bacteria resistant to anti-biotics. Seeks to educate the public, health profession-als worldwide on dangers of abusing antimicrobial agents.

25017. American Academy of Implant Dentistry, c/o Dr John P. Winiewicz, Exec Dir, 515 Washington St, Box 2002, Abington, MA 02351; (617) 878-7990. Interest in dentistry, particularly implant dentistry. Provides col-lection of technical papers without charge. Inquiries about specialized problems handled through a con-sulting service. Holds annual meetings for members, supports research projects, provides public educa-tion.

25018. American Antiquarian Society, 185 Salisbury St, Worcester, MA 01609; (617) 755-5221. Sponsors sever-al fellowship competitions. Interest in colonial New England, American history. Research facilities open to researchers, graduate students with letter of refer-ence. Factual questions answered, referrals made.

25019. American Association of Variable Star Observers, 187 Concord Ave, Cambridge, MA 02138; (617) 354-0484. Interest in variable stars that change in bright-ness, solar observations. Answers inquiries, provides data for a fee, provides stellar observation materials and charts for fees.

25020. American Family Foundation, Box 336, Weston, MA 02193; (617) 893-0930. Interest in destructive cul-tism, implications of cult membership, cults and the law, techniques of manipulation. Provides general reference services, conducts seminars, publishes ma-terials, permits onsite use of collection. Donations re-quested.

25021. American Geriatrics Society, c/o Dr Knight Steel, Coordinator, Boston Univ Medical Center, 75 East Newton St, Boston, MA 02118; (617) 247-5019. Interest in clinical medicine, geriatrics. Answers inquiries free from health professionals within limits, accredits CME courses, publishes materials.

25022. American Institute for Archaeological Research, P.O. Box 6068, Newburyport, MA 01950; (617) 465-9247. Nonprofit org that conducts research in archeol-ogy, anthropology, related fields, (especially stone-work). Provides reference services, conducts semi-nars, distributes publications, permits onsite study. Services free to members, at cost to others.

25023. American Institute for Economic Research, Great Barrington, MA 01230; (413) 528-1216. Nonprofit org that conducts research principally on monetary eco-nomics. Interest in economics and finance, particular-ly monetary policies and their effects. Answers inqui-ries, distributes publications, permits onsite use of collections.

25024. American Institute of Management, 45 Willard St, Boston, MA 02169; (617) 472-0277. Research org inter-ested in all aspects of management at corporate policy level, development of a conceptual framework for an-

alyzing management. Answers inquiries, makes re-ferrals free, conducts seminars and training programs for a fee.

25025. American Jewish Historical Society, c/o Nathan M. Kaganoff, Librarian, 2 Thornton Rd, Waltham, MA 02154; (617) 891-8110. Interest in history of Jews in America. Answers inquiries; provides bibliographic, duplication services; makes referrals, interlibrary loans; permits onsite use of collection.

25026. American Legal Studies Association, c/o Dept of Legal Studies, Univ of Mass., Hampshire House, Am-herst, MA 01003; (413) 545-2000. Assn of legal studies teachers. Interest in law, legal studies, law and socie-ty, law and literature. Answers inquiries, conducts seminars, distributes publications, makes referrals. Some services offered at cost.

25027. American Meteorological Society, 45 Beacon St, Boston, MA 02108; (617) 227-2425. Interest in atmos-pheric and related oceanic and hydrologic sciences. Provides general reference services, indexing and ab-stracting, distributes publications for a fee.

25028. American Minor Breeds Conservancy, Box 225, Hardwick, MA 01037; (617) 724-3223. Nonprofit mem-bership org interested in preservation of rare breeds of livestock, animal genetics, and crossbreeding. An-swers inquiries, makes referrals, conducts seminars, distributes publications. Services primarily for mem-bers.

25029. American Society for Gastrointestinal Endoscopy, P.O. Box 1565, (13 Elm St) Manchester, MA 01944; (617) 927-8330. Interest in research and development, training in fiberoptic instrumentation in gastroenter-ology, gastrointestinal endoscopy. Conducts semi-nars and workshops, distributes publications. Serv-ices free to members, for a fee to others.

25030. American Society of Abdominal Surgeons, c/o Blaise F. Alfano, M.D., Executive Secretary, 675 Main St, Melrose, MA 02176; (617) 665-6102. Interest in ab-dominal surgery basic sciences, surgical anatomy, pa-thology, and physiology. Answers inquiries, provides consulting services, conducts courses for fees. Serv-ices available to physicians.

25031. American Society of Law & Medicine, c/o A. Ed-ward Doudera, J.D., Executive Director, 765 Com-monwealth Ave, 16th Fl., Boston, MA 02215; (617) 262-4990. Society conducts continuing medicolegal education programs involving interface of law, medi-cine, and health care. Answers inquiries, makes refer-rals, generally without charge, sells publications.

25032. American Soviet Cultural Exchange, 151 Coolidge Ave, Ste 609, Watertown, MA 02172; (617) 924-0713. Nonprofit org promoting unofficial cultural ex-changes between peoples of U.S. and U.S.S.R. Pro-vides general reference services, and translations, conducts seminars and workshops. Some services subject to a fee.

25033. American Tuberous Sclerosis Association, P.O. Box 44, Rockland, MA 02370; president, (617) 878-5528, (800) 446-1211. Works to combat tuberous sclerosis through education, genetic research, and assistance to victims and their families. Provides general reference services, promotes legislation, publishes materials, participates in forums.

25034. American Vecturist Association, P.O. Box 1204, Boston, MA 02104; (617) 277-8111. Interest in transportation tokens, urban transportation history, transportation fare structures. Provides general reference services, sells publications.

25035. Aphasia Research Center, Boston Univ, 150 South Huntington Ave, Boston, MA 02130; (617) 232-9500. Interest in brain function in language and related higher processes. Answers inquiries from investigators doing related research.

25036. Appalachian Mountain Club, 5 Joy St, Boston, MA 02108; (617) 523-0636. Interest in mountains and mountaineering, especially in New England, rock climbing, skiing, canoeing, camping, conservation, natural history. Provides general reference services; nonmembers may use material in the library, but services primarily for members.

25037. Archaeological Institute of America, P.O. Box 1901, Kenmore Station, Boston, MA 02215; (617) 353-9361. Interest in archaeology and research in allied disciplines of art, history, anthropology, classics, philology, numismatics. Questions answered, referrals made to members, sponsors annual meeting, provides student counseling.

25038. Army Intelligence Center and School, Fort Huachuca & Fort Devens, Commander, USAISD, U.S. Army Intelligence School, Attn: ATSI-EDT-L (Library), Fort Devens, MA 01433; (617) 796-3413. Interest in military science, cryptology, electronics, military intelligence, electronic warfare, military communications. Limitations on reference services provided to non-DoD or those without security clearances.

25039. Army Materials and Mechanics Research Center, Attn: DRXMR-PL, Building 36, Watertown, MA 02172; (617) 923-5460. Interest in materials research, composites, physical and mechanical metallurgy, structural mechanics, ceramic materials, polymers, etc. Provides general reference services, info resources available to other govt activities on cooperative basis.

25040. Army Natick Research and Development Center, Kansas St, Natick, MA 01760-5000; (617) 651-4248. Interest in air-drop technology, biology, chemistry, clothing, engineering, food engineering, medical science, packaging technology. Library services primarily for U.S. Army Natick R&D Center personnel, limited access open to others by special arrangement.

25041. Art and Crafts Materials Institute, 715 Boylston St, Boston, MA 02116; (617) 266-6800. Assn of manufacturers of art materials that conducts certification program to insure safety, quality of children's art materials. Answers inquiries, distributes program, booklet.

25042. Arthur D. Little, Inc. Acorn Park, Cambridge, MA 02140; (617) 864-5770. Interest in all branches of science, technology, economics, and management. Provides consulting services on contract basis. Use of library by nonclients decided on individual basis. Literature-searching, related services performed at service/time rates.

25043. Arthur and Elizabeth Schlesinger Library on the History of Women in America, Radcliffe College, 10 Garden St, Cambridge, MA 02138; (617) 495-8647. Collects manuscripts and printed materials on American women, 1820-present, conducts oral history projects, programs. Provides general reference services, distributes publications, permits onsite use of collections. Fees charged for some services.

25044. Artificial Intelligence Laboratory, MIT, 545 Technology Square, Cambridge, MA 02139; (617) 253-6773. Lab interested in artificial intelligence, robotics, machine vision, human vision, expert systems, knowledge engineering, computer architecture, computational linguistics, natural language processing. Distributes publications.

25045. Artists Foundation, 110 Broad St, Boston, MA 02110; (617) 482-8100. Public, nonprofit org that awards fellowships to practicing Mass. artists, administers various programs. Provides general reference services, conducts seminars, distributes publications. Except for seminars and publications, services free.

25046. Association of Arab-American University Graduates, 556 Trapelo Rd, Belmont, MA 02178; (617) 484-5483. Promotes Arab-American understanding, develops professional cooperation. Provides general reference services, conducts seminars, operates a speakers bureau, distributes publications, permits onsite use of collection. Services provided for a fee.

25047. Association of Medical Rehabilitation Directors and Coordinators, 87 Elm St, Framingham, MA 01701; (617) 877-0517. Assn of professionals in rehabilitation medicine and programs, interested in rehabilitation centers, programs, and services. Provides general reference services, conducts annual conference. Services free, but primarily for members.

25048. Astrophysical Observatory, 60 Garden St, Cambridge, MA 02138; (617) 495-7461. Interest in astronomy, radio astronomy, gamma-ray and X-ray astronomy, astrophysics, geophysics, satellite geodesy, etc. Performs general reference services, library performs online searches.

25049. Atlantic Center for the Environment, 39 S Main St, Ipswich, MA 01938; (617) 356-0038. Provides ecology and wildlife preservation education and general reference services; conducts research, workshops, summer courses; distributes publications; permits onsite study. Services free to members, at cost to others.

25050. Austen Fox Riggs Library, Austen Riggs Center, Main St, Stockbridge, MA 01262; (413) 298-5511. Interest in psychoanalysis, psychiatry, psychology, and related fields. Permits limited onsite use of collection by professionals, other qualified persons.

25051. Avco-Everett Research Laboratory, Avco Corp., 2385 Revere Beach Parkway, Everett, MA 02149; (617) 389-3000, (617) 381-4617 (Library). Interest in magnetohydrodynamics and magnetohydrodynamic power generation, plasma physics, reentry physics, and gas dynamics, hypersonic aerodynamics. Answers technical inquiries, makes interlibrary loans whenever possible.

25052. Behavioral Research Council, Great Barrington, MA 01230; (413) 528-1216. Scientific nonprofit org that conducts research in methods of inquiry, including hard sciences and behavioral and social sciences. Answers inquiries, sells publications.

25053. Bolt Beranek and Newman Inc., 10 Moulton St, Cambridge, MA 02238; (617) 491-1850. Interest in architectural technologies, noise control, info sciences, transportation planning, acoustics, wide area networks, etc. Answers inquiries, makes interlibrary loans. No charge for reasonable requests, usually limited to Boston area.

25054. Boston & Maine Railroad Historical Society Collection, c/o Special Collections, Lydon Library, Univ of Lowell, 1 Univ Ave, Lowell, MA 01854; (617) 452-5000. Interest in railroad economics, history, engineering, and technical aspects of railroading. Provides general reference services, permits onsite study. Services free, except for photocopies.

25055. Bostonian Society, 206 Washington St, (Library: 15 State St, 3rd fl), Boston, MA 02109; (617) 242-5614 (Library), (617) 242-5655 (Museum). Interest in history of Boston. Answers inquiries, provides reference, duplication services, makes referrals, permits onsite use of collection by approved researchers.

25056. Cabot Corp., Concord Rd, Billerica, MA 01821; (617) 663-3455. Interest in carbon black, its manufacture, properties, applications; technology of rubber, paint, ink, and plastics; white pigments and fillers. Provides general reference services, permits onsite study, makes interlibrary loans.

25057. Cell Culture Center, MIT, 40 Ames St E17-321, Cambridge, MA 02139; (617) 253-6430. Engaged in large-scale production of animal cells and viruses for use by natl researchers. Interest in tissue culture, cell culture, virology. Answers inquiries, makes referrals free. Laboratory use by local researchers permitted.

25058. Center for Action on Endangered Species, 175 West Main St, Ayer, MA 01432; (617) 772-0445. Interest in endangered wildlife and plants, conservation, environmental education, etc. Provides general reference services, conducts seminars, distributes publications, permits onsite study. Fee for some services.

25059. Center for Birth Defects Information Services, Dover Medical Building, Box 1776, Dover, MA 02030; (617) 785-2525. Maintains computerized service to aid in diagnosis and management of birth defects, gives training courses for new users.

25060. Center for Earth and Planetary Physics, Div of Applied Sciences, Harvard Univ, Pierce Hall, Cambridge, MA 02138; (617) 495-2814. Interest in physical oceanography, physics and chemistry of the upper and lower atmospheres, dynamical meteorology, etc. Conducts seminars open to the public.

25061. Center for Firesafety Studies, Worcester Poly Institute, Institute Rd, Worcester, MA 01609; (617) 793-5593. Conducts research and offers graduate work in fire protection engineering. Provides general reference services, conducts seminars, permits onsite use of collection. Services provided at cost.

25062. Center for Instructional Technology, Room 412 DG, Northeastern Univ, Boston, MA 02115; (617) 437-2150. Interest in instructional technology, innovation in education, curriculum design, faculty development. Publishes materials, permits onsite use of collection by the general public.

25063. Center for International Affairs, Harvard Univ, 1737 Cambridge St, Cambridge, MA 02138; (617) 495-4420. Interest in U.S. relations with Latin America, Canada, Japan, Europe, and Africa, intl monetary policy, growth of transnatl systems. Library available for onsite use by Harvard faculty, established scholars.

25064. Center for Latin American Development Studies, Boston Univ, 745 Commonwealth Ave, Boston, MA 02215; (617) 353-4030. Interest in research on employment policies, foreign private investment policies, intl trade policies of Latin American countries. Provides info, conducts seminars, distributes publications free on exchange basis, permits onsite study. Services available to those with scholarly interest.

25065. Center for Law and Health Sciences, Boston Univ Law School, 765 Commonwealth Ave, Boston, MA 02215; (617) 353-2904. Interest in education, research in areas where law and medicine interface, including child abuse, mental health law, patient rights, human experimentation. Provides general reference services and consulting, conducts seminars, permits onsite study. Services provided at cost.

25066. Center for Medical Manpower Studies, Dept of Economics, Northeastern Univ, 301 Lake Hall, Boston, MA 02115; (617) 437-3640. Estimates employment and training effects of alternative natl health insurance plans. Interest in medical economics, natl health insurance. Answers inquiries, distributes publications.

25067. Center for Meteorology and Physical Oceanography, Dept of Earth, Atmospheric and Planetary Sciences, Room 54-1712, MIT, Cambridge, MA 02139; (617) 253-2281. Interest in dynamic meteorology, synoptic meteorology, physical oceanography, etc. Provides general reference services, conducts seminars, distributes publications, permits onsite use of collection. Services provided for a fee.

25068. Center for Middle Eastern Studies, Harvard Univ, 1737 Cambridge St, Cambridge, MA 02138. Interest in Middle Eastern languages and literatures, their history, doctrines, institutions, law, philosophy, and science, government, politics, problems. Answers inquiries, conducts academic programs, makes referrals.

25069. Center for Policy Alternatives, School of Engineering, MIT, One Amherst St E40-202, Cambridge, MA 02139; (617) 253-1667. Policy analysis group interested in technology transfer, safety regulation, productivity, office automation, labor, consumer needs. Provides reference services, permits onsite use of collections. Services free, except publications.

25070. Center for Population Studies, School of Public Health, Harvard Univ, 9 Bow St, Cambridge, MA 02138; (617) 495-2021. Interest in research on demography, regional development, income distribution, mortality, other related topics. Provides general reference services, conducts conferences, distributes publications, permits onsite study. Some services provided free.

25071. Center for Rehabilitation Research and Training in Mental Health, Boston Univ, Sargent Coll of Health Professions, 1019 Commonwealth Ave, Boston, MA 02215; (617) 353-3549. Develops research and training. Interest in mental health, rehabilitation. Provides general reference services, conducts seminars, distributes publications. Services, for fees, on request.

25072. Center for Research in Children's Television, Graduate School of Education, Harvard Univ, Larsen Hall, 4th Fl, Cambridge, MA 02138; (617) 495-3541. Interest in effects of television on children and child development. Provides general reference services, distributes publications. Fees charged for consultations, other services free.

25073. Center for Research on Women, Wellesley College, Wellesley, MA 02181. Works to improve range and quality of education and work open to women. Conducts seminars, sells publications, makes referrals, permits onsite study, provides assistance in child care.

25074. Center for Science and International Affairs, School of Govt, Harvard Univ, 79 John F. Kennedy St, Cambridge, MA 02138; (618) 495-1400. Interest in arms control, intl security, military science. Answers inquiries, provides reference services, conducts seminars and workshops, permits onsite use of collections. Services free to researchers.

25075. Center for Technology, Environment, and Development, Clark Univ, 950 Main St, Worcester, MA 01610; (617) 793-7283. Consortium of research groups interested in hazard and risk analysis. Provides general reference services, conducts seminars, distributes

publications, permits onsite use of collections. Services free, except for copying, mailing, and some publications.

25076. Center for the Study of Children's Literature, Simmons College, 300 The Fenway, Boston, MA 02115; (617) 738-2258. Offers degree programs, community education program in the field of children's literature. Provides general reference services, conducts lecture series, distributes publications, permits onsite use of collections. Services free to researchers.

25077. Center for the Study of Drug Development, Tufts Univ, 136 Harrison Ave, Boston, MA 02111; (617) 956-0070. Interest in drug development, discoveries, evaluations, and use; pharmaceutical economics. Provides general reference services, distributes publications, permits onsite use of collection. Services available, some for fees, to interested researchers.

25078. Caesareans/Support Education and Concern, 22 Forest Rd, Framingham, MA 01701; (617) 877-8266. Nonprofit org that provides info on caesarean childbirth, caesarean prevention, and vaginal birth after caesarean. Conducts research, educational programs, lectures, publishes materials for health professionals, parents. Services free, except publications.

25080. Charles H. Hurley Library, Mass. Maritime Academy, Taylors Point, Buzzards Bay, MA 02532; (617) 759-5761 ext 350. Academy educates officers for U.S. Merchant Marine, skilled professionals for maritime industry and allied marine careers. Provides general reference services, permits onsite study. Services mostly restricted to campus community.

25082. Chase Econometrics/Interactive Data Corp., c/o Director of Marketing Services, 486 Totten Pond Rd, Waltham, MA 02154; (617) 890-1234. Intl firm that provides financial info on computer time-sharing system or in microcomputer environment. Provides data and language tools, customer training and consulting services.

25083. Children in Hospitals, 31 Wilshire Park, Needham, MA 02192; (617) 482-2915. Nonprofit org that promotes education on rights of hospital patients, supportive medical care, child psychology, parent-child relationships. Answers inquiries, conducts seminars, distributes publications, makes referrals. Except publications, services free.

25084. China Trade Museum, 215 Adams St, Milton, MA 02186; (617) 696-1815. Interest in history of involvement of U.S. in China trade, Chinese export art. Provides general reference services, permits onsite use of collections by appointment. Services free, except photocopying.

25085. Committees of Correspondence, P.O. Box 232 (57 Conant St, Room 113, Danvers, MA), Topsfield, MA 01983; (617) 774-2641. Natl org of citizens concerned about drug abuse. Interest in education on drug use and abuse issues. Provides general reference services, conducts seminars, distributes publications. Services free, unless extensive.

25086. Computer Security Institute, 360 Church St, Northborough, MA 01532; (617) 393-2600. Membership org interested in computer security, data processing security, info safeguarding. Provides general reference services, conducts seminars, operates info hotline, distributes publications. Services primarily for members.

25087. Congregational Library, American Congregational Assn, 14 Beacon St, Boston, MA 02108; (617) 523-0470. Interest in history of Congregational Christian churches and United Church of Christ. Provides general reference services, distributes publication, permits onsite use of collections. Services available at cost.

25088. Conservation Law Foundation of New England, 3 Joy St, Boston, MA 02108; (617) 742-2540. Interest in all aspects of environmental law affecting New England region, especially energy, land policy, environmental health. Answers inquiries; provides advisory, litigation, administrative intervention services; makes referrals. Services free, within limits.

25089. Cooks Resources, P.O. Box 363 (1670 Washington St), Holliston, MA 01746-0363; (617) 429-6779. Interest in researching, evaluating, and appraising of stock certificates and bonds for investment value, as collectible items, or for possible market value. Prepares evaluations and reports for a fee.

25090. Copyright Clearance Center, 21 Congress St, Salem, MA 01970; (617) 744-3350. Nonprofit service org that provides to users instant permission to photocopy copyrighted material from copyright owners. Provides descriptive materials, registration form, to prospective users on request.

25091. Crime and Justice Foundation, 19 Temple Pl, 5th Fl., Boston, MA 02111; (617) 426-9800. Nonprofit org that seeks to improve and develop an understanding of the administration of criminal justice. Provides general reference services, conducts seminars, distributes publications, permits onsite study. Services free, except some publications and consulting.

25092. Cultural Survival, 11 Divinity Ave, Cambridge, MA 02138; (617) 495-2562. Nonprofit org that helps ethnic societies become successful. Interest in impact of industrial society on Third World. Provides general reference services, conducts seminars, sell publications, permits onsite study. Services generally free, but contributions appreciated.

25093. Dana-Farber Cancer Institute, 44 Binney St, Boston, MA 02115; (617) 732-3487. Nonprofit institute that conducts clinical cancer research and administers cancer programs. Interested in all aspects of cancer research. Provides general reference services, conducts seminars. Services free. Patient info is restricted.

25094. Data Resources, 29 Hartwell Ave, Lexington, MA 02173; (617) 863-5100. Commercial org interested in natl and industrial economies as applied to corporate planning, regional analysis, investments. Provides consulting and analysis services, conducts seminars, distributes publications. Services provided by subscription.

25095. Data Security Systems, 5 Keane Terrace, Natick, MA 01760; (617) 653-7101. Interest in an interdisciplinary attack on computer crime. Provides general reference services and consulting, conducts seminars, distributes publications. Services available for a fee.

25096. Digital Equipment Computer Users Society, 219 Boston Post Rd, BP02, Marlboro, MA 01752; (617) 480-3290. Interest in promotion of the exchange of info-processing related data among users of Digital Equipment Corp products. Furnishes literature, provides info, conducts seminars.

25097. Documentary Guild, Shearer Rd, Box 478, Colrain, MA 01340; (413) 625-2402. Interest in video documentaries on Soviet-American relations, dangers of nuclear war, hazards to workers at nuclear power plants, children's mime, and art shorts. Sells video documentaries and shorts.

25098. EG&G Environmental Equipment, 151 Bear Hill Rd, Waltham, MA 02154; (617) 890-3710. Interest in oceanographic acoustic systems, including side-scan sonar and seismic profiling equipment. Answers inquiries, provides consulting services, makes referrals, prepares analyses, permits onsite reference.

25099. EG&G Mason Research Institute, 57 Union St, Worcester, MA 01608; (617) 791-0931 ext 153. Multidisciplinary biomedical research laboratory in cancer research and toxicology. Interest in carcinogenesis in vitro and in vivo, mutagenesis, toxicology, pathology, etc. Provides general reference services, permits onsite use of collections. Most services provided for a fee.

25100. ENDECO, 13 Atlantis Dr, Marion, MA 02738; (617) 748-0366 Interest in vehicles and instrumentation for marine research, oceanographic data gathering equipment, electromechanical aids, etc. Answers inquiries, provides consulting services for a fee, performs testing.

25101. Harvard Economic Botany Library of Oakes Ames, Harvard Univ Herbaria, 22 Divinity Ave, Cambridge, MA 02138; (617) 495-2366. Library interested in useful plants, ethnobotany, food, nutrition, drugs, narcotics, and fuel, with emphasis on historical uses. Provides limited free reference service, self-service onsite photocopying, but no interlibrary loans made.

25102. Education Development Center, 55 Chapel St, Newton, MA 02160; (617) 969-7100. Nonprofit corp engaged in educational research and development worldwide, especially developing countries. Provides general reference services, distributes materials, publications, conducts seminars. Some services free, others at cost.

25103. Educational Parameters, P.O. Box 570, (83 Industrial Lane), Agawam, MA 01001; (413) 789-1124 or 732-4157. Interest in senior citizen education, geriatric education programs, senior service orgs, drama therapy, volunteer services. Provides general reference services, distributes publications. Fees charged according to service requested.

25104. Educational Planning Associates, 584 Chestnut St, Newton, MA 02168; (617) 964-8470. Consulting org interested in development of school desegregation plans. Provides general reference services, conducts seminars, permits onsite use of collection. Services provided at cost, primarily for school systems.

25105. Educational Records Bureau, Attn: R. Bruce McGill, President, Bardwell Hall, 37 Cameron St, Wellesley, MA 02181; (617) 235-8920. Interest in educational testing at all levels, reporting of tests, testing and admission practices, etc. Approved personnel provided access to all materials except test scores; conducts workshops, other info services for members.

25106. Educators for Social Responsibility, 23 Garden St, Cambridge, MA 02138; (617) 492-1764. Natl nonprofit org interested in teacher education and curriculum development on nuclear issues. Provides general reference services, conducts seminars, permits onsite use of collection. Services available for a fee to educators.

25108. Elastic Fabric Manufacturers Council of the Northern Textile Association, 211 Congress St, Boston, MA 02110; (617) 542-8220. Interest in elastic braid, woven elastic, braided trimmings, and power net, including set standards and procedures and test characteristics. Provides general reference services, consulting, testing. Services primarily for council members, but may be provided to others.

25109. Enablement, 14 Beacon St, Room 715, Boston, MA 02108; (617) 742-1460. Interest in clergy ministry development, theology, psychology of careers. Provides general reference services, distributes publications, permits onsite use of collections. Services available for a fee to clergy, clergy-support groups.

25111. Epidemiology Resources, P.O. Box 57 (826 Boylston St, Ste 200, Brookline, MA), Chestnut Hill, MA 02167; (617) 734-9100. Interest in occupational, medical, and environmental research on the causes of chronic and acute diseases, including cancer. Provides general reference services, conducts educational programs, distributes publications. Services available for a fee.

25112. Eunice Kennedy Shriver Center for Mental Retardation, 200 Trapelo Rd, Waltham, MA 02254; (617) 893-3500. Conducts applied social policy research in the field of mental retardation. Answers inquiries, provides advisory services, conducts seminars, evaluates data, distributes publications. Services free.

25113. Eye Research Institute of Retina Foundation, 20 Staniford St, Boston, MA 02114; (617) 742-3140. Interest in eye and vision research, neuroscience, vitreal and retinal physiology and metabolism, biomedical physics and bioengineering, psychophysics, etc. Answers inquiries, provides consulting, lends materials, permits onsite use of collection.

25114. FZ East-West Trade, P.O. Box 498, Allston, MA 02134; (617) 738-5412, 769-7779. Commercial org that analyzes Soviet Bloc industrial capabilities, conducts market research for U.S. companies. Answers inquiries, provides consulting and translation services, evaluates data, conducts seminars. Services provided at cost.

25115. Factory Mutual Research Corp., P.O. Box 9102, (1151 Boston-Providence Turnpike), Norwood, MA 02062; (617) 762-4300. Performs research and testing in areas dealing with fire and other property damage hazards. Makes interlibrary loans, permits onsite use of collection by appointment.

25116. Federation for Children with Special Needs, 312 Stuart St, Second Fl, Boston, MA 02116; (617) 482-2915. Interest in children with a variety of disabling conditions. Works to increase health professionals' awareness of needs of families with handicapped children, increase families' understanding of medical systems. Encourages collaboration between parents and professionals.

25117. Flag Research Center, 3 Edgehill Rd, Winchester, MA 01890; (617) 729-9410. Interest in political symbolism, vexillology (study of flag history and symbolism and state heraldry), flags of all eras and types. Performs general reference, translation, and artwork services, permits onsite study. Fees charged for some services.

25118. Food Engineering Laboratory, U.S. Army Natick Research and Development Center, Attn: DRDNA-WP, Natick, MA 01760; (617) 651-4778. Interest in preservation, packaging, packing materials, and methods for food and related military supplies. Answers limited specific inquiries.

25121. GCA Corp., Technology Division Library, 213 Burlington Rd, Bedford, MA 01730; (617) 275-5444 ext 4134. Environmental consulting and research org interested in air, water, solid waste pollution, industrial hygiene, urban and regional planning. Provides general reference services, makes interlibrary loans, permits onsite study by appointment.

25122. GTE Products Corp., Communication System Div, Sylvania Systems Group, 77 A St, Needham Heights, MA 02194; (617) 449-2000. Interest in aerospace, communications, detection and countermeasures, electrical and electronic engineering, guided missiles, mathematics, navigation and guidance. Makes limited interlibrary loans to outside orgs.

25123. Gay and Lesbian Advocates and Defenders, P.O. Box 218, Boston, MA 02112; (617) 426-1350. Regional homosexual rights group interested in legal defense of lesbians and gay males. Provides general reference services, conducts workshops, distributes publications, permits onsite use of collection. Services free, except some publications.

25124. GenRad, 300 Baker Ave, Concord, MA 01742; (617) 369-4400. Interest in automatic measurement of analog and digital circuits, electrical and electronic measurements and instruments, electronic circuits, components, nonelectrical measurements by electrical means. Answers inquiries.

25125. Genetic Sequence Data Bank, c/o Computer Sciences Div, Bolt Beranek and Newman, 10 Moulton St, Cambridge, MA 02238; (617) 497-2742. Interest in nucleic acid sequences. Distributes data compilations, provides magnetic tape services. Services provided for a fee.

25126. Gold Filled Association, 5 Mechanic St, Attleboro, MA 02703; (617) 222-3666. Interest in marketing and promotion of gold-filled jewelry and optical wear. Provides general reference services, conducts seminars, distributes publications. Services free or for a nominal charge.

25127. Governmental Research Association, 24 Province St, No. 853, Boston, MA 02108; (617) 720-1000. Interest in state, local, and city govt administration, especially taxation, transportation, public works, education, water supplies, and air pollution. Provides general reference, consulting, and placement services.

25128. Gravity Research Foundation, 58 Middle St, Gloucester, MA 01930; (617) 283-4543. Nonprofit foundation that encourages research on theory, effects, and applications of gravitation. Provides general reference services, distributes reprints. Services generally free, except reprints of essays.

25129. Greater New York City Chapter, Organ Historical Society, c/o John Ogasapian, P.O. Box 194, Pepperell, MA 01463; (617) 433-5784. Interest in history and preservation of American organs, especially in New York City. Provides general reference services, permits onsite use of collections. Services free, except reproductions and publications.

25130. Habitat Institute for the Environment, P.O. Box 136, (10 Juniper Rd) Belmont, MA 02178; (617) 489-3850. Nonprofit org that conducts courses in natural history and environmental issues. Provides general reference services, permits onsite use of collection. Occasional use of services free, except for courses; regular use requires membership.

25131. Handwriting Analysis Research Library, 91 Washington St, Greenfield, MA 01301; (413) 774-4667. Nonprofit org interested in graphology, handwriting analysis, penmanship. Provides general reference services, distributes publications, conducts seminars, permits onsite use of collections. Most services for a fee.

25132. Harvard Institute for International Development, 1737 Cambridge St, Cambridge, MA 02138; (617) 495-2161 (General inquiries), (617) 495-2173 (Library). Center for programs of service, research, and training related to developing countries. Interest in various aspects of public policy. Provides reference services, conducts seminars. Library services free, others subject to a fee.

25133. Harvard Laboratory of Psychophysics, 33 Kirkland St, Cambridge, MA 02138; (617) 495-3855. Interest in research on psychoacoustics, hearing, vision, and the other senses. Answers occasional inquiries, makes referrals, and distributes reprints to a select distribution list.

25134. Headache Research Foundation, c/o The Faulkner Hospital, Allandale at Centre St, Jamaica Plain, MA 02130; (617) 522-7900 (Education Div), (617) 522-6969 (Research and Patient Care Divs). Conducts research on, provides care for, headache, migraine, tension headache, stress. Answers inquiries, conducts seminars and lectures, makes referrals. Services free, except lectures and courses.

25135. Hearing Ear Dog Program, P.O. Box 213, West Boylston, MA 01583; (617) 835-3304. Nonprofit regional org that provides trained dogs to aid hearing impaired persons. Trains clients, dogs. Services provided for a fee.

25136. Henry A. Murray Research Center, Radcliffe College, 10 Garden St, Cambridge, MA 02138; (617) 495-8140. Conducts, sponsors research on changing life experiences of American women. Provides reference services, conducts seminars, permits onsite study. Data free, other services at cost, to nonprofit groups.

25137. Herb Society of America, 2 Independence Court, Concord, MA 01742-2501; (617) 371-1486. Interest in study of culinary, fragrant, dye, and economic uses of herbs, identification and culture of herbs, herbal references. Provides general reference services, lends slide-lecture program for a fee. No medical advice is given.

25138. Herman G. Dresser Library, Camp, Dresser & McKee, 1 Center Plaza, Boston, MA 02108; (617) 742-5151. Interest in environmental engineering, sanitary engineering, including water resources, sewerage, sewage treatment, waste treatment, etc. Provides general reference services, provides reprints of publications, permits onsite study by appointment. Some restrictions apply.

25139. Higgins Armory Museum, 100 Barber Ave, Worcester, MA 01606; (617) 853-6015. Interest in arms and armor, military history, medieval and renaissance art history, iron work. Provides general reference services. Library hours by appointment; museum open to the public for an admission fee.

25141. Horace Mann Bond Center for Equal Education, Integrated Education Associates, School of Education, Library Tower, Univ of Mass., Amherst, MA 01003;

(413) 545-0327. Natl center that provides research and info on race, minority education, desegration, allied subjects. Provides general reference services, conducts seminars, distributes publications, permits onsite use of collections.

25142. Human Relations Area Files Library, Univ of Mass., Harbor Campus, Boston, MA 02125; (617) 929-7000. Interest in cross-cultural research data, all aspects of culture, ethnography. Provides general reference services, permits onsite use of collections. Services free to qualified users.

25144. Inforonics, 550 Newtown Rd, Littleton, MA 01460; (617) 486-8976. Interest in library automation, data base production services for automated library, info retrieval, and publishing systems. Provides time-shared computer services for publishers, consulting services. Services for a fee, except for answers to simple inquiries.

25145. Institute for Community Economics, 151 Montague City Rd, Greenfield, MA 01301; (413) 774-5933. Non-profit corp that promotes economic justice through local control of economic development. Provides general reference services, conducts seminars, monitors loan fund. Services free, except publications, consultation, technical assistance.

25146. Institute for Defense and Disarmament Studies, 2001 Beacon St, Brookline, MA 02146; (617) 734-4216. Nonprofit research and education center interested in nuclear disarmament, peace studies, American and world military affairs. Provides general reference services, permits onsite use of collections. Services free, except copying.

25147. Institute for Foreign Policy Analysis, Central Plaza Bldg, 10th Fl, Massachusetts Ave, Cambridge, MA 02139-3396; (617) 492-2116. Nonprofit org interested in intl relations, natl security, U.S./U.S.S.R. relations, military strategy. Provides reference services, distributes publications (some free), conducts seminars. Services designed for professionals in field.

25148. Institute for Graphic Communication, 375 Commonwealth Ave, Boston, MA 02115; (617) 267-9425. Interested in graphic communication, including all aspects of visual communication, marketing. Answers inquiries, provides consulting, conference program, reference services.

25149. Institute for Invention and Innovation, 33 Broad St, Boston, MA 02109; (617) 742-7840. Interest in intellectual property, patents, copyrights, inventions, trademarks, licensing, royalties, etc. Provides general reference services, conducts seminars, distributes publications, permits onsite use of collection. Services generally on a fee basis, but may be free.

25150. Institute for New Enterprise Development, Harvard Square, Box 360, Cambridge, MA 02238; (617) 491-0203. Nonprofit corp that promotes economic development. Interest in minority and small businesses,

etc. Provides general reference services, conducts seminars, distributes publications, permits onsite study. Some services free to low-income groups, at cost to others.

25151. Institute for Responsive Education, 605 Commonwealth Ave, Boston, MA 02215; (617) 353-3309. Nonprofit org that conducts studies of, and assists citizens involved in, educational decision making. Provides general reference services, distributes info, permits onsite use of collection. Services free.

25152. Institute of Agricultural and Industrial Microbiology, Dept of Environmental Science, Univ of Mass., Marshall Hall, Amherst, MA 01003; (413) 545-2288. Interest in soil microbiology, public health bacteriology, microbial physiology, antiseptics and disinfectants, related stuidies. Answers inquiries, makes referrals, provides consulting, permits onsite use of collection.

25153. Insulated Cable Engineers Association, P.O. Box P, South Yarmouth, MA 02664; (617) 394-4424. Interest in insulated copper and aluminum conductors for electric wire and cable, fiber optic cables. Provides free general reference services, distributes publications for a fee.

25154. Inter-Society Color Council, c/o Therese R. Commerford, Secretary, U.S. Army Natick R&D Center, Attn: STRNC-ITC, Natick, MA 01760; (617) 651-5469. Interest in research studies on color, application of color standards to science, art, and industry. Provides general reference services free.

25155. Interhelp, Box 331, (277 Main St), Northampton, MA 01061; (413) 586-6311. Nonprofit org interested in psychological responses to nuclear holocaust, environmental deterioration, and human oppression. Provides general reference services, conducts seminars, distributes publications. Answers inquiries free.

25156. International Association for the Study of Traditional Asian Medicine, c/o Dr Mitchell Weiss, Dept of Psychiatry, Harvard Medical School, Cambridge Hospital, 1493 Cambridge Ave, Cambridge, MA 02139; (617) 498-1000. Nonprofit assn that promotes the study of traditional medical systems of Asia and North Africa. Answers inquiries, sponsors conferences every five years, distributes publications, makes referrals. Services free.

25157. International Association of Arson Investigators, P.O. Box 600, (25 Newton St), Marlboro, MA 01752; (617) 481-5977. Interest in arson, fire investigation, law enforcement. Provides general reference services free to fire and police departments. Publications for members only.

25158. International Data Corp., 5 Speen St, Framingham, MA 01701; (617) 872-8200. Market research and consulting firm interested in gathering, analyzing, interpreting market data in the areas of computers, communications, office automation. Offers programs on subscription basis, including reports, seminars; unlimited telephone inquiry service.

25159. International Defense and Aid Fund for Southern Africa, P.O. Box 17 (Harvard Epworth Church, 1555 Mass. Ave), Cambridge, MA 02138; (617) 491-8343. Nonprofit group that provides legal defense for political prisoners in Southern Africa and humanitarian aid for their dependents. Answers inquiries and makes referrals free; distributes publications, some at cost.

25160. International Desalination and Environmental Association, P.O. Box 387, (Topsfield Crossing, 10 S Main St), Topsfield, MA 01983; (617) 887-8101. Interest in water desalination, water reuse, waste water reclamation. Answers inquiries, conducts seminars, distributes publications. Services provided at cost.

25161. International Fund for Animal Welfare, P.O. Box 193, Yarmouth Port, MA 02675; (617) 362-4944. Nonprofit org that campaigns against needless, cruel slaughter of animals worldwide. Interest in Canadian seal hunt, whaling, endangered species, marine mammal strandings. Answers inquiries, conducts workshops. Services free.

25162. International Kitefliers Association, c/o Will Yolen, President, 31 School St/Box 27, Hatfield, MA 01038; (413) 247-9010. Interest in kite flying, hang gliding, aerodynamics of unpowered flight. Provides general reference services free; publications for a fee.

25163. International Marketing Institute, c/o Dr Jerome B. Brightman, Executive Director, 29 Garden St, Cambridge, MA 02138; (617) 547-9873. Nonprofit education, research org that promotes worldwide understanding of marketing practices, market-oriented economies, export promotion, etc. Conducts courses, provides consulting, literature-searching services. Services provided at cost.

25164. International Nutrition Communication Service, c/o Education Development Center, 55 Chapel St, Newton, MA 02160; (617) 969-7100. Provides technical support for nutrition education/communication activities in the Third World. Provides general reference services, conducts seminars, permits onsite use of collections. Services free, except consulting.

25166. International Society for Bioelectricity, P.O. Box 82, Boston, MA 02135; (617) 431-1990. Scientific society that promotes research in electrical properties of biological materials, etc. Provides general reference services, conducts seminars, permits onsite use of collection. Services free, unless extensive.

25167. International Society for Cardiovascular Surgery, 13 Elm St, Manchester, MA 01944; (617) 927-8330. Interest in cardiovascular diseases. Publishes journal, answers inquiries, conducts biennial world congresses. Services free.

25169. International Union of Immunological Societies, c/o Baruj Benacerraf, Pres, Dept of Pathology, Harvard Medical School, 25 Shattuck St, Boston, MA 02215; (617) 732-1971. Interest in immunology, immunochemistry, cellular immunology, allergy, microbial immunology, organ transplants, cancer immunology,

standardization of immunodiagnostic reagents. Provides general reference services for free.

25170. Ionics, 65 Grove St, Watertown, MA 02172; (617) 926-2500. Interest in membrane separation processes, water and waste treatment, desalination by electrodialysis, etc. Provides general reference services, makes interlibrary loans. Some services free, others at cost plus fee.

25171. John G. Wolbach Library, Harvard College Observatory, 60 Garden St, Cambridge, MA 02138; (617) 495-5488. Interest in astronomy and astrophysics research, solar physics, cosmology. Provides general reference services, photocopying, permits onsite study. Services free to the scientific community, except for photocopying.

25172. Joslin Diabetes Center, One Joslin Pl, Boston, MA 02215; (617) 732-2400. Nonprofit org interested in diabetes mellitus research, treatment, and education. Answers inquiries and provides info on research in progress. Services free, primarily for medical scientists.

25174. Kendall Whaling Museum, P.O. Box 297, (21 Everett St) Sharon, MA 02067; (617) 784-5642. Collects and exhibits artifacts, memorabilia from American and foreign whaling and seal-hunting industries. Provides reference services free, permits restricted onsite use of collections. Fees charged for programs and publications.

25176. Labor Relations and Research Center, Univ of Mass., Amherst, MA 01003; (413) 545-2893. Provides academic training to graduate students, coordinates research in labor-management relations, labor law, etc. Provides general reference services, conducts seminars, distributes publications. Most services free.

25177. Laboratory for Computer Graphics and Spatial Analysis, Graduate School of Design, Harvard Univ, 48 Quincy St, Cambridge, MA 02138; (617) 495-2526. Interest in research and development related to computer graphics and spatial analysis, automated cartography, etc. Provides general reference services, distributes computer programs and publications.

25178. Laboratory for Manufacturing and Productivity, Dept of Engineering, MIT, Building 35, 234-C, 77 Mass. Ave, Cambridge, MA 02139; (617) 253-2234. Interest in computer-aided design and manufacture, robotics, materials processing. Provides general reference services, conducts seminars, distributes publications. Services available for a fee.

25179. Latin American Scholarship Program of American Universities, 25 Mount Auburn St, Cambridge, MA 02138; (617) 495-5255. Nonprofit assn interested in scholarships for all fields of study, Latin American and Caribbean higher education. Provides general reference services, conducts seminars, permits onsite use of collection. Most services provided at cost.

25181. Lincoln Institute of Land Policy, c/o Arlo Woolery, Executive Director, 26 Trowbridge St, Cambridge, MA 02138; (617) 661-3016. Interest in research and education in land economics, agrarian reform, land tenure and taxation in developing countries. Provides general reference services, permits onsite use of collections for those involved in related work.

25184. Marine Advisory Services, M.I.T. Sea Grant Program, E38-302, MIT, Cambridge, MA 02139; (617) 253-5944. Interest in coastal zone management, ocean engineering, seafood technology. Provides general reference services, distributes publications, permits onsite study. Services free, except for some publications.

25186. Marine Science and Maritime Studies Center, Northeastern Univ, East Point, Nahant, MA 01908; (617) 581-7370. Interest in high quality running sea water systems and controlled aquarium systems for maintenance of living organisms, interstitial fauna, etc. Provides general reference services, consulting, small-vessel time and space for research. Services available to investigators.

25187. Marketing Science Institute, 1000 Massachusetts Ave, Cambridge, MA 02138; (617) 491-2060. Interest in marketing management and planning, marketing resources, marketing environment, market measurement and analysis techniques. Answers inquiries, conducts seminars, distributes publications at cost and other services free to personnel of member companies, researchers.

25188. Massachusetts Historical Commission, 80 Boylston St, Boston, MA 02116; (617) 727-8470. State agency responsible for identifying, evaluating, and protecting historic properties in Mass. Provides general reference services, conducts seminars, permits onsite use of files. Services generally free.

25189. Massachusetts Historical Society, 1154 Boylston St, Boston, MA 02215; (617) 536-1608. Interest in American history from 16th Century to present, emphasis on New England and Mass. Answers specific inquiries, provides duplication services, makes referrals, permits onsite study.

25191. Massachusetts Technology Development Corp., 84 State St, Boston, MA 02109; (617) 723-4920. Nonprofit corp that provides capital to new and expanding high-tech enterprises that can generate employment growth in Mass. Provides general reference services, management assistance. Most info services free.

25193. Medical Rehabilitation Research and Training Center, Dept of Rehabilitation Medicine, Tufts Univ School of Medicine, Tufts-New England Medical Center, 171 Harrison Ave, Box 150, (75 Kneeland St), Boston, MA 02111; (617) 956-5032. Works to improve comprehensive rehabilitation services through an integrated program of research, therapy, etc. Conducts seminars, distributes publications. Services provided at cost.

25194. Medicine in the Public Interest, 65 Franklin St, Suite 304, Boston, MA 02110; (617) 482-3288. Nonprofit org that promotes, funds, and conducts research in health care and policy studies, patient education, adverse drug reactions, ethics. Conducts seminars, distributes publications free to Congress, at cost to others.

25195. Medieval Academy of America, 1430 Massachusetts Ave, Cambridge, MA 02138; (617) 491-1622. Interest in medieval architecture, armor, fine arts, geography, heraldry, history, law, literature, music, numismatics, philosophy, all other aspects of the civilization of the Middle Ages, 500-1500 A.D. Answers inquiries, makes referrals.

25196. Merrimack Valley Textile Museum, 800 Mass. Ave, North Andover, MA 01845; (617) 686-0191. Interest in history of textile industry, textiles, machinery, labor, mill architecture, etc. Provides general reference services, conducts programs and tours, permits onsite study. Services free, except copying and exhibits.

25197. Millipore Corp., Ashby Rd, Bedford, MA 01730; (617) 275-9200, (800) 221-1975. High tech multinatl corp that makes products for analysis and purification of fluids. Interest in precision microporous filtration, etc. Performs general reference services, accepts samples for trial filtrations, conducts seminars, lends films, slides.

25198. Minor Planet Center, Smithsonian Astrophysical Observatory, 60 Garden St, Cambridge, MA 02138; (617) 495-7244. Interest in minor planets and comets, astrometric observations, orbits, ephemerides, new names of asteroids. Answers inquiries, makes referrals, publishes materials.

25200. Missile Systems Division Technical Library, Raytheon Co., 350 Lowell St, Andover, MA 01810; (617) 475-5000 ext 2741. Interest in engineering and guided missile systems and subsystems. Services limited for non-company personnel to interlibrary loans and limited issuance of documents.

25202. Multipurpose Arthritis Center, School of Medicine, Boston Univ, 80 E Concord St, Boston, MA 02118; (617) 638-5180. Interest in research in arthritis and musculoskeletal diseases. Answers inquiries, provides consulting services, conducts seminars, evaluates data. Services generally free and available to anyone with related interests.

25203. Museum of Afro-American History, P.O. Box 5, Dudley Station, (Arch. Lab., 149 Roxbury St), Roxbury, MA 02119; (617) 445-7400. Interest in New England Afro-American history, authors, civil rights, archaeology, etc. Answers inquiries, makes referrals, conducts tours, distributes publications, permits onsite use of collection. Services free to members, at cost to others.

25204. Museum of Comparative Zoology Library, 26 Oxford St, Cambridge, MA 02138; (617) 495-2475. Interest in systematic zoology, paleontology, stratigraphy, oceanography, animal behavior, animal ecology. Provides general reference services, consulting, duplication services for a fee; permits onsite use of collection.

25205. Museum of Our National Heritage, P.O. Box 519, (33 Marrett Rd) Lexington, MA 02173; (617) 861-6559. Interest in American history, Masonic history. Provides general reference services, distributes catalogs, permits onsite use of collections. Services free, except for catalogs.

25207. Naismith Memorial Basketball Hall of Fame, P.O. Box 175 (460 Alden St), Highland Station, Springfield, MA 01109; (413) 781-6500. Interest in history of basketball, including personalities, events, and equipment of the entire game at all levels. Provides general reference services, permits onsite use of collection. Services free, except photocopying.

25208. National Archives and Records Administration, Columbia Point, Boston, MA 02125; (617) 929-4500. Interest in life and public careers of Kennedy family members, life and writings of Ernest Hemingway. Provides general reference services, permits onsite study, conducts lectures. Copying services provided for a fee; museum open to public.

25209. National Association of Emergency Medical Technicians, P.O. Box 334, Newton Highlands, MA 02161-0334; (617) 894-7179. Natl assn that represents emergency medical technicians. Provides general reference services, conducts seminars, awards grants, maintains malpractice legal defense fund, accredits paramedic education programs.

25210. National Braille Press, 88 St Stephen St, Boston, MA 02115; (617) 266-6160. Nonprofit org interested in printing and publishing both hard copy and paperless braille, large type production. Provides general reference services, offers printing press services to orgs. Contract work on a fee-for-service basis.

25211. National Building Granite Quarries Association, c/o H.E. Fletcher Co., West Chelmsford, MA 01863; (617) 251-4031. Interest in granite quarrying and fabricating. Answers inquiries, provides consulting services by members. Services generally free, unless extensive.

25212. National Bureau of Economic Research, 1050 Mass. Ave, Cambridge, MA 02138; (617) 868-3900. Interest in quantitative research in natl and intl economic problems such as public and private pensions, capital formation, business cycles, taxation issues, etc. Info provided primarily through the bureau's publications; no specific policy made.

25213. National Center for Death Education, New England Institute of Applied Arts and Sciences, 656 Beacon St, Boston, MA 02215; (617) 536-6970. Interest in funeral services, embalming, thanatology, including grief psychology, suicide, and hospices. Provides reference service without charge, permits onsite use of collection. All printed materials and audio cassettes available via interlibrary loan.

25214. National Commission for Cooperative Education, 360 Huntington Ave, Boston, MA 02115; (617) 437-3778. Provides training, info on cooperative education programs. Provides general reference services, conducts seminars and workshops, distributes publications. Services free, but membership donations encouraged.

25215. National Evaluation Systems, P.O. Box 226, (30 Gatehouse Rd), Amherst, MA 01004; (413) 256-0444. Interest in test administration, occupational tests, licensing tests, educational evaluation, etc. Provides advisory, test development and administration services; conducts seminars. Fees charged for all services.

25216. National Fire Protection Association, Batterymarch Park, Quincy, MA 02269; (617) 770-3000. Interest in development of fire prevention, fire fighting, fire protection, and public education. Answers inquiries, conducts studies and literature searches for a fee, provides limited consulting services to members, sells publications, permits onsite study. Services limited.

25219. National Head Injury Foundation, Box 567, Framingham, MA 01701; (617) 879-7473. Natl clearinghouse for info on head injuries. Interest in head injuries and related disabilities, related legislation. Answers inquiries, makes referrals, distributes publications. Services free.

25221. National Pediculosis Association, P.O. Box 149, Newton, MA 02161; (617) 449-6487. Nonprofit assn that provides info on pediculosis (head lice) through public education, consumer advocacy, and by encouraging research. Provides general reference services, conducts seminars, distributes publications; info packets available for $5, memberships for $25.

25222. National Scoliosis Foundation, P.O. Box 547, Belmont, MA 02178; (617) 489-0888. Nonprofit educational org interested in scoliosis, kyphosis, lordosis, and other spinal abnormalities. Provides general reference services, distributes publications. Services free, except for audiovisuals and bulk orders. Some services limited.

25223. National Society for the Preservation of Covered Bridges, 44 Cleveland Ave, Worcester, MA 01603; (617) 756-4516. Interest in history and preservation of covered bridges. Answers inquiries free.

25224. National Spinal Cord Injury Association, 149 California St, Newton, MA 02158; (617) 964-0521. Interest in spinal cord injury, community rehabilitation, basic neuroscientific research. Provides free general reference services and low-cost pharmacy program, conducts seminars, distributes publications.

25225. Nationwide Epidemiologic Study of Child Abuse, Florence Heller Graduate School for Advanced Studies in Social Welfare, Brandeis Univ, Waltham, MA 02254; (617) 647-2927. Surveys all legally reported incidents of natl child abuse during 1968-69, studies samples, and estimates total incidence. Answers inquiries, conducts seminars, distributes publications, data tapes. Tapes available to bona fide research groups for a fee; other services free.

25226. Naval Blood Research Laboratory, School of Medicine, Boston Univ, 615 Albany St, Boston, MA 02118; (617) 247-6700. Interest in hematology, research, development, testing, methods for preservation of blood, blood products, plasma proteins, etc. Answers inquiries, provides consulting services, reprints of articles, and training.

25227. Navy Clothing and Textile Research Facility, 21 Strathmore Rd, Natick, MA 01760; (617) 651-4172. Interest in clothing and textiles for men and women, including military uniforms, battle-dress, and protective clothing. Answers inquiries or refers inquirers to other sources of info.

25228. New Alchemy Institute, 237 Hatchville Rd, East Falmouth, MA 02536. Nonprofit intl org interested in development of ecologically derived forms of energy, agriculture, appropriate technology, fish farming, etc. Distributes publications, conducts workshops. Services free or at reduced prices to membership, open to anyone.

25229. New Bedford Whaling Museum, c/o Old Dartmouth Historical Society, 18 Johnny Cake Hill, New Bedford, MA 02740; (617) 997-0046. Interest in whaling history, including whaling artifacts and ships' logs and journals, New Bedford history. Museum open to public; library answers inquiries, provides reference services, and lends microfilm.

25230. New England Anti-Vivisection Society, One Bullfinch Pl, Boston, MA 02114; (617) 523-6020. Interest in use of living animals in scientific research, effects upon those who practice it and upon society. Provides general reference services, conducts seminars, distributes publications. Services free.

25232. New England Enzyme Center, Tufts Univ School of Medicine, 136 Harrison Ave, Boston, MA 02111; (617) 956-6653. Nonprofit pilot plant involved in isolation and purification of enzymes on a large scale. Answers inquiries, makes referrals, publishes materials. Services free.

25233. New England Fire and History Museum, 1439 Main St (Rte. 6A), Brewster, MA 02631; (617) 896-5711. Interest in U.S. volunteer firefighters from Revolutionary War through 1920s, various aspects of firefighting. Provides general reference services, distributes publications. Services free, except for publications.

25234. New England Forestry Foundation, 85 Newbury St, Boston, MA 02116; (617) 437-1441. Nonprofit educational corp interested in forest management and conservation, especially for small land owners; Memorial Forest Program gifts of forested land in New England.

Provides professional, educational advice to timberland owners at cost.

25235. New England Intercollegiate Geological Conference, c/o Dr D.W. Caldwell, Secretary, Dept of Geology, Boston Univ, 725 Commonwealth Ave, Boston, MA 02215; (617) 353-2534. Interest in geology of New England, N.Y., and eastern Canada, regional geology, petrology, mineralogy, paleontology, stratigraphy, hydrology, glacial geology, coastal geomorphology. Sells guidebooks.

25236. New England Marine Research Laboratory, Battelle Memorial Institute, Washington St, Duxbury, MA 02332; (617) 934-5682. Interest in marine research, oceanography, marine microbiology, marine ecology, biomedical research algae culture, etc. Performs general reference services, consulting on a cost-reimbursement basis, permits onsite reference.

25237. New England Regional Primate Research Center, Harvard Medical School, 1 Pine Hill Dr, Southborough, MA 01772; (617) 481-0400. Interest in research of living nonhuman primates, including comparative pathology, immunology, microbiology, primatology, etc. Performs general reference and copying services, makes interlibrary loans, permits onsite use of collection.

25238. New England Sights, 18 Brattle St, Ste 255, Cambridge, MA 02167; (617) 492-6689. Org interested in location of geologic sites, coastal shore areas important in marine biology and geology, cultural and historic sites. Provides general reference services, distributes data compilations. Services for a fee.

25239. New England Wild Flower Society, Garden in the Woods, Hemenway Rd, Framingham, MA 01701; (617) 877-7630. Nonprofit org that supports education and research in conservation, botany, ecology, and horticulture of native plants. Provides general reference services, makes interlibrary loans, permits onsite study. Direct borrowing of books available to members only.

25240. North American Clinical Dermatologic Society, c/o Edmund F. Finnerty, M.D., Secretary General, 510 Commonwealth Ave, Boston, MA 02215; (617) 536-8910. Interest in dermatology research and its clinical applications. Provides consulting services to members, distributes publication.

25241. Northeast Document Conservation Center, 24 School St, Andover, MA 01810; (617) 470-1010. Nonprofit, regional center specializing in conservation of library, archival material and art on paper. Provides general reference services, sponsors workshops, distributes publications. Services available for a fee.

25242. Northeast Metric Resource Center, Univ of Mass., 920 Campus Center, Amherst, MA 01003; (413) 545-1995. Develops plans for business, industry, govt, and general public to change over to metric system. Provides general reference services, conducts seminars, permits onsite use of collections. Services provided at cost.

25243. Northern Textile Association, 211 Congress St, Boston, MA 02110; (617) 542-8220. Interest in textile manufacturing and economics, product test methods and specifications. Provides general reference services, permits onsite use of collection. Services primarily for members, but available to others on limited basis.

25245. Norton Co. Library, 1 New Bond St, Worcester, MA 01606-2698; (617) 853-1000 ext 2278. Interest in abrasives, abrasive products, ceramics, diamonds, polymers, resins, refractories, chemistry, plastics, metallurgy, etc. Makes interlibrary loans, permits photocopying, permits restricted onsite study.

25246. Nuclear Metals, Inc., 2229 Main St, Concord, MA 01742; (617) 369-5410. Interest in metal powders, titanium, metallurgy, depleted uranium components, metal extrusion, bimetallic tubular joints, superalloy powders. Provides consulting, reference, and document services on limited basis. Access governed by patent and security requirements.

25247. Nuclear Negotiation Project, Program on Negotiation, Harvard Law School, 500 Pound Hall, Cambridge, MA 02138; (617) 495-1684. Interest in nuclear crisis control, long-range global conflict resolution, Soviet-American negotiation. Answers inquiries, provides advisory services, conducts seminars, distributes publications.

25248. Oakes Ames Orchid Library, c/o Harvard Univ Herbarium, 22 Divinity Ave, Room 324, Cambridge, MA 02138; (617) 495-2360. Interest in orchid systematics, floristics, and evolution; biology, including anatomy and cytology. Provides general reference services, permits onsite study by appointment. Services, except photocopying, free to students of orchidology.

25249. Ocean Research and Education Society, 19 Harbor Loop, Gloucester, MA 01930; (617) 283-1475; (800) 447-2022 (outside Mass.). Nonprofit scientific org interested in marine biology research, whales and dolphins, ocean ecology, nautical science. Conducts sail/study courses.

25250. Optical Systems Division Library, ITEK Corp., 10 Maguire Rd, Lexington, MA 02173; (617) 276-2643. Interest in optics, photography (especially aerial reconnaissance), graphic data processing, photogrammetry. Provides general reference services and copying, lends materials to libraries.

25251. Orthodox Theological Society in America, One Oxbow Rd, Lexington, MA 02173; (617) 862-8177. Interest in Orthodox theology, history of Orthodox churches in U.S. Answers inquiries, provides literature-searching services, makes referrals. Services available at cost.

25252. Pathfinder Fund, 1330 Boylston St, Chestnut Hill, MA 02167; (617) 731-1700. Public, nonprofit foundation interested in population, family planning, intl health. Provides general reference services, distributes publications. Services free, except some publications.

25253. Pen Pals Project, International Friendship League, 22 Batterymarch St, Boston, MA 02109; (617) 523-4273. Nonprofit org that promotes understanding among people of the world through personal letter exchanges. Answers inquiries, arranges letter exchanges. Services available for a registration fee.

25254. Percy Howe Memorial Library, Forsyth Dental Center, 140 Fenway, Boston, MA 02115; (617) 262-5200 ext 244. Interest in dentistry, dental hygiene, endodontics, preventive dentistry, caries research, orthodontics. Provides general reference services, permits onsite use of collections. Some services free.

25255. Phytopathological Translations Index, c/o F.W. Holmes, Director of Shade Tree Laboratories, Univ of Mass., Amherst, MA 01003; (413) 545-2402. Interest in phytopathology and mycology, including virology, nematology, and noninfectious injuries to plants. Provides general reference services, provides duplication services at cost, permits onsite use of index.

25256. Pilgrim Society, 75 Court St, Plymouth, MA 02360; (617) 746-1620. Nonprofit org interested in Plymouth, Mass. Pilgrims, colonial history, etc. Provides reference services, conducts seminars, distributes publications, permits onsite use of collections. Services free, except research and copying.

25257. Polaroid Corp., Library and Information Services, 730 Main St, Cambridge, MA 02139; (617) 864-6000 ext 3363. Interest in chemistry, physics, engineering, photography, basic and applied research, business. Provides general reference services and translation, permits onsite use of collections. Services and collections available to employees, qualified researchers.

25258. Polymer Research Institute, Univ of Mass., Amherst, MA 01002; (413) 545-2727. Interest in polymers and plastics with specialization in physical chemistry, light scattering, birefringence, and X-ray studies, etc. Answers inquiries, makes referrals, conducts scientific meetings, provides consulting services, permits onsite study.

25259. Product Assurance Materials and Components Engineering and Test, Missile Systems Div, Raytheon Co., Hartwell Rd, Mail Stop CS1-62, Bedford, MA 01730; (617) 274-7100 ext 4301. Interest in electronic circuit and device analysis, electrical test and evaluation, chemical and metallurgical analysis. Provides general reference services at cost, classified materials excepted.

25260. Program in Science and Technology for International Security, Dept of Physics, MIT, 20A-011, Cambridge, MA 02139; (617) 253-4248. Interest in scientific and technical issues of nuclear arms limitation, defense policy. Provides reference services, conducts seminars, distributes publications, permits onsite use of collections. Services free, technical reports.

25261. Public Affairs Research Institute, 12 Frost St, Arlington, MA 02174; (617) 641-3333. Evaluates educational, social, and training programs, special education, competency testing, bilingual education. Provides consulting services, conducts research and seminars. Services primarily for local educational agencies; others provided for a fee.

25262. Public Systems Evaluation, 929 Mass. Ave, Cambridge, MA 02139; (617) 547-7620. Conducts research on innovative concepts, e.g. electronic funds transfer, computer models and applications, etc. Provides general reference services, conducts conferences, distributes publications. Services, except simple inquiries, for fees.

25263. Railway and Locomotive Historical Society, P.O. Box 1418, Westford, MA 01886. Interest in railroad history. Answers inquiries, provides reference services. Services free.

25264. Reading Machine Department, Kurzweil Computer Products, 185 Albany St, Cambridge, MA 02139; (617) 864-4700. Commercial org interested in reading machine for the blind, computer that translates print into synthetic speech, optical character recognition. Provides general reference services, distributes publications.

25265. Research Institute for Educational Problems, 29 Ware St, Cambridge, MA 02138; (617) 868-0360 Nonprofit consortium concerned with social, educational problems of school-failing children, especially those with handicapping conditions. Provides info on research free, sells publications.

25266. Research Program on Communications Policy, Room E53-402, MIT, Cambridge, MA 02139; (617) 253-3144. Interest in interaction of various communications media with society, govt, one another; new media technologies. Provides reference services, conducts seminars, distributes publications, permits onsite study. Services free, except for publications.

25268. Resolve, P.O. Box 474, (497 Common St), Belmont, MA 02178; (617) 484-2424. Nonprofit telephone counseling service. Interest in infertility, artificial insemination, fertility drugs, etc. Provides general reference services free, conducts support groups, other services on a fee basis.

25269. Robert S. Peabody Foundation for Archaeology, Phillips Academy, P.O. Box 71, Andover, MA 01810; (617) 475-0248. Interest in American archaeology. Performs general reference and consultation services, artifact identification. Onsite study permitted by appointment.

25270. Science for the People, 897 Main St, Cambridge, MA 02139; (617) 547-0370. Nonprofit org interested in social and political impacts of technology. Answers inquiries, conducts workshops, distributes publications, makes referrals. Referrals free, other services available thru membership.

25271. Sea Education Association, P.O. Box 6, Woods Hole, MA 02543. Nonprofit educational institution combining classroom studies ashore with experience at sea aboard an oceanographic sailing ship. Answers inquiries, conducts courses. Research facility available to qualified investigators.

25272. Social Investment Forum, 222 Lewis Wharf, Boston, MA 02110; (617) 723-1670. Interest in investment of capital with social goals, costs, and needs as key criteria for asset allocation. Provides general reference services, conducts seminars. Fees scaled according to ability to pay.

25273. Social Welfare Research Institute, Boston College, 515 McGuinn Hall, Chestnut Hill, MA 02167; (617) 969-0100 ext 4070. Interest in social economic research on public assistance and the economy, econometric forecasting, simulation modeling, etc. Provides general reference services, conducts seminars, distributes publications. Services free or at cost.

25274. Society for Iranian Studies, c/o Center for Middle Eastern Studies, Harvard Univ, 1737 Cambridge St, Room 521, Cambridge, MA 02138; (617) 495-7596. Interest in culture, history, and politics of Iran. Answers inquiries, distributes publications, makes referrals to other sources of info. Services free.

25275. Society for the Preservation of Colonial Culture, c/o Vincent Kehoe, Pres, 52 New Spaulding St, Lowell, MA 01851; (617) 459-9864. Interest in American history prior to 1800, Iroquois Indians, Revolutionary War, British military orgs and methods. Provides general reference services, permits onsite study by appointment. Services generally free to libraries, at cost to others.

25276. Society of Arts and Crafts, 175 Newbury St, Boston, MA 02116; (617) 266-1810. Nonprofit org that promotes contemporary American crafts. Interest in American contemporary crafts in all media. Provides general reference services, permits onsite use of collections. Sponsors, conducts seminars for a fee.

25277. Society of Fire Protection Engineers, 60 Batterymarch St, Boston, MA 02110; (617) 482-0686. Intl professional org interested in fire protection engineering. Provides info, conducts seminars, and meetings.

25278. Sophia Smith Collection (Women's History Archive), Smith College, (Alumnae Gynmasium, Levels A and B), Northampton, MA 01063; (413) 584-2700 ext 2970. Archive of women's history sources documenting status, role, and achievements of women. Provides general reference services, conducts seminars, permits onsite use only of collections. Services, except photocopying, usually free.

25279. Sprague Electric Co. Library, North Adams, MA 01247; (413) 664-4411 ext 2355. Interest in chemistry, physics, materials sciences, chemical, electrical, and mechanical engineering, electronics. Provides general reference and translation services, consulting; permits onsite use of collection.

25280. State Lobster Hatchery and Research Station, Div of Marine Fisheries, Mass. Dept of Fisheries, Wildlife and Environmental Law Enforcement, Box 9, Vineyard Haven, MA 02568; (617) 693-0060. Conducts research on commercial growing of lobsters. Interest in basic lobster biology. Answers inquiries, provides consulting services, distributes publications. Services free.

25282. Stripers Unlimited, P.O. Box 45, (880 Washington St), South Attleboro, MA 02403; (617) 761-7983. Interest in conservation, preservation of the Maryland strain of striped bass; effects of chemical pollution. Answers inquiries free.

25283. Student/Teacher Organization to Prevent Nuclear War, 636 Beacon St, Room 203, Boston, MA 02215; (617) 437-0035. Educational org of high school students and teachers committed to reducing threat of nuclear war. Provides general reference services, conducts seminars, distributes publications. Services free, except for literature.

25285. Teledyne Engineering Services, 130 Second Ave, Waltham, MA 02254; (617) 890-3350. Interest in theoretical and experimental stress analysis, metals technology, including metal fatigue, metallurgy, applied mechanics, etc. Answers inquiries, provides consulting and engineering services for a fee, makes referrals, permits onsite reference.

25287. Thorstensen Laboratory, 66 Littleton Rd, Westford, MA 01886; (617) 692-8395. Interest in engineering and pollution control for leather, fur, hide, shoe, and textile industries, testing of materials and food, chemical analyses. Provides general reference services, consulting, conducts workshops. Services provided for a fee to all users.

25288. Titanic Historical Society, P.O. Box 53, Indian Orchard, MA 01151; (413) 543-4015. Interest in 19th and 20th Century North Atlantic liners, especially those of White Star and Cunard lines. Provides general reference services, distributes publications, permits onsite use of collection. Some services free to nonprofit users.

25290. Ukrainian Research Institute, Harvard Univ, 1583 Mass. Ave, Cambridge, MA 02138; (617) 495-3341. Interest in Ukrainian history, language, and literature. Answers inquiries, provides reference services, makes referrals, permits onsite use of collections.

25291. Union of Concerned Scientists, 26 Church St, Cambridge, MA 02238; (617) 547-5552. Nonprofit org of professionals interested in nuclear power plant safety, radioactive waste disposal, alternative energy,

etc. Answers inquiries, conducts public education programs, sells publications, permits onsite use of collection.

25293. United States Committee on Large Dams, c/o Charles T. Main, Prudential Center, Boston, MA 02199; (617) 262-3200. Natl committee on large dams, interested in improvements in planning, design, construction, maintenance, and operation of large dams. Answers brief inquiries, makes referrals.

25294. Urban Educational Systems, 75 Kneeland St, Suite 1106, Boston, MA 02111; (617) 482-4477. Nonprofit research and development firm specializing in arson prevention, housing and neighborhood rehabilitation. Provides general reference services, permits onsite use of library. Work usually done on a fee basis.

25295. WEEA Publishing Center, Education Development Center, 55 Chapel St, Newton, MA 02160; (617) 969-7100, (800) 225-3088. Reviews, publishes materials to promote educational equity and economic opportunities for women in U.S. Provides general reference services, conducts seminars, sells publications, permits onsite study.

25296. Weather Services Corp., 131A Great Rd, Bedford, MA 01730; (617) 275-8860. Provides meteorological forecasting services, real time and historical weather observations via computer interface. Answers inquiries, provides consulting services, supplies real-time, historical weather data.

25297. Wet Ground Mica Association, 715 Boylston St, Boston, MA 02116. Interest in research on use of 325 Mesh Muscovite Wet Ground Mica pigment in paints and thermoplastics. Answers brief inquiries, makes referrals, distributes publications.

25298. Wheelchair Motorcycle Association, 101 Torrey St, Brockton, MA 02401; (617) 583-8614. Interest in wheelchair motorcycles and vehicle adaptation for handicapped persons, especially for off-road operation. Provides general reference services, conducts seminars, distributes publications. Services free, primarily for members.

25299. Wild Goose Association, P.O. Box 556, Bedford, MA 01730. Interest in radionavigation, radio wave propagation, Loran-C, time distribution, coordinate conversion. Answers inquiries, makes referrals free, distributes publications at cost.

25300. Williams College Center for Environmental Studies, P.O. Box 632, Williamstown, MA 01267; (413) 597-2346. Sponsors, coordinates environmental education, research, and outreach activities. Interest in various environmental concerns, including pollution, energy, agriculture, etc. Provides reference assistance and consulting, conducts conferences open to public.

25301. Williams Ethnological Collection, Univ Libraries, Special Collections, More 216, Boston College, Chestnut Hill, MA 02167; (617) 552-3282. Interest in Caribbean culture and its African derivations, emphasis on

Jamaican ethnology, history to 1940. Noncirculating collection open to scholars, photocopy facilities available. Computer searches provided by reference department.

25302. Women's International Network, c/o Fran P. Hosken, Coordinator, 187 Grant St, Lexington, MA 02173; (617) 862-9431. Nonprofit org interested in women's development, and rights, intl women's activities and achievements, women's equality, etc. Provides general reference services, conducts seminars, distributes publications, permits onsite study. Services provided for fees.

25303. Woods Hole Oceanographic Institution, McLean Lab, Ouissett Campus, Woods Hole, MA 02543; (617) 548-1400 ext 2471. Interest in oceanography, biology, chemistry, geology, geophysics, ocean engineering, physical oceanography, marine policy, etc. Provides free general reference services to contracting agencies, permits onsite study.

25304. Worcester Foundation for Experimental Biology, 222 Maple Ave, Shrewsbury, MA 01545; (617) 842-8921 ext 282. Interest in biomedical sciences, with emphasis on molecular biology, reproductive physiology, and neurophysiology and behavior. Provides general reference services, permits onsite use of collection, lends materials.

25306. World Peace Foundation, 22 Batterymarch St, Boston, MA 02109; (617) 482-3875. Interest in intl orgs, foreign affairs, regional security, U.S.-Canada relations, U.S.-South Africa relations, U.S.-Latin America relations. Answers inquiries, makes referrals free, publishes materials.

Michigan

26004. A.E. Seaman Mineralogical Museum, Mich. Technological Univ, Electrical Energy Resources Center, Houghton, MI 49931; (906) 487-2572. Museum of mineralogy and geology with 60,000 specimens. Answers inquires, provides advisory and reference services. Services are free, but only qualified professionals are permitted hands-on use of specimens and equipment.

26006. Acheson Industries, Corporate Information Center, P.O. Box 8, Port Huron, MI 48060; (313) 984-5583 ext 503. Commercial org concerned with colloidal chemistry, carbon, graphite chemistry, lubricants and electronic chemicals. Answers inquiries and provides reference services free, unless extensive—primarily for corporate personnel.

26008. African Studies Center, International Studies and Programs, Mich. State Univ, 100 International Center, East Lansing, MI 48824-1035; (517) 353-1700. Serves as focus for development of teaching and research programs in African studies at the univ, offering undergraduate and graduate courses. Provides reference, consulting, and translation services; answers inquiries.

26009. Alcohol Research Information Service, 1120 E Oakland Ave, Lansing, MI 48906; (517) 487-9276. Collects and disseminates info about alcohol and alcohol products, their manufacture, sale, and use and their relationship to health. The "8:30 Monday Morning" program is for use with junior high and high school students.

26010. American Academy of Medical Administrators, 30555 Southfield Rd, Ste 525, Southfield, MI 48076; (313) 540-4310. Encourages scientific approach to medical administration and provides communication among health care administrators. Answers inquiries. Provides consulting, publications, data compilations, and referral services. Charges made only for attendance at educational institutes or seminars.

26011. American Amateur Baseball Congress, 215 E Green, Marshall, MI 49068; (616) 781-2002. Seeks to advance amateur baseball by stimulating interest and competition and by providing sound, experienced assistance. Answers inquiries, distributes publications, provides reference services for a fee.

26012. American Athletic Association of the Deaf, c/o Martin Belsky, 1134 Davenport Dr, Burton, MI 48529. Interest in sanctioning and promotion of state, regional, and national basketball and softball tournaments for the deaf. Inquiries are answered free.

26014. American Board of Prosthodontics, c/o Dr Brien R. Lang, Secty-Treas, 1415 Folkstone, Ann Arbor, MI 48105. Certifies competence in the specialty of prosthodontics. Answers inquiries, provides advisory services, distributes publications. Services free to eligible candidates or other professional individuals or orgs.

26015. American Concrete Institute, P.O. Box 19150 (22400 West Seven Mile Rd), Detroit, MI 48219; (313) 532-2600. Promotes design, construction, and maintenance of concrete structures and manufacture and use of concrete products. Answers inquiries and makes referrals. Services to non-ACI members limited.

26016. American Hotel and Motel Association, 1407 South Harrison Rd, Ste 310, East Lansing, MI 48823; (517) 353-5500. Publishes and distributes educational materials for use in training people for hospitality industry. Conducts seminars, makes referrals, distributes publications on a fee basis.

26017. American School Band Directors' Association, Box 146, Otsego, MI 49078; (616) 694-2092. Concerned with improvement of band music education, including research in music curricula, equipment, and facilities. Answers inquiries and distributes publications. Services available for a fee.

26018. American Society of Agricultural Engineers, 2950 Niles Rd, St Joseph, MI 49085; (616) 429-0300. Interest in application of engineering principles to the production and processing of food and fiber. Answers inquiries and makes referrals. Keyword indexes of all ASAE info are available.

26019. American Society of Colon and Rectal Surgeons, 615 Griswold, No. 1717, Detroit, MI 48226; (313) 961-7880. Society of surgeons interested in diagnosis and treatment of diseases of the colon and rectum. Answers inquiries or provides referrals, sells publications. Services are primarily for members, but others will be assisted.

26021. American Society of Limnology and Oceanography, Great Lakes Research Division, Univ of Mich., Ann Arbor, MI 48109; (313) 764-2422. Studies all aspects of fresh and marine waters, water quality manpower in aquatic sciences. Answers brief inquiries, provides limited career info. Referrals made to members of the society.

26022. Amphibian BioTech, P.O. Box 4120, Ann Arbor, MI 48106; (313) 482-2213. Raises and sells anuran or urodele amphibians to research and teaching markets. Services primarily for professional biologists and potential commercial producers of amphibians, provided for a fee.

26023. Ann Arbor Railroad Technical and Historical Association, P.O. Box 51, Chesaning, MI 48616; (313) 949-0288. Concerned with all aspects of the Ann Arbor Railroad, its predecessors and subsidiaries. Answers inquiries, provides reference services free, offers publications for a fee. Requests must include a SASE.

26024. Army Tank-Automotive Command, Technical Library, Warren, MI 48090; (313) 574-6470. Inspects and tests wheeled and tracked military vehicles and their components: ballistic armor, engineering, materials, etc. Answers inquiries, makes referrals, and provides literature to Dept of Defense and other authorized agencies.

26025. Artificial Language Laboratory, 405 Computer Center, Mich. State Univ, East Lansing, MI 48824-1042; (517) 353-5399 or 353-0870. Builds communication devices for individuals with handicaps due to neuromuscular or neurological conditions. Answers inquiries, provides consulting and reference services, most for a fee.

26026. Asian Studies Center, College of International Studies and Programs, Mich. State Univ, 101 Intl Center, East Lansing, MI 48824; (517) 353-1680. Concentration on Asian studies, particularly problems of rural development, theater, East Asian history, and American-East Asian relations. Answers inquiries and provides range of reference services free.

26029. Association for Healthcare Quality, 3550 Woodland Road, Ann Arbor, MI 48104; (313) 971-9492. Promotes quality assurance activities in health care by providing a forum for exchange of ideas on such topics as systems improvement, risk management, health records, and utilization review.

26030. Association of Driver Educators for the Disabled, 33736 LaCrosse, Westland, MI 48185; (313) 525-0362. Interested in driver education for the disabled. An-swers inquiries free, provides consulting and reference services, conducts seminars and workshops. Most services subject to a fee.

26031. Auto Leather Guild, c/o Mrs. Lorraine Schultz, Director, 776 Waddington Rd, Birmingham, MI 48009; (313) 646-5250. Sponsored by tanners of automotive leather in America. Answers inquiries, provides consulting and reference services—most for free.

26032. BASF Wyandotte Corp., Corporate Research Library, P.O. Box 111, Wyandotte, MI 48192; (313) 246-6200. Corporate library of inorganic and organic chemistry, chemical engineering, management and business. Some services available free to a limited number of qualified individuals by arrangement.

26034. Bureau of Michigan History, State Archive Section, Dept of State, 3405 North Logan St, Lansing, MI 48918; (517) 373-0512. Archival data on Mich. and its local subdivisions. Answers inquiries, provides reference services, makes referrals. Services are free, except for copying.

26036. Business and Institutional Furniture Manufacturer's Association, 2335 Burton SE., Grand Rapids, MI 49506; (616) 243-1681. Provides statistical and marketing data for institutional and business furniture industry. Answers inquiries, provides reference services, distributes publications, makes referrals. Services free to members, to others for a fee.

26038. Center for Electron Optics, Mich. State Univ, Pesticide Research Center, East Lansing, MI 48824; (517) 355-0484. Performs scanning electron microscopy and x-ray analysis, scanning-transmission EM with energy loss of biologic and inert materials. Provides consulting, electron microscopy, and x-ray analysis on fee basis.

26039. Center for Health Research, College of Nursing, Wayne State Univ, 5557 Cass Ave, Detroit, MI 48202; (313) 577-4134. Conducts research into nursing theory, health manpower, staffing economics, and other health issues. Answers inquiries and provides consulting services free to some users, at cost to others.

26040. Center for Japanese Studies, Univ of Mich., 108 Lane Hall, Ann Arbor, MI 48109; (313) 764-6307. Historical library of Japanese society and culture. Approved scholars may have access to material by appointment. Staff will answer questions, suggest other sources of info, and reproduce documents.

26041. Center for Near Eastern and North African Studies, Univ of Mich., 144 Lane Hall, 204 South State St, Ann Arbor, MI 48109; (313) 764-0350. Coordinates training programs on Near East and North Africa and administers degree programs. Answers inquiries, provides free advisory and reference services.

26043. Center for Research on Utilization of Scientific Knowledge, Institute for Social Research, Univ of Mich., P.O. Box 1248, Ann Arbor, MI 48106-1248;

(313) 764-2554. Studies the processes of knowledge utilization, adoption of research-based innovations and ethical issues in the use of scientific knowledge. Answers inquiries, distributes publications, provides research and consulting services for a fee.

26044. Center for Russian and East European Studies, Univ of Mich., Lane Hall, Ann Arbor, MI 48109; (313) 764-0351. Concerned with politics, history, and culture of the Soviet Union and Eastern Europe. Answers inquiries, conducts courses and lectures.

26046. Check Collectors Round Table, c/o Charles Kemp, Secty, 481 Kirts, No. 70, Troy, MI 48084. Promotes interest in numismatics by acquisition and study of checks, drafts, and other financial instruments. Provides consulting, reference, and copying services, answers inquiries, distributes publications. Services free, except postage and publications.

26048. Childbirth Without Pain Education Association, 20134 Snowden, Detroit, MI 48235; (313) 341-3816. Provides the public with quality childbirth education and monitoring services; promotes Lamaze method by providing educational materials to those interested.

26049. Christian Association for Psychological Studies, c/o Dr J. Harold Ellens, Executive Director, 26705 Farmington Rd, Farmington Hills, MI 48018; (313) 477-1350. Nonprofit professional assn promoting theoretical and applied relationships between Christianity and psychology. Answers inquiries and provides reference services. Reference services free; fees charged for clinical services, consulting, and publications.

26050. Citizens for Better Care, 1553 Woodward Ave, Ste 525, Detroit, MI 48226; (313) 962-5968. Acts as advocate for nursing home residents in Mich. and as watchdog on legislation affecting long-term care. Answers inquiries, provides consulting and reference services, sells publications. Services are free.

26051. Climax Molybdenum Co., Technical Information Department, 1600 Huron Parkway, Ann Arbor, MI 48105 (313) 761-2300. Promotes interest in metallurgy and chemistry of molybdenum and tungsten. Answers inquiries, provides reference services, distributes publications, makes referrals. Services are free.

26053. Commission on Professional and Hospital Activities, P.O. Box 1809 (1968 Green Rd), Ann Arbor, MI 48106; (313) 769-6511; (800) 521-6210. Offers data collection and research assistance to health personnel and institutions, publishes promotional brochures describing its data collection.

26054. Community Systems Foundation, 1130 Hill St, Ann Arbor, MI 48104 (313) 761-1357. Operates intl info service for persons and orgs concerned with improving human nutrition. Provides copies of library documents. Fees charged for literature and copying services.

26055. Computer and Automated Systems Association of SME, P.O. Box 930 (One SME Dr), Dearborn, MI 48121; (313) 271-1500. Provides coverage of computers and automation in the advancement of manufacturing. CASA/SME answers inquiries and provides literature on R&D in progress.

26056. Cooperative Information Center for Hospital Management Studies, Univ of Mich., 1021 E Huron, Ann Arbor, MI 48109; (313) 764-1380. Concerned with all aspects of management and planning, design and construction of hospitals, nursing homes, and other health care facilities. Answers inquiries, provides bibliographical services.

26057. Council of Citizens with Low Vision, 1315 Greenwood Ave, Kalamazoo, MI 49007; (616) 381-9566. Advocacy group for partially sighted people involved in obtaining federal money for purchase of vision aids and eliminating architectural barriers. Membership open to persons with low vision and their families.

26060. Defense Logistics Services Center (DLSC), Public Affairs Office, Federal Center, P.O. Box 3412, Battle Creek, MI 49016-3412; (616) 962-6511 ext 6644. Disseminates logistics info for the Federal Catalog System, a supply management tool used by U.S. armed services, civilian agencies, and U.S. allies. Answers inquiries, provides reference, abstracting, and indexing services free to qualified users, at cost to others.

26061. Detroit Public Library, Labor Collection, 5201 Woodward Ave, Detroit, MI 48202; (313) 833-1440. Library collection of labor history and economics in the U.S. and foreign countries. Provides duplication services for a fee, furnishes data, lends materials, makes referrals. Fees may be charged.

26063. Dossin Great Lakes Museum, Belle Isle, Detroit, MI 48207; (313) 267-6440. Museum of ships and shipping on the Great Lakes with historical and current info on ship names, owners, and engines. Answers inquiries on specific vessels and makes referrals. No browsing allowed.

26065. Dow Chemical Co., Technical Library, P.O. Box 1704, Midland, MI 48640; (517) 636-1098. Concerned with chemistry, plastics, agriculture, engineering, physics, and biology. Makes interlibrary loans and permits onsite use of collection with staff approval.

26066. Eaton Corp., Engineering and Research Library, P.O. Box 766 (26201 Northwestern Highway), Southfield, MI 48037; (313) 354-6979. Corporate library of metallurgy, mechanical engineering, and fluid power. Answers inquiries, provides reference service, and makes interlibrary loans when material is not available from other library sources.

26067. Edison Institute, Dearborn, MI 48121; (313) 271-1620. Institute consists of Greenfield Village and Henry Ford Museum, including research library and archives. Answers inquiries. Village and museum open to the public; library and archives mainly for museum staff, but others are aided by appointment.

26068. Ehlers-Danlos National Foundation, P.O. Box 1212 (15331 Cameron), Southgate, MI 48195; (313) 282-0180. Provides emotional support to patients and their families, and education for health professionals concerning Ehlers-Danlos Syndrome. Makes referrals and distributes reprints of articles on EDS and related issues.

26069. Environmental Resource Center for Community Information, Institute of Public Affairs, Western Mich. Univ, 116 Moore Hall, Kalamazoo, MI 49008; (616) 383-3983. Investigates problems of land use, water quality, transportation, public policy, community revitalization, resource recovery. Policy and technical assistance available on a fee basis.

26071. Folklore Archive, Wayne State Univ, 448 Purdy Library Bldg., Detroit, MI 48202; (313) 577-4053. Concentrates on orally transmitted culture, including narrative, song, proverb, belief, cures, attitudes, and oral history. Answers inquiries, provides consulting, reference and reproduction services. Except for copying, all services are free.

26072. Ford Forestry Center, Route 2, Box 736, Mich. Technological Univ, L'Anse, MI 49946; (906) 524-6181 Concerned with forestry, forest soils, reclamation of mine wastes, and forest economies. Answers inquiries, provides consulting services, lends documents, conducts workshops and seminars.

26073. Francis W. Kelsey Museum of Archeology, Univ of Mich., Ann Arbor, MI 48104; (313) 764-9304. Museum of art and archeology of the ancient Mediterranean world and Near East. Open to the public. Info on objects supplied on request, photographs supplied for a fee.

26074. GMI Engineering and Management Institute, Library, 1700 West 3d Ave, Flint, MI 48502; (313) 762-7814. Library of automotive, mechanical, electrical, and industrial engineering. Answers brief inquiries, makes referrals, provides bibliographic services.

26075. General Electric Co., Carboloy Systems Department, P.O. Box 237, GPO, Detroit, MI 48232; (313) 497-5000. Conducts research into powder metallurgy, metal cutting, milling cutters, and systems tooling. Answers inquiries, provides consulting services, makes referrals.

26076. Gerald R. Ford Library, 1000 Beal Ave, Ann Arbor, MI 48109; (313) 668-2218. Repository of documents bearing on the life and career of Gerald R. Ford as congressman, vice president, and president. Museum in Grand Rapids is open to the public, with free admission to persons under age 16 and to organized school groups.

26078. Great Lakes Commission, Institute of Science and Technology Bldg, 2200 Bonisteel Blvd, Ann Arbor, MI 48109; (313) 665-9135. Concerned with conservation, development, and use of water resources of Great Lakes Basin. Answers brief inquiries, makes referrals.

26079. Great Lakes Environmental Research Laboratory, National Oceanic and Atmospheric Administration, 2300 Washtenaw Ave, Ann Arbor, MI 48104; (313) 668-2235. Concerned with limnology, ecological modeling, lake chemistry, biology, climatology. Answers specific inquiries related to work of the laboratory and provides info and consulting services.

26080. Great Lakes Fishery Commission, 1451 Green Rd, Ann Arbor, MI 48105; (313) 662-3209. Seeks to improve and perpetuate Great Lakes fishery resources in U.S. and Canada. Relies on outside agencies, but answers inquiries.

26081. Great Lakes Sugar Beet Growers Association, 320 Plaza North, Saginaw, MI 48604; (517) 792-1531. Promotes Michigan's sugar industry, educates Michigan consumers and taxpayers about importance of the industry, and supports research. Answers inquiries, provides consulting and reference services.

26082. Grosse Ile Large Lakes Research Station, Environmental Protection Agency, 9311 Groh Rd, Grosse Ile, MI 48138; (313) 675-5000. Investigates movement and ultimate fate of pollutants in large lakes, with concentration on Great Lakes. Answers inquiries and issues reports.

26084. Immortalists Society, 24041 Stratford, Oak Park, MI 48237; (313) 967-3115. Provides financial support for cryobiological and gerontological research. Answers inquiries, provides consulting and reference services, makes referrals free.

26085. Industrial Technology Institute, Information Services, P.O. Box 1485 (1101 Beal Ave), Ann Arbor, MI 48106; (313) 769-4290. Established to improve American manufacturing productivity through technological change. Activities are in areas of automated manufacturing technologies. Provides consulting and reference services on a fee basis.

26087. Information Coordinators, 1435-37 Randolph St, Detroit, MI. Commercial publishing org concerned with all aspects of psychology and sociology of work. Offers work-related abstracts and sells publications.

26088. Information Management and Processing Association, c/o Ms. Pattie Seidl, 3112 Sablin Parkway, Lansing, MI 48901; (517) 374-4122. Interest in word processing, office information processing, careers in word processing, and continuing education. Answers inquiries, conducts seminars and workshops. Services are free.

26089. Informed Homebirth, P.O. Box 3675, Ann Arbor, MI 48106; (313) 662-6857. Nonprofit org offering a full range of homebirth services. Answers inquiries, provides reference services. Fees charged for workshops and publications.

26090. Infrared Information and Analysis Center, Environmental Research Institute of Mich., P.O. Box 8618, Ann Arbor, MI 48107; (313) 994-1200 ext 214. Investigates infrared technology, with special emphasis on military applications. Qualified users are Dept of Defense and their contractors with appropriate security clearance and demonstrated need-to-know.

26091. Inland Lakes Research and Study Center, Mich. State Univ, 334 Natural Resources Bldg., East Lansing, MI 48824; (517) 353-3742. Administers grants for regional water research. Interests are inland lakes research, eutrophication, and water related issues. Conducts seminars, provides info, makes referrals. Services are free.

26092. Institute for Fisheries Research, Mich. Dept of Natural Resources, Museums Annex Bldg, North Univ Ave, Ann Arbor, MI 48109; (313) 663-3554. Conducts research into physical and chemical features of Michigan's waters and sport fisheries. Answers inquiries, provides consulting on contract basis, makes materials available free to fisheries in other states.

26094. Institute of International Agriculture, Mich. State Univ, 101 Agriculture Hall, East Lansing, MI 48824; (517) 355-0174. Promotes intl programs on campus and overseas in academic dept programs in research, teaching, and extension. Provides info on R&D, conducts seminars, makes referrals in support of MSU programs.

26095. Institute of Mineral Research, Mich. Technological Univ, Houghton, MI 49931; (906) 487-2600 Provides R&D to mineral industry, primarily in areas of exploration geology and mineralogy. Answers inquiries, makes referrals, provides reference and consulting services for a fee.

26096. Institute of Public Policy Studies (IPPS), Univ of Mich., 1516 Rackham Bldg., 915 East Washington St, Ann Arbor, MI 48109; (313) 764-3490. Carries out a broad-ranging program of research on public policy problems. Answers inquiries, provides info on research, distributes discussion papers. Small handling charge for publications.

26097. Institute of Public Utilities, Graduate School of Business Administration, Mich. State Univ, 113 Olds Hall, East Lansing, MI 48824; (517) 355-1877. Researches public utilities economics. Answers inquiries, makes referrals, distributes publications.

26098. Institute of Technological Studies, Western Mich. Univ, Kohrman Hall, Kalamazoo, MI 49008 (616) 383-6040. Promotes metric education, training, and info services. Answers inquiries or refers inquirers to other sources. Provides consulting and conducts seminars on a fee basis.

26099. Institute of Wood Research, Mich. Technological Univ, Houghton, MI 49931; (906) 487-2464. Investigates Mich. forest areas, wood technology, chemical wood processing, and economics of wood production. Provides consulting services for a fee for extensive projects.

26100. Inter-University Consortium for Political and Social Research, P.O. Box 1248, Ann Arbor, MI 48106; (313)

764-2570. Serves social scientists by providing repository for machine-readable social science data and training in basic and advanced techniques. Answers technical inquiries, provides consulting and referral services to individuals belonging to nonmember institutions.

26101. International Association for Great Lakes Research, c/o Great Lakes Research Division, Univ of Mich., Ann Arbor, MI 48109. Conducts biological, chemical, and physical research on resources and uses in the Great Lakes and other large lakes. Answers inquiries, sells back issues of journals, and sponsors conferences on Great Lakes research.

26103. International Association of Voice Identification, c/o Lonnie Smrkovski, Chairperson, 714 South Harrison Rd, East Lansing, MI 48823; (517) 332-2521 ext 514. Investigates voice identification and acoustic analysis using sound spectrography. Answers inquiries. Provides consulting and reference services free, but costs assessed when travel is required for testimony.

26104. International Dwarf Fruit Tree Association, Horticulture Dept, Mich. State Univ, East Lansing, MI 48824; (517) 355-5200. Provides education and research on dwarfing of fruit trees, fruit tree training, and tree fruitfulness. Answers inquiries, supplies info, conducts meetings, distributes publications. Membership in association is open, on a fee basis.

26105. International Institute for Visually Impaired, 1975 Rutgers Circle, East Lansing, MI 48823; (517) 332-2666. Clearinghouse on the early development and education of visually handicapped preschool children. Services include publications and consultation for teachers and parent groups, and regional meetings.

26106. International Society for Fluoride Research, P.O. Box 692 (11670 Martin Rd), Warren, MI 48090; (313) 757-2850. Conducts research on biological effects of fluoride and its physical and chemical properties. Answers inquiries, provides reference services, distributes publications, conducts conferences. Services free, except for publications.

26107. International Trumpet Guild, c/o School of Music, Western Mich. Univ, Kalamazoo, MI 42008 Promotes communication among trumpet players and seeks to improve professional levels of performance, teaching, and trumpet literature. Answers inquiries and provides reference services free, except for publications,

26108. Kresge Eye Institute, Wayne State Univ, 3994 John R. St, Detroit, MI 48201; (313) 577-1320. Performs clinical research on cell biology of the eye, eye diseases, diabetes, and eye muscle physiology. Answers inquiries, provides info and reference services to scientists and students free or at cost, depending on the service.

26109. Kresge Hearing Research Institute, Univ of Mich. Medical School, Ann Arbor, MI 48109; (313) 764-8110. Conducts research into hearing, deafness, comparative physiology of hearing and cochlear prothesis implants. Answers inquiries.

26110. L. Lee Stryker Center for Management Studies, Kalamazoo College, Kalamazoo, MI 49007; (616) 383-8436. Management center promoting development, specialized training, and management consulting. Answers brief inquiries, provides consulting for a fee, makes referrals, conducts seminars with special interest in small businesses.

26111. LOEX Clearinghouse, Univ Library, Eastern Mich. Univ, Ypsilanti, MI 48197; (313) 487-0168. Sponsors biennial National Academic Library Orientation and Instruction Conference in May, and a workshop in alternate years. Answers inquiries, provides reproduction services, makes referrals. Annual membership fee is charged.

26112. Laboratory of Subsurface Geology, Dept of Geological Sciences, Univ of Mich., 2006 C.C. Little Bldg, Ann Arbor, MI 48109; (313) 764-2434 or 764-9405. Provides info on oil and gas wells in Michigan Basin, stratigraphy, sedimentary rock, geochemistry and carbonate diagenesis. Answers inquiries, provides reference and computer services at fees to cover costs.

26113. Leader Dogs for the Blind, 1039 South Rochester Rd, Rochester, MI 48063; (313) 651-9011. One of the largest guide dog schools in the world, trains over 300 blind people annually in the use of guide dogs. No charge for the services.

26114. MSU-DOE Plant Research Laboratory, Mich. State Univ, East Lansing, MI 48824; (517) 353-2270. Concerned with plant research and devlopment, molecular biology, genetics, biochemistry, energetics and the environment. Provides info on research in progress, distributes publications. Services free, primarily for scientists in related areas.

26115. Marble Institute of America, 33505 State St, Farmington, MI 48024; (313) 476-5558. Trade org concerned with dimensional stone and marble. Answers inquiries.

26116. Mental Health Research Institute, Library, Univ of Mich., 205 Washtenaw Pl., Ann Arbor, MI 48109; (313) 764-4202. Seeks to carry out basic research on causes of mental illness and develop strategies for its prevention and cure by bringing scientists together. Answers inquiries, permits onsite use of collections.

26117. Metal Finishing Supplier Association, 1025 East Maple Rd, Birmingham, MI 48011; (313) 646-2728. Provides info on metal finishing, primarily electroplating; finishing specifications and standards. Answers inquiries, makes referrals, distributes publications. Services free, except for some publications.

26118. Michigan Association for Computer Users in Learning, P.O. Box 628, Westland, MI 48185; (313) 595-2493. Interest in instructional use of computers, computer programs, computer products. Answers inquiries and provides referrals. Services free, except for publications.

26119. Michigan Basin Geological Society, c/o Geological Survey Division, Mich. Dept of Natural Resources, P.O. Box 30028, Lansing, MI 48909; (517) 373-7860. Interest in the Michigan Basin, geophysics and petroleum. Sells publications and conducts monthly meetings (Sept.-May) and field trips.

26120. Michigan Diabetes Research and Training Center, Medical School, Univ of Mich., Box 056, Ann Arbor, MI 48109; (313) 763-5256. Concerned with diabetes research, treatment, and training for health professionals. Provides advisory and information services at cost.

26121. Michigan Memorial-Phoenix Project, Univ of Mich., North Campus, Ann Arbor, MI 48109; (313) 764-6213. Encourages and supports research in peaceful uses of nuclear energy. Answers inquiries, provides consulting, reproduction, and irradiation services. Info and library services usually free.

26122. Michigan Molecular Institute, 1910 West St Andrews Rd, Midland, MI 48640; (517) 832-5555. Promotes education and research in macromolecular science and technology, including chemistry and physics of polymers. Answers inquiries, provides consulting and information services, conducts seminars and symposia. Services free, except for consulting and symposia.

26123. Michigan Pure Water Council, 424 River St, Lansing, MI 48933; (517) 485-6125. Nonprofit, educational org crusading for unfluoridated drinking water locally, statewide, and nationwide. Distributes publications, answers inquiries free.

26124. Michigan-Canadian Bigfoot Information Center, 152 West Sherman St, Caro, MI 48723; (517) 673-2715. Info source for data on "Bigfoot" or Sasquatch. Services free, except for reproduction services and publications, and available to anyone with serious intent.

26125. Middle English Dictionary Project, Univ of Mich., 555 South Forest, Ann Arbor, MI 48109; (313) 764-8296. Project editing and publishing a dictionary of English language of the 12th-15th Centuries. Answers inquiries, distributes publications, permits onsite use of collections. Services free or at cost.

26126. Motor Vehicle Manufacturers Association of the United States, Patent and Trademark Department Library, 320 New Center Bldg, Detroit, MI 48202; (313) 872-4311. Provides info on automotive technology, including parts and accessories, and automotive history. Answers inquiries, provides reference services to assn member companies. Facilities not generally open to public, but requests from individuals considered.

26127. Mueller Brass Co., Library, 1925 Lapeer Ave, Port Huron, MI 48060; (313) 987-4000. Library concerned with copper, brass, aluminum, forgings, extrusions, and metalworking. Materials available or on loan to local industrial libraries, public libraries, and trade assns.

26128. Multiloque, 321 Parklake Ave, Ann Arbor, MI 48103; (313) 663-3690. Commercial org interested in the development of projects using gaming and simulations as a policy tool. Answers inquiries, provides consulting services and info on R&D in progress. Services available for a fee.

26129. Museum of Anthropology, Univ of Mich., Univ Museums Bldg., Ann Arbor, MI 48109; (313) 764-0485. Museum of archeology, ethnology, anthropology, the Orient, Great Lakes; Latin and North American, African, Near Eastern, and European prehistory. Technical inquiries answered, citations made for professionals. Fees may be charged.

26130. Museum of Paleontology, Univ of Mich., Washtenaw and N Univ Aves, Ann Arbor, MI 48109; (313) 764-0489. Museum of morphologic, taxonomic, and stratigraphic aspects of fossil vertebrates, invertebrates, and plants. Answers technical inquiries and performs paleontological identifications for bona fide investigators.

26131. Museum of Zoology, Univ of Mich., Ann Arbor, MI 48109; (313) 764-0476. Zoological museum of evolutionary biology, mammalogy, ornithology, herpetology, ichthyology, malacology, and entomology. Answers inquiries, provides consulting services by arrangement for research scientists.

26132. National Association of Industrial and Technical Teacher Educators, c/o Industrial Education and Technology, Central Mich. Univ, Mt. Pleasant, MI 48859. Industrial and technical teacher education assn. Answers inquiries, conducts seminars, provides info and publications. Services primarily for dues-paying members.

26133. National Association of Investment Clubs, P.O. Box 220, Royal Oak, MI 48067; (313) 543-0612. Interest in investment principles, techniques, and procedures and how to apply them on a do-it-yourself basis or an through investment club. Answers inquiries, provides reference services, conducts seminars for a fee

26134. National Association of Photo Equipment Technicians, Photo Marketing Association, 3000 Picture Pl, Jackson, MI 49201; (517) 788-8100. Concerned with photographic equipment, including audiovisual equipment, test instrumentation, repair, and video equipment. Answers inquiries, provides reference services free.

26135. National Child Safety Council, P.O. Box 1368, Jackson, MI 49204; (517) 764-6070. Promotes child safety educational programs in cooperation with educators and law enforcement agencies. Provides pamphlets, manuals, posters, and folders geared to children's levels of understanding.

26136. National Coalition of Alternative Community Schools, 1289 Jewett St, Ann Arbor, MI 48104; (313) 769-4515. Provides a network for schools, coalitions, programs, and individuals involved in alternative education. Answers inquiries, provides advisory and reference services free to members.

26138. National Council on Stuttering, P.O. Box 8171, Grand Rapids, MI 49508; (616) 241-2372. Provides information about the prevention and treatment of stuttering. Publishes booklets for clinicians on stuttering therapy, parents' guides and self-therapy. There is a charge for all materials.

26139. National Guild of Decoupeurs, 807 Rivard Blvd, Grosse Pointe, MI 48230; (313) 882-0682. Provides general and special education in art form of decoupage. Answers inquiries; provides advisory services, seminars, special tutoring sessions, and publications for a fee.

26140. National Hearing Aid Society, 20361 Middlebelt Rd, Livonia, MI 48152; (313) 478-2610, (800) 521-5247. Offers assisstance in establishing and implementing hearing aid legislation and programs. Pamphlets and other documents are distributed in answer to recurring questions, and referrals are made.

26142. National Housing Center, College of Architecture and Urban Planning, Univ of Mich., 2000 Bonisteel Blvd, Ann Arbor, MI 48109; (313) 763-1275. Concerned with housing for the elderly and govt policy bearing on it. Answers inquiries, provides technical assistance and info. Services provided at cost to all users.

26144. National Institute for Burn Medicine, 909 East Ann Street, Ann Arbor, MI 48104; (313) 769-9000. Nonprofit health care support org dedicated to resolving the burn problem by supporting programs of patient care, education, research, and prevention of burns. Produces publications and films, conducts research.

26145. National Institute of Hypertension Studies, 13217 Livernois, Detroit, MI 48238; (313) 931-3427. Conducts research into relationship of psychosocial and occupational stress and hypertension in blacks in the U.S. Answers inquiries, provides reference, library, and other services free.

26146. National Orientation Directors Association, c/o Deborah M. Schriver, President, Western Mich. Univ, 2203 Student Services, Kalamazoo, MI 49008; (616) 383-1898. Seeks to stimulate communication about orientation and encourage and assist in enhancement of orientation programs. Answers inquiries, provides reference services, conducts conferences and workshops. Services free, except for publications.

26147. National Sanitation Foundation, NSF Bldg, Ann Arbor, MI 48105; (313) 769-8010. Provides research, education, standards, and service in relation to environmental health, pollution, and safe food handling. Answers inquiries, conducts seminars, makes referrals. Consulting and testing services avilable for a fee.

26148. National Spasmodic Torticollis Association, 905 North Wilson, Royal Oak, MI 48067 Formed to serve the needs of patients with spasmodic torticollis (ST), to bring ST patients together, to make the medical profession and public more aware of disease.

26149. National Superconducting Cyclotron Laboratory, Mich. State Univ, East Lansing, MI 48823; (517) 355-9671. Investigates nuclear physics, cyclotron design, superconducting magnets. Answers inquiries and permits onsite reference.

26150. National Trappers Association, c/o Don Hoyt, Sr., Pres, 15412 Tau Rd, Marshall, MI 49068 (616) 781-3472. Interest in annual fur harvest and control of furbearing animals by trapping. Answers inquiries, provides advisory services and educational programs. Services are free.

26151. Neurospora Genetics Laboratory, Dept of Biology, 126 Olin Hall, Albion, MI 49224; (517) 629-5511 ext 388. Provides materials and methods for the use of Neurospora in teaching. Answers inquiries, provides consulting and reference services. Supplies cultures of genetic strains. Services available to biology teachers.

26152. Non-Formal Education Information Center, College of Education, Mich. State Univ, 237 Erickson Hall, East Lansing, MI 48824; (517) 355-5522. Coordinates worldwide network of persons concerned with out-of-school education programs. Answers inquiries. Advisory, reference, and publications services available for those working in areas bearing on developing countries.

26153. North American Students of Cooperation, P.O. Box 7715 (530 South St), Ann Arbor, MI 48107; (313) 663-0889. Foundation interested in aspects of cooperative economic systems, including student housing, food, and other co-ops. Answers inquiries and provides reference services to non-members at cost.

26154. North Country Trail Association, P.O. Box 300, White Cloud, MI 49349. Trail stretches 3,246 miles from vicinity of Crown Point, N.Y. to Lewis and Clark Trail in N.Dak. Answers inquiries, provides reference services and publications at cost.

26155. Nuclear Reactor Laboratory, Division of Engineering Research, Mich. State Univ, East Lansing, MI 48824-1226; (517) 353-9097. Concerned with nuclear reactor irradiations, neutron activation analysis, and radioisotope preparation. Answers inquiries, provides irradiation and isotope preparation services at nominal cost to on- and off-campus researchers.

26156. Paleopathology Association, 18655 Parkside, Detroit, MI 48221; (313) 864-7944. Undertakes studies of diseases in antiquity, including autopsies of mummies, frozen bodies, skeletons, and coprolites. Conducts seminars, provides info, distributes publications. Services available to interested scientists.

26157. Pesticide Research Center, College of Agriculture and Natural Resources, Mich. State Univ, East Lansing, MI 48824; (517) 353-9430. Conducts studies on pesticides and their effects on animals, plants, man, and the environment. Answers inquiries, conducts seminars, performs research and pesticide analysis for research programs.

26159. Polymer Institute, Dept of Chemistry and Chemical Engineering, Univ of Detroit, 4001 West McNichols Rd, Detroit, MI 48221; (313) 927-1270. Conducts and sponsors basic and applied polymer research. Answers inquiries, provides consulting services, conducts seminars on a fee basis.

26160. Proaction Institute, 203 Evergreen St, East Lansing, MI 48840; (517) 351-6566. Nonprofit org assisting communities with planning and implementation of economic development activities. Answers inquiries and provides a range of reference services, including seminars, for a fee.

26161. Quaternary Research Laboratory, Dept of Geological Sciences, Univ of Mich., 1006 C.C. Little Bldg, Ann Arbor, MI 48109; (313) 764-1473. Coordinates research activities in quaternary geology at the univ. Answers inquiries, provides advisory or reference services, makes referrals. Services free, primarily for univ-related groups.

26162. R. L. Polk and Co., 431 Howard St, Detroit, MI 48231; (313) 961-9470. Publishes city directories based on information gathered in door-to-door canvasses and engages in direct mail advertising. Answers inquiries, distributes publications and magnetic tape data compilations for a fee.

26163. R.E. Olds Museum Association, 240 Museum Dr, Lansing, MI 48933; (517) 372-0422. Museum of transportation and automobile industry with emphasis on Lansing-built vehicles, including Oldsmobile, Reo, Star, Durant, and Bates cars and Duplex and Reo trucks. Also interested in life and career of R.E. Olds. Services available to anyone.

26166. Rehabilitation Institute, Learning Resources Center, 261 Mack Blvd, Detroit, MI 48201; (313) 494-9860. Nonprofit org concerned with rehabilitation of physically handicapped persons, physical medicine and therapy. Answers inquiries, provides reference and referral services, distributes publications free.

26167. Reye's Syndrome Society, P.O. Box RS, Benzonia, MI 49616; (616) 882-5521. Nonprofit org founded in 1976 by parents of a Reye's victim to stimulate and support research into disease. Society is supported by contributions and proceeds of fund-raising events.

26168. Robotic Industries Association, P.O. Box 1366, Dearborn, MI 48121; (313) 271-7800. Membership org of robot manufacturers, distributors, users, and others active in field of robotics. Provides reference services, conducts workshops and plant tours. Except for publications, services are free.

26169. Seaway Review, Harbor Island, Maple City Postal Station, MI 49664; (616) 334-3651. Concerned with Great Lakes shipping, economics, legislation, navigation, commerce, and U.S.-Canada relations. Provides consulting, reference, and publication services on Great Lakes issues.

26170. Seismological Observatory, Dept of Geological Sciences, Univ of Mich., Ann Arbor, MI 48109; (313) 763-4069. Conducts continuous recording of seismic waves. Answers inquiries, provides consulting free on a limited basis and at a nominal fee for extensive services.

26171. Seney National Wildlife Refuge, U.S. Fish and Wildlife Service, Seney, MI 49883; (906) 586-9851 Provides limited collection of frozen wildlife specimens to educational/scientific orgs. Answers inquiries and provides advisory services to anyone with proper approval.

26172. Society for Ethnomusicology, P.O. Box 2984, Ann Arbor, MI 48106; (313) 665-9400. Org of musicologists, anthropologists, students, and institutions that disseminates knowledge of the music of the world's peoples. Answers inquiries and provides reference services at cost.

26173. Society of Manufacturing Engineers, P.O. Box 930 (One SME Dr), Dearborn, MI 48121; (313) 271-1500. Assn involved in manufacturing management and research in tool and manufacturing engineering. Answers inquiries, provides copying for a fee, makes referrals.

26174. Society of Professional Archaeologists, c/o Dr William Lovis, Museum of Anthropology, Mich. State Univ, East Lansing, MI 48824; (517) 355-3485. Seeks to define archeological professionalism and define archeological research. Answers inquiries, provides consulting services, distributes pulications. Services free, except for consulting and publications.

26175. Speech and Hearing Sciences Laboratories, Dept of Audiology and Speech Sciences, Mich. State Univ, East Lansing, MI 48824-1212; (517) 353-8780. Investigates human communication: its disorders, voice identification through spectral analysis, and effects of noise. Answers inquiries, provides consulting, conducts seminars, makes referrals. Some services provided on a fee basis.

26176. Spill Control Association of America, 17117 W Nine Mile Rd, Ste 1040, Southfield, MI 48075; (313) 552-0500. Sponsors regional seminars and membership meetings on oil and hazardous materials spills. Answers inquiries, provides reference, abstracting, indexing, and referral services at cost to nonmembers.

26177. Student Advocacy Center, 420 N 4th Ave, Ann Arbor, MI 48104; (313) 995-0477. Nonprofit, volunteer org trying to ensure that public school students have access to all school benefits regardless of social class, race, or handicaps. Answers inquiries, provides reference services, conducts seminars. Services free, contributions welcomed.

26178. Survey Research Center, Institute for Social Research, Univ of Mich., P.O. Box 1248, Ann Arbor, MI 48106; (313) 764-8365. Makes large-scale studies to describe American public and explain its collective acts in the fields of economic and organizational behavior. Answers inquiries. Research conducted on a fee basis.

26179. Transportation Research Institute, Univ of Mich., Huron Parkway and Baxter Rd, Ann Arbor, MI 48109; (313) 764-2171. Concerned with highway accident investigation, human impact tolerance, emergency medical services and related problems. Answers inquiries, provides copying services, distributes publications. Fees are charged.

26181. Unicycling Society of America, c/o Al Hemminger, Secty, P.O. Box 40534, Redford, MI 48240 (313) 537-8175. Fosters social and athletic interest in the sport of unicycling among youth and adults. Answers inquiries free for SASE.

26183. United Automobile, Aerospace, and Agricultural Implement Workers, 8000 East Jefferson Ave, Detroit, MI 48214; (313) 926-5386. Concerns include collective bargaining and labor relations in automobile, aerospace, and agricultural implement industries. Answers brief inquiries and provides union literature free.

26184. University Center for International Rehabilitation, College of Education, Mich. State Univ, 513 Erickson Hall, East Lansing, MI 48824; (517) 355-1824. Transfers info from other countries that will improve rehabilitation of disabled individuals in the U.S. Answers inquiries, provides reference services, distributes publications. Services free, except for publications.

26186. Upjohn Co., Corporate Technical Library, Kalamazoo, MI 49001; (616) 385-7814. Library of pharmaceuticals, antibiotics, prostaglandins, pharmacology, chemistry, biomedical sciences. Makes interlibrary loans. Onsite use of collection permitted with clearance from library manager.

26187. Vickers, 1401 Crooks Rd, Troy, MI 48084; (313) 280-3000. Manufacturer of hydraulic equipment for converting, transmitting, and controlling power. Answers inquiries, provides consulting services, permits limited access to library. Services generally available, depending on workload.

26188. Volunteers in Prevention, Probation, Prisons, 527 N Main St, Royal Oak, MI 48067; (313) 398-8550. Creates volunteer programs in all areas of criminal justice, crime prevention, prosecution, probation, prison, parole. Answers inquiries, provides publications and consulting services through Univ of Alabama and centers throughout the nation.

26189. W.E. Upjohn Institute for Employment Research, 300 S Westnedge Ave, Kalamazoo, MI 49007; (616)

343-5541. Concerned with manpower training, income maintenance, economic analysis, social welfare, and labor-management relations. Answers inquiries, provides advisory services, makes referrals.

26190. Walter Reuther Library, Archives of Labor and Urban Affairs, Wayne State Univ, Detroit, MI 48202; (313) 577-4024. Serves as depository for United Automobile Workers, Michigan AFL-CIO, Industrial Workers of the World and many other unions' records. Approved researchers may use collections; archival assistance provided to labor unions and related orgs.

26191. Whirlpool Technical Information Center, Research Center-Monte Rd, Benton Harbor, MI 49022; (616) 926-5325. Emphasizes engineering and development of major home appliances, such as washing machines, clothes dryers, refrigerators, etc. Permits onsite use of literature collection.

26192. William L. Clements Library of Americana, Univ of Mich., South Univ St, Ann Arbor, MI 48109; (313) 764-2347. Library of early American history from period of discovery and exploration through Civil War. Approved researchers may have access to collection (an interview is required). Mail inquiries welcome.

26193. Wilson Ornithological Society, c/o Josselyn Van Tyne Memorial Library, Univ of Mich. Museum of Zoology, Ann Arbor, MI 48109 Source of scientific study of birds and their habits. Answers inquiries, holds annual meeting, makes referrals. Services primarily for members, others assisted.

26194. Women's Justice Center, 651 East Jefferson Ave, Detroit, MI 48226; (313) 961-7073. Offers legal info and referrals, makes proposals for legislative reform, and educates women and legal community. Answers inquiries, provides reference services, conducts seminars. Services free, primarily for women in Detroit area.

Minnesota

27001. Acid Rain Foundation, 1630 Blackhawk Hills, St Paul, MN 55122; (612) 455-7719. Interest in acid rain. Provides reference and copying services; conducts conferences, seminars; permits onsite use of collection. Services mostly free.

27002. Airline Medical Directors Association, c/o John Hodgson, M.D., Secty, Mayo Clinic, E19A, Rochester, MN 55905; (507) 284-2511. Concerned with airline aviation medicine, including physiological, biological, and human factors. Answers brief inquiries or refers inquirers to member specialists.

27003. Alternative Sources of Energy, Milaca, MN 56353. Publishes reports, bibliographies on use of renewable energy sources; provides advisory, reference services; permits onsite use of library. Fee for some services.

27005. American Academy of Neurology, 2221 Univ Avenue, SE., Ste 335, Minneapolis, MN 55414; (612) 623-

8115. Org composed of neurologists, pros in related fields who share goal of continued growth and development of neurological sciences. Handles requests for info by referrals to other orgs.

27006. American Association of Cereal Chemists, 3340 Pilot Knob Rd, St Paul, MN 55121; (612) 454-7250. Publishes magazines, books on cereal grains and seeds industries, including analytical procedures; answers inquiries; makes referrals. Services provided as time permits.

27007. American Association of Electromyography and Electrodiagnosis, c/o Ella M. VanLaningham, Exec Dir, 732 Marquette Bank Bldg, Rochester, MN 55904; (507) 288-0100. Interest in electromyography. Publishes specifications, guidelines, abstracts; maintains list of fellowships available.

27008. American Board of Physical Medicine and Rehabilitation, c/o Gordon M. Martin, M.D., Exec Secty-Treas, Norwest Center, Ste 674, 21 First St SW, Rochester, MN 55902; (507) 282-1776. Concerned with physical medicine and rehabilitation. Publishes pamphlets, answers inquiries, provides consulting services, prepares specialty examinations.

27010. American Citizens Concerned for Life, 6127 Excelsior Blvd, Minneapolis, MN 55416; (612) 925-4395. Natl citizens' group engages in educational, research, and service activities to promote respect and protection for human life. Publishes catalog of educational materials on abortion, provides advisory services, conducts seminars and workshops. Services at cost.

27011. American Collectors Association, P.O. Box 35106 (4040 W 70th St), Minneapolis, MN 55435; (612) 926-6547. Nonprofit trade assn of accounts receivable collection specialists. Publishes magazine, bulletin; conducts seminars, workshops. Services mostly free.

27012. American Orthopaedic Foot and Ankle Society, c/o Dr K.A. Johnson, Mayo Clinic, 200 First St SW, Rochester, MN 55905; (507) 284-2778. Publishes journal on medical, surgical care of foot and ankle; answers inquiries; conducts seminars; distributes publication. Services free.

27013. American Otological Society, c/o Secty-Treas, 200 First St SW, Rochester, MN 55905; (507) 284-2369. Advances medical and surgical otology, the anatomy, physiology, and pathology of the ear. Answers inquiries, conducts seminars, makes referrals, records scientific programs.

27014. American Pancreatic Association, c/o Dr V.L.W. Go, Exec Secty, Gastroenterology Unit, Mayo Clinic, Rochester, MN 55901; (507) 285-5711. Publishes abstracts, indexes on research on pancreas; provides consulting services, info on research in progress. Services at cost to those with biomedical interests.

27015. American Peony Society, 250 Interlachen Rd, Hopkins, MN 55343; (612) 938-4706. Interest in tree and herbaceous peonies. Publishes bulletin, book;

conducts seminars, workshops; provides peony seed on request; lends color slides. Services free.

27016. American Phytopathological Society, c/o Mr. Raymond Tarleton, Exec V.P., 3340 Pilot Knob Rd, St Paul, MN 55121; (612) 454-7250. Interest in phytopathology, the science of plant diseases. Publishes journal, monographs, college source book of lab experiments, career brochure; makes available slides on plant pathogens, teaching films; answers inquiries and makes referrals.

27017. American Rural Health Association, c/o Jacquelyn B. Admire, Div of Epidemiology, School of Public Health, Stadium Gate 20, Univ of Minn., 611 Beacon St, SE, Minneapolis, MN 55455; (912) 681-5144. Provides research, education, technical assistance to communities developing rural health programs; acts as resource for rural health policy at natl level; sponsors annual institute.

27018. American Society of Brewing Chemists, 3340 Pilot Knob Rd, St Paul, MN 55121; (612) 454-7250. Publishes journal, reports, standards, abstracts, research summaries for brewing industry; answers inquiries; conducts seminars, workshops. Services for a fee.

27019. American Thyroid Association, c/o Colum A. Gorman, M.B., B.Ch., Secty, Mayo Clinic, 200 First St SW, Rochester, MN 55905; (507) 284-4738. Interest in thyroid gland. Publishes abstracts of papers presented at annual meeting on thyroid gland; provides advisory, consulting services; conducts seminars, courses, workshops. Services mostly free.

27020. American Underground-Space Association, c/o Donald Gillis, Exec Director, 500 Pillsbury Dr SE, Room 122, Minneapolis, MN 55455; (612) 376-5580. Interest in effective use of underground space. Publishes journal, reports, reviews; sponsors conferences, workshops, design competitions; permits onsite use of collection. Services at cost.

27022. Association for Computers and the Humanities, c/o Donald Ross, Exec Secty, English Dept., Univ of Minn., Minneapolis, MN 55455; (612) 373-2541. Explores computer applications in linguistics, history, musicology, archeology, anthropology. Publishes newsletter, provides advisory services for a fee.

27023. Association of Asphalt Paving Technologists, c/o E.L. Skok, Jr., Secty-Treas, 134 CME Bldg, Univ of Minn., Minneapolis, MN 55455-0220; (612) 373-2518. Interest in asphalt technology, pavement condition, construction and design procedures. Has collection of annual conference proceedings; answers inquiries free.

27025. Association of Halfway House Alcoholism Programs of North America, 786 E 7th St, St Paul, MN 55106; (612) 771-0933. Promotes role of residential facilities caring for alcoholics. Provides consultation to members; holds conferences, seminars, workshops; publishes newsletters, directory. Fees for services.

27026. Bakken Library of Electricity in Life, 3537 Zenith Ave S, Minneapolis, MN 55416; (612) 927-6508. Collects documents on electromagnetism in life processes. Provides reference and copying services, conducts tours, permits onsite use of collection. Services mostly free.

27027. Biological and Agricultural Sciences Information Service, 1984 Buford Ave, St Paul, MN 55416; (612) 373-0947. Commercial firm interested in agriculture, forestry, veterinary medicine, food science. Provides data base searching services for a fee.

27028. Calix Society, 7601 Wayzata Blvd, Minneapolis, MN 55426. Assn of Catholics participating in Alcoholics Anonymous. Encourages abstinence; promotes spiritual development of members. Local units must obtain approval from bishop of their diocese.

27030. Center for Death Education and Research, 1167 Social Science Building, 267 19th Ave S, Minneapolis, MN 55455; (612) 376-3641. Concerned with issues surrounding mortality; sponsors research into grief, attitudes toward death. Provides speakers, conducts symposia and workshops, offers courses by television.

27033. Center for Residential and Community Services, Univ of Minn., 207 Pattee Hall, 150 Pillsbury Dr SE, Minneapolis, MN 55455; (612) 376-5283. Interest in residential facilities caring for mentally retarded. Publishes directory, provides advisory and consulting services, permits onsite use of collection. Services for a fee.

27034. Center to Study Human-Animal Relationships and Environments, 1-117 Health Sciences, Unit A, 515 Delaware St SE, Minneapolis, MN 55455; (612) 373-8032. Conducts research and disseminates info on human-animal relationships and their effects on human well-being. Serves as regional clearinghouse; helps develop courses and programs.

27035. Charles Babbage Institute for the History of Information Processing, Univ of Minn., 104 Walter Library, 117 Pleasant St SE, Minneapolis, MN 55455; (612) 376-9336. Interest in history and evolution of computing. Provides advisory, reference services; conducts seminars, workshops; permits onsite use of collection. Services for a fee.

27036. Citizens United to Reduce Emissions of Formaldehyde Poisoning Association, R.R. 9255, Lynnwood Road, P.O. Box 148C, Waconia, MN 55387 (612) 448-5441. Provides educational materials on hazards of working in areas contaminated by formaldehyde; organizes campaigns aimed toward federal agencies responsible for hazard control.

27037. Citizens' Scholarship Foundation of America, P.O. Box 297, St Peter, MN 56082; (507) 931-1682. Nonprofit org that coordinates student aid opportunities in private sector, such as Dollars for Scholars (community-supported scholarship program awarding non-interest honor loans).

27038. Communication Research Division, School of Journalism and Mass Communication, Univ of Minn., 206 Church St SE, Minneapolis, MN 55455; (612) 373-3369. Publishes and disseminates research reports on mass communications, role of media in society; answers inquiries.

27042. Dight Institute, Univ of Minn., 400 Church St SE, Minneapolis, MN 55455; (612) 373-3792. Owns family records with follow-up genetic studies on 5-7 generations. Provides reference, consulting, counseling services; permits onsite use of collection; publishes books, pamphlets.

27044. Emotions Anonymous, P.O. Box 4245 (1595 Selby Ave), St Paul, MN 55104; (612) 647-9712. Nonprofit intl org that acts as mutual support program for emotional health, patterned after Alcoholics Anonymous. Publishes monthly magazine. Services free

27047. Family Interest Group—Head Trauma, P.O. Box 375, Excelsior, MN 55331; (612) 473-8687. Nonprofit self-help org that provides support to persons with head injury; informs public about medical advances, educational programs, need for legislation to fund programs and services.

27048. FluiDyne Engineering Corp., Library, 5900 Olson Memorial Highway, Minneapolis, MN 55422; (612) 544-2721 ext 269. Publishes reports on aerospace research, alternate uses of energy. Provides copying services, lends materials, permits onsite use of collection. Services mostly free.

27050. Grain Elevator and Processing Society, P.O. Box 15026 (301 Fourth Ave S, Ste 365), Commerce Station, Minneapolis, MN 55415-0026; (612) 339-4625. Publishes safety training programs on grain industry; provides reference services; conducts seminars, workshops, expositions, conferences. Fee for some services.

27051. Hazelden Research Services, 1400 Park Ave S, Minneapolis, MN 55404; (612) 349-9400. Publishes research reports, pamphlets, books, audiovisual materials on research on alcoholism, drug dependency. Provides advisory and consulting services, permits onsite use of collection.

27052. Hockey Hall of Fame, P.O. Box 657 (Hat Trick Ave), Eveleth, MN 55734; (218) 749-5167. Honors Americans who made contributions to ice hockey; owns skates dating back to 1850; provides reference services free. Onsite use of collection restricted to serious students.

27053. Hormel Institute, 801 16th Ave NE, Austin, MN 55912; (507) 433-8804. Engages in cooperative studies on biochemistry of lipids; owns books, journals, research data. Publishes technical reports, annual report, brochure, two journals; answers inquiries.

27054. Human Growth Foundation, P.O. Box 20253, Minneapolis, MN 55420. Natl org of volunteers concerned with dwarfism. Offers parent education and mutual support, supports research, promotes public awareness of problems of short-statured people.

27055. Immigration History Research Center, Univ of Minn., 826 Berry St, St Paul, MN 55114; (612) 373-5581. Publishes research guides on immigrants. Provides reference, copying services; conducts seminars, workshops; permits onsite use of collection. Services mostly free.

27056. Immigration History Society, c/o Minn. Historical Society, 690 Cedar St, St Paul, MN 55101; (612) 296-5662. Promotes study of immigration to U.S. and Canada. Publishes newsletter and journal, provides consulting services and info on research in progress. Services free.

27057. Industrial Fabric Association International, 345 Cedar Bldg, Ste 450, St Paul, MN 55101; (612) 222-2508. Trade assn for industrial textile industry. Publishes journals, how-to manuals, directories, research reports; provides free consulting, reference services.

27059. Infant Formula Action Coalition, 310 E 38th St, Minneapolis, MN 55409; (612) 825-6837. Campaigns to stop corps endangering health of infants. Publishes research summaries, provides advisory and reference services, conducts seminars. Fee for some services.

27060. Institute of Child Development, Univ of Minn., 51 E River Rd, Minneapolis, MN 55455; (612) 373-9852. Conducts research in developmental psychology. Answers inquiries, conducts seminars and workshops, permits onsite use of collection by arrangement.

27061. InterStudy, P.O. Box S (5715 Chrismas Lake Rd), Excelsior, MN 55331. Performs research, consulting, technical assistance in delivery of health services. Publishes reports, provides reference services, permits access to library by appointment.

27063. International Childbirth Education Association, P.O. Box 20048, Minneapolis, MN 55420; (414) 542-6138. Promotes family-centered maternity and infant care; informs public through publications, conventions, conferences, teacher training, and assistance in forming childbirth education classes. Publishes journal, directories; provides advisory, reference services. Fee for some services.

27065. International Federation of Sports Medicine, 5800 Jeff Pl, Edina, MN 55436; (612) 922-0156. Publishes quarterly bulletin on sports medicine; answers inquiries free; conducts seminars, workshops, courses, congresses; makes referrals. Fee for some services.

27066. International Rescue and Emergency Care Association, 8107 Ensign Curve, Bloomington, MN 55438; (612) 941-2926. Works for improvement of standards, techniques of emergency care; disseminates info to rescue personnel; promotes organized rescue and emergency medical care throughout world.

27068. International Society for Plant Pathology, c/o Dr Thor Kommedahl, Secty-General and Treas, Univ of Minn., 1991 Buford Circle, St Paul, MN 55108. Publishes periodicals, directories, special reports on plant pathology; provides consulting services. Services usually free.

27069. International Species Inventory System, Minn. Zoological Garden, 12101 Johnny Cake Ridge Rd, Apple Valley, MN 55124; (612) 432-9010. Computerized system on animals in captivity, with data on 60,000 species. Provides info on physiological norms for captive species on cost-recovery basis. Phone inquiries answered free.

27070. Irish American Cultural Institute, 683 Osceola Ave (2115 Summit Ave, College of St Thomas), St Paul, MN 55105; (612) 647-5678. Gives awards to arts in Ireland; sponsors Irish cultural events in U.S.; conducts projects with Irish groups. Provides reference services. Services mostly free.

27072. James Ford Bell Technical Center Library, General Mills, 9000 Plymouth Ave N, Minneapolis, MN 55427; (612) 540-2801. Publishes bimonthly bulletin on food research and development; owns books, periodicals, pamphlets, patents; makes interlibrary loans; permits onsite reference by request.

27073. Lightning & Transients Research Institute, 2531 W Summer St, St Paul, MN 55113; (612) 631-1221. Publishes reports on lightning and static effects on aircraft, rockets, power transmission system, computer electronics. Provides consulting services on annual fee basis.

27074. Limnological Research Center, School of Earth Sciences, Univ of Minn., Minneapolis, MN 55455; (612) 373-4063. Publishes technical reports, journal articles on limnological research, especially of MN lakes and wetlands. Answers inquiries or makes referrals free.

27075. Livestock Conservation Institute, 239 Livestock Exchange Bldg S, St Paul, MN 55075; (612) 457-0132. Nonprofit org that initiates methods in livestock handling, marketing. Publishes standards, research summaries; conducts seminars, workshops. Services for a fee.

27079. Mayo Foundation, Pain Management Center, Dept. of Psychiatry, 200 First St SW, Rochester, MN 55901; (507) 284-2933. Provides treatment for patients with chronic pain and associated drug dependency. Answers inquiries free, conducts seminars and workshops for a fee, conducts research.

27080. Men's Rights Association, 17854 Lyons, Forest Lake, MN 55025; (612) 464-7887. Seeks to obtain equal rights for men. Provides divorce counseling, reference services; conducts seminars, workshops; refers to attorneys. Services to members for a fee.

27081. Middle East Peace Now, P.O. Box 14492, Minneapolis, MN 55414; (612) 699-0236. Publishes bibliographies, audiovisual materials, reprints with balanced view of Middle East; conducts conferences, seminars, workshops. Services mostly free.

27082. Mineral Resources Research Center, Univ of Minn., 56 E River Rd, Minneapolis, MN 55455; (612) 373-3341. Conducts contract research on development of mineral resources, including environmental engineering, mining technology; provides training in mineral engineering.

27083. Minnesota Bureau of Mediation Services, 205 Aurora Ave, St Paul, MN 55103; (612) 296-2525. Owns bargaining case histories between Minn. employers and labor orgs, impasse resolution journals, books. Answers inquiries. Info provided only for approved research.

27084. Minnesota Center for Social Research, Univ of Minn., 2122 Riverside Ave, Minneapolis, MN 55454; (612) 373-0236. Conducts research, sponsors workshops and conferences on social sciences. Provides consulting services; publishes monographs, reports. Services provided on grant or fee basis.

27085. Minnesota Environmental Sciences Foundation, Security Bldg, Room 312, 2395 Univ Ave, St Paul, MN 55114; (612) 642-9046. Publishes materials on environmental education for schools. Provides consulting services, conducts workshops, evaluates educational programs. Services at cost.

27086. Minnesota Historical Society, 690 Cedar St, St Paul, MN 55101; (612) 296-2143. Collects manuscripts, newspapers, photos, paintings on Minn. Provides reference services, allows onsite access of collection by appointment, provides copying for a fee.

27087. Minnesota Mycological Society, c/o Erma Lechko, Corresponding Secty, 4128 Seventh St NE, Minneapolis, MN 55421; (612) 788-3945. Publishes newsletter, cookbooks, papers on mushroom hunting; conducts workshops, mushroom forays; lends materials to members; answers inquiries. Services mostly free.

27089. National Association for Gifted Children, 2070 County Road H, St Paul, MN 55112; (612) 784-3475. Serves as public advocate for needs of gifted. Promotes research, publishes journal, provides names of programs for gifted. Some materials available free, plus mailing cost.

27091. National Ataxia Foundation, 600 Twelve Oaks Center, 15500 Wayzata Blvd, Wayzata, MN 55391; (612) 473-7666. Combats all types of hereditary ataxia. Conducts research on causes and treatment, sponsors free ataxia clinics, helps ataxia victims locate medical care, provides genetic counseling.

27092. National Avionics Society, 500 E 66th St, Richfield, MN 55423; (612) 866-8800. Interest in avionics, science of electronics applied to aeronautics and astronautics. Publishes newsletter, answers inquiries, provides info on research in progress. Services free.

27093. National Coalition of Resident Councils, 3231 1st Ave S, Minneapolis, MN 55408; (612) 827-8151. Coalition of residents, resident councils from long-term-care facilities. Develops strategies to improve the residents' quality of life; addresses pertinent legislation.

27094. National Council on Family Relations, 1219 Univ Ave SE, Minneapolis, MN 55414; (612) 331-2774. Publishes research journals, newsletters, books on marriage, family life; answers brief inquiries free; provides consulting services; sponsors conferences.

27095. National Council on Family Relations, 1910 W County Road B., Ste 147, St Paul, MN 55113; (612) 633-6933. Org providing forum for members on marriage and family life; has developed online bibliographic data base. Publishes research journal, newsletters, books on marriage and family life; answers brief inquiries free; provides consulting services.

27097. National Marine Electronics Association, P.O. Box 57, Oronoco, MN 55960; (507) 367-2568. Assn of marine electronics manufacturers and dealers. Publishes magazine, audiovisual training aids; conducts workshops, technician certification programs.

27098. National Minority Business Campaign, 65 22nd Ave NE, Minneapolis, MN 55418; (612) 781-6819. Encourages purchasing from minority-owned businesses. Publishes directory, answers inquiries free, provides reference and copying services on cost basis.

27099. National Railroad Construction and Maintenance Association, 6989 Washington Ave S, Ste 200, Edina, MN 55435; (612) 941-8693; (Minn.) (800) 752-4249; (U.S.) (800) 328-4815. Assn serving railroad construction industry. Publishes newsletter, safety manual, specifications, directory; provides law assistance; conducts seminars; serves as govt relations liaison.

27100. National Wildlife Refuge Association, P.O. Box 124 (67 E Howard St), Winona, MN 55987; (507) 454-5940. Nonprofit assn seeking to increase public understanding of Natl Wildlife Refuge System. Publishes newsletter, provides free advisory services.

27104. Northfield Historical Museum, P.O. Box 372 (408 Division St), Northfield, MN 55057; (507) 646-9268. Holds documents on 1876 Northfield First Natl Bank Raid of James-Younger gang. Provides reference services, permits onsite use of collection. Services mostly free.

27106. Northwestern College of Chiropractic Library, 2501 W 84th St, Bloomington, MN 55431; (612) 888-4777. Owns books, journals, videocassettes on chiropractic topics. Provides reference and copying services, permits onsite use of collection. Services mostly free.

27110. Prader-Willi Syndrome Association, 5515 Malibu Dr, Edina, MN 55436; (612) 933-0113. Assn for parents of children who suffer from Prader-Willi Syndrome. Provides forum for exchange of ideas, sponsors annual conference, publishes educational material.

27111. Quetico-Superior Wilderness Research Center, 215 W Oxford St, Duluth, MN 55803; (218) 724-0095. Publishes technical notes on ecological effects of natural,

man-caused perturbation in northern forest. Lends herbarium, seed specimens; permits onsite use of collection by arrangement.

27113. Seminar Clearinghouse International, 630 Bremer Tower, St Paul, MN 55101; (612) 293-1044, 293-1204. Consortium of companies, govt agencies that provides info on training programs to orgs for annual fee. Producers of training programs may register their services free.

27115. Sister Kenny Institute, 800 E 28th St at Chicago Ave, Minneapolis, MN 55407; (612) 874-4463. Provides diagnostic, vocational, therapeutic services for those with neurological, musculoskeletal difficulties. Publishes research reports, films; provides advisory, reference, abstracting services.

27116. Ski for Light, 1455 W Lake St, Minneapolis, MN 55408; (612) 827-3232. Encourages sports participation by visually, mobility impaired persons. Provides advisory, reference services; conducts seminars, workshops. Services free.

27117. Social Welfare History Archives, Univ of Minn. Library, Minneapolis, MN 55455; (612) 373-4420. Collects historical records of natl, state voluntary welfare orgs, social service leaders. Provides free reference service, permits onsite use of collection by researchers.

27118. Spinal Cord Society, 2410 Lakeview Drive, Fergus Falls, MN 56537; (800) 328-8253, in Minn.; (800) 862-0179. Advocacy org that seeks cure for spinal cord injuries. Supports research program, clinical center, computerized data and referral service with toll-free phone number.

27120. Standards Engineering Society, 6700 Penn Ave S, Minneapolis, MN 55423; (612) 861-4990. Nonprofit org that promotes technical standardization. Provides advisory, reference services; conducts conferences, seminars, workshops. Services mostly free.

27121. Student Letter Exchange, c/o Wayne J. Dankert, General Manager, 910 Fourth Ave, Austin, MN 55912; (507) 433-4389. Seeks to develop intl goodwill through pen pals in schools (correspondence is in English). Answers inquiries, provides names of pen pals in U.S. and foreign schools. Services for a fee.

27122. TECHNOTEC, Control Data Corp., Tech and Info Services, P.O. Box O, Minneapolis, MN 55440; (612) 853-3575. Intl technology exchange that links 15 countries through CYBERNET network. Provides advisory, reference services; provides info on technology for sale; conducts seminars, workshops.

27123. Trumpeter Swan Society, 3800 County Rd 24, Maple Plain, MN 55359; (612) 477-4255. Intl scientific org that promotes research on Trumpeter Swan. Publishes newsletter, provides consulting services, conducts seminars. Services free.

27125. Underground Space Center, Univ of Minn., 790 Civil and Mineral Engineering Bldg, 500 Pillsbury Dr SE, Minneapolis, MN 55455; (612) 376-5341. Conducts research on underground space use. Provides advisory, reference services; conducts seminars, workshops; permits onsite use of collection. Services mostly free.

27127. Vinland National Center, P.O. Box 308 (3675 Ihduhapi Rd), Loretto, MN 55357; (612) 479-3555. Disseminates info on sports for disabled. Provides advisory, reference services; conducts conferences, workshops; permits onsite use of collection. Services mostly free.

27128. Water Resources Research Center, Univ of Minn., 866 Bioscience Center, 1445 Gortner Ave, St Paul, MN 55108; (612) 376-5668. Publishes free circulars, bulletins containing current info on state and natl water resources research projects. Provides reference and advisory services, permits onsite use of collection.

27131. World Affairs Center, Univ of Minn., 306 Wesbrook Hall, Minneapolis, MN 55455; (612) 373-3799. Publishes monthly world affairs report; conducts seminars, workshops, lectures; makes referrals; permits onsite use of collection. Services mostly free.

Mississippi

28003. American Catfish Marketing Association, P.O. Box 1609, Jackson, MS 39205; (601) 948-5938. Assn of major processors of farm-raised catfish in Miss. and Ala. Interest in farm-raised catfish, catfish markets. Provides free general reference services, distributes publications and data.

28004. American Daffodil Society, c/o Miss Leslie E. Anderson, Exec Dir, Route 3, 2302 Byhalia Rd, Hernando, MS 38632; (601) 368-6337. Interest in growth, cultivation, hybridizing, exhibition, diseases, and improvement of daffodils. Answers inquiries free, sells publications and computer printouts, rents slide sets.

28005. Aquatic Plant Management Society, P.O. Box 16, Vicksburg, MS 39180; (601) 634-3542. Interest in all aspects of aquatic vegetation management, including field operations, research, and regulation. Answers inquiries, conducts meeting, distributes publications. Services provided free to members; membership open to anyone interested in the field.

28006. Bass Research Foundation, P.O. Box 99 (Old West Point Rd), Starkville, MS 39759; (601) 323-3131. Promotes and funds research to improve America's freshwater bass fishery resources. Provides general reference services, analyzes data. Services free.

28007. Boll Weevil Research Laboratory, Agricultural Research Service, USDA, P.O. Box 5367, Miss. State, MS 39762; (601) 323-2230. Interest in elimination of boll weevil as an economic factor in cotton production, cotton plant resistance to insects, pest management. Provides general reference services, conducts seminars, distributes publications. Services free, available to interested parties.

28008. Catfish Farmers of America, P.O. Box 34 (550 High St, Room 1602), Jackson, MS 39205; (601) 353-7916. Interest in research and marketing activities on catfish. Provides general reference services, conducts seminars, distributes publications. Services free.

28009. Cobb Institute of Archaeology, Box AR, Miss. State Univ, MS 39762; (601) 325-3826. Teaches and conducts research in archeology in the Middle East and North America. Answers inquiries, provides advisory and reference services, makes referrals. Services free.

28010. Concrete Technology Information Analysis Center, U.S. Army Corps of Engineers, Waterways Experiment Station, Structures Lab; (WES-SL), P.O. Box 631, Halls Ferry Rd, Vicksburg, MS 39180; (601) 634-3264. Interest in concrete technology, portland cement. Provides general reference services, conducts seminars, distributes publications, permits onsite reference. Services available to anyone; priority given to DoD. Costs determined on individual basis.

28011. Entomological Consultant Service, 551 Hillcrest Circle, Cleveland, MS 38732; (601) 843-3204. Interest in all areas of entomology, plant pathology, weed control, environmental evaluation, etc. Provides general reference services, conducts workshops, permits onsite reference. Services provided at cost except to municipal, county govts.

28012. Gulf Coast Research Laboratory/Museum, Ocean Springs, MS 39564; (601) 875-2244. Interest in systematic biology, ichthyology, marine invertebrates. Provides limited identification of fishes, permits onsite use of all collections by qualified scientists.

28013. Gunter Library, Gulf Coast Research Lab, P.O. Box AG, Ocean Springs, MS 39564-0951; (601) 872-4253. Interest in oceanography, marine biology, ecology, biochemistry, botany, ichthyology, etc. Provides general reference services, permits onsite reference, publishes materials, provides complimentary reprints to researchers on an exchange basis.

28014. Hydraulic Engineering Information Analysis Center, U.S. Army Corps of Engineers, Waterways Experiment Station, P.O. Box 631, Halls Ferry Rd, Vicksburg, MS 39180; (601) 636-3111 ext 2608. Interest in hydraulic engineering, flood control, etc. Provides general reference services, conducts seminars, distributes publications, permits onsite reference. Services available to anyone; priority given to DoD. Costs determined on individual basis.

28015. International Association of Industrial Accident Boards and Commissions, c/o J.T. Noblin, Exec Dir, P.O. Box 79109, Jackson, MS 39236; (601) 366-4582. Interest in workmen's compensation, industrial accidents. Provides general reference services, advisory services, publishes materials. Services primarily for members; others will be assisted.

28016. Mississippi Forest Products Utilization Laboratory, Miss. State Univ, Miss. State, MS 39762; (601) 325-2116. Interest in chemical, physical, and biological properties of wood and wood products, manufacturing processes of wood. Answers inquiries, provides consulting and reference services. Services free, but limited.

28017. Mississippi Mineral Resources Institute, Univ of Miss., Univ, MS 38677; (601) 232-7320. Conducts research in mining engineering, Landsat exploration, mineral exploration, land reclamation, etc. Provides general reference services, conducts workshops, distributes publications. Services free, except for postage and handling.

28018. Mississippi Museum of Natural Science, 111 N Jefferson St, Jackson, MS 39202; (601) 354-7303. Interest in Miss. wildlife, environmental education. Provides general reference services, identifies specimens, conducts free lecture tours, offers multimedia shows and films, permits onsite reference. Services available to students in natural sciences.

28019. NOAA Data Buoy Center, NSTL Station, MS 39529; (601) 688-2800. Natl center for environmental data buoy technology. Provides technical info, assists user orgs in design of data buoys and systems. Distributes materials on request.

28020. National Highway Safety Foundation, P.O. Box 479, Ridgeland, MS 39157; (601) 856-7146. Promotes safer highway travel, highway assistance. Answers inquiries, distributes publication. Services requests require $2 to cover mail and handling costs.

28021. National Seafood Inspection Laboratory, (F/S324), National Marine Fisheries Service, NOAA, P.O. Drawer 1207 (3209 Frederic St), Pascagoula, MS 39567-0112; (601) 762-7402. Interest in fishery products technology, product standards, quality and sanitation control, bacteria and parasites, etc. Answers inquiries, conducts seminars, provides speakers, furnishes reprints, permits onsite reference, provides inspector training services.

28022. Pavements and Soil Trafficability Information Analysis Center, U.S. Army Corps of Engineers, Waterways Experiment Station, P.O. Box 631, Halls Ferry Rd, Vicksburg, MS 39180; (601) 634-2734. Interest in pavements, vehicle mobility, soil trafficability. Provides general reference services, conducts seminars, distributes publications, permits onsite reference. Services available to anyone; priority given to DoD. Costs determined on individual basis.

28023. Project for Metric Research, Dept of Science Education, Univ of Southern Miss., Box 8298, Hattiesburg, MS 39401; (601) 266-4740. Interest in methods and materials for teaching metric system or Intl System of Units. Answers inquiries, provides consulting and reference services.

28024. Research Institute of Pharmaceutical Sciences, School of Pharmacy, Univ of Miss., Univ, MS 38677; (601) 232-7484. Interest in pharmacognosy, marine biology, pharmacology, medicinal chemistry, pharma-

ceutical marketing. Answers inquiries, provides consulting services, prepares analyses, makes referrals.

28025. Social Science Research Center, Miss. State Univ, P.O. Box 5287, Miss. State, MS 39762; (601) 325-3423. Interest in public health, alcohol studies, alcoholism, traffic safety, disaster studies, population migration, sociological characteristics of the aging. Answers inquiries.

28026. Soil Mechanics Information Analysis Center, U.S. Army Corps of Engineers, Waterways Experiment Station, P.O. Box 631, Halls Ferry Rd, Vicksburg, MS 39180; (601) 636-3111 ext 2223. Interest in soil mechanics, engineering geology, related fields. Provides general reference services, conducts seminars, distributes publications, permits onsite reference. Services available to anyone; priority given to DoD. Costs determined on individual basis.

28027. South Central Poultry Research Laboratory, Agricultural Research Service, USDA, P.O. Box 5367, Miss. State, MS 39762; (601) 323-2230. Interest in research on effects of environment and management on poultry performance. Answers inquiries, provides consulting services.

28028. Southern Rural Development Center, Box 5406, Miss. State Univ, Miss. State, MS 39762; (601) 325-5843. Works with govt and univs on rural modernization. Provides general reference services and consulting, conducts seminars, permits onsite reference. Services free, except publications, primarily for Southern land-grant institutions.

28029. Tennessee-Tombigbee Archives, Archives and Museums Dept, Miss. Univ for Women, W-Box 369 (Orr Bldg, MUW Campus), Columbus, MS 39701; (601) 329-4750 ext 325. Interest in Tennessee-Tombigbee waterway history. Permits unrestricted supervised use of archival documentation, provides reproduction services for a fee. Service hours restricted.

28030. U.S. Naval Oceanographic Office, NSTL Station, Bay St Louis, MS 39522-5001; (601) 688-4597. Collects marine data, produces data products, provides data services and technical support to U.S. Navy. Offers some reference services; other services require written request, with approval and costs determined on case-by-case basis.

28031. USDA Sedimentation Laboratory, P.O. Box 1157, Oxford, MS 38655; (601) 234-4121. Interest in sediment, sedimentation, sediment transport, sediment deposition, soil erosion, hydraulics, pollution. Provides general reference services, conducts seminars, evaluates data. Services free.

28032. Water Resources Research Institute, Miss. State Univ, Miss. State, MS 39762; (601) 325-2215. Interest in agriculture, engineering, economics, forestry, oil pollution, political influences, etc. Answers inquiries, makes referrals, provides detailed info on request.

Missouri

29001. Affirmative Action, 8356 Olive Blvd, St Louis, MO 63132; (314) 991-1335, 991-1338. Commercial firm interested in implementation of affirmative action programs. Provides general reference and consulting services, conducts seminars, distributes publications. Services free to job applicants; fees charged to employers.

29002. Agricultural Chemicals Library, Mobay Chemical Corp., P.O. Box 4913 (Hawthorn Rd), Kansas City, MO 64120. Interest in pesticides, agriculture, engineering, chemistry, biology, toxicology, manufacturing, marketing, management. Provides general reference services, distributes data compilations, permits onsite reference. Services generally free, but limited.

29003. American Academy of Family Physicians, 1740 W 92nd St, Kansas City, MO 64114; (816) 333-9700. Interest in production, delivery, financing of medical services by family physicians. Provides general reference services, consulting. Services primarily for members, but available to others as time permits.

29005. American Academy of Oral Medicine, 15 Princeton Pl, St Louis, MO 63130; (314) 721-3753. Interest in oral medicine. Provides general reference services, conducts seminars, distributes publications. Services free, except for journal.

29006. American Angus Association, 3201 Frederick Blvd, St Joseph, MO 64501; (816) 233-3101. Records ancestry and production of purebred Angus cattle, maintains genetic purity, promotes breed nationwide. Provides general reference services, conducts seminars, permits onsite reference. Services free, except meetings and some publications.

29007. American Association of Bioanalysts, 818 Olive St, Ste 918, St Louis, MO 63101; (314) 241-1445. Interest in bioanalysis, clinical chemistry, microbiology, hematology, immunohematology, laboratory management, certification. Provides general reference services, conducts workshops, analyzes data. Services available only to members, special groups.

29008. American Association of Orthodontists, 460 N Lindbergh Blvd, St Louis, MO 63141; (314) 993-1700. Interest in diagnosis and correction of malocclusion, public education concerning orthodontics, continuing education for orthodontists. Provides general reference services and reproductions, permits onsite use of collections. Services at cost to nonmembers.

29010. American Association of Veterinary Lab Diagnosticians, c/o L.G. Morehouse, Secty-Treas, UMC Veterinary Medicine Diagnostic Lab, P.O. Box 6023, Columbia, MO 65205; (314) 882-6811. Interest in diagnosis of animal diseases, standardization of techniques, laboratory accreditation. Provides general reference services, distributes publications. Services free to members, at cost to others.

29011. American Board of Orthodontics, 225 S Meramec Ave, St Louis, MO 63105; (314) 727-5039. Interest in examination and certification of orthodontists, orthodontic science and furtherance of its knowledge and capabilities. Answers inquiries, conducts exams toward certification. Services available only to orthodontic practitioners.

29012. American Hereford Association, 715 Hereford Dr, Kansas City, MO 64101; (816) 842-3757. Interest in breeding, promotion, and registration of Hereford cattle. Provides general reference services, provides performance records services for participating breeders, distributes publications. Fees charged for services.

29013. American Nurses' Association, 2420 Pershing Rd, Kansas City, MO 64108; (816) 474-5720. Promotes improvement of health standards and availability of health care services; higher standards of nursing. Provides general reference services, publishes materials, statistical data. Services primarily for members of nursing profession.

29015. American Optometric Association, 243 N Lindbergh Blvd, St Louis, MO 63141; (314) 991-4100. Interest in optometry, vision, health care. Answers inquiries, makes referrals, offers single copies of pamphlets (usually free), sells pamphlets in quantity, lends films, provides materials to other groups.

29017. American Polled Hereford Association, 4700 E 63rd St, Kansas City, MO 64130; (816) 333-7731. Interest in Polled Hereford breed of cattle, R&D of breeding stock, beef cattle production and marketing. Answers inquiries, conducts seminars and workshops, distributes publications. Services free, unless extensive.

29018. American Rhinologic Society, c/o Dr Pat A. Barelli, Secty, Penn Park Medical Center, 2929 Baltimore Ave, Ste 105, Kansas City, MO 64108; (816) 561-4423. Interest in nasal reconstructive surgery, rhinology, rhinologic and reconstructive surgery as it may apply to pulmonary-cardiac and systemic health. Answers inquiries. Services at cost to all.

29019. American Soybean Association, P.O. Box 27300, St Louis, MO 63141; (314) 432-1600. Interest in soybeans, soybean products, including production, processing, legislation, market development. Provides general reference services to nonmembers as time and personnel allow.

29020. AquaScience Research Group, 1100 Gentry St, North Kansas City, MO 64116; (816) 842-5936 Commercial firm that conducts research in aquaculture, mariculture, and aquariculture, manufactures related products. Provides general reference and consulting services, conducts seminars, distributes publications, permits onsite reference. Most services for a fee.

29021. Association of Conservation Engineers, c/o William F. Lueckenhoff, Mo. Dept of Conservation, P.O. Box 180, Jefferson City, MO 65102. Interest in engineering practices in fish, wildlife, and recreation developments. Answers inquiries on conservation-related issues.

29022. Association of Women in Architecture, 7440 Univ Dr, St Louis, MO 63130. Interest in women architects' position and opportunities in the profession. Provides consulting services on employment for women architects.

29023. Beer Can Collectors of America, 747 Merus Ct, Fenton, MO 63026. Social club interested in beer can collecting, cataloging, hunting, trading, and history, other brewery-produced items. Answers inquiries, makes referrals, publishes materials. Services free.

29024. Biological Control of Insects Research Laboratory, Agricultural Research Service, USDA, P.O. Box A, Columbia, MO 65205; (314) 875-5363. Interest in biological control of insects, use of parasites, predators, and pathogens of insect pests, pest management programs. Provides general reference services, conducts seminars, distributes publications. Services free.

29025. Boehringer Ingelheim Animal Health Technical Library, P.O. Box 999 (2621 North Belt Hwy), St Joseph, MO 64502; (816) 233-2571 ext 572. Interest in veterinary medicine, including bacteriology, virology, immunology, and pharmaceutical sciences, business management. Provides general reference services, makes interlibrary loans, permits onsite reference.

29026. Bounty Information Service, c/o Charles Laun, Dir, Stephens Post Office, Columbia, MO 65215; (314) 442-0509. Interest in bounties in North America. Service conducts yearly bounty surveys, various studies for bounty removal, etc. Answers inquiries, provides reference services, lends materials. Services free.

29027. Bureau of Mines, Rolla Research Center, P.O. Box 280 (1300 Bishop Ave), Rolla, MO 65401; (314) 364-3169. Interest in cobalt and nickel from Mo. lead ores, new base metal leach systems, carbonyl recovery, alloys, coatings, etc. Answers inquiries, makes referrals, provides consulting and mineral identification services.

29028. Camp Fire, 4601 Madison Ave, Kansas City, MO 64112; (816) 756-1950. Interest in skills for young people in leadership, citizenship, interpersonal relationships, community service programs, camping. Provides general reference services, conducts seminars, distributes publications. Services generally free, except publications.

29029. Cancer Research Center, 115 Business Loop 70 West, Columbia, MO 65205; (314) 875-2255, 875-2257. Nonprofit org interested in research in cancer immunotherapy, specifically use of lymphokines, cancer detection, public education. Answers inquiries, conducts seminars, lends materials, makes referrals, permits onsite use of collection. Services free.

29030. Center for Development Technology, Dept of Engineering and Policy, Washington Univ, Box 1106, St Louis, MO 63130; (314) 889-5494. Interest in bioresources, energy conversion, environmental conservation, medicine, technological innovation. Provides consulting, conducts courses, makes referrals, permits onsite use of collection. Teaching, consulting services for a fee, other services free.

29031. Center for Metropolitan Studies, Univ of Mo., SSB Bldg, Room 362, 8001 Natural Bridge Rd, St Louis, MO 63121; (314) 553-5273. Interest in community conflict resolution, economic development and employment, financing urban services, public policy, health policy. Answers inquiries free, conducts seminars and workshops, distributes publications for a fee.

29032. Center for Urban Programs, St Louis Univ, 221 N Grand Blvd, St Louis, MO 63103; (314) 658-3934. Interest in urban affairs, political science, sociology, policy analysis, urban economics, demography, health care politics. Provides general reference services, permits onsite reference. Services generally free, except copying.

29033. Center for the Study of American Business, Washington Univ, Campus Box 1208, St Louis, MO 63130; (314) 889-5630. Research org interested in public policy, its effects on American business. Conducts natl programs, distributes publications. One copy of publication free to anyone with valid occupational interest.

29034. Center for the Study of Metropolitan Problems in Education, Univ of Mo. (School of Education Bldg, Room 359), 5100 Rockhill Rd, Kansas City, MO 64110; (816) 276-2251. Interest in urban education, including school desegregation. Provides general reference services and consulting, distributes publications, permits onsite reference. Services free, except consultations and some publications.

29035. Central Institute for the Deaf, Washington Univ, 818 South Euclid Ave, St Louis, MO 63110; (314) 652-3200. Interest in education of the deaf, speech and hearing disorders, medicine, electrical engineering, especially acoustics, psychology. Answers brief inquiries, provides consulting services, makes referrals.

29036. Children's Hospital, Library, P.O. Box 14871 (400 South Kings Hwy Blvd), St Louis, MO 63178; (314) 454-6000 ext 7312. Provides concentrated selection of pediatric and nursing literature. Provides general reference services, makes interlibrary loans. Facilities and services available to those in related fields. Photocopy facilities provided on cash, fee-for-service, basis.

29037. Church of the Nazarene, Archives, 6401 The Paseo, Kansas City, MO 64131; (816) 333-7000. Interest in Church of the Nazarene, its history and the history of its precedent religious bodies, statistics of local churches. Provides general reference services and reproductions, permits onsite use of collections. Services free to serious researchers, except reproductions..

29038. Concordia Historical Institute, 801 De Mun Ave, St Louis, MO 63105; (314) 721-5934 ext 320. Interest in history, life, and theology of American Lutheranism. Provides general reference services and translations, permits onsite reference. Fees charged for most services. Access to archives and manuscript dept limited by terms of deposit.

29039. Cook Paint and Varnish Co., Central Research Laboratory, P.O. Box 389 (1412 Knox St), Kansas City, MO 64141; (816) 391-6003 through 391-6017. Interest in analysis, performance of all types of chemical coatings, polyester resins, acrylic resins, polyisocyanate, etc. Provides general reference services, consulting for a fee. Services mainly for scientists and medical personnel.

29040. Council on Clinical Optometric Care, American Optometric Assn, 243 N Lindbergh Blvd, St Louis, MO 63141; (314) 991-4100. Interest in standards for clinical optometric care, evaluation and accreditation of optometric clinical facilities. Answers inquiries, provides consulting, conducts seminars, distributes publications, makes referrals. Some services available only to professionals.

29041. Council on Electrolysis Education, P.O. Box 11812 (911 S Brentwood Blvd, Ste 236), Clayton, MO 63105; (314) 862-2111. Interest in educational programs in electrolysis, medications, equipment, professional ethics for electrologists. Provides general reference services and consulting, conducts workshops. Services free to some, at cost to others—primarily for professionals in electrolysis.

29042. Defense Mapping Agency, Aerospace Center, 3200 S 2nd St, St Louis, MO 63118; (314) 263-4266. Interest in astronomy, astronautics, earth sciences, mathematics, computer sciences. Provides general reference and consulting services, makes loans. Services available to DMAAC personnel and, on limited basis, to others who have interlibrary cooperation with DMAAC.

29043. Disabled Citizens Alliance for Independence, Box 675 (Hwy 49 and Vine), Viburnum, MO 65566; (314) 244-3315. Nonprofit org that provides independent living services for disabled, elderly through outreach programs, community education and development. Provides general reference services, permits onsite use of collection. Info referral services free, client services only to disabled and elderly.

29044. Division of Library and Archives, Mo. Historical Society, Jefferson Memorial Bldg, Forest Park, St Louis, MO 63112-1099; (314) 361-1424. Interest in U.S. history of 18th, 19th, and 20th Centuries, with emphasis on St. Louis, Mo., and the Mississippi River. Provides general reference services, conducts seminars, permits onsite reference. Services available for a fee to adult researchers.

29045. Educational Freedom Foundation, 20 Parkland, Glendale, St Louis, MO 63122; (314) 966-3485. Interest

in freedom of education, free choice in education, parental control of education, govt support of education, etc. Provides general reference services; conducts legal defense, seminars, workshops; promotes and conducts research; distributes publications. Services free or at cost.

29046. Environmental Trace Substances Research Center, Univ of Mo., Route 3, Columbia, MO 65203; (314) 882-2151. Interest in environmental research and services on physical and chemical substances in the environment. Provides general reference services, conducts seminars, performs tests. Fees charged for services.

29047. Freedom of Information Center, Univ of Mo. School of Journalism, P.O. Box 858, Columbia, MO 65205; (314) 882-4856. Interest in govt-compiled and controlled info, methods used by economic, social, and media institutions to control flow of info. Provides general reference services, distributes publications, permits onsite use of collections. Fees charged for services.

29048. Gaylord Memorial Laboratory, RFD 1, Puxico, MO 63960; (314) 222-3531. Interest in ecology and behavior of birds and mammals, wetland ecology, larval fishes, nutrient cycling, related topics. Answers inquiries.

29049. Gazette International Networking Institute, 4502 Maryland Ave, St Louis, MO 63108; (314) 361-0475. Nonprofit org interested in poliomyelitis, paralysis, neuromuscular diseases, accessibility, etc. Provides general reference and consulting services, conducts seminars, permits onsite reference. Services except consulting, onsite use, and publications free.

29051. Health Sciences Communications Association, 6105 Lindell Boulevard, St Louis, MO 63112; (314) 725-4722. Assn for those involved in application of communications technology to health sciences education. Provides general reference services, conducts seminars, distributes publications, offers job placement services.

29052. Independent Computer Consultants Association, P.O. Box 27412, St Louis, MO 63141; (314) 997-4633, (800) 438-4222. Interest in computer-related products and services, info processing. Answers inquiries, provides consulting, conducts seminars, distributes newsletter, makes referrals. Services free.

29053. Industrial and Technical Referral Center, Univ of Mo., 1020c Engineering Bldg, Columbia, MO 65201; (314) 882-3469. Interest in engineering, business administration, applied science. Provides general reference services, lends handbooks.

29054. Information Science Group, Health Care Technology Center, Univ of Mo., 605 Lewis Hall, Columbia, MO 65211; (314) 882-4906. Interest in health care technology research, computer applications in medicine, artificial intelligence in medicine, etc. Provides general reference services, bibliographic services at cost; sells publications. Price list supplied on request.

29055. Institute for Molecular Virology, St Louis Univ School of Medicine, 3681 Park Ave, St Louis, MO 63110; (314) 664-9800 ext 401. Interest in mechanism of replication of and cell transformation by DNA and RNA viruses, human cell molecular biology. Answers inquiries, makes referrals.

29056. Institute for Theological Encounter with Science and Technology, 221 N Grand Blvd, St Louis, MO 63103; (314) 535-3300. Nonprofit org interested in value-dimension of science and technology, especially social application of discovery. Answers inquiries free for members, at cost for others.

29057. International Association of Parents and Professionals for Safe Alternatives in Childbirth, P.O. Box 429, Marble Hill, MO 63764; (314) 238-2010. Explores, examines, implements family-centered childbirth programs, promotes education on natural childbirth. Provides general reference services, conducts seminars and certification programs, distributes publications, provides consulting.

29058. International Consumer Credit Association, 243 N Lindbergh, St Louis, MO 63141-7809; (314) 991-3030. Trade assn for individuals, firms, institutions involved in providing consumer credit service. Provides general reference services and consulting, sponsors courses. No charge for telephone inquiries, consultation, or referrals.

29059. International Flying Nurses Association, c/o Darlene Sredl, Pres, P.O. Box 1247, Ballwin, MO 63022; (314) 569-7763. Interest in aviation, nursing, flying nurses. Answers inquiries, provides consulting, conducts seminars, makes referrals. Services free.

29060. International Library, Archives and Museum of Optometry, American Optometric Association, 243 N Lindbergh Blvd, St Louis, MO 63141; (314) 991-0324. Interest in ophthalmic and related visual sciences; optometry, its historical and socioeconomic aspects; optometry as a profession. Provides general reference services, permits onsite use of collections to researchers only. Services free, except reproductions.

29061. International Society for Clinical Laboratory Technology, 818 Olive St, Ste 918, St Louis, MO 63101; (314) 241-1445. Provides educational materials, services for those in medical laboratory field, encourages self-improvement. Conducts workshops at cost to members, cost-plus basis to others; distributes newsletter free to members, at subscription rates to others; makes referrals.

29062. International University Foundation, 1301 S Noland Rd, Independence, MO 64055; (816) 461-3633. Promotes education and research worldwide in intl relations, socioeconomics, history, religious trends and movements. Provides general reference services, distributes publications, makes referrals. Services free to persons in higher education.

29063. Investigative Reporters and Editors, 26 Walter Williams Hall, Univ of Mo., Columbia, MO 65211; (314) 882-3364. Nonprofit org that helps journalists find info for publication or airing, acts as resource center. Provides general reference services, consulting; conducts seminars, conferences; distributes publications; permits onsite reference. Services available to nonmembers for a fee.

29064. Lupus Foundation of America, 11921 A Olive Blvd, St Louis, MO 63141; (800) 558-0121. Promotes public awareness of lupus erythematosus, expands research and patient education, strengthens physician training. Holds annual meeting, conducts media campaign. Scholarships provided, grants available.

29065. Make Today Count, P.O. Box 222, Osage Beach, MO 65065; (314) 348-1619. Nonprofit natl org that provides self-help support groups for patients with cancer, other life-threatening illness. Sells newsletter, conducts meetings.

29066. Mallinckrodt Library, Mallinckrodt, Inc., P.O. Box 5439, St Louis, MO 63147; (314) 982-5514. Interest in chemistry, pharmacology, and closely-related subjects. Provides reference, online searching services; makes interlibrary loans; permits onsite study.

29067. Masters & Johnson Institute, 24 South Kings Hwy, St Louis, MO 63108; (314) 361-2377. Interest in research, treatment, and education within broad fields of human sexuality and reproduction. Provides psychotherapy program, consulting services; answers inquiries; conducts seminars, workshops. Some services may be provided free or at reduced rates.

29068. May Department Stores Co., Information Center, 611 Olive St, St Louis, MO 63101; (314) 342-6300. Interest in retail trade, legal and tax info concerning real property, corps, and retailing, corp and retail business finance. Provides general reference services; permits onsite use of collection, except for retail statistics, with permission. Services free.

29069. McDonnell Aircraft Library, McDonnell Douglas Corporate Library, Dept H 465, P.O. Box 516; St Louis, MO 63166; (314) 232-8519. Interest in aeronautical and aerospace sciences, aerospace medicine, engineering, electronics, space science, acoustics. Permits onsite reference, makes limited interlibrary loans. Most materials governed by security and proprietary restrictions.

29070. Medical Literature Information Center, St Mary's Hospital Medical Ed. and Research Foundation, 101 Memorial Dr, Attn: Dr G.X. Trimble, Medical Dir, Kansas City, MO 64108; (816) 753-5700. Interest in all major clinical disciplines of medicine, medical history, pharmacotherapy, clinical toxicology. Provides general reference services and reproductions, distributes data, permits onsite reference. Services free to medical staff, at cost to others.

29071. Mid-America Arts Alliance, 20 W 9th St, Ste 550, Kansas City, MO 64105; (816) 421-1388. Interest in regional development and touring of arts programs, arts management, development of TV series on arts of Mid-America. Provides general reference and consulting services, conducts workshops, distributes publications. Services generally free within five-state area.

29072. Mid-Continent Regional Educational Laboratory, 4709 Belleview Ave, Kansas City, MO 64112; (816) 756-2401. Interest in elementary and secondary school improvement systems, postsecondary institutional improvement systems. Provides general reference services, conducts seminars, distributes publications. Services usually free.

29073. Midwest Community Education Development Center, Univ of Mo. at St Louis, 8001 Natural Bridge Rd, St Louis, MO 63121; (314) 453-5746. Interest in development of community education programs in Mo. Provides general reference and consulting services, conducts seminars, distributes publications. Services free.

29074. Midwest Research Institute, 425 Wolker Blvd, Attn: Harold E. Way, Librarian, Kansas City, MO 64110; (816) 753-7600. Interest in environment, toxic substances, pollution control, solid waste management, ecological assessment, energy conservation, etc. Provides general reference services and consulting, permits onsite reference, makes interlibrary loans.

29075. Missouri Prairie Foundation, P.O. Box 200 (1110 College Ave), Columbia, MO 65205; (314) 449-3761. Interest in preservation and restoration of Mo. prairies, prairies in general. Provides general reference services, conducts seminars and workshops, distributes publications, lends materials, permits onsite study. Services free, except books and loans.

29076. Missouri State Museum, Room B-2, Capitol, Jefferson City, MO 65101; (314) 751-2854. Interest in Mo. history, natural and industrial resources, technology of visual info presentation, applied sciences. Provides general reference services and consulting, identifies objects, prepares evaluations and studies. Museum open to public.

29077. Missouri Water Resources Research Center, Univ of Mo., Sinclair Rd-Rte. 3, Columbia, MO 65201; (314) 445-8008. Interest in aquatic biology and ecology, aqueous solutions, basin systems, climatology, ground- and surface-water hydrology, lake ecology, etc. Answers inquiries, makes referrals to specialists, distributes publications at cost.

29078. Morrison Observatory, Central Methodist Coll, Fayette, MO 65248; (816) 248-3391 ext 213 or 371. Concered with all aspects of stellar atmosphere calculations, particularly abundance and turbulent velocity analyses of stellar spectra. Answers inquiries, provides consulting.

29079. Multipurpose Arthritis Center, Washington Univ, Box 8045 (660 South Euclid Ave), St Louis, MO 63110; (314) 454-3586. Interest in arthritis, lupus, immune disorders, metabolic bone disease, rehabilitative medicine. Answers inquiries, provides consulting services, conducts seminars and workshops, distributes publications. Services free, available to health professionals.

29080. Museum of the Ozarks, 603 East Calhoun, Springfield, MO 65802; (417) 869-1976. Has collection of materials reflecting lifestyle of the 1890s in the Ozarks, Springfield and Greene County history. Provides general reference services, conducts seminars aand workshops, lends materials, distributes publications, permits onsite reference. Services free.

29081. National Association for Practical Nurse Education and Service, 10801 Pear Tree Lane, Ste 151, St Louis, MO 63074; (314) 426-2662. Accredits practical nursing programs, develops curricula for practical nursing schools, sponsors seminars, workshops, and conferences. Provides technical assistance to state assns, maintains computerized record, distributes transcripts.

29082. National Association of Animal Breeders, P.O. Box 1033 (401 Bernadette Dr), Columbia, MO 65205; (314) 445-4406, 445-9541. Concerned with animal breeding, reproduction and genetics, livestock improvement, artificial insemination, animal health. Answers inquiries, makes referrals.

29083. National Association of Insurance Commissioners Library, National Association of Insurance Commissioners, 1125 Grand Ave, Kansas City, MO 64106; (816) 842-3600. Voluntary assn interested in insurance regulation, insurance law, insurance and actuarial studies generally. Provides general reference services, distributes publications. Hourly research fee charged to nongovt requesters; fees charged for reproductions, publications.

29084. National Association of Intercollegiate Athletics, c/o Dr Harry G. Fritz, Exec Dir, 1221 Baltimore Ave, Kansas City, MO 64105; (816) 842-5050. Administers a natl intercollegiate athletic program. Provides general reference services, conducts workshops and clinics, analyzes data, distributes publications. Services free to members, at cost to others.

29085. National Association of Medical Examiners, 1402 S Grand Blvd, St Louis, MO 63104; (314) 664-9800. Assn composed of medical examiners, pathologists, other licensed physicians having responsibilities in official investigations of sudden, suspicious, and violent deaths. Answers inquiries, publishes journal, makes referrals. Fees determined individually.

29086. National Association of Parents and Professionals for Safe Alternatives in Childbirth, P.O. Box 428, Marble Hill, MO 63764; (314) 238-2010. Implements and establishes family-centered childbirth programs. Provides general reference services, conducts public conferences and seminars for fees, certifies childbirth leaders and special agents, sells publications.

29087. National Bowling Hall of Fame and Museum, 111 Stadium Plaza, St Louis, MO 63102; (314) 231-6340. Natl nonprofit historic and educational org interested in bowling: its history, equipment, artifacts. Answer inquiries, publishes materials, permits onsite use of library and archives to qualified persons.

29088. National Clearinghouse, Nuclear Weapons Freeze Campaign, Nuclear Weapons Freeze Campaign, 4144 Lindell Blvd, Ste 404, St Louis, MO 63108; (314) 533-1169. Interest in organizing, fund raising, lobbying for a bilateral U.S.-Soviet freeze of nuclear weapons. Gathers info; provides training, technical assistance to activists, organizers.

29089. National Council of State Garden Clubs, 4401 Magnolia Ave, St Louis, MO 63110; (314) 776-7574. Nonprofit council interested in garden clubs, civic beauty, botanical and horticultural centers, gardening, etc. Answers inquiries, makes referrals. Services primarily for members.

29090. National Decorating Products Association, 1050 N Lindbergh Blvd, St Louis, MO 63132; (314) 991-3470. Interest in retail trade in paints, wallcoverings, window blinds, draperies, related equipment, marketing data. Provides general reference services, conducts seminars and workshops, lends materials, distributes publications, permits onsite reference. Fees charged for services.

29091. National Federation of Press Women, c/o Lois Lauer Wolfe, Exec Administrator, P.O. Box 99, Blue Springs, MO 64015; (816) 229-1666. Interest in women employed in mass communication, improvement of journalistic skills, conditions of employment, etc. Answers inquiries, conducts seminars, provides current-awareness services, offers scholarships.

29092. National Federation of State High School Associations, P.O. Box 20626 (11724 Plaza Circle), Kansas City, MO 64195; (816) 464-5400. Interest in high school athletics and activities. Answers inquiries, provides consulting services, makes referrals, permits onsite reference.

29093. National Food and Energy Council, 409 Vandiver West, Ste 202, Columbia, MO 65202; (314) 875-7155. Membership org interested in R&D relating to interdependence of food and energy. Provides general reference services, conducts workshops, distributes publications. Most services provided for a fee.

29094. National Hairdressors and Cosmetologists Association, 3510 Olive St, St Louis, MO 63103; (314) 534-7980. Promotes education in cosmetology industry, sponsors Natl Cosmetology Week, beauty shows. Answers inquiries, conducts conferences and beauty shows, sponsors courses at univs, makes referrals.

29095. National Lubricating Grease Institute, 4635 Wyandotte St, Ste 202, Kansas City, MO 64112; (816) 931-9480. Interest in grease lubrication. Answers inquiries, publishes materials, makes referrals, provides bibliographic services.

29096. National Museum of Transport, 3015 Barrett Station Rd, St Louis, MO 63122-3398; (314) 965-7998. Collection includes transportation and communication devices of historical interest. Provides general reference services, identifies documents, provides duplication services. Museum open to public for admission fee; access to library given to accredited visitors by appointment.

29097. National Prairie Grouse Technical Council, c/o Richard Cannon, Mo. Dept of Conservation, 1110 College Ave, Columbia, MO 65201. Council interested in status, ecology, biology, management problems of Greater and Lesser Prairie Chicken, Sharptailed Grouse, and Sage Grouse in North America. Answers inquiries, makes referrals, provides consulting.

29098. National Rural Health Care Association, 2220 Holmes, Kansas City, MO 64108; (816) 421-3075. Natl assn dedicated to improvement of health care services in rural areas. Provides reference services, sponsors nation's largest annual conference on rural health.

29099. North American Association of Summer Sessions, 11728 Summerhaven Dr, Creve Coeur, MO 63146; (314) 872-8406. Interest in summer sessions in higher education, including standards, programs, policies, procedures, and problems. Answers inquiries, provides abstracting and indexing services, distributes publications, makes referrals. Some services free, others at cost.

29100. Ozarks Whittlers and Woodcarvers, 1625 S Broadway, Springfield, MO 65807; (417) 865-7705. Promotes art of woodcarving through fairs, shows, and teaching. Provides general reference services and consulting, conducts seminars. Services primarily for members; others assisted by phone or with a SASE.

29101. Parents Rights in Education, 12571 Northwinds Dr, St Louis, MO 63146; (314) 434-4171. Pursues legal action in behalf of right of parents to direct and control education of their own children. Provides general reference services, conducts conferences and seminars, distributes publications. Services free, except some publications; donations appreciated.

29103. Polycystic Kidney Disease Research Foundation, 127 W 10th St, Kansas City, MO 64105; (816) 421-1869. Nonprofit research foundation interested in cause and cure of polycystic kidney disease. Works to educate social agencies and the public, assists patients in finding support groups.

29104. Pony Express Historical Association, Box 1022 (Patee House; 12th and Penn Sts), St Joseph, MO 64502; (816) 232-8206. Interest in history of transportation and communication in American West, particularly the Pony Express, career of Jesse James. Provides general reference services, conducts seminars, permits onsite use of collections. Services free, except admission to museum.

29105. Professional Secretaries International, 301 E Armour Blvd, Kansas City, MO 64111-1299; (816) 531-7010. Interest in secretarial profession. Answers inquiries, provides guidance to prospective secretaries.

29107. Purebred Dairy Cattle Association, 1722 S Glenstone Ave, Springfield, MO 65804; (417) 887-6525. Concerned with purebred dairy cattle, official production testing, showing of purebred cattle, herd health. Answers inquiries, provides reference services, makes referrals.

29108. Railway Tie Association, 314 N Broadway, St Louis, MO 63102; (314) 231-8099. Interest in wood railroad cross-ties, research on optimum cross section, length, and spacing in track of such cross-ties. Answers inquiries, provides free reference services.

29109. Ralston Purina Co., Library, Checkerboard Square, St Louis, MO 63164; (314) 982-2150, 982-2181. Interest in nutrition, veterinary medicine, biochemistry, world food supply, food sanitation, expanding interests in business and management. Makes interlibrary loans, permits onsite use of collections by appointment.

29110. Refugee Materials Center, U.S. Dept of Education, 324 E 11th St, 9th Fl, Kansas City, MO 64106; (816) 374-2276. Collection focuses on teaching materials on English as second language, bilingual education, other materials for immigrants, refugees. Provides general reference services, distributes translations, permits onsite reference. Services free to those working with refugees, immigrants.

29111. Research Reactor Facility, Univ of Mo., Columbia, MO 65211; (314) 882-4211. Produces neutron and gamma radiation to support research, radiation applications, and nuclear science. Answers inquiries, provides consulting services, permits onsite reference.

29112. Road Runners Club of America, c/o Jerry Kokesh, 1224 Orchard Village, Manchester, MO 63011; (314) 391-6712. Advocates physical fitness through running, promotes competitive running events. Provides general reference services, conducts seminars and workshops, distributes publications, selects honors recipients. Services free with SASE.

29113. Rock Island Technical Society, c/o David J. Engle, 8746 N Troost, Kansas City, MO 64155. Interest in history of Chicago, Rock Island, and Pacific Railroads, their predecessors, and other controlled lines. Provides general reference services, distributes publications. Services to nonmembers on a fee and time-available basis.

29114. Ryan Headache Center, 621 S New Ballas Rd, St Louis, MO 63141; (314) 872-8778. Interest in diagnosis and treatment of headache, headache research. Answers inquiries, provides advisory services, conducts seminars, evaluates data. Services subject to a fee.

29115. Saint Louis Zoological Park, Tissue Bank, c/o William J. Boever, Forest Park, St Louis, MO 63110; (314) 781-0900 ext 77. Provides to biomedical researchers and educators tissues from fauna in the collection that have died. Tissues available at nominal cost.

29116. Shealy Pain and Health Rehabilitation Institute, 3525 S National, Springfield, MO 65807; (417) 882-0850. Nonprofit org interested in pain, biofeedback, stress control, health maintenance, biogenics. Provides general reference services, consulting; conducts seminars, treatment and training programs; distributes publications. Fees charged to all users, except selected charity patients.

29117. Stained Glass Association of America, 1125 Wilmington Ave, St Louis, MO 63111; (314) 353-5128. Promotes advancement of stained glass craft, conducts apprenticeship program. Provides general reference services, conducts seminars, distributes publications, permits onsite reference. Services free, except some publications, but primarily for members.

29118. State Historical Society of Missouri, 1020 Lowry St, Columbia, MO 65202; (314) 882-7083. Interest in history, govt, culture, economics of Mo. (1790-present), history of Western America. Provides duplications, makes referrals, answers technical questions. Evaluates authenticity of material by request.

29119. Steel Deck Institute, P.O. Box 3812, St Louis, MO 63122; (314) 965-1741. Interest in standardization of steel decking and accessories, fire testing, diaphragm testing, fire insurance rating, building codes. Answers inquiries, provides certification of property values related to deck products to all industry manufacturers, makes referrals.

29122. U.S. Trout Farmers Association, P.O. Box 171, Lake Ozark, MO 65049; (314) 365-2478. Interest in trout culture, farming, and cooking, trout marketing and advertising, freshwater fish culture and marketing. Provides general reference services free to assn members.

29123. UMKC Affiliated Facility for Developmental Disabilities, UMKC Institute for Human Development, Univ of Mo., 2220 Holmes St, Kansas City, MO 64108; (816) 474-7770. Facility interested in training, evaluation, consultation in developmental disabilities. Provides general reference services, conducts seminars, distributes publications. Services provided at cost to professionals in the field.

29124. United States Orienteering Federation, P.O. Box 1039, Ballwin, MO 63011; (314) 394-2869. U.S. Federation interested in recreational use of topographic maps and compasses, orienteering education. Provides general reference and copying services, conducts workshops, distributes publications. Fee for some services.

29126. Weather Corp. of America, 5 American Industrial Dr, St Louis, MO 63043; (314) 878-5150. Commercial org that performs weather forecasting, related applications. Provides general reference services and consulting, provides round-the-clock weather forecasting services. Fees charged for services.

29127. Wild Canid Survival and Research Center/Wolf Sanctuary, P.O. Box 760, Eureka, MO 63025; (314) 938-5900. Nonprofit org that focuses on conservation of wolves through education, research, and captive breeding, conservation of other endangered and threatened wild canids. Answers inquiries, conducts programs and tours, permits onsite use of library. Donations of $1 must accompany all requests.

29128. Winston Churchill Memorial and Library in the United States, Westminster College, 7th St and Westminster Ave, Fulton, MO 65251; (314) 642-3361. Interest in life and times of Sir Winston Churchill, Anglo-American relations. Provides general reference services and reproductions, permits onsite use of collections. Services except reproductions generally free, primarily for scholars.

29129. World Archaeological Society, Information Center, Star Route-Box 445, Hollister, MO 65672; (417) 334-2377. Scientific org dedicated to archaeology, anthropology, art history. Provides general reference services, illustration services; distributes publications. Simple inquiries handled free with SASE, fees charged for other services.

Montana

30002. Center for Innovation, Mont. Energy Research and Development Institute, Inc., P.O. Box 3809 (505 Centennial Ave), Butte, MT 59702; (406) 434-6319. Provides technical, marketing, and management assistance to inventors and small businessmen. Publishes *New Product Booklet* and licensing packages. Answers inquiries, provides advisory services for a fee.

30003. Dog Writers Association of America, c/o Mrs. Edith E. Munneke, Secretary, 66 North McKinley Ave, Hamilton, MT 45013; (513) 863-2870. Interest in writing and editing for publications relating to dogs. Conducts annual writing contest open to all. Publishes monthly bulletin for members. Answers inquiries.

30004. Forest and Conservation Experiment Station, School of Forestry, Univ of Mont., Missoula, MT 59812; (406) 243-5521. Interest in forest and recreation resource management. Publishes quarterly journal and bulletins, answers inquiries, makes referrals and provides consulting services. Provides analytical, testing, and identification services in wood technology and soils.

30005. Great Bear Foundation, P.O. Box 2699, Missoula, MT 59806; (406) 273-2971. Interest in bear habitat preservation, management, and support of research. Publishes *Bera News*, critical reviews. Answers inquiries, makes referrals, provides free reference services.

30007. International Wild Waterfowl Association, c/o Wendi Schenmdel, Secretary/Treasurer, 217 Ridge Trail Rd, Bozeman, MT 59715; (406) 587-4464. Dedicated to the advancement of ornithological and avicultural knowledge of wild waterfowl. Provides advisory services, conducts annual conference, sells publications.

30008. Montana Energy Research and Development Institute, P.O. Box 3809 (321 West Galena St), Butte, MT 59702; (406) 782-0463. Interest in methods for utilizing and conserving western energy resources. Maintains technical library relating to MHD technology, energy conservation methods, and environmental studies. Answers inquiries, provides literature, makes interlibrary loans.

30009. Montana Geological Society, P.O. Box 844, Billings, MT 59101. Interest in geology and engineering aspects of oil fields in Mont. Maintains geological library. Publishes monthly newsletter and annual guidebook, answers inquiries. Consulting services provided by individual members on a fee basis.

30010. Montana Historical Society Library and Archives, 225 North Roberts St, Helena, MT 59620-9990; (406) 444-2681 (Library); (406) 444-4774 (Archives). Collection of Mont.-related materials. Maintains museum of paintings and a firearms collection. Publishes quarterlies and newsletters, answers inquiries, makes referrals, provides advisory services, permits onsite use of collections.

30011. Montana Land Reliance, P.O. Box 355, Helena, MT 59624; (406) 443-7027. Interest in protection and conservation of ecologically significant land. Responsible for 38,000 acres of protected ranchlands, fish and game habitat. Answers inquiries, makes referrals, provides advisory and consulting services at cost.

30013. National Center for Appropriate Technology, P.O. Box 3838 (3040 Continental Dr), Butte, MT 59702; (406) 494-4572. Interst in development of appropriate technology to aid communities in developing alternative sources of energy. Answers inquiries, provides reference services,lends materials. Services free to policymakers, community developers.

30015. Northern Plains Resource Council, 419 Stapleton Bldg, Billings, MT 59101; (406) 248-1154. Helps shape coal, energy, agriculture, and water-related policies affecting the Northern Plains. Maintains reference library on coal-related developments. Answers inquiries, makes referrals, provides consulting services.

30016. Reclamation Research Unit, Dept of Animal and Range Sciences, Mont. State Univ, Bozeman, MT 59717; (406) 994-4821. Interest in mineland reclamation, including revegetation, soils, hydrology, and administrative policy. Publishes technical reports and journal articles. Answers inquiries, provides advisory services, permits onsite use of collection. Services free.

30017. Rural Sociological Society, c/o Dr Anne S. Williams, Dept of Sociology, Mont. State Univ, Wilson Hall, Bozeman, MT 59717; (406) 994-5248. Interest in rural community organization and development. Publishes *Rural Studies Series* and related publications, makes referrals.

30019. School of Forestry, Wilderness Institute, Univ of Mont., Missoula, MT 59812; (406) 243-5361. Interest in wilderness, wild rivers, and wildland management. Publishes journal, books, and reports, makes referrals, provides printout files of roadless areas and wilderness management plans for entire National Wilderness Preservation System.

30020. Veterinary Research Lab, Mont. State Univ, Bozeman, MT 59717; (406) 994-4705. Interest in veterinary science and related subjects. Maintains complete collections of books and serials in veterinary medicine. Answers inquiries, makes referrals, provides reference services, permits onsite use of collection.

30021. Yellowstone-Bighorn Research Association, c/o Russell R. Dutch, Box 648, Red Lodge, MT 59068. Interest in geology and botany of Bighorn Basin and Beartooth Mountains. Maintains collection of 3,000 volumes, journals, and maps related to topic. Conducts field courses and research in geology and botany.

Nebraska

31002. American Aging Association, Univ of Neb. Medical Center, Omaha, NE 68105; (402) 559-4416. Interest in biological process of aging. Answers inquiries, provides free consulting and reference services.

31003. American Association for Clinical Immunology and Allergy, P.O. Box 912-DTS (114 South 39th St), Omaha, NE 68101; (402) 552-0801. Encourages study, practice, advances in clinical immunology and allergy, promotes high standards of medical ethics in these specialties. Conducts seminars, provides magnetic tape services on a fee basis, makes referrals for free.

31004. American Historical Society of Germans from Russia, 631 D St, Lincoln, NE 68502; (402) 474-3363. Interest mainly in history of Germans who immigrated first to Russia after the 1760's, then to the Americas. Provides general reference services and translation, conducts seminars, permits onsite study. Services available on payment of membership dues.

31005. Boys Town PhilaMatic Center, P.O. Box 1 (13628 Father Flanagan Blvd), Boys Town, NE 68010; (402) 498-1360. Nonprofit museum interested in worldwide coins, stamps, and paper money, philately, numismatics. Answers inquiries, identifies individual items, provides appraisals for a fee, permits onsite reference.

31006. Bureau of Business Research, Univ of Neb., 200 Coll of Business Administration, Lincoln, NE 68508; (402) 472-2334. Interest in Neb. business, including retail sales in cities and counties, population estimates. Provides bibliographic, tabulation, consultation, loan, reproduction services. Academic researchers allowed access to nonconfidential material.

31007. Center for Applied Urban Research, Univ of Neb. at Omaha, 1313 Farman on the Mall, Peter Kiewit Conference Center, Omaha, NE 68182; (402) 554-2764. Interest in research, education in urban affairs, housing, transportation, economic, demographic indicators. Provides reference and copying services, permits onsite study. Services free, except some publications and extensive reference work.

31008. Center for Rural Affairs, P.O. Box 316, Walthill, NE 68067; (402) 846-5428. Nonprofit center for agricultural research, ecology, social impact studies. Provides general reference services, conducts seminars, distributes publications, permits onsite study. Services intended primarily for Neb. residents. Fees charged for materials and copying.

31009. Center for Rural Affairs Small Farm Resources Project, P.O. Box 736 (104 Main St), Hartington, NE 68739; (402) 254-6893. Develops low-cost applications of appropriate technology to small commercial farms. Provides general reference services, conducts seminars, distributes publications. Services provided at cost.

31010. Christian Record Braille Foundation, P.O. Box 6097 (4444 South 52nd St), Lincoln, NE 68506; (402) 488-0981. Interest in services for the blind and visually-impaired. Provides library services, correspondence courses, limited scholarship assistance; conducts glaucoma screening clinics, other services. All free to the legally blind, state schools, and teachers of the blind.

31012. Contact Center, P.O. Box 81826 (Superior Industrial Park), Lincoln, NE 68501; (402) 464-0602. Natl referral link to ex-offenders, runaways, illiterates, others needing social and human services. Provides general reference services, distributes publications. Services free to subscribers; fees charged to nonsubscribers. Human service info, referrals provided free to clients.

31013. Danish Brotherhood In America, 3717 Harney St, Omaha, NE 68131; (402) 341-5049. Nonprofit org that promotes Danish culture and heritage, provides fraternal benefits and family protection. Provides general reference, genealogical, and translation services, conducts seminars, distributes publications. Services primarily for members.

31014. Department of Veterinary Science, Institute of Agriculture and Natural Resources, Univ of Neb., Lincoln, NE 68583-0905; (402) 472-2952. Interest in respiratory and enteric diseases of pigs and cattle, veterinary diagnostics, immunology, biotechnology. Provides general reference and diagnostic services, conducts seminars. Reference services free to state users.

31015. Divorce Research Institute, 3503 South 97th St, Omaha, NE 68124; (402) 393-6742. Nonprofit org interested in research in all aspects of divorce, including laws, legal precedents, statistics, etc. Provides general reference services and mediation, conducts workshops, distributes publications. Services requiring one hour or less free, other services at cost.

31016. Eugene C. Eppley Institute for Research in Cancer and Allied Diseases, Univ of Neb. Medical Center, 42d and Dewey Ave, Omaha, NE 68105; (402) 541-4238. Initiates multidisciplinary studies into the general areas of cancer induction by chemicals. Provides consulting services on limited basis.

31017. Great Plains National Instructional Television Library, P.O. Box 80669, Lincoln, NE 68501; (402) 472-2007, (800) 228-4630. Interest in instructional television courses in all subjects from the primary through college level. Answers inquiries, provides consulting services.

31018. Harold W. Manter Laboratory of Parasitology, Univ of Neb. State Museum, W-529 Neb. Hall West, Lincoln, NE 68588-0514; (402) 472-3334. Interest in animal parasitology. Lends specimens, permits onsite use of collections. Services free, by appointment.

31019. Inland Bird Banding Association, c/o Mrs John Lueshen, RFD 2, Box 26, Wisner, NE 68791; (402) 529-6679. Interest in ornithology, primarily banding of birds for collecting data on individual birds. Provides general reference services, sells publications. Services to nonmembers limited.

31020. International Halfway House Association, Information Center, P.O. Box 81826, Lincoln, NE 68501; (402) 464-0602. Provides info, assistance to operators of halfway houses, community residential treatment centers, and group homes. Provides general reference and consulting services, conducts conferences. Consulting services, seminars, some publications provided for a fee.

31021. Missouri Basin States Association, 10834 Old Mill Rd, Suite 1, Omaha, NE 68154; (402) 330-5714. Nonprofit assn that coordinates water resources development in area of the Missouri River Basin, operation and maintenance of a water accounting system. Answers inquiries, makes referrals, permits onsite reference.

31022. Museum of the Fur Trade, HC 74, Box 18, Chadron, NE 69337; (308) 432-3843. Museum of materials and methods of the North American fur trade from 1500 to 1900. Provides general reference services. Single inquiries from members answered free except for postage, other services provided at cost. Technical evaluations available.

31023. National Arbor Day Foundation, 100 Arbor Ave, Neb. City, NE 68410; (402) 474-5655. Interest in conservation and forestry, including urban forestry, trees, Tree City USA, and Arbor Day programs. Answers inquiries, distributes publications. Services free.

31024. National Association of Barber Schools, 304 South 11th St, Lincoln, NE 68508; (402) 474-4244. Promotes ethical standards for barber school operation, advancement of barber industry, barbering as a career. Answers inquiries, distributes publications, makes referrals. Services free, except publications in quantity.

31025. Nebraska Educational Television Network, P.O. Box 83111, Lincoln, NE 68501; (402) 472-3611. Interest in noncommercial television, TV engineering and programming, instructional TV. Provides general reference services (primarily to educators), provides program info to print media, conducts natl satellite teleconferences, disseminates materials.

31027. Nebraska Organic Agriculture Association, Route 1, Box 163, Marquette, NE 68854; (402) 854-3195, 854-3165. Promotes organic soil management systems, conservation, development of soil, water, other resources, proper nutrition, organic farming. Answers inquiries free as funds and personnel permit, conducts workshops. Services primarily for farmers for a fee.

31028. Nebraska State Historical Society, Box 82554, Lincoln, NE 68501; (402) 471-3270. Interest in history and anthropology of Neb. and the Central Plains. Most of collections open to public. Bibliographic references provided, factual questions answered, identifications made. Documents reproduced for nominal fees. Interlibrary, direct loans available.

31029. Phycological Society of America, c/o Dr J.R. Rosowski, Pres, School of Life Sciences, Univ of Neb., Lincoln, NE 68588. Conducts research in biochemistry, ecology, genetics, morphology, physiology of freshwater and marine algae. Provides info, advisory services, conducts seminars; distributes publications. Services except publications generally free to members.

31030. Railroad Station Historical Society, 430 Ivy Ave, Crete, NE 68333; (402) 826-3356. Interest in railroad history, railroad stations, signal towers, etc., railroad building architecture. Provides general reference and copying services. Services free and primarily for members, but others will be assisted.

31032. Stuhr Museum of the Prairie Pioneer, 3133 West Hwy 34, Grand Island, NE 68801; (308) 384-1380. Museum interested in history of central Neb., early settlement in the prairies, culture of Plains Indians, etc. Provides general reference services, conducts workshops, permits onsite study. Services free, except copying.

31033. Tractor Testing Laboratory, Univ of Neb., East Campus, Lincoln, NE 68583-0832; (402) 472-2442, 472-2421. Interest in performance of agricultural tractors. Answers inquiries, distributes tractor test data, sells publications, provides consultation services to govts on testing procedures.

31034. Universities Council on Water Resources, c/o Exec Secty, Water Resources Research Institute, 310 Agricultural Hall, Univ of Neb., Lincoln, NE 68583; (402) 472-3305. Council for education and research in all aspects of water resources. Answers general questions concerning study programs, other univ activities related to water resources, and sources of expertise.

31035. Water Resources Center, Institute of Agriculture and Natural Resources, Univ of Neb., 310 Agricultural Hall-East Campus, Lincoln, NE 68583; (402) 472-3307. Interest in water resources management, conservation, water quality, water quantity development and groundwater, related aspects. Answers specific technical inquiries, makes referrals to specialists.

31036. Western Heritage Museum, Omaha Union Station, 801 South 10th St, Omaha, NE 68108; (402) 444-5071. Interest in history of region, especially Omaha, Neb. Answers inquiries, provides prints from photographic negatives for a fee, conducts seminars, makes referrals to other sources of info.

Nevada

32004. Agricultural Research Service, Alfalfa Research Unit, USDA, Room 323A, Univ of Nev, Reno, NV 89557; (702) 784-5336. Investigates alfalfa genetics, autotetraploid genetic theory, tissue culture, interspecific crosses of Medicago species, soil pathogens, seed production, and plant breeding. Answers inquiries, distributes publications. Services free.

32005. Allie M. Lee Cancer Research Laboratory, Univ of Nev, Reno, NV 89557; (702) 784-6031. Info source on cancer research, chemotherapy, biochemistry, toxicology, narcotics, and hallucinogens. Answers inquiries, provides consulting services. Services free, unless extensive.

32006. American Academy of Neurological & Orthopaedic Medicine & Surgery, 2320 Rancho Dr, Suite 108, Las Vegas, NV 89102; (702) 385-6886. Assn for those in neurological and orthopaedic medicine and surgery. Publishes monthly newsletter, provides reference and copying services, conducts seminars, distributes publications. Most services free.

32007. American Federation for Medical Accreditation, 522 Rossmore Dr, Las Vegas, NV 89110; (702) 452-9538. Accredits medical and scientific orgs and provides continuing medical education for members. Answers inquiries, provides advisory and reference services, makes referrals. Services free.

32008. Biology Museum, Univ of Nev, Reno, NV 89557; (702) 784-6188. Studies taxonomy of Nevada flora and fauna, including angiosperms, gymnosperms, birds, reptiles, amphibians, fishes, insects, and invertebrates. Provides reference and consulting services to professionals without charge.

32009. Bureau of Mines, Reno Research Center, 1605 Evans Ave, Reno, NV 89512; (702) 784-5391. Investigates

ferric chloride leaching of galena concentrates and molten-salt electrolysis of lead chloride, gold and silver recovery from low-grade resources and other metals recovery. Answers inquiries, provides consulting and mineral identification services, makes referrals.

32010. Carnivore Research Institute, Old College, 401 W 2nd St, Reno, NV 89503. Studies the ecology, behavior, evolution, and conservation of carnivorous mammals, including toothed whales, primates, and humans. Answers inquiries, conducts conferences, distributes publications. Most services free.

32011. Desert Bighorn Council, c/o William R. Brigham, P.O. Box 1806, Carson City, NV 89702. Clearinghouse for info among agencies, orgs, and individuals studying desert bighorn sheep. Answers inquiries, provides advisory services, conducts seminars, distributes publications, makes referrals. Services free, except for publications.

32012. Desert Research Institute, P.O. Box 60220, Reno, NV 89506; (702) 673-7313. Library of hydrology, atmospheric physics and chemistry, climatology, geochemistry, biochemistry, chemistry, biology, ecology, and botany. Answers inquiries, conducts research, provides consulting services on a grant or contract basis.

32014. Environmental Monitoring Systems Laboratory, P.O. Box 15027 (944 E Harmon), Las Vegas, NV 89114; (702) 798-2648. Library with holdings on environmental monitoring, monitoring systems, and techniques for remote sensing of the environment. Makes interlibrary loans, permits onsite use of collections. Services free.

32015. Environmental Research Center, 4505 S Maryland Parkway, Las Vegas, NV 89154; (702) 739-3382. Studies environmental sciences and measurements, earth sciences, analytical chemistry, quality assurance, anthropology. Answers inquiries, provides advisory, consulting, and reference services, makes referrals. Services for a fee.

32016. International Society for the Protection of Mustangs & Burros, 11790 Deodar Way, Reno, NV 89506; (702) 972-1989. Involved in the welfare of wild horses and burros, implementation of federal protection, management and control programs of the animals, and adoption and sponsorship programs for them. Answers inquiries, distributes publications, makes referrals. Services primarily for members.

32017. International Soundex Reunion Registry, P.O. Box 2312, Carson City, NV 89701; (702) 882-6270. Intl central reunion registry for persons desiring and seeking a reunion with next-of-kin by birth. Answers inquiries, provides advisory and reference services, conducts seminars, distributes data compilations, makes referrals.

32018. Knudtsen Renewable Resources Center, 1000 Valley Rd, Reno, NV 89512; (702) 784-6763. Conducts research, offers resident instruction, and provides cooperative extension services in the area of renewable natural resources. Answers inquiries, conducts seminars, makes referrals. Services free.

32020. National Council of Juvenile and Family Court Judges, P.O. Box 8970 (Judicial College Bldg), Reno, NV 89507; (702) 784-6012. Seeks to improve juvenile justice system in the U.S. Answers inquiries, publishes a monthly, provides advisory, abstracting, and indexing services, distributes publications, makes referrals. Fee for some services.

32021. National Judicial College, Univ of Nev, Reno, NV 89557; (702) 784-6747. Provides assistance to state supreme courts and other state judicial orgs in organizing local judicial colleges and local judicial training and educational programs. Conducts judicial courses and seminars. Services provided for a fee.

32022. Nevada Historical Society, 1650 N Virginia St, Reno, NV 89503; (702) 789-0190. Library of the history of Nevada. Provides historical info to researchers.

32023. Nevada State Museum, Capitol Complex, Carson City, NV 89710. Library of prehistory, anthropology, Indians of the Great Basin, plants, vertebrates, and butterflies of Nevada. Answers inquiries, provides advisory services, distributes publications, makes referrals, permits onsite use of collections.

32024. PMS Research Foundation, P.O. Box 14574, Las Vegas, NV 89114; (702) 731-6476. Collects and disseminates info on Premenstrual Syndrome (PMS), stressing roles of nutrition, stress reduction, and exercise. Also coordinates network of support groups, conducts research, and distributes publications.

32025. Pacific Southwest Inter-Agency Committee, c/o David R. Hetzel, 1515 E Tropicana, Ste 400, Las Vegas, NV 89158. Coordinates policies, programs, and activities in regard to water and related land resources in the Pacific Southwest. Answers inquiries, makes referrals to appropriate federal, state, and other orgs or specialists.

32026. Research and Educational Planning Center, Room 201, Univ of Nev, Reno, NV 89557; (702) 784-4921. Research arm of the College of Education, interested in inservice educational training, drug abuse education, education for women, ethnic education. Answers inquiries, provides advisory services, conducts seminars, distributes publications, permits onsite use of collection.

32027. Reynolds Electrical and Engineering, Coordination and Information Center, P.O. Box 14400 (3084 S Highland), Las Vegas, NV 89114; (702) 295-0735. Repository of publicly released documents dealing with nuclear test fallout in offsite areas. Answers inquiries, provides reference, copying, and microform services, makes referrals, permits onsite use of collections. Services provided on a fee schedule.

32028. Seismological Laboratory, Mackay School of Mines, Univ of Nev, Reno, NV 89557. Investigates earthquake and volcano hazards in western Great Basin, researches test ban treaty verification and structure of crust and upper mantle. Answers inquiries and permits onsite use of collections free, provides advisory and consulting services. Services primarily for funding agencies and state agencies.

32029. Sierra Arts Foundation, P.O. Box 2814 (145 N Sierra), Reno, NV 89505; (702) 329-1324. Serves to promote, strengthen, and expand region's cultural activities and provide a home for the area's arts. Publishes a newsletter, answers inquiries, provides advisory and reference services, conducts seminars, distributes publications. Some services free.

32030. Water Resources Center, P.O. Box 60220, Reno, NV 89506; (702) 673-7361. Concerned with all aspects of water resources, particularly in arid and semiarid lands. Answers inquiries, provides consulting services, distributes publications and data compilations. Services free to sponsors, at cost to others.

32031. Weather Service Nuclear Support Office, P.O. Box 14985 (2753 S Highland), Las Vegas, NV 89114; (702) 295-1232. Investigates boundary layer meteorology, atmospheric transport and diffusion of radiological effluents; makes numerical weather forecasts. Answers inquiries, makes local data of the Nevada Test Site available, permits onsite use of collections. Library not open to public.

New Hampshire

33001. American Bonsai Society, P.O. Box 358, Keene, NH 03431; (603) 352-9034. Nonprofit org interested in bonsai art. Publishes journal, newsletter; provides advisory, reference services; conducts tours, workshops; lends materials.

33002. American Society for Environmental Education, Attn: Dr William Mayo, Wheeler Professional Park, P.O. Box 800, Hanover, NH 03755; (603) 643-3536. Promotes environmental education. Publishes books, directories, bibliographies; provides advisory services; conducts workshops, conferences. Services provided for a fee.

33003. American-Canadian Genealogical Society, P.O. Box 668 (52 Concord St), Manchester, NH 03105; (603) 622-2883. Collects civil and church records, genealogies. Provides reference, copying services; conducts seminars, workshops; permits onsite use of collection. Services available for a fee.

33004. Cold Regions Science and Technology Information Analysis Center, P.O. Box 282, Hanover, NH 03755; (603) 643-3200. Publishes reports on cold regions science and technology, bibliographies on worldwide scientific literature; provides technical advice to govt agencies; makes interlibrary loans.

33005. Concerned United Birthparents, 595 Central Ave, Dover, NH 03820; (603) 749-3744. Natl nonprofit support group for parents who gave children up for adoption. Provides advisory, reference services, info on research in progress; conducts seminars, workshops. Inquiries answered for $1; other services for members.

33006. Elm Research Institute, Harrisville, NH 03450; (603) 827-3048; (800) FOR ELMS (toll free). Nonprofit org that raises funds for research on Dutch elm disease. Publishes a newsletter, provides reference services concerning tree care. Services free to members.

33007. Forum for U.S.-Soviet Dialogue, 22 Hemlock Hill, Amherst, NH 03031; (603) 673-8639. Independent, nonpartisan org that arranges conferences at which American and Soviet delegates meet to discuss various topics. Expenses paid by participants (some financial aid available).

33009. International Society for Organ History and Preservation, P.O. Box 104 (60 Nelson Rd), Harrisville, NH 03450; (603) 827-3055. Documents history of pipe organ building. Provides advisory, reference, translation, copying services; permits onsite use of collection. Services mostly free.

33010. International Society for Terrain-Vehicle Systems, c/o Ronald A. Liston, Gen Secty, 72 Lyme Rd, Hanover, NH 03755; (603) 646-4208. Publishes journal, reports on off-road performance of motor vehicles. Provides consulting and reference services, permits onsite use of collection. Services provided at cost.

33011. Mount Washington Observatory, Gorham, NH 03581; (603) 466-3388. Owns books on history of White Mountains, journals, abstracts, indexes. Permits onsite use of collection, provides copying services, investigates specific problems on contract basis.

33012. National Arborist Association, c/o Robert Felix, Exec VP, 174 Rte 101, Bedford, NH 03102; (603) 472-2255. Publishes home study course, slides, tree care safety programs, standards, guides; answers inquiries; provides advisory services. Services free.

33013. National Motor Vehicle Research Safety Foundation, Newmarket P.O., Lee, NH 03857. Nonprofit org dedicated to preventing accidents. Provides advisory services, info on current research; conducts seminars, workshops. Services mostly free.

33014. New Hampshire Historical Society, 30 Park St, Concord, NH 03301; (603) 225-3381. Publishes museum catalogs, journal on N.H. history. Provides advisory, reference, copying services; permits onsite use of collection. Services mostly free to public.

33015. New Hampshire Radiological Health Program, Health and Welfare Bldg, Hazen Dr, Concord, NH 03301; (603) 271-4588. Owns small collection of books, journals, reports on x-ray and radioisotope shielding design, radiation detection. Answers inquiries, provides consulting services. Services free.

33016. Northeastern Forest Fire Protection Commission, c/o Richard Mullavey, Exec Dir, 10 Ladybug Lane, Concord, NH 03301. Commission composed of representatives from northeastern states, New Brunswick and Quebec, Canada. Publishes annual report, books on forest fire prevention and control; answers inquiries.

33017. Office of Small Business Programs, Univ of N.H., 110 McConnell Hall, Durham, NH 03824; (603) 862-3556. Business assistance org that publishes manuals, guides, directories for small business entrepreneurs. Provides literature searches, data analyses; sponsors business development counselors.

33018. Organ Clearing House, P.O. Box 104 (60 Nelson Rd), Harrisville, NH 03450; (603) 827-3055. Finds homes for pipe organs that might otherwise be destroyed; publishes lists of available pipe organs. Provides advisory, reference services; conducts seminars, workshops.

33019. Osteogenesis Imperfecta Foundation, c/o Gemma Geisman, P.O. Box 838, Manchester, NH 03105; (603) 623-0934. Nonprofit org that provides info on brittle bone disease. Publishes newsletter, directories, bibliographies; sponsors research. Services free to patients, professionals.

33021. Resource Policy Center, Thayer School of Engineering, Dartmouth College, P.O. Box 8000, Hanover, NH 03755; (603) 646-3551. Publishes bibliographies, technical reports, abstracts on factors governing resource availability. Provides info on research in progress. Services mostly free.

33022. Restoration of Atlantic Salmon in America, P.O. Box 164, Hancock, NH 03449; (603) 563-8051. Coordinates efforts of conservation orgs interested in restoring Atlantic salmon to rivers. Provides consulting and article writing services, info on research in progress; conducts lectures.

33023. Sea Grant Marine Advisory Program, Univ of N.H., NEC Administration Bldg, Durham, NH 03824; (603) 862-1255. Makes available info on marine activities in N.H. Provides advisory services, conducts seminars and workshops, lends materials, permits onsite use of collection. Services mostly free.

33024. Student Conservation Association, P.O. Box 550, Charlestown, NH 03603; (603) 826-5206. Nonprofit assn that offers volunteer work-education programs for high school, college, graduate students to help U.S. Dept of Interior, Dept of Agriculture, Merck Forest Foundation, Nature Conservancy accomplish needed but unbudgeted projects.

33027. Water Resources Research Center, Univ of N.H., Durham, NH 03824; (603) 862-2144. Publishes bulletins, journals, annual report, pamphlets on conservation of water resources in New Hampshire. Answers brief inquiries, makes referrals.

New Jersey

34003. Allied Corporation, Technical Information Service, P.O. Box 1021R, Morristown, NJ 07960; (201) 455-3014. Library with holdings on inorganic, organic, polymer, and agricultural chemistry. Services primarily for company employees, but others are permitted limited access to collections upon special arrangement.

34004. American Abstract Artists, 41 Sunset Dr, Summit, NJ 07901. Membership org interested in abstract art and history of abstract art in U.S. Services primarily for scholars and librarians and are limited according to time and effort required.

34005. American Accordion Musicological Society, 334 Broadway South, Pitman, NJ 08071; (609) 589-8308. Sponsors a composers' competition, exhibitions, and performances and plans intl projects. Answers inquiries, provides reference services, conducts seminars, lends materials, makes referrals. Services free.

34006. American Accordionists' Association, 580 Kearny Ave, Kearny, NJ 07032; (201) 991-5010. Sponsors competitions and concerts, commissions composers of accordion works. Answers inquiries, provides advisory services and speakers, makes referrals. Most services free.

34008. American Anorexia/Bulimia Association, 133 Cedar Lane, Teaneck, NJ 07666; (201) 836-1800. Provides services and programs for persons involved with anorexia nervosa and bulimia and aids in the education, research, cure, and prevention efforts related to these illnesses. Group meetings are free to members. Newsletter and referrals available.

34009. American Association for Cancer Education, CRTC Bldg, Room A-1020, 100 Bergen Street, Newark, NJ 07103. Professional org working to improve quality of education in field of neoplastic diseases. Encourages projects for the training of paramedical personnel and educational programs for general public, populations at risk, and patients with cancer.

34010. American Association for Music Therapy, 66 Morris Ave, Springfield, NJ 07081; (201) 379-1100. Fosters research in field of music therapy and approves programs of music therapy at institutions of higher learning. Answers inquiries, provides certification services, distributes publications.

34011. American Association for the Study of Liver Diseases, 6900 Grove Road, Thorofare, NJ 08086; (609) 848-1000. Promotes exchange of scientific info among physicians interested in liver disease and hepatic research. Conducts symposia and educational courses to improve quality of patient care.

34012. American Association of Diabetes Educators, North Woodbury Road, Box 56, Pitman, NJ 08071; (609) 589-4831. Promotes and assists development of diabetes education in the U.S. for the diabetic consumer. Fos-

ters communication and cooperation among individuals and orgs involved in diabetes education. Publishes a newsletter and journal.

34013. American Association of Foot Specialists, c/o Dr Jerome J. Erman, P.O. Box 54, Union, NJ 07083; (201) 688-1616. Source of info on podiatry, podiatric surgery, and dermatology. Answers written inquiries, provides consulting services, makes referrals.

34014. American Association of Teachers of German, c/o Dr Robert A. Govier, 523 Bldg Route 38, Cherry Hill, NJ 08034. Promotes teaching of German at all levels. Publishes a quarterly and answers questions on the teaching of German and availability of teaching materials.

34015. American Association of Veterinary State Boards, c/o Robert R. Shomer, 1680 Teaneck Rd, Teaneck, NJ 07666. Investigates state veterinary examination procedures, veterinary education, and professional conduct. Answers inquiries, provides consulting and reference services, makes referrals. Services free.

34016. American Carousel Society, c/o Ms. Mary Fritsch, 470 South Pleasant Ave, Ridgewood, NJ 07450. Interest in history of the carousel and its manufacture, carvings, and restoration. Publishes newsletter, answers inquiries, provides consulting services, distributes publications. Services primarily for members.

34017. American Celiac Society, 45 Gifford Avenue, Jersey City, NJ 07304; (201) 432-1207. Nonprofit corp formed to provide assistance to persons who are sensitive to gluten in foods. Publishes educational materials and will respond to specific questions from individuals about particular foods.

34018. American College of Osteopathic Pediatricians, c/o Theresa E. Goeke, 104 Carnegie Center, Princeton, NJ 08540. Org of osteopathic physicians certified in or have major interest in pediatrics. Publishes a newsletter. Inquiries addressed to the Executive Director are referred to the appropriate committee for reply.

34019. American Council for Healthful Living, 439 Main Street, Orange, NJ 07050; VD/STD/AIDS Hotline, (201) 674-7476. Conducts disease education programs for health educators, patients, health care professionals, and the community. Runs a number of educational programs on such topics as wellness and venereal diseases.

34020. American Council on Science and Health, 47 Maple St, Summit, NJ 07901; (201) 477-0024. Promotes scientifically balanced evaluations of chemicals, nutrition, the environment, and human health. Answers inquiries, provides advisory services and experts for media presentations, distributes publications. Most services free.

34021. American Cyanamid Company, Consumer Products Research Library, 967 Route 46, Clifton, NJ 07015; (201) 365-6321. Library of chemistry, pharmacology, cosmetics, perfumery, dermatology, microbiology, biochemistry, and pesticides. Provides ready-reference, interlibrary loan, and copying services.

34022. American Economic Foundation, Liberty Village, 3 Church St, Flemington, NJ 08822; (201) 788-6995. Concerned with simplification of economics and creation of employee/community and teacher/student education programs. Answers inquiries, operates a semantic laboratory, develops educational and training materials. Services generally provided free to contributors of $25 or more.

34023. American Electrolysis Association, 710 Tennent Rd, Englishtown, NJ 07726; (201) 536-6477. Intl certifying agency and educational resource for the field of electrology. Publishes newsletter, answers inquiries, provides advisory services and guest speakers, makes referrals. Services free.

34024. American Fine China Guild, c/o Mark Z. Segal, 860 Lower Ferry Rd, Trenton, NJ 08628. Investigates the characteristics and uses of American-made fine china dinnerware. Answers inquiries and makes referrals. Services free.

34025. American Gastroenterological Association, c/o Charles B. Slack, 6900 Grove Rd, Thorofare, NJ 08086. Fosters development and application of the science of gastroenterology by providing leadership and aid in all aspects of field. Publishes a journal, answers specific questions or refers them to appropriate members, conducts postgraduate courses.

34026. American Institute of Food Distribution, 28-12 Broadway, Fair Lawn, NJ 07410; (201) 791-5570. Supplies food industry members with useful, timely info relevant to distribution of food products. Answers inquiries, provides consulting services, distributes publication. Services provided free to members and at an hourly fee to nonmembers.

34027. American Institute of Marketing, P.O. Box X, Mantoloking, NJ 08738; (201) 899-8600. Concerned with financial planning, business forecasts, marketing research, consulting, and futures research. Answers inquiries, provides reference and copying services, distributes publications, makes referrals. Some services free.

34028. American Leprosy Missions, One Broadway, Elmwood Park, NJ 07042; (201) 794-8650. Helps support intl leprosy research and training centers in Ethiopia, India, Brazil. Provides resource materials on leprosy and how it is fought around the world. Services free to anyone. Toll-free number, (800) 543-3131, is provided for info on ALM activities.

34030. American Littoral Society, Sandy Hook, Highlands, NJ 07732; (201) 291-0055. Encourages underwater study of fishes and other marine life and fosters public awareness of the need for conservation of estuaries. Answers inquiries, provides advisory services, distributes publications, makes referrals. Most services free.

34032. American Liver Foundation, 998 Pompton Avenue, Cedar Grove, NJ 07009; (800) 223-0179. Promotes and funds research on liver disease and seeks to inform public about liver disease. Research grants are awarded to student and postdoctoral researchers. Sponsors a natl organ donor program. Most services free for physicians and other medical professionals.

34033. American Microchemical Society, c/o Leonard C. Klein, FMC Corp, Box 8, Princeton, NJ 08540. Investigates microanalysis, microchemical techniques, microelemental and microfunctional group analysis. Answers inquiries, provides consulting services, makes referrals. Fees may be charged to commercial users.

34034. American Paralysis Association, P.O. Box 187, Short Hills, NJ 07078; (800) 225-0292. Nonprofit org that funds research to cure paralysis caused by central nervous system injury or disease.

34035. American Platform Tennis Association, P.O. Box 901, Upper Montclair, NJ 07043; (201) 783-5325. Natl governing body for platform tennis. Publishes newsletter, answers inquiries, provides reference services, distributes publications. Services for a fee.

34036. American Powder Metallurgy Institute, 105 College Rd East, Princeton, NJ 08540; (609) 452-7700. Studies metal powders, powder metallurgy processes and products. Answers inquiries and makes referrals.

34037. American Society of Consulting Arborists, 315 Franklin Rd, North Brunswick, NJ 08902; (201) 821-8948. Studies biological and legal problems with trees. Publishes newsletter. Refers inquirers to local arboricultural consultants who provide info or offer services for fees.

34038. American Society of Perfumers, P.O. Box 573, West Englewood Branch, Teaneck, NJ 07666. Studies art and science of perfumery. Answers inquiries, conducts seminars, distributes publications. Most services free.

34039. American Spice Trade Association, P.O. Box 1267, Englewood Cliffs, NJ 07632; (201) 568-2163. Studies spices, seeds, and herbs and their nutritional composition. Answers inquiries free, primarily for the spice industry, but others will be assisted according to the time and effort required.

34041. American Vegan Society, P.O. Box H, Malaga, NJ 08328; (609) 694-2887. Promotes veganism as a way of life through public education. Veganism goes beyond vegetarianism, nuttism, and ovo-lactarianism into excluding all animal products such as dairy products or woolen clothing.

34042. American Wax Importers and Refiners Association, c/o Bernard Pompeo, P.O. Box 4085, Jersey City, NJ 07304. Concerned with wax importing and refining, specification, sampling, and test methods for carnauba, candelilla, and ouricury waxes. Answers inquiries or makes referrals.

34043. Archaeological Research Center and Museum, Seton Hall Univ, South Orange, NJ 07079; (201) 761-9543. Studies prehistoric archaeology of N.J. and northeastern U.S., and ethnography of Delaware Indians. Answers inquiries, provides advisory services, lends materials, permits onsite use of collections. Services free to those in field.

34044. Army Electronics Research and Development Command, Technical Library, DELSD-L, Fort Monmouth, NJ 07703; (201) 544-2235. Interest in acoustics, data processing equipment, aerospace electronics, communications equipment. Answers inquiries, makes referrals. Unclassified-unlimited publications available through National Technical Information Service. Library not open to public.

34045. Army Satellite Communications Agency, Bldg 209, Fort Monmouth, NJ 07703; (201) 532-2813. Concerned with military satellite communications systems, with emphasis on ground environment. Answers inquiries, makes referrals, provides brochures and technical fact sheets. Classified info is furnished on a need-to-know basis.

34046. Associated Technical Services, 855 Bloomfield Ave, Glen Ridge, NJ 07028; (201) 748-5673. Specializes in collections of dictionaries and translation tools in all fields of science and technology and in all languages. Provides worldwide literature-searching, consulting, abstracting, and translation services. Reference use of library is decided on an individual basis.

34047. Association for Advancement of Mental Health, 145 Witherspoon St, Princeton, NJ 08542; (609) 924-7174. Seeks to create permanent community support system for mentally handicapped adults. Programs include groups for parents, instruction in living skills, crisis assistance, and case management.

34048. Association for Computational Linguistics, c/o Dr D.E. Walker, 445 South St, Morristown, NJ 07960. Intl professional society for those interested in computational linguistics, algorithms, models, and computer systems. Answers inquiries and makes referrals based on resources available.

34049. Association for Professional Practice, 1143 East Jersey St, Elizabeth, NJ 07201; (201) 352-0060. Concerned with professional regulation and licensing with emphasis on real estate brokers, physicians, dentists, and other health professionals. Answers inquiries, provides advisory services, distributes publications, makes referrals. Services provided for a fee.

34050. Association for the Advancement of Baltic Studies, 231 Miller Rd, Mahwah, NJ 07430; (201) 529-2887. Studies Baltic area history, sociology, geography, musicology, political science, and economics. Publishes newsletter, answers inquiries, provides advisory services, distributes publications. Services provided at cost.

34051. Association of Retail Marketing Services, 412 Ocean Ave, Sea Bright, NJ 07760; (201) 842-5070. Clearinghouse for info on retail marketing programs and research on motivating retail consumer. Answers inquiries and makes referrals. Services primarily for members.

34052. Association to Advance Ethical Hypnosis, 60 Vose Ave, South Orange, NJ 07079; (201) 762-3132. Promotes ethics in hypnosis. Answers inquiries, publishes a bulletin, provides reference services, distributes publications, makes referrals.

34053. BIRTHRIGHT, 686 North Broad St, Woodbury, NJ 08096; (609) 848-1819. Provides assistance to women and girls with unplanned pregnancies by providing testing, guidance, shelter, community resource info, maternity clothes, medical care, legal advice.

34054. C. W. Thornthwaite Associates Laboratory of Climatology, RD 1 (Centerton), Elmer, NJ 08318; (609) 358-2350. Studies climatology, microclimatology, agricultural climatology, turbulence, heat and water balance, meteorological instruments. Answers inquiries, permits limited onsite use of collection by request.

34055. Campaign for U.N. Reform, 600 Valley Rd, Wayne, NJ 07470; (201) 694-6333. Works to strengthen United Nations through lobbying and educational activities, including holding congressional seminars and receptions for U.N. delegates. Answers inquiries, conducts seminars, distributes publications. Fee for some services.

34056. Carl Campbell Brigham Library, Educational Testing Service, Princeton, NJ 08541; (609) 734-5667. Library of educational and psychological tests and measurements, sociology and economics. Answers inquiries, provides advisory and reference services, permits onsite use of collection. Most services free.

34057. Celanese Plastics and Specialties Company Information Center, 26 Main St, Chatham, NJ 07928. Source of info on polymers and plastics. Provides reference services, lends materials.

34058. Center for Analysis of Public Issues, 16 Vandeventer Ave, Princeton, NJ 08542; (609) 924-9750. Nonprofit research org studying issues affecting state and local govts in N.J. and nearby states. Answers inquiries and provides advisory services free.

34059. Center for Coastal and Environmental Studies, Busch Campus, New Brunswick, NJ 08903; (201) 932-3738. Studies most phases of marine, coastal plain, and piedmont areas; their oceanography, marine biology, and coastal geomorphology. Answers inquiries, provides consulting services. Some services free.

34060. Center for Energy and Environmental Studies, 102 Engineering Quad, Princeton, NJ 08544; (609) 452-5445. Concerned with indoor air quality, technological aspects of energy conservation, nuclear energy, nuclear weapons policy. Answers inquiries, provides reference services, distributes publications. Services free.

34061. Center for U.N. Reform Education, 139 East McClellan Ave, Livingston, NJ 07039; (201) 992-8350. Acts as catalyst, coordinating agent, and resource bank for groups focusing on improving United Nations system. Answers inquiries, provides help to groups planning meetings, sponsors speakers bureau.

34062. Center for Urban Policy Research, Bldg 4051-Kilmer Campus, New Brunswick, NJ 08903; (201) 932-3134. Concerned with urban policy research, housing, urban economics. Answers inquiries, provides reference services, makes interlibrary loans. Services primarily for professionals in field.

34063. Center for the American Woman and Politics, Eagleton Institute, New Brunswick, NJ 08901; (201) 232-9384. Concerned with participation of women in politics and govt in U.S. Answers inquiries, provides advisory services, distributes publications. Services available for a fee.

34064. Center for the Study of Human Sexuality, Montclair State College, Upper Montclair, NJ 07043; (201) 893-4336. Conducts research on sexuality, behavior, aging, child growth and development and related subjects. Answers inquiries, provides consulting services to schools and agencies, makes referrals. Most services free.

34065. Center of Alcohol Studies, Rutgers Univ, New Brunswick, NJ 08903; (201) 932-4442. Collects and classifies scientific literature on alcohol and alcoholism. Answers inquiries, prepares bibliographies, and provides photocopies of abstracts and library materials for a nominal fee. Library resources available through loan and onsite use.

34067. Center of International Studies, 118 Corwin Hall, Princeton, NJ 08544; (609) 452-4851. Supports research in intl studies by faculty and students of Princeton Univ and scholars from other institutions in U.S. and abroad. Answers inquiries, conducts seminars, distributes publications. Services for professionals in field.

34068. Chester Davis Memorial Library, 5121 Park Blvd, Wildwood, NJ 08260; (609) 522-2569. Source of precancelled stamps of U.S., Canada, and Europe. Publishes a monthly, answers inquiries, provides reference services, permits onsite use of collection. Services primarily for members.

34069. Children's Liver Foundation, 7 Highland Place, Maplewood, NJ 07040; (201) 761-1111. Self-help group that provides support for parents whose children have liver diseases and funds pediatric liver research. Produces educational materials for parents, medical professionals, and public and lobbies for automatic screening for galactosemia in newborns.

34070. Chinese Language Teachers Association, Seton Hall Univ, South Orange, NJ 07040; (201) 762-4973. Conducts research on and teaching of Chinese. Publishes newsletter and provides literature-searching services free to members and at cost to others.

34071. Citizens Energy Council, Box 285 (77 Homewood Ave), Allendale, NJ 07401; (201) 327-3914. Concerned with nuclear energy hazards and alternative energy sources. Answers inquiries, provides advisory services, distributes publications. Most services free.

34072. Classic Car Club of America, P.O. Box 443, Madison, NJ 07940; (201) 377-1925. Interest in custom and limited production cars manufactured between 1925 and 1948. Publishes a magazine, answers inquiries, makes referrals. Services free and primarily for members.

34073. Colgate-Palmolive Company, Technical Information Center, 909 River Rd, Piscataway, NJ 08854; (201) 878-7574. Interest in soaps, detergents, dentifrices, fats, oils. Makes interlibrary loans. Members of scientific and technical communities may utilize public collections upon authorization by the Section Head.

34074. Commission on Archives and History of the United Methodist Church, Box 127 (36 Madison Ave), Madison, NJ 07940; (201) 822-2826. Studies United Methodist Church history and its predecesssor denominations. Answers inquiries, provides reference and duplication services, lends materials, makes referrals. Services free to some users, at cost to others.

34075. Committee for National Arbor Day, Box 333, West Orange, NJ 07052; (201) 731-0840. Promotes Arbor Day observances, tree planting, and involvement of conservationists. Answers inquiries, provides consulting services for free.

34076. Communications Managers Association, 40 Morristown Rd, Bernardville, NJ 07924. Concerned with telecommunications management, legislation, regulation, state-of-the-art telecommunications equipment and services. Answers inquiries, provides advisory services, distributes publications. Services primarily for professionals.

34077. Conservation and Environmental Studies Center, 120-13 Whitesbog Rd, Browns Mills, NJ 08015; (609) 893-9151. Nonprofit org that supports environmental education for grades K-12, including curriculum development. Provides consulting services to school districts, conducts teacher training programs and environmental study courses for students. Services provided on a fee basis.

34078. Consumer Education Research Center, P.O. Box 336, South Orange, NJ 07079; (201) 762-6714. Nonprofit org concerned with consumer protection info for purchase of goods and services. Publishes a bulletin, answers inquiries, provides advisory services and taped consumer info by telephone. Most services free.

34079. Costume Society of America, P.O. Box 761 (15 Little John), Englishtown, NJ 07726; (201) 536-6216. Provides opportunities for scholarship and exchange of info on all facets of costume, its study and preservation. Publishes a newsletter, answers inquiries, provides consulting services, distributes publications. Services primarily for members.

34081. Delaware River Basin Commission, P.O. Box 7360 (25 State Police Dr) Trenton, NJ 08628; (609) 883-9500. Oversees planning and development in the Delaware River Basin. Answers inquiries, provides reference and copying services, distributes forecasting data, makes referrals. Services free to govt agencies, citizen groups, consultants, libraries.

34083. Dow Jones Newspaper Fund, P.O. Box 300 (Route 1 at Ridge), Princeton, NJ 08540; (609) 452-2820. Encourages talented young people to enter newspaper profession. Answers inquiries, operates scholarship programs, provides info on journalism as a career. Services free.

34084. Duster Class Yacht Racing Association, c/o Tom Bryant, Secretary, 137 Balsam Rd, Pines Lake, NJ 07470. Studies dynamics and physics of wind power as it relates to sailing vessels. Answers inquiries, provides advisory services, distributes publications. Services may be subject to a fee.

34085. ERIC Clearinghouse on Tests, Measurement, and Evaluation, Educational Testing Service, Rosedale Rd, Princeton, NJ 08541. Seeks to acquire significant educational literature within area of measurement, evaluation, and research design and methodology. Like other ERIC clearinghouses, ERIC/TM abstracts and indexes documents within its areas of interest for announcement in ERIC's monthly abstract bulletin.

34086. Eagleton Institute of Politics, Neilson Campus, Rutgers Univ, New Brunswick, NJ 08901; (201) 828-2210. Involved in education and research in politics, govt, and public affairs to assist agencies and groups in dealing with issues of public importance. Provides advisory and consulting services, conducts seminars, distributes publications. Services provided on a contract or fee basis.

34087. Eastern Bird Banding Association, c/o Hannah Suthers, 4 View Point Ave, Hopewell, NJ 08525. Regional assn of professional and amateur ornithologists from East Coast of U.S. and Canada. Answers inquiries, provides consulting services to ornithologists engaged in any form of bird marking or banding. Sells netting and trapping equipment to licensed banders.

34088. Edison National Historic Site, Main St and Lakeside Ave, West Orange, NJ 07052; (201) 736-0550. Museum of career and inventions of Thomas Alva Edison and history of 19th and 20th Century technology. Laboratory and home are open to public. Archives open to those engaged in specific research. Copying services available.

34089. Education Law Center, 155 Washington St, Suite 209, Newark, NJ 07102; (201) 624-1815. Nonprofit, public-interest law firm providing free legal assistance to parents, students and their orgs. Answers inqui-

ries, provides counseling and reference services. Services generally free for education consumers in N.J. and Penn.

34090. Educational Press Association of America, Triad Bldg, Glassboro, NJ 08080; (609) 863-7349. Seeks to improve quality of educational communications and advance aims of education. Answers inquiries, provides consulting services, distributes publications, makes referrals. Services free.

34091. Educational Testing Service, Test Collection, Princeton, NJ 08541; (609) 734-5686. Archives for testing and info on tests and related services for persons engaged in research and related activities. Sells annotated bibliographies of tests. Manual searches free, computerized searches for a fee. Permits onsite use of materials to qualified individuals.

34092. Electronic Information Exchange System, 323 High St, Newark, NJ 07102; (201) 645-5211. Provides electronic mail, computerized conferencing, and electronic notebooks. Answers inquiries, provides advisory services, distributes publications. Services for those in the industry.

34093. Engelhard Corporation, Research Library, Edison, NJ 08818; (201) 321-5371. Promotes use of clay and kaolin products, catalysts, noble metals. Answers inquiries, provides reference, abstracting, indexing, and copying services. Certain services available to non-staff.

34095. Fair Lawn Technical Center Library, 2111 Route 208, Fair Lawn, NJ 07410; (201) 797-6800 ext 5338. Studies food science. Answers inquiries free.

34096. Federal Aviation Administration Technical Center, ACT 624, Atlantic City Airport, NJ 08405; (609) 484-5124. Investigates air traffic control systems, aircraft communication, guidance and safety. Answers inquiries.

34097. Fiber Society, P.O. Box 625 (601 Prospect Ave), Princeton, NJ 08540; (609) 924-3150. Studies fiber science, including polymer physics and chemistry, textile engineering and technology, and fiber morphology. Conducts semiannual technical meetings, which are open to the public.

34098. Fluid Controls Institute, P.O. Box 9036 (31 South St), Morristown, NJ 07960; (201) 829-0990. Nonprofit assn of manufacturers of devices for fluid control and fluid conditioning. Publishes a quarterly. Answers inquiries and makes referrals free.

34099. Friction Materials Standards Institute, E210 Route 4, Paramus, NJ 07652; (201) 845-0440. Technical assn made up of manufacturers of brake linings, brake shoes, and clutch facings. Answers inquiries and makes referrals.

34100. Gallup Organization, P.O. Box 628 (53 Bank St), Princeton, NJ 08542; (609) 924-9600. Investigates public attitudes and opinions on political, economic, and social issues. Approved academic users may have access to material by appointment. Data tabulations are provided for a fee, loans of published material are made, and documents are reproduced.

34101. Geophysical Fluid Dynamics Laboratory, NOAA, c/o Princeton Univ, P.O. Box 308, Princeton, NJ 08542. Studies fluid dynamics models, general circulation of ocean and atmosphere, thermal convection, experimental circulation prediction, and numerical weather prediction. Provides specific info regarding programs and projects, exchanges publications with scientific community.

34102. German Shepherd Dog Club of America, c/o Blanche Beisswenger, 17 West Ivy Lane, Englewood, NJ 07631. Concerned with German Shepherd breeding, judging standards, and showing. Answers inquiries, provides reference services, conducts dog shows, distributes publications. Most services free.

34103. Global Education Associates, 552 Park Ave, East Orange, NJ 07017; (201) 675-1409. Seeks to catalyze a transcultural, multi-issue movement for world order based on values of social and economic justice, peace, and ecological balance. Answers inquiries, provide consulting services, distributes publications. Fees charged for services.

34104. Global Learning, 40 South Fullerton Ave, Montclair, NJ 07042; (201) 783-7616. Nonprofit, educational org specializing in global education programs for teachers, churches, and community groups. Answers inquiries, provides consulting services, conducts workshops. Most services free.

34105. Gottscho Packaging Information Center, P.O. Box 909, Piscataway, NJ 08854; (201) 932-3044. Concerned with packaging graphic and structural design, laws and regulations concerning packaging, packaging materials and testing. Answers inquiries; provides reference, abstracting, indexing and copying services, often at cost.

34106. Hair Science Institute, 39 Milltown Rd, East Brunswick, NJ 08816; (201) 257-1990. Commercial org concerned with hair loss, baldness, alopecia, human nutrition, trichology, esthetics, skin care. Answers inquiries, provides advisory services, distributes publications. Fees charged for some services.

34107. Hearing and Tinnitus Help Association, P.O. Box 97, Skillman, NJ 08558; (609) 466-1202. Disseminates info on ear-related problems, with emphasis on tinnitus and a holistic approach to its treatment. Holds educational seminars and encourages research.

34108. Hobby Industry Association of America, 319 East 54th St, Elmwood Park, NJ 07407; (201) 794-1133. Interest in the buying, selling, and manufacturing of models, crafts, collectibles, and other hobby merchandise. Answers inquiries, provides advisory services, distributes publications. Services primarily for those in the business.

34109. Hoffmann-LaRoche Inc., Scientific Library, Nutley, NJ 07110; (201) 235-3091. Has holdings on drugs, pharmaceutical chemistry, vitamins, organic chemistry, pharmacology. Answers inquiries and makes referrals. Library not open to the public.

34110. Hospital Compensation Service, P.O. Box 321 (115 Watchung Dr), Hawthorne, NJ 07507; (201) 427-2221. Studies management of human resources in hospitals and nursing homes. Answers inquiries, provides consulting services, distributes publications. Simple inquiries are answered free.

34111. Hydronics Institute, 35 Russo Pl, Berkeley Heights, NJ 07922; (201) 464-8200. Trade assn for boiler and radiator industry, which tests and rates equipment and disseminates info on hydronic heating systems. Answers inquiries free, distributes publications on a fee basis.

34112. ITT Defense Communications Division Library, 492 River Rd, Nutley, NJ 07110; (201) 284-2096. Conducts research into electronic communications systems, electronic switching systems, lasers, fiber optics, orbital transmission. Answers inquiries, makes interlibrary loans, permits onsite use of collections. Services available with approval.

34114. Information Services, P.O. Box 356, Wharton, NJ 07885; (201) 366-3784. Commercial org that conducts literature searching and other info services into business, home businesses, marketing, retailing, wholesaling, management, training. Provides consulting and reference services, makes referrals. Services for a fee.

34115. Inmont Corporation Central Research Library, 1255 Broad St, Clifton, NJ 07015; (201) 365-3400. Source of info on graphic arts, finishes, coatings, polymers, plastics, color science, dispersions, emulsions, films, dyes. Provides reference services. Some materials are available for loan or onsite reference. Services provided only by prior approval.

34116. Institute for Cognitive Studies, 210 Bradley Hall, Newark, NJ 07102; (201) 648-5150. Conducts research and graduate training in cognitive psychology, perception, memory and learning. Answers inquiries and distributes reprints of journal articles free.

34117. Institute for Medical Research Library, Copewood St, Camden, NJ 08103; (609) 966-7377 ext 100. Performs medical research in microbiology, virology, oncology, cytology, cell biology, tissue culture. Answers inquiries, makes referrals, permits onsite use of collection.

34118. Institute for Political and Legal Education, R.D. 4, Box 209 (207 Delsea Dr), Sewell, NJ 08080; (609) 228-6000. Disseminates a curriculum designed to inform secondary and middle school students about citizenship, politics, govt, law. Answers inquiries, distributes publications, makes referrals. Most services free and primarily for those in the field.

34119. Institute for the Advancement of Philosophy for Children, Montclair State College, Upper Montclair, NJ 07043; (201) 893-4277. Concerned with educational research, development of curricula in philosophy for children, degree programs in philosophy education for children. Answers inquiries, provides reference services, lends materials, distributes publications.

34120. Institute of Animal Behavior, 101 Warren St, Newark, NJ 07102; (201) 648-5862. Conducts research and training in animal behavior, behavior development, social behavior. Answers inquiries, provides advisory and reference services, distributes publications. Most services free.

34121. Institute of Far Eastern Studies, Seton Hall Univ, South Orange, NJ 07079; (201) 761-9000 ext 456. Conducts Far Eastern research with emphasis on China, Japan, Korea. Answers inquiries free, provides consulting and translating services.

34122. Institute of Health Management, P.O. Box 1215 (130 Library Pl), Princeton, NJ 08540; (609) 927-7799. Nonprofit org concerned with development, implementation, assessment of health issues through education, preventive medicine, and care. Answers inquiries, provides advisory services, makes referrals. Services available at cost.

34123. Institute of Management and Labor Relations, Ryder's Lane, New Brunswick, NJ 08903; (201) 932-9513. Studies industrial relations, particularly industrial relations in N.J. since 1950. Answers inquiries, lends published materials, permits onsite use of collection.

34124. Institutional Research Program for Higher Education, Educational Testing Service, Princeton, NJ 08540; (609) 921-9000. Aids colleges in carrying out programs of self-study, evaluation, planning. Answers inquiries, provides data processing services and professional assistance. Services for colleges provided on a cost basis.

34125. Inter-American Safety Council, 33 Park Pl, Englewood, NJ 07631; (201) 871-0004. Seeks to create accident-prevention attitudes among Spanish- and Portuguese-speaking people. Answers inquiries, provides advisory and translation services, distributes publications, makes referrals. Some services free.

34127. International Intertrade Index, P.O. Box 636, Federal Square, Newark, NJ 07101; (201) 686-2382. Commercial org studying new foreign products available for import into U.S. Publishes a monthly, provides advisory services, distributes publications. Services for a fee.

34128. International Schools Services, P.O. Box 5910 (13 Rosvel Rd), Princeton, NJ 08540; (609) 452-0990. Private, nonprofit org that operates schools in remote areas on behalf of intl business. Answers inquiries, provides consulting services on a fee basis, operates a referral service for U.S. teachers and administrators seeking employment abroad.

34129. International Society of Statistical Science in Economics, P.O. Box 124, Princeton, NJ 08542; (609) 921-0611. Nonprofit org seeking to clarify statistical applications and conducting research programs on improvement of statistical methods. Answers inquiries, provides reference services, distributes publications. Some services for a fee.

34130. Interuniversity Communications Council, P.O. Box 364, Princeton, NJ 08540; (609) 734-1915. Seeks to develop, operate, and use computing and technology-related systems in higher education. Answers inquiries, provides advisory services through EDUCOM, makes referrals. Services available to colleges, univs, and higher education service orgs for a fee.

34131. Kessler Institute for Rehabilitation, Pleasant Valley Way, West Orange, NJ 07052; (201) 731-3600. Voluntary, nonprofit, nonsectarian specialty hospital serving physically handicapped children and adults by providing specialized spinal cord injury care. Answers inquiries, provides advisory and reference services, makes referrals. Simple services free.

34132. Knowledge Foundation, P.O. Box 31 (288 Main, Butler, NJ), Wanaque, NJ 07465; (201) 492-0823. Nonprofit org involved in wildlife and the environment. Publishes magazine, answers inquiries, provides reference services. Some services free.

34134. League of Lefthanders, P.O. Box 89, New Milford, NJ 07646; (201) 265-9110. Concerned with needs and problems of lefthanded persons in all areas of human endeavor—psychological, social, technological. Publishes a newsletter, answers inquiries, provides reference services, distributes publications and data compilations. Services free to members.

34135. M&T Chemicals Inc., Technical and Business Information Center, P.O. Box 1104, Rahway, NJ 07065; (201) 499-2437. Compiles data on chemistry, ceramics, organometallics, and patents. Makes interlibrary loans; other services available only to company employees.

34136. MEPCO/ELECTRA, Columbia Rd, Morristown, NJ 07960; (201) 539-2000. Info source on electronic components, all types of resistors, microcircuits, thin and thick films, plastic film, aluminum electrolytic and tantalum capacitors. Answers inquiries and permits onsite use of literature collection.

34137. MTM Association for Standards and Research, 16-01 Broadway, Fair Lawn, NJ 07410; (201) 791-7720. Conducts research, training, and certification in Methods-Time Measurement (MTM) techniques. Answers inquiries, provides advisory and training services, distributes publications. Most services free.

34138. Magnesium Elektron, RD 2, Box 251, Flemington, NJ 08822; (201) 782-5800. Investigates zirconium chemistry and all aspects of current developments in paper, paints, refractories, and oil. Pamphlets, data sheets, or samples distributed in answer to inquiries. Reference services provided without charge.

34139. Mineral Insulation Manufacturers Association, 382 Springfield Ave, Summit, NJ 07901; (201) 277-1550. Source of data on insulation, including rock, slag, glass wool, and energy conservation in heating and cooling. Answers inquiries, provides reference services, sells publications, makes referrals.

34140. Molasses Information Network, P.O. Box 9179, Morristown, NJ 07960; (201) 326-9220. Acts as an info source on uses of molasses. Answers inquiries, provides advisory services, distributes publications. Services free.

34141. Moped Association of America, 72 Summit Ave, Montvale, NJ 07645; (201) 391-1077. Assn of moped manufacturers seeking to promote use of mopeds and represent industry before govt, press, and public. Answers inquiries, provides advisory services, distributes brochures, makes referrals. Services free.

34142. Motor Bus Society, c/o Gerald L. Squire, P.O. Box 7058, West Trenton, NJ 08628. Studies history of buses and bus lines and preserves bus-related material for historical purposes. Answers brief inquiries, provides bibliographic services, reproduces photographs for a fee, permits limited onsite use of collections.

34143. Motor and Equipment Manufacturers Association, P.O. Box 439 (222 Cedar Lane), Teaneck, NJ 07666; (201) 836-9500. Investigates automotive safety components and systems, including brakes, lighting, and emission control. Answers inquiries, provides consulting services, makes referrals. Services provided free to govt agencies, at cost to commercial orgs.

34144. Municipal Arborists Urban Foresters Society, P.O. Box 1255, Freehold, NJ 07728-1255; (201) 431-7903. Concerned with all phases of urban forestry and municipal arboriculture, including street tree planting standards, tree care and maintenance. Publishes a newsletter, answers inquiries, makes referrals. Services free to arborists and urban foresters.

34145. Music Associates of America, 224 King St, Englewood, NJ 07631; (201) 569-2898. Commercial org serving music publishers and composers through distribution of info about their catalogs and published works. Answers inquiries, provides consulting services, distributes publications. Services for professionals in field of music.

34146. National Adult Education Clearinghouse, Montclair State College, Upper Montclair, NJ 07043; (201) 893-4353. Concerned with adult continuing education. Publishes a newsletter, answers inquiries, provides consulting services, permits onsite use of collection or lends material by mail. Some services provided free.

34147. National Alliance of Homebased Businesswomen, P.O. Box 306, Midland Park, NJ 07432. Membership org representing interests of homebased businesses.

Publishes a newsletter, conducts seminars, distributes model zoning regulations. Services free to members, for a fee to others.

34148. National Art Materials Trade Association, 178 Lakeview Ave, Clifton, NJ 07011; (201) 546-6400. Concerned with art materials, including paints, brushes, surfaces, airbrushes, graphic computers, and art materials industry. Answers inquiries free.

34149. National Assessment of Educational Progress, Educational Testing Service, Princeton, NJ 08541; (800) 223-0267. Provides comprehensive info on educational achievement of young Americans and adults in elementary, middle, and secondary schools. Answers inquiries, provides advisory and data tape services, distributes publications. Most services free.

34150. National Association of Accountants, 10 Paragon Dr, Box 433, Montvale, NJ 07645. Concerned with accounting, emphasizing management accounting, business decision models, and labor costs and performance. Answers inquiries, provides reference and duplication services. Services primarily for members, but provided to others for educational purposes.

34151. National Association of Commissions for Women, 336 Northfield Ave, West Orange, NJ 07052; (201) 877-3055. Studies the activities of state, county, and city commissions to assure legal, economic, and educational equality for women. Answers inquiries, provides consulting services, distributes newsletter. Services free to members, at cost to others.

34152. National Association of Noise Control Officers, 65 Prospect St, Trenton, NJ 08618; (609) 984-4161. Provides a forum for info, discussion, and study of noise control problems and promotes effectiveness of noise control methods. Answers inquiries, provides reference services, distributes publications, makes referrals. Fees charged for some services.

34153. National Association of Orthopaedic Nurses, North Woodbury Rd, Box 56, Pitman, NJ 08071; (609) 582-0111. Nonprofit org involved in public education concerning orthopaedic nursing and basic and advanced nursing education in orthopaedics. Answers inquiries, provides advisory services and speakers, distributes publications. Services free.

34154. National Association of Purchasing Management, P.O. Box 418, Oradell, NJ 07649; (201) 967-8585. Investigates purchasing, materials management, and related areas. Answers inquiries, makes referrals, provides short citation lists, permits onsite use of collection. Services primarily for members.

34155. National Cocaine Hotline, Fair Oaks Hospital, 19 Prospect St, Summit, NJ 07901; (800) 262-2463. Provides info and counseling for cocaine abusers, their friends, and families. Referrals to approved treatment centers are also provided. Phones are staffed by recovering cocaine abusers.

34156. National Council for Families and Television, 20 Nassau St, Suite 200, Princeton, NJ 08542; (609) 921-3639. Concerned with television and children, child development, critical television viewing skills. Publishes a journal, answers inquiries, provides advisory services, distributes publications. Most services are free.

34157. National Council of Acoustical Consultants, P.O. Box 359 (66 Morris Ave), Springfield, NJ 07081; (201) 379-1100. Source of info on acoustical consulting. Publishes newsletter, answers inquiries, distributes publications. Acoustical engineering services provided by members are performed at a negotiated rate.

34158. National Food and Conservation Through Swine, RR 4, Box 397 (Fox Run Rd), Sewell, NJ 08080; (609) 468-5447. Studies recycling of treated food waste in the production of hogs and proper cooking of food waste to avoid disease. Answers inquiries, provides advisory services and speakers for meetings. Services free to members, at cost to others.

34159. National Forensic Center, 17 Temple Terrace, Lawrenceville, NJ 08648; (609) 683-0550. Specializes in identification of expert witnesses, litigation consultants, and legal support specialists. Publishes newsletter, provides advisory and reference services, distributes publications. Services available for a fee.

34160. National Fragile X Syndrome Support Group, RR 8, Box 109, Bridgeton, NJ 08302;(609) 455-7508. Works toward educating medical community in diagnostic variations of Fragile X syndrome and promoting public awareness. Group responds to questions on syndrome and makes physician referrals.

34161. National Guild of Community Schools of the Arts, P.O. Box 583 (545 Cedar Lane), Teaneck, NJ 07666; (201) 836-5594. Acts as a clearinghouse for info on communications and research into dance, music, opera, and music theater. Publishes a monthly, answers inquiries, provides technical assistance, distributes publications. Some services free.

34162. National Industries for the Blind, 524 Hamburg Turnpike, Wayne, NJ 07470; (201) 595-9200. Promotes the creation of industrial employment opportunities for blind persons. Answers inquiries, provides consulting services to members or prospective members, answers inquiries, conducts rehabilitation program, makes referrals.

34163. National Institute for Rehabilitation Engineering, 97 Decker Rd, Butler, NJ 07405; (201) 838-2500. Nonprofit, clinical, research facility seeking to use today's technology to help permanently disabled people live and function independently. Answers brief inquiries free.

34165. National Juvenile Detention Association, c/o Youth Receiving Center, P.O. Box 3000, Somerville, NJ 08876. Provides training programs for all levels of juvenile detention personnel and conducts juvenile

training institutes. Publishes a newsletter, answers inquiries, provides advisory services, distributes publications. Services for those in the field.

34167. National Paperbox & Packaging Association, 231 Kings Highway East, Haddonfield, NJ 08033; (609) 429-7377. Concerned with production, marketing, and promotion of rigid paper boxes and folding cartons. Answers inquiries, provides reference services, distributes publications, lends materials. Most services free to members and at cost to others.

34168. National Premium Sales Executives, 1600 Route 22, Union, NJ 07083; (201) 687-3090. Concerned with incentive, premium, and motivational marketing. Answers inquiries, provides reference services, distributes publications. Services are free.

34169. National Religious Broadcasters, CN 1926, Morristown, NJ 07960; (201) 428-5400. Assn whose members produce religious programs for radio and television or operate stations carrying predominantly religious programs. Answers inquiries, provides consulting and reference services.

34170. Naval Air Engineering Center, Technical Library, Code 1115, Lakehurst, NJ 08733. Holdings on ground-support equipment, catapult and arresting gear, avionics, optical landing aids, propulsion, vertical take-off and landing. Answers inquiries, provides limited reference services. Services subject to security restrictions.

34171. Naval Air Propulsion Center, Technical Library, P.O. Box 7176 (1440 Parkway Ave), Trenton, NJ 08628; (609) 896-5609. Studies aerospace engineering, including theoretical and applied research and engineering development. Provides library services to Center personnel, govt contractors with special needs, and other qualified users subject to security clearance.

34172. New Eyes for the Needy, P.O. Box 332, Short Hills, NJ 07078; (201) 376-4903. Seeks to provide better vision for the poor throughout the world by soliciting used eyeglasses, frames, and artificial eyes. A brochure describing the org's program to collect needed materials is available.

34175. New Jersey Historical Society, 230 Broadway, Newark, NJ 07104; (201) 483-3939. Library of N.J. history and genealogy as well as American history. Library is open to the public; staff will answer inquiries and suggest other sources of info. Materials do not circulate.

34177. North American Blueberry Council, P.O. Box 166, Marmora, NJ 08223; (609) 399-1559. Assn of blueberry growers and marketers throughout U.S. and Canada. Answers inquiries, provides info on R&D in progress, conducts seminars, distributes publications. Services free.

34178. North American Electric Reliability Council, Research Park, Terhune Rd, Princeton, NJ 08540; (609) 924-6050. Promotes reliability and adequacy of bulk power supply of electric utility systems in North America. Answers inquiries, distributes publications, permits onsite use of collections. Services primarily for electric utilities and those in the industry.

34179. North American Thermal Analysis Society, c/o Harvey E. Bair, AT&T Labs, 600 Mountain, Murray Hill, NJ 07974. Studies thermoanalytical methods, including thermogravimetry (TG), differential thermal analysis (DTA), differential scanning calorimetry (DSC) and other forms of analysis. Answers inquiries, publishes newsletter, assists in locating experts in problem areas.

34181. Office of Population Research, Notestein Hall, Princeton Univ, 21 Prospect Ave, Princeton, NJ 08544; (609) 452-4870. Develops research programs and instruction in demography. Publishes a newsletter and a quarterly, answers inquiries, provides advisory, abstracting, and indexing services. Most services free.

34182. Oil and Hazardous Materials Spills Branch, Environmental Protection Agency, Edison, NJ 08837; (201) 321-6635. Conducts water pollution abatement research, including oil spills, hazardous material spills, and control of air pollution from spills. Answers inquiries, provides advisory services, permits onsite use of collection. Services are free.

34183. Olympic Media Information, 70 Hudson St, Hoboken, NJ 07030; (201) 963-1600. Performs and publishes info services that list, abstract, describe, and evaluate audiovisual materials in current circulation, with emphasis on those used in employee education. Provides consulting services to audio-visual users.

34184. Optical and Magnetic Components Department, Litton Industries, 200 East Hanover Ave, Morris Plains, NJ 07950; (201) 539-5500. Investigates single crystals, crystal growth, crystal quality, lasers, magnetic oxides, optical coatings, and gem stones. Answers inquiries and makes referrals.

34185. Oral Health Research Center, 110 Fuller Pl, Hackensack, NJ 07601; (201) 692-2622. Conducts research in preventive aspects of oral health, evaluates products of food and pharmaceutical industries, and provides community services. Answers inquiries, provides reference services, distributes data compilations. Fees charged.

34186. Organization of Women for Legal Awareness, 17 North Clinton St, East Orange, NJ 07019; (201) 672-5441. Legal advocacy org supporting the legal rights of women. Publishes a newsletter, answers inquiries, provides reference services, conducts workshops. Some services free.

34187. Paulsboro Laboratory Technical Information Group, Mobil Research and Development Corp., Paulsboro, NJ 08066. Source of data on petroleum processing, refining, and conversion (excluding exploration and production). Provides reference services to outsiders, makes interlibrary loans, makes referrals to other

sources of info, permits onsite use of collections by appointment.

34188. Phone-TTY Incorporated, 202 Lexington Ave, Hackensack, NJ 07601; (201) 489-7889. Nonprofit org that researches, develops, manufactures, and distributes communications equipment for the deaf and deaf-blind. Answers inquiries free, provides consulting services for a fee.

34189. Picatinny Arsenal Ammunition Museum, U.S. Army Armament R&D Center, Dover, NJ 07801. Museum of munitions of war, ammunition, and the history of Picatinny Arsenal. Answers inquiries, provides reference services, lends exhibits, permits onsite use of collections. Services free.

34190. Plastics Institute of America, Stevens Institute of Technology, Castle Point Station, Hoboken, NJ 07030. Provides graduate continuing education, fellowship support, audio courses, in-plant educational programs, and basic research support in polymer science and engineering. Answers inquiries, provides reference services.

34191. Plastics Technical Evaluation Center, U.S. Army Armament R&D Center, Building 351 North, Dover, NJ 07801. Provides technical info and data on plastic materials, adhesives, and composites of interest to Dept of Defense, its contractors and suppliers. Answers inquiries, provides technical advice and consulting services, makes referrals. Services limited to specific agencies.

34192. Point-of-Purchase Advertising Institute, 2 Executive Dr, Fort Lee, NJ 07024; (201) 585-8400. Assn of suppliers, associate suppliers, and users of point-of-purchase signs and displays. Answers brief inquiries, provides reference and consulting services. Services primarily for Institute members.

34193. Polymer Processing Institute, Stevens Institute of Technology, Hoboken, NJ 07030; (201) 420-5819. Research and info service org dedicated to advancement of polymer/plastics technology. Publishes a quarterly, answers inquiries, provides reference services, distributes publications. Services primarily for members.

34194. Population Research Library, Princeton Univ, Princeton, NJ 08540; (609) 452-4874. Conducts population research, especially its economic and sociological aspects, demography with an emphasis on fertility, nuptiality, mortality, and methodology. Provides reference services, participates in interlibrary loans through Princeton Univ Library.

34196. Princeton Child Development Institute, 300 Cold Soil Rd, Princeton, NJ 08540; (609) 924-6280. Provides education of and treatment for autistic children and young adults. Answers inquiries, provides advisory and consulting services, conducts seminars. Most services free.

34197. Princeton University Public Administration Collection, Princeton Univ Library, Princeton, NJ 08544; (609) 452-3209. Depository of documents on public administration, civil service, personnel administration, state and municipal govt. Answers inquiries, permits onsite use of collection by prior approval. Requests for service are approved only on an individual basis.

34198. Railroadians of America, c/o A.R. Ward, 689 Totowa Rd, Totowa, NJ 07512. Interest in railroad history and the collection, preservation, and maintenance of railroad memorabilia. Answers inquiries, conducts exhibits and meetings, distributes publications. Most services free.

34200. Recording for the Blind, 20 Rozel Road, Princeton, NJ 08540; (212) 517-9820. Provides recorded educational books free of charge to persons who cannot read normal printed material because of visual, physical or perceptual handicaps. Other services include a

34201. Reese Palley Gallery, Box 1983 (Park & Boardwalk), Atlantic City, NJ 08404; (609) 348-4800. Commercial org interested in modern American and English art porcelains and art glass, ceramics, wood, fibre, and other art. Answers inquiries, provides advisory services, appraises porcelain and glass. Some services free.

34202. Reflex Sympathetic Dystrophy Syndrome Association, 822 Wayside Lane, Haddonfield, NJ 08033; (609) 428-6510. Supports research into cause, treatment, and cure of reflex sympathetic dystrophy syndrome, a multisymptom syndrome affecting one or more extremities. RSDSA plans to establish a national data

34203. Revlon Research Center Library, 2121 Route 27, Edison, NJ 08817; (201) 287-7649. Library of cosmetics, perfumery, soaps, and packaging. Answers inquiries and permits onsite use of collection.

34204. Rona Pearl, 4 Hook Rd, Bayonne, NJ 07002; (201) 437-0800. Associate of E. Merck, Darmstadt, West Germany, promoting natural fish scale pearl essence and synthetic pearlescent pigments. Answers inquiries, provides technical services on use of pearl essence and pearlescent pigments.

34205. Rutgers Poultry Health Laboratory, P.O. Box 231, New Brunswick, NJ 08903; (609) 691-0360. Concerned with diagnosis of avian diseases, poultry management and health. Answers inquiries regarding bird diseases and management.

34207. Salvation Army, 799 Bloomfield Ave, Verona, NJ 07044; (201) 239-0606. Intl religious and charitable movement serving people in 85 countries around the world. Answers inquiries, provides advisory and counseling services, conducts classes and workshops. Services are free.

34208. Sandoz Library, Route 10, East Hanover, NJ 07936; (201) 386-7741. Library of pharmacology, chemistry, and medicine. Provides brief answers to inquiries and permits onsite use of collection. Services free.

34209. Sandy Hook Laboratory, NOAA, Highlands, NJ 07732; (201) 872-0200, (FTS) 342-8235. Studies abundance and distribution of groundfish, shellfish, and ichthyoplankton. Answers inquiries on laboratory activities and provides literature on its accomplishments. Permits onsite use of collections.

34210. Schiffli Lace and Embroidery Manufacturers Association, 512 23d St, Union City, NJ 07087; (201) 863-7300. Concerned with manufacture of laces and embroideries, embroidered fabrics, emblems, and appliques. Answers inquiries and provides consulting services.

34211. Scleroderma Research Foundation, Box 200 (Jobstown Rd), Columbus, NJ 08022; (609) 261-2200. Nonprofit org offering communication and support for persons and families affected by scleroderma. Answers inquiries, provides advisory services, conducts seminars. Services free.

34212. Search-A Central Registry of the Missing, 560 Sylvan Ave, Englewood Cliffs, NJ 07632; (201) 567-4040. Provides detailed info on runaway or missing individuals to law enforcement, security, medical, and social service agencies. Answers inquiries, provides consulting services, distributes publications. Services free.

34213. Secondary School Admission Test Board, c/o Dr Regan Kenyon, 20 Nassau St, Suite 314, Princeton, NJ 08542. Educational org concerned solely with elementary and secondary school admissions. Publishes a bulletin, conducts validity studies and workshops. SSAT is administered nationally by Educational Testing Service.

34214. Seeing Eye, P.O. Box 375, Morristown, NJ 07960; (201) 539-4425. Provides dog guides for the blind and training in their use. Answers inquiries, publishes a newsletter, distributes publications.

34215. Shelterforce Newspaper, 380 Main St, East Orange, NJ 07018; (201) 678-6778. Provides info to community orgs involved in tenant rights, creation of low-income housing, and neighborhood preservation. Answers inquiries for subscribers free, provides video tapes and consulting services for a fee.

34216. Shipcraft Guild, c/o Abraham Taubman, 11 College Dr, Jersey City, NJ 07305. Assn of shipmodel builders and marine artists, with membership open to all. Answers inquiries, distributes publications, makes referrals. Services primarily for members, but anyone may attend the monthly meetings.

34217. Skate Sailing Association of America, c/o Ronald Palmer, Secretary, R.D. 2, Whitehouse Station, NJ 08889. Interest in skate sailing. Publishes plans and instructions, answers inquiries, distributes publications. Services free to members and at cost to others.

34218. Society for Historical Archaeology, P.O. Box 241, Glassboro, NJ 08028. Promotes scholarly research and the dissemination of knowledge concerning historical archaeology and the application of archaeological methods to the study of history. Answers inquiries, provides advisory services, makes referrals. Services free.

34219. Society for the Encouragement of Research and Invention, P.O. Box 412 (100 Summit Ave), Summit, NJ 07901; (201) 273-1088. Encourages researchers, scientists, authors, and others of all disciplines who are distinguished by their contributions to the furtherance of research and invention. Answers inquiries, provides reference services, makes referrals. Services are free.

34220. Society for the Investigation of the Unexplained, P.O. Box 265, Little Silver, NJ 07739; (201) 842-5229. Investigates unexplained events in science, as well as mentalogy and mysticism. Answers inquiries, provides reference and copying services, distributes publications. Service fees for nonmembers.

34221. Society of Professional Management Consultants, 163 Engle St, Englewood, NJ 07631; (201) 569-6668. Serves as management consultants. Refers requesters to individual members upon submittal of a profile of requester's particular problems. Service is free and primarily for business, assns, nonprofit orgs, and govt.

34222. South Mountain Laboratories, 380 Lackawanna Pl, South Orange, NJ 07079; (201) 762-0045. Conducts drug bioassay and research on cosmetics, food additives, pharmaceuticals, and pharmaceutical aids. Provides consulting and reference services for a fee, permits onsite use of collection by govt agencies and clients.

34223. Soyfoods Association of North America, c/o Gary Barat, 170 Change Bridge Rd, Montville, NJ 07045. Engaged in production, marketing, and popularization of foods made from soybeans. Answers inquiries, provides reference services, distributes publications. Services are primarily for members.

34224. Stein Collectors International, P.O. Box 463, Kingston, NJ 08528; (201) 329-2567. Assists collectors in study, collection, and appreciation of beer steins and similar antique drinking vessels. Publishes a bulletin, answers inquiries, provides reference services, distributes publications. Services are free.

34225. Technical Insights, P.O. Box 1304, Fort Lee, NJ 07024; (201) 568-4744. Commercial publisher interested in emerging technologies. Info is provided primarily through the publications, which are available by subscription.

34226. Textile Care Allied Trades Association, 543 Valley Rd, Upper Montclair, NJ 07043; (201) 744-0090. Compiles data on commercial, industrial, institutional, and coin-operated laundering and cleaning equipment and supplies. Answers inquiries from public health officials.

34227. Textile Economics Bureau, 101 Eisenhower Parkway, Roseland, NJ 07068. Statistical agency of the man-made fiber producers of the U.S. Answers inquiries, provides reference services, distributes publications. Services for a fee.

34228. Textile Research Institute, P.O. Box 625 (601 Prospect Ave), Princeton, NJ 08542; (609) 924-3150. Collection of materials on textiles, polymers, fibers, organic chemistry, dyes, and processing. Answers inquiries, makes referrals, provides reference and duplication services for a fee, permits onsite use of collections.

34229. Thomas-Betts Company, 920 Route 202, Raritan, NJ 08869; (201) 685-1600. Repository of info on cable connectors for aluminum/copper cables, conduit supports and beam clamps, electrician's tools, and other electrical fixtures. Answers inquiries and permits onsite reference.

34230. Thrombocytopenia Absent Radius Syndrome Association, 312 Sherwood Drive, RD 1, Linwood, NJ 08221; (609) 927-0418. Provides info and support to families of children with thrombocytopenia absent radius syndrome. Acts as a clearinghouse for affected families and health professionals.

34231. Tile Council of America Research Center, P.O. Box 326 (U.S. Highway 1), Princeton, NJ 08542; (609) 921-7050. Provides methods and materials for installing ceramic tile. Answers inquiries, provides consulting services, makes referrals.

34232. Trinet, c/o Ellen Helms, 9 Campus Dr, Parsippany, NJ 07054; (201) 267-3600. Concerned with identification and measurement of business markets, including evaluation of purchasing potential and production volume of companies and industries. Offers reports, online data base.

34233. Truck Safety Equipment Institute, 222 Cedar Lane, Teaneck, NJ 07666; (201) 839-9500. Nonprofit org of North American manufacturers of motor vehicle safety equipment, promoting improved vehicle and highway safety. Answers inquiries, conducts seminars, makes referrals. Services free to members and free or at cost to others.

34234. U.S. Army Communications-Electronics Museum, Kaplan Hall, Fort Monmouth, NJ 07703; (201) 532-2445. Library of the history of military communications, with emphasis on U.S. Army Signal Corps. Answers inquiries, lends reproductions of photos and documents, permits onsite reference.

34235. U.S. Golf Association, Golf House, Far Hills, NJ 07931; (201) 234-2300. Promotes game of golf and golf courses, including uniform rules and standards. Brief answers to technical and historical inquiries are given, and onsite use of the golf museum and library is permitted.

34236. Ultrasonic Industry Association, P.O. Drawer F (300 Buckelew Ave), Jamesburg, NJ 08831; (201) 521-4441. Studies ultrasonics, ultrasonics terminology in commercial, industrial, defense, and medical applications. Conducts technical symposia and workshops at cost and makes referrals free.

34237. Unexpected Wildlife Refuge, Newfield, NJ 08344; (609) 697-3541. Concerned about wildlife preservation, with emphasis on beavers. Publishes a newsletter, answers inquiries, distributes publications. Services provided for a fee.

34238. United States Association for Blind Athletes, 55 West California Ave, Beach Haven Park, NJ 08008; (609) 492-1017. Trains, coaches, and prepares blind athletes for natl and intl competition in both winter and summer sports. Answers inquiries, provides advisory services, distributes publications. Most services are free.

34239. United States Testing Company, 1415 Park Ave, Hoboken, NJ 07030; (201) 792-2400. Conducts materials testing, chemical and microbiological analysis. Answers inquiries, provides reference and consulting services. A fee is charged for all testing services.

34240. Waksman Institute of Microbiology Library, P.O. Box 759, Piscataway, NJ 08854; (201) 932-2906. Library of microbiology, virology, immunology (nonclinical aspects), fermentation, antibiotics (nonclinical aspects), biotechnology, and molecular biology. Provides copying services on a fee basis, makes interlibrary loans, permits onsite use of collection.

34241. Wallcovering Information Bureau, P.O. Box 359 (66 Morris Ave), Springfield, NJ 07081; (201) 379-1100. Promotes greater interest in and sale of flexible wall coverings and consumer education to advance that goal. Answers inquiries, assists in locating wallcovering sources. Services are free.

34242. Water Resources Program, Princeton Univ, Princeton, NJ 08544; (609) 452-4675. Studies geohydrology, water quality engineering, quantitative aspects of surface water hydrology, geochemistry of water, and hydraulics. Answers inquiries and makes referrals.

34243. Wetlands Institute, Lehigh Univ, Stone Harbor Blvd, Stone Harbor, NJ 08247. Dedicated to research and educational programs dealing with the understanding of salt marshes and shallow water estuarine environment. Answers inquiries, conducts lectures and tours of marshlands, distributes pamphlets. Most services are free.

34244. Yesteryear Museum Archives, 20 Harriet Dr, Whippany, NJ 07981-1906; (201) 386-1920. Nonprofit org that preserves material pertaining to the history of mechanical music and sound reproduction. Answers inquiries; provides reference, magnetic tape, and video tape services; makes referrals. Some services free.

34245. Youth Environmental Society, P.O. Box 441 (23A N Main St), Cranbury, NJ 08512; (609) 655-8030. Works with youth to develop leadership through environmental action. Publishes a newsletter, answers inquiries, provides advisory services.

New Mexico

35001. Access Innovations, P.O. Box 40130, Albuquerque, NM 87196; (505) 265-3591. Interest in org, management of corporate and institutional libraries, records management, data base design, construction, indexing, data entry. Provides general reference services, conducts seminars. Fees charged for all services.

35002. Air Force Systems Command 6585th Test Group/PR, 6585th Test Group/PR, Holloman Air Force Base, NM 88330; (505) 479-6511 ext 2144. Test and evaluation facility specializing in inertial guidance navigation systems, gyroscopes, accelerometers, simulated flight conditions, etc. Answers inquiries, distributes technical reports.

35003. All Indian Pueblo Council Business Development Center, P.O. Box 6507 (2401 12th St), Albuquerque, NM 87197; (505) 242-4774. Assists individual Indians and tribes in establishing and managing their own businesses. Provides general reference services, conducts seminars, permits onsite use of library. Services available to enrolled members of federally recognized Indian tribes.

35004. American Farriers Association, P.O. Box 695, Albuquerque, NM 87103; (505) 255-3109. Interest in shoeing horses, horseshoes and related supplies and materials for shoeing horses; shoeing and forging competitions. Answers inquiries, makes referrals free with SASE.

35005. American Indian Law Center, P.O. Box 4456 (1117 Stanford St NE), Station A, Albuquerque, NM 87196; (505) 277-5462. Interest in Indian law and policy, tribal govt administration, Indian child welfare, tribal courts, etc. Provides general reference services, conducts seminars. Services available to those active in the field; some at cost.

35006. American Society for Radiologic Technologists, 15000 Central Ave SE, Albuquerque, NM 87123; (505) 298-4500. Interest in radiologic technology, including radiography, nuclear medicine, radiation therapy, and diagnostic medical sonography. Answers specific questions, makes referrals, conducts education programs for radiologic technologists, insurance programs for members.

35008. Anthropology Film Center Foundation, P.O. Box 493 (1626 Canyon Rd), Santa Fe, NM 87501; (505) 983-4127. Interest in study of visual anthropology, generation and analysis of film records of human behavior. Provides general reference services, conducts courses and seminars, distributes publications, permits onsite study. Most services provided for a fee.

35009. Archaeological Conservancy, 415 Orchard Dr, ·Sante Fe, NM 87501; (505) 982-3278. Nonprofit membership corp dedicated to preservation of significant archaeological, prehistoric sites in the U.S., usually through acquisition. Provides general reference services, permits site visits by prior appointment. Services free.

35010. Army Atmospheric Sciences Laboratory, Attn: DE-LAS-DP, White Sands Missile Range, NM 88002; (915) 678-5232. Interest in remote atmospheric sensing research, atmospheric dynamics research, aerosol physics research, electromagnetic EM propagation, etc. Provides technology transfer assistance, meteorological consulting.

35011. Bureau of Business and Economic Research Data Bank, Institute for Applied Research Services, Univ of N.M., Albuquerque, NM 87131; (505) 277-6626. Interest in economic, business, and local govt data and general social characteristics for N.M. and Southwest. Provides general reference services, up to two free hours of consulting. Fees charged for photocopies.

35012. Coronado State Monument, P.O. Box 95 (State Route 44, 1/4-mile west of Rio Grande bridge), Bernalillo, NM 87004; (505) 867-5351. Interest in prehistory of the Pueblo Indians (1300-1600), N.M. history during the Spanish Period (1500-1700). Answers brief inquiries, publishes materials. Monument open to public; guided tours available by appointment.

35013. ERIC Clearinghouse on Rural Education and Small Schools, N.M. State Univ, Box 3AP, Las Cruces, NM 88003; (505) 646-2623. Clearinghouse for research on American Indian education, rural education, Mexican-American and migrant education, etc. Answers inquiries, provides consultating services, permits onsite study, conducts workshops, sells publications.

35014. Energy Institute, N.M. State Univ, P.O. Box 3EI, Las Cruces, NM 88003; (505) 646-1745. Conducts research projects on geothermal resources, promotes geothermal development and other renewable energy sources. Provides general reference services, distributes publications. Most services free.

35015. Futures for Children, 805 Tijeras NW, Albuquerque, NM 87102; (505) 881-6616, (800) 545-6843. Nonprofit org that provides community advisory services for underprivileged in Republic of Colombia, Southwestern American Indians. Answers inquiries, distributes publications. Services free, except community advisory services, made by special agreement.

35016. Gallup Public Library, 115 West Hill Ave, Gallup, NM 87301; (505) 863-3692. Interest in social, biological aspects of Navajo, Hopi, and Zuni Indians. Provides general reference services, makes interlibrary loans, permits onsite use of collections.

35017. Geology Museum, Univ of N.M., Yale Ave NE, Albuquerque, NM 87106; (505) 277-4204. Interest in geology, paleontology, meteorites. Identifies fossils, rocks, minerals, meteorites from Southwestern U.S. for professional, amateur geologists.

35018. Historical Society of New Mexico, P.O. Box 5819, Santa Fe, NM 87502. Interest in history of N.M. Conducts annual conference (registration fee required), publishes materials, makes info referrals.

35019. Indian Arts and Crafts Association, P.O. Box 40013 (4215 Lead St SE), Albuquerque, NM 87196; (505) 265-9149. Natl nonprofit trade org that promotes Native American crafts, Southwestern Indian jewelry, Kachina dolls, Navajo weaving, pottery. Provides general reference services, conducts seminars, wholesale markets for retailers only. Services primarily for members and buyers. Fees may be charged.

35020. Inhalation Toxicology Research Institute, P.O. Box 5890, Albuquerque, NM 87185; (505) 844-2600. Conducts basic and applied research on effects of inhaled materials. Interest in toxicology, fission products, aerosols, etc. Provides general reference services, conducts seminars, permits onsite use of collection. Services free to orgs providing reciprocal services.

35021. Institute for Applied Research Services, Univ of N.M., Albuquerque, NM 87106; (505) 277-5934. Interest in economic and social development of N.M. and Southwest, research, training, assistance. Provides general reference services, permits onsite use of collections. Fees charged for extensive services.

35022. Institute for Applied Research Services Division of Government Research, Univ of N.M., Albuquerque, NM 87131; (505) 277-3305. Interest in federal, state, and local govt, especially N.M. govt, education, economics, highway traffic safety. Evaluates programs; provides consulting services, computer programming, design, and systems analysis services for a fee; sells publications.

35023. Institute of American Indian Arts Library, St Michaels Dr, College of Santa Fe Campus, Santa Fe, NM 87501; (505) 988-6356. Interest in American Indian arts and culture. Provides general reference and copying services for a fee, permits onsite study. Services primarily for the students, staff, but also provided to other Indian groups as time allows.

35024. International Foundation for Theatrical Research, P.O. Box 4526 (614 Indian School Rd NW), Albuquerque, NM 87196; (505) 843-7749. Interest in new forms of theatrical expression. Answers inquiries, provides literature-searching and copying services, distributes publications. Services available at cost.

35026. Los Alamos National Laboratory Libraries, P.O. Box 1663, MS-P362, Los Alamos, NM 87545; (505) 667-4448, 843-4448. Interest in theoretical physics and mathematics, computer science. Provides general reference services, permits onsite reference. Services free to regional libraries, federal agencies, and contractors; services provided to outsiders only on very limited basis.

35027. Lovelace Medical Foundation Library, 5200 Gibson Blvd SE, Albuquerque, NM 87108; (505) 262-7158. Interest in clinical medicine. Provides general reference and copying services primarily for scientists, medical personnel.

35028. Maxwell Museum of Anthropology, Univ of N.M., Albuquerque, NM 87131; (505) 277-4404, 277-2924 (Education Division). Interest in archaeology and ethnology of major world cultures, emphasis on American Southwest. Provides consulting services, identifies artifacts free, conducts programs, tours, and lectures. Photographic services provided for a fee. Museum open to public at no charge.

35029. Museum of New Mexico, P.O. Box 2087, Santa Fe, NM 87503; (505) 827-6450. Interest in anthropology, history, and fine arts of Southwest, folk art of the world. Collections available to researchers. Answers written inquiries, publishes materials.

35030. Museum of Southwestern Biology, Univ of N.M., Albuquerque, NM 87131; (505) 277-5340, 277-5130. Interest in research on invertebrates, vertebrates, plants of Southwestern U.S., Mex., and Holarctic region. All materials available for study by qualified scientists. Limited amount of free identification provided; large projects and impact studies conducted by contract.

35031. National Atomic Museum, P.O. Box 5400 (Building 20358), Kirtland Air Force Base, Albuquerque, NM 87115; (505) 844-4223. Interest in nuclear weapons history, energy. Answers inquiries, shows films, permits onsite use of collections. Services free.

35032. National Energy Information Center, Institute for Applied Research Services, Univ of N.M., 2500 Central Ave SE, Albuquerque, NM 87131; (505) 846-2375. Interest in all energy subjects. Provides general reference and indexing services, distributes publications. Inquiries responded to free of charge.

35034. National Indian Council on Aging, P.O. Box 2088, Albuquerque, NM 87103; (505) 242-9505. Natl org offers comprehensive services to Indian and Alaska Native elderly. Provides general reference services, technical assistance to tribes, Congress.

35035. National Information Center for Educational Media, Access Innovations, P.O. Box 40130, Albuquerque, NM 87196; (505) 265-3591, (800) 421-8711. Natl info retrieval system for audiovisual educational materials. Interest in educational media, filmstrips, records, transparencies, etc. Answers inquiries; provides consulting, reference services; cataloging, indexing, and retrieval services by subject. Services provided at cost.

35036. Naval Weapons Evaluation Facility, Kirtland Air Force Base, Albuquerque, NM 87117; (505) 844-0491. Interest in nuclear weapon safety, weapon testing and evaluation, naval aircraft testing. Provides general reference services, consulting. Services free, available only to special groups on need-to-know basis.

35037. New Mexico Energy Research and Development Institute, 457 Washington SE, Suite M, Albuquerque, NM 87108; (505) 277-3661. Interest in energy info, R&D, traditional and alternative energy systems, energy conservation, renewable energy sources. Provides general reference services, distributes publications—some free to state residents, all at cost to nonresidents.

35038. New Mexico Engineering Research Institute, P.O. Box 25, Univ Station, Univ. of N.M., Albuquerque, NM 87131; (505) 864-4644. Interest in simulated nuclear blast effects, design, testing of structures to withstand conventional and nuclear blast effects. Provides technical data, consulting services to industry, govt agencies and contractors; some reports distributed to independent orgs.

35039. New Mexico Geological Society, Campus Station, Socorro, NM 87801; (505) 835-5410. Promotes interest, research in geology and allied sciences, engineering, mining, mineral and energy exploration in region. Answers inquiries free, sells publications.

35042. New Mexico Organic Growers Association, 1312 Lobo Pl NE, Albuquerque, NM 87106; (505) 268-5504. Interest in organic farming and gardening. Answers inquiries, conducts seminars, distributes newsletter, makes referrals. Services free.

35043. New Mexico Solar Energy Institute, P.O. Box 3 SOL (Corner of Stewart and Espina), Las Cruces, NM 88003; (505) 646-2639. Interest in solar, photovoltaic, and wind energy, bioenergy, solar heating and cooling systems. Provides general reference services, conducts workshops, distributes publications. Except for copying and workshops, services free for state residents.

35044. New Mexico Tumor Registry, Univ of N.M., 900 Camino de Salud NE, Albuquerque, NM 87131; (505) 277-5541. Interest in population-based cancer data for state of N.M. and American Indian populations in Ariz. Provides general reference services, conducts seminars, distributes publications, permits onsite study. Services free, except for computer time, within restrictions.

35045. New Mexico Water Resources Research Institute, N.M. State Univ, P.O. Box 3167, Las Cruces, NM 88003; (505) 646-4337. Interest in water resources research, water cycle, conservation, augmentation of water supplies, aquatic biology and ecology, etc. Answers brief inquiries, makes referrals, publishes reports.

35046. New Mexico Wildlife Federation, 300 Val Verde SE, Albuquerque, NM 87108; (505) 265-7372. Interest in wildlife resources and natural environment management and use, conservation in N.M. Provides general reference services, conducts seminars, distributes publications, lends materials—all for a fee.

35047. Paleo-Indian Institute, Agency for Conservation Archeology, Eastern N.M. Univ, Portales, NM 88130; (505) 562-2147. Conducts archaeological, anthropological research in Mexico and Southwest. Provides general reference services, distributes publications and data compilations, permits onsite study. Info services free. Archaeological surveys performed by bid contracts.

35048. Professional Salespersons of America, 100 Maria Circle, Albuquerque, NM 87114; (505) 897-1666. Interest in sales, marketing, product info, sales as a career, standards in sales, legislation and regulations affecting sales, etc. Provides general reference services, conducts seminars, distributes publications, permits onsite study. Membership fee required.

35049. Shelton Research, P.O. Box 5235 (1517 Pacheco St), Santa Fe, NM 87502; (505) 983-9457. Independent laboratory conducting research and testing on residential heating systems, primarily for solid fuels wood and coal. Provides consulting and lecturing services, conducts annual seminars, sells publications and slide sets.

35050. Society for Pediatric Research, c/o William Berman, Jr., M.D., Secty-Treas, Dept of Pediatrics, Univ. of N.M. School of Medicine, Albuquerque, NM 87131; (505) 277-4361. Interest in pediatric research. Answers inquiries regarding membership and annual meetings.

35051. Society for the Anthropology of Visual Communication, c/o Dr Carroll Williams, President, Anthropological Film Center, P.O. Box 493, Santa Fe, NM 87501; (505) 983-4127. Interest in communication and culture, anthropology of visual communication, mass media, films, photography, TV, etc. Provides general reference and consulting services, conducts seminars. Services primarily for members; consulting provided for a fee.

35052. Southwest Research and Information Center, P.O. Box 4524, Albuquerque, NM 87106; (505) 262-1862. Public interest advocacy center that litigates, testifies at hearings, provides info on social and environmental issues in N.M. and Southwest. Provides general reference services, distributes publications, permits onsite use of collections. Services provided free to the needy, at cost to most others.

35053. Southwestern Cooperative Educational Laboratory, 229 Truman St NE, Albuquerque, NM 87108; (505) 268-3348. Operates educational projects to improve learning in multicultural settings. Interest in communication arts. Answers inquiries, provides info, disseminates materials and research findings.

35054. Tamarind Institute, Univ. of N.M., 108 Cornell Ave SE, Albuquerque, NM 87106; (505) 277-3901. Provides opportunities for artists and skilled lithographic printers to work creatively in collaboration to produce lithographs. Answers inquiries, conducts training programs and seminars, sells publications. Training programs require payment of tuition. Services limited to artists.

35055. Technology Application Center, Univ of N.M., 2500 Central Ave SE, Albuquerque, NM 87131; (505) 277-3622. Interest in transfer and utilization of remote sensing technology, aerial and satellite photography. Provides computerized searches, consulting, research, and reference services, offers short courses. Services provided to clients on fee or contract basis.

35056. Transportation Technical Environmental Information Center, Sandia National Laboratories, Albuquerque, NM 87185; (505) 844-2765. Interest in transportation environments described in engineering terms. Answers inquiries, provides referral and copying services, distributes data compilations, publications. Services free within limits.

35057. Western States Arts Foundation, 141 East Palace, Santa Fe, NM 87501; (505) 988-1166. Manages, directs, coordinates, and supports arts events and activities in western U.S. and Hawaii. Provides general reference services, conducts seminars, sells publications and mailing lists. Most info services free to artists, arts orgs in West.

35058. White Sands Missile Range Technical Library Branch, Attn: STEWS-TE-TL, White Sands Missile Range, NM 88002; (505) 678-1317. Interest in missile systems, physics, mathematics, engineering, computers. Provides general reference and copying services, permits onsite study. Services available only to DoD personnel with proper clearance.

New York

36008. A. Philip Randolph Institute, 260 Park Ave S, 6th Fl, New York, NY 10010; (212) 533-8000. Nonprofit org interested in black trade unionists, leadership development, political activists, voter registration, and education. Answers inquiries, provides advisory and reference services, distributes publications, makes referrals. Services primarily for special groups.

36010. AFS International/Intercultural Programs, 313 E 43rd St, New York, NY 10017; (212) 661-4550. Offers opportunities for students 16 to 18 to live for a year or a summer with families in different countries, to attend local school, and to participate in the activities of new communities. Answers inquiries, provides advisory services. Services free.

36011. AGWAY Corporate Library, P.O. Box 4766, Syracuse, NY 13221; (315) 477-6408. Maintains a center for applied and developmental research in crops, dairy and livestock, farm management, farm systems, and poultry. Answers inquiries, permits onsite use of collection. Services free to anyone referred from another library.

36013. APM Library of Recorded Sound, 502 E 17th St, Brooklyn, NY 11226; (718) 941-6835. Maintains holdings on the history of recorded sound, development of the phonograph, and patent history. Answers inquiries; provides advisory, reference, patent-searching, and reproduction services; distributes publications; makes referrals; permits onsite use of collections.

36014. Academy for Educational Development, 680 Fifth Ave, New York, NY 10019; (212) 397-0040. Assists schools, colleges, univs, govtal agencies, and other orgs with the improvement of their operations and educational programs and development of plans for the future. Provides consulting and reference services, makes referrals.

36016. Academy of American Poets, 177 E 87th St, New York, NY 10028; (212) 427-5665. Encourages and fosters production of American poetry by providing fellowships for poets of proven merit and by granting awards and prizes for poetic achievement. Answers inquiries, conducts classes and poetry readings, provides speakers, distributes publications, makes referrals.

36017. Academy of Orthomolecular Psychiatry, P.O. Box 372, Manhasset, NY 11030; (516) 627-1718. Seeks to further knowledge and clinical application of orthomolecular psychiatry for the alleviation of mental disorders. Provides info on research in progress, distributes publications, makes referrals.

36018. Accreditation Board for Engineering and Technology, 345 E 47th St, New York, NY 10017; (212) 705-7685. Interest in engineering education, engineering technician and technology education. Answers inquiries, makes referrals, permits onsite reference to nonconfidential info.

36019. Acid Rain Information Clearinghouse, 33 S Washington St, Rochester, NY 14608; (716) 546-3796. Interest in all aspects of acid rain, including atmospheric sciences, environmental aspects, social aspects, and engineering. Answers inquiries, provides reference and educational services, makes referrals. Services free, unless extensive.

36020. Ackerman Institute for Family Therapy, 149 E 78th St, New York, NY 10021; (212) 879-4900. Nonprofit, nonsectarian org providing research, training, and treatment through family therapy. Provides advisory services, conducts seminars and workshops, rents instructional tapes. Clinical services provided on a sliding-fee scale.

36021. Acoustical Society of America, 335 E 45th St, New York, NY 10017; (212) 661-9404. Seeks to increase and diffuse the knowledge of acoustics and promote its practical application. Answers inquiries, distributes publications, makes referrals. Services free.

36022. Actors' Equity Association, 165 W 46th St, New York, NY 10036; (212) 869-8530. Labor union for performers in the legitimate theater. Publishes monthly newsletter and answers inquiries.

36023. Adirondack Mountain Club, 172 Ridge St, Glens Falls, NY 12801; (518) 793-7737. Promotes conservation practices specifically related to the Forest Preserve of N.Y. State. Answers inquiries, conducts winter mountaineering schools and environmental workshops. Fees charged for some services, but summer ranger-naturalist program free to public.

36024. Adirondack Museum Library, Blue Mountain Lake, NY 12812; (518) 352-7312. Interest in the economic and social history of Adirondacks, their art and artists, forestry, conservation, and ecology. Researchers may have access to the collections by appointment. Inquiries answered or referrals made. Reference service available free.

36025. Adoptive Parents Committee, 210 Fifth Ave, New York, NY 10010; (212) 683-9221. Dedicated to improvement of adoption and foster care laws. Answers inquiries, provides consulting and reference services, distributes publications. Most services free.

36026. Adrenal Metabolic Research Society of the Hypoglycemia Foundation, 153 Pawling Ave, Troy, NY 12180; (518) 272-7154. Studies functional hypoglycemia and its relationship to other conditions, adrenal insufficiency, alcoholism, allergy, and nutrition. Answers inquiries, provides consulting and reference services, makes referrals, disseminates publications.

36028. Advertising Council, 825 Third Ave, New York, NY 10022; (212) 758-0400. Nonpartisan, nonprofit public service org interested in public service advertising campaigns. Answers inquiries, makes referrals, distributes publications (many free), supplies public service advertising to media on major problems facing communities and the nation as a whole.

36029. Advertising Photographers of America, 118 E 25th St, New York, NY 10010; (212) 254-5500. Seeks to promote high level of business standards and ethics within the industry. Answers inquiries, provides advisory and reference services, distributes newsletter, makes referrals. Most services free.

36030. Advertising Research Foundation, 3 E 54th St, New York, NY 10022; (212) 751-5656. Conducts advertising and advertising research, marketing and marketing research. Answers inquiries, provides consulting and analytical testing services, makes referrals. Services only to members and qualified students.

36031. Advisory Group on Electron Devices, 201 Varick St, New York, NY 10014; (212) 620-3374. Interest in electronics, electron and microwave devices. Provides info retrieval services to govt agencies and govt contractors within electron devices field, provides unclassified and nonproprietary info to contractors and potential contractors.

36032. Aesthetic Realism Foundation, 141 Greene St, New York, NY 10012; (212) 777-4490. Teaches aesthetic realism of Eli Siegel: "The world, art, and self explain each other: each is the aesthetic oneness of opposites." Conducts classes and seminars, answers inquiries, provides reference services, distributes publications. Most services free.

36033. Africa Fund, 198 Broadway, New York, NY 10038; (212) 962-1210. Helps Africans from Mozambique, Angola, Zimbabwe, South Africa, Namibia, and the Western Sahara work against civil and human injustices of colonial and white minority domination. Answers inquiries, provides reference services.

36034. African Medical & Research Foundation, 420 Lexington Ave, New York, NY 10170; (212) 986-1835. Interest in health training, public health, primary health care, and health education in East Africa, including air and ground mobile medicine. Provides consulting and reference services.

36035. African National Congress of South Africa, Observer Mission to the United Nations and Representation to the United States, 801 Second Ave, New York, NY 10017; (212) 490-3487. Works for the foundation of a free democratic state in South Africa. Answers inquiries free, distributes publications by subscription.

36036. African-American Institute, 833 U.N. Plaza, New York, NY 10017; (212) 949-5666. Works to further African development, inform Americans about Africa, and strengthen African-American understanding. Answers inquiries, distributes publications, conducts seminars, provides reference services. Services free, except for publications.

36037. Afro-American Cultural Foundation, 75 Grasslands Rd, Valhalla, NY 10595; (914) 347-4260. Interest in Afro-American history, life, and culture. Answers inquiries, provides advisory services, conducts lectures, makes referrals, permits onsite use of collections. Fee for some services.

36038. Afro-Asian Center, P.O. Box 337, Saugerties, NY 12477; (914) 246-7828. Encourages student correspondence under the direction of professional teachers on both sides of the world. Answers inquiries, distributes publications, makes referrals. Services for a fee to high school social studies teachers.

36039. Agent Orange Victims International, 27 Washington Sq North, New York, NY 10011; (212) 460-5770. Provides Vietnam veterans manifesting symptoms and effects of Agent Orange (dioxin) exposure and their families with advocacy, legal, medical, counseling, support, crisis intervention, and outreach programs. Answers inquiries, distributes publications, makes referrals free.

36040. Airport Security Council, P.O. Box 30705, JFK Intl Airport, Jamaica, NY 11430; (516) 328-2990. Responsible for development and administration of an air cargo loss prevention program. Provides advisory services, speakers, and publications. Most services free.

36041. Akwesasne Museum, Rte 37, Hogansburg, NY 13655; (518) 358-2240. Seeks to preserve, present, and perpetuate best instances of Mohawk Indian culture.

Answers inquiries; provides advisory, translation and reference services; lends materials; makes referrals; permits onsite use of collection. Services provided for nominal entrance fee.

36042. Alan Guttmacher Institute, 111 Fifth Ave, New York, NY 10003; (212) 254-5656. Independent corp for research, policy analysis, and public education, and a special affiliate of the Planned Parenthood Federation of America, Inc. Answers inquiries, provides advisory and reference services. Services primarily for family planning professionals and the media.

36043. Albany College of Pharmacy, 106 New Scotland Ave, Albany, NY 12208; (518) 445-7211. Collects info on pharmacy, including pharmacology. Answers inquiries, provides consulting and reference services, provides computer consultants for pharmacy operations, makes interlibrary loans. Extension services provided on a contract basis.

36044. Alcohol Education for Youth, 1500 Western Ave, Albany, NY 12203; (514) 456-3800. Seeks to prevent alcohol abuse among youth, with a special focus on families. Answers inquiries, provides advisory and reference services, conducts seminars, distributes publications, makes referrals. Most services free.

36045. Alcohol Education for Youth and Community, 362 State Street, Albany, NY 12210; (518) 436-9319. Provides educational services and assistance for the prevention of alcoholism. Provides speakers, films, and publications on alcohol and conducts workshops and meetings for community participants.

36046. Alcoholics Anonymous World Services, P.O. Box 459, Grand Central Station (468 Park Ave South), New York, NY 10163; (212) 686-1100. Maintains materials on history and operations of Alcoholics Anonymous, including AA groups in 110 countries. Answers inquiries, provides advisory services, makes referrals, permits onsite use of collections. Services free.

36047. Alternate Media Center, New York Univ, 725 Broadway, 4th Fl, New York, NY 10003; (212) 598-2852. Undertakes work on a project basis and sets up demonstration projects of interactive telecommunications for clients that include federal agencies, private foundations, and corporations. Provides consulting services, conducts seminars and workshops. Fee for services.

36048. Alternative Press Syndicate, Box 1347, Ansonia Station (17 west 60th St), New York, NY 10023; (212) 974-1990. Interest in alternative press, critiques of major news media, newsmakers and reporters working outside the mainstream. Answers inquiries, provides reference and microform services, makes referrals. Services free to members, for a fee to others.

36049. Alternatives to Abortion International, 46 N Broadway, Yonkers, NY 10701; (914) 423-6666. Assists persons involved in problem pregnancies and related distress by rendering personal and practical assistance. Provides consulting services and technical assistance to all emergency pregnancy service centers and groups, and conducts training and educational groups.

36050. Amalgamated Clothing and Textile Workers Union, 15 Union Sq, New York, NY 10003; (212) 242-0700. Labor union representing male apparel, textile, non-rubber footwear, and headwear industries. Answers brief inquiries, makes referrals, permits onsite use of collection by appointment only.

36051. Amateur Astronomers Association of New York City, c/o John Marshall, 1010 Park Ave, New York, NY 10028; (212) 535-2922. Nonprofit astronomical and educational institution. Answers inquiries, makes referrals, provides advice, offers lecture series by noted astronomers, conducts classes, operates an optical workshop for telescope making, offers speakers' panel of lecturers.

36052. Amazonia Foundation, P.O. Box 651, New York, NY 10023. Conducts research into special ultraviolet effect of particular interest to aeronautics and flight safety systems and development of techniques for the remote detection of environmental pollutants. Because of limited staff and resources, provides only brief answers to specific inquiries.

36053. America Israel Friendship League, 134 E 39th St, New York, NY 10016; (212) 213-8630. Seeks to foster understanding and friendship between Americans of all faiths and Israelis. Answers inquiries, provides advisory and reference services, conducts seminars, distributes publications, makes referrals. Most services free.

36054. American Academy and Institute of Arts and Letters Library, 633 W 155th St, New York, NY 10032; (212) 368-5900. Collection of literature in arts and humanities, music, art, and writing. Permits onsite use of collections by bona fide researchers with prior arrangement.

36055. American Academy of Compensation Medicine, Box 10, Island Station, Roosevelt Island, NY 10044; (212) 750-6777. Seeks to establish meaningful standards of practice and ethics in the field of compensation medicine. Answers inquiries, provides consulting services, conducts seminars.

36056. American Academy of Dental Electrosurgery, P.O. Box 374, Planetarium Station, New York, NY 10024; (212) 595-1925. Promotes instruction and research in dental electrosurgery and seeks to improve art and science of that discipline. Provides info on R&D in progress, conducts seminars, distributes publication. Services free to members.

36057. American Academy of Teachers of Singing, c/o William Gephart, 75 Bank St, New York, NY 10014; (212) 242-1836. Interest in establishing and maintaining high professional standards in the teaching of singing. Issues pronouncements from time to time on aspects of the teaching of singing and the art of singing.

Answers inquiries free, distributes publications for a fee.

36058. American Alpine Club, 113 E 90th St, New York, NY 10028; (212) 722-1628. Encourages the safe pursuit of climbing and seeks to set standards in the sound and responsible use of publicly and privately owned mountain areas. Answers brief inquiries and permits onsite use of collections. Services free.

36059. American Arab Association for Commerce and Industry, 420 Lexington Ave, Ste 2431, New York, NY 10170; (212) 986-7229. Studies U.S. relations with Middle Eastern countries, commerce between the U.S. and Middle East, and political and economic conditions. Answers inquiries; provides advisory, reference and translation services; makes referrals. Services free to members, at a fee to others.

36060. American Arbitration Association, 140 W 51st St, New York, NY 10020; (212) 484-4000. Dedicated to resolution of disputes of all kinds through the use of arbitration, mediation, democratic elections, and other voluntary methods. Answers inquiries. In-depth research is available through the library's research service. Photocopies of material may be purchased.

36061. American Association for Affirmative Action, Sheila J. Nickson, SUNY Plaza T-6, Albany, NY 12246; (518) 473-1874. Promotes affirmative action for equal opportunity in employment and education nationwide. Answers inquiries, conducts training seminars and workshops, distributes publication, makes referrals.

36062. American Association for Textile Technology, 1500 Broadway, Ste 1904, New York, NY 10036; (212) 575-8987. Develops and circulates technical knowledge, encourages research, and promotes interchange of info about textile raw materials and fiber technology. Answers inquiries, provides consulting and reference services, distributes publications, makes referrals. Some services free.

36063. American Association for the History of Medicine, c/o Edward C. Atwater, M.D., 601 Elmwood Ave, Rochester, NY 14642. Promotes research, study, interest, and writing in the history of medicine. Conducts meetings, exhibits, and the Fielding H. Garrison Lecture; awards the William H. Welch, the William Osler and the Richard H. Shryock medals. Services only to members.

36064. American Association for the International Commission of Jurists, 777 U.N. Plaza, Ste 10C, New York, NY 10017; (212) 972-0883. Seeks to familiarize American legal community with work of the Intl Commission of Jurists, represent it at the U.N., serve as an info center, and train interns. Answers inquiries, provides reference services, distributes publications, makes referrals. Most services free.

36065. American Association of Aerosol Research, Bonner Hall, Amherst, NY 14226; (716) 833-4556. Investigates particle motion in laminar or turbulent fluids, light scattering phenomena, visibility, and atmospheric optics. Answers inquiries, provides advisory services, distributes publication, makes referrals. Services available to those involved in aerosol research.

36066. American Association of Engineering Societies, 345 E 47th St, New York, NY 10017; (212) 705-7840. Provides learning resources for engineers, scientists, and managers. Answers inquiries, provides free consulting and reference services.

36067. American Association of Exporters and Importers, 11 W 42nd St, New York, NY 10036; (212) 944-2230. Represents all U.S. exporters and importers before the executive branch, Congress, Customs Service, and regulatory agencies. Answers inquiries, provides consulting and reference services, distributes publications, makes referrals. Services generally available for a fee.

36068. American Association of Fund-Raising Counsel, 24 W 43rd St, New York, NY 10036; (212) 354-5799. Promotes high standards, ethics, and principles of procedure in fund raising. Disseminates info on "giving" resources and purposes.

36069. American Association of Hospital Podiatrists, 420 74th St, Brooklyn, NY 11209; (718) 836-1017. Interest in hospital podiatry services and practices. Answers inquiries and conducts seminars. Services free.

36070. American Association of Physicists in Medicine, 335 E 45th St, New York, NY 10017; (212) 661-9404. Investigates radiation physics, thermography, ultrasound holography, computers, physics in medicine and biology, nuclear medicine, and hyperthermia. Answers inquiries and provides advisory services. Services free.

36071. American Association of Veterinary Medical Data Program Participants, VRT, Room 620, Cornell Univ, Ithaca, NY 14853; (607) 256-5454. Collects veterinary clinical data for inclusion in the Veterinary Medical Data Program. Provides data searches on animals seen by member veterinary hospitals.

36072. American Baptist Historical Society, 1106 S Goodman St, Rochester, NY 14620; (716) 473-1740. Collects writings by and about Baptists, Baptist conventions and assns in the U.S. and other parts of the world. Answers inquiries, makes referrals, furnishes location of hard-to-find bibliographic materials, permits onsite use of collection.

36073. American Boat and Yacht Council, P.O. Box 806, Amityville, NY 11701; (516) 598-0550. Promotes voluntary standards and recommended practices covering design, construction, maintenance, and equippage of boats. Answers inquiries, makes referrals.

36074. American Bureau of Metal Statistics, 420 Lexington Ave, New York, NY 10170; (212) 867-9450. Compiles nonferrous metal statistics on mine production, smelter production, refined production, consumption, inventories, imports, and exports. Answers inquiries, makes referrals, provides reference services.

36076. American Cancer Society, Medical Library, 4 W 35th St, New York, NY 10001; (212) 736-3030 ext 254. Maintains holdings in oncology, including medical, statistical, and public health aspects. Acts as clearinghouse for info on developments in field of neoplastic diseases and aids in disseminating info by direct loan or interlibrary loan of books, journals, films, reports, and articles.

36077. American Center for the Alexander Technique, 142 W End Ave, New York, NY 10023; (212) 799-0468. Teaches the Alexander Technique, a process of physiological re-education developed from discoveries of F. Matthias Alexander. Answers inquiries, provides advisory and reference services, conducts seminars, distributes publications, makes referrals. Services free, except publications.

36078. American Civil Liberties Union, 132 W 43rd St, New York, NY 10036; (212) 944-9800. Actively supports protection and extension of individual civil liberties. Answers inquiries, makes referrals, permits onsite use of literature collection when librarian is available. Photocopying available at cost.

36080. American Collegiate Retailing Association, One Lomb Memorial Dr, Rochester, NY 14618; (716) 475-2367. Encourages personal and professional development of those teaching retailing at four-year colleges and univs. Answers inquiries free, distributes reprints at cost.

36081. American Committee on Africa, 198 Broadway, New York, NY 10038; (212) 962-1210. Works to mobilize public support in the U.S. for independence and freedom in Africa. Answers inquiries, distributes literature, introduces African leaders to the American public through meetings and tours, makes referrals. Services generally free, except for publications.

36082. American Composers Alliance, 170 W 74th St, New York, NY 10023; (212) 362-8900. Seeks to protect rights of members and to promote the use and understanding of their music. Answers inquiries, provides advisory and reference services, distributes rental materials and publications, makes referrals. Info free.

36083. American Conference of Therapeutic Self-help/Self-health/Social Clubs, B-1104 Ross Towers, 710 Lodi St, Syracuse, NY 13203; (315) 471-4644. Interest in the demystification of medicine and the achievement of good health by one's self through denouncement of psychiatry, strength of body, mind and spirit, natural foods, and vitamins. Answers inquiries, provides advisory services, distributes publications. Services at cost.

36084. American Corrective Therapy Association, David Ser, 259-08 148th Rd, Rosedale, NY 11422; (212) 276-0721. Promotes medically prescribed therapeutic exercise, education, and adapted physical activities to improve the quality of life and health. Distributes publications; inquiries referred to appropriate individuals or committees.

36085. American Council for Nationalities Service, 20 W 40th St, New York, NY 10018; (212) 398-9142. Assists immigrants and refugees in adjusting to American life and becoming fully participating citizens. Provides advisory and consulting services to member agencies, other interested orgs and individuals.

36086. American Council for Voluntary International Action: InterAction, 200 Park Ave S, New York, NY 10003; (212) 777-8210. Seeks to complement and enhance effectiveness of its individual member orgs and to strengthen capacity of the private and voluntary agency community in intl development. Answers inquiries, makes referrals, permits onsite use of collections.

36087. American Council for the Arts, 570 Seventh Ave, New York, NY 10018; (212) 354-6655. Promotes communication, management improvement, and problem-solving in the arts among those who shape and implement policy. Answers inquiries, provides advisory and reference services, makes referrals. Services primarily for members, but others assisted.

36088. American Council on Germany, 680 Fifth Ave, New York, NY 10019; (212) 541-7878. Conducts fellowship programs, sponsors intl conferences, sponsors German artists in the U.S., conducts projects with American and foreign groups interested in German-American relations. Answers inquiries, distributes publications, provides speakers, makes referrals.

36089. American Council on Science and Health, 1995 Broadway, New York, NY 10023; (212) 362-7044. Promotes scientifically balanced evaluations of chemicals, the environment, and human health. Prepares and publishes reports in the areas of food safety, nutrition, health misinformation, and the effects on health of tobacco, chemicals, pharmaceuticals, and other factors.

36090. American Council on the Teaching of Foreign Languages, P.O. Box 408, Hastings-on-Hudson, NY 10706; (914) 478-2011. Dedicated to advancing the teaching of foreign languages at all levels in U.S. education and to serving the interests of the foreign language teaching profession. Answers inquiries, provides advisory services, distributes publications, makes referrals. Services free.

36091. American Craft Council, Library, 45 W 45th St, Room 201, New York, NY 10036; (212) 869-9462. Collects info on all aspects of contemporary (post-World War II) American crafts. Answers inquiries, including the location of craftspeople for commissionings and exhibitions.

36092. American Crystallographic Association, 335 E 45th St, New York, NY 10017; (212) 661-9404. Studies crystallographic properties of organic and inorganic materials. Answers inquiries, conducts seminars, makes referrals. Services primarily for members, but others assisted as time permits.

36093. American Dance Guild, 570 Seventh Ave, New York, NY 10018; (212) 944-0557. Provides a forum for exchange of ideas and methods among dancers, choreographers, teachers and students. Answers inquiries, provides advisory services, distributes publications, makes referrals. Publications sold, other services free.

36094. American Diabetes Association, 505 8th Ave, New York, NY 10018; (212) 947-9707. Conducts diabetes cure and prevention research, education of medical professionals and paraprofessionals in dealing with diabetics and education of diabetics. Answers inquiries, provides advisory and reference services, distributes publications, makes referrals.

36095. American Dog Owners Association, 1920 Route 9, Castleton, NY 12033; (518) 477-8469. Engaged in a variety of programs related to animal welfare at natl, state, and local levels. Answers inquiries, provides advisory and reference services, distributes publications, makes referrals. Services free.

36096. American Federation for Aging Research, 335 Madison Ave, New York, NY 10017; (212) 503-7600. Supports innovative investigations in biomedical basic and clinical research in aging and its associated diseases. Answers inquiries, conducts scientific meetings, distributes publications, makes referrals. Some services free.

36097. American Federation of Musicians, 1500 Broadway, New York, NY 10036; (212) 869-1330. Interest in union representation of musicians, collective bargaining, and wage scales. Answers inquiries, makes referrals.

36098. American Federation of Television and Radio Artists, 1350 Ave of the Americas, New York, NY 10019; (212) 265-7700. Labor union of the entertainment industry, interested in radio, television, slide films, nonbroadcast, phonographs, cassettes, and cable. Answers brief inquiries, provides consulting services, makes referrals.

36099. American Feline Society, 204 W 20th St, New York, NY 10011. Seeks the welfare of stray cats. Answers inquiries, provides consulting services, makes referrals. Services free.

36100. American Foundation for the Prevention of Venereal Disease, 799 Broadway, Ste 638, New York, NY 10003; (212) 759-2069. Educates public in the hope of preventing venereal diseases. Produces and disseminates educational materials and programs about venereal disease prevention.

36101. American Fur Industry, 101 W 30th St, Room 300, New York, NY 10001; (212) 736-4860. Interest in fur imports and exports, fur manufacturers, fur dressing, dyeing. Answers inquiries free, distributes booklet for a fee.

36102. American Geographical Society, 156 Fifth Ave, Ste 600, New York, NY 10010; (212) 242-0214. Dedicated to advancing the science of geography through research, and to serving as a bridge between govt, academia, and the business community. Answers inquiries, sells publications, makes referrals. Services free, except for publications.

36103. American Group Psychotherapy Association, 1995 Broadway, 14th Fl, New York, NY 10023; (212) 787-2618. Interest in group psychotherapy and research and mental health. Provides patient and training referrals, answers inquiries, distributes publications. Fees may be charged for some publications.

36105. American Guild of Organists, 815 Second Ave, Ste 318, New York, NY 10017; (212) 687-9188. National professional assn for organists and choral conductors seeking to advance the cause of organ and choral music. Answers inquiries, provides reference and tape services, conducts competitions, distributes a monthly publication, makes referrals. Services for members only.

36106. American Health Foundation, 320 E 43rd Street, New York, NY 10017; (212) 953-1900. Focuses on a preventive approach to health by conducting research and public education. A program for children in grades 1-9 has been developed which includes a medical exam and assessment of health risk factors.

36107. American Historical Print Collectors Society, 25 W 43rd St, Ste 711, New York, NY 10036; (212) 221-5900. Supports and encourages R&D of publications helpful to the appreciation and conservation of historical American prints. Answers inquiries free, conducts seminars and workshops for qualified applicants for a fee, distributes publications to members.

36108. American Home Sewing Association, 1270 Broadway, Rm 1007, New York, NY 10001; (212) 736-8820. Trade org of manufacturers, retailers, wholesalers, and sales representatives of the home sewing and craft industry. Answers inquiries, provides reference services, distributes publications, makes referrals. General info free, other services may be subject to a fee.

36109. American Horse Shows Association, 598 Madison Ave, New York, NY 10022; (212) 759-3070. Responsible for making and enforcing horse show rules, setting dates of shows, licensing judges, and keeping records of winnings of show horses. Answers inquiries, provides consulting services, distributes some publications, makes referrals. Most services free.

36110. American Industrial Health Council, 1075 Central Park Ave, Scarsdale, NY 10583; (914) 725-1492. Promotes use of the most advanced, sound scientific methods as a basis for the review and regulation of substances that may pose significant chronic health risks to people. Answers inquiries, provides advisory services, distributes publications, makes referrals. Services free.

36111. American Institute for Marxist Studies, 85 E 4th St, New York, NY 10003; (212) 982-6751. Seeks to foster Marxist scholarship in the U.S. and produce a dia-

logue among Marxist and non-Marxist scholars. Answers inquiries, provides reference services, conducts seminars, distributes publications. Services free, except publications.

36112. American Institute for Patristic and Byzantine Studies, RR 1, Box 353-A, Kingston, NY 12401; (914) 336-8797. Studies Eastern Christian culture, Byzantine civilization, and the history and theology of the Orthodox churches. Provides advisory and translation services. Services free for members; membership open to anyone.

36113. American Institute of Aeronautics and Astronautics, Technical Information Service, 555 W 57th St, New York, NY 10019; (212) 247-6500. Maintains collection of material on all aspects of aeronautics and astronautics. Answers inquiries; provides advisory, reference, abstracting, and indexing services; distributes publications. Some services free.

36114. American Institute of Certified Public Accountants, 1211 Ave of the Americas, New York, NY 10036; (1-800) 223-4155. National professional membership org of 218,000 CPAs. Answers technical inquiries, provides reference services, provides bibliographies in response to specific inquiries, makes interlibrary loans, permits onsite use of collection.

36115. American Institute of Chemical Engineers, 345 E 47th St, New York, NY 10017; (212) 705-7660. Interest in chemical engineering practices and processes, pollution control, waste management, energy resources, and technologies. Disseminates info through meetings, publications, and continuing education. Services on a cost basis, with considerable discount to members.

36116. American Institute of Mining, Metallurgical, and Petroleum Engineers, 345 E 47th St, New York, NY 10017; (212) 705-7695. Technical and professional org for individual engineers and scientists engaged in exploration for and production of minerals, and the manufacture of products from them. Answers brief inquiries from serious researchers.

36117. American Institute of Physics, 335 E 45th St, New York, NY 10017; (212) 661-9404. Membership corporation of: American Physical Society, Optical Society of America, Acoustical Society of America, Society of Rheology, American Association of Physics Teachers, American Crystallographic Association, American Astronomical Society, American Association of Physicists in Medicine and the American Vacuum Society. Answers inquiries.

36118. American Institute of Physics, Physics Manpower Data, 335 E 45th St, New York, NY 10017; (212) 661-9404. Compiles data on physics manpower, physics education statistics, including the number of undergraduate physics majors, graduate students and physics degrees granted and employment. Answers inquiries.

36119. American Institute of Stress, 124 Park Ave, Yonkers, NY 10703; (914) 963-1200. Serves as a resource and clearinghouse for info on stress-related matters. Services include a newsletter, reprints, monographs, and abstracts disseminated at minimal costs.

36120. American Insurance Services Group, Engineering and Safety Service Information Center, 85 John St, New York, NY 10038; (212) 669-0478. Collects data on loss control, risk management, fire and accident prevention, safety, health, building and fire prevention codes. Answers inquiries, provides advisory services and bulletins to insurance company subscribers. Some publications available to public.

36121. American Jewish Congress, 15 E 84th St, New York, NY 10028; (212) 879-4500. Nonprofit org interested in all aspects of minority rights, church-state relations, religious freedom, and Jewish rights around the world. Answers inquiries, provides advisory services, distributes publications, makes referrals. Services free, except publications.

36122. American Lung Association, 1740 Broadway, New York, NY 10019; (212) 245-8000. Seeks to help Americans prevent lung disease, to obtain effective treatment, and to learn to live with disabled breathing. Provides professional education. Answers inquiries, distributes publications, conducts educational programs for public and professionals.

36124. American Management Associations, 135 W 50th St, New York, NY 10020; (212) 586-8100. Studies all aspects of business management education, including administration, planning, finance, human resources, marketing, insurance, and manufacturing. Overseas visitors and students of management at graduate level or higher may obtain reference services by visiting the assn.

36125. American Medical Society on Alcoholism, 733 Third Ave, New York, NY 10017; (212) 986-4433. Serves as a meeting ground for physicians and medical students interested in the problems associated with alcohol and all other addictive drug use disorders. Sponsors and provides faculty medical seminars, for which continuing medical education credit is given.

36126. American Medical Society on Alcoholism and Other Drug Dependencies, 12 W 21st Street, New York, NY 10010; (212) 206-6770. Org of physicians with interest and experience in the field of alcoholism and other addictive drug disorders. Provides a forum for these professionals to share their experiences with one another and extend their knowledge of addictive diseases.

36127. American Medical Women's Association, 465 Grand St, New York, NY 10002; (212) 533-5104. Seeks to bring together women medical students and physicians, promote their education and training, and ensure equal opportunity to do so. Conducts continuing medical education programs and leadership workshops, provides loans to medical and osteopathic students.

36128. American Mental Health Foundation, 2 E 86th St, New York, NY 10028; (212) 737-9027. Conducts research in psychiatry, psychoanalysis, psychotherapy, and the development of a low-cost treatment method. Research findings communicated regularly to interested professionals.

36129. American Merchant Marine Library Association, One World Trade Center, Ste 2601, New York, NY 10048; (212) 775-1038. Provides library service to American seafarers. Operates the Ship's Literary Club, which distributes hardcover books to participating vessels. Library services restricted to merchant vessels and ships of the U.S. govt.

36130. American Meteor Society, State Univ Coll, Geneseo, NY 14454; (716) 245-5284. Studies meteoric astronomy, especially visual sightings, fireball analysis, coordination of worldwide observer groups, and radio scatter studies of meteors. Answers inquiries, permits onsite use of collection, Services primarily for AMS members and scientists.

36131. American Montessori Society, 150 Fifth Ave, Ste 203, New York, NY 10011; (212) 924-3209. Promotes and develops educational philosophy and principles of Maria Montessori and those consistent with her teaching strategies. Supplies pamphlets, rosters, and teacher training sites; provides research and other assistance.

36132. American Museum of Natural History, Central Park W at 79th St, New York, NY 10024; (212) 873-1300. Maintains collections in ethology, anthropology, astronomy, biology, ecology, entomology, ethnology, fossil invertebrates, and other fields. Provides reference services and interlibrary loans. Photographs and slides available for purchase. Presents courses, lectures, and films.

36133. American Music Center, 250 W 54th St, Rm 300, New York, NY 10019; (212) 247-3121. Encourages the composition of contemporary music and promotes its production, publication, distribution, and performance. Answers inquiries, provides consultation services. Library materials loaned; no restrictions on access to info or use of reference sources.

36134. American Name Society, c/o Professor Wayne H. Finke, 7 E 14th St (17-U), New York, NY 10003; (212) 929-8434. Maintains a collection of names, their etymology, meaning, and application, including scientific and geographical names and medical terminology. Answers inquiries, makes referrals to member-specialists, provides reference services, lends materials.

36135. American National Standards Institute, 1430 Broadway, New York, NY 10018; (212) 354-3311. Acts as natl coordinating institution for voluntary standardization through which interested orgs may cooperate in establishing, recognizing, and improving voluntary standards of the U.S. Answers inquiries, makes referrals.

36136. American Nature Study Society, 5881 Cold Brook Rd, Homer, NY 13077; (607) 749-3655. Seeks to advance the field of natural history interpretation and environmental education. Answers inquiries, conducts workshops, distributes publication, makes referrals. Most services free.

36137. American Numismatic Society, 155th St and Broadway, New York, NY 10032; (212) 234-3130. Seeks to advance numismatic knowledge as it relates to history, art, archaeology, and economics. Answers inquiries, provides advisory and reference services, aids in identifying material, makes referrals. Services free.

36138. American ORT Federation, 817 Broadway, New York, NY 10003; (212) 677-4400. Operates a network of vocational and technical schools on the secondary school and junior college levels in 26 countries on five continents. Distributes publications, shares expertise with other private volunteer orgs in areas of interest.

36139. American Orthopsychiatric Association, 19 W 44th St, New York, NY 10036; (212) 354-5770. Interest in mental health, preventive mental health, study, and treatment of human behavior. Answers inquiries.

36140. American Paper Institute, 260 Madison Ave, New York, NY 10016; (212) 340-0612. Interest in pulp, paper, and paperboard industry, including manufacturing, imports, intl trade, economics, and marketing services. Answers inquiries, makes referrals, permits outside use of collection by persons with proof of corporate or school affiliation.

36141. American Paper Institute, Plastics Extrusion Coaters Section, 260 Madison Ave, New York, NY 10016; (212) 340-0658. Interest in plastics, plastics extrusion on paper and paperboard. Answers inquiries, provides reference services.

36143. American Parkinson Disease Association, 116 John Street, Ste 417, New York, NY 10038; (800) 233-2732. Provides info about various services available to patients with Parkinson's disease. Makes funds available for research in new drug therapies. Awards fellowships that fund the work of senior medical researchers.

36144. American Pedestrian Association, P.O. Box 624, Forest Hills, NY 11375. Interest in pedestrian safety, health, environment, and welfare. Provides consulting and reference services, distributes publication by subscription. Services provided for a fee.

36145. American Pediatric Society, Box 49, 450 Clarkson Ave, Brooklyn, NY 11203; (718) 270-1692. Seeks to promote the study of children and their diseases, prevent illness, and promote health in childhood.

36146. American Petroleum Institute, Central Abstracting and Indexing Service, 156 William St, New York, NY 10038; (212) 587-9660. Collects data on crude oil, natural gas, petroleum refining, motor fuels, heating oils, and lubricants. Provides search services on published technical info, including patents. Computerized searches of API indexes available. Services provided on a fee basis.

36147. American Physical Society, 335 E 45th St, New York, NY 10017; (212) 682-7341. Compiles data on physics. Answers inquiries, distributes publications, makes referrals. Services primarily for members, but others assisted.

36148. American Professors for Peace in the Middle East, Community Services, 330 Seventh Ave, New York, NY 10001; (212) 563-2580. Org of those involved in Middle East education and research and who seek peace in the Middle East. Answers inquiries, provides consulting services, distributes publications, makes referrals. Most services free.

36149. American Psychoanalytic Association, 1 E 57th St, New York, NY 10022; (212) 752-0450. Interest in psychoanalysis, including education and training standards, certification, child analysis, and training facilities. Answers inquiries, makes referrals.

36150. American Psychosomatic Society, 265 Nassau Rd, Roosevelt, NY 11575; (516) 379-0191. Studies psychosomatic medicine and psychobiology, including psychophysiology, psychoendocrinology, and neurobiology of brain-body relationships. Answers inquiries.

36151. American Psychotherapy Seminar Center, 789 West End Ave, New York, NY 10025; (212) 663-4327. Seeks to provide a forum for professionals, as well as for the community at large, in the field of mental health and related areas of behavioral and social sciences. Answers inquiries, provides advisory services, makes referrals. Services primarily for professionals.

36152. American Rescue Dog Association, P.O. Box 151 (Rte 17M), Chester, NY 10918; (914) 469-4173. Provides trained German Shepherd dogs and handlers for rural, wilderness, and disaster search and rescue, as well as info on search and rescue techniques. Conducts search and rescue, provides advisory and reference services, answers inquiries, distributes publications, makes referrals.

36153. American Society for Psychical Research, 5 W 73rd St, New York, NY 10023; (212) 799-5050. Interest in psychical research. Answers inquiries, performs searches (unless extensive), supplies photocopies for a fee. Library open to members, serious researchers, and students. Facilities available to aid students with papers and reports.

36154. American Society for the Prevention of Cruelty to Animals, 441 E 92nd St, New York, NY 10128; (212) 876-7700. Seeks to develop, provide, and maintain services and facilities for promoting the welfare of animals and prevention of unnecessary sickness and suffering. Answers inquiries, provides advisory and reference services, distributes publications. Services free, except for some publications.

36155. American Society of Civil Engineers, 345 E 47th St, New York, NY 10017; (212) 705-7496. Interest in civil engineering, including aerospace transport, construction, engineering mechanics, highways, hydraulics, irrigation and drainage. Answers inquiries; provides reference, abstracting and indexing services; makes referrals.

36156. American Society of Group Psychotherapy and Psychodrama, 116 E 27th St, New York, NY 10016; (212) 725-0033. Aims to establish standards for specialists in group psychotherapy, psychodrama, sociometry, and allied methods. Answers inquiries, provides reference services, distributes publications, makes referrals. Services free, except publications.

36157. American Society of Indexers, 235 Park Ave S, New York, NY 10003; (212) 799-0970. Membership org of freelance and salaried indexers and of publishers and editors who employ indexers. Answers inquiries; provides reference, abstracting and indexing services; distributes publications; makes referrals. Services free.

36158. American Society of Interior Designers, 1430 Broadway, 22nd Fl, New York, NY 10018; (212) 944-9220. Interest in interior design. Answers inquiries, rents films, provides reference services.

36159. American Society of Journalists and Authors, 1501 Broadway, Ste 1907, New York, NY 10036; (212) 997-0947. Nationwide org of independent nonfiction writers. Operates Dial-a-Writer referral service, conducts annual nonfiction writers conference.

36160. American Society of Magazine Photographers, 205 Lexington Ave, New York, NY 10016; (212) 889-9144. Acts as a clearinghouse for info vital to the professional photographer in areas of rights, ethics, and artistic standards. Answers inquiries, provides consulting and reference services, distributes publications, makes referrals. Services primarily for members.

36161. American Society of Master Dental Laboratory Technologists, Box 248, Oakland Gardens, NY 11363; (212) 428-0075. Professional society formed to elevate educational standards of the dental technicians residing in the U.S. Answers inquiries free, conducts seminars and courses for a fee. Services available to those associated with the field.

36162. American Society of Mechanical Engineers, Bioengineering Division, 345 E 47th St, New York, NY 10017; (212) 705-7722. Conducts studies into mechanical engineering, bioengineering, biomechanical engineering. Answers inquiries, provides advisory and consulting services, distributes publications. Services provided for a fee.

36163. American Society of Mechanical Engineers, Noise Control and Acoustics Division, 345 E 47th St, New York, NY 10017; (212) 705-7054. Investigates noise control, acoustics, analytical and computational methods for modeling acoustical systems. Answers inquiries, distributes publications, makes referrals. Services provided for a fee.

36164. American Society of Mechanical Engineers, Petroleum Division, 345 E 47th St, New York, NY 10017; (212) 705-7153. Studies petroleum engineering, offshore technology, hydrocarbon processing. Answers inquiries; provides advisory, reference, abstracting, and indexing, microform and reproduction services; distributes publications; makes referrals. Services may be provided for a fee.

36165. American Society of Picture Professionals, P.O. Box 5283, Grand Central Station, New York, NY 10163-5283. Membership org of photographers, agents, designers, picture editors, researchers, librarians, curators, and historians. Answers inquiries, provides reference services, distributes publications, makes referrals. Some services free.

36166. American Thoracic Society, 1740 Broadway, New York, NY 10019; (212) 315-8700. Professional and scientific society with broad interests in respiratory diseases. Serves as the medical section of the American Lung Association. Answers inquiries from serious inquirers within the limits of available time.

36167. American Translators Association, 109 Croton Ave, Ossining, NY 10562; (914) 941-1500. Interest in translation, interpreting, and the intellectual and material interests of translators in the U.S. Answers inquiries.

36168. American Vacuum Society, 335 E 45th St, New York, NY 10017; (212) 661-9404. Studies vacuum science and technology, thin films, vacuum metallurgy, surface science, electronic materials, and processes and fusion technology. Conducts short courses, seminars, and workshops on vacuum-related topics; distributes publications. Services provided at cost.

36169. American West African Freight Conference, 50 Broadway, Ste 2100, New York, NY 10004; (212) 269-7430. Establishes freight rates between the U.S. and West Africa. Freight rates available free to members, by subscription to others.

36170. American Wine Association, c/o A. M. Buchman, 10 E 40th St, New York, NY 10016; (212) 953-0440. Interest in wine production and sales, viticulture, fed and state laws controlling the manufacture and sale of wine. Answers inquiries from all govt agencies, provides consulting services, makes referrals. Services primarily for members.

36171. American-Scandinavian Foundation, 127 E 73rd St, New York, NY 10021; (212) 879-9779. Dedicated to furthering cultural and educational exchange between the U.S. and Denmark, Finland, Iceland, Norway, and Sweden. Answers inquiries, provides reference services.

36172. Americans for Middle East Understanding, 475 Riverside Dr, Room 771, New York, NY 10115; (212) 870-2053. Seeks to create a deeper understanding of the culture, history, and current events in the Middle East. Answers inquiries, provides reference services, distributes publications, makes referrals, permits onsite use of collection. Fees may be charged.

36173. Amnesty International of the USA, 304 W 58th St, New York, NY 10019; (212) 582-4440. Works impartially for release of prisoners of conscience provided they have neither used nor advocated violence. Opposes torture and the death penalty and advocates fair and prompt trials. Answers inquiries, sells publications. General materials free.

36174. Amyotrophic Lateral Sclerosis Association, 185 Madison Ave, Ste 1001, New York, NY 10016; (212) 679-4016. Seeks to find the cause and cure of ALS, commonly known as Lou Gehrig's disease. Program encompasses funding research, services to patients, public and professional education, development of chapters, and establishment of ALS clinical service centers nationwide.

36175. Animal Medical Center Library, 510 E 62nd St, New York, NY 10021; (212) 838-8100. Provides medical and surgical care for animals, conducts clinical research of benefit to animals as well as humans, and provides postgraduate education to veterinarians. Answers inquiries, distributes publications, makes referrals, permits onsite use of collection. Services free.

36176. Anti-Defamation League of B'nai B'rith, 823 U.N. Plaza, New York, NY 10017; (212) 490-2525. Studies intergroup relations, including civil rights, race relations, education, human relations, anti-Semitism, totalitarianism, extremism, and prejudice. Answers inquiries, provides consulting services, makes referrals. Audiovisual materials available for rental or purchase.

36177. Antique Wireless Association, Holcomb, NY 14469; (716) 657-7489. Museum of the history of radio, telegraph, and other forms of electronic communication. Answers inquiries, provides films and speakers for meetings, distributes publication, makes referrals. Services free on a limited scale.

36178. Appraisers Association of America, 60 E 42nd St, New York, NY 10165 (212) 867-9775. Promotes and maintains standards of skill and ethical conduct in the profession of appraising American and European furniture and decorative arts. Answers inquiries, provides advisory and reference services, distributes publications, makes referrals. Most services free.

36179. Arbitron Ratings, 1350 Ave of the Americas, New York, NY 10019; (212) 887-1300. Conducts measurements of radio and television audiences on a local level. Answers inquiries, distributes publications, makes referrals, permits onsite use of collections. Services primarily for subscribers.

36180. Architects for Social Responsibility, 225 Lafayette St, Room 207, New York, NY 10012; (212) 334-8104.

Promotes redirection of U.S. national goals from the nuclear arms race and toward improving the built environment and quality of life. Answers inquiries, provides advisory and reference services. Services of special interest to architects and related professionals.

36181. Argus Archives, 228 E 49th St, New York, NY 10017; (212) 355-6140. Promotes humane treatment of animals and functions as a data bank in all areas of interest to the humane movement. Answers inquiries, provides reference services, distributes publications, makes referrals, permits onsite use of collections by appointment. Most services free.

36182. Arica Institute, 101 Fifth Ave, New York, NY 10003; (212) 807-9600. Teaches experimental methods designed to maximize development of human potential. Answers inquiries, provides advisory services, conducts group programs, makes referrals. Some services free.

36183. Art Dealers Association of America, 575 Madison Ave, New York, NY 10022; (212) 940-8590. Promotes interests of persons and firms dealing in works of fine art to improve stature of the business and enhance confidence of the public in responsible dealers. Answers inquiries, operates a Theft Notice Service, appraises works of fine art, distributes publications.

36184. Art Hazards Information Center, 5 Beekman St, New York, NY 10038; (212) 227-6220. Serves as clearinghouse for info on occupational health problems of artists, craftspeople, theater craftspeople, and museum conservators. Answers inquiries, provides consulting services, distributes publications, makes referrals. Some services free.

36185. Art Information Center, 280 Broadway, Room 412, New York, NY 10007; (212) 227-0282. Collects info about the work of living artists, N.Y. City gallery outlets for artists, setting up of galleries by art dealers. Answers inquiries, provides consulting services, makes referrals, permits onsite use of slide collection by appointment.

36186. Arts and Business Council, 130 E 40th St, New York, NY 10016; (212) 683-5555. Seeks to promote understanding and communication between the arts and business. Answers inquiries, provides advisory and reference services, trains corporate executives to serve as volunteer consultants to arts orgs, distributes publications, makes referrals. Services free.

36187. Asia Society, 725 Park Ave, New York, NY 10021; (212) 288-6400. Seeks to educate Americans about Asian affairs and cultures and promote effective trans-Pacific dialogue. Provides public affairs briefings, conducts intensive lecture and seminar programs.

36188. Asian Cultural Council, 280 Madison Ave, New York, NY 10016; (212) 684-5450. Supports cultural exchange in visual and performing arts between the U.S. and countries of Asia. Answers inquiries, makes referrals. Services free.

36189. Association for Advancement of Behavior Therapy, 15 W 36th St, New York, NY 10018; (212) 279-7970. Studies behavior therapy and behavior modification in clinical, research, educational, and social settings. Answers inquiries, provides consulting and reference services. Services primarily for professionals in psychiatry, psychology, and social work.

36190. Association for Birth Psychology, 444 E 82nd St, New York, NY 10028; (212) 988-6617. Studies correlation between the birth process and its impact on later personality development. Answers inquiries, provides advisory services, distributes a bulletin, makes referrals. Services may be subject to a fee.

36191. Association for Children with Retarded Mental Development, 162 Fifth Ave, 11th Fl, New York, NY 10010; (212) 475-7200. Provides retardation, behavioral, mental health, rehabilitative, vocational, residential, educational, and community services. Answers inquiries, makes referrals. Services may be provided for a fee.

36192. Association for Computing Machinery, 11 W 42nd St, New York, NY 10036; (212) 869-7440. Seeks to advance science and art of info processing and promote free interchange of info. Sells publications, conducts conferences and symposia, makes referrals.

36193. Association for Macular Diseases, 210 E 64th Street, New York, NY 10021; (212) 605-3719. Promotes education on and research into macular diseases and provides support for afflicted persons and their families. Also disseminates info on resources and encourages post-mortem donation of eyes with macular disease for research purposes.

36194. Association for Research in Vision and Ophthalmology, Jaye Henkind, C-1002, Wykagyl Station, New Rochelle, NY 10804. Collects data on intl ophthalmic research. Answers inquiries, distributes publications, makes referrals. Services free, except publications.

36195. Association for Research of Childhood Cancer, 3653 Harlem Road, Buffalo, NY 14215; (716) 838-4433. Seeks to find cures and, ultimately, prevent the types of cancer that attack children. As a parent support group AROCC aids parents of young cancer victims by distributing info on treatment, emotional problems, and patient services.

36196. Association for Union Democracy, YWCA Bldg, Room 619, Brooklyn, NY 11217; (718) 855-6650. Seeks to promote principles and practices of internal union democracy in the American labor movement by publications, conferences, education and by assisting union members whose internal union rights under the law are denied or curtailed. Answers inquiries, makes referrals.

36197. Association for Voluntary Sterilization, 122 E 42nd St, 18th Fl, New York, NY 10168; (212) 573-8350. Promotes use of safer, simpler sterilization techniques. Answers inquiries, permits onsite use of resource center, distributes info, furnishes location of hard-to-find bibliographic citations.

36198. Association for the Advancement of Blind and Retarded, 164-09 Hillside Ave, Jamaica, NY 11432; (718) 523-2222. Operates a 6-day Day Treatment Center Program for multihandicapped, blind, and severely retarded young adults. Also provides an Upstate Summer Camp Program. Answers inquiries.

36199. Association for the Advancement of Psychoanalysis, 329 E 62nd St, New York, NY 10021; (212) 752-5267. Has specialized collection of psychoanalytic literature and materials covering related fields. Answers inquiries; provides consulting and reference services; conducts lectures, seminars, and workshops; distributes publications; makes referrals. Services primarily for professionals.

36200. Association for the Advancement of Psychotherapy, 114 E 78th St, New York, NY 10021; (212) 288-4466. Interest in psychotherapy, psychotropic drugs, and psychosocial problems. Answers inquiries and provides abstracting services for psychotherapists.

36201. Association for the Study of Man-Environment Relations, P.O. Box 57, Orangeburg, NY 10962; (914) 634-8221. Studies man-environment relations, behavior and design research, and environmental psychology. Provides consulting, reference, abstracting, and indexing services. Services primarily for members.

36202. Association of Consulting Chemists and Chemical Engineers, 50 E 41st St, New York, NY 10017; (212) 684-6255. Interest in chemistry and chemical engineering. Provides, without charge, names and addresses of members specializing in particular fields of chemistry and chemical engineering. Directory is for sale.

36203. Association of Existential Psychology and Psychiatry, c/o Dr Louis De Rosis, 40 E 89th St, New York, NY 10028; (212) 348-3500. Investigates existential psychology and psychiatry. Answers inquiries, provides referral service for existential therapy. Services free, primarily for students of social science and other related fields.

36204. Association of Independent Video and Filmmakers, 625 Broadway, 9th Fl, New York, NY 10012; (212) 473-3400. Interest in film, video, television, film and video production, including financing, insurance, legal and accounting problems, and taxes. Answers inquiries, provides reference services, distributes publications, makes referrals, permits onsite use of collections. Most services free.

36205. Association of Jewish Libraries, 122 E 42nd St, New York, NY 10017; (212) 490-2280. Compiles data on Judaica libraries and bibliographies. Answers inquiries, provides advisory services, makes referrals. Services free.

36206. Association of Management Consulting Firms, 230 Park Ave, New York, NY 10169; (212) 697-9693. Acts as a central source of info on management consultants in North America who serve clients on managerial and related operating and technical problems. Answers brief inquiries free, makes referrals, permits onsite use of collection.

36207. Association of Master of Business Administration Executives, 305 Madison Ave, New York, NY 10165; (212) 682-4490. Professional assn of MBA degree holders. Answers inquiries, conducts seminars, distributes publications. Some services free to general public, but limited according to time and effort required.

36208. Association of National Advertisers, 155 E 44th St, New York, NY 10017; (212) 697-5950. Interest in advertising and marketing. Answers concise inquiries, makes referrals. Services primarily for members, but most also available to others as time and staff permit.

36209. Association on American Indian Affairs, 95 Madison Ave, New York, NY 10016; (212) 689-8720. Provides legal and technical assistance to American Indian tribes and communities at their request. Answers inquiries, distributes publications, makes referrals. Services free, except some publications.

36210. Atmospheric Sciences Research Center, 1400 Washington Ave, Albany, NY 12222; (518) 457-4604. Studies inadvertent weather modification of the atmosphere by air pollution. Answers inquiries, provides consulting services. Services provided free or for a fee, depending on the time and effort involved.

36211. Audio Engineering Society, 60 E 42nd St, Rm 449, New York, NY 10017; (212) 661-8528. Studies audio engineering. Answers inquiries free, sells publication.

36212. Aviation Development Council, P.O. Box 699, LaGuardia Airport, Flushing, NY 11371; (718) 457-7890. Serves as a mechanism for the aviation community serving the N.Y. metro region to deal with programs and problems of common interest, such as airport promotion, aircraft noise, and aviation education. Responds to brief inquiries, provides computerized statistical data.

36213. Baking Industry Sanitation Standards Committee, c/o Raymond J. Walter, 521 Fifth Ave, New York, NY 10017; (212) 687-9071. Interest in sanitation, food processing equipment, sanitary engineering, industrial hygiene, and public health. Answers inquiries, provides reference services.

36214. Benet Weapons Laboratory, Watervliet Technical Library, Attn: SMCAR-LCB-TL, Watervliet, NY 12189-5000; (518) 266-5613. Collects material on Cannons, mortars, howitzers, antitank, and anti-aircraft weapons. Accepts ALA and OCLC requests for books and journals. Normally, library does not lend technical reports, but will verify publication info and refer requests to the correct agency for purchase.

36215. Better Vision Institute, 230 Park Ave, New York, NY 10169; (212) 682-1731. Promotes interest in care of vision, public awareness of eye and vision care, contact lenses, and sunglasses. Answers inquiries, provides reference services. Services free.

36217. Biological Research Laboratories, 130 Coll Pl, Syracuse, NY 13210; (315) 423-3186. Investigates molecular biology, genetics, biochemistry, biophysics, cardiovascular and pulmonary diseases, immunology, and aging. Answers inquiries.

36218. Biological Stain Commission, Univ of Rochester Medical Center, Rochester, NY 14642; (716) 275-2751. Promotes development, standardization, and certification of biological stains. Provides consulting services.

36219. Book Industry Study Group, 160 Fifth Ave, New York, NY 10010; (212) 929-1393. Voluntary assn of publishers, manufacturers, suppliers, wholesalers, retailers, libraries, and individuals engaged in the production of books. Answers inquiries, provides reference services, distributes publications, makes referrals. Fees charged for publications.

36220. Bowne Information Systems, 777 Northern Blvd, Great Neck, NY 11021; (516) 487-0101. Commercial org that offers three computer-based services; COMSPEC, Word/One, and KEYSEARCH. Provides online access and floppy disk data to engineering and architectural specification data bases. Services provided on a contract basis.

36221. Box Office Management International, c/o Patricia Spira, 500 E 77th St, Room 1925, New York, NY 10021; (212) 570-1099. Serves as a resource center addressing mutual concerns of control and service in box office management and ticket industry. Answers inquiries, provides consulting and reference services, distributes publications, makes referrals, publicizes jobs. Some services free.

36222. Boyce Thompson Institute for Plant Research, Library, Cornell Univ, Tower Rd, Ithaca, NY 14853; (607) 257-2030. Studies botany and related subjects, such as biochemistry, entomology, agriculture, disease tolerance of plants. Makes interlibrary loans, permits onsite use of collection.

36223. Brain Research Laboratories, 550 First Ave, New York, NY 10016; (212) 340-6287. Studies diagnostic significance of brain electrical activity as related to functional impairment. Answers inquiries, distributes reprints. Services free and available to those working in the field.

36224. Brazilian Government Trade Bureau, 551 Fifth Ave, New York, NY 10176; (212) 916-3200. Commercial dept of Brazilian Consulate General in N.Y. Answers inquiries, provides advisory and reference services, distributes publication, makes referrals. Services free.

36225. Bristol Laboratories Research Library, P.O. Box 657, Syracuse, NY 13201. Collects material on pharmaceutical, medicinal and organic chemistry, microbiology, toxicology, and cancer research. Answers inquiries; use of library and its services by persons outside the company is available by registering at the Security Center.

36226. Broadcast Information Bureau, 100 Lafayette Dr, Syracuse, NY 11791; (516) 496-3355. Commercial publisher of research source books pertaining to everything available on film and tape for television. Sells publications. Film and series source books available to anyone; newsletter available only to television executives.

36227. Broadcast Music, 320 W 57th St, New York, NY 10019; (212) 586-2000. Org of music writer and publisher affiliates interested in protection of their performing rights and with service to public by making music as readily available as possible. Answers inquiries, distributes publications, makes referrals. Some services available to nonmembers.

36228. Broadcasting Foundation of America, Box 1805, Murray Hill Station, New York, NY 10156; (212) 679-3388. Produces and distributes intl audiotape material and radio programs on contemporary and historical subjects in science, education, public affairs, and the arts. Provides audiotapes for a small fee to cover tape cost.

36229. Brookhaven National Laboratory, Protein Data Bank, Brookhaven National Laboratory, Attn: T.F. Koetzle, Upton, Long Island, NY 11973; (516) 282-4384. Acts as a data bank for structural info on proteins, nucleic acids, and other biological macromolecules. Data and programs distributed to public either on magnetic tape or in the form of microfiche listings. A charge for this service.

36230. Brookhaven National Laboratory, Research Library, Upton, Long Island, NY 11973; (516) 282-3490. Maintains extensive collection of materials in physics, chemistry, biology, mathematics, applied science, instrumentation and health physics, environmental science and energy. Answers inquiries, provides reference services, makes interlibrary loans, permits onsite use of collections.

36231. Brooklyn College, Institute of Political Psychology, Bedford Ave and Ave H, Brooklyn, NY 11210; (718) 780-5485. Studies Chinese political psychology and behavior, psychology of Chinese youth and adults, research methodology for Chinese studies. Answers inquiries from academic researchers only.

36232. Brooklyn Public Library, Fire Protection Collection, Brooklyn Public Library, Grand Army Plaza, Brooklyn, NY 11238; (718) 780-7745. Interest in all aspects of the science of firefighting, flammability, fire retardancy of materials, and fire protection for the home and industry. Answers inquiries, permits onsite reference.

36233. Builders Hardware Manufacturers Association, 60 E 42nd St, Room 511, New York, NY 10165; (212) 682-8142. Interest in builders' hardware and development of product standards. Answers inquiries free within limits of time and staff.

36234. Building Stone Institute, 420 Lexington Ave, New York, NY 10170; (212) 490-2530. Interest in building stone industry, quarrying and fabrication. Answers inquiries, provides consulting services, identifies building stones, permits onsite reference.

36235. Bureau of Jewish Education Library, 2640 N Forest Rd, Getzville, NY 14068; (716) 689-8862. Maintains a collection of materials on Judaica, Hebraica and education. Answers inquiries; provides consulting, reference, duplication, and limited translation services; lends materials; makes referrals. Nominal fee charged for duplication services and a library card.

36236. Business Committee for the Arts, 1775 Broadway, New York, NY 10019; (212) 664-0600. Works to encourage new and increased support for the arts throughout the U.S. Answers inquiries, provides advisory and reference services to business, conducts awards programs. Services free, except publications.

36237. Business International Corp., 1 Dag Hammarskjold Plaza, New York, NY 10017; (212) 750-6300. Advises and assists those seeking info on problems and opportunities existing in world markets. Answers inquiries; provides advisory, reference, abstracting and indexing services; distributes publications; makes referrals. Access to the online BIDATA service is available.

36238. Business Research Institute, St John's Univ, Jamaica, NY 11439; (718) 990-6161 ext 6768. Conducts business research, including business administration, economics, and finance. Answers inquiries, provides consulting services, distributes publications. Some services free, others on a fee basis.

36239. C.L. Mauro Associates, 12 W 31st St, New York, NY 10001; (212) 868-3940. Interest in evaluation and development of products, environments, and systems responsive to user capabilities and limitations. Answers inquiries; provides consulting, design, research, and reference services; provides expert witness testimony; makes referrals.

36240. CBS News Reference Library, 524 W 57th St, New York, NY 10019; (212) 975-2877. Collects info on radio, television, and current events. Provides reference services to other libraries, makes interlibrary loans, permits onsite use of collections to researchers by arrangement. All services available outside the org at discretion of the librarian.

36241. Cadmium Council, 292 Madison Ave, New York, NY 10017; (212) 578-4750. Membership trade assn devoted to developing new applications of cadmium and expanding old ones. Answers inquiries free.

36242. Calspan Corp., Technical Information Center, Box 400 (4455 Genesee St), Buffalo, NY 14225; (716) 632-7500. Collects data on computers, transportation, automotive research, meteorology, electronics, radar, aerospace vehicles, and weapons research. Answers inquiries, makes interlibrary loans, provides microfiche copies of post-1972 NTIS reports.

36243. Canadian Consulate General, Cultural Affairs, 1251 Ave of the Americas, New York, NY 10020; (212) 586-2400. Provides info on and financial and practical assistance for presentations of the arts and culture of Canada within N.Y. City metro area. Answers inquiries, provides advisory services, distributes publications, makes referrals to other sources of info.

36244. Canadian Consulate General, Library, 1251 Ave of the Americas, New York, NY 10020; (212) 586-2400. Interest in Canadian politics, economics, business, history, literature, culture, law, and geography. Answers inquiries, provides advisory and reference services, makes referrals, permits onsite use of collections by appointment.

36245. Cancer Care, 1 Park Ave, New York, NY 10016; (212) 679-5700. Provides professional counseling and guidance to help patients and families cope with emotional and psychological consequences of cancer. Pamphlets and other documents distributed, referral made to other orgs.

36247. Cancer Hopefuls United for Mutual Support, 3310 Rochambeau Ave, New York, NY 10467; (212) 655-7566. Helps cancer survivors and their families better understand the disease and cope with resulting problems. Offers self-help sessions, crisis intervention, Phone-a-Patient and Visit-a-Patient programs, sponsorship of research, and house-hotel facilities.

36248. Caribbean Cultural Center, 408 W 58th St, New York, NY 10019; (212) 307-7420. Identifies, compiles, and disseminates info on traditions and culture of the Caribbean Basin. Answers inquiries, provides advisory and reference services, provides speakers, distributes publications, makes referrals. Although services free, donations suggested.

36249. Carrier Corp., Logan Lewis Library, Carrier Parkway, Syracuse, NY 13221; (315) 432-6306. Maintains a collection of materials on air conditioning, acoustics, electrical and mechanical engineering, and heating. Provides reference services, permits onsite reference by local scientists and students.

36250. Catalyst Information Center, 250 Park Ave S, New York, NY 10003; (212) 777-8900. Works with corps and individuals to develop career and family options. Answers inquiries, provides reference and reproduction services, distributes publications, makes referrals. Except for access to data base, services free.

36251. Catholic Medical Mission Board, 10 W 17th St, New York, NY 10011; (212) 242-7757. Provides "no cost" shipments of medical supplies to overseas medical institutions; recruitment, validation, and placement of physicians and registered nurses. Answers inquiries, provides advisory services free.

36252. Catholic Peace Fellowship, 339 Lafayette St, New York, NY 10012; (212) 673-8990. Educational and action service conducted by Roman Catholic members of the Fellowship of Reconciliation. Answers inquiries, provides consulting and draft counseling, distributes publications, makes referrals.

36253. Catholic Press Association of the U.S., 119 N Park Ave, Rockville Centre, NY 11570; (516) 766-3400. Collects data on Catholic publications and book publishers. Answers inquiries, provides reference services, conducts seminars and workshops, distributes publications.

36254. Celebrity Service, 171 W 57th St, New York, NY 10019; (212) 757-7979. Acts as a worldwide clearinghouse for info on public figures. Publishes a bulletin; answers inquiries; provides advisory, consulting, and reference services; distributes publications. Services available for a fee.

36255. Cellulose Research Institute, State Univ of New York, Syracuse, NY 13210; (315) 473-8824. Interest in cellulose and wood chemistry, wood anatomy and ultrastructure, and solid state properties of polysaccharides. Answers inquiries, provides consulting services, arranges conferences.

36256. Center for Arts Information, 625 Broadway, New York, NY 10012; (212) 677-7548. Serves as a clearinghouse and referral service for nonprofit arts on sources of services and funds for arts orgs and artists. Answers inquiries, provides advisory and reference services, distributes publications, makes referrals. Fees charged for some services.

36257. Center for Book Arts, 626 Broadway, New York, NY 10012; (212) 460-9768. Devoted to developing and promoting book arts through educational programs, publications, and exhibitions. Answers inquiries, provides advisory and reference services, makes referrals, permits onsite use of collection. Most services free.

36258. Center for Community and Environmental Development, 379 deKalb Ave, Brooklyn, NY 11205; (718) 636-3486. Provides technical assistance, advocacy planning, policy analysis, and training in urban affairs. Answers inquiries, provides advisory services, distributes publications, makes referrals. Most services free to low- or moderate-income groups that practice no discrimination.

36259. Center for Cuban Studies, 124 W 23rd St, New York, NY 10011; (212) 242-0559. Studies Cuban history, govt, economy, society, and culture since the revolution of 1960. Answers inquiries, provides advisory and reference services, distributes publications, makes referrals. Use of library is free, other services available to nonmembers for a donation.

36260. Center for Entrepreneurial Management, 83 Spring St, New York, NY 10012; (212) 925-7304. Nonprofit membership org for presidents of small growing businesses. Publishes newsletter, answers inquiries, provides advisory and reference services, conducts seminars, distributes publications, makes referrals. Services available for a fee.

36261. Center for Environmental Information, 33 S Washington St, Rochester, NY 14608; (716) 546-3796. Interest in all aspects of environmental studies, including technical, societal, regulatory, and legal issues. Answers inquiries, provides advisory and reference services, makes referrals. Services may be subject to a fee.

36262. Center for Environmental Research, Cornell Univ, 463 Hollister Hall, Ithaca, NY 14853; (607) 256-7535. Encourages university-wide interaction among faculty that address problems in man's physical, biological, and social environment. Distributes publications, attempts to answer individual requests for information.

36263. Center for Governmental Research, 37 S Washington St, Rochester, NY 14608; (716) 325-6360. Conducts research in municipal, county, and metropolitan govt, including taxation, finance, housing, criminal justice, health, manpower, social welfare, demography, and human services. Answers inquiries, distributes publications, provides consulting services.

36264. Center for Human Environments, 33 W 42nd St, New York, NY 10036; (212) 790-4551. Collects materials on social sciences and humanities impacting on relation of men and women to the environment. Answers inquiries, provides reference services, makes referrals. Services free.

36265. Center for Hyperactive Child Information, P.O. Box 406, Murray Hill Station, New York, NY 10156; (212) 679-3959. Dedicated to helping parents and teachers identify children with hyperactivity and find appropriate educational and medical help. Provides a research library, and referral service; collects articles for dissemination.

36266. Center for Inter-American Relations, 680 Park Ave, New York, NY 10021; (212) 249-8950. Provides a forum for those interested in political, social, and economic activity in the Americas. Promotes translation and publication of Latin American and Caribbean literature in the U.S., and sponsors exhibitions of art and performances of Latin American musicians.

36267. Center for Medical Consumers and Health Care Information, 237 Thompson St, New York, NY 10012; (212) 674-7105. Nonprofit org interested in health and medical issues and consumer info. Answers inquiries, provides reference services, distributes publications, makes referrals, permits onsite use of library collection. Services free.

36269. Center for Migration Studies of New York, 209 Flagg Pl, Staten Island, NY 10304; (718) 351-8800. Investigates sociological, demographic, economic, historical, and legislative aspects of human migration movements and ethnic group relations. Conducts conferences and seminars, permits onsite use of the library and archives.

36270. Center for Near Eastern Studies, 50 Washington Sq South, New York, NY 10003; (212) 598-2697. Studies history, civilization, politics, anthropology, economics, and sociology of the Arab world, Israel, Iran, and Turkey. Answers inquiries, provides consulting services, distributes publications and films, makes referrals. Some services may be subject to a fee.

36271. Center for Nonprofit Organizations, 203 W 25th St, 3rd Fl, New York, NY 10001; (212) 989-9026. Provides professional advice on starting, funding, and managing nonprofit orgs and helps existing ones advance rapidly toward their goals. Answers inquiries, provides advisory and reference services, distributes publications, makes referrals. Services available at a fee.

36272. Center for Occupational Hazards, 5 Beekman Street, New York, NY 10038; (212) 227-6220. Gathers and disseminates info about health hazards related to arts and crafts materials and facilities. Answers info requests, maintains a reference library, provides onsite assessments.

36273. Center for Packaging Education, 32 Court St, Brooklyn Heights, NY 11201; (718) 624-6157. Studies packaging, including folding boxes, cartons, corrugated boxes, shipping cartons, labels, metal cans, aerosols, glass containers, plastic containers, and blister packages. Provides consulting services, makes referrals. Services available at cost.

36274. Center for Policy Research, 475 Riverside Dr, New York, NY 10115; (212) 870-2180. Conducts research leading to the formulation and reformulation of public policy issues, especially with regard to education, incarceration, manpower, reindustrialization, environment, and aging. Answers inquiries, provides consulting services, distributes publications.

36275. Center for Radiophysics and Space Research, Space Sciences Bldg, Ithaca, NY 14853; (607) 256-4341. Studies infrared astronomy, theoretical astrophysics, lunar and planetary surfaces and atmospheres, theoretical solar system studies, exobiology and the origin of life. Answers inquiries, distributes publications. Services free to those in similar fields of research.

36276. Center for Responsive Psychology, Brooklyn Coll, Brooklyn, NY 11210; (718) 780-5960. Org of professional psychologists and students dedicated to constructive social change. Answers inquiries, provides consulting and reference services, makes referrals. Services free to those in jail, at nominal cost to students, and at modest or clerical fees to most other users.

36277. Center for Safety, 715 Broadway, New York, NY 10003; (212) 598-2156. Seeks to help the community, business, labor, industry, and govt reduce the harmful effects of hazards, to identify areas where safety and health problems exist, and to remedy them. Answers inquiries, provides services. Services for a fee to industry, labor, and govt.

36278. Center for Science and Technology Policy, 114 Liberty St, Room 501, New York, NY 10006; (212) 285-8946. Examines the role and impact of public and private policies in the generation, application, and management of science and technology. Provides advisory services, conducts seminars. Fee for some services. Research and analysis requires sponsorship.

36279. Center for Social Analysis, SUNY at Binghamton, Binghamton, NY 13901; (607) 798-2116. Promotes research in the social sciences and related disciplines through programs in intl documentations, management service, policy analysis, survey research. Answers inquiries, provides advisory and reproduction services for a fee.

36280. Center for Understanding Media, 69 Horatio St, New York, NY 10014; (212) 929-1448. Specializes in projects involving education, communication, and the arts. Conducts seminars and conferences on independent filmmaking, film and television criticism, filmmaking by young people, children's film, television festivals, and reading and alphabet reform.

36281. Center for United States-China Arts Exchange, 423 W 118th St, 1E, New York, NY 10027; (212) 280-4648. Promotes and facilitates exchanges of specialists and materials in visual, literary, and performing arts between U.S. and the People's Republic of China. Answers inquiries, provides advisory and consulting services, distributes newsletter, makes referrals. Services at cost.

36282. Center for Women in Government, 302 Draper Hall, 1400 Washington Ave, Albany, NY 12222 (518) 442-3900. Conducts research, training, and public education programs to remove barriers to the employment and promotion of women, minorities, and the disabled in public sector. Answers inquiries, provides advisory services, distributes publications. Services available for a fee.

36283. Center for the Biology of Natural Systems, c/o Dr Barry Commoner, Queens Coll, CUNY, Flushing, NY 11367. Studies the natural sciences and their use in solving practical environmental problems. Provides consulting services, makes referrals. Inquiries welcomed.

36284. Center for the Study of Aging, 706 Madison Ave, Albany, NY 12208; (518) 465-6927. Promotes education, research, and training in the fields of aging, health, and fitness. Answers inquiries, provides reference and advisory services, distributes publications, makes referrals. Services free, except publications.

36285. Center for the Study of Anorexia and Bulimia, One W 91st St, New York, NY 10024; (212) 595-3449. Nonprofit org interested in psychotherapeutic treatment of anorexia and bulimia. Answers inquiries, provides advisory and reference services, distributes publications, makes referrals. A fee for services.

36286. Center for the Study of Women and Society, 33 W 42nd St, New York, NY 10036; (212) 790-4435. Interest in women and health, women in the arts, women and work, feminist social theory, and women's studies. Answers specialized inquiries, conducts seminars, makes referrals. Services generally free to researchers and the news media.

36287. Center for the Study of the Presidency, 208 E 75th St, New York, NY 10021; (212) 249-1200. Studies the American presidency, including its relationship with Congress, with particular emphasis on organization and policymaking processes. Answers inquiries; provides free advisory, reference, abstracting, indexing and microform services; distributes publications.

36288. Central Opera Service, Lincoln Center, New York, NY 10023; (212) 799-3467. Fosters closer association among civic, community, college, and national opera companies throughout the country and assists them in improving artistic standards. Answers inquiries, provides reference services, distributes publications, makes referrals. Inquiries answered free.

36290. Cesarean Prevention Movement, PO Box 152, Syracuse, NY 13210; (315) 424-1942. Aims to reduce rate of cesarean deliveries, provide a forum for discussion, and provide a support network for women recovering from cesarean deliveries.

36291. Chamber Music America, 215 Park Ave South, New York, NY 10003; (212) 460-9030. Org of more than 1,000 members involved in chamber music. Makes direct grants of about $150,000 a year to performers. Answers inquiries, provides advisory and reference services, distributes publications, makes referrals. Services for members.

36292. Chamber of Commerce of Latin America in the United States, One World Trade Center, Ste 2343, New York, NY 10048; (212) 432-9313. Seeks promotion of trade between U.S. and Latin America. Answers inquiries or refers inquirers to other sources of info free.

36293. Champagne News and Information Bureau, 220 E 42nd St, New York, NY 10017; (212) 907-9382. Conducts educational and promotional projects on champagne. Answers inquiries, provides advisory services, conducts seminars and tasting sessions, distributes publications, makes referrals. Services free.

36294. Chase Manhattan Bank, Information Center, 1 Chase Manhattan Plaza, New York, NY 10081; (212) 552-4113. Maintains data collection on finance, banking, business, commerce, and industry, both domestic and intl. Provides fee-based research services, makes interlibrary loans, permits use of collection by bank customers with written consent. Facilities available for duplication.

36295. Chemists' Club, Library, 52 E 41st St, New York, NY 10017; (212) 679-6383. Maintains collection of material on chemistry, pure and applied. Answers brief inquiries, provides reference and duplication services, makes referrals, permits onsite use of literature collection. Services may be provided for a fee.

36296. Chemotherapy Foundation, 183 Madison Ave, New York, NY 10016; (212) 213-9292. Seeks to accelerate development of drug treatment in the control of cancer through research, clinical studies, and improved application techniques.

36297. Child Find, P.O. Box 277, New Paltz, NY 12561; (914) 255-1848. Nonprofit org that collects data on missing and abducted children. Operates national location service for parents of missing children. Children in search of their parents may call a toll-free number (800-I-AM-LOST), as may spotters of abducted children. Services free.

36298. Child Welfare League of America, 67 Irving Pl, New York, NY 10003; (212) 254-7410. Devoted to improving care and services for deprived, dependent, or neglected children, youth and their families. Persons with serious research interests may visit the library. Inquiries answered and referrals made. Services available for a fee to the membership, open to anyone.

36300. Children of Alcoholics Foundation, 540 Madison Ave, 23rd Fl, New York, NY 10022; (212) 980-5394. Seeks to serve and educate the estimated seven million children living with an alcoholic parent.

36301. Children's Blood Foundation, 424 E 62nd St, New York, NY 10021; (212) 687-1564. Supports diagnosis, treatment, research and, education in all blood diseases of infants and children. Answers inquiries, makes referrals, provides consulting services. Fees for services depend upon user's ability to pay, third-party coverage, and other insurance agencies.

36303. Children's Book Council Library, 67 Irving Pl, New York, NY 10003; (212) 254-2666. Serves as a children's trade book examination center. Sponsors biennial conference, permits onsite use of children's and professional collections.

36304. China Council, 725 Park Ave, New York, NY 10021; (212) 288-6400. Seeks to educate American public about China. Answers inquiries, provides consulting services, conducts seminars and workshops, distributes publications, makes referrals. Fees charged for formal briefing seminars and workshops and most publications.

36305. China Institute in America, 125 E 65th St, New York, NY 10021; (212) 744-8181. Studies history and culture of China and promotes cultural and educational exchange between China and the U.S. Answers inquiries, conducts seminars, makes referrals, extends library privileges to its members.

36306. Chlorine Institute, 70 W 40th St, New York, NY 10018; (212) 682-4324. Interest in all problems relating to the safe handling and use of chlorine. Makes referrals, provides bibliographic, consulting, and duplication services.

36307. Citizen Exchange Council, 18 E 41st St, Ste 1004, New York, NY 10017; (212) 889-7960. Interest in intl education, educational travel, cultural exchange, relations between U.S. and other countries, especially the Soviet Union and Eastern European nations. Answers inquiries, provides advisory and translation services, makes referrals. Some services free.

36308. Citizen Soldier, 175 Fifth Ave, Ste 1010, New York, NY 10010; (212) 777-3470. Advocacy org serving Vietnam veterans and active duty military personnel in terms of their human and constitutional rights. Answers inquiries, provides advisory services, distributes publications and TV spot announcements. Services free.

36309. Citizens Forum on Self-Government/National Municipal League, 55 W 44th St, New York, NY 10036; (800) 223-6004. Conducts research in govt and administration, including intergovernmental relations, election systems, public opinion, and civic organization. Answers inquiries, provides consulting services, distributes publications. Fee for some services.

36310. Citizens Freedom Foundation, Information Services, Box 86, Hannacroix, NY 12087; (518) 756-8014. Educational org whose purpose is to create public awareness of the dangers of destructive cults. Answers inquiries, provides advisory and reference services, conducts seminars, provides speakers, distributes publications, makes referrals. Services free.

36311. Clearinghouse on Information Education and Training Materials, 200 Huntington Hall, Syracuse, NY 13210; (315) 423-4930. Collects materials and info on availability of instructional support aids in computer science. Services available to faculty members and training institutions in librarianship, information science, documentation, and archives work.

36312. Clearinghouse on Women's Studies, 311 E 94th St, New York, NY 10128; (212) 360-5790. Interest in women's studies, including women's education, history, and vocations. Answers inquiries, provides speakers, distributes publications, makes referrals. Services generally free.

36313. Clinical Pharmacokinetics Laboratory, Millard Fillmore Hospital, Buffalo, NY 14209; (716) 845-4704. Conducts research and training in the field of pharmacokinetics. Answers inquiries, provides advisory and reference services, conducts drug assays. Services offered at cost, restricted to users formally approved by the lab.

36314. Coalition on Sexuality and Disability, 853 Broadway, Room 611, New York, NY 10003; (212) 242-3900. Seeks to improve sexual health care services for the disabled through education, training, advocacy, and networking. Publishes a newsletter, answers inquiries, provides medical advisory and reference services, distributes publications, makes referrals.

36316. Coffee, Sugar, and Cocoa Exchange, 4 World Trade Center, New York, NY 10048; (212) 938-2800. Conducts commodities futures trading, especially in coffee, sugar, and cocoa. Answers inquiries and distributes literature. Services free. Visitors Gallery open to public during trading hours.

36317. Cold Spring Harbor Laboratory, Research Library, Box 100—Library, Cold Spring Harbor, NY 11724; (516) 367-8350. Nonprofit org interested in biochemistry, molecular biology, virology, cancer, cell biology, and genetics. Answers inquiries, provides advisory and reference services, makes referrals. Services free, except copying and online searching.

36318. Collectors Club, 22 E 35th St, New York, NY 10016; (212) 683-0559. Promotes interest and knowledge of philately among its members and public through encouragement of philatelic research and exchange of info. Provides reference services free, distributes publications. Library open to public for reference by appointment.

36319. College Art Association of America, 149 Madison Ave, New York, NY 10016; (212) 889-2113. Membership org comprised of scholars, teachers, artists, critics, museum curators and administrators, art dealers, collectors, art and slide librarians, and students. Answers inquiries, provides a job placement service, distributes publications. Most services for members.

36320. College Board, 45 Columbus Ave, New York, NY 10023-6917; (212) 713-8000. Provides a variety of tests and other services for admissions, guidance, placement, and financial aid purposes in education. Answers inquiries, provides advisory and magnetic tape services, distributes publications, makes referrals. Most services and testing programs restricted.

36321. Colombia Information Service, 140 E 57th St, New York, NY 10022; (212) 421-8270. Acts as source of info on Colombia: economic development, infrastructure, housing, mining, agriculture, and foreign trade. Publishes newsletter, answers inquiries or makes referrals.

36322. Color Association of the United States, 343 Lexington Ave, New York, NY 10016; (212) 683-9531. Interest in colors, their standardization and forecasting color trends 20 to 24 months ahead. Answers inquiries, provides reference and consulting services, provides standard color cards and standard color swatches for a fee, provides color forecasts.

36323. Color in Construction News Bureau, c/o Schorr and Howard Co., 6 E 43rd St, Ste 2000, New York, NY 10017; (212) 867-8888. Provides info to the media and to orgs of building construction professionals about effective use of color, especially colored concrete products. Answers inquiries, conducts seminars, distributes data compilations and publications, makes referrals. Services free.

36324. Comics Magazine Association of America, Attn: J. Dudley Waldner, 60 E 42nd St, New York, NY 10165; (212) 682-8144. Studies history and progress of comics magazine industry, particularly with reference to its self-regulation program. Answers inquiries, makes referrals, permits limited onsite use of collection.

36325. Committee for Better Transit, P.O. Box 3106, Long Island City, NY 11103; (718) 728-0091. Dedicated to development of improved public transportation. Answers inquiries, provides consulting and reference services, makes referrals. Fees may be charged, depending on the nature and extent of services requested.

36326. Committee for Economic Development, 477 Madison Ave, New York, NY 10022; (212) 688-2063. Conducts research and formulates recommendations on: the national economy, the intl economy, education and urban development and govt. Research results and policy recommendations widely disseminated through various media.

36327. Committee for a New Korea Policy, 221 Central Ave, Albany, NY 12203; (518) 434-4037. Works in support of human rights, reduction of military tensions, and the right of Koreans to decide their own future without outside interference or control. Answers inquiries, makes referrals, permits onsite use of collection, distributes publications. Services provided at cost.

36328. Committee for the Futherance of Torah Observance, 1430 57th St, Brooklyn, NY 11219; (718) 851-6428. Interest in kosher food, kosher laws, and Jewish religious observance. Answers inquiries, provides advisory and reference services, distributes publications. Services may involve a fee.

36329. Committee for the Scientific Investigation of Claims of the Paranormal, P.O. Box 229, Central Park Station (3151 Bailey Ave), Buffalo, NY 14215; (716) 834-3222. Encourages critical investigation of paranormal and fringe-scientific claims from a responsible, scientific viewpoint and disseminates info about the results. Answers inquiries, provides advisory and reference services, distributes publications, makes referrals. Services at cost.

36330. Committee in Support of Solidarity, 275 Seventh Ave, 25th Fl, New York, NY 10001; (212) 989-0909. Studies Solidarity movement and current affairs in Poland, with emphasis on democratic opposition movements, independent trade movements, and human rights situation. Answers inquiries, distributes publications, makes referrals. Most services free.

36331. Committee on Research Materials on Southeast Asia, McGraw Hall, Ithaca, NY 14853; (607) 256-4367. Interest in the acquisition and processing of research materials on Southeast Asia by research libraries in the U.S. and Canada. Answers inquiries, distributes its publication. Services available to persons with a professional interest in Southeast Asian research materials.

36332. Committee to Halt Useless College Killings, P.O. Box 188 (126 Marion St), Sayville, NY 11782; (516) 567-1130. Compiles data and documentation on hazing incidents, deaths, and injuries in American colleges and univs. Answers inquiries, conducts seminars, distributes reprints, makes referrals. Services free.

36333. Community Action for Legal Services, Food Law Project, 335 Broadway, New York, NY 10013-9990; (212) 431-7200. Provides info on operation of federal and state food programs. Answers inquiries, provides reference services, distributes publications, makes referrals. Fee charged for publications; other services free to low-income persons and their advocates.

36334. Community Guidance Service, 120 W 58th St, New York, NY 10019; (212) 586-8160. Operates large outpatient guidance and counseling service as well as American Institute for Psychotherapy and Psychoanalyses, which offers a comprehensive curriculum for professionals. Answers inquiries, provides consulting services.

36335. Community Research Applications, 1500 Pelham Parkway, South, Bronx, NY 10461; (212) 829-1570. Nonprofit org interested in human service research, program monitoring and evaluation, child abuse, and aging. Answers inquiries, provides advisory and technical services. Services provided at cost to all users.

36336. Community Sex Information, 380 Second Ave, 5th Fl, New York, NY 10010; (212) 677-3320. Committed to providing easy access to free and accurate info about human sexuality in all of its aspects. Answers inquiries, provides advisory and reference services, operates speakers bureau and telephone info service, makes referrals. Some services free.

36337. Comprehensive Cancer Center/Institute of Cancer Research, 701 W 168th St, New York, NY 10032; (212) 694-6904. Conducts basic and clinical research on problems of cancer, cancer control and, cancer education. Answers inquiries, provides consulting services, distributes publications.

36338. Comprehensive Sickle Cell Center, 135th St and Lenox Ave, Ste 6146, New York, NY 10037; (212) 491-8074. Provides coordinated program of medical, social, and vocational services for patients with sickle cell disease, and education and research on that disease. Answers inquiries, provides consulting and reference services, distributes publications, makes referrals. Info services free.

36339. Conference Board, 845 Third Ave, New York, NY 10022; (212) 759-0900. Collects material on economics, business, labor, taxation, finance, demography, intl operations, management and personnel administration, governmental regulations, marketing, and accounting. Materials accessible to subscribing associates and university members.

36340. Congress of Racial Equality, 236 W 116th St, New York, NY 10026; (212) 316-1577. Interest in civil rights, black nationalism, culture, economic and community development. Answers inquiries, provides advisory and reference services, distributes publications, makes referrals. Services free, except publications, primarily for minorities.

36341. Congress on Research in Dance, 35 W 4th St, Room 675, New York, NY 10003; (212) 598-3459. Provides opportunities for the exchange of ideas among dance scholars and scholars working in dance-related fields. Conducts seminars and workshops, distributes publications. Services for members.

36342. Conscience and Military Tax Campaign, 44 Bellhaven Rd, Bellport, NY 11713; (516) 286-8825. Seeks congressional passage of World Peace Tax Fund Act, which would amend Internal Revenue Code to provide an alternative for taxpayers conscientiously opposed to participation in war. Answers inquiries, provides advisory services, makes referrals. Services free.

36343. Consciousness Research and Training Project, 315 E 68th St, Box 9G, New York, NY 10021. Nonprofit org interested in holistic health, meditation, stress reduction, psychology, and parapsychology. Answers inquiries, provides advisory services, makes referrals, distributes publications on a selective basis. Services free, unless extensive.

36344. Consortium for Continental Reflection Profiling, Cornell Univ, Attn: Prof S. Kaufman, Ithaca, NY 14853; (607) 256-7165. Involved in continuous seismic profiling of earth's crust and upper mantle within U.S. and analysis of the data. Answers inquiries, distributes newsletter free and data packages at cost of reproduction.

36345. Consumers Union of the United States, 256 Washington St, Mt Vernon, NY 10553; (914) 667-9400. Provides consumers with info and counsel on consumer goods and gives info on all matters relating to expenditure of family income. Publishes magazine, makes interlibrary loans, permits limited onsite reference by request.

36346. Contact Lens Association of Ophthalmologists Public Relations Council, c/o G. Peter Halberg, M.D., 40 W 77th St, New York, NY 10024; (212) 675-3333. Works with American Society for Testing and Materials and American National Standards Institute in the establishment of standardized procedures. Answers inquiries, provides advisory and reference services, distributes publications, makes referrals. Services for professionals.

36347. Cooley's Anemia Foundation, 105 E 22nd St, New York, NY 10010; (212) 598-0911. Furnishes medical supplies, provides genetic counseling, seeks to make public and medical profession aware of Cooley's anemia, and supports research aimed at treatment and eventual cure of this disease. Answers inquiries, distributes publications, makes referrals free.

36348. Cooper-Hewitt Museum, 2 E 91st St, New York, NY 10128; (212) 860-6868. Maintains collections and library devoted to historical and contemporary design. Answers inquiries, provides advisory and reference services, permits onsite use of slides and photographs of the collections, permits onsite study of collection objects by special arrangement.

36349. Coordinating Council of Literary Magazines, 2 Park Ave, New York, NY 10016; (212) 481-5245. Provides grants and services to noncommercial literary magazines and editors and, through them, contemporary American poets and fiction writers. Answers inquiries.

36350. Copyright Society of the U.S.A., 40 Washington Sq S, New York, NY 10012; (212) 598-2280. Interest in copyright law and rights in literature, music, art, the theatre, motion pictures, and other forms of intellectual property. Answers inquiries, provides reference and reproduction services, distributes a publication, makes referrals. Nonmembers assessed a fee for services.

36351. Corning Museum of Glass, Museum Way, Corning, NY 14831; (607) 937-5371. Collects objects and materials representing every aspect of art and history of glass. Answers inquiries from scholars, makes interlibrary loans. Library open to public.

36352. Corporate Data Exchange, 198 Broadway, Room 707, New York, NY 10038; (212) 962-2980. Studies stock ownership and control of largest corporations in various U.S. industries, including transportation, agribusiness, energy, banking, and Fortune 500. Provides advisory and consulting services, including company profiles, distributes data compilations, makes referrals.

36353. Council for Financial Aid to Education, 680 Fifth Ave, Room 800, New York, NY 10019; (212) 541-4050. Encourages business to provide financial support to higher education. CFAE neither collects nor disburses money. Answers inquiries, provides advisory and reference services, distributes publications. Most services free.

36354. Council for Intercultural Studies and Programs, 777 U.N. Plaza, Ste 9A, New York, NY 10017; (212) 972-9877. Provides teaching materials to aid undergraduate teachers and librarians in American colleges and univs in teaching about Asia, Africa, and Third World in general. Answers inquiries, permits onsite use of collection. Fee for publications.

36355. Council for Livestock Protection, 930 Fifth Ave, 11-H, New York, NY 10021. Conducts research in better and more humane methods of handling livestock from farm to slaughter. Answers inquiries and provides consulting services. Services free.

36356. Council on Botanical and Horticultural Libraries, c/o John F. Reed, N.Y. Botanical Garden, Bronx, NY 10458; (212) 220-8728. Seeks to initiate and improve communication between persons and institutions interested in libraries of botanical and horticultural literature. Provides consulting and reproduction services,

distributes publications. Services primarily for members.

36357. Council on Economic Priorities, 84 Fifth Ave, New York, NY 10011; (212) 691-8550. Conducts analysis and comparison of corporate social responsibility and public policy concerns in such areas as military production, hiring policies, consumerism, pollution control, foreign investments, product safety. Offers use of its files, sells its publications.

36359. Council on Family Health, 420 Lexington Ave, New York, NY 10017; (212) 210-8836. Conducts public health education programs and provides publications on family and individual health and safety needs. Published info on general health, proper medicine use, first aid in the home, child safety, and other topics is available to public on written request.

36360. Council on Foreign Relations, 58 E 68th St, New York, NY 10021; (212) 734-0400. Studies fundamental problems of foreign policy in order to increase understanding of foreign policy issues in the U.S. and abroad. Info services performed primarily to meet the research needs of the staff and members of the Council.

36361. Council on International Educational Exchange, 205 E 42nd St, New York, NY 10017; (212) 661-1414. Nonprofit assn of orgs that sponsor educational exchange programs. Answers inquiries, distributes publications (some free, some at cost), makes referrals, provides advisory services.

36362. Council on International and Public Affairs, 777 U.N. Plaza, Ste 9A, New York, NY 10017; (212) 972-9877. Promotes study and public understanding of problems and affairs of the peoples of the U.S. and other nations through conferences, research, seminars and workshops, publications, and other means. Answers inquiries, conducts seminars, sells publications, makes referrals. Services free.

36363. Council on Interracial Books for Children, 1841 Broadway, New York, NY 10023; (212) 757-5339. Seeks to counteract racist, sexist stereotypes and bias in literature and instructional materials for children. Answers inquiries, conducts clinics, provides consultants and resource specialists, distributes publications, makes referrals.

36364. Council on Municipal Performance, 84 Fifth Ave, New York, NY 10011; (212) 243-6603. Develops and uses performance measurement standards for state and local govt services and prepares guides for municipal managers. Conducts seminars, provides consulting services by negotiation, distributes publications, makes referrals. Services free to members.

36365. Council on Social Work Education, 111 Eighth Ave, New York, NY 10011; (212) 242-3800. Promotes social work education on undergraduate and graduate levels, including guidelines, curriculum development, experimentation, and research. Answers inquiries, provides consulting services, makes referrals.

36366. Country Dance and Song Society of America, 505 Eighth Ave, New York, NY 10018; (212) 594-8833. Assn dedicated to enjoyment, preservation, and study of English and American traditional dance, music, and song. Answers inquiries, provides consulting services. Services free, except extensive consulting services.

36367. Cousteau Society, 777 Third Ave, New York, NY 10017; (212) 826-2940. Dedicated to protection and improvement of life in marine environment. Answers inquiries, provides reference services, organizes lectures, makes referrals. Services free, primarily for membership.

36368. Creative Education Foundation, c/o Angelo M. Biondi, 1300 Elmwood Ave, Buffalo, NY 14222; (716) 878-6221. Interest in development of creative ability problem-solving and education in business and industry. Provides consulting services, conducts training courses and conferences. Fees charged for services.

36369. Dag Hammarskjold Library, United Nations, New York, NY 10017; (212) 754-7444. Interest in apartheid, arms control and disarmament, demography, intl law, treaties and conventions. Answers inquiries, provides bibliographies, indexes, reproduction service, online searches in UNBIS data base.

36370. Damien-Dutton Society for Leprosy Aid, 616 Bedford Ave, Bellmore, NY 11710; (516) 221-5829. Promotes education, research, rehabilitation, and care of leprosy patients in all parts of the world. Publishes a newsletter, answers inquiries, provides advisory and reference services, makes referrals. Services free.

36371. Dance Films Association, 241 E 34th St, Room 301, New York, NY 10016; (212) 686-7019. Acts as an intermediary between users, producers, and distributors of dance motion pictures and videotapes. Answers inquiries, provides consulting, assists in locating dance films. Services provided free to members, for a fee to others.

36372. Dance Notation Bureau, 33 W 21st St, 3rd Fl, New York, NY 10010; (212) 807-7899. Seeks to preserve dance heritage through graphic notation using Labanotation and other notation systems. Conducts workshops, lends Labanotation scores of dances, distributes publications, permits onsite use of collections. Services primarily for those involved in dance.

36373. Dance Theater Workshop, 219 W 19th St, New York, NY 10011; (212) 691-6500. Provides production facilities and artist sponsorship programs as well as technical services to the community of independent performing artists in N.Y. and throughout the country. Answers inquiries, provides consulting services, distributes publications, makes referrals.

36374. Deafness Research Foundation, 9 E 38th Street, 7th Fl, New York, NY 10016; (800) 535-3323. Supports research on treatment and prevention of deafness and other ear disorders. Helps sponsor National Temporal Bone Banks Program and conducts research into nerve deafness, ototoxic drugs, cochlear implants, noise, Meniere's disease, tinnitus, otosclerosis, etc.

36375. Deafness Research and Training Center, N.Y. Univ, 733 Shimkin Hall, New York, NY 10003; (212) 598-3232. Provides education and rehabilitation of deaf and multiply handicapped persons. Answers inquiries, provides consulting services, distributes publications, makes referrals. Services free.

36376. Design Institute for Physical Property Data, 345 E 47th St, New York, NY 10017; (212) 705-7332. Compiles data on a large number of industrially important chemicals and their mixtures, and disseminates it in formats useful for industrial process design. Provides reference services, distributes data compilations. Services provided for members.

36378. Direct Marketing Association, Information Central, 6 E 43rd St, New York, NY 10017; (212) 689-4977. Operates a Mail Order Action Line service for consumers that attempts to resolve their difficulties with mail order firms. Processes consumer complaints and attempts to remove consumers' names from or add their names to mailing lists, distributes publications, makes referrals.

36379. Direct Marketing Educational Foundation, 6 E 43rd St, New York, NY 10017; (212) 689-4977. Dedicated to improving the quality and increasing the scope of direct mail marketing education at the univ level. Answers inquiries, provides speakers, distributes teaching aids. Most services free.

36381. Downtown Research and Development Center, 1133 Broadway, Ste 1407, New York, NY 10010; (212) 206-7979. Studies and reports on downtown and urban problems and solutions in an effort to provide a focus for recycling cities and towns. Provides reference services, conducts multiclient studies, conducts seminars, sells publications.

36382. Dramatists Guild, 234 W 44th St, New York, NY 10036; (212) 398-9366. Professional assn of playwrights, composers, and lyricists in the U.S. Provides business counseling, answers queries on dramatists, producers, lawyers, agents, contracts, royalties, grants, copyright, contests, conferences, workshops and theater; makes referrals.

36383. Drug Information Center, 462 Grider St, Buffalo, NY 14215; (716) 898-3927. Interest in drugs and dissemination of drug info, including adverse reactions, allergies, chronic toxicity, and poisoning in infants and children. Answers inquiries, provides consulting and reference services free to scientists and health professionals.

36384. Drug and Alcohol Council, 396 Alexander St, Rochester, NY 14607; (716) 244-3190. Nonprofit org interested in preventive education and primary intervention in alcohol and drugs. Answers inquiries, provides advisory services, distributes publications, makes referrals. Services free, except extended programs.

36385. Dun & Bradstreet Business Library, 99 Church St, New York, NY 10007; (212) 285-7304. Collects materials on business with emphasis on credit and marketing. Collection open to public for reference purposes. Services include bibliographic assistance, answers to inquiries, referrals and simple data transcriptions. Copying services available for a fee.

36386. Dysautonomia Foundation, 370 Lexington Ave, New York, NY 10017; (212) 889-0300. Sponsors fund raising activities, allocates money for research, and provides info about Familial Dysautonomia. Answers inquiries, distributes publications, makes referrals. Services free to physicians, patients, and parents of afflicted children.

36387. EIC/Intelligence, 48 W 38th St, New York, NY 10018; (800) 223-6275. Collects materials on all aspects of environmental pollution, conservation, and management. Answers inquiries, provides consulting, reference, and document-retrieval services.

36388. ERIC Clearinghouse on Information Resources, Syracuse Univ, Syracuse, NY 13210; (315) 423-3640. Provides educational community with up-to-date info and access to materials in the fields of educational media and technology and library and info science. Answers inquiries, distributes publications, makes referrals, permits onsite use of collections.

36389. ERIC Clearinghouse on Urban Education, 525 W 120th St, New York, NY 10027; (212) 678-3437. Collects, maintains, and disseminates info about urban and minority children and youth. Answers inquiries, provides consulting and reference services, distributes publications, makes referrals.

36390. Early American Industries Association, P.O. Box 2128, Empire State Plaza Station, Albany, NY 12220-0128; (518) 473-1748. Studies early American industry and tools. Answers inquiries, provides consulting and reference services, makes referrals. Services, except publications, usually free.

36391. East Asian Institute, 913 Intl Affairs Bldg, 420 W 118th St, New York, NY 10027; (212) 280-2591. Collects data on China, Japan, and Korea. Inquiries referred to institute members for reply.

36392. Eastfoto, 25 W 43rd St, Room 1008, New York, NY 10036; (212) 921-1922. Collects photographs of all aspects of life in Albania, Bulgaria, Czechoslovakia, East Germany, Hungary, Yugoslavia, Poland, Rumania, and China. Onsite use of collection permitted by appointment; original photos may be rented for reproduction.

36393. Eastman Kodak, Department of Information Services, Research Labs, Rochester, NY 14650; (716) 477-4310. Collects materials that deal with photography, emphasizing scientific aspects. Provides limited reference services, makes interlibrary loans and referrals, permits onsite use of collection by arrangement.

36394. Ecological and Toxicological Association of the Dyestuffs Manufacturing Industry, 1075 Central Park Ave, Scarsdale, NY 10583; (914) 725-1492. Represents dye producers in matters relating to health and environmental impacts of dyes in distribution, us,e and disposal.

36397. Educational Film Library Association, 45 John St, Ste 301, New York, NY 10038; (212) 227-5599. Natl clearinghouse for info about nontheatrical 16mm films and other nonprint media. Answers inquiries, provides advisory services, distributes publications, makes referrals. Services intended for members only.

36398. Educational Products Information Exchange Institute, c/o Teachers Coll, Columbia Univ, P.O. Box 27, New York, NY 10027; (516) 283-4922. Seeks to provide educational consumers with info and evaluative services that enable them to select materials, equipment, and systems that best meet the needs of learners. Answers inquiries, provides consulting services, distributes publications. Services primarily for members.

36399. Edward S. Harkness Eye Institute, 635 W 165th St, New York, NY 10032; (212) 694-2916. Collects materials on ophthalmology. Answers inquiries, provides reference and copying services, permits onsite use of collections. Services free, except copying, available to nonstaff with approval from director's office.

36400. Embroiderer's Guild of America, 6 E 45th St, 13th Fl, New York, NY 10017; (212) 986-0460. Interest in all types of embroidery and related subjects, including design, crewel, gold work, ecclesiastic embroidery, black work, white work, etc. Answers inquiries, provides reference services, conducts classes and correspondence courses, distributes publications, makes referrals.

36401. Engineering Information, 345 E 47th St, New York, NY 10017; (212) 705-7600. Produces and distributes two data bases covering important developments in engineering and related technology from worldwide sources of the published literature. Search service provides access to the data bases and hundreds of others via major online vendor services.

36402. Engineering Societies Library, 345 E 47th St, New York, NY 10017; (212) 705-7611. Maintains holdings in engineering and related physical sciences, including chemical, civil, electrical, and electronic. Answers inquiries, provides consulting and reference services, makes referrals. Fees charged for some services.

36404. Environmental Action Coalition, 417 Lafayette Street, New York, NY 10003; (212) 677-1601. Disseminates info on ecological and environmental issues and cleanup efforts. Has curriculum and audiovisual materials, a library and resource center for environmental research and local govt technical assistance and advisory councils.

36406. Environmental Defense Fund, 475 Park Ave S, New York, NY 10016; (212) 686-4191. Promotes economically and environmentally sound alternatives to destructive practices with respect to energy, toxic substances, wildlife, and water resources. Public education efforts include press, radio and television interviews, and publication of informational brochures.

36407. Equitable Life Assurance Society, Technical Information Center/Library Services, 1285 Ave of the Americas, New York, NY 10019; (212) 554-4064. Info resource for all data processing areas; specializes in computer literacy. Answers inquiries, conducts research, makes referrals. Services for EDP community, American Library Assn, Special Libraries Assn, ACM, AFIPS, ASIS, LOMA, TIME, ASTD and others.

36408. Eulenspiegel Society, P.O. Box 2783, Grand Central Station, New York, NY 10163; (212) 695-0550. Studies role of fantasy in sexuality, principally the elements of dominance and submission. Answers inquiries, provides advisory services, distributes publications. Some services free, others at cost.

36409. Explorers Club, 46 E 70th St, New York, NY 10021; (212) 628-8383. Collection of material on exploration, with particular emphasis on scientific disciplines and related subjects. Provides reference services, makes interlibrary loans, permits onsite use of collection by responsible researchers by appointment, provides intl info service.

36410. Eye-Bank for Sight Restoration, 210 E 64th St, 10th Fl, New York, NY 10021; (212) 980-6700. Provides ophthalmic surgeons with eye tissue for sight-restoring corneal transplants, research and medical education. Answers requests from general public for info on corneal transplants.

36412. Fairchild Republic Co., Technical Information Center, Conklin St, Farmingdale, NY 11735; (516) 531-3497. Collects material on aerospace sciences. Makes interlibrary loans free.

36414. Family Service America, 44 E 23rd St, New York, NY 10010; (212) 674-6100. Provides technical assistance to its 275 member agencies and works for development of family-oriented policies and practices in public and private institutions. Other activities include research on family problems, training of professionals, publicaton of educational materials.

36415. Fashion Institute of Technology, Library, 227 W 27th St, New York, NY 10001; (212) 760-7780. Promotes interest in the fashion business and industry, fashion buying and merchandising, fashion illustration and design. Answers inquiries, provides advisory, reference and microform services, makes referrals, permits onsite use of collections. Most services free.

36416. Federation of Historical Bottle Clubs, 20 Church Ave, Ballston Spa, NY 12020. Seeks to promote activities toward the betterment of antique bottle, jar, and insulator collecting. Answers inquiries, provides ad-

visory services, conducts shows, makes referrals. Services may be provided for a fee.

36418. Federation of the Handicapped, 211 W 14th St, New York, NY 10011; (212) 206-4250. Provides vocational rehabilitation and support programs for adults with physical and mental handicaps, including diagnosis and evaluation, skills training, sheltered employment, home employment, job placement, counseling and followup.

36419. Fertility Research Foundation, 1430 Second Ave, Ste 103, New York, NY 10021; (212) 744-5500. Seeks to identify probable reasons for infertility and provide appropriate treatment and emotional support that will lead to pregnancy. Answers inquiries, provides consulting and reference services, distributes publications, makes referrals. Simple services free.

36420. Field Foundation, 100 E 85th St, New York, NY 10028; (212) 535-9915. Interest in race relations, special aspects of child welfare, poverty, some issues of civil liberties, and peace. Answers inquiries regarding scope and procedures of the Foundation's activities.

36421. Fight for Sight, 139 E 57th St, New York, NY 10022; (212) 751-1118. Encourages students of medicine to study ophthalmology or consider ophthalmic research as a future career. Provides postdoctoral research fellowships and grants-in-aid. Answers inquiries, disseminates published material, makes referrals.

36422. Film Library Information Council, P.O. Box 348, Radio City Station, New York, NY 10101-0348; (212) 708-9533. Interest in nontheatrical films, videotapes, and other nonprint materials suitable for public library, museum, school, and community use. Answers inquiries by mail.

36423. Film/Video Arts, 817 Broadway, New York, NY 10003; (212) 673-9361. Media arts resource center for N.Y. State, providing region's film and video communities with services and training. Conducts seminars for a fee, makes referrals, lends material and equipment, provides postproduction facilities and financial assistance for film rentals.

36424. Financial Analysts Federation, 1633 Broadway, Ste 1402, New York, NY 10019; (212) 957-2860. Professional org of investment and security analysts. Answers brief questions relating to the profession and professional development free, sponsors seminars, provides checklist of criteria for corporate financial reporting.

36425. Finderhood, 49 W 37th St, New York, NY 10018; (212) 840-2423. Acts as intl clearinghouse for finder's fee opportunities. Answers inquiries, provides advisory services, distributes publications. Services primarily for members.

36426. Flexographic Technical Association, 95 W 19th St, Huntington Station, NY 11746; (516) 271-4224. Interest in printing, engraving, plates, inks, artwork, solvents, packaging, and graphic arts industries. Answers inquiries, provides advisory and reference services, distributes publications, makes referrals. Some publications free and others sold at cost.

36427. Fly Without Fear, 310 Madison Ave, New York, NY 10017; (212) 697-7666. Self help program for people suffering from aviaphobia, or who are unnecessarily anxious aboard airplanes. Members board static aircraft, take taxi flights on runways, and every third month take a short "conditioning flight" in order to practice techniques and acquire new attitudes.

36428. Food and Drug Research Laboratories, P.O. Box 107, Route 17C, Waverly, NY 14892; (607) 565-8131. Conducts basic research directed toward detection and assessment of environmental hazards for both man and animal. Conducts research and provides consulting services, all on a fee basis.

36429. Footwear Council, 51 E 42nd St, New York, NY 10017; (212) 581-7737. Interest in the history, manufacture, and marketing of shoes. Answers inquiries, provides advisory services, makes referrals, permits on-site use of collection. Services free.

36430. Ford Foundation, 320 E 43rd St, New York, NY 10017; (212) 573-5000. Seeks to identify and contribute to the solution of problems of national and intl importance. Many publications distributed free, some for sale. Films available for sale and rental.

36431. Foreign Medical School Information Center, 1 E Main St, Bay Shore, NY 11706; (516) 665-8500. Compiles info on all foreign medical schools (except those in certain countries without formal exchange policies). Answers inquiries, provides consulting and reference services, makes referrals.

36432. Foreign Policy Association, 205 Lexington Ave, New York, NY 10016; (212) 481-8450. Works to develop, through education, an informed, thoughtful, and articulate public opinion on major issues of foreign policy. Provides info primarily through its publications.

36433. Formaldehyde Institute, 1075 Central Park Ave, Scarsdale, NY 10583; (914) 725-1492. Conducts health and toxicity studies on formaldehyde. Answers inquiries, provides advisory and reference services, distributes publications, makes referrals. Services available to consumers, special interest groups and companies.

36434. Fortune Society, 39 W 19th St, New York, NY 10011; (212) 206-7070. Seeks to change conditions in penal institutions, works for improved treatment of ex-offenders. Answers inquiries from penal institutions, provides counseling, training, education, reference, and referral services free to ex-offenders.

36435. Foundation Center, 79 Fifth Ave, New York, NY 10003; (212) 620-4230. Collects data on philanthropic foundations, charitable trusts and grants, philanthropy in the U.S. and in principal foreign countries. Provides free library reference service, special services to

institutions and orgs needing up-to-date info, toll-free telephone referrals.

36437. Foundation for Alternative Cancer Therapies, Box HH, Old Chelsea Station, New York, NY 10011; (212) 741-2790. Distributes info about nontoxic therapies for cancer, supports biological and nutritional research, and works to eliminate carcinogens from the environment. Answers inquiries, provides advisory services, distributes publications, makes referrals. Most services free.

36438. Foundation for Child Development, 345 E 46th St, Room 700, New York, NY 10017; (212) 697-3150. Conducts research and policy studies affecting the young child. Answers inquiries.

36439. Foundation for Children with Learning Disabilities, 99 Park Ave, 6th Fl, New York, NY 10016; (212) 687-7211. Appropriates grants to support model demonstration programs across the country that benefit children with learning disabilities and their families. Publishes magazine, answers inquiries free or refers inquirer to other sources of info.

36440. Foundation for Ethnic Dance, 17 W 71st St, New York, NY 10023; (212) 877-9565. Supports research and teaching and sponsors the Matteo EthnoAmerican Dance Theatre, a professional dance company that tours nationally and internationally. Answers inquiries, provides advisory and reference services, makes referrals. Services may be subject to a fee.

36441. Foundation for Interior Design Education Research, 322 Eighth Ave, Ste 1501, New York, NY 10001; (212) 929-8366. Administers a voluntary plan for special accreditation of programs of interior design education offered at institutions of higher learning in the U.S. and Canada. Answers inquiries, provides consulting services, distributes publications, makes referrals. Most services free.

36442. Foundation for Research in the Afro-American Creative Arts, P.O. Drawer I, Cambria Heights, NY 11411. Collects info on black music, American music, and African music. Answers inquiries free, distributes publications for a fee.

36443. Foundation for the Extension and Development of the American Professional Theatre, 165 W 46th St, Ste 310, New York, NY 10036; (212) 869-9690. Offers comprehensive arts management expertise and one-on-one consultancies, workshops, seminars, and publications to professional theatres, dance companies, and performing arts centers. Answers inquiries, distributes publications, makes referrals. Services available at a fee.

36444. Foundation for the Peoples of the South Pacific/Pacific Islands Association, 200 W 57th St, Room 808, New York, NY 10019; (212) 757-8884. Conducts development programs in the islands of the Pacific Ocean and Pacific Islands Assn, and sponsors seminars on South Pacific issues in the U.S. Answers inquiries, provides advisory and consulting services, distributes publications, makes referrals.

36445. Foundation for the Study of Wilson's Disease, 5447 Palisade Ave, Bronx, NY 10471; (718) 430-2091. Studies Wilson's disease and educates public and the medical community about this hereditary disorder in which excessive and lethally toxic amounts of copper accumulate in the liver and brain. Fact sheet on the disease and an article reprint available from the foundation.

36446. Foundation of Thanatology, 630 W 168th St, New York, NY 10032; (212) 694-3685. Interest in scientific and humanistic inquiries, as well as application of knowledge to the psychological aspects of dying, reactions to death, loss and grief, and recovery from bereavement. Answers inquiries, distributes publications, makes referrals.

36447. Fragrance Foundation, 116 E 19th St, New York, NY 10003; (212) 725-2755. Interest in fragrances, perfumes, scent-impregnated objects, including candles, pomanders, sachets, and incense. Answers inquiries, distributes publications. Services free. Use of the library is restricted to the membership.

36448. Franciscan Institute, St Bonaventure Univ, St Bonaventure, NY 14778; (716) 375-2105. Acts as a center for research, publication, and teaching related to Franciscan movement. Answers inquiries, provides free advisory, reference, and translation services, distributes publications, permits onsite use of collections.

36449. Franklin D. Roosevelt Library, Hyde Park, NY 12538; (914) 229-8114. Maintains holdings on the administration and times of Franklin D. Roosevelt and the career and times of Eleanor Roosevelt. Inquiries answered, bibliographic services provided, interlibrary loans made, holdings may be duplicated for a small fee.

36450. French Institute — Alliance Francaise, Library, 22 E 60th St, New York, NY 10022-1077; (212) 355-6100. Collection of literature, history, and art of France and French-speaking countries. Answers inquiries, provides reference and reproduction services, permits onsite use of book and periodical collection. Services free, except copying.

36451. Friends of Animals, 11 W 60th St, New York, NY 10023; (212) 247-8077. Seeks prevention of cruelty to and exploitation of animals through education, publication, and other activities. Answers inquiries, distributes documentary films.

36452. Friends of Cast Iron Architecture, 235 E 87th St, Room 6C, New York, NY 10128; (212) 369-6004. Investigates identification and preservation of cast iron architecture. Answers inquiries, provides advisory and reference services, distributes publications, makes referrals. Services free, unless extensive.

36453. Friends of the Origami Center of America, 15 W 77th St, New York, NY 10024; (212) 496-1890. Seeks to preserve, disseminate, and stimulate origami (paperfolding) as an art, a craft, a therapy, and a satisfying form of recreation. Answers inquiries, provides consulting services, distributes publications, makes referrals. Services primarily for members.

36455. Fund for Multinational Management Education, 680 Park Ave, New York, NY 10021; (212) 535-9386. Promotes better understanding of the role of private enterprise in intl economic development. Conducts seminars, conferences, and managerial training courses, distributes publications, makes referrals. Services available primarily to institutions.

36456. Fund for New Priorities in America, 122 E 42nd St, New York, NY 10017; (212) 697-2282. Sponsors conferences on Capitol Hill in cooperation with Members of Congress on a variety of national policy issues. Distributes reprints of conference proceedings for a nominal fee. Single copies available to members of Congress free.

36457. Fund for Open Information and Accountability, 339 Lafayette St, New York, NY 10012; (212) 477-3188. Nonprofit org dedicated to protecting public's right to know about govt's activities and to hold it accountable for them. Publishes newsletter, answers inquiries, provides advisory and reference services, makes referrals, distributes publications. Services free.

36458. Fund for Peace, c/o Dr James F. Tierney, 345 E 46th St, New York, NY 10017; (212) 661-5900. Conducts research and public education on global problems that threaten human survival, such as the threat of nuclear war and needless expansion of conventional weapons. Answers inquiries.

36460. Garden Club of America, 598 Madison Ave, New York, NY 10022; (212) 753-8287. Serves its member clubs in fields of conservation, horticulture, and flower arranging. Copy of environmental education packet is available free to teachers and librarians.

36461. Gelatin Manufacturers Institute of America, 516 Fifth Ave, Room 507, New York, NY 10036. Conducts research in manufacture and usage of gelatin. Answers inquiries or refers inquirers to other sources of info free.

36462. General Foods Corp., Technical Center Library, White Plains, NY 10625; (914) 335-6185. Collects materials on food science and technology, including biochemistry, nutrition, chemistry, and chemical engineering. Makes interlibrary loans, permits onsite use of collection by qualified scientists and librarians.

36463. General Library of the Performing Arts, 111 Amsterdam Ave, New York, NY 10023; (212) 870-1600. Library of the performing arts, including dance, drama, and music. Provides ready reference, presents free programs, makes interlibrary loans, permits onsite use of collections. Services free, except library card, for which non-state residents must pay a nominal fee.

36464. Geriatric Study and Treatment Program, HN314, 550 First Ave, New York, NY 10016; (212) 340-5700. Interest in Alzheimer's disease and related disorders. Answers inquiries, provides advisory services and info on research in progress, distributes publications, makes referrals. Services provided at cost to some users, free to others.

36465. German Information Center, 950 Third Ave, New York, NY 10022; (212) 888-9840. Provides info on political, economic, social, and cultural developments in Federal Republic of Germany. Answers inquiries, provides advisory services, distributes publications, makes referrals, permits onsite use of collections. Services free.

36466. Gerontological Research Information Program, Brockway Hall, Syracuse Univ, Syracuse, NY 13244; (315) 423-4683. Serves users in fields of gerontological and geriatric information. Info is retrieved manually, via computerized databases and through a networking system with other aging centers, libraries, and persons in the field of aging. Also develops curriculum materials.

36467. Ginseng Research Institute, Main St, Box 42, Roxbury, NY 12474; (607) 326-7888. Correlates research info, supervises and conducts tests, and dispenses general and specific info on ginseng and related species. Answers inquiries, provides advisory and reference services, distributes publications, makes referrals. Services provided at cost.

36468. Girl Scouts of the USA, 830 Third Ave, New York, NY 10022; (212) 940-7500. Interest in the informal education of girls 5-17, emphasizing career and personal development as well as service to others. Answers inquiries, provides consulting services, disseminates info the general public and to Congress.

36469. Glass Art Society, P.O. Box 1364, Corning, NY 14830. Promotes collection, exhibition, and appreciation of objects made with glass. Answers inquiries, provides reference services, distributes journal, makes referrals. Most services free.

36470. Glenn H. Curtiss Museum of Local History, Lake and Main St, Hammondsport, NY 14840; (607) 569-2160. Collects material on aviation history, aviation at Hammondsport, and Glenn H. Curtiss' accomplishments. Answers inquiries (mailed inquiries should include a SASE for reply), permits onsite use of collection by appointment to serious researchers.

36471. Global Development Studies Institute, Attn: John P. Rorke, Millbrook School, Millbrook, NY 12545; (914) 677-8261. Seeks to further awareness in American students of interdependent nature of the earth's population and foster rational development of man. Distributes model curricula, publications, and teaching materials for a fee, permits onsite use of collection free.

36472. Global Perspectives In Education, 218 E 18th St, New York, NY 10003; (212) 475-0850. Works to prepare American students for responsible national citizenship in an increasingly interconnected and rapidly changing global age. Answers inquiries, provides consulting services.

36473. Glycerine and Oleo Chemical Association, c/o Theodore E. Brenner, 475 Park Ave S, New York, NY 10016; (212) 725-1262. Studies glycerine, fatty acids, and other oleo chemicals, including production, disposition, applications, and raw materials. Answers inquiries.

36474. Gold Information Center, 900 Third Ave, New York, NY 10022; (212) 688-0474. Provides general info about gold, and is a nontechnical research facility on gold. Answers inquiries, provides reference services, distributes publications, makes referrals. Some services free.

36475. Graphics Philately Association, c/o Mark Harris Winnegrad, 1450 Parkchester Rd, Bronx, NY 10462; (212) 829-7548. Promotes collection and study of any philatelic material pertaining to graphic arts. Answers inquiries or refers inquirers free (SASE required for mail inquiries), sells publications.

36476. Gravure Research Institute, 22 Manhasset Ave, Fort Washington, Long Island, NY 11050; (516) 883-6670. Interest in graphic arts technology and printing industry in general, with particular coverage of gravure processes and equipment. Provides reference, consulting, and translating services to sponsor members and other graphic arts research institutes only.

36477. Great Lakes Laboratory, 1300 Elmwood Ave, Buffalo, NY 14222; (716) 878-5422. Conducts basic and applied limnological research on water quality of Great Lakes, with emphasis on environmental toxicology and chemistry of contaminants. Answers inquiries, provides reference and consulting services, distributes publications, makes referrals.

36478. Grumman Aerospace Corp., Technical Information Center, S Oyster Bay Rd, Mail Stop L-01-35, Bethpage, NY 11714; (516) 575-3912. Interest in aeronautics, astronautics, and electronics. Answers brief inquiries, makes interlibrary loans.

36479. Guardians of Hydrocephalus Research Foundation, 2618 Ave Z, Brooklyn, NY 11235; (718) 743-4473. Dedicated to research in cause and treatment of hydrocephalus. Operates lab in Dept of Neurology at N.Y. Univ Medical Center, in which info from clinical and research facilities is provided for better diagnosis and treatment of hydrocephalus.

36480. Guide Dog Foundation for the Blind, 371 E Jericho Turnpike, Smithtown, NY 11787; (516) 265-2121. Provides trained dogs for qualified blind persons. No charge for service, which includes a guide dog, four weeks of training in dog's use and care, board and lodging while the student is in residence at the foundation's training center, and a followup program.

36482. Guiding Eyes for the Blind, 611 Granite Springs Rd, Yorktown Heights, NY 10598; (914) 245-4024. Provides independent mobility to qualified blind persons through use of highly trained guide dogs. Voluntary tuition fee requested from students, who receive the dog, followup services, and food and lodging while participating in the training program.

36483. Guild of Book Workers, 521 Fifth Ave, New York, NY 10175; (212) 757-6454. Natl org representing several hand-book-crafts, binders, restorers, illuminators, calligraphers, and decorated paper makers. Answers inquiries, provides advisory and consulting services, conducts tours, distributes publications. Services primarily for members.

36484. Gummed Industries Association, 380 N Broadway, Jericho, NY 11753; (516) 822-8948. Trade assn of U.S. converters of water-activated tape and other gummed products. Answers inquiries, makes referrals. Brochures and pamphlets mailed upon inquiry.

36485. H.H. Franklin Club, c/o C.C. Nash, Cazenovia Coll, Cazenovia, NY 13035; (315) 841-4956. Seeks to form bond among people interested in air-cooled automobiles, particularly Franklins, and to be of service to them. Provides technical assistance to Franklin owners, conducts seminars, permits onsite use of collections. Services free to members and at cost to others.

36486. Hadassah, The Women's Zionist Organization of America, 50 W 58th St, New York, NY 10019; (212) 355-7900. Interest in Zionism, Israel, and world Jewish affairs. Provides info and referral services, conducts seminars, disseminates a periodical and other literature, provides media relations and limited research accessibility.

36487. Halcon SD Group, Information Center, 2 Park Ave, New York, NY 10016; (212) 689-3000 ext 2465. Collects materials on chemistry, including chemical processes, engineering, and organic chemistry. Answers inquiries as time permits, makes referrals, permits limited onsite use of collection.

36488. Hall of Fame of the Trotter, 240 Main St, Goshen, NY 10924; (914) 294-6330. Collects, classifies, and preserves archives, records, relics, and other items relating to origin and development of the standardbred horse. Answers inquiries, provides consulting and reference services, conducts tours and lectures, distributes publication. Services free.

36489. Health Insurance Association of America, 919 Third Ave, New York, NY 10022; (212) 486-5520. Trade assn for insurance companies writing health insurance coverages in the U.S. Answers inquiries, provides consulting services, prepares analyses, makes referrals.

36491. Health Policy Advisory Center, 17 Murray St, New York, NY 10007; (212) 267-8890. Monitors and interprets the health system for change-oriented groups of health workers, consumers, professionals, and stu-

dents. Advocates changes that will make low-cost, high-quality health services available to all; emphasizes disease prevention and an end to discrimination.

36492. Helen Keller International, 15 W 16th St, New York, NY 10011; (212) 620-2100. Seeks to alleviate problems associated with blindness overseas. Answers inquiries, provides consulting services to foreign govts and voluntary agencies, supplies training aids for ophthalmologists, social workers, nutritionists, nurses, medical assistants, and mothers.

36493. Helen Keller National Center for Deaf-Blind Youths and Adults, 111 Middle Neck Rd, Sands Point, NY 11050; (516) 944-8900. Provides rehabilitation of deaf-blind youths and adults, professional personnel training, and deaf-blind research. Answers inquiries, provides advisory and professional training services, makes referrals.

36494. Helen S. Kaplan Center for Sexual Disorders, 30 E 76th St, New York, NY 10021; (212) 249-2914. Interest in evaluation and treatment of sexual disorders. Provides wide range of medical and psychological diagnostic and treatment services for sexual disorders, as well as professional training. Services provided on a fee basis.

36495. Helsinki Watch Committee, 36 W 44th St, New York, NY 10036; (212) 840-9460. Observes human rights practices in the 35 countries signatory to 1975 Helsinki Accords. Answers inquiries, distributes publications, makes referrals. Services generally free.

36496. Hemochromatosis Research Foundation, PO Box 8569, Albany, NY 12208; (518) 489-0972. Seeks to increase awareness among medical community that hereditary hemochromatosis is one of the most common genetic disorders, to promote research aimed at identifying its cause. Provides informative brochures, counseling, and referrals to local physicians.

36497. Hispanic Society of America Library, 613 W 155th St, New York, NY 10032; (212) 926-2234. Nonprofit org of Hispanic authors, artists, composers, and scholars that maintains a free public museum and reference library. Answers inquiries, distributes publications, permits onsite use of collections. Most services free.

36498. Histamine Research Society of North America, c/o Dr Margaret A. Reilly, Rockland Research Institute, Orangeburg, NY 10962; (914) 359-1050 ext 2382. Society composed of scientists interested in histamine research. Answers inquiries free, on a limited basis.

36499. Hudson Photographic Industries, Box 227, Irvington on Hudson, NY 10533; (914) 591-8700. Interest in audiovisual equipment, photographic equipment, film repair systems, rear projection screens, splicers and splicing tapes, unbreakable-nonglass mirrors. Answers inquiries, makes referrals.

36500. Huguenot Historical Society, P.O. Box 339 (18 Broadhead Ave), New Paltz, NY 12561; (914) 255-1660. Studies history of Huguenot immigrants to New

Paltz and other areas. Maintains six stone houses built from 1694 to 1712 and reconstructed French Church. Answers inquiries, conducts tours, distributes publications, makes referrals. Services may be subject to a fee.

36501. Human Resources Center, I.U. Willets Rd, Albertson, NY 11507-1326; (516) 747-5400. Interest in the evaluation, training, education, employer services, and rehabilitation of the handicapped. Answers inquiries, provides advisory and reference services, conducts career training programs, distributes publications, makes referrals. Services free.

36503. Human Sexuality Program, 525 E 68th St, New York, NY 10021; (212) 472-6545. Studies human sexuality, sexual dysfunction, teaching and training. Conducts training program in evaluation and treatment of sexual disorders for professionals, permits onsite use of collection. Cost of therapy sessions adjusted to income of patients.

36504. Hunter College, Health Professions Library, 425 E 25th St, New York, NY 10010; (212) 481-4326. Collects materials on all aspects of nursing profession. Provides copying services, makes interlibrary loans, permits onsite use of collection by professional persons.

36505. Huntington's Disease Foundation of America, 250 W 57th St, New York, NY 10107; (212) 757-0443. Works to help change community's attitude toward the HD patient and, in doing so, enhance lifestyle of the individual and promote better health care and treatment. Distributes publications, lends materials, makes referrals, conducts crisis intervention and advocacy services.

36506. IIT Research Institute, Reliability Analysis Center, Griffiss Air Force Base, Rome, NY 13441-5700; (315) 330-4151. Functions as focal point for recovery of reliability test data and experience info on microcircuit and related component parts. Provides technical assistance, reliability support, and engineering studies in response to direct user requests. Fees charged.

36508. INDA, Association of the Nonwoven Fabrics Industry, 1700 Broadway, New York, NY 10019; (212) 582-8401. Represents nonwoven fabrics industry and products, including medical-surgical, commercial and consumer products. Answers inquiries or refers inquirers free, distributes publications.

36509. INFORM, 381 Park Ave, S, New York, NY 10016; (212) 689-4040. Tax-exempt org analyzing impact of U.S. corps on employees, consumers, and public in areas of environmental concern. Answers inquiries, provides consulting services, distributes publications, makes referrals. Fees charged for consulting services and publications.

36510. ISO Commercial Risk Services, 160 Water St, New York, NY 10038; (212) 487-5000. Provides property and casualty insurance advisory ratemaking for participating insurers. Answers inquiries, usually by providing data and published materials, makes referrals.

Services subject to a fee, limited according to time and effort required.

36511. Illuminating Engineering Society, 345 E 47th St, New York, NY 10017; (212) 705-7926. Interest in science and art of illumination, including illuminating engineering, light and vision, measurement, color, and lighting control. Answers inquiries, distributes pamphlets and publication lists, recommends speakers for meetings.

36512. Impact on Hunger, 145 E 49th St, New York, NY 10017; (212) 750-9893. Educates public for action on issue of world hunger, local and global. Answers inquiries, provides advisory services, conducts seminars, makes referrals. Services available to communicators.

36513. Independent Citizens Research Foundation for the Study of Degenerative Diseases, P.O. Box 97, Ardsley, NY 10502; (914) 478-1862. Disseminates info on causes and prevention of chronic illnesses; underwrites research projects offering an early and practical applicability of findings to the problems of those afflicted with such illnesses.

36514. Indoor Light Gardening Society of America, 128 W 58th St, New York, NY 10019; (203) 743-3434. Promotes growing plants under artificial light, hortitherapy, and indoor gardening in general. Answers inquiries, provides advisory services, distributes publications, makes referrals. Services primarily for members.

36515. Industrial Relations Counselors, P.O. Box 1530, New York, NY 10101; (212) 541-6086. Interest in industrial and employee relations, labor relations, labor economics, and behavioral science. Answers inquiries, makes referrals.

36516. Industrial Research Institute, 100 Park Ave, Ste 2209, New York, NY 10017; (212) 683-7626. Seeks improved management of industrial research. Answers inquiries, permits onsite use of collection. Services free.

36517. Industrial Social Welfare Center, 622 W 113th St, New York, NY 10025; (212) 280-5173. Develops mental health, rehabilitation, and social services for working men and women at workplace facilities. Answers inquiries, provides advisory services, conducts seminars, distributes publications, makes referrals. Sells publications, other services free.

36518. Information Center on Children's Cultures, 331 E 38th St, New York, NY 10016; (212) 686-5522 ext 402. Interest in intercultural education, children's literature, developing countries and their children. Answers inquiries, provides advisory and reference services, distributes publications, makes referrals.

36520. Information for Policy Design, 5413 Webster Rd, Lafayette, NY 13084; (315) 677-9278. Prepares and distributes bibliographic materials on general literature of public policy, social change, and alternative futures. Answers inquiries, provides advisory services, distributes publications, makes referrals. Some services provided for a fee.

36521. Institute for Advanced Studies in Asian Science and Medicine, P.O. Box 555, Garden City, NY 11530; (516) 248-0930. Studies Chinese and other Asian science and medicine, including scientific, historical, sociological, and cultural perspectives. Answers inquiries, provides advisory and reference services, conducts acupuncture training workshops, distributes publications, makes referrals.

36522. Institute for Art and Urban Resources, 46-01 21st St, Long Island City, NY 11101; (718) 784-2084. Promotes development of low-cost studio workspace and exhibition spaces for artists. Answers inquiries, distributes publications, makes referrals to other sources of info. Services free.

36523. Institute for Basic Research in Developmental Disabilities, 1050 Forest Hill Road, Staten Island, NY 10314; (718) 494-0600. Conducts research into neuro degenerative diseases, including Alzheimer's disease and Down's Syndrome, and publishes its findings in medical and professional journals. Reprints of many of these reports available.

36524. Institute for Expressive Analysis, 325 W End Ave, New York, NY 10023; (212) 362-5085. Trains art, dance, music, and other therapists in expressive analysis. Provides advisory and consulting services, conducts seminars and workshops, makes referrals. Services available for a fee to mental health professionals.

36525. Institute for Family Research and Education, Slocum Hall, Room 110, Syracuse, NY 13210; (315) 423-4584. Prepares parents to be sex educators of their own children. Answers inquiries, conducts workshops, distributes publication, makes referrals.

36526. Institute for Human Identity, 490 W End Ave, New York, NY 10024; (212) 799-9432. Conducts psychotherapy (individual and group) with homosexual and bisexual people, research into homosexuality and training for students in clinical fields. Answers inquiries, provides psychotherapy on fee basis according to income, supplies speakers and consultants.

36527. Institute for Mediation and Conflict Resolution, 49 E 68th St, 4th Fl, New York, NY 10021; (212) 570-9400. Studies application of negotiations, mediation, and other conflict resolution techniques borrowed from labor-management field to a wide variety of intergroup and interpersonal conflicts. Provides consulting and training services for a fee.

36528. Institute for Rational-Emotive Therapy, 45 E 65th St, New York, NY 10021; (212) 535-0822. Provides training and public education in rational-emotive therapy. Provides speakers and other consulting services, conducts public and professional workshops, publishes and distributes therapy and self-help materials. Nominal fees for all services.

36529. Institute for Research in Hypnosis, Dr M.U. Kline, 45 W 67th St, New York, NY 10023; (212) 874-5290. Collects data on hypnotherapy, hypnoanalysis, and specialized psychotherapeutic services utilizing hypnotic procedures. Answers inquiries, provides consulting services, makes referrals, prepares analyses. Services available to members of the medical, psychological, and dental professions.

36530. Institute for Research of Rheumatic Diseases, Box 955, Ansonia Station, New York, NY 10023; (212) 595-1368. Publishes monographs and a newspaper which discuss relationship between treatment approaches, nutrition, stress, and development of arthritis. Promotes its holistic approach to treatment of arthritis through these publications.

36531. Institute for Sensory Research, Syracuse Univ, Syracuse, NY 13210; (315) 423-4164. Conducts research on sensory systems of animals and humans, with emphasis on the peripheral auditory, tactile, and visual systems. Answers inquiries free.

36532. Institute for Social Dance Studies, 60 W 57th St, Ste 18A, New York, NY 10019; (212) 247-7658. Grants scholarships for teacher training, develops and distributes teaching materials, and maintains a reference library. Answers inquiries, provides reference services. Services available only to professionals in social dance education, choreographers, and qualified researchers.

36533. Institute for Socioeconomic Studies, Airport Rd, White Plains, NY 10604; (914) 428-7400. Conducts research relating to such broad areas as quality of life, economic development, social motivation, poverty, urban regeneration, and problems of the elderly. Answers inquiries, provides advisory and reference services, distributes publications, makes referrals.

36534. Institute for Women and Work, 15 E 26th St, New York, NY 10010; (212) 340-2800. Conducts applied research and develops, tests, and provides educational programs to help working women fulfill their educational and career goals. Answers inquiries, provides advisory and reference services, distributes publications, makes referrals. Some services free.

36535. Institute of Chronobiology, 21 Bloomingdale Rd, White Plains, NY 10605; (914) 997-5825. Involved in research, consultation, and clinical practice in the area of human biological clocks and sleep. Answers inquiries, provides consulting and reference services, distributes publications, makes referrals. Services provided at cost.

36536. Institute of Electrical and Electronics Engineers, 345 E 47th St, New York, NY 10017; (212) 705-7900. Interest in all aspects of electrical and electronic engineering. Provides info primarily through its publications, but Director of Publishing Services will answer inquiries whenever possible or refer inquirers to the Engineering Societies Library and other headquarters offices.

36537. Institute of Environmental Medicine, 550 First Ave, New York, NY 10016; (212) 340-7300. Collects info on environmental and occupational health, environmental cancer, fate of inhaled aerosols, inhalation toxicology, and metabolism of toxic agents. Answers brief inquiries, provides consulting services, makes referrals.

36538. Institute of Environmental Program Affairs, State Univ of New York, Syracuse, NY 13210; (315) 473-8892. Provides college-wide coordination for multidisciplinary research and public service projects conducted by faculty, staff, and students at the College of Environmental Science and Forestry. Answers inquiries, provides advisory and consulting services. Limited services provided free.

36539. Institute of International Education, 809 U.N. Plaza, New York, NY 10017; (212) 883-8200. Clearinghouse for info on overseas study for U.S. nationals and U.S. study for foreign nationals at undergraduate and graduate levels. Answers inquiries, provides advisory and reference services, sells publications, makes referrals. Library not open to public.

36540. Institute of Judicial Administration, One Washington Sq Village, New York, NY 10012; (212) 598-7721. Promotes improvement in, and serves as a clearinghouse of, info on judicial administration. Answers inquiries, provides consulting and reference services, distributes publications, makes referrals. Studies, surveys, and consultation on a fee basis; publications sold at cost.

36541. Institute of Management Consultants, 19 W 44th St, Ste 810-811, New York, NY 10036; (212) 921-2885. Interest in management consulting in areas of general management, finance and accounting, intl operations, manufacturing, marketing, and administrative services. Answers inquiries or refers inquirers. Services free.

36542. Institute of Marine and Atmospheric Sciences, Convent Ave at 138th St, New York, NY 10031; (212) 690-6800. Studies oceanography, benthic ecology, phytoplankton, fisheries, Hudson River Estuary, and N.Y. Bight. Answers inquiries, provides consulting services.

36543. Institute of Noise Control Engineering, P.O. Box 3206, Arlington Branch, Poughkeepsie, NY 12603. Performs engineering and research in noise pollution control and abatement. Answers inquiries, conducts seminars, distributes publications, makes referrals. Services free, except publications.

36544. Institute of Public Administration Library, 55 W 44th St, New York, NY 10036; (212) 730-5631. Collects material on public administration, govt, public policy, city planning, housing, public finance, and civil service. Answers inquiries, provides advisory and consulting services, distributes publications. Services available to bona fide researchers.

36545. Institute of Rehabilitation Medicine, 400 E 34th St, New York, NY 10016; (212) 340-6200. Involved in physical rehabilitation training and patient care. Answers inquiries, distributes publications, makes referrals. Services primarily for groups related to health fields, provided at cost.

36546. Institute of Society, Ethics, and the Life Sciences, Hastings Center, 360 Broadway, Hastings-on-Hudson, NY 10706; (914) 478-0500. Interest in ethical, legal, and social problems concerning death and dying, control of human behavior, genetic counseling and engineering. Answers inquiries free.

36547. Institute of Store Planners, 211 E 43rd St, Ste 1601, New York, NY 10017; (212) 867-4876. Society of those involved in store planning, design, decorating, and architecture. Answers some inquiries, makes referrals, provides consulting.

36548. Insurance Information Institute, 110 William St, New York, NY 10038; (212) 669-9200. Interest in property and liability insurance. Answers inquiries free, provides reference services, permits onsite use of collection by institute members and the press, makes referrals.

36549. Intelligence for Education, 2 East Ave, Room 209, Larchmont, NY 10538; (914) 834-2606. Conducts research on educational expenditures and construction. Answers inquiries, provides advisory services, conducts research, makes referrals. Services provided at cost and primarily for educational leaders and suppliers to the market.

36550. Inter-American Association for Democracy and Freedom, c/o Frances R. Grant, 20 W 40th St, New York, NY 10018; (212) 221-6790. Seeks to create a democratic front to fight totalitarianism in all its forms and to investigate and verify violations of civil and political liberties in the Americas. Answers inquiries and provides consulting services free.

36551. InterDok Corp., P.O. Box 326 (173 Halstead Ave), Harrison, NY 10528; (914) 835-3506. Maintains published proceedings of conferences, symposia, seminars, meetings, and congresses on all subjects. Publications sold, conference proceedings acquisitions service also available to subscribers.

36552. InterFuture, 150 Nassau St, Ste 1538, New York, NY 10038; (212) 964-8861. Trains undergraduate students and enables them to carry out independent intercultural research projects in European and Third World locales. Answers inquiries, distributes publications, makes referrals. Services free, except publications.

36553. Interchurch Center, Ecumenical Library, 475 Riverside Dr, Room 253, New York, NY 10115; (212) 870-3804. Provides reference services on Christianity, missions, theology, and church history for orgs located in the Center. Answers inquiries, provides reference services, makes referrals. Services free and provided subject to availability of staff. Appointments recommended.

36554. Intercollegiate Broadcasting System, P.O. Box 592, Vails Gate, NY 12584; (914) 565-6710. Assn of 700 school, college, and univ radio stations. Answers inquiries; provides program service, engineering and management advice; makes referrals; permits onsite use of collection. Services free to members, at cost to others.

36555. Interfaith Center on Corporate Responsibility, 475 Riverside Dr, Room 566, New York, NY 10115; (212) 870-2293. Sponsored by about 220 Protestant and Roman Catholic church orgs, coordinates church proxy resolution activity. Answers inquiries, conducts research, distributes publications, makes referrals. Most services free.

36556. Interlink Press Service, 777 U.N. Plaza, New York, NY 10017; (212) 599-0867. Exclusive U.S. distributor of Inter Press Service, Rome-based private independent cooperative of journalists providing an intl wire service. Services available via a high-speed computer-based delivery system. Interlink news is also available on NEXIS. A weekly is available.

36557. International Academy of Proctology, c/o Alfred J. Cantor, M.D., N Shore Towers, 271-17V, Grand Central Parkway, Floral Park, NY 11005; (212) 631-5291. Conducts research on and treatment of diseases of the colon and accessory organs of digestion, including those of nutrition. Conducts seminars and annual medical congresses in all parts of the world. Services free to all physicians.

36558. International Advertising Association, 475 Fifth Ave, New York, NY 10017; (212) 684-1583. Interest in intl communications, including advertising, marketing, and related fields. Answers brief inquiries, provides short lists of literature citations in response to specific inquiries, makes referrals, permits onsite use of collection. Services primarily for members.

36559. International Association for Medical Assistance to Travellers, 736 Center St, Lewiston, NY 14092; (716) 754-4883. Gathers and disseminates data on health, sanitary, and climatic conditions around the world for the benefit of travelers. Answers inquiries, distributes publications, makes referrals. Services free, but donations to support research and cover printing costs welcomed.

36561. International Association for Psychiatric Research, P.O. Box 457, St James, NY 11780; (516) 246-2447. Supports research into biological aspects of mental illness, with particular emphasis on biological treatments of the mentally ill. Provides advisory services, makes referrals. Services free to National Institute of Mental Health grantees, at cost to other agencies.

36562. International Association of Laryngectomees, 777 Third Ave, New York, NY 10017; (212) 371-2900 ext 246. Provides support for rehabilitation of laryngectomees, esophageal speech; "lost chord clubs," artificial larynges. Answers brief inquiries free, disseminates publications.

36563. International Association of Milk Control Agencies, Ronald Pearce, Capital Plaza, One Winners Circle, Albany, NY 12235; (518) 457-6773. Assn of regulatory personnel dealing with price and related trade regulation in fluid milk industry. Members required to be governmental bodies. Answers inquiries free.

36564. International Business Machines Corp., Library and Technical Reports Center, Route 17C, Oswego, NY 13827; (607) 751-2121 ext 2720. Collects materials on electronics, with particular emphasis on avionics, navigation, guidance, displays, computer technology, underwater acoustics, astronautics, and circuit board technology. Makes interlibrary loans, provides nonproprietary info in response to individual requests.

36565. International Cargo Gear Bureau, 17 Battery Pl, New York, NY 10004; (212) 425-2750. Provides recognized registration, inspection, certification, documentation, design evaluation, and consultation services for materials handling equipment ashore and afloat used in shipping. Answers inquiries.

36567. International Center for the Disabled, Library/Information Center, 340 E 24th St, New York, NY 10010; (212) 679-0100 ext 307. Serves needs of disabled persons through development and implementation of exemplary rehabilitation programs that foster independence, adjustment to community life, and productivity. Answers inquiries, provides advisory and reference services, distributes publications, makes referrals.

36568. International Center of Photography, 1130 Fifth Ave, New York, NY 10128; (212) 860-1777. Museum devoted to all aspects of photography. Answers inquiries free, conducts education classes for a fee. Admission to museum on a fee basis, except school groups. Admittance to archives and resource library is by appointment only.

36569. International College of Acupuncture and Electro-Therapeutics, 800 Riverside Dr (8-I), New York, NY 10032; (212) 781-6262. Professional assn that publishes research results, provides certification for members, and disseminates info to public. Answers inquiries, provides advisory services, distributes publications, makes referrals. Most services limited to physicians, dentists, and researchers.

36570. International Commission on Microbial Ecology, c/o M. Alexander, Dept of Agronomy, Cornell Univ, Ithaca, NY 14850; (607) 256-3267. Investigates microbial ecology. Answers inquiries and provides advisory services free.

36571. International Committee Against Mental Illness, P.O. Box 898, Ansonia Station, New York, NY 10023; (914) 359-8797. Interest in psychiatry, mental illness, psychiatric rehabilitation, and education. Answers inquiries, conducts seminars, makes referrals. Services free.

36572. International Confederation of Art Dealers, 32 E 57th St, New York, NY 10022. Interest in arts and antiques, art and antique dealers, art trade and art legislation. Answers inquiries free for anyone.

36573. International Copper Research Association, 708 Third Ave, New York, NY 10017; (212) 697-9355. Research management org interested in new product technical research for world copper industry. Answers inquiries, distributes research reports. Services free.

36574. International Electrotechnical Commission, 1430 Broadway, New York, NY 10018; (212) 354-3361. Responsible for intl standardization in the electrical and electronics fields. Answers inquiries or refers inquirers free. Publications for sale.

36575. International Foundation for Art Research, 46 E 70th St, New York, NY 10021; (212) 879-1780. Devoted exclusively to research that helps art collectors make and protect solid investments. Answers inquiries, provides advisory, consulting and reference services, conducts lecture series, distributes publications, makes referrals. Services at cost.

36576. International Fund for Agricultural Development, U.N. Plaza, Room S-2955, New York, NY 10017; (212) 754-4248. Seeks to mobilize additional resources to help developing countries improve their food production and nutrition, as well as to increase the income and employment of rural poor. Answers inquiries, provides reference services, distributes publications. Services free.

36577. International Grooving and Grinding Association, P.O. Box 1750, Briarcliff Manor, NY 10510; (914) 941-8444. Interest in grooving and grinding of highways, airports, and other pavements. Answers inquiries, provides consulting and reference services, makes referrals. Services free to governmental agencies and engineering consultants.

36578. International Imagery Association, 22 Edgecliff Terrace, Yonkers, NY 10705; (914) 476-1208. Promotes imagery research in experimental, clinical, and educational fields and fosters its application. Answers inquiries, provides advisory and reference services, distributes publications, makes referrals. Services provided free to some users, at cost to others.

36579. International Institute for Bioenergetic Analysis, 144 E 36th St, No. 1A, New York, NY 10016; (212) 532-7742. Promotes research and education in the field of mental and physical health related to biological energy processes. Answers inquiries, provides advisory services, distributes publications. Inquiries answered free, other services for a fee.

36580. International Institute for the Study of Human Reproduction, Library/Information Program, 60 Haven Ave, New York, NY 10032; (212) 305-6960. Conducts applied research, teaching, and training related to methods for developing and evaluating population and family health programs. Answers inquiries, provides advisory and reference services, distributes publications, makes referrals. Fees may be charged.

36582. International Jugglers Association, c/o Rich Chamberlin, P.O. Box 29, Kenmore, NY 14217. Promotes interest in juggling and jugglers. Answers inquiries free.

36583. International Ladies' Garment Workers' Union, Research Department, 1710 Broadway, New York, NY 10019; (212) 265-7000. Collects economic and historical data about the ILGWU and women's garment industry. Approved academic researchers may have access to certain material in the collection by arrangement. Limited literature searches made for such users and inquiries answered.

36584. International Lead Zinc Research Organization, 292 Madison Ave, New York, NY 10017; (212) 532-2373. Studies lead, zinc, and cadmium in technical disciplines of metallurgy, chemistry, electrochemistry, and environmental health. Answers inquiries, provides consulting and reference services to scientists, industrial personnel, librarians, and others with a legitimate need-to-know.

36585. International League for Human Rights, 432 Park Ave S, New York, NY 10016; (212) 684-1221. Seeks to protect and advance human rights everywhere. Answers inquiries, provides advisory and reference services, distributes publications, makes referrals. Most services free.

36586. International League of Women Composers, P.O. Box 42, Three Mile Bay, NY 13693; (315) 649-5086. Seeks to obtain more commissions, recordings, and orchestral performances for women composers of serious music. Answers inquiries, provides advisory and reference services, distributes newsletter, makes referrals. Services free for noncommercial purposes.

36587. International Museum of Photography at George Eastman House, 900 East Ave, Rochester, NY 14607; (716) 271-3361. Museum of the art and technology of photography and cinematography. Answers inquiries, provides limited reference services, permits on-site use of collections by appointment. Museum makes interlibrary loans, reproduces materials, and distributes publications for a fee.

36588. International Narcotic Enforcement Officers Association, 112 State St, Albany, NY 12207; (518) 463-6232. Studies narcotics, drug addiction, drug law enforcement, drug education and treatment, depressants, stimulants, and hallucinogenics. Answers inquiries, provides consulting services, conducts seminars for law enforcement officials, medical personnel, and civic groups.

36589. International Peace Academy, 777 U.N. Plaza, New York, NY 10017; (212) 949-8480. Devoted to furthering practical skills and procedures of conflict resolution, peacekeeping, peacemaking, and peacebuilding. Newsletter available free on request, other publications for sale.

36590. International Petroleum Institute, 116 E 66th St, New York, NY 10021; (212) 772-1199. Collects data on all aspects of petroleum, including related energy studies. Provides reference services for a fee, makes referrals. Services available to anyone in the petroleum industry.

36591. International Planned Parenthood Federation, 105 Madison Ave, New York, NY 10016; (212) 679-2230. Interest in planned parenthood, contraception, maternal and child health, nutrition, population, and family life education. Answers inquiries, provides consulting services, makes referrals.

36592. International Population Program, 372 Uris Hall, Ithaca, NY 14853; (607) 256-4924. Performs research and provides training in demography and population studies. Answers inquiries; provides research, consulting and training services on a fee basis, generally for govts, intl orgs, and other groups engaged in population work.

36593. International Progeria Registry, 1050 Forest Hill Road, Staten Island, NY 10314; (718) 494-5231. Helps locate children with progeria and collecst info about this rare disease. Progeria is characterized by accelerated aging in children. Its incidence is estimated to be about one in four million births, with over one hundred cases reported worldwide since 1886.

36594. International Reports, 200 Park Ave S, New York, NY 10003; (212) 477-0003. Commercial org with interests in intl finance, local financial markets, foreign currencies, monetary trends, and world economies. Answers inquiries, provides advisory services, distributes data compilations and publications, makes referrals. Services provided for a fee.

36595. International Rescue Committee, 386 Park Ave South, New York, NY 10016; (212) 679-0010. Provides refugee relief, counseling, and resettlement. Provides resettlement info for refugees.

36596. International Research and Exchanges Board, 655 Third Ave, New York, NY 10017; (212) 490-2002. Administers academic exchange programs with countries of East Central and Southeastern Europe and the USSR on behalf of scholars in the U.S. Answers brief inquiries.

36597. International Student Service, 236 E 47th St, New York, NY 10017; (212) 319-0606. Meets incoming foreign students and scholars at their port of entry and assists in their orientation. Answers inquiries, provides consulting services, plans tours, assists in overnight accommodations, makes referrals.

36598. International Theatre Institute of the U.S., 1860 Broadway, Ste 1510, New York, NY 10023; (212) 245-3950. Promotes exchange of knowledge and practice in theatre arts. Answers inquiries, provides advisory services, organizes meetings and seminars, distributes publications, makes referrals. Services free to those having a serious interest in the theatre.

36599. International Travel Adventure Film Guild, 465 W End Ave, New York, NY 10024; (212) 724-1596. Trade assn of the live-lecture travelog business seeking to promote public awareness of live-lecture travel films. Answers inquiries, conducts seminars, distributes newsletter, makes referrals. Services primarily for dues-paying members.

36600. International Women's Tribune Centre, Resource Centre, 777 U.N. Plaza, New York, NY 10017; (212) 687-8633. Supports the work of women in developing countries and acts as an info clearinghouse. Answers inquiries, provides consulting and reference services, distributes publications, makes referrals. Services generally free to women in developing countries.

36601. Interracial Council for Business Opportunity, 800 Second Ave, Ste 307, New York, NY 10017; (212) 599-0677. Helps minority businesses get started and be competitive at the local level, and helps create minority firms large enough to compete in the mainstream of American business. Conducts management training courses and seminars, provides advisory and consulting services. Services for a fee.

36604. Jack P. Eisner Institute for Holocaust Studies, 33 W 42nd St, Room 1450, New York, NY 10036; (212) 790-4517. Conducts teaching, research, and scholarship programs in Holocaust studies. Answers inquiries, provides advisory and consulting services, conducts seminars and lectures, makes referrals. Some services free.

36605. Jackie Robinson Foundation, 80-90 Eighth Ave, New York, NY 10011; (212) 675-1511. Provides educational and scholarship assistance to minority and poor undergraduate college students. Answers inquiries or refers inquirers, provides career and personal counseling services to JRF scholars, distributes publications. Services free.

36606. Japan Foundation, 342 Madison Ave, Ste 1702, New York, NY 10173; (212) 949-6360. Conducts programs in the exchange of scholars, writers, and other professionals in Japanese studies and language programs. Conducts seminars and workshops, distributes publications.

36607. Japan Information Center, 299 Park Ave, 18th Fl, New York, NY 10171; (212) 371-8222. Compiles general and cultural info on Japan. Answers inquiries, distributes scholarship info, provides speakers for Japanese festivals offered locally in the N.Y. area, shows films about Japan.

36608. Japan Society, 333 E 47th St, New York, NY 10017; (212) 832-1155. Collects materials on all aspects of Japanese culture, with emphasis on the arts, literature, and business. Provides brief answers to inquiries, makes referrals, lends materials to members, permits onsite use of collection.

36609. Japan-United States Concert Society, 160 W 71st St, Ste 18G, New York, NY 10023; (212) 787-6983. Establishes educational aid for young artists in traditional and modern modes of expression, and creates settings in which these artists may perform or exhibit for live audiences. Answers inquiries and provides reference services free.

36610. Jewelry Industry Council, 608 Fifth Ave, New York, NY 10020; (212) 757-3075. Compiles generic facts and consumer info about diamonds, pearls, and other gemstones, gold, silver, platinum, watches, china, crystal, and jewelry of every kind. Answers inquiries, provides advisory and reference services, makes referrals. Services generally free.

36611. Jewish Braille Institute of America, Library, 110 E 30th St, New York, NY 10016; (212) 889-2525. Collects Braille materials on Judaica, liturgy, Zionism, anti-Semitism. Answers inquiries, lends books and tapes, provides reference services, distributes publications, makes referrals. Services free to any blind or visually handicapped person.

36612. Jewish Education Service of North America, 114 Fifth Ave, 4th Fl, New York, NY 10011; (212) 675-5656. Studies Jewish elementary, secondary, and adult education. Answers inquiries, provides advisory services, distributes publications, makes referrals. Fee charged for publications, other services free.

36613. Jewish Media Service, 15 E 26th St, New York, NY 10010; (212) 532-4949. National clearinghouse for review and evaluation of audiovisual materials of Jewish interest. Answers inquiries, provides advisory and reference services, screens and reviews films of Jewish interest, rents films and videos.

36614. Jewish Museum, 1109 Fifth Ave, New York, NY 10028; (212) 860-1888. Main repository in the U.S. for arts and artifacts representing Jewish culture, and the largest museum devoted to creating changing exhibitions relating to Jewish culture. Answers inquiries, conducts tours, lectures, film showings, and concerts, makes referrals, operates a museum shop.

36615. John Milton Society for the Blind, c/o Chenoweth J. Watson, 475 Riverside Dr, Room 832, New York, NY 10115; (212) 870-3335. Publishes Christian literature (primarily Protestant) in Braille, talking book, large type, and cassette format, supports church-related schools for blind children overseas. Answers inquiries, distributes publications, makes referrals. Services free.

36616. Joint Council on Economic Education, 2 Park Ave, New York, NY 10016; (212) 685-5499. Dedicated to improving the level of economic understanding among students in the nation's schools and colleges. Answers inquiries, provides consulting services, co-

sponsors in-service teacher training and workshops, participates in curriculum development.

36618. Juvenile Diabetes Foundation, 60 Madison Ave, New York, NY 10010; (800) 223-1138. Raises funds for the support of research aimed at preventing complications and finding a cure for diabetes. Educational programs and info provided for juvenile diabetics, their families, and the general public. Provides grants for laboratory and clinical research.

36619. Katharine Angell Library, N Rd, Hyde Park, NY 12538; (914) 452-9600 ext 270. Interest in the culinary arts and cooking. Answers telephone inquiries and makes interlibrary loans.

36620. Keep America Beautiful, 99 Park Ave, New York, NY 10016; (212) 682-4564. Seeks to create public awareness of the litter problem to stimulate in individuals a personal sense of responsibility for a clean, wholesome environment. Helps develop new programs and implement projects on national, state, and local levels. Info available.

36622. Kidney Disease Institute, N.Y. State Dept of Health, Empire State Plaza, Albany, NY 12201; (518) 474-4444. Conducts research on immunological aspects of renal disease. Answers inquiries, provides advisory services, conducts seminars, makes referrals. Some services may be provided at cost.

36623. LDV Electro Science Industries, 2027 Teall Ave, Syracuse, NY 13206; (315) 463-4555. Compiles data on radar, attenuators, electronic components, coupler, coaxial and stripline filters, terminations, microwave absorbers, and screw machine products. Publishes a newsletter, answers brief inquiries, makes referrals, provides consulting services for a fee.

36624. Laban/Bartenieff Institute of Movement Studies, 133 W 21st St, New York, NY 10011; (212) 255-6800. Conducts educational and research programs on human movement as nonverbal expression. Answers inquiries, provides advisory services, conducts workshops, distributes publication, makes referrals. Some services free.

36625. Labor Institute, 853 Broadway, Room 2014, New York, NY 10003; (212) 674-3322. Promotes labor education and research. Answers inquiries, provides consulting services, conducts courses, distributes publications. Fees charged for some services.

36626. Labor Research Association, 80 E 11th St, New York, NY 10003; (212) 473-1042. Studies economic and labor conditions, wages and benefits, intl labor, occupational structure, and transnational corps. Provides info primarily through its publications, classes for unionists, and study-visits to other countries.

36627. Laboratory for Experimental Medicine and Surgery in Primates, 550 First Ave, New York, NY 10016; (212) 679-8884. Interest in the use of primate animals in medical research and hepatitis testing. Answers inquiries, provides consulting services, distributes publications, makes referrals. Services provided on a cost basis with priority as follows: N.Y., northeastern U.S., U.S.

36628. Laboratory for Laser Energetics Library, 250 E River Rd, Rochester, NY 14623; (716) 275-4479. Collects material on inertial fusion, nuclear fusion, plasma physics, and lasers. Answers inquiries, provides consulting, reference, abstracting, and indexing services, makes referrals. Services primarily for univ and laboratory personnel.

36629. Laboratory of Nuclear Studies, Cornell Univ, Ithaca, NY 14853; (607) 255-4951. Conducts research in experimental and theoretical high energy particle physics. Provides info on R&D in progress, distributes publications, makes referrals. Services free, restricted to researchers and similar laboratories.

36630. Laboratory of Ornithology, Cornell Univ, Ithaca, NY 14850; (607) 256-5056. Investigates all aspects of ornithology, especially bird ecology and population biology, bird navigation, rehabilitation of injured birds and restoration to the wild. Answers inquiries, provides photographs of birds, identifies birds, makes referrals, permits onsite use of collections.

36631. Laboratory of Plasma Studies, Cornell Univ, Grumman Hall, Ithaca, NY 14853; (607) 256-4127. Investigates controlled thermonuclear fusion, high temperature plasma physics, technology and physics of high powered electron and ion beams. Answers inquiries or refers inquirers, conducts weekly seminars.

36632. Latin America Parents Association, P.O. Box 72, Seaford, NY 11783; (516) 795-7427. Assists persons seeking to adopt children from Latin America. Also has an intl relief program to aid orphanages in Latin America. Answers inquiries, provides advisory and reference services, makes referrals. Services free to present and prospective adoptive parents.

36633. Laubach Literacy International, P.O. Box 131 (1320 Jamesville Ave), Syracuse, NY 13210; (315) 422-9121. Teaches speaking, reading, and writing to illiterate adults to enable them to solve practical life problems. Answers inquiries, conducts seminars, distributes publications, makes referrals. Most services free.

36634. Lawrence D. Bell Memorial Library, P.O. Box 1, Buffalo, NY 14240; (716) 297-1000 ext 7011. Maintains holdings on rocket engines, missile and spacecraft propulsion systems, rocket propellant tanks, aircraft landing systems, and inertial instruments. Answers inquiries, makes interlibrary loans, permits onsite reference and use of microform equipment.

36637. Lead Industries Association, 292 Madison Ave, New York, NY 10017; (212) 578-4750. Collects and distributes info about uses of lead products in industry, vehicles, radioactive waste disposal, and noise barriers among other application. Services free.

36638. League for Human Rights in Divorce, P.O. Box 985, Southampton, NY 11968; (516) 283-5010. Interest in single parents' rights, children's rights, joint custody proposals, relationship of children with divorced parents, and parents undergoing divorce. Answers inquiries, provides counseling and reference services, distributes data compilations. Services free.

36639. Lee Coombe Memorial Library, 1275 York Ave, New York, NY 10021; (212) 794-7439. Collects data on neoplasia research and therapy, cancer, immunology. Answers inquiries, provides reference and reproduction services, makes interlibrary loans and referrals, permits onsite use of collections. Services primarily for the staff.

36640. Leo Baeck Institute, 129 E 73rd St, New York, NY 10021; (212) 744-6400. Serves as a research, study, and lecture center, library, archives, and museum interested in German Jewry and other German-speaking Jewries from the 18th century until its end in Nazi days. Answers inquiries, provides reference services, distributes publications. Most services free.

36641. Leukemia Society of America, 800 Second Ave, New York, NY 10017; (212) 573-8484. Provides info on leukemia, lymphomas, Hodgkin's disease, and multiple myeloma. Answers inquiries or refers inquirers to other sources of info free.

36643. Libel Defense Resource Center, 708 Third Ave, 32nd Fl, New York, NY 10017; (212) 687-4745. Nonprofit org concerned with the law of libel and privacy, libel and invasion of privacy litigation. Answers inquiries, provides advisory and reference services, distributes publications, makes referrals. Services for a fee to media professionals and litigators.

36644. Library Binding Institute, 150 Allens Creek Rd, Rochester, NY 14618; (716) 461-4380. Interest in book preservation, rebinding of used and prebinding of new library volumes, initial hardcover binding of periodicals for libraries. Answers inquiries concerning maintenance of library volumes, distributes brochures and literature.

36645. Library Information and On-line Network Systems, 20 W 53rd St, New York, NY 10019; (212) 247-5848. Interest in library automation, machine-readable library catalogs, and machine-based authority control. Answers inquiries, provides consulting services, products from the MARC data base, online cataloging, retrospective conversion services, and bibliographic products.

36646. Lifeline for Wildlife, RR 1, Box 446A, Blanchard Rd, Stony Point, NY 10980; (914) 429-0180. Private, nonprofit org interested in wildlife medicine, rehabilitation and animal rights education. Answers inquiries, provides advisory services, permits onsite use of collection, makes referrals. Services free, but donations accepted.

36647. Lindsley F. Kimball Research Institute, 310 E 67th St, New York, NY 10021; (212) 570-3000. Conducts blood research and studies intracellular RNA synthesis and transport, cellular enzymology. Answers inquiries, provides consulting services. Services available at a fee to research and industrial orgs and blood banks.

36648. Literacy Volunteers of America, 404 Oak St, Syracuse, NY 13203; (315) 474-7039. Combats adult illiteracy in the U.S. and Canada. Operates on the premise that well-trained and supported volunteers can be effective tutors of adults. Answers inquiries, provides consulting, conducts workshops for tutors, distributes publications. Most services free.

36649. Lloyd's Register of Shipping, 17 Battery Pl, New York, NY 10004; (212) 425-8050. Maintains a classification and strength of ships, including machinery and associated metallurgy. Provides advisory and reference services, distributes literature. Services generally provided at cost, except some literature.

36650. Louis Harris and Associates, 630 Fifth Ave, New York, NY 10020; (212) 975-1600. Supplies public opinion surveys. Reprints of articles prepared for the Chicago Tribune-N.Y. News Syndicate available to public. Results of surveys conducted for private clients are confidential, unless released by the client.

36651. Lutheran Council in the USA, Records and Information Center, 360 Park Ave South, New York, NY 10010; (212) 532-6350. Collects materials on history, doctrines, and practices of Lutheran Church in the U.S. and abroad. Answers inquiries, provides copying services, makes referrals. Access, by appointment, to all materials.

36652. Magazine Publishers Association, 575 Lexington Ave, New York, NY 10022; (212) 752-0055. Trade assn of consumer magazine industry. Library staff answers questions on magazine industry or makes referrals. Library primarily for members.

36653. Mannsville Chemical Products Corp., P.O. Box 230, Cortland, NY 13045; (607) 753-8700. Conducts market and commercial research concerning commodity chemicals and chemical and allied industries. Answers inquiries or refers inquirers, provides advisory and consulting services, distributes publications. Services available for a fee.

36655. March of Dimes Birth Defects Foundation, 1275 Mamaroneck Ave, White Plains, NY 10605; (914) 428-7100. Provides prenatal and perinatal care; studies genetics, congenital defects, and human teratogenesis. Answers inquiries, makes professional (not patient) referrals, provides consulting services, lends films and exhibits, permits onsite use of collection.

36656. Marine Environmental Council of Long Island, P.O. Box 55, Seaford, NY 11783; (516) 661-1278. Interest in the protection, preservation, and conservation of the marine environment. Answers inquiries; provides advisory services, speakers, audiovisual materials; makes referrals. Library open to public on request.

36657. Marine Sciences Research Center, State Univ of New York, Stony Brook, NY 11794; (516) 246-7710.

Conducts research in all aspects of coastal oceanography and environmental problems of the coastal zone. Answers to inquiries and consulting services available to professional groups, students, and researchers of N.Y. and generally provided free.

36658. Martin J. Keena Memorial Library, 86 Trinity Pl, New York, NY 10006; (212) 938-6000. Studies finances, officers, organization, and activities of companies listed on the American Stock Exchange. Provides onsite reference services, permits public use of collection.

36659. Masonic Medical Research Laboratory, Library, 2150 Bleecker St, Utica, NY 13503; (315) 735-2217. Conducts basic research on cardiac drugs, cardiovascular reflex centers, cardiac electrophysiology, neurophysiology of hypertension, and biochemsitry. Answers inquiries, provides advisory, reference and translation services, makes referrals. Services free to professionals.

36660. Master Furriers Guild of America, 101 W 30th St, New York, NY 10001; (212) 244-8570. Provides a forum for exchange of ideas and info and coordinates efforts on behalf of the fur industry. Answers inquiries, provides advisory and reference services, makes referrals. Services primarily for members.

36661. Materials Science Center, Cornell Univ, 627 Clark Hall, Ithaca, NY 14850; (607) 256-4272. Interest in materials science research, including surface science, mechanical properties of materials, optical phenomena, including tunable lasers, phase transitions, and amorphous materials. Answers inquiries, distributes publications, makes referrals. Services free.

36662. Maternity Center Association, 48 E 92nd St, New York, NY 10028; (212) 369-7300. Interest in maternity care, nurse-midwifery, prenatal parent education, and out-of-hospital birth centers. Answers inquiries, provides consulting services for a fee, makes referrals, conducts classes.

36663. Media Basics, Larchmont Plaza, Larchmont, NY 10538; (914) 834-2505. Produces a comprehensive new program of microcomputer courseware for reading skill improvement and literature enrichment, titled *Return-to-Reading.* Answers inquiries, provides advisory and consulting services for a fee.

36664. Media Center for Children, 3 W 29th St, New York, NY 10001 (212) 679-9620. Dedicated to identifying quality films and videotapes for children by evaluating them with children. Telephone inquiries answered on specific days by the Information Director. Services intended primarily for film and videotape makers and users. Fees charged.

36665. Media Network, Information Center, 208 W 13th St, New York, NY 10011; (212) 620-0878. Org of community, labor, and social activists, librarians, teachers, and others who use media for organizing and education. Answers inquiries, provides advisory and reference services, distributes publications, makes referrals. Services available for a modest fee.

36666. Medical Library Center of New York, 5 E 102nd St, New York, NY 10029; (212) 427-1630. Collects materials on the health sciences, basic clinical sciences, biology, zoology, parasitology, veterinary medicine, dentistry, and nursing. Provides copying services, makes referrals and interlibrary loans, permits onsite use of collection. Services for health science personnel.

36667. Mental Health Institute, 25 W 81st St, New York, NY 10024; (212) 787-7535. Nonprofit org for research, education, and training in the field of mental health. Answers inquiries, makes referrals, provides consulting and psychological testing services. Fees may be charged for extensive services.

36668. Mental Health Materials Center, 30 E 29th St, New York, NY 10016; (212) 889-5760. Produces educational materials in support of mental health, family life, health and human relations education programs. Answers inquiries, provides consulting services for a fee, and disseminates the center's critical reviews on a subscription basis.

36670. Merion Bluegrass Association, c/o Ms. Margaret Herbst, 230 Park Ave, New York, NY 10017; (212) 685-5917. Studies the culture of Merion Kentucky bluegrass and Merion sod. Answers inquiries or refers inquirers.

36672. Metropolitan Museum of Art, Costume Institute, Fifth Ave and 82nd St, New York, NY 10028; (212) 879-5500. Maintains a collections of costumes, urban and folk, adult and children's, from Europe, Asia, Africa, and the Americas, 16th century to the present. Qualified specialists may study original material, tours and lecture available. Exhibitions open to public.

36673. Middle East Institute, 1113 International Affairs Bldg, 420 W 118th St, New York, NY 10027; (212) 280-2584. Collects data on the Middle East and North Africa. Individual faculty members answer inquiries and provide consulting services.

36674. Mistresses Anonymous, P.O. Box 151, Islip, NY 11751. Studies psychodynamics and social dynamics of the relationship of women with married men. Answers inquiries as time permits.

36675. Mobil Oil Corp., Secretariat/Library, 150 E 42nd St, New York, NY 10017; (212) 883-2155. Collects data on the petroleum industry. Provides reference services, permits onsite use of collection by employees of agencies and orgs by appointment. Library open to public by appointment for scholarly and research purposes.

36676. Mobilization for Youth, 271 E 4th St, New York, NY 10009; (212) 677-0400. Conducts a multifaceted program dealing with poverty and social disorganization. Provides consulting services, refers requests for publications to known resources, participates in community projects.

36677. Modern Language Association of America, 62 Fifth Ave, New York, NY 10011; (212) 741-5592. Membership org of college and univ foreign language depts in the U.S. and abroad. Answers inquiries, provides advisory and reference services, sells publications, makes referrals. Services available to institutions, teachers, publishers, associations, and govt agencies.

36678. Montefiore Medical Center, Headache Unit, 111 E 210th St, Bronx, NY 10467; (212) 920-4636. Investiagtes diagnosis, treatment, research, and education in headache and facial pain. Conducts seminars, distributes data compilations, makes referrals. Services free, except usual patient fees.

36679. Morality in Media, 475 Riverside Dr, New York, NY 10115; (212) 870-3222. Clearinghouse of info on the problem of pornography; operates National Obscenity Law Center for prosecutors and other interested members of the bar. Answers inquiries, conducts seminars, provides speakers for meetings and media.

36680. Mount Sinai School of Medicine, Human Sexuality Program, 11 E 100th St, New York, NY 10029; (212) 650-6634. Conducts human sexual function and dysfunction research. Answers inquiries, provides advisory and consulting services, makes referrals. Services provided for a fee, primarily for professionals. Specialized treatment provided to patients with sexual disorders.

36681. Movie Star News, 134 W 18th St, New York, NY 10011; (212) 620-8160. Commercial org with large collection of movie star photographs, posters, and pressbooks. Answers inquiries, researches location of photographs, distributes publication and photographs, makes referrals, permits onsite use of collections. Most services provided for a fee.

36682. Muscular Dystrophy Association, 810 Seventh Ave, New York, NY 10019; (212) 586-0808. Sponsors nationwide program of patient and community services and an intl program of research grants and fellowships. Answers inquiries, provides reference services, distributes brochures, makes referrals. Literature and referral services free.

36683. Museum Computer Network, P.O. Box 434, Stony Brook, NY 11790; (516) 246-6077. Assists museums and institutions with similar interests in converting all systematic info in their files and archives from written to machine-readable form. Provides consulting services and support. Services available only to members, provided at or below cost.

36684. Museum of Broadcasting, 1 E 53rd St, New York, NY 10022; (212) 752-4690. Preserves and makes available for study selected radio and television programs from the 1920s to present. Answers members' inquiries, provides advisory and reference services, makes publications available in the library, makes referrals, permits onsite monitoring of collection.

36685. Museum of Modern Art, Department of Film, 11 W 53rd St, New York, NY 10019; (212) 708-9400. Considers motion pictures as works of art and collects motion pictures having historical or technical value. Films and related materials available to qualified researchers, inquiries answered, rental service of about 800 selected titles provided.

36687. Music Distributors Association, 135 W 29th St, New York, NY 10001; (212) 564-0251. Membership org comprised of wholesalers, distributors, and manufacturers of musical instruments and accessories. Answers inquiries free.

36688. Myasthenia Gravis Foundation, 15 E 26th St, New York, NY 10010; (212) 889-8157. Dedicated exclusively to detection, treatment, and search for a cure of the neuromuscular disease, myasthenia gravis. Answers inquiries, provides reference services, conducts seminars, distributes publications, makes referrals. Services free.

36689. Myopia International Research Foundation, 1265 Broadway, Room 608, New York, NY 10001; (212) 684-2777. Studies causes, treatment, and prevention of myopia. Answers inquiries, provides reference services, distributes publications, makes referrals. Free services available only to doctors involved in the eye disciplines and related fields.

36691. NEW/Fourth World Movement, 172 First Ave, New York, NY 10009; (212) 228-1339. Nonprofit org that works with the poorest families in society. Answers inquiries, conducts seminars, distributes publications, provides speakers. Services free, except speakers' costs.

36692. NOW Legal Defense and Education Fund, 132 W 43rd St, New York, NY 10036; (212) 354-1225. Conducts legal and education programs to end sex discrimination. Answers inquiries, supports legal and educational projects. Services free.

36693. Narcolepsy and Cataplexy Foundation of America, 1410 York Ave, Ste 2D, New York, NY 10021; (212) 628-6315. Assists patients with neurological disorders by disseminating info to public and physicians and supporting research. Produces materials on the narcolepsy syndrome and maintains a reference library for patients and physicians.

36694. National Accreditation Council for Agencies Serving the Blind and Visually Handicapped, 15 W 65th St, 9th Fl, New York, NY 10023; (212) 496-5880. Seeks improvement of management, accountability, and services provided by agencies and schools for blind and visually handicapped persons. Answers inquiries, provides free brochure, refers inquirers.

36695. National Alliance Against Racist and Political Repression, 27 Union Sq West, Room 306, New York, NY 10003; (212) 243-8555. Interest in nature and scope of racist and political repression. Publishes newsletter, distributes publications, makes referrals, permits on-site use of materials. Most services available only to affiliates, branches, and special projects.

36696. National Alliance for Family Life, 225 Jericho Turnpike, Ste 4, Floral Park, NY 11001; (516) 352-1188. Seeks to improve quality of American family life

through education, research, and certification of persons engaged in family therapy. Answers inquiries, distributes publications.

36697. National Amputation Foundation, 12-45 150th St, Whitestone, NY 11357; (212) 767-8400. Interest in amputees and rehabilitation and retraining of military service amputees, especially those of Vietnam era. Answers inquiries, provides advisory and reference services, provides assistance to amputees, makes referrals. Services free and available to amputees only.

36698. National Antique and Art Dealers Association of America, 15 E 57th St, New York, NY 10022; (212) 355-0636. Interest in ducation of public in the decorative arts; provides expertise in various disciplines of the antiques trade. Answers inquiries, conducts workshops for a fee, conducts lectures and exhibitions free, makes referrals.

36699. National Association for Female Executives, 1041 Third Ave, New York, NY 10021; (212) 371-0740. Provides tools and info needed by women in order to reach their career goals and achieve financial independence. Answers inquiries, provides advisory, resume critiquing and legal services, conducts seminars, distributes publications, makes referrals. Services for members.

36700. National Association for Poetry Therapy, 1029 Henhawk Rd, Baldwin, NY 11510; (516) 546-2295. Provides an info network to all persons interested in poetry therapy and establishes ethics and standards for the training of poetry therapists. Answers inquiries, provides advisory and reference services, conducts seminars, distributes publications. Fees charged.

36701. National Association for Practical Nurse Education and Services, 254 W 31st St, New York, NY 10001; (212) 736-4540. Accrediting agency for practical nursing schools and programs. Answers inquiries, provides advisory and reference services, conducts seminars, makes referrals. Services free, except seminars.

36702. National Association for Regional Ballet, 1860 Broadway, New York, NY 10023; (212) 757-8460. Interested in decentralized dance companies, dance company management, set and costume referral service, and choreography. Answers inquiries, provides advisory and consulting services, distributes publications, makes referrals. Some services available only to members.

36703. National Association for Visually Handicapped, 305 E 24th St, New York, NY 10010; (212) 889-3141. Prints and distributes large print textbooks, testing materials, and books for pleasure reading for the partially sighted. Serves as a clearinghouse of info for all services available for the partially sighted, answers inquiries, offers counsel and guidance.

36704. National Association for the Advancement of Colored People, 186 Remsen St, Brooklyn, NY 11201; (718) 858-0800. Promotes the advancement of colored people throughout the world, civil rights and civil liberties, intergroup relations, laws and legislation, employment, housing, and education. Answers brief inquiries, makes referrals.

36705. National Association of Concerned Veterans, Michael Gold, CUNY Veterans Affairs, 101 W 31st St, Ste 200, New York, NY 10001; (212) 947-6000 ext 388. Interest in any and all matters concerning veterans, particularly veterans of the Vietnam era. Answers inquiries, provides advisory and reference services, distributes publications, makes referrals. Services free, except copying services for nonmember users.

36706. National Association of Display Industries, 120 E 23rd St, New York, NY 10010; (212) 982-6571. Represents display industries, trade market, trade recommendations. Answers inquiries, provides advisory services, makes referrals. Services free.

36707. National Association of Fleet Administrators, 295 Madison Ave, New York, NY 10017; (212) 689-3200. Holds responsibility for operation, control, purchase, rental, and disposition of passenger car fleets. Answers inquiries, provides reference services, makes referrals, conducts surveys.

36708. National Association of Jewish Vocational Services, 386 Park Ave S, Ste 301, New York, NY 10016; (212) 685-8355. Provides services for 31 Jewish vocational service agencies throughout U.S., Canada, and Israel. Conducts seminars and workshops, distributes publications. Services available to members, and to others on a fee-for-service basis.

36709. National Association of Marine Surveyors, 86 Windsor Gate Dr, N Hills, NY 11040; (212) 895-3677. Collects materials on marine surveying and surveying technologies. Answers inquiries, conducts seminars, makes referrals. Services free, except seminars.

36710. National Association of Patients on Hemodialysis and Transplantation, 150 Nassau St, New York, NY 10038; (212) 619-2727. Dedicated to helping kidney patients adjust to emotional impact of their disease, educating the patient and public regarding kidney disease. Answers inquiries, provides consulting services, distributes publications, makes referrals. Services free.

36711. National Association of Photographic Manufacturers, 600 Mamaroneck Ave, Harrison, NY 10528; (914) 698-7603. Interest in the manufacture of image formation equipment, sensitized materials, and chemicals. Answers inquiries or makes referrals, permits onsite use of collection. Limited amount of assn's printed material available for public dissemination.

36712. National Association of Recycling Industries, 330 Madison Ave, New York, NY 10017; (212) 867-7330. Represents recycling industries; interest in resource recovery of scrap metals, paper, textiles and rubber. Answers inquiries, provides reference services, sells publications, makes referrals.

36713. National Association of Teachers of Singing, 35 W 4th St (778), New York, NY 10003; (212) 677-5651. Professional org representing those interested in singing and vocal instruction in private studios, conservatories, schools, colleges, and community life. Conducts meetings, workshops and auditions, provides speakers, distributes publications, makes awards.

36714. National Association of Women Artists, 41 Union Sq, New York, NY 10003; (212) 675-1616. Seeks to increase public cultural awareness of contributions made to fine arts by women through exhibitions, education, television, and radio programs. Answers inquiries, provides advisory and reference services, distributes publications, makes referrals. Services free.

36715. National Association on Drug Abuse Problems, 355 Lexington Ave, New York, NY 10017; (212) 986-1170. Studies interface between world of drugs and world of work using the experience and energy of the business community to find solutions to problems of drug abuse. Data bank is maintained with coded info on potential workers who are recovered drug abusers or alcoholics.

36716. National Association on Standard Medical Vocabulary, c/o Leo Wollman, M.D., 3817 Poplar Ave, Brooklyn, NY 11224-1301; (718) 449-2414. Promotes simplification of medical word usage and standardization of medical terminology. Answers inquiries, makes referrals. Services free.

36717. National Association to Aid Fat Americans, P.O. Box 43, Bellerose, NY 11426; (516) 352-3120. Promotes tolerance and understanding of fat persons and works to improve self esteem and combat discrimination. Answers inquiries, provides reference services, distributes publications, makes referrals. Most services free.

36718. National Astrological Society, c/o Barbara Somerfield, 205 Third Ave, 2A, New York, NY 10003; (212) 673-1831. Studies astrology and related areas. Answers inquiries, conducts seminars, distributes publications, makes referrals. Services may be provided for a fee.

36719. National Audubon Society, 950 Third Ave, New York, NY 10022; (212) 832-3200. Pursues research, public education, and other activities related to conservation. Answers inquiries, provides consulting, reference and reproduction services, distributes publications, makes referrals. Fees charged for some services.

36720. National Board of Review of Motion Pictures, P.O. Box 589, New York, NY 10021; (212) 535-2528. Seeks to promote an intelligent appreciation of movies and film history through its publications and annual awards. Answers inquiries, distributes publications, makes referrals. Services free to some users, at cost to others.

36721. National Bottle Museum, P.O. Box 621, Ballston Spa, NY 12020-0621; (518) 885-7589. Museum with collection of antique glass bottles, glass blowing tools for glass bottles, and glasshouse history. Answers inquiries, provides advisory and reference services, makes referrals, permits onsite use of collections. Services free.

36722. National Cancer Cytology Center, 88 Sunnyside Blvd, Ste 204, Plainview, NY 11803; (516) 349-0610. Interest in cancer research, immunology, cytology, new methods of early cancer detection, and diagnosis and professional and public education. Answers inquiries and distributes educational pamphlets.

36723. National Cartoonists Society, 9 Ebony Ct, Brooklyn, NY 11229; (212) 743-6510. Society of cartoonists who work in magazines, syndicated newspaper features, sports, advertising, illustration, animation, etc. Answers inquiries or refers inquirers.

36724. National Center for Analysis of Energy Systems, Brookhaven National Laboratory, Building 475, Upton, Long Island, NY 11973; (516) 282-2064. Conducts detailed studies of the complex interrelationships between technological, economic, social, and environmental factors that influence energy policy. Answers inquiries, makes library loans and referrals, permits onsite use of collections. Services free.

36725. National Center for Health Education, 30 E 29th Street, New York, NY 10016; (212) 689-1886. Conducts evaluations of health education, researches health education programs, provides technical assistance and info to health education projects. Technical consultation is on a fee-for-service or retainer basis.

36726. National Center for the Study of Collective Bargaining in Higher Education and the Professions, Box 322, 17 Lexington Ave, New York, NY 10010; (212) 725-3390. Maintains collection of faculty collective bargaining contracts computerized with full-text retrieval capability. Answers inquiries, provides computerized search, consulting and reference services, distributes publications, makes referrals. Fees for services.

36727. National Center on Women and Family Law, 799 Broadway, Room 402, New York, NY 10003; (212) 674-8200. Interest in poor women's family law issues such as battery, custody, divorce, and support. Provides advisory services, distributes publications, makes referrals. Services free to persons eligible for free legal services from the Legal Services Corp.

36728. National Chamber of Commerce for Women, P.O. Box 1132 (10 Waterside Plaza, Ste 6 H), New York, NY 10159; (212) 532-6408. Helps businesses grow in order to further economic and employment opportunities for women; conducts research on effects of govt, business, and organization activities on women. Answers inquiries, provides advisory and reference services, conducts seminars, distributes publications.

36729. National Coalition Against Censorship, 132 W 43rd St, New York, NY 10036; (212) 944-9899. Promotes and defends First Amendment values of freedom of thought, inquiry, and expression. Provides direct assistance in opposing censorship, stimulates and assists First Amendment-related activities of orgs, conducts meetings and conferences. Services publicly available.

36730. National Coalition for the Homeless, 105 E 22nd St, New York, NY 10010; (212) 460-8110. Committed to principle that decent shelter, sufficient food, and affordable housing are fundamental rights in a civilized society. Answers inquiries, provides info on emergency shelters, makes referrals. Services free.

36731. National Committee for an Effective Congress, 10 E 39th St, Room 601, New York, NY 10016; (212) 686-4905. Nonprofit org interested in campaign finance reform and congressional activities. Answers inquiries or refers inquirers.

36732. National Committee on United States-China Relations, 777 U.N. Plaza, Room 9B, New York, NY 10017; (212) 922-1385. Encourages understanding of China and U.S.-China relations among leading citizens and professionals of both countries. Answers inquiries, provides advisory and reference services, prepares briefing kits for visitors to China, and assists Chinese delegations to U.S.

36733. National Committee to Combat Women's Oppression, 853 Broadway, Room 1705, New York, NY 10003; (212) 260-1360. Interest in women's rights, feminism, and discrimination against women. Answers inquiries, conducts seminars, distributes publications, makes referrals. Services may be subject to a fee, availability may be restricted.

36734. National Conference of Christians and Jews, 71 Fifth Ave, Ste 1100, New York, NY 10003; (212) 206-0006. Seeks to ameliorate and ultimately eradicate intergroup prejudice. Answers inquiries, provides advisory and consulting services, conducts seminars, distributes publications, makes referrals. Most services free.

36735. National Council of Churches, Cable TV and Emerging Technologies Information Service, 475 Riverside Dr, Room 860, New York, NY 10115; (212) 870-2575. Studies cable TV and new media, especially as they affect churches. Answers inquiries, provides advisory and reference services, makes referrals. Services free, except written materials, primarily for church groups.

36736. National Council of Music Importers and Exporters, 135 W 29th St, New York, NY 10001; (212) 564-0251. Membership org open to anyone who imports musical instruments or accessories for resale to the trade, to manufacturers, and to exporters. Answers inquiries, makes referrals to out-of-country sources of info. Services free.

36737. National Council of Salesmen's Organizations, 225 Broadway, New York, NY 10007; (212) 349-1707. Represents interests of commissioned salesmen. Answers inquiries, conducts seminars and workshops. Services provided free to members and prospective members only.

36738. National Council of States on Inservice Education, 150 Marshall St, Syracuse, NY 13210; (315) 423-4167. Provides a way for state education agencies and others to examine, discuss, and disseminate info about inservice education goals, training materials, and retraining strategies. Answers inquiries, distributes publications, makes referrals. Some services free.

36739. National Council of Women of the United States, 777 U.N. Plaza, New York, NY 10017; (212) 697-1278. Works for the education, participation, and advancement of women, and acts as a forum wherein all sides of an issue are presented to women so they may make informed decisions. Answers inquiries, conducts seminars, distributes publication, makes referrals. Most services free.

36740. National Council of the Paper Industry for Air and Stream Improvement, 260 Madison Ave, New York, NY 10016; (212) 532-9000. Interest in environmental protection and pollution abatement problems of forest products industry. Answers inquiries pertaining to industry.

36741. National Council on Alcoholism, 12 W 21st St, New York, NY 10010; (212) 206-6770. Interest in alcohol and alcoholism and its psychological, medical, and sociological aspects. Answers inquiries, provides consulting and reference services, makes referrals.

36742. National Council on Art in Jewish Life, 15 E 84th St, New York, NY 10028; (212) 879-4500. Acts as source of info and resources on Jewish life in graphic and plastic art, film, television, and visual arts. Answers inquiries, provides advisory and reference services, initiates and participates in exhibits, refers commissions, distributes publications, makes referrals.

36744. National Council on Compulsive Gambling, 444 W 56th Street, Room 3207, New York, NY 10019; (212) 765-3833. Disseminates info on compulsive gambling as an illness and a public health problem. Strives to stimulate the concern of the medical profession, educators, legislators, and the criminal justice system to provide community services and medical treatment.

36745. National Dance Institute, 245 W 75th St, New York, NY 10023; (212) 724-8545. Provides dance instruction programs to public and parochial school children, deaf children, and selected groups of adults, including policemen and women. Provides advisory and consulting services, conducts dance instruction classes, distributes films. Services available at cost.

36746. National Down Syndrome Society, 70 W 40th St, New York, NY 10018; (800) 221-4602. Promotes research into and public awareness and education about Down's Syndrome. Answers inquiries, conducts seminars, distributes pamphlets and films, makes referrals. Services free, donation appreciated.

36748. National Elevator Industry, 600 Third Ave, New York, NY 10016; (212) 986-1545. Develops industry engineering standards and works with national standards writing org and governmental standards groups. Answers inquiries, provides reference services, distributes publications, makes referrals. Services free to members.

36749. National Federation of Community Development Credit Unions, 20 John St, Room 903, New York, NY 10038; (212) 513-7191. Conducts studies in community economic development, neighborhood development, low-income self-help, and community reinvestment. Provides training, management support, and economic assistance at cost to public agencies and private orgs.

36750. National Foundation for Children's Hearing, Education and Research, 928 McLean Ave, Yonkers, NY 10704; (914) 633-1505. Funds research to cure or alleviate nerve deafness, promote early detection and treatment, expand educational choices for the hearing impaired, and inform public about deafness. Services include sponsorship of a speech and hearing center, grants and publications.

36752. National Foundation for Ileitis and Colitis, 444 Park Ave S, 11th Fl, New York, NY 10016; (212) 685-3440. Supports contract research and investigator training programs for ileitis and colitis through grants; sponsors educational programs for lay and professional audiences. Answers inquiries, provides consulting and reference services, distributes publications, makes referrals.

36753. National Foundation for Jewish Culture, 122 E 42nd St, Room 1512, New York, NY, 10168; (212) 490-2280. Provides consultation, guidance, and support to Jewish communities, orgs, and individuals for activities in the field of Jewish culture. Awards fellowships and other grants to students preparing for careers in Jewish scholarship.

36754. National Foundation for Jewish Genetic Diseases, 250 Park Ave, Ste 1000, New York, NY 10177; (212) 753-5155. Supports basic medical research aimed at prevention and cure of genetic diseases that affect children of predominantly Ashkenazi Jewish heritage. Answers inquiries, provides consulting and reference services, distributes publications, makes referrals. Services free.

36755. National Gay Health Education Foundation, P.O. Box 784, New York, NY 10036; (212) 563-6313. Seeks to coordinate educational activities, develop programs, and encourage research in gay and lesbian health care issues.

36757. National Gay Task Force, 80 Fifth Ave, New York, NY 10011; (800) 221-7044. Promotes interests of male and female homosexuals and combats discrimination on the basis of sexual preference. National toll-free crisis line offers info on AIDS, assistance to victims of anti-gay violence, makes referrals.

36758. National Genetics Foundation, 555 W 57th St, New York, NY 10019; (212) 586-5800. Clearinghouse for a network of genetic counseling and treatment centers at major teaching institutions throughout U.S.

and Canada. Answers inquiries, reviews genetic histories, makes referrals to genetics centers directly or through physicians.

36759. National Handbag Association, 350 Fifth Ave, New York, NY 10118; (212) 947-3424. Interest in all subjects relating to handbags and accessories. Answers inquiries, provides advisory and reference services, distributes publications, makes referrals. Services free to member firms, buyers, and others active in the industry.

36760. National Health Council, 622 Third Ave, 34th Fl, New York, NY 10017; (212) 972-2700. Serves as nationwide focus for evaluating needs and for sharing concerns, ideas, resources, and leadership to promote and enhance the health of Americans. Answers inquiries or refers inquirers.

36761. National Health Education Committee, 865 U.N. Plaza, New York, NY 10017; (212) 421-9010. Compiles statistical info on incidence and prevalence of major killing and crippling diseases in U.S. and the mortality and disability resulting from these diseases. Answers inquiries.

36762. National Hemophilia Foundation, 19 W 34th St, Ste 1204, New York, NY 10001; (212) 563-0211. Conducts basic and clinical research, patient care and treatment, and professional and public education regarding hemophilia and related bleeding disorders. Answers inquiries, provides advisory and reference services, makes referrals, offers research fellowships. Services free.

36764. National Home Caring Council, 235 Park Ave S, New York, NY 10003; (212) 674-4990. Promotes standards for homemaker-home health aides and other in-home supportive services. Answers inquiries, provides consulting services, conducts a monitoring program. Services available for a fee.

36766. National Huntington's Disease Association, 1182 Broadway, Ste 402, New York, NY 10001; (212) 684-2781. Offers educational material on Huntington's disease, emotional support to families of Huntington's disease patients; awards research fellowships in the disease. Answers inquiries, provides advisory services, conducts seminars, distributes publications. Services free.

36767. National Institute for the Psychotherapies, 330 W 58th St, Ste 200, New York, NY 10019; (212) 582-1566. Nonprofit org providing intensive advanced training in a variety of major methods of psychotherapy and treatment. Answers inquiries; provides consulting, comprehensive psychotherapeutic and vocational counseling; conducts training programs; makes referrals. Fees on a sliding-scale basis.

36768. National Kidney Foundation, 2 Park Ave, New York, NY 10016; (212) 889-2210. Dedicated to finding answers to kidney disease while also ensuring that people with kidney problems receive the finest possi-

ble care. Answers inquiries, distributes educational materials, conducts symposia.

36769. National Knitwear and Sportswear Association, 386 Park Ave S, New York, NY 10016; (212) 683-7520. Interest in knitwear and sportswear industries, including technology of knitting and related areas. Answers inquiries, conducts trade shows. Services available to knitting industry management and technologists.

36770. National League for Nursing, 10 Columbus Circle, New York, NY 10019; (212) 582-1022. Seeks improvement in nursing services, nursing education and nursing administration. Provides consulting and reference services, conducts workshops and seminars. Services provided on a fee basis.

36771. National Leukemia Association, Lower Concourse, Roosevelt Field, Garden City, NY 11530; (516) 741-1190. Raises funds to provide financial aid for the medical expenses of leukemia patients and promote research to help find causes of and cures for leukemia. Patient financial aid is available for drugs, lab fees, blood, x-ray therapy, and other expenses not covered by insurance.

36773. National MPS Society, 17 Kraemer Street, Hicksville, NY 11801; (516) 931-6338. Facilitates diagnosis and treatment of mucopolysaccharidosis and mucolipidosis. Helps MPS families and educates public about these rare hereditary diseases. Parent referral service puts new MPS families in touch with families who are members of the society.

36774. National Marfan Foundation, 54 Irma Ave, Port Washington, NY 11050; (516) 883-8712. Seeks to educate patients, physicians, and public about this genetic disease, support affected people and their families, and foster and develop research.

36775. National Maritime Research Center, U.S. Maritime Administration, Kings Point, NY 11024; (516) 482-8200 ext 577. Acts as a field testing, evaluation, and simulation org for products and innovations produced from research programs of Maritime Administration and maritime industry. Answers inquiries, provides advisory and reference services, makes referrals. Services for the industry.

36776. National Medical Fellowships, 234 W 31st St, 7th Fl, New York, NY 10001; (212) 714-0933. Seeks to increase number of minorities in the medical profession by providing financial assistance and info to minority groups. Answers inquiries, conducts financial planning workshops, distributes publications, makes referrals. Services for minority medical students.

36778. National Multiple Sclerosis Society, 205 E 42nd St, New York, NY 10017; (212) 986-3240. Dedicated to sponsoring research and service programs dealing with multiple sclerosis. Provides grants to research scientists to support their investigations. Medical programs include therapeutic recreation, self-help networks, clinical centers, counseling, and various services.

36779. National Music Council, 10 Columbus Circle, 13th Fl, New York, NY 10019; (212) 265-8132. Provides a forum for professional, educational, industrial, and lay musical interests in the U.S. Answers inquiries or refers inquirers to other sources of info free.

36780. National Music Publishers' Association, 205 E 42nd St, New York, NY 10017; (212) 370-5330. Interest in music publishing protection, copyright of music, and licensing of recorded music. Answers inquiries, distributes publications, conducts seminars, makes referrals, attempts to locate publishers of copyrighted music. Some services free.

36781. National Needlework Association, 230 Fifth Ave, New York, NY 10001; (212) 685-1646. Seeks to improve public understanding of needle arts and professionalize the industry. Answers inquiries, conducts seminars and trade shows, makes referrals. Services free, except seminars and workshops.

36782. National Neurofibromatosis Foundation, 70 W 40th St, New York, NY 10018; (212) 869-9034. Provides those with neurofibromatosis and their families info about the disorder and assists them in finding medical, social, and genetic counseling. Answers inquiries, conducts seminars, distributes brochure and newsletter, makes referrals. Services free, donations encouraged.

36784. National News Service, Quotation Division, 5 Beekman St, No. 728, New York, NY 10038; (212) 344-4242. Commercial org involved in publication of statistics on financial markets. Answers inquiries, provides verbal quotations and microform services, distributes data compilations and publications. Services provided for a fee.

36785. National Nuclear Data Center, Brookhaven National Laboratory, Building 197, Upton, Long Island, NY 11973; (516) 282-2902. Collects and disseminates neutron, charged particle, nuclear structure, and radioactive decay data for basic and applied research. Answers inquiries with output in tape, computer card, printout, microfiche, or graphic form. Services generally available at cost.

36786. National Organization of Social Security Claimants' Representatives, P.O. Box 794 (19 East Central Ave), Pearl River, NY 10965; (914) 735-8812. Collects data on Social Security law, Supplemental Security Income law, ethics and standards for Social Security claimants' representatives. Conducts seminars and workshops, distributes monthly publication. Services available at cost.

36787. National Outerwear and Sportswear Association, 240 Madison Ave, New York, NY 10016; (212) 686-3440. Interest in all matters concerning manufacture and marketing of men's outerwear, including design, production, sales, fashion, promotion, merchandis-

ing and company management. Answers brief inquiries, makes referrals.

36788. National Paper Trade Association, 111 Great Neck Rd, Great Neck, NY 11021; (516) 829-3070. Trade assn for the paper, plastics, and allied products distribution industry. Distributes publications for a fee to members, paper mills, advertising agencies, consulting firms, and others.

36789. National Planning Data Corp., P.O. Box 610 (20 Terrace Hill), Ithaca, NY 14851; (607) 273-8208. Commercial computer-based firm of census data and computer graphics specialists. Answers inquiries, provides computer mapping and display of census data via chloropleth maps, distributes data compilations on tape, paper, fiche, and online. Services provided at cost to all users.

36790. National Psychological Association for Psychoanalysis, 150 W 13th St, New York, NY 10011; (212) 924-7440. Trains persons with at least a master's degree or equivalent to become psychoanalysts and, as a community service, operates a low-cost referral center for psychotherapy and psychoanalysis. Answers inquiries, provides consulting services, distributes publications.

36791. National Research Council on Peace Strategy, 241 W 12th St, New York, NY 10014; (212) 675-3839. Concerned with arms control, disarmament, politics of peace, strategy for influencing public policy. Answers inquiries. Services free.

36792. National Research and Resource Facility for Submicron Structures, Cornell Univ, Ithaca, NY 14853; (607) 256-2329. Seeks to advance submicrometer fabrication technology for next generation of electronic devices. Qualified persons throughout U.S. may use microelectronic fabrication equipment onsite. Also answers inquiries, conducts seminars, distributes publications, makes referrals.

36793. National Resource Center for Paraprofessionals in Special Education, 33 W 42nd St, Room 1217, New York, NY 10036; (212) 840-1278. Promotes training and employment of paraprofessionals in education and related services for children and adults with special needs. Answers inquiries, provides advisory and reference services, distributes publications.

36794. National Sculpture Society, 15 E 26th St, New York, NY 10010; (212) 889-6960. Fosters development and appreciation of sculpture in the U.S. Answers inquiries; provides advisory services, including advice on sculpture commissions and competitions; conducts an annual exhibition; produces videotapes on sculpture available for free loan.

36796. National Self-Help Clearinghouse, 33 W 42nd Street, Room 1222, New York, NY 10036; (212) 840-1259. Disseminates info relating to self-help mutual aid groups and provides support services for such groups. Publishes a newsletter, providies info and referral services.

36798. National Shut-In Society, 225 W 99th Street, New York, NY 10025; (212) 222-7699. Offers correspondence, a network for communication, and encouragement to the chronically disabled and housebound. Through its magazine, committees, and correspondence, society seeks to build morale and encourage the housebound to develop their talents and potentials.

36799. National Soaring Museum, Harris Hill, R.D. 3, Elmira, NY 14903; (607) 734-3128. Official repository for the Soaring Society of America, interested in motorless flight, soaring, and gliding. Answers inquiries, provides advisory and reference services. Services free, dependent on staff availability.

36800. National Society of Genetic Counselors, 710 O'Neil Building, Binghamton, NY 13901; (607) 723-9692. Works to further the interests of genetic counselors, promote communications within the profession, and deal with relevant issues. Encourages inquiries about genetic counseling and issues in human genetics.

36802. National Society to Prevent Blindness, 79 Madison Ave, New York, NY 10016; (212) 684-3505. Promotes prevention of blindness through a comprehensive program of community services, education, and research. Sponsors screening and educational projects for detection of glaucoma and vision problems in young children. Provides info, referral, and advisory services.

36803. National Strategy Information Center, 150 E 58th St, New York, NY 10155; (212) 838-2912. Encourages civil-military partnership on grounds that, in a democracy, informed public opinion is necessary to a viable U.S. defense. Conducts seminars, publishes teaching materials for scholars conducting courses in natl security policy.

36805. National Tay-Sachs and Allied Diseases Association, 92 Washington Ave, Cedarhurst, NY 11516; (516) 569-4300. Acts as referral agency for the lay person and professional on all aspects of Tay-Sachs and related diseases. Answers inquiries, provides copying services and info on research in progress, distributes publications, makes referrals. Most services free.

36806. National Technical Institute for the Deaf, Staff Resource Center, P.O. Box 9887 (Johnson 2490, 1 Lomb Memorial Dr), Rochester, NY 14623 (716) 475-6823. Serves reference needs of NTID faculty and staff and distributes media adapted for deaf students. Answers inquiries, provides reference services, conducts seminars, makes referrals. Services free to NTID staff, faculty, interns, and graduate students.

36807. National Temporal Bone Banks Program, 55 E 34th St, New York, NY 10016; (212) 684-6556. Seeks to acquire human temporal bone specimens for pathological study, anatomical dissection, and surgical implan-

tation. Answers inquiries, makes referrals. Services free.

36808. National Training Center of Polygraph Science, 200 W 57th St, New York, NY 10019; (212) 755-5241. Interest in polygraphs, polygraph training, interrogation and interviewing. Answers inquiries, provides advisory and reference services, makes referrals, distributes publications. Services available to reputable persons and may be provided for a fee.

36809. National Turf Writers Association, Tony Chamblin, c/o Finger Lakes Racing Association, P.O. Box 364, Canandaigua, NY 14424; (716) 924-3232. Interest in thoroughbred horse racing and breeding, racing history. Answers inquiries and distributes publications. Services provided at cost to some users.

36810. National Urban League, 500 E 62nd St, New York, NY 10021; (212) 310-9000. Promotes civil rights and civil liberties and elimination of all forms of discrimination against blacks and other minority groups. Provides consulting services, makes referrals, permits onsite use of collection.

36812. National Video Clearinghouse, 100 Lafayette Dr, Syosset, NY 11791; (516) 364-3686. Commercial info company specializing in all facets of video program information. Answers inquiries, provides advisory and reference services, distributes publications, makes referrals. Services available for a fee.

36813. Natural Area Council, 950 Third Ave, 19th Fl, New York, NY 10022; (212) 546-9282. Assists citizens and conservation orgs seeking to preserve natural areas that have unique ecological value. Answers inquiries, provides advisory and consulting services, makes referrals. Services free.

36814. Near East Foundation, 29 Broadway, Ste 1125, New York, NY 10006; (212) 269-0600. Operates educational programs and demonstrations for raising living standards in emerging nations. Provides consulting services, permits onsite use of collection.

36815. Negative Population Growth, 16 E 42nd St, Ste 1042, New York, NY 10017; (212) 599-2020. Seeks to encourage U.S. and other countries to put into effect natl programs of population control. Answers inquiries, provides advisory services, distributes publications, makes referrals. Services free.

36816. Negotiation Institute, 230 Park Ave, New York, NY 10169; (212) 986-5555. Teaches negotiation process through public seminars and tape presentations, computer software, and print. Answers inquiries, provides advisory and reference services, makes referrals.

36817. Netsuke Dealers Association, P.O. Box 714, New York, NY 10028; (212) 427-4682. Studies antique Japanese art, particularly netsuke and related arts. Answers inquiries; provides appraisal, evaluation, and purchase consultation services; makes referrals. Fee for appraisals and a commission for purchase consultations. Other services free.

36818. New Day Films, c/o Jim Daigle, 853 Broadway, Ste 1210, New York, NY 10003; (212) 477-4604. Produces and distributes films about changing roles of women and men in society. Answers inquiries, rents and sells films, distributes film catalog. Services free, except film rental or sales.

36820. New Jewish Agenda, 149 Church St, Ste 2N, New York, NY 10007; (212) 227-5885. Promotes economic justice, peace in the Middle East and Central America, and nuclear disarmament. Conducts conferences and seminars, distributes publications, permits use of its collection. Newsletter goes to members and subscribers. Many services free.

36821. New Music Distribution Service, 500 Broadway, New York, NY 10012; (212) 925-2121. Musician-run, nonprofit org for the distribution of all independently produced recordings of new music, new jazz, and electronic music. Answers inquiries, provides advisory services, distributes publications, makes referrals.

36822. New York Academy of Sciences, 2 E 63rd St, New York, NY 10021; (212) 838-0230. Interest in all aspects of science, including anthropology, biochemistry, biophysics, engineering, environmental sciences, geology, instrumentation, mathematics, microbiology, organometallic chemistry, psychology, biological and medical sciences. Makes referrals to academy sections.

36823. New York Center for Law and the Deaf, 110 W 34th St, Ste 909, New York, NY 10001; (212) 564-1316. Counsels deaf persons with legal questions and problems, helps lawyers and human service professionals communicate with their deaf clients and learn about their needs and concerns. Provides free consulting and reference services, makes referrals.

36826. New York Foundation for Otologic Research, 920 Park Ave, New York, NY 10028; (212) 988-3100. Conducts medical and surgical research on unsolved hearing problems. Answers inquiries, conducts seminars, lends films illustrating surgical procedures. Services free to medical schools, hospitals, and lay groups interested in the subject matter.

36827. New York Genealogical and Biographical Society, Library, 122 E 58th St, New York, NY 10022-1939; (212) 755-8532. Seeks to discover, procure, preserve, and perpetuate whatever may be related to genealogy and family history and biography. Answers inquiries and provides advisory and consulting services on a limited basis, distributes publications. Services may be provided for a fee.

36828. New York Historical Society, 170 Central Park West, New York, NY 10024; (212) 873-3400. Maintains collections on American history through the 19th century, particularly that of N.Y. City and State. Library open to public, but is primarily for the use of researchers. Access to manuscripts and rare books is given only by special permission.

36829. New York Institute of Clinical Oral Pathology, 1300 York Ave, New York, NY 10021; (212) 472-4414. Sponsors research in oral pathology, particularly in the correlation of clinical findings, x-ray examinations, and histopathological evidence. Conducts courses for a fee and conferences free, makes referrals. Services limited to physicians and dentists.

36831. New York Public Library at Lincoln Center, Performing Arts Research Center, 111 Amsterdam Ave, New York, NY 10023; (212) 870-1670. Collects materials on the performing arts, including dance, drama, and music. Provides materials for in-depth research in all formats, reproduction services; makes interlibrary loans.

36832. New York Public Library, Science and Technology Research Center, Fifth Ave at 42nd St, New York, NY 10018; (212) 930-0576. Maintains a collection of materials on chemistry, physics, geology, aeronautics, meteorology, nuclear sciences, mathematics, engineering, astronomy, biophysical sciences, and other areas of science and technology. Answers inquiries, makes referrals, permits onsite use of collections.

36834. New York State Natural Food Associates, 132 Beech Rd, E Aurora, NY 14052; (716) 652-5500. Seeks to educate public to awareness of better health through natural, organically grown products and make those products readily available. Publishes newsletter, answers inquiries, provides advisory services, makes referrals, certifies organic growers. Services free.

36836. New York Stock Exchange, Regulatory Services Division, 55 Water St, New York, NY 10041; (212) 623-2095. Assists investing public with problems they are experiencing with member orgs of the N.Y. Stock Exchange. Responds to complaints received from public and to general inquiries on the securities industry.

36837. New York-New Jersey Trail Conference, 232 Madison Ave, New York, NY 10016; (212) 696-6800. Dedicated to the maintenance, protection, and expansion of the regional trail system in N.Y. and New Jersey. Answers inquiries free, sells publications.

36838. Newsletter Clearinghouse, P.O. Box 311 (44 W Market St), Rhinebeck, NY 12572; (914) 876-2081. Intl center for the newsletter industry. Answers inquiries, provides consulting services, distributes publications. Services primarily for subscribers, but others assisted.

36839. Newspaper Features Council, Ward Castle, Comly Ave, Rye Brook, NY 10573; (914) 939-3919. Provides a forum for cartoonists, columnists, writers, editors, and syndicates to exchange views on problems and developments in the newspaper features business. Answers inquiries, provides some research info, sells pamphlets, makes referrals.

36840. No-Load Mutual Fund Association, 11 Pennsylvania Plaza, Ste 2204, New York, NY 10001; (212) 563-4540. Collects data on no-load mutual funds, including money market funds, income funds, balanced funds, growth funds, and tax-exempt funds. Answers inquiries, conducts seminars and workshops. Services available for a fee.

36841. Non-traditional Employment for Women, 105 E 22nd St, Room 710, New York, NY 10010; (212) 420-0660. Serves as a training and placement program for women who want blue-collar jobs. Answers inquiries; provides skills training, job referral, placement and advisory services; conducts seminars; makes referrals. Services free to low-income or disadvantaged women who meet guidelines.

36842. North American Congress on Latin America, 151 W 19th St, 9th Fl, New York, NY 10011; (212) 989-8890. Conducts research projects on the nature of Latin American relations with the U.S. and on the political economy of the Americas. Answers inquiries, distributes publications, makes referrals, performs research on contract basis.

36844. North American Vegetarian Society, Information Department, P.O. Box 72, Dolgeville, NY 13329; (518) 568-7970. Nonsectarian, nonprofit educational org promoting vegetarianism, food reform, and feeding world population through better land use. Answers inquiries, conducts conferences, seminars and workshops, distributes publications.

36845. Northeastern Loggers' Association, P.O. Box 69, Old Forge, NY 13420; (315) 369-3078. Interest in logging, sawmilling, and forest management. Provides consulting and document services, makes referrals.

36846. Norwegian Information Service in the U.S., 825 Third Ave, New York, NY 10022-7584; (212) 421-7333. Compiles data on Norway, Norwegian affairs, culture and cultural life in Norway, and Norwegian American relations. Answers inquiries, lends materials, distributes publications, makes referrals. Services free.

36847. Nuclear Freeze Political Action Committee, 1780 Broadway, Ste 1200, New York, NY 10019; (212) 479-2566. Supports candidates for public office who will work for a comprehensive, verifiable, and bilateral nuclear weapons freeze. Answers inquiries and evaluates data. Info is free.

36848. Nuclear Information and Records Management Association, 210 Fifth Ave, New York, NY 10010; (212) 683-9221. Nonprofit org that represents nuclear utilities, architect engineers, nuclear steam supply system vendors, and others interested in the management of nuclear records. Answers inquiries, provides consulting services, makes referrals. Services may be provided for a fee.

36849. Nuclear and Plasma Science Society, 345 E 47th St, New York, NY 10017; (212) 705-7900. Promotes close cooperation and exchange of technical info among its members and affiliates studying nuclear and plasma sciences. Answers inquiries, distributes publications, makes referrals. Services primarily for members.

36850. Nurses' Educational Funds, 555 W 57th St, New York, NY 10019; (212) 582-8820. Grants scholarships to registered nurses for advanced study in nursing degree programs. Answers inquiries, makes referrals. Services free. Scholarships limited to members of American Nurses Association.

36851. Nutrition Foundation, 489 Fifth Ave, New York, NY 10017; (212) 687-4830. Interest in nutrition research and education. Answers inquiries, provides publications to students, teachers, and professionals in limited quantities.

36852. OPEN DOOR Student Exchange, P.O. Box 1150, Valley Stream, NY 11582; (516) 825-8485. Manages exchange programs for U.S. high school students in 30 countries in Europe, Latin America, the Middle East and Asia. Answers inquiries, conducts seminars. Info is free. Opportunities to host foreign students are free; opportunities to live and study abroad require fees.

36853. Occidental Chemical Corp., Technical Information Center, Occidental Research Center, Niagara Falls, NY 14302; (716) 773-8531. Collects data on organic and polymer chemistry, halogens, phosphorus, electrochemistry, thermoplastics, polyurethane foams, paints, and coatings. Answers inquiries, provides copying services, makes interlibrary loans, permits onsite use of collection. Most services free.

36854. Office and Professional Employees International Union, Research Department, 265 W 14th St, Room 610, New York, NY 10011; (212) 675-3210. Interest in all aspects of labor unionism, labor-management relations, federal and state legislation, and federal, state, and municipal labor dept activities affecting white-collar employees. Answers brief inquiries, provides consulting and limited reference services.

36855. Office of Tibet, 801 Second Ave, New York, NY 10017; (212) 867-8720. Studies Tibet, its culture, history, politics, ethnology, and current events. Answers inquiries, provides reference services, distributes publications and films, provides speakers, makes referrals. *NewsTibet* is a complimentary newsletter, but donation requested to defray costs.

36856. One to One, One World Trade Center, 105th Fl, New York, NY 10048; (212) 938-5300. Advocacy org for institutionalized retarded and disabled people. Promotes the movement of individuals from institutions to less restrictive environments and fosters community support by working through the media, volunteer programs, and related activities.

36857. Oral History Research Office, Box 20, Butler Library, Columbia Univ, 535 W 114 St, New York, NY 10027; (212) 280-2273. Conducts interviews with persons prominent in their field or with eyewitnesses to important events. Answers inquiries, provides consulting and research services on a fee basis, permits onsite reference of materials.

36858. Organization for Flora Neotropica, c/o N.Y. Botanical Garden, Bronx, NY 10458; (212) 220-8628. Maintains inventory of spontaneous plant resources of the neotropics. Analyzes data, sells publications. Services available to qualified governmental, library, and research orgs.

36859. Osborn Laboratories of Marine Science, The Boardwalk at W 8th St, Brooklyn, NY 11224; (718) 266-8500. Studies fish life, including optimum conditions for fish and invertebrate life in captivity. Answers inquiries, provides consulting, testing and analytical services, makes referrals, identifies organisms and causes of diseases.

36860. PENorth American Center, 568 Broadway, New York, NY 10012; (212) 334-1660. Assn of writers, editors, and translators who have demonstrated creative accomplishment. Answers inquiries, sponsors panels and conferences, distributes publications. Services free, except publications.

36861. PHP Self-Help Clearinghouse, 104 N Parkway West, Plainview, NY 11803. Support org for patients with pseudohypoparathyroidism (PHP) and their families. Offers current info on research findings and info on how to start a local org.

36862. Package Designers Council, P.O. Box 3753, Grand Central Station, New York, NY 10017; (212) 682-1980. Group of consultants who specialize in package and product design and other visual expressions of the corporate image. Answers inquiries, provides advisory and reference services, makes referrals. Services free.

36863. Packaged Facts, 274 Madison Ave, New York, NY 10016; (212) 532-5533. Specializes in providing back-dated newspaper and magazine clippings from current to past 30 years or more. Analyzes data and provides market studies and reports, both custom-tailored and syndicated. Services available on a project-by-project basis.

36864. Paget's Disease Foundation, P.O. Box 2772, Brooklyn, NY 11202; (718) 596-1043. Seeks to inform patients and medical professionals about diagnosis and treatment of Paget's disease of the bone; fosters research into causes and prevention of disease. Answers inquiries, provides advisory services, distributes publications, makes referrals. Services free.

36865. Pain Treatment Center, 622 W 168th St, New York, NY 10032; (212) 694-7114. Provides clinical care for patients with chronic pain, offers training for residents and fellows; conducts clinical and basic research in pain. Answers inquiries, provides advisory services, makes referrals. Clinical services available by physician referral only.

36866. Paleontological Research Institution, 1259 Trumansburg Rd, Ithaca, NY 14850; (607) 273-6623. Collects specimens from the fields of vertebrate and invertebrate paleontology, micropaleontology, paleobiology, palynology, and paleobotany. Provides reference and consulting services free for some and for a fee for others, permits onsite use of collections by qualified researchers.

36867. Pan American World Airways, Reference Library, 200 Park Ave, New York, NY 10166; (212) 880-1917. Interest in business and economics of air transportation, travel, and govt regulatory agencies. Answers inquiries, provides reference, indexing and reproduction services, makes direct and interlibrary loans. Some services available only by appointment.

36868. Parapsychology Foundation, 228 E 71st St, New York, NY 10021. Encourages research and experimentation in broad areas of paranormal phenomena. Provides reference services, permits onsite use of collection. Services free, except copying.

36869. Parents of Premature and High Risk Infants International, 33 W 42nd St, Attn: Maureen Lynch, New York, NY 10036 (212) 840-1259. Seeks to provide info, referrals, and support to parent groups, families, and professionals interested in infants who require special care at birth. Answers inquiries, provides advisory and reference services, lends materials, distributes publications, makes referrals. Most services free.

36871. Parkinson's Disease Foundation, 640 W 168th Street, New York, NY 10032; (212) 923-4700. Dedicated to research into cause, prevention, treatment, and cure of Parkinson's disease and related conditions. Maintains laboratories and grants postdoctoral and student fellowships. Has established a Brain Bank, where brains donated by deceased Parkinson patients are studied.

36872. People to People Sports Committee, 98 Cuttermill Rd, Great Neck, NY 11021; (516) 482-5158. Promotes intl friendship through sponsorship of sports competition with foreign countries, donation of sports equipment and providing coaches to developing nations. Answers inquiries and provides advisory services. Services at cost to qualified orgs.

36873. Peregrine Fund, 159 Sapsucker Woods Rd, Ithaca, NY 14850; (607) 256-4114. Conducts field and lab research on birds of prey. Publishes a newsletter, answers inquiries, provides advisory services, conducts seminars, distributes publications, makes referrals. Services free, donations appreciated.

36874. Performing Artists for Nuclear Disarmament, 225 Lafayette St, No. 207, New York, NY 10012; (212) 431-7921. Seeks to inform performing arts community about dangers of the arms race and nuclear war, and encourage performing artists to take action in this area. Answers inquiries, provides advisory services, makes referrals, provides performers for other disarmament groups' events.

36875. Performing Arts Management Institute, 408 W 57th St, New York, NY 10019; (212) 245-3850. Interest in management of cultural institutions and programs in every area of the arts. Provides advisory services, conducts seminars and informational programs. Services available for a fee.

36876. Perlite Institute, 45 W 45th St, New York, NY 10036; (212) 382-0070. Studies properties and uses of perlite, including its use as an insulating material when used as an aggregate to produce light weight, insulating concrete and plaster and as loose fill insulation. Answers brief inquiries, makes referrals, provides consulting and duplication services.

36877. Peruo Associates, 55 W 14th St, New York, NY 10011; (212) 243-4795. Commercial org interested in alternative energy architecture, solar energy utilization, and energy conservation design and analysis. Answers inquiries; provides consulting, architectural and systems design. Services provided at cost.

36878. Pfizer, Agricultural Division, 235 E 42nd St, New York, NY 10017; (212) 573-2323. Investigates drugs, their metabolism, potentiation and toxicity. Answers inquiries, provides technical literature. Services free, but decision to provide service to a specific user is made at company's option. Services primarily for customers and govt agencies.

36879. Philips Laboratories, Research Library, 345 Scarborough Rd, Briarcliff Manor, NY 10510; (914) 945-6195. Collection of material on imaging tubes, solid state devices, physics, metallurgy, electrooptics, crystallography, electrical and mechanical engineering, and computer systems. Photocopying is available for interlibrary loans. Library open to members by appointment only.

36880. Philosophy of Education Society, c/o Emily Robertson, 258 Huntington Hall, Syracuse Univ, Syracuse, NY 13210; (315) 423-3343. Interest in the philosophy of education. Answers brief inquiries, makes referrals.

36881. Physicians for Automotive Safety, P.O. Box 430, armonk, NY 10504; (914) 273-6446. Enlists special skills of the medical profession in control of mortality and morbidity resulting from traffic accidents. Encourages use of automobile restraints, especially protective devices for infants and children, and seeks to increase public understanding of the safe car.

36882. Physicians for Social Responsibility, 225 Lafayette St, Ste 207, New York, NY 10012; (212) 226-6767. Investigates consequences of nuclear weapons and nuclear war, the social, psychological and health-care effects of nuclear arms race, and civil defense. Answers inquiries, provides advisory and reference services, distributes publications, makes referrals. Some services free.

36883. Pierce-Arrow Society, c/o Bernard J. Weis, 135 Edgerton St, Rochester, NY 14607. Interest in the restoration, preservation, and maintenance of Pierce-Arrow automobiles. Answers inquiries, provides reference services, distributes publications, makes referrals. Services free to members.

36884. Pierpont Morgan Library, 29 E 36th St, New York, NY 10016; (212) 685-0008. Possesses the most extensive collection of medieval and Renaissance manuscripts in North America. Answers inquiries; provides reference services and microfilms, photographs and color slide copies of materials in the collections; makes referrals; permits onsite use of collections.

36885. Pills Anonymous, P.O. Box 473, Ansonia Station, New York, NY 10023;. Self-help group with 12-step approach based on that of Alcoholics Anonymous for people with drug dependency. Holds meetings at which members discuss their problems and the steps they are taking to solve them.

36886. Planned Parenthood Federation of America, Educational Resources Clearinghouse, 810 Seventh Ave, New York, NY 10019; (212) 541-7800. Provides info on family planning, reproductive health, contraception, population, sexuality, and family life. Answers inquiries, distributes some publications, makes referrals. Services available for a nominal reimbursement fee.

36887. Planned Parenthood Federation of America, Katharine Dexter McCormick Library, 810 Seventh Ave, New York, NY 10019; (212) 603-4637. Collects materials on voluntary fertility control, including contraception, abortion, and sterilization. Established researchers and public may use the collection directly, obtain answers to questions, and receive bibliographic assistance.

36888. Plastic Bottle Information Bureau, 355 Lexington Ave, New York, NY 10017; (212) 503-0680. Serves as public relations program for plastics industry. Answers inquiries, distributes publications, makes referrals. Services free, unless extensive.

36889. Plum Island Animal Disease Center, P.O. Box 848, The Library, Greenport, NY 11944; (516) 323-2500. Investigates recognition and diagnosis of animal diseases foreign to U.S. Answers inquiries. Library use restricted to center personnel; however, referrals made to other libraries.

36890. Poetry Society of America, 15 Gramercy Park, New York, NY 10003; (212) 254-9628. Collects American poetry. Society may be consulted on questions concerning its poet membership and their publications; library may be used for reference purposes. Services free.

36891. Poets & Writers, 201 W 54th St, New York, NY 10019; (212) 757-1766. Provides info to writers, editors, publishers, sponsors of literary events, and others interested in contemporary literature. Answers inquiries, provides advisory services, distributes publications, makes referrals. Most services free.

36892. Polytechnic Institute of New York, Libraries, 333 Jay St, Brooklyn, NY 11201; (718) 643-4446. Collects materials on every aspect of aeronautics, astronautics, and aerodynamics. Answers inquiries, makes referrals, provides reference, bibliographic and copying services. Makes interlibrary loans, permits onsite reference.

36893. Polytechnic Institute of New York, Polymer Research Institute, 333 Jay St, Brooklyn, NY 11201; (718)

643-5470. Conducts research and instruction in polymer science and engineering. Answers inquiries or refers inquirers to other sources of info. Services free.

36894. Polytechnic Institute of New York, Transportation Training and Research Center, 333 Jay St, Brooklyn, NY 11201; (718) 643-5272. Offers research, training, and advanced degrees in transportation planning, public transportation, transportation finance and economics. Answers inquiries, provides advisory services, makes referrals. Simple services free, research and analysis work on a contract basis.

36896. Population Council, One Dag Hammarskjold Plaza, New York, NY 10017; (212) 644-1300. Promotes family planning as a policy response to high population growth. Conducts and funds research on contraceptive methods and social policy, assists govt agencies in developing countries, provides professional training opportunities and fellowships.

36897. Population Information Network, U.N. Secretariat, New York, NY 10017; (212) 754-3186. Works to improve flow of population info among members by helping strengthen their own services, develop standards, and establish new centers. Answers inquiries, provides consulting and reference services, makes referrals, distributes publications. Most services free.

36898. Population Resource Center, 622 Third Ave, New York, NY 10017; (212) 687-6020. Encourages public and private sector leaders to consider population factors in their policy decisions. Analyzes demographic trends and their relationship to jobs, family, women, the elderly, minority groups, education, and social services.

36899. Post-Secondary Advisory and Referral Service for Students and Institutions, 322 Eighth Ave, New York, NY 10001; (212) 499-3700. Clearinghouse for info about educational opportunities for minority and underprivileged students. Answers inquiries, provides advisory, counseling and reference services, distributes publications, makers referrals. Services provided free to students and schools.

36900. Potsmokers Anonymous, 316 E Third Street, New York, NY 10009; (212) 254-1777. Offers nine-week course designed to help pot smokers who have been unable or unwilling to stop. It is an educational program, not a treatment. Small groups meet for two hours, once a week. Fee for the course. Intensive programs also available.

36901. Practicing Law Institute, 810 Seventh Ave, New York, NY 10019; (212) 765-5700. Provides continuing legal education programs covering 140 different topics in corporate and commercial law. Conducts seminars and conferences for fees, sells books and audio cassettes, rents or sells video cassettes. Services available to practicing attorneys and allied professionals.

36902. Predex Corp., E 54th St, New York, NY 10022; (212) 319-6400. Compiles data on exchange rates, interest rates, econometrics, technical analysis. Answers inquiries, provides consulting and reference services, distributes publications. Daily updates of all Predex forecasts and views available on Reuters and Telerate. Services for a fee.

36903. Primary Mental Health Project, 575 Mt. Hope Ave, Rochester, NY 14620; (716) 275-2547. Provides a unique program for early detection and prevention of school adjustment problems. Answers inquiries, conducts training seminars and workshops, distributes publications and manuals at cost. Some publications limited to special groups.

36904. Private Agencies Collaborating Together, 777 U.N. Plaza, New York, NY 10017; (212) 697-6222. Promotes collaboration among development orgs worldwide, makes grants to private, nonprofit, nongovernmental orgs for implementation of projects in developing countries; provides technical assistance. Answers inquiries, distributes publications, makes referrals. Services free.

36905. Program in International Agriculture, Cornell Univ, 261 Roberts Hall, Ithaca, NY 14853; (607) 256-2283. Promotes education and research directed at training of students from both the U.S. and abroad for active, productive careers in world agriculture. Answers inquiries, distributes publications. Some services available to public.

36906. Project Smart, Cornell Univ, Upson Hall, Ithaca, NY 14853; (607) 256-4117. Concerned with development and evaluation of automatic info storage and retrieval methods. Answers inquiries, provides consulting services, provides indexing services on a prototype basis, conducts seminars, makes referrals. Services at cost.

36907. Psychology Society, 100 Beekman St, New York, NY 10038; (212) 285-1872. Encourages use of psychology in the solution of human problems. Answers inquiries, provides counseling and translation services, conducts seminars, makes referrals. Services free, except seminars and translations. Inquiries from students writing papers discouraged.

36908. Public Affairs Committee, 381 Park Ave South, New York, NY 10016; (212) 683-4331. Interest in social, economic, and intergroup topics, physical and mental health, family relations, drug and alcohol abuse. Answers inquiries, usually by suggesting Public Affairs pamphlets.

36909. Public Education Association, Library, 20 W 40th St, New York, NY 10018; (212) 354-6100. Studies public education in the U.S. with particular emphasis on N.Y. City. Answers inquiries, provides reference and reproduction services, lends materials, makes referrals. Most services free.

36910. Public Health Research Institute of the City of New York, 455 First Ave, New York, NY 10016; (212) 578-0823. Collects materials on virology, genetics, microbiology, biochemistry, and molecular biology. Answers inquiries, provides copying services, makes referrals, lends materials. Services primarily for scientific and medical personnel and libraries.

36911. Public Relations Society of America, Research Information Center, 845 Third Ave, New York, NY 10022; (212) 826-1776. Provides info on public relations. Answers inquiries or refers inquirers. Services to non-members available within limits of time and staff for a fee.

36912. Public Securities Association, 40 Broad St, New York, NY 10004; (212) 809-7000. Org of banks and broker/dealers in mortgage-backed securities, U.S. securities, federal agency securities, and state and local govt securities. Answers inquiries, provides advisory services, distributes publications, makes referrals. Services may be provided for a fee.

36913. Pulp Chemicals Association, 60 E 42nd St, New York, NY 10165; (212) 697-4816. Interest in pulp and paper industry, chemicals, chemical industry, by-products, tall oil, sulfate turpentine, fatty acids, and resins. Answers inquiries, conducts seminars, makes referrals. Services free.

36914. Radio Advertising Bureau, Marketing Information Center, 485 Lexington Ave, New York, NY 10017; (212) 599-6666. Collects materials on advertising, marketing, sales promotion, retail trade, and demographics in radio industry. Answers inquiries, provides advisory and reference services, makes referrals, distributes publications and taped copies of radio commercials. Some services free.

36916. Recording Industry Association of America, 888 Seventh Ave, New York, NY 10106; (212) 765-4330. Trade assn for the American recording industry, interested in manufacture, sales, and distribution of prerecorded products. Answers inquiries, provides reference services, distributes publications, makes referrals. Services free, except special reports.

36917. Rehabilitation International, USA, 1123 Broadway, New York, NY 10010; (212) 620-4040. Natl voluntary agency dedicated to improving services to disabled people throughout the world. Provides technical assistance, consultation, and counseling to orgs and individual members interested in developing programs for the disabled. Rents or sells films, distributes publication.

36918. Religious Public Relations Council, 475 Riverside Dr, Ste 1031, New York, NY 10115; (212) 870-2013. Studies communications, public relations, news writing, public info, radio, television. Answers inquiries, distributes publications, makes referrals. Services primarily for members.

36919. Remove Intoxicated Drivers, P.O. Box 520, Schenectady, NY 12301; (518) 372-0034. Monitors enforcement of drunken driving laws, lobbys for legislation, aids victims of drunken driving accidents, and conducts public education programs on the subject. Answers questions, conducts workshops, lends materials, maintains a speakers bureau, makes referrals.

36920. Rensselaer Polytechnic Institute, Center for Architectural Research, School of Architecture, Troy, NY 12181; (518) 266-6461. Interest in facilities planning and design, architecture, development and delivery of built environments. Distributes most publications free and permits onsite use of collection.

36921. Rensselaer Polytechnic Institute, Molten Salts Data Center, Cogswell Laboratory, R-306, Troy, NY 12181; (518) 266-6337. Evaluates data on molten salts. Answers inquiries, provides consulting and reference services, conducts seminars. Services provided on a cost basis.

36922. Rensselaerville Institute, Rensselaerville, NY 12147; (518) 797-3783. Interest in new approaches to critical social problems. Activities include forums, meetings, research studies, and demonstration projects. Answers inquiries, provides consulting services, distributes publications. Services provided at cost.

36923. Reproductive Freedom Project, 132 W 43rd St, New York, NY 10036; (212) 944-9800. Conducts nationwide litigation either directly or in conjunction with American Civil Liberties Union affiliates and cooperating attorneys in reproductive freedom. Answers inquiries, acts as a legal resource, distributes publications, makes referrals. Some services free.

36924. Reproductive Rights National Network, 17 Murray Street, 5th Fl, New York, NY 10007; (212) 267-8891. Supports the right to abortion and birth control, childcare and lesbian rights, and opposes sterilization abuse and the Human Life Amendment.

36925. Research Center for Religion and Human Rights in Closed Societies, 475 Riverside Dr, Ste 448, New York, NY 10115; (212) 870-2481. Translates and analyzes official and samisdat (underground) documents and articles on attitudes and practices of communist parties, with an emphasis on religious issues. Answers inquiries, makes referrals. Services free to subscribers of the quarterly and to supporters.

36927. Research Institute for the Study of Man, Library, 162 E 78th St, New York, NY 10021; (212) 535-8448. Collects info on anthropology, history, economics, and demography of the non-Hispanic Caribbean. Provides copying for a fee, permits onsite use of collection.

36929. Research to Prevent Blindness, 598 Madison Ave, New York, NY 10022; (212) 752-4333. Provides financial support for eye research directed at finding controls, cures, and prevention for common blinding diseases. Provides grants to departments of ophthalmology to increase their eye research capability and productivity. Special awards made to provide incentives.

36930. Retarded Infants Services, 386 Park Ave South, New York, NY 10016; (212) 889-5464. Devoted to physical well-being and development of the retarded child and sound mental health of the parents. Provides consulting services, makes referrals.

36931. Risk and Insurance Management Society, 205 E 42nd St, New York, NY 10017; (212) 286-9292. Interest in management of risk and employee benefits programs to preserve corporate assets and profits, insurance and loss control. Answers inquiries, provides advisory and reference services, distributes publications, makes referrals. Some services may be subject to a fee.

36932. Rochester Institute of Technology, Technical and Education Center of the Graphic Arts, 1 Lomb Memorial Dr, Rochester, NY 14623; (716) 475-2791. Collects materials on printing, photography, and applied art aspects of graphic arts and communication. Answers inquiries, provides literature-searching, testing, and copying services on a fee basis.

36933. Rockefeller Archive Center, Rockefeller Univ, Pocantico Hills, North Tarrytown, NY 10591; (914) 631-4505. Maintains records of Rockefeller Univ, Rockefeller Foundation, Rockefeller Brothers Fund, Rockefeller family, related nonprofit orgs and .persons associated with them. Answers inquiries, makes referrals. Most services free to qualified scholars.

36935. Rose F. Kennedy Center for Research in Mental Retardation and Human Development, 1410 Pelham Parkway South, Bronx, NY 10461; (212) 430-2413. Mental retardation research center investigating developmental neurobiology and behavior and genetics. Answers inquiries, provides advisory services, conducts seminars, makes referrals. Services free.

36936. Roswell Park Memorial Institute, Center for Crystallographic Research, 666 Elm St, Buffalo, NY 14263; (716) 845-2365. Studies crystallography and light scattering, with emphasis on protein and other biologically important substances. Answers inquiries, makes referrals, provides consulting services and x-ray diffraction analyses, permits onsite reference.

36937. Roswell Park Memorial Institute, Grace Cancer Drug Center, 666 Elm St, Buffalo, NY 14263; (716) 845-5759. Studies cancer chemotherapy, development of new compounds, preclinical toxicology, drug metabolism and metabolizing enzymes, drug resistance, and biochemical effects of chemotherapeutic drugs. Answers inquiries, provides consulting services to professionals.

36938. Royal Oak Foundation, 41 E 72nd St, New York, NY 10021; (212) 861-0529. Promotes preservation of Anglo-American architectural heritage through sponsorship of cultural exchanges between the U.S. and United Kingdom. Answers inquiries, provides advisory and reference services, conducts exhibits and tours, provides speakers, distributes publications.

36939. Rudolf Steiner Library, RD 2, Box 215 (Harlemville), Ghent, NY 12075; (518) 672-7690. Investigates Goethean science, etheric (formative forces) physics, cosmology, holistic medicine, biodynamic agriculture, three-fold social order, western esoterocism, and the nature of cognition. Answers inquiries, provides reference services, makes referrals. Services free.

36941. S.I. Newhouse School of Public Communications, Syracuse Univ, Syracuse, NY 13210; (315) 423-4004. Interest in educational television and audio facilities production and design, message design, use of media for public service purposes and training. Answers inquiries and provides consulting services. Services provided by individual faculty members; fees may be charged.

36942. SLE Foundation, 95 Madison Ave, New York, NY 10016; (212) 685-4118. Raises funds for research grants, provides info and services to Lupus patient,s and educates public about Lupus. Patient services include self-help groups, orientation meetings, referrals, publications, and counseling.

36943. SESAC, 10 Columbus Circle, New York, NY 10019; (212) 586-3450. Licenses performances of copyrighted music by broadcast and nonbroadcast users of music and the mechanical and synchronization uses of its repertory. Answers inquiries, provides advisory services, maintains a speakers bureau, makes referrals. Services free.

36944. Salomon Brothers Center for the Study of Financial Institutions, 90 Trinity Pl, New York, NY 10006; (212) 285-6100. Focuses on objective analysis of the ongoing revolution in financial institutions and markets. Collection open to public. Documents in the collection can be reproduced.

36945. Salvation Army Archives and Research Center, 145 W 15th St, New York, NY 10011; (212) 620-4392. Maintains holdings on the Salvation Army, social service orgs, religion, William and Evangeline Cory Booth, and American history. Answers inquiries, provides reference, microform and copying services, distributes publications, makes referrals. Most services free.

36946. Scenic Hudson, 9 Vassar St, Poughkeepsie, NY 12601; (914) 473-4440. Dedicated to preservation of the natural and cultural resources of the Hudson Valley, with particular attention to Hudson Highlands. Answers inquiries, provides free advisory and reference services, makes referrals.

36947. Schomburg Center for Research in Black Culture, 515 Lenox Ave, New York, NY 10037; (212) 862-4000. Collects works by or about peoples of African descent, with emphasis in humanities and social sciences. Answers reference inquiries, participates in interlibrary loan. Collection primarily for onsite use. Reproductions generally available.

36948. Schuyler Otis Bland Memorial Library, U.S. Merchant Marine Academy, Kings Point, Long Island, NY 11024; (516) 482-8200 ext 503. Interest in marine engineering, nautical science, maritime history, ships and shipping industry, maritime training, oceanography, and ocean technology. Answers inquiries or refers inquirers, makes interlibrary loans, permits onsite use of collection.

36951. Scientists' Institute for Public Information, 355 Lexington Ave, New York, NY 10017; (212) 661-9110. Seeks to provide means for impartial communication of info about scientific topics of concern to nonspecialists. Puts reporters in touch with scientists who can answer their questions about scientific topics in the news.

36952. Scipio Society of Naval and Military History, 143 Cove Rd, Oyster Bay, NY 11771; (516) 922-3918. Promotes and encourages historical research in military and naval history. Provides consulting and reference services, conducts seminars, lectures, and audiovisual presentations, makes referrals. Services free, although a modest donation may be requested.

36953. Scoliosis Association, 1 Penn Plaza, New York, NY 10119; (212) 845-1760. Seeks to educate public about spinal deviations. Helps and sponsors smaller clubs throughout the country and supports an early detection and screening program.

36954. Securities Industry Association, Public Information Division, 120 Broadway, New York, NY 10271; (212) 608-1500. Trade assn that represents nation's leading stock brokerage and investment banking firms. Answers inquiries free, distributes publications on a fee basis. Other services available for members, govt, and press.

36956. Sex Information and Education Council of the United States, 80 Fifth Ave, Ste 801, New York, NY 10011; (212) 929-2300. Collects data on human sexuality throughout the life cycle, sex education, sexuality and disability. Answers inquiries, provides reference services, disseminates bibliographies, makes referrals.

36957. Sherry Institute of Spain, 220 E 42nd St, New York, NY 10017; (212) 907-9381. Conducts educational and promotional projects on sherry. Answers inquiries, provides advisory and reference services, conducts seminars and tasting sessions, distributes publications, makes referrals. Services free.

36958. Sino-American Amity Fund, 86 Riverside Dr, New York, NY 10024; (212) 787-6969. Interest in educational opportunities, including scholarships and fellowships, available to Chinese students, especially Catholic ones. Provides advisory and reference services, conducts lectures and social events. Services intended primarily for Chinese students from abroad.

36959. Skin Cancer Foundation, 475 Park Ave S, New York, NY 10016; (212) 725-5176. Interest in cancer of the skin, the world's most prevalent malignancy. Places advertisements in national magazines, makes public service announcements, publishes brochures, posters, and newsletters, holds seminars and screening clinics.

36960. Sleep-Wake Disorders Center, 111 E 210th St, Bronx, NY 10467; (212) 920-4841. Provides diagnosis

and treatment of sleep disorders and conducts research. Answers inquiries, provides consulting services, makes referrals. Services free, except clinical evaluation.

36961. Slovak-American Cultural Center, P.O. Box 291, New York, NY 10008; (212) 461-7789. Studies Slovak culture. Answers inquiries, conducts seminars and workshops. Services free.

36962. Smithsonian Institution, Archives of American Art, 41 E 65th St, New York, NY 10021; (212) 826-5722. Maintains holdings on history of art in the U.S., original and secondary source materials about painters, sculptors, craftsmen, collectors, dealers, critics, art historians, museums, societies, and institutions. Qualified scholars may use collections.

36963. Soap and Detergent Association, 475 Park Ave South, New York, NY 10016; (212) 725-1262. Represents manufacturers of over 90 percent of soaps and detergents produced in the U.S. each year. Answers inquiries, makes referrals, permits onsite use of collection.

36964. Social Psychiatry Research Institute, 150 E 69th St, New York, NY 10021; (212) 628-4800. Conducts research in community and transcultural psychiatry. Provides consulting services, video tapes and audio cassettes of seminars in psychiatry, and conducts seminars. All services provided for a fee, available to mental health groups.

36965. Society for Adolescent Psychiatry, c/o Veronica Matthes, 542 Baldwin Ave, Baldwin, NY 11510; (516) 379-1787. Interest in adolescent psychiatry. Answers inquiries, makes referrals. Services available to professionals working in the field of adolescence, to public service groups, and to the news media.

36966. Society for Clinical and Experimental Hypnosis, c/o Marion Ken, 129-A Kings Park Dr, Liverpool, NY 13088; (315) 652-7299. Investigates hypnosis and its application to medicine, dentistry, and psychology. Provides consulting, training, and reference services to bona fide researchers and practitioners, as well as general info to public.

36967. Society for Pediatric Radiology, c/o Beverly P. Wood, M.D., Radiology Dept, Univ of Rochester Medical Center, Rochester, NY 14642; (716) 275-2297. Interest in all pediatric radiology, including ultrasound, CT, nuclear medicine. Answers inquiries free.

36968. Society for Photographic Education, Box 1651, FDR Post Office, New York, NY 10150. Promotes photography education at college and univ levels and the art of photography. Answers inquiries, provides advisory services, makes referrals. Services free.

36969. Society for Sex Therapy and Research, c/o Don Sloan, MD, 215 E. 73rd St, New York, NY 10021. Collects info on sex therapy, education, and research. Answers inquiries, provides advisory services, conducts seminars, makes referrals. Services free.

36970. Society for the Preservation and Appreciation of Antique Motor Fire Apparatus in America, P.O. Box 450, Eastwood Station, Syracuse, NY 13206. Sponsors annual gatherings of antique fire apparatus with demonstrations, contests, and seminars. Answers inquiries, provides consulting and reference services. Individual members permit onsite appreciation of their collections. Services free. Magazine and roster for members.

36971. Society for the Rehabilitation of the Facially Disfigured, 550 First Ave, New York, NY 10016; (212) 340-5400. Maintains Institute of Reconstructive Plastic Surgery at N.Y. Univ Medical Center; aids clinics at Univ Hospital, Manhattan Eye, Ear and Throat Hospital, Bellevue Hospital, and N.Y. Veterans Administration Hospital. Answers brief inquiries, makes referrals.

36973. Society for the Right to Die, 250 W 57th St, New York, NY 10107; (212) 246-6973. Supports the right to die a dignified death without use of heroic measures to futilely prolong the dying process. Objectives pursued through legislation, judicial action, and education. Info available at the community level to foster formation of local citizen groups.

36974. Society of Authors' Representatives, P.O. Box 650, Old Chelsea Station, New York, NY 10113; (212) 741-1356. Assn of literary agents whose members engage in the business of marketing literary and dramatic properties. Answers inquiries. Inquiries concerning specific literary properties should be directed to individual members. Does not recommend individual member agents.

36975. Society of Clinical and Medical Electrologists, 701 Seventh Ave, New York, NY 10036; (212) 757-6300. Currently developing competency-based national exams for those practitioners wishing to be certified as clinical electrologists or medical electrologists. Answers inquiries, provides advisory and reference services, makes referrals. Services free.

36976. Society of Cosmetic Chemists, 1995 Broadway, 17th Fl, New York, NY 10023; (212) 874-0600. Interest in cosmetics, including product development, manufacturing, and quality control. Answers inquiries, maintains list of employment opportunities, makes referrals. Services free.

36977. Society of Marine Consultants, P.O. Box 72, Rockville Centre, NY 11571; (516) 379-4640. Seeks to provide marine industry with a reliable source of professionally qualified consultants in all areas of marine expertise. Answers inquiries, provides advisory services, makes referrals. Society's services free, consultants charge for their services.

36978. Society of Motion Picture and Television Engineers, 862 Scarsdale Ave, Scarsdale, NY 10583; (914) 472-6606. Assn for the exchange and dissemination of technical info on motion picture and television engineering, preparation of American and intl standards, and the conduct of technical conferences and seminars. Answers inquiries, provides reference services, distributes publications.

36979. Society of Naval Architects and Marine Engineers, One World Trade Center, Ste 1369, New York, NY 10048; (212) 432-0310. Interest in naval architecture, marine, ocean, and allied engineering, including hull structure, hydrodynamics, ship machinery, ship operation, ship production, and marine systems. Provides reference services, makes referrals.

36980. Society of Nuclear Medicine, 475 Park Ave South, New York, NY 10016; (212) 889-0717. Studies diagnostic, therapeutic, and investigational use of radio-pharmaceuticals, radionuclides, and isotopes. Answers inquiries, conducts seminars and workshops, distributes publications.

36981. Society of Professional Investigators, 1120 E 31st St, Brooklyn, NY 11210; (718) 377-8240. Interest in law enforcement, police science, and investigations. Answers inquiries, provides advisory and reference services, distributes publication, makes referrals. Services free, primarily for members.

36982. Society of Rheology, 335 E 45th St, New York, NY 10017; (212) 661-9404. Dedicated to development of the science of deformation and flow of matter. Answers inquiries, sponsors technical meetings open to interested participants and relevant short courses associated with these meetings.

36983. Society of Stage Directors and Choreographers, 1501 Broadway, 31st Fl, New York, NY 10036; (212) 391-1070. Independent labor union representing directors and choreographers in the U.S. and other countries working in the professional American theater. Answers questions from public at no charge, conducts seminars and workshops for members and their guests.

36984. Society of Telecommunications Consultants, One Rockefeller Plaza, Ste 1410, New York, NY 10020; (212) 582-3909. Resource for all firms, institutions, and orgs seeking competent telecommunications consulting assistance. Answers inquiries, provides speakers for meetings, conducts seminars. Services free.

36985. Society of the Plastics Industry, 355 Lexington Ave, New York, NY 10017; (212) 573-9400. Interest in all plastics materials, machinery, mold makers, and custom and proprietary molders. Answers inquiries, makes referrals, provides reference services.

36988. Sovfoto, 25 W 43rd St, Room 1008, New York, NY 10036; (212) 921-1922. Collects photographs of the Soviet Union. Onsite use of collection permitted; original photos may be rented for reproduction.

36989. Soviet Jewry Research Bureau, 10 E 40th St, New York, NY 10016; (212) 679-6122. Acts as the major coordinating agency for American activity and policy on behalf of Jews in the Soviet Union. Answers inquiries, provides advisory and reference services, distributes publications, makes referrals. Services free, except publications.

36990. Space Settlement Studies Project, Niagara Univ, NY 14109; (716) 285-1212 ext 552. Interest in application of the social sciences and related disciplines to the study of social and cultural development of human civilization in extraterrestrial space habitats. Answers inquiries, distributes publications. Services free.

36992. Special Libraries Association, 235 Park Ave S, New York, NY 10003; (212) 477-9250. Society of librarians and info managers employed in business, industry, govt, museums, assns, etc. Answers inquiries, pamphlets available that describe services and facilities. Info on careers available.

36993. Sports for the People Center for Athletes Rights and Education, 834 E 156th St, Bronx, NY 10455; (212) 665-6812. Provides info, education, and counseling to high school and college athletes, their parents, teachers, and coaches concerning atheletes' rights. Answers inquiries, provides advisory and reference services, distributes publications, makes referrals. Services free.

36994. Stationery and Office Equipment Board of Trade, 341 Madison Ave, 10th Fl, New York, NY 10017; (212) 687-8790. Trade assn for the stationery and office products industry. Answers inquiries, provides financial counseling and credit advisory services, evaluates data. Services primarily for members, but others assisted.

36995. Statistical Office of the United Nations, U.N., New York, NY 10017; (212) 754-1234. Provides intl statistical info, develops systems, standards and classifications, provides technical cooperation to developing countries. Info is provided in publications, computer tapes, computer printouts, microfiches, letters, and in response to telephone calls.

36996. Steamship Historical Society of America, 414 Pelton Ave, Staten Island, NY 10310; (718) 727-9583. Collects materials on history of steam and power-driven vessels, primarily U.S. and Canadian registry, past and present, including ocean, Great Lakes, and rivers vessels. Answers inquiries, makes referrals, permits onsite use of collections, sells copies of photos.

36997. Stepfamily Foundation, 333 West End Ave, New York, NY 10023; (212) 877-3244. Serves the increasing numbers of people living in step relationships, people who remarry or are considering remarriage where children are involved. Answers inquiries, provides counseling and reference services, distributes publications, provides speakers. Services may be subject to a fee.

36998. Sterling Drug, Medical Library, 90 Park Ave, 5th Fl, New York, NY 10016; (212) 972-6256. Collects data on medicine, pharmacology, drugs, pharmaceutical manufacturing, and therapeutics. Makes interlibrary loans.

36999. Sterling-Winthrop Research Institute Library, Columbia Turnpike, Rensselaer, NY 12144; (518) 445-8260. Maintains collection of info on chemistry, pharmacology, biochemistry. Answers inquiries, makes interlibrary loans or provides limited duplication services in lieu of loan, permits onsite use of collection by arrangement.

37002. Swedish Information Service, 825 Third Ave, New York, NY 10022; (212) 751-5900. Provides a central source of info about Sweden for persons and orgs in North America, including education, labor, environment, energy, literature, art, politics, etc. Answers inquiries, provides advisory and reference services, distributes publications, makes referrals.

37005. Taft Institute for Two-Party Government, 420 Lexington Ave, New York, NY 10170; (212) 682-1530. Seeks to increase understanding of the principles and processes of American govt, primarily through its seminars for elementary and secondary teachers. Answers inquiries, provides advisory services, distributes publications. Services primarily for teachers.

37006. Tanker Advisory Center, 1742 Second Ave, Ste 238, New York, NY 10128; (212) 628-7686. Conducts a course on petroleum tankship operations. Answers inquiries, provides advisory services, distributes data compilations and publications, makes referrals. Services available for a fee.

37007. Teachers & Writers Collaborative, 5 Union Sq West, 5th Fl, New York, NY 10003; (212) 691-6590. Sends creative writers and other artists into schools to discover new ways to teach writing to young people. Answers inquiries, conducts workshops, distributes publications, makes referrals.

37008. Technical Association of the Graphic Arts, P.O. Box 9887, Rochester, NY 14623-0887; (716) 272-0557. Seeks to advance the science and technology of graphic arts and closely related industries. Conducts annual technical conference, distributes publications.

37009. Technical Library Service, 213 W 35th St, New York, NY 10001; (212) 736-7744. Interest in engineering: civil, chemical, aeronautical, electrical, industrial, mechanical, and nuclear. Provides reference, document delivery, and consulting services on a fee basis.

37010. Technological American Party, 147 W 42nd St, Room 603, New York, NY 10036; (212) 947-0949. Seeks to have as many people as possible fully understand technology of today with emphasis on electronics. Answers inquiries, provides advisory and reference services, distributes publication, makes referrals. Services free, except publication.

37011. Technology Transfer Institute, One Penn Plaza, Ste 1411, 250 W 34th St, New York, NY 10119; (212) 947-2648. Conducts industrial study missions to Japan and other Asian countries, affording U.S. managers opportunities to observe Japanese manufacturing strategies. Answers inquiries, provides consulting, reference, translation, and advertising services, makes referrals.

37013. Television Information Office, 745 Fifth Ave, New York, NY 10151; (212) 759-6800. Interest in nontechnical aspects of television, especially social and cultural aspects. Public may use the collection and accompanying services by appointment. Questions answered and referrals made. Staff provides consulting services for specific research.

37014. Tensolite Co., Old Post Rd, Route 9A, Buchanan, NY 10511; (914) 737-5600. Interest in the design, testing, and development of high-temperature specialty wires and cable, coaxial cable and military specifications. Answers brief inquiries for industry and govt agencies regarding wire and cable problems, makes referrals to other sources of information.

37015. Tesla Coil Builders Association, RD 3, Box 181 Amy Lane, Glen Falls, NY 12801; (518) 792-1003. Acts as focal point for gathering info and data on Tesla coils. Answers inquiries, provides advisory services, distributes publication, makes referrals. Services free, except publication.

37016. Textile Distributors Association, 45 W 36th St, New York, NY 10018; (212) 563-0400. Studies textile trade practices. Answers inquiries, provides advisory services, conducts seminars, symposia, and workshops, makes referrals.

37017. Textron, Spencer Kellogg Division, Research Center Library, P.O. Box 210 (4201 Genesee St), Buffalo, NY 14225; (716) 852-5850. Interest in protective coatings, polyurethane, alkyd and epoxy resins. Provides reference services to local technical libraries or other orgs, permits onsite reference by special permission, makes interlibrary loans.

37019. Theatre Communications Group, 355 Lexington Ave, New York, NY 10017; (212) 697-5230. Natl service org for the nonprofit professional theatre. Provides research, advisory, and referral services; library is available by appointment for use by theatre personnel. General info free, publications for sale.

37020. Thematic Indexes of Renaissance Polyphony, c/o Dr Harry Lincoln, SUNY at Binghamton, Binghamton, NY 13901; (607) 798-2436. Devises data processing and computer techniques by which 16th-century Italian polyphonic, anonymous works can be identified and borrowings cited. Answers inquiries, provides magnetic tape services and printing of musical themes, distributes reprints. Services available at cost.

37021. Thermal Insulation Manufacturers Association, John M. Barnhart, P.O. Box 686, Mount Kisco, NY 10549; (914) 241-2284. Interest in commercial or industrial thermal insulation. Answers inquiries, makes referrals.

37022. Thomas J. Watson Research Center Library, P.O. Box 218, Yorktown Heights, NY 10598; (914) 945-1415.

Collects materials on all aspects of electronic data processing research and engineering, with emphasis on computer technology. Permits onsite reference of nonproprietary material, makes interlibrary loans. Searching of online data bases limited to research staff.

37023. Tinker Foundation, 645 Madison Ave, New York, NY 10022; (212) 421-6858. Awards grants and fellowships to support important research, with a geographical focus on South America, Central America, Spain, and Portugal. Answers inquiries, makes referrals, distributes publications. Services free.

37024. Tobacco Merchants Association of the United States, Howard S. Cullman Library, 1220 Broadway, Ste 705, New York, NY 10001; (212) 239-4435. Collects material on the tobacco industry. Answers inquiries, provides reference services and trademark searching services for a fee, permits onsite use of collection.

37025. Tourette Syndrome Association, 41-02 Bell Blvd, Bayside, NY 11361; (212) 224-2999. Investigates symptomatology, diagnosis, and treatment of Tourette Syndrome and any related psychiatric dysfunctioning. Answers inquiries, provides advisory and reference services, offers advocacy, maintains a listing of volunteer assns, distributes publications, refers patients.

37027. Tracers' Reunion Registry, 39 Broadway, New York, NY 10006; (212) 558-6550. Reunites adult adoptees with their biological parents. Answers inquiries, provides advisory services for a fee.

37028. Translation Research and Instruction Program, SUNY at Binghamton, Binghamton, NY 13901; (607) 798-6763. Interest in translator training in all subject areas. Operates Translation Referral Service, which makes resources available to the general public.

37029. Travel Companion Exchange, P.O. Box 833, Amityville, NY 11701; (516 454-0880). Provides a medium where single, divorced, separated, and widowed single travelers can find a travel companion. Answers inquiries, matches single travelers with a partner, distributes publications. Services provided to dues-paying members only.

37030. Travel Holiday, Travel Bldg, Floral Park, NY 11001; (516) 352-9700. Commercial publishing org seeking to inform and educate traveling consumer on all facets of travel, whether it be for pleasure or business. Answers inquiries and distributes publications to members by subscription.

37031. Trilateral Commission, 345 E 46th St, New York, NY 10017; (212) 661-1180. Encourages closer cooperation among the three democratic industrialized regions of North America, Western Europe, and Japan. Answers inquiries, distributes brochures free and task force reports for a small fee.

37032. Tropical Timber Information Center, State Univ of New York, Syracuse, NY 13210; (315) 470-6879. Assists that segment of the wood industry interested in tropical hardwoods. Distributes reports, conducts regular academic and special short courses in identification of tropical woods and a survey of the properties of those woods, identifies wood samples. Services for a fee.

37033. Tube Packaging Council of North America, 118 E 61st St, New York, NY 10021; (212) 935-1290. Promotes the use of collapsible tubes, metal, laminate, and plastic. Answers inquiries, provides reference services, distributes publications. Services free.

37034. Tubular Exchanger Manufacturers Association, 25 N Broadway, Tarrytown, NY 10591; (914) 332-0040. Sponsored by tubular exchanger manufacturers, seeks to maintain high-level design and manufacturing standards. Answers inquiries and sells publications.

37035. Tunison Laboratory of Fish Nutrition, Cortland, NY 13045; (607) 753-9391. Conducts research and development of practical type diets for fish, dietary protein and amino acid, carbohydrate and mineral requirements. Provides diagnostic and other info on fish nutrition to federal, state, univ, and private interests.

37036. Twentieth Century Fund, 41 E 70th St, New York, NY 10021; (212) 535-4441. Sponsors research projects on public policy issues. Answers inquiries or refers inquirers to other sources of info within limits of available staff and time.

37037. U.S. Military Academy, Library, U.S. Military Academy, West Point, NY 10996. Museum of military art and science, USMA history, and U.S. Army history. Answers inquiries, provides reference services, makes interlibrary loans, permits onsite use of collections. Most services free.

37038. U.S. Servas Committee, 11 John St, New York, NY 10038; (212) 267-0252. Promotes peace through understanding and friendship, using means of short homestays. Answers inquiries, makes referrals free. Some publications available only to members. Costs and arrangements for all travel and visits abroad are responsibility of the traveler.

37039. U.S.-Arab Chamber of Commerce, One World Trade Center, Ste 4657, New York, NY 10048; (212) 432-0655. Investigates economies of member nations of the Arab League, their commercial ties and relations between Arab countries and the U.S. Answers inquiries, provides consulting, reference, and translation services, distributes publications, makes referrals. Services free.

37040. Unicyclists Association of America, c/o Jean Paul Jenack, 67 Lion Lane, Westbury, Long Island, NY 11590; (516) 334-2123. Correspondence group of unicyclists worldwide exchanging news and info on the sport of unicycling. Answers inquiries (SASE should accompany all mail inquiries). Services free.

37041. Union College, Character Research Project, Union Coll, 266 State St, Schenectady, NY 12305; (518) 370-6012. Interest in research, product development, dissemination in areas of family life, personality, cognitive, moral and character development. Responds to brief inquiries, provides consulting services and product development for a fee, distributes catalog on request.

37042. Unipub/Info Source International, 205 E 42nd St, New York, NY 10017; (212) 916-1659. U.S. source for publications of the United Nations system and other intl orgs. Answers inquiries, distributes catalogs and publication lists free, sells publications.

37043. United Cerebral Palsy Associations, 66 E 34th St, New York, NY 10016; (212) 481-6300. Conducts programs dealing with cerebral palsy, including research, prevention, management, treatment,and rehabilitation. Answers inquiries, distributes publications, conducts workshops, makes referrals. Services available through local orgs, free or at minimal cost.

37045. United Lightning Protection Association, 34 May St, Webster, NY 14580. Interest in lightning protection. Answers inquiries, provides consulting services. Services free.

37046. United Nations Association of the USA, 300 E 42nd St, New York, NY 10017; (212) 697-3232. Studies U.S. policy in relation to United Nations and other intl and multilateral organizations. Answers inquiries, provides basic information on U.S. participation in United Nations.

37047. United Nations Centre on Transnational Corporations, 2 U.N. Plaza, New York, NY 10017; (212) 754-3176. Serves as focal point for matters related to transnational corps; acts as secretariat to Commission on Transnational Corporations. Answers inquiries, provides advisory and reference services, makes referrals, distributes publications. Most services free.

37048. United Nations Institute for Training and Research, 801 U.N. Plaza, New York, NY 10017; (212) 754-1234. Seeks to enhance effectiveness of the United Nations, in particular the maintenance of peace and security and promotion of economic and social development. Pamphlets, promotional materials, and other documents distributed, inquiries answered or referred.

37049. United Nations, Crime Prevention and Criminal Justice Branch, U.N., Room DC II-2348, New York, NY 10017; (212) 754-4657. Assists member states with respect to all matters of crime control and criminal justice. Publishes a newsletter, answers inquiries, provides advisory services, conducts seminars. Services free, primarily for govts and agencies in crime prevention.

37050. United Neighborhood Centers of America, 232 Madison Ave, New York, NY 10016; (212) 679-6110. Acts as spokesman and liaison for 140 member agencies operating 360 centers in 80 major cities in the U.S.

Answers inquiries, provides consulting services, conducts training center courses and special studies.

37051. United Seamen's Service, One World Trade Center, Ste 1365, New York, NY 10048; (212) 775-1033. Operates seamen's centers in Bremerhaven, Naples, Genoa, Casablanca, Alexandria, Guam, Manila, Okinawa, Yokohama, Pusan, Inchon, and Diego Garcia that provide services to seafarers. Answers inquiries, provides a 24-hour hotline, distributes publications. Services free.

37052. United States Chess Federation, 186 Route 9W, New Windsor, NY 12550; (914) 562-8350. Maintains records on chess in the U.S. Answers inquiries, provides advisory services, makes referrals. Services free to members and others interested in chess development in the U.S.

37053. United States Council for International Business, 1212 Ave of the Americas, New York, NY 10036; (212) 354-4480. Serves as U.S. affiliate of the Intl Chamber of Commerce, the Intl Organization of Employers, the Business and Industry Advisory Committee to the OECD, and the ATA Carnet System. Answers inquiries, distributes publications, makes referrals. Most services free.

37054. United States Institute of Human Rights, 200 Park Ave, 13th Fl, New York, NY 10166; (212) 880-4752. Jointly sponsors seminars with American Society of Intl Law and assists persons attending the annual teaching sessions of the Intl Institute of Human Rights, Strasbourg, France. Sponsors seminars, distributes publications. Services free.

37055. United States Trademark Association, 6 E 45th St, New York, NY 10017; (212) 986-5880. Maintains a library of trademark matters on a legal and info basis and related areas of unfair competition. Permits onsite reference.

37056. United States Wheelchair Sports Fund, 1550 Franklin Ave, Ste 29, Mineola, NY 11501; (516) 294-7610. Nonprofit org for the raising and administering of funds to sponsor physically disabled athletes in intl competition. Answers inquiries, provides advisory and reference services, distributes publications, makes referrals. Most services free.

37057. United States-Japan Foundation, 560 Lexington Ave, New York, NY 10022; (212) 688-6363. Supports activities that strengthen cooperation and understanding between people of the U.S. and Japan. Answers inquiries, distributes publications, makes referrals, permits onsite use of collection. Services free.

37058. Universal Autograph Collectors Club, P.O. Box 467, Rockville Centre, NY 11571; (516) 766-0093. Studies autographs, signatures, and manuscripts. Answers inquiries, provides advisory and reference services, distributes publication, makes referrals. Services free with a SASE.

37059. Universal Coterie of Pipe Smokers, 20-37 120th St, Coll Point, NY 11356; (718) 358-0269. Promotes pipe smoking and collects literature on pipes and tobacco. Answers inquiries, provides consulting and reference services, makes referrals. Services free, by appointment only.

37061. Urban Initiatives, 530 W 25th St, New York, NY 10001. Interest in quality of the built environment and urban and environmental issues. Provides advisory services, conducts seminars, distributes publications. Services available at a fee.

37062. Value Line Data Services, 711 Third Ave, New York, NY 10017; (212) 687-3965. Provides collection, evaluation, and forecasting of economic and corporate info. Answers inquiries, provides advisory, reference, and magnetic tape services, distributes publications. Fees charged for all services.

37063. Vampire Information Exchange, c/o Eric Held, P.O. Box 328, Brooklyn, NY 11229. Investigates vampires, Dracula myth, and the occult. Publishes a newsletter, answers inquiries, provides reference and copying services, makes referrals. Services free, except newsletter.

37064. Vampire Research Center, P.O. Box 252, Elmhurst, NY 11373. Collects data on the drinking of human blood by those who believe it is beneficial to their health or who believe that it retards the aging process. Answers inquiries, provides advisory and reference services, performs serology, distributes publications. Fee for services.

37065. Vera Institute of Justice, 377 Broadway, New York, NY 10013; (212) 334-1300. Interest in crime, juvenile delinquency, drug addiction, manpower and human services delivery systems. Answers inquiries, makes referrals, reproduces documents, permits onsite use of collection.

37066. Veterans Bedside Network, 1841 Broadway, New York, NY 10023; (212) 757-8659. Nonprofit org of volunteers who use music and drama as therapy in VA hospitals. Answers inquiries, provides consulting services, produces radio programs for presentation over hospitals' closed-circuit radio systems. Services free.

37067. Videotape Production Association, 63 W 83rd St, New York, NY 10024; (212) 986-0289. Encourages use of videotape as a means of communication; provides an interchange of ideas between companies in audio-video production field. Answers inquiries, provides advisory services, provides speakers for meetings, makes referrals. Most services free.

37068. Vintage Sports Car Club of America, c/o A. S. Carroll, 170 Wetherill Rd, Garden City, NY 11530. Interest in the acquisition, preservation, restoration, maintenance, and operation of vintage sports cars. Answers inquiries or refers inquirers free, sells publications. Services to nonmembers limited according to time and effort required.

37069. Viola d'Amore Society of America, c/o Dr Myron Rosenblum, 39-23 47th St, Sunnyside, NY 11104; (212) 786-1467. Seeks to further study of the history of the viola d'amore, promote its performance, encourage composition, and make available editions of music written for it. Answers inquiries, conducts workshops, distributes publications, makes referrals. Services primarily for members.

37070. Visual Artists and Galleries Association, One World Trade Center, Ste 1535, New York, NY 10048; (212) 466-1390. Clearinghouse for licensing reproduction rights to members' works. Polices against unauthorized reproduction. Answers inquiries, provides advisory and reference services, distributes publications, makes referrals. Most services for members.

37071. Visual Studies Workshop, 31 Prince St, Rochester, NY 14607; (716) 442-8676. Offers educational programs, facilities, exhibitions, publications, and supportive services to artists, scholars, and others in the visual arts. Answers inquiries, provides advisory and reference services, lends materials, provides speakers, distributes publications. Some service free.

37072. War Resisters League, 339 Lafayette St, New York, NY 10012; (212) 228-0450. Avocates Gandhian nonviolence to create a democratic society free of war, racism, sexism, and human exploitation. Answers inquiries, distributes publications, makes referrals. Most services free.

37075. Webb Institute of Naval Architecture, Library, Crescent Beach Rd, Glen Cove, NY 11542; (516) 671-0439. Maintains collection of material on naval architecture, marine engineering, and marine history. Answers inquiries, permits onsite reference by appointment.

37076. Welding Research Council, 345 E 47th St, New York, NY 10017; (212) 705-7956. Interest in welding, its science and technology, including metallurgy, structural design and fabrication, and testing. Answers brief inquiries, makes referrals.

37077. West Point Museum, U.S. Military Academy, W Point, NY 10996-5000; (914) 938-2203. Collection of material on the history and technology of American and European weapons, arms and armor (late Middle Ages to present), and military paintings. Answers inquiries, provides advisory, reference, and reproduction services, distributes publications. Services free.

37078. Whaling Museum Society, P.O. Box 25, Cold Spring Harbor, NY 11724; (516) 367-3418. Collects info on whales and whaling. Answers inquiries, provides reference, reproduction, and graphics services, conducts seminars, makes interlibrary loans, distributes publications, makes referrals. Most services free.

37079. Women Executives in Public Relations, P.O. Box 781, Murray Hill Station, New York, NY 10156; (212) 683-5438. Nonprofit org interested in executive public

relations, corporate and nonprofit public relations, and women in business. Answers inquiries, publishes newsletter, provides advisory and reference services, makes referrals. Services primarily for members.

37080. Women for Racial and Economic Equality, 130 E 16th St, New York, NY 10003; (212) 473-6111. Promotes programs needed by working women, including child care, affirmative action and quality, nonsexist, nonracist public education. Answers inquiries, distributes publications, makes referrals. Publications available at a fee, other services free.

37081. Women in Crisis, 133 W 21st St, 11th Fl, Ste 11, New York, NY 10011; (212) 242-3081. Interest in work-related issues affecting women, including career options, assuming leadership roles, alcoholism, drug abuse, mental health problems, and legal issues. Answers inquiries, distributes publications, makes referrals. Services may be subject to a fee.

37082. Women in the Arts Foundation, 325 Spring St, Room 200, New York, NY 10013; (212) 691-0988. Works to change outdated concepts and attitudes regarding women as professional artists. Answers inquiries, conducts seminars, distributes publications, arranges gallery shows, makes referrals. Shows arranged for members only; other services free.

37083. Women's Action Alliance, 370 Lexington Ave, New York, NY 10017; (212) 532-8330. Develops educational programs and services that assist women and women's orgs in accomplishing their goals. Answers inquiries, provides advisory and reference services, distributes publications, makes referrals. Services free.

37084. Women's Economic Round Table, 866 U.N. Plaza, New York, NY 10017; (212) 688-9651. Studies national and intl economic policy. Answers inquiries, provides advisory services, conducts seminars, distributes transcripts, makes referrals. Some services free.

37085. Women's Independent Film Exchange, 50 W 96th St, New York, NY 10025; (212) 749-1250. Collects info about women filmmakers and directors in the U.S. from 1910 to 1970. Answers inquiries, provides advisory and reference services, locates films and distribution sources, makes referrals, permits onsite use of collections. Services free.

37086. Women's Occupational Health Resource Center, 600 W 168th St, New York, NY 10032; (212) 305-3924. Interest in occupational safety and health needs of women. Answers inquiries, provides consulting and reference services, distributes publications, makes referrals. Services available for a fee.

37087. Work in America Institute, 700 White Plains Rd, Scarsdale, NY 10583; (914) 472-9600. Provides organized and continuing support to all sectors of the work community, with an interest in improving the quality of working life and productivity. Research service available free to members. For nonmembers, institute provides fee-based info service and publications.

37088. Workers Defense League, 15 Union Sq, New York, NY 10003; (212) 242-0700 ext 279. Dedicated to constitutional and human rights of workers denied justice because of their economic, nationality, sex, age, or minority status. Answers inquiries, provides advisory and reference services, operates a speakers bureau, makes referrals. Services free.

37089. Working Women's Institute, 593 Park Ave, New York, NY 10021; (212) 838-4420. Devoted solely to the unique needs of women from all racial, ethnic, and economic backgrounds who work outside their homes. Answers inquiries, provides reference services and consultation on corporate policy, conducts seminars and training programs, makes referrals. Fees charged.

37090. World Conference on Religion and Peace, 777 U.N. Plaza, New York, NY 10017; (212) 687-2163. Multireligious, worldwide org interested in the many factors that threaten world peace and human dignity. Publishes newsletter, answers inquiries, distributes publications. Services available at cost, except major donors and institutional members for whom they are free.

37091. World Council of Churches, U.S. Office, 475 Riverside Dr, Room 1062, New York, NY 10115; (212) 870-2533. Seeks advancement of Christian unity through common study, witness, and service. Answers inquiries, operates study programs in field of religious liberty, administers world-mission and interchurch aid programs for the welfare and resettlement of refugees.

37092. World Crafts Foundation, 247 Center St, New York, NY 10013; (212) 966-6708. Federation of each member country's natl craft orgs that stresses crafts as an expression of cultural life. Answers inquiries, provides advisory and reference services, distributes publications, makes referrals. Except for publications, services free.

37093. World Environment Center, 605 Third Ave, 17th Fl, New York, NY 10158; (212) 986-7200. Serves natl and intl orgs, business and industry, univs and research institutions on environmental issues and policy. Publications available for sale.

37094. World Food Council, U.N. Plaza, Room S-2955, New York, NY 10017; (212) 754-4245. Promotes implementation of its resolutions and United Nations General Assembly resolutions interested in food; strives to solve world food problems. Answers inquiries, provides reference services, distributes publications. Services free.

37096. World Institute Council, Green St and East River, Brooklyn, NY 11222; (718) 383-5000. Nonprofit research and educational org that publishes and disseminates such works and ideas as it believes will lead to solutions to the urgent problems facing mankind. Answers inquiries, provides consulting services, sells publications. Services primarily for institutions.

37097. World Institute of Black Communications, c/o Adriane Jaines or Joan Logue-Henry, 10 Columbus Circle, 10th Fl, New York, NY 10019; (212) 586-1771. Seeks to educate corps, advertising agencies, and consumers of their importance to one another, especially in the African-American community. Answers inquiries, provides reference services, distributes publications, makes referrals. Services free.

37098. World Modeling Association, P.O. Box 100, Croton-on-Hudson, NY 10520; (914) 737-8512. Conducts World Model Award Competitions, World Model Scholarship Awards, and conventions in the U.S. and foreign countries. Answers inquiries, provides advisory and reference services, distributes publications, makes referrals. Some services free.

37099. World Policy Institute, 777 U.N. Plaza, New York, NY 10017; (212) 490-0010. Investigates strategic and conventional arms reductions, Soviet-American relations, European security, U.S. policy in Central America, East Asia and southern Africa. Answers inquiries, provides advisory services, distributes publications, makes referrals. Some services free.

37100. World Rehabilitation Fund, 400 E 34th St, New York, NY 10016; (212) 340-6062. Interest in rehabilitation of handicapped and disabled, especially in underdeveloped countries. Answers inquiries, provides consulting services, makes referrals.

37101. World's Fair Collectors Society, 148 Poplar St, Garden City, NY 11530; (516) 741-4884. Seeks to preserve for future generations the heritage of data relating to World's Fairs of the past. Answers inquiries, provides advisory services, conducts exhibits, shows, and sales events, distributes publications. Services free to members, for a fee to others.

37102. YIVO Institute for Jewish Research, 1048 Fifth Ave, New York, NY 10028; (212) 535-6700. Devoted to the study of Jewish life, past and present. Provides consulting, genealogical, and reference services, answers inquiries or makes referrals. Limited bibliographic service provided free; photocopies, microfilm, and reproductions of photographs may be purchased.

37103. Young Audiences, 115 E 92nd St, New York, NY 10020; (212) 831-8110. Provides professional performances in music, dance, and theater in schools through in-school performances, workshops, and residencies.

37104. Young Concert Artists, 250 W 57th St, New York, NY 10019; (212) 307-6655. Discovers extraordinary young classical musicians through the Young Concert Artists Intl Auditions each year and launches their careers as professionals. Info is for those booking YCA artists. Management services for artists who are winners of the auditions.

37105. Young Mnemonics Library, Morris N. Young, M.D., 170 Broadway, Ste 714, New York, NY 10038; (212) 233-2344. Personal library maintained by Dr. Morris N. and Mrs. Chesley V. Young concentrating on mnemonics, including memory aids and rapid calculations. Collection is available to approved researchers for reference use by appointment. Brief questions answered free.

37106. Young Social Democrats, 275 Seventh Ave, New York, NY 10001; (212) 989-0909. Interest in socialism, social democracy, and labor. Answers inquiries, conducts seminars, provides speakers, distributes publications, makes referrals. Services free, except some publications.

37107. Zinc Institute, 292 Madison Ave, New York, NY 10017; (212) 578-4750. Investigates technical and application engineering related to zinc industry. Reference services available without charge. Research conducted by the institute's associated org on a contractual basis.

North Carolina

38002. Acid Deposition Program, N.C. State Univ, 1509 Varsity Dr, Raleigh, NC 27606; (919) 737-3520. Interest in effects of atmospheric deposition on aquatic and terrestrial ecosystems, acid rain, precipitation. Provides general reference services, permits onsite reference, mails out info packets. Services free to anyone, priority given to investigators funded by program.

38003. African Heritage Center, N.C. A&T State Univ, Greensboro, NC 27411; (919) 379-7874. Interest in black culture, history, nations. Provides general reference services; conducts tours, lectures, workshops, programs; distributes publications; permits onsite study. Services generally free.

38004. Alopecia Areata Research Foundation, P.O. Box 14, Century Station, Raleigh, NC 27602-0014; president, (919) 832-3711. Raises funds for medical research into causes and cure of alopecia areata, a disease affecting an estimated 2,000,000 Americans. Foundation solicits and is supported by donations.

38005. American Association of Textile Chemists and Colorists, P.O. Box 12215, Research Triangle Park, NC 27709; (919) 549-8141. Interest in test methods for identification and analysis of textiles and for determining the colorfastness, physical, and biological properties of textiles. Answers inquiries, makes referrals.

38006. American Board of Pediatrics, 111 Silver Cedar Court, Chapel Hill, NC 27514; (919) 929-0461. Certification board that establishes qualifications, conducts examinations, and certifies those it finds qualified as specialists and subspecialists in pediatrics. Distributes publication.

38007. American Dance Festival, P.O. Box 6097, College Station, Durham, NC 27708; (919) 684-6402. Modern dance producing service org serving needs of dance, dancers, and choreographers. Provides general reference services, conducts programs, schools, and conferences, distributes publications, permits onsite reference. Services free, except schools, programs.

38008. American Society of Echocardiography, P.O. Box 2598 (1100 Raleigh Bldg), Raleigh, NC 27602; (919) 821-1435. Interest in echocardiography, ultrasonic examination of adult heart, nomenclature and standards, education and training. Answers inquiries, makes referrals free, sells publications.

38009. Appalachian Hardwood Manufacturers, P.O. Box 427 (164 S Main St, Room 408), High Point, NC 27261; (919) 885-8315. Interest in hardwood manufacturing research and development, product acceptance, forest industry operations. Provides general reference services free.

38010. Associated Master Barbers and Beauticians of America, P.O. Box 220782 (219 Greenwich Rd), Charlotte, NC 28222; (704) 366-5177. Interest in barbering, barbering education, cosmetology, professional standards in the industry, accreditation of barber colleges. Provides general reference services.

38011. Association of Official Seed Certifying Agencies, c/o Foil W. McLaughlin, Exec Vice-Pres, 3709 Hillsborough St, Raleigh, NC 27607; (919) 737-2851. Interest in production and certification of seed and vegetatively propagated material. Answers inquiries free. Publications distributed to members, associate members, and libraries only.

38012. Association of Pathology Chairmen, c/o Robert W. Prichard, MD, Secty-Treas, Dept of Pathology, Bowman Gray School of Medicine, Wake Forest Univ., Winston-Salem, NC 27103. Interest in medical school depts of pathology (education, administration, research, funding). Answers inquiries; provides consulting services; maintains liaison with regulatory agencies, educational assns, governmental agencies, and biomedical groups.

38013. Association of State Public Health Veterinarians, Dr John I Freeman, Secty, Veterinary Public Health Section, N.C. State Board of Health, Raleigh, NC 27602. Interest in veterinary public health, rural and environmental health, animal ecology as related to human health. Answers inquiries, provides consulting services, makes referrals.

38014. Brown Lung Association, Rte 1, Box 207, Julian, NC 27283; (919) 685-9574. Founded by disabled textile workers suffering from brown lung, sponsors talks at churches, senior citizen centers, and union halls; holds brown lung screening clinics in mill towns across South; helps disabled mill workers file workers' compensation claims.

38016. Canadian Studies Center, Duke Univ., 2122 Campus Dr, Durham, NC 27706; (919) 684-2765. Develops college and univ courses on Canada, offers Canadian concentrations in undergraduate, graduate degrees. Answers inquiries, provides consulting services, distributes publications, permits onsite use of library collections, conducts regional workshops and seminars.

38017. Cape Fear Technical Institute, 411 North Front St, Wilmington, NC 28401; (919) 343-0481 ext 230. Interest in handicapped and disadvantaged human resources development, vocational training. Provides general reference services, conducts seminars and marine research cruises, permits onsite reference. Services provided at cost.

38018. Center for Alcohol Studies, School of Medicine, Univ. of N.C., Medical School, Bldg Wing B, Room 332, Chapel Hill, NC 27514; (919) 966-5678. Promotes, coordinates training and research in alcohol use and abuse, alcoholism. Provides general reference and copying services, conducts seminars, distributes publications, permits onsite reference. Fees charged for reference, copying services.

38019. Center for Creative Leadership, P.O. Box P-1 (5000 Laurinda Dr), Greensboro, NC 27402; (919) 288-7210. Nonprofit educational institution devoted to leadership, leadership development, creative process, performance appraisal, etc. Provides general reference, consulting, copying services, sponsors conferences and seminars, permits onsite study.

38020. Center for Demographic Studies, Duke Univ., 2117 Campus Dr, Durham, NC 27706; (919) 684-6126. Interest in demography, human ecology, population modeling, research and analysis, population dynamics, urban and regional studies, etc. Provides general reference services, permits onsite study. Services generally free, except specialized data provision.

38021. Center for Urban and Regional Studies, Univ of N.C., 108 Battle Lane, Chapel Hill, NC 27514; (919) 962-3074. Interest in research on urban problems, including land use, residential development, water resources, law enforcement, etc. Provides advisory services, evaluates data, distributes publications. Services primarily for state and local govt, generally provided at cost.

38022. Center for the Study of Aging and Human Development, Duke Univ Medical Center, P.O. Box 3003, Durham, NC 27710; (919) 684-3176. Interest in aging and human development, with emphasis on processes and health problems of adulthood and aging. Provides general reference services, analyzes data, conducts seminars. Some fees charged.

38023. Center for the Well-Being of Health Professionals, 5102 Chapel Hill Blvd, Durham, NC 27707; (919) 489-9167. Independent, nonprofit org that seeks to prevent emotional and physical impairment among health professionals. Promotes assistance for professionals and their families, educates professionals about well-being strategies.

38025. Chemical Industry Institute of Toxicology, P.O. Box 12137, Research Triangle Park, NC 27709; (919) 541-2070. Interest in descriptive toxicology/epidemiology studies, biological mechanisms of chemical toxicity, risk assessment evaluation, etc. Provides general reference services, conducts seminars, distributes data compilations, permits onsite study. Publications may be provided for a fee.

38026. Chickasaw Horse Association, P.O. Box 8, Love Valley, NC 28677; (704) 592-7451. Interest in Chickasaw horses and their breeding. Answers inquiries, distributes publications. Services free.

38027. Child Development Research Institute, c/o Frank Porter Graham Child Development Center, Highway 54, Bypass West 071A, Chapel Hill, NC 27514; (919) 966-4121. Natl mental retardation research center. Answers inquiries, provides advisory services, conducts seminars and workshops, distributes publications, makes referrals. Services free within limits; some provided for a fee.

38028. Clinical Research Center, Duke Univ Medical Center, Box 3854, Durham, NC 27710; (919) 684-3806. Interest in clinical research, inborn errors of metabolism, endocrinology, vascular surgery, neurosurgery, gastroenterology, etc. Answers inquiries, makes referrals. Services provided to medical personnel only.

38029. Commission of Professors of Adult Education, c/o Joan Wright, Chair, Dept of Adult and Community Coll Education, Box 7607, N.C. State Univ, Raleigh, NC 27695-7607. Voluntary assn of professors of adult education in U.S. and Canada whose primary concern is to upgrade the quality of graduate instruction in adult education. Answers inquiries, makes referrals to other sources of info. Consulting services provided on negotiated-fee basis.

38030. Committee on Diagnostic Reading Tests, Mountain Home, NC 27858; (704) 693-5223. Nonprofit educational service org that develops, distributes diagnostic reading tests and teaching materials for reading instruction. Provides general reference services, conducts annual workshops, permits onsite use of collection.

38031. Cone Mills Corp., Library, 1106 Maple St, Greensboro, NC 27405; (919) 379-6215. Interest in textile technology, organic chemistry, management, personnel, marketing. Provides general reference services, permits limited onsite use of collections.

38032. Cystic Fibrosis Research Center, Box 2994, Duke Medical Center, Durham, NC 27710; (919) 684-3364. Interest in cystic fibrosis, related pediatric lung disease. Provides general reference services, conducts seminars. Services free.

38033. Family Health International, 1 Triangle Dr, Research Triangle Park, NC 27709; (919) 549-0517. Intl nonprofit org interested in research on contraception, family planning services, maternity care, primary health care. Provides general reference services, makes interlibrary loans, distributes publications, permits onsite reference. Services free.

38034. Family Mediation Association, P.O. Box 15689, Asheville, NC 28813; (704) 274-5588. Interest in theoretical, sociological, legal aspects of family mediation. Provides general reference services, conducts seminars and training program. Services free, except reprints and training program, which requires masters or law degree.

38035. Federation of Associations of Regulatory Boards, P.O. Drawer 609 (321 East Main St), Wallace, NC 28466; (919) 285-3167. Interest in regulatory boards, licensing and examination, law enforcement, drug laws, etc. Provides general reference services, consulting; conducts seminars, workshops; distributes publications. Services primarily for members, may require a fee.

38036. Felicidades Wildlife Foundation, P.O. Box 490, Waynesville, NC 28786; (704) 926-0192. Nonprofit foundation interested in rehabilitation, release of injured, orphaned wildlife. Provides general reference services, conducts workshops, distributes newsletter, permits onsite reference. Honorariums requested for workshops, teaching conducted outside Waynesville. Other services free.

38037. Forest History Society, 701 Vickers Ave, Durham, NC 27701; (919) 682-9319. Interest in all aspects of North American forest and conservation history, with interdisciplinary approaches to forestry, lumbering, forest products industries, conservation, and aesthetics. Provides general reference services, permits onsite use of collection for a fee.

38038. Foundation for Research on the Nature of Man, Box 6847, Coll Station, Durham, NC 27708; (919) 688-8241. Nonprofit org that conducts research and education in parapsychology, extrasensory perception, psychokinesis. Provides general reference services, conducts seminars and training programs, distributes publications, permits onsite reference. Some services free, some at cost.

38039. Furniture Industry Consumer Advisory Panel, P.O. Box HP-7, High Point, NC 27261; (919) 884-5000. Nonprofit org interested in furniture, including consumer affairs and ethical standards in sale and promotion of furniture. Answers inquiries, investigates complaints, conducts seminars and workshops, distributes publications. Services free, except brochure.

38040. Health Effects Research Laboratory, Office of Health Research, Environmental Protection Agency, Research Triangle Park, NC 27711; (919) 541-2281. Conducts research to detect, define, quantify health effects of environmental pollution. Answers inquiries, provides info on research in progress.

38041. Health Effects Research Laboratory/Experimental Biology Division, Office of Health Research, Environmental Protection Agency, Room L-322, Research Triangle Park, NC 27711; (919) 549-2771. Interest in non-

ionizing radio frequency, microwave, and extremely-low frequency, nonionizing radiation dosimetry, biological effects thereof. Answers inquiries, makes referrals free.

38042. Highlands Biological Station, P.O. Drawer 580, Highlands, NC 28741; (704) 526-2602. Administered by Western Carolina Univ, part of an interinstitutional program interested in botany, zoology, ecology, and biogeography of southern Appalachian region. Answers inquiries, permits onsite use of literature collection. Provides facilities for individual research projects.

38043. Highway Safety Research Center, Univ. of N.C., CTP, 197-A, Chapel Hill, NC 27514; (919) 966-2202. Conducts research on traffic accidents and their prevention, coordinates training of traffic safety personnel, evaluates safety programs. Answers inquiries, makes referrals, sells publications, permits onsite reference. Services available free to public on limited basis.

38044. Historical Foundation of the Presbyterian and Reformed Churches, P.O. Box 847, Montreat, NC 28757; (704) 669-7061. Maintains archival collections of the Presbyterian Church, Associate Reformed Presbyterian Church, and the former Presbyterian Church in the U.S. Provides general reference services, conducts seminars, permits onsite use of most of the collections by the public. Services free, except for microfilming and copying services.

38046. Institute for Coastal and Marine Resources, East Carolina Univ, Greenville, NC 27834; (919) 757-6779. Interest in all areas of coastal and marine research, including estuarine ecology, coastal zone management, marine geology, and maritime sociology and anthropology. Provides general reference services; offers translation, duplication, and interlibrary loan services for a fee.

38047. Institute for Southern Studies, P.O. Box 531 (604 West Chapel Hill St), Durham, NC 27701; (919) 688-8167. Nonprofit research, education org interested in progressive political, economic, social development in the South. Provides general reference services, distributes publications, permits onsite reference. Services free, except publications.

38048. Institute of Marine Sciences, Univ of N.C., 3407 Arendell St, Morehead City, NC 28557; (919) 726-6841. Interest in life history, taxonomy, ecology, of marine invertebrates, fishes, and fungi; oceanography of estuarine areas; geomorphology of barrier islands; coastal sedimentology; more. Provides general reference services, makes interlibrary loans, permits onsite reference.

38049. Institute of Outdoor Drama, Univ of N.C., 202 Graham Memorial Bldg 052-A, Chapel Hill, NC 27514; (919) 962-1328. Interest in outdoor drama, playwriting, fund raising, amphitheatre design, scenic design and lighting, sound equipment. Provides general reference services, lends a program of 35mm slides with text. Services generally free to in-state residents, at cost to others.

38050. Instrument Society of America, P.O. Box 12277, Research Triangle Park, NC 27709; (919) 549-8411. Interest in instrumentation and controls to industrial, lab, biophysical, marine, and space environments. Also, instrumentation for analysis, telemetry, metrology, physical and mechanical measurement, etc. Answers inquiries, makes referrals, sponsors annual conference, permits onsite use of collection.

38051. Insurance Accounting and Systems Association, P.O. Box 8857, Durham, NC 27707; (919) 683-2356. Interest in methods and procedures in insurance accounting, systems, statistics. Provides reference services, publications. Services primarily for member and prospective member companies.

38052. International Chessology Club, P.O. Box 2066, Chapel Hill, NC 27707. Postal chess club that offers chess tourneys and competitions, sanctions chess events, promotes correspondence chess. Provides general reference services, conducts seminars and workshops, distributes publications, permits onsite reference. Services subject to fees, available to serious players only.

38054. Lollipop Power, P.O. Box 1171 (304-A Weaver St), Chapel Hill, NC 27514; (919) 929-4857. Nonprofit educational feminist collective that works to overcome sex role stereotypes in the lives of children. Sells publications.

38055. Marquat Memorial Library, Army Institute for Military AssiStance, Kennedy Hall, Room 140, Fort Bragg, NC 28307; general (919) 396-9222; reference, (919) 396-6386. Interest in psychological and unconventional warfare, civil affairs, military and social sciences, terrorism, military assistance, counterinsurgency, intl relations. Provides general reference services, makes interlibrary loans, permits onsite use of collections.

38056. Metz Owners Club Register, Seven Lakes, Box 2055, West End, NC 27376. Interest in history and specifications of Metz automobiles. Provides general reference services. Fees charged for copies of more than three pages, other services free.

38057. Microelectronics Center of North Carolina, Research Program Management Division, P.O. Box 12889 (3021 Cornwallis Rd), Research Triangle Park, NC 27709; (919) 248-1842. Nonprofit org that works to develop high-tech and modern electronics industry in N.C. Answers inquiries, conducts seminars and workshops, distributes publications, makes referrals. Fees charged for services.

38058. Minerals Research Laboratory, N.C. State Univ, 180 Coxe Ave, Asheville, NC 28801; (704) 253-0371. Interest in applied research, with emphasis on nonmetallic mineral beneficiation, including froth flotation, gravity, and magnetic, plus electrostatic separa-

tion; wet and dry grinding. Performs contractual projects for individual industries, with priority given to N.C. industries.

38059. Moravian Music Foundation, 20 Cascade Ave, Winston-Salem, NC 27107; (919) 725-0651. Interest in world Moravian musical activities, hymnology, 18th-Century music. Permits onsite use of collection by qualified research scholars and students (advance arrangements required). Copying facilities available.

38060. Mossbauer Effect Data Center, Univ of N.C., Asheville, NC 28814; (704) 258-6617. Sponsored by its users, center is interested in Mossbauer spectroscopy. Provides general reference services, analyzes data, distributes data compilations, makes direct and interlibrary loans, permits onsite use of collection. Services usually provided at minimal cost.

38061. Museum of Early Southern Decorative Arts, P.O. Box 10310 (924 South Main St), Winston-Salem, NC 27108; (919) 722-6148. Researches, exhibits decorative arts of the early South. Answers inquiries, provides advisory services, conducts seminars and workshops, makes loans, permits onsite use of files. Most services free to serious scholars, usually by appointment.

38062. Museum of the Cherokee Indian, P.O. Box 770-A, Cherokee, NC 28719; (704) 497-3481. Interest in culture of the Cherokee Indian, including lore, customs, games, and religion. Provides general reference services. Museum open to the public. Appointment required for access to archives.

38065. N.C. Science and Technology Research Center, P.O. Box 12235 (Davis Dr and Cornwallis Rd), Research Triangle Park, NC 27709; (919) 549-0671. Interest in application of science and technology to problems of industry, business, and govt; physical and social sciences; biosciences; engineering; business; education. Provides general reference services, conducts seminars, distributes publications. Services provided for a fee.

38066. N.C. State Museum of Natural History/Research and Collections Section, N.C. State Museum of Natural History, P.O. Box 27647 (102 North Salisbury St), Raleigh, NC 27611; (919) 733-7451. Interest in natural history and ecology in the Southeast, emphasizing N.C., including herpetology, ichthyology, mammalogy, ornithology, mineralogy, and invertebrate zoology. Provides general reference services, operates speakers bureau, permits onsite use of collections by, and lends materials to, qualified researchers.

38067. N.C. Wildlife Federation, P.O. Box 10626 (1033 Wade Ave, No. 126), Raleigh, NC 27605; (919) 833-1923. Nonprofit state federation interested in preservation, appreciation, restoration of wildlife, natural resources. Provides general reference services, conducts seminars, distributes publications, permits onsite reference. Services free, except publications and seminars.

38068. National Association of Hosiery Manufacturers, 447 South Sharon Amity Rd, Charlotte, NC 28211; (704) 365-0913. Natl trade assn representing interests of manufacturers of all types of men's, women's, and children's hosiery products in U.S. Provides general reference services for members and to others on a time-available basis. Pamphlets and brochures distributed on a limited basis.

38069. National Association of School Music Dealers, P.O. Box 1209 (513 Gillespie St), Fayetteville, NC 28302; (919) 483-9032. Represents businesses that service school music programs. Answers inquiries, conducts seminars and workshops, distributes newsletter, makes referrals. Services free, available to members.

38070. National Athletic Trainers' Association, 1001 East 4th St, Greenville, NC 27834; (919) 752-1725. Offers scholarships, grants. Interest in athletic trainers, rehabilitation of athletes, conditioning, diet, etc. Provides general reference services and consulting, conducts symposia, distributes publications. Services primarily for members.

38071. National Center for Catastrophic Sports Injury Research, 204 Fetzer, Univ of N.C., Chapel Hill, NC 27514; (919) 962-0017. Collects, analyzes data on sports injuries resulting in death or permanent severe functional disability to recommend rule changes, safe coaching and equipment. Prepares annual reports in football fatalities, permanent paralyzing injuries from football, and catastrophic injuries in all other sports.

38072. National Climatic Data Center, Natl Environmental Satellite, Data, and Information Service, Federal Bldg, Asheville, NC 28801; (704) 259-0682. Archives U.S. govt agencies' meteorological records; builds an intl data base through data acquisition programs; makes climatological data available. Distributes data publications and summaries. Most services performed on a reimbursable basis, available to any individual or private or governmental org.

38073. National Council on Black Aging, P.O. Box 8813, Durham, NC 27707; (919) 489-2563. Interest in gerontology, special problems of aging among minorities. Provides general reference services, consulting; conducts seminars, workshops; distributes publications. Fees charged for services.

38076. National Federation of Licensed Practical Nurses, P.O. Box 11038, Durham, NC 27703; (919) 596-9609. Professional org that offers encouragement and leadership to its members and helps secure recognition for LPNs within medical community. Focuses on public education and continuing education for members. Offers info on participating educational institutions and courses.

38077. National Independent Automobile Dealers Association, 3700 Natl Dr, Ste 208, Raleigh, NC 27612; (919) 781-2350. Interest in used car market, used car sales, related legislation and regulation. Answers inquiries, distributes publications, makes referrals. Magazine

available by subscription, brochure available for SASE. Other services free.

38079. National Institute of Environmental Health Sciences, P.O. Box 12233, Research Triangle Park, NC 27709; (919) 541-3345. Conducts basic research on interaction between humans and potentially toxic or harmful agents in their environment. Research is basis for preventive programs for environment-related diseases and for action by regulatory agencies. Gives grants and awards to research orgs.

38081. National Park Service/Cape Hatteras Group, Natl Park Service, Route 1, Box 675, Manteo, NC 27954; (919) 473-2111 ext 40. Interest in early colonization and settlement of coastal N.C., coastal history, aviation, coastal ecology, conservation. Answers inquiries, makes referrals, distributes publications on a limited basis.

38082. National Press Photographers Association, P.O. Box 1146, Durham, NC 27702; (919) 489-3700. Interest in photojournalism, news photography. Answers inquiries, conducts periodic seminars on a fee basis, rents slide/tape lectures.

38083. North American Youth Sport Institute, 4985 Oak Garden Dr, Kernersville, NC 27284; (919) 784-4926. Consulting institute interested in sports and recreation for children up to 18 years old. Provides general reference services, conducts seminars, workshops, and clinics, distributes publications. Services provided for a fee.

38084. Old Time Western Film Club, P.O. Box 142, Siler City, NC 27344; (919) 742-2664. Preserves "old time" western films, history. Provides general reference services, conducts seminars and film showings, distributes publication, permits onsite reference. Services free.

38085. Organization for Tropical Studies, P.O. Box DM, Duke Station (08 Old Chemistry Bldg, Duke Univ.), Durham, NC 27706; (919) 684-5774. Interest in graduate education and research in terrestrial biology, marine biology, geography, agriculture, forestry, and tropical ecology. Answers inquiries, permits onsite use of files by qualified research workers, graduate students, etc.

38086. Pearse Memorial Library, Duke Univ. Marine Laboratory, Beaufort, NC 28516; (919) 728-2111. Interest in oceanography; marine ecology, zoology, parasitology; physiological ecology; etc. Provides general reference services, conducts seminars, makes interlibrary loans, permits onsite use of collections. Services free to some users, at cost to others.

38087. Psychical Research Foundation, P.O. Box 3356, Chapel Hill, NC 27514; (919) 968-4956. Nonprofit org that conducts research in parapsychological matters using electrical engineering and psychophysiological labs at Duke Univ. Provides general reference services, distributes data compilations and publications.

Services free, except for publications; donations appreciated.

38088. Research Triangle Institute, P.O. Box 12194, Research Triangle Park, NC 27709; (919) 541-6000. Self-supporting, nonprofit contract research corp interested in numerous areas of research ranging from air and water pollution and waste processing to alcholism, drug abuse, and cancer chemotheraphy. Also interested in satellite data interpretation, solar cells, and radar systems. Conducts research on contract basis for federal, state, and local govt departments, public service orgs.

38089. Rural Advancement Fund of the National Sharecroppers Fund, 2124 Commonwealth Ave, Charlotte, NC 28205; (704) 334-3051. Interest in agricultural training for small farmers, skill training for rural people, rural development, genetic conservation. Provides general reference services, conducts seminars and workshops, distributes publication. Services free.

38090. Social Science Data Library, Institute for Research in Social Science, Univ. of N.C., Manning Hall, Room 10, Chapel Hill, NC 27514; (919) 966-3346. Library facility for printed and machine-readable data for the social sciences. Most data sets (with the exception of those data obtained through univ membership with other archives) made available to scholars or academic institutions outside UNC community. Services available on a cost basis.

38091. Southeast Fisheries Center/Beaufort Laboratory, Natl Marine Fisheries Service, NOAA, Beaufort, NC 28516; (919) 728-4595. Interest in Menhaden (population dynamics, catch forecasts, juvenile abundance, migrations, age, growth, reproduction); offshore bottom fisheries for reef fishes; estuarine and coastal ecosystems; etc. Provides general reference services, lends biological materials, permits onsite use of collections.

38092. Southern Growth Policies Board, P.O. Box 12293, Research Triangle Park, NC 27709; (919) 549-8167. Interstate board interested in regional economic growth policies, southern U.S. economy, environmental policies, management, etc. Provides general reference services, conducts seminars, distributes publications, permits onsite reference. Services free, except publications.

38093. Southerners for Economic Justice, P.O. Box 240, Durham, NC 27702; (919) 683-1361. Nonprofit org interested in workers' rights, labor issues, economic development in the South, racial issues, occupational health and safety. Provides general reference services, conducts workshops, distributes publication. Fee for some services.

38094. Summer and Casual Furniture Manufacturers Association, P.O. Box HP-7 (223 South Wrenn St), High Point, NC 27261; (919) 884-5000. Furniture manufacturers assn interested in legislative and nonproprietary data on summer and casual furniture industry.

Answers inquiries, distributes publications. Fees charged for services.

38095. Synergetics Society, 1825 North Lake Shore Dr, Chapel Hill, NC 27514; (919) 942-2994. Interest in application of tools, methods, techniques of synergetics to any area of conflict or potential conflict, prevention of nuclear war. Distributes pamphlets and other documents, makes referrals, provides consulting, conducts seminars. Promotes use of quality programs for internships and other forms of experiential education. Answers inquiries, conducuts seminars.

38096. TVIS Educational Services, 18 Dan St, Salisbury, NC 28144. Nonprofit org of radio telegraph operators interested in homemade crystal constance wave transceivers and antennas, morse code, etc. Answers inquiries when provided with SASE.

38099. Tobacco Growers' Information Committee, P.O. Box 12046, Cameron Village Station (Flue-Cured Stabilization Corp Bldg, 1306 Annapolis Dr, Ste 111), Raleigh, NC 27605; (919) 832-3766. Represents views of tobacco farmers on public policy issues and provides info on these subjects to tobacco farmers and others in tobacco economy. Provides general reference services.

38100. Tobacco Literature Service, P.O. Box 7111 (2314 DH Hill Library), Raleigh, NC 27695-7111; (919) 737-2836. Interest in tobacco, including chemical and physical properties, climatological factors, cultural practices, diseases, economics, marketing, production, policy, genetics and varieties, harvesting and curing, more. Provides general reference services primarily for onsite faculty and staff.

38101. Tobacco Research Laboratory, Agricultural Research Service, U.S.DA, Route 2, Box 16G, Oxford, NC 27565; (919) 693-5151. Interest in tobacco plant research, breeding and genetics, control of diseases, curing and harvesting techniques, tobacco production research. Answers inquiries, distributes publications, permits onsite use of collection. Services free, limited to professionals.

38102. Toxicology Testing and Research Program, Natl Toxicology Program, Technical Information and Scientific Evaluation Group MD-18-01, P.O. Box 12233, Research Triangle Park, NC 27709; (919) 541-3418. Interest in results from Natl Toxicology Program, testing chemicals for carcinogenesis, mutagenesis, teratogenesis, and toxicity. Answers inquiries.

38103. UNC Cancer Research Center, School of Medicine, Univ. of N.C., Lineberger Cancer Research Center 237H, Chapel Hill, NC 27514; (919) 966-3036. Conducts research in cancer, viral oncology, cancer cell biology, tumor immunology, carcinogenesis, biotechnology. Provides general reference services, conducts seminars and symposia, distributes publications. Services free, except laboratory work.

38104. Upholstered Furniture Action Council, P.O. Box 2436, High Point, NC 27261; (919) 885-5065. Furniture industry trade assn interested in upholstery research, upholstering materials and methods, fire resistant materials. Provides general reference services and consulting, conducts workshops, distributes publications. Services free, except bulk publications.

38105. Water Resources Research Institute, N.C. State Univ, 225 Page Hall, Box 7912, Raleigh, NC 27695-7912; (919) 737-2815. Interest in water resources. Provides general reference services and literature searches using Water Resources Scientific Info Center data base through onsite terminal.

38106. Women-In-Action for Prevention of Violence and Its Causes, P.O. Box 2185 (305 East Main St), Durham, NC 27702; (919) 682-1431. Interest in directional counseling, resource coordination, community education, problems involving shelter, utilities, food, clothing. Answers inquiries, makes referrals. Services free.

38107. World Data Center A: Meteorology and Nuclear Radiation, Natl Climatic Data Center, Federal Bldg, Asheville, NC 28801; (704) 259-0682. Interest in meteorological observations from ships and stations, including surface and upper air synoptic observations, ozone, atmospheric electricity and chemistry, solar and nuclear radiation. Answers inquiries, assists scientists in obtaining data, reproduces data for fee.

38108. Wright Brothers National Memorial, Natl Park Service, Route 1, Box 675 (Highway 158, Kill Devil Hills, NC), Manteo, NC 27954; (919) 441-7430. Interest in Wright Brothers Natl Memorial, Visitor Center, and First Flight area. Answers inquiries free, distributes informational brochures free on a limited basis.

North Dakota

39003. Dakota Resource Council, 29 7th Ave West, Dickinson, ND 58601; (701) 227-1851. Grass roots citizens org of farmers, small businessmen concerned with preservation of viable agriculture. Provides general reference services, conducts workshops, distributes publications. Most services free to members, at cost to others.

39004. Institute for Ecological Studies, Box 8278, Univ Station, Univ of N.D., Grand Forks, ND 58202; (701) 777-2851. Interest in aspects of ecology relating to environmental problems. Answers inquiries free, provides environmental impact analysis services at cost, provides copying services at cost, permits onsite reference.

39005. Ireland Research Laboratory, Univ of N.D. Medical School, Grand Forks, ND 58202; (701) 777-3937. Interest in glucose-6-phosphatase role in regulation of blood sugar gluconeogenesis, phospholipids, biosynthesis, amino acid transport, enzymes, metabolism, cancer, histochemistry. Provides general reference services, conducts research at cost.

39006. Man-in-the-Sea Project, Dept of Physiology, School of Medicine, Univ of N.D., Grand Forks, ND

58201; (701) 777-3923. Interest in hyperbaria, high pressure, oxygen toxicity, decompression. Provides general reference services and consulting, conducts seminars, permits onsite study. Seminars, workshops, consulting available to researchers and govt agencies for a fee.

39007. North Dakota Geological Society, c/o Frances S. Bleth, P.O. Box 82, Bismarck, ND 58501; (701) 258-1807. Interest in geologic, hydrologic, engineering, and petroleum studies in N.D. Answers inquiries, makes referrals for free, sells publications. Services available to professionals.

39008. North Dakota Historical Society, c/o Sheila Robinson, Secty, Coleharbor, ND 58531; (701) 442-5335. Interest in history of N.D. and the Northern Plains, including fur trade, early military activities, settlement, coal mining, Lewis and Clark expedition. Provides general reference services free.

39009. North Dakota Indian Affairs Commission, State Capitol, 1st Fl, Bismarck, ND 58505; (701) 224-2428. Administers State Indian Scholarship Program and State Indian Development Fund. Interest in tribal govts and Indian affairs. Provides general reference services, distributes publications, permits onsite study. Services free.

39010. North Dakota Wildlife Federation, P.O. Box 66, Erie, ND 58029; (701) 967-8581. Interest in wildlife conservation in N.D.; outdoor recreation, including hunting, fishing, and trapping; conservation education. Provides general reference services, conducts conferences, distributes publication. Services free, except publication and conferences.

39011. Northern Prairie Wildlife Research Center, U.S. Fish and Wildlife Service, P.O. Box 1747, Jamestown, ND 58401; (701) 252-5363. Interest in wildlife research and conservation, waterfowl habitat research, ecology of prairie wetlands, migratory bird habitats, game bird propagation, avian physiology, plant ecology. Makes interlibrary loans.

39012. State Archives and Historical Research Library, Heritage Center, Bismarck, ND 58505; (701) 224-2668. Interest in history of N.D., Dakota Territory, and Northern Great Plains. Provides general reference services and copying, makes interlibrary loans, permits onsite reference. Services free, except copying and census searches.

Ohio

40002. AEBG Technical Information Center, N-32, Bldg 700, General Electric Co., Cincinnati, OH 45215; (513) 243-4333. Interest in air-breathing propulsion systems and related technologies, aerodynamics, instrumentation and controls, etc. Makes interlibrary loans.

40003. APEC, Miami Valley Tower, Ste 2100, Dayton, OH 45402; (513) 228-2602. Provides computer application programs for mechanical design, electrical design, and energy simulation. Answers inquiries, conducts seminars, workshops, distributes publications.

40004. Abrasive Grain Association, 712 Lakewood Center North, Cleveland, OH 44107; (216) 226-7700. Interest in abrasive grain, aluminum oxide, silicon carbide, grinding materials. Answers brief inquiries, makes referrals.

40005. Academy of Sports Psychology International, 4795 Evanswood Dr, Columbus, OH 43229; (614) 846-2275. Interest in the role of psychology in sports and athletics. Provides general reference services, conducts seminars, distributes publications, permits onsite reference, at cost.

40006. Adventures in Movement for the Handicapped, 945 Danbury Rd, Dayton, OH 45420; (513) 294-4611. Helps handicapped persons through specialized movement education. Answers inquiries free, conducts workshops, distributes publications free, except brochure at cost.

40007. Aeronautical and Astronautical Research Laboratory, Dept of Aeronautical and Astronautical Engineering, Ohio State Univ, Univ Airport, 2300 W Case Rd, Columbus, OH 43220; (614) 422-1241. Laboratory interested in education, research in aerodynamics, gas dynamics, and combustion. Provides general reference services, consulting, conducts seminars. Services at cost to aerospace industries.

40008. Aerospace Structures Information and Analysis Center, Wright Aeronautical Laboratories/FIBRA, Wright-Patterson AFB, OH 45433; (513) 255-6688. Interest in aerospace structural design and analysis. Provides general reference services, consulting, permits onsite reference. Services free to govt agencies, contractors, not available to foreign govts.

40009. Agricultural Technical Institute, Ohio State Univ, Wooster, OH 44691; (216) 264-3911. Interest in animal husbandry, livestock, agricultural business, entomology, agronomy, food marketing, etc. Provides general reference services, conducts seminars, distributes publications. Services free, except seminars, and restricted.

40010. Air Force Institute of Technology School of Engineering, Wright-Patterson AFB, OH 45433; (513) 255-4372. Interest in aerospace engineering, electrical engineering, mathematics, mechanical engineering, nuclear engineering, systems, etc. Answers inquiries, provides advisory services. Services primarily for USAF, DoD agencies.

40011. Air Force, Wright Aeronautical Laboratories, Wright-Patterson AFB, OH 45433; (513) 255-5804. Interest in aircraft, materials, flight dynamics, avionics, early warning systems, aerospace systems, related fields. Answers technical inquiries, provides consulting services to govt agencies and contractors.

40012. Airborne Law Enforcement Association, 681 W 3rd Ave, Columbus, OH 43212; (614) 222-4656. Natl nonprofit org interested in safe utilization of fixed and rotary wing aircraft in law enforcement activities. Provides general reference services, conducts seminars, distributes publications. Services free to members, at cost to others.

40013. American Academy of Osteopathy, P.O. Box 750 (12 W Locust St), Newark, OH 43055; (614) 349-8701. Interest in clinical investigation, patient care utilizing osteopathic structural diagnosis and manipulative therapy, postdoctoral education for physicians. Answers inquiries, provides reference services to osteopathic physicians.

40014. American Association for the Study of Neoplastic Diseases, c/o Dr Robert H. Jackson, Pres, 10607 Miles Ave, Cleveland, OH 44105; (216) 341-4335. Interest in causation, diagnosis, prevention, treatment of neoplastic (tumorous) diseases, cancer chemotherapy, etc. Provides free general reference services, restricted to interested professionals.

40015. American Association of Physical Anthropologists, c/o Dr Frank E. Poirier, Secty-Treas, Ohio State Univ, Lord Hall, Dept of Anthropology, Columbus, OH 43210; (614) 422-9766. Interest in physical anthropology, human and nonhuman primate evolution, human variation. Answers inquiries, publishes materials, provides career pamphlet.

40016. American Carnival Glass Association, Box 273, Gnadenhutten, OH 44629; (614) 254-9446. Interest in collection and study of old carnival glass. Answers inquiries free, distributes publication.

40017. American Casting Association, c/o Cheryl and Jean Engle, Exec Secty, 7328 Maple Ave, Cincinnati, OH 45231; (513) 931-1204. Interest in promotion of angling, fly casting, and plug casting, regulation of competition, championships. Answers inquiries, provides education, instruction, distributes publications. Services free.

40018. American Ceramic Society, 65 Ceramic Dr, Columbus, OH 43214; (614) 268-8645. Interest in ceramics, glass, refractories, porcelain enamels, composites, whitewares, analytical, crystal, and colloid chemistry, etc. Provides limited reference services, publication duplications, makes interlibrary loans, permits onsite reference.

40019. American College of Podopediatrics, 10515 Carnegie Ave, Cleveland, OH 44106; (216) 231-3300. Interest in podiatric medicine, musculoskeletal pathomechanics, gait analysis, as applied to children. Provides general reference services, consulting, conducts seminars. Services to anyone; nonmembers subject to a fee.

40020. American Conference of Governmental Industrial Hygienists, c/o William D. Kelley, Exec Secty, Bldg D-5, 6500 Glenway Ave, Cincinnati, OH 45211; (513) 661-7881. Interest in industrial hygiene and occupational health, emphasizing air contaminants, industrial ventilation, air sampling instruments, and health services in small industries. Answers inquiries, makes referrals.

40021. American Flame Research Committee, c/o Abbott A. Putnam, Secty, Battelle-Columbus Laboratories, 505 King Ave, Columbus, OH 43201; (614) 424-4902. Interest in industrial combustion of solid, liquid, and gaseous fuels. Provides general reference services, conducts meetings open to the public for a fee; other services for members only.

40022. American Gourd Society, P.O. Box 274, Mount Gilead, OH 43338; (419) 946-3302. Interest in gourds, including cultivation, history, and uses as food and for display. Answers inquiries, provides free reference services, sells publications.

40023. American Guernsey Cattle Club, P.O. Box 27410 (2105-J S Hamilton Rd), Columbus, OH 43227; (614) 864-2409. Interest in registration of Guernsey cattle, care and maintenance of pedigree files. Provides general reference services, consulting, permits onsite reference. Services free.

40025. American Industrial Hygiene Association, 475 Wolf Ledges Parkway, Akron, OH 44311; (216) 762-7294. Promotes study and control of environmental factors affecting the health of workers. Publishes materials, conducts training courses and workshops.

40026. American Institute of Plant Engineers, 3975 Erie Ave, Cincinnati, OH 45208; (513) 561-6000. Promotes engineering practice and management in plant facilities in public and private sectors. Provides general reference services, conducts seminars, distributes publications. Inquiries answered free, other services at cost.

40027. American Iron Ore Association, 514 Bulkley Bldg, 1501 Euclid Ave, Cleveland, OH 44115; (216) 241-8261. Interest in iron ore statistics, lake shipments to Great Lakes ports, iron and steel plants in U.S. and Canada, etc. Distributes publications, makes referrals. Services to nonmembers limited.

40028. American Ivy Society, P.O. Box 520 (c/o Cox Arboretum, 6733 Springboro Pike), W Carrollton, OH 45449. Interest in Ivy Hedera cultivation, description, and nomenclature, testing. Answers inquiries, provides ivy identification services, conducts convention.

40029. American Jewish Periodical Center, 3101 Clifton Ave, Cincinnati, OH 45220; (513) 221-1875. Collects Jewish-interest publications, currently microfilming all Jewish-interest periodicals, newspapers published in U.S., Canada, Latin America from 1823 to 1925, and selected publications since 1925. Lends microfilm, permits onsite use of collection, makes referrals.

40030. American Leather Chemists Association, Campus Station, Univ of Cincinnati, Cincinnati, OH 45221-0014; (513) 475-2707. Interest in chemistry, technology of skin, hide, leather, methods of sampling and ana-

lyzing leather and tanning materials. Answers inquiries, provides data base searches for a fee.

40031. American Maltese Association, c/o Marge Stuber, Secty, 886 W Spring St, Lima, OH 45805; (419) 222-7616. Interest in breeding, showing Maltese dogs, promoting ethical conduct of breeders and owners. Provides general reference services, distributes publications. Services free, except some publications.

40032. American Metal Stamping Association, 2707 Chardon Rd, Richmond Heights, OH 44143; (216) 585-8800. Interest in metal stamping, metal spinning, metal fabricating, washers, related areas. Answers inquiries, makes referrals for anyone, provides consulting to members only.

40033. American Motorcyclist Association, P.O. Box 6114 (33 Collview Ave), Westerville, OH 43081-6114; (614) 891-2425. Involved in lobbying, legislative work for motorcyclists, sanctions races, other events. Provides reference services, conducts workshops, distributes publications, permits onsite reference. Services free to members, at cost to others.

40034. American Orff-Schulwerk Association, c/o Dept of Music, Cleveland State Univ, Cleveland, OH 44115; (216) 543-5366. Promotes music education philosophy of Carl Orff. Provides general reference services, conducts workshops, sells publications, materials, permits onsite reference. Info free, most workshops open; other services for members only.

40035. American Registry of Diagnostic Medical Sonographers, 2810 Burnet Ave, Ste N, Cincinnati, OH 45219; (513) 281-8860. Interest in diagnostic medical sonography. Provides general reference services, distributes brochure free. Examinations of eligible candidates for a fee.

40036. American School Health Association, P.O. Box 708 (1521 S Water St), Kent, OH 44240; (216) 678-1601. Promotes comprehensive school health programs, health services, health instruction. Answers inquiries, provides consulting, sells publications, conducts seminars, makes referrals.

40038. American Scientific Glassblowers Society, 1507 Hagley Rd, Toledo, OH 43612; (419) 476-5478. Interest in scientific glassblowing, and related apparatus, equipment, materials. Answers inquiries, makes referrals.

40039. American Society for Nondestructive Testing, Caller No 28518, 4153 Arlingate Plaza, Columbus, OH 43228-0518; (614) 274-6003. Interest in applications, research, techniques for nondestructive testing of metals, ceramics, wood, plastics, composites, and components. Provides general reference services, duplications for a fee, sells books and films, permits onsite reference.

40040. American Society of Business Press Editors, 4196 Porter Rd, N Olmsted, OH 44070; (216) 734-9522. Interest in professional development of business press editorial personnel, trade magazines. Answers inquiries, conducts seminars, workshops, makes referrals. Fees charged for seminars, workshops, other services free.

40041. American Society of Hematology, c/o Secty, Basic Science Research, IDR 729, Children's Hospital Research Foundation, Elland and Bethesda Aves., Cincinnati, OH 45229. Interest in hematology, continuing education. Conducts meetings, prepares courses, provides reproduction services, distributes publication, lends materials. Services for a fee to professionals, students.

40042. American Society of Sanitary Engineering, P.O. Box 40362, Bay Village, OH 44140; (216) 835-3040. Interest in all aspects of sanitary engineering, sewage disposal, health as related to sanitation. Answers inquiries, makes referrals, provides reference services.

40043. Andrew W. Breidenbach Environmental Research Center, EPA, Cincinnati, OH 45268; (513) 684-7707 Interest in solid wastes, water hygiene, water pollution control, waste water treatment, toxic substances, related training. Provides general reference services, interlibrary loans, permits onsite use of collection.

40044. Applied Physiology Research Laboratory, Kent State Univ, Kent, OH 44240; (216) 672-2859. Interest in applied human physiology, effects of exercise, physical fitness. Answers inquiries, provides reference and consulting services.

40045. Archives of the History of American Psychology, c/o John A. Popplestone, Dir, Univ of Akron, Akron, OH 44325; (216) 375-7285. Interest in history of American psychology. Provides general reference services, conducts seminars, distributes publications, permits onsite reference. Services for advanced scholars at cost; some exemptions granted.

40046. Area Economics Information Center, James M. Jennings Assocs, P.O. Box 21398, Columbus, OH 43221; (614) 488-2643. Interest in regional economics, urban and regional planning, industrial development, population, etc. Provides general reference services, data bank assistance, legislative, business info, conducts seminars, training courses. Services at cost.

40047. Ashland Chemical Co. Technical Information Center, P.O. Box 2219, Columbus, OH 43216; (614) 889-3281. Interest in foundry binders, petrochemicals, specialty resins, polymers, organic chemistry. Makes interlibrary loans, permits onsite use of collections by appointment. Some publications restricted.

40048. Association for Systems Management, 24587 Bagley Rd, Cleveland, OH 44138; (216) 243-6900. Interest in management info systems, systems engineering, education, and technology. Answers inquiries, makes referrals to members, provides education guidance to universities, corporate training departments.

40049. Association of Advertising Lawyers, 5122 Heatherdowns Blvd, Toledo, OH 43614; (419) 385-9661. Promotes advertising and marketing for lawyers. Provides general reference services, conducts seminars. Services free; specific legal advice not offered.

40050. Association of African Studies Programs, c/o Bob J. Walter, Chair, 56 E Union, Athens, OH 45701; (614) 594-5542. Assn interested in coordination of teaching and research on Africa in U.S. univs, exchange programs, grants. Answers inquiries, makes referrals, usually free.

40051. Association of Railroad Advertising and Marketing, c/o Joe D. Singer, 3706 Palmerston Rd, Shaker Heights, OH 44122; (216) 751-9673. Interest in promotion of the railroad industry, improving communications in railroad industry advertising and marketing. Answers technical inquiries, makes referrals.

40052. Association of Theological Schools, P.O. Box 130, Vandalia, OH 45377; (513) 898-4654. Interest in graduate professional education in theology and for ministry. Answers inquiries free, provides advisory or consulting services for a fee.

40053. Aviation Safety Institute, P.O. Box 304, Worthington, OH 43085-0304; (614) 885-4242. Interest in aviation accident prevention, hazard identification, survival techniques, training. Provides general reference services, consulting, conducts seminars, distributes publications, permits onsite study. Services for a fee.

40054. Barium and Chemicals, P.O. Box 218 (County Rd 44), Steubenville, OH 43952; (614) 282-9776. Interest in chemical technology on barium, strontium, and other alkaline earth chemicals. Permits onsite reference upon approval of manager.

40055. Battelle Memorial Institute, Copper Data Center, Columbus Laboratories, 505 King Ave, Columbus, OH 43201; (614) 424-7679. Provides technical data and info on copper, its alloys and compounds. Answers inquiries, provides literature searches, data bulletins free. Member companies have direct access to data base; nonmember online searching possible.

40056. Battelle Memorial Institute, Technical Information Center, Project Management Division, 505 King Ave, Columbus, OH 43201; (614) 424-7697. Provides info, data on nuclear, other hazardous waste management, environmental sciences, mining engineering, etc. Answers inquiries, distributes technical reports.

40057. Bell & Howell Co., Micro Photo Division, Old Mansfield Rd, Wooster, OH 44691; (216) 264-6666. Interest in micropublishing and indexing of newspapers, periodicals, telephone directories, special and scholarly collections, 9-digit zip code info. Provides indexing and microform services for a fee, sells publications, other support products.

40058. Biomedical Engineering Center, Ohio State Univ, 2015 Neil Ave, Columbus, OH 43210; (614) 422-6018.

Interest in biomedical engineering, biomedical instrumentation, clinical engineering, rehabilitation systems. Provides general reference services, conducts seminars. Services free. Use of research facilities available by contract.

40059. Botany Herbarium, Dept of Biological Sciences, Univ of Cincinnati, 1601 Crosley Tower, Cincinnati, OH 45221; (513) 475-3741. Interest in vascular plants of Cincinnati area, lichens and mosses of Ohio and Kentucky, hepaticae of South America, mosses of North America. Makes limited loans, permits onsite use of collection. All services require permission of curator.

40060. Bowling Green Productivity and Gainsharing Institute, Bowling Green State Univ, 369 B.A. Bldg, Bowling Green, OH 43403; (419) 372-2807. Institute interested in productivity gainsharing and measurement, evaluation. Provides general reference services, conducts seminars, distributes publications, permits onsite reference. Fee for some services.

40061. Brotherhood of Locomotive Engineers, 1365 Ontario St, Cleveland, OH 44114; (216) 241-2630. Interest in railroad labor relations in the U.S. and Canada, including wages and working conditions, occupational safety and health, labor education, and occupational training. Answers inquiries.

40062. Brush Wellman Inc. Technical Library, 17876 St Clair Ave, Cleveland, OH 44110; (216) 486-4200. Interest in beryllium metallurgy, beryllium alloys, ceramics, berylliosis, prevention of beryllium toxicity. Services primarily for in-house use, but library will cooperate with qualified nonprofit orgs. No outside loans made.

40063. Canvasback Society, P.O. Box 101, Gates Mills, OH 44040; (216) 623-2040. Nonprofit society interested in Canvasback duck, wildlife preservation, management, habitat, and refuges. Answers inquiries, provides free reference services, makes library loans.

40065. Cave Research Foundation, c/o Roger E. McClure, Treas, 4700 Amberwood Dr, Dayton, OH 45424; (513) 257-3155, 233-3561. Nonprofit foundation that performs field work in cave systems, promotes karst research. Answers inquiries, provides consulting services, sells publications. Services free.

40066. Cemented Carbide Producers Association, 712 Lakewood Center North, Cleveland, OH 44107; (216) 226-7700. Interest in cemented tungsten carbide. Answers inquiries, makes referrals.

40067. Center for Archival Collections, Bowling Green State Univ Library, 5th Fl., Bowling Green, OH 43403; (419) 372-2411. Center interested in northwest Ohio history, geography, sociology, political science, etc. Provides general reference services, conducts research, permits onsite study. Services free, except reproductions.

40068. Center for Community Education, Kent State Univ, 405 White Hall, Kent, OH 44242; (216) 672-2294. Cen-

ter provides degree programs in administration of community education. Interest in citizen involvement, adult education, interagency collaboration. Provides general reference services, consulting, conducts seminars.

40069. Center for Environmental Research Information, Environmental Protection Agency, 26 W St Clair St, Cincinnati, OH 45268; (513) 684-7562. Interest in R&D on environmental quality, pollution control technology, toxic substances control. Refers inquiries to appropriate sources of info, distributes technical reports.

40070. Center for Human Resource Research, Ohio State Univ, 650 Ackerman Rd, Ste A, Columbus, OH 43202; (614) 422-7337. Interest in age and employment, careers, labor economics, manpower studies, working women. Provides general reference services, conducts seminars, distributes publications, permits onsite study. Services at cost.

40071. Center for Medieval and Renaissance Studies, Coll of Humanities, Ohio State Univ, 322 Dulles Hall, 230 W 17th St, Columbus, OH 43210; (614) 422-7495. Center interested in interdisciplinary studies of the Middle Ages and the Renaissance. Provides general reference services, consulting, conducts workshops, distributes publications. Services free, primarily for OSU community.

40072. Center for Nursing Research, School of Nursing, Ohio State Univ, 1585 Neil Ave, Columbus, OH 43210; (614) 422-3943. Center promotes nursing research, women's health research, etc. Provides general reference services, conducts seminars, distributes publications, permits onsite study. Services free, except copying.

40073. Center for Robotics Research, Dept of Mechanical and Industrial Engineering, Univ of Cincinnati, Mail Stop 72 (569B Baldwin Hall), Cincinnati, OH 45221; (513) 475-4862, 475-5067. Interest in research and education in robotics, computer programming, mechanical engineering. Provides general reference services (primarily for members), distributes publications.

40074. Center for Statistical Consulting, Ohio State Univ, 1958 Neil Ave, Columbus, OH 43210; (614) 422-0294. Center interested in data analysis, statistical consulting, computations, design of experimental and survey studies. Answers inquiries, provides consulting. Fees vary.

40075. Center for Unified Science Education, Capital Univ, 231 Science Hall, Columbus, OH 43209; (614) 236-6816. Interest in unified science education curriculum development, research, teaching methods. Provides general reference services, consulting, permits onsite reference. Services to interested parties; token fees may be charged.

40076. Center for the Study of Popular Culture, Bowling Green State Univ, Bowling Green, OH 43403; (419) 372-2981. Interest in popular culture of all kinds, pop music and writers. Provides general reference services, conducts seminars, distributes publications, permits free onsite reference. Services at cost.

40077. Certified Ballast Manufacturers Association, 1422 Euclid Ave, Ste 772, Cleveland, OH 44115; (216) 241-0711. Interest in ballasts for fluorescent lighting, testing of ballasts, standards and specifications. Answers inquiries, publishes materials.

40078. Charles F. Kettering Foundation Research Laboratory, 150 E S Coll St, Yellow Springs, OH 45387; (513) 767-7271. Interest in photosynthesis, nitrogen fixation, cell differentiation, instrumentation, related aspects of biochemistry, plant physiology, etc. Answers inquiries, permits onsite use of literature collection.

40079. Chemical Abstracts Service, P.O. Box 3012, Columbus, OH 43210; (614) 421-3600. Interest in all aspects of chemistry and chemical engineering. Publishes materials available by subscription, offers many online services; photocopies, or loans for a fee. Library not open to the public, but will answer inquiries, make referrals.

40080. Chemical Data Center, 3620 N High St, Columbus, OH 43214; (614) 261-7101. Interest in chemicals, chemical nomenclature, patents, safety and hazards, toxicity, and substructure. Performs computer online searches, provides info, consulting, reference services. Fees charged.

40081. Chemineer, P.O. Box 1123 (45 S Main St), Dayton, OH 45401; (513) 229-7000. Interest in fluid agitation, mixing, impellers, corrosion-resistant process equipment. Answers inquiries, provides reference, consulting services free to potential clients, for a fee to others, permits onsite reference.

40082. Children's Hospital Research Foundation, Elland and Bethesda Aves, Cincinnati, OH 45229; (513) 559-4300. Interest in medicine, pediatrics, immunology, metabolic diseases, neurology, laboratory animal science. Provides general reference services to personnel of Research Foundation, Children's Hospital and Institute for Developmental Research.

40083. Cincinnati Zoo Research C3400 Vine St, Cincinnati, OH 45220; (513) 281-4701. Research federation interested in animal reproduction, breeding, exotic animals. Provides general reference services, conducts seminars, permits onsite reference. Services free, primarily for scientific community.

40084. Citizenship Development and Global Education Program, Mershon Center, Ohio State Univ, 199 W 10th Ave, Columbus, OH 43201; (614) 422-1681. Program interested in development of global perspectives education, adult education, social studies curriculum. Answers inquiries, provides consulting services, conducts seminars. Fee for some services.

40085. Clearinghouse for Occupational Safety and Health Information, 4676 Columbia Parkway, Cincinnati, OH 45226; (513) 841-4287. Clearinghouse provides technical info support for occupational safety and health

research programs. Provides general reference services, interlibrary loans, database searches.

40086. Cleveland Clinic Foundation Department of Artificial Organs, 2020 E 93rd St, Cleveland, OH 44106; (216) 444-2470. Department interested in artificial organs, blood oxygenators, biocompatible material research, etc. Answers inquiries, conducts training classes, makes referrals, permits onsite reference.

40087. Collaborating Center for the Biological Control of Vectors of Human Diseases, c/o Dept of Entomology, Ohio State Univ, 1735 Neil Ave, Columbus, OH 43210; (614) 422-1085. Center interested in invertebrate vectors of human diseases, biological agents, infectious microorganisms, parasites, predators, biological control. Provides free general reference services, conducts short courses.

40088. Community Service, P.O. Box 243 (114 E Whiteman St), Yellow Springs, OH 45387; (513) 767-2161. Center interested in community development, planning and govt, community service, industries, etc. Permits onsite reference, sells publications, answers inquiries, provides consulting.

40089. Computer Graphics Research Group, Ohio State Univ, 1501 Neil Ave, Columbus, OH 43201; (614) 422-3416. Research laboratory for computer-generated digital imagery. Answers inquiries, provides consulting, makes referrals. Services limited, not in great volume.

40090. Concerned Relatives of Nursing Home Patients, P.O. Box 18820, Cleveland, OH 44118; (216) 321-4499. Promotes dignity and comfort for nursing home patients. Monitors nursing homes, tracks legislation, provides info. Membership restricted to those with relatives, friends in homes.

40091. Consortium of University Film Centers, c/o Audio Visual Services, Kent State Univ, Kent, OH 44242; (216) 672-3456. Nonprofit corp promotes use of film, improvements in film quality, distribution, and availability. Provides free general reference services, sells publications.

40092. Contact Lens Manufacturers Association, P.O. Box 1009, One Avelon Road, Mount Vernon, OH 43050; (800) 343-5367. Trade assn regulates standards for contact lens manufacturers. Holds periodic meetings, provides info, sponsors research, publishes directory, other member services.

40093. Coronary Club, 3659 Green Road, Room 200, Cleveland, OH 44122; (216) 292-7120. Nonprofit club provides info on preventing heart attacks and adjusting to life with a heart condition. Provides info reports, conducts meetings, for paid-up members.

40094. Cox Heart Institute, Wright State Univ School of Medicine, 3525 Southern Blvd, Dayton, OH 45429; (513) 299-7204. Interest in prevention, treatment, and mechanism of coronary artery disease, heart failure, hypertension, bioengineering. Answers inquiries, provides consulting services.

40095. Custom Roll Forming Institute, 522 Westgate Tower, Cleveland, OH 44116; (216) 333-8848. Interest in custom roll-formed shapes. Answers inquiries, provides free advisory services.

40096. DU-IT Control Systems Group, 8765 Township Rd, No 513, Shreve, OH 44676; (216) 567-2906. Corp interested in specialized wheelchairs, rehabilitation aids for physically handicapped persons. Provides general reference services, evaluations, conducts seminars, workshops. Extensive services for a fee.

40097. Decorative Laminate Products Association, c/o Patrick Weaver, Exec Dir, Hulman Bldg, 20th Floor, 120 W 2nd St, Dayton, OH 45402; (513) 228-1041. Natl assn interested in high/low-pressure, decorative, laminate-surfaced products. Provides general reference services, free to members, at a charge to others. Permits limited use of resources by written request for a fee.

40098. Department of Dairy Science, Ohio State Univ, 625 Stadium Dr, Columbus, OH 43210; (614) 422-6851. Interest in dairy science, biology, physiology, animal breeding, immunogenetics, etc. Answers inquiries, conducts seminars, distributes publications. Services free.

40099. Department of Pathology and Laboratory Medicine, Univ of Cincinnati Medical Center, 231 Bethesda Ave, Cincinnati, OH 45267; (513) 872-4542, 872-4543. Interest in necropsy and surgical pathology, laboratory medicine, immunopathology, pathology educational. Answers inquiries, provides consulting services.

40100. Department of Pharmacology, Coll of Medicine, Ohio State Univ, 5086 Graves Hall, 333 W 10th Ave, Columbus, OH 43210; (614) 422-8608. Interest in various disciplines in pharmacology, prostaglandins, cyclicnucleotides, anesthetics, etc. Answers inquiries, provides consulting, laboratory services to medical personnel, police, coroner employees for negotiated fee.

40101. Diamond Wheel Manufacturers Institute, 712 Lakewood Center North, Cleveland, OH 44107; (216) 226-7700. Interest in diamond wheels for grinding and cutting. Answers inquiries, makes referrals.

40102. Diamonite Products Manufacturing Inc., 453 W McConkey St, Shreve, OH 44676; (216) 567-2145. Interest in aluminum oxide and high alumina ceramics, electronic ceramic components, insulators, dielectric materials, etc. Answers inquiries, makes referrals, provides consulting, permits onsite study of nonproprietary info.

40103. Directorate of Engineering Standardization, Defense Electronics Supply Center, 1507 Wilmington Pike, Dayton, OH 45444; (513) 296-6531. Engineering org interested in all aspects of electronic parts standardization, provides support services for the military, defense agencies, contractors. Answers inquiries, provides consulting services.

40104. Drinking Water Research Division, Municipal Environmental Research Laboratory, EPA, Cincinnati, OH 45268; (513) 684-7201. Interest in water supply research, control technology research related to standards for drinking water. Answers inquiries. Services primarily for health departments, water utilities, consulting engineers.

40105. ERIC Clearinghouse for Science, Mathematics, and Environmental Education, Ohio State Univ, 1200 Chambers Rd, Columbus, OH 43212; (614) 422-6717. Clearinghouse collects, disseminates materials related to science, mathematics, and environmental education. Provides limited general reference services, sells publications.

40106. Educational Research Council of America, Rockefeller Bldg, Room 880, Cleveland, OH 44113; (216) 696-8222. Nonprofit R&D center interested in curriculum development in career education and social science. Provides consulting services, conducts workshops, conferences, and seminars. Services to school districts for honorarium plus expenses.

40107. Emery Industries Research Library, Emery Industries, 4900 Este Ave, Cincinnati, OH 45232; (513) 482-2157. Corp interested in chemical technology of fats, oils, fatty acids, organic chemistry, chemical engineering, testing methods, patents. Library provides reproduction services, permits onsite reference by arrangement.

40108. Entrepreneurship Institute, 3592 Corporate Dr, Ste 100, Columbus, OH 43229; (614) 895-1153. Institute assists communities in creating support networks for entrepreneurs, new businesses. Provides general reference services for a fee, consulting, conducts seminars, distributes publications.

40109. Environmental Monitoring and Support Laboratory, EPA, 3411 Church St, Newtown, OH 45244; (513) 684-8601. Interest in fish toxicology, water quality criteria, effects of effluents on aquatic life, freshwater ecosystems. Answers inquiries, distributes reprints.

40110. Environmental Quality Instructional Resources Center, Ohio State Univ, 1200 Chambers Rd, Room 310, Columbus, OH 43212; (614) 422-6717. Interest in water treatment, wastewater treatment, water quality, education, training. Provides general reference services, consulting, conducts seminars, distributes publications, permits onsite reference. Services at cost.

40111. Facing Tile Institute, Box 8880, Canton, OH 44711; (216) 488-1211. Interest in ceramic glazed brick and structural facing tile. Provides free (unless extensive) general reference services, conducts seminars, distributes publications, permits onsite reference.

40112. Fels Research Institute for the Study of Human Development, School of Medicine, Wright State Univ, Yellow Springs, OH 45387; (513) 767-7324. Interest in growth, genetics, developmental psychology, endo-crinology. Answers inquiries, provides advisory services in certain areas for a fee.

40113. Forging Industry Association, 55 Public Square, Cleveland, OH 44113; (216) 781-6260. Interest in forging industry, forgings, dies, industrial safety. Provides general reference services, conducts seminars, distributes publication. Services primarily for members, some at cost.

40114. Franz Theodore Stone Laboratory and Center for Lake Erie Area Research and Ohio Sea Grant Program, Ohio State Univ, 484 W 12th Ave, Columbus, OH 43210; (614) 422-8949. Interest in zoology, ichthyology, botany, coastal engineering, geology, resource economics, large lakes worldwide. Provides general reference services, limited consulting, identifies specimens. Onsite reference permitted only by consent of director.

40115. Frederick C. Crawford Auto-Aviation Museum, Western Reserve Historical Society, 10825 E Blvd, Cleveland, OH 44106; (216) 721-5722. Interest in transportation vehicles, emphasis on Cleveland-built cars, early aircraft, engines. Provides general reference services, reproduction. Services free, except reproductions and museum admission.

40116. Garden Forum of the Greater Youngstown Area, 123 McKinley Ave, Youngstown, OH 44509; (216) 792-7961. Interest in horticultural education, conservation, gardening, flower arranging. Provides general reference services, permits onsite reference, conducts classes, workshops, sells materials. Services free, except workshops.

40117. GenCorp Information Center, Research Division, 2990 Gilchrist Rd, Akron, OH 44305; (216) 798-2818. Interest in natural and synthetic rubber, plastics, textiles, chemistry, automotive engineering. Answers inquiries, provides database-search services, makes interlibrary loans, makes referrals.

40118. General Electric Lighting Institute, Nela Park, E Cleveland, OH 44112; (216) 266-2621. Interest in light sources, lighting applications, research, education. Answers inquiries, makes referrals, provides consulting, provides info on lighting courses and conferences.

40119. Goodyear Aerospace Corp., Dir Public Relations, 1210 Massillon Rd, Akron, OH 44315; (216) 796-2121, 796-3632. Interest in undersea warfare systems, tactical ordnance systems, radar systems, reconnaissance equipment, guidance systems, various technical and safety systems. Answers brief inquiries free, provides literature citations, makes interlibrary loans.

40120. Goodyear Atomic Corp. Technical Library, P.O. Box 628, Piketon, OH 45661; (614) 289-2331. Interest in chemistry, radiation, mathematics, nuclear physics, engineering, uranium enrichment process technology, metallurgy, industrial safety. Makes interlibrary loans. Site visits require security clearance.

40121. Goodyear Research Information Center, 142 Goodyear Blvd, Akron, OH 44316; (216) 796-3007. Interest in rubber, plastics, synthetic fibers, chemistry, physics, management, data processing, nuclear and environmental science. Answers inquiries, makes referrals, lends materials, permits onsite use of collection. Services primarily for staff.

40122. Great Lakes Historical Society, 480 Main St, Vermilion, OH 44089; (216) 967-3467. Society interested in history of Great Lakes, commerce, shipping, shipwrecks, lighthouses, yachting. Provides reference services, distributes publications, permits onsite study. Services require membership fee.

40123. Great Lakes Tomorrow, P.O. Box 1935 (6789 Brown St, Tiffany Hall), Hiram, OH 44234; (216) 569-7015. Nonprofit org that encourages public participation in decisions affecting Great Lakes. Provides general reference services, conducts seminars, permits onsite reference. Some services under contract, others free.

40124. Grinding Wheel Institute, 712 Lakewood Center, North, 14600 Detroit Ave, Cleveland, OH 44107; (216) 226-7700. Interest in grinding wheel, abrasives. Answers inquiries, makes referrals.

40125. Index to Authors in Bryophyta and Index to Bryophyte Literature of Latin America, c/o Dr Margaret Fulford, Prof. of Botany, Ret., Univ of Cincinnati, Cincinnati, OH 45221; (513) 475-3741. Interest in bryophyta, hepatica of Latin America. Answers brief inquiries free, permits onsite reference by special arrangement.

40126. Industrial Fasteners Institute, 1505 E Ohio Bldg, 1717 E 9th St, Cleveland, OH 44114; (216) 241-1482. Institute interested in mechanical fasteners, fastener technology and research. Provides general reference services, conducts seminars, distributes publications, data. Services free or at cost.

40128. Institute for Applied Interdisciplinary Research, Univ of Cincinnati, U.C. Mail Location 72, Cincinnati, OH 45221-0072; (513) 475-6131. Institute conducts applied research in crash-victim simulation, ergonomics, modeling, dynamics, robotics, accident reconstruction. Provides general reference services, conducts seminars, analyzes data. Services at cost.

40129. Institute for Development of Educational Activities, 259 Regency Ridge, Dayton, OH 45459; (513) 434-6969. Interest in primary and secondary education, learning problems, teaching, school administration. Conducts seminars and workshops, distributes publications, permits onsite use of collection. Services at cost.

40130. Institute for Environmental Education, 8911 Euclid Ave, Cleveland, OH 44106; (216) 791-1775. Nonprofit org interested in environmental, economic, energy education, emphasizing on-the-job internships for educators. Conducts training workshops, courses, provides support materials, evaluates curriculum. Services for a fee.

40131. Institute for Futures Studies and Research, Univ of Akron, 105 Fir Hill, Room 318, Akron, OH 44304; (216) 375-7887. Interest in creativity and innovation, regional and industrial change, urban futures. Provides general reference services, consulting, conducts seminars, distributes publications. Most services for a fee.

40132. Institute of Polar Studies, Ohio State Univ, 125 S Oval Mall, Columbus, OH 43210; (614) 422-6531. Research institute interested in polar regions, glaciology-geophysics, bedrock geology, glacial geology, climatology, etc. Provides general reference services, consulting, conducts seminars, permits onsite reference, distributes reports; fees may be charged for extensive services.

40133. Intermuseum Conservation Association, Allen Art Bldg, Oberlin Coll, Oberlin, OH 44074; (216) 775-7331. Interest in examination and treatment of works of art, primarily paintings, preservation of art. Answers inquiries, provides consulting, pigment analyses, conducts seminars, makes referrals. Services for member museums and public nonprofit institutions.

40134. International Anesthesia Research Society, 3645 Warrensville Center Rd, Cleveland, OH 44122; (216) 295-1124. Interest in medical practice, research in anesthesiology, analgesia. Provides general reference services, conducts seminars, distributes publications. Services primarily for anesthesiologists.

40135. International Association of Printing House Craftsmen, c/o John A. Davies, Exec V.P., 7599 Kenwood Rd, Cincinnati, OH 45236; (513) 891-0611. Interest in education of management personnel in graphic arts industry. Answers inquiries, conducts seminars, makes referrals.

40136. International Association of Quality Circles, 801-B W 8th St, Ste 301, Cincinnati, OH 45203; (513) 381-1959. Interest in quality circle concept where management and employees work to improve quality of both product and worklife. Provides general reference services, conducts seminars, distributes publications. Fee for some services.

40137. International Chemical Workers Union, ICWU Bldg, 1655 W Market St, Akron, OH 44313; (216) 867-2444. AFL-CIO affiliate interested in labor relations in chemical industry, labor legislation, labor unions. Answers inquiries, makes referrals. Extensive services for members only.

40138. International Cystic Fibrosis Association, 3567 E 49th St, Cleveland, OH 44105; (216) 271-1100. Provides research, support services on prevention, treatment, and cure of cystic fibrosis. Provides general reference services, social support, holds meetings.

40139. International Myomassethics Federation, 196 W Main St, Brewster, OH 44613; (216) 767-3297. Interest in therapeutic massage, nutrition, exercise. Provides general reference services, conducts seminars, distributes publication. Services free to members; others charged.

40140. International Naval Research Organization, 1729 Lois Ct, Toledo, OH 43613; (419) 472-1331. Interest in historical, technical studies of naval ships from all periods and nations. Provides general reference services, distributes publication, primarily for members.

40141. International Thespian Society, 3368 Central Parkway, Cincinnati, OH 45225-2392; (513) 559-1996. Promotes standards of excellence in theatre arts, interest in theatre arts in secondary schools. Answers inquiries, provides data, distributes pamphlets. Reference services, loans for members.

40142. Investment Recovery Association, c/o Mr. Robert H. Ecker, Exec Dir, 712 Lakewood Center North, 14600 Detroit Ave, Cleveland, OH 44107; (216) 226-7700. Assn interested in philosophy, methods, and procedures for the reuse or sale of a firm's surplus machinery, equipment. Provides general reference services, consulting, conducts seminars. Services, except seminars, usually restricted to members.

40143. James Leffel and Co., 426 East St, Springfield, OH 45501; (513) 323-6431. Corp manufactures, repairs hydraulic turbines. Provides free general info services, consulting, develops hydroelectric generating systems and turbines.

40144. Jewish Hospital of Cincinnati Medical Center, Cincinnati, OH 45229; (513) 569-2000. Interest in laser applications in biology and medicine, laser surgery. Answers inquiries, provides consulting. Services free to patients, scientists, for fees to industry. Fees charged for laser surgery.

40145. John Carroll University Seismological Observatory, N Park and Miramar Ave, Univ Heights, Cleveland, OH 44118; (216) 397-4361. Interest in seismology, solid earth geophysics, seismic-parameters, volcanology. Answers inquiries, makes referrals, interlibrary loans, lends data to authorized agencies, scientists.

40146. John G. White Collection of Folklore, Orientalia and Chess, Cleveland Public Library, Planning and Research, 325 Superior Ave, Cleveland, OH 44114-1271; (216) 623-2818. Collection of Middle Eastern, Oriental, African folklore, anthropology, religion, literature, history, archaeology, etc. Provides general reference services, identifies artifacts. Limited onsite use of collection, some reproductions permitted.

40147. John H. Blankenbuehler Memorial Library, Hobart Technical Center, Trade Square East, Troy, OH 45373; (513) 339-6000 ext 4603. Interest in welding engineering, welding metallurgy, chemistry, physics. Makes interlibrary loans, provides duplications, permits onsite use of collection.

40148. John H. Gifford Memorial Library and Information Center, Rubber Division, American Chemical Society, Univ of Akron, Akron, OH 44325; (216) 375-7197. Interest in chemistry and technology of natural, synthetic rubbers, elastomers, polymers. Provides free general reference services, sells materials, permits onsite use of collections. Special rates and privileges for members.

40149. Jury Verdict Research, 5325 Naiman Parkway, Ste B, Solon, OH 44149-1065; (800) 321-6910 (Toll-free), (216) 248-7960 (in Ohio, call collect). Interest in jury verdicts in personal injury cases, valuation of personal injuries, liability recovery probabilities. Provides case evaluations, analyses, verdict surveys, searches, distributes publications. Services for a fee.

40150. Kent State Center for Peaceful Change, Kent State Univ, Kent, OH 44242; (216) 672-3143. Interested in peace studies, conflict management, arbitration. Offers BA degree in Integrative Change. Provides general reference services, consulting, conducts seminars, distributes publication. Services generally available for a fee.

40151. LTV Steel Corp. Research Center Library, 6801 Brecksville Rd, Independence, OH 44131; (216) 524-5100 ext 261, 262. Interest in ferrous metallurgy, chemistry, physics, materials engineering, welding, nondestructive testing, mathematics. Provides reference services to special libraries, permits onsite study by request, makes interlibrary loans.

40152. Labor Education and Research Service, Ohio State Univ, 1810 Coll Rd, Columbus, OH 43210; (614) 422-8157. Interest in labor unions, occupational safety, collective bargaining, labor-management cooperation. Provides general reference services, conducts seminars, permits onsite use of collection. Services free, primarily for unions, graduate students.

40153. Laboratory Animal Center, Ohio State Univ, 6089 Godown Rd, Columbus, OH 43220; (614) 422-3382. Interest in procurement, housing, breeding of laboratory animals, English foxhound production, development of associated biomedical data. Answers inquiries, provides free reference services.

40154. Laboratory for Isotope Geology and Geochemistry, Dept of Geology and Mineralogy, Ohio State Univ, 125 S Oval Mall, Columbus, OH 43210; (614) 422-4304. Laboratory measures level of strontium and rubidium, dates rocks and minerals by radioactive decay determination. Provides general reference services, conducts seminars, analyzes specimens. Services free, but restricted.

40155. Lake Carriers' Association, 915 Rockefeller Bldg, Cleveland, OH 44113-1306; (216) 621-1107. Interest in Great Lakes transportation by bulk cargo ships. Provides limited reference services.

40156. Laminated Fiberglass Insulation Producers Association, c/o Thomas Associates, Inc., 1230 Keith Bldg, Cleveland, OH 44115; (216) 241-7333. Interest in lamination of various facings, fiberglass insulation used in the metal building industry. Answers inquiries, distributes publications, makes referrals. Services free.

40157. Laser Institute of America, 5151 Monroe St, Ste 118W, Toledo, OH 43623; (419) 882-8706. Professional

technical org that promotes laser technology and applications. Provides general reference services, conducts seminars, sells publications. Services for anyone, discounted prices for members.

40158. Lighter-Than-Air Society, c/o Roger L. Wolcott, Secty, 4796 Waterloo Rd, Atwater, OH 44201; (216) 325-7087. Promotes knowledge of history, science, and techniques of buoyant flight. Interest in lighter-than-air craft. Answers inquiries, provides bibliographic services, sells books at discount to members, permits onsite reference.

40159. Lincoln Electric Co., 22801 St Clair Ave, Cleveland, OH 44117; (216) 481-8100. Interest in arc welding, welded design of structures, machinery, and manufactured products. Answers inquiries, makes referrals, permits onsite reference.

40160. Liquid Crystal Institute, Kent State Univ, Kent, OH 44242; (216) 672-2654. Interest in liquid crystals structure and properties, liquid crystal display research and development. Answers brief inquiries free, consulting for a fee.

40161. Lloyd Library and Museum, 917 Plum St, Cincinnati, OH 45202; (513) 721-3707. Interest in botany, botany morphology, taxonomy, plant chemistry, medicinal plants, etc. Provides general reference services, conducts seminars, workshops, permits onsite references. Services free, except photoreproductions and publication.

40162. Machinability Data Center, Metcut Research Associates Inc., 3980 Rosslyn Dr, Cincinnati, OH 45209; (513) 271-9510. Interest in material removal, turning, milling, drilling, tapping, grinding, etc, engineering evaluation. Provides general reference services, conducts seminars, permits onsite use of collection. Answers inquiries free, other services for a fee.

40163. Magnesium Research Center, Battelle Memorial Institute, Columbus Laboratories, 505 King Ave, Columbus, OH 43201; (614) 424-4139. Interest in experimental research on magnesium alloy development, fabrication, corrosion and use. Provides general reference services, conducts research. Services for a fee.

40164. Mead Corp. Central Research Library, Corner 8th and Hickory Sts, Chillicothe, OH 45601; (614) 772-3588. Interest in packaging, paper, paperboard, pulp and pulpwood, forestry, cellulose chemistry, pollution control. Permits onsite reference, provides interlibrary loans, duplication services for libraries.

40165. Mechanized Information Center, Ohio State Univ Libraries, 1858 Neil Ave Mall, Columbus, OH 43210-1286; (614) 422-3480. Info services org provides computer-based search services, general assistance in using univ libraries. Provides general reference services, consulting, conducts lectures, seminars. Services for a fee for non-univ users.

40166. Merrell Dow Research Institute Library, 2110 E Galbraith Rd, Cincinnati, OH 45215; (513) 948-9111.

Interest in medicine, biology, chemistry, pharmaceuticals. Makes interlibrary loans, permits onsite reference with prior approval.

40167. Metal Building Manufacturers Association, 1230 Keith Bldg, Cleveland, OH 44115; (216) 241-7333. Trade assn of domestic manufacturers of metal building systems. Interest in standards, design, construction. Answers inquiries, makes free referrals.

40168. Metals Information, American Society for Metals, Metals Park, OH 44073; (216) 338-5151. Interest in all aspects of metallurgy. Provides custom online searches of database, photocopies, English translations, sells publications, permits onsite reference. Services at cost, some discounted for members.

40169. Metals and Ceramics Information Center, Battelle Memorial Institute, Columbus Laboratories, 505 King Ave, Columbus, OH 43201; (614) 424-5000. Defense research center interested in metals, ceramics, materials, and their applications. Provides general reference and consulting services, distributes reports, permits onsite reference. Bulletin available to registered orgs, other services at cost.

40170. Middle East Librarians' Association, c/o Dona S. Straley, Secty-Treas, 308 Main Library, Ohio State Univ, 1858 Neil Ave Mall, Columbus, OH 43210; (614) 422-3362. Works to improve communication, cooperation among Middle East librarians, increase access to info on the Middle East. Provides general reference services, conducts seminars. Services free, except publications to nonmembers.

40171. NLO Library, P.O. Box 39158, Cincinnati, OH 45239; (513) 738-6534 Interest in chemistry, metallurgy, nuclear technology, uranium and its compounds. Provides reference services, makes interlibrary loans of unclassified material. Library not open to public.

40172. National Anorexic Aid Society, 550 S Cleveland Ave, Ste F, Westerville, OH 43081; (614) 895-2009. Provides support groups for victims of anorexia nervosa and bulimia. Provides info, makes referrals, conducts seminars, maintains a hotline, operates clinic.

40173. National Association for Core Curriculum, c/o Dr Gordon F. Vars, Exec Secty-Treas, 316 White Hall, Kent State Univ, Kent, OH 44242; (216) 672-7977. Interest in interdisciplinary educational programs, general education, teaching. Provides general reference services, permits onsite use of collections. Services free to members; membership open.

40174. National Association for Creative Children and Adults, 8080 Springvalley Dr, Cincinnati, OH 45236; (513) 631-1777. Nonprofit org interested in personal development, commonsense problem solving, creativity. Provides general reference services at cost, conducts conferences, distributes publications, permits onsite reference by appointment.

40175. National Association of Church Personnel Administrators, 100 E 8th St, Cincinnati, OH 45202; (513) 421-

3134. Interest in church personnel administration, fair personnel practices, professional standards. Provides general reference services, consulting, conducts workshops. Fee for some services.

40176. National Association of Pattern Manufacturers, 21010 Center Ridge Rd, Cleveland, OH 44116; (216) 333-7417. Interest in pattern making, molds, model making, mock-ups. Provides general reference services, consulting, abstracting. Services primarily for members, some to nonmembers, free or at cost.

40177. National Association of Student Personnel Administrators, c/o Richard S. Stevens, Exec Dir, 160 Rightmire Hall, 1060 Carmack Rd, Columbus, OH 43210; (614) 422-4445. Interest in student personnel work in higher education, improvement of administrative effectiveness. Provides info, conducts workshops, conferences, placement service, awards meritorious recognition to graduate researchers.

40178. National Association of the Physically Handicapped, 76 Elm St, London, OH 43140; (614) 852-1664. Interest in advancement of economic, social, and physical welfare of all physically handicapped persons, improving accessibility, employment, housing, etc. Answers brief inquiries.

40180. National Association on Volunteers in Criminal Justice, Box 1326, Pyle Center, Wilmington Coll, Wilmington, OH 45177; (513) 382-6661 ext 292. Interest in improvement of juvenile and criminal justice systems through development and support of citizen participation. Provides general reference services, conducts seminars, distributes publications, permits onsite use of collection. Services for a fee.

40181. National Board of Boiler and Pressure Vessel Inspectors, 1055 Crupper Ave, Columbus, OH 43229; (614) 888-8320. Interest in engineering as applied to safety of boilers, unfired pressure vessels, nuclear vessels, safety valves. Answers inquiries, makes referrals, provides copies of data reports, makes quality control surveys and reviews, unannounced investigations.

40182. National Button Society, c/o Lois Pool, Secty, 2733 Juno Pl, Akron, OH 44313; (216) 864-3296. Promotes button collecting. Interest in buttons, button manufacturers, dealers. Provides general reference services, conducts show, permits onsite use of collection. Services primarily for members.

40183. National Euchre Players Association, P.O. Box 7138, Columbus, OH 43205; (614) 224-6237 ext 228. Nonprofit org interested in Eucre card game, card playing styles, strategies, regulations, statistical analysis. Provides free general reference services, conducts seminars, distributes publications.

40184. National Executive Housekeepers Association, Business and Professional Bldg, 414 Second Ave, Gallipolis, OH 45631; (614) 446-4800. Assn for persons employed in institutional housekeeping management in hospitals, hotels, schools, colleges, govt buildings, industrial establishments. Answers brief inquiries, provides consulting, distributes free brochure to post-secondary schools.

40185. National Heisey Glass Museum, Box 27 (169 W Church St), Newark, OH 43055; (614) 345-2932. Interest in table glass products produced by the A.H. Heisey & Co of Newark, from 1896 to 1957. Provides general reference services, conducts seminars, permits onsite study. Some services limited to members, some for a fee.

40186. National Institute for Occupational Safety and Health, U.S. Public Health Service, 4676 Columbia Parkway, Cincinnati, OH 45226; (513) 684-8326. Interest in occupational health, industrial hygiene, toxicology and hazards of industrial materials and conditions. Answers inquiries, provides consulting, makes referrals, publishes materials, conducts investigations.

40187. National Registry of Emergency Medical Technicians, P.O. Box 29233 (6610 Busch Blvd), Columbus, OH 43229; (614) 888-4484. Interest in standards of competence for emergency medical technicians, educational programs, examinations, and certification. Answers inquiries on requirements for natl EMT registration.

40188. National Regulatory Research Institute, 2130 Neil Ave, Columbus, OH 43210; (614) 422-9404. Provides technical assistance, expert policy research on issues connected with the regulation of utilities. Provides general reference services, onsite technical services, conducts seminars, distributes publications. Services at cost.

40189. National Reye's Syndrome Foundation, P.O. Box 829 (426 N Lewis), Bryan, OH 43506; (419) 636-2679, (800) 233-7393 (nationwide), (800) 231-7393 (in Ohio). Promotes research and analyses on Reye's syndrome. Provides general reference and consulting services, maintains toll-free hotline, conducts seminars, distributes publications. Services free, but donations are welcome.

40191. National Rural Crime Prevention Center, Ohio State Univ, 2120 Fyffe Rd, Columbus, OH 43210; (614) 422-1467. Conducts research, provides education in rural and farm crime prevention. Provides general reference services, conducts seminars, distributes publications. Services free, except bulk copies of publications.

40192. National Spray Equipment Manufacturers Association, 550 Randall Rd, Elyria, OH 44035; (216) 366-6808. Interest in paint spray product and process safety, paint spray equipment. Answers inquiries, analyzes data, makes referrals. Services free.

40193. National Tax Association-Tax Institute of America, 21 E State St, Columbus, OH 43215; (614) 224-8352. Nonprofit org that promotes scientific research in theory and practice of taxation. Conducts conferences, sells publications.

40194. National Water Well Association, 500 W Wilson Bridge Rd, Worthington, OH 43085; (614) 846-9355. Interest in water well drilling, hydrogeology, irrigation, water pollution control and abatement, surface engineering, water conservation. Provides technical info, conducts natl, regional expositions.

40195. National Women's Football League, c/o Daniel L. Dorman, Exec Dir, 363 E Broad St, Columbus, OH 43215-3818; (614) 221-0746. Interest in women's professional football, other women's contact sports. Provides general reference services, conducts workshops, distributes publications, permits onsite study. Fees for some publications, most other services free.

40196. National Wood Carvers Association, 7424 Miami Ave, Cincinnati, OH 45243; (513) 561-9051. Interest in woodcarving, wood sculpture and whittling. Provides general reference services, consulting, conducts seminars, distributes publication. Services free.

40197. Naval Medical Research Institute Toxicology Detachment, ASD/NMRI/TD, Wright-Patterson AFB, OH 45433; (513) 255-6058. Interest in toxicology of chemicals of Navy interest, air pollution, hyperbaric toxicity, etc. Answers inquiries.

40198. New York Central System Historical Society, P.O. Box 10027, Cleveland, OH 44110. Interest in history of New York Central Railroad Co, its subsidiaries and predecessors. Inquiries answered free. Reproduction services and publication for sale.

40199. North American Association for Environmental Education, P.O. Box 400 (5995 Horseshoe Bend Rd), Troy, OH 45373; (513) 698-6493. Professional org interested in environmental studies, communication, and education. Provides general reference services, conducts seminars, distributes publications. Fee for most services.

40200. North American Mycological Association, 4245 Redinger Rd, Portsmouth, OH 45662; (614) 354-2018. Nonprofit org interested in higher fungi, edible and poisonous mushrooms, fungi taxonomy. Provides general reference services, lends photos, conducts seminars, contests. Services free, except postage, insurance for members, schools, etc.

40201. Office of Merchant Marine Safety Great Lakes Pilotage Staff, Commander, Ninth Coast Guard District, Federal Office Bldg, 1240 E 9th St, Cleveland, OH 44199; (216) 522-3930. Interest in regulated pilotage on Great Lakes. Answers inquiries.

40202. Ohio Cooperative Wildlife Research Unit, Ohio State Univ, 1735 Neil Ave, Columbus, OH 43210; (614) 422-6112. Interest in wildlife biology, diseases, wildlife management, ecology, pollution. Provides general reference services, permits onsite use of collections. Services free to anyone, but priority given to graduate students, govt agencies.

40203. Ohio Covered Bridge Committee, 18 Elm Ave, Cincinnati, OH 45215; (513) 761-1789. Interest in timber covered bridges, especially in Ohio; engineering history. Answers inquiries and permits onsite use of collections free.

40204. Ohio Vegetable and Potato Growers Association, 35 E Chestnut, Box 479, Columbus, OH 43216; (614) 225-8947. Interest in representation, legislation, promotion and education for growers of vegetables, potatoes. Answers inquiries.

40205. Organ Recovery, 19201 Villaview Rd, Cleveland, OH 44119; (216) 531-5544. Interest in organ donation and transplantation, kidney dialysis, kidney disease, related subjects. Provides general reference services, conducts seminars and workshops. Services free.

40206. Organization Development Institute, 11234 Walnut Ridge Rd, Chesterland, OH 44026; (216) 461-4333. Seeks to educate the public on org development, technology for improving org effectiveness. Provides general reference services, conducts seminars, info exchange. Services free to members, at cost to others.

40207. Orton Memorial Library of Geology, Ohio State Univ, 155 S Oval Dr, Columbus, OH 43210; (614) 422-2428. Interest in geology, paleontology, polar region studies, physical oceanography, environmental science. Permits onsite reference, makes interlibrary loans.

40208. Owens-Corning Fiberglass Corp., Technical Data Center, Granville, OH 43023; (614) 587-7265. Interest in glass composition and melting, fibrous glass, reinforced plastics. Provides reference and library services to outsiders on individual basis.

40209. Owens-Illinois, Information Research Department, One Seagate, 1700 N Westwood Ave, Toledo, OH 43666; (419) 247-9312. Interest in glass technology, physics, chemical engineering, ceramics, metallurgy, plastics, paper products, geology, optics, computer science. Answers inquiries, provides reference services.

40210. PEI Associates Library, 11499 Chester Rd, Cincinnati, OH 45246; (513) 782-4700. Interest in environmental engineering. Provides general reference services, permits onsite use of collection. Services at cost by prior appointment or written request.

40211. Perkins Observatory Library, P.O. Box 449, Delaware, OH 43015; (614) 363-1257. Interest in astronomy, astrophysics. Answers inquiries, makes interlibrary loans, permits onsite reference by qualified persons.

40212. Philosophy Documentation Center, Bowling Green State Univ, Bowling Green, OH 43403-0189; (419) 372-2419. Interest in philosophy of science, logic, all areas of philosophical research. Provides general reference services, consulting, abstracting, duplication services. Fees may be charged.

40213. Pioneer America Society, c/o Allen Noble, Dir, Dept of Geography, Univ of Akron, Akron, OH 44325; (216) 375-7620. Interest in structures illustrating every-

day life of common man in rural pioneer America. Answers inquiries, conducts courses, lectures, distributes publications. Fee for services.

40214. Planning Executives Institute, P.O. Box 70, Oxford, OH 45056; (513) 523-4185. Intl nonprofit org interested in business, managerial planning, financial management, marketing, continuing education. Provides general reference services, conducts conferences, seminars, distributes publications. Services for a fee.

40215. Polimetrics Laboratory, Dept of Political Science, Ohio State Univ, 145 Derby Hall, 154 N Oval Mall, Columbus, OH 43210; (614) 422-1061. Interest in political science, sociology, economics, marketing, survey research, computer programming, simulation. Provides general reference services. Univ-generated data only to others for a fee.

40216. Predicasts, 11001 Cedar Ave, Cleveland, OH 44106; (216) 795-3000. Business info and market research corp. Provides studies, article delivery, online searching, conducts seminars. Fee for all services.

40217. Pro Football Hall of Fame Library/Research Center, 2121 Harrison Ave NW, Canton, OH 44708; (216) 456-8207. Serves as repository of info on pro football from 1892 to present. Answers inquiries, makes referrals, permits onsite reference. Services free, except copying, by appointment.

40218. Program for the Study of Crime and Delinquency, Ohio State Univ, 1775 Coll Rd, Columbus, OH 43210; (614) 422-7468. Interest in criminal and juvenile justice administration and policy. Provides general reference services, consulting, conducts seminars, distributes publications. Inquiries answered free, other services for a fee.

40219. Public Education Religion Studies Center, Wright State Univ, Dayton, OH 45435; (513) 873-2274. Interest in the relationship between religion and public education, emphasis on inclusion of academic study of religion and religious literature in public school curriculum. Consulting for a fee.

40220. Rapidly Solidified Materials Resource Centre, Battelle Memorial Institute, Columbus Laboratories, 505 King Ave, Columbus, OH 43201; (614) 424-5440, 424-4030. Interest in alloy development, new alloy compositions, alloy systems, applications. Distributes reports, indices, provides limited consulting services, conducts seminars. Services for subscribers only.

40221. Rathkamp Matchcover Society, c/o John C. Williams, Secty, 1359 Surrey Ct, Vandalia, OH 45377; (513) 890-8684. Interest in collection of matchcovers, matchbooks, and match booklets, history of hobby and the society. Provides general reference services, consulting, distributes publications. Some services for a fee.

40222. Refractories Research Center, Dept of Ceramic Engineering, Ohio State Univ, 2041 College Rd, Columbus, OH 43210; (614) 422-7128. Performs refractories testing, conducts research on alumina, silica, bauxite, chromite, magnesite, zircon. Provides general reference and consulting services for a fee.

40223. Resource and Referral Service, National Center for Research in Vocational Education, Ohio State Univ, 1960 Kenny Rd, Columbus, OH 43210; (614) 486-3655. Interest in education at all levels, orgs, meetings for educators. Provides general reference services, conducts workshops, training, distributes publications. Most services free, except some publications.

40224. Rhetoric Society of America, c/o Edward P.J. Corbett, Exec Secty, Ohio State Univ, Columbus, OH 43210; (614) 267-4819. Org of scholars, teachers interested in rhetoric, audience analysis, communication, stylistic analysis, oral and written composition. Answers inquiries, conducts workshops, distributes publication. Services at cost.

40225. Rutherford B. Hayes Presidential Center, Spiegel Grove, Fremont, OH 43420; (419) 332-2081. Interest in the Gilded Age, American history for the second half of 19th and early 20th Centuries. Provides advisory, reference services, including photographs, makes interlibrary loans, permits onsite reference.

40226. SDS Biotech Corp. Library and Information Services, SDS Biotech Corp., P.O. Box 348 (7528 Auburn Rd), Painesville, OH 44077; (216) 357-3475. Interest in business info, market research, competitor intelligence, agricultural chemicals, animal health, life sciences. Makes interlibrary loans, publishes materials, permits onsite reference by request.

40227. Scaffolding, Shoring, and Forming Institute, 1230 Keith Bldg, Cleveland, OH 44115; (216) 241-7333. Concerned with scaffolding, shoring, and forming safety, erection procedures. Answers inquiries, distributes publications. Services free, except bulk publications.

40228. School Science and Mathematics Association, 126 Life Science Bldg, Bowling Green State Univ, Bowling Green, OH 43403-0256; (419) 372-0151. Interest in research and general info in science and mathematics education. Provides general reference services, conducts seminars, evaluates data, distributes publications. Services at cost.

40229. Science Fiction Research Association, 1226 Woodhill Dr, Kent, OH 44240; (216) 673-9164. Interest in academic research in science fiction. Provides info, conducts seminars, sells publications, makes referrals. Services upon payment of membership dues.

40230. Scientific and Technical Information Office, Wright-Patterson AFB, OH 45433; (513) 255-3601. Interest in biotechnology, bioengineering, biodynamics, aerospace toxic hazards, chemical defense, human engineering, etc. Makes referrals, provides consulting, prepares analyses or evaluations for those with legitimate need-to-know.

40231. Scripps Foundation Gerontology Center, Miami Univ, Oxford, OH 45056; (513) 529-2914. Coordinates research, teaching, and public service in the field of aging, gerontology. Offers degrees, short-term training programs, consulting.

40232. Scripps Foundation for Research in Population Problems/Gerontology Center, Miami Univ, Oxford, OH 45056; (513) 529-2812. Interest in demography of aging and internal migration, gerontology, population problems. Pamphlets and other documents distributed on request. Some materials sold.

40233. Semiconductor Chemical Transducer Resource, Electronics Design Center, Case Western Reserve Univ, Univ Circle, Cleveland, OH 44106; (216) 368-2934. Interest in solid state microelectronic transducers, process development, design, technology. Provides general reference services, consulting, conducts workshops, maintains mailing lists. Services may be provided for a fee.

40234. Services for Independent Living, 25100 Euclid Ave, No 105, Euclid, OH 44117; (216) 731-1529. Interest in housing, peer counseling, attendant care, education, and advocacy for disabled people . Provides general reference services, distributes publications, permits onsite study. Services free.

40235. Society of Carbide Engineers, Metals Park, OH 44073; (216) 338-5151. Interest in fabrication, application of multipoint carbide tools, throwaway tooling, industrial diamonds, ultrasonic machining, carbide die, part use. Provides general reference services, conducts seminars. Services free.

40236. Society of Explosives Engineers, P.O. Box 185 (6990 Summers Rd), Montville, OH 44064; (216) 474-8436. Interest in blasting, explosives, fragmentation, ground vibration, airblast. Answers inquiries, conducts conferences, distributes publications, makes referrals. Services free, except publications and conferences.

40237. Society of Municipal Arborists, c/o Robert S. Miller, Exec Secty, 7447 Old Dayton Rd, Dayton, OH 45427; (513) 854-1338. Interest in all aspects of municipal arboriculture, urban forestry. Answers inquiries, provides advisory services, distributes publications. Services free, except publications; slides loaned to members only.

40239. Society of Non-Invasive Vascular Technology, 5300 E Main St, Ste 206, Columbus, OH 43213; (614) 863-9862. Nonprofit org provides for continuing education in field of non-invasive vascular technology. Publishes materials, conducts conferences, consulting, offers certification examination.

40240. Solar Energy Information Services, P.O. Box 600 (600 E Tiffin St), Bascom, OH 44809; (419) 937-2225, (800) 537-0985. Commercial org interested in solar energy, biomass, alcohol fuels, wind energy, photovoltaics, etc. Provides general reference services, conducts seminars, distributes publications. Most services free.

40241. Sports Philatelists International, 1410 Illuminating Bldg, Cleveland, OH 44113; (216) 621-2595. Interest in postage stamps and collateral material dealing with sports and recreation. Answers inquiries, makes referrals, distributes publications. Fees may be charged; discounts may be available to members.

40242. Steel Door Institute, 712 Lakewood Center North, 14600 Detroit Ave, Cleveland, OH 44107; (216) 226-7700. Interest in swing standard steel doors and frames. Answers brief inquiries, makes referrals.

40243. Strategies for Responsible Development, Univ of Dayton, 300 Coll Park, Dayton, OH 45469; (513) 229-4641. Interest in world hunger, development, nonviolence, nuclear disarmament, social justice, migrant workers. Answers inquiries, provides consulting, conducts seminars, distributes publications, permits onsite reference. Services free.

40244. Systems Builders Association, P.O. Box 117, W Milton, OH 45383; (513) 698-4127. Interest in metal building systems, construction. Answers inquiries, provides reference services for anyone with legitimate need-to-know.

40245. Tactical Technology Center, Battelle Memorial Institute, Columbus Laboratories, 505 King Ave, Columbus, OH 43201; (614) 424-6424. Defense research org that collects, analyzes, stores, and disseminates info on technology related to tactical warfare. Answers technical inquiries, makes referrals, permits onsite reference. All services limited to DoD agencies, laboratories and subject to approval.

40246. Tanners Council Research Laboratory, Univ of Cincinnati, Cincinnati, OH 45221-0014; (513) 281-8501. Interest in leather chemistry and technology, studies on skins and hides. Answers inquiries, identifies skin or hide source of leathers and cause of defects in skin, hide, and leather.

40247. Technical Information Services Office, Univ of Dayton Research Institute, KL 505, 300 Coll Park, Dayton, OH 45469; (513) 229-3024. Interest in windshear atmospheric modeling, combustion analysis, energy conservation, thermal decomposition, study of impact mechanics. Provides general reference services, consulting, makes interlibrary loans. Services for a fee.

40248. Telecommunications Center, Ohio State Univ, 2400 Olentangy River Rd, Columbus, OH 43210; (614) 422-9678. Operates radio and TV stations; interested in radio, telecommunications. Provides general reference services, advisory and recording services, conducts seminars, distributes publications. Services free, except consulting.

40249. Timken Co. Research Library, Canton, OH 44706; (216) 497-2049. Interest in antifriction-bearing technology, alloy seamless steel tubing, electric furnace steel-making, tribology related to bearings. Answers inquiries subject to limitations.

40250. Tin Research Institute, 1353 Perry St, Columbus, OH 43201; (614) 424-6200. Interest in tin, tin alloys, compounds, including metallurgical and chemical aspects, research, statistics. Provides general reference services, consulting, technical assistance, conducts seminars.

40251. Tire and Rim Association, 3200 W Market St, Akron, OH 44313; (216) 836-5553. Interest in technical standards, primarily load ratings for tires and dimensions for the interchangeability of tires, rims, and valves. Answers inquiries.

40252. Topaz Memorial Library of Vision, Ohio State Univ, 338 W 10th Ave, Columbus, OH 43210; (614) 422-1888. Interest in optometry, ophthalmology, vision, physiological optics, geometrical optics, visual anatomy, learning disabilities, etc. Provides reference and duplication services, permits onsite use of collection.

40253. Tradecard, 7850 Olentangy River Rd, Columbus, OH 43085; (614) 846-4041. Promotes corporate, retail bartering of goods and services, development of barter economy. Provides general reference services, distributes publication. Services primarily for business, at cost.

40254. Transplex/OSU, Ohio State Univ, 142 Hitchcock Hall, 2070 Neil Ave, Columbus, OH 43210; (614) 422-2871. Interest in highway transportation systems. Provides general reference services, consulting for a fee; permits onsite study. Other services free, except duplication.

40255. U.S. Air Force Museum Research Division, Wright-Patterson AFB, OH 45433; (513) 255-3284. Interest in USAF history, emphasis on data concerning aircraft, engines, and related equipment items. Provides limited free advisory, reference services; permits onsite use of collection by prior arrangement.

40256. U.S. Industrial Chemicals Co., Technical Library, P.O. Box 429550 (11500 Northlake Dr), Cincinnati, OH 45249; (513) 530-6599. Interest in plastics, resins, polyethylene, vinyl acetate, heavy inorganic chemicals, petrochemicals, organic solvents, metallic sodium, market research. Permits onsite reference, makes interlibrary loans.

40257. Uniform Product Code Council, 7061 Corporate Way, Ste 106, Dayton, OH 45459; (513) 435-3870. Assigns Uniform Product Code identification numbers and symbols. Answers inquiries, makes referrals, provides printouts, tapes, publications. Services at cost to nonmembers.

40258. Union for Experimenting Colleges and Universities, 632 Vine St, Ste 1010, Cincinnati, OH 45202-2407; (513) 621-6444. Accredited, educational institution that offers degrees through individualized programs of study. Answers inquiries, makes referrals free.

40259. United States Potters Association, P.O. Box 63 (518 Market St), E Liverpool, OH 43920; (216) 386-4225. Interest in earthen and china table and kitchenware, ceramics, glaze research. Answers inquiries free.

40260. United States Trotting Association, 750 Michigan Ave, Columbus, OH 43215; (614) 224-2291. Interest in harness racing, trotting horses, horse breeding, racetrack operations, race and racehorse records. Provides general reference services, conducts seminars, distributes publications. Services at cost.

40261. Van de Graaff Laboratory, Dept of Physics, Ohio State Univ, 1302 Kinnear Rd, Columbus, OH 43212; (614) 422-4775. Interest in nuclear physics research, Van de Graaff accelerator, fundamental symmetry studies. Provides general reference services, conducts seminars, distributes publications. Services free on limited basis.

40263. Welded Steel Tube Institute, 522 Westgate Tower, Cleveland, OH 44116; (216) 333-4550. Interest in welded steel tubing. Answers inquiries, provides advisory services free.

40264. Willys-Overland-Knight Registry, c/o David Bell, Pres, 241 Orchard Dr, Dayton, OH 45419; (513) 294-6708. Interest in automobiles and commercial vehicles built through 1942 by the Willys-Overland Co. Provides general reference services, copying at low rates.

40265. Women's Law Fund, 1101 Euclid Ave, Ste 400, Cleveland, OH 44115; (216) 621-3443. Interest in litigation and education on behalf of plaintiffs for sex-based discrimination. Provides general reference services, limited legal representation, conducts workshops. Services free, except workshops.

Oklahoma

41002. Amateur Softball Association Research Center and Library, 2801 Northeast 50th St, Oklahoma City, OK 73111; (405) 424-5266. Sponsors natl Softball Hall of Fame, clinics, and competitions, acts as governing body for establishment of rules. Provides general reference services, conducts workshops, distributes publications, permits onsite study. Services free, except extensive copying.

41003. American Association of Petroleum Geologists, P.O. Box 979 (1444 South Boulder Ave), Tulsa, OK 74101; (918) 584-2555. Advances science of geology, especially as it relates to petroleum and gas resources. Services available only to special groups, free only to members.

41004. American Choral Directors Association, P.O. Box 6310 (502 Southwest 38th St), Lawton, OK 73506; (405) 355-8161. Promotes development of choral music performance, composition, publication, and research. Answers inquiries, conducts festivals, clinics, and workshops, distributes publications, makes referrals. Services provided at cost.

41005. American Honey Producers Association, P.O. Box 368, Minco, OK 73059; (405) 352-4126. Interest in apiculture. Refers any inquirer to sources of info for return postage only.

41006. American Institute of Discussion, P.O. Box 103 (1210 Northwest 9th St), Oklahoma City, OK 73101; (405) 235-9681. Interest in techniques of small group discussion, conduct of conferences and training programs, specialized programming. Answers inquiries free, provides consulting services on negotiated-fee basis.

41007. American Peanut Research and Education Society, 376 Ag Hall, Okla. State Univ, Stillwater, OK 74078; (405) 624-6423. interested in production, harvesting, curing, storing, and processing of peanuts, development of improved peanut varieties. Sells publications, conducts annual meeting, makes referrals.

41008. American Registry of Clinical Radiography Technologists, 1616 South Blvd, Edmond, OK 73034; (405) 348-5071. Natl certifying org for radiography technologists. Interest in medical radiography technology. Answers inquiries, provides advisory services, conducts seminars, evaluates data, distributes publications, makes referrals. Services free.

41009. American Society of Veterinary Ophthalmology, c/o Dr A.J. Quinn, Secty-Treas, 1528 Shalamar, Stillwater, OK 74074. Interest in veterinary ophthalmology. Services primarily for members.

41010. Amoco Production Co., Research Center Library, P.O. Box 591 (41st and South Yale Sts.), Tulsa, OK 74102; (918) 664-3000. Interest in petroleum exploration and production. Answers inquiries, makes referrals and interlibrary loans, permits onsite reference by arrangement.

41011. Benham Group, P.O. Box 20400 (9400 North Broadway), Oklahoma City, OK 73156-0400; (405) 478-5353. Interest in architecture, engineering, water systems, sewage systems, flood control and drainage, highways, bridges, airports, dams, power plants. Answers brief inquiries, makes referrals, provides consulting services for a fee, permits onsite reference.

41012. Cherokee National Historical Society, P.O. Box 515 (TSA-LA-GI), Tahlequah, OK 74464; (918) 456-6007. Interest in history and culture of Cherokee Indians from prior to first contact with whites to present. Provides general reference and consulting services, permits onsite use of collections. Services free to members, at cost to others.

41013. Chisholm Trail Museum and Seay Mansion, 605 Zellers Ave, Kingfisher, OK 73750; (405) 375-5176. Preserves artifacts from Chisholm Trail, cattle drives 1867-1887, Okla. history and artifacts 1889-1930. Provides general reference services, conducts slide-tape programs and group meetings, permits onsite study. Services free, except use of auditorium.

41014. Civil Aeromedical Institute, AAC-100, FAA Aeronautical Center, Oklahoma City, OK 73125; (405) 686-4806. Interest in aviation medicine, accident investigation, aeromedical education, civil aviation safety, medical certification. Answers inquiries, provides consulting services, makes referrals. Services free.

41016. Core and Sample Library, Univ of Okla., 2725 Jenkins Ave, Norman, OK 73069; (405) 325-4386. Interest in rock cores and samples from boreholes. Lends cores and samples from Okla. to companies or individuals for nominal fee, permits onsite reference.

41017. Creek Indian Museum, Creek Council House Museum, Okmulgee, OK 74447; (918) 756-2324. Interest in Creek Indian history and artifacts, pioneer history of Okla. Answers inquiries. Museum open to the public.

41018. Crystal Synthesis Laboratory, Dept of Physics, Okla. State Univ, Stillwater, OK 74078; (405) 624-5799, 624-5796. Interest in growing perovskite or rutile structure crystals, mostly fluorides and oxides. Provides info free on growing of certain crystals, grows and sells crystals.

41019. Data Capture Technology, 5436-F South Mingo Rd, Tulsa, OK 74146; (918) 627-7521. Interest in digital tape instrumentation, oscillographs, galvanometers. Answers brief inquiries, makes referrals, provides consulting services for a fee, permits onsite use of literature collection.

41020. Energy Resources Institute Information Systems Programs, Univ of Okla., 601 Elm St, Room 129, Norman, OK 73019; (405) 325-1600. Interest in petroleum info, mineral resources, chemical analyses of rock samples, geothermal mapping. Provides database retrievals on consultation basis, responds to inquiries on data applications. Services available to govt, industry, financial institutions.

41021. FAA Aircraft Registration Branch, AAC-250, FAA Aeronautical Center, P.O. Box 25082 (6500 South MacArthur Blvd), Oklahoma City, OK 73125; (405) 686-2116. Interest in registration of U.S. civil aircraft, recordation of liens and ownership conveyances, leases, title, etc. Records open to public, title search room is maintained for reviewing records.

41023. Five Civilized Tribes Museum, Agency Hill, Honor Heights Dr, Muskogee, OK 74401; (918) 683-1701. Interest in history and cultures of Cherokee, Chickasaw, Choctaw, Creek, and Seminole tribes. Answers inquiries free. Museum open to the public for admittance fee.

41024. Gas Processors Association, 15 East 5th, Tulsa, OK 74103; (918) 582-5112. Interest in experimental research in light hydrocarbons, gas processing, development of standards. Provides general reference services, conducts seminars, distributes data and publications. Services usually provided at cost to members, higher fees to nonmembers.

41026. Geophysical Society of Tulsa, c/o William O. Heap, Pres, Seismograph Service Corp., P.O. Box 1590, Tulsa, OK 74102. Interest in geophysical exploration, seismic, gravitometer, and magnetometer exploration, petroleum exploration. Answers limited inquiries, makes referrals, sells publications.

41027. Institute for Energy Development, P.O. Box 19243 (10017 S Pennsylvania Ave), Oklahoma City, OK 73144; (405) 691-4449, (800) 654-3824. Continuing education company specializing in programs and publications for the petroleum industry. Provides info on programs free. Conducts professional recertification and continuing education courses for credit.

41028. International Porcelain Artist Teachers Organization, c/o Mary Nokes, Board Secty, 4125 NW 57th St, Oklahoma City, OK 73112; (405) 946-7121. Interest in art of china painting, enamels and porcelain, matte and glass painting, gold agata etching, acid etching, etc. Answers inquiries, provides consulting services, conducts seminars, distributes publications, makes referrals. Services free, except publications and seminars.

41029. International Professional Rodeo Association, P.O. Box 615 (American Fidelity Bldg), Pauls Valley, OK 73075; (405) 238-6488. Sanctioning and governing body for professional rodeo worldwide. Provides general reference services, conducts workshops. Some services restricted to specific groups, all provided free.

41030. Interstate Oil Compact Commission, P.O. Box 53127 (900 Northeast 23d St), Oklahoma City, OK 73152; (405) 525-3556. Interest in oil and gas conservation, engineering, production methods, fundamental geology, research in well spacing, underground storage, etc. Answers inquiries, makes referrals, permits use of collection.

41031. John W. Keys Speech and Hearing Center, Dept of Communication Disorders, Coll of Health, Univ of Okla. Health Sciences Center, P.O. Box 26901, Oklahoma City, OK 73190. Interest in speech, language, and hearing disorders. Provides general reference services, conducts seminars. Services generally provided on a fee basis, available to patients, professionals.

41032. Kerr Industrial Applications Center, Southeastern Okla. State Univ, Station A, Box 2584, Durant, OK 74701; (405) 924-6822. Serves as industrial applications center and technical info resource for the public. Interest in aerospace categories. Provides general reference services, distributes publications, permits onsite reference. Most services provided for a fee.

41033. Museum of the Great Plains, P.O. Box 68 (Elmer Thomas Park; 601 Ferris), Lawton, OK 73502; (405) 353-5675. Interest in history of Great Plains region, with emphasis on archeology of the Paleo-Indian and Plains Archaic cultures, ethnology of Indian cultures.

Members, students, and scholars allowed access to collections.

41034. National Association of Legal Assistants, 1420 South Utica, Tulsa, OK 74104; (918) 587-6828. Nonprofit assn of legal assistants that sets standards, provides continuing education, certification. Provides general reference services, conducts seminars and Certified Legal Assistant program, sells publications. Services free, except seminars, workshops, publications.

41035. National Association of Mature People, P.O. Box 26792, Oklahoma City, OK 73126; (405) 848-1832. Natl nonprofit org that works to improve life for elderly people. Provides general reference services, programs, publications, social activities, counseling, Social Security and Medicare info, and discounts on prescriptions, insurance, travel.

41036. National Association of Royalty Owners, 119 North Broadway, P.O. Box C, Ada, OK 74820; (405) 436-0034. Nonprofit trade assn for oil and gas royalty owners, mineral owners. Answers inquiries, conducts seminars, distributes publications, makes referrals. Seminars and publications provided at cost to members, at higher fee for others. Referral services free.

41037. National Clearinghouse of Rehabilitation Training Materials, 115 Old USDA Bldg, Stillwater, OK 74078; (405) 624-7650. Exchanges ideas, info, training materials for staff development, in-service training and continuing education in rehabilitation. Provides general reference services, distributes publications free, provides copying services at cost. Some materials available on loan basis.

41039. National Cowboy Hall of Fame and Western Heritage Center, 1700 Northeast 63d St, Oklahoma City, OK 73111; (405) 478-2250. Museum that preserves story of Western migration in U.S. through Western art, history, literature, and motion pictures, rodeos, ranching. Answers inquiries, provides limited reference and copying services, permits onsite use of library. Services free, except copying.

41040. National Institute for Petroleum Energy Research Library, P.O. Box 2128, Bartlesville, OK 74005; (918) 337-4371. Interest in R&D on production of petroleum and natural gas, studies of substitute fuels, etc. Provides general reference services, makes interlibrary loans, permits onsite study. Services free as time permits.

41041. National Severe Storms Laboratory, NOAA Environmental Research Laboratories, 1313 Halley Circle, Norman, OK 73069; (405) 360-3620. Interest in severe storm dynamics, forecasting, hazards, radar, etc. Provides info to govt agencies, provides meteorological data to researchers, exchanges publications, responds to requests for info.

41042. National Square Dance Convention, c/o Howard B. Thornton, Dir of Info, 2936 Bella Vista, Midwest City,

OK 73110; (405) 732-0566. Liaison org of square dance clubs and dancers that directs annual natl square dance convention. Answers inquiries, conducts seminars and workshops, makes referrals. Services free.

41043. National Wrestling Hall of Fame, USA Wrestling, 405 West Hall of Fame Ave, Stillwater, OK 74075; (405) 377-5242, 377-5243. Nonprofit org interested in promotion of freestyle, Greco-Roman, and collegiate wrestling. Provides general reference services, conducts tours, distributes publications, permits onsite use of collections. Services free.

41044. Oklahoma Geophysical Observatory, Univ of Okla., P.O. Box 8, Leonard, OK 74043-0008; (918) 366-4152. Interest in seismology, earth tide gravimetry, geoelectricity, geomagnetism, seismicity of Okla. Provides general reference and copying services, performs computer searches, permits onsite study. Most services free, except for large quantities of reproductions.

41045. Palomino Horse Breeders of America, P.O. Box 580488; (204 SE 3rd Ave), Tulsa, OK 74158; (918) 748-8806. Interest in Palomino horse history, registration, preservation of purity, improvement of breeding, horse shows. Provides general reference services, conducts seminars, distributes data and publications, permits onsite reference. Services free, except some publications.

41046. Palynology Research Center, Stovall Museum of Science and History, Univ of Okla., Norman, OK 73019; (405) 325-4711. Interest in palynology, geology, stratigraphy, morphology, taxonomy, aerobiology, archeology. Answers technical inquiries, provides literature-searching services. Fees may be charged to industrial users.

41047. Plains Indians and Pioneer Historical Foundation, P.O. Box 1167 (2009 Williams Ave), Woodward, OK 73801; (405) 256-6136. Foundation interested in local and family history of Northwest Okla. Provides free general reference services, conducts tours, permits onsite reference.

41048. Research and Development Institute of the United States, P.O. Drawer 700270, Tulsa, OK 74170; (918) 627-1181. Interest in R&D in all subjects. Answers inquiries, makes referrals, provides consulting services. Services provided on a fee basis, except as otherwise provided in govt contracts.

41049. Robert S. Kerr Environmental Research Laboratory, Environmental Protection Agency, P.O. Box 1198, Ada, OK 74820; (405) 332-8800. Interest in water pollution, water quality, effects of pollutants on soil and ground ecology, soil treatment systems. Provides general reference services, permits onsite use of collection. Services mainly for lab personnel.

41050. Rodeo Historical Society, National Cowboy Hall of Fame, 1700 Northeast 63d St, Oklahoma City, OK 73111; (405) 478-2250. Interest in rodeo producers, managers, and performers, Wild West shows, Western heritage and culture. Answers inquiries, provides reference services, distributes publications. Services free.

41051. Samuel Roberts Noble Foundation, Biomedical Division, Box 2180, Ardmore, OK 73402; (405) 223-5810. Interest in basic biomedical research on degenerative and malignant diseases. Provides general reference services, distributes publications, permits onsite use of collection. Services available to libraries, other orgs, and qualified scientists.

41052. Seminole Nation Museum, Box 1532 (6th St and Wewoka Ave), Wewoka, OK 74884; (405) 257-5580. Museum interested in history of Seminole Indians after their removal from Florida, black freedmen, white pioneers from oil boom period 1920-1930. Answers inquiries, conducts seminars, permits onsite reference. Services free.

41053. Society of Economic Paleontologists and Mineralogists, P.O. Box 4756 (3530 East 31st St), Tulsa, OK 74159-0756; (918) 743-9765. Interest in paleontology, sedimentary petrology. Conducts seminars and workshops, distributes publications. Services available for a fee.

41054. Society of Exploration Geophysicists, Box 3098 (3707 East 51st St), Tulsa, OK 74101; (918) 743-1365. Interest in exploration geophysics. Answers inquiries, makes referrals, provides career info. Services limited; assistance provided to public if possible.

41055. Sweet Adelines, P.O. Box 470168 (5334 East 46th St), Tulsa, OK 74147; (918) 622-1444. Sponsors regional and intl competitions for quartets and choruses. Answers inquiries free, seminars, workshops, schools limited to members, publications available by subscription.

41056. Thomas Gilcrease Institute of American History and Art, 1400 Gilcrease Museum Rd, Tulsa, OK 74127; (918) 582-3122. Museum interested in discovery and development of the New World. Provides general reference services, distributes publication, permits study. Services free, except for copying and microfilm. Appointments requested for use of library.

41057. University of Oklahoma Geology Library, 830 Van Vleet Oval, Room 103, Norman, OK 73019; (405) 325-6451. Interest in geology, paleontology, palynology, mineralogy, geophysics, geochemistry, petroleum geology, mineral resources. Permits onsite use of collections, provides limited reference services. Interlibrary loans available.

41058. Vegetable Research Station, Okla. Agricultural Experiment Station, Okla. State Univ, 13711 South Mingo Rd, Bixby, OK 74008; (918) 369-2441. Interest in vegetable crop research, fertility, evaluation of varieties, herbicides, and insect damage and control. Answers inquiries, makes referrals.

41059. World Neighbors, 5116 N Portland Ave, Oklahoma City, OK 73112; (405) 946-3333. Private org that assists cooperative self-help programs in developing nations worldwide. Interest in food production, family planning, leadership training, public health, development of small industries.

Oregon

42001. 1000 Friends of Oregon, 300 Willamette Bldg, 534 SW 3d St, Portland, OR 97204; (503) 223-4396. Nonprofit org dedicated to implementation of Oregon's land use laws. Provides legal and technical advice and info to local governments and citizens. Services free, except for magazine and newsletter.

42002. American Rhododendron Society, c/o Paula L. Cash, Exec Secty, 14885 Southwest Sunrise Lane, Tigard, OR 97224; (503) 639-2817. Interest in growing and propagating rhododendrons and azaleas, plant breeding, seed distribution program. Answers inquiries free, sells publications. Services available to anyone through affiliated chapters.

42003. American Tapestry Alliance, Route 2, Box 570-D, Chiloquin, OR 97624; (503) 783-2507. Primary interest is history of American tapestry. Holdings include slide archive of tapestries woven in America. Services free to members only, but available to all with serious interest in field.

42004. American Tinnitus Association, P.O. Box 5, Portland, OR 97207; (503) 248-9985. Collects and disseminates information, raises funds for research, and conducts educational programs for tinnitus management. Free advisory and reference services, except for seminars and workshops.

42006. American-Nepal Education Foundation, c/o Hugh B. Wood, Exec Director, Box ANEF, Oceanside, OR 97134; (503) 842-4024. Provides limited scholarship aid to Nepalese. Holdings include books, periodicals, and reports covering nearly all materials published on Nepal in English (and some other languages) up to 1960. Reference services available.

42007. Aprovecho Institute, 80574 Hazelton Rd, Cottage Grove, OR 97624; (503) 942-9434. Intl assn of specialists concerned with simple technologies suitable for use in rural areas, particularly Third World. Free info, advisory services for a fee. Publications available.

42008. Association for Computer-Based Systems for Career info, Univ of Ore., 1787 Agate St, Eugene, OR 97403; (503) 686-3872. Develops standards for state-based career info systems. Programs include publications exchange clearinghouse and annual conferences. Services available to members and states starting new systems.

42009. Association of Environmental Scientists and Administrators, 2718 Southwest Kelly St, Ste C-190, Portland, OR 97201; (503) 635-3680. Promotes public debate of policy issues related to environment. Answers inquiries, conducts workshops, distributes issue briefs. Services generally free.

42010. Association of Official Racing Chemists, P.O. Box 19232, Portland, OR 97219. Intl assn of chemists analyzing official samples collected at racing events (excluding human) for detection and identification of drugs. Answers brief inquiries and makes referrals. Extensive services provided only to racing industry.

42011. Bonneville Power Administration, P.O. Box 3621 (1500 Northeast Irving, Ste R100), Portland, OR 97208; (503) 230-4171. Interest in electric generating power systems, marketing of electric power, energy conservation. Publishes issue alerts, answers inquiries, permits onsite reference to all library materials.

42012. Career info System, Univ of Ore. Library, 1787 Agate St, Eugene, OR 97403; (503) 686-3872. Compiles career info for schools and social agencies to improve career choices of students and clients. Services provided at cost to consortium members in 16 states. Special reports provided for program planners and other professionals.

42013. Center for Performance Assessment, c/o Dr Richard J. Stiggins, NW Regional Educational Lab, 300 SW 6th Ave, Portland, OR 97204; (503) 248-6800 ext 351 (in Ore.); (800) 547-6339 (outside Ore.). Interest in tests requiring application of skills and knowledge to solve real-world problems in real-life or simulated testing situations. Provides publications and reference services, permits onsite use of collection.

42014. Center for Urban Education, 0245 Southwest Bancroft St, Portland, OR 97201; (503) 221-0984. Nonprofit group that helps individuals and orgs engage more effectively in community change. Has special collections on ethnic heritage, refugee resettlement, and info technology. Some services free.

42015. Center for the Study of Women in Society, Univ of Ore., Eugene, OR 97403; (503) 686-5015. Interest in sociological and historical studies of women, sex roles, sexism, women and work, feminist theory. Provides reference services and publications. Free services, primarily for faculty, students, and local users.

42016. Center on Human Development Rehabilitation Research and Training Center in Mental Retardation, Univ of Ore., Clinical Services Bldg, Eugene, OR 97403; (503) 686-3585. Conducts research and provides training relevant to rehabilitation of mentally retarded citizens. Publishes technical reports, reviews, monographs, audiovisual materials for a fee.

42017. Collier State Park Logging Museum, Route 2, Box 450, Chiloquin, OR 97624; (503) 783-2471. Privately sponsored museum interested in forestry and logging. Collections of logging equipment and logging camp artifacts accessible to public.

42018. Columbia River Maritime Museum, 1792 Marine Dr, Astoria, OR 97103; (503) 325-2323. Interest in maritime history, with emphasis on Pacific Northwest and its general history. Holdings include artifacts, prints, paintings, manuscripts, photos. Reference services free, unless extensive.

42019. Division of Special Programs, English Language Institute, Ore. State Univ, Corvallis, OR 97331; (503) 754-2464. Provides technical and scientific English language training to meet a student's language requirements for functioning within a particular scientific field, home agency, or national industry. Services generally free.

42020. E. C. Brown Foundation, 300 Southwest 6th, Portland, OR 97204; (503) 295-0203. Interest in family life, health, and sex education, primarily the production of educational films on these subjects. Films distributed by Perennial Education, Evanston, IL 60202.

42021. ERIC Clearinghouse on Educational Management, Univ of Ore., Eugene, OR 97403; (503) 686-5043. Gathers and disseminates knowledge about educational management and facilities; connects producers and users of such knowledge. Answers inquiries, provides computerized info retrieval.

42022. Environmental Protection Agency, Narragansett Environmental Research Laboratory, Hatfield Marine Science Center, Newport, OR 97365; (503) 867-4040. Conducts research on aquatic ecosystems to improve scientific basis for criteria of regulatory decisions involving control of waste discharges. Provides research info, distributes some publications.

42023. Environmental Remote Sensing Applications Laboratory, Ore. State Univ, Corvallis, OR 97331; (503) 754-3056. Partially sponsored by NASA. Interests include development of remote sensing technology applications to problem solving in natural resource management and land use. Provides info, sometimes lends materials.

42024. Fir and Hemlock Door Association, 1500 Yeon Bldg, Portland, OR 97204; (503) 224-3930. Interests include fir and hemlock wood panel doors, industry standards, product info. Provides reference services and distributes publications, primarily to construction and production industries.

42025. Food Toxicology and Nutrition Laboratory, Dept of Food Science and Technology, Ore. State Univ, Corvallis, OR 97331; (503) 754-4193. Conducts research on effects of food toxins and carcinogens on rainbow trout. Holdings include microscopic slide collection. Permits onsite use of collection. Free reference services on a time-available basis.

42026. Forelaws On Board, 19142 South Bakers Ferry Rd, Boring, OR 97009; (503) 637-3549. Seeks to stop nuclear power development through intervention in licensing, petition, and legislative action. Works for responsible licensing of radiological and chemical waste disposal sites. Services free.

42027. Forensic Mental Health Associates, P.O. Box 12951, Salem, OR 97309; (503) 581-6115. Private org promoting research, training, and treatment in regard to victims and perpetrators of sexual abuse. Provides consulting and training for a fee.

42028. Forest Industries Management Center, Univ of Ore., Eugene, OR 97403; (503) 686-3335. Interest in marketing and general management of forest products companies, corporate strategy and long-range planning. Answers inquiries, provides consulting and reference services, some at cost.

42029. Forestry, Conservation Communications Association, c/o Donald W. Pfohl, Pres, 2600 State St, Salem, OR 97310; (503) 378-2503. Frequency coordinator in forestry conservation radio service. Publishes *FCAA News and Views* (quarterly). Answers inquiries.

42030. Hatfield Marine Science Center, Library, Ore. State Univ, Newport, OR 97365; (503) 867-3011. Special collection concentrating on marine science, including marine biology, aquaculture, fish culture, fish diseases. Search, photocopy, and microform services available for a fee.

42031. Hemangioma Support Group, 6349 North Commercial, Portland, OR 97217; (503) 289-6295. Formed by parents of children with hemangioma—birth defect which varies from small birthmark to large tumor. Has file and list of doctors and clinics specializing in hemangioma.

42032. Holt International Childrens Services, P.O. Box 2880, (1195 City View), Eugene, OR 97402; (503) 687-2202. Nonprofit org that provides permanent families for homeless children in developing nations. Publishes magazine, answers inquiries free.

42033. Industrial Forestry Association, c/o Norman E. Bjorklund, Exec Vice-Pres, 225 Southwest Broadway, Room 400, Portland, OR 97205; (503) 222-9505. Operates large, nonprofit forest tree nurseries and tree improvement program; sponsors and certifies private forests as tree farms in western Wash. and Ore. Informational services free.

42034. Institute of Recreation Research and Service, Dept of Leisure Studies and Services, College of Human Development and Performance, Univ of Ore., Eugene, OR 97403; (503) 686-3602. Involved in research and community services concerning leisure activities, including therapeutic recreation. Services free, except for some publications, primarily for Oregon residents, but others will be assisted.

42035. Institute on Aging, Portland State Univ, P.O. Box 751, Portland, OR 97207; (503) 229-3952. Federally sponsored program that offers education, conducts research, and provides training in aging. Wide range of publications and reprints available. Services free, unless extensive.

42036. International Council for Computers in Education, c/o Lynn Grimes, Conference/Outreach, Univ of Ore., 1787 Agate St, Eugene, OR 97403; (503) 686-4414. Nonprofit, intl org of educators dedicated to improved instructional use of computers. Publishes journal, answers inquiries, makes referrals.

42037. International Institute of Fisheries Economics and Trade, Dept of Agricultural and Resource Economics, Ore. State Univ, Corvallis, OR 97331; (503) 754-2942. Assn interested in factors affecting intl trade in seafoods and fisheries policy questions. Reports and reference services available, often at cost.

42038. International Plant Protection Center, Ore. State Univ, Corvallis, OR 97331; (503) 754-3541. Helps emerging nations develop increased agricultural efficiency through technical assistance and research to achieve improved control of weeds. Services free only to noncommercial requesters in less developed countries.

42039. International Weed Science Society, c/o Larry C. Burrill, Secty-Treas, Gilmore Annex, Ore. State Univ, Corvallis, OR 97331; (503) 754-3541. Interests include weeds and weed control; herbicides. Answers inquiries, provides info on R&D in progress, makes referrals. Services free as time of volunteer staff allows.

42040. Kresge Hearing Research Laboratory, Dept of Otolaryngology, Ore. Health Sciences Univ, Sam Jackson Park Rd, Portland, OR 97201; (503) 225-8032. Conducts clinical research on ear and its related problems for hearing in humans. Interests include tinnitus and acoustical overload. Has computerized data on tinnitus patients. Services free, except to patients.

42041. League of Oregon Cities, P.O. Box 928 (1021 Court St NE), Salem, OR 97308; (503) 588-6466. Interest in city government: planning and zoning, public administration, municipal finance, public works. Has library of city ordinances, maps, unevaluated data. Answers inquiries, provides reference services.

42042. Middle East Studies Certificate Program, Portland State Univ, P.O. Box 751 (724 Southwest Harrison St), Portland, OR 97207; (503) 229-4029. Interest in the Middle East. Holdings include materials in Iranian, Arabic, Turkish, and Hebrew. Answers inquiries from researchers, provides consulting and reference services, makes referrals and interlibrary loans.

42043. Minerals and Materials Research Albany Center, Bureau of Mines, P.O. Box 70 (1450 Queen Ave SW), Albany, OR 97321; (503) 967-5809. Interest in minerals thermochemistry, appraisal of critical minerals from Northwestern and Alaskan resources. Publishes reports, answers inquiries, provides consulting and mineral identification services.

42044. Mobility International U.S.A., P.O. Box 3551 (132 East Broadway), Eugene, OR 97403; (503) 343-1284. Nonprofit org that helps place disabled persons into travel and educational exchange programs in U.S. and abroad. Some info available on tape and in braille. Services primarily for disabled and their families.

42045. National Association for Chronic Epstein-Barr Virus Groups, P.O. Box 230108, Portland, OR 97223; (503) 684-5261. Nonprofit clearinghouse for info on chronic Epstein-Barr Virus and myalgic encephalomyelitis. Goals include funding research, educating public and health professionals, finding treatments, and establishing nationwide support groups.

42046. National Association of Timetable Collectors, c/o Jeff Asay, Secty, 5 Offenbach Pl, Lake Oswego, OR 97034. Promotes the hobby of collecting transportation timetables, including railroad, airline, transit, bus, and steamship schedules. Monthly and quarterly publications available. Answers inquiries free.

42047. National College of Naturopathic Medicine, 11231 Southeast Market St, Portland, OR 97216; (503) 255-4860. Four-year institution that grants Doctor of Naturopathic Medicine (N.D.) degree. Trains primary care physicians with emphasis on natural therapeutics. Conducts seminars for community and health care professionals.

42048. National Council on Education for the Ceramic Arts, P.O. Box 1677, Bandon, OR 97411; (503) 347-4394. Professional org that promotes education in ceramic arts. Publishes newsletter and journal. Informational services included in membership; available to others for a fee.

42049. National Psoriasis Foundation, 6415 Southwest Canyon Court, Ste 200, Portland, OR 97221; (503) 297-1545. Nonprofit org that disseminates info about psoriasis. Interested in research and treatment. Wide range of reference and informational services available, usually for free.

42051. North American College of Acupuncture, P.O. Box 12128, Salem, OR 97309. Interest in Chinese medical philosophy of acupuncture and research on use of minicomputers to perform Chinese diagnostic procedures. Publishes course material. Services generally free with background in anatomy and physiology.

42052. Northwest Coalition for Alternatives to Pesticides, P.O. Box 375 (454 Willamette St, Ste 201), Eugene, OR 97440; (503) 344-5044. Coalition of primarily rural-based member groups in Pacific Northwest that encourages citizen participation in government programs concerning pesticide spraying. Services free or a minimal charge, except for publications.

42053. Northwest Film Study Center, 1219 Southwest Park Ave, Portland, OR 97208; (503) 221-1156. Provides film and video resource info, sponsors exhibitions of domestic and foreign films, offers advisory and reference services. Some services may be subject to a fee.

42054. Northwest Regional Educational Laboratory, 300 Southwest 6th Ave, Portland, OR 97204; (503) 248-6800. Nonprofit org that assists education, government, county agencies, business, and labor in improving quality and equality in educational programs and processes. Answers inquiries, provides related materials.

42055. Nutrition Research Institute, Ore. State Univ, Corvallis, OR 97331; (503) 754-3561. Dedicated to advancement of nutrition knowledge and its effective application to improvement of health and welfare of mankind. Sponsors seminars, symposia, and workshops, publishes newsletter and symposia monographs.

42056. Oak Creek Laboratory of Biology, 104 Nash Hall, Ore. State Univ, Corvallis, OR 97331; (503) 754-3503. Interest in freshwater pollution biology, water quality requirements, industrial wastes, pesticides, acid rain. Answers inquiries, provides limited consulting services and reprints of journal articles on research results.

42057. Oceanographic Research Program, College of Oceanography, Ore. State Univ, Corvallis, OR 97331; (503) 754-3504. Interest in scientific study of all aspects of the seas. Has library and large collections of plant and animal specimens, sediment cores. Answers brief inquiries, provides consulting services for a fee, permits onsite reference.

42058. Office of Environmental Processes and Effects Research, Environmental Protection Agency, 200 SW 35th St, Corvallis, OR 97333; (503) 757-4601. Interest in effects of environmental pollutants on terrestrial and aquatic ecosystems; behavior, effects, and control of pollutants in lakes and river systems. Answers inquiries on EPA research, permits onsite use of library resources.

42059. Oregon Environmental Council, 2637 Southwest Water St, Portland, OR 97201; (503) 222-1963. Interests include environmental concerns in Oregon: planning, population, pollution, wildlife, natural resources, and energy. Publishes bimonthly magazine, answers inquiries, provides consulting services.

42060. Oregon Historical Society, 1230 Southwest Park Ave, Portland, OR 97205; (503) 222-1741. Interests include regional, state, and local history. Has over 17 million books, photos, maps, films, manuscripts, and other records; museum contains over 100,000 artifacts. Reference services available for a fee.

42061. Oregon Institute of Marine Biology, Univ of Ore., Charleston, OR 97420; (503) 888-5534. Interest in marine biology, including marine algae, estuarine ecology, invertebrate embryology, marine ecology, and seabirds and marine mammals. Provides reference services.

42062. Oregon Institute of Technology, Oretech Branch Post Office, Klamath Falls, OR 97601; (503) 882-6321. Provides technical assistance in preliminary engineering design and economic feasibility studies and info dissemination for geothermal direct heat applications. Services are free.

42063. Oregon Museum of Science and Industry, 4015 Southwest Canyon Rd, Portland, OR 97221; (503) 222-

2828. Nonprofit org dedicated to science and technology education and exhibits. Publishes newsletter and research laboratory findings, answers inquiries, provides reference services to public at various charges.

42064. Oregon Productivity Center, Ore. State Univ, 100 Merryfield Hall, Corvallis, OR 97331; (503) 754-3249. Seeks to develop effective ways to improve productivity. Consulting and reference services available to manufacturing, service, or govt agencies; others assisted as time and staff permit.

42065. Oregon Regional Primate Research Center, 505 NW 185th Ave, Beaverton, OR 97006; (503) 645-1141. One of 7 federally funded centers designed to advance knowledge about human health problems through research with nonhuman primates. Public Info Office distributes pamphlets and other materials.

42066. Oregon State Library, State Library Bldg, Salem, OR 97310; (503) 378-4276. Interest in Oregon history and government, Oregon authors. Holdings include 800,000 volumes of govt documents, including Oregon State documents. Services provided primarily to public, school libraries, and state agencies.

42067. Oregon Wildlife Federation, Route 1, Box 546, Hillsboro, OR 97123. Nonprofit citizens org dedicated to protection, enhancement, and wise use of Oregon's natural resources. Services are free (postage requested), but filmstrips available only to schools and clubs.

42068. Pacific Fishery Management Council, 526 Southwest Mill St, Portland, OR 97201; (503) 221-6352. Federally funded org responsible for development of management plans for fisheries off coasts of Ore., Wash., and Cal. Answers inquiries, distributes publications. Services usually free.

42069. Pacific Northwest Research Center, P.O. Box 3708 (1571 Agate St), Eugene, OR 97403; (503) 686-5125. Nonprofit org interested in corporate, economic, and political issues in Northwest. Holdings include over 2,000 clipping files. Provides wide range of reference services. Onsite use free; other services subject to a fee.

42070. Pacific Power and Light Co., Library, 920 SW 6th Ave, Portland, OR 97204; (503) 243-4095. Interest in electrical engineering, electric utilities, business, environmental engineering, energy, telephone and water utilities. Holdings include documents, annual reports, pamphlets. Permits onsite use of collections.

42071. Philomath International Sliderule Society, P.O. Box 892, Philomath, OR 97370; (503) 758-0660. Interest in history, development, and applications of sliderule, as well as its inventor, John Napier. Provides reference services and consulting for a fee.

42072. RAIN: Journal of Appropriate Technology, 3116 North Williams, Portland, OR 97227; (503) 249-7218. Interest in new ideas about environment and community: appropriate technology, renewable energy development, community self-reliance. Substantial reference resources. Telephone inquiries answered free; other services provided for a fee.

42073. Radiation Center, Ore. State Univ, Corvallis, OR 97331; (503) 754-2341. Conducts research and instruction programs in nuclear science and nuclear engineering. Publishes annual technical reports and journal papers, answers inquiries, provides consulting services.

42074. Radiation Education Council, P.O. Box 705, Lakeview, OR 97630; (503) 947-4630 or 947-3740. Nonprofit educational group that informs public of environmental hazards associated with uranium mining. Holdings include transcripts of expert testimony, industry studies, county health studies. Permits onsite use of collections.

42075. Seafoods Laboratory, Ore. State Univ, 250 36th St, Astoria, OR 97103; (503) 325-4531. Interest in marine food science and technology; fish nutrition and utilization of fishery waste and byproducts. Answers brief inquiries, provides consulting services, permits onsite use of literature collection.

42076. Solar Energy Association of Oregon, 2637 Southwest Water Ave, Portland, OR 97201; (503) 224-7867. Promotes renewable energy development and energy conservation. Most services free, but special research, consulting, and workshops have modest cost (lower for members).

42077. University Professors for Academic Order, Publications Office, 635 Southwest 4th St, Corvallis, OR 97333; (503) 752-6512, 752-2349, or 753-7271. Promotes academic, professional, and administrative standards to ensure integrity of teaching and research professions. Provides advisory and consulting services, conducts seminars and workshops, distributes publications.

42078. Water Resources Research Institute, Ore. State Univ, Corvallis, OR 97331; (503) 754-4022. Interest in water resources, management, and quality; aquatic biology and ecology; groundwater physics and geology; weather modification; waste treatment, disposal. Answers inquiries, makes referrals, permits limited use of collection.

42079. Western Forestry and Conservation Association, 621 Southwest Morrison St, No. 529, Portland, OR 97205; (503) 226-4562. Promotes sound forest management, utilization, and conservation. Publishes books, conference and meeting proceedings, guides, handbooks, technical reports. Services for a fee.

42080. Western Rural Development Center, Ore. State Univ, 307 Extension Hall, Corvallis, OR 97331; (503) 754-3621. Interest in rural development research and extension education programs in Western U.S. Answers inquiries from anyone free, provides supportive and consulting services to land grant universities in the West.

42081. Western Wood Products Association, 1500 Yeon Bldg, Portland, OR 97204; (503) 224-3930. Interested in most aspects of lumber manufacturing and distribution. Answers inquiries, provides advisory and reference services. Much info free to public in published form.

42082. Wood Moulding and Millwork Producers Association, P.O. Box 25278 (1730 Southwest Skyline Blvd), Portland, OR 97225; (503) 292-9288. Represents manufacturers of wood mouldings, jambs, and outside door frames. Answers inquiries or refers inquireres to other sources, distributes publications and data compilations for a fee.

Pennsylvania

43001. API Standard Reference Materials, Schenley Park, Pittsburgh, PA 15213; (412) 578-2319. Interest in physical properties of hydrocarbons, organic sulfur and nitrogen compounds, reference and calibration standards. Provides standard reference material of hydrocarbons; sulfur and nitrogen compounds of very high purity for a fee.

43002. ARCO Research, Development and Engineering Library, ARCO Chemical Co., 3801 West Chester Pike, Newton Square, PA 19073; (215) 359-2000. Interest in petrochemical manufacture, polymer chemistry, petroleum refining. Maintains research library, provides access to computerized data bases (for use by special permission). Answers inquiries, provides reference services.

43003. Abrasive Engineering Society, 1700 Painters Run Rd, Pittsburgh, PA 15243; (412) 221-0909. Interest in surface finishing, abrasives and abrasive machinery, grinding. Publishes magazine, answers inquiries, provides reference services free to members, for a fee to others.

43004. Academy of Food Marketing Library, 54th St and City Line Ave, Philadelphia, PA 19131; (215) 879-7489. Interest in food marketing, merchandising, retailing. Maintains research collection (for onsite use). Publishes reference materials, Provides inquiry, consulting, reference services. Some services available to the public.

43005. Academy of Oral Dynamics, c/o Dr Joseph P. Skellchock, Secty, 2363 Philadelphia Ave, Chambersburg, PA 17201; (717) 263-2451. Interest in dentistry, oral rehabilitation. Holds data on various bite correction cases. Provides inquiry, advisory services; conducts seminars, courses. Some services for a fee.

43007. Acoustic Neuroma Association, P.O. Box 398, Carlisle, PA 17013; (717) 249-4783. Offers support, info for patients with acoustic neuromas, other benign tumors of cranial nerve. Serves as source of info for physicians; promotes research.

43008. Administrative Management Society, 2360 Maryland Rd, Willow Grove, PA 19090; (215) 659-4300. Interest in productive management of people, procedures, technology in offices. Publishes magazine, newsletters, research materials; answers inquiries; sponsors seminars, conferences on management topics.

43009. Air Brake Association, c/o Andy Pommer, Secty-Treasurer, Westinghouse Air Brake, P.O. Box 1, Wilmerding, PA 15148-0001. Interest in railroad air brake functions, related subjects; train handling. Publishes books and reports, answers inquiries, provides reference services at cost.

43011. Air Pollution Control Association, P.O. Box 2861, Pittsburgh, PA 15230; (412) 232-3444. Promotes air pollution control, adoption of reasonable performance standards. Offers publications, seminars to members to increase their knowledge of control technology, legislation, costs, administration.

43012. Air Products and Chemicals Library, P.O. Box 538, Allentown, PA 18105; (215) 481-7442. Interest in the chemical industry. Maintains info center with print, microform, AV materials (for onsite use); offers access to online data bases. Publishes newsletter, answers inquiries. Services free.

43013. Allegheny Observatory, Observatory Station, Pittsburgh, PA 15214; (412) 321-2400. Performs astronomical research. Maintains library, cataloged photographic plates (for onsite use). Publishes scholarly materials, provides consulting and reference services to researchers only.

43014. American Anti-Vivisection Society, 801 Old York Rd, Suite 204, Jenkintown, PA 19046; (215) 887-0816. Works to abolish painful animal experiments through appropriate legislation. Maintains library, answers inquiries, distributes publications. Services free.

43015. American Association of Avian Pathologists, c/o Univ of Pa., New Bolton Center, Kennett Square, PA 19348-1692. Interest in diseases of birds, particularly domestic species. Publishes journal, auto-tutorials. Provides info primarily thru its publication, but some inquiries referred to member specialists for reply.

43016. American Association of Botanical Gardens and Arboreta, P.O. Box 206, Swarthmore, PA 19081; (215) 328-9145. Serves professionals associated with botanical gardens, arboreta, garden centers; vocational, research programs. Publishes journal, newsletter, reference materials; answers inquiries. Services primarily for members.

43017. American Association of Meat Processors, P.O. Box 269, Elizabethtown, PA 17022; (717) 367-1168. Interest in meat processing. Maintains library, publishes bulletin, membership newsletter. Provides free inquiry, advisory, reference services; conducts workshops, convention, lobbying.

43018. American Association of Professional Hypnologists, P.O. Box 1112 (460 Market St, Ste 301), Williamsport, PA 17701; (717) 322-8305. Interest in all phases of hypnosis, hypnotherapy; maintains registry of hypnotherapists, hypnotechnicians. Publishes magazine, booklet; provides inquiry, advisory, reference services. Written replies require SASE.

43019. American Association of Veterinary Parasitologists, c/o Dr V.J. Theodorides, Secty-Treas, Smithkline Corp., 1600 Paoli Pike, West Chester, PA 19380; (215) 647-0900. Interest in veterinary parasitology. Publishes abstracts of papers presented at annual convention, answers brief inquiries, makes referrals.

43020. American Brittle Bone Society, 1256 Merrill Drive, Marshallton, West Chester, PA 19382; (215) 692-6248. Promotes welfare of patients suffering from brittle bone disease (osteogenesis imperfecta). Promotes research and public awareness, conducts conferences.

43021. American Canal Society, 809 Rathton Rd, York, PA 17403; (717) 843-4035. Promotes preservation, restoration, and appreciation of U.S. canals. Maintains library of print, and AV materials. Publishes bulletin and guide, provides free inquiry, reference services for members.

43022. American Carbon Society, c/o The Stackpole Corp, St Marys, PA 15857; (814) 781-1234. Promotes engineering, research in field of carbon. Publishes journal and abstracts. Answers inquiries, conducts seminars and conferences, distributes publications. Services primarily for members, but others assisted.

43023. American Cavy Breeder's Association, c/o George W. Long, Secty-Treas, RD 2, Box 180A, Zionsville, PA 18092; (215) 967-2085. Interest in cavy (guinea pig) breeding, marketing, use as exhibition and lab animals. Publishes newsletter and guide. Answers inquiries free; other services for members only (membership open to public).

43024. American Cleft Palate Educational Foundation, 331 Salk Hall, Univ of Pittsburgh, Pittsburgh, PA 15261; (412) 681-9620. Works with cranio-facial anomalies, cleft lip, and palate. Publishes reference material; provides inquiry, advisory, and reference services; conducts seminars. Services, provided at cost, primarily for professionals and parents.

43025. American College Admissions Advisory Center, 2401 Pennsylvania Ave, Ste 1051, Philadelphia, PA 19130; (215) 232-5225. Interest in educational and career counseling, educational communications. Provides inquiry, advisory, consulting, and reference services, conducts seminars and workshops. Services at cost.

43026. American College of Laboratory Animal Medicine, c/o C. Max Lang, Secty-Treas, Dept of Comparative Medicine, Hershey Medical Center, Penn. State Univ, Hershey, PA 17033. Specialty board for education, training, and research in lab animal medicine. Administers certification exams, publishes scholarly materials, conducts seminars and forums.

43027. American College of Physicians, 4200 Pine St, Philadelphia, PA 19104; (215) 243-1200, (800) 523-1546. Natl professional assn of internists that sponsors continuing education and self-evaluation programs, holds scientific meetings. Produces and distributes publications, public info films. Serves members, govt, and private sector.

43028. American College of Veterinary Pathologists, c/o Dr Helen Acland, Secty-Treas, 382 W State Rd, Kennett Square, PA 19348; (215) 444-3432. Works in comparative and clinical vet pathology. Consults on animal studies involving toxicity, drug evaluation, and carcinogenicity. Conducts certification exams, publishes journal, answers inquiries. Services primarily for members.

43029. American College of Veterinary Surgeons, c/o Dr William J. Donawick, Univ of Penn. School of Veterinary Medicine, New Bolton Center, 382 W State Rd, Kennett Square, PA 19348; (215) 444-5800. Certifying agency for veterinary surgeons. Publishes journal and directory, answers inquiries free, conducts seminars for a fee.

43030. American Dahlia Society, c/o Stanley Johnson, Trustee, 406 Franklin Ave, Cheltenham, PA 19012. Interest in dahlias: cultivation, classification, care. Maintains library of print, AV materials. Publishes bulletin, answers inquiries, provides consulting services. Services free.

43031. American Diopter and Decibel Society, c/o E.A. Rittenhouse, Exec Secty, 522 Walnut St, McKeesport, PA 15132; (412) 672-7486. Interest in postgraduate education in ophthalmology, otolaryngology. Publishes proceedings, books; answers inquiries; conducts conferences, seminars, demonstrations. Services free to members, at cost to others.

43032. American Electronic Laboratories, P.O. Box 552 (Richardson Rd, Colmar, PA), Lansdale, PA 19446; (215) 822-2929. Interest in electronic warfare, communications, data processing; has reference collection. Answers inquiries, permits onsite reference.

43033. American Entomological Society, 1900 Race St, Philadelphia, PA 19103; (215) 561-3978. Fosters, conducts, publishes research on systematics, ecology, morphology of insects. Library for onsite use; answers inquiries on a limited basis. Services available to all, but on limited basis.

43034. American Friends Service Committee, 1501 Cherry St, Philadelphia, PA 19102; (215) 241-7000. Aids refugees, war victims; developing nations; U.S. poor, urban minorities, seasonal farm workers. Has archives. Publishes bulletin, answers inquiries, maintains speakers bureau. Services free.

43035. American Friends Service Committee National Action, Research on the Military Industrial Complex, 1501 Cherry St, Philadelphia, PA 19102; (215) 241-7175. Interest in U.S. foreign policy (especially Central America, South Africa, arms trade, military/industrial complex). Maintains collection of research materials. Publishes print and AV materials, answers inquiries, sells publications.

43036. American Indian Research and Resource Institute, P.O. Box 576, Gettysburg Coll, Gettysburg, PA 17325; (717) 334-3131. Studies history, culture of American Indians (especially in eastern U.S.). Holds reference collection, publishes research. Provides inquiry and consulting services, conducts seminars. Services free, primarily for tribal groups.

43037. American Institute for Property and Liability Underwriters, 720 Providence Rd, Malvern, PA 19355-0770; (215) 644-2100. Administers natl exams, certification, code of ethics for property, liability insurance industry. Publishes educational materials. Provides inquiry, advisory services; conducts seminars, workshops. Some services free.

43039. American Institute of Medical Climatology, 1023 Welsh Rd, Philadelphia, PA 19115; (215) 673-8368. Promotes bioclimatology, biometeorology. Organizes, conducts, correlates pertinent studies on relationship of weather, climate, and life. Sponsors seminars and lectures, offers consulting services.

43040. American Laryngological Association, c/o Eugene N. Myers, M.D., Secty, Eye and Ear Hospital, 230 Lothrop St, Ste 1115, Pittsburgh, PA 15213; (412) 647-2110. Interest in study of larynx, nose, nasal sinuses and their pathology. Publishes technical reports, answers inquiries, conducts seminars and workshops. Services free.

43041. American Law Institute-American Bar Association, Committee on Continuing Professional Education, 4025 Chestnut St, Philadelphia, PA 19104; (215) 243-1600. Furthers continuing legal education of members of Bar. Publishes educational materials (print, AV), conducts legal education courses, permits onsite use of library with prior permission.

43042. American Mushroom Institute, 907 East Baltimore Pike, Kennett Square, PA 19348; (215) 388-7806. Promotes cultivated mushrooms; fosters research programs for the industry, maintains statistics. Publishes newsletter and promotional materials, answers inquiries.

43043. American Musicological Society, 201 S 34th St, Philadelphia, PA 19104; (215) 898-8698. Org of scholars who study, teach music. Publishes journal, newsletter, directory, scholarly materials; answers inquiries. Most services free to members, others interested in musicology.

43044. American Myalgic Encephalomyelitis Society, 494 Meadow Lane, Gulph Mills, PA 19406; (215) 688-3832. Supports research on myalgic encephalomyelitis; gives support, help, info to patients; educates medical profession; raises funds to combat the disease.

43046. American Philatelic Society, P.O. Box 8000 (100 Oakwood Ave), State Coll, PA 16801; (814) 237-3803. Interest in philately, postal history. Maintains reference collection of postage stamps and library (for onsite use). Publishes journal and books, answers inquiries, identifies material. Some services for a fee.

43047. American Philosophical Society Library, 105 S 5th St, Philadelphia, PA 19106; (215) 627-0706. Interest in history of early U.S.; science, business, economics; American Indian linguistics. Has collection of print, graphic, microform, AV materials (for onsite use). Publishes journals, provides inquiry services, conducts seminars. For scholars only.

43048. American Schools of Oriental Research, 4243 Spruce St, Philadelphia, PA 19104; (215) 222-4643. Sponsors and supports historical, archaeological research (especially in Near East). Has small collection of books and periodicals; publishes journals, newsletter, and monographs; answers inquiries.

43049. American Society for Adolescent Psychiatry, 24 Green Valley Rd, Wallingford, PA 19086; (215) 566-1054. Fosters info exchange among psychiatrists of adolescents and stimulates research into nature, problems of adolescence. Publishes journal, newsletter, and directory, conducts seminars and meetings. Services at cost.

43051. American Society of Testing Materials, 1916 Race St, Philadelphia, PA 19103; (215) 299-5400. Promotes standardization of specifications, testing of materials, products, systems, and services. Has library of technical, scientific data and periodicals; publishes journals, technical materials, consumer info; answers inquiries.

03052. American Society of Testing Materials, Committee on Industrial Water, 1916 Race St, Philadelphia, PA 19103; (215) 299-5400. Develops voluntary standards, related techonology for water and water-formed deposits. Publishes manuals, standards, technical reports; answers inquiries; makes referrals.

43053. American Society of Testing Materials, Committee on Plastics, 1916 Race St, Philadelphia, PA 19103; (215) 299-5400. Establishes and publishes standards for plastics, including test methods. Answers brief inquiries, permits onsite use of collection.

43054. American Society of Mammologists, c/o Dr Gordon L. Kirkland,Jr., Secty-Treas, Vertebrate Museum, Shippensburg Univ, Shippensburg, PA 17257. Interest in mammology (anatomy, systematics, ecology, physiology, life history, and distribution). Publishes journal and research materials, answers inquiries. Services free, available for nonprofit purposes.

43055. American Society of Psychopathology of Expression, c/o Dr Irene Jakab, Chairman, Western Psychiatric Institute and Clinic, 3811 O'Hara St, Pittsburgh, PA 15213; (412) 624-2132. Multidisciplinary org of psychiatrists, psychologists, art therapists, art critics, artists, and sociologists interested in expression through artistic activities. Provides free consulting and reference services.

43056. American Studies Association, c/o Univ of Penn, 307 College Hall, Philadelphia, PA 19104; (215) 898-5408. Promotes study of U.S. culture. Publishes scholarly and reference materials, answers inquiries, conducts seminars, conventions, and conferences. Services free, except publications and conferences.

43057. American Swedish Museum. 1900 Pattison Ave, Philadelphia, PA 19145; (215) 389-1776. Interest in history of Swedish people in America. Permits onsite use of collection of artifacts, art, and literature. Publishes newsletter and bibliography, answers inquiries, conducts workshops. Services free.

43058. American Veterinary Dental Society, c/o Dr Colin Harvey, Secty, 3850 Spruce St, Philadelphia, PA 19104. Furthers education in veterinary dentistry. Publishes newsletter; provides inquiry, advisory, reference services; conducts seminars, workshops. Some services free, others for a fee.

43059. Annenberg School of Communication Library, 3620 Walnut St, Philadelphia, PA 19104; (215) 898-7027. Interest in theory, research in communication; history, technology of communication. Holdings available for onsite use, loan (fee charged). Publishes reference materials, provides reference services.

43060. Antique Automobile Club of America, P.O. Box 417 (501 W Governor Rd), Hershey, PA 17033; (717) 534-1910. Interest in history, technology, maintenance of antique cars. Maintains library, archives (print, AV, magnetic tape materials). Publishes magazine, answers inquiries, lends films to affiliates.

43061. Applied Research Laboratory, P.O. Box 30, State Coll, PA 16804; (814) 865-6621. Undertakes research in underwater acoustics, fluids engineering, propulsion, sonar, hydrodynamics, ultrasonics. Maintains research library, publishes technical reports. Much info is classified, unavailable to outsiders.

43062. Aquarian Research Foundation, 5620 Morton St, Philadelphia, PA 19144; (215) 849-3237. Research, educational org that encourages new age of love, peace. Publishes newsletter, print and AV materials; provides inquiry, advisory, reference services; conducts lectures. Most services free.

43063. Associated Services for the Blind, 919 Walnut St, Philadelphia, PA 19107; (215) 627-0600. Produces materials in Braille, large type, audio for visually impaired. Makes available sensory aid devices; provides training in use. Offers inquiry, referral services; publishes reference materials, newsletter. Runs sensory aids store.

43064. Association for Children and Adults with Learning Disabilities, c/o Jean S. Petersen, Exec Director, 4156 Library Rd, Pittsburgh, PA 15234; (412) 341-1515. Interest in learning disabilities. Publishes magazine, books, abstracts, and indexes, provides reference

services, conducts seminars. Services free (except publications).

43065. Association for Vital Records and Health Statistics, c/o Patricia W. Potrzebowski, State Health Data Center, Pa. Dept of Health, Box 90, Harrisburg, PA 17108; (717) 783-2548. Represents U.S. states, territories regarding vital, health statistics systems. Publishes newsletter, directory. Provides inquiry and advisory services, conducts seminars. Services free to members, at cost to others.

43066. Association for the Advancement of Sports Potential, P.O. Box 185 (Doe Run Rd), Unionville, PA 19375; (215) 347-1641, (800) 223-7014. Funds research in equine, human sports medicine. Has library of research and reference materials (for onsite use), data bank, films. Publishes technical reports, data; provides inquiry, consulting, reference services at cost.

43067. Association of College Honor Societies, 1411 Lafayette Parkway, Williamsport, PA 17701; (717) 323-7641. Coordinates college, univ honor societies. Publishes list of member societies (single copy free), answers inquiries.

43068. Association of Commercial Mail Receiving Agencies, 221 North Cedar Crest Blvd, Allentown, PA 18104; (215) 820-5518. Trade assn for mail receivers, allied business services. Publishes newsletter, reference materials; provides inquiry, consulting services; conducts workshops. Fee for some services.

43069. Association of Concert Bands, P.O. Box 71, Greentown, PA 18426; (717) 857-0830. Promotes community wind, percussion music orgs (in U.S., abroad). Publishes magazine, newsletter, directory, project reports; provides inquiry, advisory services; conducts conferences. Services free to members.

43070. Association of Food and Drug Officials, PO Box 3425, York, PA 17402; (717) 757-2888. Promotes, enforces uniform food and drug, consumer protection laws. Members are officials responsible for enforcement of laws, regulations in the field. Sponsors annual conference; monitors USDA legislative, enforcement activities.

43071. Association of Information Systems Professionals, 1015 N York Rd, Willow Grove, PA 19090; (215) 657-6300. Promotes methods, techniques on info processing in office environment. Publishes periodicals, research materials, and AV programs, answers inquiries, conducts workshops, maintains speakers bureau.

43072. Association of Iron and Steel Engineers, Gateway III, Ste 2350, Pittsburgh, PA 15222; (412) 281-6323. Interest in tech, engineering aspects of production, processing of iron, steel. Publishes magazine and yearbook, answers brief inquiries from steel industry or accredited orgs.

43073. Association of Life Insurance Medical Directors of America, c/o Dr Frank T. Mansure, Secty, P.O. Box

7378, Philadelphia, PA 19101; (215) 472-5000. Seeks to advance science of medicine as applied to insurance. Publishes journals, studies, directory; answers inquiries.

43074. Association of Overseas Educators, c/o William J. Edner, 147 North 4th St, Hughesville, PA 17737. Org of educators who have taught or lectured abroad; interested in intl education. Has small collection of print, AV, machine-readable materials; publishes newsletter (for members only).

43075. Association of Professional Vocal Ensembles, 1830 Spruce St, Philadelphia, PA 19103; (215) 545-4444. Serves professional vocal ensembles. Sponsors internships, conferences, and workshops, publishes magazine, provides inquiry, reference, and referral services. Some services for a fee.

43076. Association of Voluntary Action Scholars, Human Development Bldg, S-126, Attn: Dr Drew Hyman, Penn State Univ, Univ Park, PA 16802; (814) 863-2482. Interest in citizen participation, voluntary activity. Publishes journal, newsletter; provides inquiry, reference services; conducts conventions, workshops; permits onsite use of collections. Some services free, others at cost.

43077. Automatic Identification Manufacturers, 1326 Freeport Rd, Pittsburgh, PA 15238; (412) 782-1624. Trade assn of automatic identification industry. Compiles basic trade info; offers free inquiry, referral services; conducts seminars; distributes publications, slide sets. Fee for some services.

43078. Aviation Distributors and Manufacturers Association, 1900 Arch St, Philadelphia, PA 19103; (215) 564-3484. Interest in manufacture, distribution of general aviation parts, supplies, accessories. Publishes directories, answers inquiries. Aviation education info free.

43079. BCR National Laboratories, P.O. Box 278 (350 Hochberg Rd), Monroeville, PA 15146; (412) 327-1600. Research org for coal industry. Has print, AV materials; publishes reference, research materials; answers inquiries. Limited time available for nonmembers of corp.

43080. Balloon Club of America, c/o Peter Pellegrino, Pres, 351 Eagle Rd, Newton, PA 18940; (215) 968-2425. Interest in flying, operating free balloons. Publishes magazine, answers inquiries, provides consulting services. Services usually free.

43081. Behavior Therapy and Research Society, c/o Temple Univ Medical School and Medical Coll of Pa./EPPI, Henry Ave, Philadelphia, PA 19129; (215) 849-0607. Research, therapy org of psychiatrists, psychologists. Interest in all aspects of behavior therapy, behavior modification. Publishes journal and directory, provides free referral service.

43082. Bethlehem Steel Corp., Schwab Information Center, Martin Tower, Bethlehem, PA 18016; (215) 694-3325. Interest in all aspects of steel industry. Maintains research library with print, microform materials; has access to online services (for onsite use). Provides reference, newspaper clipping services.

43083. Betz Laboratories, 4636 Somerton Rd, Trevose, PA 19047; (215) 355-3300. Specialty chemical corp working in industrial water systems, related energy management areas. Maintains reference library (print, microform, online materials); permits onsite use by researchers. Publishes handbook, reports.

43084. Bicycle Network, P.O. Box 8194, Philadelphia, PA 19101; (215) 222-1253. Publishes info on developments in bicycle transportation, pedal technology. Provides clipping, inquiry, advisory, abstracting services; conducts seminars, workshops. Services provided at cost.

43085. Big Brothers/Big Sisters of America, 230 North 13th St, Philadelphia, PA 19107; (215) 567-2748. Federation of agencies that provide children with mature, stable, adult friends to provide guidance, understanding. Provides technical assistance, consultation to agencies. Publishes newsletter, answers inquiries.

43086. Bio-Dynamic Farming and Gardening Association, P.O. Box 550, Kimberton, PA 19442; (215) 327-2420. Promotes biodynamic method of agriculture to improve nutrition, health. Publishes reports on agribiology, especially testing of soils, composts, produce. Sponsors conferences; consulting, testing services provided for a fee.

43087. Biological Abstracts, BioSciences Information Service (BIOSIS), 2100 Arch St, Philadelphia, PA 19103-1399; (215) 587-4800, (800) 523-4806. Interest in research literature of life sciences. Publishes abstract journals, indexes; leases magnetic tape on-line, offline services. Provides descriptive user aids, educational programs, free newsletters.

43088. Black Music Association, 1500 Locust St, Ste 1905, Philadelphia, PA 19102; (215) 545-8600. Org of musicians, music industry members interested in protecting, preserving, perpetuating black music; expanding black music market. Publishes newsletter, conducts seminars and annual conference.

43089. Brandywine Conservancy, P.O. Box 141 (U.S. 1 and Route 100), Chadds Ford, PA 19317; (215) 388-7601. Preserves significant natural, historic resources. Maintains data bank on local watershed, reference library, museum. Publishes handbooks, technical materials; answers inquiries; provides planning, management services; conducts field trips, slide talks. Fee for services.

43090. Brodart On-Line Support Services, 500 Arch St, Williamsport, PA 17705; (717) 326-2461. Maintains on-line data base on 1+ million volumes in English (including availability). Provides inquiry, microform services; provides complete on-line acquisition; conducts workshops. Services available for a fee.

43091. Bureau of Mines Pittsburgh Research Center, Documents Library, P.O. Box 18070, Pittsburgh, PA 15236; (412) 675-6657. Undertakes mine health, safety studies. Maintains reference collection (for onsite use), answers inquiries. Services free.

43092. Bushy Run Research Center, 4400 Fifth Ave, Pittsburgh, PA 15213; (412) 327-1020. Interest in mammalian toxicity of synthetic organic chemicals by all portals of entry. Maintains research library, answers brief inquiries free, provides consulting on cost basis. Services to colleagues only.

43093. CALM, P.O. Box 281 (225 Haverford Ave), Narberth, PA 19072; (215) 667-7508 Offers legal aid to lesbian mothers: free local custody litigation, natl consultation. Provides inquiry and reference services, conducts workshops. Services free (except court costs), chiefly for lesbian, gay parents.

43094. CCCO: An Agency for Military and Draft Counseling, 2208 South St, Philadelphia, PA 19146; (215) 545-4626. Offers counseling, other services to conscientious objectors. Publishes newsletter, handbook; answers inquiries; provides consulting, referral services; trains military, draft counselors.

43095. Calgon Corp., Information Center, Box 1346, Pittsburgh, PA 15230; (412) 777-8205. Interest in industrial chemistry of water treatment, water-based processes. Has reference library of print, microform materials; access to data bases (permits onsite use). Answers inquiries, provides reference services.

43096. Cancer Guidance Institute, 5604 Solway St, Pittsburgh, PA 15217; (412) 521-2291. Assists people affected by cancer. Provides 24-hour hotline for Pittsburgh area, speaker service, workshops, conferences, publications; refers inquirers to other agencies.

43097. Cardeza Foundation for Hematologic Research, Tocantins Memorial Library, 1015 Walnut St, Philadelphia, PA 19107; (215) 928-8474. Interest in all facets of hematology. Maintains reference collection (for onsite use).

43098. Carnegie Hero Fund Commission, 606 Oliver Bldg, Pittsburgh, PA 15222; (412) 281-1302. Makes awards for acts of heroism involving extraordinary life risk. Has collection of data, investigative reports on acts of heroism. Publishes annual reports and lists of awards, answers inquiries.

43099. Catalog of Fossil Spores and Pollen, Coal Research Section, College of Earth and Mineral Sciences, 517 Deike Bldg, Penn State Univ, Univ Park, PA 16802; (814) 865-7232. Undertakes, facilitates research in fossil spores and pollen, palynological systematics, paleopalynology. Has reference collection (for onsite use); publishes research, reference materials (for sale).

43100. Center for Administration of Legal Systems, Duquesne Univ, School of Business and Administration, Pittsburgh, PA 15282; (412) 434-6244. Researches law administration; legal systems, answers inquiries, provides consulting services; conducts seminars. Services available to all; provided at cost to nonprofit orgs.

43101. Center for Air Environment Studies, Intercollege Research Programs, 226 Fenske Laboratory, Penn State Univ, Univ Park, PA 16802; (814) 865-1415. Researches air environment (especially pollution), effects on biosystems. Maintains research collection of print, microform materials (for onsite use); publishes reference, research materials; answers inquiries.

43102. Center for Educational Diagnosis and Remediation, 104 CEDAR Bldg, Penn State Univ, Univ Park, PA 16802; (814) 865-1881. Promotes training of psychologists interested in, knowledgeable about, education, psychology. Provides inquiry, consulting services; clinical programs. Some fees for evaluations. Clinic services available on referral basis.

43103. Center for Information and Computer Science, Mart Library, Bethlehem, PA 18015; (215) 861-3000. Interest in properties and transmission of info, info systems, humans in communication process, artificial intelligence, robotics. Publishes reports, answers inquiries, provides consulting services free or for a fee.

43104. Center for Japanese Studies, Lewisburg, PA 17837; (717) 524-1450. Interest in Japan: history, foreign relations, literature, anthropology. Has library of books, periodicals, TV programs (for onsite use). Publishes books, answers inquiries free, provides advisory services on cost basis.

43105. Center for Jewish Community Studies, c/o Temple Univ, 1017 Gladfelter Hall, Philadelphia, PA 19122; (215) 787-1459. Explores history, contemporary life of Jewish people; undertakes research, educational projects. Maintains library, archives for onsite use. Publishes newsletter, research. Fee for some services.

43106. Center for Photobiology, Health Sciences Center, Temple Univ, 3322 North Broad St, Philadelphia, PA 19140; (215) 221-3924. Researches cutaneous oncology, photobiology, phototherapy. Publishes scholarly materials; provides inquiry, consulting, research services; conducts seminars. Some services for a fee.

43107. Center for Quality of Working Life, Capitol Campus, Middleton, PA 17057; (717) 948-6053. Interest in quality of working life, organizational effectiveness. Maintains library, has access to data bases. Publishes newsletter, provides inquiry services, conducts workshops. Fee for some services.

43108. Center for Studies in Criminology and Criminal Law, 37th and Spruce Sts, 4th Fl, Philadelphia, PA 19104; (215) 898-7411. Conducts research in criminology. Has library for onsite use. Publishes bibliographies and research materials, answers inquiries. Services free, available to graduate students and professionals.

43109. Center for Women and Sport, Sports Research Institute, White Bldg, Penn State Univ, Univ Park, PA 16802; (814) 865-7591. Researches physiology, psychology, sociology, biomechanics of female response to vigorous exercise, competitive sport. Provides inquiry, advisory services; conducts workshops, conferences. Fee for some services.

43110. Center for the History of American Needlework, Carlow Coll, 3333 Fifth Ave, Pittsburgh, PA 15213; (412) 578-6016. Interest in needle, textile arts. Has research library, slide registry, collection of needlework. Publishes newsletter, catalogs, AV materials; Provides inquiry and reference services, traveling exhibits, speakers. Fee for some services.

43111. Center for the Interaction of Animals and Society, Dept of Clinical Studies, Univ of Penn School of Veterinary Medicine, 3800 Spruce St, Philadelphia, PA 19104; (215) 898-4695. Conducts research into interrelationships between people and animals; applies this knowledge in clinical, consulting services. Provides free inquiry, advisory, reference services.

43112. Center for the Study of Federalism, Temple Univ, Gladfelter Hall, 10th Fl, Philadelphia, PA 19122; (215) 787-7784. Promotes, studies federalism as practical means of organizing political power. Maintains archive (onsite use permitted); publishes journal, studies, research materials; provides consulting services for a fee.

43113. Chase Econometric Associates, 150 Monument Rd, Bala Cynwyd, PA 19004; (215) 667-6000. Makes, publishes econometric forecasts. Maintains collection of historical, forecast data bases. Provides inquiry, consulting, magnetic tape services; conducts seminars, workshops. Services for a fee.

43114. Choice Communities, 1427 Vine St, 4th Fl, Philadelphia, PA 19102-1099; (215) 568-6715. Commercial consulting firm working in racially integrated, multifamily housing management, equity investment. Provides inquiry, advisory, consulting services for a fee.

43115. Church and Synagogue Library Association, P.O. Box 1130, Bryn Mawr, PA 19010; (215) 853-2870. Serves church, synagogue libraries. Publishes magazine and bibliographies, answers inquiries, provides consulting services. Most services free, some at cost.

43116. Clark Kerr Apple Variety Museum, Coll of Agriculture, 7 Tyson Bldg, Penn State Univ, Univ Park, PA 16802. Interest in pomology; apple varieties, cultivars; germplasm. Collects Colonial-era apple cultivars, answers inquiries free, supplies budwood only to other univ, research personnel.

43117. Coal Research Section, Coll of Earth and Mineral Sciences, 517 Deike Bldg, Penn State Univ, Univ Park, PA 16802; (814) 865-6545. Undertakes research to characterize U.S. coals, carbon. Maintains data base, samples for research. Publishes research materials, answers inquiries, conducts seminars. Services for a fee.

43118. Colorcon, Moyer Blvd, West Point, PA 19486; (215) 699-7733. Interest in coatings, colorings for food and drugs. Maintains color library, lake mixtures. Publishes technical materials; provides inquiry, consulting services; conducts practical seminars (no charge).

43119. Colt Industries, Crucible Research Center Library, P.O. Box 88, Pittsburgh, PA 15230; (412) 923-2955. Interest in stainless, tool, alloy steels; high-temperature alloys, materials; magnetic materials; titanium, its alloys; powder metallurgy. Has library of print, AV materials; access to online data bases.

43120. Combustion Institute, 5001 Baum Blvd, Pittsburgh, PA 15213; (412) 687-1366. Nonprofit scientific society concerned with combustion, flame, explosion phenomena. Publishes journal, proceedings of biennial symposia; answers inquiries.

43121. Communications Media Research Center, School of Library and Information Sciences (135 North Bellefield), Pittsburgh, PA 15260; (412) 624-5234. Identifies impact of various types of info in interactive, intelligent environments. Publishes research, reference materials; provides inquiry, advisory services; conducts seminars. Services at cost.

43122. Congress of Neurological Surgeons, c/o Joseph C. Maroon, M.D., Secty, Presbyterian-Univ Hospital, Pittsburgh, PA 15213. Interest in neurological surgery, allied specialties. Maintains reference library. Publishes journal, proceedings of annual meeting, newletter, directories; distributes brochures, some public relations materials.

43123. Conoco Coal Research Division, 4000 Brownsville Rd, Library, PA 15129; (412) 854-6688. Interest in fuel technology, especially coal, its chemistry, marketing, conversion. Has library of print, microform holdings (available for onsite use); answers brief inquiries. Publications usually for corporate use only.

43124. Cooperative Work Experience Education Association, P.O. Box 324, Newtown, PA 18940; (215) 968-8018. Promotes coop vocational education, work experience programs, on-the-job training. Publishes newsletter; provides program development, operation, evaluation, staff improvement services; conducts workshops. Most services free.

43125. Cornucopia Project, 33 E Minor St, Emmaus, PA 18049; (215) 967-5171. Concerned with future of U.S. food system. Maintains computerized data base. Publishes newsletter, print, AV materials; provides inquiry, advisory services; conducts seminars. Most services free.

43126. Council for Chemical Research, P.O. Box AJ (1011 Brookside Rd, Wescosville, PA), Allentown, PA 18106; (215) 395-4550. Nonprofit assn of companies, univs that promotes cooperative activities on behalf U.S. chemical industry, funds basic research in chemistry, chemical engineering. Answers inquiries.

43127. Council on Career Development for Minorities, 62 Highland Ave, Bethlehem, PA 18017; (215) 868-1421. Performs research in career planning, placement for college graduates. Maintains collection of technical reports, literature, data; publishes journals, reference, research materials (some limits on distribution).

43128. Council on Hotel, Restaurant, and Institutional Education, Human Development Bldg Room S-208, Penn State Univ, Univ Park, PA 16802; (814) 863-0586. Interest in organized education for mass housing, feeding industries (hotels, restaurants, clubs, hospitals, schools, in-plant feeding). Publishes newsletter, journal, and directory, answers inquiries. Fees sometimes charged.

43129. Council on Tall Buildings and Urban Habitat, c/o Fritz Engineering Laboratory No. 13, Lehigh Univ, Bethlehem, PA 18015; (215) 861-3515. Studies, reports on all aspects of tall bldgs. Maintains data base. Publishes scholarly, reference materials; answers inquiries; conducts seminars, conferences. Most services free.

43130. Curtis Institute of Music, Library, 1726 Locust St, Philadelphia, PA 19103; (215) 893-5265. Serves school to train young musicians for performance careers. Has library of music scores, recordings, books, journals; archives (with papers of musicians). Answers some inquiries, makes interlibrary loans.

43131. Cystic Fibrosis and Pediatric Pulmonary Centers, 230 North Broad St, Philadelphia, PA 19102; (215) 448-7766. Researches pediatric pulmonary disease, cystic fibrosis. Maintains library, data bases. Publishes reference materials; provides inquiry, education, consulting services; conducts seminars. Services free, for health professionals.

43132. Dairy Society International, 7185 Ruritan Dr, Chambersburg, PA 17201; (717) 375-4392. Promotes dairy industry, world milk markets. Clearinghouse for technical info, promotional materials; maintains library. Publishes periodicals, provides inquiry and consulting services. Services free to members, at cost to others.

43133. Daniel Baugh Institute of Anatomy, Jefferson Medical College, Dept of Anatomy, 1020 Locust St, Philadelphia, PA 19107; (215) 928-7820. Conducts, publishes research; offers training in birth defects. Provides inquiry and consulting services, conducts seminars, distributes publications. Services provided at cost.

43134. Data and Research Technology Corp., 1102 McNeilly Ave, Pittsburgh, PA 15216; (412) 563-2212. Commercial org providing info, computerized data bases. Publishes magazine, books, articles, reference materials; provides inquiry, advisory, consulting, reference services; conducts seminars. Services provided for a fee.

43135. Deer Research Facility, Agricultural Experiment Station, 324 Henning Bldg, Penn State Univ, Univ Park, PA 16802; (814) 863-3665. Interest in white-tailed deer (basic biology, nutrition, physiology, behavior, growth rate, breeding). Answers inquiries, provides consulting services. Services free.

43136. Defense Logistics Agency Technical Data Management Office, Defense Industrial Supply Center, 700 Robbins Ave, Philadelphia, PA 19111; (215) 697-2757. Interest in technical data on hardware for armed services; weapon systems. Publishes reference materials; provides consulting, reference services; permits on-site use of collection. Services free, for govt agencies.

43137. Deltiologists of America, 10 Felton Ave, Ridley Park, PA 19078; (215) 521-1092. Interest in antique picture postcard collecting. Maintains reference library. Publishes bulletin, reference materials; provides inquiry, consulting, reference services. Services primarily for members; send SASE with queries.

43138. Dental Laboratory Conference, 1918 Pine St, Philadelphia, PA 19103; (215) 546-2313. Assn of dental labs seeking to improve technical standards of industry and develop better, more efficient lab management. Publishes magazine, provides inquiry and advisory services. Most services free.

43139. Department of Energy Coal Preparation Branch, Pittsburgh Energy Technology Center, P.O. Box 10940, Pittsburgh, PA 15236; (412) 675-5706. Interest in processing, preparation of raw coal. Maintains extensive coal washability data bank. Publishes technical materials, answers inquiries. Services free.

43140. Department of Energy, Division of Coal Fired Magnetohydrodynamics, Pittsburgh Energy Technology Center, Coal Utilization Branch, Box 10940, Pittsburgh, PA 15236; (412) 675-6000. Administers R&D program for proof-of-concept demonstration of magnetohydrodynamic (MHD) electrical power generation. Publishes technical, research materials; answers inquiries; conducts seminars, workshops.

43141. Department of Pathology, Univ of Pittsburgh School of Medicine, 3550 Terrace and DeSoto St, Pittsburgh, PA 15261; (412) 624-2441. Works in experimental pathology. Keeps large colony of inbred, congenic, recombinant rats; maintains reference library. Answers inquiries from the scientific community free of charge.

43142. Department of Pharmacology, Univ of Pittsburgh School of Medicine, Pittsburgh, PA 15261; (412) 624-2531. Interest in all aspects of pharmacology. Answers inquiries, provides consulting and reference services, makes referrals. Services available to members of the scientific, professional communities.

43143. Developmental Disabilities Center, c/o Temple Univ, RHA, 9th Fl, Philadelphia, PA 19122; (215) 787-1356. Provides training, research on developmentally disabled. Publishes research; provides inquiry, advisory services; conducts seminars, workshops. Fee for some services.

43144. Devereux Foundation, P.O. Box 400, Devon, PA 19333; (215) 964-3000. Network of day, residential treatment centers for emotionally, mentally handicapped. Publications list available. Provides inquiry, advisory services; conducts seminars. Services at cost.

43145. E. I. du Pont de Nemours and Co., Marshall Laboratory Library, P.O. Box 3886 (3500 Grays Ferry Ave), Philadelphia, PA 19146; (215) 339-6314. Interest in paint, coatings; adhesives; analytical, organic, polymer chemistry. Maintains research collection, has access to computerized data bases. Lends materials, except unpublished internal info.

43146. Early American Society, 2245 Kohn Rd, Box 8200, Harrisburg, PA 17105; (717) 657-9555. Interest in U.S. social history (1600-1899), especially architecture; furnishings; decorating; arts, crafts. Publishes magazine, answers inquiries, conducts tours. Most services free.

43148. Educational Commission for Foreign Medical Graduates, 3624 Market St, Philadelphia, PA 19104; (215) 386-5900. Sponsors foreign medical graduates entering U.S. for graduate medical education. Administers exams, reviews qualifications, certifies candidates. Provides free inquiry, advisory services.

43149. Emergency Care Research Institute, 5200 Butler Pike, Plymouth Meeting, PA 19462; (215) 825-6000. Interest in evaluation, testing of medical devices, equipment, systems. Maintains reference library, data base. Publishes magazine, reference materials; provides inquiry, consulting services and accident investigations. Some services for a fee.

43150. Emulsion Polymers Institute, Lehigh Univ, Sinclair Laboratory, Bethlehem, PA 18015; (215) 758-3000. Researches emulsion polymers, latexes, coatings. Publishes reference, teaching materials; provides inquiry, consulting, reference services; conducts seminars; permits onsite use of collection. Services available at cost.

43151. Encyclopaedia Cinematographica, Audio-Visual Services, 203 Special Services Bldg, Penn State Univ, Univ Park, PA 16802; (814) 865-6315. Encyclopedia of 16mm films in biological, social, technical sciences. Most films silent, but accompanied by printed documents. Publishes catalogs (with rental fees); provides onsite access to collection, screening facilities.

43152. Ensanian Physicochemical Institute, P.O. Box 98, Eldred, PA 16731; (814) 225-3296. Researches gravitation, its relation to the sciences; extraterrestrial civilizations; many other fields. Owns research collection; publishes journal, proceedings; provides inquiry, reference, consulting services.

43153. Environmental Coalition on Nuclear Power, 433 Orlando Ave, State College, PA 16801; (814) 237-3900. Seeks to replace nuclear power with safer sources. Has extensive reference collection. Publishes magazine, reference materials; Provides inquiry, advisory, reference, and litigation services, speakers; conducts workshops. Services free or at cost.

43154. Erie National Wildlife Refuge, U.S. Fish and Wildlife Service, RD 1, Wood Duck Lane, Guys Mills, PA 16327; (814) 789-3585. Interest in migratory birds, mammals, other wildlife. Answers inquiries, provides consulting services, permits onsite use of (small) collection. Services free.

43155. Escherichia coli Reference Center, Dept of Veterinary Science, 105 Animal Industry Bldg, Penn State Univ, Univ Park, PA 16802; (814) 863-2167. Handles serological identification of Escherichia coli (E. coli). Maintains computerized data base. Publishes technical reports, reference materials; provides inquiry and consulting services, antisera and cultures, onsite training services.

43156. Faculty Exchange Center, 952 Virginia Ave, Lancaster, PA 17603; (717) 393-8985. Interest in intl, natl teaching exchanges on college, univ levels; faculty housing exchanges. Publishes directory with house exchange supplements. Services free to faculty of member institutions.

43157. Federation of Societies for Coatings Technology, 1315 Walnut St, Philadelphia, PA 19107; (215) 545-1506. Professional technical society interested in testing, formulation, manufacture of paints, coatings, allied products. Has research, reference materials; publishes journal, directory; answers inquiries.

43158. Fels Center of Government, 39th and Walnut Sts, Philadelphia, PA 19104; (215) 898-8218. Conducts academic programs in public policy analysis; energy management, policy. Has research collection, some computerized data. Publishes discussion papers, research reports. Most info provided thru publications (for sale).

43159. Fire Retardant Chemicals Association, 851 New Holland Ave, Box 3535, Lancaster, PA 17604; (717) 291-5616. Promotes fire safety thru chemical technology. Publishes newsletter, info materials; provides inquiry, consulting, reference services; conferences, workshops. Services free, except publications.

43160. Foote Mineral Co. Research and Development Has library, Route 100, Exton, PA 19341; (215) 363-6500. Interest in lithium, vanadium, manganese; alloys, inorganic and organic chemistry, minerals. Publishes journal, technical materials; makes interlibrary loans; permits onsite reference by request.

43161. Footwear Industries of America, 3700 Market St, Ste 303, Philadelphia, PA 19104; (215) 222-2282. Interest in all aspects of footwear industry (especially U.S. manufacturers, suppliers). Maintains library, lab for footwear testing. Publishes newsletter, manual, statistics (some available to nonmembers).

43162. Foundation for the Study of Cycles, 124 S Highland Ave, Pittsburgh, PA 15206; (412) 441-0652. Promotes time series analysis, especially of cycles, rhythmic fluctuations. Has research collection (for onsite use), data analyses. Publishes journals and research materials, answers inquiries.

43163. Fox Chase Cancer Center, 7701 Burholme Ave, Philadelphia, PA 19111; (215) 728-2711. Conducts clinical research on cancer-related virus infections in man.

Has research library, access to online data bases. Publishes research, info materials; answers inquiries; offers free phone consulting to local MDs.

43164. Franklin Institute Weather Center, Benjamin Franklin Parkway at 20th St, Philadelphia, PA 19103; (215) 448-1246. Interest in meteorology, meteorology education. Has collection of weather instruments, some climatological data; library, AV materials. Offers lectures to school groups, others. Weather info provided to Museum visitors only.

43166. Friends Historical Library, Swarthmore, PA 19081; (215) 447-7496. Interest in history of Religious Society of Friends, U.S. peace movement. Has print, microform, AV, MS materials. Publishes reference materials. Library primarily for research use; most genealogical inquiries referred elsewhere.

43167. Frost Entomological Museum, Dept of Entomology, 106 Patterson Bldg, Penn State Univ, Univ Park, PA 16802; (814) 863-2863. Interest in entomology, especially taxonomy. Collects specimens for onsite use, loan. Publishes bulletin, provides inquiry, consulting, and reference services, conducts seminars. Services free to researchers.

43168. Fulbright Association of Alumni of International Educational and Cultural Exchange, P.O. Box 1042, Bryn Mawr, PA 19010; (215) 645-5038. Interest in intl exchange, Fulbright grantee experience. Publishes newsletter, directories, research; provides inquiry services; conducts seminars. Fee for some services.

43169. Fund for an OPEN Society, 1427 Vine St, 4th Fl, Philadelphia, PA 19102; (215) 568-6715. Combats racial discrimination by providing financially advantageous mortgage loans for pro-integration housing moves. Publishes newsletter, answers inquiries free, provides advisory and consulting services for a fee.

43170. Fund-Raising Institute, Box 365, Ambler, PA 19002-0365; (215) 628-8729. Commercial org interested in fundraising techniques, philanthropy. Has computer programs for fundraising, recordkeeping, planned giving. Publishes newsletter, conducts workshops. Services at cost to all users.

43171. Fusarium Research Center, Dept of Plant Pathology, Coll of Agriculture, 211 Buckhout Laboratory, Penn State Univ, Univ Park, PA 16802; (814) 865-9773. Identifies, furnishes, stores cultures of Fusarium (fungus genus) for researchers. Maintains collection of isolates, directory of researchers. Publishes reference and research materials, answers inquiries. Services free.

43172. General Electric Co., Space Systems Division Library, P.O. Box 8555 (GE Space Technology Center; King of Prussia, PA), Philadelphia, PA 19101; (215) 354-4700. Research collection (for onsite use) on aerospace, energy; computer, environmental science. Publishes research, reference materials; provides inquiry, consulting, reference services to corps, govt agencies, scholars.

43173. George S. Cox Medical Research Institute, Univ of Pa. Hospital, 809 Maloney Bldg, HUP G1, Philadelphia, PA 19104; (215) 662-3165. Researches diabetes mellitus, aortic tissue metabolism, hormonal regulation of carbohydrate metabolism, diabetic polyneuropathy (peripheral nerve studies). Publishes reports, answers technical inquiries.

43174. Gichner Mobile Systems, P.O. Box B, Dallastown, PA 17313; (717) 244-7611. Manufactures military vehicles, similar equipment. Maintains collection of standards, specifications (available for onsite use). Provides inquiry, consulting services. Some access restricted; some services for a fee.

43175. Graphic Arts Technical Foundation, 4615 Forbes Ave, Pittsburgh, PA 15212; (412) 621-6941. Interest in printing, graphic arts industry. Has print, AV materials. Publishes research, training materials. Provides plant audits, lab services; reference, consulting services. Conducts seminars, training programs.

43176. Gray Panthers, 311 S Juniper St, Philadelphia, PA 19107; (215) 545-6555. Combats age discrimination; proposes alternatives in health care, housing, transportation, employment, the media. Sponsors grassroots activities, conferences, legislative action, task forces.

43178. Guillain-Barre Syndrome Support Group, PO Box 262, Wynnewood, PA 19096; (215) 649-7837. Provides mutual support for victims of Guillain-Barre syndrome (disease of unknown cause involving extreme muscle weakness). Patients attend group meetings to share experiences, discuss problems, hear lectures by physicians.

43179. Gulf Oil Corp., Business Research Library, P.O. Box 1166 (Gulf Bldg, Room 141; 439 Seventh Ave), Pittsburgh, PA 15230; (412) 263-6040. Interest in petroleum, energy (business, finance, management, economics). Has periodicals, extensive vertical files; provides access to data bases, reference services. Services primarily for Gulf Oil employees; others served by appointment.

43181. HRN, 1926 Arch St, Philadelphia, PA 19103; (215) 299-2900. Research, consulting firm interested in corporate social responsibility, public policy planning. Publishes reports and abstracts, answers inquiries, permits some onsite use of collection. Services for a fee.

43182. Hahnemann Medical College and Hospital Laboratory of Human Pharmacology, 235 N 15th St, Philadelphia, PA 19102; (215) 448-8237. Researches metabolism, potentiation, toxicity of drugs. Publishes reports, answers inquiries, provides consulting services. Fees may be charged for extensive services.

43183. Hammermill Paper Co., P.O. Box 1440 (East Lake Rd), Erie, PA 16533; (814) 456-8811. Interest in pulp; paper manufacture, processing; printing; specialty, converting papers (research, engineering, business).

Maintains reference library (for onsite use by local residents), answers inquiries.

43184. Harry A. Cochran Research Center, Temple Univ School of Business Administration, Speakman Hall, Room 6, Philadelphia, PA 19122; (215) 787-5187. Interest in applied economics, health administration, business research. Publishes journal and research reports, provides consulting services, conducts seminars. Services free or on cost basis.

43185. Hawk Mountain Sanctuary Association, Rte 2, Kempton, PA 19529; (215) 756-6961. Promotes understanding, conservation of birds of prey, other wildlife. Maintains collection of specimens, computerized data on hawk migration (for onsite use). Publishes newsletter, provides inquiry services, conducts educational, research programs.

43186. Henry Phipps Institute of Medical Genetics, Dept of Human Genetics, Univ of Pa., 195 Medical Laboratories Bldg, Philadelphia, PA 19104; (215) 243-5172. Interest in developmental, molecular, biochemical, population genetics; immunogenetics; cytogenetics. Answers inquiries free without restriction.

43187. Hershey Museum of American Life, P.O. Box 170 (west end of Hersheypark Arena), Hershey, PA 17033; (717) 534-3439. Educates public about daily life of Native, immigrant Americans; maintains museum. Answers inquiries, lends materials, permits onsite use of collections. Fee for some services.

43188. Historical Society of Pennsylvania, 1300 Locust St, Philadelphia, PA 19107; (215) 732-6200. Interest in Pa. state, local history. Has print, microform, MS, AV materials (permits some onsite use). Publishes magazine, research materials; provides inquiry, reference services. Museum free.

43189. Hoist Manufacturers Institute, 1326 Freeport Rd, Pittsburgh, PA 15238; (412) 782-1624. Establishes, publishes specifications for overhead hoists. Answers inquiries, provides reference services. Services free, except for publications; available primarily to industry, govt.

43190. Human Energy Research Laboratory, Univ of Pittsburgh, 242 Trees Hall, Pittsburgh, PA 15261; (412) 624-4387. Operates fitness center; conducts teaching, research in exercise physiology, cardiac rehabilitation, sports medicine. Publishes research. Provides inquiry, reference services; conducts seminars. Services free.

43191. Human Relations Area Files, Univ of Pittsburgh, Hillman Library, Pittsburgh, PA 15260; (412) 624-4449. Provides material for research in human sciences (sociology, psychology, anthropology, human biology, geography). Maintains set of coded HRAF files (most in microfiche) for onsite use. No phone or mail inquiries.

43192. Hunt Institute for Botanical Documentation, Pittsburgh, PA 15213; (412) 578-2434. Researches history of plant sciences. Has library, archives of print, graphic materials (for onsite use). Maintains data base on early botanical literature. Publishes journal, scholarly materials. Most services free.

43193. Hysterectomy Educational Resources and Services Foundation, 501 Woodbrook Ln, Philadelphia, PA 19119; (215) 247-6232. Provides info on options to hysterectomy, oophorectomy; options in treatment for pelvic disorders; aftereffects of hysterectomy. Provides free phone counseling, maintains lending library, sponsors conferences.

43194. INA Corporation Archives, CIGNA Corp., 1600 Arch St, Gallery Level, Philadelphia, PA 19103; (215) 241-3293. Has archives of Insurance Co of N. America; CIGNA Corp, subsidiaries: files, microforms, AV materials. Publishes guide, provides inquiry and reference services. Available to researchers; some restrictions.

43195. Indian Rights Association, 1505 Race St, Philadelphia, PA 19102; (215) 563-8349. Interest in American Indian affairs. Publishes newsletter, answers inquiries.

43196. Industrial Health Foundation, 34 Penn Circle West, Pittsburgh, PA 15206; (412) 363-6600. Works in industrial hygiene; occupational health, safety; analytical testing. Has reference collection. Publishes journal, proceedings, reference materials. Services primarily for members; provided to others by contract.

43198. Industrial Truck Association, 1326 Freeport Rd, Pittsburgh, PA 15238; (412) 782-1624. Develops standards, safety practices for powered industrial lift trucks. Answers brief inquiries, develops recommended engineering practices.

43199. Information for Industry, 229 S 18th St, Philadelphia, PA 19103; (215) 875-2300. Commercial org that works in corporate strategy (especially mergers, acquisitions). Maintains merger, acquisition data base. Publishes journals, conducts conferences and workshops. Services for a fee.

43200. Institute for Briquetting and Agglomeration, c/o Walter W. Eichenberger, Exec Director, P.O. Box 794 (2615 W 10th St), Erie, PA 16512; (814) 838-1133. Interest in briquetting, similar processing of particulate matter such as ores, coal. Publishes newsletter, proceedings; answers inquiries; provides physical, chemical testing services, consulting for a fee.

43201. Institute for Modernization of Land Data Systems, P.O. Box 1552, Lancaster, PA 17603; (717) 394-7247. Promotes development, use of govt-operated land data systems. Publishes research, reference materials; provides inquiry, reference services; conducts seminars, conferences, workshops. Some services free.

43202. Institute for Policy Research and Evaluation, N253 Burrowes Bldg, Penn State Univ, Univ Park, PA 16802; (814) 865-9561. Undertakes research in human resources, science policy, population. Has research collection. Publishes reports, working papers; conducts research on cost-contract basis.

43203. Institute for Research on Land and Water Resources, Land and Water Research Bldg, Penn State Univ, Univ Park, PA 16802; (814) 863-0291. Interdisciplinary research program on natural resource problems. Has research collection of print, database, remote sensing materials. Publishes newsletter and reports, answers inquiries. Some services on fee basis.

43204. Institute for Scientific Information, 3501 Market St, Philadelphia, PA 19104; (215) 386-0100, (800) 523-1850. Provides bibliographic access to worldwide literature in wide range of fields. Maintains data bases, library. Publishes reference materials, provides special services, conducts seminars and workshops. All services for a fee.

43207. Institute for the Study of Civic Values, 1217 Sansom St, Ste 600, Philadelphia, PA 19107; (215) 922-8960. Undertakes research on impact of public, private institutions on neighborhood stability; community participation, development. Provides inquiry, consulting services; conducts seminars. Most services for a fee.

43208. Institute for the Study of Human Issues, 210 S 13th St, Philadelphia, PA 19107; (215) 732-9729. Conducts research in social sciences, humanities, medicine. Has data, reference collections; publications; films available. Provides inquiry, consulting, reference services; conducts lectures, seminars. Most services at cost.

43209. Institute of Building Sciences, CMU, Dept of Architecture, DH Bldg, Room 1325, Pittsburgh, PA 15213; (412) 268-2350. Interest in urban planning, building sciences. Maintains reference library, computer programs, graphic equipment. Publishes research; provides inquiry, consulting services; conducts seminars, workshops. Some services free.

43210. Institute of Neurological Sciences, Univ of Penn School of Medicine, 452 Medical Education Bldg, Philadelphia, PA 19104; (215) 898-8754. Emphasizes multidisciplinary approach to research, training in study of nervous system. Publishes directories, provides inquiry and consulting services, conducts seminars. Services free.

43211. Institute on Aging, 1601 N Broad St, Room 206, Philadelphia, PA 19122; (215) 787-6970. Develops multi-, inter-disciplinary research, education, training, community service related to aging. Provides inquiry, research, consulting services; conducts seminars.

43212. Institutes for the Achievement of Human Potential, 8801 Stenton Ave, Philadelphia, PA 19118; (215) 233-2050. Works on improved human brain function (especially of brain-injured, very young children). Publishes periodical, research; provides inquiry, consulting services, usually at cost.

43213. Intercollegiate Studies Institute, 14 S Bryn Mawr Ave, Bryn Mawr, PA 19010; (215) 525-7501. Promotes good citizenship, preservation of liberty. Publishes journals, reports; provides inquiry, reference services; conducts institutes, study groups; operates lecture bureau. Membership free.

43214. International Astronomical Union Commission on Documentation and Astronomical Data, c/o W.D. Heintz, Pres, Dept of Astronomy, Swarthmore Coll, Swarthmore, PA 19081. Establishes policy for astronomical documentation, data centers, networks. Reports published commercially.

43215. International College of Podiatric Laser Surgery, 399 N York Rd, Warminster, PA 18974; (215) 443-8209. Promotes use of laser in podiatry. Promotes research, sponsors courses and scientific progs. Board certifies members, organizes natl referral service for new patients.

43216. International Committee for the Anthropology of Food and Food Habits, c/o Miss Margaret L. Arnott, Pres, 324 S 21st St, Philadelphia, PA 19103; (215) 732-0694. Network of scholars (especially anthropologists) seeking to collect data on food habits. Publishes newsletter, answers inquiries, conducts symposia. Services available to scholars; send SASE with inquiries.

43217. International Federation of Organic Agriculture Movements, c/o Nancy Nickum Bailey (Bulletin in English), Rodale Research Center, R.D. 1, Box 323, Kutztown, PA 19530; (215) 683-6383. Nonprofit org working on organic agriculture, intl agriculture, appropriate technology. Publishes journal in English, Spanish, and German, answers inquiries, conducts intl research conferences.

43218. International Federation of Otorhinolaryngological Societies, c/o James B. Snow, Jr., M.D., Chairman, Univ of Pa. School of Medicine, 3400 Spruce St, Philadelphia, PA 19104; (215) 662-2653. Promotes educational programs in otorhinolaryngology for medical students, residents around the world. Publishes specifications, answers inquiries, provides consulting services. Services free to institutions.

43219. International Foundation for Genetic Research, 400 Penn Center Blvd, Pittsburgh, PA 15235; (412) 823-6380. Funds research on genetic disorders; advocates efforts to improve care of persons with genetic disorders. Provides inquiry, advisory, reference services; distributes publications. Services free.

43220. International Legal Defense Counsel, 1420 Walnut St, Ste 315, Philadelphia, PA 19102; (215) 545-2428. Provides counsel for Americans jailed abroad, or involved with intl civil law problems. Provides inquiry and advisory services, conducts seminars. Some services free; usual attorney fees for legal work.

43221. International Library Information Center, c/o Dr Richard Krzys, Univ of Pittsburgh School of Library and Information Sciences, Pittsburgh, PA 15260; (412)

624-5235. Provides primary source materials for intl, comparative studies in library science, documentation. Provides info for library science visitors to, from U.S.

43222. International Myopia Prevention Association, R.D. 5, Box 171, Ligonier, PA 15658; (412) 238-2101. Promotes prevention, control of myopia through public, professional education efforts. Supports inclusion of myopia prevention in education of optometrists; development of natl system of myopia prevention clinics.

43223. International Precious Metals Institute, c/o Exec Secty, Government Bldg, ABE Airport, Allentown, PA 18103; (215) 266-1570. Serves precious metals community. Publishes journal, proceedings, directory; answers inquiries; conducts conferences, workshops; permits onsite use of collections. Most services free.

43224. International Society for Animal Rights, 421 S State St, Clarks Summit, PA 18411; (717) 586-2200. Opposes exploitation, suffering of animals. Maintains library, film collection. Publishes magazine, reference materials; provides inquiry, reference services; conducts symposia; loans films. Services provided at cost.

43225. International Strabismus Association, c/o Robert D. Reinecke, M.D., Wills Eye Hospital, 9th and Walnut Sts, Philadelphia, PA 19107; (215) 928-3149. Interest in strabismus, eye movements. Publishes citations journal, distributed free to medical, scientific community.

43226. Joint Committee on Powder Diffraction Standards, 1601 Park Ln, Swarthmore, PA 19081; (215) 328-9400. Collects, edits, publishes (print, microform, machine-readable), distributes powder diffraction data for identification of crystalline materials. Answers inquiries, sells publications.

43227. Jones and Laughlin Steel Corp., Graham Research Laboratory, 900 Agnew Rd, Pittsburgh, PA 15230; (412) 884-1000. Interest in iron, steel technology; metallurgy; materials science. Has research library, with access to computerized data bases. Answers inquiries. Library not open to the public.

43228. Kafka Society of America, TUzip 022-35 (Humanities Bldg, HB-330; Broad and Montgomery Sts), Temple Univ, Philadelphia, PA 19122; (215) 787-8270. Fosters literary research on Franz Kafka. Maintains library. Publishes newsletter, answers inquiries, provides reference services, conducts seminars and workshops. Services free to members; info to others on written request.

43230. Krautkramer-Branson, P.O. Box 350 (Mifflin County Industrial Park), Lewistown, PA 17044; (717) 242-0327. Interest in ultrasonic nondestructive testing; practical applications of ultrasound. Provides inquiry, consulting, and reference services, permits some onsite use of reference library. Services free, unless extensive.

43231. Laboratory for Human Performance Research, Intercollege Research Programs, Penn State Univ, Univ Park, PA 16802; (814) 865-3453. Interest in human applied physiology (especially related to exercise, stress). Publishes scholarly materials; provides inquiry, advisory services; conducts seminars. Most services free, primarily for researchers.

43232. Laboratory for Research on the Structure of Matter, Univ of Penn, 3231 Walnut St, K1, Philadelphia, PA 19104; (215) 898-8571. Undertakes research in materials science, materials engineering. Publishes scholarly materials, answers inquiries, conducts seminars. Info provided only as incidental service; faculty provide consulting services on cost basis.

43233. Lancaster Cleft Palate Clinic, 24 N Lime St, Lancaster, PA 17602; (717) 394-3793. Serves children with cleft lips, palates; other anomalies of cranial- facial structures. Has data banks. Provides inquiry, counseling, and reference services, conducts seminars. Services primarily for professionals; fees negotiated.

43234. Learning Research and Development Center, LRDC Bldg, Univ of Pittsburgh, 3939 O'Hara St, Pittsburgh, PA 15260; (412) 624-4800. Researches psychology of learning, curriculum and instruction, educational evaluation, social aspects of learning, design of educational environments. Maintains research collection. Publications list available.

43236. Lincoln Zephyr Owner's Club, c/o Francis L. Olweiler, 2107 Steinruck Rd, Elizabethtown, PA 17022 Promotes preservation, restoration of Lincoln Zephyr, Lincoln automobiles. Maintains small reference collection. Publishes magazine and directory, answers inquiries, provides consulting services.

43237. Little League Baseball, P.O. Box 3485 (U.S. Route 15 South), Williamsport, PA 17701; (717) 326-1921. Provides baseball, softball programs for youth. Operates museum; has films, videos. Publishes newsletter, reference materials, catalogs; provides inquiry, advisory, training services. Most services free.

43240. Marriage Insurance Institute, P.O. Box 9874, Philadelphia, PA 19140; (215) 423-3105. Promotes, publishes research to lower divorce, separation rates. Provides inquiry, consulting services; conducts workshops. Services free (except travel expenses), available mainly to groups.

43241. Material Handling Institute, Department of Education, 1326 Freeport Rd, Pittsburgh, PA 15238; (412) 782-1624. Trade assn for material handling equipment industry. Publishes magazine, educational and technical literature, AV materials; provides inquiry, reference services; conducts workshops. Most services free.

43242. Media Information Service, Baum Bldg, 818 Liberty Ave, Pittsburgh, PA 15222; (412) 288-9401. Facilitates contact between journalists and members of health, medical professions. Serves newspapers, TV and radio stations in western Pa. Provides inquiry, reference services; conducts seminars, workshops. Services free.

43243. Medical College of Pennsylvania Archives and Special Collections on Women in Medicine, 3300 Henry Ave, Philadelphia, PA 19129; (215) 842-7124. Maintains library, archives, resource center on history of women in medicine (for onsite use). Publishes newsletter, provides limited reference services, prepares exhibits, lends AV materials. Some services at cost.

43244. Mellon Institute Rail Systems Center, Carnegie-Mellon Univ, 4400 Fifth Ave, Pittsburgh, PA 15213; (412) 578-2960. Interest in intercity, urban rail transport; people mover technology. Publishes technical reports, provides advisory services, conducts seminars and workshops, performs research on contract basis.

43245. Meteorological Research Facilities, Dept of Meteorology, Walker Bldg, Room 503, Penn State Univ, Univ Park, PA 16802; (814) 865-6172. Maintains collection of weather records since 1890 (for onsite use); current data computerized. Publishes articles and technical reports, answers inquiries, conducts daily TV weather program. Services free.

43246. Michael Fund / International Foundation for Genetic Research, 400 Penn Center Blvd, Ste 830, Pittsburgh, PA 15235; (412) 823-6380. Supports, disseminates research on the prevention, cure of Down's Syndrome, other chromosomal disorders. Promotes better care, treatment for children and adults with birth disorders.

43247. Mid-Atlantic Council of Watershed Associations, 2955 Edge Hill Rd, Huntingdon Valley, PA 19006; (215) 657-0830. Interest in conservation education (especially on flood plains, erosion control, water pollution). Publishes newsletter, provides inquiry and consulting services. Services available to all; most free to members.

43248. Middle East Research Institute, 3808 Walnut St, Philadelphia, PA 19104; (215) 898-6077. Researches politics, economics of Middle East, north Africa. Has library, data bases. Provides inquiry, consulting, training services; conducts conferences, briefings. Some services for members only; some for a fee.

43249. Mine Safety and Health Administration, Pittsburgh Health Technology Center, 4800 Forbes Ave, Pittsburgh, PA 15213; (412) 621-4500. Interest in applied engineering in the health field, including areas of dust, ventilation, physical agents, toxic materials; mine emergency operations. Provides technical assistance to mining industry.

43250. Mine Safety Appliances Co., Library, 600 Penn Center Blvd, Pittsburgh, PA 15235; (412) 273-5131. Interest in industrial hygiene, safety (especially in mining); space capsule atmosphere instrumentation; sound, noise measurement, control. Maintains reference library, has access to data bases.

43251. Miniature Figure Collectors of America, 102 St Pauls Rd, Ardmore, PA 19003. Interest in military history; miniature figures, dioramas. Has collection of slides, printed materials (for onsite use). Publishes journal, newsletter, answers inquiries. Has annual public exhibition.

43252. Monell Chemical Senses Center, 3500 Market St, Philadelphia, PA 19104; (215) 243-6666. Multidisciplinary research institute for study of chemical senses in lower animals, humans. Library focuses on chemical senses. Publications list available; answers inquiries.

43253. Monorail Manufacturers Association, 1326 Freeport Rd, Pittsburgh, PA 15238; (412) 782-1624. Interest in in-plant underhung crane, monorail systems. Publishes specifications. Inquiries answered by assn or referred to member companies.

43254. Moravian Church, Northern Province, 69 W Church St, Bethlehem, PA 18018; (215) 867-7566. Interest in Moravian Church: history, practices, doctrines. Publishes magazine and books, answers brief inquiries, makes referrals.

43255. Moravian Historical Society, Nazareth, PA 18064. Works on history of Moravian Church in North America. Maintains library, museum. Publishes journal, answers inquiries (mail requests should include SASE), permits some use of collections.

43256. Motorcycle Safety Foundation Information Resource Center, P.O. Box 120, Chadds Ford, PA 19317; (215) 388-1555. Seeks to reduce motorcycle accidents, injuries. Publishes magazine, consumer info, technical material; provides inquiry, consulting services; permits onsite use of reference collection. Fee for some services.

43257. Movement for a New Society, New Society Publishers, 4722 Baltimore Ave, Philadelphia, PA 19143; (215) 726-6543. Promotes nonviolent fundamental social change. Publications catalog available. Provides inquiry, advisory services; conducts seminars, workshops. Most services free.

43258. Museum Applied Science Center for Archaeology, Univ of Penn, Univ Museum Fl, 33rd and Spruce Sts, Philadelphia, PA 19104; (215) 898-4058. Interest in use of physical science techniques in archaeology (archaeometallurgy, archaeozoology, paleobotany, paleopathology, archaeometry, dendrochronology). Publishes journal, provides inquiry and indexing services.

43259. Museum of Anthropology, Penn State Univ, Univ Park, PA 16802; (814) 865-3853. Interest in archeology, ethnology (especially of Mexico, Afghanistan, Polynesia, U.S.); ceramics from around the world. Answers inquiries, permits onsite use of collection by public without charge.

43260. NASA Industrial Applications Center, 710 L.I.S. Bldg, 135 North Bellefield Ave, Pittsburgh, PA 15260;

(412) 624-5211. Promotes application of new technologies to industrial, academic problems. Provides consulting, reference services; access to online data bases; electronic publishing. Services at cost (if not restricted).

43261. National Academy of Education, LRDC Bldg, Univ of Pittsburgh, Pittsburgh, PA 15260; (412) 624-0221. Promotes scholarly inquiry and discussion on ends, means of education in U.S. and abroad. Publications list available. Provides inquiry, advisory services.

43262. National Adoption Exchange, 1218 Chestnut St, Philadelphia, PA 19107; (215) 925-0200. Natl network to match children waiting for adoption with parents to adopt them. Specializes in children with special needs (minority children, those with disabilities, those 7-15 years old). Registry is by agencies.

43264. National Association of Childbearing Centers, R.D. 1, Box 1, Perkiomenville, PA 18074; (215) 234-8068. Supports development of birth centers as alternative to hospitals, home for childbirth. Offers phone info, consultation services; conducts workshops; provides written, AV materials. Info available on running a birth center.

43265. National Association of Diaper Services, 2017 Walnut St, Philadelphia, PA 19103; (215) 569-3650. Represents professional diaper services. Publishes newsletter, reports; answers brief inquiries; provides consulting, testing services; prepares analyses. Services at cost.

43266. National Association of Professional Word Processing Technicians, 110 W Byberry Rd, E2, Philadelphia, PA 19116; (215) 698-8525. Certifies professional word processors for minimal fee; answers inquiries.

43267. National Association of Rocketry, 182 Madison Dr, Elizabeth, PA 15037; (412) 384-6490. Concerned with model rocketry activities, especially standards for safe equipment and manufacture. Sponsors contests, certifies records. Publishes journal, provides free inquiry and advisory services.

43268. National Association of Watch and Clock Collectors, 514 Poplar St, Columbia, PA 17512; (717) 684-8261. Interest in antique clocks, watches. Reference library, museum open to public; has data bank, lending library for members. Publishes bulletin and catalogs, answers inquiries, makes referrals for members and news media.

43269. National Automotive Radiator Service Association, c/o Doug Verney, Exec Director, P.O. Box 267 (320 Godshall Dr), Harleysville, PA 19438; (215) 256-4246. Interest in automotive radiators, air conditioners. Publishes magazine and newsletter, answers inquiries, makes referrals.

43270. National Center for Juvenile Justice, 701 Forbes Ave, Pittsburgh, PA 15219; (412) 227-6950. Interest in legal system and children. Maintains computerized data bases, publishes scholarly materials. Provides in-

quiry, consulting, and reference services, permits onsite use of collections. Most services at cost.

43271. National Center for the Study of Corporal Punishment and Alternatives in the Schools, 833 Ritter Annex, Temple Univ, 13th and Columbia Sts, Philadelphia, PA 19122; (215) 787-6091. Conducts research, disseminates info on corporal punishment in schools. Provides inquiry, advisory, and reference services, conducts workshops, permits onsite use of collection. Most services for a fee.

43272. National Child Nutrition Project, 101 N 33rd St, Philadelphia, PA 19104; (215) 662-1024. Works to improve nutrition for the poor. Publishes breastfeeding manual (print, tapes); provides inquiry, consulting services; distributes materials for a fee; conducts seminars.

43273. National Coalition Against the Death Penalty, 1501 Cherry St, Philadelphia, PA 19102; (215) 241-7118. Info, resource center for work against capital punishment. Publishes newsletter, directory, and reference materials, answers inquiries, conducts seminars. Services free, except some publications.

43274. National Committee for Clinical Laboratory Standards, 771 East Lancaster Ave, Villanova, PA 19085; (215) 525-2435. Develops, publishes standards and guidelines for clinical lab medicine and for manufacturers of clinical lab equipment. Answers inquiries, conducts seminars. Services for a fee.

43275. National Diabetes Research Interchange, 2401 Walnut St, Ste 408, Philadelphia, PA 19103; (215) 222-6374. Procures, distributes human tissue that may be useful in diabetes, other medical research. Scientists conducting medical research may submit requests for specific types of human tissue.

43276. National Federation of Abstracting and Information Services, 112 South 16th St, 12th Fl, Philadelphia, PA 19102; (215) 563-2406. Represents abstracting, indexing services. Publishes newsletter, technical reports; answers inquiries; conducts seminars, conferences; operates consulting bureau. Fee for some services.

43277. National Flag Foundation, Flag Plaza, Pittsburgh, PA 15219; (412) 261-1776. Promotes appreciation of U.S. flag: history, display, protocol, courtesy. Has art collection; publications list available. Provides inquiry, reference services. Fee for some services.

43278. National Foundation for Peroneal Muscular Atrophy, c/o Robert S. Krutsick, Univ City Science Center, 3624 Market St, Philadelphia, PA 19104; (215) 387-2255. Sponsors research on peroneal muscular atrophy (Charcot-Marie-Tooth disease) to define varieties, develop treatments, correct related genetic defects.

43279. National Frozen Food Association, P.O. Box 398, Hershey, PA 17033; (717) 534-1601. Serves frozen food field, including distributors, packers, brokers, suppliers, warehousers. Publishes magazine, directories, cookbook; provides inquiry, advisory, reference services. Services primarily for the industry.

43280. National Hazards Control Institute, P.O. Box 667, Easton, PA 18042; (215) 258-7045. Commercial org working in hazardous materials handling. Publishes print, AV materials; provides inquiry, advisory, consulting services; conducts workshops. Fee for some services.

43281. National Obesity Research Foundation, c/o David L. Margules, Temple Univ, Weiss Hall 867, Philadelphia, PA 19122; (215) 787-8841. Disseminates info on obesity, its causes, effects, remedies. Funds research efforts, sponsors annual meeting, publishes newsletter to provide obesity info otherwise not readily available to public.

43282. National Organization for Albinism and Hypopigmentation, 919 Walnut St, Room 400, Philadelphia, PA 19107; (215) 627-3501. Benefits persons, families with albinism, hypopigmentation. Provides info, support; promotes public, professional education; encourages research, funding for diagnosis, treatment. Conducts conferences, assists local groups.

43283. National Printing Ink Research Institute, Center for Surface and Coatings Research, Lehigh Univ, Sinclair Laboratory, Bethlehem, PA 18015; (215) 758-3000. Researches printing inks; printing, graphic arts. Maintains research library for onsite use. Publishes reference, research materials; provides inquiry, reference services; conducts workshops. Services at cost.

43284. National Railway Historical Society, P.O. Box 2051 (312-314 Empire Bldg), Philadelphia, PA 19103. Works on history of railroad transportation. Collects materials for natl railroad library; film library. Publishes bulletin, scholarly materials; provides inquiry, reference services; conducts seminars. Services free, restricted availability.

43285. National Society of Genetic Counselors, c/o Deborah L. Eunpu, Pres, Clinical Genetics, Children's Hospital of Philadelphia, 34th and Civic Center Blvd, Philadelphia, PA 19104; (215) 596-9802. Serves genetic counselors; has computerized list of members. Publishes newsletter; provides inquiry, advisory, counseling services; conducts seminars, workshops. Fee for some services.

43286. National Support Center for Families of the Aging, PO Box 245, Swarthmore, PA 19081; (215) 544-3605. Nonprofit org that helps families cope with responsibilities to older relatives; helps persons with their own aging process. Makes referrals, offers publications and leadership training. No phone inquiries.

43287. National Yokefellow Prison Ministry, P.O. Box 207 (112 Old Trail North), Shamokin Dam, PA 17876; (717) 743-7832. Serves spiritual, emotional, physical needs of jailed persons, ex-offenders. Publishes newsletter, provides consulting services, conducts conferences, workshops, and eetings. Most services free.

43289. Newborn Rights Society, Box 48, St Peters, PA 19470; (215) 323-6061. Gathers, disseminates info on medical procedures possibly unnecessary, harmful to the newborn: circumcision, silver nitrate eye drops, some infant feeding methods. Publishes reprints.

43290. Newcomen Society of the United States, 412 Newcomen Rd, Exton, PA 19341; (215) 363-6600. Interest in history, achievement of steam, steam technology. Maintains research library (print and graphic materials), exhibit hall. Publishes reference materials, answers inquiries. Visitors welcome weekdays.

43291. Noise Control Laboratory, Coll of Engineering, 213 Engineering Unit E, Penn State Univ, Univ Park, PA 16802; (814) 865-2761. Interest in noise control in machinery; acoustics. Publishes reports, provides inquiry and consulting services. Hourly rates charged for use of some facilities. Services primarily for Pa. industries.

43292. North American Association of Christians in Social Work, P.O. Box 90, St Davids, PA 19087. Follows concerns of social workers from evangelical Christian point of view. Publishes periodicals, directories, monographs; provides inquiry, advisory services; conducts workshops. Most services free.

43293. North American Native Fishes Association, 123 W Mount Airy Ave, Philadelphia, PA 19119; (215) 247-0384. Interest in nongame, game fish. Publishes journal, research and reference materials; provides inquiry, reference services; conducts seminars; distributes publications. Fee for some services.

43294. Northeast Regional Center for Rural Development, 104 Weaver Bldg, Penn State Univ, Univ Park, PA 16803; (814) 865-0455. Regional center for rural development research, training. Publishes reports, proceedings; answers inquiries; conducts research, training, extension activities. Services generally free to land-grant univs, govt agencies.

43295. Nuclear Reactor Facility, Penn State Univ, Univ Park, PA 16802; (814) 865-6351. Undertakes academic training, research in nuclear engineering. Has research collection, access to computerized data bases. Answers inquiries, provides consulting and identification (radiation exposure) services.

43296. Nuclide Corp., Technical Publications, 642 East College Ave, State College, PA 16801; (814) 238-0541. Works in mass spectrometry, gas chromatography. Has research materials. Publishes reports, standards and specifications, newsletter; provides inquiry, consulting services and custom analyses (for a fee).

43297. Nutrition Information and Resource Center, Benedict House, Penn State Univ, Univ Park, PA 16802; (814) 865-6323. Collection of nutrition reference, resource materials (print, AV, software), staffed by people trained in nutrition. Materials available for review onsite only. Questions answered in person, by phone, or by mail.

43298. Oncology Nursing Society, 3111 Banksville Rd, Ste 200, Pittsburgh, PA 15216; (412) 344-3899. Interest in oncological nursing. Publishes journal, books, standards; provides inquiry, advisory services; conducts seminars, workshops. Services free, except seminars and publications, primarily for health professionals.

43299. Ore Deposits Research Section, College of Earth and Mineral Sciences, 235 Deike Bldg, Penn State Univ, Univ Park, PA 16802; (814) 865-7573. Researches deposits of metallic ores, geothermal energy. Maintains computerized data base for research use. Provides inquiry, advisory, analytical services at cost to public.

43300. PALINET and Union Library Catalogue of Pennsylvania, 3401 Market St, Ste 262, Philadelphia, PA 19104; (215) 382-5104. Maintains union catalogs with online data bases. Available for personal use without fee. Provides training, documentation, consultation services for members; also training, consultation for microcomputer use in libraries.

43301. PCR: Film and Video in the Behavioral Sciences, Audio-Visual Services, 203 Special Services Bldg, Penn State Univ, Univ Park, PA 16802; (814) 863-3103. Collects, rents, sells 16mm films, videotapes on behavioral sciences. Publishes catalogs, guides. Producers invited to submit films, videos. Visiting scholars have access to collection, screening facilities.

43302. PPG Industries, Glass Research Center, P.O. Box 11472 (Guys Run Rd, Harmarville, PA), Pittsburgh, PA 15238; (412) 665-8566. Interest in science, technology of glass. Has research materials, patents (for onsite use by appointment). Publishes journal, answers inquiries, makes interlibrary loans.

43303. Paleobryozoological Research Laboratory, Dept of Geosciences, College of Earth and Mineral Sciences, 412-413 Deike Bldg, Penn State Univ, Univ Park, PA 16802; (814) 865-1293. Serves researchers on fossil, living bryozoans. Maintains bibliographic data base, small collection of type/figured specimens. Provides inquiry, consulting services; permits onsite use of collection. Some services free.

43304. Parenteral Drug Association, Avenue of the Arts Bldg, Ste 1407, Philadelphia, PA 19107; (215) 735-9752. Interest in parenteral (injectable), sterile technology for drugs. Publishes newsletter, journal, AV materials; provides inquiry, reference services; conducts seminars. Services chiefly for institutions; provided at cost.

43305. Peace Collection, Swarthmore College, Swarthmore, PA 19081; (215) 447-7557. Repository, research library for materials on peace, pacifism, women's history, nonviolent social change. Has research collection for onsite use, answers inquiries. Most services free, available to scholars.

43306. Pennsylvania Dutch Folk Culture Society, Lenhartsville, PA 19534; (215) 562-4803. Interest in Pa. Dutch. Maintains museums; genealogical, folklore library. Provides inquiry, ref, magnetic tape services; conducts tours; distributes publication. Services free to members.

43307. Pennsylvania Historical and Museum Commission, William Penn Memorial Museum and Archives Bldg, Harrisburg, PA 17120; (717) 787-2891. Maintains Pa. state archives; promotes Pa. history. Has printed materials, periodicals, AV materials, artifacts, museum specimens. Publishes journal and reference materials, answers inquiries. Fee sometimes charged.

43308. Pennsylvania Railroad Technical and Historical Society, c/o James J.D. Lynch, Jr., Secty, P.O. Box 389, Upper Darby, PA 19082. Furthers scholarship, interest in Pennsylvania Railroad. Publishes quarterly magazine, answers inquiries, conducts annual meeting. Services primarily for members; others served as time permits.

43309. Pennsylvania Resources and Information Center for Special Education, 200 Anderson Rd, King of Prussia, PA 19406; (215) 265-7321. Interest in special education: techniques, materials, training. Maintains research collection for onsite use. Publishes newsletter, provides inquiry, advisory, and reference services to public on fee basis.

43310. Pennsylvania Transportation Institute, Research Bldg B, Penn State Univ, Univ Park, PA 16802; (814) 863-3953. Interest in all aspects, modes of transportation. Has research library, with special collections. Publishes research and annual report, answers brief reference inquiries, makes interlibrary loans.

43311. Pennsylvania Transportation Institute, Automotive Safety Research Program, Research Bldg B, Penn State Univ, Univ Park, PA 16802; (814) 865-1891. Undertakes research in tire-pavement friction, braking systems, diesel engine cold starting, electric vehicles. Has research collection. Publishes technical reports, answers inquiries, provides search services for a fee.

43313. People's Medical Society, 14 E Minor St, Emmaus, PA 18049; (215) 967-2136. Encourages active involvement by patients in their own medical care. Offers advice to health-care users about reducing costs, improving quality and safety of care. Publishes newsletter, other materials.

43314. Perelman Antique Toy Museum, 270 S 2nd St, Philadelphia, PA 19106; (215) 922-1070. Collects, researches antique toys. Has collection of early American toys, banks (permits onsite use). Publishes articles, provides free inquiry, advisory, and reference services.

43315. Pharmaceutical Information Center, Joseph W. England Library, 42nd St and Woodland Ave, Philadelphia, PA 19104; (215) 596-8967. Interest in all aspects of drugs; foreign, domestic drug identification; history of pharmacy. Maintains research library, provides online services, answers inquiries, provides info to health professionals.

43317. Phipps Conservatory, Schenley Park, Pittsburgh, PA 15213; (412) 255-2375. Interest in ornamental plants; has plant specimens. Answers brief inquiries, provides consulting services. Open to public during scheduled hours; also presents seasonal shows (admission fee charged).

43318. Phoenix Society, 11 Rust Hill Rd, Levittown, PA 19056; (215) 946-4788. Mutual support org for burn victims, their families. Has AV, print materials; publishes magazine, books; provides inquiry, advisory, reference services; maintians speakers bureau. Most services free.

43320. Photographic Society of America, 2005 Walnut St, Philadelphia, PA 19103; (215) 563-1663. Interest in amateur photography; several photographic collections available for exhibit. Publishes journal, answers inquiries, permits onsite use of reference collection. Services available to all; mostly free to members.

43321. Pipe Fabrication Institute, 1370 Old Freeport Rd, Pittsburgh, PA 15238; (412) 781-4600. Promotes technical advancement, standardization in pipe fabrication industry. Publishes standards and technical bulletins, answers inquiries, provides consulting services.

43322. Pittsburgh Energy Technology Center, U.S. Dept of Energy, P.O. Box 10940, Pittsburgh, PA 15236; (412) 675-6128. Interest in new processes for producing clean energy from coal. Performs contracted research. Publishes technical reports and proceedings, answers inquiries, provides speakers. Fee for some services.

43323. Pittsburgh Institute of Legal Medicine, 1519 Frick Bldg, Pittsburgh, PA 15219; (412) 281-9090. Interest in medical-legal education, forensic sciences. Publishes bulletin, scholarly materials; provides inquiry, consulting, reference services; sponsors seminars. Services for a fee, primarily for professionals.

43324. Population Issues Research Center, 21 Burrowes Bldg, Penn State Univ, Univ Park, PA 16802; (814) 865-0486. Undertakes demographic research. Has working collection of books, periodicals, reports; data archive. Publishes research, answers inquiries, provides consulting services. Services free, available to researchers.

43325. Presbyterian Historical Society, 425 Lombard St, Philadelphia, PA 19147; (215) 627-1852. Researches history of Presbyterian, Reformed churches in U.S. Has library; archives of printed, microform, AV materials. Publishes journal, research materials; provides inquiry, authentication services.

43326. Print Club, 1614 Latimer St, Philadelphia, PA 19103; (215) 735-6090. Encourages printmaking. Has collection of prints, photos; archives; reference library. Publishes journal, catalogs; provides inquiry,

reference services; conducts seminars, exhibitions. Services free or at cost.

43327. Project Management Institute, P.O. Box 43, Drexel Hill, PA 19026; (215) 622-1796. Promotes professionalism in project management; research, exchange on techniques. Publishes journal, research and reference materials; conducts seminars, symposia; provides certification, training for project managers.

43328. Quaker Collection, Haverford, PA 19041-1392 Covers history, religious thought, biography, fiction relating to Society of Friends. Has books, journals, manuscripts, AV materials. Publishes reference materials, answers inquiries, permits onsite use of collection.

43329. Rack Manufacturers Institute, 1326 Freeport Rd, Pittsburgh, PA 15238; (412) 782-1624. Trade assn for rack manufacturing industry; compiles basic trade info. Free inquiry, referral services. Conducts seminars, workshops; distributes publications, slide sets.

43330. Radiation Research Society, 925 Chestnut St, 7th Fl, Philadelphia, PA 19107; (215) 574-3153. Interest in radiation characteristics, effects, hazards, dosimetry. Publishes journal, newsletter, abstracts of annual meeting. Free referral services.

43331. Refractories Institute, 3760 One Oliver Plaza, Pittsburgh, PA 15222; (412) 281-6787. Promotes interests of manufacturers, consumers of refractory products. Publishes magazine, manuals, and directories, answers inquiries, makes referrals.

43332. Regenerative Agriculture Association, 222 Main St, Emmaus, PA 18049; (215) 967-5171. Works for long-term viability of U.S. farming resources, security of future food supply. Conducts program of publishing; research; direct service to producers, consumers; public education; advocacy. Answers inquiries.

43333. Regional Science Association, Univ of Pa., 3718 Locust Walk, Philadelphia, PA 19174; (215) 387-0681. Promotes regional analysis; related spatial, areal studies (especially using mathematical models, quantitative methods, analytical techniques). Maintains reference collection. Publishes journal, proceedings for a fee.

43334. Rehabilitation Research and Training Center in Aging, Univ of Pa. Hospital, Box 590 (3400 Spruce St), Philadelphia, PA 19104; (215) 662-2487. Serves rehabilitation, aging, mental health networks. Maintains film library, data bases. Publishes newsletter, research; provides inquiry, consulting services and workshops. Fee for some services.

43336. Research Center on the Materials of the Artist and Conservator, Mellon Institute, Carnegie-Mellon Univ, 4400 Fifth Ave, Pittsburgh, PA 15213; (412) 578-3329. Interest in care, treatment of museum objects; chemistry of artists' materials, materials used in conservation. Publishes research and reference materials, answers inquiries, makes referrals.

43337. Research Institute of Information Science and Engineering, Box 7551, Pittsburgh, PA 15213; (412) 624-5205. Promotes research in info science, engineering; conducts educational programs for info professionals. Publishes journal and proceedings, answers inquiries about manpower needs.

43338. Research Instruments, 615 E Carson St, Pittsburgh, PA 15203; (412) 431-4600. Interest in lab R&D equipment, specialized computer parts. Publishes indexes; locates hard-to-find lab equipment instruments, components for a fee or on contract basis.

43339. Research for Better Schools, 444 N 3rd St, Philadelphia, PA 19123; (215) 574-9300. Works with educational agencies of 5 states, D.C. to improve school, classroom practice. Collections available for onsite use. Publishes reports, monographs; provides consulting services; conducts seminars, workshops.

43340. Resistance Welder Manufacturers' Association, 1900 Arch St, Philadelphia, PA 19103; (215) 564-3484. Interest in resistance welding: equipment, components, supplies, specifications, education. Publishes manual, articles, and standards, answers brief inquiries, conducts annual welding school.

43341. Robotics Institute, Schenley Park, Pittsburgh, PA 15213; (412) 578-3818. Undertakes advanced R&D in robots, intelligent machine systems. Facilitates transfer of technology to U.S. industry. Publishes technical reports. Services free to sponsors, some orgs; at others to cost.

43342. Rockwell International Corp., Technical Information Center, General Industries Operations, 400 N Lexington Ave, Pittsburgh, PA 15208; (412) 247-3095. Interest in engineering, instrumentation, metallurgy. Has print and microform materials, access to data bases. Publishes journal, standards, and specifications, answers inquiries. Services free, available only to corps, univs.

43343. Rolls-Royce Owners Club, P.O. Box 2001, Mechanicsburg, PA 17055. Interest in Royce, Rolls-Royce, Bentley cars. Maintains reference collection. Publishes magazine, reference materials; answers inquiries; provides consulting, reference services. Services primarily for members.

43344. Ruffed Grouse Society, 1400 Lee Dr, Coraopolis, PA 15108; (412) 262-4044. Improves environment for ruffed grouse, woodcock, other wildlife. Publishes newspaper (for members only), technical reports; provides inquiry, reference services; conducts workshops. Most services free.

43345. Rural American Women, Rte 2, Box 235, Kempton, PA 19529; (215) 756-6362. Develops skills of rural people to deal with local communities, absentee institutions. Answers inquiries, permits onsite use of collections. Services free, except publications.

43346. Sadtler Research Laboratories, 3316 Spring Garden St, Philadelphia, PA 19104; (215) 382-7800. Maintains reference spectra for various organic, inorganic compounds. Provides contract analytical services. Publishes research materials, answers inquiries, provides consulting and reference services for a fee.

43347. School of Living, Deep Run Farm, R.D. 7, Box 388, York, PA 17402; (717) 755-2666. Promotes decentralism, rural revival. Maintains reference library, info clearinghouse. Publishes journal, conducts workshops, provides consulting services. Fee for some services; send SASE with requests for written response.

43348. School of Medicine, Johnson Research Foundation, Alfred N. Richards Bldg, Philadelphia, PA 19104; (215) 243-8796. Interest in biophysics, physical biochemistry, cellular physiology. Maintains research library.

43349. School of Veterinary Medicine, Comparative Cardiovascular Studies Unit, Univ of Penn, 3800 Spruce St, Philadelphia, PA 19104; (215) 898-8585. Interest in comparative cardiology, cardiac toxicology. Maintains research collection, answers brief inquiries. Extensive services for staff members only.

43350. Science Products, Box A, Southeastern, PA 19399; (215) 687-3731. Interest in special instruments and aids for the blind, visually limited. Publishes print and audio catalogs, answers inquiries, provides consulting services, conducts seminars. Services generally free. Special instruments, aids are sold.

43351. Scleroderma International Foundation, 704 Gardner Center Rd, New Castle, PA 16101; (412) 652-3109. Provides support for patients with scleroderma (or progressive systematic sclerosi—chronic, degenerative disease of connective tissue). Supports research, especially on dimethyl sulfoxide (DMSO) treatment.

43352. Scott Paper Co., Technology Library and Technical Information Service, Scott Plaza 3, Philadelphia, PA 19113; (215) 522-6410. Interest in pulp and paper, packaging (chemistry, engineering). Has research collection and access to computerized data bases. Makes interlibrary loans; library open to visitors by appointment.

43353. Shalom Center, c/o Reconstructionist Rabbinical College, Church Rd and Greenwood Ave, Wyncote, PA 19095; (215) 576-0800. Applies Jewish history, religious tradition to halting nuclear arms race, preventing nuclear holocaust. Publishes newsletter, provides inquiry and reference services, conducts workshops. Services free.

43354. Shelving Manufacturers Association, 1326 Freeport Rd, Pittsburgh, PA 15238; (412) 782-1624. Fosters, advances, protects interests of steel shelving industry. Publishes directories, specifications; answers inquiries; conducts seminars, workshops. Fee for some services.

43355. Social Science Computer Research Institute, 5R01 Forbes Quadrangle, Pittsburgh, PA 15260; (412) 624-5560. Interest in computer program implementation for social science data management, retrieval, analysis. Has data sets. Publishes newsletter and reports, answers inquiries, provides computer program implementation services. Services usually for a fee.

43356. Social Science Data Center, Univ of Penn, 390 McNeil Bldg CR, 3718 Locust Walk, Philadelphia, PA 19104; (215) 898-6454. Undertakes quantitative studies in social science; has data sets, codebooks. Provides advisory services, permits onsite use of collection. Services primarily for univ members, affiliates; others served by prior arrangement.

43357. Society for Industrial and Applied Mathematics, 1405 Architects Bldg, 117 S 17th St, Philadelphia, PA 19103; (215) 564-2929. Interest in applied mathematics. Publishes journals, monographs (for sale in hard copy or microform), answers inquiries, conducts meetings and special conferences.

43358. Society for the Advancement of Continuing Education for Ministry, 855 Locust St, Collville, PA 19426; (215) 489-6358. Interest in continuing education of clergy, laity (Protestant, Roman Catholic, Jewish). Publishes newsletter and regional guides, answers inquiries, provides consulting services. Fees sometimes charged.

43359. Society for the Scientific Study of Sex, c/o Ms. Deborah Weinstein, Exec Director, P.O. Box 29795, Philadelphia, PA 19117; (215) 782-1430. Promotes scientific study of sexuality. Publishes journal, newsletter; conducts meetings. Data base lists professionals in the field. Info made available primarily thru publications, meetings; answers mail inquiries.

43360. Society for the Study of Breast Disease, c/o Gordon F. Schwartz, M.D., 1015 Chestnut St, Ste 510, Philadelphia, PA 19107; (215) 627-8487. Studies breast diseases; serves as natl forum for advances, controversies. Publishes proceedings, answers inquiries, conducts courses and workshops. Services provided at cost, primarily for health professionals.

43361. Society of Automotive Engineers, 400 Commonwealth Dr, Warrendale, PA 15096; (412) 776-4841. Interest in wide range of topics on automobiles, aircraft, spacecraft, engines. Publishes journal, technical materials; provides inquiry, reference services. Computer-aided search service available commercially.

43362. Sourceworks, 1505 Sylvania House, Juniper and Locust Sts, Philadelphia, PA 19107; (215) 546-0437. Provides technical assistance in grassroots neighborhood development. Maintains reference library for onsite use. Publishes newsletter, provides inquiry, consulting, and reference services.

43363. Sports Medicine Center, Dept of Orthopedic Surgery, School of Medicine, E7 Weightman Hall, Univ of Penn, 235 South 33rd St, Philadelphia, PA 19104; (215) 662-4090. Maintains natl registry of football head and neck injuries; evaluates rules, equipment, coaching techniques. Publishes research, conducts seminars and workshops. Services available to researchers.

43364. Sports Research Institute, 109 Sports Research Bldg, Penn State Univ, Univ Park, PA 16802; (814) 865-9543. Conducts, publishes research on competitive sports, especially women in sports, safety in sports. Provides inquiry, advisory, consulting services; conducts seminars, workshops. Services for a fee.

43365. St. Charles Borromeo Seminary Library, Archives and Historical Collections, St Charles Seminary, Overbrook, Philadelphia, PA 19151; (215) 839-3760. Interest in U.S. Catholic history, religious history in general. Has print materials (access by prearrangement); maintains museum of religious Americana. Publishes journal, answers inquiries.

43366. St. Christopher's Hospital for Children, Pulmonary and Cystic Fibrosis Center, 2600 N Lawrence St, Philadelphia, PA 19133; (215) 427-5183. Conducts research on cystic fibrosis. Publishes research, reference materials; provides inquiry, reference, training services; conducts seminars. Services free.

43367. Steel Structures Painting Council, 4400 Fifth Ave, Pittsburgh, PA 15213; (412) 578-3327. Interest in surface preparation, painting, and coating of structural steel. Publishes journal, manuals, standards, other reference materials; conducts workshops.

43368. Stein Research Center, Jefferson Medical College, 920 Chancellor St, Philadelphia, PA 19107; (215) 928-7800. Interest in developmental, reproductive biology. Publishes research, provides inquiry and advisory services, conducts seminars. Services free to investigators, at cost to others.

43369. Strawbridge Observatory, Haverford College, Haverford, PA 19041; (215) 896-1291. Has collection of materials on astronomy, astrophysics. Answers brief inquiries, makes interlibrary loans.

43370. Structural Stability Research Council, Fritz Engineering Laboratory No. 13, Lehigh Univ, Bethlehem, PA 18015; (215) 861-3519. Interest in design, behavior of frames, columns, and other compression elements. Maintains technical library. Publishes technical materials, newsletter; provides inquiry, advisory services to researchers.

43371. Sun Co., Library and Information Service, P.O. Box 1135, Marcus Hook, PA 19061; (215) 447-1723. Interest in petroleum chemistry. Maintains library: patents, reference materials, online data bases.

43372. Technical Advisory Service for Attorneys, 428 Pennsylvania Ave, Fort Washington, PA 19034; (215) 643-5252, (800) 523-2319. For-profit org that provides scientific, technical experts to attorneys, others. Has computerized roster of experts. Answers inquiries, provides consulting and reference services. Fee charged if expert is provided.

43373. Television Center, Hahnemann Univ School of Medicine, Broad and Vine Sts, Philadelphia, PA 19102; (215) 448-8572. Interest in continuing medical, patient education by TV. Has collection of medical education video tapes produced at univ. Sells video tapes; makes TV studio available for special seminars.

43374. Train Collectors Association, P.O. Box 248, Strasburg, PA 17579; (717) 687-8976. Collects antique and modern toy trains, related items. Maintains library. Publishes magazine, directory; provides inquiry, reference services; conducts seminars; permits onsite use of library. Services free, available primarily to members.

43376. U.S. Army Military History Institute, Carlisle Barracks, PA 17013-5008; (717) 245-3611. Interest in U.S. military history, especially land warfare. Has print, AV, microform materials. Publishes magazine and reference materials, answers inquiries, provides reference services.

43377. U.S. Navy, Naval Damage Control Training Center, U.S. Naval Base, Philadelphia, PA 19112; (215) 897-5652. Interest in all aspects of naval damage control. Maintains research collections. Services available to DoD personnel; to others by authority of Chief of Naval Personnel.

43378. USDA Eastern Regional Research Center, Agricultural Research Service, 600 E Mermaid Lane, Philadelphia, PA 19118; (215) 223-6595. Researches postharvest technology, agricultural products. Maintains library for onsite use. Publishes research materials, answers specific inquiries on research programs. Reference services limited.

43379. United Humanitarians, P.O. Box 14587, Philadelphia, PA 19115; (215) 750-0171. Offers free veterinarian services to pet owners on public welfare, social security. Promotes humane treatment of animals, especially pets. Publishes magazine. Services free, except publications.

43380. United Steelworkers of America, 5 Gateway Center, Pittsburgh, PA 15222; (412) 562-2400. Union for basic steel, allied ferrous and nonferrous metals industries. Maintains files of current contracts, financial info on steel corps. Publishes magazine, answers inquiries, permits some onsite use of collection.

43381. Urban Archives Center, Samuel Paley Library, Philadelphia, PA 19122; (215) 787-8257. Interest in all aspects of modern Philadelphia. Has collection of print, AV, taped materials; manuscript collections (for onsite use). Publishes journal, guides; provides inquiry, advisory, reference services. Most services free.

43382. Victorian Society in America, East Washington Square, Philadelphia, PA 19106; (215) 627-4252. Interest in all aspects of Victorian era in U.S., Europe. Publishes newsletter, magazine, reference materials; conducts seminars, workshops. Fee for some services.

43383. Waste Water Renovation and Conservation Research Project, Institute for Research on Land and Water Resources, Penn State Univ, Univ Park, PA 16802; (814) 863-0291. Interest in water renovation, conservation by disposal of municipal sewage effluent on agricultural, forest, disturbed lands. Publishes reports and newsletter, answers inquiries, makes referrals.

43384. Westinghouse Water Reactor Divisions, Information Resource Center, Westinghouse Electric Corp., P.O. Box 355 MNC209 (Northern Pike at Haymaker Rd, Monroeville, PA), Pittsburgh, PA 15230; (412) 374-4200. Interest in nuclear science, technology. Has research collection of print, microform, AV materials; provides limited outside reference services; makes interlibrary loans.

43385. Wharton Econometric Forecasting Associates, Univ of Penn, One Univ City, 3624 Science Center, Philadelphia, PA 19104; (215) 386-9000. Develops econometric models to supply current and long-term forecasts, simulations. Provides special econometric services, consulting, access to data banks. Services to members. Special reports available for purchase.

43386. Wheelmen, c/o David R. Gray, Publications Chairman, 39 Squirrel Rd, Doylestown, PA 18901; (215) 345-0282. Promotes riding, collecting, restoring antique bicycles and tricycles; research on their history. Collects catalogs, manuals; publishes magazine, newsletter; answers inquiries. Services free, primarily for members.

43388. Wildlife Preservation Trust International, 34th St and Girard Ave, Philadelphia, PA 19104; (215) 222-3636. Supports captive breeding of endangered species; their reintroduction in the wild. Publishes newsletter, journal, promotional materials; answers inquiries free; provides films, lecturers.

43389. Wistar Institute of Anatomy and Biology, 36th and Spruce Sts, Philadelphia, PA 19104; (215) 243-3700. Interest in virology; viral oncology; arteriosclerosis, atherosclerosis; aging, cellular development; vaccines. Maintains research library, has access to data bases. Provides consulting services on contract basis.

43390. Women Strike for Peace, 145 S 13th St, Philadelphia, PA 19107; (215) 923-0861. Lobbies, educates public on arms control and disarmament, foreign policy, nuclear war. Publishes magazine and newsletter, conducts workshops. Provides speakers and info on grassroots organizing.

43391. Women for Sobriety, Box 618, Quakertown, PA 18951; (215) 536-8026. Runs self-help program for women alcoholics. Publishes newsletter (available by subscription), promotional materials; provides inquiry service; conducts seminars, workshops.

43393. Women's International League for Peace and Freedom/U.S. Section, 1213 Race St, Philadelphia, PA 19107; (215) 563-7110. Works for world peace, freedom, disarmament; U.S. budget reform; elimination of racism, sexism, oppression. Publishes magazine, studies, policy papers; answers inquiries.

43394. Women's Law Project, 112 S 16th St, Ste 1012, Philadelphia, PA 19102; (215) 564-6280. Conducts litigation for women's legal rights. Maintains resource files; publications list available. Provides inquiry, consulting, counseling services; conducts seminars. Fee for some services.

43395. World Game Projects, 3701 Chestnut St, Philadelphia, PA 19104; (215) 967-3125. Encourages proper use of renewable resources. Maintains library, files, inventory of global energy and food resources. Publishes print, AV materials; provides inquiry, consulting services; conducts seminars, workshops. Most services at cost.

43396. World Methodist Historical Society, Box 460, Mont Alto, PA 17237; (717) 749-5132. Auxiliary of World Methodist Council for study of world history of Methodism. Publishes journal, research, reference materials; Conducts regional conferences in Methodist history; distributes publications.

43397. World Resources Inventory, 3701 Chestnut St, Philadelphia, PA 19104; (215) 387-0220. Researches energy, food production, consumption for all countries. Publishes print, machine-readable materials; provides advisory, consulting services; conducts workshops. Services for a fee.

43398. Zoological Record, BioSciences Information Service, 2100 Arch St, Philadelphia, PA 19103-1399; (215) 587-4800, (800) 523-4806. Interest in pure zoology, especially systematics, subject coverage. Publishes in print, online forms; Offers descriptive user aids, educational programs, free newsletter.

Rhode Island

44001. Adolf Meller Co., P.O. Box 6001, Providence, RI 02904; (401) 331-3717. Interest in sapphire products, laser crystals, maser crystals, alumina powders, optical crystals, halide products, laser products. Publishes data sheets, answers brief inquiries, makes referrals, provides consulting services free to bona fide scientific researchers.

44002. American Mathematical Society, P.O. Box 6248 (201 Charles St), Providence, RI 02940; (401) 272-9500. Interest in mathematics. Maintains MATHFILE computerized data base. Publishes journals, bulletins, reviews, answers inquiries, makes referrals, makes available current and back publications and indices.

44003. American Sail Training Association, Newport Harbor Center, 365 Thames St, Newport, RI 02840; (401) 846-1775. Promotes opportunities for young people to go to sea aboard deepwater sailing vessels through sponsorship and organization of sail training cruises and races. Answers inquiries, provides advisory services. Except for certain publications, info services are free.

44004. Atlantic Offshore Fishermen's Association, 174 Bellevue Ave, Ste 209, Newport, RI 02840; (401) 849-3232. Provides forum for discussion of issues affecting commercial fisheries of Atlantic coast from Maine to North Carolina. Publishes background papers, answers inquiries. Services primarily for members, but others will be assisted; fees may be charged.

44005. Behavior Research Institute, 240 Laban St, Providence, RI 02909; (401) 944-1186. Residential school/treatment center for children and adults with severe behavior disorders. Administers individualized behavior modification and special ed programs. Answers inquiries, assists parents in developing a school in their local community. Fees charged for services.

44006. Earthrise, P.O. Box 120 (503 1/2 Chalkstone Ave), Annex Station, Providence, RI 02901; (401) 272-7145. Interest in R&D in such areas as architecture and global environmental trends. Answers inquiries, provides design and consulting services, conducts simulation games. Services provided for a fee.

44007. Foster Parents Plan, 155 Plan Way, Warwick, RI 02887; (401) 738-5605. Provides health, nutrition, education, and community development assistance to children and their families within context of community needs in 21 developing countries, emphasis on Third World. Answers inquiries, distributes publication, makes referrals to other sources of info.

44008. Institute of Management Sciences, 290 Westminster St, Providence, RI 02903; (401) 274-2525. Professional org of managers, educators, and practicing mgmt scientists interested in development and application of scientific methods and concepts in management. Answers inquiries or refers inquirers free to other sources of info, publishes journal and reports.

44009. International Center for Marine Resource Development, c/o Main Library, Univ of R.I., Kingston, RI 02881; (401) 792-2938. Resource on problems of small-scale fishery development. Has about 13,000 documents, technical reports, and books from govts and intl agencies. Answers inquiries, distributes publications, permits onsite use of collection. Services generally free.

44010. International Tennis Hall of Fame, 194 Bellevue Ave, Newport, RI 02840; (401) 849-3990. Honors persons who have contributed to sport of tennis, conducts tournaments. Has special library on tennis and personalities, collects tennis memorabilia. Answers inquiries, permits use of library by appointment. Services free primarily to researchers, but others will be assisted.

44011. Isochem Products Co., 99 Cook St, Lincoln, RI 02865; (401) 723-2100. Interest in epoxy resins, silicones, polyester, urethanes and foams, missiles and aerospace formulations, resin strippers, disintegrators. Publishes technical data sets and books, answers brief inquiries, provides wide range of technical data on products.

44012. Manufacturing Jewelers and Silversmiths of America, The Biltmore Plaza, Providence, RI 02903; (401) 274-3840. Trade assn interested in jewelry, silverware, and allied item manufacturing. Publishes newsletter, magazine, and technical reports, answers inquiries, provides advisory and reference services. Services may be provided for a fee.

44013. Marine Awareness Center, Marine Advisory Service, Univ of R.I., Narragansett, RI 02882-1197; (401) 792-6211. Provides students and teachers and public with marine-oriented curricula and audiovisual materials. Has extensive collection of marine-related materials on microfiche. Answers inquiries, provides consulting service to schools, distributes publications. Most services free.

44014. National Marine Educators Association, P.O. Box 666, Narragansett, RI 02882; (401) 783-0838. Sponsors Natl Marine Education conferences and fosters development of local and regional marine education conferences and workshops. Has computerized database of marine-related magazine articles. Answers inquiries, provides advisory and consulting services, often at cost.

44015. National Sea Grant Depository, Pell Marine Science Library Bldg, Univ of R.I., Narragansett Bay Campus, Narragansett, RI 02882; (401) 792-6114. Interest in development and use of U.S. salt and fresh waters, including such topics as aquaculture, coastal zone management, law of the sea. Publishes *Sea Grant Publications Index.* Performs online literature searches when supplied with keywords. Services free.

44016. Naval Underwater Systems Center Technical Library, Newport, RI 02841-5047; (401) 841-4338, 841-4421. Interest in underwater acoustics, deep water ranges, propulsion, antisubmarine fire control systems, antisubmarine warfare, undersea surveillance, acoustic torpedoes. Has collection of 500,000 items, many with security classification. Provides library services for contractors.

44017. Northeast Fisheries Center Narragansett Laboratory, National Marine Fisheries Service, NOAA, South Ferry Rd, Narragansett, RI 02882; (401) 789-9326. Researches early life history of fish as scientific input to fisheries management and conservation practices. Has literature collection, fish collections, plankton data archives, satellite imagery archive. Answers inquiries about lab's work, permits onsite use of collections.

44018. Population Studies and Training Center, Brown Univ, Providence, RI 02912; (401) 863-2668. Provides training for graduate students in population studies and organizational framework for coordinating multidisciplinary research activities in population at univ. Has demographic library, publishes technical reports, answers inquiries. Services free to qualified researchers.

44019. Primate Behavior Laboratory, Dept of Psychology, Brown Univ, Providence, RI 02912; (401) 863-2511. Interest in research with nonhuman primates; care, breeding, and procurement of nonhuman primates. Publishes Directory of Graduate Programs in Primatology and Primate Research, answers inquiries, distributes publications. Services free to those engaged in research on nonhuman primates.

44020. Rhode Island Historical Society, Library, 121 Hope St, Providence, RI 02906; (401) 331-8575. Interest in R.I. history, history and genealogy of New England. Has over 1 million pieces of manuscript material, photos, engravings, films. Provides reference service by mail and brief genealogical searches for a small fee, offrers copying through interlibrary loan for a fee.

44021. Rhode Island State Library, State House, Providence, RI 02903; (401) 277-2473. Interest in history and govt of R.I. Has U.S govt documents, R.I. state documents, and publications on political and socioeconomic history of region. Provides legislative reference services, authenticates documents. Collection open to general public.

44022. Robotics Research Center, Univ of R.I., 212 Kelley Hall, Kingston, RI 02881; (401) 792-2514. Involved in robotics research and education and technology transfer through cooperation with industry. Answers inquiries, provides advisory and consulting services, provides info on research in progress, distributes publications. Services may be provided for a fee.

44023. Scleroderma Information Exchange, 106 Quaker Drive, West Warwick, RI 02893; (401) 822-3130. Nonprofit org for individuals with scleroderma, their families, friends, and other interested persons. Serves both as support group and clearinghouse for scleroderma info. Provides referrals to self-help groups throughout U.S., answers inquiries.

44024. Snell Memorial Foundation, P.O. Box 733, Wakefield, RI 02880; (401) 789-5410. Interest in head protection and head protective devices. Has over 250 periodical titles, books, reports. Answers inquiries, provides consulting services. Most services free.

44025. U. S. Yacht Racing Union, Box 209 (Goat Island Marina Bldg, 2nd Fl), Newport, RI 02840; (401) 849-5200. Governing body for sport of sailing, including one-design and offshore racing at all levels. Answers inquiries, provides advisory services, distributes publications and computer scoring programs, makes referrals to other sources of info. Services for a fee to members and yachting press.

44026. Volunteers in Action, 229 Waterman St, Providence, RI 02906; (401) 421-6547, 421-7472. Interest in volunteerism, volunteer training and opportunity. Holdings include Community Skillsbank, Board of Directors Registry. Publishes newsletter, answers inquiries, provides advisory and reference services, distributes publications. Services free.

44027. Water Resources Center, Univ of R.I., Bliss Hall, Kingston, RI 02881; (401) 792-2267. Interest in research and training in all phases of water resources: detection of water pollutants, removal of pollutants from groundwater, acid rain sources and effects on water quality, etc. Publishes technical reports on water resources research projects, answers inquiries.

South Carolina

45001. Alston Wilkes Society, P.O. Box 363 (2215 Devine St), Columbia, SC 29202; (803) 799-2490. Provides counseling and guidance, job assistance, housing; offers consulting services on community residential programs; provides grievance arbitrators. Services free.

45002. Association for Education in Journalism and Mass Communication, 1621 Coll St, Univ of S.C., Columbia, SC 29208-0251; (803) 777-2005. Nonprofit org of college and univ journalism, mass communication professors that provides advisory services, conducts workshops, sells mailing labels, provides career info free.

45003. Belle W. Baruch Institute for Marine Biology and Coastal Research, Univ of S.C., Columbia, SC 29208; (803) 777-5288; Field Laboratory: Georgetown, SC 29442; (803) 546-3623. Owns baseline data for meteorological, tidal, sediment, phytoplankton, spartina, zooplankton, benthos, nekton, and bird measurements; publishes technical reports; provides consulting services. Services free to some users.

45005. Charleston Naval Shipyard Technical Library, Naval Base, Charleston, SC 29408; (803) 743-3843. Owns books, journals, technical reports on shipbuilding technology, mechanical, electrical, civil, and marine engineering. Makes interlibrary loans, permits onsite reference to collection.

45006. Department of Agriculture Cotton Quality Research Station, Agricultural Research Service, USDA, P.O. Box 792, Clemson, SC 29631; (803) 656-2488. Owns small collection of books, periodicals, reports on research necessary to develop methods, techniques, instruments for accurate measures of quality in cotton. Answers inquiries.

45007. Department of Biology and Pharmacognosy, Coll of Pharmacy, Medical Univ of S.C., 171 Ashley Ave, Charleston, SC 29425; (803) 792-3111. Publishes reports, articles, reviews on pharmacognosy, synthesis of natural products. Answers brief inquiries, provides consulting services to local physicians, industry.

45008. Department of Environmental Systems Engineering, Rhodes Research Engineering Center, Clemson Univ, Clemson, SC 29634-0919; (803) 656-3276. Publishes reports, journals for water and waste water treatment plant operators. Answers inquiries, provides reference and consulting services, develops training programs and materials.

45009. Florence Air and Missile Museum, P.O. Box 1326 (Highway 301), Florence, SC 29503; (803) 665-5118. Partially sponsored by local govt, collects and displays planes and missiles, space artifacts. Publishes brochure. Open every day, admission charged.

45011. Industrial Diamond Association of America, P.O. Box 11187 (3008 Millwood Ave), Columbia, SC 29211; (803) 252-5646. Publishes bulletins, technical reports, handbooks, specifications, conference papers, film list on industrial diamonds. Conducts conferences, seminars, workshops for a fee.

45013. International Association for Identification, P.O. Box 90259, Columbia, SC 29290. Owns books on sciences of identification, including historical items. Publishes monthly news. Services for law enforcement personnel, but answers brief inquiries from others.

45014. International Primate Protection League, P.O. Box 760, Summerville, SC 29484; (803) 871-2280. Concerned with conservation, protection of nonhuman primates. Publishes newsletter, answers inquiries, makes referrals to other sources of info. Services free.

45015. International Studies Association, Byrnes International Center, Univ of S.C., Columbia, SC 29208; (803) 777-2933. Represents intl interdisciplinary studies scholars, practitioners, institutions. Publishes reports, directories, abstracts, bibliographies; provides consulting, abstracting services.

45016. Marine Biomedical Research Program, Medical Univ of S.C., P.O. Box 12559 (Fort Johnson), Charleston, SC 29412; (803) 795-7490. Publishes journals, annual review series on invertebrate pathology, experimental parasitology, compatative pathobiology. Answers inquiries, provides consulting services on a cost basis.

45017. National Association for Campus Activities, P.O. Box 11489 (749 1/2 Saluda Ave), Columbia, SC 29211; (803) 799-0768. Helps member higher education institutions produce campus activities. Publishes newsletter with job listings, provides reference services, conducts seminars, workshops, and conferences.

45018. National Council of Engineering Examiners, P.O. Box 1686, Clemson, SC 29633; (803) 654-6824. Publishes quarterly bulletin, annual yearbook, engineering exam questions. Conducts surveys, distributes pamphlets on engineering, land surveying registration requirements.

45019. National Drilling Federation, P.O. Box 11187 (3008 Millwood Ave), Columbia, SC 29211; (803) 252-5646. Provides forum for drilling contractors, manufacturers to accomplish common goals. Publishes standards and technical reports, conducts seminars and conferences. Services free.

45020. National Wild Turkey Federation, P.O. Box 530 (770 Augusta Rd), Edgefield, SC 29824; (803) 637-3106. Interest in American wild turkey conservation. Publishes magazine, newsletters; provides consulting, reference services; conducts seminars, workshops. Services mostly free.

45021. Phillips Fibers Corp. Technical Research Center, P.O. Box 66 (I-85 at Ridge Rd), Greenville, SC 29602; (803) 242-6600. Distributes technical publications on manmade fiber technology, owns standards and specifications, engineering catalogs, patents. Answers inquiries, refers inquirers to other sources of info free.

45022. Platt Saco Lowell Corp., P.O. Box 2327 (Greenville Highway), Greenville, SC 29602; (803) 859-3211. Owns patents, periodicals, newspapers on textile machinery, industrial robots. Publishes reports and standards, provides free consulting services, permits onsite use of collection.

45023. Research Planning Institute Library, 925 Gervais St, Columbia, SC 29201; (803) 256-7332. Consulting firm involved in environmental sciences. Owns topographic and nautical maps, publishes technical reports, permits onsite use of collection. Services provided for a fee.

45024. Santee National Wildlife Refuge, U.S. Fish and Wildlife Service, Rt. 2, P.O. Box 66, Summerton, SC 29148; (803) 478-2217. Publishes brochures on waterfowl management, waterfowl banding, wood duck production. Answers inquiries, makes referrals to other sources of info. Services free.

45025. South Carolina Department of Archives and History, P.O. Box 11,669 (1430 Senate St), Capitol Station, Columbia, SC 29211; (803) 758-5816. Preserves state, local govt records, conducts historic site preservation. Provides microfilming services, provides photocopies for a fee, allows onsite access to collection.

45026. South Carolina Historical Society, 100 Meeting St, Charleston, SC 29401; (803) 723-3225. Publishes books on South Carolina history; owns manuscripts, photos, architectural drawings. Provides copying services, permits onsite use of collection. Services free to members, others preparing publications.

45027. South Carolina Sea Grant Consortium, 221 Fort Johnson Rd, Charleston, SC 29412; (803) 795-6350 ext 203. Publishes bulletins, technical reports, research summaries on South Carolina's marine resources. Provides advisory services, conducts seminars and workshops. Services mostly free.

45028. SouthEastern Exchange of the U.S., P.O. Box 11181, Columbia, SC 29211; (803) 799-1234. Acts as regional connector for adoption agencies. Publishes resource packages, provides advisory services, permits onsite use of collection. Services mostly free.

45029. Steel Joist Institute, 1205 48th Ave North, Suite A, Myrtle Beach, SC 29577. Publishes technical digests, specifications and load tables for steel joists, joist girders. Provides advisory services, info on research in progress. Services free.

45030. United States Collegiate Sports Council, c/o Blatt PE Center, Suite 202, Univ of S.C., Columbia, SC 29208; (803) 777-7991. Sponsors summer, winter World University Games involving About 100 nations. Owns records on intl univ sports programs, publishes directory of games committees, answers inquiries.

45031. Water Resources Research Institute, Clemson Univ, Rhodes Research Center, Clemson, SC 29631; (803) 656-3271. Publishes circulars, bulletins, papers on subjects such as water cycle, hydrology, irrigation, water stream pollution instrumentation. Answers inquiries, conducts research for a fee.

South Dakota

46001. American Indian Culture Research Center, c/o Blue Cloud Abbey, P.O. Box 98, Marvin, SD 57251; (605) 432-5528. Nonprofit org that educates and informs non-Indian public on culture and philosophy of the Indian. Provides general reference services, conducts seminars, permits onsite use of collection. Fee for some services.

46002. American Musical Instrument Society, c/o Shrine to Music Museum, 414 East Clark St, Vermillion, SD 57069; (605) 677-5306. Promotes the study of the history, design, and use of musical instruments in all cultures and from all periods. Answers inquiries free.

46003. Archaeological Society of South Dakota, c/o Archeology Laboratory, Augustana Coll, 2032 South Grange Ave, Sioux Falls, SD 57105; (605) 336-5493. Interest in archeology, anthropology, and prehistory of South Dakota. Provides general reference services, analyzes data, conducts seminars, distributes publications. Services free, except for ublications.

46004. Archaeology Laboratory, Univ of S.D., Vermillion, SD 57069; (605) 677-5401. Interest in archeology and anthropology of eastern South Dakota. Provides general reference services, evaluates and analyzes data, conducts seminars, distributes publications and data compilations, permits onsite use of collections. Services generally available for a fee.

46005. Center for Western Studies, Augustana Coll, Sioux Falls, SD 57197; (605) 336-4007. Interest in the exploration, settlement, and development of America west of the Mississippi, particularly upper Great Plains. Provides general reference services, makes interlibrary loans, permits onsite use of collections. Services free.

46006. Devereaux Library, S.D. School of Mines and Technology, Rapid City, SD 57701; (605) 394-2418. Interest in science and engineering, with emphasis on geology and paleontology (especially of the Black Hills and Badlands of S.D.), atmospheric sciences, metallurgy, and mining. Provides reference, interlibrary loan, and computer-searching services.

46007. Earth Resources Observation Systems Library, EROS Data Center, U.S. Geological Survey, Sioux Falls, SD 57198; (605) 594-6511 ext 172. Interest in remote sensing of earth resources, including technology, applications, and programs. Library open to the public for reference. Interlibrary loan available by request.

46008. H.C. Severin Insect Museum, Department of Plant Science, S.D. State Univ, Brookings, SD 57006; (605) 688-5121. Interest in insects, especially insects in S.D. Provides general reference services, permits onsite use of collections. Services free. Some services restricted to permanent staff members of other established institutions.

46009. Institute of Atmospheric Sciences, S.D. School of Mines and Technology, Rapid City, SD 57701; (605) 394-2291. Interest in air quality, numerical cloud models, cloud physics, weather modification, radar meteorology, atmospheric electricity, etc. Answers inquiries, provides info on institute's research. Services free.

46010. Institute of Indian Studies, Univ of S.D., Box 133, Vermillion, SD 57069; (605) 677-5209. Nonacademic dept concerned with contemporary affairs, religion, history, etc. of Northern Plains Indians; alcoholism among Indians. Provides general reference services, makes direct and interlibrary loans, permits onsite use of collections. Services free, primarily for Indian tribes and individuals.

46011. Museum of Geology, S.D. School of Mines and Technology, Rapid City, SD 57701; (605) 394-2467. Interest in vertebrate fossils of western S.D., minerals of Black Hills, vertebrates, paleontology. geology. Provides reference and consulting services, conducts tours and lectures, lends materials to qualified museums, permits onsite use of collections.

46013. North American Baptist Conference Archives, 1321 West 22nd St, Sioux Falls, SD 57105; (605) 336-6805. Interest in development of corporate Baptist agencies, institutions, and activities in area of culture change, including education, medical and agricultural services, religious leaders, etc. Provides general reference services, permits onsite use of collections. Most services free.

46014. Office of American Indian Research Project, Univ of S.D., Dakota Hall, Room 16-18, Vermillion, SD 57069; (605) 677-5208. Interest in oral history of Native Americans of the Northern Great Plains, and oral history of South Dakota. Provides general reference services, conducts seminars, distributes publications. permits onsite use of the collection. Services free.

46015. South Dakota Conservation Commission, Anderson Bldg, Room 304, 445 East Capitol, Pierre, SD 57501; (605) 773-3258. Interest in natural resources conservation and development in S.D., programs of conservation districts, administration of irrigation soil/water compatibility permits. Answers brief inquiries, makes referrals, provides conservation district supervisors with necessities.

46016. South Dakota Historical Resource Center, State Historical Society, Soldiers Memorial Bldg, Pierre, SD 57501; (605) 224-3615. Provides general reference services about S.D. history; permits onsite use of collection. Photos, book excerpts, and newspaper items duplicated at cost. No loans.

46018. South Dakota State Historical Society, Memorial Bldg, Pierre, SD 57501; (605) 773-3615. Interest in S.D., western American and American Indian history and ethnology. Provides general reference services, makes interlibrary loans, permits onsite use of collections. Services free, except for copying services and postage on interlibrary loans.

46019. Water Resources Institute, S.D. State Univ, Brookings, SD 57007; (605) 688-4910. Interest in water supply, economics, and quality, waste disposal practices affecting ground-water quality, evapotranspiration, lake production, soil moisture, irrigation, subsurface drainage, etc. Answers technical inquiries, performs water analysis for a nominal fee.

Tennessee

47001. Acid Deposition Data Network Project, Environmental Sciences Division, Oak Ridge Natl Lab, P.O. Box X (Bldg 1505), Oak Ridge, TN 37831; (615) 574-7819. Interest in acid rain, acid precipitation, acid deposition assessments and analyses. Provides general reference services, distributes compilations. Assistance often restricted.

47002. Agriculture-Veterinary Medicine Library, Univ of Tenn., A-113 Veterinarian Teaching Hosp, Knoxville, TN 37916; (615) 974-7338. Interest in agricultural biology, economics, engineering, and extension, animal science, food technology, forestry, etc. Provides general reference services for a fee

47003. American Association for State and Local History, 708 Berry Rd, Nashville, TN 37204; (615) 383-5991. Interest in historical orgs, museums, historical archives and libraries. Answers inquiries, distributes career info, produces educational programs, provides speakers when expenses paid.

47004. American College of Apothecaries, 874 Union Ave, Memphis, TN 38111; (901) 528-6037. Interest in continuing education for pharmacists, pharmacy management, drug info. Provides general reference and consulting services, conducts seminars, distributes publications. Services primarily for members; some provided to others for a fee.

47005. American Economic Association, 1313 21st Ave S, Ste 809, Nashville, TN 37212; (615) 322-2595. Interest in economics. Provides info, publishes materials, provides computerized data base services.

47006. American Educational Films, P.O. Box 8188, Nashville, TN 37207; (615) 868-2040. Interest in educational films on science, history, public health and safety, art, and social awareness. Rents and sells films; previews provided for purchase consideration.

47007. American Massage and Therapy Association, c/o J.C. Bowling, Exec Secty, P.O. Box 1270, Kingsport, TN 37662; (615) 245-8071. Interest in scientific massage therapy. Provides general reference services free, advisory services and seminars for a fee; approves course of study for training.

47008. American Museum of Science and Energy, 300 S Tulane Ave, Oak Ridge, TN 37830; (615) 576-3218. Provides educational materials and support in energy, environment, communications, science education. Provides general reference services and training, conducts seminars, distributes publications, permits onsite reference. Services either free or at cost.

47009. Analytical Chemistry Division, Oak Ridge Natl Lab, P.O. Box X, Oak Ridge, TN 37830; (615) 483-8329 ext 3-1472. Interest in analytical, bioanalytical chemistry, analytical instrumentation, mass spectrometry, nuclear and radiochemistry. Provides general reference services, distributes publications. Research services provided at cost to non-DoE personnel, subject to approval.

47010. Archival Center for Radiation Biology, Special Collections Div, James D. Hoskins Library, Univ of Tenn., Knoxville, TN 37919; (615) 974-4480. Manuscript repository for research materials in field of radiation biology. Answers inquiries, provides copying services, permits onsite use of collection. Services free.

47011. Association for Christian Training and Service, 1001 18th Ave, South, Nashville, TN 37212; (615) 329-9973. Training agency interested in encouragement of churches in southeastern U.S. to identify and respond to urban and rural problems. Provides consulting, makes referrals, conducts training and leadership programs.

47012. Association of Engineering Geologists, c/o N.M. Ravneberg, 5313 Williamsburg Rd, Brentwood, TN 37027; (615) 377-3578. Interest in advancement of the science of engineering geology. Answers inquiries, distributes publications, makes referrals. Services free, except publications.

47013. Atmospheric Turbulence and Diffusion Division, NOAA/ARL, P.O. Box E, Oak Ridge, TN 37830; (615) 576-1236. Research org interested in atmospheric turbulence, diffusion, deposition, transport of environmental pollution, air/surface interaction. Research reports made available upon request.

47014. Better Lawn and Turf Institute, c/o Dr E.Roberts, Dir, P.O. Box 108 (County Line Rd), Pleasant Hill, TN 38578; (615) 277-3722. Interest in seed and lawn technology, practical lawn crafts and instructions, culti-

vars. Answers inquiries, provides consulting services, distributes publications.

47015. Biomedical Computing Technology Information Center, Medical Center, R-1302, Vanderbilt Univ., Nashville, TN 37232; (615) 322-2385. Serves field of biomedicine, nuclear medicine by collecting, evaluating, and disseminating info in computing technology. Provides general reference services, participates in seminars and meetings, distributes materials. Services available by mutual exchange.

47016. Center for Energy and Environmental Information, Information Center Complex, Oak Ridge Natl Lab, P.O. Box X, Oak Ridge, TN 37830; (615) 574-7763. Research org interested in energy and environmental policy, energy conservation, energy economics, etc. Answers inquiries, conducts limited computer searches, makes referrals, permits onsite use of library.

47017. Center for Information on Internal Dosimetry of Radiopharmaceuticals, Oak Ridge Associated Universities, P.O. Box 117, Oak Ridge, TN 37830; (615) 576-3448. Collects, interprets, correlates info on radiation doses from radiopharmaceuticals. Answers inquiries.

47018. Center for Nuclear Studies, Memphis State Univ, Bldg 1, South Campus, Memphis, TN 38152; (901) 454-2687. Trains nuclear reactor operators, technical staff, and management personnel, provides technical assistance and R&D. Provides general reference and consulting services, conducts seminars, distributes publication. Services primarily for nuclear energy industry, provided at cost.

47019. Center for Productivity, Innovation, and Technology, Chattanooga State Technical Community Coll, 4501 Amnicola Highway, Chattanooga, TN 37406; (615) 697-4411. Interest in computer-aided design, industrial productivity, computer numerical control machining, robotics, factory automation. Provides general reference and consulting services, conducts seminars and training programs. Services provided at cost.

47020. Center for Southern Folklore, P.O. Box 40105 (1216 Peabody Ave), Memphis, TN 38104; (901) 726-4205. Nonprofit org that documents rapidly disappearing folk and ethnic traditions in southern U.S. Provides general reference services and consulting, conducts workshops, distributes publications, permits limited onsite study. Fees charged for research services.

47021. Center in Environmental Toxicology, School of Medicine, Vanderbilt Univ., Nashville, TN 37203; (615) 322-2262. Interest in toxicology, including food additives, fungal toxins, neurotoxins, heavy metal intoxication, pesticides. Answers inquiries, provides consulting. Initial services free; charges may be made for continuing or scheduled services.

47022. Certified Consultants International, Box 573, Brentwood, TN 37027; (615) 377-1306. Nonprofit professional assn that certifies new behavioral and social science practitioners. Answers inquiries free.

47023. Chemical Effects Information Center, Oak Ridge Natl Lab, P.O. Box X, Bldg 2001, Oak Ridge, TN 37830; (615) 576-7568. Provides info support to the scientific community concerning health and environmental effects of chemical pollutants. Prepares reviews and assessment reports, develops specialized databases, coordinates workshops.

47024. Clearinghouse for Elementary and Secondary Aging Education, Tenn. Tech Univ., Box 5042, Cookeville, TN 38505; (615) 528-3433. Interest in aging, aging education, intergenerational programs. Provides general reference and consulting services, conducts seminars, distributes publications, permits onsite use of collections. Newsletter and most responses to inquiries free; fees charged for other services.

47025. College Media Advisers, c/o Prof. R.E. Spielberger, Journalism Dept, Memphis State Univ., Memphis, TN 38152; (901) 454-2403. Interest in advancement of guidance standards for, and improved quality of, college student media. Provides advisory services, conducts seminars, distributes publications, lends materials, makes referrals. Services primarily for members; a fee for others.

47026. Controlled Fusion Atomic Data Center, Oak Ridge Natl Lab, P.O. Box X, Bldg 6003, Oak Ridge, TN 37830; (615) 574-4704. Interest in controlled thermonuclear research, collisions involving charged and neutral particles with gases and surfaces. Provides general reference services, permits onsite use of collection. Services available to govt agencies, contractors, research institutions, industry.

47027. Country Music Association, P.O. Box 22299 (7 Music Circle North), Nashville, TN 37202; (615) 244-2840. Nonprofit org that promotes country music around the world. Interest in country music industry, recording production. Provides general reference services, conducts seminars and workshops, distributes publications. Services for members only.

47028. Country Music Foundation Library/Media Center, 4 Music Square East, Nashville, TN 37203; (615) 256-7008. Interest in country music, Anglo-American folk song, sound recording technology, copyright, historical recordings. Provides general reference services, permits onsite reference. Services available by appointment, some provided at cost.

47029. D. M. Steward Manufacturing Co., P.O. Box 510 (36th and Jerome Sts), Chattanooga, TN 37401; (615) 867-4100. Interest in technical ceramics and ferrites, especially those used in magnetic applications, electrical insulation, dielectric applications. Answers brief inquiries, provides consulting services for a fee, permits onsite use of collection.

47030. Defense Industrial Plant Equipment Center, Airways Blvd, Memphis, TN 38114; (901) 775-6501. Inter-

est in management of DoD general reserve portion of the industrial plant equipment inventory. Provides general reference and consulting services, permits onsite reference. Services available within Freedom of Info guidelines.

47031. Division of Cardiovascular Diseases, Dept of Medicine, Univ. of Tenn. Coll of Medicine, 951 Court Ave, Memphis, TN 38163; (901) 528-5759. Interest in circulation in both health and disease, electrophysiology, hypertension, medical education, thromboembolism, sodium, vascular reactivity, echocardiography. Provides consulting services, makes referrals. Services free, available to scientific community.

47032. Ecological Society of America, c/o H.R. Delcourt, Botany Dept, Univ. of Tenn., Knoxville, TN 37996. Interest in ecology, environmental sciences, population regulation, ecosystem research, pollution research, resource utilization. Provides vocational guidance and career info, makes referrals to specialists.

47033. Electron Microscopy Society of America, c/o F.L. Ball, Council Secty, 1128 East Northfield Blvd, Murfreesboro, TN 37130. Interest in electron, scanning, and transmission microscopy. Provides general reference services, conducts conferences and seminars, distributes publications. Services free, except conference proceedings.

47034. Environmental Mutagen Information Center, Information Center Complex, Oak Ridge Natl Lab, P.O. Box Y, Bldg 9224, Oak Ridge, TN 37830; (615) 574-7871. Collects, systematizes, and distributes info on mutagenesis of environmental agents. Conducts literature searches. Services free to agencies and contractors participating in program.

47035. Environmental Teratology Information Center, Information Division, Oak Ridge Natl Lab, P.O. Box Y, Bldg 9224, Y-12, Oak Ridge, TN 37830; (615) 574-7871. Collects, organizes, disseminates info on testing and evaluation of chemical, biological, and physical agents for teratogenic activity. Provides searching services, makes referrals, permits onsite study. Services free, available on a mutual exchange basis. Data base available online.

47036. Frank H. McClung Museum, Univ. of Tenn., Circle Park, Knoxville, TN 37996; (615) 974-2144. Interest in Tenn. archeology, folk history, fine arts, natural history, and early local architecture. Provides literature citations, identifies specimens, makes referrals, lends materials, permits onsite study.

47037. Hazardous Materials Information Center, Information Center Complex, Oak Ridge Natl Lab, P.O. Box X, Bldg 2001, Oak Ridge, TN 37830; (615) 574-7796. Provides info support in assessing environmental impact of nuclear energy technologies and radioactive waste management and disposal. Provides computerized literature searches free to sponsoring agencies and contractors; others charged at cost.

47038. Highlander Research and Education Center Resource Center, RFD 3, Box 370, New Market, TN 37820; (615) 933-3444. Nonprofit org that conducts research on community problems of Appalachia and rural South. Provides general reference services, conducts seminars and workshops, permits onsite reference. Fee for some services. Visitors by appointment only.

47039. Information Center for Internal Exposure, Health and Safety Research Division, Oak Ridge Natl Lab, Oak Ridge, TN 37830; (615) 574-6261. Interest in estimation of dose received from radionuclides. Provides general reference services, primarily for govt agencies, their contractors; limited assistance to others provided.

47040. Institute for Public Policy Studies, Vanderbilt Univ., 1208 18th Ave, South, Nashville, TN 37212; (615) 322-8505. Interest in interdisciplinary problem-oriented research on public policy. Provides free general reference services, conducts seminars and workshops, distributes publications.

47041. International Association for Bear Research and Management, c/o Dr Michael Pelton, Dept of Forestry, Wildlife, and Fisheries, Univ. of Tenn., Box 1071, Knoxville, TN 37901-1071; (615) 974-8842. Intl org of scientists, managers, and lay persons interested in bear biology, care, and management. Answers inquiries, provides advisory services, conducts seminars and conferences, makes referrals. Services free.

47042. International Center for Health Sciences, Meharry Medical Coll, Box 69-A, Nashville, TN 37208; (615) 327-6279, 327-6280. Serves as intl training and advisory corps in maternal and child health and nutrition planning in developing countries. Answers inquiries, makes referrals.

47043. International Courtly Literature Society, c/o Prof. J.H. McCash, Treas, Dept of Foreign Languages, Middle Tenn. State Univ., Murfreesboro, TN 37132; (615) 898-2981. Promotes study and criticism of medieval literature of Western Europe, medieval Latin literature, vernacular lyric poetry, romances. Answers inquiries, sells publication, makes referrals.

47044. International Hot Rod Association, P.O. Box 3029, Bristol, TN 37620; (615) 764-1164, 764-1165. Establishes standards and sponsors natl drag racing events in the U.S. Provides general reference and consulting services, conducts seminars and workshops, permits onsite use of collection. Services provided free to members, for a fee to others.

47045. John F. Kennedy Center for Research on Education & Human Development, George Peabody Coll for Teachers, Box 40 (21st Ave and Edgehill), Nashville, TN 37203; (615) 322-8240. Interest in mental retardation. Answers inquiries, produces and disseminates material on research. Most publications free, video tape cassettes, slide shows can be rented or purchased. Services directed to scientists and practitioners.

47046. K-25 Information Resource Center, Union Carbide Corp., Nuclear Division, P.O. Box P, Oak Ridge, TN 37830; (615) 483-8611 ext 3-3264. Interest in chemistry, physics, engineering, metallurgy, mathematics, statistics, spectroscopy, materials, etc. Provides reference services, makes interlibrary loans, permits onsite reference by those with need-to-know.

47047. Log Home Guide Information Center, Muir Publishing Co., Exit 447, Interstate 40, Hartford, TN 37753; (615) 487-2256, (800) 345-5647. Interest in residential/commercial log housing construction, interior decoration appropriate to log homes. Provides general reference services, conducts seminars and workshops, distributes publications, permits onsite reference. Services free, except publications.

47048. Lower Mississippi Valley Flood Control Association, 2602 Corporate Ave, Ste One, Memphis, TN 38132; (901) 398-1613. Interest in water resources, flood control, levee systems, bank stabilization, drainage, navigation. Answers inquiries, makes referrals to member orgs.

47049. Memphis Pink Palace Museum and Planetarium, 3050 Central Ave, Memphis, TN 38111; (901) 454-5600. Interest in history, natural history of Mid-South, especially Central Mississippi Valley. Provides general reference services, permits onsite use of collections. Services free, available by appointment.

47052. Museum of Tobacco Art and History, 800 Harrison St, Nashville, TN 37203; (615) 242-9218. Interest in tobacco-related art, artifacts and historical materials. Provides general reference services, conducts tours and lectures, lends materials. Services free by appointment.

47053. National Association for the Advancement of Black Americans in Vocational Education, 200 Cordell Hull Bldg, Nashville, TN 37219; (615) 741-1716. Interest in advancement of blacks and other minorities in vocational education. Provides general reference services, conducts workshops. Referrals, inquiries free, other services provided at cost.

47054. National Association for the Craniofacially Handicapped, P.O. Box 11082 (409 Chestnut St), Chattanooga, TN 37401. Provides financial aid, general reference, and other services free to the craniofacially handicapped.

47055. National Association of Institutional Laundry Managers, c/o Ronald C. Gasser, Exec Dir, 7105 Peach Ct, Brentwood, TN 37027; (615) 373-4924. Interest in operation and management of institutional laundries. Answers inquiries, provides laundry testing services, conducts programs and trade show, makes referrals.

47056. National Caves Association, c/o Barbara Munson, Secty-Treas, Rte 9, Box 106, McMinnville, TN 37110; (615) 668-3925. Interest in U.S. show or commercial caves and caverns. Answers inquiries, distributes publications. Services free.

47057. National Cotton Batting Institute, 1918 North Parkway, Memphis, TN 38112; (901) 274-9030. Interest in cotton batting. Answers inquiries, makes referrals, permits onsite reference.

47058. National Cottonseed Products Association, P.O. Box 12023, Memphis, TN 38182-0023; (901) 324-4417. Interest in processing of cottonseed and sunflower seed, use of cottonseed and sunflower seed products for food and feed. Answers inquiries free.

47059. National Hardwood Lumber Association, P.O. Box 34518, Memphis, TN 38184-0518; (901) 377-1818. Encourages research in management and utilization of hardwoods, lumber. Provides general reference services; inspects, measures, grades, and certifies hardwood lumber; conducts program, courses.

47060. National Kerosene Heater Association, First American Center, No. 15, Nashville, TN 37238; (615) 254-1961. Promotes safety and efficiency in kerosene heaters marketed in U.S. Provides general reference services, conducts seminars, workshops. Services to nonmembers for a fee.

47061. National Oak Flooring Manufacturers Association, 804 Sterick Bldg, Memphis, TN 38103; (901) 526-5016. Interest in installation, finishing, and maintenance of hardwood floors. Answers inquiries, rents or sells audiovisual materials, sells publications, conducts classes.

47062. National Storytelling Resource Center, P.O. Box 112 (Slemons House; Fox St), Jonesboro, TN 37659; (615) 753-2171. Interest in storytelling art and technique. Provides general reference services, conducts seminars and workshops, sells and rents materials, distributes publications, permits onsite use of collections. Except for publications, materials and services free.

47063. Northern Nut Growers Association, 4518 Holston Hills Rd, Knoxville, TN 37914; (615) 524-0416. Interest in North American nut-bearing trees and their cultivation, nut products. Answers inquiries, conducts seminars, distributes publications. Services free, except publications.

47064. Nuclear Data Project, Oak Ridge Natl Lab, P.O. Box X, Oak Ridge, TN 37830; (615) 574-4699. Responsible for collecting and evaluating nuclear structure data from radioactive decay and nuclear reactions. Provides general reference services, sells publications, lists.

47065. Nuclear Safety Information Center, Oak Ridge Natl Lab, P.O. Box Y, Oak Ridge, TN 37830; (615) 574-0391. Interest in info generated by nuclear facilities, nuclear power plants. Provides general reference and consulting services, permits onsite reference. Services free to sponsoring agencies and contractors; at cost to others.

47066. Oak Ridge Associated Universities, Information Services, P.O. Box 117, Oak Ridge, TN 37830; (615)

576-3146. Performs research tasks in energy, health, and environment, ranging from structure of the atom to large animal metabolism. Answers inquiries, makes referrals, permits onsite study by appointment. Services generally free.

47067. Oak Ridge National Laboratory Library System, Oak Ridge Natl Lab, P.O. Box X, Oak Ridge, TN 37830; (615) 574-6744. Interest in energy, nuclear science and engineering, chemistry, physics, metallurgy, biological sciences, environmental sciences. Provides general reference services, permits onsite reference. Access to some reports may be restricted.

47068. PT Boats, P.O. Box 109 (663 S Cooper St, Ste 4), Memphis, TN 38104; (901) 272-9980. Nonprofit org that works to preserve PT (patrol torpedo) boats; interested in model shipbuilding, naval history. Provides general reference services, distributes publications, permits onsite use facilities. Services primarily for PT veterans and families, may be provided for a fee.

47069. Parents Experiencing Perinatal Death, P.O. Box 38445, Germantown, TN 38138; (901) 372-5102. Volunteer group that provides emotional support and info to other parents whose babies have died prematurely. Provides info, operates 24-hour telephone service, conducts workshops.

47070. Pediatric Research Laboratory, Dept of Pediatrics, Center for the Health Sciences, Univ. of Tenn., 956 Court Ave, Room B-318, Memphis, TN 38163; (901) 528-5930. Interest in immunology, lymphocyte differentiation, nephrology, developmental aspects of renal function, gastroenterology lipids, bilirubin, infectious diseases, Pneumocystis carinii. Answers inquiries, provides consulting free.

47071. Radiation Shielding Information Center, Oak Ridge Natl Lab, P.O. Box X, Oak Ridge, TN 37830; (615) 574-6176. Interest in shielding protection from radiation from reactors, weapons, radioisotopes, and accelerators. Provides general reference services, conducts seminars, publishes materials. Services available to scientific and technical personnel.

47072. Remote Technology Corp., 114 Union Valley Rd, Oak Ridge, TN 37830; (615) 483-0228. Specializes in applying robotics techniques to hazardous industries, especially nuclear industry. Provides general reference and consulting services, distributes publications. Except for consulting, services generally free.

47073. Sickle Cell Information Center, Center for the Health Sciences, Univ. of Tenn., 800 Madison Ave, Memphis, TN 38163; (901) 528-5808, 386-9751. Interest in sickle cell anemia, studies on history of the disease in all its variant forms, clinical manifestations and anatomical lesions in hemoglobinopathies. Answers inquiries, provides reference services. Services provided at cost.

47074. Society of Behavioral Medicine, Box 8530 (Austin Peay Psychology Bldg, Ste 416; Circle Dr), Univ. Station, Knoxville, TN 37996; (615) 974-5164. Fosters continued development of high quality behavioral medicine, health psychology, psychosomatic medicine, biosocial medicine. Provides general reference services, conducts seminars, distributes publications. Nonmembers charged fees for services.

47076. Southern Baptist Historical Library and Archives, 901 Commerce, Ste 400, Nashville, TN 37203. Interest in church history of Southern Baptist Convention and other Baptist groups. Answers inquiries, makes referrals, provides research assistance, identifies documents, lends publications, permits onsite reference.

47077. Southern Cypress Manufacturers Association, 805 Sterick Bldg, Memphis, TN 38103; (901) 525-8221. Interest in tidewater red cypress, red cypress wood standards and mill products, including floors and ceilings. Answers inquiries free, sells publications.

47078. Southern Weed Science Society, c/o Pres, Uniroyal Chemical, 3035 Dir's Row, Ste 420, Memphis, TN 38131; (901) 345-3175. Interest in weed science, plant protection, herbicides, pesticides, weed control. Answers inquiries, sells publications, permits onsite reference. Services primarily for professionals.

47079. Space Institute Library, Univ. of Tenn., Tullahoma, TN 37388-8897; (615) 455-0631. Interest in aerospace, electrical, mechanical, and metallurgical engineering, applied mathematics and computer science, physics. Makes interlibrary loans.

47080. Surface Design Association, 331 E Washington St, Fayetteville, TN 37334; (615) 433-6804. Promotes interest in printing and dyeing fabrics, fabric design. Provides general reference and consulting services, conducts conferences and workshops, distributes publications. Services available for a fee.

47081. TVA Norris Branch Library, Tenn. Valley Authority, Norris, TN 37828; (615) 632-1665. Interest in forestry, natural resources, aquatic sciences, wildlife. Provides general reference services, makes loans, permits onsite use of collection. Interlibrary loan and reference services free.

47082. Tennessee Cooperative Fishery Research Unit, Tenn. Technological Univ., Box 5063, Cookeville, TN 38501; (615) 528-3093, 528-3094. Conducts research, education, and extension activities involving fish and environmental problems. Provides general reference and consulting services, distributes publications, lends materials, permits onsite reference. Services generally provided at cost.

47083. Tennessee Earthquake Information Center, Memphis State Univ., 3904 Central Ave, Memphis, TN 38152; (901) 454-2007. Provides background info on occurrence of regional earthquakes, their causes and consequences; earthquake prediction. Provides general reference services, distributes data, permits onsite use of collection. Services often provided at cost.

47084. Tennessee Historical Society, War Memorial Bldg, Nashville, TN 37219; (615) 741-2660. Interest in natural, aboriginal, and civil history of Tenn. Provides free general reference services, conducts seminars and workshops, distributes publication, permits onsite reference upon payment of membership fee.

47085. Tennessee State Library and Archives, Library and Archives Bldg, Seventh Ave N, Nashville, TN 37219; (615) 741-2764, 741-2561. Interest in history of Tenn. and Southeast, genealogy of Southern families. Provides general reference and copying services, permits onsite reference.

47086. Toxicology Data Bank, Information Center Complex/Information Division, Oak Ridge Natl Lab, P.O. Box X (Bldg 2001), Oak Ridge, TN 37830; (615) 574-7587. Interest in toxicology research. Provides general reference services.

47087. Toxicology Information Response Center, Oak Ridge Natl Lab, P.O. Box X, Bldg 2024, Room 53, Oak Ridge, TN 37830; (615) 576-1743. Intl center for toxicology and related toxicology info services. Compiles materials for a fee; offeres data and literature searches, bibliographic services.

47089. Urban Observatory of Metropolitan Nashville University Centers, Tenn. State Univ., Downtown Campus, Ste B, 10th and Charlotte, Nashville, TN 37203; (615) 251-1121. Nonprofit research org interested in urban and rural studies on various topics. Sells publications, provides consulting services for a fee, makes referrals.

47090. VA Medical Media Production Service, Veterans Administration Hospital, 1030 Jefferson Ave, Memphis, TN 38104; (901) 577-7279. Interest in medical illustrations depicting abnormal and typical aspects of disease. Permits onsite library reference, provides consulting services to qualified persons, publishes materials.

47091. Vanderbilt Television News Archive, Heard Library, Vanderbilt Univ., Nashville, TN 37240-0007; (615) 322-2927. Interest in television network news programs; has extensive collection of tapes. Provides general reference services, lends materials, distributes publication, permits onsite reference. Services available for a fee.

47092. W.R. Grace, Planning Services Library, Agricultural Chemicals Group, P.O. Box 277 (100 North Main), Memphis, TN 38101; (901) 522-2385. Interest in agriculture, fertilizers, animal nutrition, agricultural statistics and economics. Provides general reference services, permits onsite use of collections free to professionals or serious students.

47093. Water Resources Research Center, Univ. of Tenn., 428 South Stadium Hall, Knoxville, TN 37996; (615) 974-2151. Interest in water-related research, including related physical, chemical, and biological aspects; economics, recreation, legal issues, water policy and management. Answers inquiries, provides advisory services, makes referrals.

Texas

48005. Academy for Sports Dentistry, 12200 Preston Road, Dallas, TX 75230. Promotes mouth and teeth protection in athletics. Concerned with prevention of dental injuries and other aspects of sports dentistry, and promotes use of mouthguards.

48006. Action for Research into Multiple Sclerosis, P.O. Box 1028, Houston, TX 77251-1028; (800) 872-2767. Nonprofit org founded to further research into cause, treatments, and cure for multiple sclerosis. Maintains computerized library of latest research info, demographic survey of MS population that serves as a data base, and toll-free number for free info and counseling.

48007. Aerospace Medical Division Headquarters, STINFO Office, (RDO), AFSC, Brooks Air Force Base, TX 78235; (512) 536-2838. Interest in aerospace medicine, environmental toxicology. Museum of Flight Medicine is located at Division Headquarters. Answers inquiries concerning status and location of research projects at Aerospace Medical Division labs.

48008. Air Force Human Resources Laboratory, Library, Brooks Air Force Base, TX 78235; (512) 536-2651. Interest in personnel system procedures, concepts, and simulation models; personnel management. Publishes technical reports. Literature collection accessible for onsite use.

48009. Alternative Energy Institute, W Tex. State Univ, Box 248, Canyon, TX 79016; (806) 656-3904. Involved in education, research, feasibility studies, development, and testing of alternative energy systems. Answers inquiries, provides advisory and consulting services, evaluates wind turbines at Wind Test Center for a fee, provides info on R&D in progress.

48010. American Academy of Gold Foil Operators, 2514 Watts Rd, Houston, TX 77030; (713) 664-3537. Seeks to encourage treatment of carious lesions with cohesive gold. Answers inquiries, provides advisory and reference services, distributes publications. Services free, except for reprints and postage.

48011. American Association for Respiratory Therapy, 1720 Regal Row, Ste 112, Dallas, TX 75235; (214) 630-3540. Dedicated to serving needs of health professionals working in field of respiratory care. Provides continuing education opportunities, info about advances in the field, and forum for discussion.

48012. American Association of Stratigraphic Palynologists, c/o John A Clendening, Pres., Amoco Production Co., P.O. Box 3092, Houston, TX 77253; (713) 556-3549. Interest in palynology, especially its stratigraphic applications, palynological taxonomy, Kerogen analysis, organic maturation analysis, phytoplank-

ton, oceanography, paleoecology. Answers inquiries or refers them to other sources as time permits.

48013. American Bandmasters Association, 2019 Bradford Dr, Arlington, TX 76010; (817) 261-8629. Org of professional, educational, and military bandmasters, musical instrument manufacturers, and others who contribute to perpetuation of concert band music. Questions answered by ABA Research Center at Hornbake Library, Univ of Md., College Park, MD 20742.

48014. American Brahman Breeders Association, 1313 La Concha Lane, Houston, TX 77054; (713) 795-4444. Interest in American Brahman cattle; zebu cattle (bos indicus) of the world. Holdings include a registry of Brahman breed. Publishes monthly journal. Answers inquiries, makes referrals, permits onsite use of collection.

48015. American College of Emergency Physicians, P.O. Box 619911, Dallas, TX 75261-9911; (214) 659-0911. Interest in emergency medicine and emergency medical services. Publishes monthly journal and newsletter; publications list available. Services directed toward members, but available to others.

48017. American Goat Society, c/o W. Hamrick, Sec-Treas., Route 2, Box 112, DeLeon, TX 76444; (817) 893-6431. Promotes purebred dairy goats and maintains purebred dairy goat registry. Answers inquiries, provides reference services, distributes publications for a fee.

48018. American Heart Association, 7320 Greenville Ave, Dallas, TX 75231; (214) 750-5300. Natl voluntary agency dedicated to reduction of premature death or disability from cardiovascular diseases and stroke. Publication lists available. Staff answers specific questions or make referrals; library provides reference services and permits onsite use by professionals.

48020. American Literary Translators Association, P.O. Box 830688, Univ of Tex. at Dallas, Richardson, TX 75083-0688; (214) 690-2093. Seeks to provide essential services to literary translators from all languages and to create a professional forum for exchange of ideas on art and craft of translation. Reference services primarily for members, but others assisted; fees may be charged.

48021. American Malacological Union, c/o Mrs. C.E. Boone, Recording Secty, 3706 Rice Blvd, Houston, TX 77005; (713) 668-8252. Interest in mollusks and their shells, living and fossil; taxonomy; parasitology; medical malacology; commercial fisheries; conservation and related pollution problems. Inquiries referred to specialists within org.

48022. American Paint Horse Association, P.O. Box 18519 (North of Ft Worth on I-35W at Golden Triangle Blvd), Ft Worth, TX 76118; (817) 439-3400. Maintains registry of American Paint Horse; records and maintains pedigree and bloodline info of Paint Horses. Provides statistical data, brochures, pamphlets, resource photographs, and diagrams; conducts pedigree and performance research.

48023. American Political Items Collectors, c/o J.D. Hayes, Secty-Treas., P.O. Box 340339, San Antonio, TX 78234; (512) 655-5213. Interest in collection and preservation of political Americana: political items (pins, ribbons, etc.) from 1789 to present. Publishes quarterly journal, answers inquiries, provides reference services. Except for answering inquiries, services restricted to members.

48024. American Productivity Center, 123 N Post Oak Ln, Houston, TX 77024; (713) 681-4020. Designs, develops, and administers programs to help improve productivity of orgs in public and private sectors. Has significant technical library. Publishes issue papers, answers inquiries, distributes publications. Some services subject to a fee.

48025. American Quarter Horse Association, P.O. Box 200 (2701 I-40 East), Amarillo, TX 79168; (806) 376-4811. Interest in American Quarter Horses, including registration and promotion. Holdings include computerized file with info on about 2 million Quarter Horses. Fees charged for some services. General info available.

48026. American Society for Medical Technology, 330 Meadowfern Dr, Houston, TX 77067; (713) 893-7072. Interest in medical technology, clinical laboratory science. Publishes newsletter and journal. Answers inquiries, provides advisory and reference services, operates placement service. Services free and primarily for members, but others assisted.

48028. Americans for Human Rights and Social Justice, P.O. Drawer 6258, Ft Worth, TX 76115. Seeks to educate public about corrections and prison needs, bring about prison reform, improve ex-offenders' rights, aid inmate families. Holdings: Criminal Justice-Prison Data Collection that includes 21,000 newspaper articles. Services free, except for photocopying.

48029. Amon Carter Museum, P.O. Box 2365 (3501 Camp Bowie Blvd), Ft Worth, TX 76113; (817) 738-1933. Interest in history of western U.S., and American art and photography. Has research library of American newspapers, prints and negatives covering history of American photography, extensive fine arts photo collection. Answers inquiries; services free, except for reproductions.

48030. Anderson Clayton Foods, Technical Information Services, 3333 N Central Expressway, Richardson, TX 75080; (214) 231-6121. Interest in food industry and trade, food science and technology, packaging science and technology. Holdings include collection of materials on these areas. Makes interlibrary loans.

48031. Applied Research Laboratories, Univ of Tex., P.O. Box 8029 (10,000 Burnet Rd), Austin, TX 78713-8029; (512) 835-3200. Conducts applied R&D for govt agencies, mainly those of Dept of Defense. Interest in radio science. Provides consulting services, distrib-

utes publications, permits onsite use of collections. Services usually available only to qualified users and are provided free.

48032. Archaeology Research Program, Dept of Anthropology, Southern Methodist Univ, Dallas, TX 75275; (214) 692-2941. Interest in contract archaeological research, recording, and preservation of archaeological resources and cultural information in Texas, the Southeast, the Southwest. Answers inquiries, provides advisory, consulting, reference, and literature-searching services, generally under contract.

48033. Architecture Research Center, Coll. of Architecture and Environmental Design, Tex. A&M Univ, Coll Station, TX 77843; (409) 845-3061, 845-1249. Applies univ resources to solving practical problems associated with professions of architecture, construction, planning, landscape, and environmental design in general. Provides info on R&D in progress free, sells publications.

48034. Archives of the Episcopal Church, P.O. Box 2247 (606 Rathervue Pl), Austin, TX 78768; (512) 472-6818. Interest in history of Episcopal Church. Holdings include archival records, manuscript collections, pamphlets, photographs; has small library. Permits onsite use of collections, provides reference and reproduction services, makes referrals to other sources of info.

48035. Army Air Defense Artillery School Library, P.O. Box 5040, Ft Bliss, TX 79916; (915) 568-5781. Interest in U.S. Army missiles research, air defense materials, military history and science. Publishes *Air Defense* magazine (monthly). Answers inquiries, provides reference services, permits onsite use of collection. Services free to military personnel, military dependents.

48036. Army Institute of Surgical Research, Ft Sam Houston, San Antonio, TX 78234; (512) 221-2720. Interest in burns, renal failure, trauma, surgical physiology, post traumatic metabolism-infection. Maintains data base on burn patients. Answers inquiries, provides advisory and consulting services.

48037. Arnold Air Society, c/o Wm. Morley, Exec. Administrator, Emerald Bay Professional Center, Bullard, TX 75757; (214) 825-2885. Professional honorary service org of selected Air Force Reserve Officers Training Corps (ROTC) cadets from leading colleges. Has photo collection, publishes periodicals. Answers inquiries or refers inquirers to other sources of info free.

48038. Associated Locksmiths of America, 3003 Live Oak St, Dallas, TX 75204; (214) 827-1701. Nonprofit trade assn interested in physical security field. Answers inquiries, provides consulting and reference services, publishes monthly magazine. Services provided on a selective basis, free or for a fee, depending on type of info requested.

48039. Association for Retarded Citizens, P.O. Box 6109 (2501 Ave J), Arlington, TX 76011; (817) 640-0204. Promotes welfare of nation's retarded citizens, and educates public about causes, prevention, and hopes for cures. Answers inquiries, provides reference and literature-searching services, distributes publications.

48041. Association of Allergists for Mycological Investigations, c/o W.J. Raymer, MD, Pres, 444 Hermann Professional Bldg, Houston, TX 77025; (713) 797-0900. Interest in mold allergy, including air analysis; improvement in allergen preparation; fungi in the etiology of respiratory allergic diseases. Provides consulting service primarily for physicians, but also available to others.

48042. Association of American Feed Control Officials, c/o B.J. Sims, Secty, P.O. Box 3160, Coll Station, TX 77841; (409) 845-1121. Interest in animal feed ingredient definitions; rules and regulations covering labeling of animal feeds. Answers inquiries, provides short lists of literature citations in response to specific inquiries.

48043. Association of Commercial Record Centers, P.O. Box 2741 (700 N. San Jacinto), Houston, TX 77002; (713) 224-6248. Interest in professional standards for management of commercial, off-site record storage centers; information management. Answers inquiries, permits onsite use of collections. Services available upon payment of membership fee.

48044. Association of Visual Science Librarians, c/o Coll of Optometry Library, Univ of Houston, Houston, TX 77004; (713) 749-2411. Fosters development of individual libraries, develops means of making vision info available, and develops services, standards, and guidelines for vision science libraries. Answers inquiries, provides reference services, some at cost.

48045. Baylor College of Medicine Influenza Research Center, Dept of Microbiology and Immunology, 1200 Moursund Ave, Houston, TX 77030; (713) 799-4469. Conducts research in acute respiratory illnesses of humans, primarily common cold and influenza. Has collection of research data results. Answers inquiries, provides reference services, conducts seminars. Services free.

48046. Beefmaster Breeders Universal, 6800 Park Ten Blvd, Ste 290 West, San Antonio, TX 78213; (512) 732-3132. Interest in Beefmaster cattle, cattle breeding and marketing. Answers inquiries, conducts seminars and field days, distributes literature free, offers quality control programs to membership.

48047. Bell Helicopter Textron, P.O. Box 482 (Tex. Hwy 10), Ft Worth, TX 76101; (817) 280-3608. Interest in aircraft structures, aerospace and aeronautical engineering. Answers brief inquiries, makes interlibrary loans, provides limited duplication services.

48049. Benign Essential Blepharospasm Research Foundation, 755 Howell St, Beaumont, TX 77706; (713) 892-1339. Promotes awareness of and research on condition, and gives support to those afflicted with it. Provides info on treatments and on current research, and helps organize local support groups.

48050. Birth Defects-Genetics Center, Baylor College of Medicine, Houston, TX 77030; (713) 791-3261. Conducts research into causes of birth defects and development of improved treatment techniques. Answers inquiries, provides consulting services, makes referrals to other sources of info. Except for simple inquiries, services provided on a fee basis.

48051. Boy Scouts of America, National Council, 1325 Walnut Hill Lane, Irving, TX 75038-3096; (214) 659-2280. Maintains special collection of early books on scouting. Library primarily for use of National Office of Boy Scouts of America, but some interlibrary loans are made and onsite use of collection by students and others is permitted by arrangement.

48052. Brazosport Museum of Natural Science, 400 College Dr, Lake Jackson, TX 77566; (409) 265-7831. Interprets Texas Gulf and coastal regions and educates public by exploration of natural sciences and preservation and conservation of natural resources. Answers inquiries, provides advisory services, conducts seminars and tours, permits onsite use of collections.

48053. Callier Center for Communication Disorders, Univ of Tex. at Dallas, 1966 Inwood Rd, Dallas, TX 75235; (214) 783-3000. Interest in education, physiology (auditory and speech), psychoacoustics, audiology, speech pathology, electrophysiology of auditory system. Answers inquiries, provides advisory services for cost of handling and postage.

48054. Center for Allergy and Immunological Disorders, Baylor College of Medicine, 1200 Moursund Ave, Houston, TX 77030; (713) 791-4219. Diagnoses and treats humans with allergic and immunologic diseases. Answers inquiries, provides consulting services for a fee.

48055. Center for Education and Research in Free Enterprise, Tex. A&M Univ, College Station, TX 77843; (409) 845-7722. Seeks to identify market solutions to financial and economic problems in America through education and research. Conducts seminars and workshops, provides info on research in progress, distributes publications, permits onsite use of collections. Some services free, others for a fee.

48056. Center for History of Engineering and Technology, Dept of Civil Engineering, College of Engineering, Tex. Tech Univ, P.O. Box 4089, Lubbock, TX 79409; (806) 742-3591. Focuses on identification, documentation, preservation, and interpretation of historic architectural and engineering works. Answers inquiries, provides reference and computer-search services free to serious researchers in limited volume.

48057. Center for Lithospheric Studies, Univ of Tex. at Dallas, P.O. Box 830688, Richardson, TX 75083-0688; (214) 690-2445. Interest in geophysics research, lithosphere, seismology, gravity, and magnetics. Answers inquiries, provides info on research in progress, makes referrals to other sources of info. Services free.

48058. Center for Private Enterprise, Hankamer School of Business, Baylor Univ, Ste 215, Waco, TX 76798; (817) 755-3766. Interest in entrepreneurship education; public policy issues concerned with the relationship between public and private sectors; small business. Services intended primarily for students, teachers, and entrepreneurs, but available to anyone; some may be provided at cost.

48059. Center for Studies in Aging, N Tex. State Univ, Box 13438, NT Station, Denton, TX 76203; (817) 788-2765. Interest in gerontology; long-term care (nursing home and housing) administration. Answers inquiries free, provides consulting services on a fee basis, permits onsite use of collection.

48060. Center for Trace Characterization, Tex. A&M Univ, College Station, TX 77843; (409) 845-2341. Interest in all aspects of analytical chemistry; automation of chemical instrumentation. Has complete library of organic mass spectra; bibliography on nuclear activation analysis. Answers inquiries, provides consulting services.

48061. Center for the Study of Motor Performance, Coll of Health, Physical Education, Recreation, and Dance, Tex. Woman's Univ, P.O. Box 23717, Denton, TX 76204; (817) 387-4587. Interest in human behavior during exercise, exercise physiology, biomechanics, motor learning, sports psychology. Answers inquiries, provides advisory and reference services. Services generally provided free.

48062. Charles E. Stevens American Atheist Library Archives, P.O. Box 2117 (2210 Hancock Dr), Austin, TX 78768; (512) 458-1244, 458-1245, 458-1246. Interest in atheism, agnosticism, humanism, objectivism, rationalism, secularism, free thought, and other iconoclastic, nonreligious beliefs. Publishes books, booklets, catalogs. Answers inquiries, provides reference and duplication services, permits onsite use of reference library.

48063. Chihuahuan Desert Research Institute, P.O. Box 1334 (Honors Hall, SRSU Campus), Alpine, TX 79831; (915) 837-8370. Nonprofit org devoted to natural science in Chihuahuan Desert. Interest in desert ecosystem studies, status of endangered species, biological control of rangeland weeds. Answers inquiries, provides clearinghouse services for research on desert. Services available for a fee.

48064. Children's Nutrition Research Center, Baylor College of Medicine and Tex. Children's Hospital, Medical Towers Bldg, Ste 601, 6608 Fannin St, Houston, TX 77030; (713) 791-4675, 799-6006. Seeks to determine dietary standards and measure nutritional status in children and in pregnant and lactating women. Answers inquiries, provides advisory services, provides info on research in progress. Services provided at cost.

48065. Christian Medical Society, P.O.B. 689 (1616 Gateway Blvd), Richardson, TX 75080; (214) 783-8384. Professional fellowship of physicians and dentists whose members believe their fields offer unique opportunities for ministry. Publishes newsletters, directories, reprints. Answers inquiries, makes referrals to other sources of info. All services free, except seminars.

48066. Citrus Center, Tex. A&I Univ, P.O. Box 1150, Weslaco, TX 78596; (512) 968-2132. Interest in citrus culture and production, plant physiology and pathology, soil science, and pecans. Answers inquiries, provides advisory services, permits onsite use of collection. All services free.

48067. Clearinghouse for Earth Covered Buildings, P.O. Box 9428, Ft Worth, TX 76107; (817) 335-2883. Nonprofit org interested in earth-covered buildings and dwellings. Answers inquiries, provides advisory services, normally for free. SASE requested for written replies and printed materials.

48068. Coastal Ecosystems Management, 3600 Hulen St, Ft Worth, TX 76107; (817) 731-3727. Commercial org of scientists providing a systems, task-oriented approach to ecological assessments, pollution identification, and environmental planning. Has computerized file of environmental data. Most reference services provided for a fee.

48069. College Assn for Language, Learning, and Educational Disabilities, P.O. Box Z, E Tex. Station, Commerce, TX 75428; (214) 886-5932. Membership of postsecondary and adult professionals working with learning disabled. Publishes newsletter, books, directories, R&D summaries. Answers inquiries, provides reference services. Fee charged for publications.

48070. College English Association, c/o E.J. Cooper, Exec. Dir, Univ of Houston Downtown Coll, One Main St, Houston, TX 77002. Professional org of scholar-teachers devoted to English language and literature and related humanities. Answers brief inquiries free, provides consulting services, makes referrals.

48071. College Sports Information Directors of America, c/o F. Nuesch, Secty, Sports Information Dir, Tex. A&I Univ, Kingsville, TX 78363. Interest in sports public relations and sports publicity. Publishes monthly newsletter and annual directory, answers inquiries, provides consulting and reference services, permits onsite use of collection. Referral services provided at cost to nonmembers.

48072. Compucon C.A.P.E. Systems and Services, Compucon, Inc., P.O. Box 809006, Dallas, TX 75380-9006; (214) 680-1000. Commercial org involved in computerized package and warehouse utilization design. Holdings include computer programs for in-house, turnkey installations, with worldwide timesharing available. Answers inquiries, provides consulting and reference services, generally for a fee.

48073. Computer Aided Manufacturing-International, 611 Ryan Plaza Dr, Arlington, TX 76011-8098; (817) 860-1654. Nonprofit membership formed to further cooperative research and development efforts of companies with common interest in computer aided design and manufacturing (CAD/CAM). Answers inquiries, publishes reports, reprints. Reference services available at cost.

48074. Confederate Research Center, Hill Junior Coll, P.O. Box 619, Hillsboro, TX 76645; (817) 582-2555. Interest in military history of Confederacy, Texas, U.S., and Civil War. Has extensive historical holdings; publications list available. Answers inquiries, makes interlibrary loans, distributes publications. Services for a fee.

48075. Conference of Public Health Laboratorians, P.O. Box 9083 (1100 W 49th St), Austin, TX 78766; (512) 458-7318. Professional society that promotes advances in public health laboratories. Interest in clinical microbiology, environmental chemistry. Answers inquiries, provides advisory services, conducts seminars. Services free.

48076. Conservation and Production Research Laboratory, Agricultural Research Service, USDA, P.O. Drawer 10, Bushland, TX 79012; (806) 378-5721. Interest in soil and water conservation, weed control, entomological studies, fertilizer research, crop improvement, crop production economics, sunflower germplasm. Publishes research papers, answers inquiries.

48077. Cooling Tower Institute, P.O. Box 73383, Houston, TX 77273; (713) 350-1995. Interest in technology, design, performance, and maintenance of water cooling towers. Tests cooling towers and analyzes results, provides speakers for meetings, conducts annual technical meetings.

48078. Cotton Insects Research Laboratory, Agricultural Research Service, USDA, P.O. Box 1033, Brownsville, TX 78520; (512) 542-2516. Interest in research on insects, with emphasis on pests of cotton. Answers inquiries, distributes techical reports and reprints, makes referrals to other sources of info. Services free.

48079. Cowboy Artists of America Museum Foundation, P.O. Box 1716 (1550 Bandera Hwy), Kerrville, TX 78028; (512) 896-2553. Exhibits contemporary art of American West and serves as resource center on works of members of Cowboy Artists of America. Holdings include first editions and manuscripts on early range cattle industry and Western art. Reference services provided at cost to all users.

48080. Dallas Seismological Observatory, Dept of Geological Sciences, Southern Methodist Univ, Dallas, TX 75275; (214) 692-2760. Interest in seismology, heat flow, general geophysics. Holdings include seismological data and records. Publishes technical reports and journal articles, answers inquiries, provides consulting services.

48081. DeGolyer and MacNaughton Library, One Energy Square, Dallas, TX 75206; (214) 368-6391. Interest in petroleum and natural gas engineering, geology, minerals, energy. Makes interlibrary loans, provides duplication services for a fee, permits onsite use of collection. Services available to petroleum industry and other energy-related interests.

48082. Department of Microbiology and Infectious Diseases, Southwest Foundation for Research and Education, P.O. Box 28147, San Antonio, TX 78284; (512) 674-1410. Conducts basic research in infectious diseases. Interest in microbiology, virus-cancer relationship, herpes viruses, hepatitis, retinoblastoma, mechanisms of aging. Answers inquiries, distributes newsletter. Services to professionals free, except lab procedures.

48083. Department of Poultry Science, Tex. A&M Univ, College Station, TX 77843; (409) 845-1931. Interest in poultry nutrition and genetics, avian physiology, food technology, avian diseases, turkey production. Answers inquiries, provides reference services. Services free and primarily for poultry industry, food science, and commercial game bird personnel.

48084. Department of Veterinary Physiology and Pharmacology, Coll of Veterinary Medicine, Tex. A&M Univ, Veterinary Medicine Bldg, College Station, TX 77843; (409) 845-7261. Interest in veterinary physiology and pharmacology. Answers inquiries, provides consulting, reference, and literature-searching services, makes direct and interlibrary loans. Some services free, others on a cost basis.

48085. Department of Virology and Epidemiology, Baylor College of Medicine, Houston, TX 77030; (713) 799-4444. Interest in virology, including viral infections, genetics, and vaccines. Publishes technical reports, journal articles, reprints. Answers inquiries, provides advisory, reference, research, services.

48086. Division of Applied, Experimental and Engineering Psychologists, c/o M.H. Strub, Secty, U.S. Army Research Institute Field Unit, P.O. Box 6057, Fort Bliss, TX 79916; (915) 568-4491. Promotes R&D and evaluation of psychological principles relating human behavior to characteristics, design, and use of environments and systems within which humans work and live. Answers inquiries, distributes newsletter. Services primarily for members, but others assisted.

48088. Escapees, Route 5, Box 310, Livingston, TX 77351; (409) 327-8873. Club for persons interested in living and traveling for extended periods in recreational vehicle. Publishes newsletter, books, technical reports, directories, reprints. Services provided for a fee, except for answers to general inquiries and referral services.

48089. Evaluation, Dissemination, and Assessment Center for Bilingual Education, 7703 N Lamar Blvd, Austin, TX 78752; (512) 458-9131. Provides products for children in bilingual multicultural programs. Publishes textbooks and other resource materials, makes referrals to other sources of info. Info services free, except for publications.

48090. Federation of State Medical Boards of the U.S., 2630 W Freeway, Ste 138, Ft Worth, TX 76102; (817) 335-1141. Promotes uniform systems and methods of medical licensure and discipline in U.S., and serves as informational source for state medical and osteopathic licensing boards. Reference services free to member boards and selected govt agencies; others are charged.

48091. Fikes Hall of Special Collections & DeGolyer Library, Central Univ Libraries, Southern Methodist Univ, Dallas, TX 75275; (214) 692-3231. Interest in Western history and history of transportation, especially railroad. Publications list with prices available. Reference service available without charge; photocopying and other duplication services available for a fee.

48092. Food Protein Research and Development Center, Tex. A&M Univ, F.M. Box 183 (Main Campus), College Station, TX 77843; (409) 845-2741. Interest in basic and applied research on extraction and processing of vegetable oils and isolation, characterization, production, and utilization of oilseed proteins in human foods. Answers inquiries, provides reference services. Services free, except consulting.

48093. Forest Genetics Laboratory, Tex. A&M Univ, College Station, TX 77843; (409) 846-6236. Interest in genetic improvement of forest trees, especially growth rate, form, drought resistance, and wood quality. Has extensive collection of wood samples, pollen specimens, and forest tree seed. Answers brief inquiries.

48094. Forest Pest Management Laboratory, Dept of Entomology, Tex. A&M Univ, College Station, TX 77843; (409) 845-3825. Interest in development and evaluation of forest pest management tactics, especially those involving such behavioral chemicals as pheromones. Answers inquiries, provides advisory services, distributes publications. Services free.

48095. Forest Products Laboratory, P.O. Box 310, Lufkin, TX 75901; (713) 632-6666. Interest in all aspects of wood use. Maintains computerized data base of primary and secondary forest products industry in Texas. Answers inquiries, performs physical and biological testing of wood and wood products, permits onsite reference.

48096. Foundation for Education and Research in Vision, 1016 La Posada, Ste 174, Austin, TX 78752. Promotes scientific research in field of vision, including scholarships for advanced studies in visual sciences and funding for specific research projects; and educates public on importance of functional vision and on what constitutes adequate vision.

48097. Galveston Marine Geophysics Laboratory, Institute for Geophysics, Univ of Tex., 4920 N Interstate Hwy 35, Austin, TX 78751-2789; (512) 451-6468. Conducts research in geophysics; has capabilities for multichannel seismic profiling at sea, in ocean bottom seismic observations, and in land seismograph network observations. Has extensive data and tape holdings. Answers inquiries, provides reference services. Copying may require a fee.

48098. General Libraries Film Library, Univ of Tex. at Austin, Drawer W, Univ Station (Education Annex, G-12; San Jacinto and 20th Sts), Austin, TX 78713-7448; (512) 471-3572. Interest in educational films on wide variety of subjects, chiefly at college level. Has about 3,000 16mm films. Publishes media handbooks that explain proper utilization and production of simple audiovisual aids. Rents films; provides free reference and referral services.

48099. Geological Information Library of Dallas, One Energy Square, Ste 100, 4925 Greenville Ave, Dallas, TX 75206; (214) 363-1078, (800) 442-5259. Nonprofit org interested in geosciences, specializing in energy resources, with worldwide coverage. Total archival material exceeds 20 million items. Nonmembers may use data for a fee; research service available at an hourly rate. Publications for sale.

48100. Gravity Map Service, P.O. Box 146 (2116 Thompson Rd), Richmond, TX 77469; (713) 342-2883. Commercial org with interest in Bouguer gravity data and gravity maps for most oil producing states within continental U.S. Has Bouguer gravity data bank (computerized). Answers inquiries, provides consulting services, analyzes data. Services for a fee.

48101. Health Facilities Research Program, Research Center, College of Architecture and Environmental Design, Tex. A&M Univ, College Station, TX 77843; (409) 845-2216. Interest in research in all areas of built environment, including man's interaction with it. Answers inquiries, provides advisory services for a fee.

48102. High Plains Research Foundation, HC01-Box 117, Plainview, TX 79072; (806) 889-3316. Interest in agricultural production research under irrigation with plants. Answers inquiries free.

48103. Horticultural Crops Production & Marketing Systems Research, Agricultural Research Service, USDA, P.O. Box 267 (3 1/4 mi. West on E Hwy 83), Weslaco, TX 78596; (512) 968-4026. Interest in etiology and epidemiology of postharvest diseases of horticultural crops. Publications list available. Technical data and other info provided on request. Consulting services limited according to time and effort required.

48105. INTERTECT Disaster Information-Sharing System, P.O. Box 10502 (3511 N Hall St, Ste 106), Dallas, TX 75207; (214) 521-8921. Professional org that specializes in problems associated with disaster relief, with primary emphasis on Third World. Has library collections and computerized data bases. Correspondence, referrals, and onsite use of collections provided free; fees charged for other services.

48106. Independent Living Research Utilization Project, P.O. Box 20095 (6910 Fannin St, No. 207), Houston, TX 77225; (713) 797-0200. Seeks to improve dissemination and use of results of research programs and demonstration projects in field of independent living for individuals with disabilities. Publishes newsletter, sourcebook, reports; reference services for a fee.

48107. Innovation, Creativity, and Capital Institute, Univ of Tex. at Austin, 2815 San Gabriel, Austin, TX 78705; (512) 478-4081. Natl center for study of innovation, creativity, and capital. Studies designed to develop alternatives for private sector action aimed at regional and natl goals. Provides advisory and consulting services, distributes publications. Services available at cost.

48108. Institute for Aerobics Research Library, 12200 Preston Rd, Dallas, TX 75230; (214) 239-7223. Interest in aerobics research, including exercise testing, body composition, skinfold thickness, physical fitness, and exercise physiology; preventive and rehabilitative medicine. Answers inquiries, permits onsite use of collection. Services free, unless extensive.

48109. Institute for Disaster Research, Coll of Engineering, Tex. Tech Univ, P.O. Box 4089, Lubbock, TX 79409; (806) 742-3476. Conducts basic and applied research in general area of disaster mitigation, with special emphasis on wind engineering. Has photo collection of wind-damaged structures, computer listing of tornado events. Services generally provided for a fee to engineers, but others assisted.

48110. Institute for Rehabilitation and Research Information Service Center, P.O. Box 20095, Houston, TX 77225; (713) 797-5947. Interest in rehabilitation and physical medicine, particularly pediatric rehabilitation, respiratory diseases, spinal cord injuries, amputees, and neurological disorders. Answers inquiries, provides copying services, permits onsite use of collection for free.

48111. Institute for Storm Research, 3600 Mt. Vernon, Houston, TX 77006; (713) 529-4891. Conducts research on a contract basis for govt agencies and private orgs, interest in meteorology, storm research, oceanography, hydrodynamics. Has research library. All services provided at cost.

48112. Institute of Criminal Justice Studies, Southwest Tex. State Univ, San Marcos, TX 78666-4610; (512) 245-3030. Interest in prevention or control of crime and delinquency, criminal justice, safety, school violence, substance abuse, child abuse. Answers inquiries, provides advisory services. Services free to Tex. orgs, at cost to others.

48113. Intercultural Development Research Association, 5835 Callaghan Rd, San Antonio, TX 78228; (512) 684-8180. Interest in equal educational opportunity, education for ethnic and racial minorities, multicultural and bilingual education, community mental health.

Has resource library of bilingual and early childhood materials. Services available at cost.

48114. International Airline Passengers Association, P.O. Box 660074 (800 W Airport Freeway, Ste 1120), Dallas, TX 75266-0074; (214) 438-8100. Interest in enhancement of safety, convenience, comfort, and economy of air travel; aviation regulations of FAA and govts worldwide; consumer rights. Answers inquiries, permits onsite use of collection. Services primarily for members, but others are assisted, sometimes for a fee.

48115. International Boundary & Water Commission, United States & Mexico, 4110 Rio Bravo, El Paso, TX 79902; (915) 541-7300. Interest in administration of treaties and other agreements with Mexico regarding intl land and water boundaries. Publishes bulletins with statistical info. Answers inquiries, makes referrals.

48116. International Brangus Breeders Association, 9500 Tioga Dr, San Antonio, TX 78230; (512) 696-8231. Interest in Brangus cattle, including records, breed improvement programs, and promotions. Publishes monthly journal and handbook. Answers inquiries, provides advisory and promotion services, often for free.

48117. International Center for Arid and Semi-Arid Land Studies, Tex. Tech Univ, P.O. Box 4620, Lubbock, TX 79409; (806) 742-2218. Interest in arid and semi-arid lands development, technology, agriculture, history, climatology, people, economics, etc. Library is major repository for info on southern Great Plains and adjoining areas. Pamphlets and other documents distributed in answer to inquiries.

48118. International Center for the Solution of Environmental Problems, 3818 Graustark, Houston, TX 77006; (713) 527-8711. Demonstrates or implements solutions to parts of environmental problems. Interest in such areas as meteorology, oceanography, urbanization, and climate change. Publishes journal, technical reports; answers inquiries; provides advisory services. Most services provided at cost, some free.

48119. International Communication Association, P.O. Box 9589, Austin, TX 78766; (512) 454-8299. Professional org interested in interdisciplinary research on human communication and human relations. Various publications available. Inquiries referred to member specialists.

48120. International Facility Management Association, 11 Greenway Plaza, Houston, TX 77046. Attempts to further understanding of facility management; cultivates cooperation and represents facility management to orgs, management, and the public. Publishes newsletter and annual directory. Reference services provided free to members, at cost to others.

48121. International Mobile Air Conditioning Association, 3003 LBJ Freeway, Ste 219, Dallas, TX 75234; (214) 647-2038. Interest in automotive air conditioning and other mobile applications of air conditioning. Answers inquiries, prepares analyses and evaluations. Services for nonmembers limited according to time and effort required.

48122. International Municipal Signal Association, P.O. Box 8249 (6213 Ft Worth Ave), Ft Worth, TX 76112; (817) 429-8638. Interest in public safety systems, including installation and maintenance procedures. Answers inquiries, provides reference services, distributes publications. Services free, except for publications, to anyone involved in public safety.

48123. International Oil Scouts Association, P.O. Box 2121 (326 E 5th St), Austin, TX 78768; (512) 472-3357. Interest in exploratory wells drilled and current and cumulative production of petroleum and gas in energy fields discovered in U.S., Canada, and 30 foreign countries. Provides reference services, distributes publications. All services to nonmembers provided on a fee basis.

48124. International Society of Certified Electronics Technicians, 2708 W Berry St, Ste 8, Ft Worth, TX 76109; (817) 921-9101. Administers Certified Electronics Technician exam program for audio, antenna, communications, radar, computer, industrial, medical, and radio-TV technicians. Answers inquiries, provides reference services, distributes publications. Services free and primarily for members; others are assisted.

48125. International Television Association, 6311 N O'Connor Rd, Ste 110, Irving, TX 75039; (214) 869-1112. Nonprofit org that serves needs of professional video communicator. Has 72 chapters and 10 intl affiliates. Answers inquiries, provides employment info, conducts annual intl conference and regional conferences, distributes publications for a fee to nonmembers.

48126. International Youth Exchange Division, International Collegiate Sports Foundation, P.O. Box 866, Plano, TX 75074; (214) 424-8227. Interest in U.S. collegiate and univ sports tours abroad and reciprocal agreements for hosting foreign collegiate and university athletes in America. Provides advisory and consulting services at cost to any org, college, scouting groups.

48127. Investment Casting Institute, 8521 Clover Meadow Dr, Dallas, TX 75243; (312) 341-0488. Seeks to advance investment casting process (lost wax) and further interests of investment casting industry. Publishes handbook, technical reports, reprints. Answers inquiries, conducts conferences, distributes publications. Some services free.

48128. J.M. Dawson Church-State Research Center, Baylor Univ, Box 380 (Tidwell Bible Bldg, Rooms 205 and 208), Waco, TX 76798; (817) 755-1510. Interest in historical, legal, social science, and theological studies on church and state; religious liberty; ecumenics; interfaith relations. Has extensive vertical file containing church-state archival materials. Permits onsite use of collections free.

48130. Jerry Lewis Neuromuscular Disease Research Center, Dept of Neurology, Baylor College of Medicine, Houston, TX 77030; (713) 790-4629, 790-5971. Conducts basic and clinical research and provides patient care. Answers inquiries, conducts seminars, makes referrals to other sources of info. Services free to patients and professionals.

48131. Keratorefractive Society, P.O. Box 145, Denison, TX 75020; (214) 465-7311. Interest in radial keratotomy, keratorefraction, cornea, refraction. Holdings include computer-based data collection, patient registry, math model. Publishes quarterly journal, technical reports. Some reference services available to members only; general info provided to public for SASE.

48132. LAUNCH, The Coalition of LD Adults, c/o Dept of Special Education, E Tex. State Univ, Commerce, TX 75428; (214) 886-5937. Natl self-help group working for welfare of learning disabled adults. Publishes newsletter, books, directories, reprints. Answers inquiries, provides advisory and reference services, evaluates and analyzes data, conducts seminars and workshops. Services free.

48133. Latin American Studies Association, c/o Institute of Latin American Studies, Univ of Tex. at Austin, Austin, TX 78758; (512) 471-6237. Promotes education on Latin America through more effective teaching, training, and research. Answers inquiries, provides consulting services, conducts natl meetings, seminars, and workshops. Services free, except for some publications and registration for natl meetings.

48134. Linguistics Research Center, Univ of Tex., P.O. Box 7247, Univ Station (Harry Ransom Center, Room 3.342; Univ Campus), Austin, TX 78713-7247; (512) 471-4566. Interest in computational, historical, and descriptive linguistics. Engages in automatic language processing, including computer-based bibliography compilation. Services for persons outside univ community limited; fees charged.

48136. Living Bank International, P.O. Box 6725 (3927 Essex Lane), Houston, TX 77265; (713) 528-2971, (800) 528-2971. Dedicated to helping persons who, after death, wish to donate a part or all parts of their bodies for purposes of transplantation, therapy, medical research, or anatomical studies. Answers all inquiries by distributing publications; provides 24-hour telephone referral service.

48137. Lunar and Planetary Institute, 3303 NASA Rd No. 1, Houston, TX 77058-4399; (713) 486-2135, 486-2172. Permanent center for advanced research on problems in lunar and planetary science. Has Lunar and Planetary Literature Data Base; Planetary Image Center with spacecraft photos and maps. Publishes bulletin and reports, answers inquiries. Services free, primarily for univ researchers.

48138. Lyndon Baines Johnson Library, Austin, TX 78705; (512) 482-5137. Interest in career, presidential administration, and times of Lyndon Baines Johnson. Persons who wish to use Library's resources granted access upon written application. Inquiries answered, bibliographic service provided. Some materials available by interlibrary loan.

48139. M. D. Anderson Hospital & Tumor Institute Research Medical Library, 6723 Bertner Ave, Houston, TX 77030; (713) 792-2282. Interest in oncology, cancer chemotherapy, radiobiology. Has access to relevant computerized data bases. Answers inquiries, provides reference and duplication services, permits onsite reference by faculty and students, Texas residents, and visitings scholars.

48140. Meat Processing and Marketing Research Unit, Agricultural Research Service, USDA, P.O. Box ED, College Station, TX 77841; (409) 260-9258. Interest in all aspects of packaging, unitization, marketing, and transportation of perishable agricultural products, with emphasis on handling livestock and livestock products. Answers inquiries, distributes reprints and bulletins. Services generally free.

48141. Mended Hearts, 7320 Greenville Ave, Dallas, TX 75231; (214) 750-5442. Affiliation of persons throughout U.S. who have undergone heart surgery; has chapters in many states. Publishes quarterly journal, pamphlets; answers inquiries; provides advice services to persons anticipating or recovering from heart surgery and to their families.

48143. Meteoritical Society, c/o D. Bogard, Secty, SN4, Geochemistry, Johnson Space Center, Houston, TX 77058; (713) 483-2296. Interest in meteorites, meteoroids, comets, shock metamorphism, lunar science. Publishes descriptions of newly recovered meteorites, short research reports. Answers inquiries, provides consulting services, sometimes for a fee.

48144. Meyer Center for Developmental Pediatrics, Baylor College of Medicine, Tex. Children's Hospital, 6621 Fannin St, Houston, TX 77030; (713) 791-4234. Provides hospital-based multidisciplinary diagnostic services and prescribes appropriate educational and habilitative programs for children from birth to 12 years with developmental disabilities. Provides consulting services to physicians, agencies, and school districts on a fee basis.

48145. Microelectronics and Computer Technology Corp., Library, 9430 Research Blvd, Austin, TX 78759; (512) 343-0860. Supports R&D projects on a fifth-generation computer. Interest in human interface with computers, computer-aided design, advanced computer architecture, artificial intelligence. Reference services available by appointment or through interlibrary loan.

48146. Middle East Resource Center, Univ of Tex., SSB 3.122, Austin, TX 78712; (512) 471-3881. Interest in Middle Eastern studies, political science, geography, anthropology, archeology, and architecture of Middle East; Islam, Judaism, and Christianity. Fees charged for film rental and for advisory, consulting, translation, and reproduction services; other services free.

48147. Mothers Against Drunk Drivers, 669 Airport Freeway, Ste 310, Hurst, TX 76053; (817) 268-6233. Provides grassroots leadership to create major social change in attitude and behavior of Americans toward impaired driving. Publishes newsletters, training materials, audiovisuals, victim info pamphlets. Answers inquiries, makes referrals. Services free.

48148. NASA Lunar Sample Inventory, Lyndon B. Johnson Space Center, NASA, Code SN2, Houston, TX 77058; (713) 483-3274. Interest in availability of lunar samples for scientific research, physical data, and history. Has over 90,000 entries of computerized specific lunar sample data. Answers inquiries or refers inquirers to other sources of info. Services free.

48149. NASA Technical Library, JM2, Lyndon B. Johnson Space Center, NASA, Houston, TX 77058; (713) 483-4048. Interest in development, testing, and operation of manned spacecraft; life, physical, and social sciences related to manned exploration of space. Permits onsite reference by qualified govt agencies and their contractors; provides computerized searches to authorized users.

48150. NASA Toxicology Laboratory, Health Services Division, DD6, Lyndon B. Johnson Space Center, NASA, Houston, TX 77058; (713) 483-5281. Interest in spacecraft atmospheres, atmospheric chemical analysis, toxicology of atmospheric contaminants, chemical hazards from spacecraft payloads. Reference services available to scientists, specialists, and graduate students interested in inhalation toxicology.

48152. National Alliance for Safe Schools, 501 N Interregional, Austin, TX 78702; (512) 396-4987. Nonprofit org that helps schools and school districts maintain safe and secure learning environments. Has cross-indexed, constantly-updated data base of sources on school crime and violence and its prevention. Most reference servicess provided at cost.

48153. National Association for Ambulatory Care, Prestonwood Tower, Ste 1017, 5151 Beltline Rd, Dallas, TX 75240; (214) 788-2456. Trade org for freestanding (independent) emergency and ambulatory care center industry. Has computerized data base on industry, statistical data. Publishes monthly newsletter, technical reports. Reference services free to members, for a fee to others.

48154. National Association for Ambulatory Care, 5151 Beltline Road, Prestonwood Towers, Ste 1017, Dallas, TX 75240; (214) 788-2456. Sets standards for emergency clinics not physically contiguous with a hospital. Provides guidelines for their operation, promotes public awareness of such clinics, and maintains liaison between assn and medical peer groups, insurance industry, govt, and other interested parties.

48155. National Association of Board of Examiners for Nursing Home Administrators, 111 W Anderson Lane, Ste 200, Austin, TX 78752; (512) 454-4806. Interest in nursing home administration; licensing, educational and professional standards, and code of ethics for nursing home administrators. Answers inquiries, provides reference services, distributes publications. Services primarily for members, but others assisted.

48156. National Association of Corrosion Engineers, P.O. Box 218340 (1440 S Creek Dr), Houston, TX 77218; (713) 492-0535. Interest in corrosion and environmental attack on metal and nonmetal materials of construction; mechanical, chemical, and electrochemical control measures. Literature searching and duplication services available for a fee, onsite use of literature permitted.

48157. National Association of Women in Construction, P.O. Box 181068, Ft Worth, TX 76118; (817) 877-5551. Interest in women in construction industry, including architecture, general construction, subcontracting, material supplying, construction engineering. Publishes monthly newsletter, answers inquiries.

48158. National Cutting Horse Association, P.O. Box 12155 (4704 Hwy 377), Ft Worth, TX 76116; (817) 244-6188. Records achievements of and promotes interest in the cutting horse. Publishes monthly magazine, answers inquiries, provides advisory services, conducts seminars and workshops, permits onsite use of collections. Services free.

48159. National Electronic Service Dealers Association, 2708 W Berry St, Ste 5, Ft Worth, TX 76109; (817) 921-9061. Federation of state assns that serve business, management, and technical needs of electronic service dealers. Has reference library of consumer electronics; publishes magazine, newsletter. Answers inquiries or refers inquirers to other sources of info.

48160. National Heart and Blood Vessel Research and Demonstration Center Communications Core, Baylor College of Medicine, 1200 Moursund St, Room 176B, Houston, TX 77030; (713) 790-2702. Conducts basic and clinical research as well as public and professional education in prevention and treatment of cardiovascular disease. Answers inquiries, provides advisory services and info on research in progress, distributes publications. Most services free.

48161. National Home Fashions League, P.O. Box 58045 (107 World Trade Center), Dallas, TX 75258; (214) 747-2406. Promotes educational interchange among executives in interior furnishings industry and helps inform consumers about home furnishings. Answers inquiries, makes referrals to other sources of info. Services free.

48162. National Network of Learning Disabled Adults, Special Education Dept, E Tex. State Univ, Binnion Hall, Room 221, Commerce, TX 75428-1907; (214) 886-5932, 886-5937. Nonprofit org of and for learning disabled (LD) adults. Primary purpose is to form network of communications for LD adults and their self help groups; NNLDA works to coordinate efforts of these groups. Maintains speakers bureau.

48163. National Oleander Society, c/o E.M. Koehler, Corresponding Secty, P.O. Box 3431, Galveston Island, TX 77552. Interest in research on development, improvement, and preservation of oleanders (Nerium) of all kinds, including cultivation and hybridization. Publishes newsletter and brochures, answers inquiries, provides consulting services. Services free; requests should include SASE.

48164. National Opera Association, Route 2, Box 93, Commerce, TX 75428; (214) 886-3830. Aims to promote greater appreciation, more performances, and increased composition of opera. Publishes newsletter, journal, directory. Answers inquiries or refers inquirers to other sources of info free; sells publications, data compilations, and mailing lists and labels.

48165. National Pesticide Telecommunications Network, P.O. Drawer 2031, San Benito, TX 78586-2031; (800) 858-7378; (512) 399-5352. Provides info and pesticide residue lab services to prevent pesticide accidents. Maintains library of pesticide reference materials, cross-reference file of technical info on pesticides, and file of people and orgs with an interest in pesticides.

48166. National Quarter Horse Registry, P.O. Box 247, Raywood, TX 77582; (409) 587-4341. Interest in Bloodline quarter horse registration. Publishes information folders, answers inquiries, investigates registration of horses. Services provided for a fee to all users.

48167. National Spill Control School, Corpus Christi State Univ, 6300 Ocean Dr, Corpus Christi, TX 78412; (512) 991-8692. Trains people in noncredit spill prevention and control for oil, hazardous materials, and hazardous waste; develops training materials and sessions in safe handling and containment of those materials. Answers inquiries. Reference services available, sometimes for a fee.

48168. National Stripper Well Association, c/o G. Michel, Exec. V.P., Box 3373, Abilene, TX 79604; (915) 672-5225. Compiles data and info relative to stripper well (one capable of producing an average of 10 barrels of oil or less per day) segment of domestic oil producing industry. Publishes annual survey, makes referrals to other sources of info. Services free.

48169. National Wildflower Research Center, 2600 FM 973 North, Austin, TX 78725; (512) 929-3600. Seeks to stimulate, underwrite, and carry out research in propagation, cultivation, conservation, preservation, and use of wildflowers and other native and naturalized plants. Answers inquiries, provides reference services for free.

48170. Natural Fibers Information Center, Bureau of Business Research, Univ of Tex., P.O. Box 7459, Univ Station, Austin, TX 78713; (512) 471-1063. Contract agency of Natural Fibers and Food Protein Commission of Texas. Interest in marketing, merchandising, and economic aspects of Texas natural fibers industry. Answers technical inquiries and provides consulting, literature-searching, and duplication services for a fee.

48171. Nondestructive Testing Information Analysis Center, Southwest Research Institute, P.O. Drawer 28510 (6220 Culebra Rd), San Antonio, TX 78284; (512) 684-5111 ext 2362. Collects, analyzes, maintains, and disseminates info in field of nondestructive testing. Publishes newsletter, data handbooks, specialized technical reports. Answers inquiries and prepares custom bibliographies. Computerized literature retrieval available for a fee.

48172. North Texas Back Institute, 3801 W 15th St, Ste 100, Plano, TX 75075; (214) 867-2720. Interest in evaluation, treatment, and prevention of back pain; physical and occupational therapy; spine and body mechanics; relaxation, yoga, and pain control. Answers inquiries for free; other services provided on a fee basis.

48173. Numismatics International, c/o Wm. B. Thompson, Pres., P.O. Box 30013, Dallas, TX 75230; (214) 361-7543. Encourages and promotes science of numismatics by specializing in areas and nations other than U.S. Publishes monthly bulletin, books; answers inquiries; conducts seminars, workshops. Services at cost to members, other numismatic orgs, and, on occasion, others.

48174. Odessa Meteor Crater, 1204 TCB Bldg, Odessa, TX 79761; (915) 332-1666. Interest in meteoritics and Odessa meteor craters. Has small collection of books, periodicals, and reports; publishes pamphlet on Odessa meteor craters. Answers inquiries, permits onsite use of collection. Services free.

48175. Oral History Association, P.O. Box 13734, NTSU Station, Denton, TX 76203; (817) 565-3385. Seeks to advance practice and use of oral history. Publishes quarterly newsletter, technical reports, directories. Answers inquiries, provides advisory, reference, and literature-searching, services. Services free, except for seminars and publications.

48176. Pan American Health Organization Field Office, U.S.-Mexico Border, 6006 N Mesa, Ste 700, El Paso, TX 79912; (915) 581-6645. Coordinates public health affairs between U.S. and Mexico. Publishes directories, bibliographies, data compilations. Answers inquiries, provides reference, abstracting and indexing services, distributes publications. Services free to special groups.

48177. Panhandle-Plains Historical Museum, P.O. Box 967, W. T. Station, Canyon, TX 79016; (806) 655-7191. Interest in history, archaeology, paleontology, art, ethnology, and clothing and textiles of U.S. southern Great Plains. Extensive collections open to public. Reference service generally available at no cost; technical consultations available.

48178. Parents of Children with Down's Syndrome, P.O. Box 35268, Houston, TX 77035; (713) 463-1833. Provides support and information to parents of children with Down's Syndrome and promotes well-being of Down's Syndrome patients. Activities and services include parent visitations, speakers bureau, mothers' coffee groups, and lending library of books and periodicals.

48179. Pate Museum of Transportation, P.O. Box 711 (U.S. Hwy 377 b/w Ft Worth and Cresson), Ft Worth, TX 76101; (817) 332-1161. Interest in transportation history. Holdings include classic, antique, special-interest automobiles; exhibit of aircraft; antique railroad car; 1,500-volume library.

48180. Permian Basin Geophysical Society, P.O. Box 361, Midland, TX 79702. Promotes geophysics, especially as it relates to petroleum industry, and sponsors scholarships in geophysics. Answers inquiries, conducts seminars and meetings. Services primarily for members, but others assisted. Nonmembers charged for data compilations.

48181. Petroleum Equipment Suppliers Association, 9225 Katy Freeway, Ste 401, Houston, TX 77024; (713) 932-0168. Interest in petroleum equipment, supplies, and services used in drilling and producing segments of petroleum industry. Answers inquiries free, sells directory.

48182. Physical Anthropology Laboratory, Dept of Anthropology, Univ of Tex., Austin, TX 78712; (512) 471-4367. Interest in skeletal identification, primate biology. Has reference and teaching collection of human skeletons, baboon skeletons, and skeletons of various other primates. Answers inquiries, provides consulting services, permits onsite use of collections. Services generally free.

48183. Plant Resources Center, Dept of Botany, Univ of Tex., Austin, TX 78712; (512) 471-5262. Interest in systematic botany, vascular plants of the Southwest U.S. and Latin America, rare and endangered species, comparative phytochemistry, cytogenetics. Holdings include over 900,000 research specimens. Research services free, except to profitmaking corps.

48184. Political Research, Tegoland at Bent Tree, 16850 Dallas Parkway, Dallas, TX 75248; (214) 931-8827. Provides commercial info service on govts worldwide to subscribers. Publishes directories and encyclopedia. Answers inquiries, provides reference services, distributes publications, schedules appointments with U.S. public officials. Services available by subscription.

48185. Population Research Center Library, Univ of Tex., 1800 Main Bldg, Austin, TX 78712; (512) 471-5514. Interest in demographic research in Texas, Southwest U.S., Mexico, Latin America, and Europe; trends of intl labor force. Holdings include over 75 percent of all known censuses in the world. Answers inquiries, provides reference services.

48186. Ranching Heritage Center Museum, Tex. Tech Univ, P.O. Box 4499 (Indiana Ave and 4th St), Lubbock, TX 79409; (806) 742-2498. Consists of 31 relocated and reconstructed structures that reflect development of ranching and livestock industries in southwestern U.S. Has research files, photos. Permits onsite inspection by public, answers inquiries related to areas of interest.

48187. Red Angus Association of America, P.O. Box 776 (4201 Stemmons), Denton, TX 76202-0776; (817) 387-3502. Interest in Red Angus cattle and their registration. Publishes *Amereican Red Angus* (monthly). Answers inquiries, provides reference services, conducts cattle registration. Services to nonmembers for a fee.

48188. Remote Sensing Applications Unit, International Center for Arid and Semi-Arid Land Studies, Tex. Tech Univ, Lubbock, TX 79409; (806) 742-2218. Interest in remote sensing, aerial photographs, topographic maps, Skylab and Landsat data. Has collections of aerial photos, topographic maps. Answers inquiries, permits onsite use of collections. Fees charged for consulting and research services.

48189. Research Council on Structural Connections, c/o K.H. Frank, Secty, Civil Engineering ECJ 4.9, Univ of Tex., Austin, TX 78712; (512) 471-7259. Sponsors research, develops guides to design criteria, and publishes specifications applied to structural steel connections. Publishes numerous research reports, answers brief inquiries.

48190. Research and Development Associates for Military Food and Packaging Systems, 103 Biltmore Dr, Ste 106, San Antonio, TX 78213; (512) 344-5773. Interest in food products and packaging, food serving and feeding equipment, armed forces and industrial relations. Answers inquiries, provides advisory and reference services, permits onsite use of collection. Services free, unless extensive.

48191. Research and Training Center in Mental Retardation, Tex. Tech Univ, P.O. Box 4510, Lubbock, TX 79409; (806) 742-3131. Interest in work potential of mentally retarded, rehabilitation counseling and service delivery system, community adjustment and training, multiply handicapped. Publishes technical reports, training packages. Services provided at cost to some, free to others.

48192. Rob and Bessie Welder Wildlife Foundation, P.O. Box 1400, Sinton, TX 78387; (512) 364-2643. Interest in wildlife and wildlife-related research, natural history, ornithology, conservation education, botany, zoology. Has extensive library and wildlife refuge. Answers inquiries, distributes publications, permits onsite use of collections. Services free, except for publications.

48193. Runaway Hotline, P.O. Box 12428, Austin, TX 78711; (800) 231-6946; in Tex., (800) 392-3552. Volunteer-staffed, toll-free, 24-hour info and referral service. Runaways, throwaways, and homeless youth ages 17 and under may call to obtain food, shelter, medical help, counseling, and related services in area they are calling from.

48194. Santa Gertrudis Breeders International, P.O. Box 1257 (State Hwy 141 West), Kingsville, TX 78363; (512) 592-9357. Interest in purebred Santa Gertrudis cattle. Holdings include in-house computer record system with animal performance data. Publishes directories, brochures; answers inquiries free.

48195. Shuttle Earth Viewing Imagery Facility, Space Shuttle Earth Observations Project, Johnson Space Center, NASA/Code SC5, Houston, TX 77058; (713) 483-6369. Interest in remote sensing of earth resources. Has collection of remote sensing data (imagery) from NASA spacecraft and aircraft; microfilm of U.S. acquired Landsat data. Answers inquiries related to NASA-acquired imagery, available for purchase from EROS Data Center, Sioux Falls, SD.

48196. Society of American Value Engineers, 220 N Story Rd, Ste 114, Irving, TX 75061; (214) 986-5171. Interest in value engineering, value management, and value analysis; energy, resource, and manpower conservation. Answers inquiries, provides advisory, reference, and reproduction services, distributes publications. Services may be provided at cost.

48197. Society of Diagnostic Medical Sonographers, 10300 N Central Expressway, Bldg 1, Ste 276, Dallas, TX 75231; (214) 369-4332. Interest in ultrasound, diagnostic ultrasound, sonography, medical sonography, ultrasound technology, medical sonography education standards. Publishes newsletter, professional journal, directories; answers inquiries; distributes publications. Services free, except for publications.

48198. Society of Independent Professional Earth Scientists, 4925 Greenville Ave, Ste 170, Dallas, TX 75206; (214) 363-1780. Interest in independent professional earth scientists, including geologists, geophysicists, and petroleum engineers. Publishes newsletter and bulletins. Provides names, addresses, and specialties of member earth scientists to users of earth science consultants.

48199. Society of Professional Well Log Analysts, 6001 Gulf Freeway, Ste C-129, Houston, TX 77023; (713) 928-8925. Seeks to advance science of formation evaluation through well logging techniques to locate, evaluate, and exploit oil, gas, and other naturally occurring minerals. Sells publications, conducts seminars for a fee.

48200. Sociologists for Women in Society, c/o J.S. Chafetz, Dept of Sociology, Univ of Houston, Houston, TX 77004; (713) 749-4976. Interest in women's studies, sociology of sex and gender, women in sociology. Answers inquiries, provides job market info. Services free.

48201. Southwest Aviculture Foundation Reference Library, 99 Windmill Rd, San Antonio, TX 78231. Seeks preservation of world's birdlife through preservation of their natural habitats, educational campaigns in bird conservation, and funding of studies. Answers inquiries by mail only; reference services provided at cost.

48202. Southwest Collection, Tex. Tech Univ, Box 4090 (Math Bldg, Room 106), Lubbock, TX 79409; (806) 742-3749. Regional archival repository and library, center for research, devoted to perpetuating heritage of American Southwest. Answers inquiries, provides reference services and referrals to other sources of info. Services generrlly free, except for photocopies and microfilm reproductions.

48203. Southwest Educational Development Laboratory, 211 E 7th St, Austin, TX 78701; (512) 476-6861. Private, nonprofit educational R&D institution concerned with behavioral and social research, educational development, providing assistance to institutions with regionally identified problems and needs. Distributes some publications free, others at cost; permits onsite use of collections.

48204. Specialty Advertising Association International, c/o H.T. Olson, Pres., 1404 Walnut Hill Lane, Irving, TX 75038; (214) 258-0404. Interest in specialty advertising (use of articles of merchandise on which the advertising message is printed). Publishes booklets, research brochures, reprints; answers inquiries; sponsors annual conventions and expositions and educational programs.

48205. Stored-Product Insects Research Laboratory, Agricultural Research Service, USDA, Route 7, Box 999, Beaumont, TX 77706; (409) 752-5221. Interest in research on control of stored-product insects in rice and export facilities, including chemical control, pheromones, and host plant resistance. Answers inquiries, provides consulting services for govt agencies.

48206. Tatsch Associates, P.O. Box 622, Fredericksburg, TX 78624; (512) 997-8785. Commercial org interested in research on origin, evolution, and present characteristics of earth's mineral resources. Answers inquiries; provides consulting and reference services and info on research in progress; distributes publications. All services free; books sold at cost.

48207. Tektite Research, P.O. Box X, Univ Station (Geology Bldg, 5th Fl), Austin, TX 78712; (512) 471-1534. Interest in tektites. Permits onsite reference upon approval of satisfactory references. Reprints of some research accomplished available.

48208. Texas Archeological Research Laboratory, Univ of Tex., Balcones Research Center, 10100 Burnet Rd, Austin, TX 78758; (512) 835-3036. Interest in archaeology of Texas and adjacent regions. Houses more than one million specimens, primarily from prehistoric and historic sites in Texas. Scientific and academic personnel may have access to collections and records.

48209. Texas Archives for Geological Research Paleobiology Collection, Tex. Mem Museum, Univ of Tex., 2400 Trinity St, Austin, TX 78705; (512) 471-5302. 471-1604. Interest in paleobiology, paleobotany, malacology, systematics, zoological types, botanical types. Has 3.6 million-specimen paleontological collection with locality file and catalog; coverage is intl. Reference services generally free, professional services available.

48210. Texas Historical Commission, P.O. Box 12276 (1511 Colorado St), Austin, TX 78711; (512) 475-3092. Interest in historic preservation, historic and archaeological sites in Texas, historic shipwrecks off Texas coast, revitalization of small cities with historic downtown areas. Publishes newsletter, directories, catalogs; answers inquiries. A fee is charged for some reference services.

48211. Texas Instruments Inc. Library Acquisitions Center, P.O. Box 225936 MS-112 (13500 N Central Expressway), Dallas, TX 75265; (214) 995-2494. Interest in electronics, electronic systems, and components; solid state physics and chemistry; solid state devices; semiconductor materials (integrated circuits). Answers inquiries, permits onsite use of collection by prior arrangement for serious research.

48212. Texas Instruments Minicomputer Information Exchange, P.O. Box 2909, M/S 2200 (12501 Research Blvd), Austin, TX 78769; (512) 250-7151. Promotes exchange of info between users and company. Has library of software, hardware designs. Services free to members (membership free and available to anyone). Reproductions of programs and other material furnished at cost.

48213. Texas Real Estate Research Center, Tex. A&M Univ, College Station, TX 77843; (409) 845-2031. Interest in real estate research and education, land value studies, real estate marketing, housing studies. Publishes quarterly magazine, research reports; answers inquiries;, provides reference services. Services free, except for publications.

48214. Texas System of Natural Laboratories, 106 E 6th St, No. 150, Austin, TX 78701; (512) 477-4925. Clearinghouse charged with aiding scientists in search of field research plots in Texas. Answers inquiries, provides advisory and reference services, provides info on availability of specific research sites. Services free to Texas general academic institutions; at cost to others.

48215. Texas and Southwestern Cattle Raisers Foundation, 1301 W 7th St, Ft Worth, TX 76102; (817) 332-7064. Goals are to preserve heritage of cattle industry, provide answers to public inquiries, encourage cattle raising careers, promote beef cattle technology through research grants. Has library, museum, training center, and theater; extensive archives. Most services free.

48216. Textile Research Center, P.O. Box 5888, Lubbock, TX 79417; (806) 742-3587. Interest in textile research on fiber processing, fabric development, and biochemistry of cotton, wool, mohair, and manmade fibers. Publishes monthly tech/news bulletin, answers inquiries. Services provided on a fee or contract basis.

48217. Thermodynamics Research Center, Tex. Engineering Experiment Station, Tex. A&M Univ, College Station, TX 77843; (409) 845-4940 Interest in properties of chemical compounds, primarily organic, of interest to petroleum and chemical industries. Publishes loose-leaf data sheets semiannually. Provides reference and consulting services for a fee.

48218. U.S. Livestock Insects Laboratory, Agricultural Research Service, USDA, P.O. Box 232, Kerrville, TX 78029-0232; (512) 257-3566. Site of research program conducted by entomologists, chemists, microbiologists, and engineers to solve problems caused by arthropods that parasitize livestock. Answers inquiries concerning veterinary entomology.

48219. U.T. Culture Collection of Algae, Dept of Botany, Univ of Tex., Austin, TX 78712; (512) 471-4019. Interest in preservation of strains of algae that have been used in research; isolation and characterization of new strains of algae for research. Answers inquiries, provides consulting services, provides living cultures of algae for research on cost basis.

48220. U.T. Genetics Institute, Univ of Tex., Austin, TX 78712; (512) 471-5420. Organized research unit in support of graduate education, interested in research and graduate training in many areas of genetics, including human genetics, biochemical and molecular genetics, somatic cell genetics, immunogenetics, population genetics. Answers inquiries, makes referrals.

48221. U.T. Radiocarbon Laboratory, Univ of Tex. at Austin, Balcones Research Center, 10100 Burnet Rd, Austin, TX 78758; (512) 835-3010. Interest in radiocarbon dating. Performs radiocarbon dating for recognized research units and persons on a collaborative basis, not as a routine service, and usually at cost.

48222. USAF Forensic Toxicology Section, USAF Epidemiological Laboratory, Brooks Air Force Base, TX 78235-5000; (512) 536-3671. Interest in atomic absorption, gas chromatography, high-performance liquid chromatography, GLC/mass spectrometry, infrared and ultraviolet spectrophotometry. Answers inquiries, provides reference services to govt agencies, performs forensic toxicologic exams for Air Force.

48223. USAF Strughold Aeromedical Library, USAF School of Aerospace Medicine, Brooks Air Force Base, TX 78235; (512) 536-3321. Interest in aviation and space medicine, aircraft accidents, escape and survival techniques. Publishes technical reports, answers inquiries. Services primarily for personnel of the school, but may be provided to others through interlibrary loan.

48224. United States-Mexico Border Health Association, 6006 N Mesa, Ste 700, El Paso, TX 79912; (915) 581-6645. Serves as clearinghouse for exchange of public health info along Mexican-American border and as a center for health statistics. Interested in diseases of all types, from mental health to sexually transmitted diseases.

48225. Veterinary Toxicology and Entomology Research Laboratory, Agricultural Research Service, USDA, Box

GE, College Station, TX 77841; (409) 260-9372. Interest in livestock toxicology; control of insects attacking livestock; toxic plants. Publishes reports, answers inquiries.

48226. Wadley Institutes of Molecular Medicine, 9000 Harry Hines Blvd, Dallas, TX 75235; (214) 351-8111. Interest in cancer, lung, and blood disease diagnosis, treatment, and research; new drug synthesis and development; blood banking; interferons. Answers inquiries, provides consulting services for a fee, makes referrals and interlibrary loans. Services provided to medical personnel only.

48227. William Beaumont Army Medical Center, William Beaumont Army Medical Center, El Paso, TX 79920; (915) 569-2233. Interest in analytical and clinical medicine (applied and research) related to soldiers, retirees, and their dependents. Answers brief inquiries; provides consulting services to U.S. govt agencies; permits onsite use of collections by Center affiliates, personnel, and retirees.

48228. Willys Overland Jeepster Club, c/o J. Sherwin, Secty-Treas., P.O. Box 12042, El Paso, TX 79913. Nonprofit org interested in preservation, restoration, and maintenance of Willys Overland Jeepsters (produced from 1948 to 1951). Publishes monthly newsletter. Answers mailed inquiries accompanied by SASE.

48229. Women in Communications, P.O. Box 9561, Austin, TX 78766; (512) 346-9875. Interest in women in communications, including broadcasting, newspapers, magazines, advertising, public relations, public information, free-lance writing, and communications education. Publishes directory, career booklet; answers inquiries. Services free, except for publications.

48230. World Biological Society, 3615 Carson Dr, Amarillo, TX 79109; (806) 355-9369. Interest in research in genetic engineering. Holdings include 100,000 artifacts; publications include books and R&D summaries. Answers inquiries, provides advisory services and info on R&D in progress, distributes publications and data compilations. Services free.

48231. Young Peoples' Logo Association, 1208 Hillsdale Dr, Richardson, TX 75081; (214) 783-7548. Promotes computers in education and Logo as learning language. Explores microelectronics, including robots, computerized toys and appliances, artificial intelligence, and their impact on everyday life. Answers inquiries, provides reference services, often for free.

Utah

49002. Ancient Studies/Religious Studies Center, Brigham Young Univ, 4012 HB11, Provo, UT 84602; (801) 378-3498. Interest in ancient religion, history; classical languages, literature; Egyptology; ancient Judaica; Coptic. Answers inquiries, conducts seminars, evaluates data, makes interlibrary loans, permits onsite use of collection. Fee for some services.

49003. Association of Consulting Toxicologists, P.O. Box 2546 (360 E 4500 S No. 3), Salt Lake City, UT 84107; (801) 263-2282. Assists persons requiring expertise in pharmacology and toxicology by providing consultation, lab research, special investigations, literature search and review, administrative support. Services for a fee.

49004. Bacchus Works, Aerospace Division, Hercules, Inc, P.O. Box 98 (8400 West 5400 S, Salt Lake County), Magna, UT 84044; (801) 250-5911 ext 2544. Commercial org interested in chemical propulsion, solid rocket motors and propellants, explosives (as propellant ingredients), graphite fibers, etc. Provides general reference services, makes loans, permits onsite use of collections by some with security classification. Most services free, available to U.S. govt agencies, contractors, some univs.

49005. Bee Biology and Systematics Laboratory, Agricultural Research Service, USDA, Utah State Univ, UMC 53, Logan, UT 84322; research, (801) 750-2525; collection, (801) 750-2526. Interest in bee biology, systematics, introductions, pollination; parasite control; predators; larval stages; Hymenoptera. Provides general reference services, conducts seminars, permits onsite use of collections, distributes publications. Services free.

49006. Center for Atmospheric and Space Sciences, Utah State Univ, UMC-34, Logan, UT 84322; (801) 750-2961. Interest in atmospheric research, measurements, instrument development; rocketborne research of aurora borealis, other atmospheric phenomena; atmospheric emissions; etc. Provides general reference services, analyzes data. Services free, available to most persons.

49007. Center for Human Toxicology, Dept of Biochemical Pharmacology and Toxicology, Coll of Pharmacy, Univ of Utah, Skaggs Hall, Room 38, Salt Lake City, UT 84112; (801) 581-5117. Interest in biomedical pharmacology, toxicology in man. Provides general reference services, evaluates data. Most services available to physicians, medical scientists, lawyers, law enforcement officials at cost.

49009. Charles Redd Center for Western Studies, Brigham Young Univ, 4069 HBLL, Provo, UT 84602; (801) 374-4048. Interest in history, economics, sociology, literature, folklore, political science, anthropology of the American West; Utah; Mormons. Monographs sold through Signature Books, Midvale, UT 84047. Oral history tapes, transcripts available in Brigham Young Univ library on interlibrary loan.

49010. Church of Jesus Christ of Latter-Day Saints, 50 E N Temple, Salt Lake City, UT 84084; (801) 531-2745. Interest in history of the Church of Jesus Christ of Latter-Day Saints of Utah. Provides general reference services, permits onsite use of collections within guidelines. Researchers must be approved by administration. Fees charged for photocopying.

49011. Computer-Assisted Language Learning and Instruction Consortium, 3078 JKHB, Brigham Young Univ, Provo, UT 84602; (801) 378-6533. Clearinghouse for info pertaining to high technology in the teaching, learning of natural languages. Provides general reference services, evaluates data, conducts seminars. Services primarily for those involved in teaching languages, provided at cost.

49012. Cystems, c/o Judge John Farr Larson, 2877 E 4430 S, Salt Lake City, UT 84117; (801) 278-7325. Assists local, state, federal govt agencies to improve human services through computerized management techniques. Provides general reference services, conducts seminars, evaluates data, distributes publications. Services free, unless extensive.

49013. Dugway Proving Ground Technical Library, Dugway Proving Ground, UT 84022; (801) 831-3565. Interest in biological and chemical defense, weapons systems and operations, environmental and engineering tests, ecology, safety, aerosols, decontamination, micrometeorology, rickettsia, protective clothing, etc. Provides general reference services, makes interlibrary loans. Services available to govt agencies, qualified contractors, non-govt orgs.

49014. Ecology Center, Utah State Univ, UMC-52, Logan, UT 84322; (801) 750-2555. Promotes research, graduate training, extended action, in ecology. Provides general reference services, conducts seminars, makes interlibrary loans, permits onsite use of collection. Services primarily for professional researchers, govt officials, business executives. Some fees charged.

49015. Economics Research Institute, Utah State Univ, Eccles Business Bldg, Room 607, Logan, UT 84322; (801) 750-2297. Interest in natural resources planning, use, conservation, econometrics, manpower studies, public finance and money studies, economics of public land policy, mineral resources (oil, shale, coal). Provides general reference services, research conducted on grant basis.

49016. Energy Law Center, Coll of Law, Univ of Utah, Salt Lake City, UT 84112; (801) 581-5881. Engages in comprehensive interdisciplinary analysis of energy development with law as the focus. Conducts conferences, distributes publications. Services provided on a subscription basis.

49017. Exceptional Child Center, Utah State Univ, Logan, UT 84322; (801) 750-1980. Interest in special education, psychology, curriculum material. Conducts computer software evaluations for special education programs, conducts seminars. Most services free; Utah, Nev, Wyo referrals given priority.

49018. Exemplary Center for Reading Instruction, 3310 S 2700 East, Salt Lake City, UT 84109; (801) 486-5083. Interest in teaching reading, language arts; diagnosis, instruction in reading for reading programs; dissemination of info concerning language instruction. Provides general reference services, conducts seminars, permits onsite use of collection. Services free to some.

49019. Family History and Genealogical Research Center, Brigham Young Univ, 4500 HBLL, Provo, UT 84602; (801) 378-4388. Interest in family history and genealogy, concentrating on British Isles, Canada, Continental Europe, Scandinavia, U.S. Provides general reference services, genealogical and family history research; evaluates data. Services available at cost.

49020. Family and Demographic Research Institute, Coll of Social Sciences, Brigham Young Univ, Provo, UT 84602; (801) 378-2948. Conducts research concerning social-psychological, emotional, spiritual welfare of the family. Provides general reference services, conducts seminars, evaluates data, distributes publications. Services provided for a fee.

49021. Forest Service, Regional Forester, USDA, Federal Bldg, 324 25th St, Ogden, UT 84401; (801) 625-5352. Interest in management of forest, rangelands in Utah, southern Idaho, western Wyo, Nev; timber, range, soils, watershed, wildlife habitat management; fire, insect, disease control; etc. Provides general reference services, presents exhibits, slide talks, films.

49022. Genealogical Indexing Associates, P.O. Box 102, West Bountiful, UT 84087; (801) 295-3898. Interest in indexing of biographical sketches arranged by states. Provides searches of computerized indexes, printouts of results; distributes publications. Services available at cost.

49023. Genealogical Library, Church of Jesus Christ of Latter-day Saints, 50 E N Temple St, Salt Lake City, UT 84150; (801) 531-2331. Preserves, makes available records of genealogical value from all parts of the world. Provides general reference services, suggestions, limited copying services by mail; permits onsite use of collections. Services free. Library does not do genealogical research for individuals.

49024. Human Performance Research Center, Coll of Physical Education, Brigham Young Univ, Provo, UT 84601; (801) 378-3981. Interest in muscle biochemistry, energy expenditure, exercise, body composition, cardiovascular studies, enzyme chemistry, blood lipid levels. Answers inquiries, provides advisory services. Services free, unless extensive.

49025. Intermountain Cystic Fibrosis-Pediatric Gastrointestinal Center, Dept of Pediatrics, School of Medicine, Univ of Utah, 50 N Medical Dr, Salt Lake City, UT 84132; (801) 581-8227. Interest in research, education in cystic fibrosis, other digestive diseases and pediatric gastroenterology. Provides general reference services, conducts seminars, evaluates data. Some services free, restricted to families with afflicted children.

49026. Mental Retardation Association of America, 221 E Third S, Ste 214, Salt Lake City, UT 84111; (801) 328-1575. Seeks to improve quality of life for mentally retarded, developmentally disabled children, adults.

Promotes research on prevention of mental retardation. Represents state, local concerns at federal level by assuring quality programing, new services. Sponsors annual convention.

49027. Mental Retardation Association of Utah and America, 211 E 300 S St, Ste 212, Salt Lake City, UT 84111; (801) 328-1575. Nonprofit advocacy org for mentally retarded persons. Provides advisory services, conducts seminars, evaluates data. Services free.

49028. Middle East Center, Univ of Utah, Bldg 413, Salt Lake City, UT 84112; (801) 581-6181. Interest in Middle Eastern languages, literatures, culture, history, archaeology, politics, economics, social institutions, religion, geography, philosophy. Provides general reference services, conducts seminars, distributes publications.

49029. Mormon History Association, P.O. Box 7010, Univ Station, Brigham Young Univ, Provo, UT 84602. Interest in Mormon past, from inception in N.Y. to current intl status. Conducts occasional seminars, sponsors annual convention, distributes publications. Services free, except publications.

49030. Mountain Plains Regional Resource Center, Utah State Univ, UMC68, Logan, UT 84322; (801) 750-2015. Interest in special education, education of the handicapped, technology in special education, etc. Provides general reference services, evaluates data, conducts seminars. Services free, available to area education agencies, consumers working through state depts of education.

49031. Musicians National Hot Line Association, 277 E 6100 S, Salt Lake City, UT 84107; (801) 268-2000. Nonprofit org that seeks to increase employment of musicians, related occupations. Has natl center for employment info, education of musicians. Provides computer data-based searching and matching, operates a telephone hotline, makes referrals. Services primarily for members.

49032. North American Weather Consultants, Technical Library, 1521 E 3900 S, Ste 103, Salt Lake City, UT 84124; (801) 278-2672. Commercial org providing air quality, meteorological consulting, operational program services. Library provides reference services as time permits; makes direct, interlibrary loans.

49033. Poisonous Plants Research Laboratory, Agricultural Research Service, USDA, 1150 E 14th N, Logan, UT 84321; (801) 752-2943. Interest in investigation of poisonous plants; development of methods to prevent livestock losses from these plants. Answers inquiries from veterinarians, livestockmen, federal land management agencies, univs, others.

49034. School Management Study Group, 860 18th Ave, Salt Lake City, UT 84103; (801) 532-5340. Nonprofit natl action org interested in educational issues, such as school reform, building programs, integration, management, policy development, etc. Provides general reference services, conducts seminars, research, training programs. Fee for some services.

49035. Utah Geological Association, P.O. Box 11334, Salt Lake City, UT 84147. Interest in geology of Utah. Answers inquiries, conducts seminars and field trips, distributes publications, makes referrals.

49036. Utah Heritage Foundation, 355 Quince St, Salt Lake City, UT 84103; (801) 533-0858. Interest in architectural history of Utah; management, preservation, acquisition, resale of historic properties. Provides general reference services, conducts seminars, lends materials. Services may be subject to a fee.

49037. Utah State Historical Society, 300 Rio Grande, Salt Lake City, UT 84101; (801) 533-5755; library, (801) 533-5808. Interest in Utah history, Mormons, the West, Great Basin prehistory, paleontology. Answers brief mail, telephone inquiries; provides general reference services; permits onsite use of collections.

49039. Utah Water Research Laboratory, Utah State Univ, UMC 82, Logan, UT 84322; (801) 750-3168. Interest in water resources in arid climates. Provides general reference services for some fees.

49040. Watershed Science Unit, Coll of Natural Resources, Utah State Univ, Logan, UT 84322; (801) 750-2547. Interest in forest, range hydrology, modeling, impact of man's activities on forest or range land hydrologic cycles, land management. Provides general reference services, conducts seminars, analyzes data. Fee for some services.

49041. Western States Water Council, 220 S 200 East, Salt Lake City, UT 84111; (801) 521-2800. Interest in state, regional, natl water policy, including water rights, resource planning, development, quality, conservation. Answers inquiries, conducts meetings, sponsors symposia, disseminates publications.

Vermont

50001. American Society of Dowsers, Danville, VT 05828-0024; (802) 684-3417. Nonprofit society interested in dowsing, including the search, with or without a device, for tangible targets such as water, gas, oil, missing persons, and for intangible targets such as earth energies. Answers inquiries, provides some reference services for moderate fees.

50002. Ayrshire Breeders' Association, Brandon, VT 05733; (802) 247-5774. Interest in ayrshire breed of dairy cattle. Has computer data base for breed genealogy, production records, and Type Traits data. Publishes reports and *The Ayrshire Digest,* answers inquiries free.

50003. Barre Granite Association, Box 481 (51 Church St), Barre, VT 05641; (802) 476-4131. Interest in granite monuments, granite working techniques and equipment, granite quarrying. Answers inquiries, provides

advisory and consulting services, makes referrals to other sources of info. Fee for some services.

50004. Center for Arab and Islamic Studies, P.O. Box 543, Brattleboro, VT 05301; (802) 257-0872. Nonprofit org that strives to promote understanding and friendship between American and Islamic people. Has library on Middle Eastern affairs, in English and Arabic. Answers inquiries, provides advisory, copying, and translation services, distributes publications. Services provided at cost.

50005. Center for Studies in Food Self-Sufficiency, P.O. Box 1397, Burlington, VT 05402; (802) 863-3204. Interest in food self-sufficiency, energy utilization, agriculture, land use, environmental conservation. Publishes technical reports, answers inquiries, evaluates data. Services primarily for Vt. region, but may be available to others for a fee.

50006. Ephemera Society, North American Office, 124 Elm St, Bennington, VT 05201; (802) 442-6873. Promotes collection, preservation, presentation of ephemera, including their sociological and historical applications and value as aesthetic and typographical records. Answers inquiries, provides advisory services, distributes publications. Services free, except postage.

50007. Experiment in International Living, School for International Training, Kipling Rd, Brattleboro, VT 05301; (802) 257-7751. Interest in cross-cultural studies, foreign languages, intl management, intl service careers, peace studies, English as a second language. Has resource files on 2,000 social service orgs. Answers inquiries, permits onsite use of collection for free; other services at cost.

50008. Fire Safety Institute, P.O. Box 674, R.D. (2 Cider Mill Rd), Middlebury, VT 05753; (802) 462-2663. Nonprofit org involved in fire safety research, education, and info. Has special fire safety library of about 2,500 items, computerized data base. Answers inquiries or refers inquirers to other sources of info free; permits onsite use of collection. Fees for some services.

50009. Gardens for All/The National Association for Gardening, 180 Flynn Ave, Burlington, VT 05401; (802) 863-1308. Nonprofit org dedicated to helping people be successful food gardeners. Publishes books and monthly magazine, answers inquiries, provides advisory services and info on research in progress. Services free to members, at cost to others.

50010. Green Mountain Club, Box 889 (43 State St), Montpelier, VT 05602; (802) 223-3463. Nonprofit org founded to build and maintain Long Trail, which follows Green Mountains from Mass. to Canadian border. Publishes guide book, pamphlets, brochures; answers inquiries; provides advisory and reference services. Services free, except publications.

50011. Green River Tools By Hand & Foot, Ltd., P.O. Box 611 (5 Cotton Mill Hill Rd), Brattleboro, VT 05301; (802) 254-2388. Research division of Green River

451 · INSTANT INFORMATION

Tools, which imports and tests human-powered tools for garden and small farm use. Answers inquiries, provides consulting, reference, and literature-searching services, distributes publications. Services at cost if extensive.

50012. Maple Research Laboratory, Dept of Botany, Univ of Vt., 225 Marsh Life Science Bldg, Burlington, VT 05405-0086; (802) 656-2930. Conducts research and educational programs centered around sugar maple tree and its products. Has maple research library and 500 bacterial cultures (restricted to scientists at other research institutions). Answers inquiries, distributes publications. Services provided at cost.

50013. Merck Forest Foundation, Rupert, VT 05768; (802) 394-7836. Interest in forest land management and related subjects, such as wildlife and its problems, logging practices, and plantings, maple sugaring, and small-scale farming. Answers inquiries, conducts ed programs for schools and organized groups and summer camp program.

50014. National Institute of American Doll Artists, c/o Mirren Barrie, R.I. Box 328, Waterbury, VT 05677. Interest in original dolls designed and made by artists, some of which are one-of-a-kind. Publishes quarterly newsletter. Brochure with list of artists available for large SASE.

50015. New England Coalition on Nuclear Pollution, P.O. Box 545 (American Bldg, 3rd Fl, 67 Main St), Brattleboro, VT 05301; (802) 257-0336. Intervenes in state and federal regulatory proceedings relating to nuclear power plants; sponsors the Great New England Energy Show. Has resource center, answers inquiries, distributes publications. Services free.

50016. Northeastern Bird-Banding Association, c/o Vt. Institute of Natural Science, Attn: Sarah B. Laughlin, Secty, Woodstock, VT 05091; (802) 457-2779. Interest in bird banding and field research on birds, bird migration studies. Publishes quarterly journal, answers inquiries or refers inquirers to other sources of info free, conducts research grant program for students of ornithology.

50017. Recognition Technologies Users Association, P.O. Box 2016 (Battenkill Bldg, Routes 11 and 30), Manchester Center, VT 05255; (802) 362-4151. Interest in data scanning and capture by optical character recognition, optical mark recognition, optical bar recognition, voice recognition. Publishes newsletter and annual buyer's guide, answers inquiries, makes referrals. Services for a fee.

50018. Terrarium Association, Box 276, Newfane, VT 05345. Promotes terrarium gardening and maintains terrarium displays in libraries and other public places. Has history and photo files; how-to video tapes for rent. Publishes pamphlets and brochures, answers inquiries. Services free, except for publications and tapes.

50019. Vermont Historical Society, Pavilion Bldg, 109 State St, Montpelier, VT 05602; (802) 828-2291. Formed to preserve, protect, and display Vermont's past. Maintains two museums and awards grants for Vermont projects; has research library; publishes quarterly and bimonthly periodicals. Answers inquiries, provides limited literature-searching and duplication services.

50021. Vermont Maple Industry Council, Extension Service, Morrill Hall, Univ of Vt., Burlington, VT 05401; (802) 656-2990. Interest in maple syrup and sugar production and marketing, including promotion, education, and research. Answers inquiries, provides educational and promotional info either directly or through Univ of Vt. Extension Service, makes referrals to other sources of info.

50022. Vermont Natural Resources Council, 7 Main St, Montpelier, VT 05602; (802) 223-2328. Concerned with educational and governmental relations aspects of environmental protection and wise land use. Publishes quarterly magazine, periodic reports; answers inquiries; permits onsite use of collection. Services free.

50023. Vermont Water Resources Research Center, School of Natural Resources, Univ of Vt., Aiken Center, Burlington, VT 05405; (802) 656-4280. Interest in water for recreational use, limnology, measurement of watershed runoff, groundwater management. Publishes technical reports, reports for general public; answers inquiries; provides research services.

50024. Volunteers for Peace, Tiffany Rd, Belmont, VT 05730; (802) 259-2759. Recruits American volunteers for service in intl workcamps abroad; provides info to potential host communities in U.S. Publishes newsletter and International Workcamp Listing (both annual), answers inquiries, provides free advisory services.

Virginia

51004. A/C Pipe Producers Association, 1600 Wilson Blvd, Ste 1008, Arlington, VA 22209; (703) 841-1556. Central clearinghouse for info on asbestos-cement water and sewer pipe. Answers inquiries; provides advisory, reference, referral services, seminars, publications; evaluates data. Services available to members and interested groups, some at cost.

51005. Academy of Model Aeronautics, 1810 Samuel Morse Dr, Reston, VA 22090; (703) 435-0750. Promotes modeling as recognized sport, charters clubs, sponsors competitions in model aircraft flying, keeps natl and world records. Answers inquiries; provides consulting, film library services; offers liability protection, publications. Services provided at cost.

51006. Accrediting Commission on Education for Health Services Administration, 1911 N Fort Myer Dr, Ste 503, Arlington, VA 22209; (703) 524-0511. Interest in health services administration education, graduate education in health administration, planning, policy. Answers inquiries, makes referrals, permits onsite use of collection. Services free to specialists, others at discretion of ACEHSA.

51007. Adhesive and Sealant Council, 1500 N Wilson Blvd, Arlington, VA 22209; (703) 841-1112. Interest in adhesives and sealants in solid or liquid form, raw materials for adhesives and sealants, including rubber and plastics. Conducts seminars, permits onsite reference, makes info referrals.

51008. Agricultural Research Service, Tobacco Insects Investigations Laboratory, USDA, 400 N 8th St, Richmond, VA 23240; (804) 771-2551. Conducts research on control of insects that attack stored tobacco. Answers inquiries, provides consulting services and assistance in obtaining USDA publications, makes referrals.

51009. Air Traffic Control Association, 2020 N 14th St, Ste 410, Arlington, VA 22201; (703) 522-5717. Nonprofit, professional org of individuals and corporations concerned with continuing safety, reliability, efficiency of U.S. air traffic control system. Provides info free to persons interested in air traffic control system, its operational problems, and related matters.

51010. Air Conditioning and Refrigeration Institute, 1501 Wilson Blvd, Arlington, VA 22209; (703) 524-8800. Trade assn that develops, establishes standards for air conditioning and refrigeration equipment and components. Answers inquiries, provides reference and referral services, seminars, workshops, publications. Services available to members, schools, other trade assns, govt.

51011. Alliance for Perinatal Research and Services, P.O. Box 6358, Alexandria, VA 22306; (703) 765-6300. Disseminates info on childbirth, breastfeeding, women's health, children's health, parenting. Answers inquiries, provides advisory, consulting, reference services, seminars and workshops, publications. Services available at cost.

51013. Ambulatory Pediatric Association, 1311A Dolley Madison Blvd, McLean, VA 22101; (703) 556-9222. Assn, composed of 10 regional groups, interested in pediatrics (teaching, practice, research). Answers inquiries, provides reference and referral services, conducts seminars and workshops, distributes publications. Services to anyone, some free only to members.

51014. American Academy for Cerebral Palsy and Developmental Medicine, P.O. Box 11083, Richmond, VA 23230; (804) 355-0147. Interest in cerebral palsy and related handicapping conditions in children, such as developmental disabilities, myelomeningocele, and muscle diseases. Conducts courses and scientific plenary sessions, sponsors research.

51016. American Academy of Physician Assistants, 1117 N 19th St, Ste 300, Arlington, VA 22209; (703) 525-4200. Natl assn of physician assistants interested in physician assistant training, continuing medical education,

health manpower, health care delivery. Answers inquiries, provides consulting services and info referrals, permits onsite use of collection.

51018. American Alliance for Health, Physical Education, Recreation, and Dance, 1900 Association Dr, Reston, VA 22091; (703) 476-3400. Comprised of related assns, provides info on sports, dance, health and safety education, recreation for the handicapped. Answers inquiries; provides advisory, reference, placement services; conducts seminars; permits onsite use of collections. Services for a fee.

51019. American Apparel Manufacturers Association, 1611 N Kent St, Ste 800, Arlington, VA 22209; (703) 524-1864. Interest in apparel manufacturing for consumers, military, and space personnel; textiles and textile machinery; other equipment, supplies, services furnished apparel manufacturers. Answers inquiries, makes info referrals, lends films and books to nonmembers for a fee.

51020. American Art Therapy Association, 1980 Isaac Newton Square S, Reston, VA 22090; (703) 437-6012. Interest in all aspects of art therapy, guidelines for clinical and academic training, professional ethics for practitioners in field. Answers inquiries, provides advisory and reference services, distributes publications. Services to anyone, nonmembers subject to a fee.

51022. American Association for Counseling and Development, 5999 Stevenson Ave, Alexandria, VA 22304; (703) 823-9800. Interest in professional guidance; counseling; human development in schools, colleges, community orgs, govt, industry, business, and private practice. Literature collection open to the public for onsite use. Consulting, referral, limited bibliographic services provided.

51023. American Association for Laboratory Accreditation, 2045 N 15th St, Ste 1000, Arlington, VA 22201; (703) 528-0072. Primary natl general laboratory accreditation system in private sector, accredits all testing laboratories in 11 fields. Answers inquiries or refers inquirers free, conducts seminars, lab accreditations, and certifications for fees.

51024. American Association for Leisure and Recreation, 1900 Association Drive, Reston, VA 22091; (703) 476-3472. Supports and provides guidance to members in development of leisure programs; nurtures conceptualization of a philosophy of leisure. Sponsors educational programs, maintains a library.

51025. American Association of Anatomists, c/o William P. Jollie, Secty-Treas, P.O. Box 101, MCV Station, Richmond, VA 23298; (804) 786-9477. Interest in descriptive and experimental research in gross anatomy, anthropology, embryology, endocrinology, genetics, histology, neurology, other biological and medical sciences. Publishes monthly journal, quarterly newsletter, directory; answers inquiries concerning assn free.

51026. American Association of Blood Banks, 1117 N 19th St, Ste 600, Arlington, VA 22209; (703) 528-8200. Professional org for those engaged in blood banking. Collects blood, conducts inspection and accreditation program, training programs. Provides public info, regulatory updates. Labs exchange info on rare blood and blood diseases, antibodies, typing, cross-matching, compatibility testing, research.

51027. American Association of Healthcare Consultants, 1235 Jefferson Davis Hwy, Room 602, Arlington, VA 22202; (703) 979-3180. Provides analysis of need for hospital facilities, consults on hospital facilities planning, financial feasibility, construction, and equipment, hospital management, medical staff relations, more. Provides consulting and referral services, certification program, education programs.

51028. American Association of Pastoral Counselors, 9508A Lee Hwy, Fairfax, VA 22031; (703) 385-6967. Org of pastors and other religious-oriented professionals that sets standards for training in pastoral counseling, certifies persons and accredits insitutions in field. Answers inquiries, provides advisory and reference services, distributes publications. Most services free.

51029. American Association of Port Authorities, 1010 Duke St, Alexandria, VA 22314; (703) 684-5700. Interest in port administration, construction, and maintenance, ship channels and harbors, port facilities, estuarine ecology, oil spillage and ship sewage, coastal zone management. Answers inquiries free, sells publications. Services primarily for members, but others assisted.

51030. American Association of School Administrators, 1801 N Moore St, Arlington, VA 22209; (703) 528-0700. Interest in elementary and secondary education, including curriculum evaluation, planning, discipline, public relations, more. Answers inquiries, provides advisory and reference services, permits onsite use of collections. Some services provided at cost.

51031. American Association of Tissue Banks, 1117 N 19th St, Arlington, VA; (703) 528-0663. Establishes standards for retrieval, preservation, and distribution of transplantable tissues, encourages development of regional tissue banks, undertakes educational programs to stimulate donation of tissues and improve efficiency of tissue banking. Inquiries answered.

51032. American Astronautical Society, 6060 Tower Ct, Alexandria, VA 22304; (703) 751-7721. Interest in astronautics, utilization of space, spacecraft, space flight, astrodynamics, bioastronautics, navigation, propulsion, orbits, trajectories, solar physics, radiation, more. Answers inquiries, conducts symposia, makes info referrals. Materials available for purchase.

51033. American Automobile Association, 8111 Gatehouse Rd, Falls Church, VA 22047; (703) 222-6466 (Library). Interest in travel, traffic engineering and safety, pedestrian protection and safety, hotels, motels, automobiles, highway planning, road maps, vacation planning, insurance, business management. Answers inquiries, provides referrals and other services, permits onsite reference.

51034. American Blood Commission, 1117 N 19th St, Ste 501, Arlington, VA 22209; (703) 522-8414. Dedicated to assuring a safe and adequate blood supply available to all at reasonable cost. Answers inquiries, provides advisory and reference services, conducts seminars, distributes publications. Some services may be provided at cost.

51037. American Boiler Manufacturers Association, 950 N Glebe Rd, Ste 160, Arlington, VA 22203; (703) 522-7350. Promotes welfare of boiler industry, improves its services to the public. Answers inquiries or refers inquirers to other info sources free, conducts seminars by invitation, sells publications.

51038. American Boxwood Society, P.O. Box 85 (Blandy Experimental Farm, Univ of Va.), Boyce, VA 22620; (703) 837-1758. Intl boxwood registration authority interested in propagation, care, and usage of boxwoods, boxwood fungus diseases. Answers inquiries, provides R&D info, permits onsite use of collection, sells publications. Services free to members, others assisted.

51039. American Canoe Association, P.O. Box 248 (7217 Lockport Pl), Lorton, VA 22079; (703) 550-7523. Governing body for natl and intl canoe competition in U.S. Answers inquiries; provides reference services, workshops, publications, videotapes, films; permits onsite use of collections. Services free, except publications, film rentals, etc.

51040. American Cemetery Association, 5201 Leesburg Pike, Ste 1111, Falls Church, VA 22041; (703) 379-5838. Interest in cemetery management, administration, financing, maintenance, operations, sales techniques. Answers inquiries, provides reference services, conducts workshops, distributes publications. Fees for some services, lower rate for members.

51041. American Chamber of Commerce Executives, 1454 Duke St, Alexandria, VA 22314; (703) 836-7904. Interest in enhancement of personal growth, development, and management effectiveness of chamber of commerce execs. Answers inquiries, conducts seminars, distributes publications, makes info referrals. Services at cost to nonmembers.

51042. American Child Care Services, P.O. Box 548 (532 Settlers Landing Rd), Hampton, VA 23669; (804) 722-4495. Private foundation interested in child care and early childhood education and development. Provides educational cassette tapes for personnel within child care field, employment info.

51043. American Chiropractic Association, 1916 Wilson Blvd, Arlington, VA 22201; (703) 276-8800. Interest in human spine, its anatomy and pathology, diagnosis of spinal ailments, manipulative therapy and physiotherapy, chiropractic theory, chiropractic management. Answers general inquiries, makes info reterrals. Bibliographic service free to professional societies, at cost to others.

51044. American Cocoa Research Institute, 7900 Westpark Dr, Ste 514, McLean, VA 22101; (703) 790-5011. Center for technical cocoa problems. Disseminates scientific and educational info relating to culture, growing, handling, and distribution of cocoa plants, products. Finances cocoa research. Answers inquiries, lends materials, permits onsite use of collection. Services free to researchers.

51045. American College of Radiology, 1891 Preston White Dr, Reston, VA 22091; (703) 648-8900. Advances science of radiology, represents radiologists. Services include publications, ed accreditation, seminars, professional placement, and mgmt consultation.

51046. American Committee for South Asian Art, 3222 Brookings Ct, Fairfax, VA 22031; (703) 591-1193. Interest in art and archeology of India, Nepal, Pakistan, Sri Lanka, and Bangladesh, including Buddhist, Hindu, Jain, and Moslem monuments. Answers inquiries, provides info on current research, distributes publications. Some services free, others subject to membership fee.

51047. American Concrete Pipe Association, 8320 Old Court House Rd, Vienna, VA 22180; (703) 821-1990. Interest in design, manufacture, and installation of precast concrete pipe and box sections for sanitary and storm sewers, culverts, other uses. Answers inquiries or refers inquirers to other sources of info free.

51048. American Congress on Surveying and Mapping, 210 Little Falls St, Falls Church, VA 22046; (703) 241-2446. Interest in the broad field of surveying and mapping, including geodesy, cartography, field and photogrammetric surveying, related land data and mapping systems. Answers inquiries; provides pamphlets on careers, listings of colleges and universities offering courses in those disciplines.

51049. American Defense Preparedness Association, 1700 N Moore St, Ste 900, Arlington, VA 22209; (703) 522-1820. Interest in all weapons systems, including artillery, bombs, warhead, and artillery ammunition, combat and tactical vehicles, electronics, fire control instruments, missiles small arms, etc. Provides consulting, reference services to govt agencies.

51050. American Dental Trade Association, 4222 King St, Alexandria, VA 22302; (703) 379-7755. Trade assn of manufacturers and distributors of dental products. Evaluates data, distributes publications, makes referrals to other sources of info. Services primarily for members, but educational, govtal institutions assisted.

51051. American Diabetes Association, 1660 Duke St, Alexandria, VA 22314; (703) 549-1500; (800) 232-3472. Created to fight diabetes through education and research. Uses volunteers to organize educational, screening programs and conduct fund raising activi-

ties to support research. Conducts symposia and patient education programs, publishes journals.

51052. American Driver and Traffic Safety Education Association, 123 N Pitt St, Ste 509, Alexandria, VA 22314; (703) 836-4748. Interest in driver, pedestrian, and traffic safety education in schools, colleges. Provides consulting services on state driver and safety education conferences. Services limited by time available.

51054. American Federation of Information Processing Societies, 1899 Preston White Dr, Reston, VA 22091; (703) 620-8900. Interest in all aspects of info processing related to development and application of computer and data processing, including all new uses of computers, software. Answers inquiries; provides resources, expert witnesses, panel seminars.

51055. American Feed Industry Association, 1701 N Fort Myer Dr, Arlington, VA 22209; (703) 524-0810. Interest in animal and poultry feeds, feed production, marketing, animal nutrition. Answers inquiries, provides info on industry, makes info referrals.

51056. American Gas Association Library, 1515 Wilson Blvd, Arlington, VA 22209; (703) 841-8400. Collects info on natural gas transmission and distribution, gas industry and technology, appliance research, liquefied natural gas, pipelines, energy in general. Answers inquiries; provides reference, referral, other services; permits onsite use of collections by appointment.

51057. American Gear Manufacturers Association, 1901 N Fort Myer Dr, Ste 1000, Arlington, VA 22209; (703) 525-1600. Specializes in gears, including generating equipment, lubrication, standards, measuring methods, metallurgy and materials, and nomenclature. Sells standards.

51058. American Geological Institute, 4220 King St, Alexandria, VA 22302; (703) 379-2480. Interest in earth sciences, geological education, including curriculum improvement, computer-based bibliographic services, geoscience news. Answers written inquiries about its programs and publications, makes referrals. Bibliographic data base, GeoRef, provides online access to geological literature of the world.

51060. American Group Practice Association, 1422 Duke Street, Alexandria, VA 22314; (703) 838-0033. Represents group practice physicians, promotes development of high standards of care for medical group practices. Monitors legislation; accredits group practices; provides reference services, management workshops, patient education materials.

51061. American Helicopter Society, 217 N Washington St, Alexandria, VA 22314; (703) 684-6777. Interest in helicopters, VTOL/STOL aircraft. Answers inquiries, makes referrals, provides reference services.

51062. American Holistic Medical Association, 6932 Little River Turnpike, Annandale, VA 22003; (703) 642-5880. Nonprofit physicians org that seeks to expand use of holistic medicine, establish standards for new concepts of therapy, and provide new tools for practitioners. Answers inquiries, provides advisory and reference services, conducts workshops, distributes publications. Services available to health professionals for a fee.

51063. American Horticultural Society, 7931 E Boulevard Dr, Alexandria, VA, Mount Vernon, VA 22121; (703) 768-5700. Nonprofit org that promotes better understanding of gardening and its impact on our lives and environment. Answers inquiries, provides consulting services, conducts seminars, distributes publications, permits onsite use of collections.

51064. American Industrial Arts Association, 1914 Assn Dr, Reston, VA 22091; (703) 860-2100. Assn of educators, guidance counselors, curriculum specialists, business people interested in educational programs dealing with development of technological literacy, industrial arts. Answers inquiries, provides reference services.

51065. American Institute for Cancer Research, 500 N Washington St, Falls Church, VA 22046; (703) 237-0159. Nonprofit org that informs public on how to reduce risk of cancer and how to detect early signs. Concentrates on holistic methods, diet, stress reduction, nutrition, informs public about unethical practitioners and groups. Also supports various types of cancer research, sponsors conferences.

51066. American Intellectual Property Law Association, 2001 Jefferson Davis Hwy, Ste 203, Arlington, VA 22202; (703) 521-1680. Interest in patent, trademark, copyright, intellectual property, technology transfer, invention, and innovation. Answers inquiries, conducts seminars, evaluates data, and distributes publications. Services free to govt agencies, at cost to others.

51067. American Intraocular Implant Society, 3700 Pender Dr, Ste 108, Fairfax, VA 22030; (703) 591-2220. Nonprofit org that disseminates info concerning intraocular lens implantation, ophthalmic surgery, cataract extraction. Answers inquiries, provides advisory and referral services, conducts seminars, distributes publications. Services free to members.

51068. American Judges Association, 300 Newport Ave, Williamsburg, VA 23185; (804) 253-2000. Interest in judges, courts, law, judicial education. Answers inquiries.

51070. American Life Lobby, P.O. Box 490 (Route 6, Box 162-F), Stafford, VA 22554; (703) 659-4171. Nonprofit org involved in research, dissemination of materials pertaining to life, family, related issues such as abortion, infanticide, euthanasia, sex education, birth control. Answers inquiries, provides referrals, workshops, publications. Services free, except cost of materials.

51071. American Movers Conference, 2200 Mill Rd, Alexandria, VA 22314; (703) 838-1931. Interest in interstate moving industry. Answers inquiries for consumer assistance and general industry info, sponsors research, distributes consumer publications, makes referrals to other sources of info. Services free to members, may be provided for a fee to others.

51072. American Needlepoint Guild, 2431 Poe Lane, Petersburg, VA 23803; (804) 732-9140. Seeks to advance participation in and encouragement of interest in art and history of needlepoint. Answers inquiries; provides advisory, reference services; distributes correspondence courses, publications, conducts workshops, exhibitions. Services primarily for members, others assisted as time permits.

51074. American Paralysis Association, Research Division, 7655 Old Springhouse Rd, McLean, VA 22102; (703) 556-7782. Supports research directed toward a cure for paralysis caused by spinal cord injury, head injury, and stroke. Answers inquiries, sponsors workshops, evaluates data, provides info on current research, publishes newsletter. Services free.

51075. American Physical Therapy Association, 1111 N Fairfax St, Alexandria, VA 22314; (703) 684-2782. Works to improve physical therapy education, practice, and research, sets standards, participates in preparation and revision of licensure examinations, accredits educational programs. Supplies info and advice to members, institutions, agencies, other assns; conducts conference, courses.

51077. American Pipe Fittings Association, 8136 Old Keene Mill Rd, Springfield, VA 22152; (703) 644-0001. Natl trade org representing U.S. manufacturers of different types of pipe fittings and pipe hangers and supports. Interested in pipe fittings industry technology, standards, promotion. Answers inquiries, provides reference services, makes info referrals.

51078. American Press Institute, 11690 Sunrise Valley Dr, Reston, VA 22091; (703) 620-3611. Conducts management development and product quality improvement seminars for daily and weekly newspapers of U.S. and Canada. Answers inquiries. Services primarily for professional newspaper personnel. Journalism students may not attend seminars, but may receive other services.

51079. American Production and Inventory Control Society, 500 W Annandale Rd, Falls Church, VA 22046-4274; (703) 237-8344. Interest in production planning, production control, inventory management, materials management, physical distribution. Answers inquiries, makes referrals, permits onsite use of collection of technical reports, newsletters, bibliographies, pamphlets, etc.

51080. American Society for Cybernetics, c/o Stephen Ruth, V.P., Dept of Decision Sciences, George Mason Univ, Fairfax, VA 22030; (703) 323-2738. Interest in current developments in cybernetics and related fields, including epistemology, neurophysiology, artificial intelligence, more. Answers inquiries, holds conferences, conducts seminars, distributes publications, makes info referrals. Services available at cost.

51081. American Society for Horticultural Science, Attn: Cecil Blackwell, Exec Dir, 701 N Saint Asaph St, Alexandria, VA 22314; (703) 836-4606. Interest in breeding and genetics of crop plants, growth and development, postharvest physiology of plants, food science, horticulture, pomology, viticulture, insecticides, fungicides, herbicides, growth-regulator chemicals. Answers brief inquiries, sells publications.

51082. American Society for Industrial Security, 1655 N Fort Myer Dr, Ste 1200, Arlington, VA 22209; (703) 522-5800. Natl society of protection professionals interested in all aspects of business security, including white collar crime, terrorism, computer security, privacy, etc. Answers inquiries; provides reference, referral services; conducts seminars, exhibitions. Most services provided to nonmembers within limits.

51083. American Society for Personnel Administration, 606 N Washington St, Alexandria, VA 22314; (703) 548-3440. Specializes in personnel administration, industrial relations, human resource management, employee relations. Provides consulting services, info referrals; conducts conferences, workshops, seminars. Consulting services primarily for members, seminars open to all.

51084. American Society for Photogrammetry and Remote Sensing, 210 Little Falls St, Falls Church, VA 22046; (703) 534-6617. Promotes photogrammetry and remote sensing (sciences of making reliable measurements by means of photography or sensors using other parts of the energy spectrum). Answers inquiries; provides advisory, employment, info services; conducts seminars; distributes publications. Most services free, non-members assisted.

51085. American Society for Psychoprophylaxis in Obstetrics, 1840 Wilson Blvd, Ste 204, Arlington, VA 22201; (703) 524-7802. Membership org for physicians, childbirth educators, parents, interested in Lamaze method of childbirth, obstetrics, parenting, family-centered maternity care. Answers brief inquiries, provides speakers, physician referrals, teacher training and certification program, parenting program.

51086. American Society of Agricultural Consultants, 8301 Greensboro Dr, Ste 470, McLean, VA 22101; (703) 356-2455. Specializes in agribusiness, agricultural consultants. Provides advisory and consulting services, makes referrals to other sources of info. Fees may be charged for services.

51087. American Society of Consultant Pharmacists, 2300 Ninth St S, Ste 503, Arlington, VA 22204; (703) 920-8492. Natl group of pharmacists providing pharmacy and nondispensing consultant pharmacist services to long-term care facilities and other institutions. Answers inquiries, conducts seminars, distributes publications. Services mostly free.

51088. American Society of Extra-Corporeal Technology, 1980 Isaac Newton Square S, Reston, VA 22090; (703) 435-8556. Promotes profession of perfusion and life-support technology, utilized in the interest of providing better patient care. Answers inquiries, provides info referrals, distributes publications. Services free, except publications, available to members, students, manufacturers.

51089. American Society of Military Comptrollers, P.O. Box 91, Mount Vernon, VA 22121; (703) 780-6164. Specializies in military comptrollership, financial management, accounting, finance, budgeting, auditing, cost analysis, electronic data processing, management analysis. Conducts conventions and seminars, distributes publication. Services generally free.

51090. American Textile Machinery Association, 7297 Lee Hwy, Ste N, Falls Church, VA 22042; (703) 533-9251. Interest in textile machinery, textiles, dyeing of fabrics. Answers inquiries, provides consulting services, makes referrals, lends materials. The American Textile Machinery Exhibition-Intl held every two years.

51091. American Tobacco Co., Research and Development Library, P.O. Box 899 (13101 N Enon Church Rd, Chester, VA), Hopewell, VA 23860; (804) 748-4561. Interest in tobacco, biochemistry, engineering, mathematics, physics, plant physiology, production quality control, ecology. Answers brief inquiries, permits limited onsite use of collection by arrangement.

51092. American Trucking Associations, 2200 Mill Rd, Alexandria, VA 22314; (703) 838-1870 (Public Relations); (703) 838-1880 (Library). Interest in transportation, particularly by motor carriers, highway construction, motor equipment, motor carrier statistics and research, trucking, legislative and regulatory matters. Answers inquiries, provides reference and consulting services, permits onsite reference by appointment only.

51093. American Vocational Association, 2020 N 14th St, Arlington, VA 22201; (703) 522-6121. Org of educators interested in all areas of vocational education, including agricultural, business education, home economics, health occupations, industrial arts, employment and training programs. Answers inquiries, makes info referrals, permits onsite use of collection.

51094. American Waterways Operators, 1600 Wilson Blvd, Ste 1000, Arlington, VA 22209; (703) 841-9300. Interest in transportation provided by towboats, tugboats, barges, self-propelled freighters and tankers, etc. on 25,543 miles of commercially navigable waterways of U.S. Answers inquiries, lends materials.

51095. American Wind Energy Association Data Center, 1516 King St, Alexandria, VA 22314; (703) 684-5196. Trade assn for wind energy industry. Promotes application and use of wind energy conversion systems as a renewable, nonpolluting energy source. Answers inquiries, sells publications, conducts seminars, permits onsite use of collection. Most services free.

51096. American Wood Preservers Bureau, P.O. Box 6085 (2772 S Randolph St), Arlington, VA 22206; (703) 931-8180. Conducts quality assurance program on preservatively-treated wood products. Provides advisory services, issues and implements quality assurance standards on preserved wood products, distributes standards. Services may be provided for a fee.

51097. Animal Health Institute, P.O. Box 1417-D50 (119 Oronoco St), Alexandria, VA 22313; (703) 684-0011. Assn of animal health and nutrition products industry. Answers inquiries, provides statistics, makes referrals. Services primarily for members, but also provided to academic institutions, govt agencies, press, interested assns.

51098. Anti-Friction Bearings Manufacturers Association, 1235 Jefferson Davis Hwy, Ste 704, Arlington, VA 22202; (703) 979-1261. Interest in ball bearings, roller bearings, balls and rollers for bearings. Holds technical info and statistics on imports, exports, and U.S. production. Answers inquiries free, sells publications.

51099. Architectural Woodwork Institute, 2310 S Walter Reed Dr, Arlington, VA 22206; (703) 671-9100. Specializes in architectural woodwork, including promotion of its use, quality standards, cost estimating systems, and cost accounting for architectural woodwork firms. Provides reference, document services to members, architects, engineers, specification writers.

51101. Armed Forces Communications and Electronics Association, 5641 Burke Centre Parkway, Burke, VA 22015; (703) 425-8500; (800) 336-4583. Involved in development, design, production, maintenance, and operation of communications, command and control, intelligence systems, electronics, computer sciences, teleprocessing, and photographic equipment. Answers govt, military, and industry inquiries.

51102. Army Engineer School Hotline, U.S. Army Corps of Engineers, Attn: ATZA-TD-P, Fort Belvoir, VA 22060-5291; (703) 664-3646, 354-3646; (800) 336-3095 ext 43646 (WATS: outside Va. only). Hotline is a 24-hour telephone answering service that records questions or problems to U.S. Army Engineer School. Answers legitimate inquiries or refers inquirers to other info sources. Services free to all branches, components of military.

51103. Army Foreign Science and Technology Center, 220 Seventh St NE, Charlottesville, VA 22901; (804) 296-5171 ext 513. Provides army with foreign scientific and technical info on all subjects of interest to ground forces research and development (no U.S. info). Answers inquiries, provides reference services, makes interlibrary loans (only for authorized govt agencies). Some reports sold to public.

51104. Army Logistics Management Center, Army Materi-al Command, Fort Lee, VA 23801; (804) 734-3500. Largest AMC school, trains interns, top and middle managers, journeymen for AMC work force and logis-

tics community of army and Dept of Defense. Provides advisory, instructional services to DoD, other govt agencies; makes interlibrary loans and provides other library services as time permits.

51105. Army Quartermaster Center Museum, Army Quartermaster Corps, Fort Lee, VA 23801; (804) 734-1854. Museum of artifacts related to history of Army Quartermaster Corps, including uniforms, heraldic insignia, chevrons, flags, subsistence, mortuary, etc. Answers inquiries, provides advisory and reference services, evaluates data, permits onsite use of collections. Services free to all.

51106. Army Transportation Museum, Fort Eustis, VA 23604; (804) 878-3603. Resource center specializing in history of U.S. Army transportation from Revolutionary War to present, history of Fort Eustis and area. Answers inquiries; provides reference, referral, reproduction services; permits onsite use of collection. Services generally free.

51107. Arthritis Information Clearinghouse, Natl Institute of Arthritis, Diabetes, and Digestive and Kidney Diseases, Natl Institutes of Health, P.O. Box 9782 (1700 N. Moore St), Arlington, VA 20892; (703) 558-8250. Helps health professionals locate print and audiovisual educational materials concerned with arthritis and related diseases. Distributes publications, conducts searches of data base, other bibliographic sources. Services free, available to health care professionals only.

51109. Asbestos Information Association/North America, 1745 Jefferson Davis Hwy, Ste 509, Arlington, VA 22202; (703) 979-1150. Group of asbestos companies in U.S. and Canada working together to inform public about the asbestos industry, asbestos and health. Answers inquiries; provides advisory, reference, other services; sells publications; permits onsite use of collection. Services free.

51110. Associated Telephone Answering Exchanges, Information Services, 320 King St, Ste 500, Alexandria, VA 22314; (703) 684-0016. Trade assn for live telephone answering service industry. Interested in live and automated systems, marketing, industry statistics. Answers recurrent questions with prepared info packets. Provides limited additional reference services, conducts seminars. Services available for a fee.

51111. Associated Writing Programs, c/o Old Dominion Univ, Norfolk, VA 23508; (804) 440-3839. Provides info on creative writing for writers, teachers, and students, and degree programs in writing. Answers inquiries; provides advisory, consulting, placement services; conducts seminars; distributes publications. Placement available to writers, teachers, students; other services available to anyone.

51112. Association for Communication Administration, 5105 Backlick Rd, Ste E, Annandale, VA 22003; (703) 750-0534. Interest in higher education in the communication arts and sciences, including advertising, film, journalism, public relations, theater. Answers inquiries, provides consulting services for program review, conducts seminars, distributes publications, permits onsite use of collection. Services available for a fee.

51114. Association for Education and Rehabilitation of the Blind and Visually Impaired, 206 N Washington St, Alexandria, VA 22314; (703) 836-6060. Interest in education and rehabilitation of the visually handicapped. Publishes monthly Job Exchange, answers inquiries, conducts seminars and workshops, makes referrals. Services free.

51116. Association for Research and Enlightenment, Library, P.O. Box 595 (67th and Atlantic Ave), Va. Beach, VA 23451; (804) 428-3588. Disseminates readings of Edgar Cayce (1877-1945), a psychic who, by entering into a self-induced state of unconsciousness, claimed he had access to info on virtually any subject. Answers inquiries, provides reference services, conducts workshops, distributes publications, permits onsite use of collections. Info available to anyone.

51117. Association for Supervision and Curriculum Development, Resource Information Service, 225 N Washington St, Alexandria, VA 22314; (703) 549-9110. Collects info on educational supervision, curriculum, and instruction. Answers inquiries or refers inquirers to other sources of info, permits onsite use of collection free to all; other services available to members.

51118. Association for the Advancement of Health Education, 1900 Assn Dr, Reston, VA 22091; (703) 476-3440. Interest in all areas related to health education. Answers inquiries; provides advisory, reference, referral services; conducts seminars; sells publications. Some services free.

51120. Association for the Advancement of Medical Instrumentation, 1901 N Fort Myer Dr, Ste 602, Arlington, VA 22209; (703) 525-4890. Interest in medical instrumentation, including aspects of technology, applications, education, service, maintenance, standards. Answers inquiries, makes referrals.

51121. Association for the Education and Rehabilitation of the Blind and Visually Impaired, 206 N Washington St, Alexandria, VA 22314; (703) 548-1884. Nonprofit membership org founded for orgs, individuals involved in the field of blindness. Provides a forum for exchange of ideas; provides leadership through seminars, workshops, conferences.

51122. Association of American Pesticide Control Officials, c/o Harry K. Rust, Secty, Div of Product and Industry Regulation, Va. Dept of Agriculture and Consumer Service, P.O. Box 1163, Richmond, VA 23209; (804) 786-3798. Tracks enforcement of laws and regulations concerned with registration, labeling, distribution, sale, use, and custom application of pesticides. Answers inquiries, makes referrals relating to regulatory and enforcement work of member agencies.

51124. Association of American Physicians and Surgeons, 5201 Lyngate Court, Burke, VA 22015; (703) 425-6300.

Surgeons and physicians united for purpose of analyzing the profession's problems, protecting the practice of private medicine, educating physicians and public to defeat schemes that would destroy free-choice system of medical care. Lobbies Congress.

51125. Association of Data Processing Service Organizations, 1300 N 17th St, Ste 300, Arlington, VA 22209; (703) 522-5055. Trade assn of computer services industry. Works to protect industry from unlawful competition and unwise govtl regulations and legislation, improve industry standards and management performance. Answers inquiries or refers inquirers to other info sources.

51126. Association of Earth Science Editors, c/o American Geological Institute, 4220 King St, Alexandria, VA 22302. Professional assn of editors and publications managers of principal North American earth-science journals and fed and state geological surveys. Info services limited, but will attempt to answer inquiries directly or by referral to appropriate AESE members.

51127. Association of Former Intelligence Officers, 6723 Whittier Ave, Ste 303A, McLean, VA 22101; (703) 790-0320. Nonpartisan org that believes "a responsive intelligence service is vital to security of U.S." Interested in U.S. security, intelligence systems and services. Provides research, lecture material, speakers, writers on intelligence matters for educational forums, civic groups, TV, radio.

51128. Association of Governmental Appraisers, 4201 John Marr Dr, Ste 233, Annandale, VA 22003; (703) 941-8878. Membership org of employees of govtl and quasi-govtl agencies who require an understanding of appraisal theory and practice. Answers inquiries, provides reference services, conducts seminars, has 24-hour job referral service, permits onsite use of collection. Services generally free to anyone.

51129. Association of Labor-Management Administrators and Consultants on Alcoholism, 1800 N Kent St, Ste 907, Arlington, VA 22209; (703) 522-6272. Interest in occupational alcoholism and employee assistance programs. Answers inquiries, provides referral services, conducts seminars and workshops, distributes publications. Most services are free.

51130. Association of Medical Illustrators, 2692 Huguenot Springs Rd, Midlothian, VA 23113; (804) 794-2908. Interest in field of medical illustration, accredited schools of medical illustration. Answers inquiries or refers inquirers to other sources of info.

51131. Association of Official Analytical Chemists, 1111 N 19th St, Ste 210, Arlington, VA 22209; (703) 522-3032. Interest in analytical chemistry, other methods of analysis for beverages, foods, food additives, vitamins, drugs, any product or substance affecting public health, environment, economic protection of the consumer. Answers inquiries, makes referrals, provides reference services.

51133. Association of University Anesthetists, c/o Edward D. Miller, Jr., M.D., Secty, Dept of Anesthesia, Univ of Va. Medical School, P.O. Box 238, Charlottesville, VA 22908. Interest in anesthesia, physiology, pharmacology, biomedical engineering, biochemistry, surgery, medicine. Publishes directory, answers inquiries, provides consulting services. Services at cost.

51134. Autometric, Skyline I, Ste 1308, 5205 Leesburg Pike, Falls Church, VA 22041; (703) 998-7606. Interest in photogrammetric mapping, remote sensing, aerial surveying, computer-graphic processing, digital graphic info systems, more. Answers inquiries, provides consulting and product services, conducts seminars and workshops, analyzes data. Services provided for a fee.

51135. Babcock and Wilcox Co., Library, Utility Power Generation Div, P.O. Box 1260 (3315 Old Forest Rd), Lynchburg, VA 24505; (804) 385-2475. Resource center on nuclear power reactors, nuclear engineering, nuclear physics, chemistry, energy and technology. Answers inquiries, provides reference services, makes interlibrary loans, permits onsite use of collections by appointment only. Services free, offered on time-available basis.

51136. Blandy Experimental Farm—Orland E. White Arboretum, P.O. Box 175, Boyce, VA 22620; (703) 837-1758. Resource center for agriculture, botany, horticulture. Holdings include a large collection of living plants, records of 17,000 plant species planted at the farm. Answers brief inquiries, makes referrals, lends materials. Extensive services provided only to noncommercial orgs, individuals.

51137. Boat/U.S. Foundation for Boating, Safety Reference Resource Center, 880 S Pickett St, Alexandria, VA 22304; (703) 823-9550. Nonprofit org for boating safety education and research. Answers inquiries, operates nationwide toll-free number to provide info on boat courses, distributes boating safety materials, makes info referrals, permits onsite use of collections by appointment.

51138. Boone and Crockett Club, 205 S Patrick St, Alexandria, VA 22314; (703) 548-7727. Interest in big game hunting in North America, conservation of big game animals, study of their habitats and natural history, predator-prey relations, travel. Holds computerized archives of North American big game trophy data. Answers inquiries, makes info referral.

51139. Brick Institute of America, 11490 Commerce Park Dr, Ste 300, Reston, VA 22091; (703) 620-0010. Interest in brick masonry construction and design. Answers inquiries, provides advisory services, permits limited onsite use of collection, sells and distributes publications. Services available to professionals.

51140. Cable Television Information Center, 1800 N Kent St, Arlington, VA 22209; (703) 528-6836. Assists local officials in making decisions about public policy issues related to cable television: financial feasibility, regula-

tion, municipal uses, more. Answers inquiries free, provides advisory services on implementation of cable television, conducts seminars, distributes publications for a fee.

51141. Cast Iron Soil Pipe Institute, 1499 Chain Bridge Rd, Ste 203, McLean, VA 22101; (703) 827-9177. Interest in cast iron plumbing pipes, research and development in the drain, waste, and vent plumbing field, cast iron fittings and products. Answers inquiries, provides free advisory services, distributes publications, makes referrals to other info sources.

51142. Center for Consumer Health Education, 1900 Assn Dr, Reston, VA 22091; (703) 860-9090. Nonprofit center that promotes self-responsibility for health, with interest in preventive medicine, self-care, minimizing risks of major diseases, etc. Provides consulting services, evaluates health programs, offers training programs, distributes publications. Services free or at cost.

51143. Center for Energy and Environmental Management, P.O. Box 536 (11726) Winterway Lane), Fairfax, VA 22030; (703) 250-5900. Nonprofit org that provides products and services aimed at improving energy and environmental specialty management process. Answers inquiries; provides advisory, reference, other services; conducts conferences, courses, seminars; evaluates data. Services provided for a fee.

51144. Center for Oceans Law and Policy, School of Law, Univ of Va., Charlottesville, VA 22901; (804) 924-7441. Specializes in oceans law and policy, coastal and polar areas, ocean resources development, energy policy, boundary delimitation, naval security. Answers inquiries, provides consulting services, conducts seminars, distributes publications, permits onsite use of collections. Most services free, available to all.

51145. Center for Palladian Studies in America, c/o School of Architecture, Univ of Va., P.O. Box 5643, Charlottesville, VA 22905; (804) 924-6448. Nonprofit org seeks to define "Palladianism," to discover American "Palladian" buildings and to present its findings to the public. Answers inquiries; conducts scholarly studies, seminars, lectures; distributes publications. Services available to dues-paying members (membership open).

51146. Century Research Corp., 4113 Lee Hwy, Arlington, VA 22207; (703) 527-5373. Interest in human-factors engineering, motivation research, systems analysis, programmed instruction, highway safety, attitude and opinion assessment, more. Answers inquiries; provides consulting, reference, referral services—free to scientists if mutually beneficial. Students assisted.

51148. Children's Hospice International, 501 Slaters Lane, No 207, Alexandria, VA 22314; (703) 556-0421. Promotes hospice support through pediatric care facilities; encourages inclusion of children in hospices, home care programs; promotes public and professional awareness of hospice care for children; coordinates support for families of terminally ill children; provides info on resources.

51149. Chocolate Manufacturers Association of the U.S., 7900 Westpark Dr, Ste 514, McLean, VA 22102; (703) 790-5011. Engages in research to improve manufacturing procedures and techniques, public relations programs, govt relations activities affecting chocolate manufacturing operations. Answers inquiries, distributes publications, permits onsite use of library.

51150. Citizens Clearinghouse for Hazardous Wastes, P.O. Box 926, Arlington, VA 22216; (703) 276-7070. Nonprofit org that provides citizen groups, individuals, municipalities with info to assist them in dealing with hazardous waste problems. Answers inquiries; provides consulting, reference, other services; distributes publications. Services generally free.

51152. Colonial Williamsburg Foundation Research Center, Drawer C (Henry and Francis Sts), Williamsburg, VA 23187; (804) 229-1000 ext 2275. Devoted to 18th-century Virginia, American and British history, agriculture, architecture, demography, 18th-century music, Virginia colonial records. Answers inquiries, provides use of library resources. Open to scholars (appointment preferred).

51153. Commission on Accreditation for Law Enforcement Agencies, 4242B Chain Bridge Rd, Fairfax, VA 22030; (703) 352-4225. Nonprofit corp that promotes professional excellence in law enforcement through accreditation. Standards for accreditation were developed with cooperation of natl and intl law enforcement assns. Answers inquiries, provides info on commission activities, serves as liaison for applicant and accredited agencies, distributes publications.

51154. Committee for Purchase from the Blind and Other Severely Handicapped, Crystal Square 5, Ste 1107, 1755 Jefferson Davis Hwy, Arlington, VA 22202; (703) 557-1145. Directs procurement of selected products and services by fed govt to qualified workshops for the blind and other severely handicapped, to establish fair market price for these products, services. Answers inquiries, makes referrals.

51155. Community Associations Institute Research Foundation, 1423 Powhatan St, Ste 8, Alexandria, VA 22314; (703) 548-8600. Gathers info and initiates research on emerging issues related to management of condominiums, housing cooperatives, community assns. Answers inquiries, provides referrals and info on current research, conducts seminars, distributes publications. Some services subject to a fee.

51156. Compressed Gas Association, 1235 Jefferson Davis Hwy, Arlington, VA 22202; (703) 979-0900. Interest in safe handling, storing, transporting of chemical and natural gases in gaseous, liquid, or solid form, including atmospheric gases, hydrocarbons, poisonous gases. Answers inquiries, sells publications, makes referrals. Services free.

51157. Computer Law Association, c/o Administrator, 9520 Lee Hwy, Ste A, Fairfax, VA 22031; (703) 591-7014. Studies legal problems related to computer and communications technology, software protection, taxation. Answers inquiries, conducts seminars, provides resume clearinghouse for members, makes referrals, sells transcripts. Services for lawyers, companies in field, but may be available to anyone.

51158. Computer Measurement Group, 101 S Whiting, No 302, Alexandria, VA 22304; (703) 370-3979. Assn of professionals in data processing concerned with productivity and technology of computer performance and evaluation. Answers inquiries; provides reference, referral services; conducts meetings, annual conference. Services provided at cost.

51159. Conservation Resources International, 8000 H Forbes Pl, Springfield, VA 22151; (703) 321-7730. Commercial consulting firm interested in preservation of library, archive, museum, and individual collections, specialized equipment for preservation of historic materials. Answers inquiries, provides advisory, consulting, referral services. Except for consultations, services free.

51160. Conservative Alliance, 1001 Prince St, Ste 100, Alexandria, VA 22314; (703) 684-3980. Nonprofit org concerned with Soviet human rights violations; statistics on—and effects of—U.S. trade with and aid to Communist govts. Answers inquiries, provides reference and referral services, distributes publications. Services free to public. Some data available at a fee to Congress, congressional candidates.

51161. Construction Products Manufacturers Council, 1600 Wilson Blvd, Arlington, VA 22209; (703) 522-0613. Assn of building products manufacturers. Answers inquiries, provides info, reference services. Construction marketing seminars held annually.

51162. Construction Specifications Institute, 601 Madison St, Alexandria, VA 22314; (703) 684-0300. Dedicated to improvement of communications, specifications, and building practices in construction industry through service, education, and research. Answers inquiries, provides reference and educational services, makes info referrals.

51163. Consumer Bankers Association, 1300 N 17th St, Arlington, VA 22209; (703) 276-1750. Interest in retail banking in commercial banks, other federally insured depository institutions, including savings and loan assns, mutual savings banks, credit unions. Answers inquiries, makes referrals, provides reference services. Primarily for members or persons in retail banking.

51164. Continental Quilting Congress, P.O. Box 561 (1604 Palm Springs Dr), Vienna, VA 22180; (703) 938-3246. Nonprofit org that promotes quilting as an art form. Answers inquiries; provides reference, referral services; conducts conventions, seminars, and workshops; sponsors quilt shows. Services may be provided for a fee.

51165. Council for Accreditation of Counseling and Related Educational Programs, c/o American Assn for Counseling and Development, 5999 Stevenson Ave, Alexandria, VA 22304; (703) 823-9800. Independent org that works with colleges and univs offering counselor education and related programs so they might achieve full accreditation status. Answers inquiries, conducts accreditation program, distributes publications. Primarily for professionals, others assisted within limits.

51166. Council for Exceptional Children, Department of Information Services, 1920 Assn Dr, Reston, VA 22091; (703) 620-3660. Interest in education of gifted and handicapped children, special education. Answers inquiries; provides advisory, reference, referral services and computer searches; conducts workshops; distributes publications. Onsite use of collection free; users charged for other products, services.

51167. Council of American Building Officials, 5205 Leesburg Pike, Ste 201, Falls Church, VA 22041; (703) 931-4533. Specializes in building code coordination; energy conservation and its enforcement in buildings; model codes, regulations, and standards; solar energy. Answers inquiries; sells, distributes publications; offers "Certified Building Official" examination. Services free.

51168. Council of Better Business Bureaus, 1515 Wilson Blvd, Arlington, VA 22209; (703) 276-0100. Intl assembly of Better Business Bureaus. Coordinates member activities, issues trade practice codes, administers arbitration program, disseminates consumer info, tracks business legislation. Answers inquiries, provides advisory services free, distributes publications.

51169. Council of the Southern Mountains, P.O. Box 1188, Clintwood, VA 24228; (703) 926-4495. Nonprofit org interested in Appalachia, labor disputes, health and safety of mine, mill, and factory workers, welfare reform, compensation programs. Answers inquiries, makes info referrals, operates bookstore. Many services free or at cost.

51170. Council on America's Military Past, U.S.A., c/o Col. Herbert Hart, USMC-Ret, P.O. Box 1151, Fort Myer, VA 22211; (202) 479-2258. Nonprofit org interested in identification, location, restoration, preservation of old military units, installations and their history, traditions. Answers inquiries, conducts conferences and field trips, distributes publications. Services generally free.

51171. Data Use and Access Laboratories, 1515 Wilson Blvd, Ste 607, Arlington, VA 22209; (703) 525-1480. Nonprofit org that helps people use publicly available data. Provides online access to 1980 Census, reference and guidance to public data sources for a fee; conducts data searches; assists users with data access, tabulation, and analysis; develops software for special applications; provides training, conducts seminars, more.

51172. Defense Advanced Research Projects Agency, Technical Information Office, 1400 Wilson Blvd, Arlington, VA 22209; (202) 694-5919. U.S. agency that funds and manages basic weapons research and exploratory development. Answers inquiries, conducts classified meetings, conducts seminars and workshops, permits onsite use of collection. Services available to govt agencies and defense industry on need-to-know basis.

51173. Defense Logistics Studies, Information Exchange, Fort Lee, VA 23801; (804) 734-4255. Interest in logistics, logistics management, resources and operations related to military personnel and materiel. Permits onsite use of collection; provides extensive reference services to authorized personnel, selective info services in area of logistics to qualified and registered customers.

51174. Defense Technical Information Center, U.S. Dept of Defense, Cameron Station, Bldg 5, Alexandria, VA 22304; (202) 274-6871 (Registration); (202) 274-7633 (Public information). Central depository within Dept of Defense for interchange of scientific, technical research info. Available to U.S. govt agencies, other authorized persons. Unclassified/unlimited-distribution reports provided to NTIS for further distribution to general public.

51175. Department of Agriculture, Division of International Forestry, Forest Service, USDA, Plaza W, Room 101, 1735 N Lynn St, Rosslyn, VA 22209; (703) 235-2743. Engaged in forestry and related sciences, U.S. training of foreign natls in field of forestry, science and technology agreements with France, Federal Republic of Germany, Spain, People's Republic of China, Brazil. Answers inquiries, permits onsite use of collection.

51176. Department of Defense, Explosives Safety Board, Hoffman Bldg I, Room 856C, 2461 Eisenhower Ave, Alexandria, VA 22331; (703) 325-0152. U.S. agency that studies explosives, chemical munitions safety, ammunition handling, storage, magazine design, layout, barricade design, transportation, disposal of hazardous materials, etc. Answers public inquiries; provides advisory, consulting services to Dept of Defense, other authorized entities.

51177. Department of the Army, Applied Technology Laboratory, Fort Eustis, VA 23604; (804) 878-2208. Info center devoted to subsonic aeronautics, particularly helicopters and other V/STOL aircraft and related fields. Answers inquiries, makes referrals, provides reference services to govt personnel and contractors.

51178. Department of the Army, Casemate Museum, P.O. Box 341, Fort Monroe, VA 23651; (804) 727-3973. Interest in Fort Monroe history, including the site of confinement of Confederate president, Jefferson Davis; the battle of the Monitor and Merrimack; and U.S. Army's Coast Artillery Museum. Answers inquiries, permits onsite use of collections. Services free to anyone.

51179. Department of the Interior, Geological Survey, U.S. Geological Survey, 101 Natl Center, Reston, VA 22092; (703) 860-7411. Survey's duties include identifying nation's land, water, energy, and mineral resources, investigating natural hazards, conducting natl mapping program. Info services are listed in *A Guide to Obtaining Information* from USGS. Public Inquiries Offices sells books, maps.

51180. Department of the Navy Amphibious Museum, U.S. Naval Amphibious Base, Little Creek, Norfolk, VA 23520; (804) 464-8130. Museum devoted to amphibious history, amphibious warfare strategy and technology. Holds U.S. Navy and amphibious artifacts and memorabilia, books. Answers inquiries free; museum is open to public.

51181. Division of Parapsychology, Dept of Behavioral Medicine and Psychiatry, School of Medicine, Univ of Va. Medical Center, P.O. Box 152, Charlottesville, VA 22908; (804) 924-2281. Interest in parapsychology, psychokinesis, telepathy, precognition, clairvoyance, reincarnation, near-death and out-of-body experiences, hauntings, more. Answers inquiries, provides consulting services, conducts seminars, info referrals. Services only for scientists and students in field.

51182. Division of Substance Abuse Medicine, Medical Coll of Va. Hospital, P.O. Box 109, Richmond, VA 23298; (804) 786-9914. Interest in treatment, research, and training in substance abuse, chronic pain, and iatrogenic drug addiction. Answers inquiries, provides consulting services, makes referrals.

51184. Door and Hardware Institute, 7711 Old Springhouse Rd, McLean, VA 22102-3474; (703) 556-3990. Specializes in builders' hardware (locks, latches, hinges, metal and hollow core doors), govt and industrial standards, marketing techniques and practices. Answers inquiries, provides reference services, conducts management and technical training, conducts seminars, permits onsite use of collection.

51185. Dry Color Manufacturers' Association, 206 N Washington St, Ste 202, Alexandria, VA 22314; (703) 684-4044. Interest in color pigments, including organic pigment colors and lakes, inorganic chemical pigments and earthen colors, toxicity of pigments, pollution problems. Answers inquiries, makes info referrals, provides speakers on subjects in technical and other areas of pigment manufacturing industry.

51186. ERIC Clearinghouse on Handicapped and Gifted Children, Council for Exceptional Children, 1920 Assn Dr, Reston, VA 22091; (703) 620-3660. U.S.-funded clearinghouse that disseminates info on education of children, including the gifted, abused, and handicapped, for whom special methods, techniques, and materials are necessary. Answers inquiries, provides reference services, permits onsite use of collection. Sells publications.

51187. Educational Research Service, 1800 N Kent St, Arlington, VA 22209; (703) 243-2100. Provides member school administrators and boards with research to aid in effective decisionmaking for both long-range and day-to-day operations. Answers inquiries, provides reference services, sells publications. Services primarily for administrators and membership.

51188. Environmental Mutagen Society, Attn: Peggy Hinton, 1340 Old Chain Bridge Rd, Ste 300, McLean, VA 22101; (703) 790-1745. Promotes study of mutagens in human environment, sponsors research, disseminates info on health problems related to mutagens, food additives, pesticides, drugs. Answers inquiries, provides research info, conducts seminars, distributes publications, permits onsite use of collection. Services free.

51189. Farm Credit Administration, Congressional and Public Affairs Division, 1501 Farm Credit Dr, McLean, VA 22102; (703) 883-4056. Independent U.S. agency that supervises Federal Land Banks, Federal Intermediate Credit Banks, related assns through which funds obtained from sale of bonds to private investors are made available to farmers, ranchers, rural homeowners, etc. Answers inquiries, makes referrals.

51190. Federal Procurement Data Center, General Services Administration, 4040 Fairfax Dr, Ste 900, Arlington, VA 22203; (703) 235-1326. Tracks obligations of fed procurement dollars exceeding $10,000 (civilian agencies) or $25,000 (defense) from 1979 to present. Answers inquiries, distributes quarterly report and special computer-generated reports. Services free, except special reports.

51191. Federal Software Exchange Center, Natl Technnical Info Service, 5285 Port Royal Rd, Springfield, VA 22161; (703) 487-4848. U.S.-sponsored center that promotes sharing of common-use computer programs and related documentation among fed agencies, with distribution available to private sector. Answers inquiries, distributes publications, makes referrals to sources of software. Services available at cost.

51193. Flight Safety Foundation, 5510 Columbia Pike, Arlington, VA 22204; (703) 820-2777. Interest in aviation safety. Answers inquiries; provides consulting, reference, literature-searching services generally free to members and educational institutions, at nominal cost to others.

51194. Forecasting International, 1001 N Highland St, Arlington, VA 22201; (703) 527-1311. Commercial org interested in all areas of technological forecasting and technology assessment, especially as applied to corporate or govt planning. Provides consulting services and info referrals, distributes publications. Most services provided for a fee.

51195. Freestanding Ambulatory Surgery Association, 700 N Fairfax St, Ste 520, Alexandria, VA 22314; (703) 836-8808. Nonprofit natl org of freestanding ambulatory surgical centers. Acts as advocate and representative of industry, works to educate public about benefits of outpatient surgery, has developed standards and accredits ambulatory surgical facilities.

51196. Gas Appliance Manufacturers Association, 1901 N Moore St, Ste 1100, Arlington, VA 22209; (703) 525-9565. Interest in residential, commercial, industrial gas appliances and equipment, electric and oil-fired water heaters, equipment used in production, transmission, and distribution of natural gas, oil-fired warm air furnaces. Answers inquiries, permits onsite use of literature collection by appointment.

51197. Geographic Names Office, Natl Mapping Div, U.S. Geological Survey Natl Center, Mail Stop 523, 12201 Sunrise Valley Drive, Reston, VA 22092; (703) 860-6331. Conducts research on standardization of geographic names, domestic and foreign, for fed govt usage. Answers inquiries, provides info and referrals, permits onsite use of files. Services free, except use of data base, magnetic tapes, microfiche, spiral-bound books.

51198. Geologic Inquiries Group, Geologic Div, U.S. Geological Survey, 907 Natl Center, 12201 Sunrise Valley Drive, Reston, VA 22092; (703) 860-6517. Interest in physical, historical, environmental, lunar, and marine geology, geophysics, geochemistry, mineral and energy resources, volcanoes, earthquakes, tectonics, geologic mapping in U.S. Answers inquiries, including questions on availability of published geologic maps, or refers inquirers to other sources of info free. Furnishes single copies of selected reference materials.

51199. Geologic Names Committee, Geologic Div, U.S. Geological Survey, U.S. Geological Survey Natl Center, Mail Stop 902, 12201 Sunrise Valley Dr, Reston, VA 22092; (703) 860-6511. Maintains files on use of all geologic names of rock units in use in U.S., their age, distribution, correlation, character. Answers inquiries, lends magnetic tape, supplies printouts from GEONAMES data base. Service free, sells publications.

51200. Geological Survey, Office of International Hydrology, Water Resources Div, U.S. Geological Survey, 470 Natl Center, 12201 Sunrise Valley Dr, Reston, VA 22092; (703) 860-6548. Federal office responsible for planning and direction of Water Resources Division's activities in foreign countries. Provides training for foreign natls in techniques of water resource investigations. Answers inquiries, permits onsite use of collections. Services free.

51201. Geological Survey, Public Affairs Office, 119 Natl Center, 12201 Sunrise Valley Dr, Reston, VA 22092; (703) 860-7444. Serves news media with info regarding activities, programs, and interests of Geological Survey. Provides news and feature releases, photographs, other visuals on current scientific and technical subjects relating to programs, interests of Geological Survey.

51202. Geoscience Information Society, c/o American Geological Institute, 4220 King St, Alexandria, VA 22302; (703) 371-2480. Interest in info processing and management in earth sciences. Provides info on publications free; many other services available to members.

51203. Glass Packaging Institute, 6845 Elm St, Ste 209, McLean, VA 22101; (703) 790-0800. Interest in glass containers and closures, including manufacture, handling, use, packaging, end use product areas (beverages, drugs, cosmetics, etc.). Answers inquiries, lends materials, permits onsite use of collection by researchers. Some requests not served because of limited staff.

51204. Government Suppliers Association, P.O. Box 6232, McLean, VA 22106; (703) 533-9445. Conducts mass marketing to fed govt concerns, utilizing readily available resources and agencies to provide govt supplies. Answers inquiries, provides marketing services, evaluates data. Services available for fees to providers of services or products to govt.

51205. Graphic Arts Employers of America, c/o Printing Industries of America, 1730 N Lynn St, Arlington, VA 22209; (703) 841-8150. Interest in industrial relations in graphic arts industries. Answers inquiries; provides advisory, consulting, reference, referral services; conducts seminars, workshops; distributes publications; analyzes data. Cost and availability of services decided on case-by-case basis.

51206. Graphic Communications Association, 1730 N Lynn St, Ste 604, Arlington, VA 22209; (703) 841-8160. Interest in computer applications in graphic communications industry, management info systems, etc. Answers inquiries; provides advisory, consulting, referral services; conducts seminars, tutorials. General inquiries and referrals provided free, other services for a fee.

51207. Group Practice Information Service, 1422 Duke St, Alexandria, VA 22314; (703) 838-0033. Interest in group practice of medicine, including external and internal factors affecting it, socioeconomic aspects of health care. Answers inquiries; provides advisory and reference services, info referrals; distributes publications; evaluates data; permits onsite use of collections.

51208. Hampton Roads Maritime Association, P.O. Box 3528 (236 E Plume St), Norfolk, VA 23514; (804) 622-2639. Nonprofit assn that is voice of maritime industry. Interested in all aspects of port operation, development, improvements, statistics, origin and destination of each vessel, hazardous cargo, tariffs, regulation and law. Info provided free to nonmembers if purpose is in best interest of assn.

51209. Hardwood Plywood Manufacturers Association, P.O. Box 2789 (1825 Michael Faraday Dr), Reston, VA 22090; (703) 435-2900. Interest in hardwood plywood and veneer, including manufacture, testing, inspecting, selling, and use. Answers inquiries. Assn members and govt agencies given preference in obtaining services.

51210. Health Activation Network, P.O. Box 923, Vienna, VA 22180; (703) 281-3830. Nonprofit group that concentrates on establishing programs for wellness and for individuals to become more aware of health rights and responsibilities. Answers inquiries, provides advisory services, conducts seminars and workshops. Services provided at cost.

51211. Health Physics Society, 1340 Old Chain Bridge Rd, Ste 300, McLean, VA 22101; (703) 790-1745. Interest in radiation-related sciences, primarily as they affect man, health physics. Answers inquiries free or refers inquirers to other sources of info.

51212. Helicopter Association International, 1619 Duke St, Alexandria, VA 22314-3406; (703) 683-4646. Trade assn of civil helicopter operators, manufacturers, suppliers dedicated to advancing civil helicopter industry. Answers inquiries; provides reference, consulting, referral services; distributes publications, data; sponsors annual trade exposition. Services primarily for members, but others assisted.

51214. Highlands Center, Univ of Va. Medical Center, Dept of Neurology, BRH, Charlottesville, VA 22908; (804) 924-5401. Focuses on treatment of epilepsy and its consequences. Clinics throughout state serve as ongoing sources of research and treatment. Hospital unit also maintained. Provides info, referral service for Virginia.

51215. Historic American Buildings Survey Foundation, P.O. Box 1702, Alexandria, VA 22313; (703) 241-0611. Nonprofit org that provides funding and support to Historic American Buildings Survey and its programs. Answers inquiries, conducts seminars and workshops, sponsors exhibits, provides research info, distributes publications. Services primarily for members, others assisted. Fees charged for some services.

51216. Historical Evaluation and Research Organization, T.N. Dupuy Associates, 10392 Democracy Lane, Fairfax, VA 22030; (703) 591-3674. Interest in natl security policy, military history, analysis of military combat experience, simulation of combat, storage and retrieval of social science info. Provides research, consulting services on cost basis to anyone.

51217. Hotaling Associates/International, 2255 Cedar Lane, Vienna, VA 22180; (703) 560-4496. Commercial org that provides info on development, use of basic materials such as aggregates, asphalt, brick, cement, ceramics, masonry, steel, wood for engineered constructions. Answers inquiries; provides court testimony, expert witnesses, reference services; conducts seminars. Services provided for a fee.

51218. Human Life and Natural Family Planning Foundation, 5609 Broadmoor St, Alexandria, VA 22310; (703) 836-3377. Promotes natural family planning, including basal body temperature method, ovulation method, sympto-thermal method, periodic abstinence. An-

swers inquiries, provides advisory and reference services, distributes publications, permits onsite use of collection. Services free.

51219. Human Resources Research Organization, 1100 S Washington St, Alexandria, VA 22314; (703) 549-3611. Applies behavioral and social science principles and techniques to improve training, education, and operational performance of individuals and groups. Answers inquiries.

51220. Human Sciences Research, Westgate Research Park, 7710 Old Springhouse Rd, McLean, VA 22101; (703) 893-5200. Interest in social and behavioral sciences research, especially as it relates to race relations, community needs and services, social systems and and social change, energy conservation, health care delivery. Sells copies of technical reports.

51221. Industrial Designers Society of America, 1360 Beverly Rd, McLean, VA 22101; (703) 556-0919. Interest in product design and product systems; industrial, consumer packaging; exhibition design, graphics, interiors, space planning. Answers inquiries; provides advisory and reference services primarily for members, but others assisted.

51222. Industrial Heating Equipment Association, 1901 N Moore St, Arlington, VA 22209; (703) 525-2513. Represents major segments of industrial heat processing industry, including industrial furnaces, industrial ovens, combustion equipment, atmosphere generators, induction and dielectric heaters, industrial heaters, and fuel saving and heating devices. Answers inquiries, provides reference services.

51223. Infilco Degremont Inc., P.O. Box 29599 (2828 Emerywood Parkway), Richmond, VA 23229; (804) 281-7600. Interest in sanitary engineering processes and equipment; manufacture of water, waste water, water reuse; ion exchange systems. Answers inquiries, lends visual aids on request. Lab available for water testing.

51224. Institute for Alternative Futures, 1405 King St, Alexandria, VA 22314; (703) 684-5880. Nonprofit org that performs futures research, aids Congress and state legislatures in legislative foresight. Answers inquiries; provides advisory, consulting, reference services; conducts seminars; distributes publications. All services free to nonprofit groups that cannot pay, for a fee to others.

51225. Institute for Business and Community Development, Univ of Richmond, Special Programs Bldg, Richmond, VA 23173; (804) 285-6495. Interest in management development, org development, management by objectives, leadership. Provides training, consulting, problem diagnosis services to orgs for a fee, conducts public seminars on variety of applied management topics.

51226. Institute for Computer Applications in Science and Engineering, Mail Stop 132C, NASA Langley Research Center, Hampton, VA 23665; (804) 827-2513. Conducts research in application of computer science and applied mathematics to physical problems in science and engineering. Conducts seminars, distributes publications, makes info referrals. Services free, except some seminars.

51227. Institute of Chartered Financial Analysts, Univ of Va., P.O. Box 3668, Charlottesville, VA 22903; (804) 977-6600. Interest in financial analysis as it relates to investments, ethical standards for financial analysts. Provides education on investments, ethical standards for candidates and members.

51228. Institute of Early American History and Culture, Swem Library, Coll of William and Mary, P.O. Box 220, Williamsburg, VA 23187; (804) 229-2771. Interest in early American studies (U.S., Canada, and West Indies before 1815), historical writing and criticism, papers of John Marshall. Provides advisory services primarily for scholars, public agencies. Does not provide routine reference services.

51229. Institute of Textile Technology, Textile Information Center, P.O. Box 391, Rt. 250 West, Charlottesville, VA 22902; (804) 296-5511. Interest in textile technology, dyeing, apparel manufacture, polymers, manmade fibers, cotton. Answers inquiries, provides reference and referral services, permits onsite use of collections. Services generally free.

51230. Intellectual Property Notes, 2001 Jefferson Davis Hwy, Arlington, VA 22202; (703) 521-1669. Interest in patents, trademarks, copyrights, relevant legislation, inventions, technology transfer, trade secrets, technology licensing. Answers inquiries, provides advisory and reference services, conducts seminars, evaluates data. Services free, unless extensive.

51231. Inter-American Foundation, 1515 Wilson Blvd, Rosslyn, VA 22209; (703) 841-3800. Independent govt corp that supports self-help efforts of poor people in Latin America and Caribbean by providing fellowships to students, grants to private, indigenous orgs that initiate development projects throughout the region. Distributes publications free.

51232. Interior Design Educators Council, P.O. Box 8744, Richmond, VA 23226. Seeks to improve quality of teaching of interior design and professional level of interior design practice. Answers inquiries from public without charge.

51233. International Apple Institute, P.O. Box 1137 (6707 Old Dominion Dr, Room 210), McLean, VA 22101; (703) 442-8850. Interest in fresh and processed apple industry from grower through distribution. Answers inquiries, provides educational materials, makes referrals. Services primarily for members, but also available to educators, professionals, govt.

51235. International Association of Satellite Users and Suppliers, P.O. Box DD (6845 Elm St), McLean, VA 22101; (703) 759-2094. Seeks to improve govt and business understanding and use of satellite technology and to promote trade to foreign countries through direct consultation and financial assistance. Answers inquiries, provides info, conducts seminars, distributes publications. Services available, within limits, to nonmembers.

51236. International Bank Note Society, 4307 Granada St, Alexandria, VA 22309; (703) 780-5295. Org with chapters in U.S., England, Canada, and Australia interested in educational, scientific, and historical studies of worldwide bank notes and paper currencies. Answers inquiries free concerning paper money. Auctions open to members only are conducted by mail.

51237. International Bottled Water Association, 113 N Henry St, Alexandria, VA 22314; (703) 683-5213. Promotes use of bottled drinking water, quality assurance and growth of bottled water worldwide. Answers inquiries, provides reference services, conducts seminars, distributes publications. Services free, except publications.

51238. International Business Forms Industries, 1730 N Lynn St, Arlington, VA 22209; (703) 841-9191. Trade assn serving companies that manufacture business forms or forms-related products. Provides equipment surveys, sales indexes, training courses. Answers inquiries, provides consulting and reference services for members, conducts seminars, permits onsite use of collection. Most services for a fee.

51239. International Communications Industries Association, 3150 Spring St, Fairfax, VA 22031; (703) 273-7200. Natl trade assn of firms in video, microcomputer, and audiovisual industry. Answers inquiries, makes referrals, conducts annual convention and exhibits of latest communications technology.

51240. International Council for Health, Physical Education, and Recreation, 1900 Assn Dr, Reston, VA 22091; (703) 476-3462. Interest in health, physical education, sports, and recreation education. Answers brief inquiries, makes referrals to other sources of info.

51241. International Dental Health Foundation, 11800 Sunrise Dr, Ste 832, Reston, VA 22091; (703) 476-6110. Interest in prevention of dental caries and periodontal disease, microbiologically monitored and modulated periodontal therapeutics, known as the Keyes system. Answers inquiries, provides advisory and magnetic tape services, distributes publications. Services to laymen, professionals for a fee.

51242. International Fortean Organization, P.O. Box 367, Arlington, VA 22210-0367. Interest in crypto-scientific subjects, particularly philosophy and history of science and phenomenological interpretation of science, subjects unexplainable by conventional science. Answers inquiries or refers inquirers to other info sources. Services free, unless extensive.

51243. International Frozen Food Association, 1700 Old Meadow Rd, McLean, VA 22102; (703) 821-0770. Promotes intl trade of frozen foods and acts as an info clearinghouse. Answers inquiries; provides reference and referral services, info on research in progress;

conducts seminars and workshops; distributes publications. Services at cost to nonmembers.

51245. International League Against Epilepsy, Off of Secty General, Dept of Neurology, Univ of Va. Medical Center, Charlottesville, VA 22908; (804) 924-5669. Seeks to advance and disseminate knowledge about epilepsy, has commissions on antiepileptic drugs and on classification and terminology. Answers inquiries, provides advisory services, distributes publications, conducts seminars. Services for a fee.

51246. International Microwave Power Institute, 301 Maple Ave W, Ste 520, Vienna, VA 22180; (703) 281-1515. Worldwide scientific org devoted to domestic, industrial, medical, scientific, other noncommunications applications of microwave power. Provides info on microwave standards, safety, and frequency interference; distributes publications, research info; makes referrals. Services free to members, for a fee to others.

51247. International Society of Transport Aircraft Traders, 1925 N Lynn St, No 304, Arlington, VA 22209; (703) 522-8332. Interest in airline aircraft appraisal standards, used airline aircraft, aircraft sales, transport aircraft. Answers inquiries, provides advisory and reference services, conducts seminars, distributes publications. Services for a fee.

51248. International Teleconferencing Association, 1299 Woodside Dr, Ste 101, McLean, VA 22102; (703) 556-6115. Interest in teleconferencing, video conferencing, audio-audiographic conferencing, computer conferencing. Answers inquiries; provides advisory, reference, referral, services; conducts seminars, workshops. Services for a fee.

51249. Interstate Carriers Conference, 2200 Mill Rd, Alexandria, VA 22314; (703) 838-1950. Natl coordinating point and promotional arm for irregular-route common and contract carriers. Represents its members before Congress, fed agencies. Answers inquiries; provides advisory, reference, referral services; distributes publications. Services free to members, at cost to others.

51250. Izaak Walton League of America, 1701 N Fort Myer Dr, No 1100, Arlington, VA 22209; (703) 528-1818. Nonprofit org that combats water and air pollution, promotes citizen involvement in environmental protection projects, instigates litigation to protect vital natural areas. Conducts conferences, sells publications, makes referrals. Services free.

51251. Kosh Louis die Lurito & Associates, 1400 N Uhle St, Arlington, VA 22201; (703) 528-3772. Holds collection of annual reports to stockholders for all public utilities in U.S. since 1946 and computerized analyses of those companies earnings, rates, etc. over same period. Provides consulting services on fee basis. Academic users may have limited access to files.

51252. Laboratory of Nocturnal Cognition, Blue Ridge Hospital, Charlottesville, VA 22901; (804) 924-2365.

Interest in sleep and dream research, content analysis of dreams. Answers inquiries free. Services primarily for scientists, officials of fed agencies.

51253. Lazar Institute, 6726 Lucy Lane, McLean, VA 22101; (703) 821-0900. Nonprofit org that analyzes and evaluates public sector programs. Provides info services, evaluates and analyzes data, sells publications. Services free if related to research in progress.

51254. Learning Technology Institute, 50 Culpeper St, Warrenton, VA 22186; (703) 347-0055. Conducts research and development into use of computers in instruction, interactive media-based instruction delivery systems, instructional software, videodisc, more. Answers inquiries; provides referral, advisory, consulting services; conducts seminars. Services for a fee.

51255. Manufacturers Standardization Society of the Valve and Fittings Industry, 127 Park St NE, Vienna, VA 22180; (703) 281-6613. Produces standards and codes concerning valves, pipe fittings, and pipe hangers for commercial/industrial pressure piping. Answers specific technical inquiries, makes referrals.

51256. Marine Corps League, 956 N Monroe St, Arlington, VA 22201; (703) 524-1137. Seeks to preserve traditions, promote interests of U.S. Marine Corps, to fit its members for civilian life. Answers inquiries, provides advisory and reference services, conducts seminars, distributes publications, permits onsite use of collection. Services primarily free and for members, but others assisted.

51257. Marine Environment and Resources Research and Management System, Va. Institute of Marine Science, Gloucester Point, VA 23062; (804) 642-2111. Provides info on marine environment for researchers, managers, with emphasis on waters and coastal zone of Va. Answers inquiries; provides advisory, reference, microfiche duplication services. Some services provided at cost.

51258. Mariners Museum Library, Museum Dr, Newport News, VA 23606; (804) 595-0368. Devoted to naval architecture, marine history, ships. Answers limited inquiries, provides reference services, permits onsite use of collection. Services free, except copying.

51260. Mental Health Association Information Service, 1021 Prince St, Alexandria, VA 22314; (703) 684-7722. Natl org that promotes mental health, prevention of mental illness, and improved care and treatment of mentally ill. Answers inquiries or refers inquirers to other info sources, distributes publications. Services free, with some restrictions.

51261. Microneurography Society, c/o Dr Dwain Eckberg, Secty, Cardiovascular Physiology, Veterans Administration Medical Center, 1201 Broad Rock Blvd, Richmond, VA 23249; (804) 230-0001 ext 2606. Interest in research applications of microneurography in humans, neuroscience, nerve activity. Answers inquiries, conducts seminars. Services free.

51262. Military Family Resource Center, Armed Services YMCA of the USA, 6501 Loisdale Court, Ste 1107, Springfield, VA 22150; (703) 922-7671; (800) 336-4592. Nonprofit org that serves as intl clearinghouse in support of family advocacy in military, in such areas as child care, military careers, counseling. Answers inquiries, provides reference services, conducts workshops, permits onsite use of collections. Services free to practitioners.

51263. Mine Safety and Health Administration, Office of Information and Public Affairs, U.S. Dept of Labor, Ballston Tower No 3, Room 601, 4015 Wilson Blvd, Arlington, VA 22203; (703) 235-1452. Interest in coal, metal, and nonmetal mine health and safety. Publishes annual reports, mine injury and worktime statistics, safety manuals, instruction guides, health and safety standards pertaining to mineral industries. Answers inquiries.

51264. Mitre Corp., Washington Information Services Department, 1820 Dolley Madison Blvd, McLean, VA 22102; (703) 883-6481. U.S.-funded contract research center interested in systems engineering management, with special emphasis on militiary communications, command, control, and intelligence systems, environmental problems, more. Answers inquiries, provides reference services, makes interlibrary loans.

51265. Motorcycle Industry Council, Government Relations Office, 1235 Jefferson Davis Hwy, Ste 1410, Arlington, VA 22202; (703) 521-0444. Represents manufacturers, distributors of motorcycles, parts, and accessories; generates industry statistics; analyzes legislative and regulatory actions at state and fed levels. Answers inquiries, distributes publications. Most services free.

51266. Museum of the Confederacy, 1201 E Clay St, Richmond, VA 23219; (804) 649-1861. Governed by Confederate Memorial Literary Society, specializes in documents, artifacts pertaining to Confederate States of America, Civil War. Answers inquiries, provides photos and transparencies, makes referrals. Services for serious scholars.

51267. Music Educators National Conference, 1902 Assn Dr, Reston, VA 22091; (703) 860-4000. Interest in all aspects of music education. Sells publications, answers brief inquiries.

51268. NTL Institute for Applied Behavioral Science, 1501 Wilson Blvd, Ste 1000, Arlington, VA 22209; (703) 527-1500. Focal agency for experience-based learning programs and for developing new profession of laboratory education. Interested in behavioral science, group dynamics, etc. Answers inquiries; provides consulting, referral services; permits onsite use of collection; conducts seminars, training.

51270. National Aeronautics and Space Administration, Visitor Center, Langley Research Center, Off of Aeronautics and Space Technology, NASA, Mail Stop 480, Hampton, VA 23665; (804) 865-2855. Center for aeronautical research, spaceflight research, planetary exploration and earth resource monitoring from space. Holds over 40 exhibits, including Apollo 12 command module, moon rock, space suit, etc. Answers inquiries on programs, open to the public.

51271. National Alliance for the Mentally Ill, 1901 N Ft Myer Dr, Arlington, VA 22209; (703) 524-7600. Coalition of local support groups for mentally ill and their families. Provides info on mental illness, support for rights of patients and families, help in starting local groups. Promotes research, works to educate public and public officials, offers referrals.

51273. National Alliance of Senior Citizens, 2525 Wilson Blvd, Arlington, VA 22201; (703) 241-1533. Serves senior citizens by advocating control of inflation, development of senior citizen self-help programs, anticrime policies. Monitors consumer affairs and economic trends, provides expert testimony on current issues, establishes local senior citizen chapters.

51274. National Aloe Science Council, 1299 Woodside Dr, Ste 101, McLean, VA 22102; (703) 556-9656. Clearinghouse for info on aloe vera. Answers inquiries, provides advisory and reference services, conducts seminars. Services provided at cost.

51275. National Art Education Association, 1916 Assn Dr, Reston, VA 22091; (703) 860-8000. Promotes visual arts education in schools, museums, univs and meaningful art education for everyone. Answers inquiries; provides advisory, reference, placement services; conducts conferences, seminars; distributes publications; permits onsite use of collection. Some services for members only.

51276. National Association for Girls and Women in Sport, 1900 Assn Dr, Reston, VA 22091; (703) 476-3450. Recommends, implements athletic training programs at all educational levels; plans convention programs; disseminates info pertaining to the profession of athletic training and career education in field; maintains speakers bureau.

51277. National Association for Independent Living, 633 S Washington St, Alexandria, VA 22314; (703) 836-0850. Info source for projects fostering increased independence for disabled individuals. Answers inquiries, conducts seminars and workshops, distributes newsletter, makes referrals to other sources of info. Seminars and workshops usually open to all, other services restricted to NRA members.

51278. National Association for Sports and Physical Education, 1900 Assn Dr, Reston, VA 22091; (703) 476-3413. Formed to improve total sport and physical education experience in U.S., focusing on sport psychology, sociology, kinesiology. Sponsors conferences and workshops, provides consultation for members, involved in curriculum development of physical education on all levels.

51279. National Association of Alcoholism and Drug Abuse Counselors, 951 S George Mason Dr, Arlington, VA 22204; (703) 920-4644. Promotes prevention, treatment, and control of alcoholism and drug abuse, certification and professional education of alcoholism and drug abuse counselors. Answers inquiries; provides advisory, referral services; conducts seminars, workshops, conferences; publishes magazine. Some services free.

51280. National Association of Bedding Manufacturers, 1235 Jefferson Davis Hwy, Ste 601, Arlington, VA 22202; (703) 979-3550. Interest in govt specifications on fed and state laws pertaining to construction and performance of mattresses, mattress flammability and toxicity regulations. Provides consulting services, referrals to other info sources. Services free to members, at cost to others.

51281. National Association of Biology Teachers, 11250 Roger Bacon Dr, Reston, VA 22090; (703) 471-1134. Interest in biological science education, including classroom and laboratory instruction, facilities, professional education of biology teachers at high school and college levels. Answers inquiries.

51282. National Association of Brick Distributors, 1750 Old Meadow Rd, McLean, VA 22102; (703) 893-4010. Interest in sales, product distribution, marketing, education, and transportation related to clay products industry. Answers inquiries, provides advisory and reference services, conducts seminars, distributes publications. Some services free, others at cost.

51283. National Association of Chain Drug Stores, P.O. Box 1417-D49 (413 N Lee St), Alexandria, VA 22313; (703) 549-3001. Tracks pharmacy, health care legislation, retail regulations and legislation, cosmetics, security, general retailing, industry education. Answers inquiries free.

51284. National Association of Dental Assistants, 3837 Plaza Dr, Fairfax, VA 22030; (703) 273-3906. Serves needs of professionals employed by dentists, including office personnel. Promotes increased professional stature of dental assistants through education, provides members with benefits normally limited to specialized groups, conducts job exchange service.

51285. National Association of Dental Laboratories, 3801 Mount Vernon Ave, Alexandria, VA 22305; (703) 683-5263. Acts as liaison for dental laboratory industry in relations with dental profession and govt agencies. Through separate agencies, it certifies dental lab technicians and facilities. Answers inquiries, supplies career info, statistical and analytical business data.

51286. National Association of Educational Office Personnel, 1902 Assn Dr, Reston, VA 22091; (703) 860-2888. Interest in all facets of educational office personnel work, including certification and professional standards. Answers inquiries, provides consulting and reference services, makes referrals.

51287. National Association of Government Communicators, 80 S Early St, Alexandria, VA 22304; (703) 823-4821. Purpose is to improve govt communications by fostering high standards of professionalism. Interested in freedom of info. Answers inquiries, conducts workshops and training sessions, maintains job bank for members, makes referrals. Services on cost basis.

51288. National Association of Mail Service Pharmacies, 510 King St, Ste 420, Alexandria, VA 22314; (703) 684-8242. Represents the mail service pharmacy industry. Assists and informs consumers of mail service pharmacies' services, generally used by elderly, retired, chronically ill, immobile, or isolated persons and those heavily burdened by drug expense. Services free.

51289. National Association of Personnel Consultants, 1432 Duke St, Alexandria, VA 22314; (703) 684-0180. Assn for private employment agency business interested in employment, manpower programs, consumerism. Operates education and certification programs for field. Distributes publications free or at cost. Answers inquiries, provides free consulting, reference services to researchers.

51290. National Association of Private Residential Facilities for the Mentally Retarded, 6269 Leesburg Pike, Ste B-5, Falls Church, VA 22044; (703) 536-3311. Seeks to improve quality of private residential services for developmentally disabled Americans through fed legislation, regulation. Answers inquiries; provides advisory, reference, referral services; conducts seminars; distributes publications; permits onsite use of collection. Most services free.

51291. National Association of Professional Insurance Agents, 400 N Washington St, Alexandria, VA 22303; (703) 836-9340. Interest in clear definitions of property and casualty insurance policies, dispute mechanisms available to policyholders within the insurance industry and through state regulators' offices. Answers inquiries, provides reference services. Services free, available to private individuals only.

51292. National Association of Retail Druggists, 205 Daingerfield Rd, Alexandria, VA 22314; (703) 683-8200. Promotes independent retail pharmacy business, represents and protects members, encourage high standards in field. Answers inquiries; provides advisory, referral services; conducts seminars, meetings; distributes publications. Services at cost to nonmembers.

51294. National Association of Schools of Art and Design, 11250 Roger Bacon Dr, No 5, Reston, VA 22090; (703) 437-0700. Professional accrediting agency for art in higher education. Answers brief inquiries, makes referrals.

51295. National Association of Schools of Music, 11250 Roger Bacon Dr, No 5, Reston, VA 22090; (703) 437-0700. Interest in music in higher education, accreditation of schools and depts of music. Answers inquiries, makes referrals, provides consulting services to members and nonmember institutions.

51296. National Association of Schools of Theatre, 11250 Roger Bacon Dr, Ste 5, Reston, VA 22090; (703) 437-0700. Interest in evaluation and accreditation of theater education programs. Identifies accredited theater education programs, sells directory for $1.

51297. National Association of Secondary School Principals, 1904 Assn Dr, Reston, VA 22091; (703) 860-0200. Intl assn of secondary school administrators that represents members on all educational issues, coordinates 50 state assns of secondary school administrators, sponsors conferences. Answers inquiries, provides consulting services, performs research. Services free to members, at cost to others.

51298. National Association of State Boards of Education, 701 N Fairfax St, Ste 340, Alexandria, VA 22314; (202) 624-5845. Interest in activities of state boards of education in their role as policymaking body in several states. Answers brief inquiries, provides consulting services, makes referrals to other sources of info.

51299. National Association of State Mental Retardation Program Directors, 113 Oronoco St, Alexandria, VA 22314; (703) 683-4202. Membership org that serves as natl spokesman for state agencies serving mentally retarded, handicapped. Conducts seminars and conferences, provides communications network, distributes publications. Primarily for member state agencies, but public inquiries answered.

51300. National Association of State Outdoor Recreation Liaison Officers, c/o Art Buehler, Exec Dir, P.O. Box 731, Richmond, VA 23206; (804) 786-2556. Interest in land and water conservation funds. Provides reference and congressional liaison services.

51301. National Association of Temporary Services, 119 S Saint Asaph St, Alexandria, VA 22314; (703) 549-6287. Interest in temporary-help service industry, temporary-help employment, part-time work, office and clerical workers, and medical, industrial, and technical professionals. Answers inquiries, provides reference, referral services. Info free.

51302. National Association of the Remodeling Industry, 1901 N Moore St, Ste 808, Arlington, VA 22209; (703) 276-7600. Trade assn of home improvement products and building supplies manufacturers, remodeling contractors, lenders, similar firms in home improvement industry. Answers inquiries, compiles industry statistics, distributes publications, makes referrals.

51303. National Automobile Dealers Association Communications Group, 8400 Westpark Dr, McLean, VA 22102; (703) 821-7010. Interest in new car and truck dealers, automobile sales and service, consumer affairs. Answers inquiries or refers inquirers to other sources of info free.

51304. National Board for Certified Counselors, c/o American Assn for Counseling and Development, 5999 Stevenson Ave, Alexandria, VA 22304; (703) 823-9800. Offers natl certification to professional counselors based on a credential-oriented review and exam. Answers inquiries or refers inquirers free, conducts generic certification programs for counselors for fee, distributes publications.

51305. National Captioning Institute, Department of Research, 5203 Leesburg Pike, 15th Floor, Falls Church, VA 22041; (703) 998-2400. Nonprofit org that captions television programs for the hearing impaired. Answers inquiries, distributes publications. Info services free.

51306. National Cartographic Information Center, Natl Mapping Div, U.S. Geological Survey, 507 Natl Center, 12201 Sunrise Valley Dr, Reston, VA 22092; (703) 860-6045. Collects, organizes, distributes info about availability of maps and charts, aerial and space photography, geodetic control, and digital data for U.S. Accepts orders for aerial photographs, out-of-print Geological Survey maps, digital terrain data, more— all for a fee.

51307. National Center for Employee Ownership, 927 S Walter Reed Dr, Room 1, Arlington, VA 22204; (703) 979-2375. Nonprofit org interested in employee ownership, including Employee Stock Ownership Plans, worker participation, producer cooperatives. Answers inquiries; provides initial consulting, research, reference services; conducts seminars and workshops; distributes publications. Services for a fee.

51308. National Center for State Courts Library, 300 Newport Ave, Williamsburg, VA 23185; (804) 253-2000. Interest in all facets of judicial administration and court management on state, local levels. Answers inquiries or refers inquirers; provides research, reference services; permits onsite use of collection; distributes publications. Services available to court personnel, others served as time permits.

51309. National Center for the Thermodynamic Data of Minerals, U.S. Geological Survey, Natl Center, Stop 959 12201 Sunrise Valley Dr, Reston, VA 22092; (703) 860-6911. Evaluates all published literature on thermodynamic, physical, and thermochemical properties of minerals. Provides reference and referral services, distributes publications. Fees for some services.

51310. National Center on Institutions and Alternatives, Office of Public Information, 814 N St Asaph St, Alexandria, VA 22314; (703) 684-0373. Nonprofit org that develops, promotes strategies to reduce number of persons involuntarily institutionalized in nursing homes, hospitals, prisons, etc. Answers inquiries, provides advisory and reference services, conducts seminars, distributes publications, permits onsite use of collection. Services free.

51311. National Chronic Pain Outreach Association, 8222 Wycliffe Court, Manassas, VA 22110; (703) 368-7357.

Natl network of self-help groups offering emotional support and practical help to individuals and families coping with any chronic pain situation. Answers inquiries; provides advisory, reference, referral services; conducts seminars, distributes publications. Services free.

51313. National Chrysanthemum Society, c/o Galen L. Goss, Secty, 5012 Kingston Dr, Annandale, VA 22003; (703) 941-1791. Interest in chrysanthemums. Answers inquiries free, sells publications (reduced prices to members), lends slide sets to anyone for a fee.

51314. National Clearinghouse for Bilingual Education, 1555 Wilson Blvd, Ste 605, Rosslyn, VA 22209; (703) 522-0710; (800) 336-4560. U.S.-funded org interested in bilingual education, languages, ethnic/linguistic minority groups, culture. Answers inquiries; provides reference services, info on current research, technology; conducts seminars; distributes publications; permits onsite use of collections. Services free.

51315. National Clearinghouse for Family Planning Information, P.O. Box 12921 (1700 N Moore St), Arlington, VA 22209; (703) 558-7932. U.S.-funded clearinghouse that offers info on contraception, family planning, reproductive health, human sexuality, sexuality education. Answers inquiries, distributes publications, makes referrals to other sources of info. Services free.

51317. National Clearinghouse for Primary Care Information, 8201 Greensboro Drive, Ste 600, McLean, VA 22102; (703) 821-8955. Provides info services to support planning, development, delivery of ambulatory health care to urban and rural areas where there are shortages of medical personnel and services. Primary audience is health care practitioners, but others assisted.

51318. National Coal Resources Data System, Branch of Coal Resources, Geologic Div, U.S. Geological Survey, 956 Natl Center, 12201 Sunrise Valley Dr, Reston, VA 22092; (703) 860-7464. Interest in coal resources; coal geochemistry, geology, and petrology; trace elements in coal. Answers brief inquiries free, extensive inquiries answered at cost. Permits remote computer terminal access of coal data at cost.

51319. National Composition Association, c/o Printing Industries of America, 1730 N Lynn St, Arlington, VA 22209; (703) 841-8165. Interest in typesetting, typography, photocomposition, printing, graphic arts, data base management, design. Answers or refers inquiries; conducts conferences, conventions, seminars; distributes publications. Services for a fee, primarily for members, but others assisted.

51320. National Computer Graphics Association, 2722 Merrilee Dr, Ste 200, Fairfax, VA 22031; (703) 698-9600. Org of individuals and major corporations dedicated to developing and promoting computer graphics, its use in industry, govt, science, arts. Distributes publications on a varying fee basis. Resource Center avail-

able to members, press, and public for info on computer graphics.

51321. National Concrete Masonry Association, P.O. Box 781 (2302 Horse Pen Rd), Herndon, VA 22070; (703) 435-4900. Interest in all aspects of concrete masonry and building construction. Answers inquiries free, provides advisory services and structural computer feasibility studies, distributes publications. Fees are charged for publications and structural computer feasibility studies.

51322. National Contract Management Association, 6728 Old McLean Village Dr, McLean, VA 22101; (703) 442-0137. Interest in contract management, all forms of contracting with govt agencies, including procurement, production, quality control, contract negotiation, administration, more. Answers inquiries, conducts workshops and conducts seminars, produces educational materials for contract management.

51323. National Council for a Responsible Firearms Policy, 7216 Stafford Rd, Alexandria, VA 22307; (202) 785-3772. Interest in regulation of private possession and acquisition of guns and ammunition, caution in private firearms possession. Provides press releases, copies of congressional testimony, reprints of articles. Answers inquiries free within limits of time and staff.

51324. National Council of Teachers of Mathematics, 1906 Assn Dr, Reston, VA 22091; (703) 620-9840. Intl org intersted in all aspects of mathematics education, including teacher prep, methodology, research. Answers inquiries; makes referrals; sells reprints, microfilms, publications.

51325. National Defense Transportation Association, 727 N Washington St, Ste 200, Alexandria, VA 22314-1976; (703) 836-3303. Interest in transportation and logistics generally, with emphasis on defense transportation, emergency transportation planning, procedures, and activities. Answers inquiries, makes referrals, provides consulting services, prepares analyses and evaluations for authorized persons.

51327. National District Attorneys Association, 708 Pendleton St, Alexandria, VA 22314; (703) 549-9222. Promotes cooperation among county and prosecuting attorneys in order to effect strict, honest law enforcement and efficient local govt. Answers inquiries; provides advisory, reference, referral services; conducts seminars; distributes publications. Services provided at cost to those in field.

51329. National Future Farmers of America Organization, P.O. Box 15160 (Natl FFA Center, 5632 Mount Vernon Hwy), Alexandria, VA 22309; (703) 360-3600. Nonprofit natl org for high school vocational agriculture and agribusiness students. Provides incentive awards for agribusiness careers, intl agricultural work exchange programs.

51330. National Hospice Organization, 1901 N Fort Myer Dr, Ste 902, Arlington, VA 22209; (703) 243-5900.

Membership org of hospice programs whose goal is to provide quality care for terminally ill and support for their families. Answers inquiries, provides research findings, conducts seminars, distributes publications and locator service for U.S. hospices, permits onsite use of library on approval. Services free.

51332. National Institute for Certification in Engineering Technologies, 1420 King St, Alexandria, VA 22314; (703) 684-2835. Certification body for engineering technicians and technologists who voluntarily apply for certification. Certification programs are competency-based, require examination. Answers inquiries concerning programs, distributes publications. Info services free.

51333. National Institute for Public Policy, 8408 Arlington Blvd, Fairfax, VA 22031; (703) 698-0563. Nonprofit org interested in public policy issues relating to strategic defense and nuclear weaponry. Answers inquiries, lends materials, distributes publications. Services available at cost to anyone. Request for onsite use of research facility considered on case-by-case basis.

51334. National Institute of Governmental Purchasing, 115 Hillwood Ave, Falls Church, VA 22046; (703) 533-7300. Interest in govtal purchasing standards, specifications, practices, bids, and contracts (U.S. and Canada). Answers inquiries; provides consulting, referral services; offers public purchasing courses, certification program for public purchasing. Services primarily for members.

51335. National Institute of Victimology, 2333 N Vernon St, Arlington, VA 22207; (703) 528-8872. Provides technical assistance and monitors legislative and programmatic developments affecting victims and witnesses of crimes. Answers inquiries, provides consulting services, conducts seminars, distributes publications. Most services for a fee.

51336. National Insurance Consumer Organization, 344 Commerce St, Alexandria, VA 22314; (703) 549-8050. Nonprofit org that serves as a consumer advocate on public policy matters, advises consumers on how to buy insurance, works for reform of unfair industry practices, marketplace abuses. Members provided one telephone consultation per year, other services.

51337. National Legal Research Group, 2421 Ivy Rd, Charlottesville, VA 22906; (804) 977-5690. Commercial org that specializes in legal research and comparative legal analysis on questions of domestic and intl law, regulation. Answers inquiries, provides advisory services. Specific legal research only for members of the bar; distributes publications available to all, for a fee.

51338. National Licensed Beverage Association, 309 N Washington St, Alexandria, VA 22314; (703) 683-6633. Interest in state and fed beverage alcohol laws and regulations, laws regulating small businesses. Answers inquiries, provides free reference and referral services, sells publications.

51339. National Lime Association, c/o Kenneth Gutschick, Exec Dir, 3601 N Fairfax Dr, Arlington, VA 22201; (703) 243-5463. Org Studies all aspects of lime technology, including manufacture, method of tests, specifications, and all uses in chemical, structural, highway, and agricultural fields. Answers inquiries or refers inquirers to other info sources.

51340. National Mental Health Association, 1021 Prince St, Alexandria, VA 22314-2971; (703) 684-7722. Citizens voluntary org of local and state chapters committed to improved care and treatment of mentally ill people, and prevention of mental disorders. Answers inquiries, provides referrals, distributes publications. Some services subject to a fee.

51342. National Milk Producers Federation, 1840 Wilson Blvd, 4th Floor, Arlington, VA 22201; (703) 243-6111. Provides dairy farmer-owned cooperatives with a voice in natl public policy. Answers inquiries, evaluates data, distributes publications, makes referrals to other sources of info. Services free

51343. National Moving and Storage Association, 124 S Royal St, Alexandria, VA 22314; (703) 549-9263. Interest in moving and warehousing, with emphasis on small business operations. Answers inquiries; provides reference services, public and career info, referrals to other info sources; conducts seminars, training programs.

51344. National Ocean Service, Atlantic Marine Center, NOAA, 439 W York St, Norfolk, VA 23510; (804) 441-6616. Interest in cartography, photogrammetry, hydrography, geodesy, tides and currents, coasts and harbors. Answers inquiries, sells Natl Ocean Service publications, maps, charts.

51345. National Office Products Association, 301 N Fairfax St, Alexandria, VA 22314; (703) 549-9040. Interest in office and institutional supplies, stationery, furniture, machines, and equipment. Publishes industry reports, membership directory, buyers' guide. Answers inquiries, provides reference services.

51346. National Office for Social Responsibility in the Private Sector, 208 N Washington St, Alexandria, VA 22314; (703) 684-1041. U.S. Dept of Justice office that examines linkages between public and private resources in areas affecting juvenile justice, youth employment training. Answers inquiries; provides consulting, technical assistance; conducts seminars. Services free or on a contract basis.

51347. National Pasta Association, 1901 N Fort Myer Dr, Rosslyn, VA 22209; (703) 841-0818. Interest in pasta and related products, development of pasta industry. Answers inquiries, conducts seminars and workshops, sells publications. Many services primarily for members, but some info available to public.

51348. National Perinatal Association, 1311 A Dolley Madison Blvd, Ste 3A, Mclean, VA 22101; (703) 556-9222. Promotes perinatal health through fostering delivery of optimal care, education, and research, and natl policy. Sponsors annual clinical conference, serves as education and legislation resource center.

51349. National Pest Control Association, 8100 Oak St, Dunn Loring, VA 22027; (703) 573-8330. Interest in structural pest control, control of pest birds, rodents, insects. Answers inquiries, provides consulting and reference services, conducts workshops, distributes publications, permits onsite use of collection. Services available primarily to members, consumer info program offered to the layman.

51350. National Preservation Institute, P.O. Box 1702, Alexandria, VA 22313; (703) 241-0611. Nonprofit corp that provides educational programs and technical assistance in management, restoration, preservation, documentation of historic properties. Answers inquiries, provides technical info and assistance, issue identification, mediation services. Services at cost.

51351. National Printing Equipment and Supply Association, 6849 Old Dominion Dr, Ste 200, McLean, VA 22101; (703) 734-8285. Member companies engaged in building, manufacturing, selling, importing for sale, and distributing of machinery, equipment, and supplies used in the graphic arts industry. Provides inquirers with free copy of its directory of member companies and their products.

51352. National Public Services Research Institute, 123 N Pitt St, Alexandria, VA 22314; (703) 548-3444. Conducts research, development in public service fields, including safety and health (especially highway safety, energy conservation). Answers inquiries, provides R&D info, conducts seminars. Info, publications free; other services to anyone on contract basis.

51353. National Radio Astronomy Observatory, Edgemont Rd, Charlottesville, VA 22901; (804) 296-0211. Maintains library, computers, staff, in Charlottesville. Radio telescopes located at Green Bank, W.Va., Kitt Peak, Ariz., and near Socorro, N.M. Answers specific inquiries about radio astronomy observations, theory, techniques. Welcomes use of facilities by all radio astronomers.

51354. National Recreation and Park Association, 3101 Park Center Dr, Alexandria, VA 22302; (703) 820-4940. Nonprofit service, educational, research org dedicated to improving quality of life through better recreation and leisure opportunities. Provides technical assistance to affiliated orgs amd local communities, provides info on public policy, innovations, research in the field.

51356. National Rehabilitation Association, 633 S Washington St, Alexandria, VA 22314; (703) 836-0850. Interest in rehabilitation of all persons with disabilities. Answers inquiries, conducts seminars, training institutes, periodic forums on specific rehabilitation problems. Emphasis given to interprofessional and interagency cooperation.

51359. National School Boards Association, 1680 Duke St, Alexandria, VA 22314; (703) 838-6722. Interest in concerns and needs of school boards, school board members, and state school board assns. Answers inquiries; provides consulting, literature-searching services; makes referrals; permits onsite use of collection. Info provided within limits of time and staff.

51360. National School Public Relations Association, 1501 Lee Hwy, Arlington, VA 22209; (703) 528-5840. Interest in public relations for educators, educational improvement, school-community relations. Answers inquiries; provides advisory, consulting, reference services; conducts workshops; distributes publications; permits onsite use of collection. Charges for services, primarily for members, but others assisted.

51361. National School Volunteer Program, 701 N Fairfax St, Ste 320, Alexandria, VA 22314; (703) 863-4880. Nonprofit org that promotes citizens participation, volunteerism to supplement activities that benefit schools, students, communities. Answers inquiries, provides advisory and reference services, conducts seminars and workshops, distributes publications. Services free, primarily for members.

51362. National Slag Association, 300 S Washington St, Alexandria, VA 22314; (703) 549-3111. Nonprofit assn that conducts, stimulates research in the field of mineral aggregates and their end products, with particular emphasis on slag. Disseminates info pertaining to production, processing, properties, and uses of steel industry slags. Answers inquiries free.

51363. National Society of Professional Engineers, Washington Engineering Center, 1420 King St, Alexandria, VA 22314; (703) 684-2800. Promotes professional (rather than technical) aspects of engineering, engineering salaries, ethics, education, careers, etc. Answers inquiries, provides free advisory and reference services, conducts seminars and workshops, sells publications.

51364. National Society of Public Accountants, 1010 N Fairfax St, Alexandria, VA 22314; (703) 549-6400. Interest in public accounting and fed income taxation. Answers brief inquiries, provides reference services, prepares analyses, makes referrals.

51365. National Spa and Pool Institute, 2111 Eisenhower Ave, Alexandria, VA 22314; (703) 838-0083. Interest in swimming pool, spa, and hot tub construction, including industry standards, technical activities, public and govt relations, pool design, ethics. Answers inquiries, distributes publications, conducts seminars, conventions, and expositions.

51366. National Sporting Library, c/o Judith Ozment, Librarian, P.O. Box 1335, Middleburg, VA 22117; (703) 687-6542. Research library devoted to field sports, their social significance, with emphasis on horses, related sports. Special collections date from 1550 to present. Answers inquiries, provides reference services, permits onsite use of collection. Services free, except copying.

51367. National Study of School Evaluation, 5201 Leesburg Pike, Falls Church, VA 22041; (703) 820-2727. Nonprofit natl group of educators that develops materials to evaluate elementary and secondary schools. The evaluation process includes all aspects of the school. Answers inquiries regarding use of materials and procedural questions relating to institutional evaluation.

51368. National Technical Information Service, Dept. of Commerce, 5285 Port Royal Rd, Springfield, VA 22161; (703) 487-4600. Central source for public sale of govt-sponsored research, reports, analyses. Selected Research in Microfiche provides paid subscribers with full texts of research reports, bibliographic data file available for lease, other specialized services for sale.

51369. National Therapeutic Recreation Society, c/o Natl Park and Recreation Assn, 3101 Park Center Dr, Alexandria, VA 22302; (703) 820-4940. Interest in therapeutic recreation. Answers inquiries, provides advisory and reference services, conducts seminars, conferences, and workshops, distributes publications. Nonmembers charged for some publications.

51370. National Turkey Federation, 11319 Sunset Hills Rd, Reston, VA 22090; (703) 435-7206. Trade assn representing natl turkey industry. Interested in production, promotion, marketing of turkeys. Answers inquiries, evaluates data, makes referrals. Services free on limited basis.

51371. National Venture Capital Association, 1655 N Fort Myer Dr, Ste 700, Arlington, VA 22209 (202) 528-4370. Promotes a broader understanding of importance of venture capital to vitality of U.S. economy and the free flow of capital to young companies. Answers inquiries, distributes directory, makes referrals to other sources of info. Services free.

51372. National Vocational Guidance Association, c/o American Assn for Counseling and Development, 5999 Stevenson Ave, Alexandria, VA 22304; (703) 823-9800. Specializes in vocational, career, and educational guidance, student and adult counseling services. Provides brief answers to technical inquiries.

51373. National Water Safety Congress, 5313 Dunbar Lane, Burke, VA 22015; (703) 323-6347. Nonprofit agency of professionals and others interested in water safety. Answers inquiries, conducts professional development seminars. Services primarily for govt agencies, but also available to others, free.

51375. National Wholesale Druggists Association, P.O. Box 238 (105 Oronoco St), Alexandria, VA 22313; (703) 684-6400. Trade assn for wholesalers of pharmaceuticals and over-the-counter medications. Conducts annual operating surveys, collects other industry statistics. Answers inquiries, conducts workshops, distributes publications. Services free to members, for a nominal fee to others.

51376. Natural Disaster Resource Referrals Service, P.O. Box 2208, Arlington, VA 22202; (703) 920-7176. Commercial org that provides in-depth info on many aspects of natural hazards and disasters, including hurricanes, earthquakes, fires, recovery. Answers inquiries, provides advisory amd reference services, conducts training programs, lends materials. Services provided for a fee.

51377. Nature Conservancy, 1800 N Kent St, Ste 800, Arlington, VA 22209; (703) 841-5300. Natl conservation org that engages in identification and preservation of ecological diversity through protection of natural areas. Answers inquiries, provides conservation assistance, distributes publications, makes referrals. Charge for some services, on limited basis.

51378. Naval Electronic Systems Engineering Center, Portsmouth, P.O. Box 55 (Norfolk Naval Shipyard; Building 74, 2nd Floor), Portsmouth, VA 23705; (804) 396-7688. Interest in fleet and shore electronics. Answers inquiries, provides advisory and reference services, makes interlibrary loans, permits onsite use of collection. Services free, with real need.

51379. Naval Medical Command, Industrial Hygiene Branch, Occupational and Preventive Medicine Service, Norfolk Naval Shipyard, Portsmouth, VA 23709; (804) 396-3280. Interest in industrial hygiene, dust, fumes, particles, heavy metals, adhesives, household chemicals, solvents, irritants, emulsifiers, occupational medicine. Answers inquiries, provides consulting services to Tidewater Region Navy facilities.

51380. Naval Mine Warfare Engineering Activity, Technical Library, Code 322, Yorktown, VA 23691-5076; (804) 887-4671; (Autovon) 953-4671. Interest in underwater mines, destructors, depth charges, surface-deployed mine countermeasures (excluding magnetic), associated equipment. Answers inquiries, provides reference services, makes referrals. Reproductions of microfilm and microfiche available when not classified.

51381. Naval Research Scientific Information Office, Off of Naval Research, Ballston Tower No 1, 800 N Quincy St, Arlington, VA 22217; (202) 696-4108. Conducts research for Navy in environmental sciences, physical sciences, engineering, mathematical, biological, medical, psychological sciences, ocean science. Answers inquiries, makes referrals to other sources of info.

51382. Naval Surface Weapons Center, Technical Library Division, Mail Code E23, Dahlgren, VA 22448; (703) 663-8351. Devoted to electronics, explosives, weaponry, aeronautics, aerodynamics, astronautics, chemistry, plastics, physics, metallurgy, lasers, radiation as they relate to warfare. Answers inquiries, provides reference services to govt agencies and authorized contractors.

51383. Navy Acquisition, Research and Development Information Center, Naval Ocean Systems Center, 5001 Eisenhower Ave, Alexandria, VA 22333-0001; (202) 274-9315. Tracks Navy acquisition related to research, development, test, and evaluation. Answers inquiries, makes referrals, permits onsite use of collection. Services free, available to authorized agencies.

51384. Network Users Association, 2111 Eisenhower Ave, Ste 400, Alexandria, VA 22314; (703) 683-8500. Nonprofit org that promotes development, availability of effective info systems networks. Informs members of networking technology, fosters dialogue between computer network suppliers and users. Answers inquiries, conducts seminars, evaluates data. Some services free, others at cost to members.

51385. Newport News Shipbuilding and Dry Dock Co., Technical Information Center, 4101 Washington Ave, Newport News, VA 23607; (804) 380-2610. Collects info on many aspects of engineering, mathematics, physics, data processing, cryogenics, all fields of chemistry, technical writing, machinery, more. Also serves as depository for unclassified NASA and DTMB reports. Provides reference services, onsite use of collection.

51386. Night Vision and Electro-optics Laboratory, Public Affairs Office, Army Electronics Research and Development Command, Attn: DELNV-PA, Fort Belvoir, VA 22060; (703) 664-5066. Interest in image intensification, far infrared (thermal imaging), laser technology. Answers inquiries or refers inquirers to other info sources free. Services available to anyone requesting unclassified defense info, classified info is issued on need-to-know basis.

51387. North American Academy of Manipulative Medicine, c/o Stephen M. Levin, M.D., Secty-Treasurer, 5021 Seminary Rd, Alexandria, VA 22311; (703) 931-0233. Affiliated with Intl Federation of Manual Medicine. Interested in manipulative medicine, manual medicine. Answers inquiries, conducts seminars. Services available only to medical and ancillary health service personnel, vendors.

51388. North American Benthological Society, c/o Albert C. Hendricks, Secty, Univ Center for Environmental Studies and Biology Dept, Polytechnic Institute and State Univ, Blacksburg, VA 24061. Interest in benthos, aquatic, bottom-living organisms, aquatic ecology, invertebrates, including especially aquatic insects. Answers inquiries, provides reference and referral services, conducts meetings, distributes publications. Reference services only for members, other services free to anyone.

51390. Office of Naval Research, Biological Sciences Program, Dept of the Navy, 800 N Quincy St, Arlington, VA 22217; (202) 696-4760. Interest in research in biological sciences, especially cellular responses to toxic and stressful environments, cellular and behavioral immunology, molecular biology directed at understanding biological phenomena at molecular level and biotechnology. Answers inquiries.

51391. Opticians Association of America, P.O. Box 10110 (10341 Democracy Lane), Fairfax, VA 22030; (703) 691-8355. Interest in prescription optics, eyeglasses and contact lenses, low-vision aids, sunglasses, artificial eyes, safety and sports eyewear. Answers brief inquiries on work of opticians, makes info referrals.

51393. Pain Management Center, Dept of Anesthesiology, Univ of Va. Medical Center, P.O. Box 293, Charlottesville, VA 22908; (804) 924-5581. Has diagnostic and therapeutic capabilities in the study of acute pain. Answers inquiries; provides advisory, reference, referral services; provides info on current research, conducts seminars; distributes publications. Services free, except seminars.

51394. Painting and Decorating Contractors of America, 7223 Lee Hwy, Falls Church, VA 22046; (703) 534-1201. Natl trade assn that serves contractors in the painting industry. Provides legal, legislative, educational, management info for membership; conducts regional and natl conferences, workshops; cosponsors natl apprentice training program; distributes publications and other materials.

51396. Parent Educational Advocacy Training Center, 228 S Pitt St, Room 300, Alexandria, VA 22314; (703) 836-2953. Nonprofit org that provides support services for parents of handicapped children. Answers inquiries; provides consulting, reference, info referral services; conducts workshops for parents and educators. Consulting services provided on a sliding-fee scale, workshops and team training free.

51397. Passive Solar Industries Council, 125 S Royal St, Alexandria, VA 22314; (703) 683-5003. Trade assn of major building industry orgs, utilities, others interested in passive solar design, products, projects, industry activities and resources. Distributes publications. Does not have resources to respond to other inquiries from public or to provide library services.

51399. Personnel Accreditation Institute, P.O. Box 19648 (606 N Washington St), Alexandria, VA 22320; (703) 684-8327. Grants accreditation to generalists and specialists in personnel and human resources field based on written examination and verified current full-time professional experience in field. Answers inquiries free. Testing services for qualified persons provided for a fee.

51400. Philip Morris U.S.A. Research Center, P.O. Box 26583 (4201 Commerce Rd), Richmond, VA 23261; (804) 274-2877. Specializes in organic chemistry, physics, packaging, tobacco chemistry and technology and the composition and chemistry of cigarette smoke. Answers inquiries, provides reference and bibliographic services, permits onsite use of collection by appointment.

51401. Piedmont Environmental Council, P.O. Box 460 (28-C Main St), Warrenton, VA 22186; (703) 347-2334. Nonprofit org that seeks to preserve the rural character of counties in Piedmont Virginia. Answers inquiries, provides advisory services, conducts seminars, evaluates data, makes referrals to other sources of info. Services free to members, to the public for a fee.

51402. Porcelain Enamel Institute, 1911 N Fort Myer Dr, Ste 1009, Arlington, VA 22209; (703) 527-5257. Interest in porcelain enamel as applied to metal substrates, including steel, aluminum, and others, ceramic metal systems, porcelain enamel test methods. Answers inquiries, makes referrals, provides reference services for a fee, permits onsite use of collection.

51403. Powered Ultralight Manufacturers Association, 7535 Little River Turnpike, Ste 350, Annandale, VA 22003; (703) 642-5859. Promotes ultralight vehicle industry by developing an airworthiness standard and vehicle certification program for ultralight vehicle manufacturers. Disseminate info to members, represents membership before govt. Answers inquiries from public without charge.

51404. Presidential Classroom for Young Americans, 441 N Lee St, Alexandria, VA 22314; (703) 683-5400. Introduces high school juniors and seniors to fed govt through intensive one-week sessions held in Washington, D.C. Also conducts program for teachers, college students. Students must be approved by schools. Tuition paid by student, school, or scholarships.

51405. Project HOPE, c/o People-to-People Health Foundation, Health Sciences Education Center, Carter Hall, Millwood, VA 22646; (703) 837-2100. Foundation runs Project HOPE, formerly a hospital ship, now a land-based medical education program in developing nations. Also operates research center that seeks solutions to health care issues in U.S. Answers inquiries; provides reference services, pamphlets, promotional services.

51406. Public Administration Service, 1497 Chain Bridge Rd, Ste 202, McLean, VA 22101; (703) 734-8970. Provides consulting, research on planning, management of foreign and domestic govtal operations, conducts training programs in rural development, provides assistance in planning, implementing projects in public works, budgeting, finance. Answers inquiries.

51407. Recreation Vehicle Industry Association, P.O. Box 2999 (1896 Preston White Dr), Reston, VA 22090; (703) 620-6003. Natl trade assn of recreation vehicle manufacturers, suppliers. Follows legislation, marketing, standards related to industry. Answers inquiries, provides advisory and reference services, makes referrals. Services free.

51408. Rehabilitation Engineering Center, Univ of Va., P.O. Box 3368 Univ Station (Towers Off Bldg, 1224 W Main St), Charlottesville, VA 22903; (804) 977-6730. Sponsored by U.S., center specializes in research on wheelchair mobility, including seating and body supports. Answers inquiries; provides advisory, consulting, reference, referral services; conducts seminars; permits onsite use of collection. Services available at cost to qualified users.

51409. Relocation Counseling Center of America, 8200 Greensboro Dr, McLean, VA 22102; (703) 790-8300. Independent org that offers info packets on living and working in Washington, D.C., metro area. Answers inquiries, provides advisory and reference services, conducts seminars, distributes publications. Services for a fee.

51410. Renewable Energy Institute, 1516 King St, Alexandria, VA 22314; (703) 683-7795. Sponsored by energy interests, org examines trade laws affecting transfer of energy technologies to developing countries, changing relationships among utilities, energy industries, consumers, govt. Answers inquiries, conducts seminars, distributes publications. Many services free.

51411. Reynolds Metals Co., Technical Information Services Library, P.O. Box 27003 (4th and Canal Sts.), Richmond, VA 23261; (804) 788-7409. Interest in aluminum and alloys, alumina, bauxite, metallurgy, corrosion, castings, wrought products, production, packaging, standards, chemicals, natural resources relating to aluminum. Answers inquiries, provides reference services, permits onsite use of collections on need-to-know basis.

51412. Rice Millers Association, Crystal Gateway One, Ste 302, 1235 Jefferson Davis Hwy, Arlington, VA 22202; (703) 920-1281. Acts as liaison between rice milling industry and U.S. and foreign govts, arbitrates industry disputes, promotes interests of rice industry through other activities. Answers inquiries, makes referrals, distributes publications free.

51413. Risks International, P.O. Box 115 (120 S Royal St), Alexandria, VA 22313; (703) 836-6126. Tracks terrorist incidents against business worldwide, including kidnappings, assassinations, facility attacks, bombings, hijackings. Answers inquiries; provides advisory, security consulting, reference services; distributes publications. Services for a fee.

51414. Safety Society, 1900 Assn Dr, Reston VA 22091; (703) 476-3431. Promotes development of safety concepts and behaviors among its members, sponsors natl conferences, safety programs that focus on educational aspects of traffic safety, emergency preparedness, injury control, sports safety.

51415. Safety of Explosive Ordnance Databank, Naval Surface Weapons Center/DL (Code E52), Dahlgren, VA 22448; (703) 663-7201. Provides safety info on naval weapons systems. Answers inquiries, provides reference and literature-searching services, permits onsite use of collection. Services available only to U.S. military personnel.

51416. Salt Institute, 206 N Washington St, Alexandria, VA 22314; (703) 549-4648. Interest in uses of salt, including highway construction and maintenance, manufacturing, industry, and marketing, chemicals, water treatment, human nutrition, agriculture. Answers inquiries, supplies literature.

51417. Scandinavian Documentation Center, 5827 Columbia Pike, Ste 306, Falls Church, VA 22041; (703) 845-

0115. Follows science research activities in North America and Scandinavia. Answers inquiries; serves as exchange center for nonclassified technical documents, other material between North America and Scandinavia.

51418. Screen Printing Association International, 10015 Main St, Fairfax, VA 22031; (703) 385-1335. Assn of printers, suppliers, and graphic arts educators interested in screen printing and related subjects. Answers inquiries free, distributes publications free to members and at cost to nonmembers, conducts seminars and workshops on a fee basis to all.

51419. Search Corp., 655 Mine Ridge Rd, Great Falls, VA 22066; (703) 759-3560. Commercial org that specializes in technology transfer info. Interest in location of new products and processes, advanced and emerging technology, patent monitoring. Answers inquiries, provides advisory, consulting, reference services. Services provided for a fee.

51420. Ski Industries America, 8377-B Greensboro Dr, McLean, VA 22102; (703) 556-9020. Natl trade assn for suppliers of consumer ski products. Answers inquiries, conducts seminars and workshops, distributes publications, makes referrals. Services generally available to nonmembers for a fee.

51421. Society for Health and Human Values, 1311A Dolly Madison Blvd, Ste 3A, McLean, VA 22101; (703) 556-9222. Promotes inclusion of humanities disciplines in curricula of health professional schools, especially medicine and nursing. Conducts seminars, distributes publications. Services for a fee.

51422. Society for Industrial Microbiology, 1401 Wilson Blvd, Arlington, VA 22209; (703) 527-6776. Professional assn dedicated to advancement of microbiological sciences, especially as applied to industrial materials, processes, products, associated problems (oil spills, waste disposal, etc.). Answers inquiries, conducts seminars and placement service. Services free, except publications.

51423. Society for Marketing Professional Services, 801 N Fairfax St, Alexandria, VA 22314; (703) 549-6117. Interest in marketing of professional services in architectural, engineering, interior design, planning, and construction management fields. Answers inquiries; provides advisory, consulting, reference services; conducts seminars, workshops; distributes publications. Services free to members.

51424. Society for Optical and Quantum Electronics, P.O. Box 245, McLean, VA 22101; (703) 642-5835. Provides info on lasers, nonlinear optics, fiber optics, integrated optics, laser photochemistry, laser spectroscopy. Conducts conferences and short courses on a fee basis, makes referrals to other sources of info free.

51425. Society for Private and Commercial Earth Stations, 709 Pendleton St, Alexandria, VA 22314; (703) 549-6990. Trade assn of satellite earth station industry, serves as a clearinghouse for issues affecting the in-

dustry and associated technology. Answers inquiries, conducts seminars, distributes publications, makes referrals. Services provided free to members, for a fee to others.

51426. Society of American Florists, 901 N Washington St, Alexandria, VA 22314; (703) 836-8700. Natl trade assn representing flower growers, wholesalers, retailers, interested in floriculture, ornamental plants, flowers. Answers inquiries, provides reference services, conducts seminars, distributes publications. Services provided at cost.

51427. Society of American Wood Preservers, 7297 Lee Hwy, Unit P, Falls Church, VA 22042; (703) 237-0900. Natl trade assn that serves water-borne wood preservers. Lobbies Congress, fed agencies; assists members with specifications, code and insurance matters; informs of prospective legislation. Distributes publications, makes referrals free. Audiovisual presentations, other services for a fee.

51428. Society of Data Educators, c/o Coll of Business Administration, IDS, James Madison Univ, Harrisonburg, VA 22807. Interest in computer info systems, computer instruction at all levels (grammar school through univ). Answers inquiries; provides advisory services; conducts seminars, workshops, CDE certification program; distributes publications. Services for a fee.

51429. Society of Packaging and Handling Engineers, Reston International Center, 11800 Sunrise Valley Dr, Reston, VA 22091; (703) 620-9380. Interest in packaging, related handling of consumer, industrial, and military products. Answers inquiries, conducts seminars and workshops, distributes publications, makes referrals. Services for a fee.

51430. Society of Photographic Scientists and Engineers, 7003 Kilworth Lane, Springfield, VA 22151; (703) 642-9090. Interest in imaging science and technology, preservation of photographic films. Answers inquiries, conducts seminars and workshops, assists orgs in preserving photographic films, distributes publications, makes referrals. Services for a fee.

51431. Society of Underprivileged and Handicapped Children, 5910 Farrington Ave, Alexandria, VA 22304; (703) 823-0008. Provides rehabilitation, prostheses, specialized aids, occupational therapy, foster care for handicapped children, others. Answers inquiries, provides consulting services, conducts seminars, distributes publications, permits onsite use of collections. Services free to handicapped, their families, social workers.

51432. Special Industrial Radio Service Association, 1700 N Moore St, Ste 910, Rosslyn, VA 22209; (703) 528-5115. Coordinates frequencies for all U.S. "special industrial" radio licenses. In most cases, applicants must submit a SIRSA recommendation with other FCC forms before they are granted a license. Answers inquiries, provides advisory and reference services only to members, for fees.

51433. Speech Communication Association, 5105 Backlick Rd, Annandale, VA 22003; (703) 750-0533. Interest in speech communication, theory and practice, including interpersonal, public, mass, intl communication, related areas. Answers inquiries, provides advisory and reference services, distributes publications, permits onsite use of collection. Services generally free.

51434. Speech Research Laboratory, Speech and Hearing Center, Univ of Va., 109 New Cabell Hall, Charlottesville, VA 22903; (804) 924-7107. Interest in speech, hearing, language processes and their dysfunction, computer applications in communication disorders. Provides reference and consulting services, permits onsite use of collections.

51435. Stockholder Sovereignty Society, P.O. Box 7273, Alexandria, VA 22307; (703) 521-9709. Promotes rights, priviledges, and influence of stockholders in corporate decisions and elections. Answers inquiries, provides advisory and reference services, publishes quarterly news report. Services free, except the quarterly.

51440. Tactical Energy Systems Laboratory, U.S. Army Belvoir Research and Development Center, Fort Belvoir, VA 22060; (703) 664-5830. Conducts research in electric power generation, utilization, and transmission (military), electric vehicular propulsion, environmental control technology (heaters, air conditioners, microclimate cooling, etc.). Answers inquiries related to its programs.

51441. Tayloe Murphy Institute, Univ of Va., Dynamics Bldg, 4th Floor, 2015 Ivy Rd, Charlottesville, VA 22903-1780; (804) 971-2661. Serves business, education, and govt in Va. as research and info center. Records populations, income statistics, consumer behavior in state, more. Also serves as State Data Center, provides access to 1970 and 1980 Census computer tapes for Va. Library open to public.

51442. Technical Services Corp., 9022-C Telegraph Rd, Lorton, VA 22079; (703) 550-8282. Interest in standardization engineering, automatic data processing, technical writing, cataloging and data dissemination. Answers inquiries; provides consulting, data processing services, technical assistance, training; distributes catalogs; makes referrals. Most services for a fee.

51443. Telecommunications and Telephone Association, P.O. Box 2387, Arlington, VA 22202; (703) 521-1089. Also known as Telephone Users Assn, represents consumer interests in telephone rate cases and other telecommunication matters, provides info on telecommunications. Answers inquiries if accompanied by a SASE. Charges may be imposed to cover costs.

51444. Trout Unlimited, 501 Church St NE., Vienna, VA 22180; (703) 281-1100. Nonprofit conservation org interested in trout, salmon, and steelhead fishery resource management, trout research, conservation, air and water pollution, cold water fisheries resource-habitat. Answers brief inquiries, makes referrals to other info sources.

51445. Truck Trailer Manufacturers Association, c/o Charles J. Calvin, Pres, 1020 Princess St, Alexandria, VA 22314; (703) 549-3010. Interest in truck trailers, cargo containers. Makes referrals, provides reference services.

51446. U.S. Animal Health Association, 6924 Lakeside Ave, Ste 205, Richmond, VA 23228; (804) 266-3275. Coordinates activities among animal health orgs and serves as animal health clearinghouse among the assn, food-producing industries, and veterinary profession. Answers inquiries, distributes publications, makes referrals. Services free, except publications.

51447. U.S. Army Engineer Museum, ATZA-PTSP-M (Building 1000; 16th St and Belvoir Rd), Fort Belvoir, VA 22060-5054; (703) 664-6104. Museum is an element of U.S. Army Engineer Center and Fort Belvoir, specializing in history of U.S. Army Corps of Engineers, Belvoir's fort and plantation. Answers inquiries, provides referral and reference services, permits onsite use of collections. Services free to researchers.

51448. U.S. Homeopathic Association, 6560 Backlick Rd, Ste 211, Springfield, VA 22150; (703) 569-5300. Interested in field of homeopathy, homeopathic medicine. Answers inquiries; provides advisory, reference, referral services; conducts seminars; distributes publications; provides info on current research. Services generally free.

51449. U.S. Parachute Association, 1440 Duke St, Alexandria, VA 22314; (703) 836-3495. Promotes safety in parachuting, competitive sport parachuting; documents all record attempts in field. Answers inquiries, provides advisory and reference services, conducts seminars, permits onsite use of collections. Services may be free or at cost.

51450. United Fresh Fruit and Vegetable Association, N Washington at Madison, Alexandria, VA 22314; (703) 836-3410. Trade assn serving produce industry, consumers. Promotes use of fresh fruits and vegetables through public service announcements, films, newsletters, workshops for food service professionals, newspaper columns, articles, leaflets, distribution of recipes, etc. Publication list available.

51452. United Way of America, Information Center, 701 N Fairfax St, Alexandria, VA 22314; (703) 836-7100. Assn of autonomous United Ways across U.S., Canada, and overseas, interested in management of social and human services, volunteerism, fundraising. Provides computer-assisted subject searches of holdings, lends studies, makes referrals.

51454. VOLUNTEER: The National Center for Citizen Involvement, 1111 19th St, Ste 500, Arlington, VA 22209; (703) 276-0542. Works with natl network of community orgs, others to improve quality and quantity of volunteer services in U.S. Disseminates info, provides training, leadership development activities, initiates model programs, conducts surveys, provides consultation, maintains library.

51455. Valentine Museum, 1015 E Clay St, Richmond, VA 23219; (804) 649-0711. Collection of books, manuscripts, photographs etc. related to history of Richmond and surrounding region. Open to public by appointment. Staff will answer technical questions and authenticate documents by appointment. Consultation, duplication services also available.

51456. Vinifera Wine Growers Association, P.O. Box P, The Plains, VA 22171; (703) 754-8564. Interest in culture of European wine grape varieties in U.S., modernization of state wine laws, wine making, marketing. Answers inquiries, provides free advisory and reference services, conducts seminars, sells publications.

51457. Virginia Cooperative Fish and Wildlife Research Unit, 100 Cheatham Hall, Va. Polytechnic Institute and State Univ, Blacksburg, VA 24061; (703) 961-5927. Publicly funded unit that conducts fish and wildlife research, trains graduate students for fish and wildlife profession. Answers inquiries, provides info services, distributes publications, conducts seminars, permits onsite use of collections. Simple requests answered free.

51459. Virginia Historical Society, P.O. Box 7311 (428 N Blvd), Richmond, VA 23221; (804) 358-4901. Collection of manuscripts, journals, maps and more related to Va. and American history, including materials dating from 1590. Researchers, students assisted in using collections onsite. No mail order research services, though referrals made to other info sources. Photocopies sold.

51461. Virginia Institute of Marine Science, Gloucester Point, VA 23062; (804) 642-2111. Interest in all phases of seafood, commercial and sport fishing industries, development of fisheries, other marine resources, Chesapeake Bay, more. Answers inquiries, provides referral and consulting services, conducts courses and lectures, permits onsite reference, identifies animals, plants.

51462. Virginia Institute of Marine Science, Aquaculture Data Base, Gloucester Point, VA 23062; (804) 642-2111 ext 298. U.S.-funded terminal-searchable system of aquaculture info that is part of Lockheed DIALOG system. Entries to system provided by Virginia Institute of Marine Science. Each search includes printout with complete bibliographic info. Fee charged for each search.

51463. Virginia Institute of Marine Science, Marine Education Materials System, Dept of Advisory Services, VIMS-Sea Grant Marine Education Center, Gloucester Point, VA 23062; (804) 642-7169. Provides educational info on marine and fresh water environments for use by educators. Answers inquiries, provides advisory and consulting services, conducts seminars, distrib-

utes publications, permits onsite use of collection. Services generally free; primarily for educators, but others assisted.

51464. Virginia Poultry Breeders Club, c/o Tommy Stanley, Secty, Route 1, P.O. Box 551, Ashland, VA 23005; (804) 798-8111. Interest in breeding, preservation, and improvement of purebred poultry, education of the public about poultry. Answers inquiries free if SASE is provided.

51466. Vocational Industrial Clubs of America, P.O. Box 3000 (Route 15), Leesburg, VA 22075; (703) 777-8810. Represents students enrolled in trade and industrial, technical, and health occupations programs in public schools. Answers inquiries, provides advisory services, conducts seminars and conference, distributes publications. Info free, seminars and publications available for a fee.

51467. Volunteers in Technical Assistance, P.O. Box 12438 (1815 N Lynn St, Ste 200), Arlington, VA 22209-8438; (703) 276-1800. Nonprofit org that provides low-income people with locally available resources, technical assistance, with emphasis on agriculture, business, education, housing, etc. Answers inquiries, provides consulting services, referrals. Services free in developing countries, for a fee to others.

51468. War Memorial Museum of Virginia, 9285 Warwick Blvd, Huntington Park, Newport News, VA 23607; (804) 247-8523. Devoted to military history. Holds books, films, weapons, uniforms, posters, insignia, vehicles, accoutrements related to every major U.S. military involvement. Answers inquiries, provides research assistance.

51470. Water Resources Scientific Information Center, Water Resources Div, U.S. Geological Survey, 425 Natl Center, 11300 Sunrise Valley Drive, Reston, VA 22092; (703) 860-7455. Disseminates info on water-related research, including water policy, water pollution, water quality, water supply, etc. Center's resources provided to other research/info orgs. Online access to data base available on Dept. of Energy's RECON system, and through commercial orgs.

51472. Water and Sanitation for Health Project, Coordination and Information Center, c/o CDM & Assoc, 1611 N Kent St, Room 1002, Arlington, VA 22209; (703) 243-8200. U.S.-funded org that provides short-term technical consulting assistance to AID and AID-assisted developing countries and orgs. Answers inquiries; provides advisory, consulting, reference, translation services. Permits onsite use of collections. Public assisted free with AID approval.

51473. Western Dredging Association, 1911 N Fort Myer Dr, Ste 601, Arlington, VA 22209; (703) 524-6367. Intl engineering society dedicated to advancement of dredging technology, such related areas as harbor and waterway construction, environmental effects of dredging, etc. Answers inquiries, provides advisory services. Services, when extensive, provided at cost to nonmembers.

51474. Wilson's Disease Association, P.O. Box 489 (1737 Fort Henry Court), Dumfries, VA 22026; (703) 221-5532. Interest in symptoms, treatment, and current research in Wilson's disease, Menkes' disease, and other disorders of copper metabolism, copper content of foods. Answers inquiries, provides advisory and referral services, permits onsite use of collections. Services free.

51475. Wire Reinforcement Institute, 8361A Greensboro Dr, McLean, VA 22102; (703) 790-9790. Assn dedicated to promotion of welded wire fabric as reinforcement for concrete through scientific research and engineering. Answers inquiries; provides consulting services, info on R&D in progress; conducts workshops; distributes publications.

51476. Woman Activist, 2310 Barbour Rd, Falls Church, VA 22043; (703) 573-8716. Nonprofit org involved with issues of concern to women, including research, program development, report writing, polling, legislative liaison. Answers inquiries, provides consulting services, conducts workshops, distributes publications. Charge for some services, primarily for women; others assisted.

51477. Women and Mathematics Education, c/o Education Dept, George Mason Univ, 4400 Univ Dr, Fairfax, VA 22030; (703) 323-2421. Interest in mathematical education of women and girls, nonsexist education. Answers inquiries free, distributes materials at cost. Services available to those concerned with promotion of mathematics education for women and girls.

51478. Women in Community Service, 1900 Beauregard St, Ste 108, Alexandria, VA 22311; (703) 671-0500. Coalition of women's volunteer orgs that coordinates community programs to combat poverty in U.S., with emphasis on services to young women. Answers inquiries from both Job Corps prospects, potential volunteers. Services free, available in more than 200 communities.

51479. World Federation for Mental Health, 1021 Prince St, Alexandria, VA 22314-2932. Coordinates activities of mental health orgs worldwide. Interest in mental health services and advocacy, promotion of optimal function, aging, abused children, victims of discrimination. Answers inquiries, provides advisory services, conducts seminars, distributes publications, makes referrals.

Washington

52003. Abernathy Salmon Technology Center, U.S. Fish and Wildlife Service, 1440 Abernathy Rd, Longview, WA 98632; (206) 425-6072. Interest in development of fish cultural methods, salmon hatchery operations, marking of salmon, effects of salmon raceway types on young salmon, salmon diets, selective breeding program of salmon, density and growth rates. Answers inquiries, permits onsite use of collections.

52004. Abundant Life Seed Foundation, P.O. Box 772 (1029 Lawrence St), Port Townsend, WA 98368; (206) 385-5660. Interest in acquisition, propagation of Pacific Northwest plants and seed, particularly older, nonhybrid, and endangered species. Answers inquiries; provides consulting, advisory, reference services; conducts workshops, seminars. Services for a fee.

52005. Agriculture Research Center, Wash. State Univ, Pullman, WA 99163; (509) 335-4563. Interest in general agriculture, agronomy, animal science, food science, entomology, forestry, horticulture, rural sociology, veterinary science, soil science, human nutrition, family studies, interior design, textiles. Answers inquiries, makes referrals, provides consulting services.

52006. Albrook Hydraulics Laboratory, College of Engineering, Wash. State Univ, Pullman, WA 99164; (509) 335-4546. Interested in hydraulics, fluid mechanics, hydromechanics, hydrology, dams, water supply, watershed precipitation, runoff, estuaries, sedimentation, slurry pipelines, floating breakwaters, floods, more. Answers brief inquiries, provides consulting services for a fee, permits onsite reference by request.

52008. American Council on Rural Special Education, Western Wash. Univ, Bellingham, WA 98225; (206) 676-3000. Concerned with needs of rural educators, parents, students. Operates job referral service, conducts special education conferences, sells audio cassette and rural in-service modules. Services for a fee.

52009. American Holistic Medical Association, 2727 Fairview Ave E, Ste D, Seattle, WA 98102; (206) 322-6842. Founded to provide physicians and health professionals with education in principles of holistic health and medicine. Conducts natl conference annually, continuing medical education programs and certification programs in nutrition, exercise, self-regulation, and other selected topics.

52010. American Plywood Association, P.O. Box 11700, Tacoma, WA 98411; (206) 565-6600. Interest in engineering research and quality validation of western softwood, southern pine plywood, and other types of wood-based structural panels, basic properties and use of plywood, conservation, forestry management. Answers inquiries; provides referrals, reference services.

52011. Applied Physics Laboratory, Univ of Wash., 1013 NE 40th St, Seattle, WA 98105; (206) 543-1300. Researches underwater and atmospheric acoustics, ocean physics and engineering, Arctic technology, acoustic lenses, unmanned underwater research vehicles, Arctic oceanography. Answers inquiries, provides consulting services, conducts research at cost to all users. Permits onsite reference.

52012. Association for Persons with Severe Handicaps, 7010 Roosevelt Way NE, Seattle, WA 98115; (206) 523-

8446. Promotes quality education and life for persons with severe handicaps from birth through adulthood; serves as advocate for handicapped in legal proceedings. Answers inquiries; provides reference, referral services, seminars, data, publications. Services free to members, at cost to others.

52014. Battelle Memorial Institute, Office of Hazardous Waste Management, Project Management Division, 601 Williams Blvd, 4th Fl, Richland, WA 99352; (509) 943-5504. Interest in toxic and hazardous substances, including physical, chemical, commercial, toxicological aspects, with emphasis on water pollution. Answers inquiries or refers inquirers to other info sources, conducts research, offers consulting services on a cost-plus basis.

52015. Behavioral Alcohol Research Laboratory, Dept of Psychology, Univ of Wash., Seattle, WA 98195; (206) 545-1395. Research org that studies prevention, treatment of alcohol abuse using simulated cocktail lounge in which drinking behavior can be observed and studied. Answers inquiries, provides advisory and referral services, conducts seminars, evaluates data. Services free to anyone.

52016. Boeing Company, Technical Libraries, P.O. Box 3707, M/S 74-60, Seattle, WA 98124; (206) 237-8314. Technical libraries devoted to aeronautics, missiles, space flight, engineering, electronics, computer technology, more. Makes interlibrary loans of unclassified, nonproprietary materials by arrangement.

52017. Boise Cascade Corporation, Pulp and Paper Research Library, 909 W 7th St, Vancouver, WA 98600; (206) 695-4477 ext 113. Interest in pulp and paper technology and chemistry, engineering. Answers inquiries, provides reference services, makes referrals to other info sources. Services free to anyone.

52018. Center for Quantitative Science in Forestry, Fisheries, Wildlife, Univ of Wash., 3737 15th Ave NE, Seattle, WA 98195; (206) 543-1191. Interest in ecosystem modeling, animal population dynamics and population estimation, systems analysis of north Pacific fisheries, modeling of fisheries and forest resources. Answers brief inquiries. Results of completed research free to anyone.

52019. Center for Research in Oral Biology, Univ of Wash., Health Sciences Center B-530, SM-42, Seattle, WA 98195; (206) 543-5599. Conducts investigations and studies relating to cause, prevention, diagnosis, and treatment of dental diseases and conditions. Answers inquiries, provides advisory service and info on current research, conducts seminars. Services available to anyone; fees charged to commercial users.

52020. Center for Studies in Demography and Ecology, Dept of Sociology, Univ of Wash., Savery Hall, DK-40, Seattle, WA 98195; (206) 543-5035. Resource center on demography, human ecology, and vital statistics, with emphasis on study of fertility, city structure, and U.S. historical data. Answers specific inquiries, makes referrals, permits onsite use of collection. Services available to serious researchers only.

52021. Center for Urban Horticulture, Univ of Wash., GF-15, Seattle, WA 98195; (206) 543-8616. Center for research and education on functional use of plants to maintain and enhance urban environments and utilization of plants in landscape situations. Answers inquiries, distributes educational materials and other publications free.

52022. Charles R. Conner Museum, Wash. State Univ, Pullman, WA 99164; (509) 335-1977. Conducts research and instruction in natural history and systematics of vertebrates, including birds, mammals, reptiles, and amphibians. Answers inquiries free, lends materials. Research collections open to qualified scientists and students; public display museum open to all.

52023. Coastal Washington Research and Extension Unit, Rte 1, Box 570, Long Beach, WA 98631; (206) 642-2031. Interest in cranberry culture, postharvest physiology and storage of cranberries, weed control, fertilizers. Answers inquiries; provides advisory, reference, abstracting, indexing services and publications; evaluates data. Services free to anyone.

52024. Copyright Information Services, 440 Tucker Ave, Friday Harbor, WA 98250; (206) 378-5128. Interest in application of copyright law to educators, librarians, industrial training specialists. Answers inquiries; provides consulting and reference services, training sessions, publications, referrals. Services for a fee, primarily for specialists.

52025. Cox Group, P.O. Box 175 (246 E Bartlett Rd), Lynden, WA 98264; (206) 398-7073. Assists qualified, professional scientists and inventors in research, development, marketing, and financing of inventions. Answers inquiries; provides advisory, referral, copying services; evaluates data. Services free to scientists and inventors, but contributions welcomed.

52026. Cybele Society, Peyton Bldg, Ste 414, Spokane, WA 99201; (509) 838-2332. Natl medical org for maternity care professionals that promotes benefits of family-centered maternity care and assists providers through publications, consultation, and educational programs. Answers inquiries. Services available to providers of maternal/newborn care; fees charged for some services.

52027. Delta Society, 212 Wells Ave South, Ste C, Renton, WA 98055; (206) 226-7357. Intl educational, research, and service org that provides info on relationships between people, animals, and environment. Answers inquiries; provides consulting, reference services; permits onsite use of collection. Services for a fee.

52028. Drug Information Center, College of Pharmacy, Wash. State Univ, Wegner Hall, Room 155, Pullman, WA 99164-6510; (509) 335-1402. Interest in pharmacology, biopharmaceutics, clinical pharmacy, adverse drug reactions, drug interactions, foreign drug identification, medical and herbal therapies. Answers patient and professional inquiries free of charge, commercial firms for a fee.

52030. Emergency Response Institute, 1819 Mark St NE, Olympia, WA 98506. Interest in emergency preparedness education, survival, outdoor recreation safety, search and rescue, civil defense education, aviation crash survival. Answers inquiries, provides consulting services, conducts workshops, distributes handbooks. Services generally available for a fee.

52031. Energy Business Association of Washington, Maritime Bldg, Ste 300A, 911 Western Ave, Seattle, WA 98104; (206) 622-7171. Interest in energy-efficient home construction techniques, solar and renewable resource technologies and professions. Answers inquiries, provides advisory and reference services, conducts seminars, distributes publications and data. Consumer info services free.

52032. Fairhaven College Outback Program, Western Washington Univ, Bellingham, WA 98225; (206) 676-3680. Provides education through experience and experimentation in organic agriculture, animal husbandry, and "soft" technology. Facilities include farm where projects are carried out. Answers inquiries about program, makes referrals to other info sources. Services free.

52033. Federation of Western Outdoor Clubs, 1516 Melrose Ave, Seattle, WA 98122; (206) 621-1696. Interest in subjects relating to environment, wilderness management, politics of environmental protection, wilderness preservation. Answers inquiries as time permits, makes referrals, permits onsite use of collection by bona fide scholars and environmentalists.

52034. Fisheries Research Institute, College of Ocean and Fishery Sciences, WH-10, Univ of Wash., Seattle, WA 98195; (206) 543-4650. Interest in Alaskan, international North Pacific, and Soviet fisheries, dynamics of aquatic populations, management of commercial and sport fisheries, more. Answers brief inquiries, provides consulting services for a fee. Results of completed research available at nominal copying charge.

52035. Fred Hutchinson Cancer Research Center, 1124 Columbia St, Seattle, WA 98104; (800) 4-CANCER. Comprehensive cancer center that engages in wide range of research. Answers inquiries, provides consulting and reference services, permits onsite use of collections. Services generally free to health professionals from Pacific Northwest. Toll-free service provides info, referrals to public.

52036. Friday Harbor Laboratories, Univ of Wash., Friday Harbor, WA 98250; (206) 378-2165. Conducts research in marine sciences, especially marine biology, experimental and comparative embryology of marine invertebrates. Answers reference questions, does computerized searching for a fee. Makes interlibrary loans and permits onsite use of collections.

52037. Friends of Mineralogy, c/o Raymond Lasmanis, V.P., Geology and Earth Resources Division, Dept of Natural Resources, Olympia, WA 98504; (206) 459-6372. Nonprofit org interested in geology, mineralogy, mineral collectors and collections, mineral specimens. Answers inquiries, conducts seminars and workshops, distributes publications, makes referrals to other info sources.

52038. Gluten Intolerance Group of North America, P.O. Box 23053, Seattle, WA 98102; Newsletter Editor (206) 325-6980. Org of health professionals and patients suffering from gluten-sensitive diseases (sprue and dermatitis herpetiformis). Advises its members on diet, disseminates info on celiac sprue research, product and drug info, and new recipe ideas. Membership is by fee.

52039. Halibut Association of North America, 309 Maritime Bldg, 911 Western Ave, Seattle, WA 98104; (206) 623-0102. Membership org of halibut dealers in Wash., Alaska, and British Columbia. Promotes halibut products; undertakes research, public education, advertising programs to increase the use of halibut products by public.

52040. Hanford Technical Library, Battelle-NW Technical Information Section, P.O. Box 999, Richland, WA 99352; (509) 376-5451. Interest in nuclear science, engineering, applied physics, chemistry, metallurgy, radiological sciences, biological sciences, ecology, pollution. Answers inquiries; provides reference, consulting, referral services; permits onsite use of collection by arrangement.

52041. USAF Survival School, Public Affairs Division, Headquarters, 3636th Combat Crew Training Wing (Survival) (ATC), Fairchild Air Force Base, WA 99011; (509) 247-2367. Conducts all U.S. Air Force survival training. Aircrew members, other personnel are prepared to survive in any environment through basic training in all climes and in water. Answers inquiries, makes referrals. Limited unclassified materials available to public.

52042. Historical Society of Seattle and King County Museum, 2700 24th Ave E, Seattle, WA 98112; (206) 324-1125. History museum covering Seattle, Alaska, and Pacific Northwest regional history of 18th and 19th Centuries, including maritime, transportation, aeronautics, and fashion. Answers inquiries; provides reference, copying services. Museum open seven days, library by appointment only. Fees charged.

52043. Honeywell Marine Systems Division, Honeywell, Inc., 5303 Shilshole Ave NW., Seattle, WA 98107; (206) 789-2000 ext 1650 or 1375. Resource for info on marine systems, acoustics, signal processing, computer science, marine engineering, sonar, marine technology, sonics and ultrasonics. Answers inquiries, makes interlibrary loans. Services free, unless extensive.

52044. Institute for Food Science and Technology, College of Ocean and Fishery Sciences, Univ of Wash., Seattle, WA 98195; (206) 543-4281. Engages in teaching and research in food science and technology, especially fish technology, food microbiology, food engineering, food toxins and carcinogens. Answers inquiries, provides consulting services, conducts seminars. Info free, other services for a fee.

52045. Institute for Movement Therapy, 1607 13th Ave, Seattle, WA 98122; (206) 329-8680. Interest in dance and movement therapy, kinesthetics, psychotherapy, stress control, self-awareness. Answers inquiries, provides consulting and referral services, conducts workshops and courses. Services for a fee.

52046. Institute of Environmental Sciences Solar Radiation Committee, c/o Albert R. Lunde, Committee Chairman, Boeing Co, 2-5615 MS 86-01, P.O. Box 3999, Seattle, WA 98124. Interest in terrestrial and space solar radiation, both spectral and total. Examines effects of solar radiation on materials, spacecraft, space flight through lab simulation. Answers inquiries and provides advisory services for free, within limits.

52047. International Association for the Study of Pain, 909 NE 43rd Street, Room 204, Seattle, WA 98105; Executive Officer (206) 547-6409. Nonprofit assn that fosters research of pain mechanisms and syndromes, helps improve management of acute and chronic pain, promotes education and training in field of pain. Refers patients to pain clinics.

52048. International Association of Women Police, P.O. Box 15207, Wedgewood Station, Seattle, WA 98115. Interest in women law enforcement officers, police procedures and techniques, forensic science, police and community relations, discipline and labor relations in police orgs, police management. Answers inquiries accompanied by SASE.

52049. International Foundation for Homeopathy, 2366 Eastlake Ave E, Ste 301, Seattle, WA 98102; Executive Director (206) 324-8230. Nonprofit org that promotes better understanding of health and disease through homeopathy by increasing public education, R&D, education of professionals in use of homeopathy and founding of a homeopathic medical college.

52050. International Pacific Halibut Commission, P.O. Box 95009 (Oceanography Teaching Bldg, Room 250, Univ of Wash.), Seattle, WA 98145; (206) 634-1838. Jointly maintained by govts of Canada and U.S., interested in Pacific halibut, fisheries management, conservation. Conducts research, publishes results, recommends regulations to govts of two countries.

52051. International Radio Club of America, P.O. Box 21074, Seattle, WA 98111; (206) 784-5145. Devoted to listening for distant radio stations on medium-wave broadcast band (510-1630 kHz). Answers inquiries, conducts seminars and workshops, distributes publications. Services primarily for members, but provided at cost to others.

52052. International Society for Optical Engineering, P.O. Box 10 (1022 19th St), Bellingham, WA 98227; (206) 676-3290. Interest in optical and electro-optical engineering, instrumentation, and applications in medicine, astronomy, industry. Answers inquiries or refers inquirers to other sources of info.

52053. International Stop Continental Drift Society, Star Route Box 38, Winthrop, WA 98962; (509) 996-2576. Seeks to establish alternatives to plate tectonics and continental drift theories and arrest crustal plate motions, sea-floor spreading and plate subduction. Answers inquiries, evaluates data, makes referrals. Services for a fee.

52054. Interspecies Communication, 273 Hidden Meadow, Friday Harbor, WA 98250; (206) 378-5186. Nonprofit org that conducts research on man-animal communication and relationships. Other interests: music, whales, dolphins, Shamanism. Answers inquiries; provides advisory, consulting, reference services and data. Permits onsite use of collection. Services available for a fee.

52055. James R. Slater Museum of Natural History, Univ of Puget Sound, Tacoma, WA 98416; (206) 756-3189. Interest in flora and fauna of northwestern U.S., northwestern Canada, and Alaska; mammals, birds, reptiles, amphibians, and some marine invertebrates. Provides consulting, reference services; lends specimens to scientists working in related fields.

52057. Laboratory of Radiation Ecology, College of Ocean and Fishery Sciences, Univ of Wash., Seattle, WA 98105; (206) 543-4257. Studies distribution, concentration, effects of radionuclides in aquatic environments; radioecology of coral atolls; radiation chemistry; biogeochemistry of transuranic elements in western Pacific Ocean, Alaska, Puget Sound. Answers inquiries, provides consulting services.

52058. Magic Lantern Society of the United States and Canada, 819 14th St NE, Auburn, WA 98002; (206) 833-7784. Interest in magic lanterns and other vintage kinetic-type optical devices, magic lantern manufacturers, lantern slide makers, and lantern slide artists. Answers inquiries; provides seminars, publications, magic lantern shows, reference services, referrals. Services available at cost.

52059. Middle East Resource Center, Univ of Wash., 318 Thomson Hall (DR-05), Seattle, WA 98195; (206) 543-7236. Focuses on Middle East, Near East, north Africa. Answers inquiries; provides advisory, consulting, reference, referral services; conducts seminars, workshops; lends materials. Services free, except for consulting. Loan of materials restricted to Northwest.

52060. Movari, P.O. Box 21963, Seattle, WA 98111; (206) 322-6110. Researches and disseminates info about nonsmokers' rights and methods to develop and implement smoke-free work policies worldwide. Answers inquiries; provides consulting, reference, advisory, referral services, publications; analyzes data; conducts workshops. Services for a fee.

52061. Mycological Herbarium, Dept of Plant Pathology, Wash. State Univ, Pullman, WA 99164; (509) 335-3732. Resource center on fungi, plant taxonomy, toxicology, plant pathology. Holds about 70,000 fungal specimens. Lends materials, permits onsite use of collections. Services free to anyone connected with a univ or research lab.

52062. National Association for the Deaf-Blind, 12573 SE 53d Pl, Bellevue, WA 98006; (206) 747-2611. Nonprofit advocacy org that seeks to further educational, rehab, and employment opportunities for deaf-blind. Answers inquiries; provides free advisory and reference services, info on current research, referrals to other sources of info.

52063. National Association to Keep and Bear Arms, P.O. Box 78336 (8434 Rainier Ave S), Seattle, WA 98178; (206) 725-5888. Devoted to retaining right of American citizens under Constitution to keep and bear arms. Answers inquiries, distributes publications. Services available for a fee.

52064. National Rental Service Association, c/o Keelers Home Nursing Supply, 2009 W Lincoln Ave, Yakima, WA 98902; (509) 452-6542. Assn of companies that rent, sell medical and party equipment. Answers inquiries; conducts annual convention with seminars and exhibits of party and medical supplies; distributes publications, data compilations; makes referrals. Services primarily for members, but others assisted.

52066. Northwest Institute of Acupuncture and Oriental Medicine, P.O. Box 31639 (144 NE 54th St), Seattle, WA 98103; (206) 525-6887. Nonprofit org devoted to bringing practice of acupuncture and Oriental medicine into American society to complement Western healing arts. Answers inquiries; conducts seminars, clinical training programs; provides advisory, reference services. Services free, except courses.

52067. Northwest Pulp and Paper Association, 1300 114th Ave SE, Ste 110, Bellevue, WA 98004; (206) 455-1323. Promotes pulp and paper industry of Ore., Wash., and Alaska, including environmental, energy, and economic issues, legislation and public education. Answers inquiries, makes referrals.

52068. Northwest Regional Calibration Center, 300 120th Ave NE, Building No 6, Bellevue, WA 98005; (206) 455-1999. Conducts calibration and testing services for a variety of oceanographic research and water quality instruments. Answers inquiries; provides advisory, consulting, calibration, testing services; conducts seminars, workshops. Services provided at cost.

52069. Northwest Regional Foundation, E 525 Mission, Spokane, WA 99202; (509) 484-6733. Nonprofit corp that develops community education programs aimed at increasing awareness of contemporary problems. Answers inquiries, provides consulting, and refer-

ence services, conducts seminars, evaluates data. Services free.

52070. Northwest Sports Medicine Foundation, 1551 NW 54th St, Ste 200, Seattle, WA 98107; (206)782-3383. Nonprofit org that fosters development and implementation of programs in preventive and sports medicine, treatment of sports-related injuries, greater appreciation of athletics. Answers inquiries; provides advisory and referral services, conducts seminars. Services provided at cost.

52071. Northwest Women's Law Center, 119 S Main St, Ste 330, Seattle, WA 98104; (206)682-9552. Works to secure equal rights for women, provides legal representation for sex discrimination cases, sponsors educational programs on women's legal rights. Answers inquiries, provides reference and referral services, conducts seminars. Services free, except seminars.

52072. Nuclear Radiation Center, Wash. State Univ, Pullman, WA 99164; (509) 335-8641. Interest in radiation research, nuclear power and the environment, nuclear power plant operator training, neutron activation analysis, coal liquefaction research, geochemistry. Answers inquiries, provides consulting services, conducts seminars. Some publications free, others at cost.

52073. Nuclear Reactor Laboratories, Univ of Wash., Mail Stop FD-10, Seattle, WA 98195; (206) 543-4170. Conducts research on neutron physics, radiation shielding, devices for neutron spectrum measurements, bionuclear applications, two-phase flow, reactor safety analysis, radiation dosimetry, neutron radiography. Performs complete activation analysis services, irradiation services for a fee.

52075. Pacific Coast Oyster Growers Association, 1437 Elliott Ave W, Seattle, WA 98119; (206) 281-4010. Interest in oyster production, import, export, processing, and shipping; federal, state, and local rules, regulations, and authority over operations of oyster business. Answers inquiries.

52076. Pacific Northwest Regional Health Sciences Library Service, Univ of Wash., SB-55 (Warren G. Magnuson Health Sciences Center, 1801 NE Pacific St), Seattle, WA 98195; (206) 543-8262. Regional Medical Library that coordinates development of a health info network within region and provides backup info services. Provides consulting, reference, and interlibrary loan services; conducts workshop. Services available to health care professionals on cost-recovery basis.

52077. Pacific Northwest Waterways Association, P.O. Box 61473 (915 Broadway, Ste 300), Vancouver, WA 98666; (206) 699-4666. Nonprofit membership corp dedicated to comprehensive planning and development of water and related land resources of the region. Distributes publications, makes referrals. Reference sources, speakers available without charge.

52078. Pacific Science Center, 200 Second Ave North, Seattle, WA 98109; (206) 625-9333. Examines methods, meaning, role, impact, and potential of science and technology in modern society. Conducts educational programs for schools and individuals. Exhibits open to public for admission fee.

52079. Pain Center, School of Medicine, Univ of Wash., 1959 NE Pacific St, Seattle, WA 98105; (206) 543-3236. Engaged in study and treatment of pain, especially chronic pain. Provides consulting services, conducts seminars. Referral by a physician necessary for clinical evaluation.

52080. Particle Information Services, 34467 Hood Canal Dr NE, Kingston, WA 98346; (206) 638-2034. Studies fine particle technology, particle sizing, particle counting, dust calibration standards. Answers inquiries, provides reference services, sells calibrated fine particles for various purposes.

52081. Polar Science Center, Applied Physics Laboratory, Univ of Wash., 4057 Roosevelt Way NE, Seattle, WA 98105; (206) 543-6613. Conducts basic, applied, theoretical, experimental research in physical sciences and provides operations support for Arctic oceanographic field research. Answers inquiries; provides advisory, referral services; permits onsite use of collections. Services at cost.

52082. Primate Information Center, Regional Primate Research Center SJ-50, Univ of Wash., Seattle, WA 98195; (206) 543-4376. Provides literature-based info on living, nonhuman primates to scientists studying these animals for themselves or as surrogates for humans. Answers inquiries, makes referrals, prepares topical bibliographies available on a fee basis.

52083. Primate Supply Information Clearinghouse, Regional Primate Research Center SJ-50, Univ of Wash., Seattle, WA 98195; (206) 543-5178. Provides communications channels needed by American institutions holding and using nonhuman primates to share animals and other materials such as blood specimens, tissues, cadavers. Answers inquiries on primate supply; provides matching, advertising, and referral services.

52084. Program for Appropriate Technology in Health, 130 Nickerson St, Seattle, WA 98109; (206) 285-3500. Committed to development, promotion, introduction of technology for primary health care programs in developing countries. Answers inquiries; provides advisory, reference, abstracting, referral services; evaluates data; distributes publications. Services generally free to program administrators.

52085. Puget Sound Naval Shipyard Engineering Library, Code 202.5, Bremerton, WA 98314; (206) 476-2767. Resource center on naval architecture, engineering, pure and applied sciences, naval history. Makes interlibrary loans of nonclassified materials (no fee for copying).

52086. Puget Sound Power and Light Company, Puget Power Bldg, Bellevue, WA 98009; (206) 454-6363. Concerned with electric utility engineering, economics, and management. Answers inquiries; provides advisory, reference, literature-searching, copying, microform services, and info on current R&D; makes referrals to other info sources. Services free to anyone.

52087. Radical Women, 3815 Fifth Ave NE, Seattle, WA 98105; (206) 632-1815. Interest in women's role in society, economic status, social and political issues including race, sexual orientation, labor, rights of young people and elderly. Answers inquiries, provides reference and referral services, distributes publications. Services free.

52088. Rainier Brewing Company Quality Control Laboratories, 3100 Airport Way S, Seattle, WA 98134; (206) 622-2600. Interest in all aspects of beer and beer brewing: raw materials and analysis, including yeast and hops, process, fermentation, equipment, by-products, chemistry, flavor, stability, consumption. Permits onsite reference.

52089. Red Cedar Shingle & Handsplit Shake Bureau, 515 116th Ave NE, Ste 275, Bellevue, WA 98004; (206) 453-1323. Devoted to red cedar shingles, machine-grooved red cedar shingles, rebutted-rejointed red cedar shingles, handsplit-resawn, tapersplit, and straight-split red cedar shakes. Answers technical inquiries.

52090. Rockwell Hanford Operations, Energy Systems Group, P.O. Box 800, Richland, WA 99352; (509) 376-6898. Operates Basalt Waste Isolation Program and provides nuclear support services for Hanford nuclear reactor site. Answers inquiries; provides reference, referral services, info on R&D, publications. Permits onsite use of report collection. Services free to most users.

52091. Small Business Development Center, College of Business and Economics, Wash. State Univ, 180 Nickerson St, Ste 310, Seattle, WA 98109; (206)464-5450. Provides assistance to small businesses in Wash. Answers inquiries, provides advisory, consulting, and reference services, conducts workshops, performs innovation assessments. Services available to Wash.-based small businesses. Fee for some services.

52093. Survival Education Association, 9035 Golden Givens Rd, Tacoma, WA 98445; (206) 531-3156. Provides educational programs to teach survival and self-reliancy for wilderness, man-made and natural disasters; search and rescue training; survival medicine; more. Answers inquiries, provides advisory services, distributes publications. Services provided at cost.

52094. Tissue Banking and Distribution Program, Regional Primate Research Center SJ-50, Univ of Wash., Seattle, WA 98195; (206) 543-6999. Provides nonhuman primate tissues, blood samples, and cadavers to biomedical scientists for educational purposes (limited species available: Macaca and Papio). Answers inquiries; prepares and ships fresh, frozen, and fixed tissues for a fee plus shipping cost.

52095. Treaty Research Center, Univ of Wash., Seattle, WA 98195; (206) 543-8030. Mission is to establish and maintain data bank on as many as possible of the world's treaties since 1900. Answers inquiries; provides custom printouts, reference services; permits onsite use of collection. Charges for some services.

52096. Tree Fruit Research Center, Wash. State Univ, 1100 N Western, Wenatchee, WA 98801; (509) 663-8181. Researches deciduous tree fruit production, with special capabilities in nutrition, soil and pest management, fruit storage, marketing. Answers inquiries, evaluates data, provides info on R&D in progress. Services free, restricted to fruit growers and affiliated industries.

52097. U.S. Columbia Basin Project, Bureau of Reclamation, U.S Dept of the Interior, P.O. Box 815 (C St NW and Division), Ephrata, WA 98823; (509) 754-4611. Interest in Columbia Basin project's development for irrigation, power, flood control, fish and wildlife, and recreation enhancement. Answers inquiries involving general and technical info on Columbia Basin Project, permits onsite use of collection.

52098. U.S. Forestry Sciences Laboratory, U.S. Forest Service, 1133 N Western Ave, Wenatchee, WA 98801; (509) 662-4315. Conducts research on upper slope mixed conifer forests of interior Northwest, focusing on reforestation environments, site productivity. Provides advisory and referral services, info on current research; hosts workshops; distributes publications. Services free.

52099. U.S. Pacific Marine Center, National Ocean Service, NOAA, 1801 Fairview Ave E, Seattle, WA 98102; (206) 442-7657. Interest in hydrography, cartography, photogrammetry, geodesy, tides and currents. Answers inquiries relating to availability of National Ocean Service products, lends motion pictures.

52100. U.S. Spokane Research Center, Bureau of Mines, E 315 Montgomery Ave, Spokane, WA 99207; (509) 484-1610. Conducts research to improve mine design, safety, and efficiency and techniques for evaluating risk potential of different mining operations. Library open to public, Mon.-Fri. Publications available for public viewing. Inquiries referred to appropriate sources.

52101. United Indians of All Tribes Foundation, Center Three, P.O. Box 99253, Discovery Park, Seattle, WA 98199; (206) 328-2850. Offers consulting, field training to Indian education projects serving Native American students in Wash., Ore., Idaho, Alaska. Provides consulting, seminars, publications; permits onsite use of collection. All inquiries answered free, but priority given to Indian Education Act grantees.

52104. Washington People First, P.O. Box 381 (505 Broadway, Room 5), Tacoma, WA 98401; (206) 272-2811. Promotes self-help and self-advocacy for people with developmental disabilities. Answers inquiries, provides advisory and reference services, distributes publications. Services free, except for postage, available to disabled, their families, professionals.

52107. Washington State Chimney Sweep Guild, P.O. Box 31851, Seattle, WA 91803; (206) 630-5337. Assn of professional chimney sweeps that encourages fire safety in home and safety of on-the-job members. Promotes certification of chimney sweeps. Answers inquiries; conducts continuing education courses, public education campaigns; makes referrals. Services free.

52108. Washington State Historical Society, 315 N Stadium Way, Tacoma, WA 98403; (206) 593-2830. Resource center on history of Wash. and Pacific Northwest. Answers inquiries; provides reference, literature-searching, referral services; conducts seminars, workshops; distributes publications. Permits onsite use of collections. Charges for copying.

52109. Westinghouse Hanford Company, P.O. Box 1970, Richland, WA 99352; (509) 376-5101. Interest in liquid metal fast breeder reactors, fusion materials research. Public Relations Office answers brief inquiries. Requests for technical documents made through U.S. Energy Dept's Technical Information Center.

52110. Weyerhaeuser Company, Technical Information Center, WTC/TIC, Tacoma, WA 98477; (206) 924-6267. Interest in forestry and forest products, chemicals, aquaculture, energy, construction, horticulture. Answers inquiries, makes reciprocal interlibrary loans. Services free, except for postage, for employees and Wash. Library Network. Available to public by appointment.

52111. Whatcom Museum of History and Art, 121 Prospect St, Bellingham, WA 98225; (206) 676-6981. Maintains collections and exhibits of artifacts, fine art and photoarchives related to Northwest regional history, art. Answers inquiries, provides copying and referral services, permits onsite use of collections. Services free, unless for commercial purposes.

52112. Wood Technology Laboratory, College of Engineering, Wash. State Univ, Pullman, WA 99164; (509) 335-4916. Devoted to wood science, technology, adhesion, nondestructive testing, timber construction, timber physics. Answers inquiries; provides advisory, referral, copying services; conducts workshops; permits onsite use of collections. Services free, except copying.

52113. World Concern, Box 33000 (19303 Fremont Ave N), Seattle, WA 98133; (206) 546-7201. Private intl relief agency that develops, administers, and implements self-help programs in Third World and acts as a sending agency for professionals overseas. Answers inquiries, provides advisory services, distributes publications. Services free, unless extensive.

52114. Yakima Agricultural Research Laboratory, Agricultural Research Service, USDA, 3706 W Nob Hill Blvd, Yakima, WA 98902; (509) 575-5877. Interest in research on insects of fruits, vegetables, and field crops; pesticide residues; isolation, identification, and synthesis of insect attractants. Answers inquiries, provides research info, evaluates data. Services free.

West Virginia

53003. American Association of Zoological Parks and Aquariums, Oglebay Park, Wheeling, WV 26003; (304) 242-2160. Promotes zoological institutions for public education. Publishes monthly newsletter and magazine; answers inquiries; conducts conferences, seminars, and workshops; makes referrals to other sources of info.

53004. American Canal and Transportation Center, P.O. Box 310, Shepherdstown, WV 25443; (304) 876-2464. Commercial org with interest in canals, transportation history, industrial archeology. Holdings include canal boat models, prints. Publishes numerous books, provides consulting services, evaluates data, distributes publications. Services provided at cost.

53005. American Committee to Advance the Study of Petroglyphs and Pictographs, P.O. Box 260 (1100 Washington St), Harpers Ferry, WV 25425; (304) 535-6977. Interest in petroglyphs; pictographs; study, documentation, conservation, preservation, and interpretation of rock art. Answers inquiries; provides advisory, reference, literature-searching services; distributes publications. Services may be provided for a fee.

53006. Appalachia Educational Laboratory, Inc., P.O. Box 1348 (1031 Quarrier St), Charleston, WV 25325; (304) 347-0400. Conducts R&D in early childhood and parenting, career decisionmaking, and basic skills; provides educational services in problem identification, dissemination, and technical assistance and training to educators; offers consulting services to regional, state, or local education agencies.

53007. Appalachian Geological Society, P.O. Box 2605, Charleston, WV 25329. Interest in geology and technology relating to exploration for and recovery of petroleum and natural gas. Answers inquiries, conducts seminars and workshops, sells publications. Except for publications, services free.

53008. Appalachian Trail Conference, P.O. Box 236, Harpers Ferry, WV 25425; (304) 535-6331. Interst in administration and preservation of Appalachian Trail (covering 14 states and 2,106 miles from Maine to Georgia); hiking. Publishes bimonthly magazine, guidebooks, and other publications for trail users and maintainers. Answers inquiries.

53009. Autism Services Center, 101 Richmond St, Huntington, WV 25702; (304) 525-8014. Interest in public education, advocacy, training, and consultation concerning autism. Has autism library; publishes reprints, brochure; answers inquiries; provides adviso-

ry, reference services. Some services free; consultation and other services provided under contract.

53011. Automobile License Plate Collectors Association, c/o Gary Brent Kincade, Secty-Treas, P.O. Box 712, Weston, WV 26452; (304) 842-3773. Promotes interest in collecting of motor vehicle license plates. Answers inquiries, provides reference services, distributes publications, makes referrals to other sources of info. Int convention held each June.

53012. Brooks Bird Club, 707 Warwood Ave, Wheeling, WV 26003. Interst in surveys of plant and bird life in W.Va., including breeding birds and hawks, counts, bird banding. Answers inquiries, distributes data compilations and publications, permits onsite use of collection. Services free, except for publications.

53013. Eastern Professional River Outfitters Association, c/o Willis H. Hertig, Jr., Box 127, Barboursville, WV 25504. Organized to advance safety on rivers, improve quality of river trip experience, and to promote, advance, and conserve wilderness and wildlife areas of Eastern U.S. Answers inquiries free, conducts seminars and workshops for a fee.

53014. Fenton Art Glass Collectors of America, Inc., P.O. Box 384, Williamstown, WV 26187; (304) 375-6196. Interest in American-made glass, Fenton art glass. Has small number of previous catalogs of Fenton Art Glass Co. Publishes *The Butterfly Net* (bimonthly), answers inquiries, makes referrals to other sources of info. Services free.

53015. Fish Health Research Laboratory, U.S. Fish and Wildlife Service, Box 700, Kearneysville, WV 25430; (304) 725-8461. Interest in bacterial, viral, and parasitic diseases of fishes; basic studies on immune response of fishes. Provides Fish Disease Leaflets (series of information leaflets issued irregularly), and reference antisera for identification of fish pathogens.

53016. Forestry Sciences Laboratory, U.S. Forest Service, P.O. Box 152, Princeton, WV 24740; (304) 425-8106. Interest in forestry and forest products. Holdings include 1,200 bound volumes of mags, 60 periodical subs, 10,000 reports; data on markets for forest and wood products and forestry. Answers inquiries, permits onsite use of collection.

53017. Foundation for Science and the Handicapped, 236 Grand St, Morgantown, WV 26505; (304) 293-5201. Interest in concerns, rights, and methods of facilitation of physically handicapped individuals to education, training, and employment opportunities in fields of science. Answers inquiries, provides advisory services—sometimes for a fee.

53018. Job Accomodation Network, PO Box 468, Morgantown, WV 26505; (304) 293-7186, (800) 526-7234. Database of info on how individual tasks can be done by persons with limitations. Enables employers to discuss with one another how they have made accomodations for handicapped employees. Service free to employers in return for info—data forms are provided—on accomodations they have made.

53019. Mathematics Research Library, Mathematics Bldg, W.Va. Univ, Morgantown, WV 26506; (304) 293-6011. Interest in pure mathematics, particularly number theory, geometry, combinatorial analysis, and theory of special functions. Makes interlibrary loans, provides duplication services through university library, permits onsite reference to materials.

53020. Morgantown Energy Technology Center, U.S. Dept of Energy, P.O. Box 880 (3610 Collins Ferry Rd), Morgantown, WV 26505; (304) 291-4620. Interest in development of technology, equipment, and materials for processes for producing gas, oil, and electricity from coal, and for extraction of oil and gas. Publishes technical reports, answers inquiries, provides info on R&D in progress. Services generally free.

53021. National Peach Council, P.O. Box 1085 (103 N Coll St), Martinsburg, WV 25401; (304) 267-6024. Interest in peaches, primarily freestones. Publishes *Peach Times* (monthly), answers inquiries free, provides consumer info.

53022. National Scrip Collectors Association, P.O. Box 29, Fayetteville, WV 25840; (304) 574-0105. Interest in metal and paper scrip issued by coal, lumber, and manufacturing companies; history of scrip-issuing companies. Answers inquiries, provides reference services. Catalog available for a fee, other services free upon payment of membership dues.

53023. North Central West Virginia Center for Independent Living, Coordinating Council for Independent Living, P.O. Box 677 (1000 Van Voorhis Rd), Morgantown, WV 26507; (304) 599-3636. Facilitates availability, accessibility, and coordination of services for severely disabled, while encouraging and supporting full participation of disabled in their community. Services free to disabled persons and for a negotiated fee to agencies, businesses, and orgs.

53024. Water Research Institute, W.Va. Univ, Morgantown, WV 26506; (304) 293-2757. Interest in acid mine drainage, hydrologic data on W.Va. Answers brief inquiries, makes referrals.

53025. West Virginia Department of Culture and History Library, Archives and History Division, W.Va. Dept of Culture and History, Cultural Center, Capitol Complex, Charleston, WV 25305; (304) 348-0230. Interest in govt and history of W.Va, culture of Appalachian region, U.S. history, Civil War history. Holdings include state archives, documents, county court records. Answers inquiries, permits onsite use of collections. Fees charged for copying services.

53026. West Virginia and Regional History Collection, Colson Hall, Downtown Campus, W.Va. Univ, Morgantown, WV 26506; (304) 293-3536. Interest in history, sociology, economics, literature, art, and music of the southern Appalachians, especially W.Va.

Wisconsin

54003. Alverno College, Research Center on Women, 3401 S 39th St, Milwaukee, WI 53215; (414) 647-3723. Owns print, audiovisual resources on all aspects of women's lives. Provides reference services, lends materials, permits onsite use of collection. Services free.

54004. American Academy of Allergy and Immunology, 611 E Wells St, Milwaukee, WI 53202; (414) 272-6071. Publishes journal on allergy and clinical immunology, newsletter, abstracts, monographs, patient education materials. Offers consultation service, conducts seminars.

54006. American Council for Elementary School Industrial Arts, c/o Dr Roger Schaefer, VTAE District One, 620 W Clairmont Ave, Eau Claire, WI 54701-1098. Publishes newsletter, reports, bibliographies, directories on industrial arts. Provides consulting, reference services. Publications available to nonmembers at cost.

54007. American Fern Society, c/o Dr W.C. Taylor, Secty, Milwaukee Public Museum, 800 W Wells St, Milwaukee, WI 53233; (414) 278-2760. Publishes newsletter and quarterly journal on ferns; answers inquiries; refers inquirers to other sources of info. Services free, available to nonmembers as staff and time permit.

54008. American Forensic Association, c/o James W. Pratt, Secty, Univ of Wisc., River Falls, WI 54022; (715) 425-3198. Enforces code of ethics for univ forensic programs. Publishes journal, reviews, directories, bibliographies; answers inquiries; conducts seminars. Services provided at cost.

54009. American Geriatric Education Society, 5685 North Shore Dr, Milwaukee, WI 53217; (414) 962-4820. Nonprofit corp that publishes group leader discussion guides, pamphlets on such topics as loneliness, decisions, goals. Provides advisory services.

54011. American Medical Electroencephalographic Association, 850 Elm Grove Rd, Elm Grove, WI 53122; (414) 797-7800. Promotes clinical medical electroencephalography. Sponsors scientific meetings, maintains registry of certified EEG technicians and technologists, establishes certification procedures.

54012. American Orthoptic Council, c/o Leslie Lennarson, C.O./C.O.T., Secty-Treas, 3914 Nakoma Rd, Madison, WI 53711; (608) 233-1747. Interest in orthoptic profession, including training, examination, certification of orthoptists. Publishes journal and brochure, answers inquiries, provides consulting services.

54013. American Poultry Historical Society, c/o Louis C. Arrington, Secty-Treas, Poultry Science Dept, 1675 Observatory Dr, Room 260, Univ of Wisc., Madison, WI 53706; (608) 262-9764. Publishes newsletter and books on poultry industry. Answers inquiries, arranges for limited literature searches. Services provided at cost. Individual members own artifacts.

54014. American Society for Laser Medicine and Surgery, 425 Pine Ridge Blvd, Ste 203, Wausau, WI 54401; (715) 845-9283. Provides info on medical applications of laser. Provides advisory, consulting, reference, magnetic tape services; conducts seminars and workshops; lends materials. Services for a fee.

54016. American Society for Quality Control, 230 W Wells St, Milwaukee, WI 53203; (414) 272-8575. Interest in quality control in aerospace, automotive, chemical, electronics, biomedical, drugs, textile, food industries. Publishes journals, available for a fee; answers inquiries.

54017. American Society of Agronomy, 677 S Segoe Rd, Madison, WI 53711; (608) 274-1212. Nonprofit scientific org that jointly sponsors, with Crop Science Society of America and Soil Science Society of America, annual meeting. Publishes journals, abstracts, monographs, slides.

54018. American Society of Plant Taxonomists, c/o Dr Neil A. Harriman, Secty, Dept of Biology, Univ of Wisc., Oshkosh, WI 54901; (414) 424-3077. Publishes journal, monographs, directories, on systematic botany. Answers inquiries free, sells publications.

54019. American Wheelchair Bowling Association, c/o Daryl L. Pfister, Exec Secty-Treas, N54 W 15858 Larkspur Lane, Menomonee Falls, WI 53051; (414) 781-6876. Provides info on wheelchair bowling. Provides advisory, reference, literature-searching services; conducts seminars, workshops. Services primarily for members.

54020. Applied Biochemists Laboratory Services, P.O. Box 225 (5300 W County Line Rd), Mequon, WI 53092; (414) 242-5870. Manufactures chemicals for aquatic weed control. Formulates products for wastewater treatment, provides advisory services, permits onsite use of collection. Most services free.

54021. Applied Population Laboratory, Dept of Rural Sociology, Univ of Wisc., 316 Agricultural Hall, Madison, WI 53706; (608) 262-1515. Conducts research on demographic aspects of public issues, particularly at state, local level. Provides advisory and reference services, conducts workshops, permits onsite use of collection.

54022. Association for the Development of Religious Information Systems, Dept of Sociology, Anthropology, and Social Work, Marquette Univ, Milwaukee, WI 53233; (414) 224-6838. Promotes coordination among religious info services by discussing mutual interests, exploring feasibility of proposed projects. Publishes newsletter, directory.

54023. Association of College, University and Community Arts Administrators, 6225 Univ Ave, Madison, WI 53705-1099; (608) 233-7400. Org of those presenting performing arts. Publishes books, directories; provides advisory, reference services and speakers; conducts workshops. Services for a fee.

54025. Beloit College, Logan Museum of Anthropology, Beloit, WI 53511; (608) 365-3391 ext 305. Maintains archeological, ethnological collection including specimens from American Indian cultures of Southwest. Approved researchers allowed access to collection. Provides copying services.

54026. Biotron, Univ of Wisc., 2115 Observatory Dr, Madison, WI 53706; (608) 262-4900. Interest in controlled environment facilities for research. Publishes journals, provides consulting services, conducts seminars and workshops. Most services free to investigators.

54027. Brown Swiss Cattle Breeders' Association of the U.S.A., P.O. Box 1038 (800 Pleasant St), Beloit, WI 53511; (608) 365-4474. Owns official herdbook for registered Brown Swiss cattle. Publishes monthly bulletin, provides reference services, conducts seminars and workshops. Fees charged for research.

54028. Center for Biotic Systems, Institute for Environmental Studies, Univ of Wisc., 511 WARF Bldg, 610 N Walnut, Madison, WI 53706; (608) 262-9937. Conducts research in ecosystem analysis. Publishes reports, provides advisory services, conducts seminars and workshops, permits onsite use of collection. Services free.

54029. Center for Environmental Communications and Education Studies, Univ of Wisc., 433 N Murray St, Madison, WI 53706; (608) 262-2116. Interest in science and technology communications. Publishes research reports (copies available for a fee), provides consulting and reference services, permits onsite use of collection.

54030. Center for Great Lakes Studies, Univ of Wisc., Milwaukee, WI 53204; (414) 649-3000. Develops understanding of Great Lakes, impacts of technological and social trends. Publishes reports, bibliographies; permits onsite use of collection by scientists, students.

54031. Center for Interactive Programs, Univ of Wisc. Extension, 610 Langdon St, No. 728, Madison, WI 53703; (608) 262-4554. Publishes conference papers, books on teleconferencing. Provides advisory services, conducts seminars and workshops. Fee for most services.

54032. Center for Lake Superior Environmental Studies, Univ of Wisc., Superior, WI 54880; (715) 394-8315. Publishes research summaries on Lake Superior basin. Provides advisory, reference, copying services; conducts seminars, workshops; permits onsite use of collection. Services at cost to nonsponsoring agencies.

54033. Center for Mass Media Research, College of Journalism, Marquette Univ, 1135 W Kilbourn Ave, Milwaukee, WI 53233; (414) 224-7132. Analyzes role of mass media in society, with emphasis on energy and environment. Provides info on research. Services primarily for educational institutions, provided at cost.

54038. Committee for Economic Growth of Israel, P.O. Box 2053 (5301 N Ironwood Rd), Milwaukee, WI 53201; (414) 961-1000 ext 403. Provides info on business opportunities in Israel and U.S. Provides advisory, reference services. Initial services free, ongoing services for a fee.

54039. Conservation Education Association, c/o Robert Darula, Exec Secty/Treas, Univ of Wisc.-Green Bay, Green Bay, WI 54301-7001; (414) 465-2397. Concerned with conservation and environmental education. Publishes quarterly newsletter, answers inquiries, makes referrals to other sources of info.

54040. Construction Industry Manufacturers Association, 111 E Wisc. Ave, Milwaukee, WI 53202; (414) 272-0943. Issues technical publications on power cranes and excavators, hydraulic excavators, and telescoping boom cranes. Publishes standards, handbook, equipment ratings, safety manuals.

54041. Cookware Manufacturers Association, P.O. Box J, Walworth, WI 53184; (414) 275-6838. Publishes guide to cookware and bakeware. Answers inquiries free, distributes publication for a fee.

54043. Credit Union National Association, P.O. Box 431 (5710 W Mineral Point Rd), Madison, WI 53701; (608) 231-4170. Owns memorabilia relating to credit union movement. Publishes technical reports. Provides consulting, reference services; permits onsite use of collection. Services for members, researchers, students.

54045. Crop Science Society of America, 677 S Segoe Rd, Madison, WI 53711; (608) 274-1212. Society closely affiliated with American Society of Agronomy, Soil Science Society of America. Publishes journal on crop science, monographs, books, reports; answers inquiries.

54047. Endometriosis Association, P.O. Box 92187, Milwaukee, WI 53202; (414) 962-8972. Assn of women with endometriosis (inflammation of uterus lining) that operates as peer support network. Maintains data bank of individuals' experiences. Provides crisis assistance and technical assistance to researchers.

54048. Environmental Remote Sensing Center, Institute for Environmental Studies, Univ of Wisc., 1213 Meteorology/Space Science, 1225 W Dayton St, Madison, WI 53706; (608) 263-3251. Conducts research in environmental remote sensing. Publishes reports, journals. Provides advisory services, info on research in progress. Most services free.

54049. Environmental Toxicology Center, Univ of Wisc.-Madison, Infirmary, Room 309, Madison, WI 53706; (608) 263-4580. Promotes interdisciplinary research in environmental toxicology. Conducts seminars, provides info on research in progress. Services free.

54050. Experimental Aircraft Association, Wittman Airfield, Oshkosh, WI 54901-3065; (414) 426-4800. Intl nonprofit org dedicated to aviation education and re-search. Owns over 200 aircraft. Publishes magazines and films, conducts seminars and workshops.

54053. Food Research Institute, Univ of Wisc., 1925 Willow Dr, Madison, WI 53706; (608) 263-7777. Publishes reports on food-borne disease agents, food additives, toxic components of food. Answers inquiries, provides advisory services to supporting agencies in govt, industry.

54054. Forest Products Research Society, 2801 Marshall Court, Madison, WI 53705; (608) 231-1361. Publishes journal, bibliographies, slide-tape series on wood waste for industrial energy. Provides literature surveys and abstracts, sponsors conferences. Fees for most services.

54055. Geophysical and Polar Research Center, Univ of Wisc., 1215 W Dayton St, Madison, WI 53706; (608) 262-1921. Publishes technical reports on Antarctic glaciology and geophysics. Provides consulting services free to nonprofit orgs, at cost to others; lends equipment.

54056. Industrial Perforators Association, 710 N Plankinton Ave, Ste 333, Milwaukee, WI 52303; (414) 271-2263. Publishes designer's, specifier's, and buyer's handbook for perforated metals. Provides literature-searching services, answers inquiries. Services free.

54057. Institute for Environmental Studies, Univ of Wisc., 15 Science Hall, 550 N Park St, Madison, WI 53706; (608) 263-3185. Owns data on environmental impact of coal-fired power plants. Publishes research reports and symposia proceedings, answers inquiries, permits onsite reference of collection.

54058. Institute for Fluitronics Education, P.O. Box 106 (1000 Grandview Dr), Elm Grove, WI 53122; (414) 782-0410. Conducts courses, seminars on fluid power technology. Publishes books, standards, research summaries and bibliographies; provides advisory, literature-searching services for a fee.

54060. Institute for Research on Poverty, Univ of Wisc., Social Science Bldg, 1180 Observatory Dr, Madison, WI 53706; (608) 262-6358. Conducts research on poverty. Publishes newsletter and books, provides consulting and reference services, permits onsite use of collection.

54061. Institute of Paper Chemistry, Division of Information Services, P.O. Box 1039 (1043 E South River St), Appleton, WI 54912; (414) 734-9251. Conducts research on paper industry. Publishes bulletin and conference proceedings. Provides consulting, reference, copying, translation services; conducts seminars; permits onsite use of collection.

54062. Instrumentation Systems Center, College of Engineering, Univ of Wisc., 735 Engineering Research Bldg, 1500 Johnson Dr, Madison, WI 53706; (608) 263-1550. Conducts research on instrumentation. Publishes specifications; provides consulting, reference services; permits onsite use of collection. Services for a fee.

54063. International Bone Marrow Transplant Registry, Medical College of Wisc., P.O. Box 26509, Milwaukee, WI 53226; (414) 257-8325. Aims to improve success rate of bone marrow transplantation by maintaining statistical center for clinical data. Maintains list of bone marrow transplant teams. Publishes newsletter.

54064. International Crane Foundation, Route 1, P.O. Box 230C, Shady Lane Rd, Baraboo, WI 53913; (608) 356-9462. Conducts research on propagation, conservation of wild, captive cranes. Provides advisory, reference services, conducts seminars and tours, permits onsite use of collection.

54065. International Horn Society, c/o Ruth Hokanson, Exec Secty, 1213 Sweet Brier Rd, Madison, WI 53705; (608) 233-6336. Conducts horn competitions. Awards grants and scholarships, commissions composers. Publishes newsletter and journal, conducts workshops. Services for a fee.

54068. Justice System Training Association, P.O. Box 356, Appleton, WI 54912; (414) 731-8893. Conducts natl psycho-motor skill design instructor training seminar. Provides advisory, reference services; lends materials. Services to criminal justice agencies for a fee.

54069. Kevin Parsons and Associates, P.O. Box 356, Appleton, WI 54912; (414) 731-6903. Serves as consultant in litigation involving use of force by law enforcement personnel. Conducts training programs, provides advisory and reference services to justice system agencies, law firms.

54070. Kissel Kar Klub, P.O. Box 305 (147 N Rural), Hartford, WI 53027; (414) 673-7002. Assists owners of surviving Kissel-built motor cars and trucks in authentic restorations and in locating parts. Provides consulting, copying services. Most services free.

54071. Laboratory for Surface Studies, Univ of Wisc., Milwaukee, WI 53201; (414) 963-5765. Publishes technical papers on subjects such as electron, ion, and photon induced desorption, auger electron spectrometry. Provides advisory services for a fee.

54073. Lazy Eye, Ltd., 1521 Folsom St, Eau Claire, WI 54703; (715) 832-9943. Nonprofit org that promotes home screening eye kit (10 cents plus postage), booklet used to educate parents to test their children for amblyopia — dimness of sight. Helps communities start detection programs.

54074. League Against Nuclear Dangers, Rte 1, Rudolph, WI 54475; (715) 423-7996. Publishes newsletter, books, technical reports, data compilations, reprints on hazards of nuclear power. Provides reference services, distributes publications for a fee.

54075. Lithium Information Center, Dept of Psychiatry, Univ of Wisc., 600 Highland Ave, Madison, WI 53792; (608) 263-6171. Collects lithium-related literature. Publishes journal and reviews, provides advisory and reference services and info on research in progress. Services for a fee.

54077. Maledicta: The International Research Center for the Study of Verbal Aggression, 331 S Greenfield Ave, Waukesha, WI 53186-6492; (414) 542-5853. Analyzes offensive language in all cultures. Publishes journal, books, reviews, bibliographies; provides advisory, reference services. Most services free.

54078. Mass Communications Research Center, School of Journalism and Mass Communication, Univ of Wisc., Vilas Communication Hall, Madison, WI 53706; (608) 262-3642. Analyzes data on mass communication. Publishes journal and reviews, answers inquiries free, provides advisory services, permits onsite use of collection. Most services at cost.

54080. Materials Science Center, 1103 Engineering Research Bldg, 1500 Johnson Dr, Univ of Wisc., Madison, WI 53706; (608) 263-1795. Industrial consortium that owns books on subjects such as polymer science, thin film electronic devices. Publishes reports and books, provides free consulting services.

54082. McArdle Laboratory for Cancer Research, Center for Health Sciences, Univ of Wisc., Madison, WI 53706; (608) 262-2177. Owns journals, reference books on cancer research. Publishes research papers in journals, books. Access to reading room restricted, but permission for limited use may be obtained.

54083. Medical Electronics Laboratory, Medical School, Univ of Wisc., 1300 Univ Ave, Madison, WI 53706; (608) 262-1326. Sponsored by Natl Institutes of Health, designs medical electronic instruments. Publishes journal, permits onsite use of collection. Services free to govt, univ agencies.

54085. Milwaukee School of Engineering Applied Technology Center, P.O. Box 644, Milwaukee, WI 53201; (414) 277-7398. Publishes newsletters, technical reports, research summaries on product design, development, testing. Conducts seminars, symposia on hydraulics, pneumatics. Services at cost.

54086. Model Railroad Industry Association, P.O. Box 72, Cedarburg, WI 53012; (414) 377-3078. Publishes newsletter, booklets for members on hobby of model railroading. Answers inquiries free, provides advisory services, distributes brochures to libraries, schools, clubs.

54087. National Association for Retired Credit Union People, P.O. Box 391 (5910 Mineral Point Rd), Madison, WI 53701; (608) 238-4286. Membership assn that helps credit unions serve senior consumers. Helps credit union members plan retirement, publishes retirement planning booklets. Most services free.

54088. National Association of Breweriana Advertising, 2343 Met-To-Wee Lane, Wauwatosa, WI 53226; (414) 257-0158. Nonprofit org of hobby collectors, dealers who collect info on American brewery advertising. Publishes newsletter, provides free advisory services.

54089. National Board of Fur Farm Organizations, 450 N Sunny Slope Rd, Ste 120, Brookfield, WI 53005; (414) 786-4242. Nonprofit corp that represents mink and fox farmers. Publishes bibliography and conference proceedings, provides free reference services.

54090. National Center for Home Equity Conversion, 110 E Main, Madison, WI 53703; (608) 256-2111. Nonprofit org that promotes research to convert home equity into retirement income. Publishes technical reports, reviews, and bibliographies, provides advisory services, conducts seminars. Services at cost.

54091. National Christmas Tree Association, 611 E Wells St, Milwaukee, WI 53202; (414) 276-6410. Publishes journal, directories, research summaries and bibliographies. Provides consulting, reference services; sponsors Christmas tree marketing conference. Fee charged nonmembers.

54092. National Coalition of Gay Sexually Transmitted Disease Services, P.O. Box 239, Milwaukee, WI 53201; (414) 277-7671. Nonprofit membership org encourages communication among gays' service providers. Maintains liaison with Centers for Disease Control; gives info to medical, scientific, gay communities.

54093. National Fishery Research Laboratory, U.S. Fish and Wildlife Service, P.O. Box 818 (2630 Fanta Reed Rd), La Crosse, WI 54602-0818; (608) 783-6451. Owns research reports on Upper Miss. River System. Publishes journals, answers inquiries. Provides consulting, reference services, permits onsite use of collection.

54094. National Fluid Power Association, 3333 N Mayfair Rd, Ste 311, Milwaukee, WI 53222; (414) 778-3344. Publishes books, fluid power curriculum guide, standards. Provides reference services and indexes for fluid power products, conducts seminars. Fee for some services.

54095. National Funeral Directors Association, 135 W Wells St, Milwaukee, WI 53203; (414) 276-2500. Publishes books, bibliographies, audiovisual material; provides advisory, reference services; conducts seminars and workshops. Most services free.

54096. National Geriatrics Society, 212 W Wisc. Ave, 3rd Floor, Milwaukee, WI 53203; (414) 272-4130. Interest in care of geriatric patients in nursing homes. Publishes newsletter and U.S. nursing care requirements, answers inquiries, refers inquirers free to other sources of info.

54098. National Police Chiefs and Sheriffs Information Bureau, P.O. Box 92007 (152 W Wisc. Ave, Ste 727), Milwaukee, WI 53202; (414) 272-3853. Owns materials on law enforcement, rehabilitation. Publishes natl directory of law enforcement administrators and correctional agencies. Provides reference services. Most services free.

54099. National Registration Center for Study Abroad, 823 N 2nd St, Lower Lobby, Milwaukee, WI 53203; (414)

278-0631. Info office of foreign univs, language institutes, short-term study centers offering programs in Latin America, Britain, Ireland, Europe. Provides advisory, reference services; conducts seminars, workshops; permits onsite use of collection.

54100. National Telemedia Council, 120 E Wilson St, Madison, WI 53703; (608) 257-7712. Seeks to improve electronic media programming. Provides advisory services, conducts seminars and workshops, permits onsite use of collection. Services for a fee.

54101. National Wildlife Health Laboratory, 6006 Schroeder Rd, Madison, WI 53711; (608) 264-5411. Detects and controls disease in wildlife populations; conducts research. Provides disease diagnostic service to federal, state, commercial resource managers; conducts workshops.

54102. Office Technology Management Association, 9401 W Beloit Rd, Ste 101, Milwaukee, WI 53227; (414) 321-0880. Publishes magazine, glossary, brochures on word processing and office automation. Conducts conferences, seminars, workshops. Fee for most services.

54103. Old Songs Library, Society for the Preservation and Encouragement of Barber Shop Quartet Singing in America, P.O. Box 575 (6315 Third Ave), Kenosha, WI 53140; (414) 654-9111. Encourages music appreciation. Provides reference and copying services, conducts workshops, permits onsite use of sheet music collection. Services at cost to nonmembers.

54104. Omnion Power Engineering Corp., Route 3, P.O. Box 44A, Mukwonago, WI 53149; (414) 363-4088. Conducts research on use of solar, industrial waste energy sources. Manufactures power conditioning equipment. Provides consulting and reference services at cost.

54105. Organization of American Kodaly Educators, c/o Dr Robert Perinchief, Exec Secty, Music Dept, Univ of Wisc.-Whitewater, Whitewater, WI 53190; (414) 472-1341. Promotes Zoltan Kodaly (emphasizes importance of folk music in teaching music). Participates in intl conferences, conducts seminars and workshops. Most services free.

54107. Power Company Midwest, P.O. Box 96 (Berg Bldg, Highways 59 and 83), Genesee Depot, WI 53127; (414) 968-3188. Manufactures wood laminated propeller blades for small wind energy conversion systems. Publishes directory, specifications; provides advisory, reference services. Fee for most services.

54108. Power Crane and Shovel Association, 111 E Wisc. Ave, Ste 1700, Milwaukee, WI 53202; (414) 272-0943. Bureau of Construction Industry Manufacturers Assn that publishes technical bulletins, standards on power and hydraulic cranes, shovels, excavators. Answers inquiries, makes referrals.

54110. Progressive Foundation, 315 W Gorham St, Madison, WI 53703; (608) 256-4146. Fosters public awareness of implications of nuclear technology. Provides reference services; conducts seminars, workshops; operates speakers bureau. Most services free.

54112. River Studies Center, Univ of Wisc., Cowley Hall, La Crosse, WI 54601; (608) 785-8239. Studies historical features associated with upper Miss. River. Provides advisory, reference, copyingo services; conducts seminars, workshops. Services for a fee.

54114. Science for the Handicapped Association, c/o Univ of Wisc.-Eau Claire, Eau Claire, WI 54701; (715) 836-4164. Disseminates info for handicapped. Publishes newsletter and bibliography, provides reference services, conducts seminars and workshops. Services free; contributions welcomed.

54115. Society for Nonprofit Organizations, 6314 Odona Rd, Ste 1, Madison, WI 53719; (608) 274-9777. Natl org for those serving nonprofit orgs. Provides advisory, reference, and copying services, conducts seminars and workshops, permits onsite use of collection. Services for a fee.

54116. Society of North American Goldsmiths, 2849 St Ann Dr, Green Bay, WI 54301; (414) 465-6680. Provides advisory, reference, copying services; conducts workshops and intl exhibitions on metalsmithing; provides audiovisual materials. Most services restricted to members.

54117. Society of Wood Science and Technology, P.O. Box 5062, Madison, WI 53705; (608) 264-5796. Publishes journal, newsletter and reviews on wood products; conducts seminars. Administrative inquiries answered free, technical inquiries for a fee.

54118. Soil Science Society of America, 677 S Segoe Rd, Madison, WI 53711; (608) 273-8080. Affiliated with American Society of Agronomy, Crop Science Society of America. Interest in soil testing and plant analysis. Publishes journal, books, glossary; answers inquiries.

54119. Solar Energy Laboratory, Univ of Wisc., Engineering Research Bldg, Madison, WI 53706; (608) 263-1586. Publishes technical reports on solar energy applications. Answers brief inquiries. Provides bibliographic services; consulting services by arrangement with staff members.

54122. U.S. Department of Agriculture, Forestry Sciences Laboratory, U.S. Forest Service, P.O. Box 898, Rhinelander, WI 54501; (715) 362-7474. Conducts research on genetics, physiology, maximum-biomass production, ecophysiology, biotechnology. Provides advisory services and conducts workshops. Services free.

54123. U.S. Department of Agriculture, Stored-Product Insects Research Laboratory, Univ of Wisc., Dept of Entomology, Madison, WI 53706; (608) 262-3795. Conducts research on control of stored-product insects, including insect sex attractants, insect behavior and reproductive biology. Answers inquiries, provides consulting services.

54124. Universal Foods Corp., Technical Information Center, Research and Development Dept, 6143 N 60th St, Milwaukee, WI 53218; (414) 535-4307. Owns literature collection on fermentation industry, food technology, biochemistry, biotechnology. Makes interlibrary loans, permits onsite use of collection. Services free unless extensive.

54126. Wisconsin Innovation Service Center, College of Business and Economics, Univ of Wisc., 402 McCutcan Hall, Whitewater, WI 53190; (414) 472-1365. Provides low-cost commercial feasibility evaluation of inventions and new product ideas. Provides advisory services, but no assistance in obtaining patents.

54127. Wisconsin Regional Primate Research Center Library, Univ of Wisc., 1223 Capitol Court, Madison, WI 53706; (608) 263-3512. Owns rare books, primate slides and vocalizations. Provides free reference services, lends materials, sells reproductions, distributes publication to researchers in primatology.

54128. Women's Studies Research Center, Univ of Wisc., 209 N Brooks St, Madison, WI 53715; (608) 263-2051. Owns materials on motherhood, including how viewed in art, literature. Provides advisory services, conducts seminars, permits onsite use of collection. Services free to community women.

54129. World Council of Credit Unions, P.O. Box 391 (5810 Mineral Point Rd), Madison, WI 53701; (608) 231-7130. Interest in credit unions worldwide. Publishes journals, answers inquiries, provides consulting and reference services. Services primarily for members, researchers, and students.

54130. Yerkes Observatory Library, P.O. Box 258, Williams Bay, WI 53191; (414) 245-5555. Owns star charts. Provides reference and copying services, makes interlibrary loans, permits onsite use of collection. Most services free, restricted to those with proper credentials.

54132. ZIMPRO, Military Rd, Rothschild, WI 54474; (715) 359-7211. Org concerned with design of waste treatment plants using wet air oxidation. Provides reference services, permits onsite use of collection by arrangement. Services free.

54133. Zoological Museum, Dept of Zoology, Lowell Noland Bldg, Univ of Wisc., Madison, WI 53706; (608) 262-3766. Interest in zoology. Permits onsite use of collection on ornithology, mammalogy, ichthyology, herpetology, osteology, paleontology, malacology, slides and tissue fragments.

Wyoming

55001. American Association of Wildlife Veterinarians, P.O. Box 950 (1174 Jackson St), Laramie, WY 82070; (307) 742-6638 Publishes newsletter on wildlife veterinary medicine; answers inquiries; provides advisory services; conducts seminars and meetings. Services free.

55002. American Heritage Center Archives, Univ of Wyo., P.O. Box 3334, Univ Station, Laramie, WY 82071; (307) 766-6384 Owns manuscripts, photos, printed materials on all aspects of American West. Answers inquiries; provides advisory, reference services; permits onsite use of collection.

55003. American Heritage Center Petroleum History Research Division, Univ of Wyo., P.O. Box 3334, Univ Station, Laramie, WY 82071; (307) 766-4114. Interest in history of geological sciences. Publishes reports, answers inquiries, provides reference and copying services for a fee, lends materials, permits onsite use of collection.

55005. Buffalo Bill Memorial Association, P.O. Box 1000 (8th St), Cody, WY 82414; (307) 587-4771. Operates Buffalo Bill Historical Center. Permits onsite use of collection, researches small arms in response to specific requests. Fees charged.

55006. Foundation for North American Wild Sheep, 802 Canyon Ave, Cody, WY 82414; (307) 527-6441. Publishes periodical on wild sheep. Provides advisory and reference services, info on research, and permanent marking pins to fish and game depts. Services mostly free.

55007. Frontier Taxidermists, P.O. Box 3024 (3424 E Pershing Blvd), Cheyenne, WY 82001; (307) 632-3686. Interest in taxidermy. Owns specimens, films, photos, pamphlets, books, data; answers inquiries; makes referrals; permits onsite use of collection.

55008. Great Plains Lore and Natural History, P.O. Box 6204, Sheridan, WY 82801; (307) 672-5858. Collects stories, recordings on American West. Provides advisory services; conducts seminars, workshops; permits onsite use of collection. Services for a fee.

55009. Institute for Policy Research, Univ of Wyo., P.O. Box 3925, Univ Station, Laramie, WY 82081; (307) 766-5141. Owns state, federal publications on applied social and economic research. Publishes research reports; provides census info for Wyo. and Wyo.-oriented socioeconomic data at cost.

55010. Laramie Project Office, Library, U.S. Dept of Energy, P.O. Box 1189 (365 N 9th St), Laramie, WY 82070; (307) 721-2201. Publishes technical reports, journals on oil shale, tar sand, underground coal gasification; provides reference services; permits onsite use of collection. Services free.

55011. National Association for Outlaw and Lawman History, c/o Western Research Center, Univ of Wyo., P.O. Box 3334, Laramie, WY 82071. Collects, distributes info on history of law and order in American West. Works against laws that hamper genealogical research. Services available to membership, open to everyone.

55012. National Council of State Consultants in Elementary Education, c/o Anna M. Kitchener, Ph.D., Wyo. State Dept of Education, Hathaway Bldg, Cheyenne, WY 82002. Answers inquiries on elementary education program planning and development. Publishes reports of annual meetings; provides consulting, reference, and literature-searching services.

55013. National Park Service Research Center, Univ of Wyo., P.O. Box 3166, Univ Station, Laramie, WY 82071; (307) 766-4227. May 20-Oct. 15 address: P.O. Box 170; Moran, Wyo. 83013; (307) 543-2463. Provides info free on basic, applied research in biological, physical, social sciences; publishes research report, list of articles published by investigators. Lab available to researchers.

55014. Rocky Mountain Herbarium, Univ of Wyo., P.O. Box 3165, Univ Station, Laramie, WY 82071; (307) 766-2236. Open to botanical experts and graduate students, identifies plants submitted by ranchers, county agents, institutions, federal agencies. Loans specimens free.

55016. Wyoming Agricultural Experiment Station, Univ of Wyo., P.O. Box 3354, Univ Station, Laramie, WY 82071; (307) 766-3667. Answers inquiries on Western agriculture; publishes research reports, monographs, bulletins; provides consulting services; conducts seminars. Services free.

55017. Wyoming Catastrophic Information Network, P.O. Box 662, Cheyenne, WY 82003; (307) 635-9246. Gathers and disseminates info on social services, research hospital services available to victims of catastrophic illness. Puts victims in contact with orgs that can provide assistance.

55018. Wyoming Geological Association, P.O. Box 545, Casper, WY 82602; (307) 234-8245. Publishes periodical, field conference guidebooks, reports on geology. Answers inquiries, provides reference services. Most services free.

55019. Wyoming State Archives, Museums and Historical Department, Public Information Office, Barrett Bldg, Cheyenne, WY 82002; (307) 777-7014. Publishes newsletter on Wyo. history; owns photos, manuscripts, correspondence, maps, state and local govt records; provides onsite access to collection; provides reference, copying services.

55020. Wyoming Water Research Center, Univ of Wyo., P.O. Box 3067, Univ Station, Laramie, WY 82071; (307) 766-2143. Owns documents pertaining to Wyo. and hydrology; publishes research reports; provides limited literature-searching services; permits onsite reference of collection.

Puerto Rico/Virgin Islands

60001. Association of Island Marine Laboratories of the Caribbean, c/o Dept of Marine Sciences, Univ of P.R., Mayaguez, PR 00708; (809) 832-4040. Seeks to increase interest in marine sciences in the Caribbean and tropical Atlantic through meetings, improved relations, and cooperative research progs. Services free, except for publication.

60002. Caribbean Research Institute, College of the V.I., St. Thomas, VI 00801; (809) 774-9200 ext 1259. Interest in Caribbean resources, culture, history, economics, politics, agriculture, ecology, Caribbean-American relations. Provides advisory, microform, magnetic tape services, generally at cost.

60003. Institute of Puerto Rican Culture, Biblioteca Gen de P.R., 500 Ave Ponce de Leon, San Juan, PR 00906; (809) 724-2680. Promotes local culture, maintains intl exchange program. Interest in area history and art. Provides reference, literature-searching, indexing services; analyzes data. Except for copying, services free.

60004. Institute of Tropical Forestry, U.S. Forest Service, P.O. Box AQ, Rio Piedras, PR 00928; (809) 753-4335. Interest in tropical forestry, forest products utilization, timber management, ecosystems management. Provides consulting, orientation, and document services; permits onsite use of collection.

60005. Institute of Tropical Meteorology, Box 22931, Univ of P.R. Station, Rio Piedras, PR 00931; (809) 764-0000

ext 2387. Interest in tropical meteorology. Answers inquiries, makes interlibrary loans, permits onsite use of collection.

60006. Natural History Society, P.O. Box 1036, San Juan, PR 00936; (809) 753-5593. Interest in area conservation, flora and fauna, water and air pollution control, astronomy, population control, archaeology, more. Provides current-awareness services; conducts lectures, workshops, field and camping trips. Services free.

60007. Technical Information Center (Puerto Rico), Engineering Research Center, Univ of P.R., Mayaguez, PR 00708; (809) 832-4040. Interest in engineering, technology, related areas. Answers inquiries; provides reference, literature-searching services. Services available on request at cost to industry, commerce, professionals, professors, students, and intl orgs.

60008. Tropical Agriculture Research Station, Agricultural Research Service, USDA, P.O. Box 70, Mayaguez, PR 00709; (809) 834-2435. Conducts research on plant breeding, agronomy, horticulture. Interest in beans, maize, sweet potatoes, and tomatoes, and the introduction of new crops. Operates winter nursery program for U.S. crops. Provides advisory services, plant propagation material. Most services free.

Canada

61001. Addiction Research Foundation, 33 Russell St, Toronto, Ont M5S 2S1; (416) 595-6100. Conducts specialized research, educational, development programs in Ont. on prevention and treatment of dependence on drugs, alcohol. Provides general reference services, distributes publications, permits onsite reference. Services free to Ont. residents, for a fee to others.

61003. Agricultural Institute of Canada, 151 Slater St, Ste 907, Ottawa, Ont K1P 5H4; (613) 232-9459. Interest in all areas of agriculture, particularly professionalization in agriculture, agrology, and scientific manpower and research. Answers inquiries free (time permitting), makes referrals, sells back copies of journals, scientific papers.

61004. Alberta Department of the Environment Air Quality Control Branch, Pollution Control Div, Oxbridge Pl, 9820 106th St, Edmonton, Alberta T5K 2J6; (403) 427-5893. Interest in air pollution control, air monitoring, source emission sampling, calibration of instruments, meteorology, data review, Alberta Clean Air Act. Answers inquiries, makes referrals. Services free.

61005. Allergy Information Association, 25 Poynter Dr, Room 7, Weston, Ont M9R 1K8; (416) 244-4805. Helps allergy sufferers achieve more productive lives by disseminating info about special products, recent scientific discoveries; provides patient education. Publishes newsletter, cookbooks, info kits; answers inquiries; provides advisory, reference, other services; conducts seminars and workshops. Most services free.

61006. American Magnolia Society, c/o C.E. Tubesing, Secty-Treas, 9280 No 3 Rd, Richmond, B.C. V7A 1V9. Interest in classification, breeding, and culture of magnolia and magnoliaceae, primarily as ornamental plants. Answers inquiries, provides info on research in progress, makes referrals. Services primarily for members, but available to others.

61007. Arctic Institute of North America, Univ Library Tower, 2500 Univ Dr, NW, Calgary, Alberta, T2N 1N4; (403) 284-7515. Interest in all aspects of arctic, subarctic, and low-temperature regions. Provides general reference services, conducts seminars, distributes publications, permits onsite study. Services that require staff study or labor performed at cost.

61009. Arts Carousel/Arts With The Handicapped Foundation, Box 342, Station P, Toronto, Ont M5S 2S8. Interest in improving quality of life for handicapped through visual arts, drama, creative writing. Answers inquiries; provides advisory, reference, other services; conducts seminars and workshops. Fees, if any, based on ability to pay. Services available chiefly to physically handicapped, but others served.

61010. Association for Preservation Technology, Box 2487, Station D, Ottawa, Ont K1P 5W6; (613) 238-1972. Interest in preservation of historic resources, rehabilitation, reuse of historic structures; history of building technology. Answers inquiries; provides consulting, reference, other services; produces, distributes publications; offers training courses in various aspects of preservation/rehabilitation field. Fees may apply.

61011. Association of Canadian Medical Colleges, 151 Slater St, Ste 1120, Ottawa, Ont K1P 5N1; (613) 237-0070. Promotes advancement of academic medicine in Canada through review and development of standards for medical education, relevant natl policy and agency representation, fostering of research. Answers inquiries; provides data evaluation, referral, other services. Most services free.

61012. Association of Exploration Geochemists, P.O. Box 523, Rexdale, Ont M9W 5L4. Interest in utilization and study of element dispersion cycles and patterns applied to geochemical prospecting in the exploration phase of economic geological activities. Answers inquiries, makes referrals free, sponsors intl and regional symposia, sells journal.

61013. Atlantic Geoscience Society, c/o Nova Scotia Dept of Mines and Energy, P.O. Box 1087, Halifax, Nova Scotia B3J 2X1. Acts as communications liaison among geologists in industry, univs, and govt institutions in Atlantic Canada. Produces newsletter, holds seminars; fees may apply. Answers inquiries free.

61014. Atlantic Salmon Federation, Box 429, St Andrews, N.B. E0G 2X0; (506) 529-8889. Interest in Atlantic salmon catch statistics, technical and general info, conservation programs, research, educational grants, operation of the Salmon Research Center. Answers inquiries, provides limited consulting services, makes referrals, permits onsite reference. Services free.

61015. Bell Canada Telephone Historical Collection, 1050 Beaver Hall Hill, Rm 820, Montreal, Que H2Z 1S4; (514) 870-7088. Interest in history of telecommunications in Canada with emphasis on Bell Canada. Provides reference and copying services, lends materials, makes referrals to other info sources, permits onsite use of collections. Most services free.

61016. Biosystematics Research Institute, Agriculture Canada, Central Experimental Farm, Ottawa, Ont K1A 0C6; (613) 994-5309. Provides Natl Identification Service for Canada on fungi, vascular plants, insects, arachnids, nematodes. Answers inquiries, distributes publications, permits onsite use of collections, identifies organisms, makes direct and interlibrary loans. Services free, usually restricted to govt agencies, univs, other institutions; services to individuals offered on limited basis.

61017. Braille Authority of North America, c/o D.E. Bogart, Secty, Canadian Natl Institute for the Blind, 1929 Bayview Ave, Toronto, Ont M4G 3E8; (418) 486-2609. Responsible for approving and adopting changes in all existing braille codes in use both in U.S. and Canada. Answers technical inquiries, provides consultation, some research related to braille code compatability.

61018. Bruce Trail Association, P.O. Box 857, Hamilton, Ont L8N 3N9; (416) 529-6821. Concerned with maintenance and use of Bruce Trail, extending from Niagara Falls northwest to Tobermory on Bruce Peninsula. Publishes manuals, guides, calendars, promotional materials; answers inquiries; provides advisory, reference and referral services; conducts seminars, workshops. Most services free.

61019. Canada Defence Research Board Scientific Information Centre, Defence and Civil Institute of Environmental Medicine, P.O. Box 2000 (1133 Sheppard Ave W), Downsview, Ont M3M 3B9; (416) 633-4240. Conducts human behavioral and biosciences research for military and civil natl requirements. Interest in aviation medicine, aircraft accident investigation, life support systems, etc. Provides reference and copying services, makes interlibrary loans, permits onsite study. Services free.

61020. Canada Grains Council, 760-360 Main St, Winnipeg, Manitoba R3C 3Z3; (204) 942-2254. Interest in Canadian grains and grain products, market development. Answers inquiries; provides advisory, referral, other services; conducts seminars, workshops; distributes publications. Services primarily for grain industry, but others assisted; fees may apply.

61021. Canada Institute for Scientific and Technical Information Library, Natl Research Council of Canada, Bldg M-55, Montreal Rd at Blair Rd, Ottawa, Ont K1A OS2; (613) 993-2013. Interest in scientific, technical, and medical info. Provides general reference and computerized info retrieval services, makes interlibrary loans, permits onsite study. Fees for some services; only interlibrary loan and photocopy services available to users outside Canada.

61022. Canada's Sports Hall of Fame, Exhibition Pl, Toronto, Ont M6K 3C3; (416) 595-1046. Interest in history of sports in Canada. Permits onsite use of materials by qualified researchers.

61023. Canada-Japan Trade Council, 75 Albert St, Ste 903, Ottawa, Ont K1P 5E7; (613) 233-4047. Interest in trade relations between Canada and Japan; mercantile, economic, social, cultural info on Canada and Japan. Answers inquiries, conducts seminars and workshops, distributes publications, makes referrals to other sources of info. Services free, except publications.

61024. Canadian Arctic Resources Committee, 46 Elgin St, Rm 11, Ottawa, Ont K2P 5K6; (613)236-7379. Interest in environment, energy resources, transportation, natural resources conservation, economic development in Arctic regions of northern Canada. Answers inquiries; provides advisory, reference, other serv-

ices; conducts seminars, workshops; permits onsite use of collections. Most services free.

61025. Canadian Asbestos Information Centre, 1130 Sherbrooke St W, Ste 410, Montreal, Que H3A 2M8; (514) 844-3956. Interest in research, development of safe asbestos products; occupational, environmental health; promotion of safe use of asbestos; biological research. Answers inquiries, provides advisory and reference services, permits onsite use of collections. Most services free.

61026. Canadian Association for Laboratory Animal Science, 2627 Morley Trail, NW, Calgary, Alberta T2M 4G6; (403) 284-2928. Interest in laboratory animal science. Provides general reference services, consulting; conducts seminars; distributes publications, training manuals, and materials. Services free, except publications, materials.

61027. Canadian Association of Anatomists, c/o Dr M.H.L. Gibson, Secty, Dept of Anatomy, Faculty of Medicine, Univ. of Manitoba, Winnipeg, Manitoba R3E 0W3; (204) 786-3652. Promotes anatomy teaching, research in Canadian dental, medical, veterinary schools. Answers inquiries, provides advisory and referral services, conducts seminars, distributes newsletter. Services free, available only to health profession, students interested in career guidance.

61028. Canadian Association of Chiefs of Police, 1908-112 Kent St, Ottawa, Ont K1P 5P2; (613) 233-1106. Interest in advancement of professionalism in policing; promotion of progressive practices in crime prevention, detection. Answers inquiries, makes referrals to other info sources. Services free. Publications at cost, restricted to law enforcement, criminal justice, security agencies.

61029. Canadian Association of Gastroenterology, 3755 Chemin de la Cote Ste-Catherine, Montreal, Que H3T 1E2; (514) 738-3675. Interest in diseases of alimentary tract, liver and biliary tree, pancreas. Answers inquiries, provides advisory and reference services, conducts seminars and workshops. Most services free.

61030. Canadian Association of Optometrists, 77 Metcalfe St, Ste 207, Ottawa, Ont K1P 5L6; (613) 238-2006. Federal coordinator of activities of 10 Canadian provincial Optometric Assns in areas of public info, political activity, communications. Publishes journal, answers inquiries, provides reference and copying services. Most services free.

61031. Canadian Association of Social Workers, 55 Parkdale Ave, Ottawa, Ont K1Y 1E5; (613) 728-1865. Encourages development of high standards, special studies, and research to strengthen social work profession. Publishes, distributes reports, quarterly; answers inquiries; participates in seminars, symposia. Most services free.

61032. Canadian Ceramic Society, 2175 Sheppard Ave E, Ste 110, Willowdale, Ont M2J 1W8; (416) 491-2886.

Seeks to advance ceramic arts and sciences, encourages study and research in ceramic field. Provides general reference services, conducts conferences and correspondence course, distributes publications. Services free, except course and publications, but primarily for members.

61033. Canadian Coordinating Council on Deafness, 116 Lisgar, Ste 203, Ottawa, Ont K2P OC2; (613) 232-2611. Coordinating body for Canadian groups lobbying govt for rights of deaf, hearing impaired. Answers inquiries, provides advisory and reference services, conducts seminars and workshops, distributes publications and data compilations. Most services free.

61034. Canadian Council of the Blind, 220 Dundas St, Ste 610, London, Ont N6A 1H3; (519) 433-3946. Nonprofit org that works for rehabilitation of blind Canadians. Answers inquiries; provides advisory, reference, magnetic tape services; distributes publications. Services free.

61035. Canadian Council on Animal Care, 151 Slater St, Ste 1105, Ottawa, Ont K1P 5H3; (613) 238-4031. Interest in surveillance of care and use of research animals in biology, medicine, psychology, and agriculture. Provides general reference services, consulting services free; conducts onsite assessment of animal care facilities and procedures.

61036. Canadian Council on Social Development, P.O. Box 3505, Station C (55 Parkdale Ave), Ottawa, Ont K1Y 4G1; (613) 728-1865. Natl nonprofit org that promotes social policies (income security, housing, etc.) based on principle of social justice for all. Provides general reference services, conducts conferences and seminars, distributes publications, makes restricted interlibrary loans.

61037. Canadian Diabetes Association, 78 Bond St, Toronto, Ont M5B 2J8; (416) 362-4440. Interest in diabetes research, care, and education. Publishes reports, studies, pamphlets; answers inquiries; provides advisory, reference services; conducts seminars, workshops; operates natl film lending library. Most services free.

61038. Canadian Energy Research Institute, 3512 33rd St NW, Calgary, Alberta T2L 2A6; (403) 282-1231. Carries out studies, investigations, projects related to energy and energy policy in Canada. Answers inquiries; provides advisory, consulting services; conducts seminars and workshops; produces, distributes publications. Services for a fee.

61039. Canadian Film Institute, National Film Library of Canada, 150 Rideau St, Ottawa, Ont K1N 5X6; (613) 232-6727. Interest in scientific films in all physical, biological, engineering, and social areas. Provides general reference services, lends/rents films, sells catalogs, performs research and consulting on contract basis. Answers to inquiries, referrals free; services in Canada only.

61040. Canadian Folk Music Society, Box 4232, Station C (1314 Shelbourne St SW), Calgary, Alberta T2T 5N1. Promotes, publishes, and enhances performance of Canadian folk music. Publishes folk festival directory, bulletins; answers inquiries; provides advisory, reference services; conducts seminars and workshops; distributes records and publications. Most services free.

61041. Canadian Forestry Association, 185 Somerset St, Ste 203, Ottawa, Ont K2P 0J2; (613) 232-1815. Natl federation of provincial forestry assns interested in forestry, conservation, natl resource utilization. Answers inquiries, conducts seminars and programs, distributes publications, makes referrals. Services primarily for member provincial forestry assns; most free.

61042. Canadian Hearing Society, Information Services Department, 271 Spadina Rd, Toronto, Ont M5R 2V3; (416) 964-9595. Provides testing, interpreters, rehab, other services to deaf and hard of hearing people. Answers inquiries, distributes publications, provides advisory and reference services, conducts seminars and workshops. Most services free.

61043. Canadian Institute of Mining and Metallurgy, 1130 Sherbrooke St W, Ste 400, Montreal, Que H3A 2M8; (514) 842-3461. Promotes progressive development of Canada's mineral industries. Answers inquiries, publishes materials, makes referrals free.

61044. Canadian Institute of Resources Law, BioSciences Bldg, Rm 430, Univ of Calgary, Calgary, Alberta T2N 1N4; (403) 282-9197. Undertakes, promotes research, education, publication on the law relating to Canada's natural resources. Answers inquiries; provides advisory, research services; conducts conferences and short courses; produces, distributes publications; permits onsite use of collections. Some services subject to fees.

61045. Canadian Institute of Steel Construction, 201 Consumers Rd, Ste 300, Willowdale, Ont M2J 4G8; (416) 491-4552. Interest in structural steel, its applications in design, fabrication, and erection; computer cost analysis. Answers inquiries, provides other info services free.

61046. Canadian International Grains Institute, 1000-303 Main St, Winnipeg, Manitoba R3C 3G7; (204) 949-5344. Seeks to maintain and develop markets for Canadian grain. Conducts short courses for invited participants from Canadian grain industry and selected customer countries; distributes books at cost to all users.

61047. Canadian Jewish Congress, National Archives, 1590 Ave Docteur Penfield, Montreal, Que H3G 1C5; (514) 931-7531. Interest in all aspects of Jewish community in Canada. Answers inquiries, provides advisory, reference, and referral services, distributes publications, permits onsite use of collections by appointment. Most services free.

61048. Canadian Lung Association, 75 Albert St, Ste 908, Ottawa, Ont K1P 5E7; (613) 237-1208. Nonprofit org for research, education, prevention, control of respiratory disease. Answers inquiries, makes referrals to other info sources, distributes publications, permits onsite use of collection. Services free.

61049. Canadian Nuclear Association, 111 Elizabeth St, Toronto, Ont M5G 1P7; (416) 977-6152. Corporate membership org interested in development of nuclear energy for peaceful uses in Canada and abroad. Sponsors public affairs info program, publishes materials, answers inquiries, permits onsite use of library. Services primarily for members.

61050. Canadian Nuclear Society, 111 Elizabeth St, 11th Fl, Toronto, Ont M5G 1P7; (416) 977-6152. Acts as forum for info exchange relating to nuclear energy among diverse specialists. Answers inquiries; provides info, referral services; conducts conferences, seminars, workshops; distributes publications. Services primarily for members.

61051. Canadian Orthoptic Society, 6411 Nelson Ave, No 303, Burnaby, B.C. V5H 3J4; (604) 522-2193. Maintains and improves standards, honor, and integrity of orthoptics as branch of ophthalmology; fosters natl interest in orthoptics. Answers inquiries, provides advisory and reference services, conducts seminars and workshops. Most services free.

61052. Canadian Paraplegic Association National Office, Library, 520 Sutherland Dr, Toronto, Ont M4G 3V9; (416) 422-5640. Collection emphasizes spinal cord injury, rehabilitation, and resettlement. Answers inquiries, provides advisory and reference services, distributes publications. Most services free.

61053. Canadian Pharmaceutical Association, 104-1815 Alta Vista Dr, Ottawa, Ont K1G 3Y6; (613) 523-7877. Interest in pharmacy, drug info, patient info, economic aspects of pharmaceutical services. Answers inquiries, provides reference services and info on old and new drug products.

61054. Canadian Physiological Society, c/o Dept of Medical Physiology, Univ of Calgary, Calgary, Alberta T2N 4N1; (403) 220-4587. Interest in physiology, medicine. Answers inquiries, provides advisory services, conducts seminars and workshops. Services free to affiliated professional orgs, at cost to commercial orgs.

61055. Canadian Plains Research Center, Univ of Regina, Regina, Sask. S4S 0A2; (306) 584-4015. Maintains computerized info system to record published and current research info relevant to Canadian Plains region. Answers inquiries; provides info on research in progress; organizes conferences, workshops, seminars; distributes data compilations and publications; makes referrals to other sources of info; permits onsite use of collection. Fees for all services.

61056. Canadian Red Cross Society Library, 95 Wellesley St, E, Toronto, Ont M4Y 1H6; (416) 923-6692, ext 232.

Interest in Canadian Red Cross, Intl Red Cross, intl humanitarian law. Answers inquiries, makes interlibrary loans, makes referrals to other info sources, permits onsite use of collection. Services free to Canadians directly or through division offices, to others through their natl Red Cross.

61057. Canadian Research Institute for the Advancement of Women, P.O. Box 236, Station B (151 Slater St, Ste 408), Ottawa, Ont K1P 6C4; (613) 563-0681. Interest in research into women's experience in Canada. Answers inquiries, conducts seminars and workshops, distributes publications, makes referrals to other sources of info. Most services free.

61058. Canadian Society for Chemical Engineering, 151 Slater St, Ste 906, Ottawa, Ont K1P 5H3; (613) 233-5623. Interest in chemical engineering. Answers inquiries; conducts meetings, development program, annual conference; publishes materials; makes referrals.

61059. Canadian Society of Petroleum Geologists, 206 Seventh Ave SW, No 505, Calgary, Alberta T2P 0W7; (403) 264-5610. Nonprofit technical society interested in geological earth sciences, current exploration technology for fossil fuels, other energy resources. Answers inquiries, conducts seminars and conferences for nominal registration fee.

61060. Canadian Tax Foundation Library, 130 Adelaide St W, Toronto, Ont M5H 3P5; (416) 863-9784. Interest in Canadian taxation; intl taxation; federal, provincial revenues and expenditures. Answers inquiries, provides referral and reference services, conducts conferences, permits onsite use of collections. Most services free.

61061. Canadian Teachers' Federation, G.G. Croskery Memorial Library, 110 Argyle Ave, Ottawa, Ont K2P 1B4; (613) 232-1505. Interest in all areas of education: teachers, economics, industrial relations, legislation. Provides general reference services, evaluates data, distributes publications, makes interlibrary loans, permits onsite study. Services free, except reproductions, but primarily for members.

61062. Canadian Wood Council, 85 Albert St, Ottawa, Ont K1P 6A4; (613) 235-7221. Natl federation of Canadian forest products assns. Interest in wood engineering, fire performance research, fire regulations, forest products. Provides general reference services, distributes publications. Fees for publications.

61063. Canadian Wood Energy Institute, 85 Curlew Dr, Don Mills, Ont M3A 2P8; (416) 445-6296. Promotes safe, efficient use of solid fuel as energy source; acts as info clearinghouse. Answers inquiries; conducts training courses on installation, operation, maintenance of solid fuel appliances; sponsors, manages annual trade show and conference; provides reference services. Services available to members, fees may apply.

61064. Center for Applied Mathematical Research, Centre de Recherche de Mathematiques Appliquees, Univ de Montreal, C.P. 6128 (Pavillon, 5620 rue Darlington), Montreal, Que H3C 3J7; (514) 343-7501. Interest in applied mathematics, development of mathematics as means for advancement of scientific knowledge and engineering. Answers inquiries; provides advisory, referral services; conducts seminars and workshops; produces, distributes publications. Services for a fee.

61065. Center for Research in Human Relations, 2715 Chemin Ste-Catherine, Montreal, Que H3T 1B6; (514) 738-8076. Conducts research on training of religious congregations and rehabilitation of criminals, relations between psychological science and theological and moral sciences. Conducts seminars, permits onsite study. Services free, available primarily to students from Univ of Montreal.

61066. Centre for Resource Studies, Queen's Univ., Kingston, Ont K7L 3N6; (613) 547-5957. Studies problems of mineral resource policy in Canada. Answers inquiries; provides advisory, consulting, and reference services; conducts seminars and workshops; distributes data compilations, publications; permits onsite use of collections. Services free to sponsors, at cost to others.

61067. Centre of Criminology, Univ of Toronto, John P. Robarts Research Library, Rm 8001, 130 St George St, Toronto, Ont M5S 1A1; (416) 978-7124. Research and teaching center interested in all aspects of criminology, with special reference to Canadian society. Provides general reference services, permits onsite library reference, conducts seminars, distributes publications. Most services free, fees for detailed services.

61068. Chalk River Nuclear Laboratories Technical Information Branch, Atomic Energy of Canada, Ltd., Chalk River, Ont K0J 1J0; (613) 687-5581. Interest in nuclear technology, heavy water reactors, radioisotopes, accelerators. Provides general reference services, permits onsite reference by appointment. Services free to AECL and contractors, at cost to other Canadians. Use by non-Canadians permitted only by special agreement.

61069. Chemical Institute of Canada, 151 Slater St, Ste 906, Ottawa, Ont K1P 5H3; (613) 233-5623. Natl assn of chemists, chemical engineers, and chemical technologists in Canada. Interest in chemistry, chemical engineering, chemical technology, and chemical education in Canada, pollution control. Answers inquiries free, publishes materials.

61071. Department of Anaesthesia Research, McGill Univ, McIntyre Medical Bldg, 3655 Drummond St, Montreal, Que H3G 1Y6; (514) 392-3004. Interest in neurophysiological, neurohumoral, and neuropharmacological research, especially on synaptic transmission in mammalian central nervous system. Answers inquiries, lends material, distributes publications, makes referrals to other info sources, permits onsite use of collection. Services primarily for special groups, but others assisted.

61072. Ecology House, 12 Madison Ave, Toronto, Ont M5R 2S1; (416) 967-0577. Acts as urban demonstration, resource centre for conservation. Answers inquiries; provides limited consulting, reference services; conducts workshops, seminars, courses, personalized training sessions, slide shows, tours, exhibits; distributes publications; permits onsite use of collection. Most services free or at cost.

61073. Energy Probe Research Foundation, 100 Coll St, Univ. of Toronto, Toronto, Ont M5G 1L5; (416) 978-7014. Interest in social, environmental, economic impacts of energy policies. Answers inquiries; provides advisory services; conducts research, seminars, workshops; distributes publications; makes referrals to other info sources. Services for a fee.

61074. Equine Behavior Study Circle, c/o Dr. S.E. Cregier, N American Coordinator and Editor, Univ of Prince Edward Island, Charlottetown, P.E.I. C1A 4P3; (902) 892-4121, ext 229. Provides intl forum for info exchange on equine behavior, training, breeding, health. Answers inquiries; provides advisory and reference services; conducts seminars, meetings, tours; produces, distributes publications. Services free to members, at cost to others. Inquirers must furnish return postage.

61075. Evan Shute Foundation for Clinical and Laboratory Research, 10 Grand Ave, London, Ont N6C 1K9; (519) 432-1884. Nonprofit center for preventive medicine involved in study of nutrition; acts as world headquarters for medical use of alpha tocopherol (vitamin E) in humans. Answers inquiries, provides advisory, consulting and reference services, distributes publications. Publications and dosage schedules free to physicians, research personnel.

61076. Forintek Canada Corp., Western Lab, 6620 NW Marine Dr, Vancouver, B.C. V6T 1X2; (604) 224-3221; Eastern Lab, 800 Montreal Rd, Ottawa, Ont K1G 3Z5; (613) 744-0963. Interest in research in sawmilling, seasoning, wood machining, plywood, composite products, adhesives, energy, other wood sciences. Answers inquiries, provides consulting services, conducts seminars and meetings, permits onsite study, distributes publications (some free.)

61077. Geotechnical Research Centre, McGill Univ, 817 Sherbrooke St W, Montreal, Que H3A 2K6; (514) 392-4751. Conducts integrated, multidisciplinary research studies of geotechnical engineering and environmental problems inherent in land management. Provides management, advisory, consulting services; produces, distributes publications; conducts seminars. Fee for some services.

61078. Hockey Hall of Fame, Exhibition Pl, Toronto, Ont M6K 3C3; (416) 595-1345. Interest in history of hockey, especially in Canada and U.S., but not excluding hockey anywhere. Sells publications, permits onsite use of materials by qualified researchers.

61079. Information Retrieval System for Social Sciences of Leisure and Sport, Faculty of Human Kinetics and Leisure Studies, Univ of Waterloo, Waterloo, Ont N3B 2Z1; (519) 885-1211 ext 2560. Computerized, online data base and documentation center that collects literature on leisure and sport. Answers inquiries, provides advisory and reference services, conducts seminars and workshops, permits onsite use of collection. Services free to students and faculty members, at cost to others.

61080. Informetrica, P.O. Box 828, Station B (130 Slater St, 11th Fl), Ottawa, Ont K1P 5P9; (613) 238-4831. Involved in economic consulting and comprehensive forecasts of Canadian economic activity to 2005 and beyond. Answers inquiries; provides consulting services; provides natl, provincial forecasts; conducts executive briefings, training programs, workshops; evaluates data. Fees for all services.

61081. Institute for Hydrogen Systems, 2480 Dunwin Dr, Mississauga, Ont L5L 1J9; (416) 828-7700. Interest in hydrogen and hydrogen-related technologies; thermochemical and electrochemical technologies, systems analysis, application development for hydrogen. Answers inquiries, provides advisory, consulting and reference services, permits onsite use of collection. Fees for some services.

61082. Institute for Research on Public Policy, P.O. Box 3670, Halifax S, Nova Scotia B3J 3K6; (902) 424-3801. Promotes informed public debate on issues of major public interest, participation in public decisionmaking; finds practical solutions to important public policy problems. Answers inquiries, provides advisory and reference services, conducts seminars and workshops; produces aand distributes publications. Fees may apply.

61083. Institute of Air and Space Law, Faculty of Law, McGill Univ, 3690 Peel St, Montreal, Que H3A 1W9; (514) 392-6721. Interest in air and space law research, education; economics of air transport. Provides advisory services, conducts courses, seminars, and symposia, permits onsite use of collection. Services for a fee to those with professional interest in subject.

61084. Institute of Law Research and Reform, 402 Law Centre, Univ of Alberta, Edmonton, Alberta T6G 2H5; (403) 432-5291. Interest in law research directed to law reform primarily at provincial state level. Provides info on research, distributes publications, permits onsite use of collection. Services free, limited by time, priorities, and cost.

61085. International Air Transport Association, IATA Bldg, 2000 Peel St, Montreal, Que H3A 2R4; (514) 844-6311. Acts as spokesman for air transport industry in its relations with govts and governmental orgs. Answers inquiries, distributes free certain booklets and pamphlets, and annual report.

61086. International Arthurian Society, North American Branch, c/o Hans R. Runte, Secty-Treas, Dept of French, Dalhousie Univ, Halifax, Nova Scotia B3H 4H8. Interest in literature and history, legend of King Arthur. Answers inquiries free.

61087. International Center for Research on Bilingualism, Pavillon Casault, 6e etage sud, Cite Universitaire, Que, Que G1K 7P4; (418) 656-3232. Research center interested in bilingualism, sociolinguistics, linguistic rights, psycholinguistics, language teaching didactics. Provides general reference services, permits onsite study. Services free, except photocopying.

61088. International Civil Aviation Organisation, 1000 Sherbrooke St W, Montreal, Que H3A 2R2; (514) 285-8219. United Nations specialized agency that establishes intl regulations concerning all aspects of civil aviation. Answers inquiries, sells publications, makes referrals free.

61089. International Confederation for Plastic and Reconstructive Surgery, c/o Dr. J.P. Bosse, 3875 St Urbain, Ste 602, Montreal, Que H2W 1V1. Confederation of natl societies of plastic surgeons worldwide primarily concerned with info exchange; interested in plastic, reconstructive surgery. Serves as advisory headquarters to members of constituent natl societies, which pay a subscription rate.

61090. International Council for Distance Education, c/o Athabasca Univ, 12439 52 Ave, Edmonton, Alberta T6H 0P5; (403) 435-2817. Interest in education at a distance, correspondence education, educational technology. Distributes publication, makes referrals to other info sources. Services primarily for members, but also available to others for fee, time and resources permitting.

61091. International North Pacific Fisheries Commission, 6640 NW Marine Dr, Vancouver, B.C. V6T 1X2; (604) 228-1128. Interest in conservation of the fisheries resources of north Pacific Ocean. Answers inquiries, evaluates data, makes referrals. Publications free, available preferably on exchange basis.

61092. International Pacific Salmon Fisheries Commission, Box 30 (549 Columbia St), New Westminster, B.C. V3L 4X9; (604) 521-3771. Interest in Pacific salmon fisheries, Fraser River sockeye and pink salmon. Makes interlibrary loans, permits onsite use of collection. Services free to students and other fisheries agencies.

61093. Investment Dealers Association of Canada, 33 Yonge St, Ste 350, Toronto, Ont M5E 1G4; (416) 364-6133. Interest in investment securities industry. Publishes and distributes reports, studies; answers inquiries; makes referrals. Most services free.

61094. J.W. Crane Memorial Library of Geriatrics and Gerontology, Canadian Geriatrics Research Society, 351 Christie St, Toronto, Ont M6G 3C3; (416) 537-6000. Interest in geriatrics and gerontology, biomedical and social science aspects of aging. Provides general reference and consulting services, distributes publications, makes interlibrary loans, permits onsite reference. Services free, except reproductions.

61095. Leisure Studies Data Bank, Dept of Recreation, Univ of Waterloo, Waterloo, Ont N2L 3G1; (519) 885-1211 ext 6354. Interest in recreation and health studies; data analysis, archive, and storage; leisure activities, fitness and tourism. Pubishes *Canadian Atlas of Recreation and Exercise.* Answers inquiries, provides advisory and consulting services. permits onsite use of collections. Services for a fee.

61096. Maritime Resource Management Service Information Records Centre, P.O. Box 310, Amherst, Nova Scotia B4H 3Z5; (902) 667-7231. Interest in land use, resource planning and development, engineering. Provides general reference and consulting services, conducts seminars and workshops, distributes data compilations, permits onsite use of collections. Services at cost of materials.

61097. McGill Cancer Centre, Faculty of Medicine, McGill Univ, McIntyre Medical Sciences Bldg, 3655 Drummond St, Montreal, Que H3G 1Y6; (514) 392-3033. Interest in molecular biology of DNA tumor viruses, immune reactions against tumors, related cancer research. Provides general reference services, conducts seminars, teaches postsecondary courses, distributes publications. Services free.

61098. McGill Subarctic Research Station, McGill Univ, P.O. Box 790, Schefferville, Que G0G 2T0; (418) 585-2489. Interest in various aspects of subarctic environmental studies. Conducts courses and colloquia, distributes publications, makes interlibrary loans, permits onsite reference. Services free, except courses and publications, but available primarily to resident researchers.

61099. Micromedia, 144 Front St W, Toronto, Ont M5J 1G2; (416) 593-5211. Provides document delivery services, including Canadian natl, provincial, and territorial govt documents, newspapers, business periodicals. Maintains index of periodicals, govt documents; distributes publications. Catalog available on request; services for a fee.

61100. Migraine Foundation, 390 Brunswick Ave, Toronto, Ont M5R 2Z4; (416) 920-4916. Dedicated to research, education, and info dissemination about migraine and related disorders. Answers inquiries, provides advisory and reference services, conducts seminars, produces and distributes publications. Most services free.

61101. Mining Association of Canada, 350 Sparks St, Ste 705, Ottawa, Ont K1R 7S8; (613) 233-9391. Natl org of mining industry, works to project industry views on a natl scale to govt depts and the public. Provides general reference services, conducts annual meetings, publishes materials, makes interlibrary loans. Services free.

61102. Montreal Neurological Institute, 3801 Univ St, Montreal, Que H3A 2B4; (514) 284-4651. Interest in the neurosciences, including neuromuscular disorders, spinal disorders, computer tomography, brain metabolism and chemistry. Provides advisory, consulting, reference, and computer search services, distributes publications, permits onsite use of collections. Services at cost to other research or investigative groups with mutual interests.

61103. National Association for Research in Science Teaching, c/o Dr. Wm G. Holliday, NARST-EDCI, Univ of Calgary, Calgary, Alberta T2N 1N4; (403) 284-7485. Interest in promotion of research in science teaching and dissemination of findings, science education, and curriculum. Answers inquiries, publishes material.

61104. National Association of Antique Automobile Clubs of Canada, 27 Queen St E, Ste 404, Toronto, Ont M5C 2M6; (416) 362-1369. Coordinates activities of antique automobile hobby clubs in Canada. Interest in antique automobiles, Canadian automobiles. Provides general reference and consulting services, distributes publication. Services for auto clubs, historians, etc. Fees for copying, other services free.

61105. National Research Council of Canada Atlantic Research Laboratory, 1411 Oxford St, Halifax, Nova Scotia B3H 3Z1; (902) 429-6450. Interest in marine biology and algology, chemistry, marine algae, mycology, lichenology, metallurgy. Provides general reference, consulting, and translation services, permits onsite reference. Services primarily for staff, to others at discretion of librarian.

61106. North-South Institute, 185 Rideau St, Ottawa, Ont K1N 5X8; (613) 236-3535. Interest in professional policy research of multilateral cooperation, especially relations between industrialized and developing countries. Answers inquiries, provides advisory and consulting services, conducts seminars and workshops, distributes publications. General inquiries free for nonprofit users, fees for other services.

61107. Northwest Atlantic Fisheries Organization, P.O. Box 638, Dartmouth, Nova Scotia B2Y 3Y9; (902) 469-9105. Interest in scientific study of principal marine resources of the northwest Atlantic Ocean, including hydrography, marine life management. Answers inquiries; provides advisory, reference services; conducts seminars and workshops; produces, distributes publications, data compilations. Services free, generally available only to representatives of member countries.

61108. Oak Manor Farms, c/o T. Nimmo, Intl Marketing, R.R. 1, Tavistock, Ont N0B 2R0; (519) 662-2385. Involved with growing, storing, processing, shipping of certified organically-grown grains, grain products. Answers inquiries; provides advisory and reference services; conducts seminars, workshops, farm inspections; distributes publications. Most services free.

61109. Ocean Engineering Information Centre, Memorial Univ of Newfoundland, St John's, Newfoundland A1B 3X5; (709) 737-8377. Interest in cold ocean engineering, ice research, offshore hydrocarbon development in northern waters. Provides info search, maintains collection on related subject matter. Primarily for use of sponsors; other requests handled on limited basis by contractual arrangement, time permitting. Charges for copying materials.

61110. Oldtime Country Music Club of Canada, c/o B. Fuller, Secty, 1421 Gohier St, St Laurent, Que H4L 3K2; (514) 748-7251. Interest in oldtime country and western music, bluegrass, traditional music, etc. Provides general reference services, sponsors concerts and family get-togethers, distributes publication, permits access to library. Many services free to members, and membership is invited.

61111. Ontario Centre for Auto Parts Technology, 63 Church St, 2nd Fl, St Catherine's, Ont L2R 3C4; (416) 688-2600. Helps Ont. auto supplier base become more competitive by improving productivity, quality. Answers inquiries, provides advisory, consulting, and reference services, conducts seminars and workshops. Services generally for a fee, usually only to auto industry, but others assisted.

61114. Ontario Tree Improvement and Forest Biomass Institute, Ont. Ministry of Natural Resources, Maple, Ont L0J 1E0; (416) 832-2761. Interest in biomass production for traditional forest products and energy, intensive forest management, silviculture, tree breeding, tree physiology, forest ecology, forest soils. Answers inquiries free, publishes materials.

61115. Parents of Multiple Births Association of Canada, 283 Seventh Ave S, Lethbridge, Alberta T1J 1H6; (403) 328-9165. Interest in social, medical aspects of multiple births. Produces, distributes publications; answers inquiries; provides advisory, reference services to parents with multiple births and those working with them. Fees may apply.

61116. Planetary Association for Clean Energy, 100 Bronson Ave, Ste 1001, Ottawa, Ont K1R 6G8; (613) 236-6265. Facilitates implementation of clean energy systems on local, regional, continental, and global scale. Answers inquiries; provides advisory, consulting and reference services; conducts seminars and workshops; produces, distributes publications; permits onsite use of collections. Fees based on ability to pay. Services available to anyone; members given priority.

61117. Pollution Probe Foundation, 12 Madison Ave, Toronto, Ont M5R 2S1; (416) 926-1907. Addresses Canadian environmental issues through investigation, info, and education. Answers inquiries; provides advisory, reference, referral services; conducts seminars, workshops, lectures, and slide/tape shows; produces, distributes publications; permits onsite use of collections. Most services free.

61118. Prairie Agricultural Machinery Institute, P.O. Box 1900 (No 5, Hwy West), Humboldt, Saskatchewan S0K 2S0; (306) 682-2555. Interest in improving design, aiding in selection, use of agricultural machinery in prairie provinces. Answers inquiries; provides advisory and reference services; conducts seminars and workshops; produces, distributes publications. Most services free.

61119. Quebec Asbestos Mining Association, 1130 Sherbrooke St W, Rm 410, Montreal, Que H3A 2M8; (514) 842-0382. Interest in mining and milling of asbestos. Answers inquiries, publishes materials. Services free.

61120. Quebec Association for Quaternary Research, Assn Queoise pour l'Etude du Quaternaire, c/o Jean-Marie M. Dubois, Sec-Treas, Dept de Geographie, Univ de Sherbrooke, Sherbrooke, Que J1K 2R1; (819) 565-4571. Interest in quaternary research in Canada, especially in Quebec; physical and paleo environments in Quebec. Answers inquiries; conducts conferences, seminars, workshops; distributes publications. Most services free.

61121. Renewable Energy in Canada, 334 King St E, Ste 208, Toronto, Ont M5A 1K8; (416) 947-9552. Interest in renewable energy resources; technology transfer related to residential low-energy construction, retrofit. Answers inquiries; provides advisory, referral, consulting services; conducts seminars and workshops; produces, distributes publications. Services for a fee.

61123. Royal Astronomical Society of Canada, National Library, 136 Dupont St, Toronto, Ont M5R 1V2; (416) 924-7973. Interest in astronomy. Provides reference services, publishes materials, permits onsite use of collection. Direct loans only to members.

61124. Royal Botanical Gardens, Box 399, Hamilton, Ont L8N 3H8; (416) 527-1158. Scientific, cultural institution interested in horticulture, plant taxonomy, floral art, breeding, pathology of ornamentals. Provides info services, distributes publications, conducts lectures and seminars, permits onsite study. Services available to all; special programs for members.

61125. Ryerson Polytechnical Institute Nutrition Information Service, Dept of Food, Nutrition, Consumer and Family Studies, Ryerson Polytechnical Institute, 350 Victoria St, Rm L192, Toronto, Ont M5B 1E8; (416) 979-5000 ext 6903. Collects, disseminates food, nutrition info to educate public. Answers inquiries, provides advisory and reference services, conducts seminars and workshops, distributes publications, permits onsite use of collections. Most services free.

61126. Social Science Data Archive, Dept of Sociology-Anthropology, Carleton Univ, Loeb Bldg, Rm A715, Colonel By Dr, Ottawa, Ont K1S 5B6; (613) 231-7426. Interest in social science data, public opinion surveys, Statistics Canada census data. Provides general reference services, data documentation, processing services; permits onsite study. Services free to Carleton community, for a fee to others.

61127. Society of Toxicology of Canada, Societe de Toxicologie du Canada, c/o Dr G. Krip, Exec Dir, P.O. Box 517, Beaconsfield, Que H9W 5V1. Promotes advancement of toxicology in Canada by providing a forum for contact and communication among toxicologists. Answers inquiries, provides advisory services, conducts annual symposium. Services available only to researchers in field.

61128. Sport Information Resources Centre, 333 River Rd, Ottawa, Ont K1L 8H9; (613) 746-5357. Provides sport, phys ed, recreation info services to orgs throughout world. Publishes sport bibliographies, indexes; answers inquiries; provides reference, literature-searching. Permits onsite use of collections. Most services free.

61129. Stock Market Information Service, P.O. Box 120, Station K, Montreal, Que H1N 3K9; (514) 256-9487. Interest in stocks and bonds of unknown value; traces present status, exact value, collection value of old stocks and bonds issued by companies, govts anywhere in the world since 1850. Maintains in-house computer data base; answers inquiries, provides consulting services. Services for a fee.

61130. Surgical Infection Society, c/o J.L. Meakins, MD, Secty, Dept of Surgery, Rm S10.30, Royal Victoria Hospital, 687 Pine Ave W, Montreal, Que H3A 1A1; (514) 842-2423. Interest in research, causes, treatment of surgical infections; clinical care; biotechnology. Answers inquiries; conducts research, conferences, seminars, workshops; makes referrals to other info sources. Services primarily for members, others assisted.

61131. The Biomass Energy Institute, 1329 Niakwa Rd, Winnipeg, Manitoba R2J 3T4; (204) 257-3891. Accumulates, classifies, disseminates info on biomass energy, biotechnology. Provides general reference and consulting services, conducts seminars, distributes publications, permits onsite study. Services free, except publications; regular use of services requires membership.

61132. Traffic Injury Research Foundation of Canada, 171 Nepean St, 6th Fl, Ottawa, Ont K2P 0B4; (613) 238-5235. Interest in behavioral and medical factors relevant to road safety: alcohol and drug effects, driver education, etc. Answers inquiries, evaluates data, distributes publications. All services at cost, limited by time and personnel availability.

61134. Welding Institute of Canada, Institut de Soudage du Canada, 391 Burnhamthorpe Rd E, Oakville, Ont L6J 6C9; (416) 845-9881. Interest in welding research into consumables, processes, and materials technology, quality control. Provides general reference services, makes interlibrary loans, permits onsite reference by members. Services free to corporate membership, fees to others.

61135. West Coast Environmental Law Association (Canada), 207 W Hastings St, Ste 1001, Vancouver, BC V6B 1H7; (604) 684-7378. Provides legal advice to individuals and orgs with environmental problems, advocates environmental law reform, conducts educational, environmental activities. Answers inquiries; provides advisory, consulting, and reference services; conducts seminars, workshops; produces, distributes publications, permits onsite use of collection. Most services free.

61136. Westminister Institute for Ethics and Human Values, Westminster Coll, 361 Windermere Rd, London, Ont N6G 2K3; (519) 673-0046. Interest in legal philosophy, ethics issues. Answers inquiries, conducts seminars, workshops, and adult education courses, distributes publications, permits onsite use of collections. Fees for some services.

61137. World Federation of Hemophilia, 1155 Dorchester Blvd, W, Ste 1517, Montreal, Que H3B 2J6; (514) 866-0442. Interest in development and improvement of diagnosis, treatment, rehabilitation, education, and research in hemophilia. Provides general reference, consulting services; conducts congresses, symposia, training, and regional workshops; distributes publications. Services free.

61138. World Leisure and Recreation Association, 559 King Edward St, Ottawa, Ont K1N 6N7; (212) 697-8783. Interest in leisure and recreation administration and research, leisure activities, leadership training, parks, physical education. Provides general reference and consulting services, conducts intl exchange, training programs, conferences, etc. Fees for extensive services.

61140. Yukon Conservation Society, Box 4163, Whitehorse, Yukon Y1A 3T3; (403) 668-5678. Interest in environmental planning and policy, protection of northern environment; wildlife and natural areas management. Answers inquiries, provides reference services, publishes travel guides. Most services free.

Organization Index

A. Philip Randolph Institute (NY), 36008
A.E. Seaman Mineralogical Museum (MI), 26004
A.O. Smith Corp. Library (WI), 54001
A/C Pipe Producers Association (VA), 51004
AAI Corp. Technical Library (MD), 24010
ABC-Clio Information Services (CA), 05018
AC-CU-MET (AL), 01001
ACCION International/AITEC (MA), 25003
ACTION Management Information Systems (DC), 10021
AFL-CIO, Community Services Department (DC), 10022
AFL-CIO, Department for Professional Employees (DC), 10023
AFS International/Intercultural Programs (NY), 36010
AGWAY Inc., Corporate Library (NY), 36011
AMC Cancer Research Center and Hospital Medical Library (CO), 07006
APEC (OH), 40003
API Standard Reference Materials (PA), 43001
APM Library of Recorded Sound (NY), 36013
ARCO Metals Co., Technical Information Center (IL), 17002
ARCO Research, Development & Engineering Library (PA), 43002
ARTS Computer Products (MA), 25004
ASA Education Foundation (IL), 17003
ASM Division of Aquatic and Terrestrial Microbiology (LA), 22001
AT International Library (DC), 10024
AXIOS (CA), 05019
Abalone Alliance (CA), 05020
Abernathy Salmon Technology Center (WA), 52003
Abrasive Engineering Society (PA), 43003
Abrasive Grain Association (OH), 40004
Abt Associates (MA), 25005
Abundant Life Seed Foundation (WA), 52004
Acacia Group (MD), 24012
Academy for Educational Development (NY), 36014
Academy for Educational Development, Clearinghouse on Development Communication (DC), 10025
Academy for Educational Development, Systems Services Division (DC), 10026
Academy for Implants and Transplants (IL), 17004
Academy for Sports Dentistry (TX), 48005
Academy for State & Local Government (DC), 10027
Academy for State & Local Government, International Center (DC), 10028
Academy of American Franciscan History (MD), 24013
Academy of American Poets (NY), 36016
Academy of Dentistry International (CA), 05021
Academy of Food Marketing Library (PA), 43004
Academy of General Dentistry (IL), 17005
Academy of Hospital Public Relations (CA), 05022
Academy of Model Aeronautics (VA), 51005
Academy of Oral Dynamics (PA), 43005
Academy of Orthomolecular Psychiatry (NY), 36017
Academy of Parapsychology and Medicine (CO), 07008

Academy of Science Fiction, Fantasy, and Horror Films (CA), 05023
Academy of Scientific Hypnotherapy (CA), 05024
Academy of Sports Psychology International (OH), 40005
Accent on Information (IL), 17006
Access Innovations (NM), 35001
Accreditation Association for Ambulatory Health Care (IL), 17007
Accreditation Board for Engineering and Technology (NY), 36018
Accreditation Council for Services for Mentally Retarded & Other Developmentally Disabled Persons (DC), 10029
Accrediting Commission on Education for Health Services Administration (VA), 51006
Acheson Industries Corporate Information Center (MI), 26006
Acid Deposition Data Network Project (TN), 47001
Acid Deposition Program (NC), 38002
Acid Rain Foundation (MN), 27001
Acid Rain Information Clearinghouse (NY), 36019
Ackerman Institute for Family Therapy (NY), 36020
Acoustic Emission Technology Corp. Technical Library (CA), 05026
Acoustic Neuroma Association (PA), 43007
Acoustical Society of America (NY), 36021
Action for Children's Television (MA), 25006
Action for Research into Multiple Sclerosis (TX), 48006
Action on Smoking & Health (DC), 10030
Actors' Equity Association (NY), 36022
Adaptive Environments Center (MA), 25007
Addiction Research Foundation (CAN), 61001
Adhesive and Sealant Council (VA), 51007
Adhesives Manufacturers Association (IL), 17008
Adirondack Mountain Club (NY), 36023
Adirondack Museum Library (NY), 36024
Administration for Children, Youth & Families (DC), 10031
Administrative Conference of the U.S. (DC), 10032
Administrative Management Society (PA), 43008
Administrative Office of the U.S. Courts (DC), 10034
Adolf Meller Co. (RI), 44001
Adoptee/Natural Parent Locators International (CA), 05027
Adoptees in Search (MD), 24014
Adoptive Parents Committee (NY), 36025
Adrenal Metabolic Research Society of the Hypoglycemia Foundation (NY), 36026
Adult Film Association of America (CA), 05028
Advanced Technology Publications (MA), 25008
Adventures in Movement for the Handicapped (OH), 40006
Advertising Council (NY), 36028
Advertising Photographers of America (NY), 36029
Advertising Research Foundation (NY), 36030
Advisory & Learning Exchange (DC), 10035
Advisory Council on Historic Preservation (DC), 10036

Alabama Cooperative Fishery Research Unit (AL), 01007

Alabama Cooperative Wildlife Research Unit (AL), 01008

Alabama Department of Forensic Sciences (AL), 01010

Alabama Geological Survey (AL), 01011

Alabama Historical Commission (AL), 01012

Alabama Humanities Resource Center (AL), 01013

Alabama Law Institute (AL), 01014

Alabama Legislative Reference Service (AL), 01015

Alabama Soil and Water Conservation Committee (AL), 01016

Alabama Solar Energy Association (AL), 01017

Alabama Wildlife Federation (AL), 01018

Alan Guttmacher Institute (NY), 36042

Alaska Agricultural Experiment Station (AK), 02001

Alaska Center for the Environment (AK), 02002

Alaska Cooperative Fishery Research Unit (AK), 02003

Alaska Cooperative Wildlife Research Unit (AK), 02004

Alaska Department of Transportation and Public Facilities (AK), 02005

Alaska Geographic Society (AK), 02006

Alaska Geological Society (AK), 02007

Alaska Historical Commission (AK), 02008

Alaska Historical Library Collection (AK), 02009

Alaska Historical Society (AK), 02010

Alaska Historical and Transportation Museum (AK), 02011

Alaska State Council on the Arts (AK), 02012

Alaska State Museum (AK), 02013

Alban Institute (DC), 10055

Albany College of Pharmacy (NY), 36043

Alberta Department of the Environment Air Quality Control Branch (CAN), 61004

Albrook Hydraulics Laboratory (WA), 52006

Alcohol & Drug Problems Association of North America (DC), 10056

Alcohol Education for Youth (NY), 36044

Alcohol Education for Youth and Community (NY), 36045

Alcohol Research Information Service (MI), 26009

Alcohol Studies Unit (IA), 19002

Alcohol, Drug Abuse, and Mental Health Administration (MD), 24018

Alcoholics Anonymous World Services (NY), 36046

Alcolac Research Library (MD), 24019

Alden Research Laboratory (MA), 25014

Alexander Graham Bell Association for the Deaf (DC), 10057

Alexander Lindsay Junior Museum (CA), 05040

Alfred I. DuPont Institute Medical Library (DE), 09003

All Indian Pueblo Council, Business Development Center (NM), 35003

All-America Selections (IL), 17013

Allegheny Observatory (PA), 43013

Allergy Information Association (CAN), 61005

Alliance For Justice (DC), 10058

Alliance for Engineering in Medicine and Biology (MD), 24020

Alliance for Environmental Education (DC), 10059

Alliance for Perinatal Research and Services (VA), 51011

Alliance for the Prudent Use of Antibiotics (MA), 25015

Alliance of American Insurers (IL), 17014

Alliance of Information and Referral Systems (IN), 18004

Alliance to Save Energy (DC), 10060

Allie M. Lee Cancer Research Laboratory (NV), 32005

Allied Corp., Technical Information Service (NJ), 34003

Allied Industrial Workers of America (WI), 54002

Alloy Phase Diagram Data Center (MD), 24021

Alopecia Areata Research Foundation (NC), 38004

Alston Wilkes Society (SC), 45001

Alternate Lifestyles (GA), 14005

Alternate Media Center (NY), 36047

Alternative Energy Collective (CA), 05041

Alternative Energy Institute (TX), 48009

Alternative Press Syndicate (NY), 36048

Alternative Schools Network (IL), 17015

Alternative Sources of Energy (MN), 27003

Alternative Technologies Association (IN), 18005

Alternatives to Abortion International (NY), 36049

Aluminum Association (DC), 10061

Aluminum Recycling Association (DC), 10062

Alverno College Research Center on Women (WI), 54003

Alzheimer's Disease and Related Disorders Association (IL), 17016

Amalgamated Clothing and Textile Workers Union (NY), 36050

Amalgamated Flying Saucer Clubs of America (CA), 05042

Amana Heritage Society (IA), 19003

Amateur Astronomers Association of New York City (NY), 36051

Amateur Athletic Foundation, L.A. Organizing Committee (CA), 05043

Amateur Athletic Union of the United States (IN), 18006

Amateur Chamber Music Players (DC), 10063

Amateur Softball Association Research Center and Library (OK), 41002

Amazonia Foundation (NY), 36052

Ambulatory Pediatric Association (VA), 51013

America Israel Friendship League (NY), 36053

America the Beautiful Fund (DC), 10064

America's Society of Separated and Divorced Men (IL), 17017

American Abstract Artists (NJ), 34004

American Academy and Institute of Arts and Letters, Library (NY), 36054

American Academy for Cerebral Palsy and Developmental Medicine (VA), 51014

American Academy of Actuaries (DC), 10065

American Academy of Allergy and Immunology (WI), 54004

American Academy of Child Psychiatry (DC), 10066

American Academy of Compensation Medicine (NY), 36055

American Academy of Dental Electrosurgery (NY), 36056

American Academy of Dental Practice Administration (AZ), 03004

American Academy of Dental Radiology (GA), 14006

American Academy of Environmental Engineers (MD), 24022

American Academy of Facial Plastic & Reconstructive Surgery (DC), 10067

American Academy of Family Physicians (MO), 29003

American Academy of Forensic Sciences (CO), 07013

American Academy of Gold Foil Operators (TX), 48010

American Academy of Implant Dentistry (MA), 25017

American Academy of Judicial Education (DC), 10068

American Academy of Medical Administrators (MI), 26010

American Academy of Medical Directors (FL), 13005

American Academy of Medical Preventics (CA), 05044

American Academy of Neurological & Orthopaedic Medicine & Surgery (NV), 32006

American Academy of Neurology (MN), 27005

American Academy of Ophthalmology (CA), 05045

American Academy of Optometry (DC), 10069

American Academy of Oral Medicine (MO), 29004

American Academy of Osteopathy (OH), 40013

American Academy of Otolaryngology-Head and Neck Surgery (DC), 10070

American Academy of Pediatrics (IL), 17018

American Academy of Periodontology (IL), 17019

American Academy of Physical Medicine and Rehabilitation (IL), 17020

American Academy of Physician Assistants (VA), 51016

American Academy of Podiatric Sports Medicine (MD), 24023

American Academy of Psychiatry and the Law (MD), 24024

American Academy of Sports Physicians (CA), 05046

American Academy of Teachers of Singing (NY), 36057

American Academy of Thermology (DC), 10071

American Academy of the History of Dentistry (MD), 24025

American Accordion Musicological Society (NJ), 34005

American Accordionists' Association (NJ), 34006

American Accounting Association (FL), 13006

American Advertising Federation Career Information (DC), 10072

American Aging Association (NE), 31002

American Agricultural Economics Association (IA), 19004

American Agricultural Economics Documentation Center (DC), 10073

American Agriculture Movement (DC), 10074

American Airship Association (DC), 10075

American Alfalfa Processors Association (KS), 20001

American Allergy Association (CA), 05047

American Alliance for Health, Physical Education, Recreation, and Dance (VA), 51018

American Alpine Club (NY), 36058

American Amateur Baseball Congress (MI), 26011

American Angus Association (MO), 29005

American Animal Hospital Association, Public Relations Department (IN), 18007

American Anorexia/Bulimia Association (NJ), 34008

American Anthropological Association (DC), 10076

American Anti-Vivisection Society (PA), 43014

American Antiquarian Society (MA), 25018

American Apparel Manufacturers Association (VA), 51019

American Arab Association for Commerce and Industry (NY), 36059

American Arbitration Association (NY), 36060

American Architectural Manufacturers Association (IL), 17021

American Archives Association (DC), 10077

American Art Therapy Association (VA), 51020

American Assembly for Men in Nursing (IL), 17022

American Assembly of Collegiate Schools of Business (DC), 10078

American Association for Adult & Continuing Education (DC), 10079

American Association for Affirmative Action (NY), 36061

American Association for Artificial Intelligence (CA), 05049

American Association for Automotive Medicine (IL), 17023

American Association for Cancer Education (NJ), 34009

American Association for Clinical Chemistry (DC), 10080

American Association for Clinical Immunology and Allergy (NE), 31003

American Association for Counseling and Development (VA), 51022

American Association for Crystal Growth (CA), 05050

American Association for Dental Research (DC), 10081

American Association for Health Promotion (CA), 05051

American Association for Higher Education (DC), 10082

American Association for Hospital Planning (DC), 10083

American Association for Laboratory Accreditation (VA), 51023

American Association for Laboratory Animal Science (IL), 17024

American Association for Leisure and Recreation (VA), 51024

American Association for Marriage & Family Therapy (DC), 10084

American Association for Maternal and Child Health (CA), 05052

American Association for Medical Systems & Informatics (DC), 10085

American Association for Music Therapy (NJ), 34010

American Association for Protecting Children (CO), 07014

American Association for Rehabilitation Therapy (AR), 04025

American Association for Respiratory Therapy (TX), 48011

American Association for State and Local History (TN), 47003

American Association for Textile Technology (NY), 36062

American Association for Vocational Instructional Materials (GA), 14007

American Association for World Health U.S. Committee for the World Health Organization (DC), 10086

American Association for the Advancement of Science, Library (DC), 10087

American Association for the Advancement of Science, Project on the Handicapped in Science (DC), 10088

American Association for the Advancement of Slavic Studies (CA), 05053

American Association for the History of Medicine (NY), 36063

American Association for the International Commission of Jurists (NY), 36064

American Association for the Study of Headache (IL), 17025

American Association for the Study of Liver Diseases (NJ), 34011

American Association for the Study of Neoplastic Diseases (OH), 40014

American Association of Aerosol Research (NY), 36065

American Association of Airport Executives (DC), 10089

American Association of Anatomists (VA), 51025

American Association of Avian Pathologists (PA), 43015

American Association of Bible Colleges (AR), 04026

American Association of Bioanalysts (MO), 29006

American Association of Black Women Entrepreneurs (DC), 10090

American Association of Blood Banks (VA), 51026

American Association of Botanical Gardens & Arboreta (PA), 43016

American Association of Cereal Chemists (MN), 27006

American Association of Certified Orthoptists (FL), 13007

American Association of Children's Residential Centers (DC), 10091

American Association of Colleges for Teacher Education (DC), 10092

American Association of Colleges for Teacher Education, ERIC Clearinghouse on Teacher Education (DC), 10093

American Association of Colleges of Nursing (DC), 10094

American Association of Colleges of Osteopathic Medicine (MD), 24026

American Association of Colleges of Pharmacy (MD), 24027

American Association of Colleges of Podiatric Medicine (MD), 24028

American Association of Community & Junior Colleges (DC), 10095

American Association of Dental Schools (DC), 10096

American Association of Dental Victims (CA), 05054

American Association of Diabetes Educators (NJ), 34012

American Association of Electromyography and Electrodiagnosis (MN), 27007

American Association of Endodontists (IL), 17026

American Association of Engineering Societies (NY), 36066

American Association of Exporters and Importers (NY), 36067

American Association of Foot Specialists (NJ), 34013

American Association of Fund-Raising Counsel (NY), 36068

American Association of Healthcare Consultants (VA), 51027

American Association of Homes for the Aging (DC), 10097

American Association of Hospital Dentists (IL), 17027

American Association of Hospital Podiatrists (NY), 36069

American Association of Housing Educators (KS), 20002

American Association of Immunologists (MD), 24029

American Association of Individual Investors (IL), 17028

American Association of Law Libraries (IL), 17029

American Association of MESBICS (DC), 10098

American Association of Meat Processors (PA), 43017

American Association of Medical Assistants (IL), 17030

American Association of Motor Vehicle Administrators (DC), 10099

American Association of Museums (DC), 10100

American Association of Neurological Surgeons (IL), 17031

American Association of Neuroscience Nurses (IL), 17032

American Association of Nurse Anesthetists (IL), 17033

American Association of Nurse Attorneys (MD), 24030

American Association of Nurserymen (DC), 10101

American Association of Occupational Health Nurses (GA), 14008

American Association of Oral and Maxillofacial Surgeons (IL), 17034

American Association of Orthodontists (MO), 29007

American Association of Pastoral Counselors (VA), 51028

American Association of Pathologists (MD), 24031

American Association of Petroleum Geologists (OK), 41003

American Association of Physical Anthropologists (OH), 40015

American Association of Physicists in Medicine (NY), 36070

American Association of Physics Teachers (MD), 24032

American Association of Poison Control Centers (DC), 10102

American Association of Port Authorities (VA), 51029

American Association of Professional Hypnologists (PA), 43018

American Association of Psychiatric Services for Children (DC), 10103

American Association of Public Health Dentistry (GA), 14010

American Association of Religious Therapists (FL), 13008

American Association of Retired Persons, Institute of Lifetime Learning (DC), 10104

American Association of Retired Persons, National Gerontology Resource Center (DC), 10105

American Association of Retired Persons, Widowed Persons Service (DC), 10106

American Association of School Administrators (VA), 51030

American Association of School Librarians (IL), 17035

American Association of Sex Educators, Counselors & Therapists (DC), 10107

American Association of State Highway & Transportation Officials (DC), 10108

American Association of Stratigraphic Palynologists (TX), 48012

American Association of Suicidology (CO), 07017

American Association of Teachers of German (NJ), 34014

American Association of Textile Chemists and Colorists (NC), 38005

American Association of Tissue Banks (VA), 51031

American Association of University Administrators (DC), 10109

American Association of University Affiliated Programs for Persons with Developmental Disabilities (MD), 24033

American Association of University Women, Educational Foundation Library (DC), 10110

American Association of University Women, Public Policy Department (DC), 10111

American Association of Variable Star Observers (MA), 25019

American Association of Veterinary Lab Diagnosticians (MO), 29008

American Association of Veterinary Medical Data Program Participants (NY), 36071

American Association of Veterinary Parasitologists (PA), 43019

American Association of Veterinary State Boards (NJ), 34015

American Association of Wildlife Veterinarians (WY), 55001

American Association of Zoo Keepers (KS), 20003

American Association of Zoo Veterinarians (GA), 14011

American Association of Zoological Parks and Aquariums (WV), 53003

American Astronautical Society (VA), 51032

American Astronomical Society (DC), 10112

American Athletic Association of the Deaf (MI), 26012

American Auto Racing Writers and Broadcasters Association (CA), 05055

American Automatic Control Council (AZ), 03005

American Automobile Association (VA), 51033

American Aviation Historical Society (CA), 05056

American Bamboo Society (CA), 05057

American Bandmasters Association (TX), 48013

American Bankers Association Library (DC), 10113

American Baptist Historical Society (NY), 36072

American Bar Association, Information Services (IL), 17036

American Bar Association, Mental Disability Legal Resource Center (DC), 10114

American Bar Association, Section of Family Law (IL), 17037

American Bar Association, Standing Committee on Lawyer Referral Service (IL), 17038

American Bar Association, Traffic Court Program (IL), 17039

American Battle Monuments Commission (DC), 10116

American Beekeeping Federation (FL), 13009

American Behcet's Foundation (CA), 05058

American Bladesmith Society (MD), 24034

American Blood Commission (VA), 51034

American Board of Dental Public Health (FL), 13010

American Board of Medical Specialties (IL), 17041

American Board of Orthodontics (MO), 29009

American Board of Orthopaedic Surgery (IL), 17042

American Board of Pathology (FL), 13011

American Board of Pediatrics (NC), 38006

American Board of Physical Medicine and Rehabilitation (MN), 27008

American Board of Prosthodontics (MI), 26014

American Boarding Kennels Association (CO), 07018

American Boat and Yacht Council (NY), 36073

American Boiler Manufacturers Association (VA), 51037

American Bonsai Society (NH), 33001

American Boxwood Society (VA), 51038

American Brahman Breeders Association (TX), 48014

American Brittle Bone Society (PA), 43020

American Bryological and Lichenological Society (IL), 17043

American Buckskin Registry Association (CA), 05059

American Budgerigar Society (CT), 08008

American Bureau of Metal Statistics (NY), 36074

American Burn Association (AZ), 03007

American Bus Association (DC), 10118

American CB Radio Association (CT), 08009

American Camellia Society (GA), 14012

American Camping Association (IN), 18008

American Can Co., Technical Information Center (IL), 17044
American Canal Society (PA), 43021
American Canal and Transportation Center (WV), 53004
American Cancer Society, Medical Library (NY), 36076
American Canoe Association (VA), 51039
American Carbon Society (PA), 43022
American Carnival Glass Association (OH), 40016
American Carousel Society (NJ), 34016
American Casting Association (OH), 40017
American Catfish Marketing Association (MS), 28003
American Catholic Philosophical Association (DC), 10119
American Cavy Breeder's Association (PA), 43023
American Celiac Society (NJ), 34017
American Cemetery Association (VA), 51040
American Center for the Alexander Technique (NY), 36077
American Ceramic Society (OH), 40018
American Cetacean Society (CA), 05060
American Chain Association (DC), 10120
American Chamber of Commerce Executives (VA), 51041
American Chemical Society (DC), 10121
American Chemical Society, Women Chemists Committee (DC), 10122
American Child Care Services (VA), 51042
American Chiropractic Association (VA), 51043
American Choral Directors Association (OK), 41004
American Citizens Concerned for Life (MN), 27010
American Civil Liberties Union (NY), 36078
American Civil Liberties Union, Foundation National Prison Project (DC), 10123
American Cleft Palate Educational Foundation (PA), 43024
American Clinical and Climatological Association (MD), 24035
American Coal Ash Associates (DC), 10124
American Coalition of Citizens with Disabilities (DC), 10125
American Cocoa Research Institute (VA), 51044
American Coke and Coal Chemicals Institute (VA), 51045
American Collectors Association (MN), 27011
American College Admissions Advisory Center (PA), 43025
American College Health Association (MD), 24036
American College Testing Program (IA), 19005
American College Theatre Festival (DC), 10126
American College of Apothecaries (TN), 47004
American College of Cardiology Extended Learning (MD), 24038
American College of Chest Physicians (IL), 17045
American College of Emergency Physicians (TX), 48015
American College of Foot Orthopedists (DC), 10127
American College of Health Care Administrators (MD), 24039

American College of Laboratory Animal Medicine (PA), 43026
American College of Legal Medicine (IL), 17046
American College of Nuclear Physicians (DC), 10128
American College of Nurse-Midwives (DC), 10129
American College of Obstetricians & Gynecologists, Resource Center (DC), 10130
American College of Osteopathic Pediatricians (NJ), 34018
American College of Physicians (PA), 43027
American College of Podiatric Radiologists (FL), 13012
American College of Podopediatrics (OH), 40019
American College of Preventive Medicine (DC), 10131
American College of Radiology (VA), 51045
American College of Sports Medicine (IN), 18009
American College of Surgeons (IL), 17048
American College of Veterinary Pathologists (PA), 43028
American College of Veterinary Surgeons (PA), 43029
American Collegiate Retailing Association (NY), 36080
American Committee for International Conservation (DC), 10132
American Committee for South Asian Art (VA), 51046
American Committee on Africa (NY), 36081
American Committee on East-West Accord (DC), 10133
American Committee to Advance the Study of Petroglyphs and Pictographs (WV), 53005
American Compensation Association (AZ), 03008
American Composers Alliance (NY), 36082
American Concrete Institute (MI), 26015
American Concrete Pavement Association (IL), 17049
American Concrete Pipe Association (VA), 51047
American Concrete Pumping Association (CA), 05061
American Conference of Governmental Industrial Hygienists (OH), 40020
American Conference of Therapeutic Selfhelp/Selfhealth/Social Clubs (NY), 36083
American Congress of Rehabilitation Medicine (IL), 17050
American Congress on Surveying and Mapping (VA), 51048
American Correctional Association (MD), 24041
American Corrective Therapy Association (NY), 36084
American Council for Capital Formation (DC), 10134
American Council for Construction Education (DC), 10135
American Council for Drug Education (MD), 24042
American Council for Elementary School Industrial Arts (WI), 54006
American Council for Healthful Living (NJ), 34019
American Council for Nationalities Service (NY), 36085
American Council for University Planning & Academic Excellence (DC), 10136
American Council for Voluntary International Action: InterAction (NY), 36086

American Foundrymen's Society (IL), 17066
American Friends Service Committee (PA), 43034
American Friends Service Committee, National
  Action/Research on the Military Industrial Complex
  (PA), 43035
American Fuchsia Society (CA), 05067
American Fur Industry (NY), 36101
American Gas Association Library (VA), 51056
American Gastroenterological Association (NJ), 34025
American Gear Manufacturers Association (VA),
  51057
American Genetic Association (DC), 10159
American Geographical Society (NY), 36102
American Geological Institute (VA), 51058
American Geophysical Union (DC), 10160
American Geriatric Education Society (WI), 54009
American Geriatrics Society (MA), 25021
American Goat Society (TX), 48017
American Gold Association (CA), 05068
American Gourd Society (OH), 40022
American Graduate School of International
  Management (AZ), 03010
American Group Practice Association (VA), 51060
American Group Psychotherapy Association (NY),
  36103
American Guernsey Cattle Club (OH), 40023
American Guild of Organists (NY), 36105
American Handwriting Analysis Foundation (CA),
  05069
American Hardboard Association (IL), 17067
American Hardware Manufacturers Association (IL),
  17068
American Health Care Association Department of
  Research & Education (DC), 10161
American Health Foundation (NY), 36106
American Health Planning Association (DC), 10162
American Health and Wellness Association (FL),
  13016
American Heart Association (TX), 48018
American Helicopter Society (VA), 51061
American Herb Association (CA), 05070
American Hereford Association (MO), 29010
American Heritage Center Archives (WY), 55002
American Heritage Center, Petroleum History
  Research Division (WY), 55003
American Hibiscus Society (FL), 13017
American Hiking Society (DC), 10163
American Historic & Cultural Society, Honor America
  Program (DC), 10164
American Historical Print Collectors Society (NY),
  36107
American Historical Society of Germans from Russia
  (NE), 31004
American Holistic Medical Association (VA), 51062
American Holistic Medical Association (WA), 52009
American Holistic Nurses Association (CO), 07019
American Home Economics Association (DC), 10165
American Home Lighting Institute (IL), 17069
American Home Sewing Association (NY), 36108
American Homebrewers Association (CO), 07020

American Honey Producers Association (OK), 41005
American Horse Council (DC), 10166
American Horse Protection Association (DC), 10167
American Horse Shows Association (NY), 36109
American Horticultural Society (VA), 51063
American Hospital Association (IL), 17070
American Hospital Management Systems Society
  (IL), 17071
American Hot Dip Galvanizers Association (DC),
  10168
American Hotel and Motel Association (MI), 26016
American Humor Studies Association (MD), 24047
American Hypnotists' Association (CA), 05071
American Indian Archaeological Institute (CT), 08011
American Indian Consultants (AZ), 03011
American Indian Culture Research Center (SD), 46001
American Indian Historical Society (CA), 05072
American Indian Law Center (NM), 35005
American Indian Research & Resource Institute (PA),
  43036
American Industrial Arts Association (VA), 51064
American Industrial Health Council (NY), 36110
American Industrial Hygiene Association (OH),
  40025
American Institute for Archaeological Research (MA),
  25022
American Institute for Cancer Research (VA), 51065
American Institute for Conservation of Historic &
  Artistic Works (DC), 10169
American Institute for Design and Drafting (MD),
  24048
American Institute for Economic Research (MA),
  25023
American Institute for Marxist Studies (NY), 36111
American Institute for Patristic and Byzantine Studies
  (NY), 36112
American Institute for Property & Liability
  Underwriters (PA), 43037
American Institute for Research Project Talent Data
  Bank (CA), 05073
American Institute of Aeronautics and Astronautics,
  Technical Information Service (NY), 36113
American Institute of Architects (DC), 10170
American Institute of Baking (KS), 20004
American Institute of Biological Sciences (DC), 10171
American Institute of Certified Public Accountants
  (NY), 36114
American Institute of Chemical Engineers (NY), 36115
American Institute of Cooperation (DC), 10172
American Institute of Discussion (OK), 41006
American Institute of Food Distribution (NJ), 34026
American Institute of Homeopathy (DC), 10173
American Institute of Maintenance (CA), 05074
American Institute of Management (MA), 25024
American Institute of Marketing (NJ), 34027
American Institute of Medical Climatology (PA),
  43039
American Institute of Merchant Shipping (DC), 10174
American Institute of Mining, Metallurgical, and
  Petroleum Engineers (NY), 36116

American Nurses' Association (MO), 29011
American ORT Federation (NY), 36138
American Occupational Medical Association (IL), 17088
American Occupational Therapy Association (MD), 24058
American Oil Chemists' Society (IL), 17089
American Optometric Association (MO), 29012
American Orchid Society (FL), 13019
American Orff-Schulwerk Association (OH), 40034
American Ornithologists' Union (DC), 10185
American Orthopaedic Foot and Ankle Society (MN), 27012
American Orthopaedic Society for Sports Medicine (IL), 17090
American Orthopsychiatric Association (NY), 36139
American Orthoptic Council (WI), 54012
American Osteopathic Academy of Sclerotherapy (CA), 05084
American Osteopathic Association (IL), 17091
American Osteopathic College of Dermatology (GA), 14014
American Osteopathic College of Rehabilitation Medicine (IL), 17092
American Otological Society (MN), 27013
American Paint Horse Association (TX), 48022
American Pancreatic Association (MN), 27014
American Paper Institute (NY), 36140
American Paper Institute, Plastics Extrusion Coaters Section (NY), 36141
American Paralysis Association (NJ), 34034
American Paralysis Association, Research Division (VA), 51074
American Parkinson Disease Association (NY), 36143
American Patent Research Corp. (DC), 10186
American Peanut Research and Education Society (OK), 41007
American Pedestrian Association (NY), 36144
American Pediatric Society (NY), 36145
American Peony Society (MN), 27015
American Petroleum Institute (DC), 10187
American Petroleum Institute, Central Abstracting and Indexing Service (NY), 36146
American Pharmaceutical Association (DC), 10188
American Philatelic Society (PA), 43046
American Philosophical Society Library (PA), 43047
American Physical Fitness Research Institute (CA), 05086
American Physical Society (NY), 36147
American Physical Therapy Association (VA), 51075
American Physiological Society (MD), 24059
American Phytopathological Society (MN), 27016
American Pipe Fittings Association (VA), 51077
American Planning Association (DC), 10190
American Plant Life Society (CA), 05087
American Platform Tennis Association (NJ), 34035
American Plywood Association (WA), 52010
American Podiatric Medical Association (DC), 10191
American Police Center and Museum (IL), 17093
American Political Items Collectors (TX), 48023

American Polled Hereford Association (MO), 29013
American Polygraph Association (MD), 24060
American Porphyria Foundation (AL), 01022
American Poultry Historical Society (WI), 54013
American Powder Metallurgy Institute (NJ), 34036
American Press Institute (VA), 51078
American Prevention Institute (CA), 05088
American Printing House for the Blind, Department of Educational Research (KY), 21003
American Production and Inventory Control Society (VA), 51079
American Productivity Center (TX), 48024
American Professors for Peace in the Middle East, Community Services (NY), 36148
American Prosthodontic Society (IL), 17095
American Protestant Correctional Chaplains' Association (GA), 14015
American Protestant Health Association, College of Chaplains (IL), 17096
American Psychiatric Association (DC), 10192
American Psychoanalytic Association (NY), 36149
American Psychosomatic Society (NY), 36150
American Psychotherapy Seminar Center (NY), 36151
American Public Health Association (DC), 10193
American Public Health Association, Clearinghouse on Infant Feeding & Maternal Nutrition (DC), 10194
American Public Power Association (DC), 10195
American Public Transit Association (DC), 10196
American Public Welfare Association (DC), 10197
American Public Works Association, Information Service (IL), 17097
American Pulpwood Association (DC), 10198
American Quarter Horse Association (TX), 48025
American Rabbit Breeders Association (IL), 17098
American Radio Relay League (CT), 08013
American Rafting Association (GA), 14016
American Railway Car Institute (IL), 17099
American Railway Engineering Association (DC), 10199
American Recreation Coalition (DC), 10200
American Red Cross Blood Services (DC), 10201
American Red Cross Library (DC), 10202
American Register of Lithium Babies (CA), 05089
American Registry of Clinical Radiography Technologists (OK), 41008
American Registry of Diagnostic Medical Sonographers (OH), 40035
American Registry of Medical Assistants (CT), 08014
American Rescue Dog Association (NY), 36152
American Reye's Syndrome Association (CO), 07026
American Rheumatism Association Medical Information System (CA), 05090
American Rhododendron Society (OR), 42002
American River Touring Association (CA), 05091
American Rivers Conservation Council (DC), 10203
American Road & Transportation Builders' Association (DC), 10204
American Rose Society (LA), 22003
American Running & Fitness Association (DC), 10205
American Rural Health Association (MN), 27017

American Sail Training Association (RI), 44003

American School Band Directors' Association (MI), 26017

American School Food Service Association (CO), 07028

American School Health Association (OH), 40036

American Schools of Oriental Research (PA), 43048

American Science Fiction Association (AZ), 03012

American Scientific Glassblowers Society (OH), 40038

American Seed Research Foundation (DC), 10206

American Seed Trade Association (DC), 10207

American Shore and Beach Preservation Association (CA), 05092

American Short Line Railroad Association (DC), 10208

American Shortwave Listeners Club (CA), 05093

American Ski Federation (DC), 10209

American Social Health Association (CA), 05095

American Social Health Association, Herpes Resource Center (CA), 05096

American Society & Academy of Microbiology (DC), 10210

American Society for Adolescent Psychiatry (PA), 43049

American Society for Artificial Internal Organs (FL), 13020

American Society for Clinical Nutrition (MD), 24061

American Society for Concrete Construction (IL), 17100

American Society for Cybernetics (VA), 51080

American Society for Deaf Children (MD), 24063

American Society for Engineering Education (DC), 10211

American Society for Enology and Viticulture (CA), 05097

American Society for Environmental Education (NH), 33002

American Society for Environmental History (CO), 07029

American Society for Gastrointestinal Endoscopy (MA), 25029

American Society for Geriatric Dentistry (IN), 18012

American Society for Handicapped Physicians (LA), 22004

American Society for Head and Neck Surgery (CA), 05098

American Society for Horticultural Science (VA), 51081

American Society for Hospital Engineering (IL), 17101

American Society for Hospital Food Service Administrators (IL), 17102

American Society for Hospital Marketing and Public Relations (IL), 17103

American Society for Hospital Materials Management (IL), 17104

American Society for Hospital Personnel Administration (IL), 17105

American Society for Industrial Security (VA), 51082

American Society for Information Science (DC), 10212

American Society for Laser Medicine and Surgery (WI), 54014

American Society for Medical Technology (TX), 48026

American Society for Microbiology (DC), 10213

American Society for Nondestructive Testing (OH), 40039

American Society for Nursing Service Administrators (IL), 17106

American Society for Parenteral and Enteral Nutrition (MD), 24064

American Society for Personnel Administration (VA), 51083

American Society for Pharmacology and Experimental Therapeutics (MD), 24065

American Society for Photogrammetry and Remote Sensing (VA), 51084

American Society for Psychical Research (NY), 36153

American Society for Psychoprophylaxis in Obstetrics (VA), 51085

American Society for Quality Control (WI), 54016

American Society for Radiologic Technologists (NM), 35006

American Society for Surgery of the Hand (CO), 07030

American Society for Testing & Materials (PA), 43051

American Society for Testing & Materials, Committee on Industrial Water (PA), 43052

American Society for Testing & Materials, Committee on Plastics (PA), 43053

American Society for Training & Development (DC), 10214

American Society for the Prevention of Cruelty to Animals (NY), 36154

American Society of Abdominal Surgeons (MA), 25030

American Society of Agricultural Consultants (VA), 51086

American Society of Agricultural Engineers (MI), 26018

American Society of Agronomy (WI), 54017

American Society of Allied Health Professions (DC), 10215

American Society of Andrology (CO), 07032

American Society of Anesthesiologists, Library Museum (IL), 17107

American Society of Appraisers (DC), 10216

American Society of Artists (IL), 17108

American Society of Association Executives, Information Central (DC), 10217

American Society of Bariatric Physicians (CO), 07033

American Society of Biological Chemists (MD), 24066

American Society of Bookplate Collectors and Designers (CA), 05100

American Society of Brewing Chemists (MN), 27018

American Society of Business Press Editors (OH), 40040

American Society of Certified Engineering Technicians (KS), 20005

American Society of Cinematographers (CA), 05101

American Society of Civil Engineers (NY), 36155

American Society of Clinical Hypnosis (IL), 17109

American Society of Clinical Pathologists (IL), 17110

American Society of Consultant Pharmacists (VA), 51087

American Society of Consulting Arborists (NJ), 34037

American Society of Contemporary Medicine and Surgery (IL), 17111

American Society of Contemporary Ophthalmology (IL), 17112

American Society of Dentistry for Children (IL), 17113

American Society of Dowsers (VT), 50001

American Society of Echocardiography (NC), 38008

American Society of Electroencephalographic Technologists (IA), 19008

American Society of Electroplated Plastics (DC), 10218

American Society of Extra-Corporeal Technology (VA), 51088

American Society of Farm Managers and Rural Appraisers (CO), 07035

American Society of Golf Course Architects (IL), 17114

American Society of Group Psychotherapy and Psychodrama (NY), 36156

American Society of Heating, Refrigerating & Air-Conditioning Engineers (GA), 14017

American Society of Hematology (OH), 40041

American Society of Hospital Pharmacists (MD), 24067

American Society of Human Genetics (MD), 24068

American Society of Ichthyologists and Herpetologists (FL), 13021

American Society of Indexers (NY), 36157

American Society of Interior Designers (NY), 36158

American Society of Internal Medicine (DC), 10219

American Society of International Law Library (DC), 10220

American Society of Journalists and Authors (NY), 36159

American Society of Landscape Architects (DC), 10221

American Society of Law & Medicine (MA), 25031

American Society of Limnology and Oceanography (MI), 26021

American Society of Lubrication Engineers (IL), 17115

American Society of Magazine Photographers (NY), 36160

American Society of Mammalogists (PA), 43054

American Society of Master Dental Laboratory Technologists (NY), 36161

American Society of Mechanical Engineers, Bioengineering Division (NY), 36162

American Society of Mechanical Engineers, Noise Control and Acoustics Division (NY), 36163

American Society of Mechanical Engineers, Petroleum Division (NY), 36164

American Society of Military Comptrollers (VA), 51089

American Society of Music Arrangers (CA), 05102

American Society of Neuroradiology (IL), 17116

American Society of Notaries (DC), 10222

American Society of Parasitologists (CO), 07036

American Society of Perfumers (NJ), 34038

American Society of Picture Professionals (NY), 36165

American Society of Plant Physiologists (MD), 24069

American Society of Plant Taxonomists (WI), 54018

American Society of Plastic and Reconstructive Surgeons (IL), 17117

American Society of Professional Ecologists (IN), 18014

American Society of Psychopathology of Expression (PA), 43055

American Society of Questioned Documents Examiners (CA), 05104

American Society of Safety Engineers (IL), 17118

American Society of Sanitary Engineering (OH), 40042

American Society of Sugar Beet Technologists (CO), 07037

American Society of Transplant Surgeons (IL), 17119

American Society of Transportation and Logistics (KY), 21004

American Society of Travel Agents (DC), 10223

American Society of Veterinary Ophthalmology (OK), 41009

American Society on Aging (CA), 05105

American Sociological Association (DC), 10224

American Sod Producers Association (IL), 17120

American Solar Energy Society (CO), 07038

American Soviet Cultural Exchange (MA), 25032

American Soybean Association (MO), 29015

American Speech-Language-Hearing Association (MD), 24070

American Spice Trade Associatio (NJ), 34039

American Spinal Injury Association (IL), 17121

American Statistical Association (DC), 10225

American String Teachers Association (GA), 14018

American Student Dental Association (IL), 17122

American Studies Association (PA), 43056

American Swedish Museum (PA), 43057

American Symphony Orchestra League (DC), 10226

American Tapestry Alliance (OR), 42003

American Tax Reduction Movement (CA), 05106

American Tax Token Society (CO), 07039

American Textile Machinery Association (VA), 51090

American Textile Manufacturers Institute (DC), 10227

American Theological Library Association (IL), 17123

American Thoracic Society (NY), 36166

American Thyroid Association (MN), 27019

American Tinnitus Association (OR), 42004

American Tobacco Co., Research and Development Library (VA), 51091

American Translators Association (NY), 36167

American Trauma Society (MD), 24071

American Truck Historical Society (AL), 01023

American Trucking Associations (VA), 51092

American Tuberous Sclerosis Association (MA), 25033

American Tunaboat Association (CA), 05107

American Type Culture Collection (MD), 24072

American Underground-Space Association (MN), 27020

American Urological Association (MD), 24073

American Vacuum Society (NY), 36168

American Vecturist Association (MA), 25034

American Vegan Society (NJ), 34041
American Veterans Committee (DC), 10228
American Veterinary Dental Society (PA), 43058
American Video Association (AZ), 03013
American Viticultural Area Association (CA), 05108
American Vocational Association (VA), 51093
American Vocational Education Research Association
  (IL), 17124
American Water Resources Association (MD), 24074
American Water Ski Association (FL), 13022
American Water Works Association (CO), 07040
American Waterways Operators (VA), 51094
American Wax Importers and Refiners Association
  (NJ), 34042
American Welding Society (FL), 13023
American West African Freight Conference (NY),
  36169
American Wheelchair Bowling Association (WI),
  54019
American Wilderness Alliance (CO), 07041
American Wind Energy Association Data Center
  (VA), 51095
American Wine Association (NY), 36170
American Wire Producers Association (DC), 10229
American Wood Preservers Bureau (VA), 51096
American Wood-Preservers' Association (MD), 24075
American Youth Hostels (DC), 10230
American Youth Work Center (DC), 10231
American-Canadian Genealogical Society (NH),
  33003
American-Nepal Education Foundation (OR), 42006
American-Scandinavian Foundation (NY), 36171
Americans for Customary Weight and Measure (ME),
  23001
Americans for Democratic Action (DC), 10232
Americans for Effective Law Enforcement (IL), 17125
Americans for Energy Independence (DC), 10233
Americans for Human Rights and Social Justice (TX),
  48028
Americans for Indian Opportunity (DC), 10234
Americans for Middle East Understanding (NY),
  36172
Americas Behavioral Research Corp. (CA), 05109
Amerind Foundation (AZ), 03014
Amistad Research Center (LA), 22005
Amnesty International of the U.S.A. (NY), 36173
Amoco Production Co. Research Center Library (OK),
  41010
Amon Carter Museum (TX), 48029
Ampex Corp., Technical Information Services (CA),
  05110
Amphibian BioTech (MI), 26022
Amusement and Music Operators Association (IL),
  17126
Amyotrophic Lateral Sclerosis Association (NY),
  36174
Analytical Chemistry Division (TN), 47009
Ancient Astronaut Society (IL), 17127
Ancient Studies/Religious Studies Center (UT), 49002
Anderson Clayton Foods Technical Information
  Services (TX), 48030

Andrew W. Breidenbach Environmental Research
  Center (OH), 40043
Andrus Gerontology Center (CA), 05113
Animal Behavior Society (LA), 22006
Animal Damage Control Program (DC), 10235
Animal Health Institute (VA), 51097
Animal Medical Center Library (NY), 36175
Animal Parasitology Institute (MD), 24076
Animal Protection Institute (CA), 05114
Animal Rights Network (CT), 08015
Animal Welfare Institute (DC), 10236
Animal-Human Nutrition and Postharvest Sciences
  Staff (MD), 24077
Ann Arbor Railroad Technical and Historical
  Association (MI), 26023
Annenberg School of Communication Library (PA),
  43059
Antarctic Marine Geology Research Facility and Core
  Library (FL), 13024
Antarctica Project (DC), 10237
Anthropology Film Center Foundation (NM), 35008
Anti-Defamation League of B'nai B'rith (NY), 36176
Anti-Friction Bearings Manufacturers Association
  (VA), 51098
Antique Automobile Club of America (PA), 43060
Antique Wireless Association (NY), 36177
Antitrust Division (DC), 10238
Aphasia Research Center (MA), 25035
Appalachia Educational Laboratory, Inc. (WV), 53006
Appalachian Geological Society (WV), 53007
Appalachian Hardwood Manufacturers (NC), 38009
Appalachian Mountain Club (MA), 25036
Appalachian Regional Commission (DC), 10239
Appalachian Trail Conference (WV), 53008
Appleton-Whittell Research Ranch Sanctuary (AZ),
  03015
Applied Biochemists Laboratory Services (WI), 54020
Applied Computer Research (AZ), 03016
Applied Physics Laboratory (WA), 52011
Applied Physiology Research Laboratory (OH), 40044
Applied Population Laboratory (WI), 54021
Applied Research Laboratories (TX), 48031
Applied Research Laboratory (PA), 43061
Applied Stochastics Laboratory (IN), 18015
Appaloosa Horse Club (ID), 16002
Appraisers Association of America (NY), 36178
Appropriate Technology Program (DC), 10240
Aprovecho Institute (OR), 42007
AquaScience Research Group (MO), 29016
Aquarian Research Foundation (PA), 43062
Aquatic Plant Management Society (MS), 28005
Aquatic Research Institute (CA), 05115
Aquatic Weed Program (FL), 13025
Arabian Horse Owners Foundation (AZ), 03017
Arabian Horse Registry of America (CO), 07042
Arbitron Ratings, Public Relations (NY), 36179
Archaeological Conservancy (NM), 35009
Archaeological Institute of America (MA), 25037
Archaeological Research Center and Museum (NJ),
  34043
Archaeological Society of South Dakota (SD), 46003

Archaeology Laboratory (SD), 46004
Archaeology Research Program (TX), 48032
Architects for Social Responsibility (NY), 36180
Architectural & Transportation Barriers Compliance Board (DC), 10241
Architectural Woodwork Institute (VA), 51099
Architecture Research Center (TX), 48033
Architecture and Engineering Performance Information Center (MD), 24078
Archival Center for Radiation Biology (TN), 47010
Archives of Traditional Music (IN), 18016
Archives of the American Lutheran Church (IA), 19009
Archives of the Episcopal Church (TX), 48034
Archives of the History of American Psychology (OH), 40045
Arctic Environmental Information and Data Center (AK), 02014
Arctic Institute of North America (CAN), 61007
Area Business Databank (KY), 21005
Area Cooperative Educational Services Library (CT), 08017
Area Economics Information Center (OH), 40046
Argonne National Laboratory, Energy Software Center (IL), 17129
Argus Archives (NY), 36181
Arica Institute (NY), 36182
Arizona Commission of Agriculture and Horticulture (AZ), 03018
Arizona Commission on the Arts (AZ), 03019
Arizona Cooperative Fishery Research Unit (AZ), 03020
Arizona Cooperative Wildlife Research Unit (AZ), 03021
Arizona Department of Library, Archives, and Public Records (AZ), 03022
Arizona Game and Fish Department (AZ), 03023
Arizona Historical Society Library (AZ), 03024
Arizona Oil and Gas Conservation Commission (AZ), 03025
Arizona Solar Energy Commission (AZ), 03026
Arizona State Museum (AZ), 03027
Arizona Wildlife Federation (AZ), 03028
Arizona-Sonora Desert Museum (AZ), 03029
Arkansas Agricultural Experiment Station (AR), 04028
Arkansas Arts Council (AR), 04029
Arkansas Audubon Society (AR), 04030
Arkansas Bureau of Environmental Health Services, Radiation Control, and Emergency Management Programs (AR), 04031
Arkansas Forestry Commission (AR), 04032
Arkansas Game and Fish Commission (AR), 04033
Arkansas Genealogical Society (AR), 04034
Arkansas Geological Commission (AR), 04035
Arkansas History Commission (AR), 04036
Arkansas Museum of Science and History (AR), 04037
Arkansas Natural and Scenic Rivers Commission (AR), 04038
Arkansas State Library (AR), 04039
Arkansas State University Museum (AR), 04040

Arlin J. Brown Information Center (VA), 51100
Armed Forces Communications and Electronics Association (VA), 51101
Armed Forces Institute of Pathology (DC), 10242
Armed Forces Radiobiology Research Institute Library (MD), 24079
Armenian Educational Foundation (CA), 05116
Armour Research Center Library (AZ), 03030
Arms Control & Foreign Policy Caucus (DC), 10243
Arms Control Association (DC), 10244
Army Aeromedical Research Laboratory (AL), 01025
Army Air Defense Artillery School Library (TX), 48035
Army Applied Technology Laboratory (VA), 51177
Army Armor School Library (KY), 21006
Army Atmospheric Sciences Laboratory (NM), 35010
Army Ballistic Research Laboratory (MD), 24080
Army Casemate Museum (VA), 51178
Army Chemical Research and Development Center, Technical Library (MD), 24081
Army Combat Developments Experimentation Command (CA), 05117
Army Corps of Engineers (DC), 10245
Army Electronics Research and Development Command, Technical Library (NJ), 34044
Army Engineer School Hotline (VA), 51102
Army Foreign Science and Technology Center (VA), 51103
Army Institute of Dental Research (DC), 10246
Army Institute of Surgical Research (TX), 48036
Army Intelligence Center and School (AZ), 03031
Army Intelligence Center and School, Fort Huachuca & Fort Devens (MA), 25038
Army Joint Medical Library (DC), 10247
Army Logistics Management Center (VA), 51104
Army Materials and Mechanics Research Center (MA), 25039
Army Medical Bioengineering Research and Development Laboratory, Library (MD), 24082
Army Medical Research Institute of Infectious Diseases Library (MD), 24083
Army Missile Laboratory (AL), 01026
Army Natick Research and Development Center (MA), 25040
Army, Office of the Chief of Engineers (AR), 04041
Army Quartermaster Center Museum (VA), 51105
Army Satellite Communications Agency (NJ), 34045
Army Tank-Automotive Command, Technical Library (MI), 26024
Army Transportation Museum (VA), 51106
Army Tropic Test Center (FL), 13026
Arnold Air Society (TX), 48037
Arrow (DC), 10248
Art Council Aids (CA), 05118
Art Dealers Association of America (NY), 36183
Art Hazards Information Center (NY), 36184
Art Information Center (NY), 36185
Art Libraries Society of North America (AZ), 03032
Art Museum Association of America (CA), 05119
Art and Crafts Materials Institute (MA), 25041
Arthritis Foundation (GA), 14022
Arthritis Information Clearinghouse (VA), 51107

Association for Professional Practice (NJ), 34049

Association for Recorded Sound Collections (DC), 10260

Association for Research and Enlightenment Library (VA), 51116

Association for Research in Vision and Ophthalmology (NY), 36194

Association for Research of Childhood Cancer (NY), 36195

Association for Retarded Citizens (TX), 48039

Association for Small Business Advancement (MD), 24091

Association for Supervision and Curriculum Development, Resource Information Service (VA), 51117

Association for Systems Management (OH), 40048

Association for Union Democracy (NY), 36196

Association for Vital Records & Health Statistics (PA), 43065

Association for Voluntary Sterilization (NY), 36197

Association for Women Geoscientists (CA), 05130

Association for Women in Computing (MD), 24092

Association for Women in Science (DC), 10261

Association for Workplace Democracy (DC), 10262

Association for the Advancement of Baltic Studies (NJ), 34050

Association for the Advancement of Blind and Retarded (NY), 36198

Association for the Advancement of Health Education (VA), 51118

Association for the Advancement of Medical Instrumentation (VA), 51120

Association for the Advancement of Psychoanalysis (NY), 36199

Association for the Advancement of Psychology (DC), 10263

Association for the Advancement of Psychotherapy (NY), 36200

Association for the Advancement of Sports Potential (PA), 43066

Association for the Anthropological Study of Play (IL), 17133

Association for the Care of Children's Health (DC), 10264

Association for the Development of Religious Information Systems (WI), 54022

Association for the Education and Rehabilitation of the Blind and Visually Impaired (VA), 51121

Association for the Study of Afro-American Life and History (DC), 10265

Association for the Study of Man-Environment Relations (NY), 36201

Association of Academic Health Centers (DC), 10266

Association of Advertising Lawyers (OH), 40049

Association of African Studies Programs (OH), 40050

Association of Allergists for Mycological Investigations (TX), 48041

Association of American Chambers of Commerce in Latin America (DC), 10267

Association of American Feed Control Officials (TX), 48042

Association of American Geographers (DC), 10268

Association of American Law Schools (DC), 10270

Association of American Medical Colleges (DC), 10271

Association of American Pesticide Control Officials (VA), 51122

Association of American Physicians and Surgeons (VA), 51124

Association of American Plant Food Control Officials (KY), 21008

Association of American Railroads (DC), 10272

Association of American Railroads, Hazardous Materials Section (DC), 10274

Association of American Railroads, Research & Test Department (DC), 10275

Association of American State Geologists (FL), 13030

Association of Applied Insect Ecologists (CA), 05131

Association of Arab-American University Graduates (MA), 25046

Association of Asphalt Paving Technologists (MN), 27023

Association of Audio-Visual Technicians (CO), 07047

Association of Balloon and Airship Constructors (CA), 05132

Association of Bank Holding Companies (DC), 10276

Association of Birth Defect Children (FL), 13031

Association of Bridal Consultants (CT), 08019

Association of Canadian Medical Colleges (CAN), 61011

Association of Catholic Colleges & Universities (DC), 10277

Association of Clinical Scientists (CT), 08020

Association of College Honor Societies (PA), 43067

Association of College Unions International (IN), 18020

Association of College and Research Libraries (IL), 17134

Association of College, University, and Community Arts Administrators (WI), 54023

Association of Collegiate Schools of Architecture (DC), 10278

Association of Commercial Mail Receiving Agencies (PA), 43068

Association of Commercial Record Centers (TX), 48043

Association of Concert Bands (PA), 43069

Association of Conservation Engineers (MO), 29017

Association of Consulting Chemists and Chemical Engineers (NY), 36202

Association of Consulting Foresters (MD), 24093

Association of Consulting Toxicologists (UT), 49003

Association of Data Processing Service Organizations (VA), 51125

Association of Driver Educators for the Disabled (MI), 26030

Association of Earth Science Editors (VA), 51126

Association of Engineering Geologists (TN), 47012

Association of Environmental Engineering Professors (GA), 14023

Association of Environmental Scientists and Administrators (OR), 42009

Association of Executive Search Consultants (CT), 08021

Association of Existential Psychology and Psychiatry (NY), 36203

Association of Exploration Geochemists (CAN), 61012

Association of Family and Conciliation Courts, Research Unit (CO), 07048

Association of Federal Investigators (DC), 10279

Association of Food & Drug Officials (PA), 43070

Association of Former Intelligence Officers (VA), 51127

Association of Former Members of Congress (DC), 10280

Association of Governing Boards of Universities and Colleges (DC), 10281

Association of Governmental Appraisers (VA), 51128

Association of Halfway House Alcoholism Programs of North America (MN), 27025

Association of Home Appliance Manufacturers (IL), 17135

Association of Human Resource Systems Professionals (CA), 05133

Association of Independent Video and Filmmakers (NY), 36204

Association of Information Systems Professionals (PA), 43071

Association of Interpretive Naturalists (MD), 24094

Association of Iron & Steel Engineers (PA), 43072

Association of Island Marine Laboratories of the Caribbean (PR), 60001

Association of Jesuit Colleges & Universities (DC), 10282

Association of Jewish Libraries (NY), 36205

Association of Labor-Management Administrators and Consultants on Alcoholism (VA), 51129

Association of Life Insurance Medical Directors of America (PA), 43073

Association of Lunar and Planetary Observers (CA), 05134

Association of Management Consultants (IL), 17136

Association of Management Consulting Firms (NY), 36206

Association of Master of Business Administration Executives (NY), 36207

Association of Maximum Service Telecasters (DC), 10283

Association of Medical Illustrators (VA), 51130

Association of Medical Rehabilitation Directors and Coordinators (MA), 25047

Association of National Advertisers (NY), 36208

Association of Official Analytical Chemists (VA), 51131

Association of Official Racing Chemists (OR), 42010

Association of Official Seed Analysts (IL), 17137

Association of Official Seed Certifying Agencies (NC), 38011

Association of Oil Pipe Lines (DC), 10284

Association of Operating Room Nurses (CO), 07049

Association of Overseas Educators (PA), 43074

Association of Pathology Chairmen (NC), 38012

Association of Petroleum Re-refiners (DC), 10285

Association of Physical Fitness Centers (MD), 24095

Association of Professional Vocal Ensembles (PA), 43075

Association of Railroad Advertising and Marketing (OH), 40051

Association of Railway Museums (ME), 23002

Association of Records Managers and Administrators (KS), 20006

Association of Rehabilitation Nurses (IL), 17138

Association of Research Libraries, Center for Chinese Research Materials (DC), 10286

Association of Research Libraries, Systems & Procedures Exchange Center (DC), 10287

Association of Retail Marketing Services (NJ), 34051

Association of Science-Technology Centers (DC), 10288

Association of Sleep Disorders Centers (CA), 05135

Association of Specialized and Cooperative Library Agencies (IL), 17139

Association of State & Territorial Solid Waste Management Officials (DC), 10289

Association of State Public Health Veterinarians (NC), 38013

Association of Surgical Technologists (CO), 07051

Association of Systematics Collections (KS), 20007

Association of Teachers of Maternal and Child Health (IL), 17140

Association of Theological Schools (OH), 40052

Association of Trial Lawyers of America (DC), 10290

Association of Trial Lawyers of America, Products Liability--Medical Malpractice Exchange (DC), 10291

Association of University Anesthetists (VA), 51133

Association of University Architects (CA), 05136

Association of Visual Science Librarians (TX), 48044

Association of Voluntary Action Scholars (PA), 43076

Association of Wall & Ceiling Industries-International (DC), 10292

Association of Western Hospitals (CA), 05137

Association of Women in Architecture (MO), 29018

Association on American Indian Affairs (NY), 36209

Association on Third World Affairs (DC), 10293

Association to Advance Ethical Hypnosis (NJ), 34052

Association to Unite the Democracies (DC), 10294

Asthma & Allergy Foundation of America (DC), 10295

Astro-Science Laboratory (CA), 05138

Astronomical League (AZ), 03034

Astronomical Society of the Pacific (CA), 05139

Astrophysical Observatory (MA), 25048

Athletes United for Peace (KS), 20008

Athletic Institute (FL), 13034

Atlantic Center for the Environment (MA), 25049

Atlantic Council of the United States (DC), 10296

Atlantic Geoscience Society (CAN), 61013

Atlantic Oceanographic and Meteorological Laboratory (FL), 13035

Atlantic Offshore Fishermen's Association (RI), 44004

Atlantic Salmon Federation (CAN), 61014

Atlantic States Marine Fisheries Commission (DC), 10297

Atmospheric Sciences Research Center (NY), 36210
Atmospheric Turbulence and Diffusion Division
(TN), 47013
Atomic Energy Levels Data Center (MD), 24098
Atomic Industrial Forum (MD), 24099
Atomic Transition Probabilities Data Center (MD),
24100
Audio Engineering Society (NY), 36211
Audio-Digest Foundation (CA), 05140
Audubon Council of Connecticut (CT), 08022
Austen Fox Riggs Library (MA), 25050
Autism Services Center (WV), 53009
Auto Leather Guild (MI), 26031
Automatic Identification Manufacturers (PA), 43077
Automation Industries/Sperry Products Division
(CT), 08023
Autometric (VA), 51134
Automobile License Plate Collectors Association
(WV), 53011
Automotive Dismantlers and Recyclers Association
(DC), 10298
Automotive Parts and Accessories Association (MD),
24101
Automotive Service Councils (IL), 17141
Avco-Everett Research Laboratory (MA), 25051
Avenues (CA), 05141
Aviation & Fire Management Staff (DC), 10299
Aviation Data Service (KS), 20009
Aviation Development Council (NY), 36212
Aviation Distributors & Manufacturers Association
(PA), 43078
Aviation Safety Institute (OH), 40053
Ayrshire Breeders' Association (VT), 50002

**BASF Wyandotte Corp., Corporate Research Library (MI),
26032**
BCR National Laboratories (PA), 43079
Babcock and Wilcox Co. Library (VA), 51135
Bacchus Works (UT), 49004
Bakery Equipment Manufacturers Association (IL),
17142
Bakery, Confectionery, and Tobacco Workers
International Union (MD), 24102
Baking Industry Sanitation Standards Committee
(NY), 36213
Bakken Library of Electricity in Life (MN), 27026
Balloon Club of America (PA), 43080
Balloon Federation of America (IA), 19010
Baltimore & Ohio Railroad Historical Society (MD),
24103
Balzekas Museum of Lithuanian Culture (IL), 17143
Bank Administration Institute (IL), 17144
Bank Marketing Association Information Center (IL),
17145
Barium and Chemicals (OH), 40054
Barre Granite Association (VT), 50003
Barren Foundation (IL), 17146
Barrier Islands Coalition (DC), 10303
Bass Anglers Sportsman Society of America (AL),
01027
Bass Research Foundation (MS), 28006

Battelle Memorial Institute, Copper Data Center
(OH), 40055
Battelle Memorial Institute, Office of Hazardous
Waste Management (WA), 52014
Battelle Memorial Institute, Technical Information
Center (OH), 40056
Batterers Anonymous (CA), 05143
Battery Council International (IL), 17147
Bay Area Center for Law and the Deaf (CA), 05144
Bay Beach Wildlife Sanctuary (WI), 54024
Baylor College of Medicine, Influenza Research
Center (TX), 48045
Beatrice/Hunt-Wesson Foods (CA), 05145
Becker and Hayes (CA), 05146
Beckman Instruments Research Library (CA), 05147
Bee Biology and Systematics Laboratory (UT), 49005
Bee Breeding and Stock Center Laboratory (LA),
22008
Beefmaster Breeders Universal (TX), 48046
Beer Can Collectors of America (MO), 29019
Beet Sugar Development Foundation (CO), 07053
Behavior Genetics Association (CO), 07054
Behavior Research Institute (RI), 44005
Behavior Therapy & Research Society (PA), 43081
Behavioral Alcohol Research Laboratory (WA), 52015
Behavioral Research Council (MA), 25052
Behavioral Research Institute (CO), 07055
Behavioral Therapy Institute (CA), 05148
Belding Heminway Co. (CT), 08024
Belgian American Educational Foundation (CT),
08025
Bell & Howell Co., Micro Photo Division (OH), 40057
Bell Canada, Telephone Historical Collection (CAN),
61015
Bell Helicopter Textron (TX), 48047
Belle W. Baruch Institute for Marine Biology and
Coastal Research (SC), 45003
Beloit College Logan Museum of Anthropology (WI),
54025
Beltsville Human Nutrition Research Center (MD),
24105
Benet Weapons Laboratory, Watervliet Technical
Library (NY), 36214
Benham Group (OK), 41011
Benign Essential Blepharospasm Research
Foundation (TX), 48049
Benthic Invertebrate College (CA), 05149
Bernan Associates, Government Publications Service
(MD), 24106
Bernice P. Bishop Museum Library (HI), 15001
Bethesda Pain Control Program (MD), 24107
Bethlehem Steel Corp., Schwab Information Center
(PA), 43082
Better Hearing Institute (DC), 10304
Better Lawn and Turf Institute (TN), 47014
Better Sleep Council (MD), 24108
Better Vision Institute (NY), 36215
Betz Laboratories (PA), 43083
Bibliographical Center for Research (CO), 07056
Bicycle Manufacturers Association of America (DC),
10305

Brown Swiss Cattle Breeders' Association of the U.S.A. (WI), 54027

Bruce Trail Association (CAN), 61018

Brush Wellman Inc. Technical Library (OH), 40062

Buffalo Bill Memorial Association (WY), 55005

Builders Hardware Manufacturers Association (NY), 36233

Building Development Counsel International (DC), 10317

Building Officials and Code Administrators International (IL), 17153

Building Owners & Managers Association, International Research Department (DC), 10318

Building Stone Institute (NY), 36234

Burbank Public Library, Warner Research Collection (CA), 05172

Bureau of African Affairs (DC), 10319

Bureau of Applied Research in Anthropology (AZ), 03036

Bureau of Business Research (NE), 31006

Bureau of Business and Economic Research (MD), 24112

Bureau of Business and Economic Research Data Bank (NM), 35011

Bureau of East Asian and Pacific Affairs (DC), 10320

Bureau of Economic Analysis (DC), 10321

Bureau of Economic and Business Affairs (DC), 10322

Bureau of Economic and Business Affairs, Office of East-West Trade (DC), 10323

Bureau of Educational Measurements (KS), 20010

Bureau of Engraving & Printing Public Affairs Section (DC), 10325

Bureau of European Affairs (DC), 10326

Bureau of Health Care Delivery and Assistance (MD), 24113

Bureau of Health Care Delivery and Assistance, Division of Maternal and Child Health (MD), 24114

Bureau of Health Professions (MD), 24116

Bureau of Higher and Continuing Education (DC), 10327

Bureau of Human Rights and Humanitarian Affairs (DC), 10328

Bureau of Indian Affairs (DC), 10329

Bureau of Industrial Economics (DC), 10330

Bureau of InterAmerican Affairs (DC), 10331

Bureau of International Organization Affairs (DC), 10332

Bureau of Jewish Education Library (NY), 36235

Bureau of Land Management (DC), 10333

Bureau of Marine Research (FL), 13039

Bureau of Michigan History, State Archive Section (MI), 26034

Bureau of Mines, Alaska Field Operations Center (AK), 02015

Bureau of Mines, Avondale Research Center (MD), 24118

Bureau of Mines, Denver Research Center (CO), 07063

Bureau of Mines, Division of Industrial Minerals (DC), 10334

Bureau of Mines, Helium Operations (DC), 10335

Bureau of Mines, Office of Technical Information (DC), 10336

Bureau of Mines, Pittsburgh Research Center, Documents Library (PA), 43091

Bureau of Mines, Reno Research Center (NV), 32009

Bureau of Mines, Rolla Research Center (MO), 29023

Bureau of Motor Carrier Safety (DC), 10337

Bureau of Near Eastern and South Asian Affairs (DC), 10338

Bureau of Oceans and International and Scientific Affairs (DC), 10339

Bureau of Politico-Military Affairs (DC), 10340

Bureau of Prisons Library (DC), 10341

Bureau of Prisons, National Institute of Corrections (DC), 10342

Bureau of Public Affairs (DC), 10343

Bureau of Reclamation (DC), 10344

Bureau of Social Science Research (DC), 10345

Bureau of the Census (DC), 10346

Bureau of the Census, Agriculture Division (DC), 10350

Bureau of the Census, Center for International Research (DC), 10347

Bureau of the Census, Industry Division (DC), 10351

Bureau of the Census, Information Services Program (DC), 10348

Bureau of the Census, International Statistical Programs Center (DC), 10349

Bureau of the Mint (DC), 10352

Burn Institute (CA), 05173

Burndy Library (CT), 08027

Bushy Run Research Center (PA), 43092

Business & Professional Women's Foundation, Resource Center (DC), 10353

Business Advisory Council on Federal Reports (DC), 10354

Business Committee for the Arts (NY), 36236

Business Council for International Understanding Institute (DC), 10355

Business Council of Georgia (GA), 14024

Business Exchange (CA), 05174

Business Executives for National Security (DC), 10356

Business History Conference (IL), 17154

Business International Corp. (NY), 36237

Business Research Division (CO), 07064

Business Research Institute (NY), 36238

Business and Institutional Furniture Manufacturer's Association (MI), 26036

C&I/Girdler Library (KY), 21009

C.G. Jung Institute Library (CA), 05175

C.I.T. Jet Propulsion Lab (CA), 05176

C.L. Mauro Associates (NY), 36239

C.W. Thornthwaite Associates Laboratory of Climatology (NJ), 34054

CALM (PA), 43093

CBS News Reference Library (NY), 36240

CCCO: An Agency for Military & Draft Counseling (PA), 43094

CONDUIT (IA), 19011

CORPUS (IL), 17155

CSR Power Information Center (DC), 10358
Cable Television Information Center (VA), 51140
Cabot Corp. (MA), 25056
Cactus and Succulent Society of America (CA), 05177
Cadmium Council (NY), 36241
Cal Poly School of Architecture and Environmental Design (CA), 05178
Calendar Reform Foundation (MD), 24120
Calgon Corp. Information Center (PA), 43095
California Academy of Sciences, J.W.M., Jr. Memorial Library (CA), 05181
California Academy of Sciences, Science Museum (CA), 05179
California Academy of Sciences, Steinhart Aquarium (CA), 05180
California Air Resources Board (CA), 05182
California Committee of Two Million (CA), 05183
California Cooperative Fishery Research Unit (CA), 05184
California Date Administrative Committee (CA), 05185
California Historical Society Library (CA), 05186
California Institute of Technology, Seismological Laboratory (CA), 05187
California Inventors Council (CA), 05188
California Medical Clinic for Headache (CA), 05189
California Primate Research Center (CA), 05190
California Radiological Society (CA), 05191
California Raisin Advisory Board (CA), 05192
California Redwood Association (CA), 05193
California Self-Help Center (CA), 05194
California Spanish Language Data Base (CA), 05195
California State Archives (CA), 05196
California State Indian Museum (CA), 05198
California State Library (CA), 05199
California Strawberry Advisory Board (CA), 05200
California Water Resources Association (CA), 05201
Calix Society (MN), 27028
Callaway Gardens (GA), 14025
Callier Center for Communication Disorders (TX), 48053
Calorie Control Council (GA), 14026
Calspan Corp., Technical Information Center (NY), 36242
Calvert Marine Museum (MD), 24121
Cambridge Scientific Abstracts (MD), 24122
Camera M.D. Studios Library Division (FL), 13040
Camp Fire (MO), 29024
Campaign for U.N. Reform (NJ), 34055
Can Manufacturers Institute (DC), 10361
Canada Defence Research Board, Scientific Information Centre (CAN), 61019
Canada Grains Council (CAN), 61020
Canada Institute for Scientific and Technical Information, Library (CAN), 61021
Canada's Sports Hall of Fame (CAN), 61022
Canada-Japan Trade Council (CAN), 61023
Canadian Arctic Resources Committee (CAN), 61024
Canadian Asbestos Information Centre (CAN), 61025

Canadian Association for Laboratory Animal Science (CAN), 61026
Canadian Association of Anatomists (CAN), 61027
Canadian Association of Chiefs of Police (CAN), 61028
Canadian Association of Gastroenterology (CAN), 61029
Canadian Association of Optometrists (CAN), 61030
Canadian Association of Social Workers (CAN), 61031
Canadian Ceramic Society (CAN), 61032
Canadian Consulate General, Cultural Affairs (NY), 36243
Canadian Consulate General, Library (NY), 36244
Canadian Coordinating Council on Deafness (CAN), 61033
Canadian Council of the Blind (CAN), 61034
Canadian Council on Animal Care (CAN), 61035
Canadian Council on Social Development (CAN), 61036
Canadian Diabetes Association (CAN), 61037
Canadian Energy Research Institute (CAN), 61038
Canadian Film Institute, National Film Library of Canada (CAN), 61039
Canadian Folk Music Society (CAN), 61040
Canadian Forestry Association (CAN), 61041
Canadian Hearing Society, Information Services Department (CAN), 61042
Canadian Institute of Mining and Metallurgy (CAN), 61043
Canadian Institute of Resources Law (CAN), 61044
Canadian Institute of Steel Construction (CAN), 61045
Canadian International Grains Institute (CAN), 61046
Canadian Jewish Congress, National Archives (CAN), 61047
Canadian Lung Association (CAN), 61048
Canadian Nuclear Association (CAN), 61049
Canadian Nuclear Society (CAN), 61050
Canadian Orthoptic Society (CAN), 61051
Canadian Paraplegic Association, National Office Library (CAN), 61052
Canadian Pharmaceutical Association (CAN), 61053
Canadian Physiological Society (CAN), 61054
Canadian Plains Research Center (CAN), 61055
Canadian Red Cross Society, National Office Library (CAN), 61056
Canadian Research Institute for the Advancement of Women (CAN), 61057
Canadian Society for Chemical Engineering (CAN), 61058
Canadian Society of Petroleum Geologists (CAN), 61059
Canadian Studies Center (NC), 38016
Canadian Tax Foundation Library (CAN), 61060
Canadian Teachers' Federation, G.G. Croskery Memorial Library (CAN), 61061
Canadian Wood Council (CAN), 61062
Canadian Wood Energy Institute (CAN), 61063
Cancer Care (NY), 36245
Cancer Center Communications Program (IL), 17156

Cancer Control Society (CA), 05202

Cancer Guidance Institute (PA), 43096

Cancer Hopefuls United for Mutual Support (NY), 36247

Cancer Information Service (FL), 13041

Cancer Research Center (IL), 17157

Cancer Research Center (MO), 29025

Cancer Research Center of Hawaii (HI), 15002

Cancer Research Institute (CA), 05203

Cancer Research Laboratory (CA), 05151

Center for Research in Management (CA), 05152

Cancer Research Project (CA), 05204

Canine Companions for Independence (CA), 05205

Canvasback Society (OH), 40063

Cape Fear Technical Institute (NC), 38017

Capitol Historical Society (DC), 10362

Capitol Services Incorporated (DC), 10363

Cardeza Foundation for Hematologic Research (PA), 43097

Career Guidance Foundation, College Catalog Library (CA), 05206

Career Information System (OR), 42012

Career Research Systems (CA), 05207

Caribbean Conservation Corp. (FL), 13042

Caribbean Cultural Center (NY), 36248

Caribbean Research Institute (PR), 60002

Carl Campbell Brigham Library (NJ), 34056

Carl Vinson Institute of Government (GA), 14028

Carnation Research Laboratories Library (CA), 05208

Carnegie Hero Fund Commission (PA), 43098

Carnegie Institution of Washington, Rock Information System (DC), 10364

Carnivore Research Institute (NV), 32010

Carpet & Rug Institute (GA), 14029

Carriage Association of America (ME), 23004

Carrier Corp., Logan Lewis Library (NY), 36249

Carrier Reports (ME), 23005

Cartographic & Architectural Archives Branch (DC), 10365

Cartographic Information Center (LA), 22009

Carver Research Foundation (AL), 01030

Cast Iron Soil Pipe Institute (VA), 51141

Catalog of Fossil Spores & Pollen (PA), 43099

Catalyst Information Center (NY), 36250

Catfish Farmers of America (MS), 28008

Catholic Biblical Association of America (DC), 10366

Catholic Medical Mission Board (NY), 36251

Catholic Peace Fellowship (NY), 36252

Catholic Press Association of the U.S. (NY), 36253

Cave Research Foundation (OH), 40065

Cecil and Ida Green Pinon Flat Observatory (CA), 05209

Ceilings and Interior Systems Contractors Association (IL), 17158

Celanese Plastics and Specialties Co. Information Center (NJ), 34057

Celanese Technical Center (KY), 21010

Celebrity Service (NY), 36254

Cell Culture Center (MA), 25057

Cello Corp. (MD), 24124

Cellulose Research Institute (NY), 36255

Cemented Carbide Producers Association (OH), 40066

Center for Action on Endangered Species (MA), 25058

Center for Afro-American Studies (CA), 05210

Center for Aging (AL), 01031

Center for Agricultural and Rural Development (IA), 19012

Center for Air Environment Studies (PA), 43101

Center for Alcohol Studies (NC), 38018

Center for Allergy and Immunological Disorders (TX), 48054

Center for Alternatives to Animal Testing (MD), 24125

Center for Analysis of Public Issues (NJ), 34058

Center for Applied Gerontology (FL), 13043

Center for Applied Linguistics (DC), 10367

Center for Applied Mathematical Research (CAN), 61064

Center for Applied Mathematics (MD), 24126

Center for Applied Research in the Apostolate (DC), 10369

Center for Applied Urban Research (NE), 31007

Center for Arab and Islamic Studies (VT), 50004

Center for Archival Collections (OH), 40067

Center for Arid and Tropical New Crop Applied Science and Technology (AZ), 03037

Center for Arts Information (NY), 36256

Center for Astrophysics and Space (CA), 05211

Center for Atmospheric and Space Sciences (UT), 49006

Center for Attitudinal Healing (CA), 05213

Center for Auto Safety (DC), 10370

Center for Biotic Systems (WI), 54028

Center for Birth Defects Information Services (MA), 25059

Center for Book Arts (NY), 36257

Center for Business and Economic Research (KY), 21011

Center for Business and Economic Research (AL), 01032

Center for Chemical Physics, Electrolyte Data Center (MD), 24128

Center for Children's Books (IL), 17159

Center for Chinese Studies (CA), 05214

Center for Climacteric Studies (FL), 13044

Center for Coastal and Environmental Studies (NJ), 34059

Center for Community Development (CA), 05215

Center for Community Development and Design (CO), 07065

Center for Community Education (OH), 40068

Center for Community and Environmental Development (NY), 36258

Center for Community and Regional Planning (KS), 20011

Center for Community and Social Concerns (IL), 17160

Center for Computer/Law (CA), 05216

Center for Consumer Health Education (VA), 51142

Center for Nonprofit Organizations (NY), 36271
Center for Nuclear Studies (TN), 47018
Center for Nursing Research (OH), 40072
Center for Occupational Hazards (NY), 36272
Center for Oceans Law and Policy (VA), 51144
Center for Packaging Education (NY), 36273
Center for Palladian Studies in America (VA), 51145
Center for Peace Studies (DC), 10382
Center for Performance Assessment (OR), 42013
Center for Photobiology (PA), 43106
Center for Policy Alternatives (MA), 25069
Center for Policy Research (NY), 36274
Center for Policy and Law in Education (FL), 13048
Center for Population Options International Center
  on Adolescent Fertility (DC), 10383
Center for Population Studies (MA), 25070
Center for Private Enterprise (TX), 48058
Center for Process Studies (CA), 05223
Center for Productivity, Innovation, and Technology
  (TN), 47019
Center for Public Representation (WI), 54034
Center for Quality of Working Life (PA), 43107
Center for Quantitative Science in Forestry, Fisheries,
  Wildlife (WA), 52018
Center for Radar Astronomy (CA), 05224
Center for Radiation Research (DC), 10384
Center for Radiophysics and Space Research (NY),
  36275
Center for Rehabilitation Research and Training in
  Mental Health (MA), 25071
Center for Renewable Resources/Solar Lobby (DC),
  10385
Center for Research Libraries (IL), 17164
Center for Research and Education (CO), 07068
Center for Research for Mothers and Children (MD),
  24136
Center for Research in Ambulatory Health Care
  Library Resource Center (CO), 07069
Center for Research in Children's Television (MA),
  25072
Center for Research in Human Relations (CAN),
  61065
Center for Research in Law and Justice (IL), 17165
Center for Research in Mining and Mineral Resources
  (FL), 13049
Center for Research in Oral Biology (WA), 52019
Center for Research on Judgment and Policy (CO),
  07070
Center for Research on Utilization of Scientific
  Knowledge (MI), 26043
Center for Research on Women (MA), 25073
Center for Residential and Community Services
  (MN), 27033
Center for Responsive Governance (DC), 10387
Center for Responsive Psychology (NY), 36276
Center for Robotics Research (OH), 40073
Center for Rural Affairs (NE), 31008
Center for Rural Affairs, Small Farm Resources
  Project (NE), 31009
Center for Russian and East European Studies (MI),
  26044

Center for Safety (NY), 36277
Center for Science and International Affairs (MA),
  25074
Center for Science and Technology Policy (NY), 36278
Center for Science in the Public Interest (DC), 10388
Center for Sickle Cell Disease (DC), 10711
Center for Social Analysis (NY), 36279
Center for Social Organization of Schools (MD), 24137
Center for Social Research in the Church (IL), 17166
Center for Solar Energy Applications (CA), 05226
Center for Southern Folklore (TN), 47020
Center for Statistical Consulting (OH), 40074
Center for Strategic and International Studies (DC),
  10389
Center for Studies in Aging (TX), 48059
Center for Studies in Criminology & Criminal Law
  (PA), 43108
Center for Studies in Demography and Ecology (WA),
  52020
Center for Studies in Food Self-Sufficiency (VT),
  50005
Center for Studies in Higher Education (CA), 05227
Center for Studies of Antisocial and Violent Behavior
  (MD), 24138
Center for Study of Multiple Birth (IL), 17167
Center for Survey Research (CA), 05228
Center for Sutton Movement Writing (CA), 05229
Center for Technology, Environment, and
  Development (MA), 25075
Center for the Advancement of Human
  Communications (CT), 08030
Center for the American Woman and Politics (NJ),
  34063
Center for the Biology of Natural Systems (NY), 36283
Center for the Environment and Man (CT), 08031
Center for the History of American Needlework (PA),
  43110
Center for the Interaction of Animals & Society (PA),
  43111
Center for the Partially Sighted (CA), 05231
Center for the Study of Aging (NY), 36284
Center for the Study of Aging and Human
  Development (NC), 38022
Center for the Study of American Business (MO),
  29029
Center for the Study of Anorexia and Bulimia (NY),
  36285
Center for the Study of Children's Literature (MA),
  25076
Center for the Study of Comparative Folklore and
  Mythology (CA), 05232
Center for the Study of Crime, Delinquency, and
  Corrections (IL), 17171
Center for the Study of Deserts and Oceans (AZ),
  03041
Center for the Study of Drug Development (MA),
  25077
Center for the Study of Ethics in the Professions (IL),
  17172
Center for the Study of Evaluation (CA), 05233
Center for the Study of Federalism (PA), 43112

Chemical Industry Institute of Toxicology (NC), 38025
Chemical Institute of Canada (CAN), 61069
Chemical Propulsion Information Agency (MD), 24142
Chemical Search Service (IL), 17176
Chemical Specialties Manufacturers Association (DC), 10398
Chemineer (OH), 40081
Chemists' Club Library (NY), 36295
Chemotherapy Foundation (NY), 36296
Cherokee National Historical Society (OK), 41012
Chesapeake Bay Foundation (MD), 24143
Chesapeake Bay Institute (MD), 24144
Chesapeake Biological Laboratory (MD), 24145
Chessie System Railroads, Public Relations and Advertising Department (MD), 24146
Chester Davis Memorial Library (NJ), 34068
Chevron Oil Field Research, Technical Information Services (CA), 05238
Chevron Research Co. Library (CA), 05239
Chicago & North Western Historical Society (IL), 17177
Chicago Academy of Sciences (IL), 17178
Chicago Board of Trade, Information (IL), 17179
Chicago Council on Fine Arts (IL), 17180
Chicago Historical Society Research Collections (IL), 17181
Chicano Studies Research Library (CA), 05240
Chickamauga & Chattanooga National Military Park (GA), 14033
Chickasaw Horse Association (NC), 38026
Chihuahuan Desert Research Institute (TX), 48063
Child Abuse Listening Mediation (CA), 05241
Child Amputee Prosthetics Project (CA), 05242
Child Development Research Institute (NC), 38027
Child Find (NY), 36297
Child Health Association Program (CO), 07072
Child Welfare League of America (NY), 36298
Child, Youth, and Family Services (CA), 05243
Childbirth Without Pain Education Association (MI), 26048
Children in Hospitals (MA), 25083
Children of Alcoholics Foundation (NY), 36300
Children's Blood Foundation (NY), 36301
Children's Book Council Library (NY), 36303
Children's Bureau, Clearinghouse on Child Abuse & Neglect Information (DC), 10399
Children's Campaign for Nuclear Disarmament (CT), 08032
Children's Cancer Research Institute (CA), 05244
Children's Defense Fund (DC), 10400
Children's Foundation (DC), 10401
Children's Hospice International (VA), 51148
Children's Hospital Library (MO), 29032
Children's Hospital, Department of Adolescent & Young Adult Medicine (DC), 10402
Children's Hospital Research Foundation (OH), 40082
Children's Hospital of L.A. Hotline (CA), 05246
Children's Legal Rights Information & Training Program (DC), 10403

Children's Literature Center (DC), 10404
Children's Liver Foundation (NJ), 34069
Children's Memorial Hospital, Division of Genetics (IL), 17182
Children's Nutrition Research Center (TX), 48064
Children's Rights of America (FL), 13053
Children's Theatre Association of America (DC), 10406
China Council (NY), 36304
China Institute in America (NY), 36305
China Trade Development Corp. of Chicago (CA), 05247
China Trade Museum (MA), 25084
Chinese Historical Society of America (CA), 05248
Chinese History Center (HI), 15004
Chinese Language Teachers Association (NJ), 34070
Chinese for Affirmative Action (CA), 05249
Chisholm Trail Museum (KS), 20014
Chisholm Trail Museum and Seay Mansion (OK), 41013
Chlorine Institute (NY), 36306
Chocolate Manufacturers Association of the U.S. (VA), 51149
Choice Communities (PA), 43114
Christian Association for Psychological Studies (MI), 26049
Christian Medical Society (TX), 48065
Christian Record Braille Foundation (NE), 31010
Chronic Epstein-Barr Virus Support Group (IL), 17183
Church & Synagogue Library Association (PA), 43115
Church of Jesus Christ of Latter-day Saints (UT), 49010
Church of the Nazarene Archives (MO), 29033
Cincinnati Zoo Research Department (OH), 40083
Circus World Museum (WI), 54037
Citizen Exchange Council (NY), 36307
Citizen Soldier (NY), 36308
Citizen/Labor Energy Coalition (IL), 17184
Citizens Action League (CA), 05250
Citizens Against Nuclear War (DC), 10407
Citizens Clearinghouse for Hazardous Wastes (VA), 51150
Citizens Energy Council (NJ), 34071
Citizens Forum on Self-Government/National Municipal League (NY), 36309
Citizens Freedom Foundation, Information Services (NY), 36310
Citizens United to Reduce Emissions of Formaldehyde Poisoning Association (MN), 27036
Citizens for Better Care (MI), 26050
Citizens for Decency Through Law (AZ), 03042
Citizens for the Treatment of High Blood Pressure (DC), 10408
Citizens' Energy Project, Publications Division (DC), 10409
Citizens' Research Foundation (CA), 05251
Citizens' Scholarship Foundation of America (MN), 27037
Citizenship Development and Global Education Program (OH), 40084
Citrus Center (TX), 48066

Combined National Veterans' Association of America (MD), 24150

Combustion Engineering Power Systems Library (CT), 08036

Combustion Institute (PA), 43120

Comet Information Center (AL), 01034

Comics Magazine Association of America (NY), 36324

Commerce Department Library (DC), 10424

Commercial Development Association (DC), 10425

Commission of Fine Arts (DC), 10426

Commission of Professors of Adult Education (NC), 38029

Commission on Accreditation for Corrections (MD), 24151

Commission on Accreditation for Law Enforcement Agencies (VA), 51153

Commission on Accreditation of Rehabilitation Facilities (AZ), 03044

Commission on Archives and History of the United Methodist Church (NJ), 34074

Commission on Civil Rights (DC), 10427

Commission on Peace Officer Standards and Training (CA), 05261

Commission on Presidential Scholars (DC), 10428

Commission on Professional and Hospital Activities (MI), 26053

Committee for Better Transit (NY), 36325

Committee for Economic Development (NY), 36326

Committee for Economic Growth of Israel (WI), 54038

Committee for Freedom of Choice in Medicine (CA), 05262

Committee for National Arbor Day (NJ), 34075

Committee for National Security (DC), 10429

Committee for Purchase from the Blind and Other Severely Handicapped (VA), 51154

Committee for Single Adoptive Parents (MD), 24152

Committee for a New Korea Policy (NY), 36327

Committee for the Futherance of Torah Observance (NY), 36328

Committee for the Preservation of the Tule Elk (CA), 05263

Committee for the Preservation of the White House (DC), 10430

Committee for the Scientific Investigation of Claims of the Paranormal (NY), 36329

Committee in Support of Solidarity (NY), 36330

Committee of Small Magazine Editors and Publishers (CA), 05264

Committee on Diagnostic Reading Tests (NC), 38030

Committee on Noise as a Public Health Hazard (MD), 24153

Committee on Research Materials on Southeast Asia (NY), 36331

Committee on the Present Danger (DC), 10450

Committee to Halt Useless College Killings (NY), 36332

Committees Of Correspondence (MA), 25085

Commodity Credit Corp (DC), 10451

Commodity Management Division (DC), 10452

Common Carrier Bureau (DC), 10453

Communication Research Center (KS), 20015

Communication Research Division (MN), 27038

Communications Managers Association (NJ), 34076

Communications Media Research Center (PA), 43121

Communications Satellite Corp. Central Library (DC), 10454

Community Action for Legal Services, Food Law Project (NY), 36333

Community Analysis Research Institute (CA), 05265

Community Artists Project (AZ), 03045

Community Associations Institute Research Foundation (VA), 51155

Community Economics (CA), 05266

Community Environmental Council (CA), 05267

Community Guidance Service (NY), 36334

Community Health Centers Program (MD), 24154

Community Nutrition Institute (DC), 10456

Community Organization for Drug Abuse, Mental Health, and Alcoholism Services (AZ), 03046

Community Relations Service of the Department of Justice (MD), 24156

Community Research Applications (NY), 36335

Community Service (OH), 40088

Community Sex Information (NY), 36336

Community Systems Foundation (MI), 26054

Company of Fifers and Drummers (CT), 08037

Comparative Cardiovascular Studies Unit (PA), 43349

Comparative Education Center (IL), 17191

Comparative Legislative Research Center (IA), 19015

Compassionate Friends (IL), 17192

Composite Can and Tube Institute (DC), 10457

Comprehensive Cancer Center (CA), 05268

Comprehensive Cancer Center/Institute of Cancer Research (NY), 36337

Comprehensive Sickle Cell Center (NY), 36338

Compressed Gas Association (VA), 51156

Comptroller of the Currency (DC), 10459

Compucon C.A.P.E. Systems and Services (TX), 48072

Computer & Business Equipment Manufacturers Association (DC), 10460

Computer-Aided Manufacturing International (TX), 48073

Computer-Assisted Language Learning and Instruction Consortium (UT), 49011

Computer Graphics Research Group (OH), 40089

Computer Institute (DC), 10461

Computer Law Association (VA), 51157

Computer Measurement Group (VA), 51158

Computer Security Institute (MA), 25086

Computer and Automated Systems Association of SME (MI), 26055

Comsat Laboratories, Technical Library (MD), 24158

Concern (DC), 10462

Concerned Relatives of Nursing Home Patients (OH), 40090

Concerned United Birthparents (NH), 33005

Concordia Historical Institute (MO), 29034

Concrete Reinforcing Steel Institute (IL), 17193

Concrete Sawing & Drilling Association (GA), 14035

Concrete Technology Information Analysis Center (MS), 28010

Cosanti Foundation (AZ), 03048
Cosmetic, Toiletry & Fragrance Association (DC), 10481
Costume Society of America (NJ), 34079
Cotton Belt Rail Historical Society (AR), 04044
Cotton Insects Research Laboratory (TX), 48078
Cotton Quality Research Station (SC), 45006
Cotton Research Center of Agricultural Research Service (AZ), 03049
Council for Accreditation of Counseling and Related Educational Programs (VA), 51165
Council for Adult and Experiential Learning (MD), 24165
Council for Advancement & Support of Education (DC), 10482
Council for Agricultural Science and Technology (IA), 19016
Council for American Private Education (DC), 10483
Council for Chemical Research (PA), 43126
Council for Educational Development & Research (DC), 10484
Council for Educational Freedom in America (MD), 24166
Council for Exceptional Children Department of Information Services (VA), 51166
Council for Financial Aid to Education (NY), 36353
Council for Intercultural Studies and Programs (NY), 36354
Council for International Exchange of Scholars (DC), 10485
Council for Livestock Protection (NY), 36355
Council for Planning and Conservation (CA), 05275
Council for Research in Music Education (IL), 17197
Council for Responsible Nutrition (DC), 10486
Council for a Livable World (DC), 10487
Council for the Advancement of Science Writing (IL), 17198
Council for the Development of French in Louisiana (LA), 22015
Council of Administrators of Special Education (IN), 18029
Council of American Building Officials (VA), 51167
Council of Better Business Bureaus (VA), 51168
Council of Biology Editors (MD), 24167
Council of Chief State School Officers, Resource Center on Sex Equity (DC), 10488
Council of Citizens with Low Vision (MI), 26057
Council of Communication Societies (MD), 24168
Council of Economic Advisers (DC), 10489
Council of Engineers and Scientists Organizations (CA), 05276
Council of Graduate Schools in the U.S. (DC), 10490
Council of Independent Colleges (DC), 10491
Council of Logistics Management (IL), 17200
Council of Professional Associations on Federal Statistics (DC), 10492
Council of State Administrators of Vocational Rehabilitation (DC), 10493
Council of State Governments (KY), 21013
Council of State Governments (KY), 21014
Council of State Housing Agencies (DC), 10494

Council of State Planning Agencies (DC), 10495
Council of the Southern Mountains (VA), 51169
Council of Tree & Landscape Appraisers (DC), 10496
Council on America's Military Past, U.S.A. (VA), 51170
Council on Botanical and Horticultural Libraries (NY), 36356
Council on Career Development for Minorities (PA), 43127
Council on Chiropractic Education (IA), 19017
Council on Clinical Optometric Care (MO), 29036
Council on Economic Priorities (NY), 36357
Council on Electrolysis Education (MO), 29037
Council on Environmental Quality (DC), 10497
Council on Family Health (NY), 36359
Council on Foreign Relations (NY), 36360
Council of Graphological Societies @ 16004
Council on Hemispheric Affairs (DC), 10498
Council on Hotel, Restaurant & Institutional Education (PA), 43128
Council on International Educational Exchange (NY), 36361
Council on International Nontheatrical Events (DC), 10499
Council on International and Public Affairs (NY), 36362
Council on Interracial Books for Children (NY), 36363
Council on Library Resources (DC), 10500
Council on Municipal Performance (NY), 36364
Council on Postsecondary Accreditation (DC), 10501
Council on Rehabilitation Education (IL), 17202
Council on Social Work Education (NY), 36365
Council on Synthetic Fuels (DC), 10502
Council on Tall Buildings & Urban Habitat (PA), 43129
Counselor Training Center (AZ), 03050
Country Dance and Song Society of America (NY), 36366
Country Music Association (TN), 47027
Country Music Foundation, Library/Media Center (TN), 47028
Court Club Enterprises (AZ), 03051
Court Counselor Program (IL), 17203
Cousteau Society (NY), 36367
Cowboy Artists of America Museum Foundation (TX), 48079
Cox Group (WA), 52025
Cox Heart Institute (OH), 40094
Crash Research Institute (AZ), 03052
Creative Arts in Education (CT), 08048
Creative Communications (WI), 54042
Creative Education Foundation (NY), 36368
Credit Research Center (IN), 18030
Credit Union National Association (WI), 54043
Creek Indian Museum (OK), 41017
Crime Prevention Coalition (DC), 10503
Crime and Justice Foundation (MA), 25091
Criminal Justice Reference and Information Center (WI), 54044
Crop Science Society of America (WI), 54045

Department of Appllied Mechanics and Engineering Science (CA), 05289

Department of Atmospheric Sciences (IL), 17211

Department of Biology and Pharmacognosy (SC), 45007

Department of Botany (DC), 10517

Department of Commerce (DC), 10518

Department of Communication Disorders and Speech Science (CO), 07086

Department of Communicology (FL), 13059

Department of Dairy Science (OH), 40098

Department of Defense Explosives Safety Board (VA), 51176

Department of Energy Coal Preparation Branch (PA), 43139

Department of Energy Division of Coal Fired Magnetohydrodynamics (PA), 43140

Department of Entomology (AR), 04045

Department of Entomology and Applied Ecology (DE), 09018

Department of Environmental Systems Engineering (SC), 45008

Department of Fisheries and Allied Aquacultures (AL), 01036

Department of Geosciences (AZ), 03054

Department of Higher and Adult Education (AZ), 03055

Department of History of Science & Technology (DC), 10519

Department of Invertebrate Zoology (DC), 10520

Department of Marine Science (FL), 13060

Department of Mechanical and Aerospace Engineering (DE), 09019

Department of Microbiology and Infectious Diseases (TX), 48082

Department of Microbiology and Public Health (CA), 05290

Department of Mineral Sciences (DC), 10521

Department of Nutritional Sciences (CA), 05291

Department of Ocean Engineering (FL), 13061

Department of Orthopaedic Surgery Biomechanics Laboratory (IA), 19020

Department of Paleobiology (DC), 10522

Department of Pathology (PA), 43141

Department of Pathology and Laboratory Medicine (OH), 40099

Department of Pharmacology (FL), 13062

Department of Pharmacology (OH), 40100

Department of Pharmacology (PA), 43142

Department of Pharmacology and Experimental Therapeutics (IL), 17212

Department of Poultry Science (TX), 48083

Department of Psychology, Developmental Program (CA), 05292

Department of Rural Sociology Research (LA), 22018

Department of Social & Cultural History (DC), 10523

Department of State Library (DC), 10524

Department of State Visa Office (DC), 10525

Department of Vertebrate Zoology (DC), 10526

Department of Veterinary Medicine (ID), 16005

Department of Veterinary Physiology and Pharmacology (TX), 48084

Department of Veterinary Science (NE), 31014

Department of Virology and Epidemiology (TX), 48085

Department of the Interior Western Technical Office (CO), 07087

Department of the Youth Authority, Division of Research (CA), 05293

Dermatology Foundation (IL), 17213

Desert Bighorn Council (NV), 32011

Desert Botanical Garden (AZ), 03056

Desert Fishes Council (CA), 05294

Desert Protective Council (CA), 05295

Design Institute for Physical Property Data (NY), 36376

Design International (CA), 05296

Detroit Public Library, Labor Collection (MI), 26061

Development Group for Alternative Policies (DC), 10527

Development Resources (DC), 10528

Developmental Disabilities Center (PA), 43143

Developmental Training Center (IN), 18032

Devereaux Library (SD), 46006

Devereux Foundation (PA), 43144

Diabetes Research and Training Center (IL), 17214

Diamond Wheel Manufacturers Institute (OH), 40101

Diamonite Products Manufacturing Inc. (OH), 40102

Dight Institute (MN), 27042

Digital Equipment Computer Users Society (MA), 25096

Direct Marketing Association, Information Central (NY), 36378

Direct Marketing Educational Foundation (NY), 36379

Direct Relief International (CA), 05297

Directorate of Engineering Standardization (OH), 40103

Directors Guild of America (CA), 05298

Disability Rights Center (DC), 10532

Disability Rights Education and Defense Fund (CA), 05299

Disabled American Veterans (DC), 10533

Disabled Citizens Alliance for Independence (MO), 29039

Disaster Research Center (DE), 09020

Disclosure (MD), 24175

Disease Detection Information Bureau (IL), 17215

Displaced Homemakers Network (DC), 10534

Distilled Spirits Council of the U.S. (DC), 10535

Distribution Sciences (IL), 17216

Division of Applied, Experimental, and Engineering Psychologists (TX), 48086

Division of Astronomical Sciences (DC), 10536

Division of Behavioral & Neural Sciences (DC), 10537

Division of Biological Control (CA), 05300

Division of Biotic Systems and Resources (DC), 10530

Division of Biomass Energy Technology (DC), 10538

Division of Cardiovascular Diseases (TN), 47031

Division of Employment & Unemployment Analysis (DC), 10539

Division of Fishery Research (DC), 10540
Division of Forest Fire & Atmospheric Sciences
   Research (DC), 10541
Division of Geothermal & Hydropower Technologies
   (DC), 10542
Division of Industrial Prices & Price Indexes (DC),
   10543
Division of International Forestry (VA), 51175
Division of International Prices (DC), 10544
Division of Lab Animal Medicine (CA), 05301
Division of Library and Archives (MO), 29040
Division of Materials Research (DC), 10545
Division of Molecular Biosciences (DC), 10531
Division of Monthly Industry Employment Statistics
   (DC), 10546
Division of Ocean Energy Technology (DC), 10547
Division of Ocean Sciences (DC), 10548
Division of Parapsychology (VA), 51181
Division of Perinatal Biology (CA), 05302
Division of Perinatal Medicine at Yale (CT), 08054
Division of Physics (DC), 10549
Division of Polar Programs (DC), 10529
Division of Refuge Management (DC), 10550
Division of Special Programs English Language
   Institute (OR), 42019
Division of Substance Abuse Medicine (VA), 51182
Division of Water Resources (NJ), 34082
Division of Wildlife Research (DC), 10551
Divorce Research Institute (NE), 31015
Do It Now Foundation (AZ), 03057
Doctors Ought to Care (GA), 14037
Document Engineering Co. (CA), 05303
Document Room, Hart Senate Office Building (DC),
   10552
Documentary Guild (MA), 25097
Dog Writers Association of America (MT), 30002
Domestic Technology International (CO), 07088
Door Operator and Remote Controls Manufacturers
   Association (IL), 17218
Door and Hardware Institute (VA), 51184
Dorr-Oliver (CT), 08055
Dossin Great Lakes Museum (MI), 26063
Dow Chemical Co., Technical Library (MI), 26065
Dow Jones Newspaper Fund (NJ), 34083
Downtown Research and Development Center (NY),
   36381
Dramatists Guild (NY), 36382
Drinking Water Research Division (OH), 40104
Drug Abuse Warning Network (MD), 24177
Drug Enforcement Administration (DC), 10554
Drug Information Analysis Service (CA), 05305
Drug Information Center (NY), 36383
Drug Information Center (WA), 52028
Drug Information and Pharmacy Resource Center
   (FL), 13063
Drug and Alcohol Council (NY), 36384
Dry Color Manufacturers' Association (VA), 51185
Dry Lands Research Institute (CA), 05306
Ducks Unlimited (IL), 17219
Dude Ranchers Association (CO), 07089

Dugway Proving Ground Technical Library (UT),
   49013
Dun & Bradstreet Corp., Business Library (NY), 36385
Duster Class Yacht Racing Association (NJ), 34084
Dwight D. Eisenhower Library (KS), 20016
Dysautonomia Foundation (NY), 36386
Dystonia Medical Research Foundation (CA), 05307

E-Systems, ECI Division (FL), 13064
E.C. Brown Foundation (OR), 42020
E.I. du Pont de Nemours & Co.: Marshall Laboratory
   Library (PA), 43145
EEG Systems Laboratory (CA), 05308
EG&G Environmental Equipment (MA), 25098
EG&G Mason Research Institute (MA), 25099
EG&G Washington Analytical Services Center (MD),
   24178
EIC/Intelligence (NY), 36387
ENDECO (MA), 25100
ENKI Research Institute (CA), 05309
EPA National Enforcement Investigations Center
   (CO), 07090
ERIC Clearinghouse for Junior Colleges (CA), 05310
ERIC Clearinghouse for Science, Mathematics, and
   Environmental Education (OH), 40105
ERIC Clearinghouse on Educational Management
   (OR), 42021
ERIC Clearinghouse on Elementary and Early
   Childhood Education (IL), 17220
ERIC Clearinghouse on Handicapped and Gifted
   Children (VA), 51186
ERIC Clearinghouse on Higher Education (DC), 10555
ERIC Clearinghouse on Information Resources (NY),
   36388
ERIC Clearinghouse on Reading and Communication
   Skills (IL), 17221
ERIC Clearinghouse on Rural Education and Small
   Schools (NM), 35013
ERIC Clearinghouse on Tests, Measurement, and
   Evaluation (NJ), 34085
ERIC Clearinghouse on Urban Education (NY), 36389
Eagle Valley Environmentalists (IL), 17222
Eagleton Institute of Politics (NJ), 34086
Earl Warren Legal Institute (CA), 05311
Early American Industries Association (NY), 36390
Early American Society (PA), 43146
Earth Resources Observation Systems Library (SD),
   46007
Earthmind (CA), 05313
Earthquake Engineering Research Institute (CA),
   05314
Earthrise (RI), 44006
East Asian Institute (NY), 36391
East-West Academy of Healing Arts (CA), 05315
East-West Center (HI), 15005
East-West Cultural Center (CA), 05316
Eastern Bird Banding Association (NJ), 34087
Eastern Professional River Outfitters Association
   (WV), 53013
Eastfoto (NY), 36392

Eastman Kodak Co., Information Services (NY), 36393
Eaton Corp. IMS Division Library (CA), 05317
Eaton Corp., Engineering and Research Library (MI), 26066
Ecological Society of America (TN), 47032
Ecological and Toxicological Association of the Dyestuffs Manufacturing Industry (NY), 36394
Ecology Action Educational Institute (CA), 05318
Ecology Center (CA), 05319
Ecology Center (UT), 49014
Ecology Center of Southern California (CA), 05320
Ecology House (CAN), 61072
Economic Botany Library of Oakes Ames (MA), 25101
Economic Development Administration (DC), 10556
Economic Research Council (MD), 24179
Economic Research Service (DC), 10557
Economic Research Service, International Economics Division (DC), 10558
Economic Statistics Bureau of Washington (DC), 10559
Economics Research Institute (UT), 49015
Ecotope (WA), 52029
Edison Electric Institute (DC), 10560
Edison Institute (MI), 26067
Edison National Historic Site (NJ), 34088
Educanetic Consulting Associates (GA), 14038
Education & Research Institute (DC), 10561
Education Commission of the States Clearinghouse (CO), 07091
Education Department Information Branch (DC), 10562
Education Development Center (MA), 25102
Education Law Center (NJ), 34089
Education Voucher Institute (CA), 05321
Educational Commission for Foreign Medical Graduates (PA), 43148
Educational Film Library Association (NY), 36397
Educational Foundation for Nuclear Science (IL), 17223
Educational Freedom Foundation (MO), 29041
Educational Media Center (CO), 07092
Educational Parameters (MA), 25103
Educational Planning Associates (MA), 25104
Educational Press Association of America (NJ), 34090
Educational Products Information Exchange Institute (NY), 36398
Educational Records Bureau (MA), 25105
Educational Research Council of America (OH), 40106
Educational Research Service (VA), 51187
Educational Testing Service. Test Collection (NJ), 34091
Educational and Industrial Testing Service (CA), 05322
Educators for Social Responsibility (MA), 25106
Edward L. Ginzton Physics Laboratory (CA), 05323
Edward S. Harkness Eye Institute (NY), 36399
Ehlers-Danlos National Foundation (MI), 26068
Eighteenth Century Short Title Catalogue for North America (LA), 22019

Eisenhower Foundation (DC), 10563
Eisenhower Institute for Historical Research (DC), 10564
Elastic Fabric Manufacturers Council of the Northern Textile Association (MA), 25108
Electric Auto Association (CA), 05324
Electric Power Research Institute (CA), 05325
Electrical Generating Systems Association (FL), 13065
Electricity Consumers Resource Council (DC), 10565
Electron Microscopy Society of America (TN), 47033
Electronic Data Processing Auditors Association (IL), 17224
Electronic Industries Association (DC), 10566
Electronic Industries Association, Joint Electron Device Engineering Councils (DC), 10567
Electronic Industries Foundation (DC), 10568
Electronic Information Exchange System (NJ), 34092
Electronic Music Consortium (IN), 18033
Electronics Research Laboratory (CA), 05326
Electronics Technicians Association, International (IN), 18034
Eli Lilly and Co. Scientific Library (IN), 18035
Elm Research Institute (NH), 33006
Elmer E. Rasmuson Library (AK), 02017
Elsa Wild Animal Appeal (CA), 05327
Embroiderer's Guild of America (NY), 36400
Embry-Riddle Aeronautical University (FL), 13066
Emergency Care Research Institute (PA), 43149
Emergency Committee for American Trade (DC), 10569
Emergency Programs Information Center (MD), 24180
Emergency Response Institute (WA), 52030
Emery Industries Research Library (OH), 40107
Emotional Health Anonymous (CA), 05328
Emphysema Anonymous (FL), 13067
Employee Relocation Council (DC), 10570
Employment & Training Administration, Office of Public Affairs (DC), 10571
Employment and Training Administration, Bureau of Apprenticeship and Training (DC), 10572
Emulsion Polymers Institute (PA), 43150
Enamel Guild West (CA), 05329
Encyclopaedia Cinematographica (PA), 43151
End Violence Against the Next Generation (CA), 05330
Endocrine Society (MD), 24181
Endometriosis Association (WI), 54047
Energenics Systems (DC), 10574
Energy Business Association of Washington (WA), 52031
Energy Inc. Technical Info Services @16006
Energy Information Administration (DC), 10575
Energy Institute (NM), 35014
Energy Law Center (UT), 49016
Energy Probe Research Foundation (CAN), 61073
Energy Resources Center (IL), 17225
Energy Resources Institute, Information Systems Programs (OK), 41020
Energy and Mineral Resources Research Institute (IA), 19021

Energy and Self-Reliance Center (IA), 19022
Engelhard Corp. Research Library (NJ), 34093
Engine Manufacturers Association (IL), 17226
Engineering and Industrial Experiment Station (FL), 13069
Engineering Experiment Station (AZ), 03059
Engineering Experiment Station (AR), 04046
Engineering Information (NY), 36401
Engineering Research Center (CO), 07093
Engineering Societies Library (NY), 36402
Engineering-Science (CA), 05331
Eno Mining Corp. (NV), 32013
Enoch Pratt Free Library (MD), 24183
Ensanian Physicochemical Institute (PA), 43152
Entomological Consultant Service (MS), 28011
Entomological Research Collection (IN), 18036
Entomological Society of America (MD), 24184
Entrepreneurs Alliance (CA), 05332
Entrepreneurship Institute (OH), 40108
Enviro-Med Laboratories (LA), 22020
Environic Foundation International (IN), 18037
Environmental & Energy Study Conference (DC), 10576
Environmental Action (DC), 10577
Environmental Action Coalition (NY), 36404
Environmental Action Resource Service (CO), 07094
Environmental Alternatives (KY), 21016
Environmental Center (HI), 15006
Environmental Coalition on Nuclear Power (PA), 43153
Environmental Communications (CA), 05333
Environmental Defense Fund (NY), 36406
Environmental Design & Research Center (CA), 05334
Environmental Design & Surveys Branch (DC), 10579
Environmental Education Group (CA), 05335
Environmental Educators (DC), 10580
Environmental Fund (DC), 10581
Environmental Law Institute (DC), 10582
Environmental Management Association (FL), 13070
Environmental Monitoring Systems Laboratory (NV), 32014
Environmental Monitoring and Support Laboratory (OH), 40109
Environmental Mutagen Information Center (TN), 47034
Environmental Mutagen Society (VA), 51188
Environmental Policy Institute (DC), 10583
Environmental Protection Agency (OR), 42022
Environmental Quality Instructional Resources Center (OH), 40110
Environmental Remote Sensing Applications Laboratory (OR), 42023
Environmental Remote Sensing Center (WI), 54048
Environmental Research Laboratory (AZ), 03060
Environmental Resource Center for Community Information (MI), 26069
Environmental Resources Center (GA), 14039
Environmental Teratology Information Center (TN), 47035
Environmental Toxicology Center (WI), 54049

Environmental Toxicology Library (CA), 05336
Environmental Trace Substances Research Center (MO), 29042
Ephemera Society North American Office (VT), 50006
Epidemiology Resources (MA), 25111
Epilepsy Concern International Service Council (FL), 13071
Epilepsy Foundation of America (MD), 24186
Equal Employment Advisory Council (DC), 10584
Equal Employment Opportunity Commission Library (DC), 10585
Equine Behavior Study Circle (CAN), 61074
Equitable Life Assurance Society of the U.S. Technical Information Center (NY), 36407
Equity Policy Center (MD), 24187
Erie National Wildlife Refuge (PA), 43154
Escapees (TX), 48088
Escherichia coli Reference Center (PA), 43155
Esperantic Studies Foundation (DC), 10586
Esperanto Information Center (CA), 05337
Eterna International (IL), 17227
Ethics & Public Policy Center (DC), 10587
Ethiopian Community Center (DC), 10588
Ethnic American Art Slide Library (AL), 01037
Eugene C. Eppley Institute for Research in Cancer and Allied Diseases (NE), 31016
Eugene V. Debs Foundation (IN), 18038
Eulenspiegel Society (NY), 36408
Eunice Kennedy Shriver Center for Mental Retardation (MA), 25112
European Communities Commission Information Service (DC), 10589
Evaluation, Dissemination, and Assessment Center for Bilingual Education (TX), 48089
Evan Shute Foundation for Clinical and Laboratory Research (CAN), 61075
Evapotranspiration Laboratory (KS), 20017
Everglades National Park (FL), 13072
Exanimo Press (CO), 07096
Exceptional Child Center (UT), 49017
Executime Systems (IL), 17228
Exemplary Center for Reading Instruction (UT), 49018
Expanded Shale, Clay, and Slate Institute (MD), 24188
Experiment in International Living (VT), 50007
Experimental Aircraft Association (WI), 54050
Expertise Institute (FL), 13073
Exploratorium (CA), 05338
Explorers Club (NY), 36409
Export-Import Bank of the United States (DC), 10590
Extension Service, Deputy Administrator for Natural Resources & Rural Development (DC), 10591
Extensions for Independence (CA), 05339
Eye-Bank for Sight Restoration (NY), 36410
Eye Research Institute of Retina Foundation (MA), 25113

F.A.C.E. (MD), 24189
FAA Aircraft Registration Branch (OK), 41021
FMC Corp. Central Engineering Laboratories Library (CA), 05340

FMC Corp. Tech Library (CA), 05341
FZ East-West Trade (MA), 25114
Fabricating Manufacturers Association (IL), 17229
Facing Tile Institute (OH), 40111
Factory Mutual Research Corp. (MA), 25115
Faculty Exchange Center (PA), 43156
Fair Lawn Technical Center Library (NJ), 34095
Fairchild Republic Co., Technical Information Center (NY), 36412
Fairchild Tropical Garden (FL), 13074
Fairhaven College Outback Program (WA), 52032
Families Anonymous (CA), 05342
Families in Action National Drug Information Center (GA), 14040
Family Health International (NC), 38033
Family Helpline (WI), 54051
Family History and Genealogical Research Center (UT), 49019
Family Interest Group--Head Trauma (MN), 27047
Family Mediation Association (NC), 38034
Family Service America (NY), 36414
Family Survival Project for Brain-Damaged Adults (CA), 05344
Family Television Research and Consultation Center (CT), 08058
Family and Demographic Research Institute (UT), 49020
Far West Lab for Educational Research and Development (CA), 05345
Farallones Institute (CA), 05346
Fargo Co. (CA), 05347
Farm Credit Administration, Congressional and Public Affairs Division (VA), 51189
Farm Labor Research Committee (DC), 10592
Farm and Industrial Equipment Institute (IL), 17230
Farmers Home Administration (DC), 10593
Farrel Company (CT), 08059
Fashion Institute of Technology, Library (NY), 36415
Fathers' Rights of America (CA), 05348
Fats and Proteins Research Foundation (IL), 17231
Federal Aviation Administration Technical Center (NJ), 34096
Federal Bar Association (DC), 10594
Federal Bureau of Investigation, National Crime Information Center (DC), 10595
Federal Communications Commission (DC), 10596
Federal Correctional Institution (KY), 21017
Federal Crop Insurance Corporation (DC), 10597
Federal Deposit Insurance Corp. (DC), 10598
Federal Election Commission (DC), 10599
Federal Election Commission, National Clearinghouse on Election Administration (DC), 10600
Federal Emergency Management Agency (DC), 10601
Federal Energy Regulatory Commission, Office of Public Information (DC), 10602
Federal Grain Inspection Service (DC), 10603
Federal Highway Administration, National Ridesharing Information Center (DC), 10604
Federal Home Loan Bank Board (DC), 10605

Federal Information Centers (DC), 10606
Federal Judicial Center (DC), 10607
Federal Labor Relations Authority (DC), 10608
Federal Legal Information Through Electronics (CO), 07097
Federal Library & Information Center Committee (DC), 10609
Federal Maritime Commission (DC), 10610
Federal Mediation & Conciliation Service (DC), 10611
Federal Procurement Data Center (VA), 51190
Federal Railroad Administration. National Test Center (CO), 07098
Federal Reserve System Board of Governors (DC), 10612
Federal Reserve System, Division of Consumer & Community Affairs (DC), 10613
Federal Software Exchange Center (VA), 51191
Federal Trade Commission, Public Reference Branch (DC), 10614
Federal Trade Commission, Office of Consumer Education (DC), 10615
Federal Voting Assistance Program (DC), 10616
Federal-State Agricultural Weather Service (Florida) (FL), 13075
Federation for American Immigration Reform (DC), 10617
Federation for Children with Special Needs (MA), 25116
Federation of American Scientists (DC), 10618
Federation of American Societies for Experimental Biology (MD), 24190
Federation of Associations of Regulatory Boards (NC), 38035
Federation of Historical Bottle Clubs (NY), 36416
Federation of National Associations (DC), 10619
Federation of Organizations for Professional Women (DC), 10620
Federation of Societies for Coatings Technology (PA), 43157
Federation of State Medical Boards of the U.S. (TX), 48090
Federation of Western Outdoor Clubs (WA), 52033
Federation of the Handicapped (NY), 36418
Feldenkrais Guild (CA), 05349
Felicidades Wildlife Foundation (NC), 38036
Fels Center of Government (PA), 43158
Fels Research Institute for the Study of Human Development (OH), 40112
Feminist Alliance Against Rape (DC), 10621
Feminist History Research Project (CA), 05350
Fennell Orchid Co., Orchid Jungle (FL), 13076
Fenton Art Glass Collectors of America. (WV), 53014
Fermi National Accelerator Laboratory, Technical Information Group (IL), 17232
Fernbank Science Center Library (GA), 14041
Fertility Research Foundation (NY), 36419
Fertilizer Institute (DC), 10622
Fiber Society (NJ), 34097
Fibonacci Association (CA), 05351
Fibre Box Association (IL), 17233

Forest Service, Office of Information (DC), 10643
Forest Service, Watershed & Air Management Staff Unit (DC), 10644
Forest and Conservation Experiment Station (MT), 30003
Forest, Wildlife, and Range Experiment Station @16007
Forestry Sciences Laboratory (WV), 53016
Forestry Sciences Laboratory (WI), 54122
Forestry, Conservation Communications Association (OR), 42029
Forging Industry Association (OH), 40113
Forintek Canada Corp. (CAN), 61076
Formaldehyde Institute (NY), 36433
Fort Carson, Museum of the Army in the West (CO), 07101
Fort Larned, Historical Society Santa Fe Trail Center (KS), 20019
Fort Logan, Mental Health Center (CO), 07102
Fortune Society (NY), 36434
Forum for Resources on Federal Lands Foundation (CT), 08060
Forum for U.S.-Soviet Dialogue (NH), 33007
Forward Lands (DE), 09021
Foster Parents Plan (RI), 44007
Foundation Center (NY), 36435
Foundation for Alternative Cancer Therapies (NY), 36437
Foundation for American Communications (CA), 05357
Foundation for Child Development (NY), 36438
Foundation for Children with Learning Disabilities (NY), 36439
Foundation for Cooperative Housing (DC), 10645
Foundation for Education and Research in Vision (TX), 48096
Foundation for Ethnic Dance (NY), 36440
Foundation for Glaucoma Research (CA), 05358
Foundation for Health Research (CA), 05359
Foundation for Interior Design Education Research (NY), 36441
Foundation for North American Wild Sheep (WY), 55006
Foundation for Public Affairs Resource Center (DC), 10646
Foundation for Research in the Afro-American Creative Arts (NY), 36442
Foundation for Research on the Nature of Man (NC), 38038
Foundation for Science and the Handicapped (WV), 53017
Foundation for the Extension and Development of the American Professional Theatre (NY), 36443
Foundation for the Peoples of the South Pacific/Pacific Islands Association (NY), 36444
Foundation for the Study of Cycles (PA), 43162
Foundation for the Study of Wilson's Disease (NY), 36445
Foundation of Thanatology (NY), 36446
Foundry Equipment & Materials Association (DC), 10647

Four Corners Geological Society (CO), 07103
Fox Chase Cancer Center (PA), 43163
Fragile X Foundation (CO), 07104
Fragrance Foundation (NY), 36447
Francis Bacon Library (CA), 05360
Francis I. Proctor Foundation for Research in Ophthalmology (CA), 05361
Francis W. Kelsey Museum of Archeology (MI), 26073
Franciscan Institute (NY), 36448
Frank H. McClung Museum (TN), 47036
Frank J. Seiler Research Lab (CO), 07105
Franklin D. Roosevelt Library (NY), 36449
Franklin Institute Weather Center (PA), 43164
Franz Theodore Stone Laboratory and Center for Lake Erie Area Research and Ohio Sea Grant Program (OH), 40114
Fred Hutchinson Cancer Research Center (WA), 52035
Fred R. Crawford Witness to the Holocaust Project (GA), 14044
Frederick C. Crawford Auto-Aviation Museum (OH), 40115
Free Congress Research & Education Foundation, Child & Family Protection Institute (DC), 10648
Freedom of Information Center (MO), 29043
Freedom of Information Clearinghouse (DC), 10649
Freer Gallery of Art (DC), 10650
Freestanding Ambulatory Surgery Association (VA), 51195
French Institute/Alliance Francaise, Library (NY), 36450
Friction Materials Standards Institute (NJ), 34099
Friday Harbor Laboratories (WA), 52036
Friedreich's Ataxia Group in America (CA), 05363
Friends Committee on National Legislation (DC), 10651
Friends Historical Library (PA), 43166
Friends of Animals (NY), 36451
Friends of Cast Iron Architecture (NY), 36452
Friends of Mineralogy (WA), 52037
Friends of the Earth (CA), 05364
Friends of the Origami Center of America (NY), 36453
Friends of the River (CA), 05365
Friends of the Sea Otter (CA), 05366
Frontier Nursing Service (KY), 21018
Frontier Taxidermists (WY), 55007
Frontlash (DC), 10652
Frost Entomological Museum (PA), 43167
Fulbright Association of Alumni of International Educational & Cultural Exchange (PA), 43168
Fund for Human Ecology (CA), 05367
Fund for Multinational Management Education (NY), 36455
Fund for New Priorities in America (NY), 36456
Fund for Open Information and Accountability (NY), 36457
Fund for Peace (NY), 36458
Fund for an OPEN Society (PA), 43169
Fund-Raising Institute (PA), 43170
Furniture Industry Consumer Advisory Panel (NC), 38039

Fusarium Research Center (PA), 43171
Fusion Bonded Coaters Association (IL), 17236
Future Aviation Professionals of America (GA), 14045
Futures Group (CT), 08061
Futures Industry Association (DC), 10654
Futures Network (MD), 24197
Futures for Children (NM), 35015

GCA Corp., Technology Division Library (MA), 25121
GMI Engineering and Management Institute, Library (MI), 26074
GTE Products Corp. (MA), 25122
Gallaudet College National Academy (DC), 10655
Gallup Organization (NJ), 34100
Gallup Public Library (NM), 35016
Galveston Marine Geophysics Laboratory (TX), 48097
Gamblers Anonymous (CA), 05368
Garden Centers of America (DC), 10656
Garden Club of America (NY), 36460
Garden Forum of the Greater Youngstown Area (OH), 40116
Gardens for All, the National Association for Gardening (VT), 50009
Gas Appliance Manufacturers Association (VA), 51196
Gas Processors Association (OK), 41024
Gas Research Institute, Technical Communications (IL), 17238
Gaucher's Disease Registry (CA), 05369
Gauss Scientific Society (CA), 05370
Gay and Lesbian Advocates and Defenders (MA), 25123
Gaylord Memorial Laboratory (MO), 29044
Gazette International Networking Institute (MO), 29045
Gelatin Manufacturers Institute of America (NY), 36461
Gem Village Museum (CO), 07106
Gemological Institute of America (CA), 05371
GenCorp Information Center (OH), 40117
GenRad (MA), 25124
Genealogical Indexing Associates (UT), 49022
Genealogical Library (UT), 49023
General Accounting Office (DC), 10657
General Aviation Manufacturers Association (DC), 10658
General Conference of Seventh-day Adventists, Department of Public Affairs & Religious Liberty (DC), 10659
General Dynamics Corp., Convair Div. Research Library (CA), 05372
General Electric Co., Carboloy Systems Department (MI), 26075
General Electric Co., Lanham Center Operations (MD), 24198
General Electric Co., Lighting Business Group (OH), 40118
General Electric Co., Space Systems Division Library (PA), 43172

General Foods Corp., Technical Center Library (NY), 36462
General Libraries Film Library (TX), 48098
General Library of the Performing Arts (NY), 36463
General Services Administration, Consumer Information Center (DC), 10660
General Services Administration, Office of Public Affairs (DC), 10661
Genetic Sequence Data Bank (MA), 25125
Genetics Society of America (MD), 24199
Geodex International Inc. (CA), 05373
Geographic Names Office (VA), 51197
Geologic Inquiries Group (VA), 51198
Geologic Names Committee (VA), 51199
Geological Information Library of Dallas (TX), 48099
Geological Society of America (CO), 07107
Geological Survey (VA), 51179
Geological Survey, Office of International Hydrology (VA), 51200
Geological Survey, Public Affairs Office (VA), 51201
Geology Museum (NM), 35017
Geomet Technologies (MD), 24200
Geophysical Fluid Dynamics Laboratory (NJ), 34101
Geophysical Institute (AK), 02018
Geophysical Society of Tulsa (OK), 41026
Geophysical and Polar Research Center (WI), 54055
George S. Cox Medical Research Institute (PA), 43173
Georgia Conservancy (GA), 14047
Georgia Council on Moral & Civic Concerns (GA), 14048
Georgia Department of Archives & History (GA), 14049
Georgia Historical Society (GA), 14050
Georgia Humanities Resource Center (GA), 14051
Georgia Institute of Technology Bioengineering Center (GA), 14052
Georgia Solar Coalition (GA), 14053
Geosat Committee (CA), 05374
Geoscience Information Service (CA), 05375
Geoscience Information Society (VA), 51202
Geotechnical Research Centre (CAN), 61077
Geothermal Resources Council (CA), 05376
Geothermal World Corp. (CA), 05377
Gerald R. Ford Library (MI), 26076
Geriatric Study and Treatment Program (NY), 36464
German Information Center (NY), 36465
German Shepherd Dog Club of America (NJ), 34102
Germplasm Resources Laboratory (MD), 24201
Gerontological Information Center (CA), 05378
Gerontological Research Information Program (NY), 36466
Gerontological Society of America (DC), 10663
Gesell Institute of Human Development (CT), 08062
Gesneriad Society International (IN), 18040
Get Oil Out! (CA), 05379
Ghost Research Society (IL), 17239
Giannini Foundation of Agricultural Economics Library (CA), 05380
Gichner Mobile Systems (PA), 43174

HUD Office of the Special Advisor for Disability Issues (DC), 10672
HUD USER (MD), 24211
Habitat Institute for the Environment (MA), 25130
Hadassah, The Women's Zionist Organization of America (NY), 36486
Hagley Museum and Library (DE), 09022
Hahnemann Medical College & Hospital Laboratory of Human Pharmacology (PA), 43182
Hair Science Institute (NJ), 34106
Halcon SD Group, Information Center (NY), 36487
Halibut Association of North America (WA), 52039
Hall Laboratory of Mammalian Genetics (KS), 20023
Hall of Fame of the Trotter (NY), 36488
Hammermill Paper Co. (PA), 43183
Hampton Roads Maritime Association (VA), 51208
Hancock Library of Biology and Oceanography (CA), 05386
Handgun Control (DC), 10673
Handweavers Guild of America (CT), 08064
Handwriting Analysis Research Library (MA), 25131
Handy-Cap Horizons (IN), 18042
Hanford Technical Library (WA), 52040
Hardwood Plywood Manufacturers Association (VA), 51209
Harold W. Manter Laboratory of Parasitology (NE), 31018
Harry A. Cochran Research Center (PA), 43184
Harry S. Truman Library (MO), 29049
Harvard Institute for International Development (MA), 25132
Harvard Laboratory of Psychophysics (MA), 25133
Haskell Laboratory for Toxicology and Industrial Medicine (DE), 09023
Haskins Laboratories (CT), 08065
Hastings Research (CA), 05387
Hatfield Marine Science Center Library (OR), 42030
Haviland Maritime Library (MD), 24212
Hawaii Volcanoes National Park (HI), 15007
Hawaiian Academy of Science (HI), 15008
Hawaiian Botanical Society (HI), 15009
Hawaiian Historical Society (HI), 15010
Hawaiian Sugar Planters' Association (HI), 15011
Hawk Mountain Sanctuary Association (PA), 43185
Haynes-Apperson Owners Club (IN), 18043
Hazardous Materials Control Research Institute (MD), 24213
Hazardous Materials Information Center (TN), 47037
Hazelden Research Services (MN), 27051
Headache Research Foundation (MA), 25134
Headquarters, USAF Survival School (WA), 52041
Health & Energy Institute (DC), 10674
Health Activation Network (VA), 51210
Health Care Exhibitors Association (CT), 08066
Health Care Financing Administration (DC), 10675
Health Effects Research Laboratory (NC), 38040
Health Effects Research Laboratory, Experimental Biology Division (NC), 38041
Health Facilities Research Program (TX), 48101
Health Insurance Association of America (NY), 36489
Health Occupations Students of America (DC), 10676

Health Physics Society (VA), 51211
Health Policy Advisory Center (NY), 36491
Health Sciences Communications Association (MO), 29050
Heard Museum of Anthropology and Primitive Art (AZ), 03063
Hearing Ear Dog Program (MA), 25135
Hearing Industries Association (DC), 10677
Hearing and Tinnitus Help Association (NJ), 34107
Heartlife (GA), 14055
Hebraic Section (DC), 10678
Heifer Project International (AR), 04049
Helen Keller International (NY), 36492
Helen Keller National Center for Deaf-Blind Youths and Adults (NY), 36493
Helen Kellogg Institute for International Studies (IN), 18044
Helen S. Kaplan Center for Sexual Disorders (NY), 36494
Helicopter Association International (VA), 51212
Helsinki Watch Committee (NY), 36495
Hemangioma Support Group (OR), 42031
Hemlock Society (CA), 05389
Hemochromatosis Research Foundation (NY), 36496
Henry D. Altobello Children and Youth Center (CT), 08067
Henry Francis du Pont Winterthur Museum (DE), 09024
Henry Phipps Institute of Medical Genetics (PA), 43186
Herb Information (AZ), 03064
Herb Society of America (MA), 25137
Herbert Hoover Presidential Library (IA), 19026
Hereditary Disease Foundation (CA), 05390
Herman G. Dresser Library (MA), 25138
Herpes Resource Center (CA), 05392
Hershey Museum of American Life (PA), 43187
Hertzler Research Foundation Library (KS), 20024
Higgins Armory Museum (MA), 25139
High Blood Pressure Information Center (MD), 24214
High Energy Physics Laboratory (CA), 05393
High Frontier (DC), 10679
High Plains Research Foundation (TX), 48102
Higher Education Research Institute (CA), 05394
Highlander Research and Education Center, Resource Center (TN), 47038
Highlands Biological Station (NC), 38042
Highlands Center (VA), 51214
Highway Loss Data Institute (DC), 10680
Highway Research Information Service (DC), 10681
Highway Safety Research Center (NC), 38043
Highway Users Federation for Safety and Mobility (DC), 10682
Hip Society (CO), 07108
Hispanic Society of America, Library (NY), 36497
Histamine Research Society of North America (NY), 36498
Historic American Buildings Survey Foundation (VA), 51215
Historic Hawai'i Foundation (HI), 15012
Historic House Association of America (DC), 10683

Historical Evaluation and Research Organization (VA), 51216

Historical Foundation of the Presbyterian and Reformed Churches (NC), 38044

Historical Pictures Service (IL), 17244

Historical Society of Delaware (DE), 09025

Historical Society of New Mexico (NM), 35018

Historical Society of Pennsylvania (PA), 43188

Historical Society of Seattle and King County Museum (WA), 52042

History of Earth Sciences Society (DC), 10684

Hobby Industry Association of America (NJ), 34108

Hocker International Federation (CT), 08068

Hockey Hall of Fame (MN), 27052

Hockey Hall of Fame (CAN), 61078

Hoffman Pilot Center (CO), 07109

Hoffmann-LaRoche Inc. Scientific Library (NJ), 34109

Hoist Manufacturers Institute (PA), 43189

Holly Society of America (MD), 24215

Hollywood Archives (CA), 05395

Holt Atherton Center for Western Studies (CA), 05396

Holt International Childrens Services (OR), 42032

Home & School Institute (DC), 10685

Home Ventilating Institute (IL), 17245

Homosexual Information Center (CA), 05398

Honeywell Marine Systems Division (WA), 52043

Hoover Institution on War, Revolution, and Peace (CA), 05399

Hopkins Marine Station (CA), 05400

Horace Mann Bond Center for Equal Education (MA), 25141

Horizons for the Blind (IL), 17246

Hormel Institute (MN), 27053

Hormone Research Laboratory (CA), 05401

Horn Point Environmental Laboratories (MD), 24216

Horseless Carriage Club of America (CA), 05402

Horticultural Crops Production & Marketing Systems Research (TX), 48103

Horticultural Crops Research Laboratory (CA), 05403

Horticultural Research Institute (DC), 10686

Hospital Compensation Service (NJ), 34110

Hospital Research and Educational Trust (IL), 17247

Hot Springs National Park (AR), 04050

Hotaling Associates/International (VA), 51217

House Committee on Agriculture (DC), 10687

House Committee on Appropriations (DC), 10688

House Committee on Armed Services (DC), 10689

House Committee on Banking, Finance and Urban Affairs (DC), 10690

House Committee on Education and Labor (DC), 10691

House Committee on Energy and Commerce (DC), 10692

House Committee on Foreign Affairs (DC), 10693

House Committee on Government Operations (DC), 10694

House Committee on House Administration (DC), 10695

House Committee on Interior and Insular Affairs (DC), 10696

House Committee on Merchant Marine and Fisheries (DC), 10697

House Committee on Public Works and Transportation (DC), 10698

House Committee on Rules (DC), 10699

House Committee on Science and Technology (DC), 10700

House Committee on Small Business (DC), 10701

House Committee on Standards of Official Conduct (DC), 10702

House Committee on Veterans' Affairs (DC), 10703

House Committee on Ways and Means (DC), 10704

House Committee on the Budget (DC), 10705

House Committee on the District of Columbia (DC), 10706

House Committee on the Judiciary (DC), 10707

House Committee on the Post Office and Civil Service (DC), 10708

House Ear Institute George Kelemen Library (CA), 05404

Housing Assistance Council (DC), 10709

HoverClub of America (IN), 18045

Hoya Society International (GA), 14056

Hudson Institute (IN), 18046

Hudson Photographic Industries (NY), 36499

Huguenot Historical Society (NY), 36500

Human Development Program, University Affiliated Facility (KY), 21021

Human Ecology Action League (IL), 17249

Human Ecology Research Foundation (IL), 17250

Human Energy Research Laboratory (PA), 43190

Human Environment Center (DC), 10714

Human Factors Society (CA), 05405

Human Growth Foundation (MD), 24217

Human Growth Foundation (MN), 27054

Human Lactation Center (CT), 08069

Human Life and Natural Family Planning Foundation (VA), 51218

Human Nutrition Information Service (MD), 24218

Human Performance Research Center (UT), 49024

Human Relations Area Files (CT), 08071

Human Relations Area Files (IA), 19027

Human Relations Area Files (MA), 25142

Human Relations Area Files (PA), 43191

Human Resources Center (NY), 36501

Human Resources Development Center (AL), 01038

Human Resources Management Corp. (MD), 24219

Human Resources Research Organization (VA), 51219

Human Rights Internet (DC), 10715

Human Sciences Research (VA), 51220

Human Sexuality Program (CA), 05406

Human Sexuality Program (NY), 36503

Humane Society of the United States (DC), 10716

Humanities Exchange (FL), 13097

Humor Communication Co. (MD), 24220

Hunger Project, Communications and Information Department (CA), 05407

Hunt Institute for Botanical Documentation (PA), 43192

Information Handling Services (CO), 07110
Information Industry Association (DC), 10727
Information Management and Processing Association (MI), 26088
Information Retrieval Research Laboratory (IL), 17262
Information Retrieval System for Social Sciences of Leisure and Sport (CAN), 61079
Information Science Group (MO), 29054
Information Services (NJ), 34114
Information Systems Security Association (CA), 05416
Information for Industry (PA), 43199
Information for Policy Design (NY), 36520
Information for the Partially Sighted (MD), 24231
Information on Demand (CA), 05417
Information/Documentation (DC), 10729
Informed Homebirth (MI), 26089
Informetrica (CAN), 61080
Inforonics (MA), 25144
Infrared Information and Analysis Center (MI), 26090
Inhalation Toxicology Research Institute (NM), 35020
Inland Bird Banding Association (NE), 31019
Inland Lakes Research and Study Center (MI), 26091
Inmont Corp., Central Research Library (NJ), 34115
Innovation International (CT), 08075
Innovation, Creativity, and Capital Institute (TX), 48107
Innovative Learning (MD), 24232
Insect Attractants, Behavior, and Basic Biology Laboratory (FL), 13100
Insect Control and Research (MD), 24233
Institute for Advanced Studies in Asian Science and Medicine (NY), 36521
Institute for Advanced Study of the Communication Processes (FL), 13101
Institute for Aerobics Research Library (TX), 48108
Institute for Alternative Agriculture (MD), 24234
Institute for Alternative Futures (VA), 51224
Institute for Antiquity and Christianity (CA), 05418
Institute for Applied Interdisciplinary Research (OH), 40128
Institute for Applied Research Services (NM), 35021
Institute for Applied Research Services, Division of Government Research (NM), 35022
Institute for Art and Urban Resources (NY), 36522
Institute for Association Management (IL), 17263
Institute for Basic Research in Developmental Disabilities (NY), 36523
Institute for Behavioral Genetics (CO), 07111
Institute for Behavioral Research (GA), 14059
Institute for Briquetting & Agglomeration (PA), 43200
Institute for Business and Community Development (VA), 51225
Institute for Certification of Computer Professionals (IL), 17264
Institute for Child Behavior Research (CA), 05419
Institute for Child Study (IN), 18052
Institute for Child Study (MD), 24235
Institute for Coastal and Marine Resources (NC), 38046
Institute for Cognitive Studies (NJ), 34116

Institute for Community Economics (MA), 25145
Institute for Comprehensive Planning (IN), 18053
Institute for Computational Research in Engineering (KS), 20026
Institute for Computer Applications in Science and Engineering (VA), 51226
Institute for Contemporary Studies (CA), 05420
Institute for Creation Research (CA), 05421
Institute for Defense and Disarmament Studies (MA), 25146
Institute for Development of Educational Activities, Inc (OH), 40129
Institute for Disaster Research (TX), 48109
Institute for Ecological Studies (ND), 39004
Institute for Energy Development (OK), 41027
Institute for Environmental Education (OH), 40130
Institute for Environmental Health Studies (IN), 18054
Institute for Environmental Management (IL), 17265
Institute for Environmental Studies (WI), 54057
Institute for Expressive Analysis (NY), 36524
Institute for Family Research and Education (NY), 36525
Institute for Fisheries Research (MI), 26092
Institute for Fluitronics Education (IL), 17266
Institute for Fluitronics Education (WI), 54058
Institute for Food Science and Technology (WA), 52044
Institute for Food and Development Policy (CA), 05422
Institute for Foreign Policy Analysis (MA), 25147
Institute for Futures Studies and Research (OH), 40131
Institute for Graphic Communication (MA), 25148
Institute for Human Identity (NY), 36526
Institute for Hydrogen Systems (CAN), 61081
Institute for Information Management (CA), 05423
Institute for Interconnecting and Packaging Electronic Circuits (IL), 17267
Institute for Invention and Innovation (MA), 25149
Institute for Lifestyle Improvement (WI), 54059
Institute for Local Self-Reliance Information (DC), 10730
Institute for Marine Information (CA), 05424
Institute for Mathematical Studies in the Social Sciences (CA), 05425
Institute for Mediation and Conflict Resolution (NY), 36527
Institute for Medical Research Library (NJ), 34117
Institute for Mining and Minerals Research (KY), 21022
Institute for Modernization of Land Data Systems (PA), 43201
Institute for Molecular Virology (MO), 29055
Institute for Molecular and Cellular Evolution (FL), 13102
Institute for Movement Therapy (WA), 52045
Institute for Neuroscience and Behavior (DE), 09026
Institute for New Enterprise Development (MA), 25150
Institute for Palestine Studies (DC), 10731

Institute of International Education, Communications Division (NY), 36539
Institute of Judicial Administration (NY), 36540
Institute of Laboratory Animal Resources (DC), 10741
Institute of Law Research and Reform (CAN), 61084
Institute of Logopedics (KS), 20029
Institute of Makers of Explosives (DC), 10742
Institute of Management Consultants (NY), 36541
Institute of Management Sciences (RI), 44008
Institute of Management and Labor Relations (NJ), 34123
Institute of Marine Science Library (AK), 02021
Institute of Marine Sciences (NC), 38048
Institute of Marine and Atmospheric Sciences (NY), 36542
Institute of Materials Science (CT), 08077
Institute of Mineral Research (MI), 26095
Institute of Molecular Biophysics (FL), 13106
Institute of Navigation (DC), 10743
Institute of Neurological Sciences (PA), 43210
Institute of Noetic Sciences (CA), 05444
Institute of Noise Control Engineering (NY), 36543
Institute of Nuclear Materials Management (IL), 17274
Institute of Outdoor Drama (NC), 38049
Institute of Paper Chemistry, Division of Information Services (WI), 54061
Institute of Polar Studies (OH), 40132
Institute of Psychiatric Research (IN), 18056
Institute of Public Administration, Library (NY), 36544
Institute of Public Policy Studies (IPPS) (MI), 26096
Institute of Public Utilities (MI), 26097
Institute of Puerto Rican Culture (PR), 60003
Institute of Recreation Research and Service (OR), 42034
Institute of Rehabilitation Medicine (NY), 36545
Institute of Risk Management Consultants (CA), 05445
Institute of Scrap Iron and Steel (DC), 10744
Institute of Shortening & Edible Oils (DC), 10745
Institute of Social and Economic Research (AK), 02022
Institute of Society, Ethics, and the Life Sciences (NY), 36546
Institute of Store Planners (NY), 36547
Institute of Technological Studies (MI), 26098
Institute of Textile Technology Textile Information Center (VA), 51229
Institute of the Rockies (MT), 30005
Institute of Transportation Engineers (DC), 10746
Institute of Transportation Studies Library (CA), 05446
Institute of Tropical Agriculture and Human Resources (HI), 15014
Institute of Tropical Forestry (PR), 60004
Institute of Tropical Meteorology (PR), 60005
Institute of Urban and Regional Development (CA), 05447
Institute of Water Resources/Engineering Experiment Station (AK), 02023
Institute of Wood Research (MI), 26099

Institute on Aging (OR), 42035
Institute on Aging (PA), 43211
Institutes for the Achievement of Human Potential (PA), 43212
Institution for Tuberculosis Research (IL), 17275
Institutional Research Program for Higher Education (NJ), 34124
Instrument Society of America (NC), 38050
Instrumentation Systems Center (WI), 54062
Insulated Cable Engineers Association (MA), 25153
Insulation Contractors Association of America (DC), 10747
Insurance Accounting and Systems Association (NC), 38051
Insurance Information Institute (NY), 36548
Insurance Institute for Highway Safety (DC), 10748
Intellectual Property Notes (VA), 51230
Intelligence for Education (NY), 36549
Inter-American Association for Democracy and Freedom (NY), 36550
Inter-American Bar Foundation (DC), 10749
Inter-American Commission on Human Rights (DC), 10750
Inter-American Council for Medical Assistance, Education & Research (GA), 14064
Inter-American Development Bank (DC), 10751
Inter-American Foundation (VA), 51231
Inter-American Nuclear Energy Commission (DC), 10752
Inter-American Press Association (FL), 13107
Inter-American Safety Council (NJ), 34125
Inter-American Tropical Tuna Commission (CA), 05448
Inter-Financial Association (CA), 05449
Inter-Society Color Council (MA), 25154
Inter-University Consortium for Political and Social Research (MI), 26100
Inter-University Seminar on Armed Forces and Society (IL), 17276
InterDok Corp. (NY), 36551
InterFuture (NY), 36552
InterStudy (MN), 27061
Interchurch Center, Ecumenical Library (NY), 36553
Intercollegiate Broadcasting System (NY), 36554
Intercollegiate Studies Institute (PA), 43213
Intercultural Development Research Association (TX), 48113
Interfaith Action for Economic Justice (DC), 10753
Interfaith Center on Corporate Responsibility (NY), 36555
Interfaith Center to Reverse the Arms Race (CA), 05450
Intergovernmental Health Policy Project (DC), 10754
Interhelp (MA), 25155
Interior Design Educators Council (VA), 51232
Interlink Press Service (NY), 36556
Intermediate Technology (CA), 05451
Intermountain Cystic Fibrosis-Pediatric Gastrointestinal Center (UT), 49025
Intermuseum Conservation Association (OH), 40133

Internal Revenue Service Library (DC), 10755
Internal Revenue Service, Public Affairs Division (DC), 10756
Internal Revenue Service, Statistics of Income Division (DC), 10757
International Academy at Santa Barbara, Environmental Studies Institute (CA), 05452
International Academy of Biological Medicine (AZ), 03066
International Academy of Cytology (IL), 17277
International Academy of Proctology (NY), 36557
International Advertising Association (NY), 36558
International Affiliation of Independent Accounting Firms (FL), 13108
International Agency for Apiculture Development (IL), 17278
International Air Transport Association (CAN), 61085
International Airline Passengers Association (TX), 48114
International Anesthesia Research Society (OH), 40134
International Apple Institute (VA), 51233
International Arthurian Society North American Branch (CAN), 61086
International Association of Clerks, Recorders, Election Officials and Treasurers (LA), 22023
International Association for Aquatic Animal Medicine (MD), 24237
International Association for Bear Research and Management (TN), 47041
International Association for Dental Research (DC), 10758
International Association for Enterostomal Therapy (CA), 05454
International Association for Financial Planning (GA), 14065
International Association for Great Lakes Research (MI), 26101
International Association for Hydrogen Energy (FL), 13109
International Association for Identification (SC), 45013
International Association for Mathematical Geology (KS), 20032
International Association for Medical Assistance to Travellers (NY), 36559
International Association for Orthodontics (IL), 17279
International Association for Personnel Women (CA), 05455
International Association for Philosophy of Law and Social Philosophy (KS), 20033
International Association for Psychiatric Research (NY), 36561
International Association for the Physical Sciences of the Ocean (CA), 05456
International Association for the Study of Pain (WA), 52047
International Association for the Study of Traditional Asian Medicine (MA), 25156

International Association of Arson Investigators (MA), 25157
International Association of Assessing Officers (IL), 17280
International Association of Auditorium Managers (IL), 17281
International Association of Business Communicators Communication Bank (CA), 05457
International Association of Campus Law Enforcement Administrators (CT), 08079
International Association of Cancer Victims and Friends (CA), 05459
International Association of Chiefs of Police (MD), 24238
International Association of Cooking Schools (DC), 10759
International Association of Educators for World Peace (AL), 01040
International Association of Electrical Inspectors (IL), 17282
International Association of Fire Chiefs (DC), 10760
International Association of Fire Fighters (DC), 10761
International Association of Fish & Wildlife Agencies (DC), 10762
International Association of Geophysical Contractors (CO), 07117
International Association of Hospital Central Service Management (IL), 17283
International Association of Hydrological Sciences (DC), 10763
International Association of Ice Cream Manufacturers (DC), 10764
International Association of Industrial Accident Boards and Commissions (MS), 28015
International Association of Laryngectomees (NY), 36562
International Association of Machinists and Aerospace Workers (DC), 10765
International Association of Marine Science Libraries and Information Centers (FL), 13110
International Association of Milk Control Agencies (NY), 36563
International Association of Milk, Food, and Environmental Sanitarians (IA), 19031
International Association of Parents and Professionals for Safe Alternatives in Childbirth (MO), 29057
International Association of Plumbing and Mechanical Officials (CA), 05460
International Association of Printing House Craftsmen (OH), 40135
International Association of Pupil Personnel Workers (MD), 24239
International Association of Quality Circles (OH), 40136
International Association of Satellite Users and Suppliers (VA), 51235
International Association of Telecomputer Networks (FL), 13111

International Association of Tool Craftsmen (IA), 19032

International Association of Voice Identification (MI), 26103

International Association of Women Police (WA), 52048

International Association on Water Pollution Research & Control (GA), 14066

International Astronomical Union Commission on Documentation & Astronomical Data (PA), 43214

International Aviation Theft Bureau (MD), 24240

International Bank Note Society (VA), 51236

International Bicycle Touring Society (CA), 05461

International Biotoxicological Center (CA), 05462

International Bird Rescue Research Center (CA), 05463

International Bone Marrow Transplant Registry (WI), 54063

International Bottled Water Association (VA), 51237

International Boundary & Water Commission, United States & Mexico (TX), 48115

International Brangus Breeders Association (TX), 48116

International Bridge, Tunnel, and Turnpike Association (DC), 10766

International Buckskin Horse Association (IN), 18057

International Bundle Branch Block Association (CA), 05464

International Business Forms Industries (VA), 51238

International Business Machines Corp., Library and Technical Reports Center (NY), 36564

International Cancer Research Data Bank Program (MD), 24241

International Cargo Gear Bureau (NY), 36565

International Center for Aquaculture (AL), 01041

International Center for Arid and Semi-Arid Land Studies (TX), 48117

International Center for Dance Orthopaedics and Dance Therapy (CA), 05465

International Center for Health Sciences (TN), 47042

International Center for Marine Resource Development (RI), 44009

International Center for Research on Bilingualism (CAN), 61087

International Center for Research on Women (DC), 10768

International Center for the Disabled, Information Center (NY), 36567

International Center for the Solution of Environmental Problems (TX), 48118

International Center of Photography (NY), 36568

International Chemical Workers Union (OH), 40137

International Chessology Club (NC), 38052

International Childbirth Education Association (MN), 27063

International City Management Association (DC), 10769

International Civil Aviation Organisation (CAN), 61088

International Clearinghouse on Science and Mathematics Curricula Developments (MD), 24242

International Cogeneration Society (DC), 10770

International College of Acupuncture and Electro-Therapeutics (NY), 36569

International College of Applied Nutrition (CA), 05466

International College of Podiatric Laser Surgery (PA), 43215

International Commission on Ilumination, U.S. National Committee (MD), 24243

International Commission on Microbial Ecology (NY), 36570

International Commission on Radiation Units and Measurements (MD), 24244

International Committee Against Mental Illness (NY), 36571

International Committee for the Anthropology of Food & Food Habits (PA), 43216

International Communication Association (TX), 48119

International Communications Industries Association (VA), 51239

International Concerns Committee for Children (CO), 07118

International Confederation for Plastic and Reconstructive Surgery (CAN), 61089

International Confederation of Art Dealers (NY), 36572

International Conference of Building Officials (CA), 05467

International Conference of Police Chaplains (CT), 08080

International Consultants Foundation (MD), 24245

International Consumer Credit Association (MO), 29058

International Copper Research Association (NY), 36573

International Coroners and Medical Examiners Association (IL), 17284

International Cotton Advisory Committee (DC), 10771

International Council for Computers in Education (OR), 42036

International Council for Development of Underutilized Plants (CA), 05468

International Council for Distance Education (CAN), 61090

International Council for Health, Physical Education, and Recreation (VA), 51240

International Council for Small Business (GA), 14067

International Council of Associations of Surfing (FL), 13112

International Council of Societies of Pathology (MD), 24246

International Council on Education for Teaching (DC), 10772

International Courtly Literature Society (TN), 47043

International Crane Foundation (WI), 54064

International Cystic Fibrosis Association (OH), 40138

International Masonry Institute (DC), 10789
International Material Management Society (IL), 17290
International Meteorology Aviation and Electronics Institute (CO), 07120
International Microwave Power Institute (VA), 51246
International Mobile Air Conditioning Association (TX), 48121
International Monetary Fund Bureau of Statistics (DC), 10790
International Municipal Signal Association (TX), 48122
International Museum of Airlines (MD), 24255
International Museum of Photography (NY), 36587
International Museum of Surgical Science and Hall of Fame (IL), 17291
International Museum of the Horse (KY), 21023
International Myomassethics Federation (OH), 40139
International Myopia Prevention Association (PA), 43222
International Narcotic Enforcement Officers Association (NY), 36588
International Naturopathic Association (CA), 05476
International Naval Research Organization (OH), 40140
International North Pacific Fisheries Commission (CAN), 61091
International Numismatic Society (DC), 10791
International Nutrition Communication Service (MA), 25164
International Occultation Timing Association (IL), 17292
International Oceanographic Foundation (FL), 13114
International Oil Scouts Association (TX), 48123
International Ozone Association (CT), 08082
International Pacific Halibut Commission (WA), 52050
International Pacific Salmon Fisheries Commission (CAN), 61092
International Palm Society (CA), 05477
International Paper Company, Southlands Experiment Forest (GA), 14069
International Peace Academy (NY), 36589
International Personnel Management Association (DC), 10792
International Petroleum Institute (NY), 36590
International Pipe Association (IL), 17293
International Planned Parenthood Federation (NY), 36591
International Plant Protection Center (OR), 42038
International Polka Association (IL), 17294
International Population Program (NY), 36592
International Porcelain Artist Teachers Organization (OK), 41028
International Precious Metals Institute (PA), 43223
International Primate Protection League (SC), 45014
International Prisoners Aid Association (KY), 21024
International Professional Rodeo Association (OK), 41029
International Progeria Registry (NY), 36593

International Project for Soft Energy Paths (CA), 05478
International Radio Club of America (WA), 52051
International Reading Association (DE), 09027
International Reference Organization in Forensic Medicine and Sciences (KS), 20034
International Remote Sensing Institute (CA), 05479
International Reports (NY), 36594
International Rescue Committee (NY), 36595
International Rescue and Emergency Care Association (MN), 27066
International Research Center for Energy and Economic Development (CO), 07121
International Research and Exchanges Board (NY), 36596
International Resource Development (CT), 08083
International Resources Consultants (DC), 10793
International Rett's Syndrome Association (MD), 24256
International Right of Way Association (CA), 05480
International Road Federation (DC), 10794
International Rural Water Resources Development Laboratory (MD), 24257
International Sand Collector's Society (CT), 08084
International Sanitary Supply Association (IL), 17295
International Schools Services (NJ), 34128
International Sculpture Center (DC), 10795
International Seal, Label, and Cigar Band Society (AZ), 03067
International Silo Association (IA), 19033
International Slurry Seal Association (DC), 10796
International Society for Animal Rights (PA), 43224
International Society for Astrological Research (CA), 05481
International Society for Bioelectricity (MA), 25166
International Society for Cardiovascular Surgery (MA), 25167
International Society for Chronobiology (MD), 24258
International Society for Clinical Laboratory Technology (MO), 29061
International Society for Fluoride Research (MI), 26106
International Society for Geothermal Engineering (CA), 05482
International Society for Labor Law & Social Security (DC), 10797
International Society for Optical Engineering (WA), 52052
International Society for Organ History and Preservation (NH), 33009
International Society for Pediatric Neurosurgery (IL), 17296
International Society for Plant Pathology (MN), 27068
International Society for Stereology (IN), 18060
International Society for Terrain-Vehicle Systems (NH), 33010
International Society for the Arts, Sciences, and Technology (CA), 05483
International Society for the Protection of Mustangs & Burros (NV), 32016
International Society of Appraisers, Ltd. (IL), 17297

Jackson Laboratory (ME), 23008

James Ford Bell Technical Center Library (MN), 27072

James K.K. Look Laboratory of Oceanographic Engineering (HI), 15016

James Leffel and Co. (OH), 40143

James R. Slater Museum of Natural History (WA), 52055

Janus Information Facility (CA), 05491

Japan Economic Institute (DC), 10817

Japan Foundation (NY), 36606

Japan Information & Culture Center (DC), 10818

Japan Information Center (NY), 36607

Japan Society (NY), 36608

Japan-America Society of Washington (DC), 10819

Japanese-American Citizens League (CA), 05492

Japanese-American Cultural and Community Center (CA), 05493

Japan-United States Concert Society (NY), 36609

Jerry Lewis Neuromuscular Disease Research Center (TX), 48130

Jet Propulsion Lab Library (CA), 05494

Jewelry Industry Council (NY), 36610

Jewish Braille Institute of America Library (NY), 36611

Jewish Education Service of North America (NY), 36612

Jewish Hospital of Cincinnati Medical Center (OH), 40144

Jewish Media Service (NY), 36613

Jewish Museum (NY), 36614

Joan Staats Library (ME), 23009

Job Accomodation Network (WV), 53018

Jobs in Energy (DC), 10820

John Carroll University Seismological Observatory (OH), 40145

John F. Kennedy Center for Research on Education & Human Development (TN), 47045

John G. White Collection of Folklore, Orientalia, and Chess (OH), 40146

John G. Wolbach Library (MA), 25171

John H. Blankenbuehler Memorial Library (OH), 40147

John H. Gifford Memorial Library and Information Center (OH), 40148

John Howard Association (IL), 17306

John Milton Society for the Blind (NY), 36615

John W. Keys Speech and Hearing Center (OK), 41031

John and Mable Ringling Museum of Art (FL), 13117

Johnson Controls Corporate Information Center/Library (WI), 54067

Johnson Research Foundation (PA), 43348

Joint Agricultural Weather Facility (DC), 10822

Joint Center for Environmental and Urban Problems (FL), 13118

Joint Center for Political Studies (DC), 10823

Joint Commission on Accreditation of Hospitals (IL), 17307

Joint Committee on Powder Diffraction Standards (PA), 43226

Joint Committee on Printing, Congressional Record Index Office (DC), 10824

Joint Council on Economic Education (NY), 36616

Joint Council on Educational Telecommunications (DC), 10825

Joint Highway Research Project (IN), 18061

Jojoba Growers Association (AZ), 03069

Jones & Laughlin Steel Corp., Graham Research Laboratory (PA), 43227

Jonsson Comprehensive Cancer Center, Information Service (CA), 05814

Josephine D. Randall Junior Museum (CA), 05495

Joslin Diabetes Center (MA), 25172

Journalism Association of Community Colleges (CA), 05496

Judah L. Magnes Memorial Museum, Western Jewish History Center (CA), 05497

Judicial, Fiscal & Social Branch (DC), 10827

Jules Stein Eye Institute (CA), 05498

Julie Moore & Associations (CA), 05499

Jury Verdict Research (OH), 40149

Justice Library (DC), 10828

Justice System Training Association (WI), 54068

Juvenile Diabetes Foundation (NY), 36618

K-25 Information Resource Center (TN), 47046

Kafka Society of America (PA), 43228

Kaiser Aluminum and Chemical Corp. Library (CA), 05500

Kaiser Engineers Hanford Co. Library (WA), 52056

Kansas Cosmosphere and Discovery Center (KS), 20037

Kansas Crop Improvement Association (KS), 20038

Kansas State Historical Society (KS), 20039

Kansas State Library (KS), 20040

Kansas University Affiliated Facility (KS), 20041

Katharine Angell Library (NY), 36619

Keeneland Library (KY), 21026

Keep America Beautiful (NY), 36620

Kempe National Center for the Prevention and Treatment of Child Abuse and Neglect (CO), 07124

Kendall Whaling Museum (MA), 25174

Kennedy Institute of Ethics Library (DC), 10829

Kennedy Space Center Library (FL), 13119

Kent State Center for Peaceful Change (OH), 40150

Kentucky Derby Museum (KY), 21028

Kentucky Historical Society Library (KY), 21029

Kentucky Research and Services (KY), 21030

Kentucky State Library Services (KY), 21031

Kenya Pyrethrum Information Centre (IL), 17308

Keratorefractive Society (TX), 48131

Kerr Industrial Applications Center (OK), 41032

Kessler Institute for Rehabilitation (NJ), 34131

Kestrel Institute (CA), 05501

Kevin Parsons and Associates (WI), 54069

Key Collectors International (AZ), 03070

Kidney Disease Institute (NY), 36622

Kinnetic Laboratories (CA), 05502

Kinsey Institute for Research in Sex, Gender, and Reproduction (IN), 18062

Kinship (DC), 10830

Kissel Kar Klub (WI), 54070

Kitt Peak National Observatory Library (AZ), 03071

Klipsch and Associates (AR), 04051
Knowledge Foundation (NJ), 34132
Knudtsen Renewable Resources Center (NV), 32018
Kosh Louiselle Lurito & Associates (VA), 51251
Krautkramer-Branson (PA), 43230
Kresge Eye Institute (MI), 26108
Kresge Hearing Research Institute (MI), 26109
Kresge Hearing Research Laboratory (OR), 42040

L-5 Society (AZ), 03072
L. Lee Stryker Center for Management Studies (MI), 26110
LAUNCH, The Coalition of LD Adults (TX), 48132
LDV Electro Science Industries (NY), 36623
LOEX Clearinghouse (MI), 26111
LTV Steel Corp., Research Center Library (OH), 40151
Laban/Bartenieff Institute of Movement Studies (NY), 36624
Labor Education and Research Service (OH), 40152
Labor Institute (NY), 36625
Labor Occupational Health Program (CA), 05503
Labor Relations and Research Center (MA), 25176
Labor Research Association (NY), 36626
Laboratory Animal Center (OH), 40153
Laboratory for Applications of Remote Sensing (IN), 18063
Laboratory for Atmospheric Probing (IL), 17310
Laboratory for Atmospheric and Space Physics (CO), 07126
Laboratory for Comparative Biochemistry (CA), 05504
Laboratory for Computer Graphics and Spatial Analysis (MA), 25177
Laboratory for Experimental Medicine and Surgery in Primates (NY), 36627
Laboratory for Human Performance Research (PA), 43231
Laboratory for Isotope Geology and Geochemistry (OH), 40154
Laboratory for Laser Energetics Library (NY), 36628
Laboratory for Manufacturing and Productivity (MA), 25178
Laboratory for Radiation and Polymer Science (MD), 24263
Laboratory for Research on the Structure of Matter (PA), 43232
Laboratory for Surface Studies (WI), 54071
Laboratory of Exocrine Physiology (AL), 01043
Laboratory of Limnology (WI), 54072
Laboratory of Medical Genetics (AL), 01044
Laboratory of Molecular Genetics (MD), 24264
Laboratory of Molecular Hematology (MD), 24265
Laboratory of Nocturnal Cognition (VA), 51252
Laboratory of Nuclear Studies (NY), 36629
Laboratory of Ornithology (NY), 36630
Laboratory of Plasma Studies (NY), 36631
Laboratory of Radiation Ecology (WA), 52057
Laboratory of Subsurface Geology (MI), 26112
Laboratory of Tree-Ring Research (AZ), 03073
Lacrosse Foundation (MD), 24266
Lake Carriers' Association (OH), 40155

Lake Michigan Federation (IL), 17311
Lake Ponchartrain Laboratories (LA), 22026
Laminated Fiberglass Insulation Producers Association (OH), 40156
Lancaster Cleft Palate Clinic (PA), 43233
Land Development Institute, Ltd. (DC), 10831
Land Improvement Contractors of America (IL), 17313
Landscape Architecture Research & Information Clearinghouse (DC), 10832
Laramie Project Office Library (WY), 55010
Laser Institute of America (OH), 40157
Latin America Parents Association (NY), 36632
Latin American Scholarship Program of American Universities (MA), 25179
Latin American Studies Association (TX), 48133
Laubach Literacy International (NY), 36633
Laurence-Moon-Biedl Syndrome Network (MD), 24267
Law Enforcement Standards Laboratory (MD), 24268
Law Engineering Testing Company (GA), 14071
Law of the Sea Institute (HI), 15017
Lawrence Berkeley Laboratory Isotopes Project (CA), 05505
Lawrence D. Bell Memorial Library (NY), 36634
Lawyers' Committee for Civil Rights Under Law (DC), 10833
Lazar Institute (VA), 51253
Lazy Eye, Ltd. (WI), 54073
Lead Industries Association (NY), 36637
Leader Dogs for the Blind (MI), 26113
Leadership Conference on Civil Rights (DC), 10834
League Against Nuclear Dangers (WI), 54074
League for Human Rights in Divorce (NY), 36638
League for International Food Education (DC), 10835
League of American Wheelmen (MD), 24269
League of Historic American Theatres (DC), 10836
League of Lefthanders (NJ), 34134
League of Oregon Cities (OR), 42041
League of Women Voters Education Fund (DC), 10837
League to Save Lake Tahoe (CA), 05506
Learning Corp. of America (IL), 17314
Learning Exchange (IL), 17315
Learning Research & Development Center (PA), 43234
Learning Resources Network (KS), 20042
Learning Technology Institute (VA), 51254
Lebanese Information & Research Center (DC), 10839
Lee Coombe Memorial Library (NY), 36639
Lefthanders International (KS), 20043
Legal Economic Evaluations (CA), 05507
Legal Services Corporation, Public Affairs Office (DC), 10840
Legal Services for Children (CA), 05508
Legislative & Diplomatic Branch (DC), 10841
Leisure Studies Data Bank (CAN), 61095
Leo Baeck Institute (NY), 36640
Lepidopterists' Society (CA), 05509
Les Amis du Vin (MD), 24270
Let's-Play-To-Grow (DC), 10842

Letterman Army Institute of Research (CA), 05510
Lettumplay (DC), 10843
Leukemia Society of America (NY), 36641
Libel Defense Resource Center (NY), 36643
Libraries Museum Reference Center (DC), 10844
Library Binding Institute (NY), 36644
Library Information Services (CA), 05511
Library Information and On-line Network Systems (NY), 36645
Library of Congress, Exchange & Gift Division (DC), 10847
Library of Congress, Exhibits Office (DC), 10848
Library of Congress, Information Office (DC), 10849
Library of Congress, New Serial Titles Section (DC), 10851
Library of Congress, Science & Technology Division (DC), 10852
Library of International Relations (IL), 17316
Library of the National Museum of American Art & National Portrait Gallery (DC), 10853
Life Insurance Marketing and Research Association (CT), 08086
Life of the Land (HI), 15018
Lifeline for Wildlife (NY), 36646
Lighter-Than-Air Society (OH), 40158
Lighting Research Institute (DC), 10854
Lightning & Transients Research Institute (MN), 27073
Lightning Protection Institute (IL), 17317
Lillian Paley Center for the Visual Arts (CA), 05512
Limnological Research Center (MN), 27074
Lincoln Continental Owners Club (AZ), 03074
Lincoln Electric Co. (OH), 40159
Lincoln Institute of Land Policy (MA), 25181
Lincoln Owners Club (IL), 17318
Lincoln Zephyr Owner's Club (PA), 43236
Lindsley F. Kimball Research Institute (NY), 36647
Linguistic Society of America (DC), 10855
Linguistics Research Center (TX), 48134
Linus Pauling Institute of Science and Medicine (CA), 05513
Lipid Research Clinic (DC), 10856
Liquid Crystal Institute (OH), 40160
Lister Hill Library of the Health Sciences (AL), 01045
Lister Hill National Center for Biomedical Communications (MD), 24271
Literacy Volunteers of America (NY), 36648
Lithium Information Center (WI), 54075
Little League Baseball (PA), 43237
Little People of America (CA), 05514
Litton Industries Guidance and Control Systems (CA), 05516
Livestock Conservation Institute (MN), 27075
Living Bank International (TX), 48136
Lloyd Library and Museum (OH), 40161
Lloyd's Register of Shipping (NY), 36649
Lockheed-Georgia Company Technical Information Department (GA), 14072
Log Home Guide Information Center (TN), 47047
Logistics Management Institute (MD), 24272
Lollipop Power (NC), 38054

Lombardi Cancer Research Center (DC), 10857
Los Alamos National Laboratory Libraries (NM), 35026
Los Angeles Communications Law Program (CA), 05517
Los Angeles Rubber Group Foundation (CA), 05518
Louis Harris and Associates (NY), 36650
Louisiana Agricultural Experiment Station (LA), 22027
Louisiana Arts and Science Center (LA), 22028
Louisiana Cooperative Fishery Research Unit (LA), 22029
Louisiana Cooperative Wildlife Research Unit (LA), 22030
Louisiana Geological Survey (LA), 22031
Louisiana Historical Association (LA), 22032
Louisiana Oil Marketers Association (LA), 22034
Louisiana Universities Marine Consortium (LA), 22035
Louisville Twin Study (KY), 21032
Lovelace Medical Foundation Library (NM), 35027
Lovely Lane Museum (MD), 24273
Low Temperature Physics Laboratory (KS), 20044
Lowe's Syndrome Association (IN), 18064
Lowell Observatory (AZ), 03075
Lower Mississippi Valley Flood Control Association (TN), 47048
Luckey Laboratories (CA), 05519
Ludwig von Mises Institute (AL), 01046
Lumberman's Museum (ME), 23010
Lunar and Planetary Institute (TX), 48137
Lunar and Planetary Laboratory (AZ), 03076
Lupus Foundation of America (GA), 14073
Lupus Foundation of America (MO), 29064
Lupus Network (CT), 08087
Luso-American Education Foundation (CA), 05520
Lutheran Council in the U.S.A., Records and Information Center (NY), 36651
Lyndon Baines Johnson Library (TX), 48138

M&T Chemicals Inc. Technical and Business Information Center (NJ), 34135
M. D. Anderson Hospital & Tumor Institute Research Medical Library (TX), 48139
MAP International Learning Resource Center (GA), 14074
MDS Industry Association (DC), 10858
MEGA Systems (GA), 14075
MEPCO/ELECTRA (NJ), 34136
MSA Research Corp. (PA), 43238
MSU-DOE Plant Research Laboratory (MI), 26114
MTM Association for Standards and Research (NJ), 34137
Machinability Data Center (OH), 40162
Machinery and Allied Products Institute (DC), 10859
Magazine Publishers Association (NY), 36652
Magic Lantern Society of the United States and Canada (WA), 52058
Magnavox Electronic Systems Corp. Library (IN), 18065
Magnesium Elektron (NJ), 34138

May Department Stores Co. Information Center (MO), 29068

Mayo Foundation Pain Management Center (MN), 27079

McArdle Laboratory for Cancer Research (WI), 54082

McCook Research Laboratories Library (IL), 17329

McDonnell Aircraft Library (MO), 29069

McGill Cancer Centre (CAN), 61097

McGill Subarctic Research Station (CAN), 61098

Mead Corp. Central Research Library (OH), 40164

Meat Laboratory (KY), 21033

Meat Machinery Manufacturers Institute (DC), 10871

Mechanical Contractors Association of America (MD), 24282

Mechanized Information Center (OH), 40165

Meckler Publishing (CT), 08092

Media Alliance (CA), 05528

Media Basics (NY), 36663

Media Center for Children (NY), 36664

Media Information Service (PA), 43242

Media Network, Information Center (NY), 36665

Medic Alert Foundation International (CA), 05530

Medical College of Georgia Comprehensive Sickle Cell Center (GA), 14079

Medical College of Pennsylvania Archives & Special Collections on Women in Medicine (PA), 43243

Medical Electronics Laboratory (WI), 54083

Medical Group Management Association (CO), 07129

Medical Library Association (IL), 17330

Medical Library Center of New York (NY), 36666

Medical Literature Information Center (MO), 29070

Medical Media Production Service (TN), 47090

Medical Passport Foundation (FL), 13122

Medical Rehab Research and Training Center (CO), 07130

Medical Rehabilitation Research and Training Center (MA), 25193

Medical Rehabilitation Research and Training Center in Spinal Cord Dysfunction (AL), 01048

Medical Research Laboratories (CT), 08093

Medical-Dental-Hospital Bureaus of America (IL), 17331

Medication Information Service (CA), 05531

Medicine in the Public Interest (MA), 25194

Medieval Academy of America (MA), 25195

Medieval Institute (IN), 18066

Meiklejohn Civil Liberties Institute (CA), 05532

Mellon Institute Rail Systems Center (PA), 43244

Memorial Cancer Research Foundation of Southern California (CA), 05533

Memorial Library (WI), 54084

Memphis Pink Palace Museum and Planetarium (TN), 47049

Men's Garden Clubs of America (IA), 19039

Men's Rights (CA), 05534

Men's Rights Association (MN), 27080

Mended Hearts (TX), 48141

Menninger Foundation Professional Library (KS), 20045

Mennonite Library and Archives (KS), 20046

Mental Health Association Information Service (VA), 51260

Mental Health Information Service (CA), 05535

Mental Health Institute (NY), 36667

Mental Health Law Project (DC), 10872

Mental Health Materials Center (NY), 36668

Mental Health Research Institute , Library (MI), 26116

Mental Research Institute (CA), 05536

Mental Retardation Association of America (UT), 49026

Mental Retardation Association of Utah and America (UT), 49027

Mental Retardation Research Center (CA), 05537

Menu—The International Software Database (CO), 07131

Merck Forest Foundation (VT), 50013

Merion Bluegrass Association (NY), 36670

Merit Systems Protection Board (DC), 10873

Merrell Dow Research Institute Library (OH), 40166

Merrimack Valley Textile Museum (MA), 25196

Metal Building Manufacturers Association (OH), 40167

Metal Finishing Supplier Association (MI), 26117

Metal Lath/Steel Framing Association (IL), 17332

Metals Information (OH), 40168

Metals and Ceramics Information Center (OH), 40169

Meteor Crater Museum of Astrogeology (AZ), 03077

Meteoritical Society (TX), 48143

Meteorological Research Facilities (PA), 43245

Metro-Help National Runaway Switchboard (IL), 17333

Metropolitan Museum of Art, Costume Institute (NY), 36672

Metz Owners Club Register (NC), 38056

Mexican American Community Services Agency (CA), 05538

Meyer Center for Developmental Pediatrics (TX), 48144

Miami Geological Society (FL), 13124

Miami Serpentarium Laboratories (FL), 13125

Michael Fund / International Foundation for Genetic Research (PA), 43246

Michigan Association for Computer Users in Learning (MI), 26118

Michigan Basin Geological Society (MI), 26119

Michigan-Canadian Bigfoot Information Center (MI), 26124

Michigan Diabetes Research and Training Center (MI), 26120

Michigan Memorial-Phoenix Project (MI), 26121

Michigan Molecular Institute (MI), 26122

Michigan Pure Water Council (MI), 26123

Microbeam Analysis Society (CA), 05539

Microbiological Associates (MD), 24284

Microelectronics Center of N.C. (NC), 38057

Microelectronics and Computer Technology Corp. Library (TX), 48145

Microform Reading Room (DC), 10874

Micromedia (CAN), 61099

Microneurography Society (VA), 51261

Mid Atlantic States Arts Consortium (MD), 24285

Morality in Media (NY), 36679
Moravian Church, Northern Province (PA), 43254
Moravian Historical Society (PA), 43255
Moravian Music Foundation (NC), 38059
Morgantown Energy Technology Center (WV), 53020
Morikami Museum of Japanese Culture (FL), 13128
Mormon History Association (UT), 49029
Morris Animal Foundation (CO), 07135
Morrison Observatory (MO), 29078
Mortgage Bankers Association of America Library (DC), 10882
Morton Collectanea (FL), 13129
Moss Landing Marine Laboratories (CA), 05543
Mossbauer Effect Data Center (NC), 38060
Mote Marine Laboratory (FL), 13130
Mothers Against Drunk Drivers (TX), 48147
Motion Picture Association of America (DC), 10883
Motion Picture, Broadcasting & Recorded Sound Division (DC), 10884
Motor Bus Society (NJ), 34142
Motor Vehicle Manufacturers Association of the United States, Patent and Trademark Department Library (MI), 26126
Motor and Equipment Manufacturers Association (NJ), 34143
Motorcycle Industry Council Government Relations Office (VA), 51265
Motorcycle Safety Foundation Information Resource Center (PA), 43256
Motorcycle Safety Foundation Research Department (CA), 05544
Mount Cuba Astronomical Observatory (DE), 09028
Mount Desert Island Biological Laboratory (ME), 23021
Mount Sinai Pain Center (FL), 13131
Mount Sinai School of Medicine, Human Sexuality Program (NY), 36680
Mount Washington Observatory (NH), 33011
Mount Wilson and Las Campanas Observatories Library (CA), 05545
Mountain Administrative Support Center Library Division (CO), 07136
Mountain Plains Regional Resource Center (UT), 49030
Movari (WA), 52060
Movement for a New Society (PA), 43257
Movie Star News (NY), 36681
Mueller Brass Co. Library (MI), 26127
Multi-Focus (CA), 05546
Multiloque (MI), 26128
Multipurpose Arthritis Center (MA), 25202
Multipurpose Arthritis Center (AL), 01052
Multipurpose Arthritis Center (MO), 29079
Municipal Arborists Urban Foresters Society (NJ), 34144
Munsell Color (MD), 24286
Murphy Center for the Codification of Human and Organizational Law (MD), 24287
Muscular Dystrophy Association (NY), 36682
Museum Applied Science Center for Archaeology (PA), 43258

Museum Computer Network (NY), 36683
Museum Consultants International (DC), 10886
Museum of Afro-American History (MA), 25203
Museum of Anthropology (MI), 26129
Museum of Anthropology (PA), 43259
Museum of Arts and Sciences (FL), 13132
Museum of Broadcasting (NY), 36684
Museum of Comparative Zoology Library (MA), 25204
Museum of Contemporary Art (IL), 17340
Museum of Early Southern Decorative Arts (NC), 38061
Museum of Geology (SD), 46011
Museum of Geoscience (LA), 22037
Museum of Independent Telephony (KS), 20048
Museum of Invertebrate Paleontology (KS), 20049
Museum of Modern Art, Department of Film (NY), 36685
Museum of Natural History (KS), 20050
Museum of New Mexico (NM), 35029
Museum of Northern Arizona (AZ), 03080
Museum of Our National Heritage (MA), 25205
Museum of Paleontology (MI), 26130
Museum of Science and Industry (FL), 13133
Museum of Science and Space Transit Planetarium (FL), 13134
Museum of Southwestern Biology (NM), 35030
Museum of Systematic Biology (CA), 05547
Museum of Tobacco Art and History (TN), 47052
Museum of Vertebrate Zoology (CA), 05548
Museum of Western Colo (CO), 07137
Museum of Zoology (MI), 26131
Museum of the Cherokee Indian (NC), 38062
Museum of the City of Washington (DC), 10887
Museum of the Confederacy (VA), 51266
Museum of the Fur Trade (NE), 31022
Museum of the Great Plains (OK), 41033
Museum of the Ozarks (MO), 29080
Music Associates of America (NJ), 34145
Music Critics Association (MD), 24288
Music Distributors Association (NY), 36687
Music Division (DC), 10888
Music Educators National Conference (VA), 51267
Music Industry Educators Association (FL), 13135
Music Resource Center (DE), 09029
Musical Box Society, International (IN), 18068
Musicians National Hot Line Association (UT), 49031
Muslim Bibliographic Center (CO), 07138
Mutilation Data Center (CA), 05549
Myasthenia Gravis Foundation (NY), 36688
Mycological Herbarium (WA), 52061
Myopia International Research Foundation (NY), 36689
Mystic Seaport Museum/G.W. Blunt White Library (CT), 08095

NAHB Research Foundation (MD), 24289
NASA Ames Research Center Library (CA), 05550
NASA Computer Software Management & Information Center (GA), 14081
NASA Industrial Application Center (CA), 05551

National Association for Drama Therapy (CT), 08098

National Association for Female Executives (NY), 36699

National Association for Foreign Student Affairs (DC), 10914

National Association for Gifted Children (MN), 27089

National Association for Girls and Women in Sport (VA), 51276

National Association for Hearing and Speech Action (MD), 24298

National Association for Home Care, Research Division (DC), 10915

National Association for Human Development (DC), 10916

National Association for Independent Living (VA), 51277

National Association for Outlaw and Lawman History (WY), 55011

National Association for Poetry Therapy (NY), 36700

National Association for Practical Nurse Education and Service (MO), 29081

National Association for Practical Nurse Education and Services (NY), 36701

National Association for Regional Ballet (NY), 36702

National Association for Research in Science Teaching (CAN), 61103

National Association for Retired Credit Union People (WI), 54087

National Association for Rural Mental Health (MD), 24299

National Association for Search & Rescue (DC), 10917

National Association for Sickle Cell Disease (CA), 05561

National Association for Sickle Cell Disease (CA), 05562

National Association for Sport and Physical Education (VA), 51278

National Association for State Information Systems (KY), 21035

National Association for Visually Handicapped (NY), 36703

National Association for the Advancement of Black Americans in Vocational Education (TN), 47053

National Association for the Advancement of Colored People (NY), 36704

National Association for the Advancement of Humane Education (CT), 08099

National Association for the Cottage Industry (IL), 17345

National Association for the Craniofacially Handicapped (TN), 47054

National Association for the Deaf-Blind (WA), 52062

National Association for the Education of Young Children (DC), 10918

National Association of Accountants (NJ), 34150

National Association of Activity Therapy & Rehabilitation Program Directors (DC), 10919

National Association of Alcoholism and Drug Abuse Counselors (VA), 51279

National Association of Allied Health Schools (IN), 18069

National Association of Animal Breeders (MO), 29082

National Association of Anorexia Nervosa and Associated Disorders (IL), 17346

National Association of Antique Automobile Clubs of Canada (CAN), 61104

National Association of Architectural Metal Manufacturers (IL), 17347

National Association of Area Agencies on Aging (DC), 10920

National Association of Area Labor-Management Committees (MD), 24300

National Association of Atomic Veterans (IA), 19042

National Association of Barber Schools (NE), 31024

National Association of Bedding Manufacturers (VA), 51280

National Association of Biology Teachers (VA), 51281

National Association of Black Accountants (DC), 10921

National Association of Black-Owned Broadcasters (DC), 10922

National Association of Board of Examiners for Nursing Home Administrators (TX), 48155

National Association of Boards of Pharmacy (IL), 17348

National Association of Breweriana Advertising (WI), 54088

National Association of Brick Distributors (VA), 51282

National Association of Broadcasters (DC), 10923

National Association of Business & Educational Radio (DC), 10924

National Association of Chain Drug Stores (VA), 51283

National Association of Childbearing Centers (PA), 43264

National Association of Church Personnel Administrators (OH), 40175

National Association of College & University Business Officers (DC), 10925

National Association of College Admissions Counselors (IL), 17349

National Association of Commissions for Women (NJ), 34151

National Association of Community Health Centers (DC), 10926

National Association of Composers-USA (CA), 05563

National Association of Concerned Veterans (NY), 36705

National Association of Corrosion Engineers (TX), 48156

National Association of Cosmetology Schools (DC), 10927

National Association of Counsel for Children (CO), 07141

National Association of Counties (DC), 10928

National Association of County Engineers (IA), 19043

National Association of County Planning Directors (DC), 10929

National Association of Real Estate Investment Trusts (DC), 10946

National Association of Realtors Department of Economics & Research (DC), 10947

National Association of Recycling Industries (NY), 36712

National Association of Regional Councils (DC), 10948

National Association of Regulatory Utility Commissioners (DC), 10949

National Association of Rehabilitation Facilities (DC), 10950

National Association of Relay Manufacturers (IN), 18070

National Association of Retail Druggists (VA), 51292

National Association of Retired Federal Employees (DC), 10951

National Association of Rocketry (PA), 43267

National Association of Royalty Owners (OK), 41036

National Association of School Music Dealers (NC), 38069

National Association of School Nurses (ME), 23022

National Association of School Security Directors (MD), 24303

National Association of Schools of Art and Design (VA), 51294

National Association of Schools of Music (VA), 51295

National Association of Schools of Public Affairs & Administration (DC), 10952

National Association of Schools of Theatre (VA), 51296

National Association of Secondary School Principals (VA), 51297

National Association of Securities Dealers (DC), 10953

National Association of Service Merchandising (IL), 17358

National Association of Small Business Investment Companies (DC), 10954

National Association of Social Workers (MD), 24304

National Association of State Approved Colleges & Universities (DC), 10955

National Association of State Aviation Officials (DC), 10956

National Association of State Boards of Education (VA), 51298

National Association of State Departments of Agriculture (DC), 10957

National Association of State Mental Health Program Directors (DC), 10958

National Association of State Mental Retardation Program Directors (VA), 51299

National Association of State Outdoor Recreation Liaison Officers (VA), 51300

National Association of State Units on Aging (DC), 10959

National Association of State Universities & Land-Grant Colleges (DC), 10961

National Association of Student Financial Aid Administrators (DC), 10962

National Association of Student Personnel Administrators (OH), 40177

National Association of Teachers of Singing (NY), 36713

National Association of Temporary Services (VA), 51301

National Association of Timetable Collectors (OR), 42046

National Association of Towns & Townships (DC), 10963

National Association of Trade & Technical Schools (DC), 10964

National Association of Underwater Instructors (CA), 05570

National Association of Urban Flood Management Agencies (DC), 10965

National Association of Watch & Clock Collectors (PA), 43268

National Association of Wheat Growers (DC), 10966

National Association of Wholesaler-Distributors (DC), 10967

National Association of Women Artists (NY), 36714

National Association of Women Business Owners (IL), 17360

National Association of Women Highway Safety Leaders (MD), 24305

National Association of Women in Construction (TX), 48157

National Association of the Deaf (MD), 24306

National Association of the Physically Handicapped (OH), 40178

National Association of the Remodeling Industry (VA), 51302

National Association on Drug Abuse Problems (NY), 36715

National Association on Standard Medical Vocabulary (NY), 36716

National Association on Volunteers in Criminal Justice (OH), 40180

National Association to Aid Fat Americans (NY), 36717

National Association to Keep and Bear Arms (WA), 52063

National Asthma Center LUNG LINE Information Service (CO), 07142

National Astrological Society (NY), 36718

National Ataxia Foundation (MN), 27091

National Athletic Health Institute (CA), 05571

National Athletic Trainers' Association (NC), 38070

National Atomic Museum (NM), 35031

National Audubon Society (NY), 36719

National Automobile Dealers Association Communications Group (VA), 51303

National Automobile Theft Bureau (IL), 17361

National Automotive Parts Association (GA), 14082

National Automotive Radiator Service Association (PA), 43269

National Avionics Society (MN), 27092

National Biomedical Research Foundation (DC), 10968

National Center for Toxicological Research (MD), 24323

National Center for Urban Ethnic Affairs (DC), 10995

National Center for Youth Law (CA), 05574

National Center for the Prevention and Control of Rape (MD), 24324

National Center for the Study of Collective Bargaining in Higher Education and the Professions (NY), 36726

National Center for the Study of Corporal Punishment & Alternatives in the Schools (PA), 43271

National Center for the Thermodynamic Data of Minerals (VA), 51309

National Center on Arts & the Aging (DC), 10996

National Center on Institutions and Alternatives Office of Public Information (VA), 51310

National Center on Women and Family Law (NY), 36727

National Chamber of Commerce for Women (NY), 36728

National Child Nutrition Project (PA), 43272

National Child Safety Council (MI), 26135

National Child Support Enforcement Reference Center (MD), 24325

National Christmas Tree Association (WI), 54091

National Chronic Pain Outreach Association (VA), 51311

National Chrysanthemum Society (VA), 51313

National Citizens' Coalition for Nursing Home Reform (DC), 10998

National Classification Management Society (MD), 24326

National Clay Pipe Institute (DC), 10999

National Clean Air Coalition (DC), 11001

National Clearing House of Rehabilitation Training Materials (OK), 41037

National Clearinghouse Library (DC), 11002

National Clearinghouse for Alcohol Information (MD), 24327

National Clearinghouse for Bilingual Education (VA), 51314

National Clearinghouse for Commuter Programs (MD), 24328

National Clearinghouse for Family Planning Information (VA), 51315

National Clearinghouse for Legal Services (IL), 17362

National Clearinghouse for Primary Care Information (VA), 51317

National Clearinghouse on Marital Rape (CA), 05575

National Clearinghouse, Nuclear Weapons Freeze Campaign (MO), 29088

National Cleft Palate Association (KS), 20054

National Climate Program Office (MD), 24329

National Climatic Data Center (NC), 38072

National Coal Association (DC), 11003

National Coal Resources Data System (VA), 51318

National Coalition Against Censorship (NY), 36729

National Coalition Against the Death Penalty (PA), 43273

National Coalition for Jail Reform (DC), 11004

National Coalition for Marine Conservation (GA), 14083

National Coalition for the Homeless (NY), 36730

National Coalition of Alternative Community Schools (MI), 26136

National Coalition of Gay Sexually Transmitted Disease Services (WI), 54092

National Coalition of Independent College & University Students (DC), 11005

National Coalition of Resident Councils (MN), 27093

National Coalition on Television Violence (IL), 17363

National Coalition to Ban Handguns (DC), 11006

National Cocaine Hotline (NJ), 34155

National College of Naturopathic Medicine (OR), 42047

National Collegiate Athletic Association (KS), 20055

National Commission for Cooperative Education (MA), 25214

National Commission on Working Women (DC), 11007

National Committee For Adoption (DC), 11008

National Committee for Citizens in Education (MD), 24331

National Committee for Clinical Laboratory Standards (PA), 43274

National Committee for Prevention of Child Abuse (IL), 17364

National Committee for Responsive Philanthropy (DC), 11009

National Committee for an Effective Congress (NY), 36731

National Committee on Certification of Physician's Assistants (GA), 14084

National Committee on Cultural Diversity in the Performing Arts (DC), 11010

National Committee on Uniform Traffic Laws and Ordinances (IL), 17365

National Committee on United States-China Relations (NY), 36732

National Committee on the Treatment of Intractable Pain (DC), 11011

National Committee to Combat Women's Oppression (NY), 36733

National Committee, Arts with Handicapped (DC), 11012

National Communications System (DC), 11013

National Community Education Association Clearinghouse (DC), 11014

National Composition Association (VA), 51319

National Computer Graphics Association (VA), 51320

National Concrete Masonry Association (VA), 51321

National Confectioners Association (IL), 17367

National Conference of Christians and Jews (NY), 36734

National Conference of Commissioners on Uniform State Laws (IL), 17368

National Conference of Lieutenant Governors (KY), 21037

National Conference of State Legislatures (CO), 07149

National Drilling Federation (SC), 45019
National Earthquake Information Center (CO), 07151
National Ecumenical Coalition Office of Public Information (DC), 11044
National Education Association Instruction & Professional Development (DC), 11045
National Education Program (AR), 04054
National Electrical Manufacturers Association (DC), 11046
National Electronic Distributors Association (IL), 17372
National Electronic Service Dealers Association (TX), 48159
National Elevator Industry (NY), 36748
National Employee Services and Recreation Association (IL), 17373
National Endowment for the Arts (DC), 11047
National Endowment for the Arts Office for Special Constituencies (DC), 11048
National Endowment for the Humanities (DC), 11049
National Energy Information Center (DC), 11050
National Energy Information Center (NM), 35032
National Energy Research and Information Institute (CA), 05577
National Entrepreneurial Development Center (FL), 13137
National Environmental Health Association (CO), 07152
National Environmental Satellite, Data, and Information Service (DC), 11051
National Euchre Players Association (OH), 40183
National Evaluation Systems (MA), 25215
National Executive Committee for Guidance (DC), 11052
National Executive Housekeepers Association (OH), 40184
National Eye Institute, Office of Scientific Reporting (MD), 24340
National Eye Research Foundation (IL), 17374
National Family Business Council Resource Center (IL), 17375
National Farmers Organization (IA), 19045
National Farmers Union Office of National Coordinator (CO), 07154
National Federation of Abstracting & Information Services (PA), 43276
National Federation of Community Broadcasters (DC), 11053
National Federation of Community Development Credit Unions (NY), 36749
National Federation of Independent Business (CA), 05578
National Federation of Licensed Practical Nurses (NC), 38076
National Federation of Local Cable Programmers (DC), 11054
National Federation of Parents for Drug-Free Youth (MD), 24341
National Federation of Press Women (MO), 29091

National Federation of State High School Associations (MO), 29092
National Federation of the Blind (MD), 24342
National Fertilizer Library (AL), 01053
National Fertilizer Solutions Association (IL), 17376
National Field Archery Association (CA), 05579
National Film Information Service (CA), 05580
National Fire Protection Association (MA), 25216
National Fishery Research Laboratory (WI), 54093
National Flag Foundation (PA), 43277
National Flight Data Center (DC), 11055
National Fluid Power Association (WI), 54094
National Flute Association (IN), 18071
National Food Processors Association (DC), 11056
National Food and Conservation Through Swine (NJ), 34158
National Food and Energy Council (MO), 29093
National Football League Players Association (DC), 11057
National Forensic Center (NJ), 34159
National Forest Products Association Information Center (DC), 11058
National Foundation for Advancement in the Arts (FL), 13138
National Foundation for Asthma (AZ), 03081
National Foundation for Asthma (AZ), 03082
National Foundation for Cancer Research (MD), 24343
National Foundation for Children's Hearing, Education and Research (NY), 36750
National Foundation for Ileitis and Colitis (NY), 36752
National Foundation for Jewish Culture (NY), 36753
National Foundation for Jewish Genetic Diseases (NY), 36754
National Foundation for Peroneal Muscular Atrophy (PA), 43278
National Foundation of Wheelchair Tennis (CA), 05581
National Foundation to Fight Political Corruption (CA), 05582
National Fragile X Syndrome Support Group (NJ), 34160
National Frozen Food Association (PA), 43279
National Funeral Directors Association (WI), 54095
National Future Farmers of America Organization (VA), 51329
National Gallery of Art (DC), 11059
National Gallery of Art Center for Advanced Study in the Visual Arts (DC), 11060
National Garden Bureau (IL), 17377
National Gay Health Education Foundation (NY), 36755
National Gay Task Force (NY), 36757
National Genealogical Society (DC), 11061
National Genetics Foundation (NY), 36758
National Geodetic Information Center (MD), 24344
National Geothermal Information Resource (CA), 05583
National Geriatrics Society (WI), 54096
National Geriatrics Society (WI), 54097

National Golf Foundation (FL), 13139
National Grain & Feed Association Library & Information Center (DC), 11062
National Grange (DC), 11063
National Guild of Community Schools of the Arts (NJ), 34161
National Guild of Decoupeurs (MI), 26139
National Hairdressers and Cosmetologists Association (MO), 29094
National Handbag Association (NY), 36759
National Hansen's Disease Center (LA), 22039
National Hardwood Lumber Association (TN), 47059
National Hazards Control Institute (PA), 43280
National Head Injury Foundation (MA), 25219
National Health Council (NY), 36760
National Health Education Committee (NY), 36761
National Health Federation (CA), 05584
National Health Federation (CA), 05585
National Health Information Clearinghouse (DC), 11065
National Health Law Program (CA), 05586
National Health Planning Information Center (MD), 24345
National Health Policy Forum (DC), 11066
National Health Screening Council for Volunteer Organizations (MD), 24347
National Hearing Aid Society (MI), 26140
National Hearing Association (IL), 17378
National Heart and Blood Vessel Research and Demonstration Center Communications Core (TX), 48160
National Heart, Lung and Blood Institute, Sickle Cell Diseases Branch (MD), 24348
National Heart, Lung, and Blood Institute, Public Inquiries and Reports Branch (MD), 24349
National Heisey Glass Museum (OH), 40185
National Hemophilia Foundation (NY), 36762
National Highway Safety Foundation (MS), 28020
National Highway Traffic Safety Administration Associate Administrator for Enforcement (DC), 11067
National Home Caring Council (NY), 36764
National Home Fashions League (TX), 48161
National Home Study Council (DC), 11068
National Hormone and Pituitary Program (MD), 24351
National Hospice Organization (VA), 51330
National Hot Rod Association (CA), 05587
National Housewares Manufacturers Association (IL), 17379
National Housing Center (MI), 26142
National Housing Law Project (CA), 05588
National Housing Rehabilitation Association (DC), 11069
National Human Studies Film Archive (DC), 11070
National Huntington's Disease Association (NY), 36766
National Hurricane Center (FL), 13140
National Ichthyosis Foundation (CA), 05589
National Immigration, Refugee & Citizenship Forum (DC), 11071

National Independent Automobile Dealers Association (NC), 38077
National Indian Council on Aging (NM), 35034
National Indian Health Board (CO), 07155
National Indian Law Library (CO), 07156
National Indian Training and Research Center (AZ), 03083
National Industrial Transportation League (DC), 11072
National Industries for the Blind (NJ), 34162
National Information Center for Educational Media (NM), 35035
National Information Center for Handicapped Children & Youth (DC), 11073
National Information Standards Organization (MD), 24352
National Initiative for Glaucoma Control (DC), 11074
National Injury Information Clearinghouse (MD), 24353
National Institute for Burn Medicine (MI), 26144
National Institute for Certification in Engineering Technologies (VA), 51332
National Institute for Citizen Education in the Law (DC), 11075
National Institute for Management Research (CA), 05590
National Institute for Music Theater (DC), 11076
National Institute for Occupational Safety & Health (GA), 14086
National Institute for Occupational Safety and Health (OH), 40186
National Institute for Petroleum Energy Research Library (OK), 41040
National Institute for Public Policy (VA), 51333
National Institute for Rehabilitation Engineering (NJ), 34163
National Institute for Urban Wildlife (MD), 24354
National Institute for Work & Learning (DC), 11077
National Institute for the Conservation of Cultural Property (DC), 11078
National Institute for the Foodservice Industry (IL), 17380
National Institute for the Psychotherapies (NY), 36767
National Institute of Allergy and Infectious Diseases, Office of Research Reporting and Public Response (MD), 24355
National Institute of American Doll Artists (VT), 50014
National Institute of Arthritis, Diabetes, Digestive and Kidney Diseases (MD), 24356
National Institute of Building Sciences (DC), 11079
National Institute of Child Health and Human Development, Office of Research Reporting (MD), 24357
National Institute of Dental Research, Public Inquiries and Reports Section (MD), 24358
National Institute of Education Educational Reference Center (DC), 11080
National Institute of Education Publications & Administrative Management Division (DC), 11081

National Institute of Environmental Health Sciences (NC), 38079
National Institute of Governmental Purchasing (VA), 51334
National Institute of Handicapped Research (DC), 11082
National Institute of Hypertension Studies (MI), 26145
National Institute of Independent Colleges & Universities (DC), 11083
National Institute of Judicial Dynamics (CO), 07157
National Institute of Mental Health, Division of Biometry and Epidemiology (MD), 24359
National Institute of Mental Health, Project Sleep (MD), 24360
National Institute of Neurological and Communicative Disorders and Stroke (MD), 24361
National Institute of Oilseed Products (DC), 11084
National Institute of Victimology (VA), 51335
National Institute on Aging, Information Office (MD), 24362
National Institute on Drug Abuse, Office of Science (MD), 24363
National Institutes of Health, Cancer Information Clearinghouse (MD), 24364
National Institutes of Health, Division of Public Information (MD), 24365
National Institutes of Health, Research Resources Information Center (MD), 24366
National Insurance Consumer Organization (VA), 51336
National Intercollegiate Flying Association (CA), 05591
National Interfaith Coalition on Aging (GA), 14087
National Interreligious Service Board for Conscientious Objectors (DC), 11085
National Inventors Foundation Library (CA), 05592
National Investor Relations Institute (DC), 11086
National Italian American Foundation (DC), 11087
National Judicial College (NV), 32021
National Juvenile Detention Association (NJ), 34165
National Kerosene Heater Association (TN), 47060
National Kidney Foundation (NY), 36768
National Knitwear and Sportswear Association (NY), 36769
National LP-Gas Association (IL), 17381
National Labor Relations Board (DC), 11088
National League for Nursing (NY), 36770
National League of Cities (DC), 11089
National Legal Aid & Defender Association (DC), 11090
National Legal Center for the Public Interest (DC), 11091
National Legal Research Group (VA), 51337
National Leukemia Association (NY), 36771
National Library Service for the Blind and Physically Handicapped (DC), 11092
National Library of Medicine (MD), 24368
National Licensed Beverage Association (VA), 51338
National Lime Association (VA), 51339
National Live Stock and Meat Board (IL), 17382

National Lubricating Grease Institute (MO), 29095
National Lupus Erythematosus Foundation (CA), 05593
National Lupus Erythematosus Foundation (CA), 05594
National MPS Society (NY), 36773
National Magnetic Fusion Energy Comp Center (CA), 05154
National Marfan Foundation (NY), 36774
National Marine Educators Association (RI), 44014
National Marine Electronics Association (MN), 27097
National Marine Exhaust Research Council (IL), 17383
National Marine Fisheries Service, Auke Bay Fisheries Laboratory (AK), 02026
National Marine Fisheries Service, Kodiak Investigations (AK), 02027
National Marine Manufacturing Association (IL), 17384
National Maritime Research Center (NY), 36775
National Measurement Laboratory, Center for Analytical Chemistry (DC), 11093
National Measurement Laboratory, Molecular Spectra Data Center (MD), 24369
National Measurement Laboratory, Office of Standard Reference Data (MD), 24370
National Meat Association (DC), 11094
National Mediation Board (DC), 11096
National Medical Association (DC), 11097
National Medical Fellowships (NY), 36776
National Mental Health Association (VA), 51340
National Merit Scholarship Corp. (IL), 17385
National Meteorological Center (MD), 24371
National Migraine Foundation (IL), 17386
National Milk Producers Federation (VA), 51342
National Minority Business Campaign (MN), 27098
National Motor Vehicle Research Safety Foundation (NH), 33013
National Moving and Storage Association (VA), 51343
National Multi Housing Council (DC), 11098
National Multiple Sclerosis Society (NY), 36778
National Museum of African Art Library (DC), 11099
National Museum of American Art (DC), 11100
National Museum of American History Library (DC), 11101
National Museum of Natural History Library (DC), 11102
National Museum of Natural History National Anthropological Archives (DC), 11103
National Museum of Transport (MO), 29096
National Music Council (NY), 36779
National Music Publishers' Association (NY), 36780
National Native American Coop (AZ), 03084
National Needlework Association (NY), 36781
National Network in Solidarity with the Nicaraguan People (DC), 11104
National Network of Learning Disabled Adults (TX), 48162
National Network of Youth Advisory Boards (FL), 13141
National Neurofibromatosis Foundation (NY), 36782

National Research and Resource Facility for Submicron Structures (NY), 36792

National Resource Center for Consumers of Legal Services (DC), 11122

National Resource Center for Paraprofessionals in Special Education (NY), 36793

National Restaurant Association (DC), 11123

National Reye's Syndrome Foundation (OH), 40189

National Reye's Syndrome Foundation (OH), 40190

National Rifle Association of America (DC), 11124

National River Academy of the USA (AR), 04055

National Roofing Contractors Association (IL), 17392

National Rural Crime Prevention Center (OH), 40191

National Rural Electric Cooperative Association Library (DC), 11125

National Rural Health Care Association (MO), 29098

National Rural Housing Coalition (DC), 11126

National Safe Transit Association (IL), 17393

National Safety Council Campus Safety Association (IL), 17394

National Safety Council Library/Safety Research Information Service (IL), 17395

National Safety Council Research Department (IL), 17396

National Safety Management Society (CA), 05596

National Sanitation Foundation (MI), 26147

National Sash and Door Jobbers Association (IL), 17397

National School Boards Association (VA), 51359

National School Orchestra Association (CO), 07163

National School Public Relations Association (VA), 51360

National School Volunteer Program (VA), 51361

National Science Foundation, Division of Civil & Environmental Engineering (DC), 11127

National Science Foundation, Division of Electrical, Computer & Systems Engineering (DC), 11128

National Science Foundation, Division of Industrial Science & Technological Innovation (DC), 11129

National Science Foundation, Division of Mechanical Engineering & Applied Mechanics (DC), 11130

National Science Foundation, Public Information Branch (DC), 11131

National Science Teachers Association (DC), 11132

National Scoliosis Foundation (MA) , 25222

National Scrip Collectors Association (WV), 53022

National Sculpture Society (NY), 36794

National Sea Grant College Program (MD), 24375

National Sea Grant Depository (RI), 44015

National Seafood Inspection Laboratory (MS), 28021

National Security Industrial Association (DC), 11133

National Seed Storage Laboratory (CO), 07164

National Self-Help Clearinghouse (NY), 36796

National Senior Citizens Law Center (CA), 05597

National Serials Data Program (DC), 11134

National Severe Storms Laboratory (OK), 41041

National Sheriffs' Association (DC), 11135

National Shooting Sports Foundation (CT), 08101

National Shut-In Society (NY), 36798

National Sisters Vocation Conference (IL), 17398

National Slag Association (VA), 51362

National Soaring Museum (NY), 36799

National Social Science & Law Center (DC), 11136

National Society for Children & Adults with Autism (DC), 11137

National Society for Medical Research (DC), 11138

National Society for the Preservation of Covered Bridges (MA), 25223

National Society of Genetic Counselors (NY), 36800

National Society of Genetic Counselors (PA), 43285

National Society of Professional Engineers (VA), 51363

National Society of Public Accountants (VA), 51364

National Society of the Sons of the American Revolution Genealogy Library (KY), 21041

National Society to Prevent Blindness (NY), 36802

National Soft Drink Association (DC), 11139

National Solid Wastes Management Association (DC), 11140

National Soybean Processors Association (DC), 11141

National Spa and Pool Institute (VA), 51365

National Space Institute (DC), 11142

National Space Science Data Center (MD), 24376

National Spasmodic Torticollis Association (MI), 26148

National Speakers Association (AZ), 03085

National Speleological Society (AL), 01054

National Spill Control School (TX), 48167

National Spinal Cord Injury Association (MA), 25224

National Sporting Goods Association (IL), 17399

National Sporting Library (VA), 51366

National Spray Equipment Manufacturers Association (OH), 40192

National Square Dance Convention (OK), 41042

National Standards Association (MD), 24377

National Standards Council of American Embroiderers (IL), 17400

National Stone Association (DC), 11143

National Storytelling Resource Center (TN), 47062

National Strategy Information Center (NY), 36803

National Stripper Well Association (TX), 48168

National Stroke Association (CO), 07165

National Student Speech Language Hearing Association (MD), 24378

National Study of School Evaluation (VA), 51367

National Stuttering Project (CA), 05598

National Sudden Infant Death Syndrome Clearinghouse (DC), 11144

National Sudden Infant Death Syndrome Foundation (MD), 24379

National Superconducting Cyclotron Laboratory (MI), 26149

National Support Center for Families of the Aging (PA), 43286

National Task Force on Prostitution (CA), 05599

National Tax Association-Tax Institute of America (OH), 40193

National Taxpayers Union(-RET-)458 (DC), 11145

National Tay-Sachs and Allied Diseases Association (NY), 36805

National Technical Association (DC), 11146

National Technical Information Service (VA), 51368

Naval Weapons Center Library Division (CA), 05606
Naval Weapons Evaluation Facility (NM), 35036
Navy Acquisition, Research and Development
    Information Center (VA), 51383
Navy Amphibious Museum (VA), 51180
Navy Clothing and Textile Research Facility (MA),
    25227
Navy Memorial Museum (DC), 11166
Navy Naval Historical Center Operational Archives
    (DC), 11167
Navy Naval Intelligence Support Center Library
    (DC), 11168
Navy Submarine Force Library and Museum (CT),
    08106
Navy Underwater Sound Reference Detachment (FL),
    13144
Navy/Government-Industry Data Exchange Program
    (CA), 05607
Near East Foundation (NY), 36814
Near East Section (DC), 11169
Nebraska Educational Television Network (NE),
    31025
Nebraska Organic Agriculture Association (NE),
    31027
Nebraska State Historical Society (NE), 31028
Negative Population Growth (NY), 36815
Negotiation Institute (NY), 36816
Nematology Research Laboratory (LA), 22040
Neoteric--USA (IN), 18073
Nephrology Division (DC), 11170
Netsuke Dealers Association (NY), 36817
Network Users Association (VA), 51384
Neurospora Genetics Laboratory (MI), 26151
Neutron Activation Analysis Laboratory (KS), 20058
Nevada Historical Society (NV), 32022
Nevada State Museum (NV), 32023
New Alchemy Institute (MA), 25228
New Bedford Whaling Museum (MA), 25229
New Call to Peacemaking (IN), 18074
New Day Films (NY), 36818
New England Anti-Vivisection Society (MA), 25230
New England Coalition on Nuclear Pollution (VT),
    50015
New England Enzyme Center (MA), 25233
New England Fire and History Museum (MA), 25233
New England Forestry Foundation (MA), 25234
New England Intercollegiate Geological Conference
    (MA), 25235
New England Marine Research Laboratory (MA),
    25236
New England Regional Primate Research Center
    (MA), 25237
New England Sights (MA), 25238
New England Wild Flower Society (MA), 25239
New Eyes for the Needy (NJ), 34172
New Games Foundation (CA), 05608
New Hampshire Historical Society (NH), 33014
New Hampshire Radiological Health Program (NH),
    33015
New Hope Pain Center (CA), 05609
New Jersey Historical Society (NJ), 34175

New Jewish Agenda (NY), 36820
New Mexico Energy Research and Development
    Institute (NM), 35037
New Mexico Engineering Research Institute (NM),
    35038
New Mexico Geological Society (NM), 35039
New Mexico Organic Growers Association (NM),
    35042
New Mexico Solar Energy Institute (NM), 35043
New Mexico Tumor Registry (NM), 35044
New Mexico Water Resources Research Institute
    (NM), 35045
New Mexico Wildlife Federation (NM), 35046
New Music Distribution Service (NY), 36821
New Orleans Society for Adolescent Psychiatry (LA),
    22041
New Ventures (MD), 24389
New Windsor Service Center, SERRV Program (MD),
    24390
New York Academy of Sciences (NY), 36822
New York Center for Law and the Deaf (NY), 36823
New York Central System Historical Society (OH),
    40198
New York Foundation for Otologic Research (NY),
    36826
New York Genealogical and Biographical Society,
    Library (NY), 36827
New York Historical Society (NY), 36828
New York Institute of Clinical Oral Pathology (NY),
    36829
New York Public Library at Lincoln Center,
    Performing Arts Research Center (NY), 36831
New York Public Library, Science and Technology
    Research Center (NY), 36832
New York State Natural Food Associates (NY), 36834
New York Stock Exchange, Regulatory Services
    Division (NY), 36836
New York-New Jersey Trail Conference (NY), 36837
Newborn Rights Society (PA), 43289
Newcomen Society of the United States (PA), 43290
Newport Aeronautical Sales (CA), 05610
Newport News Shipbuilding and Dry Dock Co.
    Technical Information Center (VA), 51385
NewsBank (CT), 08108
Newsletter Clearinghouse (NY), 36838
Newspaper Features Council (NY), 36839
Night Vision and Electro-optics Laboratory Public
    Affairs Office (VA), 51386
Nimitz Library (MD), 24391
Nitinol Technology Center (MD), 24392
No-Load Mutual Fund Association (NY), 36840
Noble Oil Laboratories (CA), 05611
Noise Control Laboratory (PA), 43291
Non Destructive Testing Management Association
    (CA), 05612
Non-Ferrous Founders' Society (IL), 17408
Non-Formal Education Information Center (MI),
    26152
Non-traditional Employment for Women (NY), 36841
Nondestructive Testing Information Analysis Center
    (TX), 48171

Nuclear Assurance Corp. (GA), 14088
Nuclear Control Institute (DC), 11175
Nuclear Data Project (TN), 47064
Nuclear Free America (MD), 24395
Nuclear Free Zone Registry (CA), 05617
Nuclear Freeze Political Action Committee (NY), 36847
Nuclear Information & Resource Service (DC), 11176
Nuclear Information and Records Management Association (NY), 36848
Nuclear Metals (MA), 25246
Nuclear Negotiation Project (MA), 25247
Nuclear Physics Laboratory (CO), 07172
Nuclear Radiation Center (WA), 52072
Nuclear Reactor Facility (PA), 43295
Nuclear Reactor Laboratories (WA), 52073
Nuclear Reactor Laboratory (MI), 26155
Nuclear Regulatory Agency Public Document Room (DC), 11177
Nuclear Regulatory Commission Office of Public Affairs (DC), 11178
Nuclear Safety Information Center (TN), 47065
Nuclear Science Center (LA), 22042
Nuclear Science Center (AL), 01056
Nuclear Test Effects and Geologic Data Bank (CA), 05618
Nuclear and Plasma Science Society (NY), 36849
Nuclide Corp.: Technical Publications (PA), 43296
Numismatics International (TX), 48173
Nurses' Educational Funds (NY), 36850
Nutrition Co. (FL), 13145
Nutrition Foundation (NY), 36851
Nutrition Information & Resource Center (PA), 43297
Nutrition Research Institute (OR), 42055
Nutrition Today Society (MD), 24396
Nutting Memorial Library (ME), 23025

OEF International (DC), 11179
OPEN DOOR Student Exchange (NY), 36852
OPERA America (DC), 11180
Oak Creek Laboratory of Biology (OR), 42056
Oak Manor Farms (CAN), 61108
Oak Ridge Associated Universities, Information Services (TN), 47066
Oak Ridge National Laboratory Library System (TN), 47067
Oakes Ames Orchid Library (MA), 25248
Oakland Museum, Natural Sciences Department (CA), 05619
Obesity Foundation (CO), 07173
Occidental Chemical Corp., Technical Information Center (NY), 36853
Occupational Safety & Health Review Commission (DC), 11181
Ocean Engineering Information Centre (CAN), 61109
Ocean Research and Education Society (MA), 25249
Oceanic Institute (HI), 15020
Oceanic Society (CA), 05620
Oceanographic Research Program (OR), 42057
Odessa Meteor Crater (TX), 48174

Odyssey Institute Corp. (CT), 08113
Office Technology Management Association (WI), 54102
Office and Professional Employees International Union (NY), 36854
Office for Civil Rights (DC), 11183
Office for Protection from Research Risks (MD), 24397
Office of Acid Deposition, Environmental Monitoring & Quality Assurance (DC), 11184
Office of Air & Radiation (DC), 11185
Office of Air Quality and Nuclear Energy (LA), 22043
Office of American Indian Research Project (SD), 46014
Office of American Studies (DC), 11186
Office of Arid Lands Studies (AZ), 03089
Office of Aviation Medicine (DC), 11187
Office of Aviation Policy & Plans (DC), 11188
Office of Beneficiary Services, Health Care Financing Administration (MD), 24398
Office of Bilingual Education & Minority Languages Affairs (DC), 11189
Office of Building Energy Research & Development (DC), 11190
Office of Business Liaison (DC), 11191
Office of Business Loans (DC), 11192
Office of Civil Rights (DC), 11193
Office of Civilian Radioactive Waste Management (DC), 11194
Office of Communication & Education Services (DC), 11195
Office of Compliance & Consumer Assistance (DC), 11196
Office of Computer Software and Systems (DC), 11197
Office of Earthquakes, Volcanoes, and Engineering (AK), 02029
Office of Educational Research and Improvement (DC), 11198
Office of Elementary and Secondary Education (DC), 11199
Office of Endangered Species (DC), 11200
Office of Environmental Processes and Effects Research (OR), 42058
Office of Family Assistance (DC), 11201
Office of Folklife Programs (DC), 11202
Office of Fusion Energy (DC), 11203
Office of Grants and Program Systems (DC), 11204
Office of Health Maintenance Organizations (MD), 24399
Office of Health Planning (MD), 24400
Office of Human Development Services, Administration on Aging (DC), 11205
Office of Industrial Programs (DC), 11206
Office of Information & Consumer Affairs (DC), 11207
Office of Information Resources Management (DC), 11208
Office of Information, Department of Labor (DC), 11209
Office of International Affairs & Energy Emergencies (DC), 11210

Oregon Museum of Science and Industry (OR), 42063
Oregon Productivity Center (OPC) (OR), 42064
Oregon Regional Primate Research Center (OR), 42065
Oregon State Library (OR), 42066
Oregon Wildlife Federation (OR), 42067
Organ Clearing House (NH), 33018
Organ Recovery (OH), 40205
Organic Acidemia Association (KS), 20059
Organization Development Institute (OH), 40206
Organization for Flora Neotropica (NY), 36858
Organization for Tropical Studies (NC), 38085
Organization for Use of the Telephone (MD), 24406
Organization of American Kodaly Educators (WI), 54105
Organization of American States Library (DC), 11263
Organization of American States, Pan American Highway Congresses (DC), 11264
Organization of Chinese American Women (DC), 11265
Organization of Women Architects and Design Professionals (CA), 05621
Organization of Women for Legal Awareness (NJ), 34186
Oriental Healing Arts Institute (CA), 05622
Oriental Institute (IL), 17416
Orientation/Media International (CA), 05623
Orlando Science Center (FL), 13147
Orphan Voyage (CO), 07174
Orthodox Theological Society in America (MA), 25251
Orthomolecular Medical Society (CA), 05624
Orton Dyslexia Society (MD), 24407
Orton Memorial Library of Geology (OH), 40207
Osborn Laboratories of Marine Science (NY), 36859
Oscar Getz and Bardstown Historical Museums (KY), 21045
Osteogenesis Imperfecta Foundation (NH), 33019
Ouachita River Valley Association (AR), 04056
Out-of-Home Measurement Bureau (CT), 08115
Outboard Boating Club of America (DC), 11267
Outdoor Circle (HI), 15021
Outdoor Power Equipment Institute (DC), 11268
Overeaters Anonymous (CA), 05625
Overseas Citizens Services (DC), 11269
Overseas Development Council (DC), 11270
Overseas Sales and Marketing Association (IL), 17417
Owens-Corning Fiberglas Corp., Technical Data Center (OH), 40208
Owens-Illinois, Information Research Department (OH), 40209
Owner Builder Center (CA), 05626
Ozark Folk Center (AR), 04057
Ozarks Whittlers and Woodcarvers (MO), 29100

P.K. Yonge Library of Florida History (FL), 13148
PALINET & Union Library Catalogue of Pennsylvania (PA), 43300
PCR: Film & Video in the Behavioral Sciences (PA), 43301
PEI Associates Library (OH), 40210
PEN American Center (NY), 36860

PHP Self-Help Clearinghouse (NY), 36861
PKU Parents (CA), 05627
PMS Research Foundation (NV), 32024
PPG Industries Glass Research Center (PA), 43302
PT Boats (TN), 47068
PYRAMID (CA), 05628
PYRAMID (MD), 24408
Pacific Biomedical Research Center (HI), 15022
Pacific Coast Entomological Society (CA), 05629
Pacific Coast Oyster Growers Association (WA), 52075
Pacific Fisheries Development Foundation (HI), 15023
Pacific Fishery Management Council (OR), 42068
Pacific Gas and Electric Co. Corporate Library (CA), 05630
Pacific Grove Museum of Natural History (CA), 05631
Pacific Information Inc. (CA), 05632
Pacific Maritime Association (CA), 05633
Pacific Northwest Regional Health Sciences Library Service (WA), 52076
Pacific Northwest Research Center (OR), 42069
Pacific Northwest Waterways Association (WA), 52077
Pacific Power and Light Co. Library (OR), 42070
Pacific Science Association (HI), 15024
Pacific Science Center (WA), 52078
Pacific Seabird Group (CA), 05635
Pacific Southwest Forest and Range Experiment Station (CA), 05636
Pacific Southwest Inter-Agency Committee (NV), 32025
Pacific Studies Center (CA), 05637
Pacific Submarine Museum (HI), 15025
Pacific Telecommunications Council (HI), 15026
Package Designers Council (NY), 36862
Packaged Facts (NY), 36863
Packaging Institute, U.S.A. (CT), 08116
Packaging Machinery Manufacturers Institute (DC), 11271
Packard Automobile Classics (CA), 05638
Paget's Disease Foundation (NY), 36864
Pain Center (WA), 52079
Pain Clinic (IL), 17418
Pain Control Center (GA), 14089
Pain Management Center (VA), 51393
Pain Treatment Center (NY), 36865
Pain and Back Rehabilitation Program (FL), 13149
Painting and Decorating Contractors of America (VA), 51394
Paleo-Indian Institute, Agency for Conservation Archeology (NM), 35047
Paleobryozoological Research Laboratory (PA), 43303
Paleontological Research Institution (NY), 36866
Paleontological Society (DC), 11272
Paleopathology Association (MI), 26156
Palo Alto Medical Foundation Library (CA), 05639
Palomino Horse Breeders of America (OK), 41045
Palynology Research Center (OK), 41046
Pan American Association of Ophthalmology (CA), 05640

Phillips Fibers Corp.. Technical Research Center (SC), 45021
Philomath International Sliderule Society (OR), 42071
Philosophy Documentation Center (OH), 40212
Philosophy of Education Society (NY), 36880
Phipps Conservatory (PA), 43317
Phobia Society of America (MD), 24414
Phoenix Art Museum (AZ), 03091
Phoenix Society (PA), 43318
Phone-TTY Inc. (NJ), 34188
Photoduplication Service (DC), 11292
Photographic Society of America (PA), 43320
Phycological Society of America (NE), 31029
Physical Anthropology Laboratory (TX), 48182
Physicians Forum (IL), 17423
Physicians for Automotive Safety (NY), 36881
Physicians for Social Responsibility (NY), 36882
Physics Library (CA), 05654
Phytochemical Society of North America (FL), 13153
Phytopathological Translations Index (MA), 25255
Picatinny Arsenal Ammunition Museum (NJ), 34189
Piedmont Environmental Council (VA), 51401
Pierce-Arrow Society (NY), 36883
Pierpont Morgan Library (NY), 36884
Pilgrim Society (MA), 25256
Pills Anonymous (NY), 36885
Pilot Guide Dog Foundation (IL), 17424
Pima Air Museum (AZ), 03092
Pioneer America Society (OH), 40213
Pioneer Fund (CA), 05655
Pipe Fabrication Institute (PA), 43321
Pittsburgh Energy Technology Center (PA), 43322
Pittsburgh Institute of Legal Medicine (PA), 43323
Plains Indians and Pioneer Historical Foundation (OK), 41047
Planetary Association for Clean Energy (CAN), 61116
Planetary Society (CA), 05656
Planned Parenthood Federation of America, Educational Resources Clearinghouse (NY), 36886
Planned Parenthood Federation of America, Library (NY), 36887
Planning Executives Institute (OH), 40214
Plant Physiology Institute (MD), 24415
Plant Physiology Institute, Hydrology Laboratory (MD), 24416
Plant Physiology Institute, Plant Stress Laboratory (MD), 24417
Plant Protection and Quarantine Library (MD), 24418
Plant Resources Center (TX), 48183
Plastic Bottle Information Bureau (NY), 36888
Plastics Institute of America (NJ), 34190
Plastics Technical Evaluation Center (NJ), 34191
Platt Saco Lowell Corp. (SC), 45022
Plum Island Animal Disease Center (NY), 36889
Poetry Center (AZ), 03093
Poetry Society of America (NY), 36890
Poets & Writers (NY), 36891
Point-of-Purchase Advertising Institute (NJ), 34192
Poisonous Plants Research Laboratory (UT), 49033
Polar Science Center (WA), 52081

Polaroid Corp., Library and Information Services (MA), 25257
Police Executive Research Forum (DC), 11294
Police Foundation Communications Office (DC), 11295
Policy Research Institute, Health Futures Project (MD), 24419
Polimetrics Laboratory (OH), 40215
Polish American Historical Association (IL), 17425
Political Research (TX), 48184
Pollution Probe Foundation (CAN), 61117
Polycystic Kidney Disease Research Foundation (MO), 29103
Polymer Institute (MI), 26159
Polymer Processing Institute (NJ), 34193
Polymer Research Institute (MA), 25258
Polytechnic Institute of New York, Libraries (NY), 36892
Polytechnic Institute of New York, Polymer Research Institute (NY), 36893
Polytechnic Institute of New York, Transportation Training and Research Center (NY), 36894
Polyurethane Manufacturers Association (IL), 17426
Pony Express Historical Association (MO), 29104
Popular Rotorcraft Association (CA), 05657
Population Association of America (DC), 11296
Population Council (NY), 36896
Population Crisis Committee (DC), 11297
Population Food Fund (LA), 22045
Population Genetics Laboratory (HI), 15027
Population Information Network (NY), 36897
Population Institute (DC), 11298
Population Issues Research Center (PA), 43324
Population Reference Bureau (DC), 11299
Population Research Center Library (TX), 48185
Population Research Laboratory (CA), 05658
Population Research Laboratory (KS), 20060
Population Research Library (NJ), 34194
Population Resource Center (NY), 36898
Population Studies and Training Center (RI), 44018
Porcelain Enamel Institute (VA), 51402
Portland Cement Association (IL), 17427
Post-Secondary Advisory and Referral Service for Students and Institutions (NY), 36899
Post-Tensioning Institute (AZ), 03094
Postal Rate Commission (DC), 11300
Postharvest Documentation Service (KS), 20061
Potash & Phosphate Institute (GA), 14091
Potato Board (CO), 07178
Potency Restored (MD), 24420
Potential Gas Agency (CO), 07179
Potomac Institute (DC), 11301
Potsmokers Anonymous (NY), 36900
Powder Actuated Tool Manufacturers Institute (IL), 17428
Power Company Midwest (WI), 54107
Power Conversion Products Council International (IL), 17429
Power Crane and Shovel Association (WI), 54108
Power Marketing Administration (DC), 11302
Power Tool Institute (IL), 17430

Powered Ultralight Manufacturers Association (VA), 51403

Poynter Center (IN), 18077

Practising Law Institute (NY), 36901

Practitioner Reporting System, United States Pharmacopeial Convention (MD), 24422

Prader-Willi Syndrome Association (MN), 27110

Prairie Agricultural Machinery Institute (CAN), 61118

Predex Corp. (NY), 36902

Predicasts (OH), 40216

Premenstrual Syndrome Action (CA), 05659

Presbyterian Historical Society (PA), 43325

Preservation Office (DC), 11303

President's Commission on White House Fellowships (DC), 11304

President's Committee on Employment of the Handicapped (DC), 11305

President's Committee on Mental Retardation (DC), 11306

President's Council on Physical Fitness and Sports (DC), 11307

Presidential Classroom for Young Americans (VA), 51404

Pressure Sensitive Tape Council (IL), 17431

Prestressed Concrete Institute (IL), 17432

Pretrial Services Resource Center (DC), 11308

Prevention-Intervention Center for Alcohol and Other Drug Abuse (WI), 54109

Price Gilbert Memorial Library (GA), 14092

Price-Pottenger Nutrition Foundation (CA), 05660

Primary Mental Health Project (NY), 36903

Primate Behavior Laboratory (RI), 44019

Primate Information Center (WA), 52082

Primate Supply Information Clearinghouse (WA), 52083

Princeton Child Development Institute (NJ), 34196

Princeton University Public Administration Collection (NJ), 34197

Print Club (PA), 43326

Privacy Journal (DC), 11309

Private Agencies Collaborating Together (NY), 36904

Private Islands Unlimited (CA), 05661

Private Radio Bureau (DC), 11310

Pro & Con Screening Board (IL), 17433

Pro Football Hall of Fame, Library/Research Center (OH), 40217

Proaction Institute (MI), 26160

Produce Marketing Association Information Center (DE), 09030

Product Assurance Materials and Components Engineering and Test (MA), 25259

Product Safety Association (CA), 05662

Productivity Institute (AZ), 03095

Professional Convention Management Association (AL), 01057

Professional Engineering Institute (CA), 05663

Professional Engineers of Colorado (CO), 07180

Professional Grounds Management Society (MD), 24423

Professional Photographers of America (IL), 17434

Professional Rodeo Cowboys Association, National Media Department (CO), 07181

Professional Salespersons of America (NM), 35048

Professional Secretaries International (MO), 29105

Professional and Technical Consultants Association (CA), 05664

Proficiency Examination Review (MO), 29106

Profit Sharing Council of America (IL), 17435

Profit Sharing Research Foundation (IL), 17436

Program for Appropriate Technology in Health (WA), 52084

Program for Collaborative Research in the Pharmaceutical Sciences (IL), 17437

Program for Neural Sciences (IN), 18078

Program for the Study of Crime and Delinquency (OH), 40218

Program in International Agriculture (NY), 36905

Program in Science and Technology for International Security (MA), 25260

Progressive Foundation (WI), 54110

Project Concern International (CA), 05665

Project HOPE (VA), 51405

Project Jonah (CA), 05667

Project Management Institute (PA), 43327

Project Smart (NY), 36906

Project for Metric Research (MS), 28023

Project on Linguistic Analysis (CA), 05668

Promoting Enduring Peace (CT), 08118

Property Loss Research Bureau (IL), 17438

Psoriasis Research Association (CA), 05669

Psychical Research Foundation (NC), 38087

Psychological Abstracts Information Service (DC), 11311

Psychology Society (NY), 36907

Public Administration Service (VA), 51406

Public Affairs Committee (NY), 36908

Public Affairs Information (DC), 11312

Public Affairs Research Institute (MA), 25261

Public Broadcasting Service (DC), 11313

Public Citizen Congress Watch (DC), 11314

Public Citizen Critical Mass Energy Project (DC), 11315

Public Citizen Health Research Group (DC), 11316

Public Citizen Tax Reform Research Group (DC), 11317

Public Education Association, Library (NY), 36909

Public Education Religion Studies Center (OH), 40219

Public Gaming Research Institute (MD), 24424

Public Health Entomology Laboratory (IN), 18079

Public Health Research Institute of the City of New York (NY), 36910

Public Health Service, Centers for Disease Control (GA), 14094

Public Information, Department of the Treasury (DC), 11319

Public Inquiries, Department of Energy (DC), 11320

Public Lands Institute (DC), 11322

Public Law Education Institute (DC), 11323

Public Management Institute (CA), 05670

Public Policy Research Organization (CA), 05671

Public Relations Society of America, Research Information Center (NY), 36911
Public Securities Association (NY), 36912
Public Systems Evaluation (MA), 25262
Publishing Office (DC), 11324
Pueblo Grande Museum (AZ), 03096
Puget Sound Naval Shipyard Engineering Library (WA), 52085
Puget Sound Power and Light Co. (WA), 52086
Pulp Chemicals Association (NY), 36913
Puppeteers of America (CA), 05672
Purebred Dairy Cattle Association (MO), 29107
Puritan-Bennett Corp. (KS), 20062
Pyrotechnics Guild International (MD), 24426

Quaker Collection (PA), 43328
Quality Bakers of America Cooperative (CT), 08119
Quality Circle Institute (CA), 05673
Quality of Working Life and Human Resource Management (CA), 05674
Quantum Chemistry Program Exchange (IN), 18080
Quantum Institute (CA), 05675
Quantum Metrology Group (MD), 24427
Quaternary Research Laboratory (MI), 26161
Quebec Asbestos Mining Association (CAN), 61119
Quebec Association for Quaternary Research (CAN), 61120
Quetico-Superior Wilderness Research Center (MN), 27111
Quill and Scroll Society (IA), 19050

R.E. Gibson Library (MD), 24429
R.E. Olds Museum Association (MI), 26163
R.H. Lowie Museum of Anthropology (CA), 05677
R.L. Polk and Co. (MI), 26162
R.M. Hutchins Center for Study of Democratic Institutions (CA), 05676
R.P. Foundation Fighting Blindness (MD), 24428
RAIN: Journal of Appropriate Technology (OR), 42072
RARE (DC), 11325
Rachel Carson Council (MD), 24430
Racing Driver's Club (CA), 05678
Rack Manufacturers Institute (PA), 43329
Radiation Center (OR), 42073
Radiation Chemistry Data Center (IN), 18081
Radiation Education Council (OR), 42074
Radiation Research Laboratory (IA), 19051
Radiation Research Society (PA), 43330
Radiation Shielding Information Center (TN), 47071
Radical Women (WA), 52087
Radio Advertising Bureau, Marketing Information Center (NY), 36914
Radio Astronomy Lab (CA), 05156
Radio Technical Commission for Aeronautics (DC), 11326
Radio Television News Directors Association (DC), 11327
Radiological Society of North America (IL), 17439
Railroad Retirement Board (IL), 17440

Railroad Station Historical Society (NE), 31030
Railroadians of America (NJ), 34198
Railway Engineering Maintenance Suppliers Association (FL), 13154
Railway Tie Association (MO), 29108
Railway and Locomotive Historical Society (MA), 25263
Rainier Brewing Co. Quality Control Laboratories (WA), 52088
Ralston Purina Co. Library (MO), 29109
Ranching Heritage Center Museum (TX), 48186
Rand Corp. Library (CA), 05679
Rapidly Solidified Materials Resource Centre (OH), 40220
Raptor Research Foundation (FL), 13155
Rare Book & Special Collections Division (DC), 11328
Rare-Earth Information Center (IA), 19052
Rathkamp Matchcover Society (OH), 40221
Raytheon Co. Engineering Library (CA), 05680
Reactor Radiation Division (MD), 24431
Reading Is Fundamental (DC), 11329
Reading Machine Department (MA), 25264
Reading Reform Foundation (AZ), 03097
Real Estate Data (FL), 13156
Reclamation Research Unit (MT), 30016
Recognition Technologies Users Association (VT), 50017
Recording Industry Association of America (NY), 36916
Recording for the Blind (NJ), 34200
Recovery, The Association of Nervous and Former Mental Patients (IL), 17441
Recreation Management Staff Unit (DC), 11330
Recreation Resources Center (WI), 54111
Recreation Vehicle Industry Association (VA), 51407
Red Angus Association of America (TX), 48187
Red Cedar Shingle & Handsplit Shake Bureau (WA), 52089
Redwood Inspection Service (CA), 05681
Reese Palley Gallery (NJ), 34201
Reflex Sympathetic Dystrophy Syndrome Association (NJ), 34202
Refractories Institute (PA), 43331
Refractories Research Center (OH), 40222
Refrigeration Research Foundation (MD), 24432
Refugee Materials Center (MO), 29110
Regenerative Agriculture Association (PA), 43332
Regional Cancer Foundation (CA), 05682
Regional Science Association (PA), 43333
Regional Social Science Data Archive (IA), 19053
Registry of Interpreters for the Deaf (MD), 24434
Regulatory Information Service Center (DC), 11331
Rehabilitation Engineering Center (VA), 51408
Rehabilitation Engineering Program (IL), 17442
Rehabilitation Engineering Society of North America (DC), 11332
Rehabilitation Institute of Chicago, Learning Resources Center (IL), 17443
Rehabilitation Institute, Learning Resources Center (MI), 26166

Robotic Industries Association (MI), 26168
Robotics Institute (PA), 43341
Robotics Research Center (RI), 44022
Rochester Institute of Technology, Technical and
    Education Center of the Graphic Arts (NY), 36932
Rock Island Technical Society (MO), 29113
Rockefeller Archive Center (NY), 36933
Rockwell Hanford Operations (WA), 52090
Rockwell International Corp., Technical Information
    Center (CA), 05690
Rockwell International Corp., Technical Information
    Center (PA), 43342
Rocky Mountain Association of Geologists (CO),
    07184
Rocky Mountain Forest and Range Experiment
    Station (CO), 07185
Rocky Mountain Herbarium (WY), 55014
Rocky Mountain Hydraulic Lab (CO), 07186
Rocky Mountain Mineral Law Foundation (CO),
    07187
Rodel (DE), 09031
Rodeo Historical Society (OK), 41050
Roeding Park Zoo (CA), 05691
Rogers Corp. Lurie Library (CT), 08120
Rolf Institute (CO), 07188
Rolls-Royce Owners Club (PA), 43343
Rona Pearl (NJ), 34204
Roof Coatings Manufacturers Association (IL), 17447
Roper Center (CT), 08121
Rose F. Kennedy Center for Research in Mental
    Retardation and Human Development (NY), 36935
Rosenstiel School of Marine and Atmospheric Science
    (FL), 13158
Roswell Park Memorial Institute, Center for
    Crystallographic Research (NY), 36936
Roswell Park Memorial Institute, Grace Cancer Drug
    Center (NY), 36937
Rotary Natural Science Center (CA), 05692
Royal Astronomical Society of Canada National
    Library (CAN), 61123
Royal Botanical Gardens (CAN), 61124
Royal Oak Foundation (NY), 36938
Rubber Manufacturers Association (DC), 11342
Rudolf Steiner Library (NY), 36939
Rudolph Matas Medical Library (LA), 22047
Ruffed Grouse Society (PA), 43344
Runaway Hotline (TX), 48193
Rural Advancement Fund of the National
    Sharecroppers Fund (NC), 38089
Rural America (DC), 11343
Rural American Women (PA), 43345
Rural Education Association (CO), 07189
Rural Electrification Administration (DC), 11344
Rural Sociological Society (MT), 30017
Russell Cave National Monument (AL), 01058
Russian and East European Institute (IN), 18085
Rutgers Poultry Health Laboratory (NJ), 34205
Rutherford B. Hayes Presidential Center (OH), 40225
Ryan Headache Center (MO), 29114

Ryerson Polytechnical Institute, Nutrition
    Information Service (CAN), 61125
Ryukyu Philatelic Specialist Society (CA), 05693

**S.I. Newhouse School of Public Communications (NY),
36941**
S.L.E. Foundation (NY), 36942
SAFE Association (CA), 05694
SANE, Committee for a Sane Nuclear Policy (DC),
    11345
SCM Corp., Organic Chemicals Technical Library
    (FL), 13159
SCM Pigments Division, Research Center Library
    (MD), 24440
SDS Biotech Corp. Library and Information Services
    (OH), 40226
SEARCHLINE (IL), 17448
SESAC (NY), 36943
SHARE (IL), 17449
SRI International, Artificial Intelligence Center (CA),
    05698
SRI International, Chemical Information Services
    (CA), 05695
SRI International, Computer Science Laboratory
    (CA), 05696
SRI International, Library and Research Information
    Services Department (CA), 05699
SRI International, Life Sciences Division (CA), 05697
Saber Laboratories (CA), 05700
Sacramento Valley Museum Association (CA), 05701
Sadtler Research Laboratories (PA), 43346
Safety Society (VA), 51414
Safety of Explosive Ordnance Databank (VA), 51415
Saint Louis Zoological Park Tissue Bank (MO), 29115
Salinity Laboratory (CA), 05702
Salk Institute for Biological Studies (CA), 05703
Salmon Unlimited (IL), 17451
Salomon Brothers Center for the Study of Financial
    Institutions (NY), 36944
Salt Institute (VA), 51416
Salvation Army (NJ), 34207
Salvation Army, Archives and Research Center (NY),
    36945
Samuel Roberts Noble Foundation, Biomedical
    Division (OK), 41051
San Diego Museum of Man (CA), 05704
San Diego Natural History Museum, Library (CA),
    05705
San Francisco Crafts and Folk Art Museum, Reference
    Library (CA), 05706
San Francisco Port Commission (CA), 05707
San Francisco Society for the Prevention of Cruelty to
    Animals (CA), 05708
Sandoz Library (NJ), 34208
Sandy Hook Laboratory (NJ), 34209
Sanitary Engineering and Environmental Health
    Research Laboratory (CA), 05709
Sansum Medical Research Foundation (CA), 05710
Santa Barbara Museum of Natural History (CA),
    05711

Santa Fe Railway Historical Society (CA), 05712
Santa Gertrudis Breeders International (TX), 48194
Santee National Wildlife Refuge (SC), 45024
Sar-assist (CT), 08122
Savannah Science Museum (GA), 14096
Save the Children Library (CT), 08123
Save-the-Redwoods League (CA), 05713
Scaffolding, Shoring, and Forming Institute (OH), 40227
Scandinavian Documentation Center (VA), 51417
Scenic Hudson (NY), 36946
Schiffli Lace and Embroidery Manufacturers Association (NJ), 34210
Schomburg Center for Research in Black Culture (NY), 36947
School Management Study Group (UT), 49034
School Science and Mathematics Association (OH), 40228
School for Workers Library (WI), 54113
School of Forestry Wilderness Institute (MT), 30019
School of Living (PA), 43347
Schuyler Otis Bland Memorial Library (NY), 36948
Science Editors (KY), 21046
Science Fiction Research Association (OH), 40229
Science Products (PA), 43350
Science for the Handicapped Association (WI), 54114
Science for the People (MA), 25270
Scientific Apparatus Makers Association (DC), 11348
Scientific Manpower Commission (DC), 11349
Scientific and Technical Information Office (OH), 40230
Scientific, Economic & Natural Resources Branch (DC), 11350
Scientists Center for Animal Welfare (MD), 24441
Scientists' Institute for Public Information (NY), 36951
Scipio Society of Naval and Military History (NY), 36952
Scleroderma Information Exchange (RI), 44023
Scleroderma International Foundation (PA), 43351
Scleroderma Research Foundation (NJ), 34211
Scoliosis Association (NY), 36953
Scoliosis Research Society (IL), 17452
Scope Research and Development (LA), 22048
Scott Paper Co., Library & Technical Information Service (PA), 43352
Screen Actors Guild (CA), 05714
Screen Manufacturers Association (IL), 17453
Screen Printing Association International (VA), 51418
Scripps Clinic and Research Foundation (CA), 05715
Scripps Foundation Gerontology Center (OH), 40231
Scripps Foundation for Research in Population Problems, Gerontology Center (OH), 40232
Scripps Marine Geological Collection (CA), 05716
Scripps Physical and Chemical Oceanographic Data Facility (CA), 05717
Scripps Zooplankton Invertebrate Collection (CA), 05718
Sea Education Association (MA), 25271
Sea Grant Marine Advisory Program (NH), 33023
Sea Grant-Marine Advisory Service (CT), 08124
Sea Shepherd Conservation Society (CA), 05719

Seafoods Laboratory (OR), 42075
Search Corp. (VA), 51419
Search Group (CA), 05720
Search-A Central Registry of the Missing (NJ), 34212
Seaway Review (MI), 26169
Second Harvest (AZ), 03098
Second Harvest, Communications Department (IL), 17454
Secondary School Admission Test Board (NJ), 34213
Securities Industry Association, Public Information Division (NY), 36954
Securities Investor Protection Corp. (DC), 11351
Securities and Exchange Commission, Office of Public Affairs (DC), 11352
Sedimentation Laboratory (MS), 28031
Seeing Eye (NJ), 34214
Seismological Laboratory (NV), 32028
Seismological Observatory (MI), 26170
Selective Service System Public Affairs Office (DC), 11353
Selectrons (CT), 08125
Selenium-Tellurium Development Association (CT), 08126
Self Help for Hard of Hearing People (MD), 24443
Self-Help Center (IL), 17455
Self-Help for the Elderly (CA), 05721
Semiconductor Chemical Transducer Resource (OH), 40233
Semiconductor Industry Association (CA), 05722
Seminar Clearinghouse International (MN), 27113
Seminole Nation Museum (OK), 41052
Senate Committee on Agriculture, Nutrition, and Forestry (DC), 11354
Senate Committee on Appropriations (DC), 11355
Senate Committee on Armed Services (DC), 11356
Senate Committee on Banking, Housing and Urban Affairs (DC), 11357
Senate Committee on Commerce, Science and Transportation (DC), 11358
Senate Committee on Energy and Natural Resources (DC), 11359
Senate Committee on Environment and Public Works (DC), 11360
Senate Committee on Finance (DC), 11361
Senate Committee on Foreign Relations (DC), 11362
Senate Committee on Governmental Affairs (DC), 11363
Senate Committee on Labor and Human Resources (DC), 11364
Senate Committee on Rules and Administration (DC), 11365
Senate Committee on Small Business (DC), 11366
Senate Committee on Veterans Affairs (DC), 11367
Senate Committee on the Budget (DC), 11368
Senate Committee on the Judiciary (DC), 11369
Senate Special Committee on Aging (DC), 11370
Seney National Wildlife Refuge (MI), 26171
Sensory Aids Foundation (CA), 05723
Sensory Communication Research Lab & Rehabilitation Engineering Center for the Hearing-impaired (DC), 11371

Sequoia Natural History Association (CA), 05724
Sequoia-Turner Corp. (CA), 05725
Serial and Government Publications Division (DC), 11372
Service Corps of Retired Executives, Chapter One (DC), 11373
Services for Independent Living (OH), 40234
Sex Information and Education Council of the United States (NY), 36956
Sexaholics Anonymous (CA), 05726
Shakespeare Oxford Society (MD), 24444
Shakespeare Society of America (CA), 05727
Shalom Center (PA), 43353
Shared Parenting Association (FL), 13160
Shealy Pain and Health Rehabilitation Institute (MO), 29116
Sheep Industry Development Program (CO), 07190
Shelter Institute (ME), 23027
Shelterforce Newspaper (NJ), 34215
Shelton Research (NM), 35049
Shelving Manufacturers Association (PA), 43354
Sherman Grinberg Film Libraries (CA), 05728
Sherry Institute of Spain (NY), 36957
Shipbuilders Council of America (DC), 11374
Shipcraft Guild (NJ), 34216
Shock Wave Data Center (CA), 05157
Shore Line Interurban Historical Society (IL), 17456
Shuttle Earth Viewing Imagery Facility (TX), 48195
Sibling Information Network (CT), 08127
Sick Kids Need Involved People (MD), 24445
Sickle Cell Information Center (TN), 47073
Sidney R. Frank Group and SRF Research Institute (CA), 05729
Sierra Arts Foundation (NV), 32029
Sierra Club (CA), 05730
Signed English Project (DC), 11376
Sikorsky Aircraft Public Relations (CT), 08129
Silicon Beach Consultancy (FL), 13161
Silver Institute (DC), 11377
Silverado Museum (CA), 05731
Simon Wiesenthal Center (CA), 05732
Singer Co. Librascope Technical Library (CA), 05733
Single Service Institute (DC), 11378
Sino-American Amity Fund (NY), 36958
Sister Kenny Institute (MN), 27115
Skate Sailing Association of America (NJ), 34217
Ski Industries America (VA), 51420
Ski for Light (MN), 27116
Skidaway Institute of Oceanography Library (GA), 14097
Skin Cancer Foundation (NY), 36959
Skip Barber Racing School (CT), 08130
Slavic and East European Library (IL), 17457
Sleep Disorders Clinic (CA), 05734
Sleep Disorders Clinic and Research Center (CA), 05735
Sleep Laboratory (IL), 17458
Sleep Research Society (CA), 05736
Sleep-Wake Disorders Center (NY), 36960
Slovak-American Cultural Center (NY), 36961
Slurry Transport Association (DC), 11379

Small Business Administration, Field Offices (DC), 11380
Small Business Administration, Office of Advocacy (DC), 11381
Small Business Administration, Office of Women's Business Ownership (DC), 11382
Small Business Development Center (DC), 10713
Small Business Development Center (WA), 52091
Small Homes Council (IL), 17459
Small Motor Manufacturers Association (IL), 17460
Small-Scale Hydropower Branch (DC), 11384
Small-Scale Technology Branch (DC), 11383
Smith Mental Retardation Research Center (KS), 20064
Smith-Kettlewell Institute of Visual Sciences (CA), 05737
Smithkline Bio-Science Laboratories Library (CA), 05738
Smithsonian Institution, Office of Printing & Photographic Services (DC), 11385
Smithsonian Institution, Archives of American Art (NY), 36962
Smithsonian Institution, Environmental Research Center (MD), 24446
Snell Memorial Foundation (RI), 44024
Snow Entomological Museum (KS), 20065
Soap and Detergent Association (NY), 36963
Soaring Society of America (CA), 05739
Social Development Corp. (DC), 11386
Social Documents Collection (IA), 19055
Social Investment Forum (MA), 25272
Social Legislation Information Service (DC), 11387
Social Psychiatry Research Institute (NY), 36964
Social Science Computer Research Institute (PA), 43355
Social Science Data Archive (CAN), 61126
Social Science Data Center (PA), 43356
Social Science Data Library (NC), 38090
Social Science Research Center (MS), 28025
Social Science Research Laboratory (CA), 05740
Social Security Administration, Welfare Management Institute (DC), 11388
Social Welfare History Archives (MN), 27117
Social Welfare Research Institute (MA), 25273
Society for Adolescent Medicine (CA), 05742
Society for Adolescent Psychiatry (NY), 36965
Society for Applied Spectroscopy (MD), 24447
Society for Cinema Studies (CT), 08131
Society for Clinical and Experimental Hypnosis (NY), 36966
Society for Computer Applications in Engineering, Planning, and Architecture (MD), 24448
Society for Computer Simulation (CA), 05743
Society for Creative Anachronism (CA), 05744
Society for Epidemiologic Research (MD), 24449
Society for Ethnomusicology (MI), 26172
Society for Experimental Stress Analysis (CT), 08132
Society for General Systems Research (KY), 21047
Society for Health and Human Values (VA), 51421
Society for Historical Archaeology (NJ), 34218

Society for Industrial & Applied Mathematics (PA), 43357
Society for Industrial Microbiology (VA), 51422
Society for Information & Documentation, Federal Republic of Germany (DC), 11389
Society for Intercultural Education, Training & Research (DC), 11390
Society for Investigative Dermatology (CA), 05745
Society for Iranian Studies (MA), 25274
Society for Marketing Professional Services (VA), 51423
Society for Neuroscience (DC), 11391
Society for Nonprofit Organizations (WI), 54115
Society for Nutrition Education (CA), 05746
Society for Optical and Quantum Electronics (VA), 51424
Society for Pediatric Radiology (NY), 36967
Society for Pediatric Research (NM), 35050
Society for Photographic Education (NY), 36968
Society for Private and Commercial Earth Stations (VA), 51425
Society for Psychophysiological Research (CA), 05748
Society for Public Health Education (CA), 05749
Society for Public Health Education (CA), 05750
Society for Range Management (CO), 07191
Society for Surgery of the Alimentary Tract (CA), 05751
Society for Technical Communication (DC), 11393
Society for Values in Higher Education (CT), 08133
Society for the Advancement of Chicanos and Native Americans in Science (MD), 24450
Society for the Advancement of Continuing Education for Ministry (PA), 43358
Society for the Advancement of Material and Process Engineering (CA), 05752
Society for the Anthropology of Visual Communication (NM), 35051
Society for the Application of Free Energy (MD), 24451
Society for the Encouragement of Research and Invention (NJ), 34219
Society for the History of Technology (DC), 11394
Society for the Investigation of the Unexplained (NJ), 34220
Society for the Preservation and Appreciation of Antique Motor Fire Apparatus in America (NY), 36970
Society for the Preservation of Birds of Prey (CA), 05753
Society for the Preservation of Colonial Culture (MA), 25275
Society for the Preservation of Old Mills (ME), 23028
Society for the Rehabilitation of the Facially Disfigured (NY), 36971
Society for the Right to Die (NY), 36973
Society for the Scientific Study of Sex (PA), 43359
Society for the Study of Breast Disease (PA), 43360
Society for the Study of Evolution (CO), 07192
Society for the Study of Reproduction (IL), 17461
Society of Actuaries (IL), 17462
Society of Allied Weight Engineers (CA), 05754

Society of American Archivists (IL), 17463
Society of American Florists (VA), 51426
Society of American Foresters (MD), 24452
Society of American Magicians, International (FL), 13162
Society of American Value Engineers (TX), 48196
Society of American Wood Preservers (VA), 51427
Society of Arts and Crafts (MA), 25276
Society of Authors' Representatives (NY), 36974
Society of Automotive Engineers (PA), 43361
Society of Behavioral Medicine (TN), 47074
Society of Biological Psychiatry (CA), 05755
Society of Carbide Engineers (OH), 40235
Society of Clinical and Medical Electrologists (NY), 36975
Society of Cosmetic Chemists (NY), 36976
Society of Critical Care Medicine (CA), 05756
Society of Data Educators (VA), 51428
Society of Diagnostic Medical Sonographers (TX), 48197
Society of Die Casting Engineers (IL), 17464
Society of Economic Paleontologists and Mineralogists (OK), 41053
Society of Exploration Geophysicists (OK), 41054
Society of Explosives Engineers (OH), 40236
Society of Eye Surgeons (MD), 24453
Society of Federal Linguists (DC), 11395
Society of Fire Protection Engineers (MA), 25277
Society of Independent Professional Earth Scientists (TX), 48198
Society of Logistics Engineers (AL), 01059
Society of Manufacturing Engineers (MI), 26173
Society of Marine Consultants (NY), 36977
Society of Motion Picture and Television Engineers (NY), 36978
Society of Municipal Arborists (OH), 40237
Society of Naval Architects and Marine Engineers (NY), 36979
Society of Non-Invasive Vascular Technology (OH), 40239
Society of North American Goldsmiths (WI), 54116
Society of Nuclear Medicine (NY), 36980
Society of Packaging and Handling Engineers (VA), 51429
Society of Photo-Technologists (CO), 07193
Society of Photographic Scientists and Engineers (VA), 51430
Society of Plastics Engineers (CT), 08134
Society of Professional Archaeologists (MI), 26174
Society of Professional Business Consultants (IL), 17465
Society of Professional Investigators (NY), 36981
Society of Professional Management Consultants (NJ), 34221
Society of Professional Well Log Analysts (TX), 48199
Society of Prospective Medicine (DC), 11396
Society of Psychologists in Addictive Behaviors (KY), 21048
Society of Real Estate Appraisers (IL), 17466
Society of Research Administrators (CA), 05757
Society of Rheology (NY), 36982

Society of Stage Directors and Choreographers (NY), 36983

Society of State Directors of Health, Physical Education, and Recreation (MD), 24454

Society of Telecommunications Consultants (NY), 36984

Society of the Plastics Industry (NY), 36985

Society of Toxicology (DC), 11397

Society of Toxicology of Canada (CAN), 61127

Society of Underprivileged and Handicapped Children (VA), 51431

Society of University Otolaryngologists (IL), 17467

Society of Vertebrate Paleontology (CA), 05758

Society of Wood Science and Technology (WI), 54117

Society to Preserve and Encourage Radio Drama, Variety, and Comedy (CA), 05759

Sociologists for Women in Society (TX), 48200

Soil Conservation Service (DC), 11398

Soil Conservation Service, National Cooperative Soil Survey (DC), 11399

Soil Conservation Society of America (IA), 19056

Soil Mechanics Information Analysis Center (MS), 28026

Soil Science Society of America (WI), 54118

Solar Energy Applications Lab (CO), 07194

Solar Energy Association of Oregon (OR), 42076

Solar Energy Industries Association (DC), 11400

Solar Energy Information Services (OH), 40240

Solar Energy Laboratory (WI), 54119

Solar Energy and Energy Conversion Laboratory (FL), 13163

Solar Rating & Certification Corp. (DC), 11402

Solar Turbines Inc., Technical Information Center (CA), 05760

Solar Use Now for Resources and Employment (CA), 05761

Solution Mining Research Institute (IL), 17468

Songwriters Resources and Services (CA), 05762

Sonia Shankman Orthogenic School (IL), 17469

Sophia Smith Collection, Women's History Archive (MA), 25278

Sourceworks (PA), 43362

South Carolina Department of Archives and History (SC), 45025

South Carolina Historical Society (SC), 45026

South Carolina Sea Grant Consortium (SC), 45027

South Central Poultry Research Laboratory (MS), 28027

South Dakota Conservation Commission (SD), 46015

South Dakota Historical Resource Center (SD), 46016

South Dakota State Historical Society (SD), 46018

South Mountain Laboratories (NJ), 34222

Southeast Archeological Center Library (FL), 13164

Southeast Asia Resource Center (CA), 05763

Southeast Fisheries Center (NC), 38091

Southeast Poultry Research Laboratory (GA), 14108

Southeastern Association of Fish and Wildlife Agencies (LA), 22049

Southeastern Exchange of the U.S. (SC), 45028

Southeastern Fish Cultural Laboratory (AL), 01060

Southeastern Fisheries Association (FL), 13165

Southeastern Geological Society (FL), 13166

Southeastern Power Administration (GA), 14098

Southern Association of Colleges & Schools, Commission on Colleges (GA), 14099

Southern Association on Children Under Six (AR), 04059

Southern Baptist Historical Library and Archives (TN), 47076

Southern Building Code Congress International (AL), 01061

Southern California Academy of Sciences (CA), 05764

Southern California Meter Association (CA), 05765

Southern Cypress Manufacturers Association (TN), 47077

Southern Forest Institute (GA), 14100

Southern Forest Products Association (LA), 22051

Southern Growth Policies Board (NC), 38092

Southern Pine Inspection Bureau (FL), 13167

Southern Poverty Law Center (AL), 01062

Southern Regional Education Board (GA), 14102

Southern Regional Research Center (LA), 22052

Southern Research Institute (AL), 01063

Southern Rural Development Center (MS), 28028

Southern Weed Science Society (TN), 47078

Southerners for Economic Justice (NC), 38093

Southwest Aviculture Foundation Reference Library (TX), 48201

Southwest Collection (TX), 48202

Southwest Educational Development Laboratory (TX), 48203

Southwest Institute for Research on Women (AZ), 03099

Southwest Louisiana Geophysical Society (LA), 22053

Southwest Parks and Monuments Association (AZ), 03100

Southwest Regional Lab for Educational Research and Development (CA), 05766

Southwest Research Station of the American Museum of Natural History (AZ), 03101

Southwest Research and Information Center (NM), 35052

Southwestern Cooperative Educational Laboratory (NM), 35053

Sovfoto (NY), 36988

Soviet Jewry Research Bureau (NY), 36989

Soy Protein Council (DC), 11403

Soyfoods Association of North America (NJ), 34223

Soyfoods Center (CA), 05767

Space Astronomy Laboratory (FL), 13168

Space Environment Laboratory (CO), 07197

Space Institute Library (TN), 47079

Space Settlement Studies Project (NY), 36990

Spangler Geotechnical Laboratory (IA), 19057

Sparks Center for Developmental and Learning Disorders (AL), 01064

Special Industrial Radio Service Association (VA), 51432

Special Libraries Association (NY), 36992

Special Olympics (DC), 11405

Special Services Center (IL), 17470

Stuhr Museum of the Prairie Pioneer (NE), 31032
Substance Abuse Librarians and Information
  Specialists (CA), 05784
Subtropical Horticulture Research Station (FL), 13170
Sulphur Institute (DC), 11412
Summer and Casual Furniture Manufacturers
  Association (NC), 38094
Sun Co., Library & Information Service (PA), 43371
Sun Foundation Center for Advancement in the
  Sciences, Art, and Education (IL), 17481
Sunkist Growers Research Library (CA), 05785
Sunlight Energy Corp. (AZ), 03104
Supersensonic Energy Technologies (CO), 07202
Supreme Court of the U.S., Office of the Clerk (DC),
  11413
Surface Design Association (TN), 47080
Surgical Eye Expeditions International (CA), 05786
Surgical Infection Society (CAN), 61130
Surratt Society (MD), 24459
Surrogate Parent Foundation (CA), 05787
Survey Research Center (CA), 05788
Survey Research Center (MI), 26178
Survival Education Association (WA), 52093
Survivors of Incest Anonymous (MD), 24461
Suzuki Association of the Americas (IA), 19061
Swedish Information Service (NY), 37002
Swedish-American Historical Society Archives (IL),
  17482
Sweet Adelines (OK), 41055
Swiss-American Historical Society (IL), 17483
Swords to Plowshares (CA), 05789
Synergetics Society (NC), 38095
System Safety Society (CA), 05791
Systems Builders Association (OH), 40244

TECHNOTEC (MN), 27122
TRANET (ME), 23029
TRW Electronics and Defense Sector, Technical
  Information Center (CA), 05792
TVIS Educational Services (NC), 38096
Tactical Energy Systems Laboratory (VA), 51440
Tactical Technology Center (OH), 40245
Taft Institute for Two-Party Government (NY), 37005
Talcott Mountain Science Center for Student
  Involvement (CT), 08138
Tall Timbers Research (FL), 13171
Tallgrass Prairie Alliance (KS), 20066
Tamarind Institute (NM), 35054
Tanker Advisory Center (NY), 37006
Tanners Council Research Laboratory (OH), 40246
Tanners' Council of America (DC), 11414
Tatsch Associates (TX), 48206
Tax Foundation (DC), 11415
Tayloe Murphy Institute (VA), 51441
Teachers & Writers Collaborative (NY), 37007
Teachers of English to Speakers of Other Languages
  (DC), 11416
Technical Advisory Service for Attorneys (PA), 43372
Technical Association of the Graphic Arts (NY), 37008

Technical Information Center (Puerto Rico) (PR),
  60007
Technical Information Services, University of Dayton
  Research Center (OH), 40247
Technical Insights (NJ), 34225
Technical Library Service (NY), 37009
Technical Marketing Society of America (CA), 05793
Technical Reference Division (DC), 11417
Technical Services Corp. (VA), 51442
Technological American Party (NY), 37010
Technology Application Center (NM), 35055
Technology Transfer Institute (NY), 37011
Technology Utilization and Industry Affairs Division
  (DC), 11418
Tektite Research (TX), 48207
Tel-Med (CA), 05794
Telecommunications Center (OH), 40248
Telecommunications Research & Action Center (DC),
  11419
Telecommunications and Telephone Association
  (VA), 51443
Teledyne Engineering Services (MA), 25285
Teledyne Ryan Aeronautical, Technical Information
  Services (CA), 05796
Telesensory Systems (CA), 05797
Television Center (PA), 43373
Television Information Office (NY), 37013
Temple School, Division Library-Archives (MO),
  29120
Tennessee Cooperative Fishery Research Unit (TN),
  47082
Tennessee Earthquake Information Center (TN),
  47083
Tennessee Historical Society (TN), 47084
Tennessee State Library and Archives (TN), 47085
Tennessee-Tombigbee Archives (MS), 28029
Tennessee Valley Authority, Land Between the Lakes
  (KY), 21049
Tennessee Valley Authority, Norris Branch Library
  (TN), 47081
Tennessee Valley Authority, Office of Agricultural
  and Chemical Development (AL), 01066
Tensolite Co. (NY), 37014
Terrarium Association (VT), 50018
Terri Gotthelf Lupus Research Institute (CT), 08139
Territorial and International Affairs (DC), 11420
Tesla Coil Builders Association (NY), 37015
Texas Archeological Research Laboratory (TX), 48208
Texas Archives for Geological Research, Paleobiology
  Collection (TX), 48209
Texas Historical Commission (TX), 48210
Texas Instruments, Library Acquisitions Center (TX),
  48211
Texas Instruments, Minicomputer Information
  Exchange (TX), 48212
Texas Real Estate Research Center (TX), 48213
Texas System of Natural Laboratories (TX), 48214
Texas and Southwestern Cattle Raisers Foundation
  (TX), 48215
Textile Care Allied Trades Association (NJ), 34226

U.S. Advisory Commission on Public Diplomacy (DC), 11433
U.S. Air Force, Forensic Toxicology Section (TX), 48222
U.S. Air Force, Historical Research Center (AL), 01069
U.S. Air Force, Museum Research Division (OH), 40255
U.S. Air Force, Strughold Aeromedical Library (TX), 48223
U.S. Air Force, Western Space and Missile Center Technical Library (CA), 05807
U.S. Animal Health Association (VA), 51446
U.S.-Arab Chamber of Commerce (NY), 37039
U.S. Arms Control and Disarmament Agency Library (DC), 11434
U.S. Army, Aviation Museum (AL), 01067
U.S. Army, Center of Military History (DC), 11435
U.S. Army, Communications-Electronics Museum (NJ), 34234
U.S. Army, Engineer Museum (VA), 51447
U.S. Army, Environmental Hygiene Agency (MD), 24465
U.S. Army, Military History Institute (PA), 43376
U.S. Army, National Infantry Museum (GA), 14105
U.S. Army, Safety Center (AL), 01068
U.S. Association for Blind Athletes (NJ), 34238
U.S. Beet Sugar Association (DC), 11436
U.S. Borax Research Corp. Research Library (CA), 05808
U.S. Botanic Garden (DC), 11437
U.S. Catholic Conference, Division of Elementary & Secondary Education (DC), 11439
U.S. Catholic Mission Association (DC), 11440
U.S. Coast Guard Academy Library (CT), 08140
U.S. Chess Federation (NY), 37052
U.S. Collegiate Sports Council (SC), 45030
U.S. Columbia Basin Project (WA), 52097
U.S. Committee for Refugees (DC), 11441
U.S. Committee on Irrigation, Drainage, and Flood Control (CO), 07207
U.S. Committee on Large Dams (MA), 25293
U.S. Conference of Local Health Officers (DC), 11442
U.S. Conference of Mayors, Labor-Management Relations Service (DC), 11443
U.S. Council for International Business (NY), 37053
U.S. Cycling Federation (CO), 07208
U.S. Divorce Reform (CA), 05826
U.S. Figure Skating Association Museum (CO), 07209
U.S. Forestry Sciences Laboratory (WA), 52098
U.S. Golf Association (NJ), 34235
U.S. Grain Marketing Research Laboratory (KS), 20067
U.S. Hide, Skin & Leather Association (DC), 11444
U.S. Gymnastics Federation (IN), 18091
U.S. Homeopathic Association (VA), 51448
U.S. Industrial Chemicals Co. Technical Library (OH), 40256
U.S. Information Agency, Office of Public Liaison (DC), 11445
U.S. Institute of Human Rights (NY), 37054

U.S. International Development Cooperation Agency, Public Affairs Office (DC), 11463
U.S. International Trade Commission Library (DC), 11446
U.S.-Japan Foundation (NY), 37057
U.S. Livestock Insects Laboratory (TX), 48218
U.S. Metric Association (CA), 05809
U.S.-Mexico Border Health Association (TX), 48224
U.S. Migratory Bird Conservation Commission (DC), 11447
U.S. Military Academy Library (NY), 37037
U.S. National Focal Point—UNEP/Infoterra (DC), 11449
U.S. Naval Institute (MD), 24469
U.S. Naval Oceanographic Office (MS), 28030
U.S. Navy, Naval Damage Control Training Center (PA), 43377
U.S. Navy, Naval Historical Center (DC), 11450
U.S. Navy, Pacific Missile Test Center Technical Library (CA), 05810
U.S. Nuclear-Free and Independent Pacific Network (CA), 05811
U.S. Olympic Committee (CO), 07210
U.S. Orienteering Federation (MO), 29124
U.S. Pacific Marine Center (WA), 52099
U.S. Parachute Association (VA), 51449
U.S. Police Canine Association (MD), 24470
U.S. Postal Service, Communications Department (DC), 11451
U.S. Potters Association (OH), 40259
U.S. Psychotronics Association (IL), 17489
U.S. Railway Association, Public Affairs Office (DC), 11464
U.S. Savings Bond Division, Office of Public Affairs (DC), 11452
U.S. Servas Committee (NY), 37038
U.S.-South Africa Leader Exchange Program (DC), 11466
U.S. Spokane Research Center (WA), 52100
U.S. Sports Academy (AL), 01070
U.S. Testing Co. (NJ), 34239
U.S. Synthetic Fuels Corp., Information Management Group (DC), 11453
U.S. Tax Court (DC), 11454
U.S. Tobacco Museum (CT), 08142
U.S. Trademark Association (NY), 37055
U.S. Travel & Tourism Administration (DC), 11455
U.S. Trotting Association (OH), 40260
U.S. Trout Farmers Association (MO), 29122
U.S. Water Conservation Laboratory (AZ), 03105
U.S. Wheelchair Sports Fund (NY), 37056
U.S. Yacht Racing Union (RI), 44025
U.T. Culture Collection of Algae (TX), 48219
U.T. Genetics Institute (TX), 48220
U.T. Radiocarbon Laboratory (TX), 48221
UCLA Map Library (CA), 05815
UFO Information Retrieval Center (AZ), 03106
UMKC Affiliated Facility for Developmental Disabilities (MO), 29123
UNC Cancer Research Center (NC), 38103

Van de Graaff Laboratory (OH), 40261
Vance Bibliographies (IL), 17498
Vanderbilt Television News Archive (TN), 47091
Varian Associates Technical Library (CA), 05828
Veach, Nicholson, Griggs Associates (IN), 18092
Vector Biology Laboratory (IN), 18093
Vegetable Research Station (OK), 41058
Vegetarian Information Service (MD), 24472
Vera Institute of Justice (NY), 37065
Vermiculite Association (GA), 14110
Vermont Historical Society (VT), 50019
Vermont Institute of Natural Science (VT), 50020
Vermont Maple Industry Council (VT), 50021
Vermont Natural Resources Council (VT), 50022
Vermont Water Resources Research Center (VT), 50023
Veteran Motor Car Club of America (CT), 08145
Veterans Administration, Research Division (DC), 11471
Veterans Bedside Network (NY), 37066
Veterans Day National Committee (DC), 11472
Veterinary Diagnostic Laboratory (IA), 19063
Veterinary Research Laboratory (MT), 30020
Veterinary Toxicology and Entomology Research Laboratory (TX), 48225
Vibration Institute (IL), 17499
Vickers (MI), 26187
Victorian Society in America (PA), 43382
Videodocumentary Clearinghouse (HI), 15029
Videotape Production Association (NY), 37067
Vietnam Veterans Agent Orange Victims (CT), 08146
Vinifera Wine Growers Association (VA), 51456
Vinland National Center (MN), 27127
Vintage Sports Car Club of America (NY), 37068
Viola d'Amore Society of America (NY), 37069
Violin Society of America (CA), 05829
Virginia Cooperative Fish and Wildlife Research Unit (VA), 51457
Virginia Historical Society (VA), 51459
Virginia Institute of Marine Science (VA), 51461
Virginia Institute of Marine Science, Aquaculture Data Base (VA), 51462
Virginia Institute of Marine Science, Marine Education Materials System (VA), 51463
Virginia Poultry Breeders Club (VA), 51464
Virology Laboratory (FL), 13174
Visibility Lab (CA), 05830
Visual Artists and Galleries Association (NY), 37070
Visual Studies Workshop (NY), 37071
Vitamin Information Bureau (IL), 17500
Vocational Industrial Clubs of America (VA), 51466
Vocational and Occupational Information, Center for Educators (CA), 05831
Voluntary Action and Information Center (MO), 29125
Volunteer: The National Center for Citizen Involvement (VA), 51454
Volunteers for Peace (VT), 50024
Volunteers in Action (RI), 44026
Volunteers in Asia (CA), 05832

Volunteers in Overseas Cooperative Assistance (DC), 11474
Volunteers in Prevention, Probation, Prisons (MI), 26188
Volunteers in Service to America (VISTA) (DC), 11475
Volunteers in Technical Assistance (VA), 51467
Von Braun Astronomical Society (AL), 01073
Voter Education Project (GA), 14111

W.E. Upjohn Institute for Employment Research (MI), 26189
W.M. Keck Lab of Hydraulics and Water Resources (CA), 05833
W.R. Grace Planning Services Library (TN), 47092
W.R. Grace and Co.Dearborn Chemical Library (IL), 17501
WEEA Publishing Center (MA), 25295
Wadley Institutes of Molecular Medicine (TX), 48226
Waikiki Aquarium (HI), 15030
Waksman Institute of Microbiology Library (NJ), 34240
Walking Association (AZ), 03109
Wallcovering Information Bureau (NJ), 34241
Walter Reed Army Medical Center, Health Physics Office (DC), 11476
Walter Reuther Library, Archives of Labor and Urban Affairs (MI), 26190
War Memorial Museum of Virginia (VA), 51468
War Resisters League (NY), 37072
Washington Office for Social Concern (DC), 11479
Washington Office on Africa (DC), 11480
Washington Peace Center (DC), 11481
Washington People First (WA), 52104
Washington State Chimney Sweep Guild (WA), 52107
Washington State Historical Society (WA), 52108
Waste Water Renovation & Conservation Research Project (PA), 43383
Water Pollution Control Federation (DC), 11484
Water Quality Association (IL), 17502
Water Quality Research Council (IL), 17503
Water Research Institute (WV), 53024
Water Resources Center (DE), 09032
Water Resources Center (LA), 22055
Water Resources Center (NE), 31035
Water Resources Center (NV), 32030
Water Resources Center (RI), 44027
Water Resources Institute (SD), 46019
Water Resources Program (NJ), 34242
Water Resources Research Center (AZ), 03110
Water Resources Research Center (AR), 04060
Water Resources Research Center (HI), 15031
Water Resources Research Center (IN), 18094
Water Resources Research Center (MN), 27128
Water Resources Research Center (NH), 33027
Water Resources Research Center (TN), 47093
Water Resources Research Institute (MS), 28032
Water Resources Research Institute (NC), 38105
Water Resources Research Institute (OR), 42078
Water Resources Research Institute (SC), 45031
Water Resources Research Institute (AL), 01074

Women for Sobriety (PA), 43391
Women in Cell Biology (CA), 05846
Women in Communications (TX), 48229
Women in Community Service (VA), 51478
Women in Crisis (NY), 37081
Women in Information Processing (DC), 11491
Women in the Arts Foundation (NY), 37082
Women Library Workers (CA), 05845
Women Strike for Peace (PA), 43390
Women's Action Alliance (NY), 37083
Women's Bureau (DC), 11492
Women's Campaign Fund (DC), 11493
Women's College Coalition (DC), 11494
Women's Economic Round Table (NY), 37084
Women's Equity Action League (DC), 11495
Women's History Research Center (CA), 05848
Women's Independent Film Exchange (NY), 37085
Women's Institute for Freedom of the Press (DC),
11496
Women's International League for Peace & Freedom
(PA), 43393
Women's International Network (MA), 25302
Women's Justice Center (MI), 26194
Women's Law Fund (OH), 40265
Women's Law Project (PA), 43394
Women's Medical Center (DC), 11497
Women's Occupational Health Resource Center
(NY), 37086
Women's Research & Education Institute (DC), 11498
Women's Sports Foundation (CA), 05850
Women's Studies Research Center (WI), 54128
Women-In-Action for Prevention of Violence and Its
Causes (NC), 38106
Wood Moulding and Millwork Producers Association
(OR), 42082
Wood Technology Laboratory (WA), 52112
Wood Truss Council of America (IL), 17508
Wood and Synthetic Flooring Institute (FL), 13176
Woodrow Wilson International Center for Scholars
Library (DC), 11499
Woods Hole Oceanographic Institution (MA), 25303
Woodstock Institute (IL), 17509
Worcester Foundation for Experimental Biology
(MA), 25304
Work in America Institute (NY), 37087
Workers Defense League (NY), 37088
Workers' Institute for Safety & Health (DC), 11500
Workforce Analysis & Statistics Division (DC), 11501
Working Women's Institute (NY), 37089
World Affairs Center (MN), 27131
World Agricultural Outlook Board (DC), 11502
World Airline Hobby Club (KY), 21058
World Archaeological Society Information Center
(MO), 29129
World Association for Public Opinion Research (CT),
08149
World Bank Publications Department (DC), 11503
World Biological Society (TX), 48230
World Concern (WA), 52113
World Conference on Religion and Peace (NY), 37090
World Council of Churches (NY), 37091

World Council of Credit Unions (WI), 54129
World Crafts Foundation (NY), 37092
World Data Center A: Coordination Office (DC),
11504
World Data Center A: Glaciology (Snow and Ice)
(CO), 07221
World Data Center A: Meteorology and Nuclear
Radiation (NC), 38107
World Data Center A: Oceanography (DC), 11505
World Data Center A: Rockets and Satellites (MD),
24477
World Data Center A: Rotation of Earth (DC), 11506
World Data Center A: Solar-Terrestrial Physics (CO),
07222
World Data Center A: Solid Earth Geophysics (CO),
07223
World Environment Center (NY), 37093
World Federalists Association (DC), 11507
World Federation for Mental Health (VA), 51479
World Federation of Hemophilia (CAN), 61137
World Federation of Public Health Associations (DC),
11508
World Food Council (NY), 37094
World Food Institute (IA), 19065
World Future Society (MD), 24478
World Game Projects (PA), 43395
World Hunger Education Service (DC), 11509
World Institute Council (NY), 37096
World Institute of Black Communications (NY), 37097
World Institute on Disability (CA), 05851
World International Nail and Beauty Association
(CA), 05852
World Leisure and Recreation Association (CAN),
61138
World Methodist Historical Society (PA), 43396
World Modeling Association (NY), 37098
World Neighbors (OK), 41059
World Peace Foundation (MA), 25306
World Peace Through Law Center (DC), 11510
World Plan Executive Council, Institute for Social
Rehabilitation (CA), 05853
World Policy Institute (NY), 37099
World Population Society (DC), 11511
World Print Council (CA), 05854
World Rehabilitation Fund (NY), 37100
World Resources Inventory (PA), 43397
World Sign Association (CO), 07224
World Wildlife Fund-U.S. (DC), 11512
World Without War Council (CA), 05855
World's Fair Collectors Society (NY), 37101
World's Poultry Science Association, U.S. Branch
(MD), 24479
Worldwatch Institute (DC), 11514
Wright Brothers National Memorial (NC), 38108
Writing Instrument Manufacturers Association (DC),
11515
Wyatt Technology Co. (CA), 05856
Wyoming Agricultural Experiment Station (WY),
55016
Wyoming Catastrophic Information Network (WY),
55017

Subject Index

Abandoned children, 34212
Abdominal surgery, 25030
Aberrant religions, 05771
See also Cults
Aborigines, 25092
Abortion, 05164, 05257, 10829, 10889, 10890, 11334, 11479, 27010, 36042, 36815, 36886, 36887, 36923, 36924, 43394, 51070
Abrasives, 10334, 25245, 40004, 40124, 43003
Abstract art, 34004
Abstracting, 34046, 43276
    biological, 43087
    scientific, 24122
Academic, *See also* Education
Academic achievement, 10685, 34149
Academic freedom, 24166, 29041, 42077
Academic guidance, 10035, 10095, 11052
    See also Counseling, Educational counseling
Academic standards, 42077
Accident investigations, 11149
Accident prevention, 05596, 05791, 10102, 11149, 17395, 17396, 34125, 36120
Accident research, 40128
Accidents, 17396, 24353, 52093
    industrial and occupational, 36055
    motor vehicle, 61132
    See also Highway safety, Industrial health and safety, Motor vehicle safety, Occupational health and safety, Safety
Acclimatization, 61007
Accordions, 34005, 34006
Accountants, 13108
    certified public, 36114
Accounting, 10657, 10713, 11373, 13006, 13105, 34150, 36114, 51364
Accounting practices, 13108
Accreditation, 10078
Acculturation, 27056
Acesulfame K, 14026
Achievement tests, 34085, 34091, 34213
    See also Educational testing
Acid rain, 05320, 05381, 07145, 10462, 25300, 27001, 36019, 38002, 42056, 42058, 43203, 47001, 50023, 54072, 61098, 61117
    See also Air pollution, Water pollution
Acoustic Neuroma, 43007
Acoustic emission, 05026, 11215
    See also Noise
Acoustic trauma, 42040
Acoustics, 04051, 05323, 05733, 05805, 07213, 08065, 17158, 17271, 25053, 29031, 34157, 36021, 36163, 43291, 52043
    underwater, 05605, 08105, 13144, 25053, 25249, 28030, 36021, 44016, 48031, 52011
Acquired Immune Deficiency Syndrome (AIDS), 05398, 36755, 54092
Acrylic resins, 29035
Acting, 08098, 10126, 36022, 36443, 40141
    See also Performing arts, Theater
Acting schools, 51296

Actors and actresses, 05714, 36022, 36098
    photographs, 36681
Actuarial mathematics, 10065
Actuaries, 10463, 17462
Acupuncture, 05315, 05556, 05622, 24194, 27106, 36569, 42051, 52066
Addams, Jane, 43166
Addictive behaviors, 21048
    See also Alcoholism, Drug abuse, Smoking
Adenine, 05504
Adenoviruses, 29055
Adhesive papers, 36484
Adhesive tapes, 17431, 36484
Adhesives, 17008, 34191, 51007
Adirondack Mountains, 36023
Administrative law, 10032, 10417
Administrative procedure, 10032, 11312
Admiralty law, 10290
Adolescence, 17469
Adolescent medicine, 05742
    See also Child health, Pediatrics
Adolescent pregnancies, 10255
Adolescent psychiatry, 22041, 36965, 43049
    See also Child psychology
Adolescent sexuality, 10383
Adoption, 05027, 05036, 05858, 07118, 07174, 10830, 10403, 10830, 10970, 11008, 24014, 24152, 24189, 25267, 32017, 33005, 34053, 36025, 36049, 36298, 36632, 37027, 42032, 43262, 45028, 51042
    international, 24189
    interracial, 24189
    records, 05858, 24014
Adoptive parents, 05027, 05858, 07118, 24152, 36025
Adrenal cortex, 36026
Adsorption, 54071
Adult education, 03055, 10079, 10104, 18019, 20042, 24165, 25103, 34146, 38029, 40068
    See also Continuing education
Adult film, 05028
Adultery, 36674
Advertising, 05838, 08028, 08115, 10072, 10614, 10971, 11373, 17078, 36029, 36179, 36208, 36558
    direct-mail, 24274, 36378, 36379
    lawyers, 40049
    magazine, 36652
    outdoor, 07224, 08115, 15021
    point-of-purchase, 34192
    public-service, 36028
    radio and television, 36684, 36914
    regulation of 10614
    specialty, 48204
Advertising art, 08142, 54088
Advertising displays, 36706
Advertising photography, 36029, 36160
Advertising research, 36030
Aerial phenomena, 03001
    See also Unidentified flying objects
Aerial photography, 05685, 10365, 19054, 22009, 24198, 25250, 42023, 48188, 51084, 51134, 51306, 54048

Agricultural resources, international, 43397
Agricultural statistics, 10350, 10603, 10781, 11408
Agriculture, 02001, 03018, 05160, 07071, 07154, 10048,
10073, 10074, 10149, 10628, 10793, 10957, 11031,
11063, 11242, 11343, 11514, 19045, 24053, 24234,
24292, 27027, 31008, 31009, 36011, 36222, 04061,
10558, 11502, 16018, 36814, 43217, 15014, 60008
    congressional committees on, 10687, 11354
    foreign, 10637
    international, 04061, 10558, 11502, 16018, 36814
    organic, 43217
    tropical, 15014, 60008
Agriculture, U.S. Department of, 10451, 10466, 10476,
10541, 10557, 10558. 10591, 10593, 10597, 10603,
10634, 10637, 11204, 11212, 11223, 11232, 11253,
11344, 11398, 11399, 11408, 11457
    See also Forest Service
Agricultural weather, 10822
Agronomy, 02001, 05160, 05163, 07012, 24415, 40009,
48076, 54017
AIDS, *See* Acquired Immune Deficiency Syndrome
Air brakes, 43009
Air cargo, 10902
Air circulation equipment, 17009, 17012
Air conditioning, 10049, 11190, 14017, 36249, 48121,
51010
Air diffusion, 17009
Air Force, U.S., 10050, 10051, 10052, 10242
Air mail, 05039
    See also Postal service
Air navigation, 11055, 11326
    See also Aviation
Air pollution, 01063, 05182, 05648, 05777, 11001,
11470, 24381, 24382, 32031, 36122, 36210, 38002,
38040, 43011, 43039, 43101, 47013, 61004
    See also Pollution
Air pollution control, 11163, 11185
Air quality, 10644, 11001, 22043
Air traffic control, 01033, 10251, 11188, 11211, 11326,
34096, 36212, 40254, 51009, 61088
Air transportation, 08129, 10053, 10901, 10902, 10956,
11072, 36867, 61085
    See also Aviation
Airborne wastes, 32031, 47013
Aircraft, 01033, 03092, 05037, 05372, 05610, 05657,
05796, 08039, 08129, 10725, 20009, 24017, 24255,
40254, 45009, 48047
    antique, 19001, 54050
    history, 48179
    law enforcement, 40012
    hijacking, 11510
    home-built, 54050
    instruments, 24386
    maintenance, 13066
    military, 01067, 05277, 34170, 40255
    parts and equipment, 43078
    registration, 41021
    rotary-wing, 51212
    security, 34096
    short- and vertical-takeoff, 51061, 51177

(Aircraft, continued)
    theft, 24240
    used, 51247
Airglow, 07010, 07161, 07222
Airline fares, 48114
Airline management, 13066
Airline passengers, 14038, 48114
Airlines, 10901, 11188, 20009, 36867
    history, 21058, 24255
    local-service, 10902
Airplanes, *See* Aircraft
Airport management, 10089
Airport security, 34096, 36040
Airports, 05446, 10054, 10089, 10251, 10725, 10956,
11188, 24017, 61088
    federal regulation of, 10251
Airships, 05132, 10075, 40119, 40158
    See also Aircraft
Airworthiness, 41021
Alabama, 01004, 01007, 01008, 01010, 01011, 01012,
01013, 01015, 01016, 01017
Alarms, burglar and fire, 10976
    See also Security systems
Alaska, 02005, 02006, 02007, 02008, 02009, 02010,
02011, 02012, 02013, 02014, 02030, 02031
Albinism, 43282
Alcohol
    abuse, 05784, 13038, 19002, 19007, 24018, 24327,
        24341, 36046, 51182, 54109
    addiction, 13141
    and diet, 51142
    driving and, 48147
    education, 36044
    fuels, 40240
    See also Alcoholism
Alcoholic beverage laws, 51338
Alcoholics Anonymous, 36046
    See also Alcoholism
Alcoholics, children of, 36300
Alcoholism, 01005, 03046, 03057, 05342, 05428, 05519,
05560, 05710, 05784, 07055, 08094, 10056, 10231,
10535, 10958, 13038, 13146, 14037, 14048, 17387,
17403, 19002, 19007, 21048, 24018, 24327, 27025,
27028, 27051, 34065, 36026, 36045, 360
    women, 43391
    prevention, 10231
Alcohols, 34065
Alexander technique, 36077
Alfalfa, 20001, 32004
Algae, 05386, 05400, 13060, 31029, 36262, 40059,
40114, 48219, 52036, 54020, 61105
Algebra, 05432, 44002
    See also Mathematics
Alkaline earth compounds, 40054
Alkyd resins, 37017
Allegory, 47043
Allergens, 48041
Allergies and allergic diseases, 03081, 03082, 05047,
07142, 10295, 17250, 24355, 25169, 31003, 34018,
36026, 48041, 48054, 54004, 61005

Biological psychiatry, 05755
Biological research, 36217
Biological rhythms, 24258, 36535
Biological stains, 36218
Biological warfare, 13003, 24081, 24083, 43377, 49013
Biology, 01063, 05160, 05495, 05547, 05703, 05846,
 10171, 10520, 11102, 25243, 27027, 32008, 35030,
 43191, 50020
    editors, 24167
    education, 51281
    aquatic, 05184, 13092, 15022, 16015, 18094, 35045,
     42078, 47093, 51388, 54030
    arctic, 02019
    cell, 05846, 24072, 25057
    desert, 32008
    developmental, 24357, 40112
    estuarine, 22035, 23003
    experimental, 24190, 25304
    marine, 02026, 05386, 05424, 05524, 05527, 05543,
     05717, 05718, 13120, 13130, 25249, 28012, 31029,
     34059, 42061, 44013, 44015, 45016, 61105
    molecular, 10531, 24066, 25304, 29055, 36217,
     40078
    perinatal, 05302
    systematic, 05547
Bioluminescence, 05180, 05725
Biomass energy, 01053, 01066, 05761, 10306, 10538,
 17235, 17238, 35014, 35043, 36283, 40240, 54122,
 61114, 61131
Biomathematics, 10307
Biomechanics, 05349, 07093, 11130, 17442, 19020,
 21057, 36162, 40058, 40128, 48061, 48172
Biomedical communications, 24271
Biomedical computer applications, 10085, 47015
Biomedical engineering, 05162, 40058
Biomedical materials, 01063
Biomedical photography, 17148
Biomedical research, 15022, 24366
Biometeorology, 43039
Biometrics, 05163, 10307, 10308, 24359
Bionics, 05326, 05405, 10071, 11332, 24020, 36387,
 40230, 40233, 54083
Biopharmaceutics, 41051, 52028
Biophysics, 10531, 11391, 24020, 36217, 43389
Biopsy, 17488
Biorheology, 05484, 36982
Biostatistics, 10307, 17445
Biostratigraphy, 10522
Biosynthesis, 05437, 39005
Biosystematics, 61016
Biotechnology, 24228, 47092
Biotic systems, 10530
Bird diseases, 34205, 43015, 48083
Bird migrations, 13155, 24402
Bird nests, 36630
Bird rescue, 05463
Bird songs, 36630
Bird banding, 05835, 17222, 31019, 34087, 50016,
 50020, 53012
Bird watching, 08022

Birds, 03101, 04030, 05065, 05199, 05463, 05753, 05835,
 08008, 08022, 10185, 10510, 10526, 10551, 13078,
 13155, 17328, 19036, 21001, 24394, 24475, 34205,
 36630, 43185, 43344, 48201,
    53012
    game, 19046, 48083
    migratory, 11222, 43154, 54024, 54101
Birds of prey, 16005, 17222, 21043, 36873
Birefringence, 25258
Birth control, 05164, 05257, 11297, 11334, 24136,
 25278, 36042, 36197, 36525, 36591, 36815, 36886,
 36887, 36923, 38033, 43062, 51070, 51218, 51315
    See also Family planning
Birth defects, 04053, 13031, 25059, 36479, 36655,
 42031, 43246, 48050
    See also Congenital abnormalities, Handicapped
    persons
Births, multiple, 61115
Bituminous coal, 10309, 11003
Bituminous sands, 07092, 22010
Black Catholics, 11108
Black consumers, 37097
Black duck, 23020
Black lung, disease 01051, 43091, 43249, 51263
Black office-holders, 10969
Black physicians, 11097
Blacks, 10985
    in labor unions, 36008
    in politics, 10969
    professional development of, 21038
Blacksmithing, 25233, 35004
Bladder diseases, 01048
Blades, hand-forged, 24034
Blasphemy, 54077
Blast-resistant structures, 48109
Blasting, 40236
Blepharospasm, 48049
Blimps, 05132, 40158
Blind athletes, 34238
Blind persons
    education, 21003, 36493, 36694, 51114, 51121
    employment, 51154
    rehabiliation, 24044, 51114, 51121
Blindness, 05167, 05384, 05472, 05498, 05723, 05737,
 07059, 10140, 17149, 17246, 17424, 24247, 24342,
 24428, 24453, 31010, 34162, 34214, 36198, 36421,
 36480, 36482, 36492, 36493, 36615, 36802, 36929,
 43063, 43350, 52062, 61034
Blood, 05504, 10201, 25226, 36647, 40041
Blood banks, 10201, 51026, 51034
Blood diseases, 01022, 13116, 24259, 24348, 24349,
 24356, 34230, 36301, 43097, 48226, 61137
    See also Hematology
Blood lipids, 10856
Blood substitutes, 61008
Blood sugar, 39005
Blowers, 17012
Blue crabs, 24216
Blue laws, 10659
Blueberries, 34177

(Choreography, continued)
films and video tapes, 36371
See also Dance
Christianity, 05019, 10934, 36553, 48146
Christians in social work, 43292
Christmas trees, 10591, 24093, 54091
Chromatography, 11093, 24124, 34113, 36218, 40079, 43051, 43346
Chromites, 40222
Chromium, 29023
Chromosome abnormalities, 43285
See also Birth defects, Genetic diseases
Chronic Epstein-Barr Virus, 17183
Chronic diseases, 05058, 07214, 10161, 17250, 24449, 25111, 29116, 36513
Chronic pain, 05609, 13131, 14089, 24107, 27079, 36865, 51311, 51393, 52047, 52079
See also Pain
Chronobiology, 24258, 36535
See also Circadian rhythms
Chrysanthemums, 51313
Church administrative, 40175
Church bells, 07171
Church communications, 36735
Church history, 05418
Church libraries, 43115
Church management, 10369
Church music, 25129, 33009
Church of Jesus Christ of Latter Day Saints, 49010, 49037
Church of the Nazarene, 29033
Church registers, 49023
Church-state relations, 10659, 11334, 29041, 37091, 40219, 48128
Churches, 36553
Churchill, Sir Winston, 29128
Cigar bands, 03067
Cigarette smoke, 05784, 10030, 52060
See also Smoking
Cigarettes, 51400
See also Smoking, Tobacco
Cinematography, 05101, 05284, 05352, 08131, 10154, 10883, 17495, 35008, 36423, 36587, 36720, 36831, 36978
See also Film, Motion pictures
Circadian rhythms, 05734, 24258, 36535, 36960
Circuits, integrated, *See* Integrated circuits
Circumcision, 43289
Circuses, 21036, 36463, 36831, 54037
Citizen action, 05250
Citizen lawsuits, 10837
Citizen participation, 10837, 10881, 30005, 36309, 40084, 52069
Citizens band radio, 08009
Citizenship education, 10652, 43207
Citizenship procedures, 36085
Citrus fruits, 05785, 13083, 48066
Civil War, 04043, 14033, 40225, 48074, 51266, 53025
aviation in, 61088

Civil defense, 10152, 10601, 11287, 36882, 48122, 51049, 52030
Civil disobedience, 05020, 05687, 18076, 37072
Civil engineering, 10793, 11127, 14071, 17432, 19043, 36155
Civil liberties, 05258, 05532, 10123, 10232, 10651, 10667, 10834, 36078, 36420, 36550, 43393, 54110
Civil rights, 01062, 05124, 05249, 05492, 05532, 10114, 10228, 10232, 10378, 10380, 10390, 10400, 10410, 10651, 10707, 10833, 10834, 10837, 10872, 10890, 10982, 11002, 11017, 11044, 11183, 11193, 11301, 11314, 11479, 14078, 14111, 36035, 36173, 36176, 36340, 36495, 36704, 36810, 36820, 52071
government commissions on, 10427, 11002
in South Africa, 36035
See also Blacks, Discrimination, Minorities
Civil service, 10150, 10792, 10907, 10951, 11218, 34197, 36544
See also Government employees
Civilization, ancient, 17127
Clairvoyance, 36329, 36868, 38038, 51181
Clams, 24216
See also Crustacea
Clarinets, 16017
Classification of government documents, 24326
Clay minerals, 18027
Clay pipes, 10999
Clay, expanded, 24188
Clays, 34093
Clean fuels, 05253, 43322
See also Alternative energy sources, Solar energy
Cleaning, 34226
Cleaning agents, 10398, 17295, 24124, 36963
fabrics, 24248
See also Soaps
Cleaning equipment, 17295
Cleft palate, 01047, 20054, 24358, 43024, 43233
Clemens, Samuel Langhorne, 08137, 29118
Climatic changes, 07082, 07159
Climatology, 03065, 05375, 05729, 07145, 13044, 17011, 24329, 24372, 24381, 24382, 25011, 25042, 29126, 33011, 34054, 35010, 38072, 38105, 48117, 49032, 49039
See also Meteorology
Climatotherapy, 43039
Clinical chemistry, 05738, 08020
Clinical laboratories, 43274
Clinical psychology, 10192
See also Psychology
Clocks, 43268
Cloisonne, 05255
Clothing, 25227, 36415, 36672, 36769, 36787, 51019
international trade, 10800
protective, 44024
Clothing workers, 36050
Cloud chambers, 05689, 29046
Cloud physics, 25011, 29046
Cloud-seeding, 49039
Clouds, 03065, 07159, 07160, 17310
See also Meteorology

Commercials, 05728
  See also Advertisements
Comminution (coal), 43139
Commissions for women, 34151
Commodities, 08029
  government regulation of, 10451, 11195
  marketing, 10781
  markets, 05174, 10654, 10966, 11191, 11195, 17179, 36316
Common carriers, 10681, 10949, 11427, 51249
Communes, 43062
Communicable diseases, 14031, 48224
  See also Diseases
Communication skills, 17221
  See also Communications, Speech, Writing
Communication, animal, 52054
Communication, multilingual, 17289
Communication, nonverbal, 36624, 36624
Communications, 05356, 05457, 07067, 10868, 13101, 36984, 37036, 48119, 51112, 54042
  aeronautic, 11326
  audiovisual, 40091, 43121
  biomedical, 24271
  business, 07045, 11086
  church, 36735
  corporate, 08030
  federal regulation of, 10453, 10596, 10868, 11234
  graphic, 51206
  intercultural, 48119
  interpersonal, 43059, 43121, 48119
  mass, 05528, 07067, 43059, 48119, 51433, 54033, 54078
  microwave, 10858, 10977, 40248
  military, 05383, 13064, 25038, 25122, 34234, 51101, 51101
  organizational, 48119
  political, 08030
  private radio, 11310
  radio, 05699, 07112, 18067, 48031, 51432
  satellite, 34045
  spacecraft, 24158, 34112
  telegraph, 10453
  visual, 35008, 35051
  See also Graphic arts, Media, Radio, TV
Communications cables, 11458
Communications disorders, 48053
Communications equipment, 05354, 48124
Communications law, 05517, 11336, 11410, 11419
Communications organizations, 24168
Communications professions for women, 48229
Communications regulation, 10283
Communications research, 08030, 08149, 20015, 25266, 27038, 43059, 43121
Communications satellites, 08013, 10454, 10480, 15026, 24158, 51235
Communications systems, 11208, 13033, 51239
Communications theory, 51433
Communicative disorders, 07086, 11137, 20029, 41031
Communism, 18085, 36111, 36803, 51160
Communist countries, 05053, 10561

Communities, utopian, 19003
Community associations, 51155
Community broadcasters, 11053
Community colleges, 05310, 10095
Community development, 01038, 05215, 05266, 05588, 07065, 08123, 10021, 10064, 10387, 10528, 10671, 10929, 10938, 10970, 10991, 11016, 11026, 11089, 11152, 11179, 11278, 17401, 17509, 20011, 21055, 25145, 28028, 29027, 29074, 36258, 36335, 36749, 40046, 40243, 43207, 43362, 51155, 51225, 52069, 61036
Community education, 10473, 11014, 40068
Community gardens, 10064, 50005, 50009
Community health services, 10926, 24154, 29098, 51317
Community involvement, 10730, 10881, 11295, 11314, 11462
Community mental health centers, 10091, 24334
Community organization, 10942, 14005, 17401, 17509, 34215, 36309
Community organizing, 05250
Community-school relations, 25104
Community service programs, 40088, 47011, 51478
Commuter airlines, 10902
Commuting, 10604, 24439
  students, 24328
Comparative education, 17191
Competition, 10614
Composers, 05563, 05762, 34145, 36082, 36382, 36943
  women, 36586
Composing (typesetting), 51319
Composite materials, 11215
Composts, 43086, 61108
Compressed gas, 51156
Comptroller of the Currency, 10459
Compulsive gambling, 05368, 36744
  See also Gambling
Compulsory military service, 10651, 11085, 11481, 43094
Computational linguistics, 34048
Computer-aided design, 05080, 05326, 05410, 07093, 14072, 17129, 24448, 25178, 36387, 38057, 40073, 43209, 47019, 48073, 48145, 51320, 54085
Computer-aided instruction, 05425, 08138, 10256, 10257, 19011, 19013, 34130, 48231, 49011, 51254
Computer-aided manufacturing, 24308, 25178, 36387, 40073, 40162, 43341, 48073, 51320, 54085
Computer chips, *See* Integrated circuits
Computer crime, *See* Computer-related crime
Computer data bases, *See* Data bases
Computer education, 51428
Computer engineering, 05696, 11128
Computer graphics, 24448, 25177, 36192, 40089, 48033, 51320
Computer industry, 10460
Computer law, 05216, 51157
Computer mapping, 17216
  See also Cartography
Computer networks, 11426, 13111, 51384
Computer professionals, 17264

Criminals, 05075, 10595
Criminology, 08043, 10224, 10740, 11295, 43108, 61067
    international, 37049
Crisis intervention, 24134
Critical-care medicine, 05756
Critical-path method, 43327
Crocheting, 36781
Crohn's Disease, 36752
Crop damage, 07150
Crop dusting, 10897
    See also Pesticides
Crop estimates, 10822
Crop insurance, 07150, 10597
Crop losses, 07150
Crop production, 11408
Crop protection, 05269
Crop rotation, 10149
Crop science, 54045
    See also Agriculture
Cross-cultural studies, 02016, 25142, 35051, 36552
Cross-cultural training, 05623, 07068, 07088, 10355, 11390
Crude oil, 10187, 10284, 10720, 36146, 36590, 43179, 48168
Crushed stone, 11143
Crustacea, 10520, 13039, 23006, 24216
Cryobiology, 17204, 40083
Cryogenics, 07136, 08049, 14017, 17204, 20044, 24317, 25051
Cryptology, 05360, 25038
Cryptozoology, 03068
Crystal growth, 05050
Crystallography, 05323, 10521, 10878, 24311, 34184, 36092, 36661, 36879, 36936, 43226
Crystals, 41018, 43232, 44001
    liquid, 25258, 40160
Cuba, 36259
Cuban-Americans, 13057
Cued speech, 10504
Culicidae, 05081, 18079, 18093
Cultivars, 24417
Cultivation, 18028
Cults, 05549, 05771, 25020, 36310
Cultural education, 10819
Cultural history, American, 10523
Cultural property, 11078
Cultural relations, 10586, 11024
Cultural resources, 07201
Cultured dairy products, 10145
Cultures (biology), 24072
Cuneiform writing, 05435
Currency, 07025, 10325, 11432, 48173
Curriculum development, 10095, 51117
Curriculums, 10078, 19013, 10970, 24242, 25102, 36472, 40105
    core, 40173
Customs (international trade), 10505, 10506, 10639, 24301
Customs-free zones, 10639
Customs Service, U.S., 10505, 10506

Cutting wheels, 40101
Cybernetics, 03059, 05405, 11391, 21047, 25052, 41048, 51080
Cyclamates, 14026
Cycles, 43162
Cycling, 05461, 07208, 10230, 24269, 37040, 43084, 43386
    See also Bicycles
Cyclones, 07160, 13140
Cypress wood, 47077
Cystic Fibrosis, 01043, 17205, 18031, 22016, 24169, 24276, 38032, 40138, 43131, 43366, 49025
Cystinosis, 05278
Cystitis, 05487
Cytodiagnosis, 17277, 17488
Cytogenetics, 01044, 05408, 08050, 43186
Cytology, 13152, 17277, 17488, 24190, 34117, 36722, 38025, 40078, 43389
    See also Cell biology

Daffodils, 28004
Dahlias, 43030
Dairies, 36011, 43132, 51342
    See also Milk
Dairy cattle, 29107, 40023, 40098, 50002
    See also Livestock
Dairy products, 05208, 10145, 10764, 10877, 17053, 17060, 17207, 17370, 17506, 24171, 29102, 43132, 51342, 54124
Damage awards (jury verdicts), 40149
Dampers, 17012
Dams, 05365, 17313, 25293, 38105, 52006
Dams, beaver, 28032
Dance, 05465, 05564, 13058, 17294, 36093, 36373, 36443, 36463, 36624, 36702, 36745, 36831, 38007, 51018
    aerobic, 05564
    ballroom, 36532
    ethnic, 36440
    films and video tapes, 36371
    See also Choreography
Dance education, 36371
Dance notation, 05229, 36372
Dance research, 36341
Dance theater, 36373
Dance therapy, 05465, 24043, 52045
Dancing, 41042
    ballroom, 05564
Danish-Americans, 31013
Danish literature, 36171
Data bases, computer, 05018, 05281, 05607, 07110, 07131, 07199, 08051, 08061, 08071, 08092, 08108, 10073, 10272, 10335, 10364, 10399, 10480, 10570, 10669, 10829, 11080, 11149, 11242, 11243, 11246, 11424, 11428, 11470, 11470, 17006, 17262, 24175, 24337, 25144, 36645, 36906, 38065, 40165, 40247, 43087, 43090, 49023, 51171, 51368
    geneological, 49023
Data evaluation, 11246
Data management systems, 10727

Engineering technicians, 20005
  accreditation, 36018
Engineers, 05276, 10023, 36066, 45018
  U.S. Army, 51102
  motion-picture, 36978
  operating, 10805
  television, 36978
Engines, 08143, 17226
  aircraft and spacecraft, 34171, 40011
English as a second language, 11416
English foxhounds, 40153
English horns, 22024
English language, 17057, 17221, 42019
English literature, 24444
Engraving, 10791, 43175
  currency, 10325
Enterostomal therapy, 05454
Enteroviruses, 48085
Entertainers, 36098
  See also Actors, Performing arts
Entertainment, 11462, 36463
  See also Performing arts
Enthalpy, 24128, 24310
Entomology, 04045, 05131, 05160, 05300, 05403,
  05629, 08040, 10640, 11102, 13084, 14109, 15001,
  17206, 18036, 18079, 20065, 24184, 28011, 30003,
  36222, 43033, 43167, 48076, 48078, 48218, 48225,
  49005, 51008
  See also Insects
Entrepreneurs, 05332, 13137, 25150, 36260, 40108
Entropy, 24310
Environmental design, 05178, 05334, 07065, 10064,
  10221, 10579, 13045, 22013, 36239
Environmental development, 36258
Environmental education, 10059, 10374, 10510, 10580,
  11325, 16020, 27085, 36136, 40105, 40110, 40130,
  40199
Environmental engineering, 11127, 14023, 17256,
  17271, 18037, 24022, 24082, 36155, 40210, 45008,
  48033, 48068
Environmental geology, 11250
Environmental health, 05709, 07152, 10193, 11066,
  11242, 11261, 11273, 11316, 14074, 17249, 17250,
  18054, 24254, 36433, 38040, 38079, 47087, 51472
Environmental history, 07029
Environmental impact statements, 11470
Environmental law, 05773, 07187, 10290, 10582,
  11163, 25088, 61044, 61135
  international, 37093
Environmental management, 11200, 13070, 51143
Environmental medicine, 36537, 61019
Environmental monitoring, 11184, 11449, 32014,
  40109, 45008, 54048
Environmental planning, 11250, 13118
Environmental policy, 10059, 10583, 10821, 11338,
  42009
Environmental protection, 05158, 05183, 05267,
  05319, 05320, 05335, 05364, 05381, 05620, 05730,
  05803, 05821, 05861, 07090, 07094, 07205, 08031,
  08045, 08102, 08124, 10466, 10497, 10576, 10577,

(Environmental protection, continued)
  10582, 10786, 10881, 11091, 11155, 11178, 11185,
  11470, 11487, 13081, 13082, 13093, 13114, 14047,
  15006, 15018, 17311, 17486, 21016, 21039, 24015,
  24143, 24430, 25049, 25075, 25130, 27100, 30019,
  33002, 34245, 35046, 36404, 36406, 36430, 36620,
  36656, 36719, 36740, 37093, 38067, 39003, 39004,
  39010, 40043, 40056, 40069, 42059, 43089, 43101,
  43125, 48118, 50022, 51150, 51250, 51300, 51377,
  51401, 60006
  congressional committees on, 11360
  international, 37093
Environmental quality, 10837, 11511
Environmental Protection Agency, U.S., 11184,
  11229, 11238
Environmental research, 03060, 17265, 24016, 29042,
  41049, 42058, 54028
Environmental sciences, 05540, 07082, 10668, 10714,
  17271
Environmental studies, 05452, 25300, 34059, 34060,
  34077, 36538, 54057
Environmental toxicology, 05604, 34020, 42058,
  47021, 47034, 47086, 48007, 54049
Enzymes, 27014, 39005
Ephemera, 50006
Ephemerides, 11506, 25198
Epics, 47043
Epidemiology, 08150, 10193, 10308, 10666, 11273,
  13085, 14094, 15002, 15027, 24449, 25111, 34020,
  36071, 40085, 48085
  mental illness, 24359
Epilepsy, 05308, 10148, 13071, 17151, 24186, 51214,
  51245, 61102
Episcopal Church, 48034
Epithets, 54077
Epoxy resin, 44011
Epoxy resins, 37017
Epstein-Barr Virus, 17183, 42045
Equal educational opportunity, 11255, 20047, 25295,
  36389, 36692, 36704
Equal employment opportunity, 10584, 10585, 10620,
  10834, 10971, 11207, 11301, 17507, 24219, 29001,
  36282, 36699, 36728, 38093, 40265, 48229
Equal Employment Opportunity Commission, 10585
Equal rights, 05845, 10378, 10620, 10834, 11044, 11492,
  11498, 17507, 24187, 25295, 27080, 34151, 34186,
  36250, 36286, 36692, 36727, 36733, 36739, 37080,
  37083, 37089, 38093, 40265, 43394, 48229, 51476,
  52071, 52087
Equine behavior, 61074
Equipment, 11148, 11166
Equivalency tests, 10144
Ergonomics, See Human-factors engineering
Erosion, 05092, 10149, 10763, 11398, 19056, 28031,
  49040
Erosion control, 07186, 43247
Erotic art, 18062
Erotic literature, 18062
Erythrocytes, 05504, 36647
Erythropoiesis, 43097

Hardwoods, 14085, 17413, 23024, 38009, 47059, 51209
Harelip, 01047, 24358, 43233
    See also Speech disorders
Harness racing, 36488, 40260
Hartshorne, Charles, 05223
Harvard graduates, 25189
Harvesting, 16018
Hawaii, 15001, 15003, 15008, 15009, 15010, 15012
Hawaiian business and industry, 15003
Hawks, 16005, 21043, 43185, 53012
Hay fever, 05047, 10295, 48054
    See also Allergies
Hayes, Rutherford B., 40225
Hazardous materials, 10274, 10275, 10337, 21051,
    24206, 24213, 24464, 34126, 34182, 36277, 36406,
    40069, 40085, 42058, 43280, 47087
    spills, 10418, 11238, 45023, 48167
    transportation, 54066
Hazardous wastes, 01006, 07090, 10289, 10418, 10462,
    10583, 11140, 11194, 11238, 11244. 11338, 21051,
    24206, 25138, 34182, 36404, 41049, 48167, 51150,
    52014
    transportation of, 54066
Hazing, fraternity, 36332
Head injuries, 24361, 25219, 27047, 43363
Head surgery, 10070
Headaches, 05189, 17025, 17386, 25134, 29114, 36678,
    61100
    See also Pain
Healing, 05315
Health
    child, 05052, 07072, 10987, 21007, 24114, 24357,
        36145
    environmental, 05709, 07152, 10193, 11066, 11242,
        11261, 11273, 11316, 14074, 17249, 17250, 18054,
        24254, 36433, 38040, 38079, 47087, 51472
    holistic, 05086, 07019
    infant, 08054, 08069, 10986, 27063, 29086, 51011
    international, 24401
    maternal, 05052, 05089, 08069, 10987, 11158,
        21007, 24114, 25078, 27063, 29057, 29086, 34053,
        36049, 36290, 36662, 38033, 47042, 51011, 51348,
        52026
    mental, *See* Mental health
    occupational, *See* Occupational health and safety
    perinatal, 51011
    prenatal, 05089
    preventive, 05088
    public, 05095, 05290, 07119, 07152, 08150, 10030,
        10086, 10131, 10162, 10193, 10263, 10675, 10754,
        10936, 11043, 11065, 11259, 11278, 11387, 11511,
        17215, 18054, 18079, 19029, 22022, 24036, 24113,
        24147, 24153, 24200, 24209, 24319, 24345, 24365,
        24400, 24454, 25070, 28025, 29125, 34020, 36071,
        36263, 36335, 36406, 36537, 36559, 36580, 36760,
        36770, 36810, 36908, 36910, 38013, 38035, 40042,
        40104, 42026, 43242, 47042, 48075, 48176, 48224,
        51472, 54036
    women's, 05485
Health and safety, occupational, *See* Industrial health

and safety, Occupational health and safety
Health care, 05078, 05444, 05584, 05585, 05665, 05794,
    07069, 07072, 07119, 07129, 07155, 10215, 10793,
    10926, 11273, 13016, 14074, 16008, 17007, 17150,
    17162, 17307, 24055, 24113, 24319, 24413, 24419,
    27061, 36106, 36760, 36761, 36764, 43313, 51027,
    51060, 51317, 52009, 52076, 52084
    ambulatory, 07069
    careers, 10676, 24116, 36504
    colleges and universities, 24036
    consumer education, 36267
    in developing countries, 11023
    international, 24401
    rural, 27017, 28028, 29098
    women in, 11158, 37086
Health and Human Services, U.S. Department of,
    10399, 10675, 11183, 11201, 11205, 11230
    See also Food and Drug Administration
Health care costs, 11066, 17331
Health care delivery, 10085, 11316, 17320, 24400
Health care financing, 10675
Health care products, 08066
Health care technology, 29054
Health clubs, 24095
Health education, 05218, 05573, 05573, 05750, 10095,
    10162, 10266, 10685, 10987, 11065, 13018, 14031,
    14032, 14074, 18069, 24154, 24347, 25268, 29050,
    36089, 36106, 36359, 36504, 40036, 40085, 42020,
    43373, 51006, 51018, 51118, 51142, 51210, 51240,
    54036
Health facility planning, 10784
Health foods, 05088, 36834
Health hazards, 04053, 11396, 14037, 14086, 24153,
    24209, 24254, 27036, 36089, 36110, 36272, 36404,
    36433, 38040, 43280
    art materials, 36184
    See also Industrial health and safety
Health information systems, 10085
Health insurance, 10066, 10138, 10754, 17150, 36489,
    51207, 51336
Health law, 05586
Health maintenance organizations, 24345, 24399
Health occupations education, 10161, 10188
Health physics, 10674, 11476, 51211
Health planning, 10162, 11396
Health policy, 10754, 10829, 36491
Health professions, 10676, 24116, 36504
Health promotion, 05051
Health research, 05359, 24366
Health sciences, 01045, 52076
Health services, 10039, 10130, 10162, 10188, 10663,
    11314, 11508
    See also Health care
Health services administration, 07069, 08066, 10085,
    10784, 10912, 13005, 17162, 17353, 24345, 24400,
    34110, 43184
Health statistics, 17150, 24147, 24320, 43065
34122, 51006
Hearing, 10304, 17420, 17471, 24070, 25133, 27013,
    34107

Historical photographs, 17244
Historical prints, 36107
Historical research, 11061
Historiography, 05223
History, 04037, 08011, 11101, 11227, 19025, 21031, 52111
   Afro-American, 25203
   American, 07077, 10164, 10523, 10846, 10909, 11101, 11111, 11186, 11256, 25018, 25205, 25231, 27056, 43365
   American newspaper, 10183
   ancient, 10376
   architectural, 15012, 36348, 61010
   art, 05166, 13117, 36884
   aviation, 03092, 05039, 05056, 05277, 08039, 10051, 10900, 19001, 21058, 24255, 36470, 38081, 38108, 40158
   business, 17154
   church, 05418
   constitutional, 24192
   early American industrial, 36390
   economic, 11350
   environmental, 07029
   Jewish, 05497, 05732, 07066, 14044, 25025, 36604, 36613, 36614, 36640, 61047
   local, 01012, 02008, 02009, 02010, 02011, 02013, 02031, 03022, 03024, 03079, 05701, 07137, 07200, 08042, 08063, 08072, 10887, 11061, 16013, 16014, 17181, 17259, 17496, 18048, 18050, 19037, 19049, 19059, 20019, 20039, 21029, 21045, 22011, 22032, 23017, 24280, 25055, 25189, 25256, 27086, 29040, 29076, 29118, 30010, 31028, 31032, 32022, 32023, 33014, 34175, 35018, 35029, 36827, 36828, 39008, 39012, 40067, 40122, 40225, 43188, 43307, 44020, 44021, 45025, 45026, 46016, 46018, 47036, 47049, 47084, 47085, 48175, 48202, 48210, 49010, 49023, 49037, 50019, 51459, 52042, 52108, 53025, 53026, 54120, 55019
   maritime, 05424, 23026, 24121, 24212, 24384, 24469, 25080, 25174, 25229, 36129, 36996, 42018, 51258
   masonic, 25205
   medical, 17080, 17291
   medieval, 36448, 36884
   military, 01067, 03031, 07101, 10051, 10863, 10880, 11167, 11287, 11337, 11435, 14033, 14105, 17335, 21006, 25139, 25275, 36828, 36952, 37037, 37077, 40255, 43251, 43376, 48074, 51170, 51178, 51180, 51216, 51447, 51468
   music, 34244
   natural, 20050, 24094
   naval, 11164, 11166, 11167, 11450, 24385, 24391, 24469, 36952, 40140
   oral, 10712, 23023, 36857
   railroad, 17099, 17174, 17177, 17258, 17338, 17456, 24103, 24146, 24208, 25263
   social, 10827
   state and local, *See* Local history
   women's, 05350, 25043, 25278, 61057
Hobbies, 03067, 03070, 05100, 05255, 05256, 05272,

(Integrated circuits, continued)
   05567, 05600, 05638, 05693, 07025, 07039, 08084, 08089, 10791, 13019, 13037, 13055, 17335, 21058, 24384, 25034, 29019, 34108, 34216, 34224, 36318, 36416, 36781, 37101, 40016, 40182, 40185, 40221, 40241, 42046, 43046, 43137, 43251, 43267, 43268, 43314, 43374, 48023, 48173, 51005, 51072, 51236, 52037, 52058, 53011, 53014, 53022, 54086, 54088
Hocker, 08068
Hockey, 27052, 61078
Hodgkin's Disease, 36641
Hog cholera, 24180
Hohokam culture, 03027, 03096
Hoists, 43189
Holding companies, bank, 10276
Holidays, 11472, 34075
Holistic medicine, 05086, 05315, 05444, 05660, 07019, 36343, 51100, 51116, 52009, 54059
Holly, 24215
Hollywood, Calif., 05395
   See also Motion pictures
Holocaust, 05732, 07066, 10678, 14044, 36604
   See also Jewish history, World War II
Holography, 11262, 51084
Home-based businesses, 17345, 34147
Home building, 24289
   See also Construction
Home-care services, 36764
Home economics, 10165, 51093
Home-equity conversion, 54090
Home health care, 10151, 10915
   See also Health care
Home improvements and repair, 05626, 11079, 25294, 51302
Home-sewing industry, 36108
Home study, 10144, 11068, 25103, 61090
Homebuilding, *See* Construction
Homebuying, *See* Real estate
Homelessness, 36730
Homemakers, displaced, 10534
Homeopathy, 10173, 27106, 51448, 52049
Homesteading, 43347, 50011
Homicide, 48112
Homosexuality, 05398, 05491, 25123, 29067, 36526, 36755, 36757, 54092
Honey, 13009, 41005
Honey bees, 04049, 22008, 24393
   See also Apiculture, Beekeeping
Honor societies, college, 43067
Hoover, Herbert, 19026
Hopi Indians, 35016
Hops, 52088
Hormone therapy, 05659, 27054
Hormones, 05401, 24181
Horn music, 54065
Hornworts, 17043
Horoscopes, 03009, 05481, 36718
   See also Astrology
Horror movies, 05023
Horse breeding, 18057, 40009

Inks, printing, 10184, 25056, 34115, 36426, 37008, 43175, 43283
Inmates, 21024
    See also Criminals, Prisons
Innovation, 03095, 05817, 48107
Insect control, 05300, 13070, 13100, 13170, 24233, 29020, 51008, 51349
    stored agricultural products, 48205
    See also Insecticides, Pesticides
Insect taxonomy, 18036
Insect vectors, 18093
Insecticides, 04045, 10398, 10640, 13084, 14109, 17308, 24015, 24124, 24233, 46008, 51081
    See also Pesticides
Insects, 03101, 04045, 05131, 05199, 05629, 10640, 13084, 13100, 14109, 20065, 24184, 43033, 43167, 46008, 48218, 54123
    cotton, 48078
    forest, 10640, 10641, 48094
    See also Entomology
Inservice education, 36738
Insider trading, 11352, 36658, 36836
Insignia, military, 25227
Insomnia, 05135, 05734, 05735, 05736, 24360, 36960
Institutional food, 07028, 17102, 43128
    See also Food service
Institutional investors, 10814, 25272, 36357, 36555
Instruction, computer-assisted, *See* Computer-assisted instruction
Instructional technology, 10025, 18003, 19013, 36388, 48098
Instrumentation, 01063, 10137, 11215, 11396, 43338, 43342, 54062
Instruments, laboratory, 38050
Instruments, musical, *See* Musical instruments
Insulated cable, 25153
Insulated wire, 37014
    See also Wire
Insulation, 05478, 07128, 07183, 10747, 18005, 24086
    laminated fiberglass, 40156
    thermal, 34139, 37021
    See also Energy conservation
Insulin, 17214, 24338, 40112
    See also Diabetes
Insurance, 07150, 08007, 08012, 08073, 08086, 10138, 17014, 17438, 29083, 36120, 36510, 36548, 36931, 38051, 43037, 43194, 51291, 51336
    automobile, 10680, 17014
    crop, 07150
    disaster, 17438
    government, 10065
    health, 10066, 10754
    legal, 11122
    liability, 17014
    life, 43073
    property, 17014, 17438
Insurance Company of North America, 43194
Insurance agents, 51291
Insurance industry, 10065, 10939
Integrated circuits, 05080, 05279, 05326, 11128, 36031,

(Integrated circuits, continued)
    40103, 40222, 40233, 48211
    See also Computers
Integrated energy systems, 11190
Integration, 10714
    See also Civil rights, Discrimination
Intellectual property, 51066, 51230
    See also Copyright
Intelligence, 10393
    government, 11168
Intelligence agents, 51127
Intelligence services, 05258, 10381
Intensive-care units, 05756
InterAmerican affairs, 10331
Intercultural communications, 48119
Intercultural relations, 11024, 11462
Intercultural studies, 36354
Interest rates, 36784, 36902
    See also Banking, Credit
Interfaith relations, 36734, 48128
    See also Religions
Interferometry, 05156
Intergalactic dust, 24376
Intergovernmental relations, 05441, 07134, 07149, 10027, 10465, 10948, 10963, 11089, 11340, 21014, 36309, 38092, 40193, 43112, 48184, 61060
Interior decorating, 29090, 36415, 48161, 51394
Interior design, 07065, 17270, 22013, 36158, 36441, 51221, 51232
Interior lighting, 17158
    See also Lighting
Interior, U.S. Department of the, 10329, 10333, 10344, 10540, 10550, 10551, 10625, 10626, 10722, 11200, 11225, 11420
    See also National Park Service
Intermediate technologies, 05451
Internal combustion engines, 17226
    See also Automobile engines
Internal medicine, 10219, 20024, 43027
    See also Medicine
Internal Revenue Service, 10755, 10756, 10757, 11361
International affairs, 10078, 10668
International agricultural development, 10558, 16018, 36814, 36905
International arbitration, 11510
International banking, 36594
International business, 03010
International conflict, 25063
International cooperation, 10294, 10569, 11210, 11507, 11510, 15005
International corporations, 10379, 10569, 10775
International cultural exchange, 10806, 11278, 11516
International development, 03047, 04061, 05422, 10041, 10042, 10296, 10314, 10786, 11179, 11270, 11278, 11474, 11503, 15005, 24187, 25003, 25063, 25064, 25075, 25132, 36086, 36138, 36369, 36455, 36897, 36814, 36995, 37031, 37048, 40243, 44007, 44009, 51467, 61106
    education, 36471
    women, 10044, 10768

(Irrigation, continued)
   See also Agriculture
Islamic civilization, 36172
Islamic studies, 03078, 07138, 48146, 50004
Islands, 05661, 10816, 14077
Isotope separation, 10384, 11251, 40120, 47046
Isotopes, 05505, 24431
Israel, 07066, 10678, 10731, 36053, 36121, 36172,
   36270, 36614, 36820, 43105, 54038
Italian-Americans, 11087
Ivory carvings, 36817
Ivy, 40028

Jaguars (automobiles), 07073
Jail reform, 11004
   See also Prisons
Jamaica, 25301
James, Jesse, 27104, 29104
Japan, 10817, 10818, 34121, 36391, 36606, 36607,
   36608, 36609, 37011, 37057, 43104
Japanese-Americans, 05492, 05493
Japanese-American relations, 10819
Japanese art, 10650
Japanese culture, 10818, 13128, 36608
Japanese gardens, 13128
Japanese language, 10819
Jazz, 05839, 10397, 10843, 20052, 22056
   dixieland, 22056
Jesuits, 10282
Jet propulsion, 05494, 18088
Jetties, 10933
Jewelry, 05371, 25126, 36178, 36348, 36610, 44012,
   54116
Jewish art, 17472, 36742
Jewish culture, 07066, 17472, 36753
Jewish dietary laws, 36328
Jewish education, 36235, 36612
Jewish history, 05497, 05732, 07066, 14044, 25025,
   36604, 36613, 36614, 36640, 43353, 61047
Jewish lawyers, 17210
Jewish libraries, 36205
Jewish literature in Braille, 36611
Jewish music, 37102
Jewish organizations, 36121
Jewish sociology, 11459
Jewish studies, 43105
Jews, 05732, 07066, 10678, 36121, 36613, 36820, 37102
   Soviet, 36989
   Canadian, 61047
Jews in America, 05497, 11459, 36053
Job market, 10990
Job discrimination, *See* Employment discrimination
Job placement, 05207, 10571, 10810, 11416
   women, 11486
Job satisfaction, 37087
   See also Employment
Jogging, 05079, 10205, 29112
   See also Physical fitness
Johnson, Lyndon Baines, 48138
Joint diseases, 05141, 07108

Joint ventures, 11020
Joints, structural, 48189
Joists, steel, 45029
Jojoba, 03037, 03069, 05611
Joseph Disease, 05475
Journalism, 05357, 05496, 05528, 10183, 10561, 11105,
   11278, 11327, 11496, 13107, 34083, 51078, 54033,
   54078
   broadcast, 47091
   earth sciences, 51126
   high-school, 19050
   horse-racing reportage, 36809
   investigative, 29063
   science, 54029
   student, 11410
Journalism education, 34083, 45002, 47025
Journalists, 36159
Jousting, 05744
Judaica, 17472
Judaism, 03078, 05732, 07066, 10678, 11459, 36121,
   36235, 36614, 48146, 61047
   See also Jews
Judges, 17074, 36540, 51068
Judgment, 07070, 37041
Judicial administration, 05235, 07139, 07157, 10034,
   10607, 10749, 10931, 11042, 11413, 17039, 17074,
   17165, 25091, 32020, 32021, 36540, 51068, 51308,
   61084
Judicial reform, 07157, 10058, 11004, 17074, 51308
Judiciary, congressional committees on, 10707
Juggling, 36582
Jukeboxes, 17126
Jung, Carl Gustav, 05175, 11291
Jungles, 13026
Junior colleges, 05310, 10095
   See also Colleges
Junkyards, automobile, 10298
Jury verdicts, 40149
Justice, criminal, *See* Criminal justice
Justice, U.S. Department of, 10238, 10341, 10342,
   10410, 10554. 10595, 10719, 10828, 11233
Juvenile assistance, 10231
Juvenile corrections, 05293, 24151, 34165, 43270
Juvenile courts, 05574, 10400, 10403, 17037, 32020
   See also Junvenile justice
Juvenile delinquency, 05075, 05293, 05574, 05576,
   07055, 10231, 10341, 10400, 10563, 11042, 17171,
   17354, 24041, 24138, 24337, 34165, 36434, 37065,
   40218, 43108, 43270, 48112, 54131
Juvenile drinking, 10231
Juvenile justice, 11004, 25091, 34165, 36540, 40218,
   43270, 49012, 51346, 54131
Juvenile justice administration, 10231, 13141

Kafka, Franz, 43228
Kampuchea, 36331
   See also Cambodia
Kansas, 20039, 20040
Kaolin, 34093
Katcinas, 35019, 35028

(Laos, continued)
   See also Southeast Asia
Large-type publications, 11092, 24231, 25210, 36694, 36703, 43063
Larynges, artificial, 36562
Laryngology, 43040
Laser medicine, 54014
Laser printers, 05283
Laser surgery, podiatric, 43215
Lasers, 03059, 04048, 05220, 05323, 05393, 05675, 05689, 05733, 10384, 11262, 24131, 25008, 25051, 34112, 34184, 35026, 36031, 36628, 36634, 40157, 44001, 51386, 51424, 52052
   in surgery, 40144, 54014
Latex, 11342, 43150
Laths, 10292
Latin America, 03039, 10267, 10498, 10750, 10751, 10752, 11263, 11264, 11278, 11325, 19018, 20012, 22014, 25003, 25064, 25179, 36266, 36292, 36550, 36555, 36632, 36842, 48065, 48133, 51231
Latin American studies, 37023
Laundering, 13172, 24248, 34226, 47055
Laurence-Moon-Biedl Syndrome, 24267
Law (jurisprudence), 01014, 05311, 07097, 07139, 10068, 10222, 10290, 10417, 10594, 10749, 10788, 10872, 10930, 10967, 10972, 11075, 11090, 11136, 11323, 17036, 17040, 17334, 17362, 17368, 21020, 25026, 32021, 36901, 43041, 51068, 51337, 61084
   American Indian, 35005
   administrative, 10032, 10417
   admiralty, 10290
   aviation, 10290, 10956, 36867, 61083
   communications, 05517, 11336, 11410, 11419
   computer, 05216, 51157
   criminal, 10290, 10740, 11295, 11510
   energy, 49016
   environmental, 05773, 07187, 10290, 10582, 11163, 25088, 61044, 61135
   family, 17037, 36727
   food, 36333
   food and drug, 10629, 34020
   Indian, 10737
   information, 05216
   international, 05855, 10220, 10524, 10638, 10715, 10749, 10785, 10788, 11284, 11507, 11510, 15017, 17316, 24391, 34103, 36064, 36369, 43220, 45015, 51144, 52095
   international environmental, 11510
   labor, 10611, 10797, 11088, 36196
   maritime, 05620, 08140, 10174, 10296, 10506, 10610, 15017, 51144
   marriage, 05826, 10084
   medical, 24030, 25031, 25065
   mental health, 10872
   military, 10228, 11287
   mining, 07132, 41030
   patent, 11243, 51066
   public interest, 10263, 10473, 10058, 10881, 10949, 11091, 11163, 11316, 11323
   railroad, 10272, 10290, 11428

(Law, continued)
   space, 61083
   tax, 10755, 11454
   telecommunication, 05216
   water, 10344
   women and, 43394
   See also Criminal justice
Law and society, 05270, 05311
Law enforcement, 01049, 05075, 05261, 07157, 08079, 10152, 10279, 10419, 10614, 11042, 11135, 11233, 11294, 11295, 13080, 17125, 17171, 24238, 24240, 24337, 25262, 36588, 40012, 48112, 51153, 51327, 54098, 61028, 61067
   community relations, 24156
   history, 55011
   standards and specifications, 24268
Law libraries, 17029
Law reform, 10400
Law schools, 10270
Lawn mowers, power, 11268
Lawns, 47014
Laws (legislative)
   federal and state, 24160
   liquor, 51338
   motor-vehicle, 17039, 51352
Lawyers, 10290, 10930, 11090, 11122, 17036, 17038
   advertising, 40049
   Jewish, 17210
   trial, 10972
Lead, 36584
Lead (metal), 36637
Lead poisoning, 14094, 24211
Leaded glass, 29117
Leadership, 05800, 10142, 10230, 11466, 36605, 3801943207, 51219, 51225
Leadership training, 16021
Leaks (journalism), 10667
Learning, 10035, 17315, 20042, 34116, 36223, 43234, 47045, 51254, 54125
   anxiety in, 10738
   See also Education
Learning disabilities, 01064, 07086, 10919, 20027, 24232, 24455, 36265, 36439, 43064, 47045, 48069, 48132, 48144, 48162
Leather, 11414, 25227, 25287, 40030, 40246
Leather industry, 11444
Lebanon, 10839
Lecithin, 18039
Lecturers, 10716
Left-handed products, 20043
Left-handedness, 20043, 34134
Legal aid, 10228, 10872, 11090, 11205, 17038
Legal assistance to prisoners, 10123
Legal assistance to the poor, 10872
Legal assistants, 41034
Legal documents, 05104
Legal education, 10068, 11075, 11510, 25026, 34118, 36901, 43041
   continuing, 36901
Legal information services, 07097

Museums, 05119, 10100, 10288, 10844, 10886, 11166, 51105
Mushrooms, 27087, 40200, 43042
Music, 05563, 05762, 07075, 10063, 10226, 10260, 10712, 10888, 11180, 13175, 17085, 17422, 36013, 36054, 36082, 36133, 36227, 36291, 36463, 36779, 36821, 36831, 36943, 37104, 43069, 43075, 43130, 48013
   African, 36442
   Afro-American, 36442, 43088
   American, 17085, 36133
   chamber, 36291
   choral, 36105, 41004, 43075
   church, 25129, 33009
   country, 36366, 47027, 47028
   electronic, 18033
   fife and drum, 08037
   folk, 05232, 11202, 18016, 36366, 40034, 47028, 61040, 61110
   horn, 54065
   jazz, 22056
   Jewish, 37102
   military, 08037
   moravian, 38059
   popular, 40076
   renaissance, 37020
   vocal, 41055
Music appreciation, 08091
Music arrangement, 05102
Music boxes, 18068
Music critics, 24288
Music education, 07075, 07163, 13135, 17197, 19061, 20052, 38069, 40034, 41004, 51267, 51295, 54105
Music history, 10888, 22056, 34244, 47028
Music publishing, 34145, 36780
Music schools, 51295
Music teachers, 14018
Musical composition, 36586, 36943
Musical instruments, 08037, 10888, 14018, 16017, 17085, 17356, 18071, 22024, 25129, 33009, 33018, 34005, 34006, 36105, 36687, 36736, 37069, 38069, 46002, 54065
Musical scores, 43130
   Braille, 11092
Musical theater, 07075, 11076, 34145, 36288, 43043
Musicians, 10843, 36097, 49031
Musicology, 10888, 17197, 36105, 38059, 43043
Musicotherapy, 10842, 10996, 34010, 37066, 40034
Muskeg, 61077
Muslims, 07138
Mussels, 51457
Mustangs, 32016
Mutagenesis, 38102
Mutagens, 47034, 47086, 51188
Mutations, 05336
Mutual funds, 10813, 36840, 37062
   See also Investments
Myalgic Encephalomyelitis, 42045, 43044
Myasthenia Gravis, 17212, 36688
Mycology, 27087, 40200, 48041

Mycorrhizae, 10640
Mycotoxins, 47021
Myocardial infarction, 40094
   See also Coronary heart diseases
Myofacial Pain Dysfunction Syndrome, 36865
Myopia, 36689, 43222
Mysticism, 36153, 36182, 36343
Mythology, 05232, 10376

Nairobi sheep disease, 36889
Names, 36134
   geographic, 10312, 17216, 51197
   geologic, 51199
Nannoplankton, 08109
Napier, John, 42071
Narcolepsy, 05082, 05135, 05734, 05735, 36693, 36960
Narcotics, 05553, 05555, 11233, 24042, 24363, 25101, 36588
   See also Drug Abuse, Drugs
National Aeronautics and Space Administration, 10895, 10896
   See also Astronautics
National Aquariam, 10905
National Archives and Records Administration, 10365, 10827, 10841, 10846, 10880. 10907, 10908, 10909, 11227, 11254, 11256, 11350
National Bureau of Standards, 10384, 11093, 11215, 11249
National defense, 05217, 10244, 10372, 10561, 10679, 11345, 25146
   See also Defense Deparament, Warfare, Weapons
National Football League, 11057
National forests, 10644
   See also Forest Service
National Highway Traffic Safety Administration, 11067, 11417, 11425
National Oceanic and Atmospheric Administration,, 11051
   See also National Weather Service
National Park Service, U.S., 11111, 11112, 11113
National parks, 05273, 11112, 11113, 11115, 11325, 55013
   congressional committees on, 10696, 11359
National security, 10156, 10356, 10372, 10381, 10389, 10429, 10450, 11133, 11242, 24326, 51333
National Weather Service, 10822
   See also Meteorology, Weather forecasting
Native American arts and crafts, 01037, 03063, 03084, 10772, 35019, 35028, 35023, 41023
Native American businesses, 35003
Native American culture, 03036
Native American history, 03088, 38062, 41012, 41017, 41033, 41047, 41052, 41056, 48177
Native Americans, 02016, 03011, 03014, 03027, 03043, 03083, 03086, 03090, 03096, 05072, 05198, 05411, 05602, 07144, 07155, 07212, 08011, 08072, 10234, 10248, 10722, 10737, 11017, 11103, 19028, 24450, 34043, 35005, 35015, 35016, 35029, 35034, 36041, 36209, 39009, 42069, 43036, 43187, 43195, 46001, 46010, 46014, 46018, 52101

Oceanographic vehicles, 36979
Oceanography, 02021, 02026, 03041, 05386, 05456, 05502, 05524, 05526, 05543, 05620, 05717, 05830, 08031, 08090, 08105, 08124, 08140, 10160, 10548, 10684, 10866, 11102, 11504, 11505, 13024, 13060, 13061, 13087, 13089, 13110, 13114, 13158, 14097, 15006, 15024, 22022, 22035, 23003, 23007, 24144, 24148, 24178, 24279, 25080, 25067, 25184, 25249, 25271, 25303, 28013, 28019, 28030, 33023, 34059, 34243, 36367, 36542, 36657, 38046, 38086, 40207, 42030, 42057, 44013, 44015, 45023, 48068, 48097, 48111, 48118, 51144, 51257, 51381, 51461, 52011, 60001
Oceans and foreign policy, 10339
Ockham, William, 36448
Oenology, 05097, 05108, 05844, 18047, 24270, 36170, 36293, 36957, 51456
Office and professional employees, 36854
Office automation, 05817, 08083, 24085, 24089, 25069, 25158, 43071, 43266, 54102
    See also Automation, Computers, Micrographics
Office buildings, 10318
Office equipment, 10460, 36994, 51345
Office machines, 05595, 10460, 11385
    See also Computers
Office management, 43008
Office products, 51345
Official secrets, 10381
    See also National security
Offshore commerce, 10610
Offshore drilling, 05502, 11050, 11107, 11242, 25184, 36164, 41020
    See also Oil exploration
Offshore structures, 07186
Ohio, 40067, 40202, 40225
Oil, 03025, 07177, 10187, 11117, 41020, 41027, 41030, 43179, 48099, 49015, 53020
    See also Petroleum
Oil and gas exploration, 07080
Oil compacts, interstate, 41030
Oil exploration, 10720, 41010, 41026, 48100, 48123, 61059
Oil fields, 05238
Oil leases, 41036
Oil recovery, 10720, 11250, 41010
Oil shale, 07092, 11116, 11453, 22010
Oil spills, 05320, 05379, 05386, 05463, 05502, 05524, 10418, 11238, 34182, 48167
    See also Hazardous wastes, Water pollution
Oil tankers, 37006
Oil wells, 36164, 48168
Oils, 10745, 34073, 40107
    vegetable, 17089, 27006
Oilseeds, 11084, 22052, 48092, 48170, 61046
Oklahoma, 41044, 41057
Old radio programs, 24204
Older Americans, 43176
    See also Aging
Oleanders, 48163
Oleic acid, 40107

Oleochemicals, 36473
Olympic games, 07210
On-the-job training, 10943, 24090, 36841
Oncogenic viruses, 24437, 25093, 39005, 54082
Oncology, 05151, 05203, 05204, 13174, 17156, 24241, 34117, 36076, 38103, 43298, 52035
    See also Cancer
Oncorhynchus, 61092
One-parent families, See Single-parent families
Onions, 07162
Open-air theaters, 38049
Open housing, 05588, 10494, 10834, 11301, 24219, 36704, 43114, 43169
    See also Civil rights, Discrimination
Open universities, 40258
Opera, 07075, 08091, 11076, 11180, 34145, 36288, 36713, 43043, 48164
Opera singers, 11180, 36288, 48164
Operating engineers, 10805
    See also Engineers
Operating rooms, 07049
    See also Surgery
Operations research, 04048, 10463, 11128, 24126, 34137, 36407, 44002, 44008, 51104, 51383
Ophthalmology, 05045, 05361, 05498, 05640, 05786, 11391, 13007, 17112, 17374, 24247, 24453, 36194, 36346, 36399, 36410, 36802, 40252, 43031, 43225, 48044, 51067
    veterinary, 41009
Opium, 25085
    See also Narcotics
Optical character recognition, 50017
    See also Optical scanning
Optical coatings, 34184
Optical discs, 24089
Optical electronics, 51424
Optical engineering, 52052
Optical equipment, 11348
Optical properties, 18023
Optical scanning, 11281, 50017
Opticians, 51391
    See also Contact lenses, Eyeglasses
Optics, 03059, 05220, 05733, 05830, 11262, 25250, 25257, 29060, 36879, 40209, 40252, 44001, 48044
Optometry, 10069, 17374, 24405, 29012, 29036, 29060, 40252, 48044, 61030
    See also Contact lenses, Eyeglasses
Oral diseases, 05288, 13010, 17019, 17026, 36829, 52019
    See also Dentistry
Oral history, 10712, 23023, 36857, 48175
    See also Folklore
Oral hygiene, 03053, 13010, 34185
Oral medicine, 29004
Oral microbiology, 52019
Oral surgery, 17034, 17407, 36056
    Oral-facial restoration, 43005, 47054
Oranges, 13083
    See also Citrus fruits
Orchestras, 07163, 10226

Pharmacology, 01063, 05254, 05305, 05437, 07176, 08117, 10253, 11391, 11397, 13062, 13063, 17212, 17437, 18035, 24065, 24067, 25077, 25304, 28024, 29066, 34109, 34208, 36043, 36225, 36313, 36428, 36998, 36999, 40100, 40166, 43152, 43182, 43315, 49003, 49007, 52028
    veterinary, 36878, 42010, 48084
Pharmacy education, 24027
Phenylketonuria, 05627, 24276
Pheromones, 48094, 54123
Philanthropy, 05382, 05670, 10721, 11009, 36353, 36430, 36435, 36933, 43076, 51452
Philately, 05693, 07039, 10325, 11257, 11451, 31005, 34068, 36318, 36475, 40241, 43046
    See also Collecting, Postage stamps
Philippine Islands, 05763, 36331
Philology, 10376
Philosophers, 40212
Philosophy, 10119, 40212
    eastern, 05316
    educational, 08133
    legal, 20033
    process, 05223
    religious, 05316, 10119
    social, 20033
Philosophy for children, 34119
Philosophy of education, 36880
Phobias, 14038, 24414, 36427
Phonetics, 05770, 07086
    See also Speech
Phonics, 03097
Phonograph recordings, 36013
Phonographs, 04051, 36013
Phonology, 08065, 13101
Phosphates, 05504, 10334, 13088, 14091, 27082
Photobiology, 10854, 24446, 43106
Photochemistry, 18081, 24309
Photocomposition, 37008, 51319
    newspapers, 10184
    See also Typesetting
Photocopying, 11385
Photogrammetry, 03059, 11168, 24344, 25250, 51048, 51084, 51134, 51179, 51344, 52099
Photographers, 05034, 17434, 36165
Photographic archives, 10909
Photographic equipment, 07193, 36568, 36711
Photographic research, 05034
Photographs, 10511, 10712, 10909, 11385, 36681
    aerial, 10365, 22009, 24198
    Eastern Europe and China, 36392
    historical, 17244
    in National Archives, 10909
    Soviet Union, 36988
Photography, 05034, 05284, 07193, 11385, 17434, 25250, 25257, 35008, 35051, 36165, 36393, 36568, 36587, 36932, 37071, 38082, 43320, 43326, 51430
    advertising, 36029
    aerial, 05685, 19054, 25250, 42023, 48188, 51084, 51134, 51306, 54048
    biological, 17148

(Photography, continued)
    biomedical, 13040, 17148
    color, 25154
    corona discharge, 07008
    high-speed, 52052
    history of, 48029
    infrared, 51386
    magazine, 36160
    space, 35055
    spaceborne, 05685, 48195, 51134, 51306, 54048
    underwater, 05171, 05259, 10866, 51084
Photography education, 36968
Photogravure, 08125
Photojournalism, 36160, 36568, 38082, 43320
Photometry, 05830, 10384
Photomicrography, 07110, 24252
Photon cross sections, 10384
Photons, 24316
Photosynthesis, 24415, 40078
Photovoltaic power, 03104, 11400, 35043
Phreatophyte control, 32025
Phycology, 31029
Physical anthropology, 11103, 40015, 48182
Physical education, 13034, 24454, 29092, 51018, 51240, 51278, 61138
Physical fitness, 01070, 03109, 05029, 05079, 05086, 05088, 05444, 05571, 05850, 08018, 10205, 10916, 11307, 13016, 13018, 13034, 17373, 24236, 29112, 36579, 38070, 40044, 43190, 48061, 48108, 49024, 51142, 51210, 61095, 61128
Physical fitness centers, 24095
Physical medicine, 17020, 27008
Physical properties, 36921, 43001
Physical rehabilitation, 36084, 43190
Physical sciences, 05495, 05699, 08024, 10059, 13147, 25243
Physical therapy, 03044, 05349, 05568, 07188, 14030, 17443, 20029, 25193, 27115, 36084, 36545, 37100, 40139, 47007, 51075
Physicians, 05819, 17423, 29003
    Afro-American, 11097
Physicians' assistants, 14084, 51016
Physicists, 36118
Physicists in medicine, 36070
Physics, 01063, 03059, 03071, 05155, 05211, 05323, 05326, 05338, 05393, 05654, 05690, 07136, 07182, 24429, 25279, 36117, 36147, 40078, 40147
    atmospheric, 03065, 07126, 25013, 25060
    atomic, 07123
    cloud, 25011, 29046
    health, 10674, 11476, 51211
    high-energy, 05155, 05393, 05774, 17232, 36629
    ice, 40132
    low-temperature, 10545, 20044, 36661
    nuclear, 05393, 05505, 07172, 17087, 24316, 24431, 40120, 40261, 47018, 47064
    particle, 05155, 05856, 07172
    plasma, 11203, 25051, 36631, 43295, 49006
    radio, 36275, 43330

Pueblo Indians, 03027, 35012, 54025
Puerto Rico, 60003
Pulmonary diseases, pediatric, 43131
Pulmonary neoplasms, 29025
Pulp, 14100, 17419, 36140, 40164, 42028, 43183, 43352, 52017, 52067, 52110
    See also Papermaking
Pulp mills, 10157
Pulpwood, 10198, 14100, 40164
Pulsars, 05211, 10112
Pumps, 54094
Puppetry, 05672, 36831
Purchasing management, 34154
Purses, 36759
Pyrethrum, 17308
Pyrolysis, 34179, 43120, 48150
Pyrotechnics, 05606, 24426, 51415

Quackery, 34020
Quadriplegia, 34034
Quadruplets, 17167
Quakers, 18074, 43166, 43328
Quality assurance, 11251
Quality circles, 05673, 40136
Quality control, 05673, 10137, 10283, 10478, 10632, 34239, 37011, 40136, 41048, 42064, 54016
Quality of life, 05674
Quantum chemistry, 18080
Quantum electronics, 05220, 05323, 05326, 11128, 51424
Quantum mechanics, 44002
Quantum metrology, 24427
Quantum theory, 43047
Quarrying, 11143, 18049, 25211, 36234, 50003
Quarter horses, 48025, 48166
Quartermaster Corps (history), 51105
Quasars, 05211, 10112
Quaternary, 61120
Quilting, 51164
Quintuplets, 17167

Rabbits, 17098
Rabies, 08150
Race cars, 05587, 05678
    See also Racing, automobile
Race relations, 22005, 36037, 36340, 36420
    See also Blacks, Civil rights, Discrimination, Integration
Racial discrimination, *See* Discrimination
Racial integration, *See* Integration
Racing
    automobile, 05165, 05587, 05678, 05769, 07198, 08130, 47044
    bicycle, 07208
    dog, 24424
    harness, 36488, 40260
    horse, 08010, 21026, 21028, 24424, 36488, 40260
    yacht, 34084, 44025
Racism, 10982, 36176, 36695, 37080
    See also Discrimination

Racketeering, 05582
Racks, 43329
Radar, 05605, 05807, 05857, 07213, 08105, 11168, 13064, 13157, 18065, 34096, 36623, 40119, 45005, 48031
    meteorological, 41041
    See also Meteorology
Radar astronomy, 05224
Radial keratotomy, 48131
Radiation, 01056, 04031, 07216, 11229, 17087, 17271, 19051, 24100, 24244, 24263, 24316, 24336, 32014, 38041, 40120, 42073, 43330, 47018, 47039, 52073, 61116
    ionizing, 18081, 24263
    nuclear, 19042, 24098, 25097, 43295
    solar, 41044
    ultraviolet, 10384
    See also X rays
Radiation chemistry, 18081
Radiation dosage, 10384, 47017
Radiation ecology, 52057
Radiation hazards, 04031, 05320, 10497, 10583, 11178, 11229, 11476, 13106, 17475, 22043, 34071, 35036, 36277, 36308, 36848, 36882, 42074, 43153, 43368, 47065, 48007, 48223, 50015
Radiation measurement, 10384, 24317, 33015
Radiation penetration, 10384
Radiation research, 10384
Radiation shielding, 33015, 47071
Radiators, 34111
    automobile, 43269
Radio, 03112, 05093, 05285, 05615, 05699, 07112, 08009, 08013, 10315, 10412, 10480, 10923, 10971, 11119, 11234, 18067, 13033, 36179, 36463, 36831, 40248, 48031, 51432, 52051
    advertising, 36914
    amateur, 38096
    college and university, 36554
    educational, 10825, 10924
    government regulation of, 10453, 10868, 11234, 11310
    history of, 24204, 36177
    minority-owned stations, 10922
    regulation, 10924
    shortwave, 34112
    See also Broadcasting
Radio astronomy, 05156, 51353
Radio equipment, 11234
    antique, 36177
Radio frequencies, 10412, 51432
Radio news, 36240
    See also Journalism
Radio operators, 03087
Radio performers, 36098
Radio physics, 36275, 43330
Radio plays, 05615, 05759
Radio programs, 10884, 36684
    old, 05615, 05759, 24204
Radio reception, 10412
Radio waves, 10283

(Recycling, continued)
  metal, 29023
  petroleum, 10285
  waste, 34126
  See also Conservation
Redwood, 05681
Redwood trees, 05193, 05713
Reefs, 10816
  artificial, 36657
Reflex Sympathetic Dystrophy Syndrome, 34202, 36865
Reforestation, 04032, 10476, 11422, 42079, 52098
  See also Forestry
Refractories, 34138, 40222, 43119, 43331, 61032
Refrigeration, 10049, 14017, 17287, 24432, 36249, 51010, 51156
Refugees, 08123, 10182, 10617, 11023, 11071, 11230, 11441, 11510, 29110, 36085, 36595, 37091
Regeneration (biology), 25224
Regional development, 25075
Regional planning, 05447, 10073, 10190, 10239, 10344, 10671, 10929, 11118, 11447, 17412, 17498, 19043, 20011, 29074, 34197, 35052, 36946, 38092, 40046, 42001, 43333, 51401
  See also Urban planning
Regional studies, 18025, 19053, 38021, 38088, 47038
Regulated industries, 40188
Regulations, 10417, 11191, 11200, 11254, 11331
  See also Law (regulation)
Rehabilitation, 05568, 10493, 10919, 11082, 11121, 11276, 11304, 11333, 14030, 17020, 17050, 17092, 17138, 17196, 17443, 20029, 29116, 31020, 34131, 36138, 36501, 36567, 37100, 40006, 41037, 48106, 48110, 48191, 51020, 51356, 51357, 51358, 61034
  aging, 43334
  centers, 03044, 10950, 34207
  counseling, 17202
  engineering, 05737, 10568, 11332, 25004, 25193, 25264, 34163, 40058, 40096, 43350, 51408, 54121
  international, 36917
  medicine, 07130, 25047, 36545
  of amputees, 36697
  of convicts, 45001
  of criminal offenders, 17306, 36434
  of deaf persons, 36375
  physical, 05683, 27008
  through horticulture, 24332
  vocational, 07130, 34162, 36418, 52012
Rehabilitation research, 25071
Rehabilitation therapy, 04025
Reincarnation, 51116, 51181
Reinforced concrete, 17193, 17444, 28010, 51475
Reinforced plastics, 40208
Reinforcement, wire, 51475
Relativity, 44002
Relaxation therapy, 29116
Relaxation training, 36427
Relays, electric, 18070
Reliability, 11251, 54016
Religion, 05019, 10055, 17123, 17166, 37090, 37091,

(Religion, continued)
  46013, 48062
  aberrant, 05771
  ancient, 49002
Religion and politics, 48128
Religious broadcasting, 34169
Religious conferences, 18082
Religious counseling, 51028
Religious education, 04026, 10282, 10983, 11439, 11479, 40052, 40219, 43358
Religious freedom, 10659, 11044, 11459, 25020, 29041, 36925, 48128
Religious information systems, 54022
Religious orders, 17398
Religious organizations, 36918
Religious philosophy, 05316, 10119
Religious therapy, 13008
Relocation, 51409
Remarriage, 36997
Remedial education, 05426, 20027, 24455, 43102
  See also Special education
Remodeling, 51302
Remote controls, 17218
Remote sensing, 05224, 05374, 05479, 05685, 05830, 11051, 13157, 18063, 19054, 24198, 25011, 32014, 36052, 42023, 43258, 47079, 48188, 48195, 51084, 51134, 51179, 54048
Renaissance period, 05744, 11059, 36884, 37020, 40071
Renal failure, 36710, 48036
Renal transplantation, 11170, 36622, 36710
  See also Kidneys
Renewable energy resources, 05267, 07088, 10240, 10385, 10409, 10538, 10547, 10574, 10583, 11246, 11315, 11384, 11386, 11489, 11514, 19022, 21030, 24161, 24436, 24451, 27003, 30008, 32018, 34225, 35037, 36261, 39003, 43153, 51095, 51410, 52031, 61121
Renovation, 51302
Rent control, 11098
Rental equipment, 52064
Repousse work, 05255
Reproduction (biology), 17146, 17461, 24136
Reproductive physiology, 25099, 36419
Reproductive rights, 36924
Reprography, 11385, 36932
Reptiles, 03101, 05180, 05199, 05653, 10526, 11488, 13021, 14096
Rescue equipment, 05694, 10917
  emergency, 27066
Research administration, 05757
Research and development, 03095, 05675, 11190, 11206, 11235, 34219, 34225, 36278, 41048
  government, 51368
  military, 25040, 51103, 51172, 51174, 51381, 51383
Research libraries, 10287
Research
  accident, 40128
  advertising, 36030
  aeromedical, 01025
  aeronautical, 21057

School-community relations, 10685, 25104, 51359, 51360, 51361
School discipline, 05330, 43271
School equipment, 36398
School health services, 24454, 40036
School integration, 11301, 25104, 25141, 29030, 36340, 36389
School libraries, 17035
School lunches, 10456, 10633, 11106, 36333
School newspapers, 11410
School nurses, 23022
School orchestras, 07163
School safety, 48152
School security, 24303
School volunteers, 51361
Schools, 10892, 51367
Schools, art, 51294
    cooking, 10759
    correspondence, 11068, 61090
    dental, 10096
    medical, 24028
    parochial, 10983, 11439, 29041
    private, 05321, 10483
    technical, 10964
    trade, 10964
    See also Education
Science, 04037, 05179, 05775, 08103, 10087, 10798, 11131, 13132, 13133, 14041, 14092, 14096, 15008, 19025, 22028, 29056, 36230, 36822, 36832, 36892, 36922, 37009, 38065, 41032, 42063, 43204, 47008, 55009
    behavioral, 05109, 07055, 07070, 43081
    computer, 05696, 10463, 10727, 11281, 16006, 17208, 17264, 36311, 43103, 44002, 48145, 51054
    computers in, 51226
    crop, 54045
    electrical, 08077
    food, See Food science
    history, 08027, 10519, 11350, 51242
    industrial, 11129
    journalism, 54029
    library, See Library science
    materials, 36661, 54080
    natural, 17178, 28018
    noetic, 05444
    nuclear, 01056, 16006, 17223, 36849, 47067
    plasma, 36849
    political, 38090, 40215, 51404
    soil, 05702, 10622, 11398, 24292, 36982, 43086, 43203, 43332, 54017, 54118
    women in, 10261
Science and society, 10618, 10829, 25069, 25270
Science and technology, 04039, 10288, 36278, 61021
    congressional committees on, 10700, 11358
Science education, 08138, 10288, 11132, 11146, 17481, 24242, 40075, 40105, 40228, 52078, 54114
Science fiction, 03012, 40229
    films, 05023
Science writing, 17198

Sciences
    atmospheric, 07145, 08082, 24372, 24382, 25011, 25042, 35010, 36210, 36542, 47079
    behavioral, 05430, 05697, 10537, 10586, 24088, 25052, 35051, 36151, 36201, 36935, 38019, 43301, 44005, 44008, 51220, 51268
    earth, 03054, 05130, 05375, 05381, 07103, 07107, 07133, 07184, 10160, 10684, 10900, 20051, 48198, 51058, 51201
    environmental, 05540, 07082, 10668, 10714, 17271
    estuarine, 45003
    forensic, 01010, 07013, 07100, 34159, 45013
    health, 01045, 52076
    information, See Information sciences
    life, 05697, 05699, 10829
    marine, See Marine sciences
    neural, 10537
    occult, 05771, 36329, 51242
    physical, 05495, 05699, 08024, 10059, 25243
    social, 05740, 07077, 10345, 11136, 19053, 25243, 38090, 40084, 43356, 49012, 51220, 61126
    soil, 11399, 61077
    space, 05211, 05550, 07197, 10852, 10900, 24429, 48137
    thermal, 18088
Scientific abstracts, 24122
Scientific apparatus, 11348
Scientific instruments, 05147, 05828, 07143
Scientific meetings, 36551
Scientific proceedings, 36551
Scientific research, 05675, 10721
Scientists, 05276, 08020, 10023, 36066
    women, 05846
Scintillation, 07213
Scleroderma, 34211, 43351, 44023
Sclerotherapy, 05084
Scoliosis, 17452, 36953
Scotus, John Duns, 36448
Scrap, 40142
Scrap metal, 10298, 10394
    recycling, 36712
Screen doors, 17453
Screen printing, 51418
Screens, window, 17453
Screenwriters, 05066
Screws, 40126
Scrip, 53022
Scuba diving, 05570, 51373
Sculpture, 05616, 10795, 10853, 11059, 11060, 11099, 11100, 36794
Sea birds, 05499, 05635, 25049
Sea grant colleges, 24279
Sea ice, 52081
Sea lampreys, 54093
Sea nettles, 24145
Sea otters, 05366
    See also Marine mammals
Sea power, 11167, 24469
    See also Wave power
Sea turtles, 10374

Vertebrate paleontology, 05758, 46011
Vertebrate zoology, 10526
Vertebrates, 05548, 05758
Vertigo, 36826
Very large-scale integration (computers), 38057
    See also Integrated circuits
Vesicular exanthema, 24180, 36889
Vesicular stomatitis, 24180
Veterans, 05789, 10144, 10228, 11276, 11471, 24150, 36308, 36705
    amputees, 36697
    atomic, 19042
    congressional committees on, 10703, 11367
    disabled, 10533
    Vietnam, 08146
Veterans Administration, 10308, 10394, 11471
Veterans Day, 11472
Veterans hospitals, 37066
Veterans' employment, 10713
Veterinarians, wildlife, 55001
Veterinary dentistry, 43058
Veterinary diagnostics, 19063
Veterinary drugs, 48042
Veterinary medicine, 05301, 05463, 05691, 05862, 07135, 11160, 11161, 16005, 17170, 17343, 17461, 18007, 19041, 19064, 22017, 22027, 24077, 24180, 24237, 25304, 27027, 29021, 29109, 30020, 31014, 34015, 34205, 36071, 36175, 36646, 36889, 36889, 38013, 43015, 43026, 43066, 43111, 47002, 48084, 51097, 51446, 54101, 55001
Veterinary ophthalmology, 41009
Veterinary parasitology, 24076, 43019
Veterinary pathology, 11161, 17343, 29008, 43028
Veterinary pharmacology, 36878, 42010, 48084
Veterinary surgery, 43029
Veterinary toxicology, 19063, 48225, 49033
Vibration, 05805, 17271, 17499, 21056, 36163
Victims of crimes, 11109, 11295, 51335
Victorian literature, 08137, 43382
Victorian period, 43382
Video, 17495, 36916, 37067
    art, 36423, 42053
    documentaries, 05469, 15029
    equipment, 03013, 51239
Video display terminals, 10567, 36031
    See also Computers
Video tapes, 05352, 10068, 10154, 13127, 24295, 36204, 36812
Videodiscs, 10480, 24089, 36812
Videotex, 10480, 36047
Vietnam, 36331
    See also Southeast Asia
Vietnam veterans, 08146, 36039
Viola d'amore, 37069
Violence, 05429, 10563, 11295, 17363, 24138, 38106
Violins, 05829, 14018
Viral carcinogenesis, 29055
Viral diseases, 05594, 48085
Viral hepatitis, 36647
Viral neoplasms, 24437, 48085

Viral vaccines, 13095
Virginia, 51457, 51459, 51468
Virology, 05204, 13085, 13174, 17157, 24072, 24264, 25057, 25255, 29055, 34117, 34240, 36317, 48082, 48085, 52035
Viruses, 08150, 27016
    oncogenic, 24437, 25093, 39005
Visas, 10525
Viscosity, 36921
Visibility, 05830
Vision, 36215, 36194, 48096
Vision aids, 05231, 34172
    impairment, 05231, 05358, 05498, 17246, 24231, 34172, 34200, 36421, 43063, 43222, 48096, 51051, 54073
    machine, 25044
Visna, 24180
Visual aids, 10025, 36499
Visual anthropology, 17433
Visual arts, 05512, 11060, 37070, 37071
    See also Arts, Graphic arts
Visual communications, 35008, 35051
Visual perception, 18078, 24340, 25113, 40252
Visually handicapped persons, 05723, 29012, 36615, 36703
    education of, 36694, 51121
    rehabilitation of, 51114, 51121
    See also Blindness, Handicapped persons
Vital statistics, 11296, 11299, 14036, 17462, 24320, 33003, 34194, 43065, 44018, 49023, 51171, 54021
Vitamin C, 05513
Vitamin E, 61075
Vitamins, 05291, 05513, 08117, 10486, 17500, 34109
Viticulture, 05097, 05108, 05844, 36170, 36293, 36957, 51456
Vivisection, 25230, 43014
    See also Humane treatment of animals
Vocal ensembles, 43075
Vocal music, 41055
    See also Opera, Singing, Songs
Vocational education, 10039, 10095, 10685, 11037, 11073, 14007, 17051, 17124, 36138, 36418, 40223, 43124, 47053, 51093, 51396, 51466
Vocational guidance, 03050, 05322, 10571, 11037, 36334, 42008, 42012, 51093, 51289, 51372
    minorities, 43127
    women, 11486
Vocational rehabilitation, 03044, 04025, 07130, 10140, 10493, 10919, 11121, 11333, 14030, 22002, 24044, 24205, 25193, 25224, 34162, 36418, 36517, 36567, 48106, 48191, 51253, 52012, 54079
Vocational services, Jewish, 36708
Voice coaches, 36057, 36713
Voice recognition, 50017
Voiceprints, 45013
Volcanoes, 02018, 02029, 07161, 07169, 07223, 10160, 15007, 10521, 15007, 32028, 51198, 51376
Voluntary organizations, 10721, 10806, 10912, 11024, 36086, 43076, 44026, 51454
Volunteer workers, 10685, 11474, 29125, 40180, 43076,

If you know of organizations that should be included in future editions of *Instant Information*, we'd appreciate your contribution. Send us a brief description of the organization, including name, address, phone number, and who to contact for further information. Send contributions to: Instant Information, % Tilden Press Inc., 1001 Connecticut Avenue NW, Washington, D.C. 20036.